Louisiana Law of Obligations

Louisiana Law of Obligations

A Methodological & Comparative Perspective

Cases, Texts and Materials

SECOND EDITION

Alain A. Levasseur

PROFESSOR OF LAW EMERITUS
PAUL M. HEBERT LAW CENTER,
LOUISIANA STATE UNIVERSITY

Nikolaos A. Davrados

ASSOCIATE PROFESSOR OF LAW
LOYOLA UNIVERSITY
NEW ORLEANS COLLEGE OF LAW

J. Randall Trahan

PROFESSOR OF LAW
PAUL M. HEBERT LAW CENTER
LOUISIANA STATE UNIVERSITY

Sandi Varnado

PROFESSOR OF LAW
LOYOLA UNIVERSITY
NEW ORLEANS COLLEGE OF LAW

CAROLINA ACADEMIC PRESS
Durham, North Carolina

ISBN   978-1-5310-2640-0 (casebound)
ISBN   978-1-5310-2641-7 (electronic)
ISBN   978-1-5310-2737-7 (looseleaf)
LCCN   2022950039

Carolina Academic Press
700 Kent Street
Durham, NC 27701
(919) 489-7486
www.cap-press.com

Printed in the United States of America

Contents

PART TWO
CONVENTIONAL OBLIGATIONS

PART THREE

QUASI-CONTRACTS

Preface

This Second Edition of *Louisiana Law of Obligations: Cases, Texts and Materials* is as innovative as the first edition of 2013 but more comprehensive as a result of the experience acquired over the last ten years.

To Part One on "Nature, Division & Kinds of Obligations" and Part Two on "Conventional Obligations," we have added a Part Three on "Quasi-Contracts."

We have structured this Second Edition around the single most original feature of a civil law system, exemplified particularly, but not exclusively, by a Civil Code. This feature is that of a hierarchy in the sources of law that establishes a ranking among those sources which are "legislation," "jurisprudence or judicial decisions," and "doctrine or legal scholarly writings." In the Louisiana Civil Code, this feature finds its *raison d'être* in the very first articles of the Code in the Preliminary Title and in Chapter 1 on General Principles.[1]

We have built the Chapters in this coursebook to reflect this foundational feature of the ranking of the sources of law. At the beginning of every Chapter we have presented the most relevant Code articles as the "primary" source of law; the articles are followed by the two "secondary" sources of law which are the jurisprudence or judicial opinions and doctrine or legal scholarly writings.[2] With respect to the Code articles in particular, we recommend that a reader of this coursebook have available a copy of the Louisiana Civil Code to better understand, and appreciate, the intricate symbiosis and connections that exist between the Books, Titles, Chapters and Articles in that Code, and, to a large extent, in other Civil Codes of civil law jurisdictions such as France and Québec. The "secondary" sources, jurisprudence and doctrine, that follow the Code articles will help readers understand how the methods of "Interpretation of Laws" can be used by the courts and doctrine to "go through the Civil Code and beyond the Civil Code."

Following each case we have offered a series of questions, some designed to direct students to the significant points of the court's analysis, particularly as regards Code articles; other questions are designed to deepen the students' understanding of civil law methodology, particularly the many principles and techniques of interpretation

---

1. See art. 1 to 4.

2. For more on Sources of Law, see *Code Napoléon or Code Portalis*, 63 Tul. L. Rev. 762 (1969); and *Deciphering a Civil Code: Sources of Law and Methods of Interpretation* (2015) (works cited).

of written sources of law with a focus on Code articles.[3] Questions beginning with paragraph numbers refer to words or concepts within those paragraph, while questions without paragraph numbers refer to the case as a whole.

Because the Louisiana civil law system is exposed to the influence of the common law system and naturally borrows from other civil law systems, we have included in this coursebook pertinent articles of other Civil Codes, extensive excerpts of doctrine/legal scholarship, many of which are very recent and that we have translated for the benefit of some readers. We have also reprinted several already existing translations. One will also find many cross references to common law legal scholarship, English and American, as well as to the U.C.C. and the Restatement of Contracts.

The result, we hope, is a work that provides students, and the legal community, with a comprehensive insight into the Louisiana Law of Obligations, Conventional Obligations and Quasi-Contracts. This work is also meant to open students' minds towards exploring and inquiring beyond the borders of their State, Louisiana first. and foremost, to find in other legal systems possible answers to issues that are not "exclusively" raised and debated within the confines of their own legal system.

A.A.L.

N.A.D.

---

3. On methods of interpretation, see *Deciphering a Civil Code: Sources of Law and Methods of Interpretation* (2015) (works cited).

Alain A. Levasseur

PROFESSOR OF LAW EMERITUS
PAUL M. HEBERT LAW CENTER, LOUISIANA STATE UNIVERSITY

Nikolaos A. Davrados

ASSOCIATE PROFESSOR OF LAW
LOYOLA UNIVERSITY, NEW ORLEANS COLLEGE OF LAW

J. Randall Trahan

PROFESSOR OF LAW
PAUL M. HEBERT LAW CENTER, LOUISIANA STATE UNIVERSITY

Sandi Varnado

PROFESSOR OF LAW
LOYOLA UNIVERSITY, NEW ORLEANS COLLEGE OF LAW

With the collaboration
of

Olivier Moreteau

PROFESSOR OF LAW
DIRECTOR, CENTER OF CIVIL LAW STUDIES
PAUL M. HEBERT LAW CENTER, LOUISIANA STATE UNIVERSITY

Nadia E. Nedzel

PROFESSOR OF LAW EMERITUS
SOUTHERN UNIVERSITY LAW CENTER

EDITOR

Cindra Fox

Works Cited

General References

Dictionary of the Civil Code, Alain A. Levasseur and Marie-Eugénie Laporte-Legais, Gérard Cornu, Association Henri Capitant, LexisNexis (2014).

French Civil Code-Code Civil Français, English-French-Arabic, Dir. Michel Séjean, LexisNexis (2020).[4]

Louisiana Pocket Civil Code, Alain A. Levasseur ed., Carolina Academic Press (2022).

Doctrine on the Louisiana Civil Code

The Law of Obligations, S. Litvinoff, *Louisiana Civil Law Treatise*, vol. 5, West Publishing Company (1992).

Louisiana Law of Conventional Obligations: A Précis, Alain A. Levasseur, Carolina Academic Press (2015).

Louisiana Law of Obligations in General: A Comparative Civil Law Perspective, A Treatise, Alain A. Levasseur, Carolina Academic Press (2020).

Louisiana Law of Obligations in General: A Précis, Alain A. Levasseur, Carolina Academic Press (2015).

Louisiana Law of Unjust Enrichment in Quasi-Contracts, Alain A. Levasseur, LexisNexis (1991).

Comparative Civil Law

Droit Civil: Les Obligations, Alex Weill & François Terré, 3ème éd. (1980).

Droit Civil: les Obligations, F. Terré, Ph. Simler, Y. Lequette, F. Chénedé, 12ème éd., Dalloz (2019). (Reprinted with permission.)

Le Droit Civil Français, C.B.M. Toullier, J.B. Duvergier rev., 6ème éd. (1846).

---

4. The articles of the F.C.C. used in this casebook are from the Civil Code of 1804 and do not reflect the 2016 revisions.

LEÇONS DE DROIT CIVIL: OBLIGATIONS, Henri et Léon Mazeaud, et al., vol. 1., François Chabas rev., 9th ed. (1998).

LES OBLIGATIONS, Jean-Louis Baudouin, Yvon Blais 4ème éd. (1993).

LES OBLIGATIONS, Jean-Louis Baudouin — Pierre Gabriel Jobin, Yvon Blais Inc., 5ème éd. (1998).

TRAITÉ DES OBLIGATIONS, Robert Pothier, 2ème éd. (1825).

TRAITÉ ELÉMENTAIRE DE DROIT CIVIL BELGE: LES OBLIGATIONS, vol. 3, 3ème éd. (1967).

TRAITÉ THÉORIQUE ET PRATIQUE DE DROIT CIVIL, G. Baudry-Lacantinerie et Louis Joseph Barde, 2ème éd. (1902).

TREATISE ON THE CIVIL LAW, Marcel Planiol Georges Ripert, Louisiana State Law Institute trans., 11th ed. (1939).

A TREATISE ON THE LAW OF OBLIGATIONS OR CONTRACTS, Robert J. Pothier, William David Evans trans. (1806).

Comparative Law

COMPARATIVE LAW OF CONTRACTS, Alain A. Levasseur, Carolina Academic Press (2008).

THE LAW OF CONTRACT, G.H. Treitel, 7th ed., Stevens & Son (1987). (Reproduced with permission of the Licensor through PLSclear.)

THE LAW OF CONTRACTS, John D. Calamari and Joseph M. Perillo, 4th ed., West Group (1998).

Restatement of the Law Second Contracts, copyright © 1981 by The American Law Institute. Reprinted with permission. All rights reserved.

Uniform Commercial Code (UCC), Article 1 copyright © 2001, Article 2 copyright © 2011 by The American Law Institute and the National Conference of Commissioners of Uniform State Laws. Reproduced by permission of the Permanent Editorial Board for the UCC. All rights reserved.

Acknowledgments

Restatement of the Law Second Contracts, copyright © 1981 by The American Law Institute. Reprinted with permission. All rights reserved.

Uniform Commercial Code Articles One and Two, copyright © 2001 and 2011 and respectively by The American Law Institute and the National Conference of Commissioners on Uniform State Laws. Reproduced with the permission of the Permanent Editorial Board for the Uniform Commercial Code. All rights . reserved.

CONTRACTS by E. Allen Farnsworth, reproduced with the permission of Aspen Publishing, 4th Edition, by Alan Farnsworth.

Part One

Of the Nature, Division & Kinds of Obligations

Chapter 1

Obligations: Principles

Louisiana Sources of Law
Louisiana Civil Code

Art. 1756. Obligations; definition.

An obligation is a legal relationship whereby a person, called the obligor, is bound to render a performance in favor of another, called the obligee. Performance may consist of giving, doing, or not doing something. (Acts 1984, No. 331, §1, eff. Jan. 1, 1985.)

Art. 1757. Sources of obligations.

Obligations arise from contracts and other declarations of will. They also arise directly from the law, regardless of a declaration of will, in instances such as wrongful acts, the management of the affairs of another, unjust enrichment and other acts or facts. (Acts 1984, No. 331, §1, eff. Jan. 1, 1985.)

Art. 1758. General effects.

A. An obligation may give the obligee the right to:

(1) Enforce the performance that the obligor is bound to render;

(2) Enforce performance by causing it to be rendered by another at the obligor's expense;

(3) Recover damages for the obligor's failure to perform, or his defective or delayed performance.

B. An obligation may give the obligor the right to:

(1) Obtain the proper discharge when he has performed in full;

(2) Contest the obligee's actions when the obligation has been extinguished or modified by a legal cause. (Acts 1984, No. 331, §1, eff. Jan. 1, 1985.)

Art. 1759. Good faith.

Good faith shall govern the conduct of the obligor and the obligee in whatever pertains to the obligation. (Acts 1984, No. 331, §1, eff. Jan. 1, 1985.)

Doctrine
Louisiana Law of Obligations in General, A Treatise
Sections 1.4.1 to 1.4.2

2. Pothier on obligations. In his *Treatise on the Law of Obligations or Contracts*, Robert J. Pothier wrote that "[T]his term OBLIGATION has two significations: in its more extensive signification, it is synonymous to *Duty* and comprises imperfect, as well as perfect Obligations. Those Obligations are called imperfect, for which we are accountable to God only; and of which no person has a right to require the performance. Such are the duties of charity and gratitude. [. . . .] The term *Obligation*, in a more proper and confined sense, comprises only perfect obligations, which are also called personal engagements, and which give the person, with whom they are contracted, a right to demand their performance; and it is this kind of Obligation which is the object of the present treatise."[1]

3. Obligations and duty. With respect to an "obligation" as giving the right to require its performance, it creates a "legal tie" between two parties allowing one, the *obligee*, to call upon the law to obtain the performance of the obligation by the other party, the *obligor*. This very specific and purely legal meaning of *obligation* or *perfect obligation* can be contrasted with a broad and most popular meaning of the same word obligation which encompasses all sorts *of duties* that the law or good morals, for example, would impose on a person. [. . . .]

4. Obligation: *vinculum juris*. In its narrow and technical legal sense derived from its Roman law origin,[3] the notion of obligation can be defined as a bond of law, "vinculum juris," meant to impose a performance on a person, the *obligor*, for the benefit of another, the *obligee*.

One can find in Justinian's Institutes the following definition of the concept of obligation:

> "*Obligatio est iuris vinculum, quo necessitate adstringimur alicuius solvendae rei, secundum nostrae civitatis iura.*"

> "An obligation is a legal bond whereby we are constrained by the need to perform something according to the laws of our state."[4]

---

1. Robert J. Pothier, *A Treatise on the Law of Obligations or Contracts*, William David Evans Trans., A. Strahan (1806), Vol. I, p. 1 ("Preliminary Title").

3. *Harpers' Latin Dictionary, Oxford Latin Dictionary*. The very etymology of the word "obligation" explains its nature. It comes from the Latin verbs 1) "*obligare*" which means to bind together, to tie up, to make legally liable and 2) "*ligare*" which also means to bind, to tie.

4. *The Institutes of Justinian*, Book III, Title XII ("De Obligationibus"), Text, Translation and Commentary J.A.C. Thomas (North Holland Publishing Co. 1975). The Institutes of Justinian were promulgated by the Emperor in 533, after the Digest. The Institutes were to be a condensed version of the Digest to be used by students in their first-year course of studies.

It is this meaning of "legal tie-vinculum juris" which is reflected in La. Civ. Code art. 1756: "an obligation is defined as a legal relationship, whereby a person, called the obligor, is bound to render a performance in favor of another, called the obligee. Performance may consist of giving, doing, or not doing something." In the *Dictionary of the Civil Code*, under "obligation," we find the following description: "In a technical meaning, the passive side of a personal right (or right to a claim, performance); bond of law (vinculum juris) whereby one or more persons, the obligor or obligors, is/are required to carry out a performance (doing or not doing something) for the benefit of one or more persons, the creditor(s) as a result of either a contract." [. . . .]

5. Obligations: essential features. From these definitions we can conclude that a perfect or civil Obligation presents three essential features: first, it is legally binding in such a way that the creditor has a right of action against his obligor to compel him to perform, i.e., to give, to do or not to do, or, when specific performance is not possible or not conceivable, to pay compensatory damages. A second feature is that an obligation is personal in the sense that it is personal to the person or the persons who are bound (as contrasted with the real obligation which is an obligation "fictitiously" attached to a thing).[6] The third feature of an obligation is that, in most instances, it has a patrimonial value, which means that it has a monetary/financial value.[7] [. . . .]

General Effects

37. General effects. La. Civ. Code **art. 1758:**

A. An obligation may give the obligee the right to:

(1) Enforce the performance that the obligor is bound to render;

(2) Enforce performance by causing it to be rendered by another at the obligor's expense;

(3) Recover damages for the obligor's failure to perform, or his defective or delayed performance.

B. An obligation may give the obligor the right to:

(1) Obtain the proper discharge when he has performed in full;

(2) Contest the obligee's actions when the obligation has been extinguished or modified by a legal cause. [. . . .]

---

6. See the distinction below.

7. <u>Every person has a patrimony</u>, a concept which is associated to the legal existence of a person who has assets and debts which enable her to enter into civil obligations with other persons who also have their own patrimony. A person, whether natural or legal, being endowed with legal personality can have only one patrimony which is also indivisible by nature. Conversely, since a patrimony belongs to a person, there cannot exist a patrimony without a person. *Dictionary of the Civil Code*, p. 423, word: patrimoine-patrimonial.

38. Particular importance of art. 1758. This broad listing of remedies and rights as well as defenses that make up La. Civ. Code **art. 1758**, is the outcome, albeit incomplete, of an inductive reasoning that led the drafters of this article to consider, as a first step, all the possible remedies available to creditors under the different kinds of existing obligations. The second step in the reasoning process consisted in inducing some **"general considerations"** or **"principal"** effects that can be looked upon as common links between the different kinds of existing obligations. In other words, **all Obligations will carry with them at least these "general effects."**

The importance and invaluable benefit of such a "general" article is to provide gap-filling resources and guidance in the event that a particular type of obligation would either fail to <u>specifically</u> provide for certain effects or would not <u>expressly</u> <u>exclude</u> some remedies. It stands as an umbrella article, which ought to be considered and used always as the general introductory article to any analysis, on the one hand, of the legal nature of the rights of an obligee who seeks the performance of the obligation owed to him and, on the other hand, of the defenses available to "an" obligor. The following developments will help illustrate the importance of this **art. 1758**.

Good Faith

39. La. Civ. Code Art. 1759: "Good faith shall govern the conduct of the obligor and the obligee in whatever pertains to the obligation."

This requirement of good faith on the part of all parties to an obligation is not a new requirement, although it lost some of its importance over the centuries. However, the specific inclusion of this requirement in a Code article has the merit of raising it to the status of a *general principle*, which, as such, <u>must</u> guide the jurist in his analysis of the whole law of Obligations. Inherited from Roman law and developed by Canon law, this fundamental **principle** of *good faith* inspires and pervades the entire law of the Civil Code and the law of Obligations in particular, as illustrated by the fact that it appears at the very beginning of **Title 3 on Obligations in general** under the title of *"General Principles."* The underlying influence of its spirit all through the Civil Code is the legal expression of moral, social, economic objectives that should never be forgotten. It will be particularly true as we look at the formation of a contract and the effects of conventional obligations.[73] [....]

40. Good faith: meaning? The problem one faces in an analysis of **art. 1759** is that there is nowhere in the Civil Code any definition of this concept of "good faith." It was likely intentional on the part of the codifiers not to attempt to give any definition of such a concept because of the ambivalence of its epistemological nature. On the other hand, it is fortunate that we do not have a definition of this concept because, like all definitions, a definition of good faith would very likely have confined the

---

73. La. Civ. Code arts. 1948–2012 [...]. See *Bloom's Incorporated v. Performance Fuels, L.L.C.*, 16 So.3d 476, 2009.

application of that definition to its literal wording thereby placing the reader in a straight jacket [sic] with little room to expand on the wording or to narrow it down.[74] [. . . .]

The breadth of **art. 1759** dictates that good faith "govern" the conduct of the parties, most importantly at the stage of formation of their contractual obligation but also, and just as importantly, at the stage of the performance or execution of their obligations.

NOTE: On "**good faith**" see the section on *Doctrine* in CHAPTER TWO — NATURAL OBLIGATIONS; and see PART TWO, CHAPTER THREE — EFFECTS OF CONVENTIONAL OBLIGATIONS, in the section on the *Comparative Law Perspective*.

Case
Eric Borcik
v.
Crosby Tugs, L.L.C.
Supreme Court of Louisiana
May 3, 2017
222 So.3d 672

CRICHTON, J.

[. . . .]

[1] We are called upon to interpret the meaning of "good faith" as used in R.S. 30:2027. The legislature has not defined "good faith" in the statute. And [. . .] it is apparent that the term "good faith" as used in this statute is not "clear and unambiguous." R.S. 1:4 We must therefore apply the secondary principles of statutory interpretation by looking to the purpose of the statute, the context of the term "good faith" within the statute, and the text of the law as a whole. [. . . .]

[. . . .]

[2] We find that a broad definition of "good faith" is necessary to uphold the purpose of the LEQA and the Louisiana Constitution's mandate. This construction promotes the purpose of the LEQA and balances competing interests of the State and the environment, employers and industry, and employees, by encouraging reporting of environmental violations and protecting employers from potential whistleblowers who are not operating in good faith. It likewise comports with the text of the law as a whole, which we have previously held is broadly intended to protect the environment. We therefore hold that the term "good faith," as used in R.S. 30:2027,

---

74. Portalis, on definitions: See "Code Napoléon or Code Portalis," XLIII TUL. L.REV. 762–774 (1969).

means an employee is acting with an honest belief that a violation of an environmental law, rule, or regulation occurred.

[. . . .]

[3] A broad definition of "good faith" in R.S. 30:2027 is also supported by the definition of "good faith" in the whistleblower context in our neighboring state. In *Wichita County v. Hart*, 917 S.W. 2d 779 (Tex. 1996), the Texas Supreme Court analyzed the Texas Whistleblower Act. The court held that the term "good faith," as used in the act, means: "(1) the employee believed that the conduct reported was a violation of law and (2) the employee's belief was reasonable in light of the employee's training and experience." [. . . .]

[. . . .]

[4] [T]he Louisiana legislature chose to include the reasonable belief standard within the statute itself. In other words, as noted above, R.S. 30:2027 already has the objective belief standard incorporated within the plain language. "Good faith" must therefore mean something different than an objective "reasonable belief," because the term would otherwise be duplicative and unnecessary, and we interpret statutes to avoid unnecessary verbiage. [. . . .] [T]he definition of "good faith" under R.S. 30:2027 we set forth here encompasses only the "honesty" standard outlined in Texas's two-part standard.[1]

[. . . .]

[5] [. . . .] The definition of "good faith" set forth herein also requires that the employee act with an "honest belief that a violation of an environmental law, rule or regulation occurred." These provisions of R.S. 30:2027(A)(1) therefore serve as additional safeguards against fabricated claims, because an employee is not protected unless the belief in the environmental violation directed by the employer is honest and reasonable.

[. . . .]

See also *Armstrong Airport Concessions v. K-Squared Restaurant, LLC*, 178 So.3d 1094 (La.App. 4 Cir. 2015).

---

1. Other whistleblower statutes have similar structures. For example, numerous federal appellate courts have remarked that the whistleblower provisions of the Sarbanes-Oxley Act, 18 U.S.C. § 1514A, which were "intended to include all good faith and reasonable reporting of fraud," rely on establishing that the complainant has both a "subjective belief that the complained-of conduct constitutes a violation of relevant law, and also that the belief is objectively reasonable in light of the factual circumstances." *Rhinehimer v. U.S. Bancorp Investments, Inc.*, 787 F.3d 797, 810–11 (6th Cir. 2015) (internal quotations omitted). See also, e.g., *Van Asdale v. Int'l Game Tech.*, 577 F.3d 989, 1000 (9th Cir. 2009) ("The plain language of this section, as well as the statute's legislative history and case law interpreting it, suggest that to trigger the protections of the Act, an employee must also have (1) a subjective belief that the conduct being reported violated a listed law, and (2) this belief must be objectively reasonable.").

Chapter 2

Natural Obligations

Louisiana Sources of Law

Louisiana Civil Code

Art. 1760. Moral duties that may give rise to a natural obligation.

A natural obligation arises from circumstances in which the law implies a particular moral duty to render a performance. (Acts 1984, No. 331, § 1, eff. Jan. 1, 1985.)

Art. 1761. Effects of a natural obligation.

A natural obligation is not enforceable by judicial action. Nevertheless, whatever has been freely performed in compliance with a natural obligation may not be reclaimed. A contract made for the performance of a natural obligation is onerous. (Acts 1984, No. 331, § 1, eff. Jan. 1, 1985.)

Art. 1762. Examples of circumstances giving rise to a natural obligation.

Examples of circumstances giving rise to a natural obligation are:

(1) When a civil obligation has been extinguished by prescription or discharged in bankruptcy.

(2) When an obligation has been incurred by a person who, although endowed with discernment, lacks legal capacity.

(3) When the universal successors are not bound by a civil obligation to execute the donations and other dispositions made by a deceased person that are null for want of form. (Acts 1984, No. 331, § 1, eff. Jan. 1, 1985.)

Doctrine
Louisiana Law of Obligations in General, A Précis
Sections 1.3.1 to 1.4.1

[A] natural obligation, although it expresses the existence of a right in a person, cannot be a ground for an action to have the natural obligation enforced. The creditor-obligee of a natural obligation has no right of action against the *natural obligor.* [. . . .]

LSA-C.C. Art. 1762 is only illustrative of the different kinds of natural obligations that may exist. [. . . .]

The use of the adjective *moral* to describe the inherent value of a natural obligation is broad enough to bring under the label of natural obligations any duty *binding* [. . .] *in conscience and according to natural justice.* [. . . .]

A natural obligation, because it is defined in part as an obligation, necessarily creates a right in an obligee. That right, however, is deprived of any action for the enforcement of the obligation which is its counterpart. In this respect, the natural obligation is to be distinguished from the civil obligation. [. . . .]

The performance of a natural of obligation is an onerous juridical act whereby the obligor intends to extinguish a previously existing debt which, for reasons of law, could not be enforced against him. Thus the contract resulting either from the promise to perform a natural obligation or from the performance itself of that obligation is an onerous contract since its cause is onerous. The moral duty which prompts the obligor to perform is inspired by the desire to extinguish a debt (albeit a moral debt) and, thereby, this duty voids the natural obligation of any gratuitous motivation. [. . . .]

The essential feature of the civil obligation, in contrast with the natural obligation is that the creditor-obligee had or has a right of action to compel the obligor to perform. [. . . .]

The substance of Article 1758 amounts to a broad survey and formulation of the types of remedies that might be available to a creditor-obligee depending on the legal nature of the civil obligation in existence and of the rights and defenses which might be available to a debtor-obligor of that civil obligation.

Louisiana Law of Obligations in General, A Treatise
Sections 1.1.1 to 1.4.2

9. La. Civ. Code art. 1757. Louisiana Civil Code **art. 1757** given above is the fountainhead of all sources of obligations. All the listed sources of obligations refer to and describe what is known as "**civil obligations**" by contrast with what is referred to as "**natural obligations**" which are defined in **art. 1760**: "**A natural obligation arises from circumstances in which the law implies a particular moral duty to render a performance.**"

On the basis of La. Civ. Code **art. 1757**, one can list the five sources of obligations as being: a) contracts or conventional obligations and other declarations of will; b) the law in the sense of legislation and custom; c) offenses; d) quasi-offenses; e) quasi-contracts or obligations arising without agreement. Taking these explicit sources in the order in which they are listed, a few words about each one of these sources and obligations will help frame the distinctions that must be made between them and, thereby, offer a brief outline of their respective areas of application. [. . . .]

Natural Obligations

28. Ambiguity. Although much has been written about the concept of "natural obligation," it still remains somewhat ambiguous. There is one certainty, however, and it is that a natural obligation, although it expresses the existence of a right in a person and, conversely, creates what appears to be an obligation on the part of another, cannot be a ground for an action to have that right enforced. The creditor-obligee of a natural obligation has no right of action against the *natural obligor*.[53]

A laudable effort of clarification and precision in legal terminology has been accomplished in the post-1984 drafting of La. Civ. Code **arts. 1760, 1761, and 1762**.

29. Concept. La. Civ. Code **art. 1760** defines a natural obligation as one arising "**from circumstances in which the law implies a particular moral duty to render a performance.**" As regards **art. 1762**,[54] by stating expressly that it merely lists examples of natural obligations, it puts an end to a controversy which had been engendered by the ambiguous language of former La. Civ. Code **art. 1758**.[55] It is clear now that La.

---

53. Already in Roman law "the chief effect of natural obligations was that, although he could not be sued for payment, a natural debtor who did pay would not be able subsequently to recover the *sum condictio indebiti. . . .*" J.A.C. Thomas, *Textbook of Roman Law*, p. 220 (North Holland 1976).

54. La. Civ. Code art. 1762: "Examples of circumstances giving rise to a natural obligation are: (1) when a civil obligation has been extinguished by a prescription or discharged in bankruptcy. (2) When an obligation has been incurred by a person who, although endowed with discernment, lacks legal capacity. (3) When the universal successors are not bound by a civil obligation to execute the donations and other dispositions made by a deceased person that are null for want of form."

55. Former La. Civ. Code art. 1758, up to the revision of 1984, read as follows: "Natural obligations are of four kinds: (1) Such obligations as the law has rendered invalid for the want of certain forms or for some reason of general policy, but which are not in themselves immoral or unjust. (2) Such as are made by persons having the discretion necessary to enable them to contract, but

Civ. Code **art. 1762** is only *illustrative* of the different kinds of natural obligations that may exist. The reader or interpreter is therefore invited to add <u>new</u> and <u>additional</u> natural obligations to those listed in **art. 1762** and to do so by calling upon methods of reasoning, *a pari ratione* in particular; whenever, from the existing circumstances, the law implies a particular moral duty to render a performance.[56] The Louisiana courts are then in a position to "fill gaps in the law" in finding and erecting "a particular moral duty" as the "reason" for creating as many natural obligations as they may believe are grounded in the general principles of law or equity and justice.[57] [. . . .]

30. Effects. A natural obligation, because it is defined, in part, as an *obligation*, necessarily creates a right in someone who, logically, should be considered as an obligee. That right, albeit in existence, is deprived of any means of action for the enforcement of the obligation that is its counterpart. It is mostly in this respect that the natural obligation must be distinguished from the civil obligation.

This and other effects, or lack thereof, of natural obligations are the subject matter of La. Civ. Code **art. 1761**: "**A natural obligation is not enforceable by judicial action. Nevertheless, whatever has been freely performed in compliance with a natural obligation may not be reclaimed. A contract made for the performance of a natural obligation is onerous.**"

The first sentence of the first paragraph of this article restates the identifying feature of the natural obligation as not susceptible of enforcement by judicial action. This feature is so traditional and so well accepted that it deserves no further comment here. [. . . .]

34. Heritability? One may wonder, for instance, whether a natural obligation is heritable and, as such, whether it is part of one's patrimony? If we assume a debt prescribed under La. Civ. Code **art. 1762-(1)**, should the obligor's heirs feel bound by the same natural obligation that the law had imposed on the now deceased obligor himself? As long as a natural obligation has a monetary value and represents the extinction of a debt, there is little doubt that, as a general rule, it should be heritable, both actively and passively. As such it should fall into the patrimonies of both the obligee and the obligor of the natural obligation. The heirs of an obligor of a natural obligation would find it in that obligor's patrimony and could possibly turn it into an onerous contract for the performance of the natural obligation. [. . . .]

---

who are yet rendered incapable of doing so by some provision of law. (3) When the action is barred by prescription, a natural obligation still subsists, although the civil obligation is extinguished. (4) There is also a natural obligation on those who inherit an estate, either under a will or by legal inheritance, to execute the donations or other dispositions which the former owner had made, but which are defective for want of form only." See *Breaux v. Breaux*, 51 So.2d 73, Supreme Court of Louisiana 1951.

56. La. Civ. Code art. 1760 [. . .].
57. La. Civ. Code art. 4 [. . .].

General Effects

37. General effects. La. Civ. Code **art. 1758**:

A. An obligation may give the obligee the right to:

(1) Enforce the performance that the obligor is bound to render;

(2) Enforce performance by causing it to be rendered by another at the obligor's expense;

(3) Recover damages for the obligor's failure to perform, or his defective or delayed performance.

B. An obligation may give the obligor the right to:

(1) Obtain the proper discharge when he has performed in full;

(2) Contest the obligee's actions when the obligation has been extinguished or modified by a legal cause. [. . . .]

38. Particular importance of art. 1758. This broad listing of remedies and rights as well as defenses that make up La. Civ. Code **art. 1758**, is the outcome, albeit incomplete, of an inductive reasoning that led the drafters of this article to consider, as a first step, all the possible remedies available to creditors under the different kinds of existing obligations. The second step in the reasoning process consisted in inducing some **"general considerations"** or **"principal"** effects that can be looked upon as common links between the different kinds of existing obligations. In other words, **all Obligations will carry with them at least these "general effects."**

The importance and invaluable benefit of such a "general" article is to provide gap-filling resources and guidance in the event that a particular type of obligation would either fail to <u>specifically</u> provide for certain effects or would not <u>expressly</u> <u>exclude</u> some remedies. It stands as an umbrella article, which ought to be considered and used always as the general introductory article to any analysis, on the one hand, of the legal nature of the rights of an obligee who seeks the performance of the obligation owed to him and, on the other hand, of the defenses available to "an" obligor. The following developments will help illustrate the importance of this **art. 1758**.

Good Faith

39. La. Civ. Code Art. 1759: "Good faith shall govern the conduct of the obligor and the obligee in whatever pertains to the obligation."

This requirement of good faith on the part of all parties to an obligation is not a new requirement, although it lost some of its importance over the centuries. However, the specific inclusion of this requirement in a Code article has the merit of raising it to the status of a *general principle*, which, as such, <u>must</u> guide the jurist in his analysis of the whole law of Obligations. Inherited from Roman law and developed by Canon law, this fundamental **principle** of *good faith* inspires and pervades the entire law of the Civil Code and the law of Obligations in particular, as illustrated by the fact that it appears at the very beginning of **Title 3 on Obligations in**

general under the title of *"General Principles."* The underlying influence of its spirit all through the Civil Code is the legal expression of moral, social, economic objectives that should never be forgotten. It will be particularly true as we look at the formation of a contract and the effects of conventional obligations.[73] [. . . .]

40. Good faith: meaning? The problem one faces in an analysis of **art. 1759** is that there is nowhere in the Civil Code any definition of this concept of "good faith." It was likely intentional on the part of the codifiers not to attempt to give any definition of such a concept because of the ambivalence of its epistemological nature. On the other hand, it is fortunate that we do not have a definition of this concept because, like all definitions, a definition of good faith would very likely have confined the application of that definition to its literal wording thereby placing the reader in a straight jacket [sic] with little room to expand on the wording or to narrow it down.[74] [. . . .]

The breadth of **art. 1759** dictates that good faith "govern" the conduct of the parties, most importantly at the stage of formation of their contractual obligation but also, and just as importantly, at the stage of the performance or execution of their obligations.

Cases

In re Atkins' Estate.
Atkins
v.
Commissioner of Internal Revenue

Circuit Court of Appeals
Fifth Circuit
February 25, 1929
30 F.2d 761

FOSTER, Circuit Judge.

[1] As appears by the decision of the Board of Tax Appeals, the question presented in this case is whether the sum of $23,625.24, representing one-half the amount of notes given by decedent to his sons, is deductible from the decedent's gross estate in the computation of federal estate taxes. The findings of fact by the board, which are set out in full, are as follows:

'Decedent, John B. Atkins, died intestate on October 28, 1923, a resident of the state of Louisiana. Prior to July, 1922, he had given his two daughters

---

73. La. Civ. Code arts. 1948–2012 [. . .]. See: *Bloom's Incorporated v. Performance Fuels, L.L.C.,* 16 So.3d 476, 2009.

74. Portalis, on definitions: See "Code Napoléon or Code Portalis," XLIII Tul. L.Rev. 762–774 (1969).

homes and cash from time to time and kept an accurate record of such gifts. He had also given one of his sons, J. B. Atkins, Jr., certain cash. He gave his two sons to understand that, when they became of age, he would give them amounts to equal the gifts he had made his daughters. On July 1, 1922, decedent executed and gave his sons promissory notes, payable to their order. The note to J. B. Atkins, Jr., was for the amount of $8,025.48, payable on or before 5 years after date. The note given to the other son, Joe F. Atkins, was for the amount of $39,225, payable on or before 10 years after date. Both notes bore interest at the rate of 6 per cent.

'Prior to Atkins' death the amount of $10,000 was paid on the note given to Joe F. Atkins. The principal of the note given to J. B. Atkins, Jr., was paid in full by the heirs on March 25, 1924. The heirs have paid the balance on the note of Joe F. Atkins in full in varying amounts, beginning July 7, 1924, and final payment being made July 1, 1926.'

[2] On these facts the board held that the notes were without consideration and not enforceable against the estate; therefore, were not deductible. It may be conceded that, if the law of Louisiana, which must govern, section 403, Revenue Act of 1921 (42 Stat. 279), is not to the contrary, the decision of the board is right. It would be useless to discuss the authorities from other states, cited and followed by the board and relied on by respondent.

[3] Petitioner contends that the decedent, having made donations of money to his other children, incurred the natural obligation to equalize his gifts to all his children, and having endeavored to do so by giving the notes to his two sons, as found by the board, that under the law of Louisiana this natural obligation was sufficient consideration for the notes, and they were enforceable one-half against his estate, as an obligation of the community.

[4] The articles of the Louisiana Civil Code dealing with natural obligations are as follows:

Art. 1757. 'Obligations are of three kinds: Imperfect obligations, natural obligations, and civil or perfect obligations.

'1. If the duty created by the obligation operates only on the moral sense, without being enforced by any positive law, it is called an imperfect obligation, and creates no right of action, nor has it any legal operation. The duty of exercising gratitude, charity and the other merely moral duties, is an example of this kind of obligation.

'2. A natural obligation is one which can not be enforced by action, but which is binding on the party who makes it, in conscience and according to natural justice.

'3. A civil obligation is a legal tie, which gives the party, with whom it is contracted, the right of enforcing its performance by law.'

Art. 1758. 'Natural obligations are of four kinds:

'1. Such obligations as the law has rendered invalid for the want of certain forms or for some reason of general policy, but which are not of themselves immoral or unjust.

'2. Such as are made by persons having the discretion necessary to enable them to contract, but who are yet rendered incapable of doing so by some provision of law.

'3. When the action is barred by prescription, a natural obligation still subsists, although the civil obligation is extinguished.

'4. There is also a natural obligation on those who inherit an estate, either under a will or by legal inheritance, to execute the donations or other dispositions which the former owner had made, but which are defective for want of form only.'

Art. 1759. 'Although natural obligations can not be enforced by action, they have the following effect:

'1. No suit will lie to recover what has been paid, or given in compliance with a natural obligation.

'2. A natural obligation is a sufficient consideration for a new contract.'

[5] The law of Louisiana regulating inheritance and the relation existing between parent and child differs greatly from that of most other states and is based on the fundamental principle of equality between children. There is the reciprocal duty of support between parent and child. Civ. Code, arts. 227, 229. Children may not be disinherited, except for just causes, which are specifically mentioned, Civ. Code, arts. 1617–1621 inclusive; and are forced heirs in the distribution of the parent's estate, Civ. Code, art. 1493. If a donation has been made to a child in excess of the disposable portion, it must be reduced by collation. This 'is founded on the equality which must be naturally observed between children and other lawful descendants.' Civ. Code, arts. 1227–1229. That equality between heirs of the same degree is a cardinal principle of the Louisiana law of inheritance is well settled in the jurisprudence of Louisiana. *Montgomery v. Chaney*, 13 La. Ann. 207; *Succession of Maltry*, 161 La. 1032, 109 So. 827.

[6] There could be no doubt that there is a moral obligation resting upon a parent to do equity between his children by equalizing his gifts to them during his lifetime. This is not seriously disputed by respondent, but a distinction is sought to be made between a moral and a natural obligation. As to this the contention is that the obligation of a parent to equalize his gifts to his children is not embraced in the four classes of natural obligations enumerated in article 1758, Civ. Code, and that they are exclusive.

[7] The administration of the law of Louisiana is not hampered by technical and unsubstantial distinctions. In the absence of a positive statute, it is the duty of her courts to apply the principles of equity, appealing to natural law and reason and received usages in support of those principles. Civ. Code, art. 21. And the maxim

'inclusio unius est exclusio alterius' is not always applicable in construing the articles of the Civil Code. As a rule of construction, announced in 1838, and followed ever since, the Supreme Court said in *Ellis v. Prevost*, 13 La. 230:

> 'The court cannot be ignorant of the mode in which our Codes were prepared and became laws. They were written by lawyers, who mixed with the positive legislation definitions seldom accurate, and points of doctrine always unnecessary. The legislature modified and changed many of the provisions relating to the positive legislation, but adopted the definitions and abstract doctrine, without material alteration; from this circumstance, as well as from the inherent difficulty of the subject, the positive provisions of our Code are often at variance with the theoretical part, which was intended to elucidate them; and whenever that occurs, we deem it a sound rule of interpretation, to disregard the doctrine, and consider the definitions modified by the clear intent of the positive enactments.'

[8] A reasonable construction of article 1758, Civ. Code, is that the four classes of natural obligations mentioned therein are illustrative, and not intended to be exclusive, and that any natural obligation is sufficient consideration for a new contract.

[9] Apparently there is no Louisiana decision expressly holding that the obligation of a parent to equalize his gifts to his children is sufficient consideration for a new contract; but this, perhaps, may be because the doctrine is so well understood that no one has heretofore raised the question in the settlement of an estate. That a natural obligation is sufficient consideration for a note is well settled by the following analogous cases: *Matthews v. Williams*, 25 La.Ann. 585, where a son gave his note in place of his father's note, which was prescribed; *Barthe v. Succession of Lacroix*, 29 La.Ann. 326, 29 Am.Rep. 330, where a note was given as a gratuity beyond his wages to an old and faithful servant, in which case the court used the expressions 'moral' and 'natural' obligations interchangeably; and *Interstate F. & B. Co. v. Irwin*, 138 La. 335, 70 So. 313, where a note was given by a bank director as a donation to make good the impairment of the capital of his bank. [. . . .]

[. . . .]

[10] Applying the law of Louisiana to the facts as found by the board, the conclusion is irresistible that a natural obligation rested on the decedent to equalize his gifts to his children; that in executing and delivering to his sons the promissory notes here in question he fulfilled that obligation; that under the law of Louisiana, which is controlling, regardless of decisions to the contrary in other states, there was sufficient consideration for the notes, and they were deductible from his gross estate in the payment of estate taxes.

[11] The petition is granted, and the judgment is reversed.

Questions

1. Paragraph 4: After you have read the three articles carefully, try to formulate, in your own terms, the legal reason or *ratio legis* that you see as a justification

for each of the three kinds of obligation. Focusing on the natural obligation, does the legal reason that you see behind Louisiana Civil Code article
1757-2 allow you to identify more or fewer examples of natural obligations
than those examples listed in Louisiana Civil Code article 1758? Read now
the new Louisiana Civil Code articles 1760 and 1762 on natural obligations.
How do these later articles match with the legal reasons you formulated when
considering the former articles on natural obligations? What comment(s) can
you make as to the role of legislation and the role of the courts in creating
law, if 'creating' is the proper word to use as contrasted with 'interpreting'
the law?

2. Paragraph 5: Here is an example of civil law methodology: can you identify
the *ratio juris* on which the court will build its reasoning from now on?

3. Paragraph 5: There is a reason why the court is referring to a series of Code
articles. That reason can be found in the *ratio legis* of the different sets of articles. Do you see any connection between these sets of articles?

4. Paragraph 6: Where do you place a moral obligation in the Louisiana Civil
Code?

5. Paragraph 6: Considering that this case long preceded the revision of the Law
of Obligations in 1984–1985, why should the defendant argue that the 1870 version of Louisiana Civil Code article 1758 is 'exclusive'?

6. Paragraph 9: What is the Court actually saying in the beginning of the first
sentence of this paragraph, and why do you think the Court is making this
statement? Could you relate the court's statements in this paragraph to a type
or kind of source of law mentioned in articles 1 to 4 in the Louisiana Civil
Code? Is the Court resorting to an *in pari materia* reasoning (La. Civ. Code
art. 13)? Do you see any *a pari ratione* reasoning?

Succession of Emanuel Harrison

Supreme Court of Louisiana
January 16, 1984
444 So.2d 1191

MARCUS, Justice.

[1] Emanuel Harrison died on February 17, 1960 without issue. He was survived
by his second wife, Aria Day Harrison, and by his legal heirs: a sister (Ida Harrison
Knox), a brother (Daniel Harrison), ten children of a predeceased brother, Minor
Harrison, and three children of a predeceased sister, Ada Harrison George. Emanuel Harrison was also survived by his foster son, John D. Harrison, whom he never
legally adopted.

[2] A few days after Emanuel's death, John D. Harrison found, in the glove com-
partment of Emanuel's car, a document which appeared to be Emanuel's will. The
document was entirely written, dated and signed in the handwriting of someone

other than Emanuel Harrison,[1] then was signed at the bottom in pencil by Emanuel Harrison. The document provided as follows:

Liberty, Miss.

Dec. 15, 1955

I, Emanuel Harrison, of East Feliciana Parish Louisiana, do make this my last will and testament, revoking all others, namely:

(1) I want all my just debts paid;

(2) I give and bequeath my 100 acres in East Feliciana Parish to John D. Harrison and his children;

(3) I also give and bequeath lot # 12 in sq. # 2 of North Baton Rouge to John D. Harrison and his children

(4) I futher [sic] give and bequeath 1/2 of all my personal property to John D. Harrison and his children.

Thus written, dated and signed in my own handwriting, at Liberty, Miss. Rt. ### 2, in East Feliciana, State of Louisiana, on this the 15 day of Dec. 1955.

Emanuel Harrison

[3] John D. Harrison brought this will to his attorney and was told that the will was invalid. However, the attorney drew up an instrument whereby Emanuel's legal heirs could confirm the donations made in the invalid will. Within a month of Emanuel's death, John D. Harrison obtained the signatures of twelve of the fifteen intestate heirs on the instrument. On February 11, 1972, one more heir (Ada Harrison Johnson) added her signature when John D. Harrison purchased her interest in Emanuel's succession. The instrument provided as follows:

March 21, 1960

The undersigned presumptive heirs of Emanuel Harrison, deceased, are fully aware of the contents of a purported last will and testament made by Emanuel Harrison dated December 15, 1955; that same is not in the handwriting of Emanuel Harrison, but was signed by him and represents his wishes with regard to his estate. We, therefore, desire that the Court give full effect to said will as though it was fully written, dated and signed by Emanuel Harrison as his legal will and testament, in consideration of the fact that John Harrison looked after him as his own child.

Aline George	Annie Belle H. Wallace
Thelma G. Payne	Catherine H. Vernon
Wilbert George	E. M. Harrison

---

1. John D. Harrison testified at trial that the handwriting was that of William Kline, Emanuel's attorney.

Cheles Price Harrison	His
James Harrison	Bro. Daniel X Harrison
(Sister) Ida Knox	Ada Harrison Johnson
Viola H. Faulkner	Feb. 11
Benjamin F. Harrison	72

[. . . .]

[4] The issues presented for our consideration are whether a natural obligation on the part of the legal heirs of Emanuel Harrison arose from the invalid will and, if so, did the March 21, 1960 instrument have the effect of discharging that obligation.

[5] The December 15, 1955 document clearly is invalid as the will of Emanuel Harrison because it fails to meet any of the forms for wills recognized under Louisiana law. The document does not qualify as an olographic will because such a will must be entirely written, dated and signed by the hand of the testator. La.Civ.Code art. 1588. Except for testator's own signature at the end of the will, the document in question was entirely written in the hand of another. Nor does the document meet any of the other forms for testaments in Louisiana.[4]

[6] However, this invalid will does create a natural obligation on the part of the intestate heirs of Emanuel Harrison under La.Civ.Code art. 1758 which provides:

Natural obligations are of four kinds:

1. Such obligations as the law has rendered invalid for the want of certain forms or for some reason of general policy, but which are not in themselves immoral or unjust.

2. Such as are made by persons having the discretion necessary to enable them to contract, but who are yet rendered incapable of doing so by some provision of law.

3. When the action is barred by prescription, a natural obligation still subsists, although the civil obligation is extinguished.

4. There is also a natural obligation on those who inherit an estate, either under a will or by legal inheritance, to execute the donations or other dispositions which the former owner had made, but which are defective for want of form only.

[7] Strictly applying the language of this code article, we find that the natural obligation of the heirs of Emanuel Harrison fits precisely into section four of the article. First, the heirs clearly fall into the category of "those who inherit an estate . . . by legal inheritance." Next, we find that the invalid will constituted a donation "which the former owner had made." Edward Knox contends that there is

---

4. The will is also invalid as a holographic will under the laws of the State of Mississippi, the place of execution according to the heading of the will. Miss.Code Ann. § 91-5-1 (Supp.1983).

doubt as to whether Emanuel Harrison believed or intended the prepared form to be his will. However, we believe that the record supports the trial judge's finding of fact that Emanuel Harrison "attempted to make a will" which "was intended to be valid pursuant to the rules on olographic wills." Therefore, we concur in the trial judge's finding and reject Knox's contention that Emanuel may not have made the will.

[8] Finally, article 1758(4) requires that the decedent's donation be "defective for want of form only." This element is also met by Emanuel Harrison's will. It contains no prohibited donations or any other substantive defects; it is invalid merely because it fails to satisfy the requirements of testamentary form. Knox argues that the formal invalidity is so severe that it amounts to a substantive defect. This argument is without merit; the defectiveness of the will in question is plainly one of form only no matter how severe the formal deficiencies.

[9] Hence, we hold that Emanuel Harrison's legal heirs have a natural obligation to execute the donations made in his will. This holding is consistent with the result reached by this court on rehearing in *Breaux v. Breaux,* 218 La. 795, 51 So.2d 73 (1951), in which we found a natural obligation on the part of a legatee to carry out the disposition made in an invalid oral will even though that disposition constituted a *fidei commissum.*

[10] A natural obligation, although it cannot be legally enforced, does have certain legal effects. La.Civ.Code art. 1759 provides:

Although natural obligations can not be enforced by action, they have the following effect[s]:

1. No suit will lie to recover what has been paid, or given in compliance with a natural obligation.

2. A natural obligation is a sufficient consideration for a new contract.

[11] The natural obligation of Emanuel Harrison's heirs acted as the cause for a new contract. That new contract was the March 21, 1960 instrument.

[12] This court must now determine the effect of that instrument. A new contract for which a natural obligation acts as "consideration" cannot be fitted into any one accepted legal category and should not be subject to any particular form. The juridical act may embody any contractual obligation the obligor sees fit. Martin, *Natural Obligations,* 15 Tul.L.Rev. 497, 511–12, 515 (1941). To discern the intended effect of the instrument, we will first look to its actual terms. The document asks that "the Court give full effect to said will." Knox argues that, since the instrument contains no language translative of title, it cannot be given the effect of transferring to John D. Harrison any interest in the succession of Emanuel Harrison. Instead, Knox urges, the instrument requests the court to probate an invalid will, an act which does not transfer title in the land to John D. Harrison. We reject this construction of the contract. The Louisiana Civil Code provides the following rule for interpretation of contracts: When there is anything doubtful in agreements, we must endeavor to ascertain what was the common intention of the parties, rather than to adhere to

the literal sense of the terms. La.Civ.Code art. 1950. *See also* art. 1945(2). We find that the clear intent of the thirteen heirs who signed the instrument was to discharge their natural obligation and carry into effect the dispositions made in the will. Accordingly, we hold that the effect of the March 21, 1960 instrument was to transfer to John D. Harrison and his children[5] the interests of the thirteen heirs[6] who signed the instrument in the property bequeathed in the will to John D. Harrison and his children. Hence, we will remand the case to the district court with instructions to the trial judge to recognize John D. Harrison and his children as transferees of the signing heirs' interests in the property and to place them into possession thereof and to close the succession.

[. . . .]

WATSON, Justice, dissenting.

[13] The majority creates a new method of transmitting property in Louisiana, that is, ordering probate of an invalid will. The instrument of March 21, 1960, is not a donation. LSA-C.C. art. 1536. If it were a donation, then the natural obligation brought about by the will, which is invalid because of a deficiency of form, would constitute *cause* for the donation and it could not be attacked or set aside for lacking cause. The act is certainly not a sale; in fact, it is a creature unknown to the law. Owners of property — who under the principle of *le mort saisit le vif* became owners the instant their ancestor died are held to transfer land by signing an instrument which asks the court to honor an invalid will. Here, the court is leap-frogging in the guise of pursuing the spirit of the 1960 instrument and ordering transfer of the property to John D. Harrison by a device not found in the Louisiana Civil Code.

[14] Therefore, I respectfully dissent.

Questions

1. Paragraph 3: Can you explain why all of these statements on and about Emanuel Harrison might be relevant as regards the existence or not of a natural obligation? What about the statements regarding John Harrison?

2. Paragraph 6: Compare La. Civ. Code art. 1758 (Code of 1870) with La. Civ. art. 1762 (current Code). Is the letter of those two articles supported by the same

---

5. Edward Knox, in brief to this court, specified as error the appeals court's decision that "apparently gave all of the signing heirs' portion of the property to John D. Harrison when the 'purported will' . . . bequeathed certain specified items [of] the decedent's property to John D. Harrison *and his children*." [Emphasis in original.] The appeals court held "the [March 21, 1960] instrument and the transfers made thereby to be legally valid and enforceable." We construe that language to uphold the instrument as written, which enacts the bequests in the will to John D. Harrison and his children. Hence, the appeals court's holding does not omit the children and is without error in this regard.

6. However, Ada Harrison Johnson's entire interest in the succession was transferred to John Harrison in the February 11, 1972 sale of that interest.

lawful reason (or *ratio legis*)? Can paragraph 9 help in identifying that reason? Are there reasons of form and substance vying with each other?

3. Paragraph 12: Notice the phrase "juridical act." What does that phrase mean? *See* La. Civ. Code art. 395 and La. Civ. Code art. 3471. What do the first four lines of this paragraph suggest about the law of contract at civil law and the court's task or responsibility to properly identify and classify a contract? What would you say, now, about Justice Watson's referring to this "act . . . as a creature unknown to the law"? What do you think that form can add to a juridical act?

State of Louisiana
v.
Allan L. Placke, et al.

Court of Appeal of Louisiana
Second Circuit
May 9, 2001
786 So.2d 889

PEATROSS, J.

[. . . .]

Facts and Procedural Background

[1] Timothy (now deceased) and Claudia Sue Conerly ("Conerlys") sued E.A. Conway Memorial Hospital (referred to herein as the "State"), a state-owned medical institution, for damages for injuries sustained by their infant daughter, Christina, during and immediately prior to her birth. After trial of the medical malpractice claim, the State was found solely liable for Christina's "catastrophic" injuries;[1] and, in its opinion, the trial court stated that actual damages were $3,041,833.75, with legal interest due from date of judicial demand until paid. This amount was then reduced to a single award of $500,000, exclusive of custodial care and interest, due to the statutory cap on recoveries in medical malpractice cases under La. R.S. 40:1299.39.

---

1. Ms. Conerly was pregnant and at full term with Christina, her sixth child, when she began hemorrhaging and was rushed to E.A. Conway Memorial Hospital. She was left unattended from her arrival at 11:15 p.m. until 6:00 a.m. the following morning. When she was examined, the baby was in fetal distress and it was determined that an emergency C-section was necessary. Rather than performing the section immediately, however, the doctors started her on a pitocin drip, which is a drug used to induce labor. Approximately an hour and a half later, the C-section was performed. Christina was born alive, but in poor condition. She suffered severe brain damage, seizure disorders, right-sided tension pneumothorax, chronic renal failure, microcephaly and other complications due to a lack of oxygen prior to birth. Christina lived to age five, at which time she weighed only 30 pounds. She could not feed herself, use the bathroom, hold her head up or sit unaided or make any sound other than to cry or coo. She had seizures, wore braces on her legs and underwent hip surgery. She died from aspirating vomit because she was unable to roll herself over. Ms. Conerly took care of Christina on a daily basis and tried to give her some quality of life.

On appeal, this court affirmed on the issue of liability, but held that each plaintiff's claim was distinct and subject to separate caps. *Timothy Conerly, et al., v. State of Louisiana, et al.,* 29,236 (La.App.2d Cir.3/3/97), 690 So.2d 980, *writ denied,* 97-0804 (La.3/13/98), 712 So.2d 864, *writ granted,* 97-0871 (La.3/13/98), 712 So.2d 859, *and rev'd by, Timothy Conerly, et al., v. State of Louisiana, et al.,* 97-0871 (La.7/8/98), 714 So.2d 709. The supreme court reversed on the cap issue alone, applying a single cap (liability and amount of damages affirmed). *Timothy Conerly, et al., v. State of Louisiana, et al., supra.*

[. . . .]

[2] On receipt of the incorrect check, Ms. Conerly's attorney disbursed the proceeds to her and filed the Satisfaction of Judgment into the record.[2] Subsequently, the State discovered that it had paid more than the amount judicially enforceable against it by statute. As previously stated, the State brought the present action to recover the amount it had overpaid and the parties filed cross motions for summary judgment. The trial court granted the State's motion and denied Defendants' motion, finding that the State was entitled to return of the overpayment because it lacked the "capacity to feel the sort of strong moral duty or duty of conscience that is required to create a natural obligation." The trial court further found that both attorneys, the law firm and Ms. Conerly were jointly and severally liable for return of the overpayment. Finally, finding that the attorneys did not act in bad faith in retaining the funds, despite their knowledge of the overpayment, the trial court required that they pay interest from the date of judgment only, rather than from the date of judicial demand. Defendants appeal and the State has answered the appeal requesting additional interest under La. C.C. art. 2303.

Discussion

[. . . .]

Natural Obligation

[3] The first inquiry in determining whether a natural obligation exists on the part of the State in the case *sub judice* is to decide if, in fact, a juridical person such as the State of Louisiana can *ever* satisfy the requirements of a natural obligation. In answering this question, we begin with the premise that no Louisiana court has ever found a juridical person to be the obligor of a natural obligation.[3] Our analysis,

---

2. The State also notes that the disbursement statement indicates deductions for attorney fees in the amount of $632,401.92 (1/3 of $1,897,205.77) and $40,000 for case costs.

3. Defendants rely on *Muse v. St. Paul Fire and Marine Insurance Company,* 328 So.2d 698 (La. App. 1st Cir.1976), in support of the proposition that feelings sufficient to support a natural obligation are imputed onto the State. Defendants misinterpret the holding of *Muse.* In *Muse,* the court determined that, while a charity hospital does not have an action for payment of medical services rendered to an indigent, the indigent, nonetheless, owes a natural obligation to the charity hospital for payment of medical services rendered. There was no finding in *Muse* regarding whether the State is capable of feeling the requisite moral duty required to owe a natural obligation.

therefore, begins with the treatises on the origin and development of the law on natural obligations. After an exhaustive review of the literature, we conclude that a juridical person such as the State of Louisiana is incapable of forming the conscious moral feeling required to have a natural obligation.

[4] The Civil Code articles on natural obligations are as follows:

Art. 1760. Moral duties that may give rise to a natural obligation.

A natural obligation arises from circumstances in which the law implies a particular moral duty to render a performance.

Art. 1761. Effects of a natural obligation.

A natural obligation is not enforceable by judicial action. Nevertheless, whatever has been freely performed in compliance with a natural obligation may not be reclaimed.

A contract made for the performance of a natural obligation is onerous.

Art. 1762. Examples of circumstances giving rise to a natural obligation.

Examples of circumstances giving rise to a natural obligation are:

(1) When a civil obligation has been extinguished by prescription or discharged in bankruptcy.

(2) When an obligation has been incurred by a person who, although endowed with discernment, lacks legal capacity.

(3) When the universal successors are not bound by a civil obligation to execute the donations and other dispositions made by a deceased person that are null for want of form.

[5] Nowhere in the Civil Code is the term "natural obligation" precisely defined and our courts have construed the listing of examples of such obligations as illustrative and not exclusive. *Gray v. McCormick*, 94-1282 (La.App. 3rd Cir.10/18/95), 663 So.2d 480; *Muse v. St. Paul Fire & Marine Insurance Company*, 328 So.2d 698 (La. App. 1st Cir.1976). The determination of whether a natural obligation exists, therefore, depends on the facts of each particular case.

[6] The concept of natural obligations subsumes the "reality" of a moral duty. Litvinoff, The Law of Obligations § 2.3, 5 Louisiana Civil Law Treatise (1992). In other words, there must exist a moral duty, described as a duty of conscience, in order for a natural obligation to arise. The moral duty is "the imperative feeling that something ought to be done or not done or given" and must be "so strongly felt by a person that his conscience will not be appeased unless he renders to another a certain performance." *Id.* Once such a duty is felt with such a compelling force, it becomes part of the "structure" of the natural obligation. *Id.*

[7] We do not believe that a juridical person such as the State of Louisiana is capable of feeling a moral compulsion so intense that it can only be appeased by

satisfaction of the duty.[4] The trial court was correct in concluding that the State of Louisiana is not capable of having a natural obligation.

[8] Assuming, *arguendo,* that there exist circumstances which would support a natural obligation on the part of a juridical person such as the State of Louisiana, such circumstances are not present in the undisputed facts of this case. Our courts have set forth four requirements which must be present in order for a duty to be considered a natural obligation:

(1) The moral duty must be felt towards a particular person, not all persons in general.

(2) The person involved feels so strongly about the moral duty that he truly feels he owes a debt.

(3) The duty can be fulfilled through rendering a performance whose object is of pecuniary value.

(4) A recognition of the obligation by the obligor must occur, either by performing the obligation or by promising to perform. This recognition brings the natural obligation into existence and makes it a civil obligation.

Litvinoff, §2.4; *Terrell v. Nanda,* 33,242 (La.App.2d Cir.5/10/00), 759 So.2d 1026; *Thomas v. Bryant,* 25,855 (La.App.2d Cir.6/22/94), 639 So.2d 378. All four requirements must exist to support a natural obligation. In the case *sub judice,* we find that at least the first two of these requirements have not been met. These two requirements provide the focus of our discussion and we begin with the second of the two requirements regarding the strength of the feeling of the moral duty by the alleged natural obligor, or, in this case, the State.

[9] Defendants argue that the trial court's focus on the subjective intent of the alleged natural obligor was incorrect. While we agree that it is not the sole criterion on which the finding of a natural obligation should be based, we do agree with the State that the intent of the alleged natural obligor is relevant to the determination of whether the alleged natural obligor felt the moral compulsion necessary to transform his moral duty into a natural obligation. In this regard, Litvinoff states that "the person's [alleged natural obligor's] belief in the existence of the moral duty is . . . as important as its reality. . . ." See also *Thomas v. Bryant, supra.* In the present case, the State has clearly expressed its intent not to have a moral duty to pay any judgment that exceeds $500,000. This intent was expressed by the State in the passage by the legislature of La. R.S. 40:1299.39, which contains the statutory cap on recovery in medical malpractice actions against the state. We can find no support in the record for the conclusion that the State experienced strong, forceful moral

---

4. There is also a question of whether or not the State's overpayment of the judgment may have constituted an *ultra vires* act, i.e., an act beyond the powers granted to the agency. In other words, we question whether the agency had the authority to pay more to Ms. Conerly than the amount for which the State was cast in judgment.

compulsion to pay Ms. Conerly an amount greater than it had decided to pay all other successful plaintiffs in medical malpractice cases.

[10] Defendants emphasize that voluntary payment of a natural obligation through error or mistake does not allow recovery of the payment. The Civil Code makes this clear.[5] This rule of law, however, is never reached if there is, in fact, no natural obligation in the first place; and, in order to find a natural obligation, as previously explained, there must exist a moral duty to pay. This is a separate and distinct inquiry from the later determination (after a natural obligation is found to exist between the two parties) of whether the erroneous payment was voluntary, although in error, and, thus, not recoverable. Litvinoff explains:

> If the conclusion is that no natural obligation arose from a certain situation, that is so because, for the lack of a clear object, the moral duty involved is not sufficiently precise to allow the court's conviction that it was the force that prompted the alleged debtor to act.

Litvinoff, § 2.6 at p. 36. Applying this logic to the present case, we conclude that a natural obligation did not arise from the trial court's assessment of actual damages in this case. This is so because there is no moral duty owing from the State to Ms. Conerly in particular that is "sufficiently precise" to support our conviction that it was the moral duty or compulsion on the part of the State which prompted the over-payment of the judgment. With no underlying natural obligation, the fact that the payment made to Ms. Conerly was made in error is irrelevant.

[11] The scenario in the case *sub judice* is different from the scenario envisioned by article 1761 and the principle that a payment on a natural obligation, even if made in error or by mistake, is not recoverable. The object of the "no recovery if paid in error" principle is to prevent a debtor who is bound by a natural obligation, i.e., feels a strong moral duty to pay a debt which is not enforceable against him, and makes payment on the debt, from later deciding that he wants the payment back. This is the situation which article 1761 is designed to prevent. See also Litvinoff, § 2.22 at p. 41.

[12] Litvinoff next explains that not every moral compulsion transforms into a natural obligation. The moral duty must be owed to a particular person and not to a class of persons in general. This is the basis for the first requirement. In the case *sub judice,* we believe it clear that, assuming the State owed a moral duty under the circumstances of this case, it would be a duty to the class of persons, generally, who are awarded actual damages in excess of the amount which the legislature has deemed can be judicially enforced against the State in a medical malpractice action. It would not be a moral duty felt by the State for the specific loss sustained by Ms. Conerly, or any other particular plaintiff.

---

5. Comment (b) to article 1761 states that "... this Article means that the performing party must have acted without outside compulsion by fraud or violence. It does not mean that his performance cannot have been induced by error. ..."

[13] Since we find that the first two requirements for the existence of a natural obligation are not met under the undisputed facts presented in this case, we conclude that the trial court correctly granted the State's motion for summary judgment. [. . . .]

[. . . .]

Questions

1. Read Louisiana Civil Code articles 2299–2305. Could some of these articles have been used by the court in this case? If you answered this question in the affirmative, would the State have recovered the same amount it paid in excess because of a mistake?

2. Paragraph 6: What do you think of these statements by the court: (1) "We do not believe that a juridical person such as the State of Louisiana is capable of feeling a moral compulsion;" (2) "The concept of natural obligation subsumes the 'reality' of a moral duty;" (3) "Assuming, arguendo, that there exist circumstances which would support a natural obligation on the part of a juridical person such as the State of Louisiana, such circumstances are not present in the undisputed facts of this case"?

3. Paragraph 8: What do you think of the court stating: "Our courts have set forth four requirements which must be present"? Shouldn't the requirements be set by the Code, as legislation? Since the courts' duty is to apply the law, is there not a danger created when courts "set forth" their own requirements? Is the court, in this case, relying too much on prior cases and doctrine (Professor Litvinoff), which are merely persuasive sources of law, and overlooking the law of the Code? Has the court carved an exception for the State out of Louisiana Civil Code article 24 and carried that exception over into "Natural Obligations" (La. Civ. Code arts. 1760–1762) when, in fact, no exception is made in the latter articles?

4. What lesson should be drawn from this case for individuals who have dealings with the State?

See also *Succession of Jones*, 505 So.2d 841 (La.App. 2 Cir. 1987).

Comparative Law Perspective
— Civil Law —
Marcel Planiol & Georges Ripert, *Traité Pratique de Droit Civil Français*

vol. 7, n° 979 at 314 & n° 982 at 316–18 (Paul Esmein rev., 2d ed. 1954)

979. Juridical foundation. The natural obligation incontestably constitutes a juridical anomaly. The lack of a sanction [for its enforcement], whatever efficacy it may have otherwise, places it at the extreme limit of the law and on the boundary of morality. [. . . .]

982. The theory of natural obligation founded on the duty of conscience. In the most diverse and the most certain cases of natural obligations (prescribed debt, annulment for incapacity, . . .), one finds a common element: the existence of a duty of conscience of the debtor toward the creditor. The natural obligation [. . .] is tied [. . .] to a moral duty in which the law recognizes a certain value up to the point of making of it an obligation deprived of the normal sanction, but without, however, adopting it fully. It is a rule of conscience that penetrates into the domain of the law while remaining yet at the law's frontier. [. . . .]

If there is a progressive assimilation of natural obligation and moral duty, there is, nonetheless, no complete concurrence between them. The separation of law from morality ought to be maintained. It follows that not every duty of conscience constitutes a natural obligation. [. . . .] Only those duties of conscience that are judged, at a given moment, by the legislature or the courts to be, at once, the most conformed to the general interest and the most [widely] acknowledged in the current general opinion of individuals are transformed into natural obligations. There are some moral obligations that are of such a nature that they are not and can never be clothed with any juridical efficacy whatsoever: the benefits that inspire thoughts of charity, of devotion, of love, even though these thoughts may be commanded by morality, can be analyzed in relation to the law only as liberalities. To the contrary, other moral obligations can, upon the refining of the public conscience, end up being recognized as natural obligations some day, even though they have not theretofore been so recognized.

Jacques Ghestin & Gilles Goubeaux, *Traité de Droit Civil: Introduction Générale*
n° 669 at 644 & n° 672 at 648 (3d ed. 1990)

A natural obligation is a moral duty that rises to the level of juridical life. The act of him who was held to this duty gives it access to the juridical world. The court must investigate the motives that led this person to act and must take into consideration whether he was inspired by the desire to accomplish his duty. Not every moral duty can be transformed into a civil obligation. But when the obligor himself recognizes the existence of the duty that weighs on him, it's a matter thereafter of helping him to accomplish this duty and also of protecting him against a return to immorality by maintaining the effects of the accomplished duty. The natural obligation [. . .] is born by the recognition by the obligor of his moral duty. Still, it's also necessary [. . .] that this duty be among those that the legislature or the courts judge to be the most imperious and the best conformed to the general interest.

Henri Mazeaud et al., *Leçons de Droit Civil: Introduction à l'Étude du Droit*
n° 362 at 473 (François Chabas rev., 10th ed. 1991)

But it is difficult to specify on what conditions a moral duty is called to the rank of natural obligation. Not every duty of conscience is a natural obligation. The perception remains that one who shows himself to be charitable does not accomplish a juridical obligation: he makes a liberality. Thus, a natural obligation presupposes in the person who accomplishes a duty of conscience an imperious sentiment that he *had* to submit himself to it, that he really was *indebted*, that he wanted to free himself from a veritable debt, and not to make a liberality. Pothier wrote: "One calls a natural obligation that which, *in the name of honor and of conscience*, obliges him who has contracted to the accomplishment of that which the contract contains."

It is necessary, then, that the person who performs consider himself to be bound.

Chapter 3

Heritable, Personal &
Real Obligations

Louisiana Sources of Law

Louisiana Civil Code

Art. 1763. Definition.

A real obligation is a duty correlative and incidental to a real right. (Acts 1984, No. 331, §1, eff. Jan. 1, 1985.)

Art. 1764. Effects of real obligation.

A real obligation is transferred to the universal or particular successor who acquires the movable or immovable thing to which the obligation is attached, without a special provision to that effect.

But a particular successor is not personally bound, unless he assumes the personal obligations of his transferor with respect to the thing, and he may liberate himself of the real obligation by abandoning the thing. (Acts 1984, No. 331, §1, eff. Jan. 1, 1985.)

Art. 1765. Heritable obligation.

An obligation is heritable when its performance may be enforced by a successor of the obligee or against a successor of the obligor.

Every obligation is deemed heritable as to all parties, except when the contrary results from the terms or from the nature of the contract.

A heritable obligation is also transferable between living persons. (Acts 1984, No. 331, §1, eff. Jan. 1, 1985.)

Art. 1766. Strictly personal obligation.

An obligation is strictly personal when its performance can be enforced only by the obligee, or only against the obligor.

When the performance requires the special skill or qualification of the obligor, the obligation is presumed to be strictly personal on the part of the obligor. All obligations to perform personal services are presumed to be strictly personal on the part of the obligor.

When the performance is intended for the benefit of the obligee exclusively, the obligation is strictly personal on the part of that obligee. (Acts 1984, No. 331, §1, eff. Jan. 1, 1985.)

Doctrine

Louisiana Law of Obligations in General, A Précis

Sections 2.1.1 to 2.1.2

On the basis of the Latin origin of this concept, LSA-C.C. **Art. 1763** defines a real obligation as a **"duty correlative and incidental to a real right."** [. . . .]

Thus a real obligation is an obligation, or a duty, owed to a person who can claim a performance because that person is the holder of a real right, i.e., a right to make a direct and immediate [fictitiously without the involvement of an intermediary person] use of a thing.

The greater or lesser use the holder of a real right can make of a thing suggests that a distinction be made between principal real rights and accessory real rights. [. . . .]

The effects of real obligations flow from two fundamental prerequisites: A) there can be no real obligation unless there is a thing in existence; B) the real obligation is transferred with the thing as its accessory. [. . . .]

The second type of obligations or rights are those held or owned by a person *vis-à-vis* another person. The creditor or holder of such an obligation holds a right *in personam,* a right against the person of the obligor who may be under an obligation to give, to do or not to do something. The nature of the performance owed by the obligor leads to draw a distinction between heritable obligations, on the one hand, and strictly personal obligations, on the other hand. [. . . .]

Every obligation is thus presumed to be heritable as to both parties which means that, being part of one's patrimony, an obligation can be transferred or passed on to one's heirs. This presumption, however, is rebuttable and can be defeated either by the terms of a contract or by the circumstances if they are such as to suggest that the nature of the legal relationship binding the parties dictates that one or both obligations are to be considered as strictly personal. (LSA-C.C. Art. 1766). [. . . .]

LSA-C.C. Art. 1766 defines a strictly personal obligation [. . .]. [. . . .]

An obligation which is classified as strictly personal is, therefore, an obligation which can be performed only by the obligor or exclusively for the benefit of the obligee-creditor. Such obligations are said to have been entered into *intuitus personae* or in contemplation of the person of either party or both of them.

Cases

Johnson

v.

Levy et al.

Supreme Court of Louisiana
January 7, 1907
43 So. 46

MONROE, J.

[1] Plaintiff alleges that in 1901 she became engaged to be married to Lazare Levy, and, whilst so engaged, was seduced by him; that he repeatedly promised to fulfill his engagement, but failed to keep his promises, and, on June 29, 1903, was put in default by formal demand, with which he refused to company; that, thereafter, plaintiff gave birth to a child, issue of her connection with said Levy, and, as a consequence of his refusal to marry her, is condemned to a life of social ostracism, disgrace, and poverty, and is injured and damaged in the sum of $20,000. She alleges that said Levy died on June 29, 1903, and that the three parties made defendants herein (who reside in the parish of Terrebonne), with six others (who reside elsewhere), brothers and sisters of decedent, have accepted his succession unconditionally, and are liable to her jointly, for the damages so sustained. Wherefore she prays for judgment against said defendants, each, for his virile share of the amount stated. [. . . .] When the case was called for trial plaintiff offered certain testimony in support of the allegations of her petition, whereupon 'counsel for defendants objected to the evidence, and to any and all other evidence to be offered on behalf of plaintiff, in support of the allegations of her petition, upon the grounds and for the reasons: First. The plaintiff sues for the breach of a marriage contract, and the same petition shows the death of the promisor, Lazare Levy, and an action instituted against his heirs. This being shown on the face of the petition, no cause of action lies against the heirs, since the action for breach of promise is an entirely personal action, and not heritable. Second. If it could be contended that the action of breach of promise of marriage can be instituted against the heirs of Lazare Levy for a recovery of pecuniary or specific damages to the person or property of the plaintiff in this case, there is no averment of damage to property, but a simple averment of damage to the feelings of the plaintiff herein, therefore * * * no evidence whatever is admissible to support the demand of the plaintiff.'

[2] The court having sustained this objection, counsel for plaintiff announced that it was 'impossible for them to proceed any further, inasmuch as they could not introduce any evidence to sustain the allegations of their petition,' and, after some discussion as to the proper course to be pursued, the court 'discharged the jury from any further consideration of the case, and ordered the plaintiff's demand dismissed, as in case of nonsuit,' and from the judgment so rendered, plaintiff has appealed.

Opinion.

[3] It has been argued here that, plaintiff having declined to proceed, the judgment appealed from is to be regarded as having dismissed the suit for want of prosecution. We are, however, of opinion that the dismissal of the suit was the logical and inevitable consequence of the exclusion of the testimony offered and to be offered, in support of plaintiff's demand, and that the appeal from the judgment of dismissal brings up that ruling for review.

[4] The obligation resulting from a marriage engagement, or promise of marriage, is personal, and not heritable, because no one but the obligee can enforce its performance, and it can be enforced against no one but the obligor. Civ. Code, art. 1996 et seq. The obligation to respond in damages for the breach of such contract springs from the contract itself, as one of the incidents of its obligations. Civ. Code, arts. 1763, 1930. Unless time be made of the essence of the contract, the obligor may comply with his obligation thereunder at any seasonable moment until he is put in default; from which it follows that, if the obligor die before compliance and before he is put in default, no action will lie to enforce compliance or to recover damages for noncompliance. In such case the obligation to respond in damages retains its status as a mere incident of the obligation to comply with the promise of marriage, and, as the principal obligation ceases to exist, its incidents cease likewise. The obligation to respond in damages may, however, lose its incidental character, and assume a new and independent form. Thus the obligee may obtain judgment against the obligor for the damages, in which event the judgment could be enforced against the heirs of the obligor should be die before satisfying the same; or the obligor may abandon his right to comply with his promise, and voluntarily bind himself to pay the damages resulting from his noncompliance, and the obligation thus assumed could be enforced against his heirs. Or (and we now come to the position of the plaintiff before the court), the right of the obligor to comply with his promise of marriage may be forfeited, and his liability for damages fixed, by certain legal proceedings. The law provides that a contract may be violated 'possively [*sic*] by not doing what was covenanted to be done, or not doing it at the time or in the manner stipulated or implied from the nature of the confract [*sic*].' Civ. Code, art. 1931. And that, in such case, 'damages are due from the time that the debtor has been put in default,' etc. Civ. Code, art. 1933. And specific provision is made as to manner of putting in default. Civ. Code, art. 1911 et seq. 'The object of the putting in default [this court has said] is to secure to the creditor his right to demand damages, or a dissolution of the contract, so that the debtor can no longer defeat this right by executing, or offering to execute the agreement. After the debtor has been put in mora, his offer to execute his engagment [*sic*] comes too late and cannot be listened to. 6 Toullier, 255.' *Moreau v. Chauvin et al.*, 8 Rob. 161; *Enders v. Gringras, Mulhaupt & Co.*, 38 La. Ann. 773; *Clover v. Gottlieb*, 50 La. Ann. 572, 23 South. 459. Plaintiff herein alleges that the promiser, Lazare Levy, was put in default; that is to say, that a demand was made upon him, as provided by law, to comply with his engagement to marry her; that he refused so to comply, and that she thereby sustained damages as set forth in

her petition, and these allegations are taken as true, for the purposes of the case as now presented.

[5] As a result of the putting in default, the obligation to marry, which could have been fulfilled by the obligor alone, became merged in the obligation to respond in damages for the nonfulfillment, since the right of the obligor to fulfill was thereby forfeited, and, considering the nature of the contract, specific performance could not have been enforced by the obligee. The obligation to respond in damages, from having been merely incidental to the other, became, therefore, the sole obligation left of the contract, and, being susceptible of fulfillment by another, as well as by the obligor, may be enforced against the heirs of the latter. In other words, the personal obligation, to marry, was resolved, by the putting in default, into the heritable obligation, to pay money, the amount of which may be determined by agreement, or suit.

[6] Counsel for defendant argue that the right of action here asserted has not survived for the reason that the damages claimed are alleged to have resulted from injury to the feelings of plaintiff, rather than to her person or property. But the law of this state affords no support for the argument. [. . . .]

[. . . .]

[7] For the reasons thus assigned, it is ordered, adjudged, and decreed that the judgment appealed from be annulled, avoided, and reversed, and this case remanded to the district court, to be there proceeded with according to law, and to the views expressed in this opinion; the costs of the appeal to be paid by the defendants, and all other costs to await the further action of the trial court.

Questions

1. Paragraph 1: According to the plaintiff, "she became engaged to be married to Lazare Levy. . . ." Where does engagement find its source if it creates an obligation? *See* La. Civ. Code arts. 1756–1757. What about Louisiana Civil Code articles 1 through 4? How does engagement fit under Louisiana Civil Code articles 1906 through 1908? What about Louisiana Civil Code articles 1914 and 1915?

2. Paragraph 4: Explain why, in your opinion, a marriage engagement or promise of marriage creates a personal and not heritable obligation. How important do you think it is that "no one but the obligee can enforce its performance and it can be enforced against no one but the obligor"? If the obligation itself, because of its personal nature, cannot be enforced, do you think it would be lawful, fair, or equitable to consider the existence of an alternative obligation as a substitute for the promise of marriage, which is personal?

3. Paragraph 4: Read Louisiana Civil Code articles 1989–1993 on "Putting in default." Do you give these articles the same meaning as the court gave? Do you read anywhere in those articles that an obligor has until he is put in default to "comply with his obligation," but that beyond a putting in default, an obligor

can no longer carry out his principal obligation and must now pay "compensatory damages"? Isn't the first sentence of Louisiana Civil Code article 1989 actually saying that an obligation can be performed after the obligor has been put in default? Under Louisiana Civil Code article 1991, why would an obligee put his obligor in default and request performance if such performance were no longer possible according to the Court in *Johnson v. Levy*? How much did the death of the promisor, Lazare Levy, weigh, if at all, in the opinion of the Court? Could you use Louisiana Civil Code articles 1873, 1875, and 1876 with some success? Do you think the fact that the plaintiff gave birth to a child had any bearing on the court's legal analysis and, ultimately, its decision?

4. Paragraph 5: What impact did the putting in default have on the nature or kind of obligation created by the promise of marriage or engagement? Should a 'putting in default' have this impact on all personal obligations? What if one promised another that he would divorce his or her spouse and then failed to do so? In that situation, could the promisee put the promisor in default and seek damages?

Bogart
v.
Caldwell

Court of Appeal of Louisiana
Second Circuit
April 30, 1953
66 So.2d 629

GLADNEY, Judge.

[. . . .]

[1] Appellant [**Fannye Mae Bogart**] is the widow of Harry Dalton Bogart, Jr., who died intestate on October 1, 1951. During the existence of the community between appellant and her late husband, the latter purchased from defendant the property known as the Strand Theater in Farmerville, paying as consideration therefor $60,000 of which $30,000 was paid in cash and the remainder payable in monthly installments. The act of sale was authentic in form and contained stipulations which gave rise to the issues that must be determined.

[. . . .]

[2] From the date of its purchase the Strand Theater has been in continuous operation, first by Bogart, and, after his death by his widow. The entire ownership of said property is presently in appellant, she having acquired the one-half interest that became part of the Henry D. Bogart, Jr. estate by reason of inheritance from her husband and through purchase from the decedent's father and mother of the interest inherited by them, decedent being without issue. Appellant, of course, as a partner of the community with her husband, owned a one-half interest in said theater in her

own right after June 30, 1951. On January 30, 1952, after being informed defendant was preparing to commence the operation of a motion picture show business in the Union Theater building in Farmerville, appellant, through her attorney, wrote defendant a letter calling to his attention provisions in the contract between him and her deceased husband, wherein it was agreed Caldwell would not open a motion picture theater in said building, and warning him she would take legal action to prevent him from doing so. The defendant, however, did on March 2, 1952, open and commence the operation of a picture show business in the Union Theater building and the operation thereof by defendant is, we presume, presently continuing. Because of this, this lawsuit was filed.

[. . . .]

[3] The defense urged is fully stated in the answer wherein it is urged that the agreement of defendant and Harry Dalton Bogart, Jr. was that defendant's use of the Union Theater building should be restricted only so long as the said Harry Dalton Bogart, Jr. should himself own the Strand Theater building and that such restrictions should terminate when the said Harry Dalton Bogart, Jr. ceased to own the Strand Theater, whether such cessation of ownership by Harry Dalton Bogart, Jr. was by sale, death or in any other manner. Appellant insists, on the other hand, that Caldwell's obligation was not one strictly personal, — that it was heritable, and inured to the benefit of the widow and heirs of Harry Dalton Bogart, Jr.

[. . . .]

[4] To be found in the act of sale between Bogart and Caldwell are the following provisions:

'The parties hereto agree that this vendor, John L. Caldwell, is the owner of another theater building in the Town of Farmerville, Louisiana, known as the Union Theater, and, as a part of the moving consideration for this sale, it is agreed that this vendor will not open or operate another moving picture show or theater in said building.

'The parties hereto agree that the agreement contained herein with reference to the operation or non-operation of a picture show in the Union Theater building by the vendor herein, shall be binding for so long as this vendee owns the property herein conveyed to him, but shall terminate in the event said vendee sells the property.'

[5] The provisions plainly imply the vendor would not open or operate another motion picture theater in the Union Theater building so long as the vendee should own the property conveyed to him, and that Caldwell's obligation would terminate in the event the vendee should sell the property. However, the latter proviso is of no consequence since defendant has admitted in his answer Bogart during his lifetime did not sell the Strand Theater. The legal issue is thus narrowed to a resolution of the question whether the death of Bogart resulted in a cessation of his ownership, and the termination of the obligation.

[6] Defendant's covenant was an obligation not to do. The contract of which the condition forms a part is, like all others, complete by the assent of the parties; the obligee has a right of which the obligor cannot deprive him and its exercise is only suspended, or may be defeated according to the nature of the condition. This right is heritable, if it is not one of those that result from an obligation designated in law as a personal one. Articles 2028, 2029, LSA:Civil Code. An obligation is strictly personal when none but the obligee can enforce its performance, or when it can be enforced only against the obligor. It is presumed to be personal as to the obligee in a contract to do or to give, when that which is to be done or given is exclusively for the personal gratification of obligee, and could produce no benefit to his heirs. Articles 1997, 2201 LSA:Civil Code. The nature and effect of a personal obligation is further explained in *Ferguson v. Thomas*, 3 Mart., N.S., 75, at pages 80, 81:

> 'The general rule is that all the obligations of the ancestor pass to his heirs, active as well as passive. The exceptions to this rule are those obligations, which result from agreements, in which the personal qualities of the person promising are to be supposed the leading motive of the contract, and where the want of them cannot be supplied by any other, or compensated by pecuniary damages. Such is the confidence we repose in our physician, who assists us in sickness; the painter whom we may desire to make family portraits; and in case of their decease, their heirs cannot demand that they shall be permitted to supply their place or perform their contract. But an engagement to ship cotton may be performed by any one, the qualities of mind are not the leading consideration that induced the contract. Pecuniary responsibility is the moving cause, because the nonperformance can be compensated in damages and no objection can be made to the heirs, on that score, where they are the creditors of the person whose engagement they seek to enforce.'

[6] The heritable obligation is one from which there arises the right of the heirs and assigns of one party to enforce the performance against the heirs of the others. Heritable obligations and stipulations give to and impose upon heirs, assigns and other representatives the same duties and rights that the original parties had and were liable to, except that beneficiary heirs can only be liable to the amount of the succession. Every obligation shall be deemed to be heritable as to both parties, unless the contrary be specially expressed or necessarily implied from the nature of the contract. Articles 1997, 2008, LSA:Civil Code.

[7] Manifestly, the obligation not to operate a competitive picture theater can by no stretching of the imagination be said to exist for the personal gratification of the obligee and it is productive of financial benefit to the heirs of the obligee. It is not the sort of personal obligation that ends with the death of the obligee. It is a heritable obligation the right to which is enforceable by the heirs of the obligee.

[8] In the confection of the act of sale there was inserted a provision the vendee was purchasing with his separate and paraphernal funds. This statement is refuted by other provisions in the act of sale, that is to say the vendee is declared to be living

with his wife, and that half of the consideration was to be paid under terms of credit. The funds used, therefore, were not obtained from the separate property of Bogart. Counsel for the defendant concede that the property acquired entered the community of acquets and gains, but they argue that the clause is material as evidence of limitation upon the obligation of Caldwell as existing only for Bogart and not for his wife or his heirs. The argument, we think, is untenable. Though there was a brief separation between appellant and her husband prior to the execution of the deed, the inference is not warranted that he intended to use this means to circumscribe his property rights to the disadvantage of his heirs upon his own death. It is conceivable that the non-operation of a rival motion picture show in a town of the size of Farmerville could make the difference between profit and loss in the operation of the Strand Theater. Caldwell in first offering the Strand Theater for sale to Bogart realized this and himself proposed that if Bogart purchased one of the shows owned by him, he would not keep the other open.

[9] The codal provisions heretofore referred to clearly show the subject obligation was not strictly a personal obligation that ceased upon the death of the obligee, but being a heritable obligation it continued in existence under the ownership of Bogart's surviving widow.

[10] Where, as in this instance, the obligation be not to do, the obligee may demand the obligor be restrained from doing anything in contravention of it in cases where he proves an attempt to do the act covenanted against. Article 1929, LSA:Civil Code. *Algiers Ry. & Lighting Company v. New Orleans Ry. & Lighting Company*, 1915, 137 La. 579, 595, 68 So. 960, 962. In the latter case it was said:

> 'Plaintiff bases its suit for injunction to prevent the defendant from doing an act which it contends may be injurious to it (plaintiff) or impair a right which it claims. And it argues that the respondent judge had no discretion in the matter, and should have issued a preliminary injunction when applied for by it, and supports its argument by reference to article 1929, C.C., which reads:

> "If the obligation be not to do, the obligee may also demand that the obligor be restrained from doing anything in contravention of it, in cases where he proves an attempt to do the act covenanted against."

> 'The foregoing article explicitly states the law with reference to obligations 'not to do'; that a remedy by injunction will lie; and in the case of *Levine v. Michel*, 35 La.Ann. 1121 (1127), we hold it to be the legal duty of the obligor to comply with the terms of the contract, and the legal right of the obligee to exact compliance; in other words, the obligee may enforce a contract not to do by specific performance. And that a violation of said contract is injurious to plaintiff and impairs a right which he claims, and is therefore a proper subject for injunction, within the very terms of article 296, C.P.'

[11] Plaintiff's reservation of her right to sue defendant for damages already suffered is proper.

[**12**] For the foregoing reasons the judgment is in error. It is, therefore, ordered, adjudged and decreed that the judgment from which appealed is avoided, annulled and reversed, and it is ordered that there be judgment in favor of plaintiff, Mrs. Fannye Mae Bogart and against the defendant, John L. Caldwell, Sr., permanently enjoining, restraining and prohibiting said defendant from the further operation of a moving picture show or theater in the Union Theater building located in the Town of Farmerville, Louisiana.

[**13**] It is further ordered that plaintiff's right to sue defendant for all damages suffered by her as a result of defendant's opening and operation of a picture show in the Union Theater building be reserved.

[**14**] It is further ordered that defendant, appellee, pay all costs incurred in this suit, including costs of the appeal.

Questions

1. Paragraphs 1–14: What was the obligation 'not to do' created in the contract between Harry Bogart and John Caldwell? Could such an obligation not to do be personal? Heritable? Why is the selection of the proper nature of the obligation not to do important?

2. Paragraph 3: Why is the defendant arguing that his obligation was restricted to Harry Bogart? To what kind of obligation is the defendant referring? Explain how the plaintiff, Fannye Mae Bogart, can make the argument that Caldwell's obligation to her husband was not strictly personal. Does the Louisiana Civil Code provide for a presumption regarding the nature of an obligation? *See* La. Civ. Code art. 1765. Which party in this case could rely on the benefit of such a presumption? What procedural consequence(s) would such a presumption have?

3. Paragraph 4: How do you read the second provision of the contract with respect to the kind of obligation that was to be created? Do the phrases "this vendee" or "said vendee" have any legal meaning? What if, instead of selling the theater, the vendee, Harry Bogart, had created a mortgage on the theater? *See* La. Civ. Code arts. 3278–3337. What about a usufruct? *See* La. Civ. Code arts. 535–629. Under either of those situations, would the vendor, Caldwell, be relieved of his obligation not to open his own theater?

4. Paragraph 8: What would be a legal effect of the theater "having entered the community of acquets and gains" resulting from the marriage of Harry and Mae Bogart? *See* La. Civ. Code arts. 2334–2369.8.

5. Assume that Harry Bogart is alive and that Caldwell, in turn, wants to sell his own theater to a third party. Can he do that or not? Explain. What if Caldwell had actually sold his theater to a third person? Could Bogart then go against the third person and prevent him or her from operating the theater he or she purchased from Caldwell? Be sure to properly identify, for the benefit of Bogart, the kind of obligation on which he should base his argument. What

if Caldwell had died before Harry Bogart: would Caldwell's heirs be bound by Caldwell's obligation to not open his theater so long as Bogart owned his theater?

St. Jude Medical Office Building Limited Partnership
·
v.
City Glass and Mirror, Inc., et al.

Supreme Court of Louisiana
May 24, 1993
619 So.2d 529

WATSON, Justice.

[....]

Facts

[1] In 1983, the St. Jude Medical Office Building Limited Partnership contracted with Spaw Glass, Inc. for construction of the St. Jude Medical Office Building, a seven-story medical office and retail complex in Kenner, Louisiana. Spaw Glass contracted with various sub-contractors. The building was completed in February of 1985. Approximately two months later, the Partnership applied to Travelers for permanent financing. On October 10, 1985, Travelers advanced $25 million on the Partnership's promissory note. The note was secured primarily by a real and chattel mortgage on the building, the underlying property, and all related land and improvements. The note and mortgage contained *in rem* language limiting Travelers' default remedy to judicial sale of the property.

[2] After closing the loan with Travelers, the Partnership discovered defects in the building's construction, including water leakage through the second floor windows, leakage through the building's skylights and ground settling damage to the sidewalks and driveways. The Partnership asked Spaw Glass and the sub-contractors to voluntarily repair their allegedly defective work. The requested repairs were never performed. At an impasse, the Partnership filed suit against Spaw Glass and the sub-contractors in February of 1988.

Facts

[3] In its original and amended petitions, the Partnership alleged that defects in the materials and workmanship of the building breached express and implied warranties of the contractor and several sub-contractors. Damages were estimated at $10 million.

original petition

[4] In March of 1990, the Partnership defaulted on its note. On June 1, 1990, Travelers filed suit in the United States District Court for the Eastern District of Louisiana. Among other relief, Travelers requested recognition of its *in rem* mortgage on the building, a judgment for the amount due on the note, and seizure and sale of the building. On November 24, 1990, the federal court entered a partial final judgment in favor of Travelers, recognizing its mortgage and awarding damages of approximately $26 million. Travelers executed on the judgment with a writ of fieri facias

P. H

directing the marshal to seize and sell the building. Travelers acquired the building at a judicial sale on October 18, 1991, for $7.5 million.

[5] [**In 1991, Travelers intervened in the Partnership's state court lawsuit against the building's contractor and subcontractors,**] alleging that it was subrogated to the Partnership's claims for construction breaches of express and implied warranties. The Partnership and several of the defendants filed exceptions of no cause of action and no right of action. The trial court sustained both exceptions and dismissed Travelers' petition with prejudice. In a well-reasoned opinion, the court of appeal affirmed the trial court judgment. 608 So.2d 236 (La.App. 5th Cir.1992). A writ was granted to review the court of appeal judgment. 613 So.2d 959 (La.1993).

Law and Analysis

[. . . .]

[6] The general Louisiana rule is that a purchaser cannot recover from a third party for property damage inflicted prior to the sale. *Prados v. South Central Bell Telephone Company,* 329 So.2d 744, 750 (La.1976); *Gumbel v. New Orleans Terminal Co.,* 197 La. 439, 1 So.2d 686 (1941); *Taylor v. New Orleans Terminal Co.,* 126 La. 420, 52 So. 562 (1910); *McCutchen v. Texas & P. Ry. Co.,* 118 La. 436, 43 So. 42 (1907); *Bradford v. Richard, et al.,* 46 La.Ann. 1530, 16 So. 487 (1894); *Clark v. Warner & Co.,* 6 La.Ann. 408 (La.1851).

[7] Travelers relies on the decision in *Aizpurua v. Crane Pool Co., Inc.* 449 So.2d 471 (La.1984), for its right to intervene in the Partnership's suit. In *Aizpurua,* the purchasers of a residence brought suit against the company that had constructed a swimming pool on the property prior to plaintiffs' purchase. At that time, LSA-C.C. art. 2011 provided:

[8] Not only the obligation, but the right resulting from a contract relative to immovable property, passes with the property. Thus, the right of servitude in favor of immovable property, passes with it, *and thus also the heir or other acquirer will have the right to enforce a contract made for the improvement of the property by the person from whom he acquired it.* (Emphasis added.)

[9] Relying on LSA-C.C. art. 2011, now repealed, *Aizpurua* decided that a subsequent purchaser was subrogated to the implied warranty of materials and workmanship in a building contract. Despite lack of privity, the purchaser of immovable property was allowed to enforce a property improvement contract made by the previous owner.

[10] In 1984, LSA-C.C. art. 2011 was repealed and was replaced by LSA-C.C. art. 1764. LSA-C.C. art. 1764 now provides:

A real obligation is transferred to the universal or particular successor who acquires the movable or immovable thing to which the obligation is attached, without a special provision to that effect.

But a particular successor is not personally bound, unless he assumes the personal obligations of his transferor with respect to the thing, and he may liberate himself of the real obligation by abandoning the thing.

[11] Official Comment (D) to this article states that Civil Code Article 2011 (1870) was suppressed because its provisions were conceptually inconsistent with other provisions of Louisiana law. It was, of course, in derogation of the general rule of non-recovery.

[12] *Aizpurua* was based on the now repealed provisions of LSA-C.C. art. 2011. The substantive changes made by LSA-C.C. art. 1764 have superceded *Aizpurua*. Travelers cannot rely on *Aizpurua*. In addition, important distinctions exist between the facts in *Aizpurua* and those in this case. In *Aizpurua*, plaintiffs purchased their residence by a conventional sale and the alleged defects in the pool's construction were hidden from them at the time of the sale. Here, Travelers purchased the building at a judicial sale and knew of the defects in the building. Under LSA-C.C. arts. 2537 and 2619, Travelers would have had no redhibition claim for hidden defects because the property was purchased at judicial sale.

[13] Applying LSA-C.C. art. 1764 to the facts of this case, the central issue is whether an action for defective construction of a building is based on a real or a personal obligation. *issue*

[14] Official Comment (f) to LSA-C.C. art. 1764 provides in pertinent part:

> Louisiana courts have held that ... damages due to the owner of a thing for its partial destruction or for an interference with the owner's rights, belong to the person who was the owner at the time of the ... destruction or interference. *These are personal rights that are not transferred to a successor by particular title without a stipulation to that effect.* (Emphasis added.)

[15] The underlying obligation here is personal and not real. As a successor, without stipulation or assignment, Travelers has no right of action to intervene in the Partnership's suit.

[....]

Questions

1. Paragraphs 1–5: After you have read the "Facts" carefully, draw a diagram of the different legal relationships or bonds of law that have been created. Can you identify some of these bonds of law as being principal and others as being secondary or accessory?

2. Paragraph 6: What is, in your opinion, the *ratio legis*, the reason or policy, for this rule? Could your choice of a *ratio* have an impact on the legal nature of the obligations created by the rule? Read now paragraph 10: Are there any differences in the legal identification of the kinds of obligations created before and after the revision of the law of Obligations in 1984?

3. Paragraph 13: In light of the above questions and your legal analysis, what would be your answer to the kind of question the court is posing here, that is, "Is an action for defective construction of a building based on a real or a personal obligation?" Do you agree with the Court's ruling?

Eagle Pipe and Supply, Inc.
v.
Amerada Hess Corporation, et al.

Supreme Court of Louisiana
October 26, 2011
79 So.3d 246

CLARK, Justice.

[....]

[1] In general, obligations are divided in the Civil Code into "strictly personal," "heritable," and "real." An obligation is strictly personal when its performance can be enforced only by the obligee, or only against the obligor. La. C.C. art. 1766. An obligation is heritable when its performance may be enforced by a successor of the obligee or against a successor of the obligor. La. C.C. art. 1765. A real obligation is a duty correlative and incidental to a real right. La. C.C. art. 1763.[46] Thus, a real obligation does not exist in the absence of a real right.

[....]

[2] The nature of a real obligation has been thus described:

Real obligations are always duties incidental and correlative of real rights. They are obligations in the sense that they are duties imposed on a particular person who owns or possesses a thing subject to a real right, and they are real in the sense that, as correlative of a real right, these obligations attach to a particular thing and are transferred with it without the need of

---

46. Former La. C.C. Art. 2012 (1870) described the methods of creating real obligations, but this article was not included in the 1984 revision of the Civil Code, having been deemed unnecessary. See La. C.C. art. 1764, Revision Comments — 1984, (g).

Former Art. 2012 provided that real obligations could be created in three ways: (1) by the alienation of immovable property, subject to a real condition, either expressed or implied by law; (2) by alienating to one person the immovable property, and to another, some real right to be exercised upon it; and (3) by the creation of a right of mortgage upon the immovable property. Former Art. 2012 also stated: "All these contracts give rise to obligations purely real on the part of those who acquire the land, under whatever species of title they possess it; they are not personally liable, but the real property is, and, by abandoning it to the obligee, they relieve themselves from all responsibility. A sale subject to a rent charge, or to a right of redemption as consideration of the sale, are examples of the first kind of obligations; servitudes, the right of use and habitation and usufruct, are examples of the second; and the several kinds of mortgages, and the creation of a rent charge, of the third."

After the 1984 revision, the effects of real obligations were continued in Art. 1764, as discussed in the body of the opinion.

an express assignment or subrogation. They are also real in the sense that the responsibility of the obligor may be limited to value of the thing. (Yiannopoulos, Predial Servitudes, at § 212, p. 407.)

[3] Both real rights and real obligations may be contrasted with personal rights. The legal right that a person has against another person to demand the performance of an obligation is called a personal right. Distinct from a real right, which can be asserted against the world, a personal right is effective only between the parties. La. C.C. art. 1758. This court has declared that "a personal right . . . defines man's relationship to man and refers merely to an obligation one owes to another which may be declared only against the obligor." *Harwood Oil & Mining Co.*, 240 La. at 651, 124 So.2d at 767, *citing Reagan [v. Murphy]*, 235 La. at 541, 105 So.2d at 214.

[. . . .]

[4] Real rights, and real obligations pass to a subsequent acquirer of the thing to which it is attached without the need of a stipulation to that effect. La. C.C. art. 1764, Revision Comments — 1984, (c).[51] A personal right, by contrast, cannot be asserted by another in the absence of an assignment or subrogation. La. C.C. art. 1764, Revision Comments — 1984, (d) and (f).[52]

[. . . .]

See also *Breaux v. Laird et al.*, 65 So.2d 907 (La. 1953); *Smith-Asekomeh v. Lafayette City-Parish Consolidated Government*, 273 So.3d 438 (La.App. 3 Cir. 2019); *Vaccari v. Vaccari*, 50 So.3d 139 (La. 2010).

---

51. La. C.C. art. 1764, Revision Comments — 1984, (c) provides:
A real obligation passes to a subsequent acquirer of the thing to which it is attached without need of a stipulation to that effect. Thus, when an estate burdened with a servitude is transferred, the real obligation that is correlative of the right of servitude is also transferred. See C.C. Art. 650(2) (Rev.1977). It is otherwise with respect to personal obligations.

52. La. C.C. art. 1764, Revision Comments — 1984, (d) and (f) provide, in pertinent part:
(d) A particular successor, that is, one who acquires a thing by particular title, is not bound by the personal obligations of his author with respect to the thing, unless he has assumed these obligations by delegation. Conversely, a particular successor does not acquire, without stipulation to that effect, any personal rights that his author has with respect to the thing. For example, if the owner of an immovable who has made a contract for its repair sells the immovable, the purchaser is not bound to perform the obligation of the owner under the repair contract unless he assumes that obligation. Conversely, the purchaser does not acquire any right under the repair contract unless such a right is assigned to him. . . .

* * *

(f) Louisiana courts have held that the indemnity due to the owner of an immovable for the expropriation of a part of that immovable, and damages due to the owner of a thing for its partial destruction or for an interference with the owner's rights, belong to the person who was owner at the time of the expropriation, destruction, or interference. These are personal rights that are not transferred to a successor by particular title without a stipulation to that effect. Rogers v. Louisiana Power and Light Co., 391 So.2d 30 (La.App. 3rd Cir.1980); Yiannopoulos, Predial Servitudes § 147 (1983).

Comparative Law Perspective

— Civil Law —

François Terré, Philippe Simler, Yves Lequette & François Chénedé, *Droit Civil: Les Obligations*

(12th ed. 2018)

673. When one of the contracting parties dies at a time when the contract has not exhausted its effects, that party's universal successors succeed him and become in his place creditors and debtors of the obligations created by the contract. A universal successor or successor by universal title is one who succeeds to the entirety or to a portion of the patrimony of the deceased: the heir, the universal legatee or the legatee by universal title [**general legatee**]. When succeeding to the active side of the obligation, the successor benefits from all the rights that result from the agreements made by his predecessor; when succeeding to the passive side of the obligation, the successor assumes all the conventional obligations of the predecessor. [. . . .]

The rule [**of heritable obligations is**] accompanied by two very useful exceptions [. . .]: "unless the contrary is expressed or results from the nature of the agreement." [. . . .]

First, the contracting parties can validly agree that the contract will terminate upon the death of one of them; for example, by stipulating that the lease is effective for the duration of the lifetime of the lessee.

Second, contracts that were concluded *intuitu personae* — that is to say in consideration of the very qualities of the contracting party, his aptitudes, his knowledge — do not extend their effects to successors. Such contracts give rise to strictly personal relations, either on the side of both parties — as is the case with the mandate which ends upon the death of the principal or of the mandatary (Article 2003) — or on the side of only one party (hiring of services, hiring of work); the death of the party whose personality had been taken into consideration — worker, architect, painter, surgeon, attorney — puts an end to the contract.

Charles Aubry & C. Rau, *Droit Civil Français*

vol. 4 (E. Bartin, 6th ed. 1942, Louisiana State Law Institute trans. 1965)

§ 299. [. . . .] Real obligations are those which do not bind the person nor the patrimony of the debtor but which are binding on him merely as a possessor of certain things or estates. Such are the obligations which the law imposes on the owner of a thing qua owner. See Articles 646, 656, 663. Such are also all obligations corresponding to real rights or to personal rights which can be asserted against successors by particular title; for example, the obligation imposed on a third possessor of a hypothecated immovable to pay or to abandon the immovable; and the obligation whereby the acquirer of a leased immovable may be bound to respect the lease. Articles 2168 and 1743.

On the contrary, personal obligations are those which bind the person and the entire patrimony of the debtor.

Chapter 4

Obligations of Result & Means

Louisiana Sources of Law[1]
Doctrine
Louisiana Law of Obligations in General, A Précis
Section 1.2.2

There exists an obligation of result whenever the performance or object of the obligation is so precisely determined as to amount to a definite result to be achieved. An obligation to give a specific thing and an obligation not to do something would be obligations of result. [. . . .]

There is an obligation of means or diligence when an obligor is expected to use the best possible means available to him, or to act with the utmost care and diligence in the performance of his obligation but without guaranteeing a definite result.

Cases
Miss Lula Mae Johnson
v.
New Orleans Public Service, Incorporated

Court of Appeal of Louisiana
Fourth Circuit
March 8, 1974
293 So.2d 203

SAMUEL, Judge.

[1] This is a suit for damages for personal injuries sustained by plaintiff as a result of a fall on a New Orleans Public Service, Inc. bus. Following trial on the merits judgment was rendered in favor of defendant, dismissing plaintiff's suit. Plaintiff has appealed.

[2] Plaintiff, a fare paying passenger on the bus, had boarded the vehicle at Orleans Avenue and Roman Street in the City of New Orleans. Shortly before the bus arrived

---

1. There are no specific articles in the Louisiana Civil Code on these two kinds of obligations. But see the below sections on "Doctrine" and the "Comparative Law Perspective."

at the stop at which she desired to get off, plaintiff got up from her seat and pulled the cord to indicate to the driver she intended to alight. She started to walk to the rear exit door. Before she reached the door she fell and injured herself. Being notified by another passenger that an accident had occurred, the driver brought his vehicle to a stop and went to plaintiff's assistance. He then resumed driving and called the police and his supervisor from the first stop at which a telephone was available. Plaintiff was taken to a hospital for examination and treatment.

[3] Testimony relative to the occurrence of the accident was given by plaintiff, Louis Hancock (an independent witness who was a passenger on the bus at the time of the accident), Joseph Reed (the defendant's driver), and a defendant claims representative who had interviewed plaintiff concerning the accident.

[. . . .]

[4] Applicable here are the following jurisprudential rules: A public carrier, while not an insurer, is required to exercise the highest degree of care for the safety of its passengers, and a mere showing of injury to a fare paying passenger establishes a prima facie case of negligence against the carrier.[1] Once a prima facie case has been established, the burden of proof is then on the defendant to show there has been no disregard of its duties and that the damage resulted from a cause which human care and foresight could not prevent.[2] In the operation of transit vehicles there is a certain amount of jerking or jolting consistent with the operation which is to be expected, should be anticipated, and for which the carrier cannot be held liable.[3]

[5] In the instant matter plaintiff clearly has established a prima facie case. There is no question that Mrs. Johnson fell on the bus and suffered injuries. However, the evidence shows the bus was traveling at a normal and reasonable rate of speed and that there was no unusual jolting as it crossed the railroad tracks, an operation which is expected and should be anticipated by passengers. We are satisfied the bus did not hit a curb and thus cause the fall in suit. The only evidence indicating the bus had hit a curb was the testimony given by the plaintiff herself, but the other testifying passenger and the bus driver effectively denied such an incident. Nor do we feel plaintiff fell as a result of slipping on worn metal on the bus floor. The only evidence to that effect is the testimony of the other passenger and, from our reading of all of his testimony, we are of the opinion he was merely speculating in an effort to find some reason for plaintiff's fall. Neither in her pleadings nor in her testimony did the plaintiff complain about any jolting as the bus went over the tracks or about

1. *Wise v. Prescott*, 244 La. 157, 151 So.2d 356; *Green v. Taca International Airlines*, La.App., 293 So.2d 198, handed down this date; *Alfred v. Benoit*, La.App., 253 So.2d 797.

2. *Wise v. Prescott*, Supra, footnote 1; *Jones v. New Orleans Public Service, Inc.*, La.App., 254 So.2d 652; *Walker v. New Orleans Public Service, Inc.*, La.App., 245 So.2d 763; *Hurst v. New Orleans Public Service, Inc.*, La.App., 235 So.2d 103; *King v. King*, 253 La. 270, 217 So.2d 395.

3. *Harris v. Shreveport Railways Company*, La.App., 83 So.2d 517; *Rhodes v. New Orleans Public Service*, La.App., 75 So.2d 549.

any slip because of the condition of the bus floor; her only complaint was that she fell because of the single jolt caused by the bus hitting a curb.

[6] Under these circumstances we agree with the trial court's conclusion that the defendant has carried its burden of proof showing it exercised its required degree of care for the safety of its passengers.

[. . . .]

Questions

1. Paragraphs 1–6: Having read the pages given here, you have read the whole case: what do you think of the sources of law used by the Court in this case? What about after re-reading the first four articles of the Louisiana Civil Code? Does that help in grounding your opinion or evaluation of the Court's use of sources of law?

2. Paragraph 4: Is there not in the Louisiana Civil Code a kind or type of contract that would fit a carrier and its liability? *See* La. Civ. Code art. 2754.

3. In which category would you place the obligation of a carrier towards its passenger: result or means? If you have ever travelled by plane, bus, or boat with other passengers, what would be their likely answer to your question about the obligation of an airline, bus company, or ship company towards their passengers?

Warner Max Alexander
v.
Alton Ochsner Medical Foundation et al.

Court of Appeal of Louisiana
Fourth Circuit
April 3, 1973
276 So.2d 794

SCHOTT, Judge.

[1] The plaintiff appeals from a judgment dismissing his suit against Alton Ochsner Medical Foundation, Ochsner Clinic and three physicians associated with those entities, Dr. Kenneth Meyer, Dr. Hurst B. Hatch, Jr. and Dr. Joseph K. Bradford. The case was tried to a jury resulting in a unanimous verdict for the defendants.

[2] In his petition, plaintiff alleged alternatively that the defendants, including the three physicians named, as well as other physicians associated with them, in the period between April 20, 1967, and May 5, 1967, violated an agreement made with him in that the treatment afforded him was not performed in accordance with the standard of professional skills and care prevailing in the community and were negligent in that they failed to exercise ordinary care and skill required of them. In this Court, plaintiff contends that the defendants failed to use various processes and facilities to minimize his pain during the course of their treatment, thereby failing

] P's complaint

to render to him treatment which the community has a right to expect and thereby violating an implied warranty existing between plaintiff as a patient and defendants.

[. . . .]

[3] On April 20, 1967, plaintiff was admitted to the defendant hospital by defendant, Dr. Hatch, who had found that the plaintiff was suffering from a spontaneous pneumothorax, a condition in which air has escaped from the lung into the space between the lung and the chest wall as a result of the rupture of a blister on the surface of the lung. This condition had first manifested itself on April 13, 1967, when plaintiff complained to Dr. Hatch that two days prior thereto he had an onset of stabbing pain in the mid sternal region, aggravated by breathing and by changing his position from lying prone. The doctor, on the basis of X-ray studies, diagnosed a 10% Pneumothorax and prescribed bed rest and medication. Plaintiff was told to return in a week or sooner if his condition worsened. When he returned on April 20, 1967, and X-ray studies revealed that the condition had worsened Dr. Hatch consulted with defendant, Dr. Kenneth Meyer, of the Surgery Department of Ochsner, whereupon the two physicians concurred that it was necessary to conduct a surgical procedure known as a thoracotomy.

[4] This procedure performed by Dr. Meyer consists of the insertion of a catheter through the wall of the chest and into the space between the lung and the interior chest wall so that air can be aspirated from that pleural space. As the air is removed the lung re-expands and becomes sealed with the result that the leakage of air from the lung is gradually eliminated. The insertion of the tube is accomplished by means of a local anethesia [*sic*] being administered, followed by an incision in the chest, the slant of which controls the direction to be followed by the catheter. A steel trocar or needle tube containing the catheter itself is then used to penetrate the chest muscle and chest wall. When the desired position is reached the trocar is removed leaving the catheter in place with the outside end of the catheter then connected to a suction apparatus.

[5] This procedure was carried out at 4:30 PM on April 20, 1967. The nursing notes show that on April 21 at 12:45 PM plaintiff was complaining of severe pain above the site of the insertion in the chest and 'cannot move legs, arms or head without pain.' Dr. Meyer testified that when this report came to his attention he examined the plaintiff, finding that he was able to turn and move with ease as he was requested to do in order for him to carry out his examination. A chest X-ray was taken and thereafter the position of the catheter was changed. The doctor explained that by this time most of the air in the pleural space had been removed but there was still fluid on the periphery of the space. The tube had to be repositioned in order to place one of the holes in the tube in the particular space where the fluid was located. He explained that in addition to the hole on the end of the catheter additional holes were placed in the catheter so as to make the removal of the air more effective. Plaintiff was seen by Dr. Hatch daily while in the hospital until May 1. By April 30 he felt that there was no more leakage from the lung so that the catheter could be removed, but on

consultation with Dr. Meyer it was decided to leave the catheter in place for a short while longer. On May 1 Dr. Hatch's responsibility for the plaintiff was assumed by defendant, Dr. Bradford, to whom it was apparent by May 2 that plaintiff's lung had re-expanded completely, so that it was time for the catheter to be removed from his chest, and this was confirmed by X-ray examination. The catheter was removed on May 4 and plaintiff was discharged from the hospital on May 5 with no problems of mobility. Dr. Meyer and Dr. Bradford both testified that the procedure followed, and the treatment administered, was in accordance with standard medical practice in the City of New Orleans. Dr. Bradford further testified that Drs. Hatch and Meyer both have the necessary training and skill to have treated plaintiff.

[....]

[6] With respect to plaintiff's position that the defendants committed a breach of contract, we are guided by the following principles enunciated in Phelps v. Donaldson, 243 La. 1118, 150 So.2d 35:

'We think the general rule universally obtaining on the subject matter is that: 'When a physician undertakes the treatment of a case he does not guarantee a cure, nor is any promise to effect a cure or even a partial healing to be implied, nor does the law raise from the fact of employment an implied undertaking to cure, but only an undertaking to use ordinary skill and care. For this reason a physician cannot be held up to a standard of civil responsibility similar to that of engineers, mechanics, and shipbuilders. of course a physician might contract specifically to cure and he would be liable on his contract for failure, but, in the absence of such a special and peculiar contract, the fact that treatment has resulted unfavorably does not even raise a presumption of want of proper care, skill, or diligence. * * *' 21 R.C.L. Sec. 36, p. 391. Also, see 70 C.J.S. Physicians and Surgeons s 57, pp. 981, 982 'A dentist, like a physician or surgeon, is not an insurer or guarantor or results, in the absence of express agreement.' 41 Am.Jur., Physicians and Surgeons, Sec. 104, p. 219.'

[7] There is no evidence of any expressed contract to cure. The testimony of defendant physicians standing alone is sufficient in this case with respect to implied warranty to show that they did use ordinary skill and care and their testimony is corroborated by the testimony of every other physician who reviewed their procedures and approved of same. Plaintiff attempts to contradict this testimony by suggesting that X-ray photographs taken by Drs. Hatch and Meyer were inadequate in that they did not reveal the depth into the chest cavity which the catheter reached. He speculates that this caused his suffering. But Dr. Leon thoroughly discredited this theory as a cause for plaintiff's problem. Plaintiff's argument that additional X-ray photographs should have been taken and that additional procedures, such as fluoroscoping and other tests, should have been implemented is not supported by any testimony, medical or lay. The real nub of the plaintiff's position seems to be that he was in pain at the beginning and continued to be in pain at the time of the trial; therefore, a breach of contract was committed by defendants who had undertaken to

treat him, but the law does not exact upon the physician a guarantee to cure anyone. Furthermore, the pain and discomfort described in the nursing note of April 21 are fully explained by Dr. Meyer who testified that a thoracotomy necessarily causes a patient to be uncomfortable as long as the catheter remains inserted and discomfort continues even after the patient is discharged from the hospital because of the incision and irritation to the lining of the lung and chest wall. Finally, the testimony of almost every physician who appeared at the trial, as well as numerous consultants to whom reference was made by those physicians, compels a conclusion that plaintiff's pain was not the result of defendants' actions but was psychogenic or emotional requiring psychiatric treatment for a cure.

[8] As to the allegations of negligence on the part of defendants, their conduct must be judged on the basis of whether they exercised that degree of skill and care which is usually possessed and exercised by practitioners of the profession in the same community, it being their duty to use reasonable care and diligence along with their best judgment in the application of their skill to the case before them. Uter v. Bone and Joint Clinic, 249 La. 851, 192 So.2d 100, and Meyer v. St. Paul Mercury Indemnity Company, 225 La. 618, 73 So.2d 781. When this test is applied to the conduct of defendants, the evidence is overwhelming to the effect that all of the physicians who are named defendants, as well as those personnel of Ochsner Clinic and the other entities who treated plaintiff, discharged their duty to him.

Questions

1. Paragraph 5: From the point of view of legal methodology, considering the authority attached to the opinion of a court [of appeal], and considering the principle of *jurisprudence constante*, is the reference to a "standard medical practice in the City of New Orleans" a "wise and proper" thing to say or an "irresponsible and unwise" thing to say?

2. Paragraph 6: What kind of obligation falls under the rule, and which one falls under the exception? What other occupations would you subject to the same rule and exception? Should there be only one policy or reason to explain and justify only one rule or should each occupation/profession be fitted with its own rule and exception? Whose interest should prevail?

Louis Henson
v.
St. Paul Fire and Marine Insurance Company

Court of Appeal of Louisiana
First Circuit
December 28, 1977
354 So.2d 612

SARTAIN, Judge.

[1] Plaintiff, Louis Henson, brought this suit against defendant, St. Paul Fire and Marine Insurance Co., as the insurer of Dr. Robert A. Peden. Plaintiff alleged that Peden negligently injured him during surgery on July 5, 1973. Suit was filed on February 19, 1976. Defendant interposed the peremptory exception of prescription. No evidence was received on the exception, the defendant choosing to rely solely on the allegations of plaintiff's petition which showed that suit was filed more than one year after the surgery. St. Paul asserted that the applicable prescriptive period was one year under either the general tort prescription of C.C. Art. 3536 or the special medical malpractice prescription of R.S. 9:5628.[1] Plaintiff relied on the doctrine of contra non valentem agere nulla currit praescriptio (no prescription runs against a person unable to bring an action) as well as the assertion that the applicable prescriptive period should be ten years under the general contract prescription of C.C. Art. 3544.

[2] For oral reasons assigned, the trial judge held that the applicable prescriptive period was one year and dismissed plaintiff's suit. We reverse and remand.

[3] With respect to the applicable prescriptive period or periods, the fact that an action may constitute a tort does not prevent its also being a breach of contract. The plaintiff in such a situation has two remedies. Federal Insurance Co. v. Insurance Company of North America, 262 La. 509, 263 So.2d 871 (1972). This court has held that in situations where a single set of circumstances gives rise to an action in both tort and contract, the claims are considered separately in determining whether they have prescribed. Jackson v. Zito, 314 So.2d 401 (La.App. 1st Cir.), writs denied 320 So.2d 551, 553 (La.1975).

[4] [After finding plaintiff's tort claim prescribed, the court addressed plaintiff's contract claim.]

[5] On the contractual claim defendant is apparently contending both that the claim has prescribed and that the plaintiff's petition has not stated a cause of action in contract. Defendant never filed an exception of no cause of action and has not used this phrase in brief or argument. However, we feel that his actual position is

---

1. The alleged offense occurred prior to the effective date of Act 808 of 1975 and Act 214 of 1976, now R.S. 9:5628.

that there is no cause of action on the contractual claim. In any event, being able to notice this issue on our own motion, we do so. C.C.P. Art. 927.

[6] Looking first to the issue of no cause of action we find that the Third Circuit has held that a medical malpractice claim cannot be considered a contractual claim unless the physician warrants or promises a particular result. Steel v. Aetna Life & Casualty, 304 So.2d 861 (La.App. 3rd Cir. 1974), writ denied 315 So.2d 144 (La.1975).[2] The Fourth Circuit has held that such a specific promise is unnecessary in order to found such an action in contract. Creighton v. Karlin, 225 So.2d 288 (La.App. 4th Cir.), writ denied 254 La. 842, 227 So.2d 590 (1969). We believe that in his petition plaintiff has sufficiently alleged the promise of a particular result to get past the no cause of action exception even under the test of the Third Circuit in Steel, above. (Plaintiff has alleged that Dr. Peden informed him that the surgery would produce a satisfactory result and warranted that no ill effects would ensue from the operation.) However, for the reasons which follow, we choose not to base our decision on this narrow ground, but rather to follow the Fourth Circuit view in Creighton, above.

[7] When a patient goes to a doctor for treatment and the doctor agrees to treat him a contract has been entered into. "Any other conclusion is difficult to reach intellectually." Steel v. Aetna Life & Casualty, 315 So.2d 144 (La.1975) (JJ. Barham and Tate concurring in writ denial); see also C.C. Art. 1816. Any other conclusion would mean that a doctor would have no contractual action against his clients if they refused to pay him. He would be relegated to a quasi contractual theory of negotiorum gestio or unjustified enrichment. Such would certainly not be a logical conclusion.

[8] Having determined that a contract exists in such a situation, we must decide what are the obligations of the doctor. "The obligation of contracts extends not only to what is expressly stipulated, but also to everything that, by law, equity or custom, is considered as incidental to the particular contract, or necessary to carry it into effect." C.C. Art. 1903. It follows naturally that the doctor's duty is that of using due care. The obligation under the contract should certainly not be less than one's duty under general tort law. Delaune v. Davis, 316 So.2d 7 (La.App. 1st Cir. 1975).

[9] We therefore agree with the conclusion of the Fourth Circuit in Creighton. This result is also in line with the modern civilian concept of obligations de moyen and with the decisions reached by the courts in both France and Quebec. The Work of the Louisiana Appellate Courts for the 1974–1975 Term Contracts in Particular, 36 La.L.Rev. 417, 421–426 (1976). It is also consistent with the rule of this circuit in attorney malpractice cases. Jackson, above. The decision of the Third Circuit appears to be an importation from the common law. See 70 C.J.S. Physicians and Surgeons s 57. It has no theoretical foundation in the civilian law of obligations. In

---

2. See Ball v. Siess, 351 So.2d 845 (La.App. 2nd Cir. 1977) recently decided by the Second Circuit, conforming to the views expressed by the Third Circuit in Steel v. Aetna Life & Casualty, 304 So.2d 861 (1974).

Steel the court relied on Phelps v. Donaldson, 243 La. 1118, 150 So.2d 35 (1963) to sustain its position. However, that case does not support the proposition asserted. In the case, although an exception of prescription was sustained as to the tort claim, trial was conducted on the contractual claim. The trial court found that a contract to straighten the plaintiff's daughter's teeth had not been proved. The Court of Appeal affirmed on the basis that the action was essentially in tort and that it had prescribed. Phelps v. Donaldson, 142 So.2d 585 (La.App. 3rd Cir. 1962). The Supreme Court, in its affirmance, followed the trial court rationale rather than that of the Court of Appeal. It was never found as a fact that the doctor performed in a substandard fashion. Apparently the plaintiff attempted to rely on the fact that her daughter's teeth were not straightened to sustain her breach of contract action. Absent proof of a contract to cure, such proof was found to be insufficient. We believe that this is the actual holding of Phelps plaintiff simply failed to prove a breach. Our decision here is not inconsistent with that holding. If plaintiff succeeds in proving a contract to cure, he will be relieved of his burden of proving substandard conduct. But if he does not prove such a contract he can still recover by proving Dr. Peden has violated his obligation of due care.

[10] We next move to the assertion that Henson's contractual claim has pre-scribed. In support of this contention defendant relies on R.S. 9:5628 (added by Act 808 of 1975 and amended by Act 214 of 1976). Although the alleged negligent act of defendant's insured occurred prior to September 12, 1975 (the effective date of Act 808), suit was instituted after this date. Defendant asserts that prescription statutes are remedial and procedural in nature and that they therefore are to be applied ret-roactively. It is true that prescription statutes may be applied to causes of action arising prior to their enactment, at least so long as a reasonable time is given for the assertion of rights, if the legislature so intends. Cooper v. Lykes, 218 La. 251, 49 So.2d 3 (1950). This is well illustrated in Mire v. Hawkins, 177 So.2d 795 (La.App. 3rd Cir. 1965), affirmed at 249 La. 278, 186 So.2d 591 (1966). There a statute specifi-cally provided for retroactive effect and included a saving clause allowing those who would be cut off by retroactive application to have one year to bring their action. Such a provision was held to be valid. However, in Act 808 the legislature did not specifically address this problem. Therefore it is our duty to ascertain the presumed legislative intent as to retroactivity.

[11] The general rule is that when a prescriptive period is changed "the time which preceded the change of legislation or altering the period of prescription, should be reckoned according to the ancient law, and that which followed according to the new law." Goddard's Heirs v. Urquhart, 6 La. 659, 674 (1834), accord 1 Planiol, Trea-tise on the Civil Law, s 248 (translation by the Louisiana State Law Institute, 1959). This solution is very equitable. In the absence of an express legislative intent to the contrary, we believe it is the rule to be followed.

[12] In applying this proportionate method to the facts of this case we find that Henson's contractual claim has not prescribed. He filed suit within six months of the effective date of Act 808. Therefore over one-half of the prescriptive period under

C.C. Art. 3544 would have had to elapse before Act 808's effective date in order for his claim to be prescribed. It had not done so.

[13] The finding by the trial judge that plaintiff's tort action had prescribed was correct. However, the plaintiff has sufficiently alleged a timely breach of contract action. We therefore reverse and remand the case to the trial court for further proceedings in accordance with law. Costs in this court are to be borne by appellee. All other costs are to await a final determination on the merits.

Questions

1. Paragraph 6: Is the court saying that, in the absence of a contract creating an obligation of result on the part of a physician, the latter can only be bound by an obligation of means? If you conclude that this is what the court is saying, can you give some reasons in support of the court's statement? Is the distinction between an obligation of result and one of means only a matter of procedure/evidence?

2. Paragraph 9: Since the civil law system of Louisiana is one of many other civil law systems, it is logical and helpful to learn from these other civil law systems through some comparative law research. Notice that the court is also looking at the common law.

3. Paragraph 13: This paragraph conveys a most important instruction to lawyers and judges: First and foremost, identify clearly, in legal terms, the source of the obligations that may have been created. These sources of obligations are legislation and custom (*see* La. Civ. Code arts. 1–4), juridical acts (mostly, but not exclusively, contracts) and juridical facts (such as torts/delicts). Note here that the trial judge identified the source of obligations as being a tort, whereas the court of appeal saw a contract. Is there any difference in the legal effects of one source versus the other, with respect to prescription, for example? *See* La. Civ. Code arts. 3492 & 3499.

Comparative Law Perspective

— Civil Law —

Obligations of Result & Means

France

Henri et Léon Mazeaud et al., *Leçons de Droit Civil: Obligations*

vol. 1, n° 21 at 13-15 (François Chabas rev., 9th ed. 1998)

21. — Determinate obligations (or obligations of result) and general obligations of prudence and diligence (or obligations of means). — This classification rests on the following observation: *Sometimes the obligor is bound to accomplish a determinate result; the obligation is strictly specified and the obligor must attain that result; at other times, on the contrary, the obligor is bound only to act with diligence and to conduct himself with prudence in order to attempt to achieve a desired result.* [**For example,**] whereas a transporter is bound to deliver the merchandise at the agreed-upon time and place, a doctor is bound only to conduct himself *with prudence and diligence* in view of obtaining the healing of the patient.

The practical interest of the distinction is most significant on the plane of proof.

It suffices for the obligee of a determinate obligation to establish that the result has not been attained. The obligee thereby demonstrates that the obligor has not performed his obligation. In order to exonerate himself, the obligor must then prove that the nonperformance proceeded from a cause that was foreign to him. For example, the transporter must establish the fault of the sender or an event of *force majeure.*

If the obligation that weighs on the obligor is only to conduct himself with prudence and diligence, an examination of the obligor's conduct becomes necessary. In fact, when the anticipated result is not attained, the obligee, in order to demonstrate that the obligation has not been performed, must prove that the obligor has not comported himself with the prudence and diligence to which he was held — fault in the classic sense. Proof of the imprudence or negligence of the obligor is at the charge of the obligee. For example, the patient must establish the imprudence or negligence of the doctor.

*Thus, in determinate obligations, it suffices for the obligee to prove that the result has not been attained, and it is up to the obligor to demonstrate a foreign cause. In obligations of prudence and diligence, the obligee must put on proof (which is [*more*] difficult) of some negligence or imprudence of the obligor.* Given the practical importance of the burden of proof, the classification is of primordial interest. [. . . .]

It is not always easy to determine if one is in the presence of a determinate obligation or a general obligation of prudence and diligence. *What is the criterion for the distinction?*

On contractual terrain, it is necessary to search out the will of the parties. Has the obligor taken the engagement of achieving the result in view of which the parties contracted? Then the obligation is determinate. Has the obligor only engaged himself to try, by prudent and diligent conduct, to achieve the result in view of which the parties concluded the contract? Then the obligation is a general obligation of prudence and diligence. In the absence of other circumstances that might permit one to discover this will, one should seek to ascertain *whether the realization of the end pursued through the contract entails some risk (alea).* When this realization is aleatory [**contains an element of risk**], one must suppose that the obligation which the obligor assumed is only of prudence and diligence, for an obligor normally does not engage himself to attain a result that he knows is aleatory. It is so with the doctor *vis-à-vis* his client: the healing is aleatory. It will therefore be admitted that, unless the parties have expressed a will to the contrary, the doctor does not engage himself to heal the patient, but to give him prudent and diligent care in order to try to heal him. When, on the contrary, the realization of the result in view of which the contract was made is not aleatory, one can normally conclude that the obligor has promised this realization. It is so with the transporter as to the delivery of the transported thing in good condition within the fixed delay. *Thus, the aleatory or non-aleatory nature of the realization of the end to be attained permits one to discover the unexpressed will of the parties.*

On extra-contractual terrain, there is no question of searching out the will of the parties. Because the obligation is imposed by law, it is the *will of the legislators* that must be detected when they have not expressed it.

Québec

Jean-Louis Baudouin, *Les Obligations*
n° 36 at 26–27 & n° 37 at 27–28 (4th ed. 1993)

An obligation of result is that for the satisfaction of which the obligor is bound to furnish to the obligee a specific result, fixed in advance. Such is, for example, the obligation of a seller (or that of a transporter) to deliver the merchandise.

An obligation of means is that for the satisfaction of which the obligor is bound to employ the best possible means and to act with prudence and diligence in view of obtaining a result, but nevertheless without making himself a guarantor of that result. Such is, for example, the obligation of a doctor toward his patient, that of a lessee to use the leased thing as a reasonable person, [...] that of an employee, [...] that of a mandatary [**agent**], [**and**] that of a borrower or depositary of a thing to stand watch over the conservation of the loaned or deposited thing. In the same fashion, the general [**tort**] obligation not to cause damage to another is an obligation of means. [....]

37. — *Consequences of the distinction* — This classification has great importance on the practical plane, both as to the prerequisites for the responsibility [**liability**] of the obligor and as to the proof [**of that responsibility**]. Regarding the prerequisites for

the responsibility of the obligor, if it's a matter of an obligation of means, only fault in the utilization of the means can engage his responsibility [**make him liable**]. For example, the simple fact that a surgical operation fails does not automatically lead to the doctor's responsibility. The patient must demonstrate that the doctor has committed fault in the means that he has utilized in order to care for him. In the same way, the occurrence of some harm, standing alone, does not, in principle, render the author of the damage responsible, if he has proved he was reasonably prudent and diligent. If it is a matter of an obligation of result, the fact that the promised result has not been attained results in the obligor's responsibility being presumed. [. . . .]

In the case of an obligation of means, the obligee, in order to cause the obligor to be held responsible, must prove that the obligor has not exercised reasonable prudence and diligence in pursuit of the end fixed [**by the parties or the law**]. The absence of that result does not, then, cause the fault of the obligor to be presumed. The burden of proving this fault rests on the obligee. To the contrary, in the case of an obligation of result, the simple [. . .] absence of the result or of the harm experienced suffices to cause the fault of the obligor to be presumed, once the very fact of nonperformance or of the occurrence of the damage has been demonstrated by the obligee. At that point, the obligor, in order to escape his responsibility, must go beyond proof of a simple absence of fault, that is, must demonstrate that the nonperformance or the harm experienced proceeded from a *force majeure*. He could not be permitted to escape his responsibility solely by putting on proof of an absence of fault. [. . . .]

This classification, to which the courts are appealing more and more often, has the merit of being simple and of permitting one to measure exactly the intensity of the obligor's obligational duty.

Chapter 5

Terms & Conditions

Louisiana Sources of Law[1]
Louisiana Civil Code

Art. 1767. Suspensive and resolutory condition.

A conditional obligation is one dependent on an uncertain event.

If the obligation may not be enforced until the uncertain event occurs, the condition is suspensive.

If the obligation may be immediately enforced but will come to an end when the uncertain event occurs, the condition is resolutory. (Acts 1984, No. 331, §1, eff. Jan. 1, 1985.)

Art. 1768. Expressed and implied conditions.

Conditions may be either expressed in a stipulation or implied by the law, the nature of the contract, or the intent of the parties. (Acts 1984, No. 331, §1, eff. Jan. 1, 1985.)

Art. 1770. Condition that depends on the whim or the will of the obligor.

A suspensive condition that depends solely on the whim of the obligor makes the obligation null.

A resolutory condition that depends solely on the will of the obligor must be fulfilled in good faith. (Acts 1984, No. 331, §1, eff. Jan. 1, 1985.)

Art. 1771. Obligee's right pending condition.

The obligee of a conditional obligation, pending fulfillment of the condition, may take all lawful measures to preserve his right. (Acts 1984, No. 331, §1, eff. Jan. 1, 1985.)

Art. 1772. Fault of a party.

A condition is regarded as fulfilled when it is not fulfilled because of the fault of a party with an interest contrary to the fulfillment. (Acts 1984, No. 331, §1, eff. Jan. 1, 1985.)

Art. 1773. Time for fulfillment of condition that an event shall occur.

If the condition is that an event shall occur within a fixed time and that time lapses without the occurrence of the event, the condition is considered to have failed.

---

1. Not all the Code articles under these titles have been reproduced.

If no time has been fixed for the occurrence of the event, the condition may be fulfilled within a reasonable time.

Whether or not a time has been fixed, the condition is considered to have failed once it is certain that the event will not occur. (Acts 1984, No. 331, §1, eff. Jan. 1, 1985.)

Art. 1775. Effects retroactive.

Fulfillment of a condition has effects that are retroactive to the inception of the obligation. Nevertheless, that fulfillment does not impair the validity of acts of administration duly performed by a party, nor affect the ownership of fruits produced while the condition was pending. Likewise, fulfillment of the condition does not impair the right acquired by third persons while the condition was pending. (Acts 1984, No. 331, §1, eff. Jan. 1, 1985.)

Art. 1776. Contract for continuous or periodic performance.

In a contract for continuous or periodic performance, fulfillment of a resolutory condition does not affect the validity of acts of performance rendered before fulfillment of the condition. (Acts 1984, No. 331, §1, eff. Jan. 1, 1985.)

Art. 1778. Term for performance.

A term for the performance of an obligation is a period of time either certain or uncertain. It is certain when it is fixed. It is uncertain when it is not fixed but is determinable either by the intent of the parties or by the occurrence of a future and certain event. It is also uncertain when it is not determinable, in which case the obligation must be performed within a reasonable time. (Acts 1984, No. 331, §1, eff. Jan. 1, 1985.)

Art. 1779. Term presumed to benefit the obligor.

A term is presumed to benefit the obligor unless the agreement or the circumstances show that it was intended to benefit the obligee or both parties. (Acts 1984, No. 331, §1, eff. Jan. 1, 1985.)

Art. 1781. Performance before end of term.

Although performance cannot be demanded before the term ends, an obligor who has performed voluntarily before the term ends may not recover the performance. (Acts 1984, No. 331, §1, eff. Jan. 1, 1985.)

Art. 1785. Performance on term.

Performance on term must be in accordance with the intent of the parties, or with established usage when the intent cannot be ascertained. (Acts 1984, No. 331, §1, eff. Jan. 1, 1985.)

Doctrine

Louisiana Law of Obligations in General, A Précis

Sections 2.2-A.1 to 2.2-B.2

LSA-C.C. Art. 1767 defines a conditional obligation as **one dependent on an uncertain event.** In this limited context one can also define a condition as being an uncertain event which may or may not occur. The contrast can now be clearly marked with the *term* which is defined in **LSA-C.C. Art. 1778** as a period of time either certain or uncertain but, in all circumstances, as a period of time bound to occur in the course of nature. [. . . .]

Suspensive and Resolutory Conditions

An obligation is subjected to a suspensive condition when it may not be enforced until the uncertain event occurs (LSA-C.C. Art 1767). Although this description of the effects of a suspensive condition states that the obligation **may not be enforced,** actually a suspensive condition has a much more drastic effect: it suspends the existence of the obligation between the parties until the uncertain event occurs and, therefore, suspends the enforcement of that same obligation. Although the bond of law has been formed, no obligation is yet in existence. [. . . .]

Whether suspensive or resolutory, a condition can be expressed in a stipulation or implied by the law, the nature of the contract, or the intent of the parties (LSA--C.C. Art. 1768). [. . . .]

A condition may be implied by the law as, for example, in **LSA-C.C. Arts. 2604 and 2605** which give a buyer a reasonable opportunity to inspect the things and to reject nonconforming things within a reasonable time. [. . . .]

A condition may also be implied from the intent of the parties whenever the circumstances are clearly indicative of consent (**LSA-C.C. Art. 1927**). [. . . .]

A condition would be unlawful or immoral whenever it would violate **LSA-C.C. Art. 7** and as is otherwise illustrated throughout the civil Code in **Articles 1519, 1968, 2030, etc.** [. . . .]

An impossible condition would contemplate the occurrence of an event which could absolutely not take place. [. . . .]

The principle governing the fulfillment or occurrence of the condition is that of the retroactivity of the effects of the condition. [. . . .]

LSA-C.C. Art. 1775 expresses the general principle in these terms: "**Fulfillment of a condition has effects that are retroactive to the inception of the obligation.**" [. . . .]

The essence of a suspensive condition is to *suspend* the effects of an existing legal relationship and, *a fortiori,* all performances flowing from the effects of that legal relationship. Through the fiction of retroactivity, there will take place a sort of creation *ab initio* or *ex tunc* of the effects of the relationship and the resulting obligation. [. . . .]

There are, obviously, some limitations to the retroactive effect of the condition. On the basis either of the good faith principle or the public records doctrine, **LSA--C.C. Art. 1775** stipulates, in part, that **"fulfillment of the condition does not impair the right acquired by third parties while the condition was pending."** [. . . .]

Another limitation to the retroactive effect of the condition is stated in these terms in **LSA-C.C. Art. 1775.** [. . . .]

The retroactive effects of a resolutory condition are basically the same as those of a suspensive condition. An interesting illustration of the impact of these effects can be found in the contract of sale with the right of redemption. Under **LSA-C.C. Art. 2567, 2572 and 2588**, the vendor and original owner of the thing sold receives it back, in theory, as if the sale had not taken place. [. . . .]

LSA-C.C. Art. 1778 describes the *term.* [. . . .]

A term is, therefore, a future and certain event which will definitely occur and which may either delay the performance of an obligation, as suggested by an *a contrario sensu* reasoning on **LSA-C.C. Art. 1777-2**, or bring an end to the performance of an existing obligation, such as put an end to a lease, for example. [. . . .]

A term is *suspensive* whenever it suspends or delays the right to demand the performance of an obligation until the term occurs. It means, therefore, that as long as the term has not occurred, the performance of the obligation cannot be demanded by the obligee, even though the obligation itself does exist. [. . . .]

An extinctive term is one which, when it occurs, brings an end to a binding commitment to perform an obligation. Once the event selected as the term occurs, the obligation which existed until then ceases to exist *ex nunc,* or prospectively. [. . . .]

A term is *certain* whenever the period of time preceding the occurrence of the event has been fixed. (**LSA-C.C. Art. 1778**). [. . . .]

A term is said to be *uncertain* only when the period of time preceding the occurrence of the definite event or term "is not fixed but is determinable either by the intent of the parties or by the occurrence of a future and certain event. It is also uncertain when it is not determinable, in which case the obligation must be performed within a reasonable time." [. . . .]

A conventional term is a term or certain event expressly or impliedly agreed upon between the parties to a contract (**LSA-C.C. Art. 1777**). [. . . .]

A legal term is a term granted or imposed by law. [. . . .]

A judicial term, also called a period of grace, is a term granted by a court to a debtor who is sued by his creditor seeking performance of the obligation. The court may grant or deny this term of grace in consideration of the particular situation of the debtor. [. . . .]

The function of an extinctive term is to bring an end to the performance of an existing obligation. Therefore, before the happening of the extinctive term, the obligation is immediately enforceable as any pure and simple obligation would be. [. . . .]

The function of a suspensive term is to delay the performance or execution of an existing obligation until a certain time after that obligation has come into existence. It follows that the parties are subjected to a dual legal status: one which relates to that period of time before the occurrence of the suspensive term and the other which concerns the period of time that follows the happening of the term. [. . . .]

It is most important to stress that, although the execution or performance of the obligation is delayed until the term occurs, the obligation itself is born and does exist in the sense that it has created rights and obligations in the parties. [. . . .]

Upon occurrence or happening of the suspensive term, the obligor's performance becomes due, and the obligee may then demand that performance. It is important to state again that the occurrence of a term has no retroactive effect; in other words, the past relationship between the parties is unaffected by the occurrence of a term.

Cases

In re Liquidation of Hibernia Bank & Trust Co.
In re Intervention of D. H. Holmes Co., Limited

Supreme Court of Louisiana
March 7, 1938
189 La. 813

FOURNET, Justice.

[1] D. H. Holmes Company, Limited, intervened in the liquidation proceedings of the Hibernia Bank & Trust Company to have its note dated March 13, 1933, for $100,000, payable to the order of the bank on June 12, 1933, declared offset against its deposit in the bank and to have the said note returned to it marked paid.

[2] The defense is that the two debts were not equally due and demandable at the time the bank was placed in liquidation on May 20, 1933, and, in reconvention, the Hibernia Bank & Trust Company, in liquidation, prayed for judgment for the balance due on the note, $57,000, with interest and attorney's fees.

[. . . .]

[3] It is provided by the Revised Civil Code that, 'when two persons are indebted to each other, there takes place between them a compensation that extinguishes both the debts,' * * * article 2207, and that 'compensation takes place * * * by the mere operation of law, even unknown to the debtors; the two debts are reciprocally extinguished, as soon as they exist simultaneously, to the amount of their respective sums,' article 2208, but *compensation takes place only between two debts,*

*having equally for their object a sum of money, * * * which are equally liquidated and demandable,'* article 2209. (Italics ours.) See, also, Brock et al. v. Pan American Petroleum Corporation, 186 La. 607, 173 So. 121; People's Bank in Liquidation v. Mississippi & Lafourche Drainage District, 141 La. 1009, 76 So. 179.

[4] We deem it unnecessary to narrate the facts, in detail, of this case following the 'banking holidays,' because we have done so many times in other cases. Suffice it to say that beginning with the morning of March 2 to the time the State Bank Commissioner took over the affairs of the bank for liquidation, on May 20, 1933, it remained on a restricted basis whereby 5 per cent. of the intervener's deposit was made available and the remaining 95 per cent. frozen and unavailable. In the interim, on March 13th, intervener's note for $100,000 matured and was renewed by the execution of a new note for the same amount, payable on June 12, 1933.

[5] The status of intervener's rights, both as a creditor by virtue of its deposit with the bank and as a debtor by virtue of its note due the bank, became fixed from the moment the bank was placed in liquidation and its affairs taken over by the State Bank Commissioner. Thomas v. Marine Bank & Trust Co., 156 La. 941, 101 So. 315; Brock et al. v. Pan American Petroleum Corporation, supra; People's Bank in Liquidation v. Mississippi & Lafourche Drainage District, supra.

[6] But counsel for intervener contend that the obstacle to the compensation in this case — the maturity date of the obligation — was removed by its letter of April 3, 1933, wherein it requested that its note be offset by its frozen account. It is their contention that the term of an obligation is in favor of the debtor and may be waived by him.

[7] In support of their contention, counsel for intervener, in their brief, quote from article 2053 of the Revised Civil Code as follows: '*The term is always presumed to be stipulated in favor of the debtor.*' But this is qualified by the following: '*Unless it result from the stipulation, or from circumstances, that it was also agreed upon in favor of the creditor.*' In the instant case all the stipulations in the body of the note are expressly stated to be in favor of the bank, and the evidence conclusively shows that that right has not been waived by the bank. (Italics ours.)

[8] In Daniel on Negotiable Instruments, 7th Ed., it is stated that 'payment (of a note) can only be made before maturity by consent of both debtor and creditor,' Vol. 3, §1416, p. 1461; §1418, p. 1464; and in Corpus Juris, that 'the maker of a note has no right to pay the same before maturity without the consent of the holder,' Vol. 8, §840, p. 603.

[9] We therefore conclude that the two debts were not equally due and demandable at the time the bank was placed in liquidation, and compensation did not take place under the express provisions of articles 2207, 2208, and 2209 of the Revised Civil Code.

[10] But it is argued by counsel for intervener that because the note was indorsed in blank by William F. Tutt, assistant cashier, that 'the negotiation must have been

made by the bank itself, and not by the liquidators. As an endorser, by the terms of the note, it became a party thereto, and the note provides that when any party goes into liquidation, the note automatically matures.'

[11] It is evident from a reading of the provisions of the note that the stipulations contained therein and relied upon by counsel were not intended for the benefit of the makers or indorsers, etc. — in the instant case, the maker — but expressly for the bank's.

[12] For the reasons assigned, the judgment of the lower court is affirmed; appellant to pay all costs.

[. . . .]

Questions

1. Paragraph 1: Please read the Code articles on "Compensation" (La. Civ. Code arts. 1893–1902), "Loan" (La. Civ. Code arts. 2891–2913) and "Deposit" (La. Civil Code arts. 2926–2945).

2. Paragraph 1: Is D. H. Holmes a creditor of Hibernia Bank to the extent that Holmes has deposited money in the bank? What is the status of Holmes *vis-à-vis* its deposit account? Conversely, what is the legal status of the Bank *vis-à-vis* Holmes?

3. Paragraph 7: Why is Holmes claiming to be a debtor? A debtor of what? What legal ground could the court have cited (what Code article) in support of its statement that "all the stipulations of the note are expressly stated to be in favor of the bank" to the extent it could apply to a term? Since a term is attached to the performance of an obligation, which party to the contract of loan above could claim the benefit of a term? If a term is a benefit to a party, could that party waive that term? Is there any legal support for your opinion in the Louisiana Civil Code?

4. Paragraph 9: Explain why the "two debts were not equally due and demandable at the time the bank was placed in liquidation. . . ." Is Louisiana Civil Code article 1894 at all relevant? Going back to the Code articles on deposit, was the Court correct in writing about "two debts"? Were there really two debts or only one? If only one debt exists, can compensation take place?

Housing Authority of the Town of Lake Arthur, La.
v.
T. Miller & Sons et al.

Supreme Court of Louisiana
April 25, 1960
120 So.2d 494

SIMON, Justice.

[1] This is a suit by plaintiff, the Housing Authority of the Town of Lake Arthur, Louisiana,[1] against defendant, T. Miller & Sons, Contractor, seeking the recovery of $8,875.41 plus 10% Attorney's fees, for damages allegedly sustained by plaintiff arising from defendant contractor's refusal to comply with its bid and to execute a public construction contract for which defendant was the low bidder in response to plaintiff's invitation for bids.

[2] The facts, as revealed by the record, show that in 1952, in order to construct the housing project and in order to be guaranteed the necessary funds therefor, plaintiff, in cooperation with the Government of the United States, in due and legal form advertised or invited bids on this project.

[3] After a thorough examination of all conditions and specifications defendant partnership submitted a bid in the amount of $223,777.77, and simultaneously supplemented its bid by a notation on the envelope under the signature of David B. Miller reading:

> 'Deduct from our base bid the sum of $11,000.00. T. Miller & Sons by David Miller.'

[4] Thus the final net bid submitted by defendant amounted to $212,777.77.

[5] Conformably with the terms of the invitation and advertisement on April 22, 1952, at 2:00 o'clock P.M. plaintiff received, opened and read aloud defendant's bid, along with others. In accordance with the advertisement, as well as the invitation to bid and the specifications set out in the project, the local Housing Authority had thirty days subsequent to the opening of the bids within which to accept or reject any and all that had been submitted. The fact that this right of thirty days within which to accept or reject was well within the knowledge of defendant and that this privilege was part of the terms and conditions to the proposed contract is made evident by the provisions of the bid[2] submitted by the defendant.

---

1. A duly established public organization created and existing under the provisions of LSA-R.S. 40:381 et seq., and domiciled in Jefferson Davis Parish, Louisiana.

2. '1. The undersigned (T. Miller & Sons) having familiarized themselves * * * with the specifications including invitation for bids * * *.

2. 'In submitting this bid, it is understood that the right is reserved by the Housing Authority of the Town of Lake Arthur to reject any and/or all bids. If written notice of the acceptance of this bid is mailed, telegraphed or delivered to the undersigned (defendant) *within thirty days after the opening thereof*, or at any time thereafter before this bid has been withdrawn, the undersigned agrees to

[6] It also appears that the invitation for bids expressly stipulated the following pertinent provision:

'No bid shall be withdrawn for a period of thirty (30) days subsequent to the opening of bids without the consent of the Housing Authority of the Town of Lake Arthur.'

[7] The record further discloses that after the opening and reading of all submitted bids, and it appearing that the defendant had submitted the lowest, a resolution was proposed and unanimously adopted by the local Housing Authority authorizing its director to accept defendant's bid and to proceed with the execution of the contract, but subject to the following pertinent condition, viz.:

'Section 4. That the foregoing action and the contract to be executed is expressly declared to be subject to the approval of the Public Housing Administration.'

[8] It further appears that by letter dated May 12, 1952, C. J. Stenzel, Director, Fort Worth Field Office of the United States Public Housing Administration, well within the thirty-day period, notified the local director that plaintiff had full power and authority to execute the construction contract with the defendant in accordance with the latter's bid, the construction to be limited to the parcels to which plaintiff had title. It also appears that this letter constituted an unqualified approval of defendant's proposed contract. For reasons not disclosed by the record, the local director failed to notify the defendant immediately of plaintiff's acceptance of the former's bid, other than is hereafter shown. However, it is shown by the testimony of the local director that prior to May 22, 1952, he made several unsuccessful telephone attempts to so notify the defendant.

[9] It is also shown that on May 22, 1952, shortly after 2:00 P.M. defendant wired the plaintiff that it was withdrawing its bid which had been submitted at 2:00 o'clock P.M. on April 22, 1952. Knowledge of the contents of this telegram was first obtained in a telephone conversation had between the local director and the defendant and before its actual receipt later that day. As a consequence of this 'phone conversation, the local director wired the defendant notifying it of the local Housing Authority's acceptance of its bid, which telegram was received at its offices the same afternoon at 3:35 P.M. on May 22, 1952.

[10] Upon defendant's refusal to execute the contract, the Housing Authority accepted the next lowest bid, which was submitted by the Lewis Lumber Company of Crowley, Louisiana, in the sum of $221,653.18. The Lewis Lumber Company constructed the housing units and was paid in full for its services in accordance with the terms of its bid. Whereupon the Housing Authority filed suit against defendant and its insurer and bondsmen to recover the difference between the bid of T. Miller

---

execute and deliver a contract in the prescribed form and furnish the required bond within 10 days after the contract is presented to him for signature.' (Italics ours.)

& Sons and that of Lewis Lumber Company, namely $8,875.41 plus 10% Attorney's fees, the latter under the provisions of LSA-R.S. 22:658.[3]

[11] The trial judge rendered judgment in favor of defendant, assigning as his reasons the following:

'The Court is of the opinion that the inserting of Section 4 of the contract by plaintiff changed the terms of the bid of defendant partnership in that it made it conditional upon its approval by a third party and was, therefore, unenforceable. See Fontenot v. Huguet (230 La. 483), 89 So.2d 45.

'However, should the above conclusion be wrong, the Court is still of the opinion that plaintiff cannot recover for the reason that the defendant partnership withdraw its offer timely and before an acceptance by plaintiff. The bids were opened at 2:00 P.M. on April 22, 1952. Shortly after 2:00 P.M. on May 22, 1952, defendant partnership withdrew its bid prior to acceptance by plaintiff. The 30 day period had expired.'

[12] Plaintiff perfected its appeal.

[13] Two principal defenses are here involved. [. . . .] The first defense is that there was no acceptance of the contractor's bid as the alleged acceptance was qualified and conditioned upon the approval of the Public Housing Authority, a third party. The second defense, urged in the alternative, is that defendant's bid was legally withdrawn after the expiration of thirty days and prior to notification of acceptance of the bid or award of the contract.

[14] The first question presented by this appeal is whether the acceptance of defendant's bid by the Housing Authority was conditional and unenforceable as found by the trial judge.

[15] LSA-R.S. 38:2211–2217 prescribe the manner in which contracts may be let for construction by any public corporation or political subdivision. Section 2212 thereof provides for the designation of the time and place that the bids will be opened and the contract let, and it further provides that the governing authority 'shall at the place and time specified open the bids and let the contract. The governing authority may reject any and all bids.' Hence, defendant contends that on the day the bids were opened it was mandatory that the Housing Authority, under the provisions

---

3. 'All insurers issuing any type of contract other than those specified in R.S. 22:656 and 22:657 shall pay the amount of any claim due any insured including any employee under Chapter 10 of Title 23 of the Revised Statutes of 1950 within sixty days after receipt of satisfactory proofs of loss from the insured, employee or any party in interest. Failure to make such payment within sixty days after receipt of such proofs and demand therefor, when such failure is found to be arbitrary, capricious, or without probable cause, shall subject the insurer to a penalty, in addition to the amount of the loss, of 12% Damages on the total amount of the loss, payable to the insured, or to any of said employees, together with all reasonable attorney's fees for the prosecution and collection of such loss, or in the event a partial payment or tender has been made, 12% Of the difference between the amount paid or tendered and the amount found to be due and all reasonable attorney's fees for the prosecution and collection of such amount. * * *'

of said Section, unconditionally accept the lowest bid or reject all the bids; that by including in the resolution of acceptance the condition that the acceptance was to be subject to the approval of the Public Housing Administration, there was neither an unqualified acceptance of the lowest bid nor a rejection of all the bids as required by law; and that any action taken by the Public Housing Administration, or anyone else, not directly a party to the advertisement and reception of bids, cannot be used as a substitute for the specific mandate statutorily prescribed.

[16] It is manifest that under the plain and unmistakable terms and conditions of the advertisement and invitation for bids, plaintiff had the unquestioned right of either accepting or rejecting defendant's bid within the period of thirty days from the date (April 22, 1952) of the opening of the bids. The defendant expressly recognized and bound itself accordingly in submitting its written bid as hereinabove referred to. It is common knowledge that a reasonable delay, in this instance a thirty-day period, is usually included in all bidding for public construction or works preceding the formal acceptance or award of the contract. This delay thus affords the parties an opportunity to investigate, among others, the moral attending risks, an adequate opportunity to investigate the ability, financial, workmanship or otherwise, of the bidder or offerer to perform the contract in an acceptable manner, not excluding the preparation of the formal contract. It must be borne in mind that this public work was being done with financial aid from the Public Housing Administration, and needless to say, the Federal Government, through its Housing Agency, would necessarily insist that the submitted bid, with all heretofore mentioned factors, be first approved by it during the thirty-day period prescribed.

[17] There can be no doubt that defendant was cognizant of the fact that the proposed contract was being financed through local and Federal public funds and that the formal approval of the proposed contract by both agencies was indispensable. This approval by the federal agency is fully established by its letter of May 12, 1952, well within the thirty-day period. Conceding the proviso of Section 4, supra, subjecting the execution of the contract to the approval thereof by the federal agency, to be a suspensive condition, it follows that once the proposed contract was approved, as it is shown to be, the condition became fulfilled, and may be deemed eliminated, thus affording plaintiff the right to accept or reject defendant's bid so long that affirmative action in either instance was exercised and accomplished within the thirty-day period mutually recognized.

[18] Our Codal Articles wisely provide that conditional obligations are such as are made to depend on an uncertain event, and is suspensive when the obligation is not to take effect until the happening of the event.[4] It is further provided that when an obligation has been contracted on condition that an event shall happen within

4. LSA-C.C. Article 2021: 'Conditional obligations are such as are made to depend on an uncertain event. If the obligation is not to take effect until the event happen, it is a suspensive condition; if the obligation takes effect immediately, but is liable to the defeated when the event happens, it is then a resolutory condition.'

a limited time, when the time he expired without the event having taken place, the condition is considered as broken.[5] Manifestly, by analogy and equal reasoning, when the condition is one performed within the limited time the condition becomes fulfilled and is binding and enforceable.

[. . . .]

[19] We now consider the second defense, whether the acceptance of plaintiff was timely. Defendant contended, and was upheld by the district court, that the thirty-day period during which plaintiff could accept or reject its bid began to run at 2:00 o'clock P.M. on April 22, the day the bids were received and opened, and ended at 2:00 o'clock P.M. on May 22. If we accept this view, plaintiff's acceptance by telegram to the defendant at about 3:30 o'clock P.M. on May 22 came too late as defendant had already withdrawn its bid at 2:02 o'clock P.M. that same afternoon. While counsel for defendant has devoted a large portion of the argument in his brief to this proposition, the authorities relied on are inapposite from a legal and factual standpoint. It cites Ratcliff v. Louisiana Industrial Life Ins. Co., 185 La. 557, 169 So. 572; and Richardson v. American Nat. Ins. Co., 18 La.App. 468, 137 So. 370, both involving insurance policy claims in which the contract provided that the policy was to be effective on the date on which it was written. Naturally, the date on which the policy was written, by the very provisions of the contract itself, would be counted in determining its enforceable term. Counsel for defendant also cites election contest cases, namely Smith v. Fitch, La.App., 194 So. 435, and Brown v. Democratic Parish Committee, 183 La. 967, 165 So. 167, in which the courts held that the delay for filing suit begins at the time of the promulgation of the election, not the day after. Clearly these cases are inapplicable and not controlling as to contracts, which are peculiarly governed by Articles 2057[6] and 2058[7] of the LSA-Civil Code.

[20] In the case at bar it is obvious to us that the provision that 'If written notice of the acceptance of this bid * * * within thirty days after the opening thereof, or at any time thereafter before this bid has been withdrawn, the undersigned agrees to execute and deliver a contract in the prescribed form and furnish the required bond within ten days after the contract is presented to him for signature,' shows that the parties clearly contemplated that both periods of time alluded to therein meant, and

---

5. LSA-C.C. Article 2038: 'When an obligation has been contracted on condition that an event shall happen within a limited time, the condition is considered as broken, when the time has expired without the event having taken place. If there be no time fixed, the condition may always be performed, and it is not considered as broken, until it is become certain that the event will not happen.'

6. 'Where a term is given or limited for the performance of an obligation, the obligor has until sunset of the last day limited for its performance, to comply with his obligation, unless the object of the contract can not be done after certain hours of that day.'

7. 'When the contract is to do the act in a certain number of days, or in a certain number of days after the date of the contract, the day of contract is not included in the number of days to be counted, and the obligor has until sunset of the last day of the number enumerated for the performance of his contract, with the exception contained in the last preceding article.'

was intended to mean thirty full days, or in the latter instance ten full days, and not a fraction of a day. It is equally clear to us that the fact that a meeting called for the hour of 2:00 o'clock P.M., after which hour the bids would be opened, read and publicly announced, was not intended as the specific time in which the thirty-day period would begin to run, this hour being one to satisfy the convenience of all interested parties and at which time the meeting would be called to order and thereafter proceed with the orderly process of business. We cannot say that because the meeting was called for 2:00 P.M. necessarily means the actual opening of the bids at that exact hour.

[21] We think, and we are supported in that view by the great weight of modern authority, that in the construction of contracts and statutes, when an act is to be performed within a specified period from or after a day named, the rule is to exclude the first day and to include the last day of the specified period.

[22] In the case here the word 'after' is used. Generally, when computing time 'after' an act, the day on which the event took place is excluded. American Jurisprudence, Vol. 52, Sections 17 and 27, pages 342 and 352.

[23] Our Code of Practice, Articles 180 and 318, in the computation of time for delays in filing pleadings, do not consider fractions of a day.

[24] Hence, the Housing Authority had thirty full days subsequent to the opening of the bids to accept or reject defendant's low bid. In effect, it had until sunset of May 22, 1952, and its telegraphed acceptance of the proposed contract between 2:00 and 3:00 o'clock P.M. on that day, which defendant admits was received by it, constituted a legal and enforceable acceptance of the contract within the thirty-day period to which defendant bound itself.

[25] In oral argument before this Court, both parties agreed that it [*sic*] plaintiff is entitled to recover in this suit, the amount of $8,875.41 sought in its petition to the district court is correct.

[. . . .]

Questions

1. Paragraph 5: What kind of term, if any, would you say the Court is referring to? What legal adjectives would you use to describe whatever term may exist? Explain your answer in proper legal language. Assuming a term exists, in whose favor is it? Does the Louisiana Civil Code lay down a presumption? What is the legal nature of the obligation entered into by the defendant, Miller & Sons? What is, in turn, the legal nature of the obligation binding the Housing Authority?

2. Paragraphs 7–8: Could you provide some important legal details on what the Court refers to summarily as "the following pertinent condition"? Do you think the Court meant "condition" in the sense of Louisiana Civil Code articles 1767–1776 or, instead, in the sense of a charge or duty? Under the facts of this case, was a condition to happen within a term? Explain.

3. Paragraph 9: Does the defendant's argument based on its computation of the time make sense? Could the defendant have found support for his argument in the Louisiana Civil Code? Note that the trial judge "rendered judgment in favor of defendant. . . ." Besides citing a case, is there any other legal authority for the trial judge's ruling?

4. Paragraph 16: In your opinion, does the Court give a fair or good explanation of the interaction between a suspensive condition and a term? Could the Court have made the distinction clearer by quoting specific Louisiana Civil Code articles? What is the Court actually saying in the following statement: "Conceding the proviso of Section 4, subjecting the execution of the contract to the approval thereof by the federal agency, to be a suspensive condition, it follows that once the proposed contract was approved . . . the condition became fulfilled, and may be deemed eliminated, thus affording plaintiff the right to accept. . . ."?

5. Paragraph 19: Read Question 3 above. What was your answer? Why is the Court, in this paragraph, saying that "while counsel for defendant has devoted . . . the authorities relied on are inapposite from a legal and factual standpoint"? Can it be said that counsel for defendant did not do his homework in not referring to the Louisiana Civil Code to begin with? Remember the Court stating that "our Codal Articles wisely provide . . ." in paragraph 18.

6. Paragraph 20: Read footnotes 6 and 7 and read Louisiana Civil Code article 1784. Do you see any major difference? Is the Court making a wise or proper application of then-existing Louisiana Civil Code articles 2057 and 2058? Would the application of Louisiana Civil Code article 1784 lead to a different result?

Holmes Brick & Salvage Co., Inc.
v.
Reo Construction, Inc.

Court of Appeal of Louisiana
First Circuit
September 2, 1971
253 So.2d 562

BLANCHE, Judge.

[1] This matter involves a controversy over a default judgment taken by plaintiff. [. . . .] [T]he following evidence was presented at the confirmation of the default:

'The evidence presented by plaintiff on confirmation consisted of the original contract which was the subject of the suit, the testimony of Mr. Philip H. Holmes, President of the plaintiff corporation, and the affidavit of Mr. Holmes previously filed in the record. The testimony of Mr. Holmes was as follows:

'According to Mr. Holmes, defendant, Reo Construction, Inc., had been hired as general contractor by the Wilberts to construct a new funeral home on the site of Wilbert's Funeral Home in Plaquemine, Louisiana. At the request of the architect for the project, plaintiff examined the Wilbert's property in Plaquemine and gave an estimate setting the price at which plaintiff would demolish and remove the two existing buildings on the Wilbert's property. Plaintiff did make an estimate which consisted of two parts, first, the charge for demolishing and removing a certain smaller building on the rear of the Wilbert property, and second, the charge for demolishing and removing the large building on the front of the Wilbert property which housed the old funeral home. Defendant was not present at this examination. The witness further stated that subsequent to the examination he sent his son, Michael Holmes, to meet with the architect, the Wilberts, and defendant, at which time Michael Holmes made it quite clear to them that any contract entered into by plaintiff would have to provide for plaintiff demolishing and removing both of the buildings.

'Mr. Holmes then explained how such an estimate is made for demolition work. According to his testimony, the usual contract entails the demolition contractor acquiring (ownership) to all or a part of the salvaged materials. It is first necessary to determine the value of the salvage to be realized from a particular building before setting any additional charge for the demolition and removal. The actual charge will then be smaller, if the value of salvaged materials is large, and vice versa.

'Mr. Holmes then identified and explained the contract which he drafted pursuant to his understanding with the parties and pursuant to the estimate, whereby plaintiff agreed to demolish and remove the two buildings in question in two designated phases. Phase #1 involved demolition and removal of the smaller building at the rear of the Wilbert property at a charge of $1,500.00, the salvaged materials to become the property of the plaintiff. Phase #2 involved the demolition and removal of the large building on the front of the Wilbert property at a charge of $4,000.00, the salvaged materials to become the property of the plaintiff. The witness explained that the second phase of the contract was to be performed at a time designated by defendant, which stipulation was included in the contract. Mr. Holmes signed the contract on behalf of plaintiff and forwarded same to Mr. Ray Roussel, who signed on behalf of defendant.

'The testimony of Mr. Holmes further indicated that Phase #1 of the contract was performed by plaintiff and payment in full was received therefor. However, he then stated that defendant never called upon plaintiff to perform Phase #2 of the contract, and that someone else demolished the large building on the front of the Wilbert property.' (Narrative of Facts, Record, pp. 15-A, 15-B)

[2] The contract was offered into evidence and under the date thereof is the following notation:

'Re: Demolition of two buildings at Wilbert's Funeral Home; Plaquemine, La. Work to be done in two phases numbered one and two.' (Exhibit P-1, Record, p. 6)

[3] Phase 2 of the contract referred to above provides:

'* * * At a time designated by you, we will demolish and remove the large building on the front of the property. Our charge for this part of the demolition is $4000.00 (four thousand dollars) payable to us upon completion.' (Exhibit P-1, Record, p. 6)

[4] Plaintiff's suit against the defendant alleges a breach of contract as a result of plaintiff's failure to call upon him to demolish the building called for in Phase 2 of the contract and by permitting the building to be removed by someone else. Damages were sought totaling $7,500 and consist of $4,000 as the agreed contract price and $3,500 as the value of the salvage materials to be derived from the performance of Phase No. 2 of the contract. The Court accepted the estimate of Mr. Holmes as to the value of the salvage material and gave plaintiff judgment as prayed for. From the default judgment in favor of plaintiff, the defendant took this appeal.

[5] The defendant contends that the setting of a time for the plaintiff's performance of Phase 2 was a suspensive condition of the contract. In support of this contention defendant cites the following articles of the Civil Code:

'Art. 2021. Conditional obligations are such as are made to depend on an uncertain event. If the obligation is not to take effect until the event happen, it is a suspensive condition; if the obligation takes effect immediately, but is liable to be defeated when the event happens, it is then a resolutory condition.'

'Art. 2043. The obligation contracted on a suspensive condition, is that which depends, either on a future and uncertain event, or on an event which has actually taken place, without its being yet known to the parties.

'In the former case, the obligation can not be executed till after the event; in the latter, the obligation has its effect from the day on which it was contracted, but it can not be enforced until the event be known.'

[6] The future and uncertain event in this case is alleged to be the defendant's designation of a time for the demolition of the building described in Phase 2 of its contract with plaintiff. We reject this interpretation in favor of plaintiff's argument that the words 'at a time designated by you' constitute the term for the performance of the contract.[1]

---

1. Articles 2048–2051 of the Civil Code are pertinent to this interpretation:
'Art. 2048. The time given or limited for the performance of an obligation, is called its Term.'

[7] In this case the parties had reached an agreement which was complete in all respects except for the time of performance. The 'event' of demolition was certain. The only element of uncertainty was that pertaining to When the demolition would become necessary. Obviously, it was to occur when the defendant's progress on the contract with Wilbert's Funeral Home reached the point where the building described in Phase 2 of the contract was available for demolition and removal.

[8] The words 'at a time designated by you' cannot be construed to mean that the defendant reserved the right to refrain from Ever designating a time. This is not a case of a contract that leaves the defendant the option of requesting the plaintiff's performance. In other words, the contract does not read 'at a time designated by you If you decide to set a time,' nor does it read 'at a time designated by you If you decide to choose us as the demolition company for Phase 2 of the contract.' Instead, the contract called for the plaintiff's performance of Phase 1 immediately and Phase 2 at a date to be determined in the future. Phase 1 was completed as contemplated by the parties; however, the plaintiff's performance of Phase 2 of the contract was never sought by the defendant. Defendant should have sought plaintiff's performance when defendant's progress of the contract with Wilbert's Funeral Home reached the point where the building described in Phase 2 was available for demolition and removal. This event was to occur, and did occur, in the course of defendant's work for Wilbert's.

[9] Since defendant did not designate a time for plaintiff's performance, we hold that plaintiff is entitled to damages for defendant's breach of Phase 2 of the contract described herein.

[....]

Questions

1. Paragraph 1: Describe in legal terms the kinds of obligations created; for example, to do v. not to do, result v. means, personal v. heritable, etc.

2. Paragraphs 2–3: Read carefully the two short excerpts from the contract. What is your understanding of the phrase "at a time designated by you"? Does that phrase signify that the contract contains a term and/or a condition? If you answered "term," what kind? If you answered "condition," what kind?

'Art. 2049. A term may not only consist of a determinate lapse of time, but also of an event, provided that event be in the course of nature, certain; if it be uncertain, it forms a condition.'

'Art. 2050. When no term is fixed by the parties for the performance of the obligation, it may be executed immediately, unless, from the nature of the act, a term, either certain or uncertain, must be implied. Thus, an obligation to pay money, without any stipulation for time, may be enforced at the will of the obligee. But a promise to make a crop of sugar is necessarily deferred, until the uncertain period when the cane shall be fit to cut.'

'Art. 2051. The term differs from the condition, inasmuch as it does not suspend the engagement, but only retards its execution.'

3. Paragraph 5: What do you think of the defendant's argument? If there exists a suspensive condition, what other adjective could you add to better describe that condition? Is the defendant wise in making this argument? *See* La. Civ. Code art. 1772.

4. Paragraph 6: Do you agree with the Court's endorsement of the plaintiff's argument? Can you describe in proper legal terms why "the event of demolition was certain"? Does it matter whether it is the obligee or the obligor of the obligation who designates the time?

5. Paragraph 8: Can you identify the kind of obligation or obligations the court might be considering when it states, basically, that the defendant had no option but to designate a time?

6. Paragraph 9: Shouldn't this statement of the Court have been grounded in at least one Louisiana Civil Code article? If you answered in the affirmative, which one? Could the outcome of the case have been the same had the Court held that there existed a suspensive condition instead of a term? Consider Louisiana Civil Code article 1772 carefully.

F. J. DeMary
v.
Louis A. Fontenot

Court of Appeal of Louisiana
Third Circuit
February 18, 1964
161 So.2d 82

FRUGE, Judge.

[1] This suit was brought to enforce an agreement made between plaintiff and the defendant for the sale of certain race horses.

[2] On August 21, 1959, at Orange, Texas, plaintiff and defendant entered into an agreement whereby plaintiff did 'sell, transfer, assign and deliver' to the defendant six particular horses. The total consideration was stated as $9,200 which, according to the agreement, was to be paid in the following manner:

> 'THE TOTAL CONSIDERATION for all of the above named Race Horses is NINE THOUSAND TWO HUNDRED ($9,200.00) DOLLARS which is payable in the manner as set out, expressly stipulated and fully agreed on as follows:

> "IN THE EVENT either of the above named Race Horses is Sold outright or is Claimed in a Race known and termed as a Claiming Race, the entire Sale Price or the Claiming Price, whichever applies, is to be surrendered to and delivered to the Seller, F. J. DeMary, at his office in the City of Orange, Orange County, Texas, and the amount so paid or surrendered to F. J. DeMary shall be applied by him on the full Purchase Price of NINE

THOUSAND TWO HUNDRED ($9,200.00) DOLLARS. ON ALL EARN-INGS at various Race Tracks where these Race Horses might be raced, the Seller, F. J. DeMary, is to receive and is to be paid an amount equivalent to Forty (40%) Per Cent of the Net Purse, meaning the Track Winning Purse, whether the Purse be for Winning, Placing, Showing or Placing Fourth, or such percentage fully applies to the winnings as commonly termed 'Across the Board' and it is understood that such payments are to be continued until the Seller, F. J. DeMary, has been paid the full Selling Price of NINE THOUSAND TWO HUNDRED ($9,200.00) DOLLARS."

[3] Plaintiff brought suit in St. Landry Parish praying for a judgment for the amount of the purchase price and that his vendor's privilege be recognized and maintained against the property. The defendant filed an untitled exception which was maintained by the district judge. From this ruling plaintiff appeals.

[. . . .]

[4] Defendant contends that since the total consideration is not to be paid until the horses are either 'claimed' or have won a race or races, such operates as a suspensive condition to the completion of the contract until the horses are raced. Plaintiff argues that this is merely a method of paying the purchase price.

[5] In considering the exception we must accept the pleaded facts of the plaintiff. In his pleading plaintiff alleges that defendant is indebted to the plaintiff, that the plaintiff received no payment whatsoever despite amicable demand for payment, and that defendant has actively breached the contract. Whether these alleged facts are true or not is a matter for the trial court to decide when trying the case on the merits. Regardless of whether the agreement contains a suspensive condition or is merely a method of payment, the facts pleaded by plaintiff show that there was an agreement and are sufficiently set forth to entitle plaintiff to a trial on the merits.

[. . . .]

[6] Defendant also contends that the agreement contains a potestative condition because the performance of the agreement is conditioned solely upon the horses being raced.

[7] 'Every obligation is null, that has been contracted, on a potestative condition, on the part of him who binds himself.' LSA-Civil Code art. 2034. 'The last preceding article is limited to potestative conditions, which make the obligation depend solely on the exercise of the obligor's will; but if the condition be, that the obligor shall do or not do a certain act, although the doing or not doing of the act depends on the will of the obligor, yet the obligation depending on such condition, is not void.' LSA-Civil Code art. 2035. In Long v. Foster & Associates, Inc., 242 La. 295, 136 So.2d 48, 53, the Supreme Court stated that 'Article 2034, because of the limitations placed on it by Article 2035, is applicable only to the Purely potestative condition, that is, one which is subject only to the Whim or pleasure of the promisor and would involve no detriment, disadvantage or inconvenience to him if he brings about or hinders the happening of the event on which the obligation depends.' (Emphasis added.)

Thus, we must determine in the present case whether the condition imposed for the payment of the price was purely potestative, depending merely on the whim or pleasure of the promisor. Actually, the issue is whether or not the legal freedom of the plaintiff was limited in any way. Here, if defendant sold the horses or if they were claimed, he had to pay the plaintiff. If defendant raced the horses a portion of the earnings would have to be paid to the plaintiff. Certainly this was a limit on defendant's legal freedom to use the property. There was therefore no purely potestative condition involved in the agreement.

[8] For the foregoing reasons the maintaining of the exception by the district court is reversed and the case is remanded for proceedings not inconsistent with this opinion.

[9] Reversed and remanded.

CULPEPPER, Judge (dissenting).

[10] I respectfully dissent from the majority decision that the exception of no cause of action must be overruled. It is my opinion that the exception of no cause of action should be sustained, because the contract contained a suspensive condition, as to a future and uncertain event, which is not alleged to have taken place. However, I think this case should be remanded to the district court, for the purpose of allowing plaintiff to amend his petition, so as to allege that the suspensive condition has been fulfilled.

[11] LSA-C.C. Art. 2043 provides that if an obligation is contracted on a suspensive condition, as to a future and uncertain event, the obligation is not due until after the event has taken place. Under the contract in question, plaintiff sold the defendant six race horses for the price of $9,200. The contract expressly states that this purchase price is not to be paid unless or until the horses either: (1) are sold outright by the defendant or (2) are claimed in a 'claiming race' or (3) win money in a race. It seems clear to me that these are suspensive conditions, the effect of which is that the purchase price does not become due unless or until one of these events takes place.

[12] Plaintiff's petition alleges only the contract and that plaintiff has not been paid the purchase price for the horses. The petition does not allege that the horses have ever won any money in a race or that they have ever been claimed in a 'claiming race' or that they have been sold outright by the defendant. Thus, under the contract, which is the law between the parties, the plaintiff has failed to state a cause of action in that he has failed to allege that any of these suspensive conditions, on which the obligation to pay the purchase price depends, have taken place.

[13] These suspensive conditions cannot be lightly brushed aside, as the majority has done, by simply stating that, regardless of whether the agreement contains a suspensive condition, the facts pleaded show that there was an agreement by the defendant to pay the purchase price. In my view, the express stipulation for payment, only in the event of certain events taking place, was of the very essence of the agreement. Horse racing is a most precarious business. The parties to this contract

didn't know whether these horses would ever win money or be claimed in a claiming race. It appears to me they clearly intended that unless and until one of these events occurred, defendant would not have to pay anything on the purchase price. (It is not disputed that a contract can provide for payment only from certain specified sources. Williams v. Ligon, La.App., 144 So.2d 131 and the cases cited therein; 40 Am.Jur. 734, Verbo Payment, Section 33.)

[14] I agree with the majority that there was no purely potestative condition in this contract. I do not think it was left entirely within the power of the defendant to determine whether or not he ever paid the purchase price. LSA-C.C. Art. 2024. I think there was an implied condition that the horses would be raced in an effort to win money or have the horses claimed. LSA-C.C. Art. 2026. However, if it is the contention of the plaintiff that there was an implied obligation on the part of the defendant to race the horses, and that defendant has prevented the fulfillment of the suspensive conditions by failing to enter the horses in a race, then in order to state a cause of action under the contract he must certainly allege such facts. (Plaintiff's counsel stated to us in oral argument that the horses actually have been raced but counsel did not state whether the horses have won any money or been claimed in a claiming race.)

[15] In his brief filed in this court, counsel for the plaintiff has, in the alternative, asked that in the event we conclude the exception of no cause of action must be sustained, we remand this case to the district court for the purpose of allowing him to amend his petition so as to allege that the suspensive conditions have taken place. I think the case should be remanded to the lower court for this purpose, in accordance with the provisions of LSA-C.C.P. Art. 934 which provides for amendment within a delay allowed by the court.

[....]

Questions

1. Paragraphs 1–15: After you have read the case, please carefully read Louisiana Civil Code article 2439 defining the contract of sale. In the instant case, was a price agreed upon? Was there an agreement as to the object of the sale, i.e., the horses and their number? Without going into any detail, was there a sale in your opinion? Look now at Louisiana Civil Code article 2456. On the basis of these two articles, where was the ownership of the horses: with the seller or with the buyer?

2. Paragraph 2: Describe in legal terms the modalities of payment of the price. Remember that the buyer is bound to pay the price, but the modalities of payment of the price may vary.

3. Paragraph 4: What do you think of the defendant's exception based on the existence of his suspensive condition theory? Would a suspensive condition affect, in this case, the formation of the contract or the performance of its obligations to pay the price by the buyer? Remember that under Louisiana Civil

Code article 2456, the ownership of the horses had passed to the buyer. What, then, is your answer?

4. Paragraph 6: Why would the defendant argue that the agreement contains a potestative condition? What kind of potestative condition? What kind of condition is the court referring to: suspensive or resolutory? Considering that the defendant had ownership of the horses and was to pay the price, if the condition affects the buyer's performance of having to pay the price, what should happen if the buyer does not pay the price? Is the condition, now, still suspensive or not?

5. Paragraphs 1–15: Including the dissenting opinion in this question, is it conceivable that the judges failed to draw the proper line between an uncertain suspensive term and a suspensive condition? Can you explain the difference(s) between the two?

Succession of Cladie J. Wade

Court of Appeal of Louisiana
Third Circuit
July 21, 2021
326 So.3d 306

PERRY, Judge.

[. . . .]

[1] [. . . .] The primary issue before this court concerns the following conditional legacies contained in Cladie's will:

> With respect to the property in Oakland, California which was owned by Theodore Harris and willed to me but placed in the name of Alma Rea Wade's name [sic] for accommodating purposes only, I will and bequeath that this property be sold and after all obligations incidental to the sale of the property have been paid, the remaining portion is to be divided equally among CARL WADE, ALMA REA WADE AND CLADIE J. WADE.
>
> . . . .
>
> If LAMA REA WADE does not sell the property in California and divide the proceeds from the sale in the manner I have previously suggested, I will and bequeath that all bequests I have made to Alma Rea Wade would be revoked and all of those bequests would go to CARL WADE. In other words, if she does not sell the property and divide the assets as requested, she is *not* to receive any bequests from me; Carl is to receive everything.

[2] Alma and Claude both sought judicial determinations [. . .] on the legality of Cladie's conditional legacies. Alma chiefly argued the condition on her legacy was

contrary to the laws or to morals in violation of Article 1519 of the Louisiana Civil Code.[3] [. . . .]

[3] Carl argued the conditional legacies are valid and clearly indicated Cladie's intent — sell the California property and receive your portion of my estate or keep the California property and receive nothing from my estate.[4] He contended such an optional bequest is not repugnant to the law or to good morals, and to not acknowledge and enforce the conditional legacies is to give no effect to Cladie's intended and rightful disposition of her estate. *See* La. Civ.Code art. 1612.

[4] Following a hearing, the trial court granted summary judgment in favor of Carl, upholding the conditional legacies contained in Cladie's will. [. . . .]

[5] On appeal, both Alma and Carl argue the trial court erred. Alma contends the trial court legally erred in upholding conditional legacies she asserts violate public policy by allowing, in effect, Cladie to bequeath property she did not own. [. . . .]

[. . . .]

[6] Concerning Cladie's conditional legacies, neither party asserts there are disputed facts. The issue before us is purely a legal one — namely, whether the conditional legacies herein are valid and enforceable.

[. . . .]

[7] [. . . .] Alma urges this court to disallow conditional legacies which seek to settle grievances with relatives or unfavorable wills by requiring legatees to alienate their own property.

[8] Carl concedes Cladie did not own the California property; however, he argues whether or not Cladie had an ownership interest is inconsequential. Carl denies Cladie was bequeathing property she did not own; instead, he insists Cladie was simply giving Alma an option to comply with her request. [. . . .] Carl argues no

---

3. In her motion for summary judgment, Alma also sought nullification of the following provision contained in an "Addendum to the Last Will and Testament of Cladie J. Wade dated August 13, 2007," which Cladie effectuated on November 17, 2009:

> The purpose for my adding this addendum is to resolve the dispute involving the property that is located at 1501 Campbell Street, Oakland, California. With respect to that property which is in the name of Theodore Harris of which I am the owner, I will and bequeath that if that property is not sold prior to my death, I want the property to be owned equally by my two children, namely: ALMA REA WADE and CARL J. WADE. Further, if the property does not sell quickly or does not sell for what my two children feel is a fair and just amount, I will and bequeath that the property will continue to be rented and after all expenses are subtracted from the monthly rental, the residue will be divided equally between my two children, ALMA REA WADE and CARL J. WADE.

> When the property in California is sold, then the proceeds will be divided equally between my two children.

4. Responding to the purported addendum to Cladie's will, Carl conceded, "Cladie did not own the property in California and for that reason the addendum to the subject Will should be reputed not written given the fact that it does contain an impossible condition, i.e., bequeathing property that Cladie did not own. La.Civ.Code Art. 1519."

effect would be given to Cladie's intended and rightful disposition of her estate if her conditional legacies were ruled invalid.

[....]

[9] We consider the conditional legacies at issue illegal and void. We cannot sanction allowing Cladie to accomplish after death that which she could not lawfully do during her life. Further, we believe to rule otherwise would result in far-reaching consequences of elevating a testator's intent over the public interest of property ownership.

[....]

[10] Since there were no forced heirs, Cladie could dispose of her property in any way she saw fit. However, the conditional legacies herein evidence Cladie sought to exert control over property not her own. To require Alma to alienate her property and share the profits with Carl grants control over property which does not belong to Cladie's estate. Simply stated, Cladie's testamentary rights cannot outweigh Alma's property ownership rights. [....]

[....]

See also *Turner v. Watson*, 912 So.2d 391 (La. 2nd Cir. 2005).

Comparative Law Perspective

— Civil Law —

Robert J. Pothier, *A Treatise on the Law of Obligations or Contracts*

vol. 1 n°s 227-232 at 130-32 & n°s 198-201 at 111-12
(William David Evans trans., 1806)

Article III

Of a Term of Payment

[227] An obligation is either contracted with a term for discharging it, or not: when it is contracted without a term, the creditor may require it to be discharged immediately; when it includes a term, he cannot require it until the term is expired.

§ I. What a Term of Payment is, and the different Kinds of it

[228] A term is a space of time granted to the debtor for discharging his obligation: there are express terms, resulting from the positive stipulations of the agreement; as where I undertake to pay a certain sum on a certain day; and also terms which tacitly result from the nature of the things which are the object of the engagement, or from the place where the act is agreed to be done. For instance, if a builder engages to construct a house for me, I must allow a reasonable time for his fulfilling his engagement. If a person at *Orleans* undertakes to deliver something to my correspondent

at *Rome*, the engagement tacitly includes the time necessary for taking the thing to *Rome*. [. . . .]

§ II. Of the Effect of a Term, and in what Respect it differs from a Condition

[230] A term differs from a condition, inasmuch as a condition suspends the engagement formed by the agreement: whereas a term does not suspend the engagement, but merely postpones the execution of it. [. . . .]

[231] A term defers the right of requiring payment until it is fully completed. Therefore if I promise to pay this year, no demand can be enforced on the last day; for that day is comprised within the term.

[232] This effect of a term, in postponing the right of requiring payment until it is expired, is common to a term of right, and to a term of grace.

A term of right has another effect which is peculiar to itself, viz. that it prevents the debt being opposed by way of compensation or set-off, until it is expired. [. . . .]

Article I

Of Suspensive Conditions, (a) and Conditional Obligations

[198] A conditional obligation, is that which is suspended by the condition under which it was contracted, and which is not yet accomplished. [. . . .]

§ I. What a Condition is, and its different Kinds

[199] A condition is the case of a future uncertain event, which may or may not happen, and upon which the obligation is made to depend.

[200] Conditions upon which an obligation may be suspended, are divided into positive and negative.

A positive condition consists in the case where a thing that may or may not happen, shall happen, as *if I marry.*

A negative condition is that, which consists in the case where something, that may or may not happen, shall not happen, as *if I do not marry.*

[201] Conditions are also distinguished into potestative, casual, and mixed.

A potestative condition is that, which is in the power of the person in whose favor the obligation is contracted; (a) as if I engage to give my neighbor a sum of money, in case he cuts down a tree which obstructs my prospect.

A casual condition is that, which depends upon accident, and is no wise in the power of the creditor, as *if such a ship shall arrive safe.*

A mixed condition is that, which depends upon the concurrence of the will of the creditor, and of a third person; as if you marry my cousin.

Robert Pothier, *Traité des Obligations*

vol. 1, n° 204 at 211-12 (2d ed. 1825)

The condition of an impossible thing [. . .] under which someone promises something renders the [**juridical**] act [**from which the promise springs**] absolutely null when that impossible thing is *in faciendo* [*i.e.*, **when it involves doing something**]. No obligation is born from such an act. [. . . .] [A]s if I have promised you a sum under this condition: *if you make a triangle without angles.* [. . . .]

When the impossible condition is *in non faciendo* [*i.e.*, **when it involves *not* doing something**], as if I have promised you a sum *if you do not stop the sun in its course*, it does not render null the obligation under which it is contracted. This condition has no effect, and the obligation is pure and simple.

C.-B.-M. Toullier, *Le Droit Civil Français*

vol. 3, n°s 481-482 at 307 (J.-B. Duvergier rev., 6th ed. 1846)

481. A condition is impossible when the accustomed order of nature is an obstacle to its accomplishment. Roman legislation gave as examples of it [i] if you touch heaven with your finger, [ii] if you drink all the water in the sea, [iii] if you give me a centaur, etc. This is a natural impossibility.

A condition that's possible in itself can become impossible by reason of some circumstance that gets added to it. For example, the condition of building a house *in three days*. This is what one calls impossibility of fact. [. . . .]

Finally, there are some impossibilities that are absolute and others that are only relative and personal. It is impossible *for me* to make a painting or a statue as Girodet or Canova could do it. [. . . .]

482. Because the Code does not explain what it means by an impossible condition, some doubt can arise. There is no doubt, however, in regard to natural impossibility and impossibility in fact. As to relative impossibility, Roman legislation determined that it does *not* annul contracts and that a stipulation is valid, even though a person engages himself to do a thing that is personally impossible for him, if it is possible for another. This determination ought to be continued under the domain of the Code, for it is founded in reason.

Gabriel Baudry-Lacantinerie et Louis Joseph Barde, *Traité Théorique et Pratique De Droit Civil*

vol. 11 (Des Obligations vol. II), nᵒˢ 809–826 at 34–49 (2d ed. 1902)

809. [. . . .] [L]et us determine the bearing of the principle formulated in the first part of Article 1179 [**"A condition, once fulfilled, has effects that are retroactive to the day on which the engagement was contracted."**]: after the occurrence of the conditional event, the situation is the same as if the obligation had arisen at the moment of the contract and had been immediately perfected. [. . . .]

The retroactive effect of a fulfilled condition [. . .] is [. . .] [a] fiction. [. . . .] [S]ince this retroactivity is a fiction, it is appropriate to use a restrictive interpretation in cases in which it is doubtful that retroactivity should be applied.

810. Inasmuch as Article 1179 is conceived in the most general terms, the principle of retroactivity is applied in the system of our Civil Code regardless whether the condition is suspensive or resolutory. [. . . .]

815. From the point of view of conditional ownership, here are the principal consequences of retroactivity:

1° When an obligation to give a certain and determined thing has been contracted subject to a suspensive condition, the creditor, once the condition is fulfilled, will been deemed to have become the owner from the very day of the contract. It follows from this that all real rights to which the alienator consents in the interval between the making of the contract and the realization of the condition will be effaced, not simply for the future, but also for the past, in such a fashion that, in the eyes of the law, they will have never existed. In fact, these real rights turn out to have emanated from a person who, at the moment at which he granted them, was not the owner.

816. 2° In an inverse sense, again in a case involving the accomplishment of a suspensive condition, the real rights granted on the thing by the acquirer *pendente conditione* turn out to have existed starting from the moment at which they were granted. [. . . .]

817. 3° In the case of an alienation under a resolutory condition, real rights constituted on the thing by the acquirer, while the condition was in suspense, are reputed, once the condition is realized, never to have arisen. [. . . .] (l) Thus, contracts whereby the acquirer under a resolutory condition has granted real rights on the alienated immovable to third persons are annihilated by the occurrence of the condition. [. . . .]

818. 4° In an inverse sense, in the same hypothetical case [**an alienation subject to a resolutory condition**], [. . .] real rights granted on the thing by the alienator *pendente conditione* turn out to have been granted by the owner and, as a result, to have been acquired from the moment of the making of the contract. [. . . .]

819. 5° When an immovable sold under a suspensive condition is seized and judicially sold at the request of one of the creditors of the seller, this seizure and this judicial sale, in the event that the condition should be realized, cannot be asserted against the conditional acquirer, if the title of the seizing creditor and those of all the other inscribed creditors are posterior in date to the transcription of the conditional sale. [. . . .]

820. If an immovable alienated under a resolutory condition has been seized and judicially sold *pendente conditione,* what will become of the seizure and the judicial sale if the event occurs? When all the mortgages that burden the immovable are for the benefit of the acquirer, the seizure and judicial sale [**are as if they**] did not happen. On the contrary, the seizure and sale subsist if there is one or there are several mortgage creditors of the alienator or of a previous owner, even if the seizing party was a creditor of the acquirer. Thus, in order for the seizure and judicial sale to be maintained, it suffices if only one of the mortgage creditors was able to effect the seizure in regard to the alienator. [. . . .]

821. 6° When an immovable sold under a suspensive or resolutory condition is possessed by a third person who is in the process of acquisitive prescription, the prescription, once the contemplated event is realized, must be assessed in relation to the contracting party for whose benefit the condition was fulfilled. It is yet another necessary consequence of the retroactive effect [**of the fulfillment of a condition**] that this effect is produced in regard to third persons as well as in regard to the parties. It follows from this that this contracting party [**the one benefitted by the fulfillment of the condition**] could invoke the causes of suspension or interruption of prescription that would have existed as to him. But he could not, on the other hand, avail himself of those that would have existed as to the other contracting party.

823. We have seen that acts of disposition are effaced by the retroactive effect of a fulfilled condition. Should this conclusion be extended to acts of administration, in particular, to leases?

Are leases granted *pendente conditione* by him who has alienated a thing under a suspensive condition retroactively annihilated by the occurrence of the condition?

Is it the same with leases passed *pendente conditione* by the acquirer under a resolutory condition?

In our opinion, these questions must be answered in the negative. The contrary solution has the consequence of rendering very difficult, if not impossible, the administration of the thing that forms the object of the contract. If leases granted by the intermediary possessor [**the alienator, in the case of a suspensive condition; the acquirer, in the case of a resolutory condition**] should fall in the event of the fulfillment of the condition, then no one would deal with him. Is it conceivable that the legislature has accepted a solution that is, from an economic point of view, so bad as this? [. . . .]

Finally, when there is doubt as to whether Article 1179 should be applied, must we not pronounce ourselves in favor of the more restrictive interpretation, inasmuch as retroactivity has the character of a fiction?

825. Should one make an exception to the principle of retroactivity when the condition is suspensive and is potestative for the debtor? Clearly this question can be posed only in relation to a condition that is *simply* potestative, that is to say, when the condition consists of an event that the debtor has the power to cause to occur or to prevent. The question could not include *a purely* potestative condition — a condition *si voluero* — since that kind of condition renders the obligation that it affects null. Art. 1174. Such being the bearing of the question, it is necessary to respond that a condition that is potestative on the part of the debtor has, when it is fulfilled, the same retroactive effect as every other condition.

Chapter 6

Conjunctive, Alternative & Facultative Obligations[1]

Louisiana Sources of Law
Louisiana Civil Code[2]

Art. 1807. Conjunctive obligation.

An obligation is conjunctive when it binds the obligor to multiple items of performance that may be separately rendered or enforced. In that case, each item is regarded as the object of a separate obligation.

The parties may provide that the failure of the obligor to perform one or more items shall allow the obligee to demand the immediate performance of all the remaining items. (Acts 1984, No. 331, §1, eff. Jan. 1, 1985.)

Art. 1808. Alternative obligation.

An obligation is alternative when an obligor is bound to render only one of two or more items of performance. (Acts 1984, No. 331, §1, eff. Jan. 1, 1985.)

Art. 1809. Choice belongs to the obligor.

When an obligation is alternative, the choice of the item of performance belongs to the obligor unless it has been expressly or impliedly granted to the obligee. (Acts 1984, No. 331, §1, eff. Jan. 1, 1985.)

Art. 1811. Obligor may not choose part of one item.

An obligor may not perform an alternative obligation by rendering as performance a part of one item and a part of another. (Acts 1984, No. 331, §1, eff. Jan. 1, 1985.)

Art. 1812. Impossibility or unlawfulness of one item of performance.

When the choice belongs to the obligor and one of the items of performance contemplated in the alternative obligation becomes impossible or unlawful, regardless of the fault of the obligor, he must render one of those that remain.

When the choice belongs to the obligee and one of the items of performance becomes impossible or unlawful without the fault of the obligor, the obligee must choose one

---

1. There are no La. Civil Code articles on "Facultative Obligations." But see the section on "Doctrine," below, and footnote 12.

2. Not all the Code articles under this title have been reproduced.

of the items that remain. If the impossibility or unlawfulness is due to the fault of the obligor, the obligee may choose either one of those that remain, or damages for the item of performance that became impossible or unlawful. (Acts 1984, No. 331, §1, eff. Jan. 1, 1985.)

Art. 1814. Obligor's liability for damages.

When the choice belongs to the obligor, if all the items of performance contemplated in the alternative obligation have become impossible and the impossibility of one or more is due to the fault of the obligor, he is liable for the damages resulting from his failure to render the last item that became impossible.

If the impossibility of one or more items is due to the fault of the obligee, the obligor is not bound to deliver any of the items that remain. (Acts 1984, No. 331, §1, eff. Jan. 1, 1985.)

Doctrine

Louisiana Law of Obligations in General, A Précis

Sections 4.1.1 to 4.3.1

Alternative Obligations

An alternative obligation requires that a choice be made between two or more items of performance so that the obligor will be released from his obligation whenever he will have carried out one of those items of performance. The essence of an alternative obligation is to place two (or more) items of performance on the same plane so that they are all *principal* items. No single item is an accessory to another. If the obligation deals with two objects, they are equally due and the performance of either one will be sufficient to extinguish the whole obligation. [....]

It is possible to see in an alternative obligation a sort of insurance granted to an obligee-creditor, a kind of guarantee of payment assuring him that at least one item of performance out of two or more will be conveyed to him. [....]

It is a presumption of the Louisiana law of obligations that, in an alternative obligation, "**the choice of the item of performance belongs to the obligor.**" [....]

The presumption that the choice belongs to the obligor is a rebuttable legal presumption since it merely protects the interest of private parties. Consequently, it is conceivable that the choice of the object of the obligation be "**expressly or impliedly granted to the obligee.**" [....]

Either party who is given the choice must make that choice in good faith. [....]

Whenever the choice of one item of performance has been made by the proper party and in due time, that item is owed in its entirety. Once selected, the item becomes the only object of an obligation which, from alternative, has now become pure and simple. The exercise of the choice extinguishes the alternative feature of the obligation. [....]

Facultative Obligation

An obligation is facultative when an obligor owes one particular principal item of performance and when, at the same time, he may be released of that performance by tendering another item as a substitute item which will take the place of the principal item of performance. The facultative obligation is thus characterized by the existence of a principal item which is the only one truly due under the obligation (this item is said to *in obligatione*) but, to that item the obligor, at the moment of performing may, of his own volition, substitute another item for his performance (this item is said to be *in facilitate solutionis*). [. . . .]

LSA-C.C. Art. 234 offers an example of a facultative obligation. Under this article a father, or a mother, who owes alimony to a child **"may offer to receive, support and maintain the child, to whom he or she may owe alimony, in his or her house . . ."** The principal obligation imposed on the father or mother is to pay alimony for the support of the child; the substitute facultative obligation available to the father or mother is to receive the child in his or her own home. This facultative obligation is available to the father or mother in response to the child's only right to alimony payments.

Louisiana Law of Obligations in General, A Treatise

Section 4.1.1

162. One or more objects: items of performance. An obligation may bear on one, two, or more objects or items of performance. **"When several different things form the object of a contract, it is either conjunctive or alternative."** [. . . .]

Conjunctive Obligations

163. Definition-Notion. [. . . .] In the words of La. Civ. Code **art. 1807, "an obligation is conjunctive when it binds the obligor to multiple items of performance that may be separately rendered or enforced. In that case, each item is regarded as the object of a separate obligation. The parties may provide that the failure of the obligor to perform one or more items shall allow the obligee to demand the immediate performance of all the remaining items."** This same obligation is defined in the *Dictionary of the Civil Code* as "an obligation by virtue of which the debtor is cumulatively bound to carry out multiple obligations."[6]

164. Items of performance. The obligation created in such a conjunctive obligation may bear either on several different items of performance or it may involve identical items of performance. Either way, the items of performance are bound in such a way as to form one universality[7] of things. [. . . .]

---

6. *Dictionary of the Civil Code*, p. 128, word: conjonctif, ive (2).

7. Universality: "2. Aggregate of things (called universality of fact) forming a collection (ex., a library) or a complex legal entity (ex., business) considered overall as a single thing (ex., in connection with a sale or a bequest) and subject to a specific legal regime." *Dictionary of the Civil Code*, p. 566, word: universalité.

166. Identical items of performance. [. . . .]

A universality of identical things or items will become the object of a conjunctive obligation when all these things or items are distinctively listed or enumerated and, yet, they are all bound together by a connecting link, a "copulative," which brings them all under one single universality.[11] Such would be the case, for instance, where an obligor (let us assume a lessee) would agree to pay his obligee (the lessor) an amount of money (the rent, which is a "universality") in four separate installments spread over a certain period of time. Each quarterly installment can be looked upon as the item of performance of a separate constituent "quarterly" obligation, each one subjected, therefore, to its own prescriptive period. However, the *whole* rent (or universality) is eventually owed, as a lessee may quickly discover should the lessor have included an acceleration clause in the contract of lease. The effect of such a clause is to trigger an anticipated maturity of the remaining installments or items of performance upon the lessee's failure to perform, i.e., to pay one installment on time. As stated above, "**the parties may provide that the failure of the obligor to perform one or more items shall allow the obligee to demand the immediate performance of all the remaining items.**"[12]

Cases

Mrs. Estelle Polmer Rabin
v.
Margaret S. Blazas and Harry Frisch

Court of Appeal of Louisiana
Fourth Circuit
September 16, 1988
537 So.2d 221

ARMSTRONG, Judge.

[1] The defendant, Harry Frisch, appeals from a judgment rendered against him for breach of an agreement to purchase real property. Frisch argues that the judgment of the trial court should be reversed because 1) the court erred in failing to rescind the agreement on the ground that he was incapable of contracting due to his age and infirmity; and 2) the court erred in awarding an amount in excess of that stated in the liquidated damages clause of the agreement. For the reasons that

---

11. Such an illustration must be distinguished from an item or an object of performance made up of multiple identical things but referred to as a single item under a general name; examples would be a "library," a "flock of sheep," etc.

12. La. Civ. Code art. 1807-2.

For details on Alternative Obligations and Facultative Obligations, see *Louisiana Law of Obligations in General, A Treatise*, Alain A. Levasseur, p. 135 to 150 (work cited).

follow, we affirm the judgment of the trial court as to the breach of contract claim against Frisch and modify as to the amount of damages awarded.

[2] On April 11, 1986 Margaret S. Blazas and defendant Frisch signed a Gertrude Gardner Realtors, Inc. document entitled "agreement to purchase or sell." They signed on the lines beneath the word "offeror" for the purchase of real property located at 801–03 Desire Street and 3401–03 Dauphine Street in New Orleans. The purchase offer was for $55,000.00, all cash. Lines 34 through 37 of the agreement provide:

> Upon acceptance of this offer, seller and purchaser shall be bound by all its terms and conditions and purchaser becomes *obligated to deposit* with seller's agent not later than 48 hours from acceptance, *10% of the purchase price* amounting to $_____ and *failure to do shall be considered a breach* thereof, *and seller shall have the right,* at sellers option, to reinstate said property for sale and *to demand liquidated damages equal to the amount of the deposit* or specific performance, *and purchaser shall,* in either event, *be liable for the agents commission, attorneys fees and costs.*

(Emphasis added.) On the line provided for the amount reflecting 10% of the purchase price, the figure $5,500.00, and the word "chek" (sic), are hand written. Alex Seidenfield is listed as both the selling and the listing agent and Gertrude Gardner is listed as the Broker. The offer was accepted by the seller, plaintiff Estelle P. Rabin, on the same date, April 11, 1986.[1]

[3] Neither Frisch nor Blazas tendered $5,500.00 to Seidenfield within forty-eight hours of the offer's acceptance as was required in the agreement. Rabin then filed this action against Frisch and Blazas alleging breach of contract as a result of their failure to deposit the same. [. . . .]

[4] After a bench trial, judgment was rendered against Frisch in the principal amount of $12,450.00, plus costs, allocated as follows: $5,500.00 for breach of contract; $5,500.00 for liquidated damages; $450.00 for lost rent on the property subject to the sale, and $1,000.00 for attorney's fees.[4, 5]

[5] By his first assignment of error defendant Frisch, an eighty year old man with hearing difficulty, argues that the contract as to him should be rescinded because, due to his age and mental infirmity, he did not have the mental capacity to contract. In support of this contention, Frisch points to the testimony of Dr. Jack C. Castrogiovanni, his internist. Dr. Castrogiovanni's deposition was admitted into evidence

---

1. *See* plaintiff's Exhibit No. 2.

4. On September 12, 1986 a default judgment was rendered against Blazas in the principal amount of $5,500.00 plus attorneys' fees in the amount of $2,000.00 and all costs. That judgment is not before us for review.

5. The trial court's judgment approved a $3,000.00 attorney's fee, but reduced it by $2,000.00, the amount assessed against Blazas in the September 12, 1986 default judgment.

over the plaintiff's objection.[6] Dr. Castrogiovanni stated that Frisch suffered from organic brain syndrome. Dr. Castrogiovanni described this disease as "characterized by recent memory loss, inability to have introspection frequently into the acts of one, progressive inability to care for one's own needs, and it's more or less like sliding scale (of degree)." However, this diagnosis was not made until September 19, 1986, more than five months after Frisch entered into the agreement in question. Moreover, although Dr. Castrogiovanni also testified that organic brain syndrome develops over a period of time (so that it could have existed six months earlier), he did not testify that Frisch had organic brain syndrome at least six months before the diagnosis was made. In any case, it is clear that Frisch has never been interdicted.

[6] Article 1925 of the Louisiana Civil Code provides:

> A noninterdicted person, *who was deprived of reason at the time of contracting, may obtain rescission of an onerous contract upon the ground of incapacity only upon showing that the other party knew or should have known that person's incapacity.*

(Emphasis added.) Thus, because Frisch has failed to prove, in the first instance, that he was deprived of reason *at the time of contracting,* the trial court was correct in not rescinding the contract as to Frisch. Moreover, even if Frisch were incapacitated he has, nevertheless, failed in his second burden of proving that "the other party", i.e., Seidenfeld, knew or should have known of such incapacity.

[7] Our review of Seidenfeld's testimony with respect to Frisch's reasoning capacity both before, as well as at, *the time of contracting,* bears this out. Seidenfeld testified that, although Frisch had difficulty hearing, he did appear to understand what he, Seidenfeld, was saying. Seidenfeld also portrayed Frisch, who owned several properties, as a man knowledgeable in real estate transactions and as having asked many questions with respect to the property he was about to purchase on April 11, 1986, the date of the sale.

[8] Before April 11, 1986, Seidenfeld met Frisch on only one other occasion, April 8 or 9, 1986. On that day, Seidenfeld met with Blazas to show her the property. According to Seidenfeld, Frisch drove Blazas to the site of the property, rolled down the car window and had a discussion with Seidenfeld about interest rates and financing and the advantage of paying cash. In short, there was nothing to put Seidenfeld on notice that Frisch suffered from any mental infirmity either before or on the day Frisch signed the agreement.

[....]

[9] It is clear under the terms of the contract that, upon failure to make the required $5,500.00 deposit, the buyer becomes liable for $5,500.00 in liquidated damages "or" specific performance — not both. This is consistent with La.Civ.Code

---

6. We need not decide the correctness of the trial court's decision to admit this testimony because, even assuming its admission was in error, our result would be the same.

art. 2007. Rabin opted to exercise the liquidated damages provision rather than to demand specific performance. However, in awarding Rabin $5,500.00 liquidated damages *plus* $5,500.00 for breach of contract, the trial court was awarding liquidated damages *and* partial specific performance. That was error.

[10] The trial court's award of $450.00 for lost rent also was error. The $5,500.00 liquidated damages clause fixes the amount of *all* damages that may be recovered under the contract. By contract, the parties substituted the liquidated sum of $5,500.00 for actual damages with the result that, upon breach, *actual* damages need not be determined and may not be awarded. Thus, in opting to exercise the liquidated damages clause, Rabin was entitled to recover $5,500.00, but no more.

[. . . .]

Questions

1. Paragraph 2: How do you read the words "terms" and "conditions" in the excerpt of the agreement? What kind of obligation is an obligation to deposit? *See* La. Civ. Code arts. 2926, *et seq.* Is failure "to do" a term or a condition? Can you fully characterize your choice in proper legal terms? Do the words "at seller's option" suggest that the seller will be the only one with the right to choose among two or more obligations that will have to be performed by the obligor/buyer? From the point of view of the latter, is that option of the seller like a suspensive condition?

2. Paragraph 9: In a prior paragraph, the Court referred specifically to Louisiana Civil Code article 1925 in support of its legal analysis. What Louisiana Civil Code article(s) should the Court have cited in this paragraph, particularly where the Court uses the preposition "or"?

See Walter J. Wadlington III, *Conjunctive, Alternative and Facultative Obligations in Louisiana*, 37 Tulane L. Rev. 67 (1962).

Stanford Latter and Robert L. Yuspeh
v.
State of Louisiana

Court of Appeal of Louisiana
First Circuit
March 12, 1993
621 So.2d 1159

PITCHER, Judge.

[. . . .]

Background

[1] According to the petition, on June 15, 1981, petitioners, Stanford Latter and Robert L. Yuspeh, submitted a bid for leasing the 13,000 square feet of their property at 2025 Canal Street, New Orleans, Louisiana, to the State of Louisiana, Department of Health and Human Resources, Office of Family Security. Subsequent thereto, petitioners were notified on August 17, 1981, that their bid had been accepted, were requested to execute the lease, and were informed that the bid would be forwarded to the Assistant Commissioner of the Division of Administration for approval.

[2] On September 1, 1981, petitioners and R.P. Guissinger, Secretary of the Department of Health and Human Resources, executed the lease of the Canal Street property. The lease provided for a term of five years commencing on November 1, 1981, and ending on October 31, 1986. The consideration of the lease was the payment of $552,499.80, payable in sixty equal installments of $9,208.33 each. The first installment under the lease was due on November 1, 1981, and the remaining installments were due on the first day of each month thereafter.[1] The lease also provided that the lessee would pay for all public utilities such as gas, water, and electricity. On April 13, 1982, the Division of Administration approved the lease, and occupancy of the leased premises began on July 15, 1982.

Facts

[3] On November 18, 1985, petitioners filed a suit for declaration judgment, "declaring the State of Louisiana to pay Seventy Three Thousand Six Hundred

---

1. The lease also provided as follows:

   [I]n the event occupancy by Lessee occurs subsequent to the first rental payment date Lessor waives any rights to rental payments for a period of thirty (30) days after Lessee actually occupies the leased premises.

   Should the Lessee be unable to obtain possession of the leased premises within sixty (60) days after Division of Administration approval of the lease, whether or not said delay is caused by the Lessor, the Lessee shall be entitled to the remission of rent for such term during which the Lessee is deprived of possession, and to reimbursement for any damages which the Lessee may suffer as a result of said deprivation of possession. In addition, should the Lessee be deprived of possession of the leased premises for a period of more than sixty (60) days, then this lease may be cancelled at the option of the Lessee.

Sixty-Six and 64/100 Dollars ($73,666.64) for past due rentals and Eight Thousand One Hundred Eighty-Nine and 58/100 Dollars ($8,189.58) for utilities petitioners paid on behalf of defendant between November 1, 1981, and July 15, 1982."[2] The State of Louisiana answered the petition, denying the allegations set forth therein and alleged that petitioners' action for past due rent had prescribed by the passage of three years and that petitioners' action for wrongful or intentional acts or abuse of right had prescribed by the passage of one year. Petitioners subsequently amended their petition on May 19, 1990.

[4] On June 29, 1990, the State reurged the peremptory exception raising the objection of prescription. After a hearing, the trial court sustained the State's peremptory exception raising prejudice.

[5] From this adverse judgment, petitioners appeal, assigning as error the trial court's sustaining of the objection of prescription. Petitioners argue that prescription does not commence to run until the end of the lease term and that, if prescription commenced to run prior to the end of the lease term, then the rental payments from July 15, 1982, through October 31, 1986, suspended or interrupted the running of prescription as to the unpaid amounts.

Prescription

[6] Although petitioners filed a petition for declaratory judgment as opposed to a petition for damages, the allegations of the petition determine the true nature of the action and the applicable prescriptive period. *Starns v. Emmons,* 538 So.2d 275, 277 (La.1989); *Hampton v. Hibernia National Bank,* 598 So.2d 502, 503 (La.App. 2nd Cir.1992); *Arceneaux v. Courtney,* 448 So.2d 197, 198 (La.App. 1st Cir.1984). The petition filed by petitioners clearly requests payment for past due rentals.

[7] LSA-C.C. article 3494(2) provides that an action for arrearage of rent is subject to liberative prescription of three years. LSA-C.C. art. 3495 provides that prescription begins to run from the day payment is exigible. *See Montiville v. City of Westwego,* 592 So.2d 390, 391 (La.1992).

[8] Petitioners argue that prescription did not begin to run until the end of the lease term. However, LSA-C.C. art. 1807 provides that an obligation is "conjunctive" when it binds the obligor to multiple items of performance that may be separately rendered or enforced. In such case, each item is regarded as the object of a separate obligation. *See Gardiner v. Montegut,* 175 So. 120, 122 (La.App.Orleans, 1937). The parties may provide that the failure of the obligor to perform one or more items shall

---

2. Thereafter, the State of Louisiana filed a dilatory exception pleading the objection of prematurity on the grounds that petitioners failed to exhaust their administrative remedies under the Louisiana Procurement Code, as set forth in LSA-R.S. 39:1673. By judgment, dated May 7, 1986, the State's exception pleading the objection of prematurity was overruled.

The State of Louisiana also filed a peremptory exception raising the objection of no cause of action. By judgment dated September 10, 1986, the trial court overruled the State's exception raising the objection of no cause of action.

allow the obligee to demand the immediate performance of all the remaining items. Comment (b) to LSA-C.C. art. 1807 provides that when a sum is owed in installments or rent is paid periodically, the running of prescription starts separately for each installment or rental payment in the absence of an acceleration clause.

[9] In the instant case, the State was to pay a lump sum of $555,499.50 for the occupancy of petitioners' premises. This amount was divided into sixty (60) equal installments of $9,208.33 plus utilities. The lease provided that "the first installment [was] due and payable on the first day of November, 1981, and the remaining installments [were] due and payable, respectively, on the 1st day of each month thereafter." Additionally, there was no acceleration clause.

[10] Therefore, the obligation was conjunctive, and each installment was a separate obligation. Prescription began to run separately for each installment as it became due. Accordingly, the past due rents from November 1, 1981 through July 15, 1982, had all prescribed by the time petitioners filed the instant suit on November 18, 1985.

[. . . .]

Questions

1. Paragraph 2: What kind of obligation is created by a lease: real, heritable, or strictly personal? *See* La. Civ. Code arts. 2668–2729. Can you identify a term or multiple terms and their kind in this contract of lease? Was the lessee, the State of Louisiana, bound by one or more than one obligation? Can you characterize it or them? Assuming that there is more than one obligation, how do these obligations relate one to another? Are they related by "and" or by "or"? Read Louisiana Civil Code articles 1815–1820 on divisible and indivisible obligations. Would you characterize the State's obligation to pay the rent in sixty installments as a divisible obligation? Is a divisible obligation the same thing as a conjunctive obligation? *See* La. Civ. Code art. 1807.

2. Paragraph 5: Why is the plaintiff, petitioner on appeal, making this argument? Is the plaintiff arguing that there was only one obligation created by the contract of lease and only one object (the full amount of the rent) and, therefore, there was only one term to consider? Is the lessor arguing here that the term is in his favor? Is the lessor an obligor, an obligee, or both simultaneously? In whose favor, the lessor or the lessee, would the presumption of art. 1779 operate?

3. Paragraph 7: What is the legal connection between a term and Louisiana Civil Code articles 3494(2) through 3495?

4. Paragraph 8: Does this paragraph help you, now, to answer Question 1 above: "Is a divisible obligation the same thing as a conjunctive obligation?" Do you see the important legal effect of a term being attached to a conjunctive and divisible obligation? What benefit did the State derive from the fact that an action by the lessor to collect rent on the first two years was not brought until

the lease had nearly expired? Aren't all prescriptive periods subject to a term? What kind? Since the State was no longer bound by any civil obligation to pay the first two years of rent, would you hold the State liable under a natural obligation? *See* La. Civ. Code art. 1762(1).

Colleene Madere and John A. Lingo
v.
Ellen M. Cole

Court of Appeal of Louisiana
First Circuit
December 21, 1982
424 So.2d 1125

SHORTESS, Judge.

[1] Colleen Madere and John A. Lingo (plaintiffs) filed suit against Ellen M. Cole (defendant) for the purchase price of a poodle puppy ($350.00), or alternatively, for dissolution of the sale and return of the puppy.

[2] Plaintiffs agreed to provide a stud for defendant's female poodle. The fee for this service was to be $150.00 cash in advance, or the pick of the litter. The litter consisted of two puppies, but one died. When the surviving puppy was six or seven weeks old, defendant brought it to the plaintiffs, but expressed a desire to keep the puppy. She was told that the puppy would ordinarily be sold for $350.00; but that since she owned the puppy's mother, she could purchase it for $250.00. Defendant wrote a check for $250.00 and left with the puppy. That evening she telephoned plaintiffs and told them that her husband would not let her pay $250.00. Plaintiff[s] . . . told her she could return the puppy and receive her money back. However, defendant did not want to return the puppy. Instead, she stopped payment on the $250.00 check and mailed another check for $150.00. Plaintiffs never negotiated the second check and filed suit.

[3] Plaintiffs have assigned the following errors: (1) the trial court erred in failing to find that a valid contract of sale was perfected; (2) the trial court erred in not enforcing said contract of sale; and (3) the trial court erred in finding that ambiguities existed in the agreement and in construing same against them.

[4] Before this controversy can be resolved, an analysis must be made of the agreements between the parties. Two distinct agreements are involved.

[5] The parties first entered into a synallagmatic or bilateral contract involving stud services. La. C.C. art. 1765. The parties had correlative obligations: (1) the defendant was obligated to either pay $150.00 or surrender the pick of the litter; and (2) the plaintiffs were obligated to provide a stud for the female poodle. The defendant's obligation was alternative. La. C.C. art. 2066. The initial option belonged to defendant. La. C.C. art. 2068. Because defendant did not pay $150.00 in advance, she apparently chose to discharge her obligation by delivering the pick of the litter.

La. C.C. art. 2067. Defendant argued that she did not know she had to give the $150.00 in advance. However, her testimony revelated that she understood that she was to bring the litter in at six weeks so that plaintiffs could choose the puppy they wanted[.]

[....]

[6] When defendant did not pay the $150.00 in advance, plaintiffs assumed that she chose to discharge her obligation by allowing them to have the pick of the litter. Defendant testified several times that this was her understanding. Thus, defendant's obligation could only be extinguished by allowing plaintiffs to keep the puppy of their choice. The choice belonged to plaintiffs. La. C.C. art. 2068. No ambiguity resulted when only one puppy survived. The obligation became pure and simple. La. C.C. art. 2070. Since one of the two puppies died without the fault of defendant, plaintiffs were obligated to accept the surviving puppy in satisfaction of the obligation. La. C.C. arts. 2071, 2072. Thus, the surviving puppy belonged to plaintiffs prior to the time that the second contract was perfected.

[7] The second contract was one of sale:

"The contract of sale is an agreement by which one gives a thing for a price in current money, and the other gives the price in order to have the thing itself.

"Three circumstances concur to the perfection of the contract, to wit: the thing sold, the price, and the consent." La. C.C. art. 2439

"The sale is considered to be perfect between the parties, and the property is of right acquired to the purchaser with regard to the seller, as soon as there exists an agreement for the object and for the price thereof, although the object has not yet been delivered, nor the price paid." La. C.C. art. 2456.

[8] When defendant gave plaintiffs a check for $250.00 and took the puppy home, a contract of sale was perfected.[1]

[9] No ambiguity existed in this sale. When the sale took place, any alleged ambiguity in the prior agreement[2] was irrelevant because the parties consented to the thing (the puppy) and the price ($250.00). La. C.C. art. 2439. The obligations of the seller were clear. La. C.C. art. 2474. Therefore, the trial judge erroneously found that ambiguities existed in the sale and erroneously construed said ambiguities against plaintiffs.

[10] Once the contract of sale had been perfected, defendant was obliged to pay the price. La. C.C. art. 2549. When she failed to do so, plaintiffs were entitled to sue to

---

1. The verbal sale of a movable is valid. La.C.C. art. 2441.
2. Defendant's testimony was inconsistent. At times she stated that she thought she could still pay $150.00 after the puppies were born. However, she also repeatedly said that her understanding was that she was to allow plaintiffs to retain their choice from the litter.

either compel the payment or to dissolve the sale. La. C.C. arts. 2551, 2561, 2564. We find that the appropriate remedy is to enforce payment of the purchase price. Therefore, the judgment of the trial court is amended, and plaintiffs are awarded $250.00.

[11] AFFIRMED, AS AMENDED.

Questions

1. Paragraphs 1–2: Identify, in legal terms, the obligation(s) of plaintiffs, Madere and Lingo, and the obligation(s) of defendant, Cole.

2. Paragraph 2: The facts are to the effect that the defendant, Ms. Cole, wanted to buy the puppy from the plaintiffs who had become the new owners of the puppy. How did the plaintiffs become owners of the puppy?

3. Paragraph 2: The defendant later sent a check for $150 that the plaintiffs did not negotiate. Was this attempt to pay $150 a valid attempt by plaintiff to exercise the initial choice of paying $150 for the stud services? Who had that initial choice? When the initial choice was made (pick of the litter), was the other option (pay $150) still available? Suppose the plaintiffs had negotiated the check and collected $150. Could such an action constitute a compromise of this dispute? Take a look at Louisiana Civil Code article 3079.

4. Paragraph 5: The Court states that the "parties had correlative obligations." Are correlative obligations defined in any article of the La. Civil Code? Does the Civil Code use the adjective "correlative" in relation to obligations created by any certain type of contract? If so, which one?

5. Paragraph 6: On what legal ground or concept of Obligations is the Court relying when it states that "Since one of the two puppies died . . ."?

6. Paragraphs 5–6, 10: Apparently the plaintiffs never "took possession" of the puppy since it had not been delivered or handed over to them by the defendant, the latter expressing a "desire to keep the puppy" and offering to pay a price of $250.00 to the plaintiffs for the puppy. When the Court ruled that the plaintiffs "are awarded $250.00 as the price for the puppy," is the Court confirming that the plaintiffs assumed it was up to the defendant to choose to discharge her obligation vis-à-vis the plaintiff, and the defendant had chosen not to pay $150.00 in advance but to give the plaintiff the pick of the litter?

7. What would have occurred had the Court stated that, in light of the plaintiffs providing a "service" to the defendant, "we imply that the choice between $150.00 and the pick of the litter is with the plaintiffs"? Who would bear the loss of the puppy: the plaintiffs or the defendant? Could the plaintiffs have asked for $150.00 in lieu of possession of the surviving puppy? Would you have advised the plaintiff to take $150.00 rather than $250.00 as full payment of the purchase price? Are the plaintiffs in a better situation because of the defendant "reneging" on her choice to hand over the puppy?

Comparative Law Perspective

— Civil Law —

Robert J. Pothier, *A Treatise on the Law of Obligations or Contracts*

vol. 1, nᵒs 245–247 at 136–37 (William David Evans trans., 1806)

Article VI

Of Alternative Obligations (b)

[245] An alternative obligation is contracted where a person engages to do, or to give several things in such a manner, that the payment of one will acquit him from all: as if I engage to give you a particular horse, or twenty guineas to build you a house, or pay you a hundred pounds.

Where a person is obliged in the disjunctive to pay one sum of money or another, he is only debtor to the amount of the least.

[246] In order to constitute an alternative obligation, it is necessary that two or more things should be promised disjunctively. Where they are promised conjunctively, there as many obligations as the things which are enumerated, [. . .] and the debtor cannot be wholly liberated without discharging them all; but where they are promised in the alternative, though they are all due, there is but one obligation which may be discharged by the payment of any of them. [. . . .]

[247] The choice belongs to the debtor [. . .] unless it is expressly agreed that it shall belong to the creditor. This is a consequence of the rule of interpretation. [. . . .] But though the debtor may elect to pay which he pleases, he cannot pay part of the one and part of the other. Therefore if the obligation is to pay ten pounds or six measures of corn, or a hundred pounds or an acre of land; he cannot give fifty pounds and half of the land, or five pounds and six measures of corn; he must either pay all the money or give the whole land, or the whole quantity of corn; so where the creditor has the choice he cannot require part of the one and part of the other.

Chapter 7

Joint, Solidary and Divisible Obligations

Louisiana Sources of Law
Louisiana Civil Code

Art. 1787. Several obligations; effects.

When each of different obligors owes a separate performance to one obligee, the obligation is several for the obligors.

When one obligor owes a separate performance to each of different obligees, the obligation is several for the obligees.

A several obligation produces the same effects as a separate obligation owed to each obligee by an obligor or by each obligor to an obligee. (Acts 1984, No. 331, §1, eff. Jan. 1, 1985.)

Art. 1788. Joint obligations for obligors or obligees.

When different obligors owe together just one performance to one obligee, but neither is bound for the whole, the obligation is joint for the obligors.

When one obligor owes just one performance intended for the common benefit of different obligees, neither of whom is entitled to the whole performance, the obligation is joint for the obligees. (Acts 1984, No. 331, §1, eff. Jan. 1, 1985.)

Art. 1789. Divisible and indivisible joint obligation.

When a joint obligation is divisible, each joint obligor is bound to perform, and each joint obligee is entitled to receive, only his portion. When a joint obligation is indivisible, joint obligors or obligees are subject to the rules governing solidary obligors or solidary obligees. (Acts 1984, No. 331, §1, eff. Jan. 1, 1985.)

Art. 1790. Solidary obligations for obligees.[1]

An obligation is solidary for the obligees when it gives each obligee the right to demand the whole performance from the common obligor. (Acts 1984, No. 331, §1, eff. Jan. 1, 1985.)

Art. 1792. Remission by one obligee.

---

1. Some of the Code articles on solidarity have been omitted.

Remission of debt by one solidary obligee releases the obligor but only for the portion of that obligee. (Acts 1984, No. 331, §1, eff. Jan. 1, 1985.)

Art. 1793. Interruption of prescription.

Any act that interrupts prescription for one of the solidary obligees benefits all the others. (Acts 1984, No. 331, §1, eff. Jan. 1, 1985.)

Art. 1794. Solidary obligation for obligors.

An obligation is solidary for the obligors when each obligor is liable for the whole performance. A performance rendered by one of the solidary obligors relieves the others of liability toward the obligee. (Acts 1984, No. 331, §1, eff. Jan. 1, 1985.)

Art. 1795. Solidary obligor may not request division; action against one obligor after action against another.

An obligee, at his choice, may demand the whole performance from any of his solidary obligors. A solidary obligor may not request division of the debt.

Unless the obligation is extinguished, an obligee may institute action against any of his solidary obligors even after institution of action against another solidary obligor. (Acts 1984, No. 331, §1, eff. Jan. 1, 1985.)

Art. 1796. Solidarity not presumed.

Solidarity of obligation shall not be presumed. A solidary obligation arises from a clear expression of the parties' intent or from the law. (Acts 1984, No. 331, §1, eff. Jan. 1, 1985.)

Art. 1799. Interruption of prescription.

The interruption of prescription against one solidary obligor is effective against all solidary obligors and their heirs. (Acts 1984, No. 331, §1, eff. Jan. 1, 1985.)

Art. 1800. Solidary liability for damages.

A failure to perform a solidary obligation through the fault of one obligor renders all the obligors solidarily liable for the resulting damages. In that case, the obligors not at fault have their remedy against the obligor at fault. (Acts 1984, No. 331, §1, eff. Jan. 1, 1985.)

Art. 1801. Defenses that solidary obligor may raise.

A solidary obligor may raise against the obligee defenses that arise from the nature of the obligation, or that are personal to him, or that are common to all the solidary obligors. He may not raise a defense that is personal to another solidary obligor. (Acts 1984, No. 331, §1, eff. Jan. 1, 1985.)

Art. 1802. Renunciation of solidarity.

Renunciation of solidarity by the obligee in favor of one or more of his obligors must be express. An obligee who receives a partial performance from an obligor separately preserves the solidary obligation against all his obligors after deduction of that partial performance. (Acts 1984, No. 331, §1, eff. Jan. 1, 1985.)

Art. 1803. Remission of debt to or transaction or compromise with one obligor.

Remission of debt by the obligee in favor of one obligor, or a transaction or compromise between the obligee and one obligor, benefits the other solidary obligors in the amount of the portion of that obligor.

Surrender to one solidary obligor of the instrument evidencing the obligation gives rise to a presumption that the remission of debt was intended for the benefit of all the solidary obligors. (Acts 1984, No. 331, §1, eff. Jan. 1, 1985.)

Art. 1804. Liability of solidary obligors between themselves.

Among solidary obligors, each is liable for his virile portion. If the obligation arises from a contract or quasi-contract, virile portions are equal in the absence of agreement or judgment to the contrary. If the obligation arises from an offense or quasi-offense, a virile portion is proportionate to the fault of each obligor.

A solidary obligor who has rendered the whole performance, though subrogated to the right of the obligee, may claim from the other obligors no more than the virile portion of each.

If the circumstances giving rise to the solidary obligation concern only one of the obligors, that obligor is liable for the whole to the other obligors who are then considered only as his sureties. (Acts 1984, No. 331, §1, eff. Jan. 1, 1985.)

Art. 1806. Insolvency of a solidary obligor.

A loss arising from the insolvency of a solidary obligor must be borne by the other solidary obligors in proportion to their portion.

Any obligor in whose favor solidarity has been renounced must nevertheless contribute to make up for the loss. (Acts 1984, No. 331, §1, eff. Jan. 1, 1985.)

Divisible and Indivisible Obligations

Art. 1815. Divisible and indivisible obligation.

An obligation is divisible when the object of the performance is susceptible of division.

An obligation is indivisible when the object of the performance, because of its nature or because of the intent of the parties, is not susceptible of division. (Acts 1984, No. 331, §1, eff. Jan. 1, 1985.)

Art. 1816. Effect of divisible obligation between single obligor and obligee.

When there is only one obligor and only one obligee, a divisible obligation must be performed as if it were indivisible. (Acts 1984, No. 331, §1, eff. Jan. 1, 1985.)

Art. 1818. Effects of indivisible obligations between more than one obligor or obligee.

An indivisible obligation with more than one obligor or obligee is subject to the rules governing solidary obligations. (Acts 1984, No. 331, §1, eff. Jan. 1, 1985.)

Art. 1820. Solidarity is not indivisibility.

A stipulation of solidarity does not make an obligation indivisible. (Acts 1984, No. 331, §1, eff. Jan. 1, 1985.)

Doctrine
Louisiana Law of Obligations in General, A Précis
Sections 3.1.1 to 4.4.2

Several Obligation

[A]n obligation is several on the part of obligors whenever each one of them is independently bound to a separate and distinct performance not owed in any manner by the other obligors. The item or items of the respective obligor's performance(s) may be to do different acts or give different things or abstain from doing something, etc. [. . . .]

The analysis of the effects of several obligations does not require any extensive treatment since a several obligation must be considered as being merely the gathering under one source of multiple but separate obligations creating as many different bonds of law as there are parties. [. . . .]

Joint Obligation

There exists a joint obligation on the part of different obligors when these obligors are bound **together** to **one** performance arising from one and the same obligation. Likewise, an obligation is joint on the part of different obligees when, together, they are entitled to just **one** performance from the obligor. As **LSA-C.C. Art. 1788** states [. . .].

The joint obligation is considered as the common rule or as the general principle of the law of obligations with multiple persons. [. . . .]

A joint obligation on the part of obligors is created whenever multiple obligors are bound **together** to perform **one** obligation. However, each one of them is bound to perform only his individual share of the whole obligation; each one of them is bound *pro numero virorum.* [. . . .]

The plurality of links or bonds of law between the obligee and the joint obligors has this consequence that the joint obligors will not necessarily be bound to the obligee under the same legal regimes. Each bond of law may be vested with a particular legal identity so that, for example, some defenses available to one obligor may not be available to others. [. . . .]

Whenever a joint obligation is indivisible in its performance, in the sense that the item of performance owed by the joint obligors is not susceptible of being divided in parts (**LSA-C.C. Art. 1789**), the rules of solidarity (**LSA-C.C. Arts. 1790 *et seq.)*** and those of indivisibility (**LSA-C.C. Arts. 1815 *et seq.*)** will apply. [. . . .]

Solidary Obligation

Solidarity must be understood both as a legal fiction and as a practical necessity. In essence, solidarity is an obstacle, a bar to the division of an obligation as a result of a particular feature attached to the bond of law binding together multiple persons. These persons can be, either multiple obligees [**and we have then an instance of active solidarity**], or multiple obligors [**and we have then an instance of passive solidarity**]. [. . . .]

The far-reaching, harsh and aleatory effects of solidarity are the reason why "**solidarity of obligation shall not be presumed. A solidary obligation arises from a clear expression of the parties' intent or from the law**" (LSA-C.C. Art. 1796). The two sources of solidarity are, thus, the law and contract. The fact that there may be two different sources of solidarity of an obligation is not an obstacle to two or more obligors being held solidarily bound for that same obligation. One solidary obligor could be bound solidarily on account of a contract whereas another solidary obligor could be bound for the same obligation because of an existing legal disposition. [. . . .]

The practical effects of active solidarity are many. First of all, each one of the solidary obligees may demand the whole performance and when that performance has been rendered to any one of them it extinguishes the obligation and releases the obligor even though the benefit of the obligation is to be divided among the multiple obligees. A second effect is that, should a solidary obligee interrupt prescription of the action against the obligor, the other solidary obligees will benefit from such an initiative. Thirdly, and reasoning *a pari ratione* on **LSA-C.C. Art. 1793**, should a solidary obligee put the obligor in default, the benefit of this action will be shared with the other solidary obligees. [. . . .]

As far as the relationship between the obligees is concerned it can be said that, in general, they divide among themselves, according to their respective rights, the performance received from the obligor. [. . . .]

LSA-C.C. Art. 1794 states that "**an obligation is solidary for the obligors when each obligor is liable for the whole performance. A performance rendered by one of the solidary obligors relieves the others of liability toward the obligee.**" This article suggests that there is, at the same time, only *one item* of performance owed, that is to say *the whole performance,* and a plurality of obligors held personally and individually for that performance regardless of whether the object or item of performance is divisible or indivisible in its performance. Thus, solidarity creates a personal bond between the obligee and each one of the solidary obligors.

This multiplicity of bonds between the solidary obligors and their obligee carries with it many important consequences. [. . . .]

Once the obligee has received the full performance of the obligation from one of the solidary obligors, the benefit of solidarity disappears with the extinction of the debt. The principle which now governs the relationship between the solidary obligors is that solidarity is not heritable, it cannot be claimed by that solidary obligor who, through his performance, extinguished the obligation. [. . . .]

The division of the debt among the obligors is not necessarily made on an equal basis. It may exist with some exceptions to an equal distribution. [. . . .]

Divisible or Indivisible Obligation

LSA-C.C. Art. 1815 states in very simple terms that:

> "An obligation is divisible when the object of the performance is susceptible of division.
>
> An obligation is indivisible when the object of the performance, because of its nature or because of the intent of the parties, is not susceptible of division."

Absolute natural indivisibility is dictated, first of all, by the law of nature and appears as the only authentic and unquestionable kind of indivisibility of an obligation. It can also be created by law making the indivisibility "fictitiously" natural. Whether actual or fictitious, absolute natural indivisibility refers to an object of an obligation which, in its performance, cannot possibly be divided in parts. [. . . .]

An obligation is relatively indivisible whenever its object, although susceptible of material or intellectual division, must be considered as being indivisible in relation to, or in light of, the *natural* objective pursued by the parties. The goal intended to be achieved by the obligor's performance is the fulfillment of an indivisible object. [. . . .]

By their contract, parties may provide for an *artificial* or *fictitious* indivisibility of an obligation which, otherwise, would be naturally divisible. The intent of the parties may be to make the *object* of the obligation or *item of performance* indivisible in its fulfillment. Conventional indivisibility strives to conceptually and artificially attach to an object a legal feature which only nature would normally impose. Regardless of the number of parties involved, the item of performance cannot be divided between them because their will has made it indivisible.

Louisiana Law of Obligations in General, A Treatise
Section 4.4.3-B

208. Effects of indivisibility on the part of the obligees: active indivisibility. Regardless of the source of indivisibility, whenever multiple obligees are owed an indivisible obligation, the item of performance can be claimed in its entirety by any one of the multiple obligees.[73] The bond of law (*vinculum juris*) binding the obligor to indivisible obligees is such that the obligor owes to each individual obligee the performance of the whole object or item of the obligation. The obligor may not give each obligee a part of an indivisible object. However, once the entire performance

---

73. La. Civ. Code art. 1790, *a pari ratione*. . . .

has been received by an indivisible obligee, it is incumbent upon that obligee to divide the object of the obligation (if it can be divided) among his co-obligees. The *commodum* (or advantage, opportunity) becomes divisible in the horizontal relationship between the obligees whereas the *vinculum*, or vertical bond of law between the obligor and his indivisible obligees, is not. [. . . .]

210. Effects of indivisibility on the part of obligors: passive indivisibility. Passive indivisibility can be looked at as a security device *naturally* or *contractually* given to an obligee by one or more obligors. Passive indivisibility vests in an obligee essentially the same rights against his indivisible obligors that passive solidarity would grant him against solidary obligors.[77] [. . . .]

211. Heritability: distinguishing feature between indivisibility and solidarity. The distinction that must be preserved between indivisibility and solidarity finds its rationale in the different sources of the bonds of law which may be created.

Indivisibility finds its *raison d'être* in the object of the obligation, the item of performance, whereas solidarity is related to the number of parties or persons to an obligation. Thus, solidarity is a matter of a number of persons/parties involved in an obligation whereas indivisibility is a feature of an obligation that pertains to the object of the obligation, the item of performance. [. . . .]

212. Indivisibility: heritable. The fundamental distinction that must be made between these two concepts is that solidarity is not heritable, whereas indivisibility is. Any and each heir of an obligee of an indivisible obligation may demand the whole performance of that indivisible obligation. The indivisibility of the obligation is an inherent and component feature of the obligation. On the other hand, the heirs or successors of a solidary obligee become <u>joint obligees</u> as is the principle governing the relationship between multiple obligees. [. . . .]

213. Solidarity: not heritable. [. . . .]

Indivisibility, therefore, prevents the division of the object of an obligation among the successors of the obligor or obligors. The reason is that indivisibility is an inherent legal feature of the object or item of performance, regardless of whether there is one obligor or multiple obligors. Thus, it is somewhat misleading to state, as broadly as La. Civ. Code **art. 1818** does, that "**an indivisible obligation . . . is subject to the rules governing solidarity obligations.**"[83] On the other hand, it is quite accurate to state, at least in this respect, that "**a stipulation of solidarity does not make an obligation indivisible.**"

---

77. On Solidarity, see *supra* Ch. 3, #129-161.
83. La. Civ. Code art. 1818. . . .

Cases

Jimmie Wilks et ux.
v.
Allstate Insurance Company et al.

Court of Appeal of Louisiana
Third Circuit
February 15, 1967
195 So.2d 390

TATE, Judge.

[. . . .]

Facts.

[1] The plaintiff wife was driving the family car when it was struck by a vehicle which negligently ran a stop sign. An employee of the garageman Jacobs was driving the other vehicle. It belonged to a customer (Calhoun) to whom Allstate had issued a liability policy. Allstate was held liable as the omnibus insurer of the garageman Jacobs or his employee, who were using the car with the consent of Calhoun, Allstate's named insured. See 177 So.2d 790 (opinion on first appeal).

[2] Allstate contends, however, that its liability is limited to one-half of the amount for which cast. Allstate relies upon an 'other insurance' clause of its policy, which provides for the apportionment of its liability when there is other insurance covering the same loss.[1] Allstate contends that immediately before the accident the garageman Jacobs himself had applied for and been granted an oral binder for a garage liability policy, which — being valid and collectible insurance — had the effect of reducing Allstate's liability proportionately under its 'pro rata' clause.

[. . . .]

'Pro rata' liability of both insurers: Treatise and decisional references.

[3] For purposes of summary judgment, we will therefore assume that at the time of the accident the tortfeasor's automobile was insured by one policy issued by Allstate to the vehicle's owner (Calhoun) and also by another policy issued to the garageman (Jacobs). We further assume that each policy had a bodily injury limit of $5,000 per person and that each contained a pro rata 'other insurance' clause. We further assume that both of these policies were applicable as 'primary' insurance.

---

1. The applicable clause of Allstate's policy reads: 'Other Insurance. If the insured has other insurance against a loss covered by Part 1 of this policy (automobile liability insurance) the company shall not be liable under this policy for a greater proportion of such loss than the applicable limit of liability stated in the declarations bears to the total applicable limit of liability of all valid and collectible insurance against such loss; provided, however, the insurance with respect to a temporary substitute automobile or non-owned automobile shall be excess insurance over any other valid and collectible insurance.'

Since the recovery from Mrs. Wilks's personal injuries was approximately $5,000, or within the limits of both policies, each insurer would be liable proportionate to its limits, i.e., for one-half of this amount (see pro rata clause set forth in footnote 1) If both insurers were joined as parties to this action. See State Farm Mutual Auto. Ins. Co. v. Travelers Ins. Co., La.App. 3 Cir., 184 So.2d 750.

[4] The defendant Allstate's position is, essentially, that, where recovery is within policy limits and two policies with pro rata clauses are each applicable, then each insurer can never be liable for more than its proportionate share of the recovery, even though the other insurer is not a party to the suit. In the present case, then, assuming the facts to be as stated previously, it is contended that the injured plaintiff can recover only $2,500 against Jacobs's insurer Allstate although the judgment against Jacobs himself is $5,000 for Mrs. Wilks's injuries, even though Allstate had issued and received premiums for policy protection up to $5,000 per person injured.

[. . . .]

[5] As we will shortly illustrate, this principle was for the most part applied in decisions where both insurers were parties, where at issue was primary-versus-pro rata liability of the insurers or the right of contribution of one insurer from another.

[6] A different principle may be applicable when the litigation concerns the claim of the insured (or the injured person under the Louisiana Direct Action Statute, LSA-R.S. 22:655) to enforce against either one of the insurers that insurer's full policy limits. This differing principle is stated at 8 Appleman, Insurance Law and Practice, Section 4913, p. 387, as follows:

> 'The liability of the co-insurers to the insured is several, and not joint, so that the policyholder may collect the full amount from either insurer, leaving the latter to its right of contribution from the other.'[6]

[. . . .]

[7] The source of much of the confusion in the field, both in the decisions cited immediately above and in the conflicting dicta in many of the decisions earlier cited, is the variable meaning attached to the common-law concept of a 'several' obligation. (See footnote 6 above.) It may therefore be advisable to discuss briefly this common-law concept and the civil law concepts most nearly equivalent.

A 'several' obligation in the common law.

[8] Under the Louisiana Civil Code, 'Several obligations are produced, when what is promised by one of the obligors, is not promised by the other, but each one promises separately for himself to do a distinct act * * *.' Article 2078.

---

6. It is to be noted that Appleman states the liability to the insured of each insurer is 'several and not joint', so therefore the insured can collect the full amount from either. The ALR annotation, to the exact contrary, states that each insurer is bound only for its pro rata portion because the liability is 'several and not joint'! 21 A.L.R.2d 611. The common law concept of a several obligation will be discussed under a separate heading below.

[9] By this definition, the obligors bound severally cannot have agreed to perform the same act. On the other hand, 'When several persons obligate themselves to the obligee by the terms In solido, or use any other expressions, which clearly show that they intend that each one shall be Separately bound to perform the whole of the obligation, it is called an obligation In solido on the part of the obligors.' Article 2082. (Italics ours.) The solidary obligation to pay the entire debt can result from different instruments, or although the obligors be obliged differently to pay the same debt, Article 2092; Hidalgo v. Dupuy, La.App. 1 Cir. 122 So.2d 639. Both of these types of obligations are to be distinguished from the 'joint' obligation of our Civil Code where several persons join in the same contract to do the same thing, Articles 2080, 2081, where all joint obligors must be joined in any suit to enforce the obligation, Articles 2085, 2087, and where each joint obligor is held liable only for his proportion of the obligation. Article 2086.

[10] See also Comment, Solidary Obligations, 25 Tul.L.Rev. 217 (1951).

[11] The 'joint and several' obligation of the common law is quite similar to the solidary obligation of the civil law in that either or both of the obligors may be sued for enforcement of the whole obligation. 4 Corbin on Contracts, Section 937 (1950); 17A C.J.S. Contracts s 355; 17 Am.Jur.2d Contracts, Section 299. However, the common-law concepts of 'joint' and of 'several' obligation differ distinctively from the Louisiana concepts denoted by the identical terms.

[12] The several obligation of the common law could not only be the legally independent promises of two obligors to perform separate and distinct acts (as with the several obligor of the Louisiana civil law); it could also denote separate promises by two obligors for the same performance (as in the Louisiana solidary obligation). Corbin, Section 925; 17A C.J.S. Contracts s 352. The joint obligation of the common law referred primarily to the ancient necessity to join all joint obligors in the same suit to enforce the obligation (as with Louisiana joint obligors); but it also included the concept that all joint obligors could each be bound for the entire performance to the obligee (rather than only for his proportional part, as with the Louisiana joint obligor). 4 Corbin, Chapter 52 ('Joint and Several Obligations'), especially Section 925; 17A C.J.S. Contracts § 353.

[13] Thus, with regard to the old common law distinctions the classification of an obligation as 'several' or 'joint' is not significant for the determination of the real question before us: Can either insurer be held for its full policy limits owed to the insured, even though another insurer has issued a policy covering the same liability? (That is, leaving the insurers to fight out between themselves any right one may have to enforce contribution from the others.) Under the common law definitions the obligation could be either joint or several and still be enforceable in full against either obligor. For purposes of the instant case, the question of whether the insurers' obligations would be termed 'joint' or 'several' by the common law judges is irrelevant.

[14] The ultimate test of whether the obligor could be held for the whole or for only a proportionate part of the obligation is essentially whether the two obligors each

promised the same (i.e., the full) performance or else whether each had promised only a different performance (i.e., to pay only its proportionate part of the liability). Corbin, Section 925.[14] In this regard, decision of this essential question is determined by an interpretation of the intention of the parties in the light of the language used and of the surrounding circumstances. 4 Corbin, Section 926; 17A C.J.S. Contracts s 350; 17 Am.Jur.2d Contracts, Section 299.

The insuring agreement of a liability insurance contract.

[15] Under the insuring agreement, the defendant Allstate agreed 'to pay on behalf of the insured all sums which the insured shall be legally obligated to pay as damages * * * arising out of the ownership, maintenance, or use of the owned automobile * * *.' This insuring agreement creates a solidary obligation with the insured, although the insured and the insurers are bound differently to perform the same obligation. LSA-C.C. art. 2082; Hidalgo v. Dupuy, La.App. 1 Cir., 122 So.2d 639, certiorari denied. Under the respective insuring clauses, each of the insurers are solidarily bound for the same debt, namely the tort liability of the insured, although of course the policy provisions limiting liability limit respectively the recovery against each insurer.

[16] Allstate persuasively argues that the pro rata clause limits the solidary liability of the insurer to and for the insured, just as the policy limits do. Allstate in effect contends that, where there is other valid and collectible insurance, the pro rata clause, where applicable, has the effect of converting its liability to its insured into joint Or several (i.e., only for the insured's proportionate share of the insured's liability) rather than joint And several (i.e., solidary with its insured's tort liability up to policy limits).

[17] We must reject this forceful argument. We hold instead that by reason of the solidary liability of each of the two insurers with the insured, the policyholder may collect the full amount from either insurer, leaving the latter to its right of contribution from the other insurer, in accord with what Appleman, Section 4913, and Clow v. National Indemnity Co., 54 Wash.2d 198, 339 P.2d 82 (1959) state is the majority rule. We thus conclude that the liability of each insurer with the insured continues to be solidary, Hidalgo v. Dupuy, cited above, and is not transmuted by the pro rata clause into only partial coverage which may be less than the policy limits for which premiums were charged.

[18] We so conclude by reason of our interpretation of the presumed intent of the parties to the insurance contract. In doing so, we take into consideration that otherwise the insured may be forced to pay a portion of the recovery against him even though (as here) such recovery is within the policy limits.

---

14. This treatise section contains an interesting discussion noting the distinction between the common-law concepts is largely irrelevant under modern statutory and jurisprudential law, since based chiefly on ancient analytical and procedural doctrines, now nearly extinct, relating to survivorship, discharge, and joinder of parties.

[. . . .]

b. Purpose of liability policy and relative resources of the insurer and the insured

[19] An automobile liability policy is issued to protect the insured against claims arising out of automobile use. Under the insuring agreement, the insurer agrees to pay on behalf of the insured damages within policy limits and to provide him with a legal defense against damage suits so arising. The insurer has readily available legal counsel and nationwide investigative resources, the benefits of both of which the insured contemplates receiving when covered by a valid policy.

[20] If we adopt Allstate's present contention, then where other insurance is potentially available, even under farfetched circumstances such as the present (see Facts above), the insured would be required to retain counsel independent of his insurer's in order to implead the alleged other insurer or else to prove the invalidity or uncollectibility of such coverage. Within the contemplation of the parties and of the purpose of the insurance contract, this burden should instead be on the insurer, which can more readily and efficiently investigate the potential liability of the other insurer and, if so indicated, implead it as a party to the litigation.

[. . . .]

c. Procedural consequences of the opposing constructions

[21] Under our interpretation of the pro rata clause, the liability of both insurers with the insured and with each other is solidary. If so, any insurer sued can implead any other alleged insurer by third party demand. LSA-C.C. Art. 2103; LSA-C.C.P. Art. 1111. A defendant insurer is generally far better able to do so than is the insured (see illustration above).

[22] On the other hand, if the obligation of each insurer is only for a proportionate part of the recovery against the insured, then the defendant insurer may not implead the other alleged insurer in order to have the validity of this other coverage finally determined in the present suit. A principal defendant may implead as third party defendant only a party 'who is or may be liable to Him for all or part of the Principal demand.' LSA-C.C.P. Art. 1111; Lanza Enterprises, Inc. v. Continental Insurance Co., La.App. 3 Cir., 129 So.2d 91 (syllabus 2), certiorari denied. Thus, the insured might not have the legal or investigative resources to institute a third party demand against some other insurer potentially liable (see illustration above), but nevertheless the defendant insured itself would be legally unable to implead such other insurer to have determined finally the validity of its coverage.

[23] Placing the duty upon the insurer (rather than the insured) to investigate, to attempt to secure contribution from, and to implead any other alleged insurer is in accord with the insured's fiduciary responsibility to protect the interests of its own insured in matters of settlement and litigation. Cf., Younger v. Lumbermen's Mutual Cas. Co., La.App. 3 Cir.,174 So.2d 672. By a contrary construction of the pro rata clause, the insurer — if unable to directly implead the alleged other insurer — is forced to raise such defense by instead using its superior investigative and legal

resources against its own insured in order to exculpate itself from liability for a portion of the policy limits set forth by the policy.

The insuring agreement of the liability insurance contract: Conclusion.

[24] In summary, we conclude that, with respect to the interests of the Insured, the pro rata clause does not entitle an automobile liability insurer to reduce below policy limits its coverage of the liability of the insured. Within the intent of the parties, the pro rata clause is simply designed to regulate contribution As between insurers which may have provided coverage which happens to apply to the same loss.

[25] As stated in a similar context, with citations from numerous jurisdictions in support: '* * * the rights of the insured must be fully protected and, hence, the pro rata clause must not be so applied as to diminish his protection under any circumstances. The reason generally advanced for this principle is that since usually the insurer fixes the amount of his premium regardless of other insurance, and if, after the loss, he happens to find other insurance which relieves him in part from his liability, it is a piece of pure good fortune for him, his principal engagement having been to pay the loss in full up to the face of his policy and that the insured, having given no promise to take out or to keep up other insurance, should not suffer by a windfall of the insurer.' Annotation, Apportionment or contribution as between specific and blanket insurance policies, 169 A.L.R. 387, 397–98.

[26] Our interpretation of the insurance policy to this effect is in accord with the usual rules of policy construction.

[....]

Questions

1. Paragraph 2: What kind or form of liability is Allstate claiming to be bound by? What should be the effect of a *pro rata* clause?

2. Paragraphs 8–14: Read with attention the comparative analysis made by Judge Tate of "a several obligation in the common law," "the joint and several obligation of the common law," and "the several obligation of the common law." How similar or different are these obligations of common law from the corresponding obligations of the Louisiana Civil Code? Does terminology matter? Was Judge Tate correct when he wrote "The source of much of the confusion in the field . . . is the variable meaning attached to the common-law concept of a several obligation"?

3. Paragraphs 15–16: What difference is there, if any, between "joint and several" and "joint or several"? Which form of liability is Allstate claiming to be bound under? Why?

4. Paragraph 18: Judge Tate "so conclude[s] [his] interpretation of the presumed intent of the parties to the insurance contract." Is this conclusion supported by Louisiana Civil Code article 1796?

5. Paragraphs 19–20: Remember the first question? Was your answer similar to or different from Judge Tate's policy statement? Do you agree with Judge Tate's views as to the *raison d'être* of an insurance contract? How far does the Court extend its understanding of its policy? *See* paragraph 21. Should a court be allowed to make legal decisions on policy grounds? Could there exist a legal ground available to the Court to hold the two insurers solidarily liable or liable *in solido* "with each other"? What do you think of Louisiana Civil Code articles 1815-2 and 1818?

William Hoefly & Joann C. Hoefly
v.
Government Employees Insurance Company, et al.

Supreme Court of Louisiana
June 21, 1982
418 So.2d 575

DENNIS, Justice.

[1] The question presented by this case is whether an automobile accident victim's uninsured motorist carrier is solidarily obliged with the tortfeasor so that the victim's timely suit against the latter interrupts prescription with regard to the insurer. The court of appeal affirmed the trial court's judgment sustaining the insurer's plea of prescription, holding that the plaintiffs' timely suit against two tortfeasors, one uninsured and another underinsured, failed to interrupt prescription because the uninsured motorist insurer and the tortfeasors were not solidary obligors. We reverse. An obligation is solidary among debtors when they are obliged to the same thing, so that each may be compelled for the whole, and when payment by one exonerates the other toward the creditor. When these characteristics result from provisions of law, as in the case of the obligation of the tortfeasor and uninsured motorist carrier, an obligation in solido exists without requiring an express declaration. Consequently, the plaintiff's timely and properly filed suit against the tortfeasors interrupted prescription as to his uninsured motorist carrier.

[2] This suit arises out of an automobile accident which occurred on November 1, 1976, when Mrs. Joann C. Hoefly was struck and injured by an automobile driven by Kim Lewiston, a minor, as Mrs. Hoefly was getting out of her own vehicle. On October 12, 1977, Mrs. Hoefly and her husband filed this suit against Neftali Rodriquez, the owner of the automobile driven by Kim Lewiston, Mrs. Margaret C. Lewiston, the mother of Kim Lewiston, and Government Employees Insurance Company, Mrs. Lewiston's liability insurer. In their original and amended petitions the plaintiffs alleged that Kim Lewiston was negligent in operating the vehicle without an operator's license, failing to maintain proper speed and control of the vehicle, and in failing to discover a defective condition in the vehicle. Plaintiffs also alleged that Rodriquez was negligent in allowing an unlicensed minor to operate the vehicle, failing to maintain the vehicle in proper working condition and in seizing the steering

wheel from the minor just before the accident. On September 5, 1980, plaintiffs filed an amended and supplemental petition naming Allstate Insurance Company, the Hoeflys' uninsured motorist carrier, as a defendant and alleging that Rodriquez was an uninsured motorist and that the insurance provided by Government Employees to Mrs. Lewiston was insufficient to pay for all of the damages sustained by plaintiffs. Allstate filed a peremptory exception of prescription which was sustained by the trial court. Plaintiffs appealed and the court of appeal affirmed. 403 So.2d 853 (La.App. 2d Cir. 1981). We granted certiorari to review the appeals court's holding that "[a]n uninsured motorist carrier is not liable in solido with the tort-feasor; therefore the filing of suit against the tort-feasor and/or his liability insurer does not interrupt prescription against the uninsured motorist carrier of the injured party." Id. p. 854–855.

[3] Allstate's plea of prescription is based on the circumstance that the accident occurred on November 1, 1976, whereas the amended and supplemental petition naming it as a defendant was not filed until September 5, 1980. It is thus urged that the action for recovery of damages sustained in a motor vehicle accident brought pursuant to uninsured motorist insurance coverage has prescribed, having been filed more than two years after the date of the accident in which the damage was sustained. La.R.S. 9:5629 (Supp.1977). The plaintiffs, however, rely upon the timely institution of their suit against Mr. Rodriquez, Mrs. Lewiston and her insurer as an interruption of prescription.

[4] In our opinion, the trial court and the court of appeal incorrectly decided that Allstate's plea of prescription should be sustained. The timely and proper filing of the suit against Mr. Rodriquez, Mrs. Lewiston and her insurer prevented the accrual of prescription against them. La.R.S. 9:5801 provides: "All prescriptions affecting the cause of action therein sued upon are interrupted as to all defendants, including minors or interdicts, by the commencement of a civil action in a court of competent jurisdiction and in the proper venue. * * * "Since the original filing of the suit interrupted prescription against Mr. Rodriquez, Mrs. Lewiston and her insurer, it also interrupted prescription against Allstate. "A suit brought against one of the debtors *in solido* interrupts prescription with regard to all." La.C.C. art. 2097. Although the court of appeal held, and Allstate contends, that the filing of suit against the tortfeasor and his liability insurer does not interrupt prescription against the uninsured motorist carrier of the injured party, we are constrained to disagree.

[5] Under Civil Code Article 2091, "[t]here is an obligation *in solido* on the part of the debtors, when they are all obliged to the same thing, so that each may be compelled for the whole, and when the payment which is made by one of them, exonerates the others toward the creditor." When an obligation fulfills this definition and contains these ingredients, the obligation is in solido. *Sampay v. Morton Salt Co.*, 395 So.2d 326 (La.1981); *Foster v. Hampton*, 381 So.2d 789 (La.1980); *Pearson v. Hartford Accident & Indemnity Co.*, 281 So.2d 724 (La.1973); *Thomas v. W. W. Clarklift, Inc.*, 375 So.2d 375 (La.1979) (Dennis, J., concurring); *Wooten v. Wimberly*, 272 So.2d 303 (La.1972) (Tate, J., concurring and Barham, J., dissenting); *Kern v. Travelers*

Insurance Co., 407 So.2d 2 (La.App. 4th Cir. 1981); *Granger v. General Motors Corp.*, 171 So.2d 720 (La.App. 3d Cir. 1965); *Hidalgo v. Dupuy*, 122 So.2d 639 (La.App. 1st Cir. 1960); The Work of the Louisiana Appellate Courts for the 1973–1974 Term-Obligations, 35 La.L.Rev. 280, 297 (1975). As we analyze the obligation in this case, it satisfies the prerequisites for a solidary obligation.[1]

[6] The tortfeasor and the uninsured motorist carrier are obliged to the same thing. A tortfeasor is obliged to repair the damage that he has wrongfully caused to the innocent automobile accident victim. La.C.C. art. 2315. Subject to conditions not granted the tortfeasor, the uninsured motorist carrier is independently obliged to repair the same damage. By effect of the uninsured motorist statute, La.R.S. 22:1406(D)(1)(a), and its insuring agreement, the plaintiffs' uninsured motorist carrier is required to pay, subject to statutory and policy conditions, amounts which they are entitled under other provisions of law to recover as damages from owners or operators of uninsured or underinsured motor vehicles. By effect of law and the terms of the insuring agreement, therefore, both the uninsured motorist carrier and the tortfeasor are obliged to the same thing. The Work of the Louisiana Appellate Courts, 1974–1975 Term-Obligations, 36 La.L.Rev. 375, 379–380 at n. 23; The Work of the Louisiana Appellate Courts for the 1967–1968 Term-Insurance, 29 La.L.Rev. 253, 257 (1969); The Work of the Louisiana Appellate Courts for the 1966–1967 Term-Insurance, 28 La.L.Rev. 372, 373–374 (1968).

[7] The tortfeasor and the uninsured motorist carrier each may be compelled for the whole. The principal result of solidarity is to prevent the division of the debt and to obligate each debtor for the whole, as if he were alone. 2 M. Planiol, Civil Law Treatise, pt. 1, no. 745 (11th ed. La.St.L.Inst. trans. 1959). This essential element of solidarity, that each debtor may be compelled for the whole, means simply that the debtor who has been sued cannot plead the benefit of division, which was invented for the benefit of sureties whereby the creditor is required to divide his action between them. This is covered expressly in Article 2094 because under the ancient law several attempts had been made to extend benefit of division to solidary co-debtors. That each debtor is held for the whole, i.e., unable to plead the benefit of division, is solidarity's most direct consequence. 2 M. Planiol, *supra*, no. 746.

---

1. Since this court has rejected the distinction between "perfect" and "imperfect" solidarity, *Foster v. Hampton, supra* at 791, we need not analyze the nature of the present obligation from this standpoint, although the exercise may prove interesting from an historical and academic perspective. See 2 M. Planiol, Civil Law Treatise, pt. 1, nos. 777–779 (11th ed. La.St.L.Inst. trans. 1959); 4 C. Aubry & C. Rau, Droit Civil Francais, §298b (6th ed. Bartin) in A. Yiannopoulos, 1 Civil Law Translations 20–21 (1965); The Work of the Louisiana Appellate Courts for the 1967–1968 Term-Insurance, 29 La.L.Rev. 253 (1969); The Work of the Louisiana Appellate Courts for the 1973–1974 Term-Obligations, 35 La.L.Rev. 291 (1975); The Work of the Louisiana Appellate Courts for the 1974–1975 Term-Obligations, 36 La.L.Rev. 375 (1976); Comment, Solidary Obligations, 25 Tul.L.Rev. 217 (1951); Comment, Prescribing Solidarity: Contributing to the Indemnity Dilemma, 41 La.L.Rev. 657 (1981).

[8] This requisite of solidarity is satisfied in the case of the uninsured motorist and the tortfeasor because neither may plead the benefit of division, as if each were alone. To permit the tortfeasor or uninsured motorist carrier to plead the benefit of division would be inimical to the legislative aim of the uninsured motorist statute. The object of that legislation is to promote full recovery for damages by innocent automobile accident victims by making uninsured motorist coverage available for their benefit as primary protection when the tortfeasor is without insurance and as additional or excess coverage when he is inadequately insured. *Bond v. Commercial Union Assur. Co.*, 407 So.2d 401, 407 (La.1981) (on rehearing); *Booth v. Fireman's Fund Ins. Co.*, 253 La. 521, 218 So.2d 580, 28 A.L.R.3d 573 (1968). The statute is to be liberally construed to carry out this objective of providing reparation for those injured through no fault of their own. *Niemann v. Travelers Insurance Co.*, 368 So.2d 1003 (La.1979); *Elledge v. Warren*, 263 So.2d 912 (La.App. 3d Cir. 1972); *Valdez v. Fed. Mut. Ins. Co.*, 272 Cal.App.2d 223, 77 Cal.Rptr. 411 (1969). The legislation cannot be construed, therefore, to benefit the insurer and the tortfeasor by requiring the accident victim to divide his action between them.

[9] The uninsured motorist carrier is obliged differently from the tortfeasor because its liability is conditioned by the tortfeasor's total or partial lack of liability insurance, the type of damage he has caused and any limits in the insurer's policy that are permitted by law. Contrary to Allstate's arguments, however, the terms and conditions which have been allowed the uninsured motorist carrier by law and by contract, while the tortfeasor is bound pure and simple, do not prevent the uninsured motorist carrier and the tortfeasor from being obliged to the same thing or being unable to plead the benefit of division. "The obligations may be *in solido*, although one of the debtors be obliged differently from the other to the payment of one and the same thing; for instance, if the one be but conditionally bound, whilst the engagement of the other is pure and simple, or if the one is allowed a term which is not granted to the other." La.C.C. art. 2092. See, *American Bank and Trust Co. v. Blue Bird Rest. & Lounge, Inc.* 290 So.2d 302 (La.1974); *Pearson v. Hartford Accident & Ind. Co.*, 281 So.2d 724 (La.1973); *Hidalgo v. Dupuy*, 122 So.2d 639 (La.App. 1st Cir. 1960).

[10] For similar reasons, the fact that the uninsured motorist carrier is bound by the combined effect of the tortfeasor's wrongful act, the uninsured motorist statute, and the carrier's delivery or issuance for delivery of automobile liability insurance, while the tortfeasor is obliged merely because of his delict, does not prevent there being an obligation in solido on the part of the debtors. The obligation may be in solido even though the obligations of the obligors arise from separate acts or by different reasons. La.C.C. arts. 2091, 2092. *Pearson v. Hartford Accident & Ind. Co., supra. Granger v. General Motors Corp., supra; Hidalgo v. Dupuy, supra; Finance Security Co. v. Williams*, 42 So.2d 310 (La.App. 1st Cir. 1949); *Kirtland v. J. Ray McDermott & Co.*, 568 F.2d 1166, 1171 (5th Cir. 1978); *Avondale Shipyards v. Vessell Thomas E. Cuffe*, 434 F.Supp. 920, 932 (E.D.La.1977); Developments in the Law, 1979–1980-Obligations, 41 La.L.Rev. 355, 357 (1981).

[11] When payment is made by either the tortfeasor or the uninsured motorist carrier the other is exonerated toward the creditor as to the solidary obligation. This is a direct consequence of each debtor being obliged to the same thing so that each may be compelled for the whole, as if he were the sole debtor. 4 C. Aubry & C. Rau, *supra*, p. 27. Moreover, the underlying purpose of both delictual responsibility and uninsured motorist coverage is to promote and effectuate complete reparation, no more or no less. Accordingly, as to the debt to which the tortfeasor and uninsured motorist carrier are solidarily obliged, payment of it by one exonerates the other toward the creditor.

[12] When an obligation by effect of law contains the requirements or fulfills the definition of Article 2091, the obligation is in solido and the law from which it results need not state that the obligation is solidary. "Article 2093 provides that '[a]n obligation *in solido* is not presumed; it must be expressly stipulated.

[13] This rule ceases to prevail only in cases where an obligation *in solido* takes place of right by virtue of some provisions of the law.'" The first paragraph of Article 2093 dealing with conventional solidarity, requires that it be expressly stipulated. But it is otherwise with regard to the second paragraph of the same article which, dealing with legal solidarity, admits it in all cases where it results from a provision of law, without requiring an express declaration. 4 C. Aubry & C. Rau, Droit Civil Francais, § 298b note 13 (6th ed. Bantin) in A. Yiannopoulos, 1 Civil Law Translations 24 (1965); *Cline v. Crescent City R. Co.,* 41 La.Ann. 1031, 6 So. 851 (1889); *Hidalgo v. Dupuy, supra; Finance Security Co. v. Williams, supra.* The previous expressions to the contrary by this court in *Wooten v. Wimberly,* 272 So.2d 303 (La.1973) and *Cox v. Shreveport Packing Co.,* 213 La. 53, 34 So.2d 373 (1948), which have received scholarly criticism, *Wooten v. Wimberly, supra* (Tate, J., concurring and Barham, J., dissenting); The Work of the Louisiana Appellate Courts, 1972–1973-Obligations, 34 La.L.Rev. 231 (1974); Note, The Nonsolidness of Solidarity, 34 La.L.Rev. 648 (1974); Comment, Prescribing Solidarity: Contributing to the Indemnity Dilemma, 41 La.L.Rev. 657, 674–676, and have been substantially undermined, *Sampay v. Morton Salt Co., supra; Foster v. Hampton, supra; Kern v. Travelers Insurance Co., supra,* are now expressly overrruled [*sic*].

[14] The solidary obligation in the present case results primarily from provisions of law, viz., the general rules of delictual responsibility, La.C.C. arts. 2315, et seq., and the uninsured motorist statute, La.R.S. 22:1406(D). Although an insurer must deliver or issue for delivery automobile liability insurance in order to be bound, the basic ingredients of the obligation are provided and required by law. Under these circumstances, the obligation is solidary by operation of law, without requiring an express declaration.

[15] Allstate argues that the conclusion we have reached will cause all effects of solidarity to be applied in uninsured motorist cases. Care should be taken by civilian attorneys and jurists to be on guard against applying one segment of the code in isolation from others. Neither the Civil Code nor the revised statutes were intended to be applied in this manner. A full delineation of the relationship between

the tortfeasor and the uninsured motorist carrier after payment of the debt owed by them solidarily is beyond the scope of this case. However, it is clear that the Civil Code recognizes that debtors, although solidarily bound for the creditor's benefit, may have differing relationships among themselves. The conclusion that debtors are solidarily bound does not alone determine the rights and obligations of the debtors in relation to each other. La.C.C. arts. 2103, 2104, 2106; 2 M. Planiol, *supra,* nos. 767–771; *Wooten v. Wimberly, supra* (Tate, J., concurring). The Work of the Louisiana Appellate Courts for the 1972–1973 Term-Obligations, 34 La.L.Rev. 231, 233 (1974).

[16] For the foregoing reasons, the judgment of the court of appeal is reversed and the case is remanded to the district court for further proceedings.

[17] REVERSED AND REMANDED.

[. . . .]

MARCUS, Justice (dissenting).

[18] There is an obligation *in solido* on the part of the debtors, when they are all obliged to the same thing, so that each may be compelled for the whole, and when the payment which is made by one of them, exonerates the others toward the creditor. La.Civ.Code art. 2091. An obligation *in solido* is not presumed; it must be expressly stipulated. This rule ceases to prevail only in cases where an obligation *in solido* takes place of right by virtue of some provisions of the law. La.Civ .Code art. 2093. I do not consider that an injured party's U/M carrier is liable *in solido* with the tortfeasor. U/M coverage is a contract whereby the insurer agrees to indemnify the insured in the event that the insured is injured by a tortfeasor who is uninsured or underinsured. There is no relationship, contractually or otherwise, between the U/M carrier and the tortfeasor. The obligation of the tortfeasor to repair the damage that he has caused is not the same as the obligation of the U/M carrier under its insurance contract. Moreover, there is no provision of law which makes the U/M carrier liable *in solido* with the tortfeasor. Compare La.Civ .Code art. 2324 which makes joint tortfeasors "answerable *in solido.*" Accordingly, I respectfully dissent.

CALOGERO, Justice, dissenting.

[19] I dissent from the majority opinion because in my view the requirements for solidarity expressed in La.C.C. art. 2091 are not met in this case; the payment by one of the debtors (uninsured motorist carrier) does not exonerate the other (tortfeasor).

[20] La.R.S. 22:1406(D)(4) does not grant the uninsured motorist carrier, which pays its insured in the appropriate case, the right of legal subrogation. To the contrary, the provision only gives the uninsured motorist carrier a right of reimbursement from "the proceeds of any settlement or judgment resulting from the exercise of any rights of recovery of such person [the insured] against any person or organization legally responsible for the bodily injury for which such payment is made." Thus, under this provision, there is no exoneration of the tortfeasor because of payment by the uninsured motorist carrier. The victim/insured may assert his claim

against the tortfeasor with a right in the uninsured motorist carrier to be reimbursed from the insured out of any recovery.

[. . . .]

BLANCHE, Justice (dissenting).

[21] Louisiana law requires all insurers to extend uninsured motorist coverage to their insureds, unless such coverage is explicitly waived by the insured. Under the uninsured motorist portion of an insurance policy, the uninsured motorist carrier contracts to indemnify the insured, in the event the insured is injured by a tortfeasor who is unable to fully respond in damages. The *sole* basis of the uninsured motorist carrier's liability to the insured remains the contract of insurance, to which the tortfeasor is *not* a party.

[22] The majority opinion correctly notes that "[a]n obligation *in solido* is not presumed; it must be expressly stipulated. This rule ceases to prevail only in cases where an obligation *in solido* takes place of right by virtue of some provisions of the law." Civil Code Art. 2093. In erroneously concluding that the relationship between the uninsured motorist carrier and the tortfeasor is one of legal solidarity, the majority completely ignores the absence of a most vital element present in all other cases of legal solidarity. There must be *some* relationship between the two parties who are to be held solidarily liable. The solidary relationship between an employer and his employees is premised upon the employment relationship which exists between these parties. A principal becomes solidarily liable with his agent by virtue of their unique relationship. The solidary relationship of a liability insurer and its insured is founded upon the vital contract of insurance which binds these two parties.

[23] In all other cases in which legal solidarity arises, there exists *some* relationship between the parties who are held solidarily liable. By contrast, there is *no* relationship, contractual or otherwise, between the uninsured motorist carrier and the tortfeasor. A solidary relationship between the uninsured motorist carrier and the tortfeasor does not exist by virtue of some provision of the law;[1] rather, it is purely the creation of the majority opinion. Such judicial legislation is beyond the bounds of our authority. By the express provisions of C.C. art. 2093, we cannot presume a solidary relationship where none is intended to exist.

[24] For the foregoing reasons, I respectfully dissent.

Questions

1. Paragraph 1: What is the main issue raised in this case?

2. Paragraph 6: Notice the first line or statement: it is a heading which is developed in the following paragraph. The whole legal analysis is based on the last

---

1. Compare C.C. art. 2324, which establishes a solidary relationship between joint tortfeasors.

two words of that sentence, "same thing." Consider the role of the persuasive authority cited by the Court.

3. Paragraph 10: What matters most, if at all: the fact that two obligors owe the same thing and hence can be held solidarily liable, or that the sources of solidarity between these two obligors can be different?

4. Paragraph 11: What is the real foundation or reason for solidarity between two obligors?

5. Paragraphs 18–24: On what grounds did the dissenting Justices dissent? What is their main concern? Do they share any concerns expressed by the majority?

Louisiana Bank and Trust Company, Crowley, Louisiana
v.
Mrs. Jewel B. Boutte et al.

Supreme Court of Louisiana
February 24, 1975
309 So.2d 274

DIXON, Justice.

[1] Louisiana Bank and Trust Company of Crowley sued Rex Rice Company, Inc. and Lake Rice Mill, Inc., claiming a balance due on promissory notes in the amount of over $600,000, and joined in the same suit defendant Matthew L. Hanagriff and three other persons under 'continuing guaranty' agreements, alleging that the defendants were liable for the debts of Rex Rice Company, Inc., the principal debtor.

[2] While the case was pending, a compromise agreement released the parties defendant with the exception of Hanagriff, who did not join the compromise agreement, and against whom the plaintiff bank reserved its rights.

[3] There was judgment in the trial court in favor of plaintiff and against defendant, which judgment was amended and affirmed in the Court of Appeal. Louisiana Bank & Trust Co. v. Boutte et al., La.App. 298 So.2d 884 (1974).

[4] We granted writs on the application of defendant Hanagriff to determine the effect of the 'continuing guaranty' agreement. Before us the defendant argues that his obligation under the contract of guaranty had prescribed; that the release of the principal debtor released the defendant, who was a surety; that the plaintiff creditor received immovable and other property in the payment of the principal debt, resulting in the full discharge of the surety under C.C. 3062; and, finally, that defendant's property had been illegally subjected to attachment.

[5] The record reveals that Rex Rice Company, Inc. was indebted to the plaintiff bank in 1962. On May 18 of that year the 'continuing guaranty' agreement was executed and signed by the four shareholders and directors of the Rex Rice Company, Inc., including the defendant Hanagriff. The complete agreement is reproduced in

footnote.[1] This suit was filed March 25, 1969, and a writ of attachment was issued, seizing Hanagriff's home.

Release of the Principal Debtor

[6] In the interval between the filing and the trial of the suit, three compromise agreements had been executed, the effect of which was to convey property from Rex Rice Company, Inc., Jack R. Smith, Mrs. Louie F. (Hattie F.) Broussard and

---

1. 'CONTINUING GUARANTY':

In consideration of the LOUISIANA BANK AND TRUST COMPANY, CROWLEY, LOUISIANA, at our request, giving or extending terms of credit to REX RICE COMPANY, INC. hereinafter called debtor, we hereby give this continuing guaranty to the said LOUISIANA BANK AND TRUST COMPANY, CROWLEY, LOUISIANA, its transferees or assigns, for the payment in full, together with all interest, fees and charges of whatsoever nature and kind, of any indebtedness, direct or contingent, of said debtor to said LOUISIANA BANK AND TRUST COMPANY, CROWLEY, LOUISIANA, up to the amount of TWO HUNDRED THOUSAND DOLLARS Dollars, [*sic*] whether due or to become due, now existing or hereafter arising. The Bank may, in its judgment, grant extensions, take and give securities, accent compositions, grant releases and discharges, make changes of any sort whatever in the terms of its contract or manner of doing business with the debtor and with other parties and securities in relation thereto. The Bank may also apply all moneys received from the debtor and others or from securities as it may think best, without in any way altering, affecting, limiting or lessening the liability of the undersigned under this Guaranty; the whole without any notice to or consent from us. The Bank shall not be bound to exhaust its recourse against the debtor or other persons or upon the securities it may hold before being entitled to payment from the undersigned of the amount hereby guaranteed. We do furthermore bind and obligate ourselves, our heirs and assigns, in solido with said debtor, for the payment of the said indebtedness precisely as if the same had been contracted and was due or owing by us in person hereby agreeing to and binding ourselves, our heirs and assigns, by all terms and conditions contained in any note or notes signed or to be signed by said debtor, making ourselves a party thereto; hereby waiving notice of any such indebtedness and of demand, presentment, protest or notice of any act to establish the liability of any party or any commercial or other paper, indebtedness or obligation covered by this guaranty; we do further waive all notice and all pleas of discussion and division and we agree to pay upon demand at any time to said Bank, its transferees or assigns, the full amount of said indebtedness up to the amount of this guaranty, together with interest, fees and charges, as above set forth, becoming subrogated in the event of payment in full by us to the claim of said Bank, its transferees or assigns, together with whatever security if any they may hold against said indebtedness.'

'It is expressly agreed that this continuing guaranty is absolute and complete, and that acceptance and notice of acceptance thereof by the Bank, are therefore unnecessary and they are hereby expressly waived, and the same shall continue in force until written notice or its discontinuance shall be served upon one of the executive officers of the said Bank, but such discontinuance shall not affect our liability on any debts and/or obligations of the debtor then existing nor the liability of any other party liable in the premises.

In faith whereof we have hereunto signed our name on this the 18th day of May, 1962.
S/ Jack R. Smith
S/ Matthew L. Hanagriff
S/ Mrs. Louie F. Broussard
S/ Mrs. Jewel B. Boutte'

Mrs. Jewel B. Boutte, the other three shareholders and directors of Rex Rice Company, Inc., to the plaintiff bank. Those parties were released from further liability. The bank reserved its rights against Hanagriff. Numerous other parties were involved in the compromise agreements, including another bank and other creditors of Rex Rice Company, Inc. Judgment was rendered against Hanagriff alone on June 7, 1973, following a trial on the merits on April 10, 1973. At the trial, it was shown that the balance due on Rex Rice Company, Inc. indebtedness to the plaintiff bank was $477,021.46, all of which had accrued following the execution of the 'continuing guaranty' agreement. Since the 'continuing guaranty' was for a sum of $200,000, the trial court rendered judgment against Hanagriff for one-fourth of that amount, because he was one of four signers. The Court of Appeal reduced the amount of the judgment against Hanagriff to $40,000 because Rex Rice Company, Inc. was also a solidary obligor, making Hanagriff's virile share one-fifth of the total, under C.C. 2103.[2]

[7] Defendant's argument that the release of the principal operated to discharge his, the surety's, liability depends upon classifying the instrument of 'continuing guaranty' as a contract of suretyship. Defendant relies on the following cases for the proposition that a surety bound In solido is a surety nevertheless: Jones v. Fleming, 15 La.Ann. 522 (1860); Lee v. City of Baton Rouge, 243 La. 850, 147 So.2d 868 (1963); Keller v. General Motors Acceptance Corp., 233 La. 320, 96 So.2d 598 (1957); Elmer Candy Co. v. Baumann, 150 So. 427 (La.App.1933); Brock v. First State Bank & Trust Co., 187 La. 766, 175 So. 569 (1937).

[. . . .]

[8] Like so many legal classifications, those of surety and solidary obligor are not mutually exclusive. Provisions for Solidary sureties are found in the Civil Code, and can be traced to Roman law. Planiol, Traite Elementaire De Droit Civil, translated by Louisiana State Law Institute, Vol. 2, No. 2351.[3]

---

2. Plaintiff has not complained of this ruling, and the question is not before us whether the contractual terms of the 'continuing guaranty' would have permitted a judgment against Hanagriff for the entire $200,000.

3. 'Sureties resemble solidary co-debtors, in their relations with the principal debtor, and in their relations between themselves: there is no division between them, and each one of them can be sued before the debtor. However this is not true solidarity, since the law accords to them the benefits of discussion and of division, benefits which are the negation of solidarity and which are refused to real solidary co-debtors.

'This contradictory explanation is explained by the historic development of suretyship. Under the Roman Fidejussio, the surety was originally a debtor as firmly bound as the principal obligor: Then there was a reaction in favor of debtors, and various benefits were accorded which provisionally improved the position of the surety. But they went too far. By relaxing the liability of the surety they injured borrowers whose credit was destroyed. Capitalists demand serious security; if not, they do not loan; and in fact, although our laws have retained the favors accumulated by the Roman law for the benefit of sureties, the practice has regulated itself otherwise and has passed them by. *It employs the very simple method of requiring the sureties to renounce, by a special clause, all their benefits which has the effect of re-establishing the ancient solidarity affaced by the Roman*

[9] Civil Code 3045[4] provides that the obligation of the surety toward the creditor, when the surety is bound In solido with the debtor, is 'regulated by the same principles which have been established for debtors In solido.'

[10] Civil Code 2106,[5] with reference to the case in which there is a principal debtor, for whose benefit the principal obligation was incurred, provides that with regard to the principal debtor, the solidary codebtors 'are considered only as his securities.' As Planiol explains in Vol. 2, No. 768:

> 'Art. 1216 (C.N. 1216; C.C. 2106) has taken care of this situation by providing that in such a case the debt should be entirely borne by the debtor who is directly concerned, and that the others are to be considered in relation to him as his *sureties* only; they have merely bound themselves in the interest of another. However, this assimilation with the surety is not true except in the relations of the co-debtors among themselves: 'with relation to him,' says Art. 1216, and not in their relations with the creditor. It is, in fact, an entirely different thing to obligate oneself as a solidary co-debtor and as a surety; the surety enjoys, against the creditor, various benefits which the solidary debtor does not enjoy.' (Emphasis added).

[11] The effect of the application of these articles is that, as between the creditor and the solidary surety, the obligations of the surety are governed by the rules of solidary obligors.

[12] The solidary surety waives the pleas of discussion and division. C.C. 3045; Brock v. First State Bank, supra, Hibernia Bank & Trust Co. v. Succession of Cancienne, 140 La. 969, 74 So. 267 (1917); Home Ins. Co. v. Voorhies Co., 168 So. 724 (La. App.1936); 2 Planiol, No. 2352. A remission to a simple surety does not discharge his co-sureties. C.C. 2205. As to solidary sureties, a remission by the creditor was held, in Elmer Candy Co. v. Baumann, supra, to have discharged the solidary co-sureties because the creditor failed to reserve his rights against the remaining sureties; otherwise, C.C. 2203[6] provides that a discharge of one solidary co-debtor discharges the others.

---

legislation. In our day simple suretyship tends to become more and more rare; almost always the sureties engage themselves solidarily with the principal debtor or between themselves. There has been a return thus, to the primitive rigor of the law.' (Emphasis added).

4. 'The obligation of the surety towards the creditor is to pay him in case the debtor should not himself satisfy the debt; and the property of such debtor is to be previously discussed or seized, unless the security should have renounced the plea of discussion, or should be bound In solido jointly with the debtor, in which case the effects of his engagement are to be regulated by the same principles which have been established for debtors In solido.'

5. 'If the affair for which the debt has been contracted In solido, concern only one of the coo bligors, [*sic*] In solido, that one is liable for the whole debt towards the other codebtors, who, with regard to him, are considered only as his securities.'

6. 'The remission or conventional discharge in favor of one of the codebtors In solido, discharges all the others, unless the creditor has expressly reserved his right against the latter.
In the latter case, he can not claim the debt without making a deduction of the part of him to whom he has made the remission.'

[13] Among the co-obligors, however, bound In solido, the legal relationships may be governed by the rules of suretyship. Both the simple surety and the solidary surety who pay the debt have a right of recourse against the principal debtor.[7] C.C. 2106; Marfese v. Nelson, 10 Orl.App. 288 (1913); 2 Planiol, No. 768, No. 2352.

[14] There are exceptions, and sometimes the relationships among solidary sureties are not governed by the rules of suretyship. A simple surety who pays the whole debt can enforce contribution against the other sureties, but Only when he has paid 'in consequence of a lawsuit instituted against him.' C.C. 3058. But a solidary surety need not await suit before paying, in order to preserve his right of contribution. There is no reason to require such a delay, since pleas of discussion and division are not available to him. Ferriday v. Purnell, 2 La.Ann. 334 (1847); Bond v. Bishop, 18 La.Ann. 549 (1866).

[15] We hold, therefore, that the compromise[8] and release of the principal debtor, Rex Rice Company, Inc., did not operate to release the solidary surety, Hanagriff.

[. . . .]

[16] The judgment of the Court of Appeal is therefore affirmed and amended, awarding plaintiff, Louisiana Bank and Trust Company, Crowley, Louisiana, judgment against defendant, Matthew L. Hanagriff, in the sum of $40,000, and there is further judgment in favor of Matthew L. Hanagriff, plaintiff in reconvention, and against Louisiana Bank and Trust Company, Crowley, Louisiana, defendant in reconvention, dissolving the writ of attachment and awarding plaintiff in reconvention damages in the sum of $100.00, all at the cost of defendant, Matthew L. Hanagriff.

[. . . .]

---

7. The right of subrogation of the surety who pays the creditor is not the only source of the solidary obligor's action against the principal debtor when he pays the creditor. A compromise and discharge of the principal debtor by the creditor might leave the simple surety, if he were forced to pay the creditor any balance, without any subrogation rights against the principal debtor because of the accessory nature of the suretyship obligation. C.C. 3035. If the principal creditor could discharge the debtor and proceed against the surety, the creditor's rights against the principal debtor having been extinguished, there would be nothing left to which the surety might become subrogated, should be become forced to pay the creditor.
The other source of the solidary surety's right of recourse against the principal debtor is 'one which is personal to him arising from the contract of suretyship . . .' 1 Planiol, No. 2354, No. 2355. It is this remedy, says Planiol, which is referred to in C.N. 2028 and C.N. 2030 (2029), the sources of our C.C. 3052 and 3053. C.C. 3053 refers to the right of subrogation granted to co-debtors In solido, a different source of the paying solidary surety's right of recourse against the principal debtor.
Therefore, when, under a contract a solidary suretyship, one is forced to pay the creditor a debt of the principal obligor, even after the creditor has discharged the principal obligor, the surety does not lose this right of recourse against the principal debtor, which has arisen from the nature of the contract of suretyship.
8. Compare 2 Planiol, No. 761: 'If one only of the co-debtors compromises with the creditor, the compromise does not bind the others and cannot be opposed by them to the creditor. (Art. 2051).' Our C.C. 3077 differs in phraseology from C.N. 2051, its source.

SANDERS, Chief Justice (concurring).

[17] In the present case, the plaintiff compromised its suit against Rex Rice Company, Inc., and others, reserving its rights against the present defendant, Hanagriff, who had executed a continuing guaranty. The main question is whether the release of Rex Rice Company discharged the defendant. I think not.

[18] Article 2203 of the Louisiana Civil Code provides:

'The remission or conventional discharge in favor of one of the codebtors In solido, discharges all the others, unless the creditor has expressly reserved his right against the latter.

'In the latter case, he can not claim the debt without making a deduction of the part of him to whom he has made the remission.'

[19] Since the compromise contained an express reservation of rights against the present defendant, he was not discharged in accordance with the exception set forth in the above article.

[20] For the reasons assigned, I respectfully concur in the decree.

BARHAM, Justice (concurring).

[21] I concur in the majority opinion under the simple finding that as between the Plaintiff-creditor and All of the original defendants, Rex Rice Company, Inc., and the four individuals who signed the continuing guaranty (including the present defendant, Hanagriff), all the defendants were Principal co-obligors.

[22] I differ from the majority in my opinion that having been presented Only with the question of the relationship between the plaintiff and The single defendant, Hanagriff, we are obliged to confine ourselves to a discussion of the law pertinent to resolving the legal rights and obligations betweeen [sic] them. Significantly, we do not have before us the proper parties for determining the legal relationship between the rice company and the four continuing guarantors. That must be resolved in another lawsuit in the absence of agreement among those parties. We cannot here decide whether the five original defendants are solidary obligors as between themselves to the extent that each is responsible for a virile portion of the debt or whether one of the five is a principal obligor who must indemnify the other four under a surety agreement. We should not even decide in this lawsuit whether, in relation to each other, the four continuing guarantors are solidary obligors or solidary sureties with a right of virile contribution among themselves.

[23] The majority opinion quotes doctrinal authority which in fact is a correct analysis of the position I have stated above. The difficulty is that the majority opinion does not clearly set forth the result which should be obtained in this suit under that doctrinal statement. The quote from 2 M. Planiol, Traite, e le mentaire [sic] de droit civil No. 768 (La.St.L.Inst. trans. (1959) is a correct statement of the law applicable to the issue between the parties to this lawsuit. However, the following translation of 7 M. Planiol and M. Ripert, Traite pratique de droit civil francais 466–67

(2me e d. Esmein, 1954) may more clearly state the position of the French in interpreting their Code Napole on [*sic*] Article 1216 (our Civil Code Article 2106):

> '§1091. Case where one of the debtors is totally liberated. The inequality in the debtors' share of the common debt may be very large. Carrying this conclusion to the farthest extreme it may even be, as it is in fact in the most recurring cases, that, given two solidary debtors, only one must fully pay the debt without the other having any share thereof.

> 'Article 1216 (of the Code Napole on [*sic*]) has foreseen such a situation in asserting that, in such a case, the debt must be entirely borne by the debtor in whose interest the debt was contracted while the other debtors, In their relation to the first one, are regarded as his sureties. They occupy such a position for having bound themselves for the full amount of the debt for the benefit of their co-debtor. This assimilation of the position of a solidary debtor to the one of a surety, however, is only valid insofar as the relation between solidary co-debtors is concerned. It is not valid concerning the relation between such debtors and the creditor. As a matter of fact, One thing is to bind oneself as Solidary debtor, and another is to bind oneself as Surety, since, From the viewpoint of his relation with the creditor, a surety enjoys certain privileges which are refused to a solidary debtor.' (Emphasis here and elsewhere supplied.)

[24] See also 1 C. Aubry & C. Rau, Droit civil francais 33 (La.St.L.Inst. transl.1965). See also 3 C. Toullier, Le droit civil francais 588 (1833).

[25] The point to be made is that the majority is wrong to conclude in this limited action we consider between the plaintiff-creditor and one continuing guarantor, Hanagriff, that Rex Rice Company, Inc., one of the defendants, is the principal debtor and that Hanagriff is a solidary surety with the three other guarantors. That relationship is to be determined between Those parties and has no bearing upon the decision we make; it is actually an intrusion by this Court into another legal relationship not yet litigated. The majority concedes from the law it cites that there may be solidary sureties who, as to third parties, may also be solidary obligors with a principal debtor. However, this occurs only when, as between the solidary sureties and the creditor, the sureties become principal debtors along with someone else.

[26] A. Weill, Droit civil, les obligations, No. 920 at 879, 880 (1971) states that '(w)hen one of the co-debtors has paid the debt, * * *' the law establishes a presumption that co-debtors distribute their responsibility among themselves according to their virile shares, or if it be so agreed, 'according to the interest which each has had in the business.' Weill then says that, '(i)n an exceptional case it can happen that there is no such contribution to be made to a co-debtor who has paid the debt, as when one of the co-debtors who has paid, alone, was directly concerned in the business (was the principal obligor) and the others are engaged Only under the title of Solidary sureties. Art. 1216 (La.C.C. art. 2106) anticipates this hypothesis.'

[27] It is my feeling that we should make very apparent that the instrument we interpret here (footnote 1 in the majority opinion), insofar as the creditor and one of the guarantors are concerned, is an agreement of co-obligation—a solidary obligation by each of the signing parties to that creditor for the full indebtedness. Their distribution of that debt Among themselves depends upon their agreement as to the interest of each in the business, even to the extent that only one of them may be concerned directly while the others are engaged only as Solidary sureties who are entitled to indemnification from the one who is the principal obligor. We cannot, and we should not, address ourselves to that issue. The continuing guaranty instrument alone on its face does not, without extrinsic evidence, permit us to make such a determination, even if it were properly before us. That act of guaranty does not unambiguously set forth a suretyship, although this is not to say that it was not intended as a suretyship by the parties.

[28] I respectfully concur.

Questions

1. Paragraph 1: How many obligors are there? Are they all equally bound? How would you apply Louisiana Civil Code article 1804 to the type of relationship that may exist between all the obligors?

2. Paragraphs 2 & 6: What is a "*compromise* agreement" and what are its effects? *See* La. Civ. Code arts. 3071–3083.

3. Paragraph 6: Can you figure out the two different distributions of the continuing guaranty of $200,000? The effect of the three compromise agreements was to convey property; thus, what could this form of payment be under the Louisiana Civil Code? *See* La. Civ. Code arts. 2655–2659.

4. Paragraphs 9–11: What important distinction is made here in the context of solidarity between sureties and a principal obligor?

5. Paragraph 12: What is remission? What are its effects? *See* La. Civ. Code arts. 1888–1892. In paragraph 4, and again in paragraph 15, the court speaks about "release." Is a release the same thing as a remission?

S & W Investment Company, Inc.
v.
Otis W. Sharp & Son, Inc.

Supreme Court of Louisiana
December 14, 1964
170 So.2d 360

HAMITER, Justice.

[1] In this suit S & W Investment Company, Inc., seeks to recover a sum expended by it for completing a swimming pool which the defendant, Otis W. Sharp and Son, Inc., had originally contracted to build but later abandoned.

[....]

[2] The swimming pool was to be built by the defendant, at a contracted price of $4725, in the patio area of a motel proposed to be constructed by plaintiff. It was understood by the parties that, in order to permit the use of plaintiff's heavy equipment nearby and to avoid the risk of damaging the pool tiling and appurtenances during erection of the buildings, the concrete shell of the pool would be provided first and the remaining work (including the installing of tiling, filter, ladders, trim, etc.) would be undertaken following the buildings' completion.

[3] The written contract dated September 12, 1961 provided in part:

'ARTICLE I. SCOPE OF WORK — The Contractor shall furnish all of the material and perform all of the work for the construction of a Swimming Pool as described below.

'ARTICLE 3. PROGRESS PAYMENTS — * * * Upon completion of shell (which is all but tile, brick, filter, deck eqpt., plum. line to building, and interior finish), amt. due $3000.00. Remainder due upon completion of pool.'

[4] Also, the contract obligated the owner to excavate the pool site, to move the excavated material, and to place the backfill around the shell.

[5] The excavation was performed by a construction company paid by plaintiff, but the work was under the direction and supervision of the defendant. The shell was completed about October 17, 1961, and on October 22, 1961 plaintiff gave to the defendant the $3000 progress payment then due (more particularly hereinafter discussed).

[6] Prior to leaving the job temporarily an employee of the defendant closed a hydrostatic pressure relief valve (which had been installed in the shell as a safety device) by inserting a plug in it, and he then commenced filling the shell with water by means of a garden hose. He was sent back to the site at least two more days for the purpose of continuing the water filling and (to quote his testimony) 'to watch that Our plumbing, pipes and the shell of the pool wasn't damaged by the equipment being used to backfill.' [....]

[7] The evidence is to the effect that the safest method of protecting the shell was to fill it with water rather than to depend on the valve. However, before a sufficient

amount of water was placed therein the filling operation was discontinued and the hose was removed from the site by defendant's employee.

[8] A heavy rainfall that occurred in early November, 1961 caused the uprooting or 'floating' of one end of the shell. Defendant's initial salvage attempts were unsuccessful, and it disclaimed any further obligation when plaintiff refused to augment the contract price.

[9] Plaintiff, thereupon, employed the services of J. Stanley Middleton, d/b/a Family Pools, to make the necessary repairs and to bring the work to operational status for the price of $3899.95. Plaintiff's claim in this suit of $2174.95 represents the difference between the amount paid to Middleton and the balance remaining under the contract with the defendant.

[10] Plaintiff cites and relies on Revised Civil Code Article 2758 which states: 'Builder furnishing materials — Destruction of work before delivery — Bearing of loss. — When the undertaker furnishes the materials for the work, if the work be destroyed, in whatever manner it may happen, previous [*sic*] to its being delivered to the owner, the loss shall be sustained by the undertaker, unless the proprietor be in default for not receiving it, though duly notified to do so.'

[11] Plaintiff contends that this defendant had obligated itself to construct a complete swimming pool — an indivisible obligation; that the progress payment of $3000, made for the benefit of the undertaker, did not relieve the latter of the responsibility of preserving the entire work until it was finished, delivered and accepted; and that, consequently, under the aforequoted codal provisions any damage thereto occurring before that time must be borne by the defendant contractor.

[12] The defendant apparently recognizes that generally, in the absence of an agreement of the parties, the risk of loss in a building contract is on the contractor until he has completed and delivered the work. This can hardly be gainsaid in view of the provisions of Article 2758.

[13] It urges, however, that this particular contract was one 'for work composed of detached pieces', to wit: (1) a shell and (2) the completion of a shell into a finished pool, all as is contemplated by Revised Civil Code Article 2761 which reads: 'Delivery of work in separate parts. — If the work be composed of detached pieces, or made at the rate of so much a measure, the parts may be delivered separately; and that delivery shall be presumed to have taken place, if the proprietor has paid to the undertaker the price due for the parts of the work which have already been completed.' It argues that under the provisions of this article there arose a presumption of delivery to and acceptance by the owner when the latter paid for that 'piece' (the shell) already completed; and that, therefore, following such payment, and pending the finishing of the entire work, the risk of loss of such 'piece' was on the owner.

[14] The Court of Appeal (as did the district court) found that, within the contemplation of the parties, the obligation undertaken by this defendant was an indivisible one; and it was inclined to the view that, under the circumstances, the provisions of Article 2758 placed the loss on the undertaker. However, a majority of its members

determined that two prior decisions, N. Levy and Son v. Paquette et al., 144 La. 244, 80 So. 269 and Industrial Homestead Association v. Charles A. Junker et al., Orleans Appeal, No. 7402, Unreported (February 13, 1919, cert. den. May 9, 1919-2 Peltier's Orleans Appeals 80) required a different holding, and they felt constrained to follow their interpretation of those decisions which was to the effect that when stage or progress payments are provided for in an otherwise indivisible building contract, and when the owner makes such payments, there arises a presumption of delivery and acceptance of the then completed portion of the work so as to place on the owner the risk of loss thereof pending performance of the entire contract.

[15] We agree with the Court of Appeal's conclusion that the obligation here was an indivisible one and that it did not constitute two obligations to do two different things. Under it, for a stipulated price, the contractor was obliged to construct and deliver a completed swimming pool — not to build a shell for a price and to finish a shell at another price.

[16] Divisible and indivisible contracts are dealt with in the Revised Civil Code Articles 2108–2116. Specifically, the first two of these articles provide: 'Divisible or indivisible — Distinguishing features. — An obligation is divisible or indivisible, according as it has for its object, either a thing which, in its delivery or a fact which, in its execution, is or is not susceptible of division, either material or intellectual.' Article 2108. 'Indivisibility under terms of obligation. — The obligation is indivisible, though the thing or the fact which is the object of it, be by its nature divisible, if the light, in which it is considered in the obligation, does not admit of its being partially executed.' Article 2109.

[17] Clearly the contract under consideration does not admit of its being only partially executed. Neither the shell by itself nor the finishing operation alone is a complete work fit for the use intended as the object of the agreement. The so-called 'detached pieces' (if a finishing operation can be considered as a 'piece') are totally interdependent and such interdependence was the principal motive of the contract. The worth of each component part is increased by its union with the other, and the absence of one renders the other virtually useless or without value.

[18] That such was the understanding of the parties is clearly evidenced by their actions at an unsuspicious time. Thus, when the defendant requested the progress payment, it did not submit a bill for the 'construction of a swimming pool shell'. Rather, the bill read:

> "OTIS W. SHARP & SON, INC.
> General Contractors
> P. O. Box 5164 2401 Rousseau St.
> New Orleans 15, La.

"Name   S & W INVESTMENT CO.   Date 10/20/61
                7525 Airline Highway
                New Orleans, La.   Bill No. 1991

"Job	SWIMMING POOL	
	7525 Airline Hwy.	
	First Request for Partial Payment	$3000.00"

[19] And the inscription on plaintiff's check issued on October 22, 1961 in payment of such bill recited: 'First Partial payment on swimming pool contract.' [....]

[20] We consider the above quoted language as evidence of the intention of the parties that neither considered the agreement as constituting two separate and severable obligations to the extent that the progress payment would settle in full one of them. The defendant's obligation, in other words, was indivisible. It was not transformed into a divisible one by the mere provision for the making of partial payments as the work progressed.

[21] Also, for the foregoing reasons, the contract cannot be considered as a conjoint one within the contemplation of Revised Civil Code Article 2063, as urged by the defendant. That article provides that a contract is conjoint when the obligations are severally comprised therein, and that the obligor may, when he wishes, force the creditor to receive them separately. Clearly the obligations undertaken by this defendant were not several and separable. They, as above shown, were totally interdependent. Obviously, for instance, the defendant could not have required the plaintiff to accept only performance of the 'finishing' work.

[22] Inasmuch as defendant's obligation was not divisible, i.e., it was not for work composed of 'detached pieces', Article 2761 is inapplicable. From which it follows that the progress payment cannot form the basis of a presumptive delivery of the work as of the time it was made; and in the absence of such delivery, as well as of an acceptance by the owner, the swimming pool construction remained at the risk of the contractor until its complete performance. Article 2758.

[23] We have carefully examined the decisions relied on by the majority of the Court of Appeal (and cited by the defendant), but we do not find that they conflict with the result reached herein by us.

[....]

[24] For the reasons assigned the judgment of the Court of Appeal is reversed and set aside, and the decree of the district court awarding to plaintiff the sum of $2174.95 is reinstated and made the judgment of this court. The defendant shall pay all costs.

Questions

1. Paragraphs 3–4: Can you identify an obligation of result? A personal/heritable obligation? An obligation to do? To give? Any term or condition?

2. Paragraphs 9–10: What kind of obligation is created by a contract for services? *See* La. Civ. Code arts. 2745–2750 and 2756–2777. Read carefully Louisiana Civil Code article 2758 as the Court refers to it in paragraph 10. Notice that the

Court does take the Louisiana Civil Code articles into consideration to support its opinion.

3. Paragraph 11: Is it in the plaintiff's interest to argue that the defendant was bound by an indivisible obligation? What benefit(s) is (are) attached to an indivisible obligation? Whose obligation was it to make progress payments? What does it mean as regards the nature of that obligation, its kind? Can an obligation be divisible on one side and indivisible on the other side?

4. Paragraph 13: Why is the defendant building its argument on the basis of Louisiana Civil Code article 2761? On what kind of obligation, divisible or indivisible, is the defendant relying?

5. Paragraphs 15–16: After stating that it agrees with the Court of Appeal's holding that the obligation of the contractor was an indivisible obligation, the Supreme Court cites some Louisiana Civil Code articles on the distinction between a divisible obligation and an indivisible one. Do you approve of all or only some of the words used by the Supreme Court in paragraph 16? From where do these legal terms come?

Bryan Ardis Frame, et al.,

v.

Shreveport Anti-Tuberculosis League, et al., State of Louisiana, Through the Department of Highways,

v.

Bryan Ardis Frame, et al.

Court of Appeal of Louisiana
Second Circuit
January 18, 1989
538 So.2d 684

LINDSAY, Judge.

[1] These are consolidated cases concerning ownership of approximately fifty-five acres of land donated in 1918 to the Shreveport Anti-Tuberculosis League for use as a tuberculosis treatment facility. The heirs of the original donor sought to revoke the donation for failure of the ultimate donee of the property, the State of Louisiana, to comply with the condition of the donation. The condition called for the property to be used as a tuberculosis sanitarium or camp or for some other equally charitable purpose.

[2] The trial court held that the heirs were entitled to ownership of approximately one-half of the property plus a sum of money deposited in the registry of the court pursuant to an expropriation of a portion of the property. The court also held that the State was entitled to retain ownership of the remainder of the tract in question. The State appealed and the heirs answered the appeal, each claiming ownership of the entire property. For the following reasons, we affirm in part and reverse in part the trial court judgment.

Facts

[3] On May 15, 1918, Colonel J.B. Ardis donated approximately fifty-five acres of land to the Shreveport Anti-Tuberculosis League for use as a tuberculosis sanitarium, subject to the following condition:

> It is agreed and understood that if said property should cease to be used for a tuberculosis sanatorium or camp or some other equally charitable purpose, the same should then revert back to the donor.

[4] Following the donation, a facility for the treatment of tuberculosis was established on the property. The facility was operated by the Shreveport Anti-Tuberculosis League for many years. On May 20, 1948, the Shreveport Anti-Tuberculosis League donated the property to the Pines Sanitoria, Inc. In that same year, the Pines Sanitoria, Inc. donated the property to the State of Louisiana. The State operated the tuberculosis treatment center on the property continuously until 1972. The facility was known as the Pines Tuberculosis Sanitarium.

[5] Due to innovations in the treatment of tuberculosis, the need for hospitalization and isolation of tuberculosis patients became less frequent. Nationally, the number of patients housed in specialized tuberculosis treatment facilities declined. The same was true of the Pines Tuberculosis Sanitarium. In early January, 1972, Governor Edwards ordered the Pines closed as a treatment facility for tuberculosis patients. The patients who were hospitalized at the Pines were transferred to other facilities or were treated on an outpatient basis.

[6] Shortly after the closure of the tuberculosis sanitarium, the State began renovations on one of the residences on the property for use as a halfway house for recovering alcoholics. The halfway house was opened in September or October, 1973.

[7] On June 7, 1973, the heirs of Colonel Ardis filed suit to revoke the donation. Bryan Ardis Frame, Caro P. Mills, Nancy Mills VanHoose and George H. Mills filed suit against the Shreveport Anti-Tuberculosis League, the Pines Sanitoria, Inc., the Louisiana Tuberculosis and Respiratory Disease Association and the State of Louisiana, claiming that the State had abandoned use of the property for any purpose and therefore ownership of the property should revert to the heirs of the donor.

[8] In the alternative, the heirs claimed that any portion of the property not being used by the State for a charitable purpose, in compliance with the donation, should be returned to them.

[. . . .]

[9] On May 6, 1974, the State of Louisiana, through the Department of Highways, filed an expropriation suit against Bryan Ardis Frame, Virginia Frame, Betsey Frame, George H. Mills, Jr., Caro P. Mills, Nancy Mills VanHoose, the Pines Sanitoria, Inc., Shreveport Anti-Tuberculosis League and the Louisiana Tuberculosis and Respiratory Disease Association. The Highway Department sought to expropriate 5.15 acres in the southern portion of the property in order to relocate U.S. Highway 80 and to build the Pines Road interchange onto I-20. [. . . .]

[. . . .]

[10] The trial court, in written reasons for judgment, cited the applicable Civil Code Articles dealing with donations[1] and concluded that the clause contained in the act of donation executed by Colonel Ardis, requiring that the property be used for a tuberculosis sanitarium, camp or other equally charitable purpose, created a right to revoke the donation for noncompliance with the condition. The court went on to cite Civil Code Articles dealing with general obligations and the divisibility of obligations. The court then reasoned that the wording of the condition allowed the donee to make alternate uses of the property and gave the donee a choice as to the method of fulfilling the condition of the donation. The court stated that because the donation provided for alternative uses of the property, the obligation created by the condition of the donation was a divisible obligation. The court resorted to Civil Code articles dealing with equity to conclude that because the obligation was divisible, it could be fulfilled on parts of the property and not fulfilled on other parts.

[11] The trial court then found that through the years the defendants had used the property in Tract 2 for tuberculosis treatment and an equally charitable purpose (the treatment of alcoholism). These uses of the property were sufficient to fulfill the condition of the donation and prevent reversion of that tract of land to the plaintiffs.

[12] The court found that after the tuberculosis sanitarium had closed there had not been sufficient use of Tract 1 to fulfill the condition of the obligation. Therefore, the court held that ownership of Tract 1 reverted to the heirs.

[13] The court also found that the State, by expropriating 5.15 acres of the property for a highway, had ceased to use this portion of the land for a charitable purpose. Therefore, the court ruled that the money paid for the property in the expropriation suit belonged to the heirs of the donor.

[14] The court found that the State, by virtue of the expropriation, separated the 0.6 acre tract and the 3.15 acre tract from the main portion of the property and thereby rendered them unusable for the charitable purposes contemplated by the condition of the donation. The court held these two pieces of property also reverted to the ownership of the plaintiffs.

[15] From this judgment, the State appealed, claiming that the trial court erred in finding that the condition was divisible and in failing to recognize that fulfillment of the condition by the use of a portion of the property would constitute fulfillment of the condition as to all the property. The State contends that the trial court should have completely rejected the heirs' claim for revocation of the donation. The heirs answered the appeal, claiming that the trial court erred in failing to declare them to be owners of the entire property.

---

1. The articles dealing with donations and obligations in effect prior to the 1985 revision are applicable to this case.

[16] The issues raised in this appeal are whether the trial court was correct in finding a conditional donation to be a divisible obligation, thereby entitling the heirs to a portion of the property, whether the trial court was correct in finding the heirs were entitled to the money from the expropriation suit and whether the heirs were entitled to ownership of the 0.6 acre tract and the 3.15 acre tract separated from the main property by virtue of the expropriation and relocation of U.S. Highway 80.

[. . . .]

Divisibility of the Conditions

[17] The trial court found that even though the State had fulfilled the condition of the donation sufficient to prevent a reversion of a portion of the property, the condition was divisible and had not been fulfilled on other portions of the property. Therefore the court found that the ownership of some portions of the original tract reverted to the heirs of the donor.

[18] The trial court reached this conclusion by reliance upon former LSA-C.C. Arts. 2108 and 2109[3] dealing with the divisibility of obligations. The trial court reasoned that because the condition of the donation allowed alternate uses of the property and permitted the donee to use the property for other than as a tuberculosis sanitarium or camp, or other equally charitable purposes, the donee had the choice of methods of fulfilling the condition and therefore the condition created a divisible obligation. By implication the trial court further reasoned that the property itself could be divided based upon whether its various parts were being used in compliance with the terms of the donation. The court then cited general rules of equity to reason that the State had fulfilled the condition on a portion of the property donated, but had failed to fulfill it on other parts. Therefore, the court found that the ownership of Tract 1, as shown on the survey map drawn by the heirs' surveyor, reverted to the heirs. The trial court also found that ownership of the two parcels of land separated from the main tract by the highway expropriation also reverted to the heirs because the State had made no use of this property since 1972.

[19] For the following reasons, we reverse this portion of the trial court judgment.

[20] The trial court erred in finding the condition to be a divisible obligation which allowed an arbitrary division of the property along a surveyor's line. In the present case, there is only one general condition, that the property be used for the treatment of tuberculosis or some other equally charitable purpose. Performance of that condition requires the heirs of the donor to allow the donee to remain in possession of all the property which was made the subject of the donation.

---

3. Art. 2108. An obligation is divisible or indivisible, according as it has for its object, either a thing which, in its delivery or a fact which, in its execution, is or is not susceptible of division, either material or intellectual.

Art. 2109. The obligation is indivisible, though the thing or the fact which is the object of it, be by its nature divisible, if the light, in which it is considered in the obligation, does not admit of its being partially executed.

[21] The condition does not require that every square inch of the property be occupied by buildings or structures used in pursuit of the purposes of the donation. Good faith use of a substantial portion of the property for the purpose intended, as occurred here, is sufficient to fulfill the condition as to all the property and to prevent the revocation of the donation.

[22] We find no other case in which a court has revoked a donation as to a portion of the property for nonfulfillment of a condition, but has upheld the donation as to other portions. In cases dealing with donations containing conditions that the property be used for a particular purpose, fulfillment of the specified condition has been sufficient to prevent revocation of the entire donation. *Board of Trustees of Columbia Road Methodist Episcopal Church of Bogalusa v. Richardson,* 216 La. 633, 44 So.2d 321 (1949); *Bonner v. Board of Trustees,* 181 So.2d 255 (La.App. 4th Cir.1965), writ denied 248 La. 915, 182 So.2d 664 (1966).

[23] We find that the State has fulfilled the condition of the donation. Therefore, ownership of the entire property remains with the State, with the exception of the tract which was expropriated for the relocation of the highway[.]

[. . . .]

[24] [W]e find that the trial court erred in holding that the condition of the donation was fulfilled only as to Tract 2, i.e., that portion of the property upon which the main treatment facility is located. Good faith use of a substantial portion of the property for the purpose intended, as occurred here, fulfills the condition as to all the property.

[25] Therefore, that portion of the trial court judgment directing that ownership of Tract 1, the 0.6 acre tract and the 3.5 acre tract be transferred to the heirs is hereby reversed and set aside. The State of Louisiana is hereby recognized as the owner of and entitled to the continued possession of the entire property.

[. . . .]

Questions

1. Paragraphs 1–2: Identify and characterize, in legal terms, the obligation(s) created and its (their) modalities. Any divisible or indivisible obligation?

2. Paragraph 3: Focusing on the quoted excerpt, do you see any condition? If you answered in the affirmative, what kind? Is there any legal meaning attached to the word "or"? Was the obligation to use the property tantamount to the granting of a right of use (*see* La. Civ. Code arts. 639 and 645) or a predial servitude (*see* La. Civ. Code arts. 646 and 652)? Was the obligation to use the property as a . . . or as a . . . a divisible obligation or an indivisible obligation? Look at paragraph 10.

3. Paragraph 10: Focus on the last two sentences. Is the Court's statement accurate? Do alternative choices create a divisible obligation, or does an alternative

obligation create a divisible obligation? Is the Court somewhat or very much "off track"?

4. Paragraph 12: What adjective would you add before the word "condition" to properly identify the type of condition referred to by the court?

5. Paragraphs 17–18: What do you think of this section's title? At the beginning of paragraph 18, the court uses the phrase "divisibility of obligations." Is this choice of phrase correct? What should have been the title of this section? Further into paragraph 18, the court states that "the condition created a divisible obligation." Isn't the court confusing "divisible obligation" with "alternative obligation"? Read Louisiana Civil Code article 1808 and compare it with Louisiana Civil Code article 1815. Do you see any difference?

Richard A. Berlier
v.
A.P. Green Industries, Inc., et al.

Supreme Court of Louisiana
April 3, 2002
815 So.2d 39

JOHNSON, Justice.

[1] We granted a writ in this case involving a settlement of an asbestos-related personal injury and wrongful death claim to determine whether the four settling defendants are solidarily liable. After reviewing the record and the applicable law, we find that the settlement constitutes a joint and indivisible obligation, and each of the defendants are bound for the full $450,000.00.

Facts and Procedural History

[2] On November 12, 1998, Richard Berlier filed a petition for damages for personal injuries resulting from occupational exposure to asbestos products. After his death on January 30, 1999, his surviving spouse and five adult children amended the petition to assert a wrongful death and survival action, as well as loss of consortium claims.

[3] On December 13, 1999, the day the case was set for trial, the plaintiffs agreed to settle their claims against four of the defendants, GAF Corporation ("GAF") [....], Turner & Newell, PLC ("T & N"), Union Carbide Corporation ("Union Carbide"), and Asbestos Claims Management Corporation ("ACMC"), for a lump sum total of $450,000 to be paid on or before March 13, 2000. At the time of the settlement, all four defendants were members of the Center for Claims Resolution ("CCR"), an organization established in 1988 to handle asbestos claims on behalf of its twenty-one member companies.[2]

---

2. The CCR is not now, and never has been, a defendant in this or any other asbestos personal injury claims, but is simply an agent charged with defending such claims against its members. In its

[4] The relationship among the various members of the CCR is controlled by the "Provider Agreement Concerning Center for Claims Resolution (the "Provider Agreement")," which was executed on September 28, 1988. The CCR is administered by a Board of Directors, and the Provider Agreement authorizes the CCR "to administer and arrange for the evaluation, settlement, payment, or defense of all asbestos-related claims." By becoming a member the CCR, the member "designates the [CCR] as its sole agent to administer and arrange on its behalf for the evaluation, settlement, payment or defense of all asbestos-related claims against [it]." The Provider Agreement, further provides that liability payments shall be apportioned to each member according to a specific share allocation matrix, that such apportionment shall establish the responsibility of each [member] for a percentage share of liability payments, and that each member shall pay in a timely manner the percentages of liability payments involved. Any disputes between the CCR and the members regarding the allocation or payment of a member's percentage of liability are to be resolved through alternative dispute resolution.

[5] The settlement reached by the parties was announced on the record as follows:

[6] William Harrison for Turner and Newell [T & N plc], GAF Corporation, National Gypsum [which later became ACMC], together with my partner, Janet McDonell for Union Carbide, put on the record on behalf of those four defendants, we have reached a full settlement with all the plaintiffs in this matter, in Berlier versus A.P. Green and that we have discussed this matter with Frank Swarr and Mr. Diaz as well as attorney for Maples and LeBlanc. We understand Your Honor will be signing an order as to the funds and we'll have the check made payable to both law firms, Mr. Diaz, and to LeBlanc, Maples. [. . . .]

[. . . .]

[7] On December 17, 1999, James McFadden of the CCR sent a letter to plaintiffs' counsel confirming the settlement, noting the lump sum amount of the settlement at the top of the letter, and providing as follows:

> This letter confirms settlement of the above-referenced matter. It is agreed and understood that this settlement fully releases all members whether or not such members are parties to these lawsuits. Furthermore, it is understood that this settlement includes any and all companion actions in this or any jurisdiction for these plaintiffs.
>
> Payment will be made in accordance with the terms of the settlement, providing a release has been executed properly and returned to the CCR. Please have the enclosed release request form completed and returned to Denise Loughran at the Center. We, in turn, will prepare the release from

---

brief, plaintiffs' counsel analogizes the CCR to that "of large corporation's in-house legal counsel, who may hire outside firms . . . to actually litigate claims brought against the corporation subject to in-house counsel's direction."

the information provided on the release form and send it to you for execution by your clients.

[8] The release, executed by the plaintiffs on January 28, 2000, provided in pertinent part as follows:

> For and in consideration of the sum of One Dollar ($1.00), and other good and valuable consideration, the receipt and sufficiency of which are hereby acknowledged, we [plaintiffs] ... release and forever discharge: Amchem Products, Inc.; Armstrong World Industries, Inc.; The Asbestos Claims Management Corporation (formerly known as National Gypsum Company) and The NGC Asbestos Disease and Property Damage Settlement Trust; CertainTeed Corporation; C.E. Thurston & Sons, Inc.; Dana Corporation; Ferodo America, Inc.; Gasket Holdings, Inc. (f/k/a Flexitallic, Inc.); GAF Corporation, J.U. North America, Inc.,; Quigley Company, Inc.; Shook & Fletcher Insulation Co.; T & N, plc; Union Carbide Corporation (f/k/a Union Carbide Chemicals & Plastics Company, Inc.); and United States Gypsum Company ... from any and all rights, ... which Releasors now have or may have in the future for personal injuries, disability, pain and suffering or death ... or any other asbestos-related diseases or condition suffered by RICHARD A. BERLIER, SR.,. ...
>
> * * *
>
> The parties understand and agree that nothing contained in this agreement shall be construed or deemed an admission of wrongdoing or of liability by any party as to any of the claims or counter-claims which have been made in the litigation. ...

[9] On March 8, 2000, the CCR sent plaintiffs' counsel a check for $250,028.46, along with a letter containing the following:

> Pursuant to the CCR's settlement with you, enclosed is a check for $250,028.46. This check represents the total of the amounts due for each of the claims in the attached listing, subject to payment at this time under the terms of the settlement agreement, less the amounts payable for each of these claims by GAF Corporation — which total $199,971.54. The CCR has billed GAF Corporation for these amounts, but GAF has to date refused to pay such billings.[3]

[10] The plaintiffs refused to cash the check and on March 17, 2000, filed a Motion to Enforce Settlement against all four defendant companies. [....]

[....]

---

3. Apparently, GAF has failed to fulfill its settlement obligations in numerous cases throughout the country, that were entered into by the CCR before GAF's membership in the CCR was terminated sometime between December 17, 1999 and April 27, 2000.

[11] On April 27, 2000, the trial court entered a judgment in favor of plaintiffs, finding that GAF, ACMC, Union Carbide, and T & N are liable, *in solido,* to plaintiff in the sum of $450,000.00. All four defendants appealed. [. . . .]

[. . . .]

[12] The appellate court then set out to decide "only the single issue presented by the appeal filed by the CCR defendants — whether the trial court properly entered judgment against all four settling defendant companies *in solido,* rather than entering judgment against GAF/G-I Holdings alone, as the Berliers orally requested at the hearing on the matter." *Id.* The court of appeal affirmed the trial court's judgment, finding that the four settling defendants were solidarily liable for the settlement as a matter of law, as expressed in *Cole v. Celotex Corp.,* 599 So.2d 1058 (La.1992). *Id.* at 1060. This court granted the writ application filed by T & N and Union Carbide. *Berlier v. A.P. Green Industries, Inc.,* 01-1530 (La.9/14/01).

Discussion

[13] The sole issue before us is whether the four defendants are solidarily obligated to pay the $450,000.00 lump sum settlement.

[14] The Louisiana Civil Code provides the framework for analyzing the types of obligations involving multiple persons recognized under Louisiana law, which are several, joint, and solidary obligations. LSA-C.C. art. 1786. In this case, the lower courts found that the four defendants are solidarily liable under the terms of the settlement.

Solidary Liability

[15] LSA-C.C. art. 1796 provides:

Solidarity of obligation shall not be presumed. A solidary obligation arises from clear expression of the parties' intent or from the law.

[16] The court of appeal found that a solidary obligation arose in this case from the law, relying on *Cole v. Celotex, supra,* in which "the Louisiana Supreme Court held that various asbestos defendants are solidarily liable for damages suffered by plaintiffs." 787 So.2d at 1060. However, the court of appeal erred in relying on *Cole,* a delictual action wherein certain defendants were found liable after a two-week trial for failing to provide a safe workplace, and the liability of the manufacturers of asbestos containing products, who settled before trial, was stipulated at trial. In this case, there was no trial on plaintiffs' tort claim as the parties settled before trial, and, the release expressly states that "nothing contained in this agreement shall be construed or deemed an admission of wrongdoing or of liability by any party. . . ." Except for the settlement, there would be no liability at all, since this case has not been tried. Whether the defendants in this case would have been solidarily liable in tort has not been, and may never be, determined. Therefore, *Cole* is inapplicable to the instant case.

[17] Thus, as solidary liability does not arise in this case from law, the only remaining issue is whether it arises from a "clear expression of the parties' intent."

A solidary obligation may arise even though the words "solidarity" or "*in solido*" are not used, as long as the parties' intent to be solidarily liable is clearly expressed. La.--C.C. art. 1796, Official Comment (b). In resolving this issue in a case involving the joint or solidary liability of six makers of a promissory note, this Court explained:

> When several persons join in the same contract to do the same thing, it produces a joint obligation on the part of the obligors. However, where several persons obligate themselves to the obligee by the terms In solido or use any other expressions that clearly show that they intend that each one shall be separately bound to perform the whole of the obligation, it is called an obligation in Solido on the part of the obligors. An obligation In solido is not presumed; it must be expressly stipulated.

[18] It is well settled that, absent additional promissory language, the words '(w)e promise to pay' in a note signed by co-makers are insufficient to constitute the express stipulation of liability In solido required by law.

[. . . .]

Several Liability

[19] The second category of obligations is that of several liability. An obligation is several for the obligors "when each of different obligors owes a separate performance to one obligee, . . ." LSA-C.C. art. 1787. The comments to this article explain that "if the performance owed by each obligor has a different object, the obligation is several, as when one obligor owes delivery of a thing and another owes payment of a sum of money." LSA-C.C. art. 1787, Official Comment (b). For example, if through the same act, two persons each bind themselves to give a different sum of money to another, the obligation is several for the obligors. Litvinoff, Treatise *supra* § 7.11. Professor Litvinoff also notes that in the typical several obligation, the performance promised by each obligor has a different object, which allows each obligor to be regarded as the passive subject of a different and separate obligation. *Id.*

[20] In the instant case, rather than separate performances, the agreement indicates that only one performance was contemplated on the part of the defendants, namely one payment of $450,000 in exchange for the plaintiffs' signing a document entitled "RELEASE," which released from liability fifteen different business entities. Also, the obligors together promised to give to the plaintiffs one sum of money, not each a different sum. It follows that the defendants' performance had only one object, the lump sum payment of $450,000, and each defendant cannot be regarded as the passive subject of a different and separate obligation. Therefore, the obligation at issue is not a several obligation.

Joint Liability

[21] The final category is that of joint obligations. In part, a joint obligation is one where different obligors owe together just one performance to one obligee, or where one obligor owes just one performance intended for the common benefit of different obligees. LSA-C.C. art. 1788. Professor Litvinoff states that an obligation would be joint for the obligors if, through the same act, they promise to give just one sum

of money to another, such as in the instant case. Litvinoff, Treatise *supra* § 7.21. In addition, a pre-revision case which the reporter of the revision committee found useful indicated that the classification of an obligation as several or joint depends upon the parties' intentions and understanding, as revealed by the language of their contract and the subject matter to which it refers. *See Nabors v. Producers' Oil Co.,* 140 La. 985, 74 So. 527, 531 (1917); LSA-C.C. art. 1788 cmt. (d). In *Nabors,* this Court stated:

> With regard to the subject-matter, the authorities agree that the contract is entire and not severable, although it embodies a conveyance or delivery of several things, if the consideration is paid in a gross sum and it is impossible to affirm that the party making the payment would have done so unless the rights he acquired should apply to all of the things mentioned.

[22] *Nabors,* 74 So. at 531. *Nabors* held that a mineral lease created a joint obligation where several lessors disposed of the mineral rights on several tracts of land for a gross price, without stating the amount paid to each lessor and without stating or designating the area of land belonging to each lessor.

[23] Although *Nabors* dealt with an obligation that is joint for the obligees (lessors), it is nevertheless instructive on whether an obligation is joint for obligors, such as in the instant case. The defendants owed one performance to the plaintiffs, namely to pay the plaintiffs a lump sum of $450,000.00, and they bound themselves for this performance through the same act, namely the settlement agreement. It would be impossible to affirm that the defendants would have agreed to pay the plaintiffs unless all the defendants were released, or whether the plaintiffs would have released all the defendants unless all the money were paid. Also, similar to *Nabors,* the plaintiffs released their rights to hold all the defendants, plus others, liable for a gross price, and there was no statement of the amount for which each defendant was responsible. Accordingly, we hold that the four defendant companies, T & N, GAF, ACMC, and Union Carbide, are jointly obligated to the plaintiffs for the full amount of the settlement.

[24] Next, to determine the effect of a joint obligation on the obligors, it is necessary to determine whether the joint obligation is divisible or indivisible, because the revision "leans heavily on the notions of divisible and indivisible obligations." Expose, *supra* § 5. If the joint obligation is divisible, neither obligor is bound for the whole performance; rather, each joint obligor is bound to perform only his portion. LSA-C.C. art. 1789. On the other hand, if the joint obligation is indivisible, the joint obligors are subject to the rules governing solidary obligors. *Id.* One of the principal applications of the rules governing solidary obligors to joint and indivisible obligors is that the obligee, at his choice, may demand the whole performance from any of the joint and indivisible obligors. *See* LSA-C.C. art. 1795. This notion that all parties who contract an indivisible debt may be liable for the whole is not new; it appears in art. 2113 of the 1870 Code, art. 2109 of the 1825 Code, and art. 122 of the 1808 Code. [. . . .] Revised article 1789 reflects a partial change in the law, but one consistent with general principle, and one that provides a practical approach to

situations where theoretical foundations could become insurmountable obstacles to fair solutions, such as in the instant case. Litvinoff, Treatise, *supra* § 7.94.

[**25**] In Louisiana, divisibility of a joint obligation depends on divisibility of the object of the performance, unlike joint obligations at common law. Litvinoff, Treatise, *supra* § 7.94; *Hincks v. Converse,* 38 La. Ann. 871 (1886). This rule is expressed in LSA-C.C. art. 1815:

> An obligation is divisible when the object of the performance is susceptible of division.

> An obligation is indivisible when the object of the performance, because of its nature *or because of the intent of the parties,* is not susceptible of division. (Emphasis added.)

[**26**] French doctrine has always held that division of an obligation cannot take place when the object of the performance is indivisible. Litvinoff, Treatise, *supra* § 7.94 (citing 7 Planiol et Ripert, *Traite pratique de droit civil francais* 413 (Louisiana State Law Institute transl., 2d ed.1954)). Combining the ideas of Charles DuMoulin and Andre d'Alciat, Planiol explains that indivisibility is derived sometimes from the nature of the object due (*ex natura*), and sometimes from the intention of the parties (*ex voluntate*). 2 Marcel Planiol & George Ripert, Treatise on the Civil Law, pt. 1 no. 782 (La.St.L.Inst.trans., 11th ed.1939). Planiol also states that indivisibility is contractual, or *ex voluntate,* when the thing which makes the object of the obligation is in all respects divisible, but the parties intend that the obligation should be executed as if it were indivisible. *Id.* at No. 787. Authorities are in agreement that money, which is the object of the obligation at issue in the instant case, is "in all respects divisible." *See, e.g., Martin v. Louisiana Farm Bureau Cas. Ins. Co.,* 94-0069, p. 5 (La.7/5/94), 638 So.2d 1067, 1069 (stating that "[t]he obligation to pay money at issue here is susceptible of division and thus provides no basis for legal subrogation"); Planiol, *supra* (remarking that nothing is more divisible than money); Saul Litvinoff, The Law of Obligations in the Louisiana Jurisprudence 599 (1979) (stating that a sum of money is divisible as a matter of fact).

[**27**] Although money, by its nature, is divisible, LSA-C.C. art. 1815 provides that an object can also be indivisible because the parties so intended. Thus, even where an object by its nature may be rendered in partes (such as a lump sum settlement for $450,000.00), it must be performed as a whole where it is indivisible because of the parties' intent. Saul Litvinoff, The Law of Obligations in the Louisiana Jurisprudence 599 (1979).

[**28**] In this case, it is apparent that the parties to the settlement agreement intended that "the obligation should be executed as if it were indivisible." If the parties had intended for the obligation to be divisible, then one would reasonably suspect that they would have determined each defendant's pro-rata portion, and each defendant would be bound for a sum certain. However, the parties never made such a determination, nor did they discuss such a method of payment. Rather, throughout their negotiations, plaintiffs and defendants proceeded as though their mutual

obligations were indivisible. At all times, the defendants acted through a single mandatary, the CCR. On the morning of trial, the four defendants, represented by one law firm, announced on the record that, "on behalf of those four defendants, we have reached a settlement with the plaintiffs." The parties contracted for one lump-sum payment of $450,000.00, and the letter sent by the defendants' mandatary confirmed the object as a single sum, $450,000.00. Plaintiffs were never informed as to how the settlement amount would be apportioned among the four defendants, and there was no indication that the amount would be paid other than by the mandatary in full. Pursuant to the agreement, plaintiffs could not release only those defendants who contributed to the settlement, but had to release, unconditionally, all four defendants, plus fifteen other business entities. Therefore, as this obligation is indivisible because of the parties' intent, it must be performed as a whole even though, by its nature, its object may be rendered in parts. Litvinoff, Obligations, *supra* at 599.

[29] Of course, this is not to say that the obligation in question is indivisible merely because it was incurred in exchange for an indivisible obligation. Aubry & Rau, *Cours de Droit Civil Francais,* Vol. IV-Sixth Edition, *translated in* 1 Civil Law Translations § 301 (La.St. L. Inst.1965) (stating that a divisible obligation does not become indivisible merely because it is correlative to an indivisible obligation from a commutative contract). Rather, it is the sum total of the facts surrounding the defendants' obligation, as discussed above, which reveals that the parties' intent was that their obligation be indivisible.

Conclusion

[30] For the reasons stated above, we find that there existed a joint and indivisible obligation which binds each of the defendants for the full $450,000.00.

[31] LOBRANO, J., concurs in the result.

[32] VICTORY, J., dissents and assigns reasons.

[33] TRAYLOR, J., dissents for reasons assigned by VICTORY, J.

VICTORY, J., dissenting.

[34] I dissent from the majority's holding that the settlement in this case constitutes a joint and indivisible obligation, binding each of the defendants for the full $450,000. Initially, however, I must point out that in my view, it is not at all clear that there is a legally enforceable settlement agreement in this case under La. C.C. art. 3071, much less a "settlement agreement wherein the parties contracted for one lump-sum payment of $450,000." Op. at 48.

[35] While I agree with the majority's finding that "there is no evidence of a 'clear expression' of the defendants' intent to be solidarily bound" under La. C.C. art. 1796, I find that, for the same reasons that the majority made that finding, there was also no evidence that the defendants intended to be solidary bound for purposes of creating a joint and indivisible obligation under La. C.C. art. 1815. Based on the same evidence, the majority finds "there is no evidence of a 'clear expression' of the defendants' intent to be solidarily bound," yet then concludes "it is apparent that the

parties to the settlement agreement intended that 'the obligation should be executed as if it were indivisible.'" However, the obligation does not meet the requirements for a joint and indivisible obligation under La. C.C. art. 1815 because there is no evidence that it *was the intent of the parties* to treat the object of the defendants' obligation, the payment of a sum of money, as an indivisible obligation. See Saul Litvinoff, *Louisiana Civil Law Treatise: The Law of Obligations,* § 9.5 (defining a conventional indivisible obligation as follows: "When an obligation would be divisible because the object of its performance is susceptible of division, the parties to a contract *may agree* that it shall be performed as if its object were invisible, which makes the indivisibility conventional, rather than natural.") Not only is there no evidence that the defendants intended the payment of the $450,000 to be divisible. The majority opinion discusses at some length the arrangements made between the defendants and the CCR clearly showing the defendants did not intend to be bound for the whole, but only for the percentage assigned in the Provider Agreement. Further, there is no evidence the plaintiffs intended the obligation to be indivisible for the defendants, as this settlement was so loosely structured that no amount was even stated on the record in open court.

[36] The reason the code articles require that both parties intend that a joint obligation be either solidary under La. C.C. art. 1796 or indivisible under La. C.C. art. 1815, is because of the onerous effects on the obligors if the obligation is characterized as either of the above. To allow the intent of just one party, the obligee, which in this case is not even discernable, to impose solidary liability on the obligors is unjust. Further, La. C.C. 1818 clearly states that "[a]n indivisible obligation with more than one obligor or obligee is subject to the rules governing solidary obligations." La. C.C. art. 1796, requiring that a solidary obligation shall not be presumed and "arises from a *clear expression of the parties' intent* or from the law" is certainly a "rule [] governing solidary obligations." By providing a lower standard in the law for what constitutes a joint and indivisible obligation under La. C.C. art. 1815, which under the majority's holding is an "apparent intent," the majority opinion renders meaningless the requirement found in La. C.C. art. 1796, made applicable by virtue of La. C.C. art. 1818, that a clear expression of intent is need to create a solidary obligation, and, creates far too much certainty in the law on which contracting parties have relied in this state for years.

[37] Therefore, I respectfully disagree with the majority's holding that the parties intended this divisible obligation be treated as if it were indivisible under La. C.C. art. 1815, and I am of the firm view that the defendants are not solidarily liable in this case, neither by virtue of La. C.C. art. 1796 nor 1815.

Questions

1. Paragraph 28: The majority states that the defendants who signed on to the settlement agreement did not "determine[] each defendant's pro-rata portion" nor even "discuss such a method of payment." Is that correct? What of the provision in the defendants' collective "Provider Agreement," alluded to in

Justice Victory's dissent, to the effect "that liability payments shall be apportioned to each member according to a specific share allocation matrix, that such apportionment shall establish the responsibility of each [member] for a percentage share of liability payments, and that each member shall pay in a timely manner the percentages of liability payments involved"? Does that provision concern (1) the "vertical" relationship between the defendants, as a group, and the payee or (2) the "horizontal" relationship among the defendants or (3) both?

2. By what criteria do the majority determine that the defendants "intended" the object of their obligation, a monetary payment, be "indivisible"? Is it anything more than "if multiple parties to a settlement that calls for a lump sum payment do not, contemporaneously with the settlement" (or, is it "in the act of settlement itself"?) "apportion the payment among themselves, then they intend that the payment be indivisible"? But wouldn't that be the typical case with a settlement? And, if it is, is there not something to Justice Victory's complaint that the majority's approach to indivisibility effectively undermines the presumption against solidarity?

3. Imagine that you are the attorney for one of multiple defendants in a pending tort suit, one that the defendants are about to settle. In the aftermath of *Berlier,* what would you advise your client regarding how the settlement should be worded? Is there not, in fact, a simple way around the rule of *Berlier*?

Gloria's Ranch, L.L.C.
v.
Tauren Exploration, Inc., Cubic Energy, Inc., Wells Fargo Energy Capital, Inc., and Exco USA Asset, Inc.

Supreme Court of Louisiana
June 27, 2018
252 So.3d 431

CLARK, Justice.

[. . . .]

Facts and Procedural History

[1] Gloria's Ranch, L.L.C. ("Gloria's Ranch") granted a mineral lease to Tauren Exploration, Inc. ("Tauren") on September 17, 2004. The lease covered 1,390.25 acres in [. . .] Caddo Parish, Louisiana ("the property"). Tauren was granted "the exclusive right to enter upon and use the land . . . for the exploration for and production of oil [and] gas . . . together with the use of the surface of the land for all purposes incident to [exploration and production] with the right of ingress and egress to and from said lands at all times for such purposes." The lease was granted for a primary term of three (3) years "and as long thereafter as oil, gas, sulphur, or other minerals is produced from [the property] or from land pooled therewith."

[2] In February 2006, Tauren transferred an undivided 49% interest in the lease to Cubic Energy, Inc. ("Cubic"). On March 5, 2007, Tauren and Cubic executed separate credit agreements with Wells Fargo Energy Capital, Inc. ("Wells Fargo").[1] Wells Fargo provided Cubic with a revolving credit facility not to exceed $20,000,000 outstanding at any time and a $5,000,000 convertible term loan. As security, Cubic mortgaged its interest in approximately 750 mineral leases, including the instant lease with Gloria's Ranch, and assigned as collateral the profits earned therefrom.

[3] In 2007, Tauren contracted with Fossil Operating Inc. ("Fossil") to commence oil and gas operations on the property. In early 2008, Fossil drilled and completed wells on Sections 9, 10, and 16 in an area known as the Cotton Valley geologic formation.[2] Fossil vertically drilled Section 16 to the Haynesville Shale formation, but completed the well only to the shallower depths of the Cotton Valley formation. Additionally, in 2008, another company, Chesapeake Operating, Inc. ("Chesapeake")[3] drilled a well, (the "Soaring Ridge 15-1 well") on a neighboring tract in the deeper Haynesville Shale formation. [. . . .] On September 1, 2009, Gloria's Ranch executed a top lease in favor of Chesapeake for the right to conduct operations on its property in Section 21. By definition and by the contract's terms, Chesapeake's lease only became effective if and when the existing 2004 lease to Tauren expired or was terminated.

[4] Effective October 30, 2009, Tauren and EXCO USA Asset, Inc. ("EXCO") entered into a purchase and sale agreement. Pursuant to the agreement, Tauren conveyed its 51% interest in the Deep Rights to EXCO. Cubic conveyed to Tauren an overriding royalty interest in Cubic's 49% interest in the Deep Rights. Simultaneously, Tauren made a cash payment to Wells Fargo and assigned to it a 10% net profits interest in the Shallow Rights and the overriding royalty interest in the Deep Rights received from Cubic. In exchange, Wells Fargo cancelled the Tauren mortgage.

[5] On December 3, 2009, Gloria's Ranch sent a letter to Tauren, Cubic, EXCO and Wells Fargo ("the defendants"), seeking to establish whether the lease was still producing in paying quantities. It was the belief of Gloria's Ranch that the lease had expired for lack of production in paying quantities. Thus, it wanted confirmation via monthly revenue and expense reports that the wells were still profitable.

[6] Tauren responded that it had miscalculated some of its expenses but assured Gloria's Ranch that the wells were still producing in paying quantities. Ultimately, on January 28, 2010, Gloria's Ranch sent written demand to the defendants, requesting

---

1. The credit agreement between Wells Fargo and Tauren is not in the record. The instant opinion, however, concerns only the mortgage and credit agreement between Wells Fargo and Cubic.

2. For purposes of this litigation, the geological strata between the surface and the base of the Cotton Valley Sands represent the "Shallow Rights." The geological strata below the base of the Cotton Valley Sands, including but not limited to the Haynesville Shale formation, represent the "Deep Rights."

3. Chesapeake is not a party to the instant litigation.

a recordable act evidencing the expiration of the lease. No response was forthcoming by any of the defendants. Accordingly, Gloria's Ranch filed suit, alleging the defendants failed to furnish a recordable act evidencing the expiration of the lease as required by La. Mineral Code arts. 206 and 207. Gloria's Ranch claimed in its petition that the lease expired for not producing in paying quantities and that the defendants' failure to release the lease caused it damages in the amount of lost bonus payments, lost rentals, and lost royalties. Additionally, it sought unpaid royalties for Section 15, which was still maintained by production from the Soaring Ridge 15H.

[....]

[7] A bench trial was held, and the trial court rendered judgment in favor of Gloria's Ranch and against Tauren, Cubic, and Wells Fargo *in solido*. It found the lease had expired as to Sections 9, 10, 16, and 21 due to lack of production in paying quantities for at least the twelve months preceding the January 28, 2010 demand and that the defendants failed to furnish a recordable act evidencing same, as required by the law.[4] The court also found that the 16-1 well was not drilled in good faith. Rather, it was drilled solely to maintain the Deep Rights for purposes of speculation. The trial court awarded damages for lost-leasing opportunities at $18,000 per acre ($22,806,000).[5] It further awarded $726,087.78 for unpaid royalties [...] pursuant to La. Mineral Code art. 140 ($242,029.26 in royalties due plus $484,058.52 in double royalties as a penalty). Attorney fees in the amount of $936,803 were also awarded.

[8] With regard to Wells Fargo's solidary liability, the trial court found that Wells Fargo breached its duty to Gloria's Ranch either to release its mortgage on the lease or to authorize Cubic to release the lease. The trial court reasoned that (1) Wells Fargo's mortgage included an assignment of the lease; (2) Wells Fargo controlled Cubic's right to release and never authorized a release; (3) Wells Fargo controlled the revenue from the lease by virtue of an assignment of revenues, a net profits interest, and a overriding royalty interest; and (4) Wells Fargo knew the lease had expired because it regularly audited Tauren and Cubic's well cost and revenue information.

[9] Tauren, Cubic, and Wells Fargo filed motions for new trial [... **and**] the trial court granted the motions, in part, reducing the damage awards by EXCO's virile portion (25%) to reflect EXCO's settlement. *See* La. C.C. art. 1804. The defendants appealed. The court of appeal affirmed the judgment [...] *Gloria's Ranch, L.L.C. v. Tauren Exploration, Inc.*, 51,077 (La. App. 2 Cir. 6/2/17), 223 So.3d 1202. Tauren, Cubic, and Wells Fargo filed writ applications. We consolidated and granted their writs to determine the correctness of the lower courts' judgments. *Gloria's Ranch, L.L.C. v. Tauren Exploration, Inc.*, 17–1518, 17–1519, 17–1522 (La. 12/15/17), 231 So.3d 639; 231 So.3d 640; 231 So.3d 642. We will address each writ application separately.

---

4. The court of appeal found the lease did not produce in paying quantities for the 18-month period prior to demand by Gloria's Ranch in January of 2010.

5. Sections 15 and 21 were excluded from this award. The trial court did not award any damages for lost-leasing opportunities for Section 15 since it was still producing or for Section 21 since Gloria's Ranch was able to lease it.

Discussion

Wells Fargo

[10] Wells Fargo challenges the lower courts' finding that it was solidarily liable with the remaining defendants for Gloria's Ranch's damages. Wells Fargo argued that it is not responsible for the obligations sued upon, as they are obligations of the mineral lessees, not of the mortgagee of a mineral lessee. Louisiana Mineral Code art. 206(A) (La. R.S. 31:206) provides:

> Except as provided in Paragraph B of this Article [not applicable herein], when a mineral right is extinguished by the accrual of liberative prescription, expiration of its term, or otherwise, the former owner shall, within thirty days after written demand by the person in whose favor the right has been extinguished or terminated, furnish him with a recordable act evidencing the extinction or expiration of the right.

Louisiana Mineral Code art. 207 (La. R.S. 31:207) provides:

> If the former owner of the extinguished or expired mineral right fails to furnish the required act within thirty days of receipt of the demand or if the former lessee of a mineral lease fails to record the required act within ninety days of its extinguishment prior to the expiration of its primary term, he is liable to the person in whose favor the right or the lease has been extinguished or expired for all damages resulting therefrom and for a reasonable attorney's fee incurred in bringing suit.

[11] Wells Fargo contends it is not an owner of the lease; it is merely a creditor with a security interest in the lease.[6] As such, Wells Fargo asserts it was improperly held responsible for any breach of the lease obligations. Gloria's Ranch, however, argues Wells Fargo is an assignee of the lease, an overriding royalty owner, and a net profits owner. It also argues that the "bundle of rights" assumed by Wells Fargo amounted to ownership under civilian law, and, accordingly, Wells Fargo is liable with the other defendants under a "control theory." Furthermore, Gloria's Ranch avers that Wells Fargo's mortgage created a cloud on its title, and Wells Fargo was properly held liable for its failure to release its mortgage. Last, Gloria's Ranch argues Wells Fargo judicially admitted to having an interest in the lease. Because Gloria's Ranch relied on this statement to its detriment, it contends Wells Fargo should be bound by its admission with no further proof of ownership required.

[....]

[12] The court of appeal rejected the argument that the lease was transferred to Wells Fargo by assignment. Because the mortgage did not transfer Cubic's working interest in the land, the court of appeal found an assignment did not occur. It held:

---

6. Wells Fargo points to the express provisions in the mortgage and credit agreements that state there is no intent on the part of Wells Fargo to assume the obligations of the mineral lease, to assume any obligation of Cubic, or to provide any benefit to a third party.

The language of the mortgage shows the purpose of the instrument was for Cubic to secure its loans with Wells Fargo by granting Wells Fargo a continuing security interest in multiple mineral leases, which included Gloria's Ranch's lease. In the event Cubic defaulted on its loans, the mortgage gave Wells Fargo the right to seize and sell the lease to satisfy the debt. As such, we find the use of the word "assign" in the Hypothecation clause does not deprive the mortgage of its character, which is to "secure the full and punctual payment and performance of the Indebtedness.["] *Gloria's Ranch L.L.C.*, 51,077 at 30–31, 223 So.3d at 1222.

[13] We agree. Wells Fargo cannot be considered an "owner" of the lease by virtue of an assignment. "The assignor transfers his entire interest in the lease insofar as it affects the property on which the lease is assigned." *Roberson v. Pioneer Gas Co.*, 173 La. 313, 319, 137 So. 46, 48 (1931). Because Cubic still maintained its working interest in the property, the assignment argument fails.

[14] However, the court of appeal did not end its analysis there. Citing La. Civ. Code art. 477, the court of appeal found merit in Gloria's Ranch's argument that Wells Fargo became an owner of the lease because it "controlled the bundle of rights that make up ownership, i.e., the rights to use, enjoy, and dispose of the lease." *Gloria's Ranch L.L.C.*, 51,077 at 31, 223 So.3d at 1222. Specifically, the court of appeal found the control Wells Fargo had over Cubic's right to conduct oil and gas operations on the property by virtue of the mortgage and the credit agreement rose to the level of ownership, providing several examples that it classified as civilian rights of "usus," "fructus," and "abusus." The court of appeal noted the following rights and provisions that it perceived as "rights of control": the credit agreement's language that directed where the loan proceeds were to be spent; Wells Fargo's right to approve the location and depth of the wells; Wells Fargo's ability to specify which workovers and completions were to be performed; Wells Fargo's requirement that Cubic provide it with financial statements, Wells Fargo's right to access Gloria's Ranch's property; Wells Fargo's overriding royalty interest and net profits interest; and Wells Fargo's requirement that Cubic obtain its written consent to release the lease. For the following reasons, we find the court of appeal committed error in holding that such rights, which are incidental to mortgage and credit agreement, rose to the level of ownership of a mineral lease.

[15] First, on a legal basis, we find no authority for superseding the ownership principles set forth in the La. Mineral Code with those of the La. Civil Code. "The provisions of [the La. Mineral] Code are supplementary to those of the Louisiana Civil Code and are applicable specifically to the subject matter of mineral law." La. Mineral Code art. 2. As such, the La. Mineral Code governs the creation, ownership, and transfer of mineral rights. Louisiana Mineral Code art. 16 provides that "[t]he basic mineral rights that may be created by a landowner are the mineral servitude, the mineral royalty, and the mineral lease." Mineral leases are created by contract. See La. Mineral Code art. 114. Ownership of the mineral lease can be transferred by assignment or sublease. See La. Mineral Code art. 127. In the instance of assignment

or sublease, "[t]o the extent of the interest acquired, an assignee or sublessee acquires the rights and powers of the lessee and becomes responsible directly to the original lessor for performance of the lessee's obligations.["] See La. Mineral Code art. 128. We do not find where the La. Mineral Code addresses or sanctions ownership of a lessee's interest via a theory of control of rights.

[16] Further, rights of ownership are distinguished from security rights in the La. Mineral Code.

[. . . .]

[17] Based on the foregoing, we find no authority for the court of appeal's holding that a mortgage and a credit agreement, which are both legally provided for in the La. Mineral Code, can be methods by which ownership of a mineral lease are conveyed simply because they assert some control over the collateral described therein. We find the "bundle of rights" controlled by Wells Fargo are not traits of ownership, but of security rights. The mortgage and credit agreement contain provisions typical of security contracts, all designed to protect the collateral.

[18] Importantly, none of the provisions of the mortgage or credit agreement convey to Wells Fargo the right to explore for and produce minerals on the property — the primary right granted in a mineral lease and the stamp of ownership thereof. *See* La. Mineral Code arts. 6 and 114. Rather, the provisions incorrectly held by the court of appeal as rights of "usus," "abusus," and "fructus" are security interests and derivative interests related to the sole goal of safeguarding the collateral (the lease). We find it unnecessary to address each provision in the contract because we find that none of the provisions convey rights of ownership, taken individually or as a whole. Rather, we will discuss broadly each category of rights as presented by the court of appeal ("fructus," "usus," and "abusus").

[19] First, we note it is customary in the oil and gas industry for a lender to (1) include restrictions on how the debtor/borrower will use the leased property, (2) require full financial information with regard to the "status of the collateral encumbered by the mortgage," (3) require that the borrower "maintain the encumbered mineral leases in force and effect," and (4) allow inspection of the premises, among other protective provisions. *See, e.g.*, Patrick S. Ottinger, *Louisiana Mineral Leases: A Treatise*, § 12–10 (Claitor's Law Book & Publishing Div., Inc. 2016).

[20] As to the contracts at issue, Cubic contractually agreed that, only upon default, it would pay to Wells Fargo the proceeds from production. This pledge of proceeds, which is authorized by La. Mineral Code art. 204, is merely a security device — not an assignment of the fructus (civil fruits) of the mortgaged property for purposes of creating ownership or holding a mortgagee liable for the obligations of its debtor. The existence of a security interest without more, does not subject a mortgagee to liability for the mortgagor's breach of the lease contract.[8] Also, the

---

8. *See* La. R.S. 10:9–402.

pledge at issue is conditional, and we find no record evidence that Cubic was ever in default or that Wells Fargo ever exercised such rights so as to trigger the assignment of the proceeds.

[21] Regarding the purported "usus" (physical use) of the property, we find the oversight rights, the right to enter the property, and the right for Wells Fargo to direct "use of the proceeds," among others, are typical rights of a secured creditor and exist for the clear purpose of insuring the maintenance of the collateral. They do not convey any rights of ownership. Rather, these rights are solely to keep the lender abreast of the debtor's ability to pay back the loan and remain informed of the collateral's condition.

[22] The last category, the alleged right of *abusus* (alienation), merits additional discussion inasmuch as Gloria's Ranch and the lower courts emphasized the provision which requires Wells Fargo's consent as a prerequisite to Cubic releasing its lease interest. First, we note that Cubic never requested Wells Fargo's consent to release the lease (or the mortgage thereof). Second, even if Wells Fargo had released its mortgage, the lease still would not have been released as it relates to Gloria's Ranch. This is because there was never any privity of contract between Wells Fargo and Gloria's Ranch. The privity of contract existed between Gloria's Ranch and its lessees pursuant to the mineral lease. A separate contractual relationship existed between Wells Fargo and Cubic in the form of a mortgage and a credit agreement. A breach of one contract does not directly impact the other contract so as to create a cause of action where one does not exist. Namely, any failure of Wells Fargo to consent to release the lease does not amount to a cause of action by Gloria's Ranch against Wells Fargo. Rather, if Cubic had requested Wells Fargo's consent (of which there is no record evidence) and Wells Fargo had withheld it, the recourse would not be for Gloria's Ranch to sue Wells Fargo. The only available recourse for Gloria's Ranch would be to sue the owners of the lease (the lessees), with whom it has privity of contract. Cubic, in the event consent had been requested and withheld, could have available to it a contractual claim against Wells Fargo in the form of indemnity, third party demand, reimbursement, or some other incidental demand. *See* La. Code Civ. P. art. 1031; *see also Nassif v. Sunrise Homes, Inc.*, 98-3193, pp. 2–3 (La. 6/29/99), 739 So.2d 183, 185. However, this obligation is distinct and separate from that owed by Cubic to Gloria's Ranch. The clause in Cubic's mortgage that requires Wells Fargo's consent to release the lease is merely a protection over its collateral, not an element of ownership. As such, Wells Fargo cannot be held solidarily liable for the obligation of an owner of the lease merely by virtue of its security interest.

[23] Gloria's Ranch also avers that if Wells Fargo had not released the mortgage, there would be a cloud on the title and no buyer would want to acquire the lease. This argument fails, though, because once the subject of the mortgage (the lease) no longer exists, the mortgage no longer exists by operation of extinction. Louisiana Civ. Code art. 3319(1) provides: "A mortgage is extinguished by the extinction or destruction of the thing mortgaged." Thus, in the event the lease was released by Cubic, the mortgage would cease to exist. There would be no mortgage, then, to

"cloud" Gloria Ranch's title. (*See also* La. Civ. Code art. 3282: "Mortgage is accessory to the obligation that it secures. Consequently, except as provided by law, the mortgagee may enforce the mortgage only to the extent that he may enforce any obligation it secures.")

[24] Additionally, we find no merit to the argument that because Wells Fargo acquired an overriding royalty interest[9] and net profits[10] interest from Tauren's interest in the lease, it somehow became an owner of the lease. These financial interests are merely passive, derivative rights given in exchange for the cancellation of Tauren's mortgage. "The owner of a mineral royalty has no executive rights; nor does he have the right to conduct operations to explore for or produce minerals." La. Mineral Code art. 81. These rights, which do not convey any authority to go onto the property, drill, explore, or otherwise perpetuate an oil and gas lease, do not amount to ownership and, thus, do not give rise to the obligations associated with ownership, such as the payment of royalties, the maintenance of production in paying quantities, or the release of the lease upon demand.

[25] In sum, we find that Wells Fargo, in its capacity as a creditor with only a security interest in the mineral lease, is not solidarily liable with its debtor, the mineral lessee, for obligations breached thereby. Wells Fargo acquired a mortgage affecting the mineral lease in addition to a net profits interest and an overriding royalty interest. These interests are solely accessory and derivative rights and do not amount to rights of ownership. Because Wells Fargo is not a "former owner" under La. Mineral Code art. 207, it cannot be held liable for any damages resulting from the failure to release the lease.

[26] With regard to the damages awarded for unpaid royalties for Section 15, we employ the same analysis. Under La. Mineral Code art. 140, quoted *infra*, the law holds a "lessee" liable for failure to pay royalties that are due. For the same reasons that we hold a creditor is not liable as a "former owner" under La. Mineral Code art. 207, we find Wells Fargo not liable for unpaid royalties as a "lessee" under La. Mineral Code art. 140. Accordingly, we reverse the judgment as to Wells Fargo.

Tauren

[27] Tauren asks this court to find that the mineral lease was horizontally divided when it conveyed its interest in the Deep Rights to EXCO. Such a finding, Tauren argues, would mean that two leases were created, and Tauren could not be held responsible for any obligations related to a lease it did not own. Thus, it argues the damages caused by the failure to release the lease(s) back to Gloria's Ranch (upon termination and demand) should be paid jointly, with each lessee being responsible

---

9. An overriding royalty is "[a]n interest in oil and gas produced at the surface, free of the expense of production, and in addition to the usual landowner's royalty reserved to the lessor in an oil and gas lease." 8 Williams & Meyers, Oil and Gas Law, Manual of Terms, p. 728 (2016).

10. A net profits interest is "[a] share of gross production from a property, measured by net profits from operation of the property." 8 Williams & Meyers, Oil and Gas Law, Manual of Terms, p. 649 (2016).

only for its own lease obligations. Tauren contends most of the damages resulted from the lost opportunity to lease the Deep Rights, over which it had no authority. Accordingly, Tauren claims it cannot be held solidarily liable for the full damages.

[28] Gloria's Ranch, on the other hand, argues Tauren and its co-defendants are each liable for the entirety of the damages for failing to release the lease. The court of appeal found Tauren solidarily liable because "the obligation of the owners of the lease to produce a recordable act evidencing the release of the lease was indivisible." *Gloria's Ranch L.L.C.*, 51,077 at 25, 223 So.3d at 1219. For the reasons that follow, we agree that the obligation to release is indivisible.

[29] An obligation is a legal relationship whereby a person, called the obligor, is bound to render a performance in favor of another, called the obligee. La. Civ. Code art. 1756. When different obligors owe together just one performance to one obligee, but neither is bound for the whole, the obligation is joint for the obligors. La. Civ. Code art. 1788. An obligation is indivisible when the object of the performance, because of its nature or because of the intent of the parties, is not susceptible of division. La. Civ. Code art. 1815. When a joint obligation is indivisible, joint obligors are subject to the rules governing solidary obligors. La. Civ. Code art. 1789. An indivisible obligation with more than one obligor or obligee is subject to the rules governing solidary obligations. La. Civ. Code art. 1818. Solidarity of obligation shall not be presumed. A solidary obligation arises from a clear expression of the parties' intent or from the law. La. Civ. Code art. 1796. When distinct obligors owe the same indivisible performance to one obligee, they are solidarily bound to that obligee, regardless of their intentions. La. Civ. Code art. 1818, Comment (b).

[30] Tauren is indisputably a "former owner" of the mineral lease because it held a 51% working interest in the Shallow Rights, as well as the surface rights and the exclusive right to drill on the property. Thus, Tauren's failure to release the lease makes it liable to Gloria's Ranch "for all damages resulting therefrom and for a reasonable attorney's fee incurred in bringing suit." La. Mineral Code art. 207. Tauren argues its own failure to release the lease should only be measured in damages commensurate to the value of the Shallow Rights. However, under the facts of this case, we find the obligation to release the lease is an indivisible obligation under the La. Civ. Code.[11] As stated earlier, La. Civ. Code art. 1815 classifies an obligation as indi-

---

11. We expressly reject Tauren's argument that the obligation to release was a divisible obligation and that it only was responsible for the failure to release the Shallow Rights. We take particular note that Tauren was the original lessee, who still owned an interest in the lease, which included the "exclusive rights to enter upon and use the land" for the "exploration for and production of oil [and] gas." Tauren retained the surface rights and the corresponding right to drill thereon. Further, the record shows that Tauren failed to disclose to EXCO, prior to its transfer of the Deep Rights, the lease's production shortcomings. Additionally, Tauren participated in the accounting manipulations in an effort to make it appear that the lease was still producing in paying quantities. These acts all led to the underlying failure to release the lease back to Gloria's Ranch, which necessitated judicial demand and the instant lawsuit. Accordingly, Tauren's acts in large part induced the other defendants not to release the lease. It cannot now attempt to escape liability by arguing the lease

visible when the object of the performance is not susceptible of division. An obligation is indivisible when the performance of the obligation cannot be divided or when partial performance would be of little or no use to the obligee. *Sweet Lake Land & Oil Co. LLC v. Exxon Mobil Corp.*, 9–1100, 2011 WL 5825791 (W.D. La. 11/16/11), *citing* 5 Saul Litvinoff, Louisiana Civil Law Treatise, Law of Obligations § 9.2 (2011). When an obligation is indivisible, all obligors must be held solidarily liable for the full performance. La. Civ. Code art. 1818.

[31] The court in *Sweet Lake, supra*, was tasked with determining whether solidary liability was appropriate in the context of a property restoration case. One of the lessees argued it should only be held liable for the restoration of the property to the extent of its fractional interest in the lease. The court disagreed, holding instead that the obligation to restore the property was an indivisible obligation because "[p]roperty is either restored or it is not." *Sweet Lake*, 2011 WL 5825791 at 5. We are influenced by the logic of this case and, likewise, find that the mineral lease at issue was either released or it was not. It is clear that the release by only one lessee, or less than all lessees, would have been of little or no use to Gloria's Ranch insofar

---

was divided such that it was only required to release the Shallow Rights while the others were obligated to release the Deep Rights.

Moreover, the record evidence reveals that the lease stopped producing in paying quantities on or around July of 2008, well before the transfer of the deep rights to EXCO. Mike Cougevan, an expert in oil and gas accounting and auditing, testified that the wells at issue were not producing in paying quantities in the 18-month period prior to the January 2010 demand by Gloria's Ranch. Additionally, Robert McGowen, a petroleum engineer, stated in his appraisal:

Production and revenue information for the 9-1, 10-1, and 16-1 indicates that none of these wells produced in paying quantities. The cost and revenue information for the wells indicates shortly after each well was drilled, it began operating at a loss that has only increased over time. By July 2008, the GR 9-1, 10-1, and 16-1 were operating at a cumulative loss and never regained profitability.

He further testified that the lease was not producing in paying quantities for "the majority of the life of the wells." He opined that the lease was not being released due to speculative purposes and in an attempt to hold the lease for unknown future activity. We note that such speculation is against the law and public policy. See, e.g., Carter v. Arkansas–Louisiana Gas Co., 36 So.2d 26 (La. 1948).

Tauren's expert, Michael McKenzie, a petroleum engineer, did not disagree with the findings of Mr. McGowen or Mr. Blunk. Rather, he found that Tauren and Cubic's "knowledge of the potential of the Haynesville Shale, and its negotiations and eventual contract with EXCO" were "consistent with the conduct of a reasonably prudent operator." Notably, the finding of the lower courts that the lease was no longer producing in paying quantities was not appealed to this court.

Thus, the lease expired in July 2008, by its own terms, which was before the 2009 transfer to EXCO. (Louisiana Mineral Code art. 133 provides: "A mineral lease terminates at the expiration of the agreed term or upon the occurrence of an express resolutory condition.") We acknowledge that the obligation to furnish a recordable act evidencing the expiration of the lease (i.e., the obligation to release the lease), for purposes of damages, is tethered to written demand by the landowner. See La. Mineral Code arts. 206 and 207, supra. However, because the lease technically expired before the purported assignment of rights, we will not entertain a theory of divisibility as a manner by which Tauren can escape liability. In finding the obligation to release to be an indivisible obligation in the context of these facts, we refuse to condone the acts of a lease owner who knows its lease is not producing, misrepresents such to the landowner, holds the lease for speculative purposes, finds a buyer at the eleventh hour before legal demand is made, and assigns the Deep Rights in an effort to divide the lease and, thereby, dispose of its liability.

as Gloria's Ranch would have been prevented from granting a new lease to another interested buyer.[12] Accordingly, we do not find it necessary to address the divisibility of the lease because we find the underlying obligation to release the lease in this case is indivisible.[13] As such, Tauren, as an owner of the lease, was properly held liable *in solido* for the damages it caused.

[**32**] Additionally, we find the unpaid royalties for Section 15 were directly attributed to Tauren and Cubic's failure to pay them; thus, Tauren cannot escape liability under any theory of divisibility. Lepow, a member and manager for Gloria's Ranch, contacted Chesapeake to inquire about the payment of royalties that were due. Lepow stated that SONRIS showed Chesapeake's Soaring Ridge 15H (which had been unitized to include Gloria's Ranch's property on Section 15) had been producing since the summer of 2008. Chesapeake informed Gloria's Ranch that Tauren and Cubic were receiving payments from the well's production. However, Lepow testified that Gloria's Ranch never received any of the royalty payments in connection with Section 15. Further, the record contains a clear admission that management knew of the obligation to pay royalties to Gloria's Ranch in connection with the Section 15 well and did not pay them. Accordingly, we find no error in the assessment of damages against Tauren for the unpaid royalties related to Section 15. We affirm the portion of the judgment as to Tauren's liability.

[. . . .]

Conclusion

[**33**] Based on the foregoing, we find the lower courts improperly held Wells Fargo liable as an "owner" under La. Mineral Code art. 207 and a "lessee" under La. Mineral Code art. 140. Thus, we reverse the judgment as to Wells Fargo. Second, we affirm the judgment of solidary liability against Tauren, finding the obligation to furnish a recordable act evidencing the release of the lease is an indivisible obligation under the facts of this case. Third, we amend the amount of damages awarded under La. Mineral Code art. 140 to reflect a maximum award of double the amount

---

12. Tauren argues Gloria's Ranch was not prevented from entering into a new lease; it claims, to the contrary, that Gloria's Ranch entered into two new leases with Chesapeake and EXCO, respectively. However, we find that both of these leases were top leases and conditioned upon the defendants' release of the lease. For instance, Gloria's Ranch entered into a lease with Chesapeake for rights associated with Section 21. The contract, however, expressly states: "This Lease is subordinate to that certain Oil, Gas, and Mineral Lease between Lessor and Tauren Exploration, Inc. dated September 17, 2004 . . . Lessee shall have no rights under this Lease so long as the Prior Lease is in effect with respect to the Leased Premises." Further, the contract between Gloria's Ranch and EXCO (and final payment in consideration thereof) was conditioned upon the release of the Tauren lease or upon a final judgment cancelling that lease.

13. Because we find the obligation to release the lease to be a singular, indivisible obligation under the circumstances of this case, we expressly reserve any judgment on whether a lease can be divided by the assignment of depths and pretermit analysis of the language of the lease relevant thereto. Our holding should be narrowly construed to the facts of this case.

of unpaid royalties. Last, we amend the amount of attorney fees awarded for work done on appeal.

[34] **REVERSED IN PART; AMENDED IN PART; AND AFFIRMED AS AMENDED.**

[35] Weimer, J., concurring in part and dissenting in part.

[36] Genovese, J., dissents in part.

Questions

1. Paragraph 1: What specific Civil Code adjective would you assign to the two terms included in the contract of lease?

2. Paragraph 2: In the granting of an "undivided 49% interest" in the lease to Cubic Energy, what "kind" of "thing" is granted, per Book II of the Civil Code?

3. Paragraph 2: If you were to assign the proper legal characterization or qualification to the contracts in existence in this case, which characterization would you assign to the credit facility and which one to the mortgage as a security? Should one be declared null, what impact, if any, would the nullity of one contract have on the other?

4. Paragraph 3: Can you identify the modality and kind of obligation existing in the Chesapeake's lease?

5. Paragraphs 10–16: Relying on the facts given in the case, what do you think of Wells Fargo challenging the lower court's finding?

6. Paragraphs 17–20: Couldn't the Court have referred to two fundamentally different rights, such as one granted by a lease and another by a mortgage? What are these different rights?

7. Paragraphs 21–25: How supportive of the two different rights identified in the question above is this long statement that characterizes the three sub-rights of ownership as *abusus*, *usus*, and *fructus*? Is the Court's statement that "Wells Fargo . . . is not solidarily liable with its debtor" well-grounded?

8. Paragraphs 27–33: What difference(s) is/are there between "solidarity" and "indivisibility"? Are indivisible obligors in the exact same relationship with each other as solidary obligors are with each other?

Gloria's Ranch, L.L.C.
v.
Tauren Exploration, Inc., Cubic Energy, Inc., Wells Fargo Energy Capital, Inc., and Exco USA Asset, Inc.

Supreme Court of Louisiana
November 4, 2020
303 So.3d 626

PER CURIAM

[1] Gloria's Ranch sued Tauren, Cubic, EXCO, and the lender, Wells Fargo, for failure to release a mineral lease when it stopped producing in paying quantities. In 2018, this court held Wells Fargo, as the lender, could not be liable as a lessee but affirmed the solidary liability of Tauren, Cubic, and EXCO. *Gloria's Ranch LLC v. Tauren Expl. Inc.,* 17-1518 (La. 9/7/18), 251 So.3d 392.

[2] The case was ultimately remanded "for the trial court to consider the effect the reversal of Wells Fargo's liability has on the award, particularly as it relates to the virile share accounted for in the EXCO settlement."[2] In the interim, Cubic declared bankruptcy, and its liability to Gloria's Ranch was discharged. Tauren is the sole remaining defendant. We now must determine who bears the loss of Cubic's insolvency.

[3] La. C.C. art. 1803 states:

> Remission of debt by the obligee in favor of one obligor, or a transaction or compromise between the obligee and one obligor, benefits the other solidary obligors in the amount of the portion of that obligor.

[4] Gloria's Ranch entered into a compromise with EXCO. By settling, Gloria's Ranch extinguished EXCO's debt. Thus, the obligation owed to Gloria's Ranch was reduced by EXCO's virile portion. When Cubic became insolvent, the issue arose as to whether Tauren should wholly bear Cubic's portion or whether Cubic's virile share should be split equally amongst Tauren and EXCO, with Gloria's Ranch absorbing the liability of the latter. This is a *res nova* issue.

[5] Louisiana Civil Code Article 1803, Revision Comment (d), states, "In case of insolvency of a solidary obligor after the obligee has remitted the debt in favor of another, the loss must be borne by the obligee." A treatise on the subject states:

> The obligee who remits[3] the debt in favor of one of his solidary obligors shares in the loss resulting from the insolvency of another by losing the

---

2. Gloria's Ranch reached a settlement with EXCO on August 13, 2014, thereby releasing EXCO as a defendant in this matter.

3. While they are separate legal concepts, remission, compromise, and transactions are given equal effect for purposes of Louisiana Civil Code article 1803. See La. Civ. Code art. 1803, Revision Comment (a).

amount the remitted obligor would have had to contribute had he not been favored by a remission of the debt.

Litvinoff and Scalise, 5 La. Civ. Law Treatise, *The Law of Obligations,* 2 ed. (2001), § 7.83.

[6] These secondary sources are instructive. We expressly hold that when an obligee remits (or compromises) the debt of one solidary obligor, he absorbs that obligor's portion of the loss caused by another solidary obligor's insolvency. Because Gloria's Ranch discharged the debt of EXCO, thus impairing the legal rights of the other solidary obligors, it should bear EXCO's portion of the loss caused by Cubic's insolvency.

[7] REVERSED and RENDERED.

Eugene Bellard
v.
American Central Ins. Co., et al.

Supreme Court of Louisiana
April 18, 2008
980 So.2d 654

WEIMER, Justice.

[. . . .]

[1] Louisiana Civil Code article 1794 defines a solidary obligation as follows:

An obligation is solidary for the obligors when each obligor is liable for the whole performance. A performance rendered by one of the solidary obligors relieves the others of liability toward the obligee.

[2] Drawing upon this definition, this court has held that a solidary obligation exists when the obligors (1) are obliged to the same thing, (2) so that each may be compelled for the whole, and (3) when payment by one exonerates the other from liability toward the creditor. *Hoefly v. Government Employees Insurance Company,* 418 So.2d 575, 576 (La.1982). [. . . .]

[. . . .]

[3] The first component of solidarity described in *Hoefly, Narcise* [*v. Illinois Central Gulf Railroad Co.,* 427 So.2d 1192 (La. 1983)], and *Williams* [*v. Sewerage & Water Board of New Orleans,* 611 So.2d 1383 (La. 1993),] is met here, as both the uninsured motorist carrier and the workers' compensation insurer are "obliged to the same thing." [. . . .]

[. . . .]

[4] The second component of solidarity is also present in this case: the uninsured motorist carrier and the workers' compensation insurer each may be compelled for the whole of their common liability. As we explained in *Hoefly,* an obligor's liability

for the whole "means simply that the debtor who has been sued cannot plead the benefit of division, which was invented for the benefit of sureties whereby the creditor is required to divide his action between them." [....]

[....]

[5] Finally, the third component of solidarity is satisfied in this case. Payment by one solidary obligor exonerates the other obligor as to the creditor. LSA-C.C. art. 1794. "This is a direct consequence of each debtor being obliged to the same thing so that each may be compelled for the whole, as if he were the sole debtor." *Hoefly*, 418 So.2d at 579. The injured employee is not allowed to obtain double recovery on those elements of damage which are coextensive.[3] *Williams*, 611 So.2d at 1388. Accordingly, as to the debt to which the employer's uninsured motorist carrier and the employer and/or its workers' compensation insurer are solidarily obliged, *i.e.*, the payment of lost wages and medical expenses, payment of the debt by one exonerates the other from liability to the creditor.

[....]

[6] Having found all of the requirements for a solidary obligation, we hold that the employer's uninsured motorist carrier and the employer and/or its worker's compensation insurer are solidary obligors, having coextensive obligations to reimburse the plaintiff for lost wages and medical expenses incurred as a result of his injury. The court of appeal erred in rejecting solidary liability because the insurers' obligations arise from separate parts of the law and because the elements of damage to be compensated by each are not identical; the courses of the debtors' obligations are irrelevant. There is an in solido obligation as to every item for which plaintiff can compel payment from either obligor.[4]

[....]

See also *Wooten v. Wimberly,* 272 So.2d 303 (La. 1972); *Steptoe v. Lallie Kemp Regional Hospital,* 618 So.2d 1008 (La.App. 1 Cir. 1993); *Steptoe v. Lallie Kemp Regional Hospital,* 634 So.2d 331 (La. 1994); *Hidalgo v. Dupuy,* 122 So.2d 639 (La.App. 1 Cir. 1960); *Armstrong Airport Concessions v. K-Squared Restaurant, LLC,* 178 So.3d 1094 (La. App. 4 Cir. 2015).

---

3. In the absence of a contract or agreement providing to the contrary, the employer and/or its workers' compensation insurer would have the right to be reimbursed for the workers' compensation benefits paid by it from any tort damages recovered from the employer's uninsured motorist carrier, thereby preventing a double recovery. LSA-R.S. 23:1101; Johnson, 425 So.2d at 227.

4. To the extent the cases relied on by the court of appeal, *Leger v. Sonnier Exterminating Company, supra,* and *Viada v. A & A Machine Works, Inc., supra,* conflict with our holding here, they were erroneous.

Comparative Law Perspective

— Civil Law —

France

Robert J. Pothier, *A Treatise on the Law of Obligations or Contracts*

vol. 1, nᵒs 287–288 at 171–73 (William David Evans trans., 1806)

§ I. What is a Divisible Obligation, and What is an Indivisible One

[287] A Divisible Obligation is that which may be divided. An Indivisible Obligation is that which cannot be divided. An Obligation is not the less divisible, though it be actually undivided; for it is sufficient to render it divisible if it is capable of being divided.

For instance, if I have singly contract[ed] to pay you a thousand pounds, this obligation is undivided; but it is divisible, because it may be divided; and in fact will be divided among my heirs, if I leave several, and die before discharging it. [. . . .]

[288] We are now to see what Obligations can be divided, and what cannot.

An obligation may be divided, and is divisible, when the thing which is the matter and object of it is susceptible of division and parts, by which it may be paid; and on the contrary, an obligation is indivisible, and cannot be divided, when the thing is not susceptible of division and parts, and can only be paid altogether.

The division in question is not a physical division [. . .] but a civil division.

There are two kinds of civil division, the one consisting in real and divided parts, the other intellectual, and undivided parts. When an acre of ground is divided into two parts by placing a fence in the middle, this is a division of the first kind: the parts of the acre, which are separated by this fence, are real and divided parts.

When a man who was proprietor of this acre of ground, or of any thing else, dies, and leaves two heirs, who continue proprietors of it, each having an undivided moiety, it is a division of the second kind; the parts which result from this division, and which belong to each of the heirs, are undivided parts, which are not real and which subsist only *in jure et intellectu.*

Things which are not susceptible of the first kind of division, may be of the second. For instance, a horse, a watch, are not susceptible of the first kind of division; for these things are not susceptible of real and divided parts, without the destruction of their substance; but they are susceptible of the second kind of division, because they may belong to several persons, in undivided parts.

Things are indivisible, when they are neither susceptible of real nor even of intellectual parts; such are for the most part, the rights of predial servitudes (a) *quæ pro parte acquire non possunt.*

The obligation of giving a thing of this nature is indivisible.

Alex Weill & François Terré, *Droit Civil: Les Obligations*

n° 948 at 1013 (3d ed. 1980)

The essential difference between indivisibility and passive solidarity is that, in the event of the death of one of the debtors of an indivisible debt, each of his heirs remains bound for the totality, while the heirs of a solidary co-debtor are bound only for their part. This difference is explained by this idea that indivisibility is connected with or is thought to be connected with the nature of the object.

In addition, indivisibility, inasmuch as it is connected with the nature of the object, does not suppose a community of interests among the debtors. As a result, it is admitted that the notion of a "reciprocal mandate" ought to be excluded and that, in this context, the secondary effects of solidarity are not produced, other than the effect regarding the interruption of prescription.

Charles Demolombe, *Cours de Code Napoléon: Traité des Contrats*

vol. 26, n° 597 at 534–35 (1880)

[I]n a solidary obligation, there exists, among the co-obligors, a juridical relation of mandate, of suretyship, or of partnership. This relation explains the reciprocal necessity in which each finds himself to advance the parts [**of the total performance**] that appertain to his co-obligors and serves, in fact, as the basis on which the entire theory of passive solidarity rests. [. . . .]

[I]n a divisible obligation, the obligors [. . .] are not obligated for each other; each of them, on the contrary, is obligated separately only for himself. And the necessity in which each finds himself of advancing the parts [**of the total performance**] that appertain to his co-obligors does not derive from some juridical relation that makes them reciprocal mandataries of each other; it derives solely from a physical or juridical impossibility [**i.e., the impossibility of rendering less than the total performance due**].

This difference is of capital importance!

What if one of many solidary co-obligors destroys, by his fault, the thing that forms the object of the obligation? The other co-obligors are not freed, for they respond for the fault of their co-obligor, that is to say, of their mandatary or partner.

But what if, on the contrary, one of many co-obligors of an indivisible obligation, by his fault, causes the thing that forms the object of that obligation to perish? The other obligors are freed, for they do not respond for each other, and the individual fault of one, insofar as the others are concerned, is a fortuitous event.

Belgium

Henri de Page, *Traité Elémentaire de Droit Civil Belge: Les Obligations*

vol. 3, n° 295 at 298–300 (3d ed. 1967)

Indivisible obligations and solidary obligations have this *common trait*: that both of them [. . .] have the effect of [**enabling one party or the other**] to escape the inconveniences of a divisible obligation with a plurality of subjects. But for the rest, the *differences* between the indivisible obligation and solidary obligation are important.

The indivisible obligation sometimes has *more intense* effects and sometimes *less intense* effects that the solidary obligation.

1° *More intense effects.* — Indivisibility — natural, but also conventional — is extended to the heirs of the multiple debtors; solidarity is not. When several multiple debtors engage themselves indivisibly, if one of these debtors happens to die, his heirs are bound indivisibly, each of them with the others debtors, as was their author-in-title [**i.e., the *de cujus***]. The creditor, then, can act *for the whole* against *any one or more of them*. Such is not the case with solidarity, where the debt of the solidary obligor *is divided* among his heirs, without solidary. From this, one can understand the utility of the clause that one encounters so frequently in practice: "the debtors engage themselves *solidarily and indivisibly*." Though this clause, at first glance, appears to be redundant, the utility of it appears in the case of the *death* of one of the solidary debtors. The heirs will no longer be held *solidarily*, but they will still be held *indivisibly*.

2° *Less intense effects.* — Indivisibility sometimes engenders effects that are less intense than those of solidarity:

a) When the indivisibility is founded on the *nature* of the object, the indivisibility does not subsist beyond this object. When an obligation to do, which is indivisible as such, is substituted, in the event of non-performance, for an obligation to pay a sum of money (damages), this latter obligation becomes divisible. [. . . .] It is otherwise in the case of solidarity. [. . . .]

b) According to the traditional opinion, solidarity presupposes an idea of *mandate* among the co-debtors, an idea that is lacking from indivisibility. It follows, then, that:

1) Whereas the putting in default of one of the solidary debtors produces an effect in regard to the others, it is not the same among the debtors of an indivisible obligation;

2) Whereas the loss of the thing due to the fault of one of the solidary debtors does not free the others, in the case of an indivisible obligation such a loss is considered to be a *cas fortuit* by relation to the other debtors and leads to their liberation.

Part Two

Conventional Obligations

Chapter 1

General Provisions

Louisiana Sources of Law
Louisiana Civil Code

Art. 1906. Definition of contract.

A contract is an agreement by two or more parties whereby obligations are created, modified, or extinguished. (Acts 1984, No. 331, § 1, eff. Jan. 1, 1985.)

Art. 1907. Unilateral contracts.

A contract is unilateral when the party who accepts the obligation of the other does not assume a reciprocal obligation. (Acts 1984, No. 331, § 1, eff. Jan. 1, 1985.)

Art. 1908. Bilateral or synallagmatic contracts.

A contract is bilateral, or synallagmatic, when the parties obligate themselves reciprocally, so that the obligation of each party is correlative to the obligation of the other. (Acts 1984, No. 331, § 1, eff. Jan. 1, 1985.)

Art. 1909. Onerous contracts.

A contract is onerous when each of the parties obtains an advantage in exchange for his obligation. (Acts 1984, No. 331, § 1, eff. Jan. 1, 1985.)

Art. 1910. Gratuitous contracts.

A contract is gratuitous when one party obligates himself towards another for the benefit of the latter, without obtaining any advantage in return. (Acts 1984, No. 331, § 1, eff. Jan. 1, 1985.)

Art. 1911. Commutative contracts.

A contract is commutative when the performance of the obligation of each party is correlative to the performance of the other. (Acts 1984, No. 331, § 1, eff. Jan. 1, 1985.)

Art. 1912. Aleatory contracts.

A contract is aleatory when, because of its nature or according to the parties' intent, the performance of either party's obligation, or the extent of the performance, depends on an uncertain event. (Acts 1984, No. 331, § 1, eff. Jan. 1, 1985.)

Art. 1913. Principal and accessory contracts.

A contract is accessory when it is made to provide security for the performance of an obligation. Suretyship, mortgage, pledge, and other types of security agreements are examples of such a contract.

When the secured obligation arises from a contract, either between the same or other parties, that contract is the principal contract. (Acts 1984, No. 331, §1, eff. Jan. 1, 1985; Acts 1989, No. 137, §16, eff. Sept. 1, 1989.)

Art. 1914. Nominate and innominate contracts.

Nominate contracts are those given a special designation such as sale, lease, loan, or insurance.

Innominate contracts are those with no special designation. (Acts 1984, No. 331, §1, eff. Jan. 1, 1985.)

Art. 1915. Rules applicable to all contracts.[1]

All contracts, nominate and innominate, are subject to the rules of this title. (Acts 1984, No. 331, §1, eff. Jan. 1, 1985.)

Doctrine

Louisiana Law of Conventional Obligations, A Précis

Articles 1-4 and 6

To a legal concept is associated a legal regime, a set of legal rules which govern a carefully described factual situation matching the proper legal concept. [....]

[T]he Louisiana civil Code has classified "contracts" under a series of "definitions" to which are attached specific legal regimes which are distributed all over the civil Code and which can be fully grasped only as a consequence of an understanding of the structure of the whole civil Code. [....]

Unilateral Contracts and Bilateral or Synallagmatic Contracts

A contract, an agreement between two parties at least, is unilateral when only one of the two parties owes an obligation to the other; only one party is a debtor whereas the other party is the creditor of that debtor. We can analogize such a unilateral contract to a "one-way street," the obligation moving in one direction only. [....]

It is most important to distinguish a "unilateral contract" from a "unilateral juridical act." In the latter case only one person is bound by her/his single will; such would be the case of an "offer" which binds the offeror only until it expires or is revoked. If it should be accepted, we will then have a "bilateral juridical act" or contract. That contract will be "unilateral" if it creates obligations on one party only, or it will be "bilateral/synallagmatic" if both parties owe obligations to each other.

---

1. Articles 1916 and 1917 have been omitted.

A bilateral or synallagmatic contract is, therefore, a "two-way street" because the obligations flow in both directions. [. . . .]

Onerous and Gratuitous Contracts

"A contract is onerous when each of the parties obtains an advantage in exchange for his obligation." LSA-C.C. Art. 1909. In such a contract, for example a contract of sale, each one of the two parties owes some performance to the other and is entitled to receiving a performance from that other party. [. . . .]

"A contract is gratuitous when one party obligates himself towards another for the benefit of the latter, without obtaining any advantage in return." LSA-C.C. Art. 1910. It is the gratuitous motivation or intent of that party who obliges herself towards another "without obtaining any advantage in return" that actually determines the nature of that contract. The typical and most common example of such a kind of contract is the "donation purely gratuitous . . . which is made without condition and merely from liberality." [. . . .]

There exist some important legal and practical reasons for this distinction between onerous and gratuitous contracts. [. . . .]

Commutative and Aleatory Contracts

This classification as it exists in the Louisiana civil Code is, we believe, problematic. [. . . .]

Louisiana civil Code of 1870: Art. 1768: "Commutative contracts are those in which what is done, given or promised by one party, is considered as equivalent to, or a consideration for what is done, given, or promised by the other." Article 1776, in its first paragraph, stated: "A contract is aleatory or hazardous, when the performance of that which is one of its objects, depends on an uncertain event." [. . . .] [T]he civil Code of Québec states in Article 1382 that "A contract is commutative when, at the time it is formed, the extent of the obligations of the parties and of the advantages obtained by them in return is certain and determinate. When the extent of the obligations or of the advantages is uncertain, the contract is aleatory." [. . . .]

It is our position that Article 1911 first does not add to the definition of bilateral/synallagmatic contract and, second, fails to emphasize the difference between a truly "commutative" contract at civil law and an aleatory contract as it is defined in LSA-C.C. Art. 1912.

What does "correlative" mean and how can its meaning fit in the definition of both LSA-C.C. Articles 1908 and 1911? [. . . .]

It is inherent in any bilateral/synallagmatic contract that each party owes to the other the performance of the object of her own obligation. [. . . .]

In a bilateral/synallagmatic contract, not only the obligations themselves are "reciprocal, correlative" as LSA-C.C. Art. 1908 states, but so are the performances by the very fact that they are inherent to the very nature of any bilateral/synallagmatic contract. Such a contract by itself can only create the reciprocity, the correlation, of the performances which are necessarily engendered by the reciprocity, or correlation of the obligations without which no performance could exist. We believe, therefore, that LSA-C.C. Art. 1911 adds absolutely nothing to Art. 1908. [....]

LSA-C.C. Art. 2982 describes in clear legal terms what an aleatory contract is: **"The aleatory contract is a mutual agreement, of which the effects, with respect both to the advantages and losses, whether to all the parties or to one or more of them, depend on an uncertain event."** The specific legal terms to focus on are that an *aleatory contract* is a *mutual agreement* which *creates effects*, i.e. advantages and losses, *vis-à-vis one or more parties*, and the occurrence of *which effects depend on an uncertain event.* [....]

Principle and Accessory Contracts

A principal contract is one which can stand on its own; it needs no legal (contractual or otherwise) support than its own to exist; it does not need to *arise* from any other contract. A contract of sale can stand on its own; so can a donation or marriage contract.

On the other hand, when a contract needs the support of another contract (or legislation), when **"it is made to provide security for the performance of [a principal] obligation"** then it is an "accessory" to the principal contract. **Article 1913** illustrates this concept of accessory contract with **"suretyship, mortgage, pledge ..."** [....]

Implied Kinds of Contracts

The rule is [...] that parties can be bound by a contract which is merely *consensual*, which results from the oral exchange of their wills. The most common *consensual* contract we enter into just about every day, and sometimes more than once, is the contract of sale of a movable thing. Such is very clearly stated in **LSA-C.C. Art. 2439 § 2: "Sale is a contract whereby a person transfers ownership of a thing to another for a price in money.**

The thing, the price, and the consent of the parties are requirements for the perfection of a sale." The binding force of "consent" is such that **"Ownership is transferred between the parties as soon as there is agreement on the thing and the price is fixed, even though the thing sold is not yet delivered nor the price paid."** (LSA-C.C. Art. 2456.)

To the contrary, and as an exception to the rule that contracts are consensual, there are instances of contracts, in the civil Code, which require a "form," a writing, for some contracts to be valid and binding. They are called *solemn* or *formal* contracts. We read, for example, in **LSA-C.C. Art. 2440** that **"A sale or promise of sale of an immovable must be made by authentic act or by act under private signature, except as provided in Article 1839."** [....]

As a general rule, contracts are negotiated between two parties who mutually agree on their reciprocal obligations and rights. [. . . .]

Such contracts resulting from a mutual agreement between the two parties are presumed to fully reflect the principles of "autonomy of the will" and "freedom of contract" which are the foundations of the law of contracts at civil law. [. . . .]

However, today, contracts are less and less negotiated on equal basis and more and more either non-negotiable at all or negotiable in part only. Such contracts are often referred to as "contracts of adhesion" or "adhesion contracts." [. . . .]

Illustrations abound: insurance contracts, electricity supply contracts, transportation contracts, etc. [. . . .]

With respect to contracts which the courts will qualify and describe as "adhesion contracts," it is the responsibility of the courts to attempt to re-establish some balance between the unequal bargaining powers of the parties, to protect the "weak" against the "strong."

Cases

Lillis

v.

Owens

Court of Appeal of Louisiana
Parish of Orleans
February 26, 1945
21 So.2d 185

McCALEB, Judge.

[1] The plaintiff is engaged in the contracting business in New Orleans and conducts his operations under the name of Brandin Slate Company. On November 18th, 1941, he entered into a written contract with the defendant, Mary Owens, under which he agreed to make certain alterations, additions and improvements to the real property of the defendant designated as Nos. 2427–29 London Avenue, New Orleans, in consideration of a price of $1890. This contract, which describes in detail the work to be performed by plaintiff, stipulates that the price of $1890 is 'to be paid in monthly installments' and further that 'Owner gives Brandin Slate Company permission to try and arrange the financing.'

[2] Alleging that, in accordance with his obligation under the aforesaid contract, he has fully performed the work required of him; that he is and has been ready and willing to deliver the building and improvements to defendant free and clear of all liens and claims for labor and material furnished by him which was used in connection with the alteration and repairs to the building and that he has made demand on defendant for the payment of the price due under the contract without avail,

plaintiff instituted suit in the Civil District Court to recover from defendant the contract price of $1890.

[3] After filing an exception of no right or cause of action which was overruled by the trial court, the defendant answered plaintiff's petition and denied the allegations of fact contained therein. She further set forth that the contract was void; that the price was exorbitant; that plaintiff's agent obtained her signature to the so-called contract through fraud and deceit and that the court should declare that she was relieved of any and all responsibility in the premises.

[4] The case thereafter proceeded to trial on the issues thus formed by the pleadings. At the outset of the hearing, counsel for defendant objected to the introduction of evidence in the case 'for the reason this contract which we submit to the Court is not a contract upon which one can be sued on for the reason everything is in blank.' After hearing argument on this objection, the court made the following ruling: 'In this so-called contract everything that involves a meeting of the minds is blank. Considering the fact that the alleged contract was in fact no contract at all and there was no meeting of the minds evidenced in that written agreement, and that the petition does not allege any demand to recover on a quantum meruit, the Court must sustain the objection and exclude all evidence. I will dismiss the case as of non-suit, so that there will be no question of res adjudicata in the event of a new suit on a quantum meruit or some other contract growing out of the same transaction.'

[. . . .]

[5] An examination of the contract, which is attached to plaintiff's petition, reveals that it was executed on a printed form of Brandin Slate Company. The work which the contractor proposed to perform under the agreement is fully detailed in typewriting, as well as the price of $1890, which the defendant agreed to pay. The only 'blanks' to be found in the document are those contained in that part of the printed form referring to the making of a down payment by the owner and the execution of a promissory note, payable in installments, to be given to the contractor for the balance to become due on the work. Obviously, it was unnecessary for the parties in the instant case to fill in those blanks, as the typewritten portion of the contract, which prevails over the printed matter, did not contemplate any down payment at all or the giving of a promissory note for the price of the work. Hence, it is difficult for us to understand how the presence of the blanks in the printed portion of the contract was pertinent to the judge's ruling that a binding contract did not exist as there was no meeting of minds by the parties.

[6] While the reason given by the judge for his statement that the contract is unenforceable because of lack of mutuality does not clearly appear from his ruling, it is evident that he was of the opinion that, because the parties stipulated that the purchase price was to be paid in monthly installments without stating the amount or the number of such installments, their failure to do so was fatal to the agreement. In other words, it is apparently the view of our brother below that an agreement to

do work for a certain price, payable in monthly installments, is not a binding contract because, inasmuch as the parties have not agreed upon the amount of such installments, it is impossible for the court to fix the method of payment of the price.

[7] We cannot agree with this view. In an agreement to alter, repair or construct a building, where the work to be done is set forth and the price to be paid is fixed, all of the essentials of a binding contract are present. The mode of payment of the price, whether in installments or otherwise, is merely an accidental stipulation. Under Article 1764 of the Civil Code, it is provided that all things not forbidden by law may legally become the subject of contracts but that different agreements are governed by different rules 'adapted to the nature of each contract to distinguish which it is necessary in every contract to consider:

'1. That which is the essence of the contract, for the want whereof there is either no contract at all, or a contract of another description. Thus a price is essential to the contract of sale; if there be none, it is either no contract, or if the consideration be other property, it is an exchange.

* * *

'3. Accidental stipulations, which belong neither to the essence nor the nature of the contract, but depend solely on the will of the parties. The term given for the payment of a loan, the place at which it is to be paid, and the nature of the rent payable on a lease, are examples of accidental stipulations.

[8] 'What belongs to the essence and to the nature of each particular description of contract, is determined by the law defining such contracts; accidental stipulations depend on the will of the parties, regulated by the general rules applying to all contracts.'

[9] Thus, it will be readily observed that the agreement under consideration contains all of the necessary elements of a binding contract, set forth in Article 1764, i.e., the work to be done by the contractor and the payment by the owner of a fixed price therefor. There is, however, an accidental stipulation contained in the agreement, which refers solely to the manner in which the price is to be paid by the owner — that is, that the parties contemplated that the owner would have the right to pay the agreed price in monthly installments. The fact that the amount of these installments is not fixed does not make the price indefinite but merely exhibits that the parties contemplated that the amount to be paid each month would be agreed upon at some future date. [....]

[10] It is well recognized that the nonperformance of an accidental stipulation does not invariably have the effect of abrogating an agreement forasmuch as such a covenant is not of the essence of a valid contract. See Andrus v. Eunice Band Mill Co., 185 La. 403, 169 So. 449 and Moore v. O'Bannon & Julien, 126 La. 161, 52 So. 253, 255. In the Moore case, which was quoted from with approval in the Andrus case, it is said: 'The stipulations relating to the erection of the mill and the making of the payments thereon pay days to be fixed are quoad [*sic*] the sale of the timber

'accidental,' being neither of the essence of the contract nor necessarily implied from its nature, but depending solely upon the will of the parties, regulated by the general rules applicable to all contracts. Civ.Code, art. 1764, par. 3. Where the parties so agree, or, in some cases, where there is no agreement to the contrary, noncompliance with accidental stipulations may furnish good cause to annul a contract.

[11] The accidental stipulation contained in the contract in this case was obviously inserted for the benefit of the defendant—for, if nothing had been covenanted by the parties respecting payment in installments, the price would become due as soon as the work had been completed by the contractor. See Civil Code, Article 2050. The provision in the contract, respecting the payment in monthly installments, does not contemplate the payment of interest to the contractor on the deferred balance of the price while the work was in progress and, therefore, the stipulation cannot in any sense be regarded as one in his favor. Hence, since the stipulation for installment payments was inserted solely for defendant's benefit, it could be waived by her. If we assume, as we must, that the contractor was unsuccessful in arranging for the financing of the job and if the parties were unable to come to an agreement respecting the amount of the contemplated monthly installments, defendant would have had the right to withdraw from the contract and have had it rescinded. But this right to withdraw from the engagement could be waived by defendant, either expressly, or impliedly by permitting the contractor to fulfill his part of the bargain without protest. In 17 C.J.S., Contracts § 443, pp. 926 and 927, we find the following:

> 'The right to rescind may be lost or waived by delay, or by words or conduct evidencing an intention not to exercise it, such as by accepting its benefits.
> * * *
>
> 'There is a waiver of the right to rescind a building contract where the contract is treated, by the party having such right, as still in force. So also a party to a building contract may waive his right to rescind the contract by not exercising such right promptly.'

[12] Hence, we conclude that, since the agreement under consideration contains all of the essential elements of a contract, i.e., the work to be done and the price to be paid, a valid contract subsists, despite the fact that it contains a provision concerning terms of payment which is vague and indefinite because the amounts of the monthly installments are not stated. [. . . .] [T]he question will be presented on the merits as to whether the defendant, in permitting plaintiff to excute [*sic*] his part of the engagement, has not waived, by her conduct or otherwise, her right to insist that she is not liable for the stipulated price on the ground that the parties contemplated that that price was to be liquidated in monthly installments and that no agreement could he reached concerning the amount of those installments. The result to be reached on this question can only be determined by the hearing of evidence.

[13] We therefore hold that the objection interposed by defendant to the hearing of any evidence in the case was erroneously sustained and it is now overruled.

[14] For the reasons assigned, the judgment appealed from is reversed and the case is remanded to the Civil District Court for further proceedings in accordance with law and consistent with the views herein expressed. The costs of this appeal are to be paid by the defendant, Mary Owens, other costs to await the final disposition of the matter.

[15] Reversed and remanded.

Questions

1. Paragraph 1: The court states that the parties "entered into a written contract." Was there a term and/or a condition? If so, what kind(s)?

2. Paragraph 4: Why is the court saying that the "alleged contract was in fact no contract at all and there was no meeting of the minds"? Would any blank in the contract lead to the court saying there was no meeting of the minds? Should a distinction be made between blanks bearing on essential elements or component parts of a contract and blanks bearing on accessory or secondary or incidental elements/component parts of a contract?

3. Paragraph 4–5: Isn't the court making a distinction here between the many elements of a contract? From paragraph 9 onward, see what the court is saying about accidental stipulations and the effect or lack thereof of these accidental stipulations not being performed.

4. Paragraph 9: Can you identify the essential elements of the contract at issue here (a construction contract, according to the court) and those that are not essential? Are the requirements listed in Louisiana Civil Code article 2756 the essential requirements the Court identified as essential in this case?

Orkin Exterminating Company
v.
James T. Foti

Supreme Court of Louisiana
October 28, 1974
302 So.2d 593

TATE, Justice.

[1] Orkin, the employer, sues its former employee Foti to enjoin him for working for two years in the pest control field in approximately the western half of Louisiana. The cause of action is based upon a clause in the employment contract by which Foti had agreed not to compete for two years in such area after his employment with Orkin was terminated. The employer complains of the grant of only a limited injunction,[1] affirmed by the court of appeal, 287 So.2d 569 (La.App.3d Cir. 1973).

---

1. The defendant Foti was enjoined from soliciting or getting business from customers of Orkin formerly contacted or serviced by him as an employee of Orkin. No appeal was taken from this ruling.

[2] We granted certiorari, 292 So.2d 241 (La.1974), in order to resolve a conflict in the intermediate court decisions interpreting the legality of agreements exacted by employers from their employees not to compete with them after the termination of an employee relationship.

1

[3] More specifically at issue is the application of La.R.S. 23:921 as amended in 1962.

[4] This statute as originally enacted in 1934 and as incorporated into the 1950 Revised Statutes provides: 'No employer shall require or direct any employee to enter into any contract whereby the employee agrees not to engage in any competing business for himself, or as the employee of another, upon the termination of his contract of employment with such employer, and all such contracts, or provisions thereof containing such agreement shall be null and unenforceable in any court'.

[5] The statute was amended by Act 104 of 1962 to add as a proviso a limited exception to this stringent blanket prohibition of non-competition agreements: 'where the employer incurs an expense in the training of an employee or incurs an expense in the advertisement of the business that the employer is engaged in', then a non-competition agreement was permitted that, at the termination of employment, the 'employee will not enter into the same business that employer is engaged over the same route or in the same territory for a period of two years.'[2]

[6] The conflict in the intermediate courts developed as to what extent the proviso had modified the original basic policy disfavoring non-competition agreements. See Comment, Agreements Not to Compete, 33 La.L.Rev. 94, 103-06 (1972).

[7] One line of decisions holds that, in view of the basic policy of the statute to which the 1962 amendment was a proviso, the terms of the amendment imported sums not usually or customarily expended in the normal course of employment — that the amendment contemplated validating a non-competition agreement only where substantial funds were spent in special training or in special advertisement of the employee himself (rather than generally of the business).

[8] The other line of cases holds that any expense incurred in training an employee, even normal supervisory assistance in breaking him in, and any expense incurred in advertising the employee's connection with the business, however nominal, validated an otherwise-prohibited non-competition agreement.

[. . . .]

---

2. The full language added to La.R.S. 23:921 by the 1962 act is: 'provided that in those cases where the employer incurs an expense in the training of the employee or incurs an expense in the advertisement of the business that the employer is engaged in, then in that event it shall be permissible for the employer and employee to enter into a voluntary contract and agreement whereby the employee is permitted to agree and bind himself that at the termination of his or her employment that said employee will not enter into the same business that employer is engaged in over the same route or in the same territory for a period of two years.'

2

[9] The basic public policy of this state disfavors non-competition agreement exacted of employees. The basic provision of La.R.S. 23:921 (see above) is a strict prohibition against any employer requiring such an agreement of his employee. Even before the 1934 statutory prohibition, the Louisiana courts had consistently held such agreements to be unenforceable. Cloverland Dairy Products Co. v. Grace, 180 La. 694, 157 So. 393 (1934); Blanchard v. Haber, 166 La. 1014, 118 So. 117 (1928). See: Comment, 33 La.L.Rev. 94 (1972); Note, 27 Tul.L.Rev. 364 (1953). In the absence of an enforceable contract to other effect, an employee has the absolute right to enter the employment of another and actively compete with his former employer. Jones v. Ernst & Ernst, 172 La. 406, 134 So. 375 (1931).

[10] As noted in Conque, 173 So.2d 241, the essential basis of these decisions 'is the right of individual freedom and of individuals to better themselves in our free-enterprise society, where liberty of the individual is guaranteed. A strong public policy reason likewise for holding unenforceable an agreement exacted by an employer of an employee not to compete after the latter leaves his employment, is the disparity in bargaining power, under which an employee, fearful of losing his means of livelihood, cannot readily refuse to sign an agreement which, if enforceable, amounts to his contracting away his liberty to earn his livelihood in the field of his experience except by continuing in the employment of his present employer.'

[11] These fundamental background principles must be borne in mind in interpreting the intent of the 1962 amendment. This provides only a limited exception to the stringent prohibition of the statute against such non-competition agreements, and to the strong and long-established public policy of this state to such effect.

[12] If the 1962 amendment is construed as by the Aetna v. Adams line of decisions, then Any expense incurred by an employer in training or advertisement entitles him to enforcement of a two-year restrictive covenant. If, however, this is the proper meaning of the amendment, then virtually any employer can qualify for the exception. This is contrary to the basic public policy incorporated by the statute. By such a construction, the 1962 amendment, which in terms merely added a proviso to the basic enactment, would in actuality have repealed it.

[13] The purpose of the limited exception permitted by the 1962 amendments could not have been to repeal the fundamental purpose of the prohibition. The basic public policy incorporated was to forbid an employer from effectively tying an employee to his present employment. Such a non-competition agreement may effectively prevent an employee from leaving his present employment in order to earn a better living in the occupation in which experienced and in the area of his livelihood.

[14] In view of the fundamental policy of the basic statute, the apparent purpose of the 1962 amendment, as stated in Conque, 'is to protect an employer only where he has invested substantial sums in special training of the employee or in advertising the employee's connection with his business.' 173 So.2d 241.

[15] If an employer extensively advertises a particular employee as the man to go to for the employer's type of services, it is not unfair to protect the employer's investment in this particularized asset by authorizing a limited non-competition agreement to prevent the advertised employee from misusing it. If an employer spends a substantial sum affording special training to an employee, it may not be unfair to protect the employer by authorizing a limited non-competition agreement to prevent the employee from using this specialized training for the benefit of another in competition with his former employer.

[16] However, as the Conque line of cases holds, normal expenses of administration and supervision — such as employee sales and training meetings, the time spent breaking in a new employee, training courses in the administrative needs of the employer itself — cannot be considered the sort of 'training' expense intended to justify the heavily disfavored non-competition agreement. Almost any employer could so tie his employees to their present employment by exacting a non-competition agreement. As Conque notes, 173 So.2d 241: 'What the legislators must have intended, it seems to us (since they did not repeal the basic prohibition against such contracts as void as against the public policy of the state), was to protect the investment of those employers who afford special training of a substantial nature to their employees, and to encourage them to do so.'

3

[17] Foti was employed almost five years by Orkin. He was first employed in Alexandria in 1968 at $500 per month. Non-competition agreements were exacted of him in 1970, when he became manager of the New Iberia office, in 1971 when he became branch manager at Monroe, then again in 1972, when he was transferred to the Louisiana district office in Alexandria at a base salary of $750 per month.

[18] Included in the three pages of the last contract, here sought to be enforced, was an agreement not to engage in the pest control business, for two years after his employment terminated, in the cities of Alexandria, Crowley, Monroe, Lafayette, Lake Charles, Natchitoches, New Iberia, Shreveport, or Ruston, or anywhere within a radius of fifty miles of the official geographical boundaries of each of these Louisiana cities.

[19] This injunctive proceeding was brought when Foti left Orkin's employ and then started his own pest control business in Opelousas. Orkin claims that its non-competition agreement is validated by sums spent in training Foti as a pest control worker and as a branch manager. (It also claims that its general expenses of advertising to improve its business are sufficient to validate the contract.)

[20] We agree with the court of appeal that the one-day service training schools in 1970, 1971, and 1972, and the supervisor's leadership conference in August, 1972 represent a type of normal administrative expense not available to validate non-competition agreements; they are not special training expenditures of a substantial nature. Likewise (even aside from the fact the expenditure occurred prior to the 1972 agreement here sought to be enforced), the $261.50 expense furnished the employee

for attending the Orkin's Manager Training School in Atlanta, Georgia, in 1970 cannot justify enjoining the employee from working for himself or another in 1973 and 1974 — the employer had long received the benefit of its investment through the employee's two years of managerial service afterwards; the amount is insubstantial in relation to the period of service;[3] and the training was primarily to benefit Orkin rather than to add a marketable talent to the employee.

[21] Likewise, Foti's on-the-job training through his experience, through the supervisory assistance initially received by him, and through his access to Orkin training manuals and technical bulletins, constitute usual and ordinary expenses of employee-utilization. They are not expenses for specialized training of the nature that could validate a non-competition agreement.

[22] As our brothers of the intermediate court correctly observed: '* * * the basic and necessary knowledge in the business of pest eradications and control was acquired by the defendant, Foti, by everyday exposure to the business during the five years he was employed by the plaintiff. We cannot envision a rule whereby a man who has learned a trade by his own ability and hard work 'on the job' would be restricted by the courts from trying to better himself by starting his own business. This would be contrary to our free-enterprise system.'

[....]

Questions

1. Paragraphs 3–5: What do you think was the policy or *ratio legis* behind La. R.S. 23:921 of 1934 with respect to non-competition clauses? What about the exception added by Act 104 of 1962? How much should the courts be involved in implementing these policies? Should the courts be given some outside guidance? *See* paragraph 9. How should a court look upon an exception?

2. Paragraph 9: Isn't it of the essence of a principle to call for exceptions? How can there be a conflict between a principle and an exception to that principle? Could it be because policies rather than rules of law are vying for their particular scope of application? What, then, are the courts to do?

---

3. Thus, specialized training involving an actual cash expenditure of $400 might be regarded as the investment of a substantial sum if the employee quit soon after receiving it. However, if the termination of the employee's services occurs two or three years later, after the employer had, so to speak, amortized its investment, then the amount so spent can be regarded as insubstantial insofar as sustaining an injunction to keep the employee from working in the field of his experience for years, even though in the interval insubstantial routine training expenditures have been incurred. But see Louisiana Office Systems, Inc. v. Boudreaux, 298 So.2d 341 (La.App.3d Cir. 1974), certiorari granted, 302 So.2d 37 (La.1974).

Cellular One, Inc.
v.
John Brent Boyd

Cellular One, Inc.
v.
Hamilton J. Lemoine

Court of Appeal of Louisiana
First Circuit
March 3, 1995
653 So.2d 30

LOTTINGER, Chief Judge.

[1] This is an appeal by defendants from the granting of a preliminary injunction enforcing a noncompetition agreement executed between plaintiff and defendants.

Facts

[2] John Boyd and Hamilton Lemoine were employed as sales representatives for Cellular One from 1989 to 1993. During the course of their employment, they signed several noncompetition and nondisclosure agreements. When Boyd and Lemoine left the employment of Cellular One in December of 1993, they had executed identical noncompetition agreements which became effective on September 1, 1993.[1]

[3] Upon leaving Cellular One both defendants went to work for Affordable Cellular, an authorized agent of Bell South Mobility. Cellular One filed this suit for injunctive relief asserting that Boyd and Lemoine were in violation of the noncompetition agreement. Cellular One sought to prevent the defendants from competing against it in the cellular telephone business and from soliciting the business of Cellular One's customers in the parishes of East Baton Rouge, West Baton Rouge, Ascension, and Livingston. The suit also sought protection against disclosure of confidential information.

[4] Following the hearing on the preliminary injunction, the trial court enjoined defendants from engaging in the radio telephone service business in the parishes of East and West Baton Rouge, Ascension, and Livingston, for a period of two years. The court further enjoined defendants from directly soliciting any Cellular One customer to transfer or purchase radio telephone services or equipment. The court also ordered that should any customer of Cellular One initiate contact with defendants, said customer shall be referred back to Cellular one and not to any other radio telephone service. The trial court then suspended that portion of the injunction which prohibited the defendants from engaging in the radio telephone service business.

---

1. Boyd was fired from Cellular One whereas Lemoine resigned.

[5] Defendants appeal, asserting that the trial court erred in:

1. enforcing a noncompetition clause in an employment at will agreement because the agreement lacks mutuality of obligation and the agreement fails to provide sufficient consideration for the employee;

2. failing to find that circumstances involving economic threats were sufficient to constitute duress;

3. failing to rule that the agreement provided for stipulated damages;

4. finding that the noncompetition clause was sufficient to meet the requirements of La.R.S. 23:921; and

5. granting a preliminary injunction because no evidence was set forth that defendants in fact violated the confidentiality or nondisclosure clauses of the agreement.

The Noncompetition Agreement

[6] The contract at issue in this suit contains several provisions which purportedly comprise the noncompetition agreement. These provisions are:

III. Commissions and Other Incentives

   D. Non-Competition Payments (NCPs):

   NCPs are payable for the term listed below even if the eligible Sales Representative leaves the employment of the company. The main exception to this statement is if the former Sales Representative is employed by or is contracted with any Radio/Telephone Service of Baton Rouge Cellular One during the time period that the NCP payments are due as per the Employee Handbook. In the event that the Sales Representative is employed by or is contracted with a Radio/Telephone Service, all NCPs are forfeited by the Sales Representative. The Sales Representative also forfeits all NCPs earned during his/her employment at Cellular One.

   . . . .

VIII. Direct Sales Non-Competition Payments (NCPs)

   NCPs are payable at 3% for 3 years for those accounts having monthly bills over $50 per month. This includes access and airtime. The 3 years is based from the date of the start of the original contract.

   Terms & Conditions: (Eligibility Requirements)

   . . . .

   6.) Should the Direct Sales Rep leave or be terminated, Cellular One will continue to fulfill its obligation to the employee, but only for as long as the former employee does not engage in business or employment with another Radio/Telephone Service entity. Also, should any customer cancel, any retractions the former employee might have qualified to receive will be applied to the noncompetition payment.

. . . .

NON-COMPETITION AGREEMENT

I agree to refrain from carrying on or engaging in a radio telephone service business similar to that of Cellular One, Inc. and/or from soliciting customers of Cellular One, Inc. within the parishes of East Baton Rouge, West Baton Rouge, Ascension and Livingston for a period of two years from separation of employment with Cellular One, Inc.

The Statutory Provision

[7] Louisiana has consistently had a strong public policy against noncompetition contracts which prohibit employees from competing with a former employer. *Orkin Exterminating Company v. Foti,* 302 So.2d 593, 596 (La.1974). Prior to 1989, La. R.S. 23:921 permitted noncompetition agreements only if the employer incurred significant or extensive expenditures in the training of the employee or the advertisement of the business. *Id.* at 597. In 1989, the legislature amended La.R.S. 23:921 and replaced this single exception. However, the public policy disfavoring noncompetition agreements is still reflected in subsection (A) of the amended statute which provides:

> Every contract or agreement, or provision thereof, by which anyone is restrained from exercising a lawful profession, trade, or business of any kind, except as provided in this Section, shall be null and void.

[8] One of the exceptions to this general prohibition is contained in subsection (C) which states:

> Any person, including a corporation and the individual shareholders of such corporation, who is employed as an agent, servant, or employee may agree with his employer to refrain from carrying on or engaging in a business similar to that of the employer and/or from soliciting customers of the employer within a specified parish or parishes, municipality or municipalities, or parts thereof, so long as the employer carries on a like business therein, not to exceed a period of two years from termination of employment.

[9] Subsection (G) lists remedies available to an employer when a former employee breaches a noncompetition agreement.

[10] Any agreement covered by Subsections B, C, D, E, or F of this Section shall be considered an obligation not to do, and failure to perform may entitled the obligee to recover damages for the loss sustained and the profit of which he has been deprived. In addition, upon proof of the obligor's failure to perform, and without the necessity of proving irreparable injury, a court of competent jurisdiction shall order injunctive relief enforcing the terms of the agreement.

[11] In amending section 921, the Louisiana Legislature expanded the use of non-competition agreements. The legislature recognized that employers have a right to protect their business investment provided they comply with the exceptions contained in the statute.

Compliance with La.R.S. 23:921

[12] In assignment of error four, defendants allege that the agreement does not meet the requirements of La.R.S. 23:921(C). Defendants assert that the agreement does not adequately define the geographical location or time limitation within which the noncompetition agreement would apply. They further assert that there is no adequate definition of the business from which they are allegedly prohibited from competing.

[13] To be valid, a noncompetition agreement may limit competition only in a business similar to that of the employer, in a specified geographic area and for up to two years from termination of employment. Public policy requires that the provisions of noncompetition agreements be strictly construed in favor of the employee. *See Pelican Publishing Company v. Wilson,* 626 So.2d 721 (La.App. 5th Cir.1993); *Comet Industries, Inc. v. Lawrence,* 600 So.2d 85 (La.App. 2nd Cir.), *writ denied,* 604 So.2d 1002 (La.1992). Accordingly, noncompetition agreements which fail to specify the "parish or parishes, municipality or municipalities, or parts thereof" wherein the employer carried on a similar business are unenforceable. *Comet Industries, Inc.,* 600 So.2d at 87. Similarly, contracts seeking to extend noncompetition agreements beyond the two year statutory limit are null and void. *Allied Bruce Terminix Companies, Inc. v. Ferrier,* 93-0561 (La.App. 1st Cir. 3/11/94); 634 So.2d 44.

[14] In this case, the contract prevents the defendants from "engaging in a radio telephone service business similar to that of Cellular One, Inc." in the parishes of East Baton Rouge, West Baton Rouge, Ascension and Livingston, for a period of two years after employment termination. The language used in the agreement to define plaintiff's business tracks the statutory language of La.R.S. 23:921(C). This language adequately defines the business from which the defendants are prohibited from competing. Further, the geographic and time limitations are clearly specified in the contract and comply with the statutory guidelines.

[15] For these reasons, we find that the noncompetition agreement meets the requirements of La.R.S. 23:921(C) and accordingly, this assignment of error is without merit.

Mutuality and Cause

[16] In assignment of error one, defendants assert that noncompetition agreements should be unenforceable in employment at will situations because of a lack of mutuality and an insufficiency of cause.

[17] Both defendants were at will employees who are now asking this Court to apply principles of "mutuality" stated in a Kentucky federal district court case,

rather than to follow the principles and policies set down by the Louisiana legisla-ture.[2] Defendants assert that "the Courts have yet to address the inequities and legal deficiencies involved in an employment agreement which encompasses no term and/or an employment at will clause and a non-competition agreement."

[18] To illustrate the potential inequities, defendants present the following exam-ple. An employer who has executed an employment agreement which contains no term and a non-competition agreement can fire the employee without cause at any time. However, the employee is restricted from any participation in his established career for two years within a limited geographic area. In the most severe circum-stances, an employer may enter into such an agreement with an employee one day, terminate the employee the following day, without cause, and thereafter, restrict the employee from participating in his profession.

[19] The inequities illustrated through defendants' example are not present in this case. Here, the defendants were employed by Cellular One as successful sales rep-resentatives for three and one half years.[3] Throughout their employment, Cellular One periodically requested the defendants and all sales representatives to execute employment agreements. These agreements were at will employment contracts con-taining noncompetition agreements. Defendants signed these agreements as a con-dition of their continued employment. Defendants now complain, after successful careers with Cellular One, that such agreements potentially establish great inequi-ties which must be addressed by this Court.

[20] After reviewing the extensive history of noncompetition agreements in Lou-isiana, we conclude that the Louisiana legislature has adequately addressed the equi-ties and inequities of such agreements. After dealing with this issue for many years, the legislature amended La.R.S. 23:921 in 1989, and expanded the use of noncom-petition agreements in Louisiana. While subsection (A) reflects the strong public policy against noncompetition agreements, the legislature made it clear, in subsec-tion (C), that "any person" may enter into such a contract with their employer pro-vided they follow the specific guidelines. The legislature has already addressed the policy considerations raised by defendants. Therefore, we are compelled to follow the unambiguous language of the statute which allows "any person", including an at will employee, to enter into a noncompetition agreement.

[21] Furthermore, we do not find that the agreement is unenforceable for lack of cause. The Civil Code defines a contract as "an agreement by two or more parties

---

2. Defendants cite *Orion Broadcasting, Inc. v. Forsythe,* 477 F.Supp. 198 (W.D.Kentucky 1979). In *Orion,* the court relied on principles of mutuality in determining that noncompetition agreements are unenforceable in at will employment situations when the employee is fired. *Id.* at 201. How-ever, the court went on to note that had Ms. Forsythe, an at will employee, voluntarily severed her employment, the noncompetition agreement would have been enforceable against her. *Id.*

3. Boyd was employed from May 17, 1989, through December of 1993. Lemoine was employed from April 20, 1989, through December of 1993.

whereby obligations are created, modified, or extinguished." La.Civ.Code art. 1906. No obligation can exist without a lawful cause, which is defined as "the reason why a party obligates himself." La.Civ.Code arts. 1966–67. The defendants signed the agreements as a condition of continued employment. Employment was the valid cause of the contract.

[22] For these reasons, we reject defendants' argument that the noncompetition agreement is unenforceable because of a lack of mutuality or insufficient cause.

Duress

[23] In assignment of error two, defendants assert that the trial court erred in failing to find that the agreement was vitiated by economic duress. Defendants argue that the threat of termination constituted economic duress.

[24] However, defendants were at will employees subject to termination at any time, for any reason. The threat of doing a lawful act does not constitute duress. La.Civ.Code art. 1962. Thus, the threat of termination, an act which Cellular One had a legal right to do, cannot constitute duress. *See Allied Bruce Terminix Company, Inc. v. Guillory,* 94-319 (La.App. 3rd Cir. 11/2/94), 649 So.2d 652; *Litigation Reprographics and Support Services, Inc. v. Scott,* 599 So.2d 922, 923 (La.App. 4th Cir.1992). Accordingly, we conclude that this assignment of error is without merit.

Stipulated Damages

[25] In assignment of error three defendants assert that injunctive relief was inappropriate and that the only remedy available to plaintiff was collection of stipulated damages.

[26] In the contract, defendants agreed to forfeit noncompetition payments upon breach of the agreement. Defendants assert that the forfeiture of these payments is stipulated damages and is the exclusive remedy available to Cellular One. Defendants contend that according to La.Civ.Code art. 2007, when stipulated damages are provided for in a contract, no other remedy is available.

[27] Even assuming that the forfeiture of the noncompetition payments constitutes stipulated damages, this case falls under a specific statute, La.R.S. 23:921(G). Subsection (G) specifies that failure of an employee to perform a noncompetition agreement entitles the employer to recover damages and "IN ADDITION, upon proof of the obligor's [employee's] failure to perform, and without the necessity of proving irreparable injury, a court of competent jurisdiction shall order injunctive relief enforcing the terms of the agreement." (Emphasis added.) After reviewing this statute, we conclude that injunctive relief was an appropriate additional remedy available to Cellular One.

[. . . .]

[28] For these reasons, we conclude that the trial court properly enjoined defendants from soliciting Cellular One customers.

Conclusion

[29] For the foregoing reasons, we affirm the judgment of the trial court issuing the preliminary injunction against defendants. Costs of this appeal are assessed against defendants.

[30] AFFIRMED.

[31] SHORTESS, J., dissents with reasons.

SHORTESS, J., dissenting.

[32] I do not agree with the result in this case. I would find this noncompetition agreement unenforceable because it lacks mutuality of obligation and because consent was vitiated by economic duress.

[33] The only noncompetition agreement signed by the parties which arguably contained any mutual benefit was the initial one, which was signed in consideration of initial employment. They did not gain anything by signing new more onerous agreements — they were allowed to hold onto what they already had. Plaintiff did not give up anything at all in consideration for a new agreement. In these economic times, continued employment is not sufficient cause for a noncompetition agreement. It is economic blackmail.

[34] The law of Louisiana never favored noncompetition agreements. The legislative permission to engage in voluntary noncompetition agreements that contain mutual benefit and sacrifice for the parties is permissible. Limited permission to make such a contract, however, does not abrogate the strong public policy against contracts which prohibit an employee from competing with a former employer. The basic premise underlying the prohibition stems from the fundamental right of individuals to seek success in our free-enterprise society. *Hawthorn, Waymouth & Carroll v. Johnson,* 611 So.2d 645, 656 (La.App. 1st Cir.1992) (Shortess, J., dissenting); *Winston v. Bourgeois, Bennett, Thokey & Hickey,* 432 So.2d 936 (La.App. 4th Cir.1983). This also is consistent with the policy of at will employment in this state.

[35] I respectfully dissent.

Questions

1. Paragraph 7: Why do you think the court starts with an express reference to "a strong public policy"? Could the court want to establish the foundations of the Louisiana Civil Code articles and statutes to which it is about to refer? If so, why?

2. Paragraph 13: How do these sentences relate to the questions above? Can you reconcile the statement of the court in this paragraph with the court's statement in paragraph 20?

3. Paragraphs 12–19: How do you understand the defendant's argument that the non-competition agreement lacks mutuality? Mutuality of what?

4. Paragraph 20: On the basis of the public policy the court referred to in paragraph 7, was the court justified in giving a broad meaning to the statutory words "any person"? Did the court create law or did it merely apply the law and its reason or *ratio*?

5. Paragraph 24: The court cites Louisiana Civil Code article 1962. Do you agree with the statement that "the threat of termination [was] an act which Cellular One had a legal right to do"? Read Louisiana Civil Code article 1962, 2nd paragraph. What does it mean that an act can be "lawful in appearance only" and thus constitute duress?

Nikola P. Vekic
v.
Dragutin Popich, Mary A. Popich & Helen Harris Popich

Supreme Court of Louisiana
October 18, 2017
236 So.3d 526

GENOVESE, Justice.

[. . . .]

Weimer, J., concurring in part and dissenting in part.

[1] I agree with my learned colleagues that this dispute is governed by the "unique and troublesome" agreement confected between these parties. [. . . .] This agreement has defied being pigeonholed with even the parties sometimes offering different analyses. [. . . .] Whether the agreement is a disguised credit sale, a lease, or something else, it would be fair to say the agreement is *sui generis*.

[. . . .]

Dr. Albert Lagraize
v.
Rachele Basler, Derrick Riley and People Speak, L.L.C.

Court of Appeal of Louisiana
Fifth Circuit
September 9, 2020
304 So.3d 102

MOLAISON, J.

[. . . .]

[1] The existence or nonexistence of a contract is a question of fact. [. . . .] The determination of the existence of a contract is a finding of fact, not to be disturbed unless clearly wrong. [. . . .] Under Louisiana law, the formation of a valid and enforceable contract requires capacity, consent, a certain object, and a lawful cause. [. . . .] The court must find there was a meeting of the minds of the parties to constitute the requirement of consent. [. . . .] Courts are obliged to give legal effect to contracts according to the intent of the parties. La. C.C. art. 2045. Parole evidence may be used to prove a vice of consent. La. C.C. art. 1848.

[. . . .]

[2] [. . . .] While the "loan agreements" are confusing documents, [. . .] it is clear that each party [. . .] consented to repaying the funds loaned for the down payments [. . .]. [. . . .]

[. . . .]

See also *Davis v. Humble Oil & Refining Company*, 283 So.2d 783 (La.App. 1 Cir. 1973), *John Jay Esthetic Salon, Inc. v. Woods*, 377 So.2d 1363 (La.App. 4 Cir. 1979), *Louisiana Smoked Products v. Savoie's Sausage and Food Products*, Inc., 696 So.2d 1373 (La. 1997), *Mark A. Gravel Properties, LLC v. Eddies' BBQ, LLC*, 139 So.3d 653 (La.App. 3 Cir. 2014), *Lafleur v. Law Offices of Anthony G. Buzbee*, P.C., 960 So.2d 105 (La.App. 1 Cir. 2007), *CDI Corporation v. Hough*, 9 So.3d 282 (La.App. 1 Cir. 2009), *Law Enforcement District of Jefferson Parish v. Mapp Construction, LLC*, 296 So.3d 1260 (La.App. 5 Cir. 2020).

Comparative Law Perspective

— Civil Law —

Alex Weill & François Terré, *Droit Civil: Les Obligations*

n° 36 at 41, n° 465 at 538, & n° 469 at 540-41 (3d ed. 1980)

Unilateral v. Synallagmatic Contracts: *Exceptio non Adimpleti Contractus*

36. Why the distinction matters. — [. . . .] In synallagmatic contracts, the obligations created at the charge of each of the parties serve reciprocally as the cause of each other. The notion of cause is altogether different in unilateral contracts. And this notion [**cause**] has considerable repercussions, not only in the formation of the contract, but also in its execution, when one of the parties does not execute his obligations, as we will see when we study the exception *non adimpleti contractus* (infra n°s 465 et seq.). [. . . .]

465. — **Principle.** — In principle, performances promised by the contracting parties must be executed simultaneously. [**For example**,] the buyer must pay the price at the same time at which he takes delivery of the thing. [. . . .]

It results from this principle that, if one of the contracting parties does not execute his performance at the moment at which he should, the other can himself refuse to execute [**his performance**] and can oppose to the demand of his fellow contracting party the exception *non adimpleti contractus*. In this fashion he does justice to himself. But he does so only in a provisional manner, for the exception *non adimpleti contractus* (or the exception of non-execution) leads only to the adjournment [**to a later date**] of the execution of the obligations, not to their disappearance.

469. — **Origin of the exception** *non adimpleti contractus*. [. . . .]

The exception [. . .] was created by the canonists and post-glossators for synallagmatic contracts. Considerations of a moral order, which inspired the former [**the canonists**], justified, in their eyes, the application in such cases of the principle *non servanti fidem non est fides servanda* . . . [1]

In a bilateral contract neither one of the parties can demand its fulfillment if it is not shown that he himself has fulfilled it or offered to fulfill it, unless his obligation is subject to a term.

---

1. Roughly translated: "He who is not ready to observe good faith is not accorded good faith."

Alain Levasseur, *Comparative Law of Contracts*
at 13–35 (2008)

Juridical Acts

Many civil law jurisdictions make a distinction between <u>juridical acts</u> and <u>juridical facts</u>. This distinction, made on the basis of the source of an obligation, has been elaborated mostly by civil law scholars, or doctrine. [. . . .]

The essence of the difference between juridical acts and juridical facts consists in the following: a <u>juridical act</u> is the expression of a <u>person's will</u> manifested with the intention to create specific legal effects by entering willingly into a bond of law. On the other hand, a <u>juridical fact</u> is an <u>event</u>, devoid of human will, which, when it occurs, brings about the existence of an obligation creative of legal effects. A typical illustration of a <u>juridical act</u> is a "<u>contract</u>" [. . .].

A tort, or delict in civil law terms, would be an example of a juridical fact. [. . . .]

The common law does not know this concept of 'juridical act.' [. . . .]

Institutes of Justinian, Book III, Title XXII "De Consensu Obligatione"

> Obligations are formed by the mere consent of the parties in the contracts of sale. [. . . .] An obligation is, in these cases, said to be made by the mere consent of the parties, because there is no necessity for any writing [. . .] the mere consent of those between whom the transaction is carried on suffices. [. . . .]

Fr. Civ. C. 1804 (revised in 2016)

Article 1101: A contract is a convention whereby one or more parties bind themselves towards one or more other parties, to give, to do or not to do something.

Article 1134 § 1: Conventions legally entered into have the effect of law for the parties [. . .].

C.C.Q. (Québec Civil Code)

Article 1378: A contract is an agreement of wills by which one or several persons oblige themselves to one or several other persons to perform a prestation [. . .].

Bilateral Contracts and Unilateral Contracts

Fr. Civ. C. 1804 (revised in 2016)

Art. 1102: A contract is synallagmatic or bilateral when the parties obligate themselves reciprocally towards each other.

Art. 1103: It is unilateral when one or more parties are bound towards one or more parties without any reciprocal obligation on the part of the latter parties.

See La. Civ. C. articles 1907–1908.

C.C.Q. (Québec Civil Code)

Art. 1380: A contract is synallagmatic, or bilateral when the parties obligate themselves reciprocally, each to the other, so that the obligation of one party is correlative to the obligation of the other.

When one party obligates himself to the other without any obligation on the part of the latter, the contract is unilateral.

Onerous Contracts and Gratuitous Contracts

Fr. Civ. C. 1804 (revised in 2016)

Art. 1105: A contract is gratuitous when one party intends to provide an advantage to the other without receiving an advantage in return.

Art. 1106: A contract is onerous when each of the parties expects to receive from the other an advantage in exchange for the advantage she herself provides.

See La. Civ. C. articles 1909–1910.

C.C.Q. (Québec)

Art. 1381: A contract is onerous when each party obtains an advantage in return for his obligation.

When one party obligates himself to the other for the benefit of the latter without obtaining any advantage in return, the contract is gratuitous.

— Common Law —

English Law

William Blackstone, *Commentaries on the Laws of England*, (1765–1769); Book II, Ch. XXX, Of Title by Gift, Grant, and Contract.

> IX. A contract, which usually conveys an interest merely in action, is thus defined: "an agreement, upon sufficient consideration, to do or not to do a particular thing." From which definition there arise three points to be contemplated in all contracts; 1. The *agreement*: 2. The *consideration*: and 3. The *thing* to be done or omitted, or the different species of contracts.
>
> *First* then it is an *agreement*, a mutual bargain or convention; and therefore there must at least be two contracting parties of sufficient ability to make a contract; [. . .].

G.H. Treitel, Q.C., *The Law of Contract*, Seventh Edition, Stevens & Sons, 1987. (Reproduced with permission of the Licensor through PLSclear.)

> A contract is an agreement giving rise to obligations which are enforced or recognized by law. The factor which distinguishes contractual from other legal obligations is that they are based on the agreement of the contracting parties [. . .] the law of contract is concerned with the circumstances in which agreements are legally binding. [. . . .]

United States Law

Restatement, 2d of Contracts (1981)

§ 1. Contract Defined.

A contract is a promise or a set of promises for the breach of which the law gives a remedy, or the performance of which the law in some way recognizes as a duty.

§ 3. Agreement Defined; Bargain Defined.

An agreement is a manifestation of mutual assent on the part of two or more persons. A bargain is an agreement to exchange promises or to exchange a promise for a performance or to exchange performances.

UCC

§ 1-201 (3): "Agreement," as distinguished from "contract," means the bargain of the parties in fact, as found in their language or inferred from other circumstances, including course of performance, course of dealing, or usage of trade as provided in Section 1-303.

§ 1-201 (12): "Contract," as distinguished from "agreement," means the total legal obligation that results from the parties' agreement as determined by [the Uniform Commercial Code] as supplemented by any other applicable laws.

Bilateral Contracts and Unilateral Contracts

Restatement, 2d of Contracts (1981)

§ 45. Option Contract Created by Part Performance or Tender

(1) Where an offeror invites an offeree to accept by rendering a performance and does not invite a promissory acceptance, an option contract is created when the offeree tenders or begins the invited performance or tenders a beginning of it.

(2) The offeror's duty of performance under any option contract so created is conditional on completion or tender of the invited performance in accordance with the terms of the offer.

Comment: a. [. . . .] Such an offer has often been referred to as an "offer for a unilateral contract." Typical illustrations are found in offers of rewards or prizes and in non-commercial arrangements among relatives and friends.

Onerous Contracts and Gratuitous Contracts

William Blackstone, *Commentaries on the Laws of England*

[G]ifts are always gratuitous, grants are upon some consideration or equivalent; [. . .]. A true and proper gift or grant is always accompanied with delivery of possession, and takes effect immediately: as if A. gives to B. 100L, or a flock of sheep, and puts him in possession of them directly, it is then a gift executed in the donee; [. . .]. But if the gift does not take effect, by delivery of immediate possession, it is then not properly a gift, but a contract; and this a man cannot be compelled to perform, but upon good and sufficient consideration. [. . . .]

I. Sale, or exchange, is a transmutation of property from one man to another, in consideration of some price or recompense in value: for there is no sale without a recompense: there must be quid pro quo.

Restatement, 2d of Contracts (1981)

§ 86. Promise for Benefit Received

(1) A promise made in recognition of a benefit previously received by the promisor from the promisee is binding to the extent necessary to prevent injustice.

(2) A promise is not binding under Subsection (1)

    (a) if the promisee conferred the benefit as a gift or for other reasons the promisor has not been unjustly enriched; or

    (b) to the extent that its value is disproportionate to the benefit.

§ 90. Promise Reasonably Inducing Action or Forbearance

(1) A promise which the promisor should reasonably expect to induce action or forbearance on the part of the promisee or a third person and which does induce such action or forbearance is binding if injustice can be avoided only by enforcement of the promise. The remedy granted for breach may be limited as justice requires.

Chapter 2

Requisites to the Formation of a Valid Agreement

Section I — Capacity to Contract

Louisiana Sources of Law

Louisiana Civil Code

Art. 1918. General statement of capacity.[1]

All persons have capacity to contract, except unemancipated minors, interdicts, and persons deprived of reason at the time of contracting. (Acts 1984, No. 331, §1, eff. Jan. 1, 1985.)

Art. 1920. Right to require confirmation or rescission of the contract.

Immediately after discovering the incapacity, a party, who at the time of contracting was ignorant of the incapacity of the other party, may require from that party, if the incapacity has ceased, or from the legal representative if it has not, that the contract be confirmed or rescinded. (Acts 1984, No. 331, §1, eff. Jan. 1, 1985.)

Art. 1921. Rescission of contract for incapacity.

Upon rescission of a contract on the ground of incapacity, each party or his legal representative shall restore to the other what he has received thereunder. When restoration is impossible or impracticable, the court may award compensation to the party to whom restoration cannot be made. (Acts 1984, No. 331, §1, eff. Jan. 1, 1985.)

Art. 1922. Fully emancipated minor.

A fully emancipated minor has full contractual capacity. (Acts 1984, No. 331, §1, eff. Jan. 1, 1985.)

Art. 1923. Incapacity of unemancipated minor; exceptions.

A contract by an unemancipated minor may be rescinded on grounds of incapacity except when made for the purpose of providing the minor with something

---

1. Articles 1919, 1924 and 1926 have not been reproduced.

necessary for his support or education, or for a purpose related to his business. (Acts 1984, No. 331, § 1, eff. Jan. 1, 1985.)

Art. 1925. Noninterdicted person deprived of reason; protection of innocent contracting party by onerous title.

A noninterdicted person, who was deprived of reason at the time of contracting, may obtain rescission of an onerous contract upon the ground of incapacity only upon showing that the other party knew or should have known that person's incapacity. (Acts 1984, No. 331, § 1, eff. Jan. 1, 1985.)

Doctrine

Louisiana Law of Conventional Obligations, A Précis

Sections 1 to 2.2.1

The concept of "capacity," in its legal sense, must be distinguished, first, from the concept of "personality" and, second, from the notions of "authority or power."

"Personality," in the sense of the civil Code, is the ability to hold rights and owe obligations. Personality is therefore proper to "persons," be they natural persons or juridical persons, i.e. legal entities, because upon birth (and even conception) or incorporation, persons are automatically holders of a "patrimony." "Patrimony" can be described as the sum total of the rights and obligations of a monetary value vested in the person. LSA-C.C. Arts. 25 and 26 clearly identify this concept of "personality" as concerns natural persons. [....]

<u>Natural personality</u> vests in any natural person the legal ability to hold rights and owe obligations as is stated in **LSA-C.C. Art. 27: "All natural persons enjoy general legal capacity to have rights and duties."** [....]

[**A**] distinction is made between "incapacity to enjoy" and "incapacity to exercise" a right.

As regards the notions of "authority or power," they are related to the concept of "Representation" as this concept is described in LSA-C.C. Arts 2985 and 2986. [....]

There exists an incapacity of enjoyment when a person is deprived of the ability to "enjoy" a particular right. **For example, under LSA-C.C. Art. 941, "A successor shall be declared unworthy if he is convicted of a crime involving the intentional killing, or attempted killing, of the decedent or is judicially determined to have participated in the intentional, unjustified killing, or attempted killing, of the decedent. An action to declare a successor unworthy shall be brought in the succession proceedings of the decedent.**

An executive pardon or pardon by operation of law does not affect the unworthiness of a successor." [....]

[I]ncapacities of enjoyment are always, and can only be, special, restricted, limited in scope, because they amount to depriving a "person" of a necessary component of her "personality" which is the ability to be a holder of all rights under the law as from conception or birth. [. . . .]

Incapacities of exercise are much more common than incapacities of enjoyment, so much so that the concept of "incapacity" is used, in general, to refer to incapacities of exercise. [. . . .]

For example, under LSA-C.C. Art. 28, **"A natural person who has reached majority has capacity to make all sorts of juridical acts, unless otherwise provided by legislation."** [. . . .]

Under LSA-C.C. Art. 395: **"A full interdict lacks capacity to make a juridical act. A limited interdict lacks capacity to make a juridical act pertaining to the property or aspects of personal care that the judgment of limited interdiction places under the authority of his curator, except as provided in Article 1482 or in the judgment of limited interdiction."** [. . . .]

As regards "minors," LSA-C.C. Art. 1919 lays down the general rule that a contract entered into by **"a person without legal capacity is relatively null and may be rescinded."** [. . . .]

LSA-C.C. Art. 1923 states that **"A contract by an unemancipated minor may be rescinded on the grounds of incapacity except when made for the purpose of providing the minor with something necessary for his support or education, or for a purpose related to his business."**

Case

Fidelity Financial Services, Inc.
v.
Edward E. McCoy

Court of Appeal of Louisiana
First Circuit
October 6, 1980
392 So.2d 118

CHIASSON, Judge.

[1] This is a suit on a promissory note defended successfully by the defendant-appellee, Edward E. McCoy, on the ground of insanity. The trial court also ordered the cancellation of a chattel mortgage which was granted by the defendant at the same time.

[2] Plaintiff-appellant, Fidelity Financial Services, Inc., appeals the judgment contending [, **among other things,**] that the lower court erred [. . .] in finding that the defendant had proven the incapacity of the defendant to have existed at the time the contract was made [. . .].

[3] The record establishes that Mr. McCoy was discharged from the U.S. Army in 1960 because of his mental condition and that he has been receiving psychiatric treatment and medication at the V.A. hospitals in New Orleans and Gulfport ever since. His wife, his son, and two other persons from the community testified that they knew and that it was commonly known in the community that defendant was mentally incapable of handling his affairs. Mr. McCoy was interdicted after the filing of this suit by judgment rendered on April 19, 1979.

[4] Plaintiff's only witness was its vice president and general manager who negotiated the loan. He testified that a car dealer, for whom he was then handling automobile financing, brought Mr. McCoy to his office to secure a loan for the purchase of a 1973 Chevrolet Malibu automobile; that he obtained all the information contained in the chattel mortgage (another car, a tractor, a T.V., and other household goods) from Mr. McCoy; that the whole transaction took about forty-five minutes; and that Mr. McCoy appeared to be normal.

[5] To annul the contract the law requires that the defendant proves he was incapacitated at the time of the contract (La.C.C. art. 1788(2)) and that it was generally known by those who saw and conversed with him or it was known to the person who contracted with him (La.C.C. art. 1788(3)). Louisiana Civil Code Article 402 has basically the same requirements.

[6] The trial court found that the defendant had established his mental incapacity; that his condition was common knowledge in the community; and that the incapacity existed at the time of the contract.

[7] Plaintiff's first specification of error is no more than an attack upon the court's evaluation of the credibility of the witnesses. We hold that the determination of the trial court is based upon a reasonable evaluation of credibility and of the evidence presented. Our review of the entire record convinces us that the trial court was correct in its findings. Arceneaux v. Domingue, 365 So.2d 1330 (La.1978).

[8] Plaintiff argues in brief it had carried its burden of proof to establish that the contract was made during a lucid interval. La.C.C. art. 1788(9). Mr. Brown was plaintiff's only witness, although the record establishes that the car dealer was present during the loan preparation and he was available as a witness. Failure of plaintiff to call this witness raises a presumption that his testimony would be unfavorable to plaintiff. Morgan v. Matlack, Inc., 366 So.2d 1071 (La.App. 1st Cir. 1979) and cases cited therein.

[9] But even without that presumption, we find that the plaintiff failed to carry its burden of proof. Although plaintiff claims it obtained all the information about the other items in the chattel mortgage from Mr. McCoy, its representative testified that he had consulted a "credit bureau" and obtained all of the financial transactions of Mr. McCoy. The record therefore is not clear as to what information Mr. McCoy furnished and what information was furnished by a third person.

[....]

Questions

1. Paragraph 3: What does it mean "commonly known in the community"? Why should this common knowledge be imputed to the plaintiff, Fidelity Financial Services, Inc.? Is there any difference between the phrases "common knowledge" and "it was generally known by those who saw and conversed with him"? Whose burden should it be to establish when something "was commonly known in the community"? Notice that the Court references, on the one hand, "two other persons from the community" and, on the other hand, that "plaintiff's only witness was its vice president. . . ." Wasn't the latter a member of that same community? So, did one more witness tilt the scale in favor of defendant?

2. Paragraph 9: Is it possible that the Court had its mind made up as regards the defendant's incapacity?

See also *Skannal v. Bamburg,* 33 So.3d 227 (La.App. 2 Cir. 2010), *infra,* and *McDonald v. Orr Motors of Little Rock, Inc.,* 256 So.3d 1132 (La.App. 2 Cir. 2018).

Section II — Consent

Louisiana Sources of Law
Louisiana Civil Code[1]

Art. 1927. Consent.

A contract is formed by the consent of the parties established through offer and acceptance.

Unless the law prescribes a certain formality for the intended contract, offer and acceptance may be made orally, in writing, or by action or inaction that under the circumstances is clearly indicative of consent.

Unless otherwise specified in the offer, there need not be conformity between the manner in which the offer is made and the manner in which the acceptance is made. (Acts 1984, No. 331, §1, eff. Jan. 1, 1985.)

Art. 1928. Irrevocable offer.

An offer that specifies a period of time for acceptance is irrevocable during that time.

When the offeror manifests an intent to give the offeree a delay within which to accept, without specifying a time, the offer is irrevocable for a reasonable time. (Acts 1984, No. 331, §1, eff. Jan. 1, 1985.)

---

1. Articles 1933, 1936, 1946, and 1947 have not been reproduced.

Art. 1929. Expiration of irrevocable offer for lack of acceptance.

An irrevocable offer expires if not accepted within the time prescribed in the preceding Article. (Acts 1984, No. 331, §1, eff. Jan. 1, 1985.)

Art. 1930. Revocable offer.

An offer not irrevocable under Civil Code Article 1928 may be revoked before it is accepted. (Acts 1984, No. 331, §1, eff. Jan. 1, 1985.)

Art. 1931. Expiration of revocable offer.

A revocable offer expires if not accepted within a reasonable time. (Acts 1984, No. 331, §1, eff. Jan. 1, 1985.)

Art. 1932. Expiration of offer by death or incapacity of either party.

An offer expires by the death or incapacity of the offeror or the offeree before it has been accepted. (Acts 1984, No. 331, §1, eff. Jan. 1, 1985.)

Art. 1934. Time when acceptance of an irrevocable offer is effective.

An acceptance of an irrevocable offer is effective when received by the offeror. (Acts 1984, No. 331, §1, eff. Jan. 1, 1985.)

Art. 1935. Time when acceptance of a revocable offer is effective.

Unless otherwise specified by the offer or the law, an acceptance of a revocable offer, made in a manner and by a medium suggested by the offer or in a reasonable manner and by a reasonable medium, is effective when transmitted by the offeree. (Acts 1984, No. 331, §1, eff. Jan. 1, 1985.)

Art. 1937. Time when revocation is effective.

A revocation of a revocable offer is effective when received by the offeree prior to acceptance. (Acts 1984, No. 331, §1, eff. Jan. 1, 1985.)

Art. 1938. Reception of revocation, rejection, or acceptance.

A written revocation, rejection, or acceptance is received when it comes into the possession of the addressee or of a person authorized by him to receive it, or when it is deposited in a place the addressee has indicated as the place for this or similar communications to be deposited for him. (Acts 1984, No. 331, §1, eff. Jan. 1, 1985.)

Art. 1939. Acceptance by performance.

When an offeror invites an offeree to accept by performance and, according to usage or the nature or the terms of the contract, it is contemplated that the performance will be completed if commenced, a contract is formed when the offeree begins the requested performance. (Acts 1984, No. 331, §1, eff. Jan. 1, 1985.)

Art. 1940. Acceptance only by completed performance.

When, according to usage or the nature of the contract, or its own terms, an offer made to a particular offeree can be accepted only by rendering a completed performance, the offeror cannot revoke the offer, once the offeree has begun to perform, for the reasonable time necessary to complete the performance. The offeree, however, is not bound to complete the performance he has begun.

The offeror's duty of performance is conditional on completion or tender of the requested performance. (Acts 1984, No. 331, §1, eff. Jan. 1, 1985.)

Art. 1941. Notice of commencement of performance.

When commencement of the performance either constitutes acceptance or makes the offer irrevocable, the offeree must give prompt notice of that commencement unless the offeror knows or should know that the offeree has begun to perform. An offeree who fails to give the notice is liable for damages. (Acts 1984, No. 331, §1, eff. Jan. 1, 1985.)

Art. 1942. Acceptance by silence.

When, because of special circumstances, the offeree's silence leads the offeror reasonably to believe that a contract has been formed, the offer is deemed accepted. (Acts 1984, No. 331, §1, eff. Jan. 1, 1985.)

Art. 1943. Acceptance not in accordance with offer.

An acceptance not in accordance with the terms of the offer is deemed to be a counteroffer. (Acts 1984, No. 331, §1, eff. Jan. 1, 1985.)

Art. 1944. Offer of reward made to the public.

An offer of a reward made to the public is binding upon the offeror even if the one who performs the requested act does not know of the offer. (Acts 1984, No. 331, §1, eff. Jan. 1, 1985.)

Art. 1945. Revocation of an offer of reward made to the public.

An offer of reward made to the public may be revoked before completion of the requested act, provided the revocation is made by the same or an equally effective means as the offer. (Acts 1984, No. 331, §1, eff. Jan. 1, 1985.)

Doctrine

Louisiana Law of Conventional Obligations, A Précis
Sections 3.1.1 to 3.1.2

An offer, in its legal and technical sense, is a firm and definite proposal to enter into a contract, of a <u>kind</u> agreed upon, under pre-arranged precise conditions. Such a definite proposal or offer, when accepted, will bring about the existence of the very contract the parties intended to enter into.

The offer must be <u>precise</u> in the sense that it must contain the "essential" component parts of the nominate or innominate contract to be entered into upon the offeree's acceptance. The civil Code does provide a few examples of the contents of a precise offer to enter into a nominate contract. We can find one in **LSA-C.C. Art.**

2439 which defines a sale as "**a contract whereby a person transfers ownership of a thing to another for a price in money.**

The thing, the price, and the consent of the parties are requirements for the perfection of a sale." [. . . .]

If an offer does not refer precisely to the "essential" component parts of the contract the parties wish to enter into, it will not qualify as an offer. [. . . .]

Under the second paragraph of LSA-C.C. Art. 1927, "**A contract is formed by the consent of the parties established through offer and acceptance.**

Unless the law prescribes a certain formality for the intended contract, offer and acceptance may be made orally, in writing, or by action or inaction that under the circumstances is clearly indicative of consent. Unless otherwise specified in the offer, there need not be conformity between the manner in which the offer is made and the manner in which the acceptance is made." [. . . .]

As regards the addressee of an offer, there are at least three possibilities: either the offer is made to a particular person, or to several persons or to the public at large. [. . . .]

If the offeror has specified a period of time for the acceptance then, according to **LSA-C.C. Art. 1928,** such "**An offer that specifies a period of time for acceptance is irrevocable during that time.**" The same Article adds that "**When the offeror manifests an intent to give the offeree a delay within which to accept, without specifying a time, the offer is irrevocable for a reasonable time.**" It follows logically that "**An irrevocable offer expires if not accepted within the time prescribed in the preceding Article.**" (LSA-C.C. Art. 1929).

In the event an offer is not irrevocable (under LSA-C.C. Art. 1928) then, under **LSA-C.C. Art. 1930** it "**may be revoked before it is accepted.**" Furthermore, "**A revocable offer expires if not accepted within a reasonable time.**" (LSA-C.C. Art. 1931). [. . . .]

LSA-C.C. Art. 1943 states that "**An acceptance not in accordance with the terms of the offer is deemed to be a counteroffer.**" Reading this Article *a contrario*, it is easy to conclude that an acceptance, pure and simple, is one which meets the terms of the offer in such a way that the "**consent of the parties has been established.**" (**LSA-C.C. Art. 1927**).

Such an acceptance is not complete and ceases to be pure and simple, or firm, whenever the offeree expresses some reservations of substance or suggests some conditions to his acceptance. There will be, then, a "counteroffer" by the offeree as stated in LSA-C.C. Art. 1943. [. . . .]

As regards the form of the acceptance, the civil Code contemplates different situations. As a general principle, "**Unless the law prescribes a certain formality for the intended contract, offer and acceptance may be made orally, in writing, or by action or inaction that under the circumstances is clearly indicative of consent.**" (LSA-C.C. Art. 1927). Likewise "**A medium or a manner of acceptance is reasonable** if it is the one used in making the offer or one customary in similar transactions at the time and place the offer is received, unless circumstances known to the offeree indicate otherwise." (LSA-C.C. Art. 1936). In other words, like an offer, an acceptance can be *express* or *tacit*. [. . . .]

Acceptance by silence, as a matter of principle, does not meet the requirements of a binding acceptance: silence is not acceptance. However, **"When, because of special circumstances, the offeree's silence leads the offeror reasonably to believe that a contract has been formed, the offer is deemed accepted."** (LSA-C.C. Art. 1942). [. . . .]

[W]hen an offer is irrevocable, it cannot be revoked by the offeror once the offeree has become aware of the offer. The offeror is bound unilaterally to keep his offer open. However, this same irrevocable offer represents a great benefit for the offeror since the **"acceptance of an irrevocable offer is effective when received by the offeror."** (LSA-C.C. Art. 1934). [. . . .]

On the other hand, when an offer is revocable, the offeree is given control over the moment of formation of the contract. As **LSA-C.C. Art. 1935** states: **"Unless otherwise specified by the offer or the law, an acceptance of a revocable offer, made in a manner and by a medium suggested by the offer or in a reasonable manner and by a reasonable medium, is effective when transmitted by the offeree."**

Cases

Ever-Tite Roofing Corporation
v.
G. T. Green et ux.

Court of Appeal of Louisiana
Second Circuit
November 2, 1955
83 So.2d 449

AYRES, Judge.

[1] This is an action for damages allegedly sustained by plaintiff as the result of the breach by the defendants of a written contract for the re-roofing of defendants' residence. Defendants denied that their written proposal or offer was ever accepted by plaintiff in the manner stipulated therein for its acceptance, and hence contended no contract was ever entered into. The trial court sustained defendants' defense and rejected plaintiff's demands and dismissed its suit at its costs. From the judgment thus rendered and signed, plaintiff appealed.

[2] Defendants executed and signed an instrument June 10, 1953, for the purpose of obtaining the services of plaintiff in re-roofing their residence situated in Webster Parish, Louisiana. The document set out in detail the work to be done and the price therefor to be paid in monthly installments. This instrument was likewise signed

by plaintiff's sale representative, who, however, was without authority to accept the contract for and on behalf of the plaintiff. This alleged contract contained these provisions:

> 'This agreement shall become binding only upon written acceptance hereof, by the principal or authorized officer of the Contractor, *or upon commencing performance of the work.* This contract is Not Subject to Cancellation. It is understood and agreed that this contract is payable at office of Ever-Tite Roofing Corporation, 5203 Telephone, Houston, Texas. It is understood and agreed that this Contract provides for attorney's fees and in no case less than ten per cent attorney's fees in the event same is placed in the hands of an attorney for collecting or collected through any court, and further provides for accelerated maturity for failure to pay any installment of principal or interest thereon when due.

> 'This written agreement is the only and entire contract covering the subject matter hereof and no other representations have been made unto Owner except these herein contained. No guarantee on repair work, partial roof jobs, or paint jobs.' (Emphasis supplied.)

[3] Inasmuch as this work was to be performed entirely on credit, it was necessary for plaintiff to obtain credit reports and approval from the lending institution which was to finance said contract. With this procedure defendants were more or less familiar and knew their credit rating would have to be checked and a report made. On receipt of the proposed contract in plaintiff's office on the day following its execution, plaintiff requested a credit report, which was made after investigation and which was received in due course and submitted by plaintiff to the lending agency. Additional information was requested by this institution, which was likewise in due course transmitted to the institution, which then gave its approval.

[4] The day immediately following this approval, which was either June 18 or 19, 1953, plaintiff engaged its workmen and two trucks, loaded the trucks with the necessary roofing materials and proceeded from Shreveport to defendants' residence for the purpose of doing the work and performing the services allegedly contracted for the defendants. Upon their arrival at defendants' residence, the workmen found others in the performance of the work which plaintiff had contracted to do. Defendants notified plaintiff's workmen that the work had been contracted to other parties two days before and forbade them to do the work.

[5] Formal acceptance of the contract was not made under the signature and approval of an agent of plaintiff. It was, however, the intention of plaintiff to accept the contract by commencing the work, which was one of the ways provided for in the instrument for its acceptance, as will be shown by reference to the extract from the contract quoted hereinabove. Prior to this time, however, defendants had determined on a course of abrogating the agreement and engaged other workmen without notice thereof to plaintiff.

issue

[6] The basis of the judgment appealed was that defendants had timely notified plaintiff before 'commencing performance of work'. The trial court held that notice to plaintiff's workmen upon their arrival with the materials that defendants did not desire them to commence the actual work was sufficient and timely to signify their intention to withdraw from the contract. With this conclusion we find ourselves unable to agree.

[7] Defendants' attempt to justify their delay in thus notifying plaintiff for the reason they did not know where or how to contact plaintiff is without merit. The contract itself, a copy of which was left with them, conspicuously displayed plaintiff's name, address and telephone number. Be that as it may, defendants at no time, from June 10, 1953, until plaintiff's workmen arrived for the purpose of commencing the work, notified or attempted to notify plaintiff of their intention to abrogate, terminate or cancel the contract.

RS

[8] Defendants evidently knew this work was to be processed through plaintiff's Shreveport office. The record discloses no unreasonable delay on plaintiff's part in receiving, processing or accepting the contract or in commencing the work contracted to be done. No time limit was specified in the contract within which it was to be accepted or within which the work was to be begun. It was nevertheless understood between the parties that some delay would ensue before the acceptance of the contract and the commencement of the work, due to the necessity of compliance with the requirements relative to financing the job through a lending agency. The evidence as referred to hereinabove shows that plaintiff proceeded with due diligence.

RS

Concl.

[9] The general rule of law is that an offer proposed may be withdrawn before its acceptance and that no obligation is incurred thereby. This is, however, not without exceptions. For instance, Restatement of the Law of Contracts stated:

'(1) The power to create a contract by acceptance of an offer terminates at the time specified in the offer, or, if no time is specified, at the end of a reasonable time.

'What is a reasonable time is a question of fact depending on the nature of the contract proposed, the usages of business and other circumstances of the case which the offeree at the time of his acceptance either knows or has reason to know.'

[10] These principles are recognized in the Civil Code. LSA-C.C. Art. 1800 provides that an offer is incomplete as a contract until its acceptance and that before its acceptance the offer may be withdrawn. However, this general rule is modified by the provisions of LSA-C.C. Arts. 1801, 1802, 1804 and 1809, which read as follows:

'Art. 1801. The party proposing shall be presumed to continue in the intention, which his proposal expressed, if, on receiving the unqualified assent of him to whom the proposition is made, he do not signify the change of his intention.

'Art. 1802. He is bound by his proposition, and the signification of his dissent will be of no avail, *if the proposition be made in terms, which evince a design to give the other party the right of concluding the contract by his assent; and if that assent be given within such time as the situation of the parties and the nature of the contract shall prove that it was the intention of the proposer to allow.* * * *

'Art. 1804. The acceptance needs (need) not be made by the same act, or in point of time, immediately after the proposition; *if made at any time before the person who offers or promises has changed his mind, or may reasonably be presumed to have done so, it is sufficient.* * * *

'Art. 1809. The obligation of a contract not being complete, until the acceptance, or in cases where it is implied by law, until the circumstances, which raise such implication, are known to the party proposing; *he may therefore revoke his offer or proposition before such acceptance, but not without allowing such reasonable time as from the terms of his offer he has given, or from the circumstances of the case he may be supposed to have intended to give to the party, to communicate his determination.'* (Emphasis supplied.)

[11] Therefore, since the contract did not specify the time within which it was to be accepted or within which the work was to have been commenced, a reasonable time must be allowed therefor in accordance with the facts and circumstances and the evident intention of the parties. A reasonable time is contemplated where no time is expressed. What is a reasonable time depends more or less upon the circumstances surrounding each particular case. The delays to process defendants' application were not unusual. The contract was accepted by plaintiff by the commencement of the performance of the work contracted to be done. This commencement began with the loading of the trucks with the necessary materials in Shreveport and transporting such materials and the workmen to defendants' residence. Actual commencement or performance of the work therefore began before any notice of dissent by defendants was given plaintiff. The proposition and its acceptance thus became a completed contract.

[12] By their aforesaid acts defendants breached the contract. They employed others to do the work contracted to be done by plaintiff and forbade plaintiff's workmen to engage upon that undertaking. By this breach defendants are legally bound to respond to plaintiff in damages. [. . . .]

[13] Plaintiff expended the sum of $85.37 in loading the trucks in Shreveport with materials and in transporting them to the site of defendants' residence in Webster Parish and in unloading them on their return, and for wages for the workmen for the time consumed. Plaintiff's Shreveport manager testified that the expected profit on this job was $226. None of this evidence is controverted or contradicted in any manner.

[. . . .]

Questions

1. Review in your mind the phase of the negotiations between the two parties here involved. Are the two parties on an equal level when entering the negotiations? Is one more knowledgeable than the other and, if so, could that have an impact on the inner meaning of the stipulations in the contract?

2. Paragraph 2: Can you identify the kinds of obligations created by the contract? For example, do you see any condition or term? Any conjunctive or alternative obligations? Any obligation to give, to do, or not to do? Can you explain why it might be important for each party to have a good understanding of the legal effects attached to these different kinds of obligations? Who is the offeror under the facts of this case? Should it matter? You will read the word "acceptance" in the first line of the quoted contract: does that necessarily mean the offeree is "the principal or authorized officer of the Contractor"? Shouldn't the offeror, in the legal sense of the term, be the party most knowledgeable in the matter?

3. Paragraph 3: Do you see any term and/or condition? If you answered in the affirmative, what kind? Do you see any impact on the revocability or not of the offer? When plaintiff "requested a credit report," was it the performance of a separate obligation totally unrelated to the roofing contract, or was it the performance of one obligation as a component part of a conjunctive obligation? Would it matter? Was it a form of commencing performance of the work as stated in the quoted contract? Would it matter?

4. Paragraphs 4–5: Look back at paragraph 3 and the question above regarding the existence (or not) of an alternative obligation. Was there only one method of acceptance or more than one? In the latter case, who had the choice of the method of acceptance? Had the method of acceptance chosen by the plaintiff been agreed to by the Greens? Was that method of acceptance an acceptance of a revocable offer or an irrevocable offer? Does it matter if the Greens are the offerors? Consider carefully the words of the last sentence of paragraph 5: "defendants had determined on a course of abrogating the agreement. . . ." Is the court saying there was an agreement, a contract, in existence? Does the court mean that the contract had been formed, perfected before the trucks reached the Greens' residence? If so, have the Greens breached a contract by which they had been bound sometime before they received what they thought was the plaintiff/contractor's acceptance? Would this mean that the Greens' offer was revocable and, therefore, accepted when the trucks were dispatched, unbeknownst to the Greens?

5. Paragraph 8: How important is the court's statement beginning with "No time limit . . ."? *See* Questions 1–3 above. Again, how important are the court's statements beginning with "No time limit . . ."? Can you now qualify the offer as revocable or irrevocable? How determinant, here, is the concept of term?

6. Paragraph 11: There was acceptance by beginning of performance consisting in "the loading of the trucks" and this acceptance occurred "before any notice of dissent by defendants was given plaintiff." The consequence is that "the proposition and its acceptance thus became a completed contract." What about checking on the Greens' credit and obtaining credit reports? Wasn't the performance of this obligation by the contractor the acceptance of the Greens' offer as being the first and necessary component part of a conjunctive obligation made up of two parts, of which dispatching the trucks was the second part?

The National Co., Inc., d/b/a The National Roofing and Siding Co.
v.
Fano J. Navarro and Anna Mae Navarro

Court of Appeal of Louisiana
Fourth Circuit
February 4, 1963
149 So.2d 648

REGAN, Judge.

[1] Plaintiff, The National Company, Inc., conducting its business under the trade name of The National Roofing and Siding Company, instituted this suit against the defendants, Fano J. and Anna Mae Navarro, endeavoring to recover the sum of $1,061.40, representing liquidated damages and expenses incurred by plaintiff as a result of defendants' alleged breach of a contract which involved the application of siding to their residence in Nashville Avenue in the City of New Orleans.

[2] The defendants answered and asserted that the document sued on was not a contract, but was merely a 'proposal', which plaintiff's agents had informed them could be withdrawn at any time by defendants prior to commencement of the work. In the alternative, they insisted that if the document is construed to be an offer, then it was withdrawn before the plaintiff accepted; therefore, there was no contract.

[3] Secondly, in the alternative, the defendants contend that the offer never ripeded [*sic*] into a contract since plaintiff failed to procure a loan for defendants to finance the work, which, under the terms of the document, it was required to do.

[4] Then, assuming the position of plaintiffs in reconvention, they maintain that the contractor was indebted to them for $100, the amount deposited when the offer was signed.

[....]

[5] The record reveals that at 7 p.m. on October 18, 1961, the defendants signed a document wherein they offered to pay plaintiff $3,488.00 to apply aluminum

siding to their residence and deposited $100 on account thereof. Prior to the signing thereof, Milton Loeb, one of plaintiff's salesmen, had visited the defendants at their residence on two previous occasions to sell the job.

[....]

[6] The offer, submitted on a form prepared by the plaintiff contractor, provided in part:

> 'This contract is binding, subject only to acceptance by an executive of the NATIONAL ROOFING & SIDING CO., who reserves the right to reject it without liability on its part.'

[7] The following day, Anna Mae Navarro testified that her brother was informed that the First Homestead would not loan the full amount which was required to pay for the renovation. This fact is disputed by plaintiff's representative, who testified that the First Homestead had approved the loan. In passing, it is of interest to merely note that neither plaintiff nor defendants adduced proof to support their respective contentions concerning the financing, when proof thereof was readily available to either.

[8] In any event, at 11 a.m. on October 19th, Miss Navarro telephoned the plaintiff's salesman, Loeb, to inform him they had changed their minds and desired to cancel the 'contract'. He was not in the office when she called so she left a message with one of plaintiff's employees to the effect that the offer was being withdrawn. Loeb obviously received the message for he returned the call at 2 p.m. Miss Navarro repeated that the offer was being withdrawn; however, Loeb advised her she could not cancel since the materials were on delivery to her home and the contract had been accepted.

[9] At 4 p.m. that same day, a small truck containing a few materials for use in application of the siding arrived at the defendants' home, and Miss Navarro refused delivery thereof.

[10] The following day, October 20th, the defendants received a letter from plaintiff informing them that the offer or contract had been accepted. This letter was postmarked 7 p.m., October 19th, which was eight hours after Miss Navarro initially notified defendant that she was withdrawing the offer.

[11] Predicated on the foregoing evidence, the trial judge reasoned that the offer never materialized into a contract because the defendants revoked their offer before the plaintiff accepted it.

[12] Counsel for plaintiff contends that the trial court erred in concluding as a matter of law that the defendants had a right to revoke their offer.

[13] The general rule relating to offer and acceptance is stated in LSA-C.C. Art. 1800, which reads:

> 'The contract, consisting of a proposition and the consent to it, the agreement is incomplete until the acceptance of the person to whom it is

proposed. If he, who proposes, should before that consent is given, change his intention on the subject, the concurrence of the two wills is wanting, and there is no contract.'

[14] While counsel for plaintiff recognizes the general rule, he insists that the offer submitted by the defendants was irrevocable until the offeree was afforded a reasonable time to accept, and points to the rationale of LSA-C.C. Art. 1809 in support thereof, which reads:

> 'The obligation of a contract not being complete, until the acceptance, or in cases where it is implied by law, until the circumstances, which raise such implication, are known to the party proposing; he may therefore revoke his offer or proposition before such acceptance, but not without allowing such reasonable time as from the terms of his offer he has given, *or from the circumstances of the case he may be supposed to have intended to give to the party, to communicate his determination.*' (Emphasis added.)

[15] This article obviously places a limitation upon the general rule that offers may be revoked any time before they are accepted, and is applicable where the offeror has expressly stated an intention to make the offer irrevocable within a stipulated period of time or where the offer is of such a nature that from its very terminology the implication is present that the offeror intended to make it irrevocable for a reasonable period of time, within which it would be necessary for the offeree to signify his acceptance.

[16] Plaintiff argues that since it was incumbent upon it to arrange for financing the work by obtaining a loan for the defendants, the offer was necessarily irrevocable until it had the opportunity to negotiate such a loan. He points out that the defendants attempted to cancel before a reasonable time elapsed within which to arrange financing.

[17] To support his argument he relies upon the rationale emanating from Ever-Tite Roofing Corp. v. Green.[1] In that case, the defendant submitted an offer to have the roof on his home replaced. This offer contained a provision to the effect that either notification by the plaintiff or the commencement of the job would constitute an acceptance. Several days after the offer was submitted, the plaintiff delivered the materials to the job preparatory to commencing performance, and discovered that the defendants had employed another contractor to perform the work.

[18] In the *Roofing* case, the defendant at no time withdrew his offer before the offeree accepted by tendering performance in conformity with the very terms of the agreement; therefore, there was a meeting of the minds when the materials were delivered and defendant's refusal of performance constituted a breach of the contract.

[19] In discussing whether the offeree had accepted timely the court stated:

---

1. La.App., 83 So.2d 449.

'Therefore, since the contract did not specify the time within which it was to be accepted or within which the work was to have been commenced, a reasonable time must be allowed therefor in accordance with the facts and circumstances and the evident intention of the parties. A reasonable time is contemplated where no time is expressed. What is a reasonable time depends more or less upon the circumstances surrounding each particular case. The delays to process defendants' application (which involved obtaining financing) were not unusual. * * *' (Parenthetical material added.)

[20] Plaintiff argues that the ratio decidendi of this case is to the effect that when an offer to perform work, which is contingent upon arranging a loan to pay for the job, is submitted to the offeree, an implication arises that the offeror intended to make his offer irrevocable until the offeree has had a reasonable time within which to negotiate a loan for the offeror.

[21] We find no merit in this contention. A case is authority for only what it actually decides, therefore we think the case holds that an offer Which has not been revoked is not revoked by implication when it is accepted within a reasonable time. The above quoted discussion was included in the opinion to counter the argument that the offer had been impliedly revoked since it was not timely accepted, because the court quoted and underlined LSA-C.C. Art. 1804, as follows:

'Art. 1804. The acceptance needs (need) not be made by the same act, or in point of time, immediately after the proposition; *if made at any time before the person who offers or promises has changed his mind, or may reasonably be presumed to have done so, it is sufficient.* * * *' (Emphasis supplied.)

[22] Thus the court refused to supply an implication of revocation when the offer contemplated arranging financing and the arrangement was completed within a week.

[23] We are of the opinion that the matter now before us is not controlled by the rationale of LSA-C.C. Art. 1809 since we do not think that the necessity for procuring financing is a circumstance from which we can supply the implication that the offeror intended to make his offer irrevocable for any period of time before acceptance.

[24] Article 1809 initially appears in the Civil Code of 1825 as Article 1803, and the language was not changed when it was incorporated in the Revised Civil Code of 1870. The article provoked our curiosity, and it was of interest to learn that it has no counterpart in the Code of 1808 or the Code Napoleon. Therefore, the redactors of the Code of 1825 were apparently influenced by Toullier's commentaries. In 6 Toullier, Book 3, Title III, Note 30, the French commentator, after discussing the general principles of offer and acceptance states that there is one case where the offer is irrevocable before the acceptance, which is when the one who had made the offer has set a determined time for the acceptance, either expressly or tacitly.

[25] Toullier cites the following example of the offer which tacitly is irrevocable for a reasonable period:

'For example, in consenting to contract with titles by the agency of third parties, who never had the mandate, I am tacitly obliged to wait for the time suitable or sufficient for ratification. I am engaged conditionally. The contract never existed if T does not ratify. If he ratifies, the ratification goes back to the date of contract, the same as the contract accomplishes a retro-active effect to the day on which the engagement has been contracted. * * * This is why the laws say that ratifications has a retroactive effect. * * *

'But in what time should T ratify in order to prevent a revocation? As soon as he would have knowledge of the contract.'

[26] Applying this example to the instant case, an executive of plaintiff who was authorized to accept the offer was apprised thereof but had not accepted before the defendants revoked. Therefore, the revocation was timely.

[27] A more modern version of the above example might exist when a custom prevails in the building trade to the effect that a subcontractor's bid to a general contractor, in the absence of a provision to the contrary, may be considered irre-vocable after it has been used in preparation of the general contractor's bid to the owner, and has been accepted by the owner prior to the attempted revocation by the subcontractor.

[28] The fact that financing was necessary before the work would be performed does not raise the implication that the offer was irrevocable until the offeree had time to procure financing. Had the offer been timely accepted and ripened into a contract, then the ability to procure financing would merely operate as a suspensive condition to suspend performance until the loan was procured, or negate the con-tract if financing was not available.

[29] Since the plaintiff failed to establish that the offeror impliedly intended to make the offer irrevocable until the defendant was afforded a reasonable opportu-nity to accept, we are of the opinion that, in conformity with the provision of Art. 1800, the offeror was entitled to withdraw his offer at any time before it was accepted, and the record conclusively establishes that it was withdrawn timely.

[. . . .]

Questions

1. Paragraphs 1–11: Was the document a mere proposal to enter into a contract later on, or was it an offer? If an offer, who was the offeror? Focus on para-graph 3. What would be your legal analysis and description? For whose benefit would it be? Here, as in the previous *Ever-Tite Roofing* case, was there any conjunctive obligation?

2. Paragraph 6: Who is the offeror here? What do you think of the first words of the excerpt: "This contract . . . acceptance"? In the introduction to the quote, we read the word "offer," but in the first quoted line, we read the phrase, "this contract." Which one is correct? What legal label would you attach to the phrase, "who reserves the right to reject it without liability"?

3. Paragraph 7: Was the so-called offer revocable or irrevocable? How was the acceptance to be given? Again, as per paragraph 11, who is the offeror and who is the offeree? Does it make sense?

4. Paragraph 17–20: How similar to, or different from, the *Ever-Tite Roofing* case are the facts and circumstances of this case? Focus on paragraph 20. How beneficial to the plaintiff is the *ratio decidendi* of the *Ever-Tite Roofing* case?

5. Paragraph 28: After you have read the Louisiana Civil Code articles on conditions (*see* La. Civ. Code arts. 1767–1776), what critical evaluation do you make of this statement by the court?

Leland H. Johnson
v.
Capital City Ford Company, Inc.

Court of Appeal of Louisiana
First Circuit
December 30, 1955
85 So.2d 75

TATE, Judge.

[1] This suit is for specific performance of a contractual obligation allegedly resulting from plaintiff's acceptance by act (without negotiation or other discussion) of an alleged offer made by newspaper advertisement to the public by defendant automobile dealer. Defendant dealer appeals from judgment of the District Court decreeing specific performance of the alleged obligation; plaintiff Johnson answered this appeal, praying for amendment of the decree.

[*proc. history*]

[2] The basic question involved is whether the newspaper advertisement in question constituted an 'offer' rather than merely an invitation to bargain. If the former, a secondary question for determination is whether any act or omission of plaintiff-acceptor-obligee waived his right to require the defendant-offeror-obligor to perform the obligation resulting from plaintiff's acceptance. If as contended by defendant the newspaper advertisement was merely an invitation to bargain, then of course defendant's objection to parol evidence as enlarging or varying a certain written contract in evidence was well founded; if, on the other hand, this newspaper advertisement constituted a continuing offer which the plaintiff accepted by such purchase, and thus as the District Court found, created a contemporaneous collateral obligation of defendant to do something in addition to the obligation embodied in the written contract, then of course such evidence was correctly admitted to prove the existence of this independent, collateral contract.

[*issue*]

[3] When the 1955 models were about to appear, defendant Ford dealer in an effort to dispose of an excessive supply of 1954 models (which were shortly to be outmoded by the 1955 Ford cars) engaged in an intensive advertising campaign by newspaper and radio, the first day's advertisement concerning which is self-explanatory:

'TWO FOR ONE. . . . For two weeks BUY A NEW '54 FORD NOW TRADE EVEN FOR A '55 FORD

Don't Wait-Buy a 1954 Ford now, when the 1955 models come out we'll trade even for your '54. You pay only sales tax and license fee. Your '55 Ford will be the same model, same body style, accessory group, etc. A sure thing for you — a gamble for us, but we'll take it. Hurry, though, this offer good only for the remainder of September.

The 1954 car must be returned with only normal wear and tear. Physical damage, such as dented fenders, torn upholstery, etc. must be charged to owner or repaired at owner's expense. No convertibles or Skyliners on this basis.

CAPITAL CITY FORD CO., INC. 1849 North St.-Dial 31721

A GREAT WAY TO SAY, 'WE TRADE YOUR WAY"

[. . . .]

[4] Plaintiff and his wife testified that in response to these newspaper and radio advertisements they went to defendant's premises on September 21st, 1954. Johnson there purchased a 1954 Ford Sedan with certain accessories; he received an allowance of $974.05 for his old car and paid boot of $1,660 in cash. Johnson executed an act of sale for the 1954 Ford purchased by him, which we will discuss below.

[5] In December, 1954, when the 1955 models were advertised, Johnson appeared at defendant's premises and requested its compliance with the newspaper offer accepted by him. At this time or soon after, Johnson or his attorney was informed that defendant's newspaper advertisements were not intended as offers, but merely as invitations to come in and bargain; that by delivery of the 1954 automobile for the consideration expressed in the executed act of sale, defendant felt it had fully complied with all obligations whatsoever to Johnson.

[6] Detailed discussion of the evidence is unnecessary, for we do not find the District Court's determination of the facts manifestly erroneous, supported as it is by sworn evidence and certain corroborating circumstances. For instance, defendant urges with considerable effect that Johnson's behavior in buying the 1954 Ford without any discussion whatsoever as to his right per the newspaper offer to exchange said model for a 1955 model, is not the usual and normal course of behavior.

[7] But what we are here concerned with is not the *usual* course of behavior, but what transpired on *this* particular occasion.

[8] Basically, when defendant urges that because *usually* and *ordinarily* a person would not behave as Johnson and his wife stated they did, in assuming without further discussion that they acquired the right to a 1955 model Ford upon their purchase of a 1954 Ford per the newspaper offer, defendant is attacking the credibility of the testimony of plaintiff and his wife, which issue the District Court with

opportunity to see and hear personally all witnesses has resolved in favor of the plaintiff. Because plaintiff's conduct was improbable does not require a holding that it did not occur as testified under oath by himself and wife and believed by the District Court, for human beings do improbable things at times.[1]

[. . . .]

[9] The advertisement denotes itself as an 'offer', the wording to a reader denotes a bona fide bargain offer, and it was certain and definite enough to constitute a legal offer, Articles 1779, 1886, LSA-Civil Code.

ruling

[10] If the automobile dealer had stated on September 17th to a specific customer: 'If you buy a 1954 automobile before October 1st, I will let you trade it even (except for license and sales tax) for a 1955 model of exactly the same model, body style, and accessories when these 1955 models come out in 60–90 days, providing you return the 1954 model with only normal wear and tear'; undoubtedly the offeree's purchase of a 1954 model before October 1st would have been a binding acceptance (without any further discussion) of the dealer's offer, creating in the dealer an obligation to furnish a 1955 model when available according to the terms of the offer.

Example

[11] In light of the legal principles above summarized, this same offer communicated to the general public by a newspaper advertisement has the same legal effect when accepted according to its terms. In the absence of any limitation in the offer solely to cash purchases, we do not feel the situation differs because plaintiff purchased the 1954 Ford by trade-in with cash boot, instead of by cash only.

Reasoning

[12] If appellant-dealer argues it did not actually intend this newspaper advertisement to constitute an offer, and therefore the advertisement did not do so, nevertheless 'The rights of plaintiff and defendant are to be tested by the actual legal consequences flowing from a sale [contract] made under the particular advertisement * * *. These consequences cannot be altered or checked because the agent of the company may have had an erroneous belief as to what the advertisement as written meant, or what it would legally convey. The advertisement controlled the rights and obligations of the parties', Maginnis v. Union Oil Company, 47 La.Ann. 1489 at pages 1495–1496, 18 So. 459, at page 461. In the Maginnis case, the purchaser's

---

1. Although E. J. Daigle, the salesman involved testified that he must have discussed the lack of application of the advertised offer, because he invariably did so, plaintiff and his wife testified unequivocally and were believed by the District Court, that no discussion whatsoever occurred concerning the right to acquire a 1955 model automobile when plaintiff purchased his 1954 Ford. And it is to be noted that by implication defendant's president admitted that the salesmen did not invariably discuss with customers whether they were interested in the bargain deal expressed by the advertisements, see testimony of J. Theron Brown, President of Defendant at Tr-16: 'Q. Well, now, was it the policy of you and your employees or your salesmen, or anyone connection with these deals, to discuss that with these people and inform them when they bought a 1954 Ford that they might not be entitled to a 1955 Ford?' 'A. *If they came in and referred to the ad* and for the purpose of discussing that particular proposition offered in the paper, yes. But that, as I understand it, was not mentioned in this particular case by the purchaser.' (Italics ours.)

acceptance at public sale of the vendor's advertised offer to sell was *held* to require conveyance not only of the land and buildings, but also of the valuable machinery therein (immovable by destination), although it was the *explicit intention* of the vendor in preparing the advertisement not to include this machinery in the offer.

[13] It must further be remembered that the words of the advertisement were of course chosen by defendant-dealer, and if any ambiguity exists as to their meaning, it must be resolved against their composer; LSA-Civil Code, Article 1957; Crummer v. Nuveen, 7 Cir., 147 F.2d 3, 157 A.L.R. 739, holding a newspaper advertisement to purchase bonds at par was an offer, rather than a mere proposal to negotiate, being complete and definite, and if ambiguous, construed against offerer.

[14] Defendant urges that plaintiff was under some duty when he appeared on defendant's premises in response to the advertised offer to indicate that he was accepting same, since defendant indicates it would have offered less trade-in value for plaintiff's old car had it known that this was a '1954–1955' deal as advertised.[3] Assuming defendant would not have allowed as much trade-in if it had thought this was a '1954–1955' deal, if there was a burden on anyone, it would seem to be upon defendant to inform the plaintiff of any conditions or modifications of the apparently bona fide offer contained in the advertisement. 'The party proposing shall be presumed to continue in the intention, which his proposal expressed, if, on receiving the unqualified assent of him to whom the proposition is made, he do not signify the change of his intention', Article 1801, LSA-Civil Code. See Loyd Mercantile Co. v. Long, 123 La. 777, 49 So. 521; Comment, (now Professor) Pascal, 'Duration and Revocability of an Offer', 1 La.Law Review 182. 'But if the doubt or obscurity [in the agreement] arise for the want of necessary explanation which one of the parties ought to have given, or from any other negligence or fault of his, the construction most favorable to the other party shall be adopted, whether he be obligor or obligee', Article 1958, LSA-C.C.

[15] Thus we have here what is denoted both in the common law and in our civil code as a unilateral contract, or an obligation created by an offer accepted by an act: the offer or exchange of a promise for an act. The execution of the act (purchase of the 1954 Ford) by plaintiff in compliance with terms of defendant's published offer constituted plaintiff's acceptance of said offer, creating defendant's duty or obligation to furnish a 1955 Ford according to the terms of the published offer. See Comment, 'The Unilateral Contract in Civil Law and in Louisiana' 16 Tulane Law Review 456.

[16] Plaintiff's *motive* in purchasing the 1954 Ford was not only to receive it for the trade-in and boot given, but also to receive the right to exchange without substantial charge this 1954 Ford for a 1955 model when the latter became available. The *cause* or consideration for what plaintiff gave the dealer, included not only the 1954

---

3. Plaintiff's answer is that he would not have bought the 1954 Ford car from defendant, even at that trade-in value given him by defendant, unless he thought he was to receive the 1955 car in exchange therefor without extra cost (except for sales tax and license) when such later model was available.

Ford but also the right to exchange it for a 1955 Ford according to the terms of the published offer. See Civil Code Article 1896: 'By the *cause* of the contract, in this section, is meant the consideration or motive for making it.'; also (Professor) Smith, 'A Refresher Course in *Cause*', 12 La.Law Review 2.

[17] The executed sale which plaintiff signed when he purchased the 1954 Ford contained within a paragraph printed at the bottom of the page:

> 'The front and back of this order comprise the entire agreement pertaining to this purchase and no other agreement of any kind, verbal understanding or promise whatsoever, will be recognized.'

[handwritten: Facts of Sale agreement]

[18] Defendant urges with considerable force that applying the rule stated in United Engineering Co. v. Durbin, La.App. 1 Cir., 68 So.2d 614, the alleged independent collateral agreement based on acceptance of the newspaper offer was so closely related to the contract for purchase of a 1954 Ford as to be 'naturally and normally' included in the written contract; therefore that parole proof should have been barred; or, that, in any event plaintiff waived his right to enforce this obligation as against defendant in view of the quoted clause.

[19] However, as pointed out above, in the present case defendant was under a duty to notify plaintiff of any modification of the newspaper offer. The omission in this contract is construed against defendant. In a very similar situation, construing a similar clause, our Supreme Court held that acceptance of an advertised order completes the contract, which is not subject to further modification by either one of the parties without the consent of the other, Kodel Radio Corporation v. Shuler, 171 La. 468, 131 So. 462. Further, the terms of this proviso limit it as the 'entire agreement pertaining to *this purchase*', which indeed was a complete contract within itself; but this purchase-sale contract, complete within itself, was nevertheless also the acceptance of an offer, creating *another* and a separate obligation.

[handwritten: Reasoning]

[20] Acceptance of an offer may of course be made by silent deed as well as by word; consent may be implied from actions under the circumstances, as well as by expressed words; but such acceptance of, founded on such consent to, an offer nevertheless creates a valid contract, and the offerer is bound by the obligation previously offered by him in exchange for the act which the obligee has performed in response to the offer, LSA-Civil Code Articles 1802, 1811, 1816; Shreveport Traction Company v. Mulhaupt, 122 La. 667, 48 So. 144; Lowy v. Builliard, La.App. 1 Cir., 17 So.2d 855; Netterville v. Police Jury, 6 La.App. 512 (1 Cir.).

[21] The record reflects that plaintiff went to defendant's premises with the perhaps naive belief that the advertisement meant just what it said; that as subsequently blazoned by heavy black headlines in large advertisement, 'TWO FOR ONE . . . Til September 30th AND THERE'S NO CATCH IN IT' [. . .]; that *everyone* who bought a 1954 Ford during the 2-week period was ipso facto entitled to exchange it for a 1955 model when such were available, according to the dealer's offer. The published offer without qualification was that plaintiff's acceptance thereof by purchase of a 1954 model entitled him to receive a 1955 model in exchange, which implicitly no more

needed discussion or formalized warranty in acceptance than does the assumption of one purchasing a new car that it will be painted rather than naked steel.

[**22**] If defendant seriously argues that despite the plain wording of the advertised offer, defendant had absolutely no intention of making a bona fide offer but was merely intending to lure customers to defendant's sales lot, or that, if a bona fide offer, the routine signing of a form document by plaintiff amounted to a waiver of substantial property rights because of small print at the bottom, not called to his attention by defendant, it may be well to recall the expression of the Ohio Supreme Court in an almost identical factual situation as reported at Meyer v. Packard Cleveland Motor Co., 106 Ohio St. 328, 140 N.E. 118, at page 121, 28 A.L.R. 986, at page 991:

> 'There is entirely too much disregard of law and truth in the business, social, and political world of to-day. * * * It is time to hold men to their primary engagements to tell the truth and observe the law of common honesty and fair dealing.'

[. . . .]

LOTTINGER, Judge (dissents)

[**23**] [**After detailing the facts and opining that certain evidence should not have been admitted, Judge Lottinger discussed the legal effect of the content of the newspaper advertisement.**] I still feel that petitioner's case must fail as, under the greater weight of authority, the newspaper advertisement was not an offer but was merely an invitation to enter into negotiations for an agreement. The rule on this particular point is stated in Volume 1, Corbin on Contracts, Section 25, page 60, as follows:

> 'It is quite possible to make a definite and operative offer to buy or to sell goods by advertisement, in a newspaper, by a handbill, or on a placard in a store window. It is not customary to do this, however; and the presumption is the other way. Neither the advertiser nor the reader of his notice understands that the latter is employed to close the deal without further expression by the former. Such advertisements are understood to be mere requests to consider and examine and negotiate; and no one can reasonably regard them otherwise, unless the circumstances are exceptional and the words used are very plain and clear.

> 'On the other hand it is very common, where one desires to excite many people to action, to offer a reward for such action by general publication in some form. Some offers must be reasonably interpreted, according to their terms and the surrounding circumstances; but action in accordance with such interpretation will close a contract.'

[**24**] It is noted that Mr. Corbin, as well as the other writers on the subject, draw a distinction between advertisements to sell merchandise and advertisements for a reward. Advertisements announcing the terms of a prize contest fall into the same category as announcements of rewards because the characteristics of both require

that they be addressed to the general public by advertising. As offers of rewards and prizes must of necessity be made by advertisements, it is well settled that they can be withdrawn only in the same manner. Advertisements relating to the sale of merchandise do not have the same characteristics and, consequently, are governed by different legal rules.

[. . . .]

[25] Of course throughout the country there are cases pro and con on the subject. Some hold newspaper advertisements by their peculiar wording to constitute offers. Others hold the advertisements to be mere invitations. In Louisiana we have certain cases holding advertisements to be binding offers, however, these cases deal with contests for prizes and with auction sales. In Schreiner v. Weil Furniture Co., La.App., 68 So.2d 149, the Court held the advertisement to be a binding offer, however, this case dealt with an advertisement announcing the rules and prizes to be awarded in a contest. A similar holding was reached in Youngblood v. Daily and Weekly Signal Tribune, 15 La.App. 379, 131 So. 604, which dealt with a newspaper subscription contest. In Maginnis v. Union Oil Co., 47 La.Ann. 1489, 18 So. 459, the offer was to sell at auction to the last and highest bidder, under terms and conditions set forth in the advertisement. These particular situations are covered by their own particular rules and statutes, and are not similar to the particular situation which is before us. Actually the question presented in the instant case is res novo in Louisiana.

[26] As stated, the greater weight of authority in this country is to the effect that a newspaper advertisement of the nature presented in this case is not an offer, but merely an invitation for the customer to make an offer.

[27] For the reasons hereinabove assigned, I respectfully dissent from the majority.

Questions

NOTE: We call your attention to the fact that the phrases "collateral obligation" and "independent, collateral contract" (paragraph 2) do not exist in the Louisiana Civil Code. These are not civil law concepts.

1. Paragraph 2–3: After you have read the first sentence of paragraph 2, make a legal analysis of the excerpt from the newspaper reproduced in paragraph 3. The purpose of making your own legal analysis is for you to make up your own mind as to the nature of the excerpt, specifically whether it is an offer or an invitation to bargain and why. Since a "sale" could be the named contract you identify as a result of your analysis, read the code articles on the contract of sale, particularly Louisiana Civil Code articles 2439, 2448, 2456, 2464. Who, in this case, could be the offeror? Why does it matter if you identify a party as the offeror?

2. Paragraph 3: Identify the kinds of obligations and/or modalities of obligations hiding behind some of the words used in the excerpt. For example, what kind

of legal modality should be associated with the phrase "For two weeks"? What about "two for one"?

3. Paragraphs 7–8: The contrast between a "usual" course of behavior and "this particular occasion" illustrates the fundamental distinction between, on the one hand, an objective standard of behavior (or an *in abstracto* standard), the standard of the average person or *bonus paterfamilias* (usually, ordinarily, per the first line of paragraph 8) and, on the other hand, a particular-individual standard (an *in concreto* standard) (*see* the last sentence of paragraph 8). Which one of these two standards would better fit the form of the plaintiff's acceptance?

4. Paragraph 11: On what grounds does the court rely to state that this is an offer? What are some of the legal consequences of this characterization?

5. Paragraph 19: Can the court's statements be easily accepted in these circumstances, where we have a well-established, professional corporate entity dealing with an average, naive consumer couple? Is the Court formulating some policy in the place of the Louisiana legislature?

Warren D. Kent, Jr.
v. Sarah Ann Sullivan Hogan, Eddie Lee Hogan and Travis Kentrell Washington

Court of Appeal of Louisiana
First Circuit
October 29, 2004
897 So.2d 68

GUIDRY, J.

[. . . .]

Facts and Procedural Background

[1] In August 2001, defendants, Sarah and Eddie Hogan, listed a 2-1/2 acre tract of land located in Tangipahoa Parish, Louisiana for sale through their real estate agent, Darita Richardson. On December 10, 2001, plaintiff, Warren Kent, Jr., offered to purchase the land for $52,500. After the Hogans indicated they were receptive to the offer, it was reduced to writing in a document labeled "Agreement To Purchase or Sell" (sometimes referred to as the "offer"), and was signed by Kent that day. By its terms, the offer expired at 3:00 p.m. on December 11, 2001, and contained the following language regarding deadlines: "Time is of the essence and all deadlines are final except where modifications, changes, or extensions are made in writing and signed by all parties."

[2] Ms. Richardson scheduled a meeting for 2:00 p.m. on December 11 to present the Hogans with the written offer. When they failed to appear, she telephoned plaintiff's real estate agent, Nadine Lagarde, and asked if plaintiff would extend the offer. Ms. Lagarde contacted plaintiff, who agreed to a two-day extension.

[3] On December 12, Ms. Richardson prepared a document labeled "Addendum To Agreement To Purchase or Sell" (hereinafter the "Addendum") that referenced the original offer, stating it was to remain binding and irrevocable until 3:00 p.m. on December 13. That afternoon she conveyed the original offer, together with the "Addendum," to the Hogans, who signed both documents sometime before 9:00 a.m. on December 13. Thereafter, at the request of Ms. Richardson, Ms. Lagarde met Mr. Hogan outside a restaurant near his home to pick up the documents. She then brought the documents to plaintiff's office, where he signed the "Addendum" sometime before 11:00 a.m.

[4] Ms. Richardson picked up the two documents at Ms. Lagarde's office sometime after 3:00 p.m. on December 13, which was after the time for expiration provided in the "Addendum." Noticing that the Hogans had not dated or timed their signatures on the "Agreement to Purchase or Sell," she arranged to meet them later that afternoon to complete that information. Before leaving her office, she made copies of the documents. When the Hogans were given the "Agreement to Purchase or Sell" to date and time, one of them wrote the date and 4:48 p.m. on the document and refused to give it back to Ms. Richardson, because they had changed their minds about the sale.

[5] It is unclear when plaintiff was informed of this development. In any event, a closing date of December 21, 2001, was set, but the Hogans failed to appear on either that date or on subsequent dates set for closing the sale. [. . . .]

[6] On January 29, 2002, plaintiff filed the instant suit for specific performance of the "Agreement To Purchase or Sell," naming Sarah and Eddie Hogan as defendants. [. . . .] Following trial, the court rendered judgment in favor of plaintiff. The court concluded that, while the verbal extension of the offer was invalid because not in the requisite written form, the actions of the Hogans in signing the "Addendum" and "Agreement To Purchase or Sell" after the expiration of the original offer constituted a counteroffer to plaintiff. The court further concluded the counteroffer was accepted by plaintiff when he signed the "Addendum" on the morning of December 13, and that the acceptance was timely received (before 3:00 p.m. on December 13) by the Hogans when the signed documents came into the hands of Ms. Lagarde, who was acting as an assistant of Ms. Richardson, the Hogans' realtor. [. . . .]

[. . . .]

Discussion

[7] [D]efendants argue the trial court erred in concluding a contract to sell was formed between the parties. Specifically, they challenge the court's finding that the Hogans' untimely acceptance of the "Agreement to Purchase or Sell" on the morning of December 13, together with their signing of the "Addendum," constituted a counteroffer to sell the property to plaintiff.

[8] A contract to sell is formed by the consent of the parties established through offer and acceptance. La. C.C. art.1927. *See also* 1 La. Prac. Real Est. § 9:3 (2000). In

the instant case, La. C.C. art.1943 is pertinent because it provides that an acceptance of an offer that is not in accordance with the terms of the offer is deemed to be a counteroffer. The time limit named in plaintiff's original offer clearly was one of the terms of that offer. Thus, the trial court reasoned that, since the Hogans signed the "Addendum" purporting to change that particular term at the same time that they attempted to accept the original offer, their actions constituted a counteroffer because it was an acceptance not in accordance with the original offer. On appeal, defendants argue this interpretation of events "invent[ed] an intent of the parties regarding offer and acceptance that neither of them ever contemplated." However, we need not decide whether the trial court's conclusion was correct, because we do not believe a contract to sell was formed between the parties, even if the Hogans' actions are deemed to be a counteroffer to plaintiff.

[9] The acceptance of an irrevocable offer is effective only when it is received by the offeror within the time named in the offer. La. C.C. art. 1934 & Official Comment (b). The rationale for this requirement has been explained as follows:

> The reason for that rule is that, when the offer is irrevocable, it is the offeror who finds himself at a disadvantage. Indeed, he is bound by the law not to revoke the offer upon the sole declaration of his will, which leaves him, so to say, at the mercy of the offeree, who may speculate on the advantage of accepting or not while the offeror is bound for a time even though circumstances subsequent to the offer show that the contract would no longer be advantageous for him.
>
> * * *
>
> Though it is quite clear that a written acceptance is received when it comes to the hands of the offeror or is otherwise in his possession that is not the only manner in which the reception of an acceptance can occur. Thus, an acceptance is received when it comes into the possession of a person authorized by the offeror to receive it, or when it is deposited in a place the offeror has indicated as the place where communications of that kind are to be deposited for him. (Footnotes omitted). Saul Litvinoff, *Consent Revisited: Offer Acceptance Option Right of First Refusal and Contracts of Adhesion in the Revision of the Louisiana Law of Obligations*, 47 La.L.R. 699, 729 (1987).

[10] Thus, for plaintiff's acceptance of the purported counteroffer to be effective, resulting in a perfected contract to sell, it must have been received by the Hogans (offerors) or a person authorized to receive it for them within the time named in the purported counteroffer, which was no later than 3:00 p.m. on December 13.

[11] The record contains no specific evidence indicating the Hogans were notified of plaintiff's acceptance within that time. This may have been because the realtors believed the verbal extension of the original offer was valid, and continued to operate as though plaintiff was the offeror who must be given notice of acceptance. Regardless of the reason the Hogans were not given actual notice within the time named, the trial court believed the notice requirement was met when Ms. Lagarde

secured plaintiff's signature on the "Addendum." The court reasoned that, since Ms. Lagarde picked up the documents from Mr. Hogan earlier that day at the request of the Hogans' realtor, Ms. Richardson, her receipt of plaintiff's acceptance was as effective as if Ms. Richardson herself had received it.

[12] We disagree that Ms. Lagarde was a person authorized to receive notice of acceptance on behalf of the Hogans. No agency relationship existed between them because there was no agreement, explicit or implied, between Ms. Lagarde and the Hogans that authorized her to act for or represent them in any capacity with regard to their immovable property. See La. R.S. 9:3891(1). Further, although the trial court seemed to consider Ms. Lagarde to be a subagent of Ms. Richardson, she could not properly be considered as such because subagencies can be created only by written agreement. *See* La. R.S. 9:3898. Nor can she be deemed a dual agent of the parties for the same reason. *See* La. R.S. 9:3897A.

[13] The record reflects that Ms. Lagarde had very limited contact with the Hogans at the time in question. She agreed to Ms. Richardson's request to pick up the documents strictly for the latter's convenience, since Ms. Lagarde lived closer to the Hogans than Ms. Richardson did. Ms. Lagarde testified that, when she met Mr. Hogan, they merely introduced themselves and exchanged the documents, without any discussion of the proposed sale. Under these circumstances, the trial court erred in imputing Ms. Lagarde's knowledge of plaintiff's acceptance to the Hogans. Accordingly, since the record does not reflect that the Hogans were notified of or in possession of plaintiff's acceptance within the time named in the purported counteroffer, the acceptance was not effective and no contract of sale was formed between the parties. *See* La. C.C. art.1934.

Conclusion

[14] For the reasons given, the judgment of the trial court ordering specific performance in favor of plaintiff is reversed. [. . . .] All costs of this appeal are to be paid by appellee, Warren Kent, Jr.

[15] REVERSED AND RENDERED.

See also *Succession of Aurianne*, 53 So.2d 901 (La. 1951), *Breaux Brothers Construction Company v. Associated Contractors*, 77 So.2d 17 (La. 1954), *Pooler Building Materials, Inc. v. Hogan*, 244 So.2d 62 (La.App. 1 Cir. 1971), *Marine Chartering (Gulf) Ltd. v. Boland Machine & Manufacturing Co., Inc.*, 273 So. 2d 316 (La.App. 4 Cir. 1973), *Bank of America, N.A. v. Teryl Emery DDS, LLC*, 2016 WL 4086776 (M.D. La. 2016).

Questions

1. Paragraphs 1–6: What are your legal observations on this "listing" on the one hand, and this "offer to purchase" on the other hand? Although not mentioned in the Civil Code, could a listing be given a legal identity as a potential juridical act? What about the offer? Notice that the listing refers to the sale of a "determined or determinable thing," the 2½ acre tract of land, and

that the offer to purchase refers to a specific price — "thing" and "price" being the two essential component parts of a sale. In most instances, it is the seller who offers a thing for a price. The Civil Code, however, does not require that the price that will be the object of the buyer's obligation be set by the seller only (e.g., in an auction, the price is set by bidding buyers). All the Civil Code requires is that the price "be fixed by the parties." When the Hogans indicated they were receptive to the offer to purchase the land for $52,500, and when the agreement was reduced to writing, did the Hogans' acceptance of the price offered by Kent form a contract of sale of the land? Since, in a contract of sale, there is one offeror and one offeree, which one of the two parties in this case was the offeror? Who was the offeror in the opinion of the court? Was there a "contract of sale" or a "contract to purchase"? Are they different?

2. Paragraphs 1–6: What Civil Code label or contractual name would you give to Darita Richardson? To Nadine Lagarde?

3. Paragraphs 7–8, 10–13: What particular item in the contract was modified? Was that item of the essence of the contract that the court has characterized as a sale? Or was it rather a non-essential item, such as a modality or accessory item? Does the requirement in the contract that "changes or extensions" be made in writing modify the nature of an accessory or non-essential item?

4. Paragraph 9: Was the so-called "offer" revocable or irrevocable? Do the "deadlines" or "extensions" help in deciding one way or the other? In this section of the opinion, the court appears to refer to the Hogans as having made a "counteroffer to plaintiff"; who is more likely to make a counteroffer, the offeror or an offeree?

Comparative Law Perspective

Alain Levasseur, *Comparative Law of Contracts*
at 37–68 (2008)

— Civil Law —

Formation of Contracts, Offer and Acceptance

See La.Civ.C. articles 1927–1928.

Fr. Civ. C. 1804 (revised in 2016)

Art. 1108: Four requirements are essential for the validity of a convention:

— the consent of the party who binds herself. [. . . .]

C.C.Q. (Québec)

Art. 1388: An offer to contract is a proposal which contains all the essential of the proposed contract and in which the offeror signifies his willingness to be bound if it is accepted.

Art. 1389: An offer to contract derives from the person who initiates the contract or the person who determines its content or even, in certain cases, the person who presents the last essential element of the proposed contract.

When is an "Acceptance" an "Acceptance" in a legal sense?

See La. Civ. C. articles 1927, 1928, 1939, 1942, 1943.

C.C.Q. (Québec)

Art. 1393: An acceptance which does not correspond substantially to the offer or which is received by the offeror after the offer has lapsed does not constitute acceptance.

It may, however, constitute a new offer.

Meeting of the minds: revocable or irrevocable offer

See La. Civ. C. articles 1935-1937.

C.C.Q. (Québec)

Art. 1392: An offer lapses if no acceptance is received by the offeror before the expiry of the specified term or, where no term is specified, before the expiry of a reasonable time; it also lapses in respect of the offeree if he has rejected it.

— Common Law —

Formation of Contracts, Offer and Acceptance

Restatement, 2d of Contracts (1981)

§ 24. Offer Defined

An offer is the manifestation of willingness to enter into a bargain, so made as to justify another person in understanding that his assent to that bargain is invited and will conclude it.

§ 26. Preliminary Negotiations

A manifestation of willingness to enter into a bargain is not an offer if the person to whom it is addressed knows or has reason to know that the person making it does not intend to conclude a bargain until he has made a further manifestation of assent.

§ 39. Counter-offers

(1) A counter-offer is an offer made by an offeree to his offeror relating to the same matter as the original offer and proposing a substituted bargain differing from that proposed by the original offer.

E. Allan Farnsworth, *Contracts* (2d ed. 1990)

§ 3.3. Offer and Acceptance.

What is an "offer"? It can be defined as a manifestation to another of assent to enter into a contract if the other manifests assent in return by some action, often a promise but sometimes a performance. By making an offer, the offeror thus confers upon the offeree the power to create a contract. [. . . .] Offer, then, is the name given to a promise that is conditioned on some action by the promisee if the legal effect of the promisee's taking that action is to make the promisee enforceable. Empowerment of the offeree to make the offeror's promise enforceable is thus the essence of an offer. [. . . .]

UNIDROIT Principles of International Commercial Contracts (2016)

Art. 2.1.2: (Definition of offer): A proposal for concluding a contract constitutes an offer if it is sufficiently definite and indicates the intention of the offeror to be bound in case of acceptance.

When is an "Acceptance" an "Acceptance" in a legal sense?

G.H. Treitel, *The Law of Contract*, Seventh Edition, Stevens & Sons, 1987. (Reproduced with permission of the Licensor through PLSclear.)

Acceptance Defined

An acceptance is a final and unqualified expression of assent to the terms of an offer. The objective test of agreement applies to an acceptance no less than to an offer. On this test, a mere acknowledgment of an offer would not be an acceptance; nor is there an acceptance where a person who has received an offer to sell goods merely replies that it is his "intention to place an order. [. . . .]

(3) Acceptance by conduct

An offer may be accepted by conduct, e.g. by dispatching goods in response to an offer to buy [. . .]. Conduct will, however, only have this effect if the offeree did the act with the intention of accepting the offer. [. . . .]

(4) Acceptance must be unqualified

A communication may fail to take effect as an acceptance because it attempts to vary the terms of the offer.

Restatement, 2d of Contracts (1981)

§ 30. Form of Acceptance Invited

(1) An offer may invite or require acceptance to be made by an affirmative answer in words, or by performing or refraining from performing a specified act, or may empower the offeree to make a selection of terms in his acceptance.

(2) Unless otherwise indicated by the language or the circumstances, an offer invites acceptance in any manner and by any medium reasonable in the circumstances.

§ 32. Invitation of Promise or Performance

In case of doubt an offer is interpreted as inviting the offeree to accept either by promising to perform what the offer requests or by rendering the performance, as the offeree chooses.

E. Allan Farnsworth, *Contracts* (2d ed. 1990)

§ 3.3 Offer and Acceptance [. . . .] What is an acceptance? It can be defined as the action (promise or performance) by the offeree that creates a contract (i.e. makes the offeror's promise enforceable). Acceptance, then, is the name given to the offeree's action if the legal effect of that action is to make the offeror's promise enforceable.

UNIDROIT Principles of International Commercial Contracts (2016)

Art. 2.1.6 (Mode of acceptance)

(1) A statement made by or other conduct of the offeree indicating assent to an offer is an acceptance. Silence or inactivity does not in itself amount to acceptance.

(3) However, if, by virtue of the offer or as a result of practices which the parties have established between themselves or of usage, the offeree may indicate assent by performing an act without notice to the offeror, the acceptance is effective when the act is performed.

Art. 2.1.11 (Modified acceptance)

(1) A reply to an offer which purports to be an acceptance but contains additions, limitations or other modifications is a rejection of the offer and constitutes a counter-offer.

(2) However, a reply to an offer which purports to be an acceptance but contains additional or different terms which do not materially alter the terms of the offer constitutes an acceptance, unless the offeror, without undue delay, objects to the discrepancy. If the offeror does not object, the terms of the contract are the terms of the offer with the modifications contained in the acceptance.

Meeting of the minds: revocable or irrevocable offer

Restatement, 2d of Contracts (1981)

§ 63. Time When Acceptance Takes Effect

Unless the offer provides otherwise,

(a) an acceptance made in a manner and by a medium invited by an offer is operative and completes the manifestation of mutual assent as soon as put out of the offeree's possession, without regard to whether it ever reaches the offeror; but

(b) an acceptance under an option contract is not operative until received by the offeror.

§ 64. Acceptance by Telephone or Teletype

Acceptance given by telephone or other medium of substantially instantaneous two-way communication is governed by the principles applicable to acceptances where the parties are in the presence of each other.

§ 66. Acceptance Must be Properly Dispatched

An acceptance sent by mail or otherwise from a distance is not operative when dispatched, unless it is properly addressed and such other precautions taken as are ordinarily observed to insure safe transmission of similar messages.

§ 67. Effect of Receipt of Acceptance Improperly Dispatched

Where an acceptance is seasonably dispatched but the offeree uses means of transmission not invited by the offer or fails to exercise reasonable diligence to insure safe transmission, it is treated as operative upon dispatch if received within the time in which a properly dispatched acceptance would normally have arrived.

UCC

§ 2-204. Formation in General

(1) A contract for sale of goods may be made in any manner sufficient to show agreement, including offer and acceptance, conduct by both parties which recognizes the existence of a contract, the interaction of electronic agents, and the interaction of an electronic agent and an individual.

(2) An agreement sufficient to constitute a contract for sale may be found even if the moment of its making is undetermined.

(3) Even if one or more terms are left open, a contract for sale does not fail for indefiniteness if the parties have intended to make a contract and there is a reasonably certain basis for giving an appropriate remedy. [. . . .]

UNIDROIT Principles of International Commercial Contracts (2016)

Article 2.1.3 (Withdrawal of offer)

(1) An offer becomes effective when it reaches the offeree.

(2) An offer, even if it is irrevocable, may be withdrawn if the withdrawal reaches the offeree before or at the same time as the offer.

Article 2.1.4 (Revocation of offer)

(1) Until a contract is concluded an offer may be revoked if the revocation reaches the offeree before it has dispatched an acceptance.

(2) However, an offer cannot be revoked

> (a) if it indicates, whether by stating a fixed time for acceptance or otherwise, that it is irrevocable; or

> (b) if it was reasonable for the offeree to rely on the offer as being irrevocable and the offeree has acted in reliance on the offer.

Section III — Vices of Consent

Louisiana Sources of Law
Louisiana Civil Code

Art. 1948. Vitiated consent.

Consent may be vitiated by error, fraud, or duress. (Acts 1984, No. 331, §1, eff. Jan. 1, 1985.)

Error

Art. 1949. Error vitiates consent.

Error vitiates consent only when it concerns a cause without which the obligation would not have been incurred and that cause was known or should have been known to the other party. (Acts 1984, No. 331, §1, eff. Jan. 1, 1985.)

Art. 1950. Error that concerns cause.

Error may concern a cause when it bears on the nature of the contract, or the thing that is the contractual object or a substantial quality of that thing, or the person or the qualities of the other party, or the law, or any other circumstance that the parties regarded, or should in good faith have regarded, as a cause of the obligation. (Acts 1984, No. 331, §1, eff. Jan. 1, 1985.)

Art. 1951. Other party willing to perform.

A party may not avail himself of his error if the other party is willing to perform the contract as intended by the party in error. (Acts 1984, No. 331, §1, eff. Jan. 1, 1985.)

Art. 1952. Rescission; liability for damages.

A party who obtains rescission on grounds of his own error is liable for the loss thereby sustained by the other party unless the latter knew or should have known of the error.

The court may refuse rescission when the effective protection of the other party's interest requires that the contract be upheld. In that case, a reasonable compensation for the loss he has sustained may be granted to the party to whom rescission is refused. (Acts 1984, No. 331, §1, eff. Jan. 1, 1985.)

Fraud

Art. 1953. Fraud may result from misrepresentation or from silence.

Fraud is a misrepresentation or a suppression of the truth made with the intention either to obtain an unjust advantage for one party or to cause a loss or inconvenience to the other. Fraud may also result from silence or inaction. (Acts 1984, No. 331, §1, eff. Jan. 1, 1985.)

Art. 1954. Confidence between the parties.

Fraud does not vitiate consent when the party against whom the fraud was directed could have ascertained the truth without difficulty, inconvenience, or special skill.

This exception does not apply when a relation of confidence has reasonably induced a party to rely on the other's assertions or representations. (Acts 1984, No. 331, §1, eff. Jan. 1, 1985.)

Art. 1955. Error induced by fraud.

Error induced by fraud need not concern the cause of the obligation to vitiate consent, but it must concern a circumstance that has substantially influenced that consent. (Acts 1984, No. 331, §1, eff. Jan. 1, 1985.)

Art. 1956. Fraud committed by a third person.

Fraud committed by a third person vitiates the consent of a contracting party if the other party knew or should have known of the fraud. (Acts 1984, No. 331, §1, eff. Jan. 1, 1985.)

Art. 1957. [omitted]

Art. 1958. Damages.

The party against whom rescission is granted because of fraud is liable for damages and attorney fees. (Acts 1984, No. 331, §1, eff. Jan. 1, 1985.)

Duress

Art. 1959. Nature.

Consent is vitiated when it has been obtained by duress of such a nature as to cause a reasonable fear of unjust and considerable injury to a party's person, property, or reputation.

Age, health, disposition, and other personal circumstances of a party must be taken into account in determining reasonableness of the fear. (Acts 1984, No. 331, §1, eff. Jan. 1, 1985.)

Art. 1960. Duress directed against third persons.

Duress vitiates consent also when the threatened injury is directed against the spouse, an ascendant, or descendant of the contracting party.

If the threatened injury is directed against other persons, the granting of relief is left to the discretion of the court. (Acts 1984, No. 331, §1, eff. Jan. 1, 1985.)

Art. 1961. Duress by third person.

Consent is vitiated even when duress has been exerted by a third person. (Acts 1984, No. 331, §1, eff. Jan. 1, 1985.)

Art. 1962. Threat of exercising a right.

A threat of doing a lawful act or a threat of exercising a right does not constitute duress.

A threat of doing an act that is lawful in appearance only may constitute duress. (Acts 1984, No. 331, §1, eff. Jan. 1, 1985.)

Art. 1963. Contract with party in good faith.

A contract made with a third person to secure the means of preventing threatened injury may not be rescinded for duress if that person is in good faith and not in collusion with the party exerting duress. (Acts 1984, No. 331, §1, eff. Jan. 1, 1985.)

Art. 1964. Damages.

When rescission is granted because of duress exerted or known by a party to the contract, the other party may recover damages and attorney fees.

When rescission is granted because of duress exerted by a third person, the parties to the contract who are innocent of the duress may recover damages and attorney fees from the third person. (Acts 1984, No. 331, §1, eff. Jan. 1, 1985.)

Doctrine

Louisiana Law of Conventional Obligations, A Précis
Sections 4.1.1 to 4.3.3

Error

LSA-C.C. Article 1949 contains a hint at providing some understanding of this concept of error: "**Error vitiates consent only when it concerns a cause without which the obligation would not have been incurred and that cause was known or should have been known to the other party.**" [. . . .]

All in all, an error consists in considering something as true when it is actually false or, conversely, in considering as false something which is actually true. [. . . .]

An error must be serious, as must the intent to enter into a contract. As stated in **LSA C.C. Art. 1949, "Error vitiates consent only when it concerns a cause without which the obligation would not have been incurred and that cause was known or should have been known to the other party.**" [. . . .]

The seriousness of an error can only bear on an essential requirement for a contract to exist. Otherwise the error would bear on an accessory element of the contract and such an error could not bring about the nullity of the contract (unless the parties have made such an accessory element a suspensive condition of their contractual obligations) as long as its essential requirements have been met. [. . . .]

There can be an error made by the parties as to the *nature* or *kind* of contract they wish to enter into. [. . . .]

For example: a party may think she is negotiating a contract of loan when the other party thinks that she will be a party to a contract of deposit. [. . . .]

The error can bear on the identity of the *thing* as the principal object of their contract. For example, in a contract of sale, the buyer may truly believe that he is buying a certain tract of land, the Laurentine Plantation, when the seller has in mind selling another and different tract of land, the Bayou Bleu Plantation. [. . . .]

Instead of bearing on the identity of the thing itself, an error can bear on **"a substantial quality of that thing"** or the **reasonable fitness** of the thing for its **ordinary use.** [. . . .]

An error can bear also on **"the cause"** of the contract or "reason why a party obligates himself" since "cause" is an essential requirement for the formation of any contract. [. . . .]

LSA-C.C. Art. 5 states that **"No one may avail himself of ignorance of the law."** Once a statute has been promulgated, no party to a contract can argue that she made an error as to the existence of that statute. Yet, one may enter into a contract under some misunderstanding of the statute, such as the nature or extent of one's rights. [. . . .]

However the civil Code provides for instances where an error of law, even though legitimate, cannot be raised as a ground for the nullity of some contracts or juridical acts. For example, under **LSA-C.C. Art. 1761:** " . . . **whatever has been freely performed in compliance with a natural obligation may not be reclaimed."** Another example of a contract that cannot be rescinded for error of law is the contract of *compromise or transaction.* **LSA-C.C. Art. 3080** states: **"A compromise precludes the parties from bringing a subsequent action based upon the matter that was compromised."** [. . . .]

"Error may concern . . . the person or the qualities of the other party" (LSA-C.C. **Art. 1950**). These are the only words in the Civil Code to address this issue of error as to the person, the other party to the contract. Such an error as to the person must, necessarily, concern a *cause* of the contract as stated at the beginning of **Art. 1950.** Contracts which might be annulled on this ground of error are most likely to be *gratuitous contracts* or, more generally, contracts entered into *intuitu personae* wherein the consideration of the person of the co-contracting party is foremost in the mind of the other party. [. . . .]

Not every error leads to the nullity of a contract. Not every kind of error listed in Art. 1950 will necessarily carry with it the nullity of the contract which is the consequence of an error. Some conditions are attached to the error made by one party in her relation with the other party and some limitations can affect the extent of the effects of the nullity of the contract. [. . . .]

The error can become a ground for nullity of the contract except when that error could be considered so excessive or negligent that it should not be excused: The equities of the situation may indeed favor the other party to the contract and justify that the contract remain binding.

In addition "A party may not avail himself of his error when the other party is willing to perform the contract as intended by the party in error." (LSA-C.C. Art. 1951). [. . . .]

Fraud

LSA-C.C. Art. 1953 describes fraud in these terms: "Fraud is a misrepresentation or a suppression of the truth made with the intention either to obtain an unjust advantage for one party or to cause a loss or inconvenience to the other. Fraud may also result from silence or inaction." [. . . .]

Fraud is not, therefore, in itself a vice of consent. It is, rather, either an action such as a misrepresentation or a false assertion meant to hide the "truth" and therefore to "induce an error," or an inaction such as a failure to act or the withholding of the "truth" so as to "induce an error." [. . . .]

As the description of fraud in Art. 1953 suggests, the material element of fraud may consist in maneuvers, a scheme, a behavior, lies, withholding information or silence, such that a reasonable person would be led to make an error. [. . . .]

On the other hand, there may exist factual circumstances which are such that maneuvers [and] schemes [. . .] ought not lead a reasonable person to make an error. Such circumstances would fall under the wording of LSA-C.C. Art. 1954-1, which provides that "the party against whom the fraud was directed could have ascertained the truth without difficulty, inconvenience, or special skill." [. . . .]

The error made by the first party must have been "substantially" induced by the fraud committed by the second party and the fraud must have been committed by that second party or someone else but with the knowledge of that second party.

In the words of LSA-C.C. Art. 1955: "Error induced by fraud need not concern the cause of the obligation to vitiate consent, but it must concern a circumstance that has substantially influenced that consent." [. . . .]

In other words, when "fraud" is established, the contract could be annulled for errors of consent other than when the "error concerns a cause without which the obligation would not have been incurred and that cause was known or should have been known to the other party." (LSA-C.C. Art. 1949.) More errors than an error as to "the cause" can become grounds for the relative nullity of the contract when those errors have been the outcome of fraud. [. . . .]

Since "fraud" may lead to error as a vice of consent if fraud itself meets the requirements above and if it induces an error "substantial" enough but lesser than an error as to the principal cause of the contract, it is logical to grant to the party victim of the fraud and error the right to seek the relative nullity of the contract for lack of free and informed consent. Under **LSA-C.C. Art. 2031, "A contract is relatively null when it violates a rule intended for the protection of private parties, as when a party lacked capacity or did not give free consent at the time the contract was made. A contract that is only relatively null may be confirmed.**

"Relative nullity may be invoked only by those persons for whose interest the ground for nullity was established, and may not be declared by the court on its own initiative." [. . . .]

In addition to, or in lieu of, the nullity of the contract, **"The party against whom rescission is granted because of fraud is liable for damages and attorney fees."** (LSA-C.C. Art. 1958). [. . . .]

Duress

Duress is made up of two component elements: a psychological element, the fear felt by a party to a contract, hence the vice of consent; and a material anti-social element consisting in the duress itself or the threats directed by the perpetrator against a party to a contract. These two component elements of duress make up its nature as described by **LSA-C.C. Art. 1959: "Consent is vitiated when it has been obtained by duress of such a nature as to cause a reasonable fear of unjust and considerable injury to a party's person, property, or reputation.**

"Age, health, disposition, and other personal circumstances of a party must be taken into account in determining reasonableness of the fear." [. . . .]

LSA-C.C. Art. 1960 states that **"Duress vitiates consent also when the threatened injury is directed against the spouse, an ascendant, or descendant of the contracting party.**

If the threatened injury is directed against other persons, the granting of relief is left to the discretion of the court." [. . . .]

LSA-C.C. Art. 1961 provides that **"Consent is vitiated even when duress has been exerted by a third person."** Indeed, what is of greater concern to the law on formation of contracts is the integrity of a party's consent, that party's freedom to contract or not to contract. [. . . .]

However, not all contracts entered into under duress are automatically relatively null. Under the circumstances described in **LSA-C.C. Art. 1963, "A contract made with a third person to secure the means of preventing threatened injury may not be rescinded for duress if that person is in good faith and not in collusion with the party exerting duress."** [. . . .]

LSA-C.C. Art. 1964 states that **"When rescission is granted because of duress exerted or known by a party to the contract, the other party may recover damages and attorney fees.**

When rescission is granted because of duress exerted by a third person, the parties to the contract who are innocent of the duress may recover damages and attorney fees from the third person."

Cases

Mrs. Joyce Deutschmann, wife of/and Frank Deutschmann

v.

Standard Fur Company, Inc.

Court of Appeal of Louisiana
Fourth Circuit
April 13, 1976
331 So.2d 219

GULOTTA, Judge.

P. H.

[1] Plaintiffs appeal from a judgment dismissing their suit for return of a $400.00 deposit on a $2,000.00 mink coat ordered by Mrs. Joyce Deutschmann from defendant. We reverse.

[2] In November, 1974, Mrs. Deutschmann placed an order with Elza Abel, president of Standard Fur Company, for a mink coat to be made by a New York furrier. Plaintiff-wife deposited with defendant the sum of $400.00 to be credited against the price of the coat. Mrs. Deutschmann specified that the coat was to be made with the furs running horizontally; that quality female continuous, not pieced together, furs be used; and, that the furs be of the same width as the furs selected by her from a model coat at Standard Fur.[1]

[3] Plaintiff testified that she refused to accept the coat for the reasons that (1) the skins of the coat were wider than the skins of the model coat at Standard Fur Company; (2) the horizontal skins were not continuous, but pieced together; and, (3) in 'letting out the skins', the pelts had been sliced and sewn back together, rather than stretched.

[4] The coat was returned by defendant to the New York furrier in an attempt to make alterations to satisfy plaintiff's complaints. After the coat had been returned from the furrier a second time, plaintiff rejected the coat and requested return of the deposit. Defendant refused and this suit followed.

[5] This case is a classic example of a misunderstanding between two parties to a purported agreement resulting in lack of consent on the part of the purchaser.

---

1. Mrs. Deutschmann further specified that the coat be belted and have no buttons. The finished coat was made with four buttons and no belt, however, this problem was rectified to Mrs. Deutschmann's satisfaction by defendant and is not an issue in this case.

LSA-C.C. arts. 1797[2] and 1798.[3] Consent on the part of Mrs. Deutschmann was lacking (LSA-C.C. art. 1812)[4] because of error of fact on the part of the purchaser which was a principal cause for making the agreement. See LSA-C.C. arts. 1821,[5] 1823[6] and 1825.[7]

[6] Our jurisprudence is well settled that a contract may be invalidated for a unilateral error as to a fact which was the principal cause for making the contract, where the other party knew or should have known it was the principal cause. LSA-C.C. art. 1845: Savoie v. Bills, 317 So.2d 249 (La.App.3d Cir. 1975); West Esplanade Shell Service, Inc. v. Breithoff, 293 So.2d 595 (La.App.4th Cir. 1974). Error as to the nature or object of a contract may be with regard to either the substance or the object of the agreement, or substantial quality of the object, or some other quality of the object if such quality is the principal cause of making the contract. Jefferson Truck Equipment Co. v. Guarisco Motor Co., 250 So.2d 211 (La.App.1st Cir. 1971).

[7] Applying the above articles and jurisprudence to the instant case, we conclude that consent was lacking and the purported agreement was vitiated because of error of fact which constituted a principal cause for making the agreement. Mrs. Deutschmann testified that she understood the coat would be made of continuous skins, i.e., horizontal pelts that were not 'pieced together' and which were 'let out' and would extend all around the coat. According to Mrs. Deutschmann, her definition of a continuous skin was, 'I mean a long continuous skin, not several short ones pieced together.' Her definition of a 'fully let out' fur was as follows: 'My understanding that they stretch the pelts instead of taking several small pieces and putting them together. If he could not have made it, I would have changed my plans.'

---

2. 'Art. 1797. Necessity for consent; proof. Art. 1797. When the parties have the legal capacity to form a contract, the next requisite to its validity is their consent. This being a mere operation of the mind, can have no effect, unless it be evinced in some manner that shall cause it to be understood by the other parties to the contract. To prevent error in this essential point, the law establishes, by certain rules adapted to the nature of the contract, what circumstances shall be evidence of such consent, and how those circumstances shall be proved; these come within the purview of the law of evidence.'

3. 'Art. 1798. Offer and acceptance. Art. 1798. As there must be two parties at least to every contract, so there must be something proposed by one and accepted and agreed to by another to form the matter of such contract; the will of both parties must unite on the same point.'

4. 'Art. 1812. Unequivocal language for express acceptance. Art. 1812. Express consent must be given in a language understood by the party who accepts, and the words by which it is conveyed must be in themselves unequivocal; if they may mean different things, they give rise to error, which, as is hereinafter provided, destroys the effect of a contract.'

5. 'Art. 1821. Error of fact. Art. 1821. That is called error of fact, which proceeds either from ignorance of that which really exists, or from a mistaken belief in the existence of that which has none.'

6. 'Art. 1823. Sufficiency of error to invalidate contract. Art. 1823. Errors may exist as to all the circumstances and facts which relate to a contract, but it is not every error that will invalidate it. To have that effect, the error must be in some point, which was a principal cause for making the contract, and it may be either as to the motive for making the contract, to the person with whom it is made, or to the subject matter of the contract itself.'

7. 'Art. 1825. Error as to motive. Art. 1825. The error in the cause of a contract to have the effect of invalidating it, must be on the principal cause, when there are several; this principal cause is called the Motive, and means that consideration without which the contract would not have been made.'

Mrs. Deutschmann further indicated that the furs used in the purchased coat were wider than the ones used in the model coat selected by her.

[8] On the other hand, Abel's (a furrier with 40 years experience) understanding, according to trade usage, of the meaning of the terms 'pieced together' and 'let out', graphically illustrates the lack of understanding between the parties. Abel admitted that plaintiff wanted a coat with continuous horizontal furs and without seams. However, he differentiated between a fur 'pieced together' with straight seams, which he defined as a pieced together coat, and furs pieced together with a 'V-type seam', which he defined as 'set up' and not 'pieced together'. According to Abel, use of a V-type seam is an acceptable method of joining skins, and, in trade jargon, is not considered piecing together. Significantly, Abel failed to communicate to plaintiff the trade usage difference between 'pieced together' and 'set up V-type seams'. Abel further testified that female skins are not long enough, i.e., 36 inches long, to be used continuously in a wrap-around horizontal fur coat, but must be pieced together.

[9] Abel failed to communicate to plaintiff that the width of horizontal skins was different from the width of vertical skins. Significantly, although the model coat shown Mrs. Deutschmann was made of vertical skins, Abel did not communicate the difference in width to plaintiff.

[10] Abel also stated that the term 'let out' means that the fur is sliced and sewn back together. A let out skin, according to Abel, is one that has been cut and then let out.

[11] Abel is the expert. He was aware that Standard Fur was unable to deliver to plaintiff that which she thought she had ordered. It was his responsibility to communicate to Mrs. Deutschmann information which, clearly, would have avoided the confusion. For reasons best known to himself, he failed to do so. Abel's lack of communication caused the misunderstanding on the part of Mrs. Deutschmann, resulting in the error of fact on the part of the purchaser which was a principal cause for making the agreement. See LSA-C.C. arts. 1812, 1821 and 1825. We find that consent was lacking in the instant case and that no agreement existed. The parties revert to the same position which they occupied prior to the purported formation of the agreement. Plaintiff is entitled to the return of her deposit.

[12] Accordingly, the judgment, of the trial court is reversed and set aside. Judgment is now rendered in favor of Mrs. Joyce Deutschmann and Frank Deutschmann, and against Standard Fur Company, Inc., in the sum of $400.00, together with legal interest thereon from date of judicial demand and for all costs.

[13] REVERSED AND RENDERED.

Questions

1. Paragraphs 2–3: The court refers to Mrs. Deutschmann as having placed an "order," and "she refused to accept the coat," and that "consent on the part of Mrs. Deustchmann was lacking. . . ." Where is the offer, if any, and if one

exists, who is the offeror? Note that the Court cites former Louisiana Civil Code articles 1797, 1798, 1812 etc. *See* La. Civ. Code arts. 1927–1952. Was there a misunderstanding between an offeror and an offeree?

2. Paragraph 6: Is the court correct to refer to the contract being invalidated for a unilateral error as to a fact? If error there was, would it make a difference if the error was about the "substance" of the thing, the coat, as opposed to the error being about a "substantial quality" of the thing? *See* La. Civ. Code arts. 1950 and 1967. Or was there an even more serious error as to the nature of contract?

3. Paragraphs 8–11: Should it matter that one party is a professional, a merchant? Is the court putting an undue burden on the furrier? If you answer in the affirmative, is there any acceptable justification? Should that justification be extended to all professionals? *See* paragraph 11. Where the court says that "Abel [the furrier] is the expert," is the court limiting its statement to this particular case of a furrier or should the court be understood as referring to all experts? Does this make any impact on whether or not there was an offeror and an offeree? In paragraphs 9–11, is the court suggesting that whoever speaks in a technical language is under a duty to make that language understandable to the average consumer? Could that duty, if any, fall under the principle of good faith in Louisiana Civil Code article 1759?

Mrs. Corinne Clohecy Wise, Widow of Daniel J. Wise,
v.
Vester Prescott et al.

Supreme Court of Louisiana
March 25, 1963
151 So.2d 356

HAWTHORNE, Justice.

[1] This suit arose out of an intersectional collision at St. Roch Avenue and North Miro Street in New Orleans, between a passenger bus owned by New Orleans Public Service, Inc., and operated by one of its employees, Harry J. Miller, Jr., and a car driven by Vester Prescott.

[....]

[2] The plaintiff, Mrs. Corinne Clohecy Wise, a fare-paying passenger on the bus, who received injuries as a result of this collision, instituted suit for damages for physical injuries, claiming that the collision was caused by the concurring negligence of both Miller, the bus driver, and Prescott, the driver of the automobile. [The trial court ruled in Mrs. Wise's favor against all defendants.]

[3] All defendants appealed to the Court of Appeal, Fourth Circuit. That court concluded at [*sic*] to Prescott and his insurer Allstate that plaintiff had entered into a transaction or compromise with these two defendants under which they had paid

plaintiff $105.00, and that this compromise barred her action against these two defendants [. . .] and [**the court**] dismissed plaintiff's suit against Prescott and All-state Insurance Company. See 142 So.2d 613.

[4] [. . . .] The [**writ**] application of Mrs. Wise was granted to review the Court of Appeal's holding that the release signed by her was a compromise which barred her action against Prescott and Allstate. [. . . .]

[. . . .]

On the Question of Liability of Public Service

[. . . .]

[5] Insofar as Public Service and Miller are concerned, the law applicable to the case was correctly stated by the Court of Appeal thus:

'The mere showing of injury to a farepaying passenger on a public conveyance and his failure to reach his destination safely establishes a prima facie case of negligence and imposes the burden on the carrier of convincingly overcoming such case. Adams v. Great American Indemnity Company, La.App., 116 So.2d 307; Johnson v. Continental Southern Lines, Inc., La.App., 113 So.2d 114, 74 A.L.R.2d 1328; Coleman v. Continental Southern Lines, Inc., La.App., 107 So.2d 69; Peters v. City of Monroe, La.App., 91 So.2d 428.

'A public carrier of passengers while not an insurer is required to exercise the highest degree of vigilance, care and precaution for the safety of those it undertakes to transport and is liable for the slightest negligence. Gross v. Teche Lines, Inc., 207 La. 354, 21 So.2d 378. The carrier must do all that human sagacity and foresight can do under the circumstances, in view of the character and mode of conveyance adopted, to prevent injury to passengers, the carrier being held liable for the slightest negligence with reference to the exercise of such care. Mire v. Lafourche Parish School Board, La., 62 So.2d 541.'

[. . . .]

[6] In view of the high degree of care required of public carriers toward their fare-paying passengers, the vigilance and prudence that must be exercised in the face of a slow sign, and the fact that the burden is on the carrier to show its freedom from negligence, we cannot say that the jury and the Court of Appeal erred in holding Public Service and Miller liable. The bus driver's complete lack of awareness of the Prescott car's approach under the circumstances of this case appears to us to be sufficient to justify the conclusion that he and Public Service failed to prove that he was maintaining the proper lookout, vigilance, and caution required at this intersection. Consequently we conclude that Public Service and Miller have not sustained the burden required under the law of overcoming the prima facie case of negligence against them.

[. . . .]

On the Validity of the Release by Mrs. Wise of Prescott and His Insurer Allstate

[7] The release in this case is a printed form, bears the signature of Mrs. Wise, and recites a consideration of 105.00.[1] Its language is broad, general, and all-inclusive, and it contains such expressions as 'release and forever discharge', 'all claims' for 'damages' 'sustained', or 'may hereafter sustain', 'consequences not now anticipated', 'all unknown and unanticipated injuries and damages'.

[8] The negligence of Prescott is conceded and is no longer an issue in the case. Prescott and his insurer, Allstate Insurance Company, seek to evade liability on the theory that no judgment can be rendered against them because all matters in dispute between them and plaintiff were settled by the release, which is a transaction or compromise and as between the parties has the force equal to the authority of the thing adjudged under Articles 3071 and 3078 of the Civil Code.

[9] Plaintiff Mrs. Wise, who was over 70 years old when the accident occurred, gave the following version relating to the procuring of the release: As a result of the collision she was thrown to the floor of the bus. Immediately afterwards she was taken to Charity Hospital, where X-rays were made and medication given her for pain. She spent the night in her apartment but did not sleep because of the pain in her head, and the medication made her 'woozy'. The next morning she was bruised and sore all over, and her face and eyes were bruised and swollen. She did not feel well enough to get around, and a neighbor came to look after her while she reclined in an easy chair. That afternoon at about 3:30 an adjuster from Allstate, on his own solicitation, came to her apartment and was admitted by the neighbor. The adjuster did not report himself to be such, and no insurance company was mentioned. This young man, who was nice and friendly, told Mrs. Wise that he came in behalf of Mr. Prescott, who had been worrying about her and felt sorry for her because of her age and wanted to give her some money to help with the X-rays and medical bills. She asked him whether this would have anything to do with the case, and he answered, 'No.' She would not have signed the document presented to her if she had known it was a release. She signed the paper which he told her was to show her thanks to Prescott and to show his good faith in representing Prescott. She could not read what was on the paper she signed because her glasses had been broken in the accident and she could not read without them. She had an extra pair but did not know where they were, and in any event her face was so swollen that she could not have gotten them on. No copy of the paper she signed was left with her.

[10] On the other hand, the adjuster's version was this: He told the plaintiff he was a claims agent for the insurance company and wanted to negotiate a settlement. Mrs. Wise accepted the $105.00 he offered her without hesitation or complaint, there was no discussion about the amount, and there was no discussion about liability or fault as the release taken denied any liability of Prescott and Allstate. He thought

---

1. Prior to instituting suit plaintiff tendered this amount of Allstate, but it was refused.

Mrs. Wise read the release because she held it in front of her long enough to do so. The entire negotiations were consummated in about 15 minutes.

[11] It is obvious that the testimony of Mrs. Wise and that of the adjuster are in conflict. This case, as stated previously, was tried before a jury. The jury pursuant to a specific question of the court found that the release was invalid, and the trial judge refused to grant defendants a new trial. The jury was called upon to deter- mine the credibility of the witnesses and the weight to be given to their testimony, and it is apparent from their finding that the release was invalid that they accepted Mrs. Wise's version of the procuring of the release.

[12] According to Mrs. Wise's testimony, accepted by the jury, she took the money in the belief that it was a gift from Prescott and that the document she signed was a receipt for the money, and she signed the document under the assur- ance that it would not have anything to do with her case. The question is whether under these facts the jury's finding that the release was invalid was correct as a matter of law.

[13] This kind of release is often called in personal injury cases a 'rush release', and is executed in a situation wherein there exists a high potential of error. Recognizing this great possibility for error inherent in rush releases, the legislatures of at least seven states have passed measures affecting their validity, and two of these have expressly labeled them as 'crimes against public policy'. Connecticut in 1959, and Vermont and Idaho in 1961, enacted statutes permitting persons receiv- ing personal injuries in accidents to repudiate and void any settlement or release entered into within 15 days of the injury.[2] Maryland enacted a similar provision in 1955 with a five-day period from the injury,[3] and North Dakota since 1943 has had a statute with a 30-day period.[4] In Massachusetts since 1950 any settlement or release obtained from a hospital patient within 15 days of the injury is null and void unless the injured party indicates his consent in writing at least five days prior to the procuring of the release.[5] Maine's similar provision enacted in 1959 provides that a settlement or release obtained within 10 days of the injury is null and void.[6]

---

2. The Connecticut statute, C.G.S.A., s 52-572a, expressly forbids the negotiation of any contract with the injured person by one having an adverse interest within 15 days of the 'tortious act'. No limitation is made as to time within which such a reprobated contract may be avoided. The Vermont statute, 12 V.S.A. 1076, provides a three-year limitation for disavowal; Idaho's, 5 Idaho Code s 29-113, provides a one-year period for disavowal.

3. 7 Annotated Code of Maryland (1957), Art. 79, s 11. A short 60-day period is allowed for voiding the release.

4. 1 North Dakota Century Code Annotated, ss 9-08-08, 9-08-09. The contract may be avoided within six months.

5. M.G.L.A., c. 271, s 44. Massachusetts classifies it under the chapter heading 'crimes against public policy'.

6. 4 Rev'd Stats of Maine (1954), c. 137, s 49-A. Maine classifies the matter also under the heading 'crimes against public policy'.

[14] Up to this time the Legislature of our state has not enacted any law to protect persons suffering personal injuries from the possibility of error inherent in quick releases, compromises, or settlements, and this court would not be justified in law in declaring a 'rush release' invalid simply because it was obtained within a very short time of the accident. In such cases, however, we feel that we are justified in recognizing that high potential for error in our consideration of all the facts and circumstances connected with the execution of this type of release.

[15] The adjuster here sought out Mrs. Wise within 24 hours of the accident, after she had spent a sleepless and painful night, while she needed someone to attend her, while she was feeling sore and miserable from the injuries she had received in the accident, and at a time when she, especially because of her age, could not reasonably have been expected to have recovered from the nervousness and upset which follow such an experience. According to the adjuster the whole conversation with Mrs. Wise lasted about 15 minutes.

[16] The facts and circumstances of the execution of the release in the instant case, in our opinion, clearly justify the finding of the jury, concurred in by the judge, that Mrs. Wise executed the release through error, and that she signed it reasonably believing it to be a receipt for a gift from Prescott and believing that it would not have anything to do with her case. Her error is one recognized under the general articles of our Civil Code on Obligations as 'Error as to the Nature of the contract' which will render it void, La.Civ.Code Art. 1841. (Italics ours.)

[17] The judgment of the Court of Appeal dismissing plaintiff's suit against Vester Prescott and Allstate Insurance Company is annulled and set aside[.] [. . . .]

Questions

1. After you have read this case carefully, can you identify the nature of the legal sources of the multiple legal relationships created herein? For example, was the source of one relationship a contract, and the source of another, a delict/tort? Or was it the law, a statute/code articles? Read some code articles on donations (La. Civ. Code arts. 1541–1551), on solidarity (La. Civ. Code arts. 1786–1806), and on compromise (La. Civ. Code arts. 3071–3083).

2. Paragraph 5: What kind of obligation is identified in the legal expression of this statement: "the mere showing of injury to a fare paying passenger . . . establishes a prima facie case of negligence"?

3. Paragraph 9: Consider very carefully the fact that the title of this paragraph and the court's legal analysis refer to two parties, "Prescott and His Insurer Allstate." Under what kind(s) of obligation(s) could any two of the following parties be bound one *vis-à-vis* another: Mrs. Wise, Prescott, the insurance company, New Orleans Public Service? Would a release or discharge have the same or different effects on the kind(s) of obligation(s) you have identified? Look carefully at Louisiana Civil Code articles 1802 and 1803. Is a release or

renunciation of solidarity the same thing as a remission of debt? What about a release of a joint obligor? A remission of debt to a joint obligor? Do you see now why you were asked, above, to read the Louisiana Civil Code articles on compromise?

4. Paragraph 12: Was it possible that Mrs. Wise made an error? If you answer affirmatively, is it error as to the nature of a legal document, the legal effects of that document, or the person of the other party to the document? What could be the impact of Louisiana Civil Code articles 3079, 3080, and 3082?

5. Paragraph 13: There is no rush release law in Louisiana, but can "facts and circumstances connected with the execution of this type of release" be indicative of error on the part of the party under pressure to grant a release? What kind of standard, *in abstracto* or in *concreto*, is the court applying here to Mrs. Wise? Could the Court have required the expert, as it did in the *Deutschmann* case, to explain to Mrs. Wise what the document was actually intended to be? Could the silence of the insurance agent amount to fraud? *See* La. Civ. Code arts. 1953–1958.

Daniel G. Griffin, d/b/a Checkwriter Service Co.
v.
Seismic Services, Inc.

Court of Appeal of Louisiana
First Circuit
February 24, 1972
259 So.2d 923

LANDRY, Judge.

[1] This appeal by plaintiff, Daniel G. Griffin (Appellant), is from the judgment of the trial court rejecting his demands against defendant, Seismic Services, Inc. (Appellee), for specific performance of a contract to sell a checkwriting machine [. . .]. The trial court rejected Appellant's demand for specific performance upon finding that Appellee's agreement to purchase a checkwriter from Appellant was vitiated by errors of fact, namely, that Michot was mistaken with regard to the make of machine offered for sale by Appellant, and as to the manufacturer whom Appellant allegedly represented. We affirm.

[2] Appellant maintains the lower court erred in the following respects[, **among others . . .**] believing the testimony of Appellee's witnesses rather than that of Appellant; [. . .] admitting parol evidence to vary the terms of a written document, namely, a purchase order signed by Michot[;] and (4) finding that any error of fact existed.

[3] It is conceded that for several years prior to August 11, 1970, Appellant was self-employed as a salesman of several types of office machines, principally checkwriters.

At one time, Appellant represented Paymaster Corporation, manufacturer of a checkwriter bearing the brand name Paymaster. Each time Appellant sold a checkwriter, he also sold or attempted to sell the purchaser a policy of insurance against fraudulent use of the machine. Michot, President of defendant corporation, also owned and controlled several other companies which he operated out of a single office. In his businesses, Michot used a Paymaster checkwriter. Approximately one or two years prior to the sale in question, Appellant called on Michot, ascertained that Michot's insurance contract on his Paymaster had another year or two to run and made some minor adjustments on the Paymaster checkwriter. Appellant did not attempt to sell Michot a new checkwriter at this time. On an undisclosed date prior to August 11, 1970, Appellant's authority to represent Paymaster Corporation was terminated. On August 11, 1970, Appellant sold Michot an F & E checkwriter for the price of $95.00, and a new insurance policy on the machine. Later that same day, Michot learned that Appellant no longer represented Paymaster, and that the machine he purchased was not a Paymaster. Michot stopped payment on the check issued to Appellant, and wrote the insurance company canceling the contract on the ground that Appellant falsely represented himself to be the agent of Paymaster Corporation.

[4] In essence, Appellant testified that approximately one week prior to the sale, he called at Michot's office and introduced himself to Michot's secretary, Paula Van Ness, as 'Dan Griffin, Checkwriter Service.' Michot was not in at the time. Approximately one week later, on August 11, 1970, he returned, introduced himself in the same manner, and was ushered into Michot's private office. He introduced himself to Michot as 'Dan Griffin, Checkwriter Service', and began his sales routine. Michot produced his old checkwriter and Appellant demonstrated certain defects in the machine, primarily, how numbers printed by the old Paymaster could be altered. Appellant then took out a new F & E checkwriter, demonstrated the machine and explained its advantages over the old Paymaster model. He answered Michot's numerous questions about the machine, and also pointed out that the F & E machine was slightly more expensive than a Paymaster. He told Michot, however, that if Michot bought the new F & E machine and renewed his insurance, Appellant would sell Michot the F & E checkwriter for $95.00 and pay the tax involved. Michot then wrote a check for $95.00 payable to Dan Griffin, Checkwriter Service, and Appellant requested Michot to sign a purchase order for the machine. At first, Michot declined to sign the order stating that it was unnecessary since he had given a check in payment. Appellant, however, insisted that a signed purchase order was required by the manufacturer of the machine, where-upon Michot signed the document which covered the sale of an F & E checkwriter. Appellant denied that he represented himself to Miss Van Ness and Michot as a representative of Paymaster Corporation. Appellant vigorously contended he made it clear to Michot that the machine involved was an F & E checkwriter, not a Paymaster.

[5] Michot's testimony, in substance, is that he is an extremely busy executive. He had used a Paymaster checkwriter in his several businesses for years and was

satisfied with the service it gave. On the day in question, his secretary informed him that a representative of Paymaster Corporation wished to see him. Plaintiff entered the office introducing himself as Daniel Griffin with Paymaster, and indicated it was time for renewal of Michot's insurance on his checkwriter. Appellant explained the advantages of the new machine, and Michot assumed it was a Paymaster. Michot did not examine the new machine. He was extremely busy at the time in that he answered several telephone and radio calls within the 15 to 20 minutes interval Griffin was present. In essence Michot testified he would not have dealt with Griffin knowing that Griffin did not represent Paymaster Corporation, and would not have knowingly purchased any checkwriter other than a Paymaster. By coincidence, the Paymaster representative called at Michot's office approximately two hours after Griffin left. Upon learning that he had not purchased a Paymaster machine, Michot called his bank and stopped payment on the check given Appellant. Michot explained that he made the check payable to Dan Griffin, Checkwriter Service, because Griffin requested it be made that way. He also stated he thought he was buying a Paymaster checkwriter when he signed the purchase order which he did not read.

[6] Miss Van Ness testified simply that when Appellant called at her employee's office, he introduced himself as a representative of Paymaster Corporation, and she in turn introduced plaintiff to Mr. Michot as a Paymaster representative.

[. . . .]

[7] Under our law and jurisprudence, a contract may be avoided for unilateral error as to the substance of some substantial quality of the subject matter of the agreement where the other party was apprised of the motive of the contract or where, from the nature and circumstances of the transaction, it must be presumed the other party was aware of the error. Jefferson Truck Equipment Co., Inc. v. Guarisco Motor Co., Inc., La.App., 250 So.2d 211, and authorities therein cited. The requisite consent to a contract is lacking where an error of fact exists. LSA-C.C. arts. 1819 and 1820. To avoid a contract, an error of fact must pertain to the principal cause for making the agreement, meaning the error must exist either as to the motive for making the agreement or the person with whom the agreement is made, or to the subject matter of the contract itself. LSA-C.C. art. 1823; Jefferson Truck Equipment Co., Inc., above. Error as to the qualities of an object serves to vitiate a contract if such qualities constitute the principal cause for making the agreement. LSA-C.C. art. 1845.

[8] We find, as did the trial court, that Michot was in error as to the person with whom he was making the agreement, and also as to the nature of the object of the agreement. We likewise agree with the implied finding of the trial court that plaintiff either knew of the mistakes under which Michot was laboring or because of the circumstances, it must be presumed plaintiff was aware of Michot's error. Under these circumstances, the error on the purchaser's part vitiates the contract.

[9] The judgment of the trial court is affirmed at appellant's cost.

[10] Affirmed.

On Rehearing

[11] Rehearing denied.

BLANCHE, Judge (dissenting)

[12] The majority correctly states the law concerning when a contract may be avoided for unilateral error but is in error for failing to consider what plaintiff, Daniel G. Griffin, knew or should have known. There is not even a suggestion by the evidence in the record that Griffin either knew or should have known that defendant's president and general manager, T. Warren Michot, wanted a Paymaster checkwriter and only a Paymaster checkwriter. Therefore, being unable to presume that Griffin was aware of Michot's error, I think the contract should not be avoided.

[13] While Michot may have been in error as to the person with whom he was dealing, he should not have been in error as to the quality of the object of the contract. The preponderance of the evidence is that Michot should have known what he was purchasing. It is uncontradicted that the qualities of both the F & E checkwriter which Michot purchased and the Paymaster checkwriter were discussed. The two machines were side by side on Michot's desk and bore distinguishable physical characteristics and lettering identifying the brand of each. Added to this is the fact that Michot signed an invoice showing that he purchased an F & E checkwriter. The majority excuses Michot for being in error as to the object of the contract by first finding that Griffin misrepresented himself as an agent of Paymaster and then finding that Michot was a very busy man, talking on the telephone and over the radio while Griffin was trying to sell him a checkwriter. If he was too busy to hear what Griffin was telling him and if he did not bother to notice the distinctly different machines placed before him and if he did not read the invoice showing the type of checkwriter he was purchasing, he should be estopped from claiming that he acted under an error because of the significant contribution he made thereto. There is no reason to excuse Michot from not reading what he signed or not seeing what he should have seen just because as an extremely busy executive he did not have sufficient time for a ninety-five dollar checkwriter deal.

[14] I am of the opinion that judgment should be rendered for the plaintiff for the purchase price of the checkwriter, and to that extent I would reverse the judgment of the district court.

Questions

1. Paragraph 1: Do you have any comment regarding the identity of the parties involved in this case? Should that identity have any bearing on the degree of knowledge expected from the parties when expressing their consent? The trial court ruled for the defendant on the ground of errors of fact: what errors of fact can you identify?

2. Paragraph 1: Could the plaintiff have been guilty of fraud? *See* La. Civ. Code art. 1953–1958. Did Michot act reasonably in light of his status?

3. Paragraph 7: Can a unilateral error lead to a contract being avoided? What does the word "unilateral" actually mean? Is it a misnomer?

4. Paragraph 8: The Court of Appeal finds "that Michot was in error as to the person. . . ." What do you think, keeping in mind the identity or status of the parties involved, was the particular feature of the "person" of the plaintiff salesman, Griffin, that was the ground of the error made by Michot? How much, if at all, did Michot contribute to his own error? In an onerous contract, such as a sale in this case, should error as to the person of the seller be as easily acceptable a ground for nullity of the contract as in a gratuitous contract such as a donation? Read Louisiana Civil Code article 1954 on fraud. Could Michot have ascertained the truth without difficulty? Even if Griffin committed no fraud but only knew that Michot was in error, should Griffin have the right to show that Michot would have had no difficulty in ascertaining the truth about the machine and, thus, about the company he now represented? What do you think now of the dissenting opinion in paragraphs 12–14?

Cynthia Fry Peironnet and Elizabeth Fry Franklin
v.
Matador Resources Company

Supreme Court of Louisiana
June 28, 2013
144 So.3d 791

KNOLL, Justice.

[. . . .]

[1] In a civilian context, the granting of relief differs depending upon whether the error is bilateral or unilateral:

> The granting of relief for error presents no problem when both parties are in error, that is, when the error is bilateral. [. . . .]

> When only one party is in error, that is, when the error is unilateral, there is theoretically no meeting of the minds, but granting relief to the party in error will unjustly injure the interest of the other party if he is innocent of the error. Louisiana courts have often refused relief for unilateral error for this reason. [. . . .] Yet, expanding the rule stated in C.C. Art. 1826 (1870), they have granted relief for unilateral error in cases where the other party knew or should have known that the matter affected by the error was the reason or principal cause why the party in error made the contract. [. . . .] French courts have taken a very similar approach. [. . . .]

[. . . .]

[2] In determining whether to grant recission, our courts have considered "whether the error was excusable or inexcusable, a distinction received by modern

civilian doctrine," granting relief when error has been found excusable [...].
[....]

[....]

Whether an error is excusable or inexcusable should be determined *in concreto*, that is, according to the circumstances surrounding a particular case, rather than according to an abstract standard. Thus, personal circumstances of the party in error, such as age, experience and profession, are to be taken into account. An error made by a professional person concerning a matter within his field of expertise would no doubt be regarded as inexcusable.

[....]

[3] So, while the Court of Appeal correctly found an error can only vitiate consent when it concerns a cause for the agreement about which the other party is aware or should have been aware, it erred in concluding its analysis there without examining further the various forms of error and the remedies and defenses provided by law. [....]

[....]

[4] Applying the modern civilian concept of inexcusable error as advanced in our contractual negligence defense to these undisputed facts, we find, as did the District Court, reasonable persons could not disagree the alleged error on the part of the plaintiffs' agents in this case was easily detectable and could have been rectified by a minimal amount of care, *i.e.*, by simply reading the document and/or by requesting simple changes to the written offer before acceptance. [....]

[....]

[5] [T]he plaintiffs' failure to question the extension, to seek clarification of the acreage covered, or to even discuss the Deep Rights demonstrates an inexcusable lack of "elementary prudence" or simple diligence that now precludes their recission of the agreement.

[6] In light of these undisputed facts, we find the plaintiffs were precluded by law from advancing a unilateral theory of error due to their own inexcusable error [...]. [....]

[....]

[7] To establish mutual error, the plaintiffs bore the burden of proving both parties were mistaken regarding the cause of their obligations as reflected in the written agreement — an eighteen month extension of the entire lease for the consideration paid. [....]

[....]

See also *Kaufman v. Audubon Ford/Audubon Imports, Inc.*, 903 So.2d 486 (La.App. 4 Cir. 2005).

Robert R. Boucher, A. C. Wilkinson, Jules R. Gueymard
v.
Division of Employment Security, Department of Labor of the State of Louisiana

Court of Appeal of Louisiana
First Circuit
November 16, 1964
169 So.2d 674

ELLIS, Judge.

[1] The three appellants, whose cases were consolidated for trial, have appealed from a ruling of the Commission affirming their discharge by J. Hadley Heard, Administrator of the Division of Employment Security, in accordance with letter of removal dated October 19, 1954 and we quote the material portion of this letter:

> "You are hereby advised that a decision has been reached to terminate your services with this Department because evidence available to this Department discloses that you submitted *a false and fraudulent claim for travel expenses* during the period May 15, 1950 — June 8, 1950. This termination will be effective at the close of business on June 24, 1953.

> "In reaching this decision, careful consideration was given to your sworn statement of June 11, 1953, along with other information and evidence available to this Department. *It was recognized that you may have received commitments for the reimbursement of funds in the approximate amount for which you submitted a false and fraudulent claim and that coercion and intimidation may have been exercised in causing you to incur expenses for which you desired reimbursement,* but the conclusion that you had submitted a false and fraudulent expense claim was inescapable. Of necessity, consideration was given to the effect of this act on public opinion and employee morale. Accordingly, your removal is considered to be for such cause as to be in the best interest of this Department.

> "As you have the right to appeal to the Civil Service Commission, there is attached for your information a copy of Chapter 13 of the Civil Service Rules.

> s/ J. Hadley Heard

> Administrator"

> (Emphasis added)

[2] The facts in the three cases under consideration are substantially and materially identical with those in the case of Colvin v. Division of Employment Security, La.App., 132 So.2d 909, which was decided by this court and in which the Supreme Court of the State of Louisiana denied certiorari. In that case, as in this, relator

had appealed from a ruling of the Commission affirming his discharge, which grew out of one of the same incidents and the charge was the same, of filing a false and fraudulent expense account. Colvin obtained a severance or separate trial from the relators herein. The facts in the Colvin case show that in the year 1950 he and relator herein, A. C. Wilkinson, were selected to attend a convention in Omaha. Both said they could not afford to make the trip and upon the assurance and insistence of Mr. Marvin A. Thames, then Administrator of the Department, that they go and their expenses would be paid by the agency as he had cleared that question with the Regional Office of the United States Department of Labor, Bureau of Employment Security, as under the agency rules in effect at that time, advance written authority was required for such a trip to be made at agency expense, they proceeded to the convention in Omaha, Nebraska. Colvin and Wilkinson returned from the Omaha trip about May 1, 1950. Subsequent to their return, the facts as they affect the relators in the case now at bar on this appeal are practically identical with those in the Colvin case, supra. This court in the Colvin case held that while the findings of fact by the Commission, when based on evidence supporting the discharge of an employee for a valid cause, are not subject to review by this court, which we must do under the law, as appellate courts are restricted upon appeals from the Civil Service Commission to questions of law, nevertheless, taking the entire testimony and facts as found by the Commission, Colvin's 'dismissal' was without valid cause for the reasons therein stated, namely that he had filed a false and fraudulent claim for travel expenses during the period May 15, 1950–June 8, 1950.

[3] While we feel that the judgment of this court in the Colvin case, supra, is controlling and decisive as the facts therein, and herein, are on all material questions of fact identical, we deem it necessary for a clear understanding of this decision that we proceed to a full discussion of these particular cases as they affect relators herein.

[4] The facts of the case as found by the Civil Service Commission, as applicable to each of the relators herein, are as follows:

'Findings of Fact

'A. Boucher

'At the time of his dismissal, Boucher had attained permanent Civil Service status as an Employment Security Claims Investigator in the State Division of Employment Security. He had served the Division meritoriously since September 5, 1946, and he has an unblemished record for character and service during this period.

'In May, 1950, Marvin E. Thames, then Administrator of the Division, requested Boucher to attend an I.A.P.E.S. Convention in Long Beach, California. Boucher refused as he was unable to afford the expense of the trip. Thames advised Boucher that the trip could be made at agency expense. Under agency rules in effect at that time, advance written authority from the Dallas Regional Office of the United States Department of Labor, Bureau of Employment Security, was required for such a trip to be made at agency expense. Thames told Boucher that the Regional Office had authorized this trip, and Boucher did not question the authority. There is no evidence that Boucher knew of the aforementioned agency rules. Thames' testimony that the Regional Office granted its authority by telephone prior to the departure of Boucher has not been contradicted. An advance of $350 for expense was authorized by Thames and received by Boucher, who then attended the Long Beach Convention. Upon their return from the convention, Thames advised Boucher that the Regional Office had withdrawn its approval, and in Boucher's presence Thames called the Dallas Office and spoke to one L. M. Crawford, who suggested that Boucher execute an expense report for a Dallas trip, which would then be approved by the Regional Office. This Boucher refused to do. Ultimately, at the suggestion of Thames, Boucher prepared a travel expense report, showing certain trips in Louisiana which actually had never been made by Boucher. Annexed to this report were receipts with which Boucher was not familiar. This report was apparently signed by Boucher, although Boucher testified that he did not think he signed it. Boucher did endorse the check issued by the Division on the strength of the report. Boucher actually spent, on the Long Beach trip, the amount reported on the false travel expense report, which was the basis of his discharge. He refunded a portion of this amount to the Division on or about December, 1950, and the balance he refunded by certified check on or about May 22, 1953, and the Division of Employment Security presently is holding this check, never having cashed same.

'B. Wilkinson

'At the time of his dismissal, Wilkinson had attained permanent Civil Service status as an Employment Security District Supervisor in the State Division of Employment Security. He had served the Division meritoriously since October 5, 1937, and he has an unblemished record for character and service during this period.

'In April, 1950, Marvin E. Thames, then Administrator of the Division, requested Wilkinson to attend a Biannual Convention of the A.S.F.S. & M.E. being held in Omaha, Nebraska. Wilkinson refused as he was unable to afford the expense of the trip. Thames advised Wilkinson that the trip could be made at agency expense; whereupon Wilkinson went on the trip to Omaha. Upon his return he was directed by Thames to render an expense account showing a trip to Dallas, Texas, not to Omaha, Nebraska, which Wilkinson did and was reimbursed by the agency for his expenses on the basis of a travel report signed by him and approved by Marvin E. Thames, showing travel to Dallas from Lake Charles covering the period 4-23-50 to 4-30-50.

[. . . .]

'Wilkinson actually spent on his trip to Omaha the amount he claimed on the false travel report he rendered showing a trip to Dallas, Texas, covering the period April 23, 1950, to April 29, 1950[...]. [....]

'C. Gueymard

'At the time of his dismissal, Gueymard had attained permanent Civil Service status as an Employment Supervisor I in the State Division of Employment Security. He had served the Division meritoriously since March 16, 1936, and he has an unblemished record for character and service during this period.

'In May, 1950, Gueymard planned a trip to Long Beach, California, in his personal automobile to attend the I.A.P.E.S. Convention [...]. [....] However, at the request of Marvin E. Thames, then Administrator of the Division, he changed his plans and drove to California by way of Dallas, Texas, instead of Houston, so as to pick up a delegate to the convention who lived in Dallas. This change in plans was requested by Thames and with the approval of the Deputy Director of the Regional Office of the Bureau of Employment Security. Gueymard was told by Thames that he could claim reimbursement of expenses from New Orleans to Dallas and return. [....]

'Upon his return from the convention and other points on the West Coast which he visited, Gueymard was advised by Thames to execute an expense report showing a trip to Dallas, Texas and include thereon expenses for four or five days in Dallas, but to show dates different from the dates he was in Long Beach, California.

'He then filed a fraudulent expense report showing a trip on June 19, 1950, claiming reimbursement for use of his personal automobile at 7$ per mile plus meals and tips incurred while on the purported trip. While the evidence shows that he did travel to Dallas on his way to California, the evidence is equally clear that he did not remain in Dallas the number of days shown on his travel report and he did not make any trip at all to Dallas on the dates shown on his travel report.

'The expense report which he filed was approved by Thames and an agency check was written and delivered to Gueymard who endorsed it back to the agency. Gueymard also paid the agency the difference between the amount of this check and the amount of his travel advance. On or about May 22, 1953, Gueymard refunded to the agency the amount he had been paid for the Dallas trip and according to the record the certified check covering the refund is being held by the Division of Employment Security which has never cashed it.'

[5] Under the above set of facts, the Commission found that the action of the employing authority in dismissing each of the relators from his employment on October 29, 1954 was for both a reasonable and legal cause.

[6] There is no dispute as to the material facts in these cases which was also true in the Colvin case. The relators herein felt they were financially unable to make the trips involved in these expense accounts — Wilkinson to Omaha and California and the other relators to California and that they only went after being assured by the Administrator of the Division, Mr. Marvin E. Thames, that he had cleared the question of expenses with the federal agency in Dallas and that they could make the trip at agency expense. [....] It is evident that Mr. J. Hadley Heard, the Administrator, who was appointed after a change in administrations, was quite familiar with the truth concerning the filing of the expense account by these relators which stated Dallas rather than Long Beach, California, for in his letter of dismissal he states '* * * that coercion and intimidation may have been exercised'. There is also positive testimony in the record that Heard was orally apologetic in talking to relators about their dismissal. He put it on the ground that he was on the hot seat and under great pressure. All in all, it doesn't appear from his testimony that he actually and really believed they were guilty of any fraud.

[7] Furthermore, everybody in the Department knew about the whole thing, there was nothing hidden and the superiors who had to approve these accounts did so despite the fact that they were familiar with the situation, and these same employees continued in their employment without any question.

[8] We believe that our discussion in the Colvin case is applicable and controlling in the cases under discussion and we quote therefrom:

> 'The basis of the decision of the Civil Service Commission in dismissing appellant was that he submitted 'a false and fraudulent claim for travel expenses.'

> '(1) Upon our examination of the term 'fraud' or 'fraudulent' we find that two elements are essential to constitute legal fraud, the intention to defraud and loss or damage or a strong probability of loss or damage. Slocomb and others v. Real Estate Bank of Arkansas, 2 Rob. 92. A mere misrepresentation or in this instance, a false or incorrect account, is not synonymous with fraud as used in the legal sense. Buxton et al. v. McKendrick et al., 223 La. 62, 64 So.2d 844.

> 'The necessity for the combination of the two elements is emphasized in L.S.A.-Civil Code article 1847 in defining fraud as applied to contracts as:

>> '"Fraud, as applied to contracts, is the cause of an error bearing on a material part of the contract, created or continued by artifice, with design to obtain some unjust advantages to the one party, or to cause an inconvenience or loss to the other."

> '(2) The uncontroverted facts present in the record and those findings of fact found by the Commission reveal that appellant had been selected to represent his agency at a meeting in Omaha, Nebraska, and that his travel expenses to attend said meeting would be paid by the agency. When he

returned from the trip he filed the questioned account, including therein the actual expenses incurred by him in his trip to Omaha, but at the insistence and order of Marvin E. Thames, the then Administrator of the Division, he represented in the account the fact that the expenses were incurred in connection with a meeting in Dallas rather than in Omaha.

'Nowhere in the record is it shown that by the submission of the account did he acquire a profit or monies to which he was not entitled, nor is there any showing that by being reimbursed caused 'an inconvenience or loss' to the agency. There is not one iota of evidence in the record to even indicate that at the time he was selected for the trip to Omaha that such expenses incurred by him on said trip were not validly authorized and there is no evidence whatever that he had conspired with the Administrator of the agency to defraud, or that appellant alone intended or by artifice conceived a plan to gain an unjust advantage by the filing of the account. Though it is true that the account so filed, showing a trip to Dallas, Texas, is false in that respect, if the misrepresentation was made without the intention to defraud on the part of appellant and if the error did not gain appellant an advantage to which he was not due, it is evident that neither of the elements of fraud have been satisfied and thus the incorrect account is not fraudulent.

'Upon his severance from the Civil Service position the record reveals that there was deducted from his accrued earnings the $206.90 which was the total amount of the items expended by him on his trip to Omaha and itemized in the erroneous account filed representing that the items of expenses covered the trip to Dallas, Texas.

'We are of the opinion that upon appellant's reinstatement in his position, upon submission of a corrected travel account itemizing the expenses incurred by him on his trip to Omaha, he would be entitled to reimbursement of the amount of his expenses, which in itself is recognition by us that the questioned account was not fraudulent.'

[....]

[9] In conclusion, we wish to add that the plan to substitute Dallas for Omaha and/or Long Beach, California, was agreed upon between Thames, the Louisiana Administrator who was indicted by the federal government for conspiring with William L. Crawford, Deputy Regional Director of the Federal Bureau of Employment Security at Dallas, Texas, to defraud the United States by means of the false reports in question[2] and the same William L. Crawford, both of whom continued in their jobs. [....]

[....]

---

2. The federal indictment against Thames was dismissed by directed verdict.

[10] Accepting the facts found by the Commission herein and additional facts which might be stated in this report as proven by this record and which are not in conflict or contradiction of the facts found by the Commission, all of which is on all fours with the facts in the Colvin case, and the reasons hereinabove given we do not believe that these relators were guilty of filing a false or fraudulent claim for travel expenses in the sense necessary to constitute legal fraud as we emphasized in the Colvin case.

[11] It is therefore ordered that the judgment appealed from is reversed, annulled, and set aside, and judgment is hereby rendered reinstating Robert R. Boucher, appellant, in his former position and there be judgment in his favor and against the Division of Employment Security for back pay from October 29, 1954 in accordance with law.

[12] It is also ordered, adjudged and decreed that there be judgment rendered reinstating A. C. Wilkinson [....]

[13] It is also ordered, adjudged and decreed that the dismissal of Jules R. Gueymard, deceased, is hereby decreed to have been illegal and that there now be judgment in favor of Mrs. Ethel Dickinson, widow of Jules R. Gueymard [....]

[14] REVERSED AND RENDERED.

Question

1. Paragraph 7: Notice how well the Court coordinates former Louisiana Civil Code article 1847 and the two required elements of fraud with the holdings of some prior cases. Do you find the same two elements of fraud in today's Louisiana Civil Code article 1953?

Priority Hospital Group, Inc.
v.
James Manning, Pathway Healthcare, LLC, Pathway Rehabilitation Hospital of Bossier, LLC, and Dan Bob Turner

Court of Appeal of Louisiana
Second Circuit
September 23, 2020
303 So.3d 1106

COX, J.

[. . . .]

[1] [T]o find fraud from silence or suppression of the truth, there must exist a duty to speak or to disclose information. [. . . .] Whether one party owes another a duty to speak depends on the nature of the relationship between the parties and the nature of the information allegedly suppressed. [. . . .]

[. . . .]

[2] To bring a claim for fraud, the plaintiff must allege that (1) there was a misrepresentation, suppression, or omission of true information; (2) the intent to obtain an unjust advantage, damage, or inconvenience to another; and, (3) the error induced by a fraudulent act must relate to a circumstance substantially influencing the victim's consent to contract. [. . . .]

[. . . .]

See also *Shelton v. Standard/700 Associates*, 798 So.2d 60 (La. 2001), *Rose v. Johnson*, 940 So.2d 181 (La.App. 3 Cir. 2006).

Curley Wilson
v.
Aetna Casualty & Surety Company
Court of Appeal of Louisiana
Third Circuit
October 30, 1969
228 So.2d 229

TATE, Judge.

[1] The plaintiff Wilson sues for personal injuries. Made defendant is the liability insurer of the motorist who struck him. The defendant appeals from adverse judgment awarding $16,658.50 to Wilson, subject to a credit of $5,000 received by him on an earlier 'release'.

[2] The substantial issue of this appeal is whether the trial court erred in overruling the defendant's exception pleading res judicata.[1] This plea is based upon Wilson's execution of this release on October 6, 1967 for $5,000, discharging the insurer from all claims arising out of the accident of May 22, 1967.

I

[3] The plaintiff contends, and the trial court held, that the release was invalid because there was no real consent of the plaintiff to the compromise, due to the intolerable physical and financial circumstances in which the plaintiff was situated and which destroyed his freedom of will. The defendant replies that this is not a cause recognized by our law for annulling a compromise. We find the defendant is correct.

[4] A valid compromise has the 'authority of things adjudged'. Civil Code Article 3078. A compromise cannot be annulled for error of law or for lesion. Id. It may, however, be rescinded for fraud or violence, as well as for error of fact as to a principal cause (motive) for making the contract, as to the person with whom it is made, or as to the subject matter of the dispute. Civil Code Articles 3078, 3079; see also, Civil Code Articles 1824–1826, 1850–1853; Cole v. Lumbermens Mutual Cas. Co., 160 So.2d 785 (La.App.3d Cir. 1963); Note, Compromise in Louisiana, 14 Tul.L.Rev. 282 (1940).

[5] The plaintiff apparently contends (a) that there was error as to the principal motive, in that he did not know his claim was worth far more than the $5,000 for which he settled it, and (b) that his will was vitiated by lack of consent through the violence or duress exercised upon him by external circumstances and by the misinformation from a third person that a lawyer could not help him. See Smith, A

---

1. We may say that the evidence supports the trial court's findings of the motorist's undoubted negligence, of Wilson's freedom from contributory negligence, and of the award for Wilson's serious permanent injuries — issues we need not discuss, in view of our holding that res judicata bars the suit.

Refresher Course in Cause, 12 La.L.Rev. 2, 9–13 (1951). (No contention is made as to any fraud or deception by the insurer's adjuster, nor as to this adjuster's participation in or knowledge of any alleged misinformation causing the plaintiff to settle his claim.)

II

[6] We accept the trial judge's findings of fact as to the circumstances surrounding the execution of the release:

> 'Plaintiff was 66 years old on the date of the accident and is classified as illiterate. He has no wife nor children and his only relatives consist of an aged and almost helpless mother and a sister who live in an adjoining parish. The only person that visited plaintiff with regularity during his 140 days in the hospital was Mrs. Lenad Enard with whom plaintiff boarded prior to the accident and who undertook to care for and nurse plaintiff when he was released from the hospital.

> 'On the Monday or Tuesday prior to the signing of the settlement on Friday, Mr. Wheeldon (defendant's adjuster) offered plaintiff $5,000.00 in settlement of the claim. Plaintiff turned this down and made a counter offer of $10,000.00. Mr. Wheeldon refused that but told plaintiff that if he changed his mind he could notify him and he would receive $5,000.00 less the amounts owed to the hospital and physicians.

> 'Prior to this time plaintiff had made an effort to get an attorney, but (for some reason or other) no attorney was consulted. Dr. Louis E. Shirley, Jr., plaintiff's physician, is of the impression that he talked to an attorney about the claim but cannot recall the attorney. Dr. Shirley did advise plaintiff that the only way he could get prompt settlement was to take the amount offered; that if plaintiff employed an attorney it would take a year or more to have the suit tried; and, further, that he would have to pay a substantial fee for the attorney and might not get a great deal more than the $5,000.00 offered.

> 'Dr. Shirley also advised plaintiff that it was time for him to be discharged from the hospital; that Charity Hospital would not accept him as a patient; that if plaintiff was not discharged from the hospital his hospital bill would increase at the rate of approximately $30.00 per day; and that medicare benefits were exhausted.

> 'Plaintiff's bill at that time was already $3,268.00, and his doctor bill was approximately $900.00, of which medicare had paid approximately $2,200.00.

> 'Plaintiff had just recently been released from traction and was then casted from his hip to his toes on his left leg, and with another cast on his right hip down to his knee, which immobilized his hip. Plaintiff was immobilized during his entire hospital stay. It is obvious that plaintiff needed nursing attention and, furthermore, that he needed physical therapy. * * *'

[7] Some additional facts of relevance include:

— The plaintiff's normal income is limited to his monthly social security payments plus whatever income he can derive from doing odd jobs around Jennings. Prior to his accident, this 66-year-old laborer received $92 monthly from social security and approximately $40 weekly from odd jobs. Since the accident he receives $97 monthly from social security, but he has been unable to accept employment.

— Signing the release and compromising his claim enabled plaintiff to pay Mrs. Enard $40 weekly — as long as the money from the settlement lasted — to care for him. Had he not been able to pay, she would have been unable to care for him, and he had no place else to stay or to be cared for in his helpless condition.

III

[8] Plaintiff's principal arguments for annulling the release arise from:

— The economic straits plaintiff faced once his discharge from the hospital became imminent. Dr. Shirley testified: 'He felt like he had no place to go.'

— The influence on plaintiff's decision to settle exerted by third persons who, plaintiff claims, had an overriding interest in an early settlement — particularly the attending physician, who said: 'I may have influenced him more than I should have. By this, I mean, I did emphasize to him that he could either get the lawyer and make the settlement in a year or two, or either he could settle and have his money to go on now.', and

— The fact that plaintiff, though he knew the advice of an attorney was desirable, did not consult one prior to making the settlement.

[9] In annulling the release, our brother at trial was noticeably moved by the difficulties of plaintiff's situation:

'(S)ince we are dealing with an illiterate, aged plaintiff with no family, who was under serious financial pressure and in the intolerable position of having to leave the hospital; having to pay a hospital bill; having to pay for future nursing care, and having only one source to raise funds, and who was not advised by any attorney, this Court holds that the release was signed in error and must be annulled. * * * (T)he more thought given to the intolerable and untenable position in which this plaintiff found himself, the more convinced this Court is that the release must be set aside.'

IV

[10] Nevertheless — despite these reasons which indicate that the plaintiff Wilson had no bargaining power to resist the defendant's offer and was instead under strong economic duress to accept it — we are unable to find that these constitute a ground recognized by our law for the rescission of a compromise.

[11] Louisiana Civil Code Articles 1851 through 1853 provide that a contract entered into under duress that would cause fear of great injury to person, reputation,

or fortune is invalid, even if the person favored by the contract did not exercise the violence or make the threats and was unaware of the duress. A compromise is subject to rescission when executed under such duress. Civil Code Article 3079.

[12] However, the contract — invalidating duress referred to is that which proceeds from a fear of force or violence which wipes out freedom of consent; it connotes an actor performing an exterior act which gives rise to the duress, rather than the entire set of objective circumstances causing the victim to act as he does. Planiol, Civil Law Treatise, Volume 1, Nos. 277, 278 (LSLI translation, 1959); Ibid, Volume 2, Nos. 1070, 1072; Aubry & Rau, Obligations, Section 343a (1 Civil Law Translations 314, LSLI translation, 1959); Holstein, Vices of Consent in the Law of Contracts, 13 Tul.L.Rev. 362 and 561 at 569–79 (1939). No doctrinal or jurisprudential authority to the contrary is cited.

[13] The duress here relied upon does not constitute a Code-recognized ground to rescind a compromise.

[14] Nor did the advice of Dr. Shirley amount to duress. There was no element of threatening the plaintiff's person or property. The doctor simply counselled the patient that settlement under the circumstances was in the latter's best interest. By itself, the bad advice of a stranger to the compromise is not ground for rescinding it. LeBlanc v. Brou, 205 So.2d 141 (La.App.1st Cir. 1967).

V

[15] The plaintiff-appellee cites numerous decisions. We find they concern situations differentiated from the present.

[16] This is not a case of error as to the nature of the contract. Civil Code Article 1841; Wise v. Prescott, 244 La. 157, 151 So.2d 356 (1963); Bergeron v. Port Allen Mortuary, Inc., 178 So.2d 442 (La.App.1st Cir. 1965). The present plaintiff knew he was executing a settlement of his claim for personal injuries, and that the document he signed was a release in full.

[17] Nor was the plaintiff in error as to the person with whom he was contracting or as to the matter in dispute. Civil Code Articles 3073, 3079; Moak v. American Auto. Ins. Co., 242 La. 160, 134 So.2d 911 (1961); Harris v. Stockman, 197 So.2d 365 (La.App.2d Cir. 1967). The plaintiff knew that Mr. Wheeldon was the defendant's adjuster, and that he himself was compromising all claims arising out of the accident causing his injury. He did not think the settlement merely for medical expenses, as in Harris, but knew that it included all claims for damages for personal injury. He received a sum noticeably in excess of accrued medical costs to him.

[18] A release may also be rescinded for error as to the principal cause or motive, i.e., 'that consideration without which the contract would not have been made.' Civil Code Article 1825; McKneely v. Turner, 193 So.2d 373 (La.App.2d Cir. 1966). The plaintiff knew that he was releasing his claim against the defendant and granting a full discharge in return for being paid $5,000 immediately. He was not acting under any error of fact as to principal cause of the contract.

[19] Error as to a material though not the principal cause may also be ground for annulment of a contract, but only if the other party knew or, from the circumstances, should have known, that the party acting in error regarded it as of the essence, as his motive. Civil Code Article 1826; Cole v. Lumbermens Mut. Cas. Co., 160 So.2d 785 (La.App.3d Cir. 1964). No evidence supports such a ground for rescission here.

[20] Nor is there any evidence to support rescission for fraud, Carter v. Foreman, 219 So.2d 21 (La.App.4th Cir. 1969), or for coercion through illegal exaction, New Orleans & N.E.R.R. Co. v. Louisiana Const. & Imp. Co., 109 La. 13, 33 So. 51.

[21] It is unfortunate that the plaintiff did not receive the advice of an attorney before he executed the release in question. However, in the absence of legal requirement that he have done so, the compromise is not invalid on that account. Further, the plaintiff was fully aware of his right to consult with an attorney, and he could have refused to sign the release until he consulted with an attorney.

VI

[22] The plaintiff was fully aware of his situation, the nature and effect of the release, and the extent of the claim compromised. His consent to the release was voluntary. We cannot annul the transaction because it was a bad bargain for him or out of sympathy for the plaintiff's desperate plight at the time he compromised his claim.

[23] The release was valid. The exception of res judicata should have been sustained, barring trial on the merits and the subsequent award of damages.

[24] The judgment of the trial court is reversed, and the plaintiff's suit is dismissed at his cost.

[. . . .]

Questions

1. Paragraphs 4–5: Read carefully Louisiana Civil Code articles 3071–3083 on compromise and, particularly, for the purpose of this case, Louisiana Civil Code article 3082. Read also the Louisiana Civil Code articles on error (arts. 1948–1952), fraud (arts. 1953–1958), and duress/violence (arts. 1959–1964). Consider Louisiana Civil Code article 1963. Could Mr. Wilson fit under this article? Would it be of any help to him? Where the article reads "not in collusion with the party exerting duress," could the hospital/doctors be that "party exerting duress"? *See* paragraph 6. What kind of duress does the Civil Code contemplate? Does it contemplate economic duress? *See* paragraph 7.

2. Paragraph 6: What kind of standard of behavior is the court applying to the plaintiff's behavior? Is this standard compatible with the plaintiff making a counteroffer? Were the doctors and/or hospital making a legitimate, lawful exercise of their rights in their dealings with the plaintiff? Could the doctors

and/or hospital be said to have abused their rights or not acted in good faith? *See* La. Civ. Code art. 1759.

3. Paragraphs 8–9: Can the plaintiff's arguments amount to grounds of error? What about duress?

4. Paragraphs 10–14: Why did the Court of Appeal overrule the trial court? Although the Court acknowledges the existence of a form of duress, why did the Court nevertheless reject it as a basis for rescission? What kind of duress does the Code recognize?

5. Paragraphs 15–21: How would you explain the rejection by the Court of the ground of error as to the nature of the contract? Error as to the person? Error as to the motive/reason? Why was there no fraud?

John C. Skannal
v.
Dennis Bamburg, Margie Dumas, Bamburg & Sligo Hills, L.L.C.

Court of Appeal of Louisiana
Second Circuit
January 27, 2010
33 So.3d 227

MOORE, J.

[1] Dennis and Margie Bamburg appeal a judgment which nullified four contracts with their former business partner, the late John C. Skannal, and awarded damages and attorney fees. After a 16-day trial, the district court found that out of nine contested contracts entered between 1996 and 2004, four — exclusive right to sell agreement (10/9/03), act of sale of membership interest in Sligo Hills LLC (2/27/04), act of sale of common stock in Sligo Enterprises Inc. (3/2/04), and mineral deed with assignment of leases (3/2/04) — occurred when Skannal lacked mental capacity to enter business transactions owing to alcohol-induced dementia, Alzheimer's disease and prostate cancer. The court also found that Skannal was "under the influence of Dennis Bamburg." For these reasons the court declared the contracts null. By a supplemental opinion, the court further found that Dennis Bamburg's dealings with Skannal constituted fraud, entitling Skannal's succession to a penalty of 25% of the purchase prices and attorney fees. By a second supplemental opinion, the court set attorney fees and fixed costs.

[2] The court rendered judgment which (1) nullified the four contracts, (2) ordered Skannal's succession to restore the purchase prices of $843,752, (3) ordered the Bamburgs to pay damages of $307,315 for fraud, attorney fees of $500,000, and costs, and (4) ordered incidental relief not contested on appeal.

[3] The Bamburgs have appealed, raising [**numerous**] assignments of error. [. . . .]

Factual Background

[4] Skannal owned a large tract of land called Sligo Plantation (said to have been in his family since the 1840s) in south Bossier Parish where he ran a livestock operation but primarily lived off his oil and gas royalties. He was retired from the state police and still was a notary public. A host of witnesses described him as reclusive, asocial, a chronic alcoholic and generally unpleasant person. Although many said he was miserly and loath to part with any of his assets, in the mid-1970s he was trying to sell a country lot on Skannal Road when he met the Bamburgs. Dennis was an Air Force vet working as a ticket agent for Delta Airlines when he called Skannal about buying the lot. The Bamburgs bought it and moved their mobile home there.

[5] According to the Bamburgs, Skannal wanted more than just a neighbor; he wanted a business partner. At Dennis's suggestion, they formed a corporation to develop part of Skannal's land into a 148-unit mobile home park called Plantation Acres. A few years later they formed another corporation, Sligo Enterprises Inc., to develop a tract that Skannal's father had subdivided but never completed, Shadow Ridge. Dennis was president, Skannal vice-president, and Margie secretary-treasurer. In both these companies, Skannal contributed the land and the Bamburgs the "sweat equity," and each held 50% of the capital stock. For many years Skannal voiced no objection to this business model, and apparently both projects were financially successful.

[6] In the early 1990s, Skannal's marriage ran aground; his wife moved out while he was at a ham radio convention in Texas, and at least two of his three children sided with their mother. This resulted in a long period of estrangement which, according to the succession, isolated Skannal and accelerated his drinking. Also, it meant that Skannal's immediate family were [*sic*] not able to provide any insight into his thoughts, motives and mental status from about 1992 on.

[7] In the mid-1990s, Skannal and the Bamburgs entered into a series of contracts to develop a large tract of Skannal's land into a golf course with an adjacent subdivision called Olde Oaks. Several different agreements were involved. Initially, Skannal contributed the land, some 332 acres with a reservation of mineral rights, and the Bamburgs paid cash for the equivalent value, $154,750, and each received an equal number of additional shares in Sligo Enterprises Inc.

[8] In February 1999, Skannal and Dennis formed another business, Sligo Hills LLC, to facilitate the project further. As before, Skannal put in a large amount of land (according to the petition, over 1,300 acres, virtually the last remnant of Sligo Plantation, but with a reservation of minerals) and the Bamburgs put in a promissory note for $533,000 (which they and Skannal agreed was an equivalent value), for a 50% interest each in the LLC.

[9] Around this time, Skannal was diagnosed with inoperable prostate cancer. He enrolled in an experimental treatment program at the Feist-Weiller Center at LSU Health Sciences Center from January 2000 through February 2003, under the direction of Dr. Richard Mansour, who saw him regularly for these critical three years.

Dr. Mansour found him to be a compliant patient who seemed to understand the nature of the experimental program.

[10] Other witnesses, however, described a man in rapid decline, physically and mentally. His office in the old plantation store was unkempt and littered with mounds of beer cans and bourbon bottles. Another person with whom Skannal did business, a fertilizer salesman named Jimmy Pete Burks, testified that by 2003 Skannal's farm was a shambles. Burks began to assist him with the farming operation, and brought him liquor anytime he wanted it. One day in August 2003, Burks found him flat on his face in the flowerbed, seriously drunk and injured in the fall. Skannal had to be hospitalized, first at Highland Hospital, then at LifeCare, and then at the psychiatric ward of Promise Hospital, where a geriatric psychiatrist, Dr. Keith Kessel, described him as delusional and combative. Dr. Kessel testified that he phoned Skannal's daughter, Elizabeth, to advise that in his current state, Skannal could be interdicted. Elizabeth testified that she conveyed this information to Dennis, but she never took any action to interdict her father.

[11] For several years, the Municipal Police Employees Retirement System ("MPERS") had been seeking to diversify its portfolio by acquiring real estate, particularly golf courses. According to MPERS's chairman, Bill Fields, Skannal (a retired state policeman) had always been eager to sell, and on two occasions had literally flagged down his red patrol car to press the issue, but Dennis was holding out. In 2000, MPERS bought a portion of the property for $6.5 million, but when the project foundered, MPERS escalated its requests in the belief that additional land for the surrounding subdivision would help the golf club. After long negotiations between Dennis and MPERS, Sligo Enterprises agreed to sell the remaining property for $4.544 million. Skannal and the Bamburgs both pocketed $2.1 million from the deal, making Sligo Enterprises even more lucrative than their prior ventures. At the closing on February 13, 2004, nobody from MPERS suspected that Skannal was an assisted living patient with multiple forms of dementia. The court did not rescind any of the MPERS contracts.

The Nullified Contracts

[12] On October 9, 2003, while Skannal was still in the psychiatric ward at Promise Hospital, Dennis brought him a document, "Exclusive Right to Sell Agreement," whereby Sligo Enterprises granted Dennis the exclusive right to sell corporate property at a 10% commission. Skannal and Dennis both signed this. When Sligo Enterprises later sold its property to MPERS, Bamburg paid himself a commission of $449,400 pursuant to the exclusive right to sell agreement, the first transaction nullified by the court.

[13] After Skannal was discharged from Promise Hospital on October 13, 2003, Burks resumed carrying him liquor. Burks testified that at Skannal's direction, he sold off the remainder of Skannal's cattle. He also testified that around this time, Skannal was earning $40,000 to $70,000 *a month* in mineral royalties. Burks admitted skimming off some of this money for his personal use, as did Elizabeth.

[14] Skannal was again hospitalized from January 14 to February 10, 2004, after which Dennis moved him to The Arbor, an assisted living center. While he was living at The Arbor, he signed the three other contracts ultimately nullified by the court.

[15] According to the Bamburgs, after the golf course deal was completed, Skannal wanted to convert his assets to cash. On February 27, 2004, Dennis drove him to the office of real estate attorney Jeff DeLaune, who had handled several of the parties' transactions. Using information supplied by Dennis, DeLaune drew up a two-page "Act of Sale of Membership Interest in Sligo Hills, LLC" whereby Skannal sold his remaining 50% interest in the LLC to the Bamburgs for $400,000, which Skannal received by check and deposited. DeLaune, his wife, and Janelle Ward, the notary, all testified that Skannal chatted with them about the business climate in Bossier, especially the riverboats, where Skannal had become a frequent patron, often losing thousands of dollars a night on the slots. These witnesses described a man perfectly aware of what the sale purported to do. They were not aware that he was in an assisted living center or diagnosed with dementia, and they agreed that no separate counsel was present to explain the deal to him. This was the second contract the court nullified.

[16] Four days later, on March 2, 2004, Dennis again drove Skannal to DeLaune's office, where DeLaune had drawn up two documents based on information provided by Dennis. The first was a two-page "Act of Sale of Common Stock of Sligo Enterprises Inc." whereby Skannal sold his remaining 2400 shares of the company to the Bamburgs for $323,752, which Skannal received by check and deposited. Second was a two-page "Mineral Deed with Assignment of Leases" whereby Skannal sold the naked ownership of all his mineral interests to the Bamburgs for $120,000, which Skannal received by check and deposited. The mineral deed was subject to Skannal's lifetime usufruct. Ms. DeLaune notarized these acts; as on the prior occasion, she and the witnesses testified that Skannal appeared sober and sentient, but they were unaware of his medical condition, and there was no other attorney present to advise him separately. These were the other two contracts nullified by the court.

Subsequent Events and Procedural History

[17] After these events, Skannal's health deteriorated rapidly. Jimmy Pete Burks was bringing him liquor all the time, and the staff at The Arbor reported that Skannal was usually drunk and ornery, fell down frequently, and could not control his bowels. Because drinking was against The Arbor's regulations, Dennis moved him to Garden Court, where the situation continued. In moments of apparent lucidity, however, he began telling Burks that "they" had robbed him blind and that he had nothing left. By "they," he meant the Bamburgs. Burks relayed this information to Elizabeth, who contacted her two brothers, A.C. and Barron. The children then revived a relationship with their moribund father, and in March 2005 they took him to attorney John Odom's office and painted the whole scenario.

[18] On March 14, Skannal filed this suit to rescind his contracts with the Bamburgs, dating back to 1999, on grounds of incapacity, error, fraud and lesion. Skannal

died in November 2005, and his son Barron (an undertaker in Texas), the succession representative, was substituted as plaintiff.

[19] By amended petitions, the succession added contracts dating back to January 1996 and demanded damages for fraud. A prodigious course of discovery and pretrial motions ensued. [. . . .]

[. . . .]

Discussion: Lack of Capacity 1st Asgn. of Error

[20] By their first assignment of error, the Bamburgs urge the court was manifestly erroneous to find that Skannal lacked capacity to engage in routine business transactions. They show that under La. C.C. art. 1918, only "persons deprived of reason" lack capacity to contract; they contend that the court applied too high a standard, relying on the succession's suggestion that Skannal could sign a contract only if he had been sober for weeks, had independent counsel, and somebody first read the document to him. They urge the proper standard is clear and convincing evidence of lack of capacity. *Meadors v. Pacific Int'l Petr.,* 449 So.2d 26 (La.App. 1 Cir.), *writ denied,* 450 So.2d 964 (1984). They argue, contrary to the defense experts' view, that Skannal was able to do many things, and do them well, after 1997. Finally, they urge that under La. C.C. art. 1926, a contract made by a noninterdicted person may be attacked after his death, on grounds of incapacity, only when the contract is gratuitous, evidences lack of understanding, or was made within 30 days of death. They submit that the succession's claims were raised after Skannal's death and meet none of the criteria of art. 1926.

[21] The succession responds that under the manifest error standard of review, considering the voluminous evidence in the entire record on which the court based its ruling, the finding should be affirmed. It contends the expert testimony overwhelmingly proved that Skannal suffered from alcohol dementia, vascular dementia and Alzheimer's disease, and these conditions deprived him of reason. It submits that the court carefully weighed the evidence, as it refused to nullify the contracts executed before 2001, and reasonably resolved the conflicting claims.

[22] All persons have capacity to contract, except unemancipated minors, interdicts, and persons deprived of reason at the time of contracting. La. C.C. art. 1918. The presumption is that all persons have capacity to contract; lack of capacity must be shown by clear and convincing evidence. *Succession of Hollis,* 43,315 (La.App. 2 Cir. 6/18/08), 987 So.2d 387, *writ denied,* 2008-1632 (La.10/24/08), 992 So.2d 1035. A contract made by a person without legal capacity is relatively null and may be rescinded only at the request of that person or his legal representative. La. C.C. art. 1919. A noninterdicted person, who was deprived of reason at the time of contracting, may obtain rescission of an onerous contract upon the ground of incapacity only upon showing that the other party knew or should have known that person's incapacity. La. C.C. art. 1925. *Succession of Hollis, supra.*

[23] The succession correctly shows that the expert evidence addressing Skannal's capacity was voluminous; this court cannot belabor the detailed, prolonged

and often repetitive testimony of Drs. Ware, Williams, Seiden, Henry and Phillips. It is sufficient to say that the succession's experts felt that Skannal lacked capacity from about 1997 on, while the Bamburgs' expert felt he retained reasonable capacity until the summer of 2004. [. . . .]

[24] Admittedly, the record presents factual anomalies that are difficult to reconcile. [. . . .]

[. . . .]

[25] Even with the anomalies so ably urged by the Bamburgs, the record is sufficient to establish by clear and convincing evidence that Skannal suffered from multiple forms of dementia, prostate cancer and habitual drunkenness that deprived him of reason at certain times. On this immense and difficult record, we cannot say the district court was plainly wrong in finding that Skannal lacked contractual capacity on October 9, 2003, February 27, 2004, and March 2, 2004, when these transactions were executed.

[. . . .]   *2nd Asgn. of Error*

Fraud

[26] By their second assignment of error, the Bamburgs urge the court erred as a matter of law in finding that fraud was proved in any of the challenged transactions. They contend that under La. C.C. art. 1953, the first element of any action for fraud is a misrepresentation, suppression, or omission of true information, and that in this enormous record "plaintiff failed to articulate any instance of misrepresentation by Bamburg to Skannal." They argue that all contracts were reduced to writing, the Bamburgs paid every dollar and fulfilled every promise, and the succession produced no evidence that they ever lied to Skannal.

[27] The succession responds that the proper standard for reviewing a finding of fraud is manifest error. *Chambers v. Kennington*, 35,079 (La.App. 2 Cir. 9/28/01), 796 So.2d 733. It contends that because of their relation of confidence, Skannal had no duty to ascertain the truth of any representations the Bamburgs may have made to him. La. C.C. art. 1954. It argues that even without evidence of specific statements, fraud may be proved by "highly suspicious facts and circumstances surrounding a transaction." *Bell v. Vickers*, 568 So.2d 160 (La.App. 2 Cir.1990). It concludes that on this record, the finding of fraud was not plainly wrong.

[28] Fraud is a misrepresentation or a suppression of the truth made with the intention either to obtain an unjust advantage for one party or to cause a loss or inconvenience to the other. Fraud may also result from silence or inaction. La. C.C. art. 1953. The basic elements of an action for fraud against a party to a contract are (1) a misrepresentation, suppression or omission of true information, (2) the intent to obtain an unjust advantage or to cause damage or inconvenience to another, and (3) the error induced by a fraudulent act must relate to a circumstance substantially influencing the victim's consent to the contract. *Shelton v. Standard/700 Associates*, 2001-0587 (La.10/16/01), 798 So.2d 60. Fraud does not

vitiate consent when the party against whom the fraud was directed could have ascertained the truth without difficulty, inconvenience, or special skill. However, this exception does not apply when a relation of confidence has reasonably induced a party to rely on the other's assertions or representations. La. C.C. art. 1954. When a claim of fraud is based on silence or suppression of the truth, the plaintiff must prove a duty to speak or to disclose information. *Greene v. Gulf Coast Bank,* 593 So.2d 630 (La.1992). Fraud need only be proved by a preponderance of the evidence and may be established by circumstantial evidence. La. C.C. art. 1957; *Succession of Hollis, supra.*

[29] The succession correctly shows that the standard of review of a finding of fraud is manifest error. *Mayfield v. Reed,* 43,226 (La.App. 2 Cir. 4/30/08), 981 So.2d 235; *Lafayette Ins. Co. v. Pennington,* 42,434 (La.App. 2 Cir. 9/19/07), 966 So.2d 136. Also, the succession correctly shows that a duty of full disclosure arose from the parties' relation of confidence, their work together in numerous business ventures over a 25-year period. Notably, Skannal was usually the "silent" partner, providing the real estate and relying on information from the Bamburgs, who performed the physical element of development and sales.

[30] As with the lack of capacity, this record provides a long procession of facts for and against the finding of fraud. The Bamburgs correctly show that for each of the annulled transactions, they paid and performed precisely as stated in the contract; that not one shred of testimony directly implicates them in a misrepresentation or suppression of the truth; and that because of the parties' long and lucrative business association, Skannal may have intended to treat them more favorably than an arm's-length buyer. On the other hand, the Bamburgs, more than anyone, knew or should have known of Skannal's deepening cognitive deficits, chronic alcoholism, and dependence on them. Moreover, the absence of direct proof of fraud likely results more from Skannal's dementia than from the purity of the Bamburgs' statements to him. The whole course of events in late 2003 and early 2004 can equally well be viewed as an elaborate scheme to "clean the man out" before his death or interdiction.

[31] Most impressive to this court is the gross inequity of the annulled contracts, particularly the mineral deed with assignment of leases. Henry Coutret, the succession's expert petroleum engineer, testified that mineral rights usually sell for 30 to 60 times their monthly production, and the sale price of $120,000 was less than 10% of fair market value. He had never heard of a sale of the naked interest only, reserving usufruct to the seller. The Bamburgs' CPA and expert in business valuation, John Walter Dean, testified that he would have used a multiple of 24, by which a fair market value was $1,133,000; even though the Bamburgs paid only $120,000, Skannal received royalties of $1,391,987 between March 2003 and his death in 2005, meaning he ultimately got a fair market value. Counting royalties from lessees as part of the purchase price is, in our view, a misleading inducement. The district court was entitled to find that this deal was so peculiar and unfavorable to Skannal that it could not have occurred in the absence of fraud.

[32] The district court was not plainly wrong to find that Dennis Bamburg committed fraud to obtain an unfair advantage over Skannal. This assignment does not present reversible error.

Undue Influence   3rd Asgn. of Error

[33] By their third assignment of error, the Bamburgs urge that the court's finding that Dennis Bamburg unduly influenced Skannal is legally flawed and manifestly erroneous. They show that under La. C.C. art. 1479, "influence" is a ground for revoking a donation inter vivos or mortis causa, and not for rescinding an onerous contract. This article also requires proof that the influence "so impaired the volition of the donor as to substitute the volition of the donee * * * for the volition of the donor." They contend that the evidence shows only that Skannal relied on their advice, which had been sound and lucrative for over 20 years, but that the irascible and determined Skannal never allowed *anyone* to usurp his own volition. They also show that the succession's own expert, Dr. Seiden, testified that Skannal was "vulnerable" to coercion, but declined to state that he was actually coerced.

[34] The succession does not directly address the Bamburgs' construction of Art. 1479, but urges that the evidence was sufficient to support the finding of undue influence.

[35] For the reasons already discussed, this court has affirmed the findings of lack of capacity and fraud, both of which would result in the rescission of the affected transactions. La. C.C. arts. 1919, 1958. With due respect to the Bamburgs' articulate argument, we conclude that even if the finding of undue influence were legally wrong, reversing it would not result in reinstating the affected transactions. We therefore pretermit this issue. We would only note that despite the literal language of Art. 1479, courts have applied the concept of undue influence to a marriage contract, *Brumfield v. Brumfield,* 477 So.2d 1161 (La.App. 1 Cir.1985), *writ denied,* 479 So.2d 922 (1985), and stated in dictum that it applied to "a deed or a contract," *Mitchell v. Bertolla,* 340 So.2d 287 (La.1976). This assignment does not present reversible error.

[. . . .]

Questions

1. Paragraph 20: This case is self-explanatory as regards fraud and undue influence such as vices of consent. Do you disagree with the court? Is drunkenness on the part of one party a sufficient ground for nullity of a contract on the basis of error? *See* paragraphs 1–24. Does the court require a certain degree of error?

2. Paragraphs 26–32: The court rules that "Dennis Bamburg committed fraud to obtain an unfair advantage over Skannal." Do you agree that the requirements for fraud were met?

3. Paragraphs 33–35: The court cites Louisiana Civil Code article 1479 in part (*see* paragraph 33) and goes on to state that this article is about undue influence.

Read Louisiana Civil Code article 1479 and you will see that it mentions the word "influence," but nowhere does it explicitly refer to the phrase "undue influence." So, did the court read and rely on the title of Louisiana Civil Code article 1479, which includes the adjective "undue"? If the court did this, then the court turned the title of the article into law in violation of La. R.S. 1:13, which provides: "*A. Headings to sections, source notes, and cross references are given for the purpose of convenient reference and do not constitute part of the law.*" Or did the court give its own interpretation of the word "influence" to mean undue influence, which the court could have done by interpreting the law? Why didn't the court look at the next article, Louisiana Civil Code article 1480, in the text of which the court would have found an express reference to undue influence? If undue influence is a vice of consent where donations are concerned, could undue influence also be a vice of consent in any contract, not just gratuitous contracts like donations? Can an *a pari ratione* reasoning be used to broaden the scope of application of undue influence?

See also *Millet v. Millet*, 888 So.2d 291 (La.App. 5 Cir. 2004); *Succession of Reeves*, 704 So.2d 252 (La.App. 3 Cir. 1997); *Succession of Hollis*, 987 So.2d 387 (La. App. 2 Cir. 2008).

Comparative Law Perspective

— Civil Law —

Alex Weill, *Droit Civil: Les Obligations*

n° 187 at 200 (1971)

187. Diverse sanctions. — 1° Insofar as fraud vitiates the consent of the victim, the normal sanction is the *relative nullity* of the contract.

2° But the fraud is also a fault that can be sanctioned by *damages*. If, despite the nullity, the victim experiences a prejudice, he can demand damages from the author of the fraud and from all those who, by their fault, have permitted or facilitated the fraud. Besides, nothing obliges the victim to demand the nullity of the contract, if he prefers to limit himself to recovering damages.

Moreover, damages constitute the sole sanction in the case of fraud caused by a third party. It is the same with the sanction for incidental [**non-material**] fraud.

3° One can conceive of still another sanction for fraud — the *refusal of nullity*. An incapable who has dissimulated his condition by means of fraudulent maneuvers will not be able to obtain the nullity of the contract on account of his incapacity.

François Terré, Philippe Simler, Yves Lequette & François Chénedé, *Droit Civil: Les Obligations*
(12th ed. 2018), translated by John Randall Trahan

§ 2. Dol

295. Definition. Dol in the formation of a contract designates all the deceptions whereby a contracting party leads his partner to make an error that causes him to contract. He who is the victim of dol is not deceived; he has been deceived. Acting on consent by means of the error that it engenders, dol is, to speak properly, not a vice of consent, but a cause of such a vice. [. . . .]

296. Relationship between dol and error. [. . . .]

1) Scope. Errors that are treated as of no consequence when they are spontaneous are sanctioned when they are provoked by the deceptions of a contracting party. [. . . .]

2) Proof. If there is dol, then the proof is easier, for such proof does not aim to establish the error directly — a purely psychological fact — but the acts that have provoked it — material facts that are ordinarily rather easy to demonstrate.

3) Sanction. Because dol always implies fault on the part of him who has committed it, the victim of it can obtain, in addition to nullification, damages with interest if nullification is not sufficient to repair completely the injury he has sustained. [. . . .]

A. The notion of dol

297. Ambivalence of the notion. The theory of dol in the Civil Code reflects a duality of conceptions: the Code makes of dol a vice of consent, but the Roman idea that dol is tantamount to a delict is not eliminated. From this comes a double approach: dol supposes, on the part of its author, an act of disloyalty at the time of the conclusion of the contract, that is, the delictual aspect (1°), from which results, in the victim, a vice of consent (2°), that is, the psychological aspect.

298. 1°) The delictual aspect. As an act of disloyalty committed by one of the contracting parties against the other, dol is a kind of civil offshoot of the penal delict of fraud. [. . . .]

299. a) The material element. [. . . .]

Maneuvers means all the machinations, all the staging, all the artifices that a person can put into operation in order to capture the consent of his partner and lead him to contract. As diverse as the mind of man is inventive, these maneuvers adapt themselves to changes in economic and social facts. [. . . .]

To maneuvers, the legislature assimilates the *lie*. This is the case not only when the lie takes a written form [. . .] but also when it does not rest on any exterior artifice. [. . . .]

Nevertheless, traditionally it was taught that not all lies are constitutive of dol. That would be so if one were to brag about one's products in an exaggerated manner.

One would then be in the presence of a dol that was tolerated by usage, which the Romans called *bonus dolus* (good dol), in contrast to *malus dolus* (bad dol), which alone was considered to be reprehensible. The solution proceeds from the idea that each person is bound to a duty to inform himself, which ought to lead him to not display such a grand naivete in regard to the affirmations of his partner and to proceed to a minimum of verification. As a fruit of excessive credulity, the error would, in some fashion, be too gross to be taken into account. The measure of tolerable dol depends on the quality of the author—the more that the authority attached to his position is great, the less his lie is permissible—as well as the quality of the victim—age, degree of education, professional competence.

[. . . .] On the other hand, the accent put onto the protection of consumers by contemporary law limits more and more the traditional tolerance of *bonus dolus*. Thus, deceptive advertising, which was long considered to be *bonus dolus*, is today punished under the cover of fighting against deceitful commercial practices.

300. Reticence. The silence of a contracting party with regard to information that is of interest to his partner can constitute dol. In other words, the legislature assimilates reticence to maneuvers and lies. [. . . .]

Thanks to the reform, doleful reticence is today consecrated by Article 1137, line 2: "Equally constitutive of dol is the intentional dissimulation by one of the contracting parties of information which he knows has a determinative character for the other party."

[. . .] [T]he jurisprudence most often sanctioned the behavior of a person who had not provoked his partner into making an error but was content to *exploit* his error. [. . . .] There is then a "failure of the obligation to contract in good faith," but there is no provoked error.

301. b) The intentional element. In order for a contract to be annulled on the ground of dol, it is necessary that the material element which we previously identified have been realized by one of the parties as part of a design to deceive the other. [. . . .]

In a case of doleful *reticence*, establishing the intentional element is more delicate. Silence kept by one of the parties can, in fact, come from ignorance, forgetfulness, or negligence rather than a will to deceive the other contracting party. Nevertheless, the judge will most often deduce the intention to deceive if he finds two things: that he who was silent knew the concealed information as well as its importance for his partner. He who keeps silence "knowingly" commits dol. This solution is today expressly consecrated by Article 1137, line 2.

302. c) The origin of dol. Dol is a cause of nullity only if it emanates from a contracting party. If it is the act of a third party, it will give rise only to damages with interest, unless the error so provoked is an error on the essential qualities of the performance or the qualities of the other contracting party. But it is then on the ground of error and not that of dol that the nullity will be pronounced. It is a classic difference from violence, which infects the contract no matter what may be its provenance.

[. . . .] Only dol emanating from a contracting party will thus be sanctioned by nullity, for it would be unjust if an innocent contracting party had to suffer for behavior that cannot be imputed to him.

From this follow several evident limits to the application of the rule. The rule is set aside when a contracting party [. . .] had been complicit in the dol or that he had inspired it. [. . . .] Or it may be that the dol emanates from his representative, from a manager of his affair whose management he has ratified, or even from a porte-fort, in which cases the dol will be assimilated to his own dol. [. . . .]

303. 2°) The psychological aspect. Maneuvers, lies, and other reticences are taken into consideration only if they have the effect of leading a contracting party into an error (a) that causes him to contract (b).

304. a) An error. The nature of this error little matters. It can be an error on the essential qualities of the performance or an error on the essential qualities of the person in the sense of Article 1132, in which case the parties would have the option of invoking the vice of error as well as that of dol. It can also be an error on the value or on the motivations. Finally, it can be an inexcusable error. Of no consequence when they are spontaneous, these errors become a cause of nullity of the contract if they have their source in the deceptions of a contracting party. The solution is posed in a very clear manner by Article 1139. [. . . .]

Nevertheless, it had been ruled that in a case of reticence, dol would be constituted only if the concealed information concerned the performance furnished by him who was silent. [. . . .]

305. b) A determinative error. In order for nullity to be pronounced, it is necessary that the error provoked by the dol have taken on a *determinative* character. Without this error, the victim of it would not have contracted.

Dol of this kind, which is called *principal*, was traditionally opposed to dol of the kind called *incidental*, that is to say, that without which the party who is the victim of it would nevertheless have agreed to contract, but on different conditions, for example, a more advantageous price. According to the classic doctrine, incidental dol would permit the victim to avail himself not of the nullity of the contract but rather of damages and interest, that is to say, in effect a diminution of the agreed-upon price.

This distinction was contested by an important part of the contemporary doctrine [. . . .] the jurisprudence finally admitted that the existence of incidental dol sufficed to ground the nullity of the contract. This solution has been consecrated by Article 1130, which provides that, like error and violence, dol vitiates consent when it is such a nature that, without it, "one of the parties would not have contracted or would have contracted on substantially different conditions." As all the commentators have noted, the distinction between principal dol and incidental dol in the classic sense is thus condemned. [. . . .]

The determinative character of dol, on the one hand, implies deceit prior to or contemporaneous with the formation of the contract and, on the other hand, must be appreciated *in concreto*. It is thus that Article 1130, line 2 provides "the determinative character [**of the error**] is evaluated with regard to the persons and to the circumstances in which consent has been given." [. . . .]

§ 3. Violence

308. Presentation. [. . . .] [T]he Ordonnance of 2016 created alongside classic violence, which sanctions a provoked constraint, a new case of violence, which sanctions an exploited dependency.

A. The classic violence: provoked restraint

309. Definition. There is violence when a person contracts under the threat of a considerable harm that gives rise within him to a sentiment of fear. Although he knows that the proposed contract is bad for him, the victim of violence nonetheless gives his consent, for he is threatened with a harm that is graver than that with which he would be threatened in case he were to refuse to engage himself.

1. The notion of violence.

310. Ambivalence of the notion. Even more than deceit, our law reproves violence that is exerted against a contracting party. One discovers in violence the same duality of structure as in dol: a civil delict for him who exerts it, a vice of consent for him who experiences it. But delict and vice differ. The delict is a threat, an act of force and not of disloyalty. The vice is no longer the error but the fear that undermines or suppresses the liberty of consent.

311. a) Delictual aspect. More grave than deceit, violence will be taken into account whether it proceeds from a contracting party or a third party. [. . . .]

312. 1) Material element. The civil law includes under this notion all the forms of threats, the most rudimentary as well as the most refined.

[. . . .] The harm threatened can be physical — a threat of death, of a blow, of kidnapping; moral — a threat to divulge this or that fact that is contrary to honor; pecuniary — a threat to deprive a person of his profession, of his lodging, of his resources.

313. 2) The unjust element. In order to be a cause of nullity, violence must be unjust. It does not suffice that the liberty of decision of the contracting party has been altered; it is necessary further that the constraint be illegitimate. [. . . .]

However, it is commonly admitted that the employment of *legal* recourse (a criminal action, a seizure) does not constitute violence and cannot, in principle, justify the nullification of the contract that is the consequence of it, for this is only the exercise of a legal right. [. . . .]

Nevertheless, it is otherwise if the employment of legal recourse is diverted from its proper end, if it becomes *abusive*. [. . . .]

314. 3) Origin of the violence. By virtue of article 1142 of the Civil Code, "violence is a cause of nullity whether it has been exerted by a party or by a third person." Thus, in contrast to dol, violence is taken into account even though it does not emanate from a contracting party. [. . . .] The difference is justified, however, from the social point of view, inasmuch as the trouble caused by violence is in itself more dangerous.

315. b) Psychological aspect: the sentiment of fear. According to Article 1140 of the Civil Code, "there is violence when a party engages himself under the pressure of a constraint that inspires him to fear that his person, his fortune, or that of one who is close to him is exposed to a considerable harm." [. . . .] Still it is necessary that this sentiment of fear exist at the moment of the conclusion of the contract and that it be sufficiently grave.

1) The moment. In order for consent to be vitiated, it is necessary that the contract have been concluded while the fear was in place. It must, therefore, have existed at the moment of the formation of the contract.

2) The gravity. In order for consent to be vitiated, the state of fear under which the contract was concluded [**must**] be sufficiently grave. Article 1140 says it indirectly by specifying that it is necessary that there be a threat of "considerable harm." This gravity can be appreciated in two ways: *in abstracto*, by reference to the abstract model of a prudent administrator, that is to say, of a reasonable man; *in concreto*, by relation to the capacity of the person concerned to resist. [. . . .] The courts seek to find out if the person who demands the nullity was *effectively* under the influence of fear. There has resulted from this a judicial individualization of violence. [. . . .]

However, there is no violence, to speak properly, when a person contracts under the influence of a drug that totally annihilates his will or where his hand has been guided by force in order to obtain his signature. In this case, in fact, consent is no longer given under the influence of fear, but is radically absent.

B. The new violence: exploited dependency

1. The state of the former law

318. The state of necessity [. . . .] On the basis of the fact that violence, in contrast to dol, is sanctioned when it proceeds from a third party, it was asked whether the contract could be annulled when the violence proceeded not from an individual, but from exterior events or circumstances. Exploiting a state of necessity in which a partner finds himself, a person profits from it in order to impose on him some particularly rigorous conditions. [. . . .]

The earliest opinion was that a constraint resulting from events should not be taken into consideration. An engagement taken under the influence of fear can be annulled only if it is provoked by violence or threat emanating from a person. [. . . .] Classic doctrine likewise considered that the state of necessity did not constitute violence, while at the same time recognizing that an engagement taken under the influence of necessity can be reduced for a partial lack of cause or even annulled for want of cause or for lack of consent, when the trouble in the mind provoked by the circumstances appeared comparable to a demented state. [. . . .]

Another opinion, more modern, assimilated the state of necessity to violence when a contracting party profited from it in order to obtain excessive advantages from his partner.

319. [. . .] **to the state of dependency.** The present harshness of social relations and of the life of business has sometimes led contracting parties to invoke violence in hypothetical cases that had not been envisioned by the authors of the Civil Code. Basing themselves on their subordinate juridical situation or their economic dependency, certain contracting parties — employees, distributers, producers — have invoked the vice of violence. It was decided that the *subordination* of the employee to his employer did not alone constitute violence susceptible of vitiating contracts passed between them. Nevertheless, violence has sometimes been found when this situation of subordination is accompanied by certain marked pressures. [. . . .] Although the law of competition and the law of consumers expressly consecrated it, the civil law showed itself to be more reserved.

[. . . .] But the study of the jurisprudence showed that the judges sometimes did not hesitate to annul contracts concluded under the influence of a state of economic necessity and psychological fragility by turning to the vices of consent in general. [. . . .]

2. The reform of 2016

320. Presentation. [. . . .]

The Chancellery made the choice here to take the state of dependency into account under the cover of violence and not of qualified lesion. [. . . .] Article 1143 of the Civil Code now provides: "There is violence as well when a party, abusing the state of dependency in which his fellow contracting party finds himself in regard to the party, obtains from him an engagement to which he would not have subscribed in the absence of such a constraint and draws from it a manifestly excessive advantage."

Three conditions emerge. [. . . .]

321. a) State of dependency. The injured party must find himself in a "state of dependency." [. . . .]

The state of dependency envisions the situation of a person "who has lost his autonomy by relation to another," with the dependency capable of being either economic or psychological. One envisions then not a mere psychological weakness of the injured contracting party but an "authentic dependency in regard to the other contracting party." Thus, it could be so in a contract concluded by a member of a cult who is under the influence thereof or yet a contract subscribed to by a person placed under the thumb of another, which rejoins the hypothesis of undue influence. [. . . .]

322. b) Determinative character. The text conditions the recognition of violence on the fact that, without the constraint resulting from this state of dependency, he who was subjected to it would not have subscribed to this engagement. [. . . .] The requirement is posed in a general manner by Article 1130.

323. c) Manifestly excessive advantage. On the recommendation of the practice and the doctrine, the legislature has, in effect, added a third condition of a quantitative kind: it is necessary that he who exploited the constraint that resulted from the state of dependency have profited from it in order to extort from his partner an advantage that is manifestly excessive. [. . . .] The excessive advantage will most often result from a disequilibrium of performances. But it could also, it seems, stem from the presence of one or several clauses that take on an abusive character.

Section IV — Object and Matter of Contracts

Louisiana Sources of Law
Louisiana Civil Code

Art. 1971. Freedom of parties.

Parties are free to contract for any object that is lawful, possible, and determined or determinable. (Acts 1984, No. 331, § 1, eff. Jan. 1, 1985.)

Art. 1972. Possible or impossible object.

A contractual object is possible or impossible according to its own nature and not according to the parties' ability to perform. (Acts 1984, No. 331, § 1, eff. Jan. 1, 1985.)

Art. 1973. Object determined as to kind.

The object of a contract must be determined at least as to its kind.

The quantity of a contractual object may be undetermined, provided it is determinable. (Acts 1984, No. 331, § 1, eff. Jan. 1, 1985.)

Art. 1974. Determination by third person.

If the determination of the quantity of the object has been left to the discretion of a third person, the quantity of an object is determinable.

If the parties fail to name a person, or if the person named is unable or unwilling to make the determination, the quantity may be determined by the court. (Acts 1984, No. 331, § 1, eff. Jan. 1, 1985.)

Art. 1975. [omitted]

Art. 1976. Future things.

Future things may be the object of a contract.

The succession of a living person may not be the object of a contract other than an antenuptial agreement. Such a succession may not be renounced. (Acts 1984, No. 331, § 1, eff. Jan. 1, 1985.)

Art. 1977. Obligation or performance by a third person.

The object of a contract may be that a third person will incur an obligation or render a performance.

The party who promised that obligation or performance is liable for damages if the third person does not bind himself or does not perform. (Acts 1984, No. 331, § 1, eff. Jan. 1, 1985.)

Third Party Beneficiary

Art. 1978. Stipulation for a third party.

A contracting party may stipulate a benefit for a third person called a third party beneficiary.

Once the third party has manifested his intention to avail himself of the benefit, the parties may not dissolve the contract by mutual consent without the beneficiary's agreement. (Acts 1984, No. 331, §1, eff. Jan. 1, 1985.)

Art. 1979. Revocation.

The stipulation may be revoked only by the stipulator and only before the third party has manifested his intention of availing himself of the benefit.

If the promisor has an interest in performing, however, the stipulation may not be revoked without his consent. (Acts 1984, No. 331, §1, eff. Jan. 1, 1985.)

Art. 1981. Rights of beneficiary and stipulator.

The stipulation gives the third party beneficiary the right to demand performance from the promisor.

Also the stipulator, for the benefit of the third party, may demand performance from the promisor. (Acts 1984, No. 331, §1, eff. Jan. 1, 1985.)

Art. 1982. Defenses of the promisor.

The promisor may raise against the beneficiary such defenses based on the contract as he may have raised against the stipulator. (Acts 1984, No. 331, §1, eff. Jan. 1, 1985.)

Doctrine

Louisiana Law of Conventional Obligations, A Précis

Sections 6.1.1 to 6.2.2 and 7.1 to 7.3.3

LSA-C.C. Art. 1971 lists the three characteristics which must be met by an object to be the object of a contract: "Parties are free to contract for any object that is lawful, possible, and determined or determinable." [. . . .]

Laws for the preservation of public order prohibit parties from entering a contract which would have an unlawful object or an immoral object. In the words of **LSA-C.C. Art. 7**: **"Persons may not by their juridical acts derogate from laws enacted for the protection of the public interest. Any act in derogation of such laws is an absolute nullity."** [. . . .]

LSA-C.C. Art. 1973 makes the determination of the object of a contract conditional upon the parties agreeing on the "kind" of object and the "quantity" of that object. Nothing is said of the "quality" of the same contractual object. In this respect, one has to refer to LSA-C.C. Art. 1860 listed in the civil Code under "Extinction of Obligations" and "Performance."

What is a "kind"? In the absence of a definition in the Civil Code, we are told by **LSA-C.C. Art. 11** that **"The words of a law must be given their generally prevailing meaning. Words of art and technical terms must be given their technical meaning when the law involves a technical matter."** In this instance, the general meaning of the word "kind" can be found in a dictionary as referring to "a class that is defined by the common attribute or attributes possessed by all of its members <flowers of all kinds>, <the kind of person who gets angry easily>." [. . . .]

A second facet of the determination of an object can be its quantity. **"The quantity of a contractual object may be undetermined"** at the time the parties enter their contract **"provided it is determinable"** at the time performance is due. [. . . .]

The determination of the quantity of an object can be left, as per the intent of the parties, to a third person. **"If the determination of the quantity of the object has been left to the discretion of a third person, the quantity of an object is determinable.**

If the parties fail to name a person, or if the person named is unable or unwilling to make the determination, the quantity may be determined by the court." (LSA-C.C. Art. 1974). [. . . .]

As far as the quality of an object or a thing might be important, even essential, to its determination, the civil Code includes a suppletive rule of law in Article 1860. [. . . .]

The law will feel the gap of "quality" of the thing when the parties fail to agree.

A third legal requirement that must be met by the object of a contract is that the object be "possible." [. . . .]

Only an object/thing that is absolutely impossible of ever existing or that existed at one time but no longer exists leads to the absolute nullity of the contract. [. . . .]

On the other hand, the impossibility could be "relative," in the sense that for personal reason(s) the obligor himself could not carry out his performance although somebody else could. [. . . .]

Such an obligor will be validly bound by the contract; he will be in breach of a "possible" object of an obligation and, thus, liable to pay compensatory damages for breach of an obligation to do something. [. . . .]

Promesse de Porte-Fort

[I]n a promesse de porte-fort the principal or third person is not bound to perform the contract entered into by the porte-fort with his co-contracting party. In a triangular porte-fort situation, the principal-third person is not aware that someone may be acting for his benefit since the porte-fort has received no instruction from "anyone" to act for a third person-principal. [. . . .]

Two effects flow from a ratification by the principal-third person of the juridical act or contract entered into between the porte-fort and the contracting party.

One first effect is that the third person-principal is now "bound to perform the contract that the porte-fort has made with his co-contracting party." [. . . .]

A second important effect of ratification is that it releases the porte-fort of any subsequent obligation; he is now out of the picture so much so that he is not liable for any breach, by the principal, of the obligations created by the ratified contract. [. . . .]

The principal is free not to ratify the contract entered into by the porte-fort with a third person. The principal cannot be compelled "to do" something, i.e. "ratify," against his will. [. . . .]

Third Party Beneficiary — Stipulation Pour Autrui

A stipulation pour autrui is a legal device bringing together three parties: one of them is called "stipulator," another "promisor," and the third "beneficiary." The interplay among these parties is such that the stipulator receives the commitment of the promisor that the latter will render a performance to the beneficiary. Thus, the beneficiary becomes an obligee, a creditor, as a consequence of the obligation created by the contract between the stipulator and the promisor. The beneficiary is, therefore, a "third party" to that contract. Yet, although a "non-party" to the contract and not represented in the contract, the beneficiary will receive "the benefit of the effects" of that contract. In a word, a stipulation for the benefit of another is "bilateral" in its creation but "triangular" in its effects. [. . . .]

The mechanism of a third party beneficiary stipulation is such that it creates a right of its own nature, the "benefit," in the sense that neither the stipulator nor the promisor ever had this right in their patrimonies to transfer it to the beneficiary. This right vested in the beneficiary is created, therefore, by a contract between the stipulator and the promisor out of their own bilateral legal relationship. Therefore, the actual vesting of this right into the patrimony of the beneficiary is contingent not only on the validity of the contract between stipulator and promisor but also on the performance of their obligations by these two parties. [. . . .]

A "stipulation" being a clause in a contract, that contract must meet all the requirements for a valid contract. The requirement of cause is the one of greater concern because the stipulator cannot use the device of a stipulation to transfer "indirectly" to the beneficiary and via the promisor a right which he, the stipulator, could not have transferred "directly" by a contract with the beneficiary himself. [. . . .]

The contract between the stipulator and the promisor must be binding between the parties as the "principal contract" which includes an accessory stipulation. Thus a stipulation pour autrui could not exist in the absence of a supporting-principal contract. This contract, whether onerous or gratuitous, must meet the requirements for the validity of any contract in addition to meeting the specific requirements of the nominate contract the parties may have intended to enter into, like a sale or a donation. This fundamental requirement of a valid principal contract explains why the subsequent enforcement by the "beneficiary" of the accessory stipulation for his benefit will depend on the performance of their obligations by the parties to the principal contract. [....]

A stipulation being a juridical act, that act must meet the requirements for any valid juridical act. [....]

A first set of effects is created by the principal contractual relationship between the stipulator and the promisor. These effects are those of the contract these parties entered into. [....]

The second set of effects bears on the accessory clause, the stipulation created by the contract. [....]

The relationship between the stipulator and the third party beneficiary is not a direct "effect" of the stipulation. It is only indirectly, through the promisor, that the stipulator is in a legal relationship with the third party. Thus the cause that prompted the creation of the stipulation is to be found in the interest or reason the stipulator has in having the promisor carry out a performance for the benefit of the third party. [....]

Should the stipulation pour autrui be lawfully revoked, the principal contract between stipulator and promisor remains in existence. [....]

A stipulation may be for a stipulator a means of performance of an obligation he owes the third party. [....]

A stipulation pour autrui can also be "gratuitous" when the stipulator wishes to make a donation to the third party through the promisor's performance. [....]

Once the third party has **"manifested his intention to avail himself of the benefit"** (Art. 1978), she is vested with **"the right to demand performance from the promisor"** (Art. 1981). [....]

The stipulation being "accessory" to the principal contract to which the third party is not a "contractual party," the obligations created by that principal contract cannot take second rank to the stipulation. The promisor has a primary interest in the performance of the obligations created by the principal contract.

Cases

Tac Amusement Company
v.
Kermit J. Henry

Court of Appeal of Louisiana
Fourth Circuit
August 3, 1970
238 So.2d 398

REDMANN, Judge.

[1] Plaintiff appeals from a judgment dismissing on the merits its suit for contractually-stipulated damages for breach of a contract.

[2] Under the contract defendant agreed that during its ten-year term 'no coin operated music boxes or other commercial music system, nor other legal coin boxes or other commercial music systems, nor other legal coin operated amusement devices will be installed or operated at (defendant's) premises except such as are installed and operated by you (plaintiff) or by such other party designated by you.'

[3] Plaintiff agreed to 'install, operate and maintain on said premises one or more coin operated music devices, and/or one or more legal coin operated amusement devices with the number and type of such being within your (plaintiff's) sole discretion and at your option.'

[4] The contract stipulated a division of the proceeds from the machines, and further provided:

> 'In event of any breach of this agreement, in addition to any other remedy which you may have, your company may elect to terminate this agreement and remove all such equipment without interference from said location and shall be entitled to liquidated damages in a sum equal to your company's average weekly share of the coin boxes prior to said breach multiplied by the number of weeks remaining in the unexpired term of this agreement.'

[5] There were other provisions unnecessary to recite here in our view of the case.

[6] The evidence shows that defendant caused the removal of the machines seven weeks after the date of the contract (although defendant denies the contract date). Plaintiff sought the 'liquidated damages' of its average weekly proceeds-share of $38.85 for each week of the remainder of the ten-year contract, said to amount to $20,430.00. (By amending petition filed after trial plaintiff voluntarily reduced its demand to $6,060.20, although the evidence supports the $38.85 weekly figures.)

[7] We note that the 'liquidated damages' may not be such. Plaintiff had costs of operation, such as providing phonograph records, maintenance and depreciation of its machines which presumably would not have been covered by the $10 weekly service charge. Furthermore, the proceeds from performance were receivable over a ten-year period and thus worth much less than the entire gross proceeds payable

at once. If the service charge truly covered only service, the 'liquidated damages' clause is rather a provision for a penalty far in excess of conceivable actual damages.

[8] More importantly, it seems altogether improbable that the performance promised by plaintiff was what defendant bargained for, the motive or cause of defendant's obligation, LSA-C.C. art. 1896. Presumably defendant either definitely wanted a music box; or he definitely wanted an amusement device; or he definitely wanted both. Plaintiff promised nothing definite, and defendant could not have exacted any definite machine nor even any definite kind of machine. C.C. art. 1886 requires an obligation to have 'for its object something determinate, at least as to its species.'

[9] Planiol observes in his Civil Law Treatise (La.Law Inst. trans.), II s 1001,

'The obligatory relationship is not formed when the object of the obligation is not determined.

'If the indefiniteness bears on the nature of the object, one does not know what thing or what fact can be demanded of the debtor. He who promised 'an animal' in reality has not promised at all, since he can free himself by furnishing to his creditor an insignificant insect. If the indefiniteness relates to the quantity, the thing being specified in its kind, the debtor again can liberate himself by offering a derisive performance: if he has promised grain or wine, without further precision, his obligation can reduce itself to a sip of wine or a grain of wheat, and the credit would be a sham.'

[10] Yet C.C. art. 2066 does authorize 'alternative' obligations, and it may be said that plaintiff obliged itself to provide one or more music boxes or, alternatively, one or more amusement devices or, further alternatively, one or more of both machines.

[11] Still a derisive performance, as Planiol names it, arguably might fill defendant's bar with music boxes and pinball machines, at plaintiff's 'sole discretion and at (its) option.' Or it might consist of one 12-record 78 r.p.m. 1930 vintage juke-box, or some trifling 'amusement device'.

[12] Thus although, as plaintiff argues, plaintiff may not have been free to perform or not perform under a potestative condition depending 'solely on the exercise of the obligor's will', C.C. art. 2035, nevertheless both the quality and the quantity of the object of plaintiff's obligation was, in our opinion, too indeterminate to meet the requirement of C.C. art. 1886, and therefore defendant's obligation was unenforceable because without cause, C.C. art. 1893.

[13] We might add that, because of the absence of any obligation on plaintiff to supply the very machines that had produced $38.85 weekly, even if defendant could be said to have had as his motivating cause only to have some indefinite kind of machine (and plaintiff did oblige itself to that) the proper measure of damages would be loss of proceeds from a minimum performance (the least productive machine) plaintiff might have provided. The so-called liquidated damages, obviously far in excess of hoped-for profit from a voluntarily maximum performance, are so far out of proportion to the only real obligation of plaintiff as to invoke C.C. art. 2464's

serious and proportionate consideration requirement, applicable generally to all contracts, Blanchard v. Haber, 166 La. 1014, 118 So. 117 (1928). The liquidated damages clause would be unenforceable even if the contract were otherwise valid.

[. . . .]

[14] The judgment appealed from is affirmed at plaintiff's cost.

[15] Affirmed.

Questions

1. Paragraphs 1–15: Please read the Code articles on Lease (La. Civil Code arts. 2668–2729) and Of the Letting Out of Labor or Industry (La. Civ. Code arts. 2745–2777). After you have the read the whole case, ask yourself the following question: Has the court given a proper legal identification to the nature of the contract for the breach of which the plaintiff is seeking contractually-stipulated damages?

2. Paragraph 3: Can you identify the kinds of obligations that fit in this description? For example, do you see any conjunctive obligation? Is/are the object(s) of these obligations sufficiently identified and determined so as to become objects of obligations? Do you see any condition? If you answered affirmatively, on whose part is the condition, the obligor or obligee? Does it matter?

3. Paragraph 8: Why is the court saying, in fact, that there is no object? How should the issue of object be dealt with in the event an obligation is alternative? *See* paragraph 10.

4. Paragraph 12: Why was defendant's obligation unenforceable? Should the court be concerned about the quality of the object to the same extent it is concerned with the quantity of that object?

5. Paragraphs 12–13: The court refers to the concept of "out of proportion" and to "serious and proportionate consideration requirement," and cites Louisiana Civil Code article 2464, which is concerned with the price in a contract of sale. Is this case dealing with a contract of sale? Why do you think the court can still say that the concepts of "out of proportion" and "serious and proportionate consideration" found in Louisiana Civil Code article 2464 are "applicable generally to all contracts"? Is "all" too broad a statement, and if so, why?

The Springs Thunder Agency, Inc.
v.
Odom Insurance Agency, Inc.
Court of Appeal of Louisiana
First Circuit
April 13, 1970
237 So.2d 96

ELLIS, Judge.

[1] Plaintiff, The Springs Thunder Agency, Inc., operated a fire and casualty insurance agency in Denham Springs, Louisiana. In early 1968, a representative of Odom Insurance Agency, Inc., the defendant, contacted Mr. Spring, plaintiff's president, relative to buying the business. After some negotiation, the sale took place, as of June 1, 1968. A written contract was entered into which contained the following pertinent language:

> 'Things Sold: Seller conveys all records and files of the agency sold to Buyer and the exclusive right to the renewals on existing active accounts of the agency. Seller further agrees, in consideration of the price and other provisions of this agreement not to engage in the fire and casualty insurance business in competition with Buyer in Livingston Parish or in any Parish adjoining Livingston Parish for a period of five (5) years from the effective date of this agreement. Nothing herein shall be construed as prohibiting Seller brokering such business through the Buyer.

← contract language

> 'Price: The price for which the agency is sold is the sum of Nine Thousand Sixteen and 71/100 ($9,016.71) Dollars which is allocated between the things sold as follows:

"Renewals of existing active accounts $4,016.71

"Covenant not to compete with Buyer   5,000.00

"Total $9,016.71"

[2] A promissory note for $9,573.36, including interest, was given for the purchase price. The note was payable in 24 installments of $398.89 each, called for 8% Interest on each installment from maturity until paid, and 10% Attorney's fee, and contained an acceleration clause.

[3] Among the accounts transferred was the Livingston Parish School Board account, which accounted for over 40% of the premium income of the agency. The School Board business was let by bids, and had been awarded to plaintiff for several years.

[4] Defendant bid on the School Board business shortly after the sale was completed, but was unsuccessful. It then demanded a reduction in the purchase price by the amount of the premiums lost. Plaintiff refused this, but did agree to an

adjustment of $261.11 for eight policies on which it had requested cancellation because of nonpayment of the premium.

[. . . .]

 [5] We find no evidence in the record to substantiate the allegation that there was any misrepresentation, or the withholding of any information by the plaintiff.

[. . . .]

[6] What plaintiff sold and what defendant bought was the present right to such future renewals as might occur. This is the sale of a hope under Article 2451 of the Civil Code, as opposed to the sale of a future thing or thing to come, under Articles 1887 and 2450 of the Civil Code. In the latter case, if the thing sold never comes into existence, the contract can have no effect. Had plaintiff sold the 'renewals' only, the sale would be governed by Article 2450. But plaintiff sold the 'right to renewals' and the failure of any or all of the accounts to renew can have no effect on the validity of the contract. See Losecco v. Gregory, 108 La. 648, 32 So. 985 (1901).

[7] Since we are of the opinion that defendant got what he paid for, we need not consider his argument relative to failure of consideration.

[8] Defendant claims, alternatively, that since interest is included in the note, the judgment appealed from is, in effect, forcing defendant to pay interest on interest. This contention is without merit under the express provisions of Article 2924 of the Civil Code. Williams v. Alphonse Mortgage Co., 144 So.2d 600 (La.App. 4 Cir. 1962).

[9] Plaintiff asks for judgment on the full amount prayed for. He claims that the credit of $261.11 offered in plaintiff's letter of October 14, 1968, was a compromise offer and should not be considered by the court in rendering its judgment. However, as we understand the letter, as explained by the testimony of plaintiff's president, these accounts were cancelled because the premiums were never paid, and, therefore, should not have been included in the gross premium income figure used in computing the purchase price.

[. . . .]

Questions

1. Paragraphs 1–2: What kind of parties are involved in this case? Should it matter? Carefully read the first paragraph of the quoted contract. How many objects are listed under "Things Sold"? How are those things related to one another? Are all of the things of the same legal nature? *See* La. Civ. Code arts. 448–475 on "Things" and "Division of Things." Now read the remainder of the quoted contract. Are the things listed under "Price" referred to in the same manner as they when are listed under "Things Sold"? Could there exist a problem of interpretation?

2. Paragraphs 1–4: What do you think the defendant bought: an existing thing or a future thing? If it is an existing thing, what is it? If it is a future thing, what is it?

3. Paragraphs 6–7: Do you agree with the court's analysis of "a future thing" (*see* La. Civ. Code arts. 1976, 1887, 2450), "a hope" (*see* La. Civ. Code art. 2451), and "an aleatory contract" (*see* La. Civ. Code art. 1912)? How would you distinguish between a hope and a future thing?

Nolton Andrepont
v.
Acadia Drilling Co., Inc., et al.
Supreme Court of Louisiana
February 24, 1969
231 So.2d 347

SANDERS, Justice.

[1] Nolton Andrepont, a tenant farmer, sued for damages to his soybean crop caused by defendants during the drilling of an oil well on the land. [. . . .]

[2] Andrepont entered into a verbal lease with the heirs of A. A. Bundick, whereby plaintiff acquired the right to farm a tract of land for a rental of twenty per cent of the crop harvested. Thereafter, the landowners executed an oil lease on the property, granting the lessee the right to use the land to explore for oil. The oil lease was duly recorded.

[3] Paragraph 8 of the lease originally read, 'The lessee shall be responsible for all damages to timber and growing crops of lessor caused by lessee's operations.' However, the words 'to timber and growing crops of lessor' were struck out. Thus the lease provided: 'The lessee shall be responsible for all damages caused by lessee's operations.'

[4] Under the lease, a drilling company drilled a well on the land in search of oil. Later, the defendants paid the landowners $125.00 for damages and received a release from them.

[5] Defendants made no payment to Andrepont, the tenant, and he brought this action ex delicto, or in tort, for damages to his growing soybean crop. In this Court he also contends he is entitled to recover under the mineral lease provision obligating the lessee to pay for all damages, asserting that the provision is a stipulation Pour autrui.

[6] When standing crops do not belong to the owner of the land, they are regarded as movables subject to separate ownership rather than as a part of the land. Such crops are treated as if they were harvested. LSA-C.C. Art. 465. See Fallin v. J. J. Stovall & Sons, 141 La. 220, 74 So. 911; Citizens' Bank v. Wiltz, 31 La.Ann. 244; Porche v. Bodin, 28 La.Ann. 761; Yiannopoulos, Civil Law Property, s 44, pp. 134–135 (1966). Such separate ownership may be derived from a variety of contractual relationships. When it is derived from a farm lease, the lease is of course subject to the law of registry insofar as third persons are concerned.

[7] LSA-R.S. 9:2721 provides:

'No sale, contract, counter letter, lien, mortgage, judgment, surface lease, oil, gas or mineral lease or other instrument of writing relating to or affecting immovable property shall be binding on or affect third persons or third parties unless and until filed for registry in the office of the parish recorder of the parish where the land or immovable is situated; and neither secret claims or equities nor other matters outside the public records shall be binding on or affect such third parties.'

[8] Under the foregoing statute, an unrecorded lease is ineffective against third persons to establish separate crop ownership. Separate ownership arising from a lease can be asserted against third persons only when the lease is recorded. LSA-R.S. 9:2721; LSA-C.C. Arts. 2264, 2266. See Minter v. Union Cent. Life Ins. Co., 180 La. 38, 156 So. 167; Summers & Brannins v. Clark, 30 La.Ann. 436; Yiannopoulos, Civil Law of Property, s 44, p. 135 (1966).

[9] In the present case, plaintiff's farm lease is unrecorded. It is a verbal contract, foreign to the public records. He cannot assert his separate ownership of the standing crop against the defendants, since they are third persons. As to them, the standing crop is considered as part of the land. LSA-C.C. Art. 465. Hence, under neither theory, can plaintiff recover crop damages from defendants.

[10] For the reasons assigned, the judgment of the Court of Appeal is affirmed.

ON REHEARING

SUMMERS, Justice

[11] Nolton Andrepont brings this action for damage to his soybean crop. He is the share crop tenant or farm lessee of Estelle Berdick Murphy who owns the land upon which the crop was grown and a portion of the minerals which underlie the tract. [. . . .]

[12] [. . . .] On original hearing in this Court, plaintiff's demands were rejected. Upon reconsideration we find that we erred. Plaintiff should recover.

[13] During 1964 Andrepont was granted a verbal lease to farm soybeans on a 35-acre tract in Acadia Parish, a condition being that he pay the landowner twenty percent of the crop as rent. Thereafter, on September 15, 1964, the land and mineral owners of the tract executed an oil and gas lease granting to the lessees the right to go upon the land to explore for and produce oil, gas and other minerals. In the printed form used to confect the lease, it was provided as a condition of the contract that 'The Lessee shall be responsible for all damages to timber and growing crops of Lessor caused by Lessee's operations.' This clause was altered by deleting the words 'to timber and growing crops of Lessor' with the result that the clause then read: 'The Lessee shall be responsible for all damages caused by Lessee's operations.'

[14] During the spring of 1965 Andrepont cultivated and planted the field in soybeans with early indications of a successful crop. Then, during July, the oil and gas lessee entered upon the land, built a board road across Andrepont's field, dug

waste pits and proceeded to drill a well in search of minerals. Construction of the road, the drill site and pits destroyed part of the crop and impaired drainage in the remainder of the soybean field. The lack of adequate drainage left water standing in the field and made it impracticable to work the crop. As a result, the remainder of Andrepont's crop was damaged by 'scalding' and excessive weeds.

[15] When the drilling operations resulted in a dry hole, defendants removed their equipment. In consideration of $125, they obtained a release from the landowner for 'her' damage as a result of their operations. In spite of Andrepont's repeated efforts to contact persons in authority at the well site to demand reparations, he was unable to do so. He received no payment from defendants, and on October 18, 1965 this suit was filed claiming damages to the crop caused by the oil and gas lessee's operations.

[16] In our initial consideration of the case, we found that the verbal farm lease, which would establish ownership of the farm lessee's share of the crop in the farm lessee and permit the crop to be classified in law as a movable, could have no effect against third persons, for the farm lease was not recorded as required by Section 2721 of Title 9 of the Revised Statutes, providing:

[17] No sale, contract, counter letter, lien, mortgage, judgment, surface lease, oil, gas or mineral lease or other instrument of writing relating to or affecting immovable property shall be binding on or affect third persons or third parties unless and until filed for registry in the office of the parish recorder of the parish where the land or immovable is situated; and neither secret claims or equities nor other matters outside the public records shall be binding on or affect such third parties.

[18] Hence we decided Andrepont could not recover for damage to the crop, which was an immovable and part of the land insofar as third parties were concerned, and only the record owner of rights in the land could assert claims for damage to the crop against third persons. We gave no consideration to Andrepont's contention that he was entitled to recover under the mineral lease provision, which he contends is a stipulation Pour autrui in his favor, obligating the lessee to pay all damages caused by its operations.

[19] We now feel that a proper disposition of this case requires a recognition that the quoted clause of the lease is a stipulation Pour autrui in favor of Andrepont. As the beneficiary of the stipulation, Andrepont has a direct right of action against the oil and gas lessee to recover for his damages, and the law of registry is inapplicable to his claim.

[20] Andrepont is not asserting 'secret claims or equities' unknown to defendants. He is seeking to enforce a benefit stipulated in his favor by the landowner lessor as a condition of a commutative contract between the landowner lessor and the oil and gas lessee. Defendants, as assignees of the oil and gas lessee, are, therefore, parties to the contract in which the stipulation is a condition; defendants are not third persons protected by the laws of registry insofar as Andrepont's claim is concerned. In reaching this conclusion, we have, in effect, paraphrased the language of Mr. Justice McCaleb writing for the Court in Mallet v. Thibault, 212 La. 79, 92,

31 So.2d 601 (1947) where a like contention was made in a different factual context. However, the principle involved in the case at bar is the same, and the Mallet decision is authority for the reasons we have expressed.

[21] Stipulations in favor of third persons (stipulation Pour autrui) are favored in our law. They are specifically authorized in broad terms in Articles 1890 and 1902 of the Civil Code.

[22] Article 1890 provides:

A person may also, in his own name, make some advantage for a third person the condition or consideration of a commutative contract, or onerous donation; and if such third person consents to avail himself of the advantage stipulated in his favor, the contract can not be revoked.

[23] Article 1902 provides:

But a contract, in which anything is stipulated for the benefit of a third person, who has signified his assent to accept it, can not be revoked as to the advantage stipulated in his favor without his consent.

[24] Professor J. Denson Smith, in a study of the history, legislation and jurisprudence which have formed the doctrine of stipulations in favor of third persons in this State, has enumerated the factors to be considered in deciding whether an advantage for a third person has been provided by contract between others. They are:

(1) The existence of a legal relationship between the promisee and the third person involving an obligation owed by the promisee to the beneficiary which performance of the promise will discharge; (2) the existence of a factual relationship between the promisee and the third person, where (a) there is a possibility of future liability either personal or real on the part of the promisee to the beneficiary against which performance of the promisee (sic) will protect the former; (b) securing an advantage for the third person may beneficially affect the promisee in a material way; (c) there are ties of kinship or other circumstances indicating that a benefit by way of gratuity was intended. See Smith, Third Party Beneficiaries in Louisiana: The Stipulation Pour Autrui, 11 Tul.L.Rev. 18, 58 (1936).

[25] The obligation created by the relationship of lessor and lessee which is pertinent to this case is expressed in the following language of Civil Code Article 2692:

The lessor is bound from the very nature of the contract, and without any clause to that effect:

3. To cause the lessee to be in peaceable possession of the thing during the continuance of the lease.

[26] Section 3203 of Title 9 of the Revised Statutes also imposes an obligation upon the lessor in favor of the lessee in these words:

Any lessor of property to be cultivated who fails to permit the lessee to occupy or cultivate the property leased, is liable to the lessee in an amount equal to the market value of the average crop that could have been grown on the land or on like land located in the immediate vicinity.

[27] Viewed in the context of the facts of this case, and upon application of the formula articulated by Smith, it is readily apparent that the legal relationship between the promisee (landowner lessor) and the third person (the farm lessee Andrepont) involved an obligation ('to cause the lessee to be in peaceable possession') owed by the promisee (landowner lessor) to the beneficiary (farm lessee) which performance of the promise (payment of all damages caused by the oil and gas lessee's operation) would discharge.

[28] Thus each requirement of the law is satisfied. The obligation imposed by the landowner lessor and undertaken by the oil and gas lessee as a condition of the lease — that is, to 'be responsible for all damages caused by Lessee's operations', constitutes a stipulation for the benefit of a third party, the farm lessee Andrepont, to pay for damage to his crop caused by the oil and gas lessee's operations.

[29] Because the inference is clear that drilling operations in a cultivated field must damage the crop and bring about a disturbance in the peaceable possession of the farm lessee, the landowner lessor is obviously interested in requiring the oil and gas lessee to undertake her obligation to indemnify the farm lessee in the event the oil and gas lessee's operations should result in a failure to maintain the farm lessee in peaceable possession of the leased premises. Otherwise the farm lessee's forthcoming claim for damages must be satisfied by her. See La.Civil Code Art. 2692 and La.R.S. 9:3203.

[30] In addition to her interest in having the oil and gas lessee discharge the obligation which she owed to the farm lessee, the relationship between the landowner and the farm lessee was sufficient to support the inference that there was a possibility of future liability either personal or real on the part of the landowner to the farm lessee against which performance of the promise would protect the landowner. This possibility of future liability stems from the very obligation the landowner was anxious to have the oil and gas lessee discharge. And the liability is the very crop damage involved here. In other words, the case at bar fits into two of the categories envisaged by Smith in formulating the rules applicable to stipulations Pour autrui.

[31] Another factor which persuades us to conclude that there was an intention to require the oil and gas lessee to repair the farm lessee's damage is the deletion from the printed oil and gas lease of the words 'to timber and growing crops of Lessor' so that the clause would read: 'The Lessee shall be responsible for all damages caused by Lessee's operations.' This deletion results in a change from the particular to the general and means that damages caused by the oil and gas lessee's operations to parties other than the lessor were clearly contemplated. And since drilling operations on the cultivated field must result in damage to the farm lessee, the farm lessee was undoubtedly intended as a beneficiary of this stipulation.

[32] Defendants' briefs suggest two principal defenses to the application of the doctrine of stipulation Pour autrui here. It is asserted that (1) the third party

beneficiary in the case at bar was not named or determinable, and (2) there was no consent to or acceptance of the benefits by the third party beneficiary.

[33] The contention that the third party was not named is without merit. Planiol gives the answer to this contention in his treatise 'Traite E le mentaire De Droit Civil', An English Translation by the Louisiana State Law Institute, Vol. 2-Part 1, No. 1236 (1959):

> Can one stipulate for undetermined persons? Yes, on the condition that the beneficiaries of the stipulation, at present undetermined, are determinable on the day on which the agreement is to have effect for their benefit. The obstacle to the effectiveness of a stipulation for another, is not therefore strictly speaking the simple present undetermined character of its beneficiaries, provided there are means to ascertain who they are when it becomes necessary to do so, but their future undetermined character, which must remain undefined, in other words, their undeterminability. * * *

[34] The principle has been recognized and has found application in the jurisprudence.

[35] A materialman, though furnishers of materials were not named as obligees in the condition of a bond in favor of the owner in a building contract, was given a right of action against the surety on the bond in Lichtentag v. Feitel, 113 La. 931, 37 So. 880 (1905). This conclusion was reached on the theory that since the bond was conditioned on the contractor's fulfilling the terms of his contract with the owner, payment of such claims by the contractor was necessary in order to fulfill the condition of the bond, and it could not be satisfied if the latter had left outstanding claims of materialmen to be paid by the owner enforceable by lien against the property. In like manner the stipulation that the oil and gas lessee would be 'responsible for all damages caused by Lessee's operations' cannot be considered as fulfilled if a farm lessee's damage claim 'caused by Lessee's operations' remains unsatisfied. To the same effect see Minden Presbyterian Church v. Lambert, 167 La. 712, 120 So. 61 (1929).

[36] A contractor removing dirt from a public road, who contracted with the public authority to maintain a nearby bridge during his operations, was deemed to have obligated himself in favor of the traveling public. Thus the Court held that a traveler whose wagon fell through the bridge could maintain a cause of action against the contractor for his damages. Lawson v. Shreveport Waterworks Co., 111 La. 73, 35 So. 390 (1903).

[37] In Volquardsen v. Southern Amusement Company, 156 So. 678 (La.App.1934) a member of a union, though unnamed, was permitted to entertain suit on a contract between the union and the defendant as a beneficiary of a stipulation in his favor made by the union with the defendant.

[38] Children in a parish, though unnamed and then undetermined, were recognized to have the right as third party beneficiaries to enforce a stipulation in their

favor contained in a contract between a parish school board and superintendent of schools with the United States. Lemon v. Bossier Parish School Board, 240 F.Supp. 709 (D.C.1965).

[39] The facts of this case readily fall within the rule of law established by these cases and expounded by Planiol. There is no problem in determining who the beneficiary of the stipulation Pour autrui is. He is the party suffering damages on the leased premises as a result of the oil and gas lessee's operations. He is in this case Andrepont, the farm lessee.

[40] Equally without merit is the argument that the third party beneficiary cannot avail himself of the stipulation in his favor for he has not consented to or accepted the stipulation. A categorical answer to this contention is found in a recent decision of this Court. Mr. Justice LeBlanc, speaking for the Court in First State Bank v. Burton, 225 La. 537, 549, 73 So.2d 453, 457 (1954), said:

> The law does not provide for an express acceptance of or consent to a stipulation pour autrui by the beneficiary nor does it prescribe and particular form of acceptance or consent. In some cases it was held that the appearance of the beneficiary as claimant in a suit before the Court is evidence of acceptance and certainly it would seem, under that jurisprudence that the claim now being asserted by Morris & Kendrick in this proceeding, regardless of any proof of their assent, is sufficient. See Muntz v. Algiers & Gretna Ry. Co., 114 La. 437, 38 So. 410; Vinet v. Bres, 48 La.Ann. 1254, 20 So. 693.

See also Twichel v. Andry, 6 Rob. 407 (La.1844); Smith, Third Party Beneficiaries in Louisiana: The Stipulation Pour Autrui, 11 Tul.L.Rev. 18, 55 (1936).

[41] As beneficiary of the stipulation, therefore, Andrepont should recover for damage to his crop. After a careful review of the evidence, the trial court awarded $1,298.25. We find no cause to disturb this award.

[42] In doing so we reject Andrepont's contention that the trial judge erroneously deducted twenty percent from the amount of the crop loss because the landowner had settled for 'her' damages. In a lease of land for part of the crop, that part which the lessor is to receive is considered at all times the property of lessor. La.R.S. 9:3204. It was, therefore, permissible for the landowner to accept a nominal amount for the damage to her share, and Andrepont cannot recover a second time for the same damage.

[43] For the reasons assigned, the judgment of the Court of Appeal is reversed. There is judgment in favor of plaintiff and against defendants for $1,298.25, with interest from date of judicial demand until paid and for all costs.

[. . . .]

Questions

NOTE: This case is a good illustration of a well-known principle at civil law according to which "no one can transfer to another a greater right than he has" (*nemo potior jure ad alium transfere potest quam ipse habet*). See the following Louisiana Civil Code articles as an illustration: 2700–2702. This principle was expressly stated in article 2010 of the Louisiana Civil Code of 1825 and article 2015 of the Louisiana Civil Code of 1870.

1. Paragraphs 1–2: Notice that the lease between the farmer and the Bundicks was oral, whereas the lease with Acadia Drilling Co. was in writing and recorded. Now read the Louisiana Civil Code articles on Lease (La. Civ. Code art. 2668, *et seq.*). Must a lease be in writing? Is there any benefit in a lease being recorded? Notice how the farmer is to pay the rent: 20% of the crop harvested. Now read Louisiana Civil Code articles 474, 480, 490, 491. Do you have any comment?

2. Paragraphs 3–5: Explain how the change in words could amount to a stipulation *pour autrui* (a stipulation for the benefit of another). How can the farmer take advantage of a contract between his landlord and Acadia Drilling, a contract to which that farmer is not a party?

3. Paragraph 6: Would Civil Code articles 463 and 474 have been relevant here and could they have been relied on by the Court?

4. Paragraphs 11–19: Do you think that, in rewriting the contract, the landlord and the oil company did intend to involve the farmer, to stipulate in his favor so as to make him a party to the contract? What could have motivated the Court to find a stipulation *pour autrui* in the rewriting of the contract?

5. Paragraphs 16–19: Read these paragraphs carefully, as they give a good explanation of the Court's interpretation of the contract in favor of the farmer. Since a stipulation for the benefit of another vests a benefit (and can never create a detriment) in the farmer, his consent is not required for the benefit to be created in his favor — in other words, one is always presumed to be willing to accept a benefit. Read Louisiana Civil Code article 1978. What is the consequence of the third-party beneficiary manifesting his intent to avail himself of the benefit?

6. Paragraphs 30–31: As the court is expanding on the rewriting of the contract, is the court giving any hint as to how the landlord and the oil company could be held liable to the farmer? What would be the source of the oil company's liability? What would be the source of the landlord's liability? Are those sources of liability different? What type of liability could exist between the landlord and the oil company?

Dr. Willie John Joseph, III, Dr. Michelle T. Brumfield, and St. Mary Anesthesia Associates, Inc.

v.

Hospital Service District No. 2 of the Parish of St. Mary, State of Louisiana, Our Lady of the Lake Hospital, Inc., Melvin Bourgeois, M.D., James Broussard, John Guarisco, Sharon Howell, Y. George Ramirez, Clifford M. Broussard, National Union Fire Insurance Company of Louisiana and Louisiana Hospital Association Malpractice and General Liability Trust

Supreme Court of Louisiana
October 15, 2006
939 So.2d 1206

WEIMER, Justice.

[1] We are called upon to determine whether a contract between a hospital and a medical corporation provides a stipulation for a third party (also referred to as a stipulation *pour autrui*) in the form of benefits for individual doctors affiliated with the medical corporation. This matter is before the court on defendants' exceptions of no right of action, which contend the doctors are not third party beneficiaries of the contract. The trial court granted defendants' exceptions and dismissed the plaintiff doctors' claims with prejudice. The court of appeal reversed and defendants filed an application for writ of certiorari. For reasons that follow, we reinstate the judgment of the trial court finding the contract at issue does not create a stipulation *pour autrui* in favor of the plaintiff doctors. Consequently, the doctors have no right of action.

Facts and Procedural Background

[2] On December 13, 1990, Hospital Service District No. 2 of the Parish of St. Mary (Hospital), operator of Lakewood Medical Center, entered into a contract with St. Mary Anesthesia Associates, Inc. (SMAA) for the purpose of obtaining general anesthesia services for the hospital's patients. The contract was signed by Raymond J. Rowell, chief operating officer of the Hospital, and Willie J. Joseph, III, M.D., president of SMAA. The contract provided for automatic annual renewal unless terminated by the Hospital for cause as defined in the contract or by SMAA giving no less than 60 days notice prior to the end of the original term or any renewal period.

[3] In November 2000, then chief operating officer of the Hospital, Clifford M. Broussard, advised SMAA that the contact would terminate within 30 days from the date of the letter because the contract was not in the Hospital's best interest.

[4] Dr. Willie John Joseph, III, Dr. Michelle T. Brumfield, and SMAA filed suit on August 19, 2003, naming as defendants the Hospital, Our Lady of the Lake Hospital, Inc., Melvin Bourgeois, M.D., James Broussard, John Guarisco, Sharon Howell,

Y. George Ramirez, Clifford M. Broussard, National Union Fire Insurance Company of Louisiana, and Louisiana Hospital Association Malpractice and General Liability Trust.

[5] Alleging breach of contract, the petitioners sought damages, including, but not limited to, past and future loss of earnings, costs of relocation and "moral damages," mental anguish, grief and anxiety on behalf of the doctors, and future loss of earnings on behalf of SMAA. Pursuant to a provision contained in the contract, plaintiffs also sought attorney fees in connection with this litigation.[2]

[6] Defendants filed exceptions of no right of action regarding the claims asserted by the doctors contending that SMAA was the only party with a real and actual interest in the contract and the doctors had no individual right to sue for a corporate loss. The doctors argued the contract expressed an intent to stipulate a benefit in favor of the doctors and that this benefit was a material consideration for the contract.

[. . . .]

[7] [. . . .] Thus, the question to be resolved is whether the contract clearly manifested an intent to stipulate a benefit for a third person. The court of appeal rejected the hospital's argument that the stipulation itself must be in writing to be valid and questioned the validity of the statement in *Fontenot v. Marquette Casualty Co.,* 258 La. 671, 247 So.2d 572 (1971), requiring a stipulation *pour autrui* to be in writing. The focus of the court's concern involved the following statement in *Fontenot*: "In Louisiana contracts for the benefit of others, or the stipulation pour autrui, must be in writing and clearly express that intent." *Fontenot,* 247 So.2d at 579. The *Fontenot* court cited former Civil Code articles 1890 and 1902 as authority for the statement.[3]

[. . . .]

Discussion

[. . . .]

[8] Collectively, the defendants contend the claims set forth in this case belong to SMAA, not the doctors/employees, thus the exception of no right of action is proper. Defendants also argue the decision of the court of appeal conflicts with this court's decision in Fontenot, as well as decisions from other appellate courts and should be overturned. They claim the stipulation *pour autrui* must be in writing and, thus an oral stipulation *pour autrui* is unenforceable.

---

2. A judgment granting the peremptory exception of prescription filed on behalf of defendants against plaintiffs and dismissing the cause of action in tort (including the intentional interference with contract and the denial of due process rights) asserted on behalf of plaintiffs was signed on July 7, 2004.

3. The substance of these articles was reproduced in LSA-C.C. art. 1978 when the Civil Code was amended in 1984. 1984 La. Acts No. 331 § 1, effective Jan. 1, 1985.

[9] It is plaintiffs' position that the court of appeal was correct in its interpretation of the *Fontenot* decision. *Fontenot* involved a reinsuring agreement[4] which is statutorily required to be in writing. Plaintiffs assert the statement in *Fontenot* requiring a stipulation *pour autrui* to be in writing is merely dicta. In this case, plaintiffs argue the benefits they were to receive were clearly contemplated by the parties to the contract and were not merely incidental. They assert the court of appeal decision is correct and should be affirmed.

[10] At the hearing on the exceptions, defendants introduced a copy of the contract dated December 13, 1990. The contract, an anesthesia service agreement, was executed by and between the Hospital and SMAA. Dr. Joseph signed the contract on behalf of SMAA, but not in his individual capacity. Dr. Brumfield is not mentioned in the contract. In the contract, SMAA was referred to as the "Contractor." The Hospital agreed to retain the Contractor to exclusively provide anesthesia services. The Hospital agreed to provide facilities, equipment, and supplies necessary and proper for the administration of anesthesia to its patients. Additionally, the Hospital agreed to recognize Dr. Joseph as a "medical specialist" providing services on behalf of the Contractor. The Hospital also agreed to recognize any employee of the Contractor (any duly licensed and qualified physician trained in delivery of anesthesia services and licensed to practice in Louisiana) as a "medical specialist" on behalf of the Contractor, SMAA.

[11] The contract further provided that the Contractor may from time to time retain the services of other physician specialists who were to comply with all of the terms and conditions of the agreement.

[12] The contract specifically provided that the Contractor was an "independent contractor" and clearly stated there was no intent to create an employer/employee relationship, a joint venture relationship, or lease or landlord/tenant relationship. The agreement was to be binding on the Hospital and Contractors, their successors and assigns.

[13] Because the plaintiff doctors were not parties to the contract, they can only avail themselves of the benefit of the Hospital/SMAA contract if they are third party beneficiaries. LSA-C.C. art. 1978 provides:

> A contracting party may stipulate a benefit for a third person called a third party beneficiary.

---

4. Reinsurance is a contract by which one insurance company agrees to indemnify another in whole or in part against loss or liability which the latter has incurred under a separate contract as insurer of a third party. *Fontenot*, 247 So.2d at 575. Reinsurance indemnifies the insurer for a loss which is actually sustained. In *Fontenot*, an insured of one insurance company filed suit claiming the contract of reinsurance between his insurer and another company contained a stipulation *pour autrui* inuring to his benefit. The court held the contract was governed by the insurance code and the contract of reinsurance did not create any right of action in third parties directly against the reinsurer. *Fontenot*, 247 So.2d at 581.

Once the third party has manifested his intention to avail himself of the benefit, the parties may not dissolve the contract by mutual consent without the beneficiary's agreement.

[14] The Revision Comments indicate this article reproduces the substance of LSA-C.C. arts. 1890 and 1902 and the law was not changed. Under Louisiana law, such a contract for the benefit of a third party is commonly referred to as a "stipulation *pour autrui.*"[5] *Paul v. Louisiana State Employees' Group Benefit Program,* 99-0897, p. 5 (La.App. 1 Cir. 5/12/00), 762 So.2d 136, 140.

[15] Under Roman law, a stipulation for a third party was unenforceable, despite the fact that the word "stipulation" comes from the Roman *stipulatio.* Nevertheless, the French and Louisiana Codes set to rest any contention that a third party could not recover on a contract merely because he was not a party to the contract. *See* discussion by Professor J. Denson Smith of the historical development of this doctrine in his article *Third Party Beneficiaries in Louisiana: The Stipulation Pour Autrui* at 11 Tul. L.Rev. 18, 18-28 (1936). Although the current Article 1978 had its underpinnings in the French Civil Code, the term *"stipulation pour autrui"* was not employed in the Louisiana Civil Code. Professor Smith, however, called the term a "well established part of our legal language." Smith, 11 Tul. L.Rev. at 23. The term remains a part of our legal language today.

[16] There has been a codal provision in Louisiana recognizing a stipulation for a third party since 1808. *See* Article 21 of the Louisiana Civil Code of 1808; *see also* Art. 1890, La. C.C. Comp. Ed., in 16 West's LSA-C.C. pp. 1076–1077 (1972).

[17] A true third party beneficiary is never a party to the contract in question; he is never a promisee. Smith, 11 Tul. L.Rev. at 33. The promisee is the stipulator and the promise runs to him and is merely in favor of the third party. *Id.*

[18] The Louisiana Civil Code recognizes that a third party beneficiary contract can exist, but provides few governing rules. *See* LSA-C.C. arts. 1978–1982. The code provides no analytic framework for determining whether a third party beneficiary contract exists. Professor Smith acknowledges that a determination of the circumstances under which a stipulation *pour autrui* will exist is the "primary question" in any given case. Smith, 11 Tul. L.Rev. at 24. Thus, the code has left to the jurisprudence the obligation to develop the analysis to determine when a third party beneficiary contract exists on a case by case basis. Each contract must be evaluated on its own terms and conditions in order to determine if the contract stipulates a benefit for a third person.[6]

---

5. BLACK'S LAW DICTIONARY 1427 (7th ed.1999), refers to stipulation *pour autrui* as a French civil law term meaning a stipulation "for other persons."

6. In *Andrepont v. Acadia Drilling Co.,* 255 La. 347, 231 So.2d 347 (1969), this court utilized the factors proposed by Professor J. Denson Smith to be considered in deciding whether an advantage for a third person has been provided by a contract between others. We recognize Professor Smith's test is an analytical tool to determine whether a stipulation *pour autrui* has been established — not a definitive analysis.

[19] Our study of the jurisprudence has revealed three criteria for determining whether contracting parties have provided a benefit for a third party: 1) the stipulation for a third party is manifestly clear; 2) there is certainty as to the benefit provided the third party; and 3) the benefit is not a mere incident of the contract between the promisor and the promisee. In applying these criteria, we ultimately rely on the words of Article 1978 that the contract must "stipulate a benefit for a third person."

[20] The most basic requirement of a stipulation *pour autrui* is that the contract manifest a clear intention to benefit the third party; absent such a clear manifestation, a party claiming to be a third party beneficiary cannot meet his burden of proof. *Paul*, 99-0897 at 7–8, 762 So.2d at 141–142; *see also, Doucet v. National Maintenance Corporation,* 01-1100, pp. 6–7 (La.App. 1 Cir. 6/21/02), 822 So.2d 60, 66. A stipulation *pour autrui* is never presumed. The party claiming the benefit bears the burden of proof. *See* LSA-C.C. art. 1831;[7] *see also Paul*, 99-0897 at 5, 762 So.2d at 140.

[21] The second factor, certainty as to the benefit provided, is a corollary of the requirement of a manifestly clear stipulation. "To create a legal obligation enforceable by the beneficiary there must be certainty as to the benefit to accrue to the beneficiary." *Berry v. Berry,* 371 So.2d 1346, 1347 (La.App. 1 Cir.), *writ denied,* 373 So.2d 511 (1979).

[22] In connection with the third requirement that the benefit cannot be a mere incident of the contract, we find pertinent the discussion of "incidental benefits" by Professor Smith, 11 Tul. L.Rev. at 28: "[N]ot every promise, performance of which may be advantageous to a third person, will create in him an actionable right. The problem is to separate the cases where an advantage has been stipulated from those where the advantage relied upon is merely an incident of the contract between the parties." Illustrative is *City of Shreveport v. Gulf Oil Corporation,* 431 F.Supp. 1 (W.D.La.1975), *aff'd,* 551 F.2d 93 (5th Cir.1977). [. . . .]

[. . . .]

In a study of the history, legislation, and jurisprudence which formed the doctrine of stipulations in favor of third persons, Professor Smith enumerated the following factors as being important in deciding whether the contract provides a benefit for a third person:
    (1) The existence of a legal relationship between the promisee and the third person involving an obligation owed by the promisee to the beneficiary which performance of the promise will discharge; (2) the existence of a factual relationship between the promisee and the third person, where (a) there is a possibility of future liability either personal or real on the part of the promisee to the beneficiary against which performance of the promise [sic] will protect the former; (b) securing an advantage for the third person may beneficially affect the promisee in a material way; (c) there are ties of kinship or other circumstances indicating that a benefit by way of gratuity was intended. See Smith, Third Party Beneficiaries in Louisiana: The Stipulation Pour Autrui, 11 Tul.L.Rev. 18, 58 (1936).
Andrepont, 231 So.2d at 350–351.

7. LSA-C.C. art. 1831 provides, in part:
    A party who demands performance of an obligation must prove the existence of the contract.

[23] In this matter, the court of appeal found administration of anesthesia service to the hospital's patients was the object of the contract and concluded that SMAA, as a juridical person only,[9] was incapable of rendering such service. The court of appeal noted there was no allegation of breach of fiduciary trust and the damages alleged were personal to the doctors. The court of appeal found the contract clearly manifested an express intent to benefit Dr. Joseph and also manifested an intent to benefit Dr. Brumfield.

[24] We disagree. Following a thorough review of the provisions of the contract, we also conclude the contract is unambiguous. However, we find there are no provisions included in the contract which establish a stipulation for the doctors in a manifestly clear manner. We find no certainty as to the benefit provided the doctors. We find any benefit to the doctors a mere incident of the contract between the Hospital and SMAA.[10]

[25] Ultimately, we find there is no benefit in the contract flowing directly to the doctors such that a benefit was stipulated in their favor. While the contract imposed certain obligations on the doctors regarding their qualifications, there was no benefit provided in the contract directly to the doctors that they could demand from the Hospital. The doctors were not to be paid by the Hospital. The doctors were not hired by the Hospital. The doctors had no right to demand employment by the Hospital. In fact, the contract specifically provided there was no intent to create an employer/employee relationship between the parties. Based on our review of the contract, there is no obligation owed by the Hospital to the individual doctors which will be discharged by performance of the contract because the contract provides no direct benefit to the doctors.

[26] While the doctors can perform the services to satisfy the contractual obligations of the corporation, there are no direct benefits flowing to the plaintiff doctors. Simply stated, in the absence of a direct benefit conferred by the contract, the doctors cannot be third party beneficiaries pursuant to LSA-C.C. art. 1978.

[27] A person may derive a benefit from a contract to which he is not a party without being a third party beneficiary. In this case, any benefit created by the contract in favor of the doctors was only incidental to their employment with SMAA.

---

9. In a footnote the court noted the fact that SMAA was a corporation was not relevant to a decision in this matter.

10. We note one exception which is not at issue in this litigation. The contract does contain a stipulation *pour autrui* in the section of the contract addressing recruitment. The Hospital agreed to pay relocation costs incurred by a second physician specialist moving to Morgan City. Thus, although the contract did provide a stipulation *pour autrui* for the benefit of a doctor to be recruited by SMAA in the form of reimbursement of relocation costs, that benefit was manifestly clear, and outlined in the recruitment provision of the contract addressing relocation costs. The contract could have included additional benefits to inure to the doctors; however, it did not do so in a manifestly clear manner. Nevertheless, after a review of the record and as acknowledged at oral argument, that provision is not at issue.

[28] The doctors contend that they benefitted from the contract because the Hospital granted them the exclusive right to provide anesthesiology services. However, a review of the contract establishes it is SMAA as the Contractor which is granted the exclusive right to provide anesthesia services. The contract provides: "HOSPITAL hereby EXCLUSIVELY retains CONTRACTOR, and CONTRACTOR hereby accepts such retention, to make available anesthesia services and to provide such other services in accordance with this agreement." Thus, SMAA is specifically and clearly granted the exclusive right to provide anesthesia services. Additionally, the contract provides SMAA can "from time to time retain the services of other physician SPECIALISTS," further indicating it is not the plaintiff doctors which have exclusivity, but rather SMAA. Based on this clause, physicians other than the plaintiff doctors could provide services on behalf of SMAA. As such, the contract does not provide the plaintiff doctors the exclusive right to provide anesthesia services at the hospital.

[29] The contract goes on to recognize, not only Dr. Joseph, but any employee of SMAA as a medical specialist for the purpose of providing anesthesia services. However, that recognition merely establishes how the obligations of the contract are to be discharged by SMAA and does not, in a manifestly clear fashion, confer a benefit on the doctors as third parties. The doctors further contend they were afforded exclusivity because the contract would be terminated if, among other reasons, Dr. Joseph's license to practice medicine were suspended, revoked, or terminated. However, the termination provision does not confer a benefit. Rather, this provision merely recognizes conditions which serve to terminate the contract. Regardless, the language from the contract, quoted above, establishes that the exclusivity provision of the contract is in favor of SMAA and not the individual doctors.

[30] Not every breach of a contract with a corporation provides a cause of action to the employees or shareholders of that corporation. In essence, the court of appeal decision created an implied right of action for employees of juridical entities to contest any contract between the employing corporation and another entity if any benefit flowed to the employee. In *Scaffidi and Chetta Entertainment v. University of New Orleans Foundation,* 04-1046 (La.App. 5 Cir. 2/15/05), 898 So.2d 491, *writ denied,* 05-0748 (La.5/6/05), 901 So.2d 1102, Scaffidi and Chetta established a corporation which entered into a contract with the University of New Orleans Foundation. The court denied the personal claims of shareholders Scaffidi and Chetta finding they were not third party beneficiaries of the contract. The court further found the cause of action belonged solely to the corporation.[11] This decision reflects an appropriate

---

11. *See also Joe Conte Toyota, Inc. v. Toyota Motor Sales, U.S.A., Inc.,* 95-1630, (La.App. 4 Cir. 2/12/97) 689 So.2d 650, *writ denied,* 97-0659 (La.4/25/97) 692 So.2d 1090, where the court affirmed the trial court judgment granting an exception of no right of action ruling that shareholders and officers of a corporation and a guarantor of corporate obligations had no right to recover for acts committed against or causing damage to a corporation. Only the corporation can sue for breach of a contract to which the corporation is a party.

reluctance to find a stipulation *pour autrui* in favor of each shareholder or officer or employee of a juridical person. Once established, the separate nature of the corporate existence must be respected.

[31] The doctors urge us to ignore the corporate status of SMAA because a medical corporation can only act through a physician. We refuse to do so. As a legal fiction, all corporations act through individuals. Dr. Joseph chose to establish a medical corporation. This separate juridical entity cannot be disregarded. *See* LSA-C.C. art. 24.[12] The breach of contract claim is a claim to be asserted by the corporation, not the employees, officers or shareholders of the corporation.

[32] Finally, we agree that the court of appeal was correct to question the requirement of a writing to establish a stipulation *pour autrui*. The statement in *Fontenot* indicating that contracts for the benefit of others must be in writing was dicta. The *Fontenot* court cited former Civil Code articles 1890 and 1902 for that proposition. Review of the former articles, as well as current articles related to a third party beneficiary contract (*See* Articles 1978–1982), indicates there is no statutory requirement that the stipulation *pour autrui* be in writing.[13]

[33] We note the statement in *Fontenot* that a stipulation *pour autrui* must be in writing was criticized by Judge Covington in his dissent in *Berry*, 371 So.2d at 1352–1353, and in Katherine Shaw Spaht & H. Alston Johnson, III, *The Work of the Appellate Courts for the 1975–1976 Term-Obligations*, 37 La. L.Rev. 332, 346–347 (1977), which he cited.

[34] Although the appellate court correctly found it unnecessary for a stipulation *pour autrui* to be in writing, these parties contracted that their entire agreement must be in writing. The contract provides: "This Agreement contains the entire understanding of the parties and shall be modified only by an instrument in writing signed on behalf of each party hereto." Thus, these parties contractually limited themselves to a written contract.

Conclusion

[35] For the foregoing reasons, the decision of the court of appeal is reversed and the judgment rendered by the district court granting defendants exceptions of no right of action is reinstated.

[36] **REVERSED. JUDGMENT GRANTING EXCEPTION REINSTATED.**

[37] JOHNSON, J., concurs in result.

---

12. LSA-C.C. art. 24 provides:
    There are two kinds of persons: natural persons and juridical persons.
    A natural person is a human being. A juridical person is an entity to which the law attributes personality, such as a corporation or a partnership. The personality of a juridical person is distinct from that of its members.
13. There is no general requirement that stipulations *pour autrui* be in writing. However, if the contract must be in writing (*See e.g.,* LSA-C.C. arts. 1536 and 2440. *See also* LSA-C.C. art.1832.), then the stipulation *pour autrui* must also be in writing.

Questions

1. In this case, the Supreme Court concludes that it was permissible for the Court of Appeal to reject and, in the end, refuse to follow the rule of *Fontenot v. Marquette Casualty Co.*, a prior Supreme Court case. *See* paragraphs 7 and 32–33. Is that correct? Why? Imagine that *Joseph* had been decided in, say, Alabama. Do you suppose that the Alabama Supreme Court would have reacted in the same way had one of the state's intermediate appellate courts refused to follow one of its precedents? Why or why not? *See generally* La. Civ. Code. arts. 1 to 4.

2. What role did "doctrine" (what an Anglo-American lawyer would call "legal scholarship") play in the *Joseph* court's interpretation of the legislation governing stipulations *pour autrui*?

3. One of the principal linchpins of the *Joseph* court's analysis involves the distinction between true third-party benefits, on the one hand, and "incidental" benefits, on the other. *See* paragraphs 22–28. What is the essence of this distinction? Does footnote 6 help? In that footnote, the *Joseph* court acknowledges that the contract between the Hospital and SMAA did, at least on one point, create a stipulation *pour autrui* in favor of the plaintiffs. What was that point? How was the part of the contract that pertained to that point different from the part of the contract on the basis of which the plaintiffs had predicated their claims?

Charles Robert McKee, IV
v.
Southfield School and the Board of Trustees of Southfield School

Court of Appeal of Louisiana
Second Circuit
January 20, 1993
613 So.2d 659

NORRIS, Judge.

[1] Defendant, Southfield School, appeals the trial court's order issuing a preliminary injunction requiring the school to deliver to Plaintiff, Charles Robert McKee IV, an official transcript of his academic record.

[2] At the time of trial, McKee was an 18-year-old high school junior at Trinity Heights Christian Academy ("Trinity") in Shreveport. Prior to his enrolling at Trinity, McKee had attended Southfield School ("Southfield") since 1987. Southfield is a private school, and McKee's attendance there was established by annual contracts executed between Southfield and McKee's father, Charles Robert McKee III. The plaintiff was not a party to these contracts.

[3] In June 1990, the summer before McKee's sophomore year at Southfield, Jeff Stokes became the new headmaster for the school. Shortly after arriving at Southfield, Stokes discovered that McKee's tuition account was $5,000.00 delinquent,

dating back several years. No payments at all were made during the preceding school year, 1989–90.

[4] In August 1990, Stokes met with McKee's father to make arrangements to bring the account up to date. At that meeting, Stokes agreed to allow McKee to continue in school provided his father begin making monthly payments of $600.00, starting in September 1990. When the school failed to receive payment, Stokes sent McKee's father a letter dated October 3, 1990 advising him that he was behind on the account. A second letter dated October 8, 1990 was sent by Stokes to McKee's father, advising him that "unless a payment of at least $1,200.00 is received by the end of October, the school will no longer enroll your son." (Southfield ex. # 1). Although McKee's father denies ever receiving this letter,[1] the school's records show receipt of a $1,200.00 payment on October 31, 1990. (Southfield ex. # 4). No payments were made in November, December, or January.

[5] In February 1991, Southfield's business manager sent a third letter to McKee's father requesting payment of $1,800.00 by the end of the month. In response to this letter, McKee's father made two $600.00 payments in February. No further payments were made. Nevertheless, McKee was permitted to complete the school year at Southfield because, as Stokes stated at trial, the Southfield Board of Trustees' policy, obviously unwritten, was to allow students with delinquent accounts to remain enrolled but to withhold all records. (R.p. 76). At the end of the school year, McKee's tuition account was more than $8,000.00 delinquent.

[6] Whether Southfield would have prevented McKee from returning for his junior year, as Stokes testified, is not known because the Southfield Board of Trustees decided to close Southfield's upper school at the end of the 1990–91 school year. (R.p. 78). As a result of the upper school's closure, in August 1991 McKee enrolled for his junior year at Trinity, another private school. As a prerequisite to enrollment, Trinity required a transcript from McKee's previous school. When McKee's father requested a transcript from Southfield, he was informed that a transcript would not be released until the outstanding debt was satisfied.

[7] Even without the transcript, McKee was allowed to attend Trinity because Trinity's principal, James Corley, believed "the kid need[ed] to be in school somewhere." (R.p. 42). However, Corley stated that the school would not be able to issue a diploma to McKee without the transcript unless he repeated the two years of courses he has already taken at the Southfield upper school. (R.p. 36). In the absence of a transcript, repetition of the courses would be the only way the school could be certain that state requirements had been met. According to Corley, a public school would have the same requirements. (R.p. 37).

[8] As a further result of his inability to produce a transcript, McKee was not allowed to play basketball for Trinity due to the eight-semester rule. This rule

---

1. Each of the three letters discussed herein was addressed to 35 Madonna Street. The McKees' correct address is 34 Madonna Street.

prohibits a student from competing in high school sports beyond his eighth semester of high school. Since McKee could not produce a transcript, he could not prove that he had been in high school for fewer than eight semesters. Thus, McKee was not permitted to play even though he had been a starter for Southfield's team in both his freshman a sophomore years.

[9] On January 29, 1992, after several failed attempts by McKee's father to settle the debt owed to Southfield and have the transcript released, McKee filed a Petition for Damages and Equitable Remedies against Southfield School and its Board of Trustees.[2] In his petition, McKee prayed for a temporary restraining order, preliminary and permanent injunctions, and damages for the interference in his participation in high school athletics. Judge C.J. Bolin, Jr. denied the temporary restraining order but on February 20, 1992 signed an order issuing a preliminary mandatory injunction requiring Southfield to deliver one official transcript to McKee. The trial court found that Southfield, by its actions and agreement to continue educating McKee, indicated that it would forego the harsh remedy of withholding the transcript. In essence, the court held that Southfield was estopped from withholding the transcript. Southfield filed a suspensive appeal. McKee did not file a response.

The Contract

[10] At trial, McKee introduced the Contract for Enrollment executed between his father and Southfield School. (Plaintiff's ex. # 1). While this contract only applied to the 1989–90 school year, McKee's father testified to the best of his memory, and Southfield did not dispute, that each of the annual contracts were of the same form. (R.p. 61). We note from the outset that McKee, while not a party to the contract, is an intended beneficiary of the agreement and is, therefore, entitled to a direct action against Southfield. La.C.C. art. 1978; *Dartez v. Dixon,* 502 So.2d 1063 (La.1987); *Litton v. Ford Motor Co.,* 554 So.2d 99 (La.App.2d Cir.1989), writ denied 559 So.2d 1353 (1990). See also *Bossier Parish School Board v. Lemon,* 370 F.2d 847 (5th Cir.), cert. denied 388 U.S. 911, 87 S.Ct. 2116, 18 L.Ed.2d 1350 (1967) (holding children of Barksdale Air Force Base personnel to be third party beneficiaries of an agreement to educate executed by the United States and Bossier Parish school system).

[11] The pertinent parts of the contract provide as follows:

Subject to the following provisions, I enroll my child in Southfield School for the 1989–1990 school year in the Ninth grade.

. . . .

I understand that . . . this contract covers the enrollment of my child in the school for the entire school year.

---

2. The Southfield Board of Trustees was never served with citation or a copy of the petition. Consequently, the trial court's judgment was issued against Southfield School only.

UPON ACCEPTANCE OF THIS CONTRACT BY THE SCHOOL THE
PARENT SHALL BE OBLIGATED FOR THE FULL TUITION FOR THE
YEAR IN THE AMOUNT OF $2,750.00.

. . . .

I understand that the school reserves the right to ask for the withdrawal of
a child at any time.

[12] The contract is silent with regard to the academic transcript. It states neither
that the school is obligated to provide a transcript nor that it is free from that obligation in the event that tuition is not paid. However, not all obligations arising out
of contract need be explicitly stated. *National Safe Corp. v. Benedict and Myrick,
Inc.,* 371 So.2d 792 (La.1979). When interpreting a contract, the court must look to
the common intent of the parties. La.C.C. art. 2045. Article 2045 of the Civil Code
further provides that:

[13] When the parties made no provision for a particular situation, it must be
assumed that they intended to bind themselves not only to the express provisions
of the contract, but also to whatever the law, equity, or usage regards as implied in a
contract of that kind or necessary for the contract to achieve its purpose.

[14] In the context of the instant contract, we find that the parties intended not
only that Southfield furnish McKee with an education in return for money, but also
that it furnish documentation of that education. While it is conceivable that one
might contract to be formally educated merely for education's sake, in this modern
era, it is far more likely that one entering into such a contract intends the education to be a springboard into the job market or into higher education. Neither of
these goals would be a likely result of formal education absent the ability to prove,
via documentation, that one had indeed been educated. Certainly, McKee's father
intended that Southfield furnish his son with documentation sufficient to show
the world that he had indeed completed a course of study at Southfield. Similarly,
Southfield surely contemplated the necessity of furnishing to McKee and its other
students written proof of their academic accomplishments. Thus, under the agreement Southfield was obligated to provide McKee with an education and written
verification of that education; McKee's father, in turn, was obligated to pay tuition
to Southfield.

[15] However, McKee's father, by his own admission, failed to perform his obligation under the contract, as written, or under the subsequent agreement to pay
back arrearages and keep tuition current. He fell behind on the monthly tuition
payments and eventually stopped making payments altogether, acquiring a delinquency of over $8,000.00. Under these circumstances, McKee's father, as a party to
the contract, would be in no position to demand further performance from Southfield. See La.C.C. art. 2013. As a third party beneficiary, McKee's rights under the
contract are subject to the terms and conditions of the contract entered into by his
father and Southfield. *Pelican Well & Tool Supply Co. v. Johnson,* 194 La. 987, 195
So. 514 (1940); *A.F. Blair Co. v. Haydel,* 504 So.2d 1044 (La.App. 1st Cir.1987). Thus,

McKee is in no better position than would be his father to demand that Southfield further perform under the contract. See La.C.C. art. 1982.

Detrimental Reliance

[16] Although McKee cannot demand performance under the contract, he may do so on the basis of detrimental reliance. In this regard, article 1967 of the Civil Code provides, in pertinent part:

> A party may be obligated by a promise when he knew or should have known that the promise would induce the other party to rely on it to his detriment and the other party was reasonable in so relying.

[17] Under this article, the court may grant either specific performance or damages. C.C. art. 1967, comment (e); *Woodard v. Felts,* 573 So.2d 1312 (La.App. 2d Cir.1991).

[18] In *A.F. Blair,* supra, the court held that a third party beneficiary may bring an action based on detrimental reliance against a principal party to a third party beneficiary contract. In that case, a bank entered into an agreement with a doctor whereby the bank would provide financing for the construction of the doctor's field house. Prior to construction, the bank furnished the construction company with a letter indicating that the bank had approved a loan sufficient to satisfy the construction contract between the doctor and the construction company. However, when the completion cost turned out to be more than originally expected, the bank refused to tender the difference. Although the court found the construction company to be a third party beneficiary of the financing agreement, it held that the company was not entitled to recovery in contract because the bank had fully performed under the contract. Nevertheless, the court remanded the case, stating that the construction company had alleged facts sufficient to state a claim in detrimental reliance.

[19] This court, in *Kethley v. Draughon Business College, Inc.,* 535 So.2d 502 (La. App. 2d Cir.1988), held that a business college instructor was entitled to recovery from the college on the basis of detrimental reliance. The instructor contracted with the college to teach one paralegal course during the fall quarter in return for a $200 per month payment. Some time later, the instructor agreed to teach two paralegal courses during the winter quarter. Although the parties had not discussed compensation for the winter quarter, the instructor assumed he would be paid $400 per month. The college maintained that it intended to pay the instructor only $200 per month since the second course was taught in a combined format.

[20] This court held that the instructor could not recover in contract because there had been no meeting of the minds. However, we permitted recovery under the theory of detrimental reliance. When the college agreed to employ the plaintiff to teach two courses, it implicitly promised that it would pay plaintiff more than he received for teaching one course. The plaintiff's reliance on this implied promise was reasonable, and he was therefore awarded damages. See also *Woodard,* supra; *Morris v. People's Bank & Trust Co.,* 580 So.2d 1029 (La.App. 3d Cir.), writs denied 588 So.2d 101, 102 (1991).

[21] In the instant case, Southfield was well aware of the considerable delinquency on McKee's tuition account. Nevertheless, Stokes agreed to allow McKee to continue pursuing his education at Southfield provided his father met the revised payment schedule. The record clearly indicates that, when McKee's father failed to abide by the revised payment schedule, the school contacted him on several occasions in an attempt to collect the sum he owed. Indeed, in a letter to McKee's father, Stokes suggested that the school might ask for McKee's withdrawal; however, Southfield never did so. Rather, it permitted McKee to attend until the end of the 1990–91 school year.

[22] When Southfield permitted McKee to continue his education, notwithstanding his father's clear failure to perform under the contract as written or as revised, it implicitly promised McKee's father that it would grant credit to McKee for the academic work he successfully completed. As the beneficiary of this promise, McKee relied upon it and continued to attend Southfield, performing the coursework required of him by Southfield teachers.

[23] Indeed, by permitting McKee to continue as a student, Southfield implicitly promised to McKee, himself, that he would receive credit toward his high school diploma if he successfully met academic requirements. Also implicit in Southfield's continued performance was that it would supply documentation of McKee's academic accomplishments. McKee was certainly reasonable in expecting this performance as the school never indicated that it might withhold his academic transcript. See *Woodard,* supra; *Kethley,* supra.

[24] McKee's reliance on Southfield's continued enrollment would undoubtedly have a detrimental effect upon him were Southfield now permitted to withhold documentation of his education at Southfield. Absent proof of his academic credits in the form of a transcript, McKee would be forced to repeat two years of high school before he could receive a diploma. It would be grossly unfair to allow a student to be lulled into thinking he would receive credit upon satisfactory completion of his coursework, and then to refuse him any evidence of ever having completed the coursework. Under these circumstances, we agree with the trial court's result and find that McKee is entitled to a transcript evidencing his academic accomplishments at Southfield.

[25] Finally, we note that the out-of-state jurisprudence cited by Southfield is inapplicable to the instant case. Of the cases cited, only one, *Fayman v. Trustees of Burlington College,* 103 N.J.Super. 476, 247 A.2d 688 (N.J.Ch.1968), has an analogous fact pattern. Yet, even *Fayman* is clearly inapposite; there, the contracting parents, not the student, sought to compel the issuance of a transcript notwithstanding their breach of the enrollment contract.

[26] In conclusion, the trial court judgment issuing a mandatory preliminary injunction requiring Southfield School to issue a transcript to McKee is affirmed. Costs are assessed to Southfield School.

[27] **AFFIRMED.**

VICTORY, Judge, dissenting.

[28] I agree with the part of the majority opinion that holds plaintiff cannot recover in contract.

[29] However, in my view, Southfield's decision to not disenroll plaintiff in February 1991 cannot be construed to imply it would certify his work in a transcript without the bill being satisfied. If Southfield's actions amount to an implied promise at all, at best, they merely imply plaintiff would not be disenrolled during the semester once it had begun.

[30] Assuming, arguendo, that detrimental reliance can be applicable to a situation where the third party beneficiary is the child of the party breaching a contract, the plaintiff failed to prove (1) he relied on Southfield's actions to his detriment, and (2) he was reasonable in so relying. Indeed, he did not even attempt to prove detrimental reliance, which was not raised by the parties in the trial court or this court.

[31] The detriment mentioned in the majority's opinion comes not from reliance on Southfield's "implied promise," but from its legal right to withhold the transcript. As the majority seems to acknowledge, if Southfield had chosen to disenroll plaintiff for breach of contract when the spring semester began, it would not have been obligated to furnish him a transcript. Plaintiff took no action relying on the school's forbearance that worked to his detriment. In fact, he stayed in the school and finished the year, which was very much to his advantage.

[32] If Southfield had disenrolled plaintiff when his father stopped paying in February 1991, he would now have no transcript and would not have completed the school year ending in May 1991. Plaintiff has not even attempted to show he could have enrolled in another school in mid-February 1991 without a certified transcript from Southfield. Because Southfield allowed plaintiff to continue in school, he has actually completed the school year, although he has no transcript. Upon payment of the outstanding bill, plaintiff will receive a transcript showing he finished the school year and received the appropriate credits for courses completed. Rather than relying on the school's actions to his detriment, the plaintiff is in a much better position having completed the full year and earned credits in the classes that he attended at Southfield, even if at this time he is unable to obtain a certified transcript due to the failure to pay the outstanding bill.

[33] Plaintiff's father acknowledged that he owed the money to Southfield and took part in discussions in early fall 1990 with Mr. Stokes, the headmaster, in an effort to reduce his debt of over $5,000 through monthly payments of $600. Plaintiff testified that he was aware of his father's financial problems and the problems with paying the school. The plaintiff never testified that he thought, or was misled into believing, that the school would furnish him a transcript just because it allowed him to finish the semester. The plaintiff would be unreasonable to rely on the school not only to continue to educate him without being paid, but to also certify his grades when they had no obligation under the contract to do so unless they were paid.

[34] In my view, this is a simple contract case in which the majority has erroneously applied the doctrine of detrimental reliance to force the non-breaching party, Southfield, to *fully* perform under the contract after repeated breaches of the contract by plaintiff's father, in whose shoes he stands under the contract.

[35] Because of this decision, schools, out of fear that they will lose the right to withhold transcripts, will be more inclined to disenroll students immediately when they fall behind on their debts to the school, a result that hurts the students and the schools.

[36] For these reasons, I respectfully dissent.

Questions

1. Paragraphs 1–9: Read these two pages and describe in legal terms the bonds, if any, between all the parties involved. Do all the obligations created have the same legal sources? How different are the legal regimes of these obligations? Was young McKee a party to any contract?

2. Paragraph 10: On what legal ground can the court rule that McKee is "entitled to a direct action"? Should this ruling be restricted to the facts of this case or should it be given a broad range of application? What kind of public policy could justify expanding or restricting the application of this ruling?

3. Paragraphs 14–15: In your opinion, did the "instant contract" really create two obligations on Southfield: one, to furnish an education and, two, to furnish documentation of that education? Are these two obligations bound together, somehow? Could they be dissociated and still bind the school, but on different grounds? Could the education received by McKee be returned to the school? What of the tuition paid by the father: could it be returned to the father? Is the documentation to serve as evidence that the father has paid the tuition, or is the documentation there to enable the school to raise a means of defense against the father when the latter fails to carry out his own obligation (*see* paragraph 15)? Do you agree with the Court's statement that "McKee is in no better position than would be his father to demand"? Would you agree that such a statement is a proper and necessary application of the principle seen above: *nemo potior jure ad alium transfere potest quam ipse habet* — in other words, the father cannot transfer to his son greater rights than he, the father, has.

4. Paragraphs 16–17: What do you think of this turnaround? Read Louisiana Civil Code article 1967.

5. Paragraphs 18–26: Where is detrimental reliance located in the Louisiana Civil Code? Notice that detrimental reliance is tied to the concept of "cause." "Cause" is a requirement for a contract. Was there a contract between the school and McKee or was the contract between the school and McKee's father? We saw above that the Court ruled the father had breached his obligation to the school by not paying his son's tuition; how can the Court now say that on

the basis of the contract his father breached, McKee nevertheless benefits from the right to make a claim because of that very contract? Doesn't that make McKee a third-party beneficiary? What did the Court say about this in paragraphs 13–14? Wouldn't the court have been wiser to give a remedy to McKee from the law of delicts/torts, Louisiana Civil Code articles 2315 and 2316 in particular?

6. Paragraphs 1–27: Is this case an "exemplary" illustration of "well-grounded legal characterization" or, on the contrary, is it an example of a "poor and error-ridden legal characterization"?

7. Paragraphs 28–36: What do you think of Judge Victory's dissenting opinion?

Mark C. Ledet

v.

Fabianmartins Construction Llc, Certain Underwriters at Lloyd's, London Subscribing to Policy No. LAL_000012346, Andrew W. Bursten, et als

Court of Appeal of Louisiana
Fifth Circuit
October 17, 2018
258 So.3d 1058

MOLAISON, J.

[. . . .]

Stipulation Pour Autrui

[1] In Louisiana, a plaintiff may sue under an insurance policy when he is a named insured, additional insured, or a third party beneficiary of the contract. *Haddad v. Elkhateeb* [. . .] (La.App. 4 Cir. 8/11/10), 46 So.3d 244, 257 n. 11, *writ denied* [. . .] (La. 11/12/10), 49 So.3d 895. Because Mr. Ledet is neither a named insured nor an additional named insured, he can only avail himself to the benefits of the Policy if he can establish that he is a third party beneficiary.[12] [. . . .] In Louisiana, such a contract for the benefit of a third party is commonly referred to as a "stipulation *pour autrui*."

[2] The Civil Code does not provide an "analytic framework for determining whether a third party beneficiary contract exists" in a particular case. *Joseph*, 939 So.2d at 1211. The Louisiana Supreme Court, however, has held that there are three criteria for determining whether contracting parties have provided a benefit for a third party and requires a review of whether: (1) the stipulation for a third party is

---

12. "A true third party beneficiary is never a party to the contract in question; he is never a promisee. The promisee is the stipulator and the promise runs to him and is merely in favor of the third party." *Joseph*, 939 So.2d at 1211, citing Smith, *Third Party Beneficiaries in Louisiana: The Stipulation Pour Autrui*, 11 Tul. L. Rev. 18, 33 (1936).

manifestly clear; (2) there is a certainty as to the benefit provided the third party; and (3) the benefit is not a mere incident of the contract between the promisor and the promisee. *Id.*, 939 So.2d at 1212. [. . . .] Each case must be decided on a case-by-case basis, and "[e]ach contract must be evaluated on its own terms and conditions in order to determine if the contract stipulates a benefit for a third person." *Joseph*, 939 So.2d at 1212 [. . .]. A stipulation *pour autrui* is never presumed, and the party claiming the benefit bears the burden of proof. *Joseph*, 939 So.2d at 1212. [. . . .]

1. Manifestly Clear Stipulation

[. . . .]

[3] [W]e disagree with Mr. Ledet's contention that the Policy's loss payment provisions stipulate a benefit in his favor because those provisions provide the Insurers with the *option* to adjust losses directly with unit owners. To the contrary, we find these provisions give to the *Insurers* the *exclusive* right to either adjust and settle covered losses directly with the Association [. . .] *or* with the unit owners. Our review of the entire Policy has revealed no provision which *entitles* the unit owners to receive direct payment for losses that may include their individual units. [. . . .] [E]ven though the Policy benefits Mr. Ledet and the other third party unit owners by providing coverage for certain types of property that may belong to them, we find that its express language . . . specifically negates the existence of a stipulation *pour autrui*, or any enforceable obligation, in favor of the individual unit owners as third party beneficiaries.

[. . . .]

2. Certainty as to the Benefit Provided

[4] [. . . .] As to this factor, we find no language in the Policy that *obligates* the Insurers to provide *any* benefit directly to individual unit owners such as Mr. Ledet. [. . . .] [W]hether the unit owners are able to recover any proceeds at all is contingent upon the extent of damage occasioned to the common elements and covered portion of the units, and is triggered *only* when the loss payment made by the Insurers to the Association exceeds the Association's cost to repair that damage.

[5] We find this benefit of the insurance proceeds to the unit owners, if any, is an indirect benefit, purely speculative [. . .]. Moreover, absent an express provision in the Policy, we find that a third party unit owner's potential entitlement to a portion of the insurance proceeds pad by the Insurers to the Association is insufficient to confer a benefit in favor of the unit owner to demand those proceeds directly from the Insurer. [. . . .]

3. Benefit Not a Mere Incident of the Contract

[. . . .]

[6] While acknowledging that Mr. Ledet does derive some benefit under the Policy, we find that any such benefit is merely incidental to the contract and is insufficient to establish a third party beneficiary relationship under the facts presented herein. To establish a stipulation *pour autrui*, the third party relationship must form

the consideration for a condition of the contract. [. . . .] Here, the plain language of the Policy, when viewed in its entirety, shows that the primary purpose of the Policy was *not to directly benefit unit owners or to insure their individual units*, but rather, was to discharge the Association's obligation under the Act and the Declaration to obtain insurance for the common elements and units against damage and loss, and to protect the Association's interests and property.

[7] Also, there mere mention of "unit owners" in the Policy does not make the unit owners third party beneficiaries. They are not individually identified in the Policy, nor is there a separately stated limit of liability for each unit owner. [. . . .] [E]ven though Mr. Ledet clearly benefits under the Policy, he is not an intended third party beneficiary with the right to make direct claims against the Insurers for individual losses; his potential benefits are merely incidental. Put another way, the Insurers did not intend to confer or obligate themselves to provide benefits to individual unit owners directly, nor was making unit owners third party beneficiaries consideration for the insurance contract.

[. . . .]

[8] In sum, following our *de novo* review, we find Mr. Ledet has failed to satisfy the three-prong test for establishing a stipulation *pour autrui* as set forth by the Supreme Court in *Joseph*[.] [. . . .]

[. . . .]

Louisiana Wetlands, LLC and New 90, LLC
v.
Energen Resources Corporation, Chevron USA, Inc., Southern Natural Gas Company, LLC, EP Energy E&P Company, LP, and Brammer Engineering, Inc.

Court of Appeal of Louisiana
First Circuit
October 4, 2021
330 So.3d 674

WOLFE, J.

[. . . .]

[1] [T]he Louisiana Supreme Court in *Eagle Pipe and Supply, Inc. v. Amerada Hess Corp.*, 2010-2267 (La. 10/25/11), 79 So.3d 246 [. . . .] clarified that the subsequent purchaser rule is a jurisprudential rule providing that a property owner "has no right or actual interest in recovering from a third party for damage which was inflicted on the property before his purchase, in the absence of an assignment or subrogation of the rights belonging to the owner of the property when the damage was inflicted." [. . . .] The supreme court clearly held that an owner's right to sue for damage to his property is a personal right and is possessed by the person who was the owner at the time the damage was caused. This personal right is not

transferred to a subsequent owner without a clear stipulation that the right has been transferred. In other words, a personal right cannot be asserted by another in the absence of a specific assignment or subrogation. [. . . .] Equally as important, real rights "pass to a subsequent *acquirer* of the thing to which it is attached without the need of a stipulation to that effect." (Emphasis added.)

[2] [. . . .] If the transferring instrument does not contain an explicit assignment of the personal right to sue for damage to the property, that right remains with the transferor. [. . . .]

[. . . .]

[3] [T]here is no evidence in the record of any written *stipulation pour autrui* (third-party beneficiary status) that conveys such a right to New 90, LLC. Third-party beneficiary status can never be presumed and the party claiming its benefit bears the burden of proof. [. . . .] The criteria for determining whether contracting parties have stipulated a benefit for a third party have been identified as: (1) the stipulation for a third party must be manifestly clear; (2) there must be certainty as to the benefit provided to the third party; and (3) the benefit must not be a mere incident of the contract. *Joseph v. Hospital Service Dist. No. 2 of Parish of St. Mary* (La. 10/15/06), 939 So.2d 1206, 1212. [. . . .]

[. . . .]

[4] See also *Eagle Pipe and Supply, Inc., v. Amerada Hess Corporation,* 79 So.3d 246 (La. 2011); *Landco Construction, LLC v. Precision Construction & Maintenance, LLC,* 290 So.3d 1185 (La.App. 1 Cir. 2019); *Salathe v. Parish of Jefferson Through Department of Sewerage,* 305 So.3d 1030 (La.App. 5 Cir. 2020); *Hargroder v. Columbia Gulf Transmission Co.,* 290 So.2d 874 (La. 1974).

[5] On **porte-forte**, see *Keybank National Association v. Perkins Rowe Associates, L.L.C.,* 2010 WL 2838373 (M.D. La. 2010).

Comparative Law Perspective

— Civil Law —

Marcel Planiol, *Treatise on the Civil Law*

vol. 2, pt. 1, n°s 1020–25 at 586–87 (Louisiana State Law Institute trans.,
11th ed. 1939)

1020. Definition

A person undertakes to answer for another when he promises that the person
whom he names will consent, as he has, to the agreement which he makes. It is generally said that the *porte-fort* or the person answering for another, obligates himself
to obtain the signature of another. Just what is the object of the obligation? The
porte-fort obligates himself to do what is necessary to obtain the signature promised; his obligation therefore has an object which is personal to him which consists
of the effort, the steps, and the sacrifices of money which he must make to persuade
the indicated person to give his consent. He is therefore bound by an obligation to
do; if he succeeds in obtaining the consent of the other, he is liberated; if he does not
succeed, he fails in his obligation and must pay damages. There is nothing in this
contrary to principle. [. . . .]

1023–1025. Comparison of the Porte-fort with the Surety

The surety is like the *porte-fort*, a person who engages himself for another; there
is, however, a characteristic difference between them. The *porte-fort* promises only
that the third person, of whom he believes himself sure, will consent to engage himself, and take upon himself the contract which has been made, to "ratify it," or to
"keep the engagement." [. . . .] The surety on the contrary, appears for someone
who immediately consents to obligate himself, or has even already done so, and he
guarantees to the creditor the execution of the debt. He undertakes to pay the debt
of another, if the debtor does not carry out his own obligation. His obligation therefore commences when that of the *porte-fort* ends.

Section V — Cause or Consideration

Louisiana Sources of Law

Louisiana Civil Code

Art. 1966. No obligation without cause.

An obligation cannot exist without a lawful cause. (Acts 1984, No. 331, § 1, eff. Jan. 1,
1985.)

Art. 1967. Cause defined; detrimental reliance.

Cause is the reason why a party obligates himself.

A party may be obligated by a promise when he knew or should have known that the promise would induce the other party to rely on it to his detriment and the other party was reasonable in so relying. Recovery may be limited to the expenses incurred or the damages suffered as a result of the promisee's reliance on the promise. Reliance on a gratuitous promise made without required formalities is not reasonable. (Acts 1984, No. 331, § 1, eff. Jan. 1, 1985.)

Art. 1968. Unlawful cause.

The cause of an obligation is unlawful when the enforcement of the obligation would produce a result prohibited by law or against public policy. (Acts 1984, No. 331, § 1, eff. Jan. 1, 1985.)

Art. 1969. Cause not expressed.

An obligation may be valid even though its cause is not expressed. (Acts 1984, No. 331, § 1, eff. Jan. 1, 1985.)

Art. 1970. Untrue expression of cause.

When the expression of a cause in a contractual obligation is untrue, the obligation is still effective if a valid cause can be shown. (Acts 1984, No. 331, § 1, eff. Jan. 1, 1985.)

Doctrine

Louisiana Law of Conventional Obligations, A Précis

Sections 5.1.1 to 5.1.2

Much has been written on the concept of cause and debates have taken place on the usefulness or not of this concept. [. . . .]

The word "causa" appears in some Roman law texts but it is clothed with many different meanings. [. . . .]

The word "causa" was actually identified with a particular "form," such as "specific words and phrases" or "the actual transfer of a thing" or "particular types of writings." The closest connection between the Roman "causa" and our civil law concept of "cause" can be found in the Roman law "stipulatio," which was a "formal" contract but which could be annulled for lack of "causa" whenever the promisor, who had carried out his obligation, would not receive in return from the stipulator the performance the latter was committed to carry out. [. . . .]

The concept of cause was turned into a "theory of cause" when the canon law lawyers did away with the formalism of Roman law to substitute to it a mere agreement as an exchange of wills between parties based on the moral obligation to fulfill one's word. As a consequence, one would be at fault for not performing that moral duty. [. . . .]

The idea of a commutative justice became a justification for one's commitment but it was a "moral" concept of justice not a "material (economic) justice."

The glossators and postglossators merged the canon law concept of cause with the Roman law exchange of wills to explain that the binding nature of an exchange of wills was due to the cause of the obligations created by the parties' wills. "Cause" was then the "end, goal, aim, purpose" (causa finalis) pursued by a party who binds herself to an obligation. [. . . .]

Thus "cause" is a component part of a contractual obligation as is clearly stated in **LSA-C.C Art. 1966** according to which: **"An obligation cannot exist without a lawful cause."** One will have noticed, in this Article, the connection between the "obligation" and the necessary requirement of its "cause." The same can be said about **LSA-C.C. Art. 1969: "An obligation may be valid even though the cause is not expressed."** [. . . .]

The contemporary theory of cause provides a justification for the binding effect of a person's will and the duty to perform legally entered into obligations; it also sets the limits of the binding effect of the will by declaring invalid obligations which have an illegal or immoral cause; it further provides some sort of guarantee to parties who are told that **"Contracts have the effect of law for the parties and may be dissolved only through the consent of the parties or on grounds provided by law. Contracts must be performed in good faith."** (LSA-C.C. Art. 1983). [. . . .]

For a *reason* to become *"the cause"* of an obligation which, in turn, will become *the cause* of the contract, it is necessary, as a first step, to identify one reason from all other reasons as being the "determinant-prevailing" reason so that it could become the cause of the contract if it is "common" and if it is lawful. [. . . .]

That a "cause" must exist does not mean that the cause must be expressly stated in the contract. [. . . .]

Even when a contract is in writing, it is not necessary that the cause be expressed as is stated in **LSA-C.C. Art. 1969: "An obligation may be valid even though its cause is not expressed."** As long as there is an exchange of consent between parties and an obligation created as a result, we must presume that the obligation was created for "a reason" common to the parties. [. . . .]

Good faith, "Offenses and Quasi-Offenses" as well as the binding nature of a will or intent lawfully communicated, either expressly or implicitly, provide legal justifications for the expanded, but questionable, definition of cause which appears in the second paragraph of **Art. 1967: "A party may be obligated by a promise when he knew or should have known that the promise would induce the other party to rely on it to his detriment and the other party was reasonable in so relying. Recovery may be limited to the expenses incurred or the damages suffered as a result of the promisee's reliance on the promise. Reliance on a gratuitous promise made without required formalities is not reasonable."** [. . . .]

If among the reasons that prompted the parties to enter into a contract there happens to be one reason of an immoral or unlawful nature, it is very likely that a court would "pick" that reason, from among many others, as the cause of the contract even though that reason may not have been the determinant or prevailing reason for the parties. It is the courts' duty to preserve and maintain public order and good morals in the performance of contracts in particular. [. . . .]

Whether shared, common or not, any unlawful or immoral reason should carry with it the absolute nullity of the act of which it meant to be the "cause."

Alain A. Levasseur and Nikolaos A. Davrados, *Detrimental Reliance: A "Re-Consideration" Forty Years Later*[1]

This "re-consideration" of the "imported" institution of "detrimental reliance," which has now existed for nearly forty years in the Louisiana Civil Code, shall identify several counter-arguments, based on the La. Civ. Code, that will demonstrate why detrimental reliance has no room under the "cover" of the civil law concept of cause. Here are four arguments that can easily be made to reject "detrimental reliance" from the La. Civil Code:

1: As the common law background of "detrimental reliance" explains, this concept finds its source and **legal** meaning in the notion of "consideration." In fact, a detriment suffered by a party may provide sufficient consideration for the enforcement of a promise at common law. Yet, La. Civ. C. art. 1967-1 states very positively, clearly, and in very few words, that **"cause is the reason why a party obligates himself."** Cause being the reason "why a party obligates himself," it is thus merged with and becomes a component part of consent[1] which is, itself, identified as a requirement for a conventional obligation or contract to exist. Furthermore, "Comment (c)" to art. 1967 adds that *under this Article, 'cause' is not 'consideration.'"* Indeed, the reason why a party binds herself in a contract need not be to obtain something in return, nor to secure an advantage for herself, and even less to act in full awareness that she or the other party will be suffering a "detriment," a loss or harm. Such reasons cannot be the "cause" of a contract. Thus, "detrimental reliance" cannot be the "cause" of a contract under art. 1967-1 and, therefore, art. 1967-2 has no place in the La. Civ. Code, even as a distorted type of cause.

2: Since detrimental reliance is based on a "detriment," a loss or harm, suffered by one party, a rapprochement can be most logically and naturally made with a **"juridical fact,"**[2] such as a tort/delict, giving rise to a source of obligations[3] separate from contract. "Cause," as a "reason,"[4] or as a legal requirement for the formation of a contract, and a contract only, would be totally irrelevant for delictual obligations.

---

1. We are referring here to Professor Saul Litvinoff's article "Still Another Look at Cause" in 48 LA.L.REV. (1987) and particularly to the section on "Detrimental Reliance" on p. 18 to 28.
   1. La. Civ. Code arts. 1927-1947.
   2. On juridical facts, see Chapter 1, §1 of *Louisiana Law of Obligations in General A Treatise.*
   3. La. Civ. C. art. 1757.
   4. La. Civ. C. art. 1967-1.

Indeed, in civil law systems, "pre-contractual liability," *i.e.,* any breach of the duty of good faith during negotiations for a contract — which would include a "promise upon which the other party relied to its detriment" — sounds in tort.[5] The civilian theory of cause is irrelevant.

3: An "acceptance," when made "orally, in writing, or by action or inaction," must be, "**under the circumstances, clearly indicative of consent.**"[6] "*Under the circumstances*"? An "offer" or "pollicitation" is an offeror's manifestation of his intent to "offer" to another person, an offeree, to enter into a contract on certain terms. An offeror can be bound to the terms of her offer, especially if the offer is irrevocable.[7] An offer to enter into a contract of sale, to be an "offer," must meet the requirements (the necessary elements — *essentialia negotii*) of La. Civ. C. art. 2439 at a minimum. An offer to enter into a contract of lease must meet, at a minimum, the requirements of an offer as listed in La. Civ. C. art. 2668. If those requirements are not made part of the offer, there cannot be any acceptance of what is obviously not an offer; therefore, there cannot be "consent," which means that there cannot exist any "cause", any "reason" that could "motivate" the parties to enter into a contract. It follows, first, that until there is a contract, the two parties involved were still only in the process of "negotiating" or "bargaining." Second, during this process of negotiating, it is possible that one of the parties incurred a damage, detriment, harm as the consequence or as the result of the other party seeking "to obtain an unjust advantage for herself . . . or to cause a loss or inconvenience to the other," *i.e.,* the party who suffered a detriment, a loss.

There arises then an issue of "fraud," and possibly of "duress" or "undue influence,"[8] in the sense of an "act . . . that causes damage to another" obliging "him by whose fault it happened to repair it."[9] The negotiating, reasonable party who suffered a detriment because of the fault or detrimental action of the other party should seek damages in a delictual or tort action. As mentioned above, "pre-contractual liability" is delictual liability (tort liability) in civil law systems.

4. One additional argument against keeping "detrimental reliance" in art. 1967 as a new[10] type of cause required for the formation of a contract is the existence in the La. Civ. C. of a fundamental "**Principle**" that governs the whole law of Obligations, whatever their source and whatever their performance, be it to "give," "to do" or

---

5. See French Civil Code articles 1112, 1112-1, and 1112-2 (revised in 2016); Québec Civil Code articles 7 and 1375; German Civil Code article 311; and Greek Civil Code articles 197-199.

6. La. Civ. C. art. 1927.

7. La. Civ. C. art. 1928.

8. La. Civ. C. art. 1953, *et seq.*

9. La. Civ. C. art. 2315A.

10. The legislative revision of 1984-85 included a new sub-paragraph 2 to art. 1967. The common law origin of detrimental reliance is, unfortunately, illustrated by the common law style of drafting the second paragraph, which contrasts so clearly with the "Romantic" style of drafting seen in the single sentence of the first paragraph on "cause."

"not to do."[11] This principle is stated using the imperative "**shall**" in art. 1759, as follows: "**Good faith shall govern the conduct of the obligor and the obligee in whatever pertains to the obligation.**"[12] When a failure to act in good faith, or a failure "not to do" unto others what others should not do to our own-self, causes a damage/detriment/harm to another, such failure obliges him by whose fault it occurred to repair it.[13] This **principle of "good faith,"** which is all pervasive throughout the Civil Code, is the only proper legal justification for granting a remedy in delict/tort to a party who suffers a detriment outside of the framework of a contractual relationship. Otherwise, we would have to assume that a contract was in existence and that the *breach* of his performance by one party "caused" a detriment to the other party, which detriment or harm is what very often occurs when an "obligor" fails to perform his contractual obligation towards his obligee. Aren't "damages measured by the loss sustained by the obligee and the profit of which he has been deprived"?[14] In this instance, "detrimental reliance" would have nothing to do with "cause [as] the reason why a party obligates himself."[15] As noted above, the parties must act in good faith during their contractual negotiations. A negotiating party violates the duty of good faith if its behavior is abusive, unreasonable, or deceptive. The Civil Code contains examples of "obligations" of parties during the negotiation phase that stem from the principle of good faith (e.g., irrevocability of offers[16] and due notice to the other party[17]). It should be clear that the duty to negotiate in good faith does not obligate the parties to conclude the contract; however, it does prevent them from taking advantage of the other party or, in bad faith, continuing negotiations they know to be meaningless. When occurring during contractual negotiations, the common law concept of "detrimental reliance" falls squarely within this ambit of "pre-contractual liability"—delictual liability in civil law systems. If it ever occurs in the post-contractual phase, including when a unilateral promise is binding on the promisor, the standard rules on the effects of obligations,[18] coupled with the principle of good faith,[19] ought to apply.

In conclusion, our Civil Code is well-equipped to deal with issues of "detrimental reliance" without the addition of foreign concepts intended to fill gaps in the common law of contract.

---

11. La. Civ. C. art. 1756.
12. On good faith, see *Louisiana Law of Obligations in General, A Treatise*, Alain A. Levasseur, § 2. good Faith: La. Civ. Code Art. 1759, p. 33, Carolina Academic Press 2020.
13. La. Civ. C. art. 2315A.
14. La. Civ. C. art. 1995.
15. La. Civ. C. art. 1967-1.
16. La. Civ. C. art. 1928.
17. La. Civ. C. art. 1941.
18. La. Civ. C. arts. 1983, *et seq.*
19. La. Civ. C. art. 1759.

Cases

W. T. West
v.
Loe Pipe Yard et al.

Court of Appeal of Louisiana
Third Circuit
December 19, 1960
125 So.2d 469

HOOD, Judge.

[1] This is an action for a money judgment instituted by W.T. West against Loe Pipe Yard, a commercial partnership composed of Bert Loe and Glen D. Loe, and against the two partners individually. Plaintiff alleges that he cashed drafts issued by defendant, Bert Loe, aggregating the sum of $5,000, and that the amount due on those drafts has never been paid. As evidence of this indebtedness he alleges that he is the holder and owner of nine drafts drawn on the account of Loe Pipe Yard in the Olla State Bank, Olla, Louisiana, by defendant, Bert Loe, a member of the partnership.

[2] Defendants admit the execution of the drafts, but they deny that they are liable to plaintiff for the amounts represented by them. They allege that the drafts were issued to obtain money or chips to be used by Bert Loe for gambling purposes, and that plaintiff is not entitled to recover because the transaction was one which is contra bonos mores.

[. . . .]

[3] One of the drafts on which plaintiff bases his claim is for the sum of $1,000 and is dated September 3, 1954. The eight remaining drafts are for the sum of $500 each, and each such draft is dated September 4, 1954. All of the drafts are made payable to 'Cash,' are signed by 'Loe Pipe Yard, by Bert Loe,' are drawn on the Olla State Bank, and bear the endorsement of W. T. West.

[4] At the time these drafts were issued, plaintiff West was the assistant manager of the Famous Corner, a gambling establishment located in Natchez, Mississippi. Some of the owners of this Mississippi gambling house also owned a substantial interest in the Plaza Club, in Concordia Parish, Louisiana, which club had been leased to one Ed Jones, and in September, 1954, it was being operated by him as a bar, restaurant and night club. On the second floor of the Plaza Club was a room, equipped with a table and chairs, which was used by customers to engage in gambling games of their own choice. Jones, the operator of the club, testified that the 'house' had no interest in the gambling activities which were conducted in the upstairs room, and that all such activities were spontaneously engaged in by customers without supervision or regulation by employees of the Plaza Club. The purpose of maintaining the room, he stated, was to attract customers and thus stimulate the sale of food and drinks.

[5] Late in the afternoon on Sunday, September 4, 1954, which was the day preceding Labor Day, plaintiff and Ike Cowan happened to be in plaintiff's automobile near a motel in Concordia Parish when they saw defendant Loe leaving the motel. Plaintiff engaged Loe in conversation and invited him to accompany plaintiff to the Plaza Club for a drink. Loe got into plaintiff's automobile and accompanied him to the Plaza Club, and after they arrived Loe began drinking.

[6] Shortly after Loe arrived at the Plaza Club, someone mentioned that a poker game either was in progress or was about to begin in the upstairs room. Loe then gave a barmaid $10 with instructions that she try to win something in the poker game, and a short time later Loe went upstairs and began to participate in the poker game himself.

[7] Loe apparently had little or no money with him, so he obtained a substantial sum from plaintiff in order to enable him to participate in the game. During the course of the game Loe borrowed additional amounts from plaintiff until he had obtained the total sum of $2,000 from him. Drafts were issued by Loe and handed to plaintiff for amounts aggregating $2,000. Plaintiff testified that he had only $1,700 in cash on his person at that time, all of which was handed to Loe in exchange for the drafts, but that he borrowed $300 from one Hal Kaizer and also handed that to defendant. After obtaining $2,000 from plaintiff, Loe then obtained $2,500 from Clifton Vetch, a participant in the poker game, and $500 from an unknown salesman who also was participating in the game. Drafts were issued by Loe each time these additional funds were obtained, and plaintiff endorsed the drafts which were given to Vetch and the salesman, guaranteeing the payment of such drafts. Plaintiff contends that he later paid Vetch and the salesman the amounts which they had advanced to defendant, and that he is entitled to recover judgment for these amounts as well as for the sum which plaintiff advanced directly.

[8] Shortly after plaintiff and defendant arrived at the Plaza Club, the owner of that establishment turned over his keys and the complete management of the club to plaintiff West, authorizing him to sell drinks to customers and to close the business up at any time he saw fit. Plaintiff then tended the bar and remained in complete charge of the Plaza Club from the time Jones left, which was late Sunday afternoon, until the gambling game broke up sometime after daylight the following morning.

[9] Defendant contends that plaintiff was one of the promoters of the gambling game in which defendant was engaged, that the drafts were given for the purpose of enabling Loe to engage in illegal gambling activities, that plaintiff had full knowledge of the purpose for which the checks were given, and accordingly that plaintiff is not able to enforce obligations evidenced by those checks.

[10] The Louisiana Constitution of 1921, Article XIX, Section 8, LSA, provides:

'Gambling is a vice and the Legislature shall pass laws to suppress it.'

[11] The Louisiana Civil Code of 1870, LSA, provides:

'Art. 1893—An obligation without a cause, or with a false or unlawful cause, can have no effect.'

'Art. 1895—The cause is unlawful, when it is forbidden by law, when it is contra bonos mores (contrary to moral conduct) or to public order.'

'Art. 2983—The law grants no action for the payment of what has been won at gaming or by a bet, except for games tending to promote skill in the use of arms, such as the exercise of the gun and foot, horse and chariot racing.'

'And as to such games, the judge may reject the demand, when the sum appears to him excessive.'

[12] The above quoted provisions of the constitution and statutes of the State have received frequent interpretation by the courts of Louisiana. It is now well settled that one who lends money to another to pay a gambling debt incurred in a transaction with which the lender was wholly unconnected may be classified as an innocent bystander to the illegal activity, and he, therefore, may maintain an action to recover the amount which he has lent. Brand v. Evans, 1927, 7 La.App. 205; Celmons v. Succession of Johnson, 1929, 10 La.App. 230, 120 So. 664; Wilson v. Sawyer, La.App.1958, 106 So.2d 831. However, one who owns or operates a gambling establishment and who lends money for the purpose of paying a gambling debt incurred in such establishment cannot recover the money lent, because he was not wholly unconnected with the illegal activity. Sampson v. Whitney, 1875, 27 La.Ann. 294; Bagneris v. Smoot, 1925, 159 La. 1049, 106 So. 561; Russo v. Russo, 1927, 5 La.App. 566; Keen v. Butterworth, La.App.1938, 185 So. 37; Russo v. Mula, La.App.1950, 49 So.2d 622; Domino v. La Bord, La.App.1957, 99 So.2d 841.

[13] In this case we have no difficulty at arriving at the conclusion that the Plaza Club was a gambling establishment, and that the owner or operator and those who promoted and participated in the gambling activities in that club were participating in an illegal activity prohibited by the above quoted provisions of the constitution and statutes of this State. Plaintiff, however, was not the owner of that establishment and he did not participate in the poker game in the sense that he did not sit at the table, have cards dealt to him, make bets, etc. An important question presented in this case, therefore, is whether plaintiff was wholly unconnected with the illegal activities in which Loe was engaged, and accordingly, whether he can be classified as an innocent bystander under the circumstances presented here.

[14] The trial judge concluded that although plaintiff was not the owner of the gambling establishment, he was in charge of it and his conduct was such that he could not be classified as an innocent bystander. [. . . .]

[15] In our opinion, the evidence amply supports the conclusion reached by the trial court. Plaintiff invited and brought the defendant to the Plaza Club, advanced him a substantial sum of money for the purpose of engaging in the poker game, and guaranteed the repayment of additional amounts borrowed by Loe from other participants in the game. Also, plaintiff accommodated those engaged in the poker

Analysis
RS w/ Facts

game by tending the bar and managing the Plaza Club from late Sunday afternoon until after daylight Monday morning. (The loans were made and guaranteed by plaintiff with the understanding that it would be necessary for him to go to the trouble and expense of driving to Olla, a distance of 75 miles, the following Tuesday in order to get the drafts cashed.) According to plaintiff's testimony, he had seen Loe on not more than two occasions prior to this and they were only casual acquaintances. We could understand plaintiff's actions in accommodating Loe to the extent shown here if plaintiff had an interest in or some connection with the poker game, but we cannot conceive of plaintiff loaning such large sums of money to a casual acquaintance, guaranteeing the payment of additional sums and otherwise accommodating defendant as he did if plaintiff, in fact, was wholly unconnected with the gambling activities which were being conducted in the Plaza Club on that occasion.

[....]

Holding

[16] In this case we conclude, as did the trial judge, that although plaintiff did not own the Plaza Club he was operating it temporarily and was in complete control of it while the poker game was being conducted there, that plaintiff was not wholly unconnected with that illegal activity, that he was not an innocent bystander, and that the trial judge correctly rejected his demands.

[....]

Questions

1. Paragraph 1: Can you identify an objective cause for the drafts? Is such an objective cause of any relevance? Is there any purpose in identifying such a cause in any contract? Is there any possible impact on the classification of contracts?

2. Paragraph 3: Does a draft or a check point to its cause? Must the cause be mentioned, indicated, or written for a draft or a check to be valid? Should the circumstances surrounding the making of a draft or a check be taken into account when identifying the cause of that draft or check? With what kind of cause, objective or subjective, are we then dealing?

3. Paragraph 9: What purpose, motive, or cause could be common to both the defendant and the plaintiff? How does a cause become common to two parties to a juridical act? Can the parties, because of who they are and the environment in which they operate, contribute to the type of cause on which a juridical act can be created? What kind of contract is a gambling contract? In this paragraph, what kind of defense is the defendant raising?

4. Paragraph 12: What do you think of this statement: "it is now well settled" and the listing of cases that follow? On what ground or grounds do the courts create, or not create, the connection on which they erect their policy on gambling? Is there any impact of the connection as created by the courts on the cause of the juridical acts of gambling? Could that impact be extended to juridical acts other than gambling contracts?

5. Where does the Court find any evidence of an unlawful cause? In paragraph 16, isn't the outcome of the case at odds with the defense of good morals in that the plaintiff, who has lost money, will not be allowed to get his money back and, thereby, will have enriched the defendant who was himself a party to this unlawful, *contra bonos mores*, gambling contract?

Davis-Delcambre Motors, Inc.
v.
Martin Simon

Court of Appeal of Louisiana
Third Circuit
June 18, 1963
154 So.2d 775

FRUGE, Judge.

[1] The plaintiff, Davis-Delcambre Motors, Inc., sued the defendant, Martin Simon, on his promissory note dated June 14, 1957 in the amount of $300.00. Defendant, by special plea, raised the defense of illegal consideration as a bar to collection on the note. From a judgment in the lower court granting plaintiff the relief prayed for, defendant has appealed.

[2] The record discloses that during the first week of June 1957, Wilmer Mitchel purchased a 1952 Chevrolet automobile from the plaintiff. The sale of the automobile was to be a cash transaction. Pursuant to this sale, Mitchel gave plaintiff two checks, in the amounts of $200 and $100, drawn on the State National Bank of New Iberia. Plaintiff attempted to cash these checks at the named bank but was informed that Wilmer Mitchel had no account. Accordingly, payment was refused. About one week later plaintiff contacted Wilmer Mitchel and threatened to have him arrested for issuing worthless checks. Subsequently Martin Simon, Mitchel's employer, issued a promissory note in the exact amount of the worthless checks.

[3] In urging lack of valid consideration, defendant argues that the note was given for an illegal consideration in that the only reason the note was given was plaintiff's forbearance in the prosecution of Mitchel for issuing worthless checks. Plaintiff, on the other hand, argues that the note was given in payment of the debt owed by Mitchel to plaintiff, and that as such was supported by good and valid consideration. [....]

[....]

[4] Counsel for defendant argues that the consideration for the note at issue was the debt of Wilmer Mitchel, and that the payment of a debt of a third person is valid consideration. In our opinion, counsel has correctly stated the law in this regard. Dauzat v. Bordelon, La.App., 145 So.2d 41; Foster & Glassell Co. v. Harrison, 168 La. 500, 122 So. 595. However, viewing the evidence and testimony as a whole we are convinced that the payment of the debt of Wilmer Mitchel was not the cause

which motivated defendant to make the note. Thus, Mr. Earl J. Davis, President and General Manager of Davis-Delcambre Motors, when questioned about the circumstances surrounding the making of the note, testified as follows:

> 'He (Wilmer Mitchel) gave us two checks, one dated that day, and the other check dated for a week to follow. Monday, morning we go to the bank to cash his check, and the check was no good, no account. And we got a hold of Mitchel, and he promised to make the checks good. And it was sometimes, oh, possibly a week or two weeks later before we was [*sic*] able to contact him again. He was working for Martin Simon. And Simon came in one afternoon and said that he was going to sign that check for Mitchel, rather, sign the note to clear Mitchel, *because I was threatening to have him locked in jail for giving me bad checks.*' (Tr. 57) (Emphasis added.)

> 'Q. Well, if Martin Simon had not given you the note, as you say you would have had Red picked up and put in jail on criminal charges.

> 'A. That's right, Wilmer T. Mitchel, 'Red' Mitchel.

> 'Q. You would have had him picked up and put in jail?

> 'A. Yes, sir.

> 'Q. And you would have filed a criminal charge of bad checks, is that right?

> 'A. Yes, sir.' (Tr. 60)

[5] The only realistic conclusion that can be drawn from the testimony of Mr. Davis is that defendant gave the note in question in consideration of plaintiff's forbearance to prosecute Wilmer Mitchel for issuing worthless checks. Accordingly, we so hold.

[6] Having determined the cause or consideration for defendant's making the note, we now turn to the question of whether such consideration is legal and valid.

[7] All contracts which have as their object that which is forbidden by law or contrary to good morals are void. LSA-C.C. Art. 1892. By the 'cause' of a contract is meant the motive or consideration for making it. LSA-C.C. Art. 1896. 'The cause is unlawful, when it is forbidden by law, when it is contra bonos mores (contrary to moral conduct) or to public order.' LSA-C.C. Art. 1895. Accordingly, it has been held that the promise of a father to pay the debt of his insolvent son in exchange for the creditor's promise not to prosecute for fraud is without a good consideration and void, as against public policy. Field v. Rogers, 26 La.Ann. 574; Perry v. Frilot, 6 Mart. (N.S.) 217; Leggett v. Pett, 1 La. 288, 297. Similarly, the courts have refused to enforce promises to pay gambling debts. Wilson v. Sawyer, La.App., 106 So.2d 831.

[8] As previously stated, the obvious consideration for the note in question was the forbearance to prosecute Mitchel for issuing a worthless check. We need not enter into any detailed discussion that such an act is a crime. See LSA-R.S. 14:71. In our opinion, it is axiomatic that the promise to suppress the prosecution of this crime is Contra bonos mores and results in rendering the note sued upon void for lack of consideration. In reaching this conclusion, we are mindful of plaintiff's

argument that R.S. 14:71 requires an intent to defraud and that such intent on the part of Mitchel was not established on the trial of this case. [. . . .]

[. . . .]

[9] For the reasons assigned, the judgment of the lower court is reversed and plaintiff's suit is dismissed; plaintiff-appellee to pay all costs of this appeal and of these proceedings.

[10] ~~Reversed~~. *Reversed*

HOOD, Judge (dissenting).

[11] I cannot agree with the conclusion reached by the majority that defendant Simon executed the note on which this suit is based 'in consideration of plaintiff's forbearance to prosecute Wilmer Mitchel for issuing worthless checks.' Simon, himself, testified at the trial that at the time he executed and delivered the note he did not know that Mitchel had signed any checks in favor of Davis and that he knew nothing about the possibility that Mitchel might have to go to jail. [. . . .]

[. . . .]

[12] I agree with the majority that if the Only consideration for a promissory note is a promise of the payee not to prosecute, then the obligation evidenced by the note is unenforceable because of a failure of consideration, whether there was or was not a valid ground for criminal prosecution. But, in a case such as the instant one, Where there was a valid consideration for the note (a stipulation pour autri), then it seems to me that the note Is enforceable although there may have been additional promises or considerations which were invalid, such as a promise to not prosecute.

[13] The majority apparently relies principally on the case of Perry v. Frilot, 6 Mart.(N.S.) 217, as authority for its holding. In my opinion that case does not support the views expressed by the majority in the instant suit, because there the son was an insolvent debtor, and the plaintiff had agreed as a part of the consideration for the father's promise to pay a portion of the debt that plaintiff would 'get the other creditors to sign; that is, that he would deceive them,' and would assist the son in fraudulently making a surrender of his effects. The Perry case was decided in 1827, and so far as I have been able to find it has never been cited or followed by any other court since that time. If it can be interpreted as supporting the views expressed by the majority in the instant suit, then I must respectfully disagree with the holding in that case.

[. . . .]

Questions

1. Paragraphs 2–3: Is the use of the word "consideration" proper here? Read the Code articles on cause. Do you read the word "consideration" anywhere? Do you see any equivalent between "objective cause" and consideration? What about "subjective cause" and consideration? Could an illegal consideration in the sense of objective cause be illegal? Read paragraph 3 in particular.

2. Paragraph 4: Notice that the Court refers to consideration in the first line, whereas in a later sentence, we read the word "cause." Is the Court using the two words interchangeably? If so, is that proper and good legal writing? Then, in paragraphs 5–6, the Court again uses the two words interchangeably, although the Court seems to favor the use of the word "consideration," particularly when it states that the question is whether such consideration is legal or valid.

3. Paragraph 7–8: Can forbearance to prosecute ever be consideration at common law? Here, the Court states: "by the 'cause' of a contract is meant the motive *or consideration* for making it. LSA-C.C. Art. 1896." However, the Court added the words *"or consideration"* to the words of the Louisiana Civil Code, which do not include "consideration." Did the Court find it necessary, useful, or without any legal consequence to equate cause to consideration? Would a common law court do likewise if the two concepts mean the same thing? In paragraph 8, is the Court giving to the word "consideration" its proper common law meaning when it is preceded by the word "obvious"? Isn't it more subjective cause that the Court had in mind? How does the Court presume the commonality of the unlawful cause or, rather, the lack of consideration (*see* the end of paragraph 8)?

4. Paragraphs 11–13: What do you think of Judge Hood's dissenting opinion? What do you think of his distinguishing the *Perry v. Frilot* case on which the majority reasoned by analogy? Could Judge Hood's opinion be considered as a warning to the Courts that there must be a limit to their role and authority to intervene in contractual relationships so as to police or regulate private contracts?

Davis-Delcambre Motors, Inc.
v.
Martin Simon

Supreme Court of Louisiana
May 4, 1964
163 So.2d 553

HAMLIN, Justice.

[. . . .]

[1] In reversing the trial court, the Court of Appeal relied on the case of Perry v. Frilot, 6 Mart., N.S., 217, which we find inapposite to the present matter. We agree with the following distinction made by Judge Hood in his able dissent in the present matter:

'The majority apparently relies principally on the case of Perry v. Frilot, 6 Mart.(N.S.) 217, as authority for its holding. In my opinion that case does not support the views expressed by the majority in the instant suit, because there the son was an insolvent debtor, and the plaintiff had agreed as a part of the consideration for the father's promise to pay a portion of the debt that plaintiff would 'get the other creditors to sign; that is, that he would deceive them,' and would assist the son in fraudulently making a surrender of his effects. * * *'

[2] Herein, the Court of Appeal found:

'* * * the obvious consideration for the note in question was the forbearance to prosecute Mitchel for issuing a worthless check. We need not enter into any detailed discussion that such an act is a crime. See LSA-R.S. 14:71. In our opinion, it is axiomatic that the promise to suppress the prosecution of this crime is contra bonos mores and results in rendering the note sued upon void for lack of consideration. * * *'

[3] The intent to defraud is an essential ingredient of the offense of issuing worthless checks, LSA-R.S. 14:71; such intent must be alleged and proved. State v. Clayton, 236 La. 1093, 110 So.2d 111; State v. McLean, 216 La. 670, 44 So.2d 698; State v. Alphonse, 154 La. 950, 98 So. 430. Herein, Wilmer Mitchel drew two checks on a bank in which he had no account; they were dated June 7, 1957, and the note allegedly given to cover the checks was executed on June 14, 1957, one week after the date of the checks. We do not find that plaintiff has proved an intent to defraud on the part of Mitchel; neither was there a sufficient lapse of time for there to be presumptive evidence of Mitchel's intent to defraud. Likewise, no written demand was made upon Mitchel to pay the dishonored checks. 'The offender's failure to pay such check, * * * within ten days after the receipt by him of written notice of its non-payment upon presentation, shall be presumptive evidence of his intent to defraud.' LSA-R.S. 14:71. We cannot presume therefore that Wilmer Mitchel was guilty of violating LSA-R.S. 14:71, without proof of his intent to defraud plaintiff. It follows that if Mitchel was not guilty of violating LSA-R.S. 14:71, Simon and Davis were not guilty of compounding a felony prohibited by LSA-R.S. 14:131.

[....]

[4] [....] We also conclude from a reading of the testimony, supra, that Davis did not make a promise to suppress the prosecution of Mitchel, and that no threats, violence or pressure were exerted upon Simon so as to vitiate his consent. See, LSA-R.C.C. Arts. 1819 and 1850.

[5] Having found that under the facts of this case, Mitchel was not guilty of the offense of issuing worthless checks with intent to defraud, that no promise to suppress the prosecution of Mitchel was made by Davis, that Simon and Davis were not guilty of compounding a felony, that no threats, violence or pressure were exerted upon Simon so as to vitiate his consent, and that Simon did affix his mark to the note involved, we approach a determination as to whether there was a valid consideration for the note. We find that the debt due by Mitchel to plaintiff for the price of the 1952 Chevrolet was sufficient consideration to support the promise of a third party, Simon, to pay. Paige v. Mesico, La.App., 144 So.2d 908; Louisiana Store &

Market Equipment Co. v. Moore, La.App., 167 So. 477. We do not find that the agreement between plaintiff and the defendant was unlawful or forbidden by law. We conclude that the consideration for the note is valid and that the note is enforceable.

[6] Because of our findings, supra, it is not necessary that we consider relator's other contentions with respect to alleged errors committed by the Court of Appeal.

[7] For the reasons assigned, the judgment of the Court of Appeal, Third Circuit, is reversed and set aside. The judgment of the trial court is affirmed. All costs are to be paid by defendant.

Holding

Question

1. Paragraphs 1–7: What is your overall evaluation of the Supreme Court opinion? Is the Supreme Court making a proper use of the common law concept of consideration? Is that concept, as used here by the Court, equivalent to the concept of objective cause at civil law?

Aaron & Turner, L.L.C.
v.
Melissa Michelle Perret and Continental Financial Group, Inc.

Court of Appeal of Louisiana
First Circuit
May 4, 2009
22 So.3d 910
On Rehearing[1]

HUGHES, J.

[1] In this action on a promissory note and mortgage, the defendant/borrower appeals a summary judgment dismissing her reconventional demand, which asserted a negligence claim against the law firm that performed the loan closing. On June 6, 2008, this court handed down an unpublished opinion in this appeal, reversing in part the decision of the trial court. The matter is now before this court on application for rehearing. Having decided the application for rehearing has merit, we grant the rehearing and render the following decision reversing the trial court judgment and remanding the matter.

Facts And Procedural History

[2] In 2001, Melissa Michelle Perret refinanced the mortgage on her home by executing a promissory note in favor of ABN AMRO Mortgage Group, Inc. (ABN) and an act of mortgage on her home to secure payment of the promissory note. Aaron & Turner, L.L.C. (Aaron & Turner), the law firm that acted as the closing agent for the

---

1. Because the original opinion rendered in this appeal was not designated for publication, we repeat herein those portions of the original opinion not changed on this rehearing.

transaction, disbursed funds to and on behalf of Ms. Perret during the transaction, acting on the belief that ABN had funded the loan.

[3] When it was discovered several years later that Aaron & Turner had never received the funds to finance the transaction from ABN, Aaron & Turner obtained the February 28, 2001 note by ostensible assignment from ABN and demanded payment from Ms. Perret of the total accumulated amount due on the note, plus late fees and interest. When Ms. Perret refused to remit the sum demanded, Aaron & Turner filed a petition in the 19th Judicial District Court on February 17, 2006, seeking to enforce the mortgage and to recover the amounts outstanding on the note, or in the alternative, to recover the amount loaned under the theory of unjust enrichment. [. . . .] By a supplemental petition, Aaron & Turner amended its petition to declare Ms. Perret to be in default on the note and sought to recover the total amount of the note, plus late fees, interest, attorney fees, and court costs. Aaron & Turner also subsequently filed a separate proceeding against Ms. Perret for executory process in a different division of the 19th Judicial District Court.[3]

[4] In response to the instant ordinary proceeding, Ms. Perret filed a motion for partial summary judgment seeking to have the trial court dismiss "all rights, claims and causes of action" premised on the February 28, 2001 mortgage and note, declare the mortgage and note null, and order cancellation of the mortgage and note. Ms. Perret subsequently filed a reconventional demand seeking compensation for mental, emotional, pecuniary damages, and losses that she allegedly sustained as result of negligence committed by Aaron & Turner in performing the February 28, 2001 loan closing.[4] Aaron & Turner, in turn, filed a motion for summary judgment seeking dismissal of the claims raised by Ms. Perret in her reconventional demand.

[5] Following a hearing on the cross motions for summary judgment, held May 14, 2007, the trial court denied Ms. Perret's partial motion for summary judgment and granted the motion for summary judgment filed by Aaron & Turner, dismissing with prejudice the claims asserted by Ms. Perret in her reconventional demand. A judgment to that effect was signed on May 29, 2007, from which Ms. Perret appeals. In this appeal, Ms. Perret contends that the trial court erred in dismissing her reconventional demand based on a finding that the note and mortgage at issue in these proceedings were enforceable.

---

3. Ms. Perret attempted to enjoin the executory proceedings without success and appealed the trial court's denial of her petition for injunctive relief to this court; however, because Ms. Perret's home was sold at sheriff's sale before this court could act on her appeal, her appeal of that judgment was dismissed as moot. *Aaron & Turner, L.L.C. v. Perret,* 2006-2433 (La.App. 1 Cir. 9/14/07), 971 So.2d 1049. Another appeal has been filed in the executory proceeding and is currently before this court on issues related to the disbursement of the sheriff's sale proceeds, which we also decide this date in *Aaron & Turner, L.L.C. v. Perret,* 2007-1425 (La.App. 1 Cir.5/4/09), ___ So.3d ___, 2009 WL 2857974 (unpublished).

4. The basis for the invalidity of the promissory note and mortgage as well as the negligence of Aaron & Turner asserted by Ms. Perret is the fact that ABN did not fund the loan and Aaron & Turner conducted the closing without ensuring that ABN had funded the loan.

[. . . .]

Discussion

[6] In granting Aaron & Turner's motion for summary judgment, and consequently denying Ms. Perret's partial motion for summary judgment, the trial court found that "consideration" was given for the note.[5] It further found that Aaron & Turner was entitled to judgment as a matter of law based on a judgment declaring the note to be valid that was rendered in the executory process suit filed by Aaron & Turner.

[. . . .]

[7] Thus, turning to the merits of the motion for summary judgment, as previously outlined, Aaron & Turner filed the motion for summary judgment to obtain dismissal of Ms. Perret's reconventional demand. The law firm "pointed out," as the basis for seeking dismissal of her reconventional demand, that Ms. Perret would not be able to establish that the note and mortgage were invalid. The trial court agreed, stating its finding in open court that "consideration" was given for the note and mortgage, and granting Aaron & Turner's motion for summary judgment.

[8] Our review of the pertinent Louisiana Civil Code articles and the record presented herein leads us to conclude that the parties and the trial court were misguided in examining the validity of the promissory note and mortgage at issue herein from the perspective of "consideration."

[9] "An obligation cannot exist without a lawful *cause*." LSA-C.C. art.1966 (emphasis added). "*Cause* is the reason why a party obligates himself." LSA-C.C. art.1967 (emphasis added).[6]

[10] The comments to Article 1967 state, in pertinent part:

> Under this Article, *"cause" is not "consideration."* The reason why a party binds himself need not be to obtain something in return or to secure an advantage for himself. An obligor may bind himself by a gratuitous

---

5. In oral reasons the trial court stated: "I don't agree with Ms. Perret's position that there was a lack of consideration. I think the funds were paid and I do think that plaintiff can proceed under this note. . . . I think, primarily based on Judge Calloway's prior ruling, plaintiff is entitled to judgment as a matter of law." When the written judgment was submitted for Judge Morvant's signature, it contained the following language: "IT IS FURTHER ORDERED, ADJUDGED AND DECREED that the defendant and plaintiff-in-reconvention, Melissa Michelle Perret *received consideration* in exchange for her execution of the note and related mortgage attached to the Petition. . . ." (Emphasis added.) However, Judge Morvant crossed out, by hand, that portion of the judgment and initialed the alteration. Nevertheless, we find it unnecessary to resolve this discrepancy in light of our disposition herein.

6. Article 1967 further provides: "A party may be obligated by a promise when he knew or should have known that the promise would induce the other party to rely on it to his detriment and the other party was reasonable in so relying. Recovery may be limited to the expenses incurred or the damages suffered as a result of the promisee's reliance on the promise. Reliance on a gratuitous promise made without required formalities is not reasonable."

contract, that is, he may obligate himself for the benefit of the other party without obtaining any advantage in return.

LSA-C.C. art.1967, Comment (c) (emphasis added).[7]

[11] Louisiana does not follow the common law tradition that requires consideration to effect an enforceable contract. Rather, the mere will of the parties will bind them, without what a common law court would consider to be consideration to support a contract, so long as the parties have a lawful "cause." The cause need not have any economic value. *Sound/City Recording Corp. v. Solberg,* 443 F.Supp. 1374, 1380 (D.C.La.1978).

[12] Unlike the common law analysis of a contract using consideration, which requires something in exchange, the civil law concept of "cause" can obligate a person by his will only. The difference has been analogized to a civilian contract-consent approach compared to a common law contract-bargain approach. Consideration is an objective element required to form a contract, whereas cause is a more subjective element that goes to the intentions of the parties. Therefore, in Louisiana law, a person can be obligated by both a gratuitous or onerous contract. *Bains v. Young Men's Christian Association of Greater New Orleans,* 2006-1423, p. 5 (La.App. 4 Cir. 10/3/07), 969 So.2d 646, 649, *writ denied,* 2007-2146 (La.1/7/08), 973 So.2d 727.

[13] In this case, each party had "cause" to enter into this contract: ABN in furtherance of its business as a money lender, and Ms. Perret in order to accomplish refinancing of her home. Ms. Perret complains only of the fact that ABN did not advance the sums it allegedly agreed to under the terms of the contract between the parties.

[14] Under Louisiana law, nonperformance of a promise constitutes a breach of an obligation, rather than a failure of cause. *See Sound/City Recording Corp. v. Solberg,* 443 F.Supp. at 1380. Louisiana Civil Code article 1986 provides the remedy for breach of an obligation to do:

> Upon an obligor's failure to perform an obligation to deliver a thing, or not to do an act, or to execute an instrument, the court shall grant specific performance plus damages for delay if the obligee so demands. If specific performance is impracticable, the court may allow damages to the obligee.

---

7. At common law, lack of consideration is a good reason to deny enforceability of a promise. In civilian systems derived from the French, such as the Louisiana system of private law, absence of cause, or unlawfulness or immorality of the cause, is a good reason to deprive an obligation of its legal effect. In the law of Louisiana a promise is enforceable when it gives rise to an obligation with a lawful cause and not because it is supported by a consideration. Moreover, in spite of some confusion created by imprecise language in the Louisiana Civil Code of 1870, it is now clearly explained that cause is not consideration. Saul Litvinoff, *Still Another Look At Cause,* 48 La. L.Rev. 3, 3, 19 (1987).

> Upon a failure to perform an obligation that has another object, such as an obligation to do, the granting of specific performance is at the discretion of the court.

[15] In the instant case, ABN failed to perform the obligation dictated under the contractual provisions to advance the loan funds. Putting aside for the moment the advancement of funds by Aaron & Turner, ABN's failure to perform (which Ms. Perret has denominated a "failure of consideration") did not nullify the contractual agreement as asserted by Ms. Perret, but rather entitled her to the recovery of damages and/or specific performance in accordance with LSA-C.C. art.1986. [. . . .]

[16] However, there *was* performance in this case, though it was made by third party Aaron & Turner. "Performance may be rendered by a third person, even against the will of the obligee, unless the obligor or the obligee has an interest in performance only by the obligor." LSA-C.C. art. 1855.[9] On this point, the supreme court has stated the following:

> In general, the creditor cannot refuse payment offered by a third person whether or not interested in the extinction of the obligation . . . A payment made by a third person and accepted by the creditor extinguishes the obligation as definitively as one effected by the debtor personally, except where the third person is legally or contractually subrogated to the rights of the creditor. In the last case, the debtor is discharged toward the original creditor, but the obligation continues to exist in favor of the third person who has been subrogated thereto.

Cox v. W.M. Heroman & Co., 298 So.2d 848, 853 (La.1974) (quoting Aubry & Rau, *Obligations, 1 Civil Law Transactions*, §§ 315–316, pp. 156–158 (1965)).

[17] Under these precepts, payment of the sums ABN was obligated to pay under the contractual terms by third party Aaron & Turner would constitute performance satisfying ABN's contractual obligation to Ms. Perret.

[18] However, the more appropriate legal question in the instant suit concerns whether there was a "meeting of the minds" or agreement to contract between ABN and Ms. Perret. The Louisiana Civil Code provides: "A contract is formed by the consent of the parties established through offer and acceptance." LSA-C.C. art.1927. Consent of the parties is necessary to form a valid contract. Where there is no meeting of the minds between the parties, a contract is void for lack of consent. *Stockstill v. C.F. Industries, Inc.*, 94-2072, p. 25 (La.App. 1 Cir. 12/15/95), 665 So.2d 802, 820, *writ denied*, 96-0149 (La.3/15/96), 669 So.2d 428.

[19] "A contract is null when the requirements for its formation have not been met." LSA-C.C. art.2029. A contract to which one party has not consented is a nullity. *See Ferguson v. Dirks*, 95-560, p. 5 (La.App. 5 Cir. 11/28/95), 665 So.2d 585, 587.

---

9. Article 1855 further provides: "Performance rendered by a third person effects subrogation only when so provided by law or by agreement."

[20] In this case, whether lender ABN consented to this contract was not established. It is undisputed that Ms. Perret signed the necessary legal documents signifying her consent, while Aaron & Turner partner William Aaron signed on behalf of ABN. In his deposition, Mr. Aaron testified that his firm was "instructed" to sign on behalf of ABN, but he was unable to recall the circumstances of that instruction. However, it appears that Aaron & Turner's only contact with respect to this transaction was with the loan broker, CFG, and that there was no direct contact with ABN. Moreover, the petition filed by Aaron & Turner stated that loan broker CFG "failed to request or obtain the funding of the loan from [ABN]." While not dispositive of the issue, the fact that ABN never funded the loan also militates in favor of a conclusion that ABN did not consent to contract with Ms. Perret. Further, the testimony presented in this case clearly indicates that Aaron & Turner did not *intend* to advance the sums disbursed at closing from its own funds, but rather did so on the mistaken belief that ABN had forwarded funds for the closing. No other pleading, deposition, answer to interrogatory, admission on file, or affidavit appearing in the record addresses the issue of whether ABN had, in fact, consented to contract with Ms. Perret.

[21] Ms. Perret's reconventional demand and subsequent motion for summary judgment sought to have the note and mortgage declared null and void. Aaron & Turner's cross motion for summary judgment sought the dismissal of Ms. Perret's reconventional demand, urging that she would be unable to prove at trial that the note and mortgage are null and void. Aaron & Turner's right to proceed under the note and mortgage is derived solely from the *assignment* thereof by ABN in its favor, which conveyed to Aaron & Turner only the rights ABN actually had in these contract documents. In order to prevail on the issue of the validity of the promissory note and mortgage and its right to executory process thereunder, Aaron & Turner must establish ABN had rights to convey in these contractual documents, i.e. that ABN had actually consented to enter into the contract with Ms. Perret. No evidence was presented to resolve this issue. Hence, we hold that the validity and enforceability of the note and mortgage have not been conclusively established in the record and that therefore Aaron & Turner was not entitled to foreclose, via summary judgment, Ms. Perret's right to a trial on the merits of her reconventional demand. Accordingly we conclude Aaron & Turner failed to show that no genuine issue of material fact remains and that it is entitled to judgment as a matter of law; summary judgment was inappropriately granted in this case.[10]

[. . . .]

---

10. Although Ms. Perret asserts the note and mortgage are void and unenforceable because she contends that consideration was not given, clearly the validity of these contractual documents has been raised and the fact that this court renders its decision citing a different possible defect (i.e. failure of consent) is of no moment, considering this court's duty to review the motion for summary judgment *de novo* using the same criteria that govern the trial court's consideration of whether summary judgment is appropriate. *See R.G. Claitor's Realty v. Rigell,* 2006-1629 at p. 4, 961 So.2d at 471–72.

[22] Based on these considerations, we conclude that the trial court erred in granting summary judgment in favor of Aaron & Turner.

Conclusion

[23] For the reasons stated herein, we grant Melissa Michelle Perret's application for rehearing, reverse the summary judgment granted by the trial court, and remand this matter for further proceedings consistent with the foregoing. All costs of this appeal are assessed to the appellee, Aaron & Turner, L.L.C.

[. . . .]

GUIDRY, J., concurring.

[24] While I agree that summary judgment was improperly granted and that the summary judgment should be reversed (as was provided in the original opinion rendered in this matter), I previously voted to deny the granting of the rehearing herein, which the majority uses to question the validity of the mortgage and note and then uses that as a basis to reverse the trial court's judgment in *Aaron & Turner, L.L.C. v. Perret,* 2007-1425 (La.App. 1st Cir.5/4/09), ___ So.3d ___, 2009 WL 2857974 (unpublished).

[25] In a very lengthy and strained construction, the majority reasons that the summary judgment should be reversed because "whether lender ABN consented to this contract was not established." Interestingly, the majority ignores the fact that no dispute has ever been raised by any party, or even the non-party ABN, regarding whether ABN consented to the transactions wherein the contractual agreements in dispute were produced. There is evidence in the record to indicate that ABN did consent, but the majority discredits this evidence based on mere allegations from the petition.

[26] Since a contract is an agreement by two or more parties creating, modifying, or extinguishing obligations, La. C.C. art.1906, it is implicitly understood that only parties to a contract may assert its relative nullity based on a defect in consent. *Dugas v. Modular Quarters, Inc.,* 561 So.2d 192, 201 (La.App. 3d Cir.1990). Further, a relative nullity may be invoked only by those persons in whose interest the ground for nullity was established, and may not be declared by the court on its own initiative. La. C.C. art.2031. The right of action to declare a relative nullity is available only to the incapable person or to one whose consent has been defective. With regard to all other persons, including the other party to the contract, the contract is valid. *Armour v. Shongaloo Lodge No. 352 Free and Accepted Masons,* 342 So.2d 600, 604 (La.1977) (Summers, J., concurring); *see also In re Quirk,* 119 B.R. 99 (W.D.La.1990).

[27] Accordingly, I find the majority's action of questioning whether ABN consented to the loan transaction as a possible basis for declaring the note and mortgage null to be inappropriate. I therefore concur in the opinion to the extent that the summary judgment is reversed. By granting rehearing and raising on its own the issue of consent, the majority provides a path to reversing the trial court's judgment

in *Aaron & Turner, L.L.C. v. Perret,* 2007-1425 (La.App. 1st Cir.5/4/09), ___ So.3d ___, 2009 WL 2857974 (unpublished).

Questions

1. Paragraphs 9–12: Do you see any implied meaning in "cause" and "cause is not consideration" being emphasized by the Court? Read and weigh carefully the statements made by the Court in paragraphs 11–12. Do you see any purpose or value in these statements? Could cause be identified as a distinct feature of the Louisiana civil law system and, beyond, of the civil law tradition in general? Do you see any legal problem in forcing the Louisiana legal concept of cause into the common law concept of consideration?

2. Paragraph 13: Can you make the connection between the Court saying that "each party had cause to enter into this contract" and the legal nature or kind of contract involved in the case? For example, since each party had a cause, does it mean that the contract is bilateral? The Court identifies the cause of each party; can each cause be the cause of the contract? In the negative, how should the Court select "the" cause of the contract? Is each cause identified here by the Court more an objective cause than a subjective cause, or vice-versa?

3. Paragraph 18: Shouldn't this issue of the meeting of the minds have been raised much earlier in the opinion by this Court? Why or why not?

4. Paragraph 21: Behind the statement by the Court that "Aaron & Turner's right to proceed under the note . . . assignment thereof by ABN," what kind of right would have to be created for Aaron & Turner to be able to proceed on that right? Is it heritable or strictly personal? Does the statement of the Court that "Aaron & Turner must establish ABN had rights to convey" help you?

James R. Carpenter
v.
Donald Lee Williams, et ux.

Court of Appeal of Louisiana
Third Circuit
March 9, 1983
428 So.2d 1314

CUTRER, Judge.

[....]

Facts

[1] In 1979, Williams was employed by Transco, a company involved in the oil exploration industry, as superintendent of Transco's base of operation in Cameron, Louisiana. Williams' employment required that he be in Cameron five days a week. Williams was living in Lafayette, Louisiana where he owned his home. Each work day he had to commute between Lafayette and Cameron, a distance of approximately 110 miles each way.

[2] Williams had no objection to making the drive each day. He owned his home in Lafayette and was satisfied with the arrangement. In September 1979, however, he received orders from Transco that he must move closer to Cameron. Williams stated that if he had not obeyed the order he would have lost the position he had and would have been transferred to offshore work.

[3] In order to comply with Transco's directive, Williams contacted Donna Fuselier, a real estate agent in Lake Charles, in an attempt to find suitable housing. The agent put Williams in touch with Carpenter, a builder in Lake Charles. Williams stated that he and his wife met with Carpenter at Carpenter's home. Williams stated that they told Carpenter of their reason for having to leave Lafayette and move to Lake Charles. Also, they discussed the possibility of Carpenter building a home for them [...]. Carpenter's estimate for this construction was higher than Williams expected and this proposal did not materialize. Williams was shown and became interested in a house that Carpenter had built for sale.

[4] On September 28, 1979, Williams met with his real estate agent and signed an offer to purchase the house. Included in the offer was the following language:

> "This offer is contingent upon buyer [defendant] *obtaining a conventional loan for $58,000. Offer is also contingent upon seller* [plaintiff] *painting outside of home and close of sale for buyer's* [Williams'] *home.*" (Emphasis ours.)

[5] Carpenter accepted the offer, with inserted conditions, on the same day.

[6] Two of the listed conditions were fulfilled. Williams obtained a loan commitment from a bank in Lake Charles and Carpenter repainted the exterior of the house. The third condition, "close of sale for buyer's home," was never fulfilled.

[7] Transco had a company policy of offering to purchase the homes of employees that were transferred. Williams began the procedure to secure Transco's offer. Two appraisers valued Williams' Lafayette home and Transco [. . .] offered an amount equal to the average of the two appraisals, $83,300.00.

[8] After Williams received a loan commitment from the Lake Charles bank, Bill Bruha, Williams' superior at Transco, informed him that the order requiring him to move to Lake Charles had been rescinded. When Transco rescinded the order Williams notified [**Transco's**] Bank of such and declined the outstanding offer that the bank had made on behalf of Transco. Williams allowed the loan commitment from the Lake Charles bank to expire and he notified his real estate agent, Donna Fuselier, of the turn of events. Williams told her that, under the circumstances, he could not purchase the house from Carpenter.

[9] Donna notified Carpenter of the situation and this suit followed. The trial judge found the agreement was unenforceable and stated in his reasons that the condition in the contract (that the sale was conditioned upon the sale of Williams' Lafayette home) was potestative and suspensive and not enforceable.

[10] From the judgment Carpenter appeals seeking an enforcement of the contract on the ground that the condition was a mixed potestative condition and Williams must make a reasonable effort to sell his Lafayette home and purchase the Lake Charles residence.

[11] Williams contends that, first, the condition is purely potestative and renders the contract unenforceable or, in the alternative, the contract was invalidated due to error for the failure of cause or motive.

[12] The issue before us is whether the buy-sell agreement, under the circumstances presented, created an enforceable contract.

[. . . .]

Failure Of Cause

[13] We have concluded that the contract, under the unusual circumstances presented, was invalidated by the failure of cause or motive for the reasons set forth hereinafter:

> "*Errors may exist as to all circumstances and facts which relate to a contract, but it is not every error that will invalidate it. To have that effect, the error must be in some point, which was a principal cause for making the contract, and it may be either as to the motive for making the contract, to the person with whom it is made, or to the subject matter of the contract itself. La.C.C. Art. 1823. The error in the cause of a contract to have the effect of invalidating it, must be on the principal cause, when there are several; this principal cause is called the motive, and means that consideration without which the contract would not have been made. La.C.C. Art. 1825. No error in the motive can invalidate a contract, unless the other party was apprised that it was the*

*principal cause of the agreement, or unless from the nature of the transaction
it must be presumed that he knew it. La.C.C. Art. 1826. . . . ." O'Neal v. Cascio*, 324 So.2d 539 (La.App. 2nd Cir.1975).

[14] We examine the facts herein in order to ascertain the applicability of these principles.

[15] Williams testified that his only reason for investigating buying a home in Lake Charles was to satisfy his employer's order that he live closer to Cameron.[1] Mr. and Mrs. Williams were content with their Lafayette home. However, rather than risk losing his job Williams undertook to comply with Transco's orders. This fact is supported by exhibits in the record which show Transco twice appraised, then bid on, Williams' Lafayette home. Transco has a policy of bidding on the homes of employees who are forced to relocate.

[16] Williams testified that he and his wife met with Carpenter in his home and discussed duplicating the Lafayette residence in Lake Charles. The Williamses said at this meeting that they told Carpenter of their reason for having to move to Lake Charles [. . . .] [**although**] Carpenter recalls no such discussion.

[. . . .]

[17] *Marcello v. Bussiere*, 284 So.2d 892 (La.1973), involved the question of whether the sale of a bar-lounge business and a related lease should be rescinded because of a vice of consent. Marcello held a lease to what had been a going concern. The Bussieres wanted to invest in a business. After some negotiations a verbal lease of the premises was entered into and the Bussieres bought the business and equipment from Marcello. Marcello had told Bussiere the lounge was closed for repairs. In fact, the lounge was closed at the time of the sale because it had lost its liquor license. Bussiere paid the utilities and insurance on the premises and undertook extensive renovations. When Bussiere was informed by the local authorities that he could not obtain a liquor license for the premises he refused to pay rent for subsequent months and stopped renovations.

[18] The Supreme Court stated:

"Error in the determining motive, or principal cause, vitiates consent and invalidates a contract. . . . .

"[T]he determining motive for the present contracts was to secure a going bar-lounge business for their [Bussiere's] continued operation. An alcoholic beverage license was of course essential for operation of the business. This determining motive, in our opinion, was either known to the seller or, from the circumstances, should have been known to him.

"Since the purchasers received no going business and could not secure a license to operate, we conclude that there was an error in the principal cause of the

---

1. Plaintiff's attorney stipulated that, if called, Mrs. Williams' testimony on this point would be substantially the same as Mr. Williams'.

contract. . . . The contracts must be rescinded. See LSA–C.C. Arts. 1821, 1822, 1846; Stack v. Irwin, supra [167 So.2d 363 (La.1969)]; Boehmer Sales Agency v. Russo, La.App. 99 So.2d 475 (1958); 19 La.L.Rev. 196, 199–200."

[19] Similar results have been reached in cases involving misunderstandings between a seller and a purchaser as to the zoning classification of a piece of property, *Ortego v. Lebert*, 406 So.2d 253 (La.App. 3rd Cir.1981); and the requirement of governmental approval of certain uses of the land which was the object of a sale; *Walker v. Don Coleman Const. Co., Inc.*, 338 So.2d 1183 (La.App. 2nd Cir.1976). In *O'Neal v. Cascio,* supra, the court rescinded a promissory note given by a client to an attorney in contemplation of legal fees to arise in the defense of an upcoming indictment. The indictment was never issued. The court stated the jury reasonably could have found that Cascio's principal cause or motive in entering the contract was to obtain legal defense. Further Cascio would not have entered the attorney-client contract or executed the note had he been aware that an indictment was not forthcoming.

[20] In these cases the parties entered a contract assuming certain facts or conditions to exist. When the assumed fact or condition was found not to exist or did not come into existence even through the act of third parties (Transco in this case), the contracts have been rescinded.

[21] With these cases in mind, we find that the principal, and only, cause or motive Williams had for entering into the buy-sell agreement with Carpenter was to comply with Transco's orders. We further find that Carpenter was aware of this fact. Thus, when Transco rescinded its order to Williams the cause or motive for entering the contract ceased to exist or failed and the contract became unenforceable. We shall affirm the judgment of the trial court.

[22] For the reasons above assigned, the judgment of the trial court is affirmed. The costs are to be paid by James R. Carpenter, plaintiff-appellant.

[23] AFFIRMED.

Questions

1. Paragraphs 1–3: After you have read the whole case, do you see any purpose in the first three paragraphs? Do you notice any possible influence on Carpenter's state of mind when he entered into the contract of sale with Williams?

2. Paragraphs 1–9: Was Carpenter fully aware and knowledgeable of Williams' situation? Did Williams disclose openly to Carpenter the predicament he was in or any circumstance that the parties should, in good faith, have regarded as a cause of the obligation?

3. Paragraphs 1–12: Was there any detrimental reliance on the part of Williams, who had followed Transco's instructions? Was the final decision by Transco contemplated in the conditions included in the offer made by Williams to Carpenter? Could Williams argue *force majeure*, impossibility of performance?

4. Paragraphs 4–12: Describe in legal terms the "inserted conditions." Is there any kind of legal connection between these so-called "conditions"?

5. Paragraphs 9–12: Do you agree with the trial court's statement that the condition was "potestative and suspensive," and hence "not enforceable"? Williams adds that the condition "is purely potestative": is this true? Explain. Could the argument be made that there occurred a "failure of cause"?

6. Paragraphs 13–14: The court refers to "these principles." What are those principles? What is a principle? Is a principle a source of law? Is the Supreme Court using the proper legal term when it refers to the case of *O'Neal v. Casio* or to the Code articles listed in this case? How would you qualify cases and code articles as sources of law in the Louisiana Civil Code?

7. Paragraphs 14–22: The court fails to mention a "principle" that should have opened its opinion and which controls the whole law of Obligations. This principle is stated in La. Civ. C. arts. 1759 and 1983; it is the principle of "good faith." Do you think Williams was well-protected by this "shield" of good faith?

First Louisiana Bank
v.
Morris & Dickson Co., LLC

Court of Appeal of Louisiana
Second Circuit
November 3, 2010
55 So.3d 815

GASKINS, J.

[. . . .]

Facts

[1] Morris & Dickson needed a package handling system for its warehouse. MMS was the low bidder and was chosen to install an Intertake Pallet Pick system. To facilitate the process, Morris & Dickson issued three purchase orders to MMS. One purchase order, # 031223–01, was for $249,853.47. A second purchase order, # 031223–02, the order at issue here, was for $196,450.50. The amount of the third purchase order was not specified.

[2] MMS was operated by Robert Eizel. MMS did not have the funds to purchase the system. Mr. Eizel approached Bank One, Bancorp South, and First Louisiana about obtaining financing. First Louisiana requested, as additional security, that the bank be included as additional payee on all payments made by Morris & Dickson to MMS.

[3] On January 15, 2004, Paul M. Dickson, vice-president of Morris & Dickson, wrote a "To Whom it May Concern" letter stating that:

Payment for the above referenced purchase order issued to Material Management Systems will be made payable to Material Management Systems and First Louisiana Bank Attn: Ron Boudreaux.

[4] The purchase order referenced in the letter was # 031223–02, for $196,450.50. The letter does not specify an addressee. Morris & Dickson wrote similar letters to Bank One for purchase orders # 031223–01, # 031223–02, and # 031223–03 and to Bancorp South for # 031223–01 and # 031223–03. Bank One did not lend money to MMS; Bancorp South and First Louisiana did. The two loans from First Louisiana are at issue in this case.

[5] The loans from First Louisiana were evidenced by promissory notes from MMS and Mr. Eizel to First Louisiana in the amounts of $50,070 and $65,072. Mr. Eizel signed as a guarantor on the loans. In order to secure the two loans, MMS also made assignments to First Louisiana of the contract purchase order from Morris & Dickson for $196,450.50. The assignments were filed in the Uniform Commercial Code Registry with the Louisiana Secretary of State.

[6] The intervenor, Ronald Tuminello, partnered with Mr. Eizel on previous business ventures. Mr. Tuminello signed as a guarantor on the loans from First Louisiana for this project. Mr. Eizel gave Mr. Tuminello a promissory note for $100,000 to secure his signature as guarantor.

[7] MMS failed to complete the work on the warehouse and Morris & Dickson took over the project. MMS also defaulted on its loan to First Louisiana. In August 2004, First Louisiana sent a demand letter to Mr. Eizel to pay both notes. In June 2005, First Louisiana obtained a default judgment against MMS and Mr. Eizel in the amounts of $51,160.57 and $64,724.16, the sums due on the notes. MMS went out of business and Mr. Eizel filed for bankruptcy. However, his debt to First Louisiana on these notes was not discharged in bankruptcy.

[. . . .]

[8] In January 2008, the trial court held a hearing and concluded that the claims against Morris & Dickson had prescribed. First Louisiana and Mr. Tuminello appealed. In *First Louisiana Bank v. Morris & Dickson Company, LLC*, 44,187 (La. App.2d Cir.4/8/09), 6 So.3d 1047, this court reversed the trial court, finding that the claim against Morris & Dickson was based on contract and not tort and was subject to the 10-year prescriptive period for contracts. The matter was remanded to the trial court for further proceedings.

[9] On remand, the trial court considered testimony and evidence adduced at the original hearing. Ron C. Boudreaux, president of First Louisiana, testified that there were two conditions for the loan to MMS. First, that the bank receive assignments of the purchase orders and second, that checks from Morris & Dickson for purchase order # 031223–02 be made payable to both MMS and First Louisiana.

[. . . .]

[10] First Louisiana argues that the trial court erred in failing to find that an obligation existed on the part of Morris & Dickson to pay First Louisiana monies toward purchase order # 031223–02, pursuant to the letter issued by Morris & Dickson dated January 15, 2004. First Louisiana also claims that the trial court erred in

finding that the bank and/or MMS were required to give notice to Morris & Dickson before the company was obligated to pay pursuant to its letter.

[11] The plaintiff in intervention, Mr. Tuminello, argues on appeal that the trial court erred by not applying the detrimental reliance provisions of La. C.C. art. 1967. He also argues that the trial court erred in finding that notice was required and/or was not given.

Contract and Notice

[12] First Louisiana urges that the letter at issue here created a conventional obligation or contract between Morris & Dickson and First Louisiana once the bank accepted Morris & Dickson's offer by making a loan to MMS. First Louisiana argues that the trial court erred in finding that express acceptance of the terms of the letter was required to form a contract between Morris & Dickson and the bank. First Louisiana contends that the "To Whom it May Concern" letter to the bank became an accessory contract to the principal contract between Morris & Dickson and MMS.

[. . . .]

[13] Closely tied with the arguments concerning whether there was a binding agreement in this matter, First Louisiana maintains that the trial court erred in finding that either the bank or MMS was required to give notice to Morris & Dickson to create an obligation on the part of the company to include the bank as a payee on checks to MMS. First Louisiana contends that Morris & Dickson knew that MMS was seeking financing for the project and Morris & Dickson had actual knowledge that MMS was dealing with First Louisiana and Bancorp South. According to First Louisiana, the letter by Morris & Dickson did not require the bank to contact the company to trigger the obligation of including First Louisiana as an additional payee on checks to MMS. These arguments are without merit.

Legal Principles

[14] A contract is an agreement by two or more persons whereby obligations are created, modified, or extinguished. La. C.C. art. 1906. A contract is formed by the consent of the parties established through offer and acceptance. Unless the law prescribes a certain formality for the intended contract, offer and acceptance may be made orally, in writing, or by action or inaction that under the circumstances is clearly indicative of consent. Unless otherwise specified in the offer, there need not be conformity between the manner in which the offer is made and the manner in which the acceptance is made. La. C.C. art. 1927.

[15] Unless otherwise specified by the offer or the law, an acceptance of a revocable offer, made in a manner and by a medium suggested by the offer or in a reasonable manner and by a reasonable medium, is effective when transmitted by the offeree. La. C.C. art. 1935. A medium or manner of acceptance is reasonable if it is the one used in making the offer or one customary in similar transactions at the time and place the offer is received, unless circumstances known to the offeree indicate otherwise. La. C.C. art. 1936.

[16] When an offeror invites an offeree to accept by performance and, according to usage or the nature or the terms of the contract, it is contemplated that the performance will be completed if commenced, a contract is formed when the offeree begins the requested performance. La. C.C. art. 1939.

[17] When commencement of the performance either constitutes acceptance or makes the offer irrevocable, the offeree must give prompt notice of that commencement unless the offeror knows or should know that the offeree has begun to perform. An offeree who fails to give the notice is liable for damages. La. C.C. art. 1941.

[18] When, because of special circumstances, the offeree's silence leads the offeror reasonably to believe that a contract has been formed, the offer is deemed accepted. La. C.C. art. 1942.

[19] The court must find that there was a meeting of the minds of the parties to constitute consent. The existence or nonexistence of a contract is a question of fact not to be disturbed unless clearly wrong. *Belin v. Dugdale*, 45,405 (La.App.2d Cir.6/30/10), 43 So.3d 272.

[. . . .]

Discussion

[20] The trial court did not err in finding that the letter at issue here does not give rise to a binding contract between Morris & Dickson and First Louisiana. The letter was not addressed to First Louisiana or any other entity. It is a "To Whom it May Concern" letter agreeing to include First Louisiana as a payee on payments to MMS for purchase order # 031223–02. Another letter, covering this same purchase order as well as two other purchase orders, was also written concerning Bank One. A third letter was written concerning Bancorp South and purchase orders # 031223–01 and # 031223–03. If these letters, without notice of acceptance of the terms, created a contract, then Morris & Dickson would have been required to include not only First Louisiana, but also Bank One on any checks issued to MMS for purchase order # 031223–02. We find that this is not the case. The letter was an offer that required acceptance and communication of that fact to Morris & Dickson in order to form a contract.

[. . . .]

[21] The trial court did not err in finding that notice of acceptance of the offer contained in the letter at issue here was necessary for the formation of a binding agreement between Morris & Dickson and First Louisiana. Because there was no showing that First Louisiana ever communicated acceptance of the offer, the trial court did not err in finding that no contract was formed between these parties. Further, if a *stipulation pour autrui* in favor of First Louisiana was intended by Morris & Dickson and MMS, there is no showing that First Louisiana manifested its intent to avail itself of the benefit.

[. . . .]

[22] The result in this case is determined solely by the distinct facts presented here. The circumstances and timing of the Morris & Dickson letter are significant in the outcome of this matter. The letter was clearly written at a time when MMS and Mr. Eizel were attempting to obtain financing from various banks. Under these facts, First Louisiana should have communicated to Morris & Dickson its acceptance of the offer in the letter and First Louisiana's performance by loaning money to MMS. The result in this case may have been different if the letter had been written at a different time in the loan process.

Detrimental Reliance

[23] Mr. Tuminello argues on appeal that the trial court erred in not applying the detrimental reliance provisions of La. C.C. art. 1967. He contends that Morris & Dickson knew that First Louisiana would not loan money to MMS without assurance from Morris & Dickson that it would make payments jointly to MMS and the bank. Mr. Tuminello claims that he would not have entered into the continuing guaranty agreement without the assurances of Morris & Dickson contained in the letter at issue here. He urges that notice is not required for detrimental reliance. He asserts that Morris & Dickson made a representation that he was justified in relying upon and that he changed his position to his detriment because of that reliance. This argument is without merit.

Legal Principles

[24] La. C.C. art. 1967 provides:

Cause is the reason why a party obligates himself.

A party may be obligated by a promise when he knew or should have known that the promise would induce the other party to rely on it to his detriment and the other party was reasonable in so relying. Recovery may be limited to the expenses incurred or the damages suffered as a result of the promisee's reliance on the promise. Reliance on a gratuitous promise made without required formalities is not reasonable.

[25] The doctrine of detrimental reliance is designed to prevent injustice by barring a party from taking a position contrary to his prior acts, admissions, representation, or silence. *Suire v. Lafayette City-Parish Consolidated Government*, 2004–1459 (La.4/12/05), 907 So.2d 37; *Belin v. Dugdale*, supra.

[26] The focus of analysis of a detrimental reliance claim is not whether the parties intended to perform, but, instead, whether a representation was made in such a manner that the promisor should have expected the promisee to rely upon it, and whether the promisee so relies to his detriment. *Suire v. Lafayette City-Parish Consolidated Government, supra.*

[27] To recover under the theory of detrimental reliance, a plaintiff must prove the following three elements by a preponderance of the evidence: (1) a representation by conduct or work; (2) justifiable reliance thereon; (3) a change in position to one's detriment because of the reliance. *Belin v. Dugdale, supra.*

[28] It is difficult to recover under the theory of detrimental reliance because estoppel is not favored in Louisiana law. Claims of detrimental reliance must be examined strictly and carefully. *Northside Furniture of Ruston, Inc. v. First Tower Loan, Inc.*, 43,736 (La.App.2d Cir.12/3/08), 999 So.2d 151; *Belin v. Dugdale, supra.*

Discussion

[29] We must first address the question of whether Mr. Tuminello's claim for detrimental reliance is properly before this court on appeal. In the trial court, Mr. Tuminello argued that he was damaged by the breach of an alleged contract between Morris & Dickson and First Louisiana to include the bank as an additional payee on checks to MMS. On remand, the trial court stated that the previous opinion of this court, denying the exception of prescription, held that any claims of detrimental reliance would have been prescribed. Therefore, the trial court's reasons for judgment on remand do not consider the merits of detrimental reliance.

[30] Morris & Dickson contends that detrimental reliance is based in tort and that the prior decision of this court found that any detrimental reliance claims in this case had prescribed. To the contrary, this court's prior opinion held that any tort claims which might be involved in the case had prescribed but that the claims presented were based in contract. Delictual actions are subject to a liberative prescription of one year. La. C.C. art. 3492. An action on a contract is governed by the prescriptive period of 10 years for personal actions. La. C.C. art. 3499; *Trinity Universal Insurance Company v. Horton*, 33,157 (La.App.2d Cir.4/5/00), 756 So.2d 637. The correct prescriptive period to be applied in any action depends upon the nature of the action; it is the nature of the duty breached that should determine whether an action is in tort or in contract. *Trinity Universal Insurance Company v. Horton, supra.* The classical distinction between "damages ex contractu" and "damages ex delicto" is that the former flow from the breach of a special obligation contractually assumed by the obligor, whereas the latter flow from the violation of a general duty to all persons. *Harrison v. Gore*, 27,254 (La.App.2d Cir.8/23/95), 660 So.2d 563, *writ denied*, 95–2347 (La.12/8/95), 664 So.2d 426.

[31] In the Louisiana Civil Code revision of 1984, La. C.C. art. 1967, which concerns cause and detrimental reliance, was enacted. This article is contained in that portion of the Louisiana Civil Code dealing with contracts. In Saul Litvinoff, *Still Another Look at Cause*, 48 La. L.Rev. 3 (1987), construing La. C.C. art. 1967, the author states that "the new article of the Louisiana Civil Code subtracts induced reliance from the quasi-delictual field and places it where it belongs, in contract."

[32] We also note that the jurisprudence holds that claims for detrimental reliance arising out of contracts are not subject to the one-year prescriptive period for torts. See *Babkow v. Morris Bart, P.L.C.*, 1998–0256 (La.App. 4th Cir.12/16/98), 726 So.2d 423. Therefore, Mr. Tuminello's detrimental reliance claim, based upon an alleged contract, has not prescribed.

[33] However, we find that Mr. Tuminello failed to carry his burden of proving a claim for detrimental reliance in this matter. In the present case, Mr. Tuminello

argues that he would not have signed as a guarantor on the loan from First Louisiana to MMS without the assurance that Morris & Dickson would include the bank as a payee on all checks issued to MMS for payment of the purchase order at issue here. Under the facts presented, we do not find that Mr. Tuminello was justified in his reliance on the "To Whom it May Concern" letter. No promises were made to Mr. Tuminello and no representation was made by Morris & Dickson in such a manner that the company should have expected Mr. Tuminello to rely upon it. The facts simply do not support the argument that the letter at issue here induced Mr. Tuminello to sign as a guarantor. Therefore, no claim for detrimental reliance has been proved in this case.

Conclusion

[34] For the reasons stated above, we affirm the decision of the trial court rejecting the claims of First Louisiana Bank and Ronald Tuminello against the defendant, Morris & Dickson Company, LLC. Costs in this court are assessed one-half to First Louisiana and one-half to Mr. Tuminello.

[35] AFFIRMED.

Questions

1. Paragraphs 2–3: How would you describe the legal nature of a purchase order: as a contract? a preliminary contract? an offer or an acceptance to purchase? Read the Code articles on offer and acceptance. Mr. Eizel signed the loans as guarantor; how is Mr. Eizel bound, if at all, with MMS? As guarantor on the loans from First Louisiana, how is Tuminello bound? Is he bound with anyone else? On what ground(s) can First Louisiana seek to enforce the provisions of "To Whom . . ."? What about Tuminello? How does detrimental reliance relate here? Can you find it in the Louisiana Civil Code?

2. Paragraph 8: Instead of looking at detrimental reliance as a tort, couldn't detrimental reliance be considered and identified as the cause of a pre-contract (like a contract to sell, *see* La. Civ. Code arts. 2623, *et seq.*, which precedes the sale) entered into by the parties before they actually enter into the contract itself? Since a pre-contract is a contract, breach of that contract would be ground for payment of contractual damages (*see* paragraph 29).

3. Paragraphs 9–10: Can you find an implicit stipulation *pour autrui*, stipulation for the benefit of a third party, in the facts or circumstances of this case?

4. Paragraphs 12–13: How can an acceptance by Morris & Dickson making a loan to MMS be tantamount to forming a contract between Morris & Dickson and First Louisiana? To what kind of accessory contract to the principal contract is First Louisiana referring? What are the different possible forms of acceptance? According to First Louisiana, what was its form of acceptance forming the accessory contract? Read the Louisiana Civil Code articles on Third Party Beneficiary (La. Civ. Code arts. 1978–1982) and evaluate this statement by First Louisiana: "the law does not provide for a particular form of acceptance

or require an express acceptance of or consent to a *stipulation pour autrui*." Focus on paragraph 13. Do you agree with the Court that "these arguments are without merit"? Go back now to questions 1 and 2. Do you have a different view?

5. Paragraphs 12–13: After you have read Louisiana Civil Code article 1978, can you explain where the Court finds this requirement that a *stipulation pour autrui* is never presumed? Return to the leading case of *Andrepont v. Acadiana Drilling*, above: what was the *Andrepont* Court's understanding of the requirements for the existence of a *stipulation pour autrui*? Didn't First Louisiana manifest some form of intent to be included, in some way, in the contract between Morris & Dickson and MMS? Didn't Morris & Dickson know that MMS would have to borrow money and thus obtain a loan? Is First Louisiana a total stranger to the contract between Morris & Dickson and MMS?

6. Paragraps 29–30: Is the Court suggesting that detrimental reliance can be relied on only in matters of contracts? The Court makes an important point here: at civil law, there are two kinds of damages, damages *ex contractu* (literally "out of a contract") or *ex delicto* (out of a delict/tort).

Fairbanks Development, LLC
v.
Charles Woodrow Johnson and Jessica Lyn Petersen
Supreme Court of Louisiana
September 30, 2021
330 So.3d 183

WEIMER, C.J., additionally concurring.

[1] I agree with my colleague's analysis. I additionally concur based on the Louisiana Civil Code concept of cause. See La. C.C. arts. 1966.[1] Under the cause concept, Jessica Petersen's payment of the funds for the purchase of the property is of no moment. The cause or reason for her purchase of the property and the placement of her name and the name of Charles Johnson, as purchasers, on the property deeds was to further the goal of her and Johnson "starting a life together," as each testified. Indeed, they were subsequently married and had children together. [. . . .]

[. . . .]

[2] In *Slimp v. Sartisky*, [. . .] (10/11/12), authored by Judge Max Tobias, Jr., [. . . .] [a]fter observing the text of La. C.C. arts. 1966 and 1967 and the comments to Article 1967, the *Slimp* court stated:

Louisiana does not follow the common law tradition that requires consideration to effect an enforceable contract. Rather, the mere will of the parties will bind them, without what a common law court would consider to

---

1. La. C.C. art. 1966 provides that "[a]n obligation cannot exist without a lawful cause."

be consideration to support a contract, so long as the parties have a lawful "cause." The cause need not have any economic value. [. . . .]

[. . . .] The Louisiana Civil Code does not adopt the common law's so-called "peppercorn"[3] theory of consideration or require something in exchange. Instead, the civil law concept of cause allows one to be obligated by that individual's will only. [. . . .] As recognized in *Slimp*:

> The difference has been analogized to a civilian contract-consent approach compared to a common law contract-bargain approach. Consideration is an objective element required to form a contract, whereas cause is a more subjective element that goes to the intentions of the parties. Therefore, in Louisiana law, a person can be obligated by both a gratuitous or onerous contract. [. . . .]

[. . . .]

George T. Luther and Jamie C. Luther
v.
Iom Company LLC (f/k/a Intra-Op Monitoring Services LLC), Dan Joachim M.D., John Partridge and Admiral Insurance Company

Supreme Court of Louisiana
October 15, 2013
130 So.3d 817

HUGHES, J.

[. . . .]

[1] The doctrine of detrimental reliance is designed to prevent injustice by barring a party from taking a position contrary to his prior acts, admissions, representations, or silence. To establish detrimental reliance, a party must prove three elements by a preponderance of the evidence: (1) a representation by conduct or word; (2) justifiable reliance; and (3) a change in position to one's detriment because of the reliance. *Suire v. Lafayette City-Parish Consolidated Government*, 2004-1459 (La.4/12/05), 907 So.2d 37, 59. Estoppels are not favored in our law; therefore, a party cannot avail himself of that doctrine if he fails to prove all essential elements of the plea. See *Wilkinson v. Wilkinson*, 323 So.2d 120, 126 (La. 1975).

---

3. Peppercorn is "[a] small or insignificant thing or amount; nominal consideration" used to support the formation of a binding contract. BLACK'S LAW DICTIONARY 1156 (7th ed. 1999). See In re SemCrude, L.P., 504 B.R. 39, 55 n.54 (Bankr. D. Del. 2013), adopted sub nom. In re Semcrude, L.P., No. 14-CV-357 (SLR), 2015 WL 4594516 (D. Del. July 30, 2015), aff'd sub nom. In re SemCrude L.P., 864 F.3d 280 (3d Cir. 2017) (quoting Chappell & Co. Ltd. v. Nestle Co. Ltd., [1960] A.C. 87 (H.L. 1959)) ("The English House of Lords has observed that '[a] peppercorn does not cease to be good consideration if it is established that the promisee does not like pepper and will throw away the corn.'").

[. . . .]

[2] [. . . .] This court has previously held that a party having the means readily and conveniently available to determine the true facts, but who fails to do so, cannot claim estoppel. See *Morris v. Friedman*, 94-2808 (La.11/27/95), 663 So.2d 19, 25). [. . . .]

[. . . .]

[3] Furthermore, equitable considerations and estoppel cannot be permitted to prevail when in conflict with positive written law. *Morris v. Friedman*, 663 So.2d at 25-26 (quoting *Palermo Land Company v. Planning Commission of Calcasieu Parish*, 561 So.2d 482, 488 (La.1990)). [. . . .]

[. . . .]

Darrell Suire

v.

Lafayette City-Parish Consolidated Government, et al.

Supreme Court of Louisiana
April 12, 2005
907 So.2d 37

CALOGERO, Chief Justice.

[. . . .]

[1] [. . . .] To establish detrimental reliance, a party must prove three elements by a preponderance of the evidence: (1) a representation by conduct or word; (2) justifiable reliance; and (3) a change in position to one's detriment because of the reliance. *Lakeland Anesthesia, Inc. v. United Healthcare of La., Inc.*, 2003-1662 (La.App. 4 Cir. 3/17/04), 871 So.2d 380, 393, *writ denied*, 2004-0969 (La. 6/25/04), 876 So.2d 864; *Babkow*, 726 So.2d at 427. Significantly, to prevail on a detrimental reliance claim, Louisiana law does not require proof of a formal, valid, and enforceable contract. [. . . .]

[2] [P]roof of a detrimental reliance claim does not require proof of an underlying contract. This is so because detrimental reliance is not based upon the intent to be bound. [. . . .] Rather, the basis of detrimental reliance is "the idea that a person should not harm another person by making promises that he will not keep." *Id.* [. . . .]

[. . . .]

[3] [. . . .] The [. . .] finding that a taking had occurred was "unquestionably supported." *Id.*

[. . . .]

Huey P. Morris and Susie T. Morris
v.
Sam J. Friedman
Supreme Court of Louisiana
November 27, 1995
663 So.2d 19

KIMBALL, Justice.

[. . . .]

[1] [. . . .] [I]t is clear that the La.C.C. art. 1967 is a substantive law, as it incorporates into the law of Louisiana a new basis for enforcement of obligations.[7] [. . . .]

[. . . .]

[2] Prior to January 1, 1985, claims based on a theory of loss from change in position due to allegedly "reasonable" reliance on factual representations made by another were framed in terms of either "detrimental reliance" (despite the lack of express codal authority for such claims), "equitable estoppel," or "promissory estoppel."[8] [. . . .]

[3] Such claims, when expressly framed in terms of detrimental reliance, were a relatively rare occurrence in Louisiana prior to the effective date of La.C.C. art. 1967. [. . . .]

[. . . .]

"Estoppel" in its various forms seems to be a doctrine of last resort. In Louisiana, no statutory material and no body of jurisprudence justifies its use. In this court we have discussed it, in modern times, only to disallow a claim that the opponent ought not to be able to make a certain claim or defense.

[. . . .]

---

7. This fact was noted by the Third Circuit in the first Morris decision, *Morris v. People's Bank & Trust Co.*, 580 So.2d 1029, 1033 (La.App. 3rd Cir.), *writ denied*, 588 So.2d 101 (La.1991) ("La.C.C. art. 1967 changed Louisiana law by incorporating detrimental reliance as a basis for enforceability of obligations.").

8. Additionally, we note that while much has been written in law review articles about the Roman law *maxim venire contra propium factum* (no one can contradict his own act) and the German legal theory of *culpa in contrahendo* (fault in contracting), see, e.g., M. Mattar, *Promissory Estoppel: Common Law Wine In Civil Law Bottles*, 4 Tul.Civ.L.Forum 72 (1988); S. Herman, *Detrimental Reliance In Louisiana Law—Past, Present, and Future(?): The Code Drafter's Perspective*, 58 Tul.L.Rev. 707 (1984); Comment, *Detrimental Reliance*, 45 La.L.Rev. 753 (1985), we can find only a few Louisiana decisions which even mention these doctrines, and only one case which specifically based recovery exclusively on either theory. See *Davilla v. Jones*, 418 So.2d 724 (La.App. 4th Cir.1982), *rev'd.* 436 So.2d 507 (La.1983). We have not located any case or commentary even addressing the application of either doctrine to an onerous promise where a positive legal requirement of form exists.

625 Labarre Road, LLC and Jim Hall
v.
Parish of Jefferson, American Alternative Insurance Company, National Union Fire Insurance Company of Pittsburgh, Pennsylvania, Safety National Casualty Corporation

Court of Appeal of Louisiana
Fifth Circuit
November 3, 2021
330 So.3d 1201

CHEHARDY, C.J.

[....]

[1] A detrimental reliance theory of recovery emanates from La. Civ. Code art. 1967, which provides [....] [that t]hree elements are necessary to establish a claim for detrimental reliance: (1) representation by conduct or word; (2) justifiable reliance; and (3) a change in position to one's detriment because of the reliance. [....] Claims of detrimental reliance must be examined strictly and carefully. [....]

[....]

[2] The Petition then alleges that the "threat of repeal of the acts" caused plaintiffs to enter into a compromise agreement "with the objecting property owners and the Jefferson Parish Council" resulting in a "reduced revised project" that "greatly reduced petitioners' earning potential in the project as originally approved." According to plaintiffs, "[a]s a result of the compromise," they were "forced to spend additional sums in the amount of $350,000 in redesigning the project in question[.]"

[3] A careful review of the Petition shows that the listed activities occurring before the Parish's "threat to revoke the ordinance[s]" are activities that would have been necessary for nearly any construction project, including the project as later modified. [....] Plaintiffs never allege that the listed activities were specific to the original plans, or that any of those activities would not have been performed if plaintiffs had known the project would be reduced in scope. Consequently, the third prong of detrimental reliance — a change in position to one's detriment because of the reliance — has not been pled with respect to the $250,000 of expenses plaintiffs allegedly incurred before learning of the potential revocation of the ordinances.

[4] [....] The additional $350,000 that plaintiffs claim to have spent as a result of the alleged "threatened action" of the Council were incurred after entering into a compromise agreement with the Council, according to the Petition. Further, plaintiffs do not allege that the compromise agreement reserved plaintiffs' right to pursue damages against the Council through litigation. Plaintiffs' allegations fail to state a detrimental-reliance cause of action against the Parish.

[....]

See also *McKee v. Southfield School*, 613 So.2d 659 (La.App. 2 Cir. 1993), *supra*.

Comparative Law Perspective

— Civil Law —

Henri Capitant, *De la Cause des Obligations*

n°s 6–7 at 15–18 (1923)

The Significance of "Cause"

7. — It is not only at the moment of the accord of wills that the idea of cause intervenes. Its importance is felt for as long as the contract has not been entirely performed. Indeed, the obligation can live only as long as it remains supported by its cause. In this respect, the cause is distinguished from the two other prerequisites that must exist in connection with the obligor for the contract to be valid: consent and capacity. It is sufficient, in fact, that consent and capacity exist at the moment at which the contract is made. It matters little that one of the other should disappear later on. For example, if the obligor becomes insane or is stricken with [**some other**] incapacity, that does not stop a previously contracted obligation from remaining valid.

It is otherwise with the cause. For the obligatory relation, once it has been formed, to continue to bind the obligor, it is necessary for the result that he desired to be realized. If it is not, the obligatory line cannot subsist; it must be ruptured.

Two additional consequences result from this notion, which [**should be . . .**] added to the preceding.

First, in a synallagmatic contract, when one of the parties demands execution of the performance that has been promised to him, he must prove [. . .] either (i) that the end desired by his adversary has already been attained, because he himself has fulfilled his own obligation, or (ii) that it is going to be attained, because he is ready to fulfill it. As result, a seller, for example, can pursue the buyer for the payment of the price only if he has already delivered or if, at the same time at which he makes the demand, he offers to deliver the sold thing. And reciprocally, [. . .] the seller [**need**] not deliver the thing to the buyer if the latter has not paid the price and if a delay has not been accorded him for the payment. In other words, in synallagmatic contracts, the reciprocal obligations contracted by the parties must be performed simultaneously or, as the Germans say, one for one. The contracting party who still has not received the performance that has been promised him can, then, assert against the enforcement suit of his adversary a defense that is called the *exceptio non adimpleti contractus*.

Finally, if, as a result of an event posterior to the creation of the obligation (fortuious [**sic**] event, *force majeure*, fault of the other party), the end pursued by the obligor cannot be realized, then he ceases to be obligated and he is freed. The obligation, in fact, disappears necessarily with its cause.

Philippe Malaurie, Laurent Aynès & Philippe Stoffel-Munck, *Les Obligations*
(10th ed. LGDJ 2018)

604. Lack of the theory of cause. — [. . . .] The ordinance [**2016 revision of the French law of obligations**] has banned such an ambiguous term [**cause**] from the Civil Code. In its first sense, that of a motive for the conventional obligation, the term cause is replaced with that of "purpose" of the contract (Article 1162). In its second sense, that of a performance obtained through the obligation (purpose of the conventional obligation), the term cause is replaced by that of "counterpart" ("contrepartie") (Article 1169). Further, the ordinance decided to no longer make the existence of the cause, in this second sense, a condition for the validity of the contract, which would be assessed separately from consent. This reform simplifies French law, bringing it close to several foreign laws, in particular German civil law systems, and restores a certain contractual security.

François Terré, Philippe Simler, Yves Lequette & François Chénedé, *Droit Civil: Les Obligations*
(12th ed. 2018)

403. Revision of 2016: the thing without the word. — By removing the reference to the word "cause", while retaining its functions, *the thing*, what is then the "contribution" of this revision? We thus understand that "cause" was not abandoned, but was rather disaggregated by the 2016 legislator, who chose to break it up into as many rules as it had functions, rather than restoring its lost coherence in recent jurisprudence and overanalytical doctrine that contributed to this loss. To use a metaphor, the 2016 revision missed the opportunity to transform the "Swiss Army knife" that cause had become — with blades so numerous and so badly identified that it became difficult to use — into a solid Opinel knife.

Alain Levasseur, *Comparative Law of Contracts*
at 79–91 (2008)

Cause and Consideration

Besides offer and acceptance, among the other legal requirements which are necessary, in both the civil law and the common law traditions, to make a contract binding and create obligations, is the requirement of "cause" at civil law and the requirement of "consideration" at common law.

See La. Civ. C articles 1966, 1967, 1969.

Fr. Civ. C. 1804 (revised in 2016)

> **Art. 1108:** Four requirements are essential for the validity of a convention:
>
> — consent of the party who binds herself;
>
> — capacity to contract;
>
> — an object which is the matter of the commitment;
>
> — a cause which justifies the commitment.
>
> **Art. 1131:** An obligation without a cause, or based on a false cause, or on an illicit cause, can have no effects.
>
> **Art. 1132:** The convention is valid although its cause is not expressly stated.

Fr. Civ. C. 2016

> **Art. 1112:** [T]he initiative, progress, and termination of pre-contractual negotiations re freely made. They must imperatively meet the requirements of good faith.
>
> > In the event of a fault committed during the negotiations, the damages for the resulting prejudice cannot be intended to compensate for the loss of the advantages expected from the non-concluded contract, nor the loss of the chance to obtain these advantages.

C.C.Q. (Québec)

> **Art. 1410:** The cause of a contract is the reason that determines each of the parties to enter into the contract.
>
> The cause need not be expressed.
>
> **Art. 1411:** A contract whose cause is prohibited by law or contrary to public order is null.

— Common Law —

William Blackstone, *Commentaries: Book II the Rights of Things*

> Having thus shown the general nature of a contract, we are, secondly, to proceed to the *consideration* upon which it is founded; or the reason which moves the party contracting to enter into the contract. "It is an agreement, upon *sufficient consideration*." The civilians hold, that in all contracts, either

express or implied there must be something given in exchange, something that is mutual or reciprocal. This thing, which is the price or motive of the contract, we call the consideration [. . .].

A consideration of some sort or other is so absolutely necessary to the forming of a contract, that a *nudum pactum* or agreement to do or pay any thing on one side, without any compensation on the other, is totally void in law; and a man cannot be compelled to perform.

G.H. Treitel, *The Law of Contract*, Seventh Edition, Stevens & Sons, 1987. (Reproduced with permission of the Licensor through PLSclear.)

In English law, a promise is not, as a general rule, binding as a contract unless it is either made under seal or supported by some "consideration." The purpose of the doctrine of consideration is to put some legal limits on the enforceability of agreements even where they are intended to be legally binding and are not vitiated by some factor such as mistake, misrepresentation, duress, or illegality. [. . . .]

The basic feature of that doctrine is the idea of reciprocity: something of value in the eye of the law" must be given for a promise in order to make it enforceable as a contract. An informal gratuitous promise therefore does not amount to a contract. A person or body to whom a promise of a gift is made from purely charitable or sentimental motives gives nothing for the promise; and the claims of such a promise are obviously less compelling than those of a person who has given (or promised) some return for the promise. [. . . .]

Restatement, 2d of Contracts (1981)

Chapter 4, Formation of Contracts — Consideration

Topic 1. The Requirement of Consideration

§ 71. Requirement of Exchange: Types of Exchange

(1) To constitute consideration, a performance or a return promise must be bargained for.

(2) A performance or return promise is bargained for if it is sought by the promisor in exchange for his promise and is given by the promisee in exchange for that promise.

(3) The performance may consist of (a) an act other than a promise, or (b) a forbearance, or (c) the creation, modification, or destruction of a legal relation.

(4) The performance or return promise may be given to the promisor or to some other person. It may be given by the promisee or by some other person.

§ 73. Performance of Legal Duty

Performance of a legal duty owed to a promisor which is neither doubtful nor the subject of honest dispute is not consideration; but a similar performance is consideration if it differs from what was required by the duty in a way which reflects more than a pretense of bargain.

§ 79. Adequacy of Consideration: Mutuality of Obligation

If the requirement of consideration is met, there is no additional requirement of (a) a gain, advantage, or benefit to the promisor or a loss, disadvantage, or detriment to the promisee; or (b) equivalence in the values exchanged; or (c) "mutuality of obligation." [....]

E. Allan Farnsworth, Contracts (2d ed. 1990)

§ 2.2. The Bargain Test of Consideration. Among the limitations on the enforcement of promises, the most fundamental is the requirement of consideration. [....] By the end of the nineteenth century, at least in the United States, the traditional requirement that the consideration be either a benefit to the promisor or a detriment to the promise had begun to be replaced by a requirement that the consideration be "bargained for." [....]

§ 2.3. What Can Constitute Consideration. Virtually anything that anyone would bargain for in exchange for a promise can be consideration for that promise. The same consideration can support a number of promises.

§ 2.11. Peppercorns and Pretense of Bargain. [....] To be practical, then, we must restate the example in this way: a donor promises to make a gift of a farm to a donee, and, in order to make the promise enforceable, the donee gives a dollar to the donor. Is the donor's promise supported by consideration? There is some authority, including the first Restatement, that it is, at least if the transaction is cast in the form of a bargain. The more modern view, however, mirrored in the Restatement Second, requires an actual bargain, not merely a pretense of bargain, and such extreme disparity in the exchange as here supposed would reveal the purported bargain to be a sham. Under this view the donor's promise is not supported by consideration.

Section VI — Conclusion on Formation of Contracts

Cases

Del Cryer

v.

M & M Manufacturing Company, Inc.

Supreme Court of Louisiana
October 4, 1972
273 So.2d 818

SANDERS, Justice.

[1] This case raises the question of whether a sale of manufacturing rights to a multipurpose heater should be rescinded upon the demand of the purchaser, because of a deficiency in the performance of the manufactured heater. [. . . .]

[2] The facts are largely undisputed. Del Cryer, a Shreveport oil operator, acquired from the inventor the manufacturing rights to the "JET-Glo Multi Purpose Heater," described in a pending patent application. He also acquired a small stock of parts and dies for the heater at a judicial sale. Subsequently, he retained the Greene Research Engineering Company, operated by George J. Greene, Jr., a mechanical engineer, to improve and test the heater for orchard heating purposes. After making improvements and testing, the Greene Research Engineering Company made a written report to Cryer that the maximum burning rate of the heater, using kerosene as fuel, was 275,000 BTUs per hour, suitable for use by outdoor laborers, for preventing fruit and vegetables from freezing, and for protecting newly poured concrete. The report stated that the tests extended over two 24-hour periods.[1]

[3] After receiving the report, Cryer contacted Thayer T. May, president of M & M Manufacturing Company, Inc., concerning the manufacture of the heater. On July 3, 1965, Cryer delivered the model heater and the Greene report to May, suggesting that he satisfy himself about the performance of the heater and determine

---

1. The report recited: 'Tests were performed on two identical, standard production heaters and extended over two 24-hour periods. All tests were performed in an unsheltered area with no provisions made for wind shielding. A standard recommended kerosene fuel (higher heating value of 19,900 Btu/lb.) was used for all tests.'

whether or not he desired to acquire the manufacturing rights.[2] May demonstrated the heater to numerous fruit and vegetable growers to determine its marketability.

[....]

[4] On August 17, 1965, by written contract, M & M Manufacturing Company, Inc., purchased the manufacturing rights to the heater from Cryer. M & M paid Cryer $12,500 in cash and agreed to pay him a royalty of $1.25 for each unit manufactured. In the sale, M & M obligated itself to manufacture a minimum of 5000 units in the first year. The sale contained no express warranty as to the capacity of the heater or its suitability for orchard heating.[3]

[5] M & M manufactured an initial group of some fifty heaters. In testing the fuel system on one of these units, M & M discovered that the heater accumulated soot so badly that in three to five hours it failed to produce sufficient heat to protect vegetation. Ultimately, the heater would go out completely.

[6] M & M then made extensive efforts to correct the soot problem, but failed. Although possessing some utility, the heater fell short of the long-burning feature needed for a superior orchard heater. Thus, considering it unmarketable, M & M abandoned its plan to manufacture the heaters.

[7] At the end of the initial contract year, Cryer brought the present suit for royalties and attorney's fees due him under the contract. M & M reconvened, seeking rescission of the sale on the grounds of error, failure of cause, and redhibitory vice.

[8] After trial on the merits, the district judge found that the heater was unsuitable for orchard heating and so imperfect that it must be supposed that a buyer

---

2. "Q. And you and Mr. May subsequently negotiated verbally and worked out the signed contract which was previously introduced in evidence, is that correct?"
"A. Well, he told me he was very much interested in something, some product, and I told him to take the heater and take the engineer's report and if he found that it was something that he was interested in why I would be happy to make a deal with him and told him the conditions of the deal that I would accept, so he takes the heater and the engineer's report, and then I didn't have any other personal contact with Mr. May then for a couple of weeks."
. . .
"Q. Did you give Mr. May ample opportunity to run any tests that he may have desired prior to the time of the execution of the contract on August 17th, 1965?
"A. Yes, sir. Mr. May had the heater about 30 days prior to the time that we made — that we closed the deal.
"Q. Did you conceal from him any knowledge that you had with reference to the operational effect of the heater?
"A. No, sir, nothing — I didn't conceal anything because I told Mr. May my occupation was an independent oil operator and that I wasn't an engineer but I did have an engineer's report on the heater and he could take it and do anything that he wanted to do with it, satisfy himself, and then if he thought that it was something he was interested in why I would be very happy to get with him and close the deal."
3. The sale, captioned "Sale of Manufacturing Rights," conveyed the manufacturing and distributing rights with "legal warranties," that is, with such warranties as are imposed by law. It also conveyed the stock of parts and dies.

would not have purchased it had he known of the defect. He denied redhibition, however, because M & M could not return the parts and dies delivered in the sale. Under Louisiana Civil Code Article 2543, he reduced the purchase price $6,250.00, the amount of the first year's royalty. On appeal, the Court of Appeal denied the reconventional demand for rescission of the sale and granted judgment in favor of the plaintiff against M & M Manufacturing Company in the sum of $6,250.00, the royalty on the guaranteed minimum of 5000 heaters for the first year, with legal interest from judicial demand until paid, and all costs. It rejected plaintiff's demand for attorney's fees. 253 So.2d 69. On application of M & M Manufacturing Company, Inc., we granted certiorari to review the judgment of the Court of Appeal denying rescission of the sale. 259 La. 1053, 254 So.2d 463 (1971).

[9] Redhibition is the avoidance of a sale because of a vice or defect in the thing sold. LSA-C.C. Art. 2520. It is based upon an implied-in-law warranty that the thing sold is free of hidden defects that render it useless or impair its use to such an extent that it must be supposed that the buyer would not have purchased it, had he known of the vice. LSA-C.C. Arts. 2475, 2476, 2520; 23 Tul.L.Rev. 120.

[10] As correctly noted by the Court of Appeal, the contested contract is a sale of the right to manufacture and distribute a heater built according to a design protected by patent law. The thing sold was an incorporeal right. LSA-C.C. Art. 460; Messersmith v. Messersmith, 229 La. 495, 86 So.2d 169 (1956); Yiannopoulos, Louisiana Civil Law Treatise: Property s 13, pp. 33–34 (1967).

[11] In the sale of an incorporeal right, the implied warranty includes existence of the right at the time of the transfer and peaceable possession of that right. LSA-C.C. Arts. 2501, 2646; Tomlinson v. Thurmon, 189 La. 959, 181 So. 458 (1938). It does not extend to a deficiency in a physical object to which the right may ultimately relate. The thing sold and warranted is the right, not the object. Ratcliff v. McIlhenny, 157 La. 708, 102 So. 878 (1925); 2 Planiol Civil Law Treatise (Translation by Louisiana State Law Institute) No. 1629, p. 904. See also Losecco v. Gregory, 108 La. 648, 32 So. 985 (1901); Succession of Mahoney, 167 La. 255, 119 So. 40 (1928); Benner v. Van Norden, 27 La.Ann. 473 (1875).

[12] We conclude that redhibition is unavailable in the present case because of the absence of warranty extending to the performance of the manufactured heater.

[13] M & M advances two additional reasons for rescinding the sale: error and failure of cause. Although the arguments are variously phrased, the pervasive issue is whether the sale should be rescinded because of error.

[14] As to error, the Louisiana Civil Code provides:

Article 1823:

"Errors may exist as to all the circumstances and facts which relate to a contract, but it is not every error that will invalidate it. To have that effect, the error must be in some point, which was a principal cause for making the contract, and it may be either as to the motive for making the contract, to the person with whom it is made, or to the subject matter of the contract itself."

Article 1825:

"The error in the cause of a contract to have the effect of invalidating it, must be on the principal cause, when there are several; this principal cause is called the Motive, and means that consideration without which the contract would not have been made."

Article 1826:

"No error in the motive can invalidate a contract, unless the other party was apprised that it was the principal cause of the agreement, or unless from the nature of the transaction it must be presumed that he knew it."

[15] In these articles, cause is identified with motive. Litvinoff, Louisiana Civil Law Treatise: Obligations s 290, pp. 522–523 (1969); Smith, A Refresher Course in Cause, 12 La.L.Rev. 2, 15 (1952). Error in the determining motive, or principal cause, of a contract vitiates consent and invalidates the contract. Error as to a subsidiary motive has no effect upon the validity of the contract. Stack v. Irwin, 246 La. 777, 167 So.2d 363 (1964); Carpenter v. Skinner, 224 La. 848, 71 So.2d 133 (1954).

[16] Some motives are readily discernible from the inherent nature of a sale. For example, an immediate end of the buyer is to acquire ownership of the thing sold. That motive characterizes the transaction. Other motives, not discernible from the inherent nature of the sale, rise to the status of principal cause only when the parties contract on that basis. Although the parties need not make the motive an express condition of the contract, it must appear from all the circumstances that the existence of the sale has been subordinated to the reality of the motive. The special motive must have been a constitutive element of the accord of wills. The reality of the motive becomes a tacit condition of the contract. LSA-C.C. Arts. 1825, 1826, 1827; Aubry & Rau, Droit Civil Francais: Obligations (An English Translation by the Louisiana State Law Institute) s 343a, p. 313; 3 Toullier, Droit Civil Francais (6th ed.) Title 3, Art. 1, ss 40–42, pp. 26–28; Litvinoff, Louisiana Civil Law Treatise: Obligations s 220, pp. 394–395 (1969); Smith, A Refresher Course in Cause, 12 La.L.Rev. 2, 10–11 (1952).[4]

[17] In his article on Cause, supra, Dr. J. Denson Smith, an eminent civil law authority, states:

"Considering the nature of the contract, realization of the principal cause or motive is understood to be the basis upon which consent is given and it therefore becomes a tacit condition of the contract. This is because the final and principal motive for assuming an obligation must lie in the obvious

---

4. The condition has also been described as "unvocalized" (8 Tul.L.Rev. 194), "undeveloped" (13 Tul.L.Rev. 363), and "implied" (Litvinoff, Louisiana Civil Law Treatise: Obligations s 212, p. 378 at f.n. 21 (1969).

end being sought, for example, obtaining ownership, or use, or services, or conferring a benefit. If this cause fails, the will is vitiated and the contract falls. At the same time, if the particular motive is not discernible by the nature of the contract it is subsidiary and does not rise to the status of a tacit condition because the other party is not chargeable with knowledge that the contract is conditioned on its realization. To be effective as a condition, the parties must contract on that basis. An example of this may be found in the rule that error as to the value of the thing purchased and sold does not vitiate consent. Although a buyer may not have bought if he had known the true value of the thing, it should be presumed that he is taking his chance — and the seller is in like position — unless the agreement is conditioned on value. All that the seller is required to know is that the buyer wants the thing being bought and sold, or supposedly so; why the buyer may want it, whether because of its supposed value or for any other reason is not the seller's concern if the parties do not contract on such basis. As the French writers put it, error will serve to invalidate consent only when it enters the contractual field. It does so tacitly if it relates to the principal cause, that is, the final and determining motive." (Footnotes omitted).

[18] The treatise of Aubry & Rau, Droit Civil Francais, supra, sets forth the principle as follows:

"... (T)he error relative to the occasional motives or to the circumstances which may have induced one or both of the parties to contract, is a cause of nullity only where, according to the common intention of the parties, the reality of these motifs constitutes a condition to which they intended to subordinate the formation or the performance of the agreement." (Footnote omitted).

[19] Finally, Toullier in Droit Civil Francais, supra, s 42, p. 28, states:

"It is by the manner in which the act is expressed, by the nature of the contract, by the object of the promise, finally by the circumstances, that one may determine what the determining motive has been, and whether the consent given has been subordinated to or conditioned on the reality of this motive as an implicit condition."

[20] In the present case, the transfer of ownership was effective. The buyer became the owner of the right to manufacture and distribute. The right conveyed is without defect. Hence, the immediate end that characterizes a sale generally was achieved.

[21] M & M asserts, however, that its motive was to secure the manufacturing rights to a long-burning, high-output heater to sell to orchardists for freeze protection. It postulates that this motive was the principal cause of the contract, and the heater's failure to fulfill these requirements is an invalidating error. Finally, conceding the seller's good faith, it asserts that the error was induced by the seller's misrepresentation that the heater possessed the essential features to protect orchards from freezing.

[22] Innocent misrepresentations may induce error when a purchaser justifiably relies upon them. When an error results from such non-fraudulent misrepresentations, the error invalidates the contract only if it bears upon the principal cause of the contract. LSA-C.C. Arts. 1823, 1825, 1845, 1847(2), 2529; Ganucheau v. Greff, La.App., 181 So.2d 854 (1966); Kardis v. Barrere, 17 La.App. 433, 136 So. 135 (1931); 12 La.L.Rev. 509.[6]

[23] Cryer was an oil operator, with no special competence in heat engineering. Both lower courts found that he was in good faith and made no misrepresentations to the buyer.[7] We adopt this factual finding.

[24] It is true that he transmitted a copy of the engineering report to the buyer when he delivered the model heater for testing. Under the circumstances, however, the transmission of the report cannot be considered as a representation of the seller that the heater met all the performance requirements of marketable orchard heater. On the contrary, the record reflects that the seller intended that the manufacturer itself test the heater and rely upon its own skill and judgment as to the heater's performance. He gave the company ample opportunity to conduct its investigation by supplying it with a working model more than a month before the sale. Apparently, the manufacturer's tests consisted only of burning the heater for short periods for demonstration purposes. Under no sound legal theory, however, is the inadequacy of these tests chargeable to the seller. See Henderson v. United States Sheet & Window Glass Co., 168 La. 66, 121 So. 576 (1929); Rocchi v. Schwabacher & Hirsch, 33 La.App. 1364 (1881).

[25] The manufacturer was aware that the heater was newly developed. The purchase of manufacturing rights to it was speculative in some degree. One who expresses an unqualified will tp [*sic*] purchase such right should be bound accordingly such rights should be bound accordingly that the purchaser's will is conditional. No basis for this knowledge appears in the record. Rather, it appears that, following the manufacturer's investigation and exercise of judgment, the seller reasonably contemplated an unconditional transaction. We find nothing in the contract or the circumstances under which it was formed to raise manufacturer's expectations for the heater to be contractual level of principal cause.

[26] In its well-written brief, the defendant relies upon several decisions of this Court dealing with error in contracts, including Stack v. Irwin, 246 La. 777, 167 So.2d 363 (1964); Carpenter v. Skinner, 224 La. 848, 71 So.2d 133 (1954); Overby v. Beach, 220 La. 77, 55 So.2d 873 (1951); and Pan American Production Co. v. Robichaux, 200 La. 666, 8 So.2d 635 (1942). We find these cases to be factually and legally inapposite.

---

6. In contrast, when error is induced by fraud, it need relate only to a "material part of the contract." LSA-C.C. Art. 1847(2); 12 La.L.Rev. 509; 33 Tul.L.Rev. 270.

7. On original hearing, the Court of Appeal stated: "In this case there was no misrepresentation present." This finding remained mained undisturbed on rehearing.

[27] We conclude, as did the Court of Appeal, that the sale is valid and that plaintiff's demand should be sustained.

[28] For the reasons assigned, the judgment of the Court of Appeal is affirmed at defendant's costs.

[29] HAMLIN, J., dissents in part with written reasons.

[30] SUMMERS, J., dissents.

[31] TATE, J., dissents in part and assigns written reasons.

HAMLIN, Justice (dissenting in part).

[. . . .]

[32] In my opinion, under the facts and circumstances of this case, justice does not demand the rescission of the instant contract and the return to M & M of the $12,500.00 it paid Del Cryer. Likewise, I do not believe that M & M is entitled to the return from Del Cryer of expenses it incurred after the negotiation of the instant contract on August 17, 1965. As I analyze the record, M & M was not as vigilant as it should have been. Equity aids the vigilant, not those who slumber on their rights. 30A C.J.S. Equity s 113, p. 32.

[33] Article 1883 of the Civil Code recites that every contract has for its object something which one or both of the parties oblige themselves to give, or to do, or not to do. Herein, M & M obligated itself to manufacture heaters and pay royalties. The contract states, "As further consideration the said M & M Manufacturing Company, Inc., is to pay unto the said Del Cryer a royalty upon each and every unit manufactured or caused to be manufactured by the said M & M Manufacturing Company, Inc., the sum of $1.25 per unit." It further recites that M & M binds itself to manufacture and produce a minimum of 5,000 units during the first year of production.

[34] Article 1891 of the Civil Code recites: "The object of a contract must be possible, by which is meant physically or morally possible. The possibility must be determined, not by the means or ability of the party to fulfill his agreement, but by the nature of the thing which forms the object of it." Herein, the object of the instant contract became physically impossible. M & M could not manufacture the 5,000 units. Under the articles of the Civil Code, reason dictates and justice demands that M & M not be assessed for the royalties prayed for by Del Cryer. I conclude that Del Cryer is not entitled to his demands.

[35] Each case has a separate life of its own. The facts and circumstances of one case are not the facts and circumstances of another; each case must be decided on its own particular facts. Cf. 30 C.J.S. Equity s 89, p. 976. A court of equity is a court of conscience; it seeks to do justice and equity between all parties; it seeks to strike a balance of convenience as between litigants; and looks at the whole situation. It does not act unless justice and good conscience demand that relief should be granted, and acts only in accordance with conscience and good faith. 30 C.J.A. Equity s 89, pp. 978–979.

[36] There is no case in the annals of Louisiana jurisprudence the facts of which are similar to those of the instant case. While both sides have cited numerous authorities, it is my view that they are not decisive of the instant case. I therefore look to Article 21 of the Revised Civil Code, the equity article in Louisiana. In addition to applying written law and jurisprudence to this matter, I would likewise apply equity.

[37] My reasons are not the same as the trial court's reasons for its judgment; however, I reach the same conclusion as the trial judge.

[38] I respectfully dissent in part.

TATE, Justice (dissenting in part).

[39] The writer agrees with most of the analysis of the scholarly majority opinion. My main disagreement with the majority is in its implied holding that the ability to manufacture a Workable orchard heater was not the principal cause or motive of the Obligation to pay royalty. I find the royalty agreement to have a separate and distinct principal cause from the sales agreement.

[40] The majority analyzed the contract as being solely a sale. Under my analysis, the contract between the seller Cryer and the buyer-manufacturer ("M&M") included at least two separate obligations: (a) the sale by Cryer to M&M for $12,500 of manufacturing rights and parts on hand pertaining to an orchard-heater; and (b) the agreement to pay $1.25 per unit royalty for each unit manufactured and to manufacture or produce at least five thousand units during the first year of production.

[41] This contract thus produced a conjunctive obligation as defined by Civil Code Article 2063, with several connected objects contained in a single writing. As stated by the Article, "This contract creates as many different obligations as there are different objects." See also Civil Law Translations, Aubry & Rau, Obligations, Section 300 (LSLI translation, 1965). In my view, the "principal cause or Motive." Articles 1824, 1825,[1] is different as to obligations (a) and (b), as set forth above.

[42] As to (a), the sale of the manufacturing rights, I agree with the majority's determination that it should not be rescinded because of any error as to principal cause. Both parties realized that this portion of the transaction was in some respects speculative and that the refined development necessary for future exploitation depended to some extent upon the manufacturer's skill. The manufacturer here took his chances that he would not be able to perfect a workable product.

[43] The sale of the right to manufacture the orchard-heater was therefore unconditional, with the buyer-manufacturer bound for the purchase price despite his inability, despite due diligence, to develop the orchard-heater into a merchantable product. The seller Cryer is thus entitled to retain the $12,500 purchase price, and

---

1. Civil Code Article 1825: "The error in the cause of a contract to have the effect of invalidating it, must be on the principal cause, when there are several; this principal cause is called the Motive, and means that consideration without which the contract would not have been made."

the buyer M&M is not entitled to recoup his expenses incurred in attempting to perfect the product.

[44] However, as to (b) — the obligation to pay royalties of $1.25 per unit and to manufacture 5000 units during the first year of production — , I believe there was an independent principal cause or Motive: the underlying assumption that, in fact, the manufacturer could perfect a merchantable unit, using due diligence (as, in fact, he could not).

[45] Although there was no misrepresentation by the buyer, the engineering report furnished by him indicated that the orchard-heater was a workable product. Certainly, the seller believed that this was so.

[46] In agreeing to manufacture 5000 units the first year, the principal cause or motive must have included the mutual belief that the manufacturer could produce a unit that would work and be merchantable. The parties, could not have contemplated, in my opinion, that the buyer M&M would have to produce 5000 unworkable units or to pay royalty for the manufacture of an unusable product.

[47] Therefore, I am unable to agree that the buyer unconditionally agreed to pay a royalty of $1.25 for 5000 units in the first year of production, whether or not it was possible to manufacture a merchantable orchard heater.

[48] Under the agreement, the buyer paid $12,500 cash for the manufacturing rights and further agreed to pay "a royalty upon each and every unit manufactured (in) . . . the sum of $1.25 per unit." The agreement concluded: "It is further agreed and stipulated between the parties that the said M&M Manufacturing Company, Inc., (the buyer) shall use due diligence and good business practices in expanding the manufacture and distribution of said heater, and the said M&M Manufacturing Company, Inc., binds itself to manufacture and produce a minimum of 5000 units during the first year of production."

[49] While the buyer unconditionally agreed (a) to pay $1.25 for each unit manufactured, (b) to use due diligence in expanding the manufacture and distribution, and (c) to manufacture and produce a minimum of 5000 units during the first year of production, it seems to me that the understood principal cause or Motive for the obligation to pay royalty was that, using due diligence, it would be possible for the buyer-manufacturer to produce a merchantable orchard-heater. If it was able to perfect the orchard-heater, then the manufacturer was unconditionally bound to produce the minimum 5000 units during the first year and to pay the royalty of $1.25 per unit.

[50] However, I am unable, in the absence of an express agreement to such effect, to hold as a matter of law that the motive or principal cause for an agreement to pay royalty for each unit manufactured does not include the ability of the manufacturer, using due diligence, to manufacture a workable and merchantable product. Since despite due diligence the manufacturer in the present case was unable to do so, this was an error as to a principal cause which invalidates the obligation to manufacture 5000 units during the first year and to pay royalties upon them. Civil Code Articles 1823, 1825.

[51] Applicable here is Civil Code Article 1827: ". . . wherever the motive is apparent, although not made an express condition, if the error bears on the motive, the contract is void. A promise to give a certain sum to bear the expenses of a marriage, which the party supposes to have taken place, is not obligatory, if there be no marriage."

[52] Although I differ with the majority opinion in this respect, I must admit the force of its reasoning that, since the principal cause for the Sale agreement did not include the belief that in fact a workable orchard-heater could be manufactured, likewise the validity of the royalty agreement was not dependent upon such as a principal cause. Nevertheless, because of the difference between the obligations included in the sale of the right to manufacture the product, if perfectable, and the obligation to manufacture it and to pay royalty upon units manufactured (which must assume that the product was perfectable), I personally find no intellectual incongruity in an analysis contrary to the majority's.

[53] In short, although there was an unconditional obligation to pay the purchase price for the right to manufacture the orchard-heater and to use due diligence in developing and merchandising same, nevertheless the conjunctive obligation to manufacture 5000 units and to pay royalty upon these units manufactured during the year was conditioned upon the existence (or not) of the principal cause of That obligation — that the manufacturer, using due diligence, Could produce a workable and merchantable product. Since this principal cause is shown not to exist, the royalty obligation should be held invalid because of error as to it.

[54] I therefore respectfully dissent.

On Rehearing

PER CURIAM.

[55]Upon reconsideration of the issues, a majority of this court reaches the same conclusion as reached on our first hearing. We therefore adopt all the factual and legal conclusions of our original opinion and reinstate it and our original decree.

[56]Original opinion and decree reinstated.

[57]HAMLIN, C.J., dissents, adhering to the views expressed in his dissent to original opinion.

[58]TATE, J., dissents and assigns additional written reasons.

[59]BARHAM, J., dissents for reasons assigned by TATE, J.

TATE, Justice (dissenting).

[60]The writer dissents in part and concurs in part. I adhere fully to the findings, legal analysis and statements of law of our original opinion in refusing to rescind the sale and in dismissing the reconventional demand praying for recission. I have reservations (as expressed in my dissent to the original opinion) to the majority holding that the ancillary minimum royalty agreement contained in the sales contract should not be rescinded on grounds of error in the Cause. Nevertheless, I find

it unnecessary to rest my present dissent upon a contrary view: because, for reasons to be stated, such minimum royalty agreement is unenforceable because its Performance (unlike the validity of the sale itself) depended upon an implied condition which contemplated that it was possible to develop a merchantable heater.

[61]The pertinent clauses of the "Sale of Manufacturing Rights" agreement executed between the parties are set forth in the footnote below.[1] As there set forth, for the purchase of the manufacturing rights, the manufacturer-buyer M & M unconditionally agreed to pay the seller Cryer the sum of $12,500 (Clause a) plus royalty of $1.25 for each unit manufacturer (Clause b). Additionally, by Clause c M & M agreed to use due diligence in expanding the manufacture and distribution of the heater and—in order to effectuate This ancillary agreement of Clause c, it is important to note—bound itself to manufacture a minimum of 5000 units during the first year of production.

[62]This sales agreement thus produced conjunctive obligations as defined by Civil Code Article 2063, with several connected objects contained in a single writing. As stated by the Article, "This contract creates as many different obligations as there are different objects." See also Civil Law Translations, Aubry & Rau, Obligations, Section 300 (LSLI translation, 1965). The minimum royalty agreement (Clause c) constituted an obligation separable in performance and enforceability from obligations of the buyer represented by Clauses a and b.

[63]I disagree with the majority view that the $6,250 minimum royalties guaranteed by Clause c should be considered as part of the price to be paid by the buyer—as if the sales price were $12,500 plus $6,250 minimum royalties. Instead, in my view, the agreement to pay such minimum royalties was, by terms of the contract, intended as a means of enforcing the ancillary agreement of the contract that the buyer use "due diligence and good business practices in expanding the manufacture and distribution of the heater." Clause c.

[64]The thrust of Clause c is that the buyer must manufacture and market the heater as quickly as possible, consistent with good business practices (but to produce at least 500 units the first year). However, the ability to manufacture a merchantable product was assumed to have existed. The agreement cannot have intended that the buyer manufacture at least 5000 heaters, whether or not it was possible to develop a heater that was economically competitive with other heaters on the market.

---

1. (a) "* * * The consideration for this sale is as follows: $12,500.00 cash paid to the said Del Cryer this date, who acknowledges the receipt thereof and grants acquittance and discharge therefor.
(b) As further consideration the said M & M Manufacturing Company, Inc., is to pay unto the said Del Cryer a. royalty upon each and every unit manufactured or caused to be manufactured by the said M & M Manufacturing Company, Inc., the sum of $1.25 per unit. * * *
(c) It is further agreed and stipulated between the parties that the said M & M Manufacturing Company, Inc., shall use due diligence and good business practices in expanding the manufacture and distribution of said heater, and the said M & M Manufacturing Company, Inc., binds itself to manufacture and produce a minimum of 5000 units during the first year of production. * * *"

[65]I should note that the record reflects that the buyer M & M used due diligence and did all possible to develop a heater as described in the patent and in the sale of manufacturing right to it. Nevertheless, despite these efforts, it proved impossible to develop a merchantable heater — one that was economically competitive with pre-existing products designed to fill the same function as the present heater.

[66]The obligation to pay minimum royalties depended upon, as an implied condition, an uncertain event: the ability to develop a merchantable heater. This condition is implied from the nature of the contract and from the presumed intent of the parties. Civil Code Article 2026.[2] (This, incidentally, is undoubtedly also an implied condition for the basis obligation of the contract to pay $1.25 royalty for each unit produced (Clause b); no obligation to pay royalties under this clause existed unless, in fact, the manufacture of heaters was commercially possible.)

[67]The minimum royalty agreement is therefore what is known in our law as a conditional obligation — one which depended on an uncertain event, namely, the ability to manufacture a merchantable heater. Article 2021.[3] The obligation to pay the minimum royalties never came into effect because the event upon which it depended never happened: by the exercise of all reasonable efforts, it was impossible for the obligor to develop to manufacture. economically feasible to manufacture. [*sic*]

[68]Civil Code Article 1891 provides: "The object of a contract must be possible, by which is meant physically or morally possible. The possibility must be determined, not by the means or ability of the party to fulfill his agreement, but by the nature of the thing which forms the object of it." See Planiol, Civil Law Treatise, Volume 2, Sections 1006, 1007 (LSLI translation, 1959).

[69]Thus, under traditional civilian principles, the unenforceability of the minimum royalty agreement can be ascribed not only to its dependence upon a suspensive condition which never came to happen, but also as resulting from the failure due

---

2. Article 2026: "Conditions are either express or implied. They are express, when they appear in the contract; they are implied, whenever they result from the operation of law, from the nature of the contract, or from the presumed intent of the parties."

3. Article 2021: "Conditional obligations are such as are made to depend on an uncertain event. If the obligation is not to take effect until the event happen, it is a suspensive condition; if the obligation takes effect immediately, but is liable to be defeated when the event happens, it is then a resolutory condition." Compare with Article 2020: "Simple obligations are such as are not dependent for their execution on any event provided for by the parties, and which are not agreed to become void, on the happening of any such event." See also Article 2043: "The obligation contracted on a suspensive condition, is that which depends, either on a future and uncertain event, or on an event which has actually taken place, without its being yet known to the parties. In the former case, the obligation cannot be executed till after the event; in the latter, the obligation has its effect from the day on which it was contracted. but it can not be enforced until the event be known." And see also Article 2045: "The dissolving condition is that which, when accomplished, operates the revocation of the obligation, placing matters in the same state as though the obligation had not existed. It does not suspend the execution of the obligation; it only obliges the creditor to restore what he has received, in case the event provided for in the condition takes place."

to impossibility of the initial responsibility for performance. The Roman maxim, "Impossibilium nulla obligatio est (There is no obligation to do impossible things)", Broom's Legal Maxims 248 (1974), expresses the principle which Gaius stated as "If we stipulate for something to be given to us, which is of such a nature that this cannot be done, it is evident that such a stipulation is void by natural law * * *." Gaius, Digest 44.7.1.9 (Scott translation, 1932). See also 2 Ripert & Boulanger, Traite de Droit Civil 182 (1952). Some reliance might also be placed upon the modern civilian *Théorie de l'imprévision* the power of the courts to hold negated an obligation when change of circumstance or impossibility voids the presuppositions or reasonable expectations of the parties, although not expressed, which formed an underlying basis for the agreement. Cf., Litvinoff, 1 Obligations, Sections 250, 297 (p. 538) (LISI Civil Law Treatise, V 1. 6, 1969).[4]

[70]In summary, the consideration for the sale itself contemplated that the development of a workable heater was somewhat speculative; the sale therefore is not invalidated by the impossibility to do so, since there was no error in the cause of the sale. On the other hand, the ancillary agreement within the sale — to use due diligence in producing and marketing the product and to produce and pay royalties upon at least 5000 units the first year — was entered into with the expectation that a merchantable heater Could be developed; when this event proved impossible of fulfillment, the obligation to pay the minimum royalties upon 5000 units the first year — which depended upon this event which did not occur — never came into existence.

[71]I agree with the district court conclusion that the plaintiff's demand for $6,250 minimum royalties should be dismissed.

[72]For these reasons, I respectfully dissent from the award to Cryer of $6,250 minimum royalties, although I concur with the dismissal of M &M's reconventional demand seeking recovery of the $12,500 price paid for the manufacturing rights.

Note

In paragraph 69, Justice Tate brings into his analysis the "*théorie de l'imprévision*" which he finds, indirectly, in French law. There would be too much to explain in a few lines about this theory. Suffice it to say that this *théorie de l'imprévision* was

---

4. Also, in modern French law, a contract such as the present is termed a Contrat de licence. 2 Roubier, Le Droit de la propriete industrielle 260 (1954); Allart, Traite the orique et pratique des brevet d'invention 217 (3rd ed. 1911). According to French jurisprudence the licensor (brevete) warrants to the licensee (licencie): (a) the existence of the patent, and (b) the industrial feasibility, that is, that the thing can be manufactured. But the Brevete does not warrant the commercial success. This means that, if the patent is real and it is possible to manufacture the thing, the commercial failure does not entitle the Licencie to resolution of the Contrat de licence. However, the Licencie who does not exploit the patent because it is a commercial failure does not breach the contract and is regarded as having done as much as he could under the contract. Paris. Feb. 4, 1958, Ann.Prop .ind.1959, 224; Trib.gr.inst.Seine, Feb. 9, 1963, Ann.prop.ind.1963, 385, both cited in Burst, Brevete et Licencie, leur rapports juridiques dans le contrat de licence 112–113 (1970).

created by the French administrative courts (*Conseil d'Etat*) to provide some protection to the State and its Agencies against financial disaster following some unforeseeable event, such as a war. This theory created by the administrative courts has never been used by the private-commercial law courts under the overall jurisdiction of the *Cour de Cassation*.

This theory found its way into the revised obligations provisions of the French Civil Code in 2016. *See* Fr.Civ.C. Art. 1195: "If a change in circumstances unforeseeable at the time of the conclusion of the contract makes performance excessively onerous for a party who had not agreed to assume the risk, the latter may request a renegotiation of the contract from its co-contracting party. That party continues to perform its obligations during the renegotiation. In the event of refusal or failure of the renegotiation, the parties may agree to the termination of the contract, on the date and under the conditions that they determine, or request by mutual agreement the judge to proceed with its adaptation. Failing agreement within a reasonable time, the judge may, at the request of the party, revise the contract or terminate it, on the date and under the conditions he sets."

Questions

1. Paragraph 1: The Court opens its opinion with the statement that "this case raises the question of whether a sale of manufacturing rights to a multipurpose heater. . . ." What kind of contract is a contract of sale? What kind of obligation does a contract of sale impose on the seller? In this particular sale, what kind of object is the Court saying is the object of the sale? If a sale is a contract of the kind you have identified, does that contract create one obligation only or two obligations? In the latter case, what kind of second obligation has been created? Since that obligation must have an object (to give something, to do something or not to do something), what is the object of this second obligation?

2. Paragraph 3: Can you more definitely identify the object of Cryer's offer to Thayer T. May? How would you qualify or describe Cryer's behavior against the background of Louisiana Civil Code article 1759? How many obligations, if more than one, did M & M owe to Cryer? If one, what kind is it? If more than one, are they somehow connected?

3. Paragraph 4: Is there one price or two or more prices for M & M to pay? How would you describe M & M's obligation to pay the price or prices: divisible or indivisible? Conjunctive or alternative?

4. Paragraphs 5–7: When M & M abandons its plan to manufacture the heaters, is it because M & M believes that the object of its obligation is to manufacture "workable and marketable heaters"? Was that object the object they bought from Cryer? What kind of error and by whom is M & M talking about? About what cause is M & M talking about?

5. Paragraph 12: According to the majority, what is or are the object(s) sold by Cryer to M & M? Do you see any good or important reason(s) in properly

identifying the object of an obligation as the Supreme Court did here? Do you agree with the Court's conclusion?

6. Paragraphs 20–21: If error there is, for that error to be a ground for nullity of a contract it must bear on the cause of the contract. Which cause did the Court identify as being the principal cause of the contract?

7. Paragraphs 49–50: Is Justice Tate alluding to the manufacture of a future object or "future thing"? If that is the case, isn't Justice Tate saying that M & M must both pay "a price or royalty per unit" and "manufacture the object"? But isn't the object bought for a price by a buyer, M & M in this case, to be sold and delivered by a seller, someone other than M & M? Isn't there something in these statements that does not fit with the law of the Louisiana Civil Code?

Law Enforcement District of Jefferson Parish
v.
Mapp Construction, LLC, et al

Court of Appeal of Louisiana
Fifth Circuit
May 29, 2020
296 So.3d 1260

GRAVOIS, J.

[. . . .]

[1] [F]or the following reasons, we find no error in the trial court's legal conclusion that the contract between Horne and Centria was a construction contract, i.e., a contract "to build" rather than a contract "of sale."

[. . . .]

Chapter 3

Effects of Conventional Obligations

Louisiana Sources of Law

Louisiana Civil Code

General Effects

Art. 1983. Law for the parties; performance in good faith.

Contracts have the effect of law for the parties and may be dissolved only through the consent of the parties or on grounds provided by law. Contracts must be performed in good faith. (Acts 1984, No. 331, §1, eff. Jan. 1, 1985.)

Art. 1984. Rights and obligations will pass to successors.

Rights and obligations arising from a contract are heritable and assignable unless the law, the terms of the contract or its nature preclude such effects. (Acts 1984, No. 331, §1, eff. Jan. 1, 1985.)

Art. 1985. Effects for third parties.

Contracts may produce effects for third parties only when provided by law. (Acts 1984, No. 331, §1, eff. Jan. 1, 1985.)

Simulation[1]

Art. 2025. Definition; simulation and counterletter.

A contract is a simulation when, by mutual agreement, it does not express the true intent of the parties.

If the true intent of the parties is expressed in a separate writing, that writing is a counterletter. (Acts 1984, No. 331, §1, eff. Jan. 1, 1985.)

Art. 2026. Absolute simulation.

A simulation is absolute when the parties intend that their contract shall produce no effects between them. That simulation, therefore, can have no effects between the parties. (Acts 1984, No. 331, §1, eff. Jan. 1, 1985.)

---

1. This topic is covered in greater length under Section IV: What Contracts Shall Be Avoided By Persons Not Parties to Them.

Art. 2027. Relative simulation.

A simulation is relative when the parties intend that their contract shall produce effects between them though different from those recited in their contract. A relative simulation produces between the parties the effects they intended if all requirements for those effects have been met. (Acts 1984, No. 331, §1, eff. Jan. 1, 1985.)

Art. 2028. Effects as to third persons. [*Amended in 2012*]

Any simulation, either absolute or relative, may have effects as to third persons.

Counterletters can have no effects against third persons in good faith. Nevertheless, if the counterletter involves immovable property, the principles of recordation apply with respect to third persons. (Acts 1984, No. 331, §1, eff. Jan. 1, 1985; Acts 2012, No. 277, §1.)

Doctrine

Louisiana Law of Conventional Obligations, A Précis
Sections 8.1.1 to 8.1.2

[A]ll contracts, regardless of their specific nature (unilateral or bilateral, onerous or gratuitous, for example), are subject to the control of two fundamental principles which are laid down in LSA-C.C. **Art. 1983: "Contracts have the effect of law for the parties and may be dissolved only through the consent of the parties or on grounds provided by law. Contracts must be performed in good faith."** These two principles are, first, the 'effect of law' of any contract and, second, the 'performance in good faith' of the obligations created by the contract.

The second set of effects triggered by a contract will depend on the kind or kinds of obligations which bind the parties. These obligations may bind one or both parties to **"render a performance . . . [which] . . . may consist of giving, doing, or not doing something."** Art. 1756. This second set of effects of a contract will be determined, therefore, by the 'giving' something, the 'doing' something or the 'not doing' something. [. . . .]

First, only the parties themselves are bound by their contract; their contract is their "law." A contract, being the *expression of the wills* of two parties, is as binding between them as "legislation," which is itself the *"expression of the legislative will,"* is binding on and between the citizens. [. . . .]

Second, [. . .] it is easy to understand why **Art. 1985** states that **"Contracts may produce effects for third parties only when provided by law."** In other words, a contract between parties A and B cannot have effects *"against"* a third person C who is not a "party" to that contract. [. . . .]

Third parties, heirs in particular, can be brought into the contract between A and B and incur obligations if they agree and if the obligations are transferable [. . . .]

Third, a corollary of the principle that a contract is the law of the parties is stated in **Art. 1983** in these words: **"Contracts . . . may be dissolved only through the consent of the parties . . . or on grounds provided by law."** [. . . .]

[I]f one party fails to perform her obligations in violation of either the trust placed in her by the other party or the duty of good faith in the performance of obligations, then the "aggrieved" party **"has a right to the judicial dissolution of the contract or, according to the circumstances, to regard the contract as dissolved. . . ."** Art. 2013 (1) [. . .].

Parties to a contract can, for lawful reasons, hide their true intent in a hidden contract, called **counterletter** because the letter and the intent of that hidden contract go against or counter to the intent of the open contract which is called a simulated contract. LSA-C.C. **Art. 2025** states that **"A contract is a simulation when, by mutual agreement, it does not express the true intent of the parties. If the true intent of the parties is expressed in a separate writing, that writing is a counterletter."**

The existence of such an Article in the civil Code emphasizes the freedom to enter into any lawful contract and the role given to the intent or will of parties to a contract. They are free, within the boundaries of the law, to contract as they wish. [. . . .]

"A simulation is absolute when the parties intend that their contract shall produce no effects between them. That simulation, therefore, can have no effects between the parties." Art. 2026. [. . . .]

"A simulation is relative when the parties intend that their contract shall produce effects between them though different from those recited in their contract. A relative simulation produces between the parties the effects they intended if all requirements for those effects have not been met." Art. 2027. [. . . .]

Art. 1983 states, in part, that **"contracts must be performed in good faith."** This Article is to the Effects of Contracts or Conventional Obligations what Art. 1759 is to the whole subject matter of Obligations. [. . . .]

It is the embodiment of the general duty of honest and fair behavior.

Comparative Law Perspective

Alain Levasseur, *Comparative Law of Contracts*
at 99–111 (2008)

Good Faith

We find in the Institutes that "the precepts of the law are, to live honestly, to hurt no one, to give every one his due". [The Institutes of Justinian, Title I, D.1. T.1 §1 and §3]. [. . . .]

Such, among others are these principles: that we should live honestly, should hurt nobody, and should render to every one his due; to which three general principles Justinian has reduced the whole doctrine of law" [W. Blackstone, Commentaries on the Laws of England in Four Books, Introduction]. [. . . .]

[T]he common law and the civil law have, in the field of contract (in civil law) or contracts (in common law), somewhat different approaches to those precepts of the law as Justinian and, centuries later, Blackstone expressed them. At civil law, the concept of "good faith" has played, for centuries, and still play, today, a major role in the *theory* of the law of contract. Most civil law systems, because of their inherent ability at elaborating theories, are referring to this single and comprehensive concept of "good faith" to cover, but not to its full civil law extent, a variety of concepts used by the common law in different contexts. Despite their variety, such concepts have nevertheless a common foundation which is to bring some 'fairness', 'equity', 'balance' to contractual transactions. [. . . .]

— Civil Law —

See La. Civ. C. articles: 1759, 1770, 1975, 1983, 2028, 2035.

Fr. Civ. C. 1804 (before the revision of 2016–2017)

> **Article 1134:** Conventions legally entered into have the effect of law for the parties.
>
> They may be revoked only by their mutual consent or on grounds provided by legislation.
>
> They must be performed in good faith.
>
> **Article 1135:** Conventions are binding not only as to what they expressly state, but also as to all that equity, usage or statute relate to an obligation according to its nature.

C.C.Q. (Québec)

> **Article 1375:** The parties shall conduct themselves in good faith both at the time the obligation is created and at the time it is performed or extinguished.
>
> **Article 1397:** A contract made in violation of a promise to contract may be set up against the beneficiary of the promise, but without affecting his

remedy for damages against the promisor and the person having contracted in bad faith with the promisor.

The same rule applies to a contract made in violation of a first refusal agreement.

Article 1426: In interpreting a contract, the nature of the contract, the circumstances in which it was formed, the interpretation which has already been given to it by the parties or which it may have received, and usage, are all taken into account.

Article 1434: A contract validly formed binds the parties who have entered into it not only as to what they have expressed in it but also as to what is incident to it according to its nature and in conformity with usage, equity or law.

Article 1452: Third persons in good faith may, according to their interest, avail themselves of the apparent contract or the counter letter; however, where conflicts of interest arise between them, preference is given to the person who avails himself of the apparent contract.

Planiol & Ripert, *Obligations*, vol. 6, LGDJ, 1952.

§ **379 quater. Good faith.** Conventions must be performed in good faith, states Article 1134. Inherited from Roman law wherein, besides the other meanings it still has today, good faith had a precise meaning only in the actions in good faith as opposed to actions based on law in the narrow sense of the word, today the concept of good faith in Article 1134 has only a more ambiguous scope of application. It means that any contracting party must act as an honest person in whatever relates to the performance of the contract. Not to act as an honest person amounts to being at fault. [....] In any case, it is useful to resort to an expression to refer to a breach of the duty of honesty which arises from the fact that one has bound himself by a contract.

Malaurie, Aynès et Stoffel-Munck, *Les Obligations*, Defrénois 2003.

764. An expanding principle. [....] Good faith, in the execution as well as in the formation of a contract, amounts to each party not betraying the confidence created by the willingness to enter into a contract; such an expectation is at the heart of the contract particularly when the contractual relationship is to last over a period of time. It is the embodiment of the general duty of honest and fair behavior, which does exist in many other branches of the law: criminal and civil procedure, [...] competition [...]; the opposite of fairness and honesty is duplicity [...] which undermines the long term expectations [...]. Good faith is the mere extension of the binding force of a contract, rather than a limitation imposed on the creditor; the latter is not required to waive his right or interest in the name of some vague juridical solidarity but, instead, to give the contract its full force to an extent compatible with his own personal interest. [....]

— Common Law —

Roger Brownsword, *Contract Law: Themes for the Twenty-First Century* (Butterworths 2000)

1.87 [. . .] [T]he case against the adoption of a general principle of good faith is that English contract law is premised on adversarial self-interested dealing (rather than other — regarding good faith dealing); that good faith is a vague idea, threatening to import an uncertain discretion into English law; that the implementation of a good faith doctrine would call for difficult inquiries into contracting parties' reasons in particular cases; that good faith represents a challenge to the autonomy of contracting parties; and, that a general doctrine cannot be appropriate when contracting contexts vary so much — in particular, harking back to the first objection, a general doctrine of good faith would make little sense in those contracting contexts in which the participants regulate their dealings in a way that openly tolerates opportunism.

1.89 The paradigm of neutrality holds: (i) that there is a strict equivalence between a general doctrine of good faith and the piecemeal provisions of English law that regulate fair dealing (we can call this 'the equivalence thesis'); and (ii) that it makes no difference whether English law operates with a general doctrine or with piecemeal provisions (we can call this 'the indifference thesis').

Restatement, 2d of Contracts (1981)

§ 205. Duty of Good Faith and Fair Dealing

Every contract imposes upon each party a duty of good faith and fair dealing in its performance and its enforcement.

Comment: *a. Meaning of "good faith."* [. . . .] The phrase "good faith" is used in a variety of contexts, and its meaning varies somewhat with the context. Good faith performance or enforcement of a contract emphasizes faithfulness to an agreed common purpose and consistency with the justified expectations of the other party; it excludes a variety of types of conduct characterized as involving "bad faith" because they violate community standards of decency, fairness or reasonableness. [. . . .]

c. Good faith in negotiation

Particular forms of bad faith in bargaining are the subjects of rules as to capacity to contract, mutual assent and consideration and of rules as to invalidating causes such as fraud and duress.

UCC

§ 1-201. General Definitions.

(20) "Good faith," except as otherwise provided in Article 5, means honesty in fact and the observance of reasonable commercial standards of fair dealing.

§1-304. Obligation of Good Faith.

Every contract or duty within [the Uniform Commercial Code] imposes an obligation of good faith in its performance and enforcement.

POSNER, Circuit Judge, 7th Circuit, United States Court of Appeals.

[....] The duty of honesty, of good faith even expansively conceived, is not a duty of candor [...]. Before the contract is signed, the parties confront each other with a natural wariness. Neither expects the other to be particularly forthcoming, and therefore there is no deception when one is not. Afterwards the situation is different. The parties are now in a cooperative relationship the costs of which will be considerably reduced by a measure of trust. So each lowers his guard a bit, and now silence is more apt to be deceptive. [....] The concept of duty of good faith like the concept of fiduciary duty is a stab at approximating the terms the parties would have negotiated had they foreseen the circumstances that have given rise to their dispute. The parties want to minimize the costs of performance. [....] The office of the doctrine of good faith is to forbid the kinds of opportunistic behavior that a mutually dependent, cooperative relationship might enable in the absence of rule. "Good faith" is a compact reference to an implied undertaking not to take opportunistic advantage in a way that could have been contemplated at the time of drafting, and which therefore was not resolved explicitly by the parties." [....] The formation or negotiation state is precontractual, and here the duty is minimized. It is greater not only at the performance but also at the enforcement stage, which is also postcontractual. [....] At the formation of the contract the parties are dealing in present realities; performance still lies in the future. [....] [W]hether we say that a contract shall be deemed to contain such implied conditions as are necessary to make sense of the contract, or that a contract obligates the parties to cooperate in its performance in "good faith" to the extent necessary to carry out the purposes of the contract, comes to much the same thing. They are different ways of formulating the overriding purpose of contract law, which is to give the parties what they would have stipulated for expressly if at the time of making the contract they had had complete knowledge of the future and the costs of negotiating and adding provisions to the contract had been zero. [....] [Market Street Associates Limited Partnership v. Dale Frey, et al., 941 F.2d 588, 1991]

Section I — Performance — Putting in Default

Louisiana Sources of Law
Louisiana Civil Code

Art. 1854. Extinction by performance.

Performance by the obligor extinguishes the obligation. (Acts 1984, No. 331, § 1, eff. Jan. 1, 1985.)

Art. 1855. Performance by a third person.

Performance may be rendered by a third person, even against the will of the obligee, unless the obligor or the obligee has an interest in performance only by the obligor. Performance rendered by a third person effects subrogation only when so provided by law or by agreement. (Acts 1984, No. 331, § 1, eff. Jan. 1, 1985.)

Art. 1856. Valid transfer of object of performance.

An obligation that may be extinguished by the transfer of a thing is not extinguished unless the thing has been validly transferred to the obligee of performance. (Acts 1984, No. 331, § 1, eff. Jan. 1, 1985.)

Art. 1857. Performance rendered to the obligee.

Performance must be rendered to the obligee or to a person authorized by him.

However, a performance rendered to an unauthorized person is valid if the obligee ratifies it.

In the absence of ratification, a performance rendered to an unauthorized person is valid if the obligee has derived a benefit from it, but only for the amount of the benefit. (Acts 1984, No. 331, § 1, eff. Jan. 1, 1985.)

Arts. 1858–1859. [omitted]

Art. 1860. Quality of thing to be given.

When the performance consists of giving a thing that is determined as to its kind only, the obligor need not give one of the best quality but he may not tender one of the worst. (Acts 1984, No. 331, § 1, eff. Jan. 1, 1985.)

Art. 1861. Partial performance.

An obligee may refuse to accept a partial performance.

Nevertheless, if the amount of an obligation to pay money is disputed in part and the obligor is willing to pay the undisputed part, the obligee may not refuse to accept that part. If the obligee is willing to accept the undisputed part, the obligor must pay it. In either case, the obligee preserves his right to claim the disputed part. (Acts 1984, No. 331, § 1, eff. Jan. 1, 1985.)

Art. 1862. Place of performance.

Performance shall be rendered in the place either stipulated in the agreement or intended by the parties according to usage, the nature of the performance, or other circumstances.

In the absence of agreement or other indication of the parties' intent, performance of an obligation to give an individually determined thing shall be rendered at the place the thing was when the obligation arose. If the obligation is of any other kind, the performance shall be rendered at the domicile of the obligor. (Acts 1984, No. 331, § 1, eff. Jan. 1, 1985.)

Art. 1863. Expenses.

Expenses that may be required to render performance shall be borne by the obligor. (Acts 1984, No. 331, § 1, eff. Jan. 1, 1985.)

Art. 1989. Damages for delay.

Damages for delay in the performance of an obligation are owed from the time the obligor is put in default.

Other damages are owed from the time the obligor has failed to perform. (Acts 1984, No. 331, § 1, eff. Jan. 1, 1985.)

Art. 1990. Obligor put in default by arrival of term.

When a term for the performance of an obligation is either fixed, or is clearly determinable by the circumstances, the obligor is put in default by the mere arrival of that term. In other cases, the obligor must be put in default by the obligee, but not before performance is due. (Acts 1984, No. 331, § 1, eff. Jan. 1, 1985.)

Art. 1991. Manners of putting in default.

An obligee may put the obligor in default by a written request of performance, or by an oral request of performance made before two witnesses, or by filing suit for performance, or by a specific provision of the contract. (Acts 1984, No. 331, § 1, eff. Jan. 1, 1985.)

Art. 1993. Reciprocal obligations.

In case of reciprocal obligations, the obligor of one may not be put in default unless the obligor of the other has performed or is ready to perform his own obligation. (Acts 1984, No. 331, § 1, eff. Jan. 1, 1985.)

Doctrine

Louisiana Law of Conventional Obligations, A Précis

Section 8.2.2

An obligor is not bound merely to carry out his performance of the principal object of his obligation. That principal performance must also be carried out on time. [. . . .]

There exists, therefore, in every obligation an element of "time," actually an obligation to perform "on time." [. . . .]

This obligation to perform on time by one party, obligor, gives the other party, obligee, the right to **"put the obligor in default"** (**Art. 1991**) so that **"damages for delay in the performance** [will be] **owed"** by the obligor to the obligee **"from the time the obligor is put in default." Art. 1989.** [. . . .]

[T]he purpose of putting an obligor in default is to inform him that the obligee cannot wait any longer for the obligor to perform his obligation. [. . . .]

The fault of the obligor is in not performing on time and, as a consequence, in causing a damage to the obligee. The damage caused to the obligee will entitle him to receive *"moratory damages,"* that is to say **"damages for delay in perform[ing] . . . ."** Art. 1989. [. . . .]

The requirement of putting an obligor in default is justified as long as the obligor could still perform and the performance would still be of benefit to the obligee. [. . . .]

[W]henever a term is fixed or clearly determinable, the mere arrival of the term will automatically put the obligor in default: **"When a term for the performance of an obligation is either fixed or clearly determinable by the circumstances, the obligor is put in default by the mere arrival of that term. In other cases, the obligor must be put in default by the obligee, but not before performance is due." Art. 1990.** [. . . .]

Where there is no term, fixed or determinable, attached to the timing of performance of his obligation by an obligor, the obligee, if he has the right to demand performance from his obligor, will have to " . . . **put the obligor in default by written request of performance, or by an oral request of performance made before two witnesses, or by filing suit for performance, or by a specific provision of the contract." Art. 1991** [. . .].

According to **Art. 1993**, **"In case of reciprocal obligations, the obligor of one may not be put in default unless the obligor of the other has performed or is ready to perform his own obligation."**

Louisiana Law of Obligations in General, A Précis
Section 7.1.1

Performance of an obligation is the normal mode of extinction of an obligation by an obligor. As **LSA-C.C. Art. 1854** states: **"Performance by the obligor extinguishes the obligation."** Performance is, thus, the fulfillment of the juridical act or fact undertaken by the obligor with the intent to discharge his obligation *vis-à-vis* the obligee as is called for by the nature of their legal relationship. [. . . .]

Therefore, performance can, or should, always be rendered by the obligor [*solvens*] although, in proper circumstances, that same performance can be rendered by a representative of the obligor, or a person concerned, such as a surety or a co-obligor, or, even, a third person, a gestor, for example. [. . . .]

A voluntary performance of his obligation by the obligor being a juridical act meant to extinguish that obligation, it is necessary that the obligor be capable of performing. [. . . .]

In the words of **LSA-C.C. Art. 1857: "Performance must be rendered to the obligee or to a person authorized by him."** [. . . .]

Therefore, a performance may be validly rendered to the obligee himself or to a third person empowered to receive the performance in the place and in the name of the obligee. [. . . .]

The object of the obligor's performance must be the very same object of the obligation entered into. There must be identity between the object of the obligation and the object or item of the performance carried out to extinguish the obligation whether that object or item be a service to be performed or a thing to be delivered. [. . . .]

A fundamental principle which governs an obligor's performance is the principle of indivisibility of that performance. In a few specific instances this principle will suffer some exceptions. [. . . .]

The indivisibility of an obligor's performance simply means that the obligor owes the entirety of the thing or item in one single performance. Unless the parties to a juridical act have provided otherwise, or unless the law states differently, an obligee-creditor cannot be compelled to receive a partial performance from his obligor. [. . . .]

The indivisibility of the performance is controlling whether the object of that performance is indivisible by nature or susceptible of division.

Cases

Rober Leon, Sr. v.
Aubin Dupre and Mrs. Aubin Dupre

Court of Appeal of Louisiana
Fourth Circuit
September 4, 1962
144 So.2d 667

McBRIDE, Judge.

[1] On November 1, 1956, plaintiff placed a music box in the Three Leaf Bar operated by defendants in St. Bernard Parish under a written agreement reading thus:

> 'I, Mr. Aubin Dupre and Mrs. Dupre, give Roger Leon permission to place his music box in my place of business 'The Three Leaf Bar'. If at any time I should have him remove it, I agree to pay him $190.00.'

[2] We gather that the music box is the usual coin-operated device placed in some types of business establishments for the amusement and entertainment of the patrons thereof. On what basis it was installed in defendants' bar we do not know.

[3] On November 10, 1956, Mrs. Dupre in writing ordered plaintiff to remove the box, which he did, whereupon he sued the defendants for the sum of $190 mentioned in the agreement. [. . . .]

[4] After a trial on the merits, the judge rendered judgment in plaintiff's favor for $50. [. . . .]

[5] Defendants agreed to pay plaintiff $190 in the event they should have plaintiff remove the music box. They had the box in their establishment but ten days, and it seems harsh that they should pay plaintiff $190. Perhaps that is why the trial judge rendered judgment in favor of plaintiff for only $50. The contract, so far as the record shows, was not entered into for any immoral purposes nor was it contrary to law, and defendants must be held to their agreement.

[6] LSA-C.C. art. 1901 recites:

> 'Agreements legally entered into have the effect of laws on those who have formed them.

> 'They can not be revoked, unless by mutual consent of the parties, or for causes acknowledged by law.

> 'They must be performed with good faith.'

[7] The parties may make their own contracts, and however unusual they may be or what drastic or unreasonable features there may be therein, they form the law between them and should be enforced so long as they do not contravene good morals or public policy. Salles v. Stafford, Derbes & Roy, Inc., 173 La. 361, 137 So. 62; Blakesley v. Ransonet, 159 La. 310, 105 So. 354; Stewart, Hyde & Co. v. Buard & Dranguet, 23 La.Ann. 201; Arkansas Fuel Oil Corporation v. Maggio, La.App., 141

So.2d 516; Oil Field Supply & Scrap Material Co. v. Gifford-Hill & Co., Inc., La.App., 16 So.2d 77 (annulled on other grounds — 204 La. 929, 16 So.2d 483); Yates v. Batteford, 19 La.App. 374, 139 So. 37, rehearing denied and amended 19 La.App. 374, 139 So. 746.

[8] For the reasons assigned, the judgment appealed from is affirmed.

[9] Affirmed.

Questions

1. Paragraphs 1–2: What types or kinds of obligations are created in this written agreement? Can you give a name to this contract? Are you surprised by the Court's statement in paragraph 2? Are the requirements for a contract met? Are the objects and the causes/motives lawful? What kind of cause are you referring to? If this is a contract, does it have a name?

2. Paragraph 5: What purpose or cause is the Court considering as "not immoral"?

3. Paragraphs 6–8: What does the Court mean by "they form the law between them and should be enforced" (*see* paragraph 7)? Does a party's "performance in good faith" (*see*, Louisiana Civil Code article 1901, now article 1983) add anything to the statement that an agreement or a contract has the effect of law for the parties? Have you encountered this requirement of good faith somewhere else in the Louisiana Civil Code? What is the bottom line of this unusually short case?

American Creosote Works
v.
Boland Machine & Mfg. Co.

Supreme Court of Louisiana
April 26, 1948
35 So.2d 749

FOURNET, Justice.

[. . . .]

[1] On August 4, 1943, the plaintiff, the American Creosote Works, entered into a contract with the defendant, Boland Machine & Manufacturing Company, a copartnership. This contract is incorporated in one of the plaintiff's order forms. According to its terms the plaintiff agreed to supply the defendant with 24 creosoted fir pilings treated by what is known as the Full Cell Bethel Process and conforming to Navy specifications No. 39P14a (meaning 13 inches in diameter 3 feet from the butt or bottom end of the tree) in four lots of six units each, i.e., six 75' long, six 80' long, six 85' long, and six 90' long, at a price of 95¢ per lineal foot, f. o. b. the plaintiff's plant at Southport in New Orleans, at which place they were to be loaded on the defendant's truck, subject to inspection and acceptance by the defendant.

Subsequently, according to a letter of August 17 confirming a telephone conversation had with the defendant, the contract was amended to provide for the loading of these pilings on the defendant's barge at the plaintiff's Southport plant wharf on Saturday, August 21, 1943. An extra charge of $25 was to be included in the purchase price under this new agreement for the barge loading.

[2] Since the plaintiff did not have these fir pilings in stock, they had to be specially ordered for treatment according to the detailed specifications and after they were processed the plaintiff, on August 20, under the provision in the contract calling for one day advance notice, notified the defendant by telephone to have a barge at its wharf so that loading might begin at seven the next morning, for delivery around noon. Accordingly, the defendant, on Friday afternoon, ordered a barge from the Bisso Coal and Towboat Company and it was tied up at the wharf ready for loading at the specified time. The actual loading was completed about eleven. The defendant, upon advice from the plaintiff, likewise asked the Bisso people to have a tug pick the barge up about noon, but before that time a fire started on the wharf of the plaintiff company and spread to the barge. When the tug did approach the wharf as instructed, the barge had been cut away from the wharf in an effort to save it and was drifting down the river enveloped in flames.

[3] The defendant denied liability, contending that under the contract title did not pass to them until the property was loaded on the barge and tendered to them or their agent for inspection and acceptance.

[4] The plaintiff, relying on Articles 1909, 2456, 2458, 2467, and 2468 of the Revised Civil Code, contends that title to these pilings passed to the defendant the moment they were treated and removed from the processing shed; in any event, that title passed when the pilings were measured, counted, and loaded on the barge.

[5] In passing on these issues, the Court of Appeal found that neither these codal articles nor the cases relied on by the defendant were applicable under the facts of this case, but concluded that title to the pilings had passed to the defendant prior to the fire inasmuch as they were, at that time, loaded on the barge furnished by the defendant in accordance with the court's construction of the contract, the fact that the defendant was not to take possession of them nutil [*sic*] a later time, i.e., around noon, being immaterial.

[6] We think the court's conclusion with respect to the inapplicability of the codal articles is correct. A mere reference to these articles will show their general tenor to be that the sale of an object is perfect and complete and the article is at the risk of the buyer as soon as there exists an agreement as to the object and price, although actual delivery has not been made and the price has not been paid, and that once the sale is perfected and completed, the only responsibility then resting on the seller is that of guarding the goods as a faithful administrator. But this rule applies only '*if the contract is one of those that purport a transfer.*' Article 1909. The contract in this case does not purport to be a transfer of the pilings to the defendant. On the contrary, its terms show very plainly that the pilings are to be transferred to the

defendant only after they have been tendered for inspection and have actually been accepted. (Italics ours.)

[7] Under this contract the plaintiff agreed to furnish the defendant with goods that had to meet certain specifications, that is, the pilings had to be of definite lengths and size and they had to be treated with creosote under a special process. While on the reverse side of this contract there is to be found, along with other printed provisions, the general stipulation that the 'Buyer agrees to receive material when and as delivered on cars at Seller's plant. It is specifically agreed that there shall be no claims of any kind after material is delivered as above,' this general stipulation is not controlling in this case for it has been abrogated by the very positive provision on the face of the contract, where all of the detailed specifications and conditions are clearly set out, that the pilings were to be subject to final inspection and acceptance by the defendant at the plaintiff's plant.

[8] The intention of the parties as to when the pilings would be transferred to the defendant is not only thus clearly shown on the face of the contract itself, but is further demonstrated by the oral and documentary evidence in the record unmistakably showing the property belonged to the plaintiff until delivery was completed and that delivery could not be completed until the defendant, who was given the right to inspect and check it, had actually inspected it and accepted it, such acceptance being evidenced by the defendant's signature on the delivery slip prepared for that purpose which constituted the defendant's acknowledgment that the goods had been received in good condition and accepted.

[. . . .]

[9] We therefore conclude that delivery was never completed under the terms of this contract and under the facts of this case and that title had not passed to the defendant at the time the pilings were destroyed by fire; consequently, their loss was at the risk of the plaintiff and not that of the defendant.

[10] For the reasons assigned, the judgment of the district court in favor of the American Creosote Works, as prayed for, and that of the Court of Appeal for the Parish of Orleans affirming the same, are reversed, and it is now ordered, adjudged, and decreed that the plaintiff's suit be dismissed at its cost.

[11] McCALEB, J., recused.

Questions

1. Paragraphs 1–2: What adjectives would you use to describe the parties involved here? Should the types of parties involved have an impact on one or some of the requirements for the formation of a contract between them? What requirements must be met for the object of the plaintiff's obligation to become "the" object of the contract? Can you identify the cause of this contract? Are there any modalities in this contract (i.e., condition, term, etc.)? What legal identification(s) can you give to the contractual requirement "subject to

inspection and acceptance"? Are "inspection" and "acceptance" conditions or are they essential elements of the formation of the contract?

2. Paragraph 3: What kinds of obligations were those of the plaintiff/seller? Is delivery by the seller (*see* Louisiana Civil Code articles 2475, 2477, 2484, and 2489) and taking delivery (*see* article 2549) by the buyer the same thing? Are delivery and possession the same thing?

3. Paragraphs 4–6: Read the new Louisiana Civil Code articles 2456, 2457, 2458, and 2467. On what ground does the Court rely to hold that ownership of the pilings had not passed? What do you think of this language used by the Court: "[T]his rule applies only 'if the contract is one of those that purport a transfer'" (*see* paragraph 6)? Didn't the contract here intend to transfer the pilings from one party to the other?

4. Paragraphs 7–10: Was there in existence a suspensive condition? In the affirmative, what are its effects as far as it could be connected to the delivery of the pilings?

Section II — Obligations to Give, to Do or Not to Do; Specific Performance

Louisiana Sources of Law
Louisiana Civil Code

Art. 1986. Right of the obligee.

Upon an obligor's failure to perform an obligation to deliver a thing, or not to do an act, or to execute an instrument, the court shall grant specific performance plus damages for delay if the obligee so demands. If specific performance is impracticable, the court may allow damages to the obligee.

Upon a failure to perform an obligation that has another object, such as an obligation to do, the granting of specific performance is at the discretion of the court. (Acts 1984, No. 331, §1, eff. Jan. 1, 1985.)

Art. 1987. Right to restrain obligor.

The obligor may be restrained from doing anything in violation of an obligation not to do. (Acts 1984, No. 331, §1, eff. Jan. 1, 1985.)

Art. 1988. Judgment may stand for act.

A failure to perform an obligation to execute an instrument gives the obligee the right to a judgment that shall stand for the act. (Acts 1984, No. 331, §1, eff. Jan. 1, 1985.)

Doctrine

Louisiana Law of Conventional Obligations, A Précis

Section 8.2.1

With respect to obligations to give and obligations to do, Article 1986 of the civil Code is clear in the distinction therein made between these two kinds of obligations.

With respect to an obligation to give, i.e. the transfer of a real right over a thing, such as the ownership of a thing to someone, specific performance may be obtained by constraint. The Code of civil procedure provides for some remedies [. . .]. [. . . .]

In addition, **Article 1988** of the civil Code gives an **"obligee the right to a judgment that shall stand for the act"** or instrument that the obligor failed to execute. So, in general, under the civil Code and the Code of civil procedure, obligations to give are susceptible of being specifically enforced.

The specific enforcement of an obligation to do is quite another matter. As **Art. 1986** states in fine, **"the granting of specific performance is at the discretion of the court."** In reality it is impossible to have an obligation to do specifically enforced for fear of infringing, a little or excessively, upon the individual freedom of the obligor. [. . . .]

One can state that if the element of *"intuitu personae"* is dominant in the kind of obligation to do under consideration, then specific performance will not be available.

On the other hand there are obligations to do which ought to be specifically enforceable. [. . . .]

Article 2501 of the Code of civil procedure which allows the use of force against someone who refuses to vacate an immovable property. Thus, as **Art. 1986** of the civil Code expresses in a wise statement, the use of force amounting to specific performance of an obligation to do **"is at the discretion of the court."**

Cases

Lee R. Centanni, M.D. v.
A. K. Roy, Inc.

Court of Appeal of Louisiana
Fourth Circuit
February 7, 1972
258 So.2d 219

CHASEZ, Judge.

[1] Plaintiff, Dr. Lee R. Centanni, instituted this suit against the defendant, A. K. Roy, Inc., a real estate agency or brokerage company, for a return of $850.00, attorney's fees and costs. The sum of $850.00 represents the amount allegedly due as a penalty for the alleged non-performance of an agreement to sell and convey certain real estate. Plaintiff's petition was later supplemented and amended to include J. Folse Roy personally as a defendant.

[. . . .]

[2] On March 30, 1967 plaintiff signed a written agreement to purchase a lot in Jefferson Parish for $8,500.00 and made a deposit of $850.00. The agreement was accepted [. . .]. The sale was to pass before Roy Price, as notary named in the agreement, on April 25, 1967.

[3] [. . . .] On the day set for the sale, plaintiff appeared at the Notary's office but the seller did not. Plaintiff then prepared and signed a document to allow an extension of time for the passage of the act of sale but the vendor did not sign it and denies any knowledge of the extension. Suffice it to say that at no time has the vendor appeared before a notary with plaintiff to transfer the lot in question to plaintiff. However, the evidence shows that although Jeff, Inc. claimed it could not sell the property in April of May of 1967 it was subsequently sold by Jeff, Inc. under an agreement arranged in September of 1967.

[4] A return of plaintiff's deposit, held by Price, was made. Plaintiff then made demand on J. F. Roy for an additional $850.00 which constitutes double the deposit as contained within the agreement to sell. Defendant has denied liability.

[. . . .]

[5] [**After ruling on plaintiff's argument regarding Louisiana mandate law, the court turned to defendant's argument that plaintiff is not entitled to damages because he failed to put defendants in formal default through process verbal.**] Defendants also contend that under the terms of the contract, if seller cannot deliver a merchantable title, then purchaser is only entitled to the return of his deposit which the defendants have returned.

[6] A demand in writing for the delivery of title and the placing in formal default is a prerequisite to the recovery of damages or to the rescission of the contract.

LSA-C.C. Article 1911 and Article 1912. However, putting in default is not required when such action would be a vain, futile and useless gesture. Poche v. Ruiz, 239 La. 573, 119 So.2d 469 (1960); Fox v. Doll, 221 La. 427, 59 So.2d 443 (1952).

[7] Defendant was sent a letter of damand [*sic*] on June 20, 1967 by Roy Price who was acting as attorney for plaintiff at that time. A subsequent demand for double return of deposit was again made on November 10, 1967 to which defendant denied liability.

[8] The defendant asserts that the property in question had an outstanding mortgage on it and the mortgagee refused to release the property and therefore he felt there was no reason for him to be present for the transfer of title to the plaintiff on April 25, 1967. J. F. Roy also testified that he had told Price of the mortgage and possible difficulties with same. This testimony is corroborated by his letter of March 31, 1967 which disclosed the true owner.

[9] Accepting for purposes of this case that the letters of demand previously herein discussed are not a formal putting in default we are convinced that no formal placing in default is required.

[10] In Poche v. Ruiz, supra, the Supreme Court held that where a title is known to be litigious a demand by purchasers for vendor to convey title is vain; futile and a useless gesture and therefore unnecessary.

[11] There is no necessity to formally put one in default when he refuses to perform or acknowledges an inability to perform. Fox v. Doll, supra.

[. . . .]

[12] In the present case where the vendor refused to pass the act of sale because of an outstanding mortgage and did not offer a merchantable title, demand by Centanni for performance is not necessary; any such attempt being vain and useless.

[13] The contractual agreement entered into contains the following specific conditions:

> 'The seller shall deliver to purchaser a merchantable title. Should the purchaser refuse to take the title because same is not merchantable, or for any defects therein, then in that event the seller is only liable for the return of the deposit made by the purchaser, anything to the contrary notwithstanding.
>
> 'In the event the seller does not comply with this agreement within the time specified, the purchaser shall have the right either to demand the return of his deposit in full plus an equal amount to be paid as penalty by the seller; or the purchaser may demand specific performance at his option.'

[14] Centanni has not refused to take title, rather defendants [. . .] have refused to offer the title. By the very terms of the agreement plaintiff is entitled to double the deposit as damages.

[15] Plaintiff, in his petition, has requested reasonable attorney's fees. However, the agreement contains no stipulation that fees for attorneys are intended other

than fees allowed for enforcing collection of the agent's commission. In such a situation as this case we have maintained that attorney's fees are not provided for, nor recoverable. See Scurria v. Russo, 134 So.2d 679 (La.App., 4th Cir., 1961). Where not specifically allowed for by law or by contract, attorney fees are not recoverable.

[16] For the reasons hereinabove set forth judgment of the lower court is affirmed in part and reversed in part and it is now ordered, adjudged and decreed that there be judgment in favor of the plaintiff, Dr. Lee R. Centanni and against the defendant, A. K. Roy, Inc., in the sum of $850.00, all with legal interest thereon from date of judicial demand, with all costs of court.

[17] Affirmed in part, reversed in part, and rendered.

Questions

1. Paragraph 1: How many parties are involved in this case? How many bilateral contracts have been entered into? Is there any issue of capacity? *See* the Louisiana Civil Code articles on "Representation and/or Mandate" (arts. 2985–3032). What kind of obligation(s) does a contract of "agency" create?

2. Paragraph 6: What is the purpose of a "putting in default"? Can this purpose explain why and when a putting in default may be unnecessary or useless? Is the possibility of putting an obligor in default contingent upon the nature of the obligation owed by that obligor? Could it be relevant, not to say important, to keep this in mind when negotiating a contract?

3. Paragraph 7–17: What kind of obligation(s) (the Court refers to them as "conditions") was or were created in the contract? Is there any benefit for a party to include such an obligation in a contract? If you answered affirmatively, which party benefits?

H. B. 'Bud' Fletcher
v.
Carol Rachou, d/ b/a La Louisianne Records and Recording Studio

Court of Appeal of Louisiana
Third Circuit
November 20, 1975
323 So.2d 163

WATSON, Judge.

[1] This suit involves disputes between a recording artist and the owner of a recording studio. H. B. 'Bud' Fletcher, the plaintiff and defendant-in-reconvention is an entertainer specializing in the telling of jokes and stories in 'Cajun'[1] dialect. The

---

1. 'Cajun' is a contraction of the word 'Acadian' used in reference to persons of Acadian descent, many of whom live in the southern part of the State of Louisiana.

defendant and plaintiff-in-reconvention is Carol Rachou who does business as La Louisianne Records and Recording Studio. At issue was Rachau's failure to make payment of royalties and Fletcher's failure to make additional recordings. The trial judge held that Rachou owed Fletcher $2,286.50 and Rachou had no valid claims against Fletcher.

[2] Fletcher has appealed, claiming that the amount due is considerably in excess of the award; and Rachou has appealed, contending that the trial court erred in rendering a money judgment in favor of Fletcher and in failing to award damages to Rachou.

[3] Prior to December 9, 1967, Fletcher made several recordings for Rachou which the latter sold successfully. The exact financial arrangement concerning these recordings is unclear from the record. On December 9, 1967, the parties entered into a written contract[2] for a five-year term which provided basically: that Fletcher would record exclusively for Rachou; that recordings would be made at 'mutually agreeable times'; that a royalty of 5% Of the retail price (which amounted to 25 cents per album) would be paid; and that payment would be made semi-annually within 45 days after June 30 and within 45 days after December 31 of each year, subject to a deduction for all advances against royalties.

[4] Significantly the recording contract did not call for the recordation of any particular number of records per year or during the term of the contract. There is no reference in the contract to royalties payable for prior recordings. The contract provides that, in the event of Fletcher's death, the royalties will thereafter be payable to his wife.

---

2. While the wording of the contract is not at issue, for ease of reference we will quote the first four paragraphs:

'1. This contract for your personal services is made between Carol J. Rachou D/B/A La Louisianne Records as the employer and you. We hereby employ to you render personal services and you agree to render such personal services exclusively for us for the purpose of recording and making records for phonograph records and/or tape recordings and other similar devices for home use.

'2. Recordings will be made at recording sessions in the studios we designate at mutually agreeable times. Compositions to be recorded shall be designated by La Louisianne Records and each recording shall be subject to our approval as satisfactory for manufacture and sale. We shall at all times have complete control of the services to be rendered by you under the specifications of this contract and you agree that your services are unique, exceptional, and extra-ordinary.

'3. For the rights herein granted and for the services to be rendered hereunder by you, we shall pay you a royalty of 5% Of the retail price of all LP albums and tape cartridges (25¢ per album for albums that retail for $4.79), manufactured and sold by us and paid for by purchaser.

'4. Payment of accrued royalties accompanied by statements shall be made semiannually, within 45 days after June 30, and within 45 days after December 31, in each year. However, we shall have the right to deduct from the amount of royalties due all advances against royalties.' (TR. 48)

[5] Pursuant to this contract, Fletcher made only one record despite attempts by Rachou and his employees to encourage additional recording. Certain recording dates were set up, but Fletcher contacted the studio on each occasion and indicated that, for some reason, usually sore throat, he would be unable to record. In an effort to encourage Fletcher to make additional records, Rachou withheld payment of royalties earned by Fletcher, but on one or two occasions gave him a check for royalties with an understanding that a new record would be made shortly thereafter.

[6] It is undisputed that, during the contract period, Fletcher did not make recordings for anyone else and that, as of the date of trial he had, to a large extent, retired from his activities as a 'Cajun' humorist.

[7] The contract between the parties expired on December 2, 1972, and, on December 6, 1973, Fletcher filed a petition alleging the existence of the contract, contending that no royalties had been paid since September 9, 1970 and that he was due an accounting and payment of all royalties. The petition was thereafter amended to claim the precise sum of $4,132.25. At no point in his petition or his amended petition did plaintiff assert a precise claim for royalties due under any prior contract on the several other records which he had made for Rachou prior to the December 9, 1967, contract.

[8] Defendant Rachou answered, denying plaintiff's claims and asserting a reconventional demand for $10,000. He claimed loss of expenses and profits from Fletcher's failure to make recordings during the contract period, as the result of which Rachou lost the sale of those records and enhancement of the value of Fletcher's other records.

[9] There is a certain lack of collision on the issues by the parties to this lawsuit, one side arguing certain issues and the other side arguing different and sometimes unrelated issues. However, following the propounding and answering of extensive written interrogatories, as well as other pre-trial activities, the matter was tried on the merits and the trial court found essentially that:

1. the parties did not contract to make any particular number of records;
2. defendant failed to make timely payment of royalties;
3. defendant admitted that he owed plaintiff $2,286.50 and such sum was due and owing;
4. defendant was not entitled to recover on the reconventional demand for alleged loss of profits, and even if he were so entitled, the proof was not sufficiently clear to arrive at any amount due; and
5. the claim for out of pocket expenses was not corroborated in the evidence and could not be allowed.

[. . . .]

[10] On appeal, Fletcher emphasizes the alleged error of the trial court in failing to hold that the royalties were continuing rather than limited to the five-year term

of the contract. Rachou contends that the court erred in ordering payment of royalties to Fletcher, who, according to Rachou, either breached the contract or failed to perform under it, thereby entitling Rachou to have the contract dissolved and also entitling him to recover damages.

[11] The issues to be decided on appeal are:

1. whether the trial court erred in awarding Fletcher $2,286.50 as past due royalties;

2. whether the trial court erred in failing to recognize that the payment of royalties is a continuing obligation; and

3. whether Rachou is entitled to:

   (a.) release from his obligation to pay royalties because of breach or non-performance of the contract by Fletcher, and

   (b.) payment of damages.

I. Royalties

[12] The trial court was correct in awarding the amount of $2,286.50 as past due royalties. Rachou concedes that this was the royalty only on the one record made under the contract. Fletcher persists in claiming royalties on all recordings made for Rachou, but this suit, as delineated by the petition and amending petition, is basically a demand for royalties due under the five-year contract of December 9, 1967, under which only one record was made. As to the prior records made by Fletcher for Rachou, the sale of which was alluded to in various interrogatories and answers to interrogatories, the trial court was not furnished any evidence concerning the agreement between the parties as to the amount of royalty, if any, payable on these records. The contract of December 9, 1967, did not relate to or refer to previous sales of records.

[13] In his testimony, Rachou admitted owing Fletcher the amount awarded by the trial court, and under the circumstances, we find no error in this award.

[14] We do not agree with the trial court, however, that the obligation to pay royalties terminated at the conclusion of the five-year contract. Certainly, since the contract did not relate to the several other records made by Fletcher for Rachou, it could have no effect on any obligation for payment of royalty under other agreements.

[15] As to the single record made under the contract, Rachou contends apparently that the five-year contract itself provides that royalties would be payable only for five years. However, there is no such provision in the contract and no legal authority has been cited for Rachou's contention. The five-year term relates to Fletcher's obligation to make records exclusively for Rachou. Fletcher contracted only that any records he made during the five years would be made for Rachou. The obligation to pay royalties on any record made under the contract continues. The contract even provides for payment of royalties to Fletcher's wife after his death.

Breach of Contract

[16] This brings us to Rachou's contention that Fletcher breached the contract and deprived him of profits. There is no evidence that Fletcher made recordings for any other person or firm during the contract period; the only indication of other professional activity by Fletcher was the testimony by the witnesses, Faulk, Fontenot, Stoma and Oliver, that Fletcher had made personal appearances at a bowling conference and Evangeline Downs Race Track and had made commercials for a dairy. (The contract related only to making records; see footnote 2). There was evidence by other witnesses, Leroy LeBlanc (professionally known as 'Happy Fats') and B. C. Fletcher (Fletcher's brother), that, during the contract period, Fletcher suffered considerable difficulties with his throat.

[17] Rachou's contention is that Fletcher breached the contract to record by only making one record in five years and that this relieved Rachou of the obligation of paying royalties and also entitled him to payment of damages. This argument presupposes the validity and enforceability of the contract between Fletcher and Rachou. It assumes that Rachou could have affirmatively required Fletcher to make recordings. The argument fails for two reasons: first, under its terms the contract calls for no particular number of records to be made; and second, a contract for personal services is not affirmatively enforceable.

[18] As to the first reason, the contract is clear; no particular number of records was required. As to the second reason, some consideration must be given to the basic nature of the contract. It was an agreement by an artist or performer to render personal services, akin to the contract of a singer to sing or a musician to play.

[19] Under the law of contracts in our sister states, a contract for personal services by an artist or a performer will not be specifically enforced by an affirmative decree.[4] Reinstatement of the Law of Contracts, s 379. According to the recognized authority in the field of contracts, Professor A. L. Corbin, there are three reasons usually given for this rule of law:

(1) difficulty of enforcing the decree and gauging the quality of the performance;

(2) strength of the American prejudice against any kind of involuntary personal servitude; and

(3) frequent close association between employer and employee and the consequent undesirability of enforcement where confidence and loyalty have been disrupted by dispute.

See Corbin on Contracts, s 1204, pp. 400–401.

---

4. A clear distinction should be made between the enforcement of a contract by an affirmative order to perform and the negative enforcement by preventing performance of similar services for another. Other considerations are involved in negative enforcement and that is not the question here because there is no assertion of recordings made by Fletcher for anyone else.

[20] In Louisiana, the courts have recognized the abrogation of personal contracts by inability to perform. Most notable are the cases in which persons have contracted for a prolonged series of dancing lessons and later have become physically incapacitated to dance. Louisiana courts have held that, under these circumstances, particularly relying on LSA-C.C. art. 2003,[5] such contracts are unenforceable. Acosta v. Cole, 178 So.2d 456 (La.App. 1 Cir. 1965), writ refused, 248 La. 432, 433, 179 So.2d 273, 274; Richardson v. Cole, 173 So.2d 336 (La.App. 2 Cir. 1965).

[21] We think the reasoning expressed in Richardson and Acosta, as well as the considerations mentioned by Professor Corbin (which we find equally persuasive in Louisiana) justify our adopting and following the rule of law that a contract for personal services is not specifically enforceable by affirmative decree.

[22] Also, the inability to perform as found in Richardson and Acosta, would, in our opinion, be an adequate basis on which the trial court could have found that Fletcher was not physically able to make additional recordings during the record period.

[23] It does not follow, however, that, becasue [*sic*] Fletcher could not be required to perform or make additional records, royalties for records recorded during the contract period were not payable. The royalties are payment for services already performed, not, as Rachou seemingly believed, dependent on future recordings.

[24] Therefore, we find that the trial court was correct in its conclusion that there was no breach of the contract on the part of Fletcher and, accordingly, Rachou was not entitled to any damages. Likewise, the trial court was correct in holding that there was not sufficient evidence to award Rachou out of pocket expenses resulting from the cancellation of recording dates by Fletcher.

[25] For the reasons assigned, the judgment of the trial court is affirmed, but it is amended to reserve to Fletcher the right to claim any additional royalties due: (1) on the one record made under the contract of December 9, 1967, but accruing subsequent to the five-year term of the contract, and (2) on recordings made under any agreement other than the contract of December 9, 1967.

[. . . .]

Questions

1. Paragraphs 1–25: Read the whole case while attempting to identify with the two main parties to the contract. Then read footnote 2. Can you identify some of the many legal features of this excerpt of the contract, for example, kinds of obligations, modalities, etc.?

---

5. The portion of art. 2003 relied on is as follows:
   '* * * if the obligation be purely personal as to the obligee who dies before performance, his heirs may recover from the obligor the value of any equivalent he may have received.'
Total disability has been analogized to death in the dancing cases and the disabled dancing student has been held to be entitled to recover the unearned portion of payment for lessons.

2. Paragraphs 4–9: What legal qualification would you give to Fletcher's obligation? What legal qualification would you give to Rachou's obligation to pay
the royalties to Fletcher's wife? Were these two obligations dependent on one
another? Could one continue to exist without the other? Why or why not?
What did Rachou contract for: a hope or a future thing? *See* La. Civ. Code arts.
1976 and 2450–2451. Would it make a difference as to Rachou's rights against
Fletcher?

3. Paragraphs 12–15: What is the ground of the disagreement between the lower
court and the Court of Appeal? Are an extinctive term and a continuous obligation compatible? Can a continuous obligation be compatible with an obligation to do? What about with an obligation to give?

4. Paragraphs 16–25: Is there a relationship between the legal nature or kind of
obligation and the right to demand specific performance? Can you illustrate
this with the case at hand?

J. Weingarten, Inc.
v.
Northgate Mall, Inc. and Pickens Bond Construction Company

Supreme Court of Louisiana
September 8, 1981
404 So.2d 896

DENNIS, Justice.

[1] We are called upon to decide whether, under the circumstances of this case,
a court should specifically enforce a lease by ordering the destruction of the major
part of a $4 million building which a shopping center developer erected in an area
reserved to its tenant for customer parking. The trial court refused to order the
building razed, but the court of appeal reversed, requiring that approximately 60%
of the building be torn down and removed within six months of the effective date
of its judgment. We reserve the judgment of the court of appeal. Although specific
performance is the preferred remedy for breach of a contract it may be withheld
by the court when specific relief is impossible, when the inconvenience or cost of
performing is greatly disproportionate to the damages caused, when the obligee has
no real interest in receiving performance, or when the latter would have a substantial negative effect on the interests of third parties. In view of the great disparity
between the cost of specific relief and the damages caused by the contractual breach,
the magnitude of the economic and energy waste that would result from the building's destruction, the substantial hardship which would be imposed on individuals
who are not parties to the contract or to this litigation, and the potential negative
effect upon the community, the circumstances and nature of this case do not permit
specific performance. Accordingly, the case will be remanded to the trial court for

proceedings necessary to the assessment and award of any damages to which the plaintiff may be entitled.

[2] The defendant, Northgate Mall, Inc., in 1967 and subsequently, developed an enclosed shopping mall on approximately 35 acres of land in Lafayette, Louisiana. In 1968, the defendant subleased space in the mall to the plaintiff, J. Weingarten, Inc., for the operation of a grocery store.

[3] In early 1978, the defendant began planning to renovate and expand the mall to counter expected competition from a new mall to be built in Lafayette. The plaintiff, upon learning of the expansion plans, informed the defendant that it wished to remodel or enlarge its own store in conjunction with the defendant's activities. Later the plaintiff sent rough plans of its enlargement to the defendant for approval. The plans would have allowed the plaintiff to extend its store front fifty feet into the parking lot adding roughly 7400 additional square feet of building area. Under the lease, the plaintiff had no contractual right to expand. The defendant's right to expand was limited to roughly 40,000 square feet, but it proposed to add slightly over 100,000 square feet. Therefore, consent of both parties was necessary under the lease to permit either party's proposed expansion. However, no written modification ever resulted from their preliminary negotiations.

[4] In February, 1979, the defendant erected a construction fence and began moving construction equipment and material onto the job site. The plaintiff alerted the defendant that it considered the defendant's activities a breach of contract and that injunctive relief would be sought if such activities did not cease. Last minute negotiations between the parties were unsuccessful, and the plaintiff filed suit on March 1, 1979 seeking preliminary and permanent injunctive relief.

[5] Pursuant to plaintiff's petition, the trial court issued a temporary restraining order prohibiting further construction activities and continued the order until March 19, 1979 when a hearing was held on plaintiff's motion to dissolve the restraining order. The trial court denied the preliminary injunction and dissolved the temporary restraining order based on its finding that Weingarten failed to show that it would sustain irreparable damage without injunctive relief. Realizing the great costs attendant to the delay of a multi-million dollar construction project, the trial court pledged itself to speedy action in the case and encouraged the plaintiff to appeal the correctness of its ruling. The plaintiff did not take an appeal as a matter of right, see La. C.C.P. art. 3612, or apply for supervisory writs. See La. C.C.P. art. 2201. The trial on the merits of the petition for a permanent injunction was not held until October 25 and 26, 1979. By this time the $4 million expansion project was virtually complete and the new stores therein were open for business.

[6] After the trial on the permanent injunction, the trial court reaffirmed its earlier finding that the plaintiff had not demonstrated that it would be irreparably harmed and could be adequately compensated monetarily. The court refused to enforce specifically a provision in the lease stipulating that an injunction to enforce

Weingarten's rights to egress and passage over the parking area occupied by the new building could be obtained without the necessity of showing irreparable harm or the inadequacy of damages. The trial court concluded the agreed remedy provision was against public policy relying on Termplan Arabi, Inc. v. Carollo, 299 So.2d 831 (La.App. 4th Cir.), writ denied 302 So.2d 29 (La. 1974).

[7] The court of appeal reversed the trial court, holding that the plaintiff was entitled to permanent injunctive relief because the agreed remedy provision was valid and because the plaintiff was irreparably harmed. J. Weingarten, Inc. v. Northgate Mall, Inc., 390 So.2d 527 (La.App.3d Cir. 1980). We granted defendant's application to consider the appropriateness of specific performance in this case. 396 So.2d 1326 (La. 1981).

[8] Northgate agreed not to erect any additional buildings in the parking area of the shopping center except within the space shown on a plat attached to the lease designated as sites for future department store and a proposed theater. The defendant also promised to maintain a ratio of six car parking spaces for each 1,000 feet of floor space in the shopping center. It further agreed that its tenant, Weingarten, would have the right to an "irrevocable non-exclusive easement" over all parking areas shown on the plat attached to the lease. In connection with the "easement," the lease provided that Weingarten "shall have the right to obtain an injunction specifically enforcing such rights and interests without the necessity of proving inadequacy of legal remedies or irreparable harm."

[9] We concur in the court of appeal's findings that Northgate breached each of the contractual provisions. Whereas the lease reserved a 39,375 square foot area for future expansion, Northgate's new building consumed over 100,000 square feet, covering part of the area reserved for customer parking and reducing the parking ratio from 5.7 spaces per 1000 square feet, in which Weingarten had acquiesced, to 5.0 spaces per 1000 square feet. However, we disagree with the court of appeal finding that the plaintiff had shown that it would be irreparably injured by the breaches of contract. The evidence fully supports the trial judge's determination that plaintiff failed to demonstrate that its injury would be irreparable or insusceptible to adequate compensation.

[10] The decisive issue presented by the breaches of contract is whether Weingarten is entitled to the substantive right of specific performance under the circumstances of this case. Specific performance may be enforced by the extraordinary remedy of injunction, among other procedural methods.[1] It is self-evident, however,

---

1. A judgment may also be issued directing a party to perform a specific act. When the party so adjudged fails to perform, the judgment may be enforced by various procedural methods including the use of distringas, an assessment for damages, and punishment for contempt all as authorized by La.C.C.P. art. 2502. In addition, La.C.C.P. art. 2504 authorizes the court to direct performance by the sheriff or another person appointed by the court, at the cost of the disobedient party. See Comment, 40 Tul.L.Rev. 340, 352 (1966).

that unless Weingarten has a substantive right to specifically enforce the obligation, neither an injunction nor any other procedural remedy may be used.[2]

[11] Plaintiff Weingarten has asked specific performance of defendant Northgate's obligation not to do something namely, not to infringe on plaintiff's contractual rights over areas reserved for parking by the lease.[3] Civil Code articles 1926 through 1929 govern the enforcement of obligations to do, or not to do.

[12] Articles 1926 and 1929 provide:

> Art. 1926. On the breach of any obligation to do, or not to do, the obligee is entitled either to damages, or, in cases which permit it, to a specific performance of the contract, at his option, or he may require the dissolution of the contract, and in all these cases damages may be given where they have accrued, according to the rules established in the following section.

> Art. 1927. In ordinary cases, the breach of such a contract entitles the party aggrieved only to damages, but where this would be an inadequate compensation, and the party has the power of performing the contract, he may be constrained to a specific performance by means prescribed in the laws which regulate the practice of the courts.

> Art. 1928. The obligee may require that any thing which has been done in violation of a contract, may be undone, if the nature of the cause will permit, and that things be restored to the situation in which they were before the act complained of was done, and the court may order this to be effected by its officers, or authorize the injured party to do it himself at the expense of the other, and may also add damages, if the justice of the case require it.

---

2. A party seeking an injunction has no standing to sue unless he has a substantive right, which the law will recognize, assertable against a defendant having a substantial adverse interest. Terrebonne Parish Police Jury v. Mathrene, 405 So.2d 314 (La. 1981); La. Hotel-Motel Ass'n Inc. v. Parish of East Baton Rouge, 385 So.2d 1193 (La. 1980); League of Women Voters of N.O. v. City of New Orleans, 381 So.2d 441 (La. 1980); Abbott v. Parker, 259 La. 279, 249 So.2d 908 (1977); Stoddard v. City of New Orleans, 246 La. 417, 165 So.2d 9 (1964). Cf., Moore, Federal Practice, s 65.17. Moreover, the injunction question appears entirely academic. If Weingarten is entitled to specific performance, its right may be enforced by other procedural methods even if an injunction is unavailable. See footnote 1, supra. Nevertheless, it should be noted that the court of appeal's conclusion that parties contractually may dispense with procedural requisites for an injunction is subject to serious question because of the effects it may have on court dockets and litigants in other cases. If Civil Code article 11 applies to public law with the same force as it does to private law, renunciation of an important rule of court, procedure may in fact be contrary to the public good. See Garro, Codification Technique and the Problem of Imperative and Suppletive Laws, 41 La.L.Rev. 1007, 1012–1015 (1981).

3. We agree with the trial court that the lease does not confer a servitude to plaintiff since defendant-lessor is not the owner of the property. See La. C.C. arts. 697, 710–14; Hawthorne Oil & Gas Corp. v. Continental Oil Co., 368 So.2d 726, 737 (La.App. 3d Cir., rev'd on other grounds, 377 So.2d 285 (La. 1979).

Art. 1929. If the obligation be not to do, the obligee may also demand that the obligor be restrained from doing any thing in contravention of it, in cases where he proves an attempt to do the act covenanted against.

[13] Since they are not models of clarity, the articles are susceptible to more than one reasonable interpretation.

[14] A literal reading of the codal language may lead one to conclude that the general rule, i.e., the one to be applied in ordinary cases, is that the breach of a contract entitles the party aggrieved only to damages; and specific performance may only be obtained where damages would be an inadequate compensation. Under this view, an obligee could only require a thing done in violation of the contract to be undone if the nature of the cause would permit, viz., in the exceptional case in which damages are an inadequate remedy. Such an interpretation is suspect, however, because of its common law overtones.

[15] Eminent Louisiana civilian commentators have argued persuasively to the contrary that these articles of the code where designed to enhance the rank of specific performance over damages as a remedy for the nonperformance of obligations to do or not to do in a manner not expressed in the comparable French articles. 2 S. Litvinoff, Obligations, s 168 in 7 Louisiana Civil Law Treatise (1975); Comment, Louisiana Law of Specific Performance: Codal Provisions and Methods of Enforcement, 40 Tul.L.Rev. 340 (1966). In their view, several circumstances support such an interpretation of the code: Article 1926 was mistranslated from the French; it should read: "On the breach of any obligation to do, or not to do, the obligee is entitled either to damages, or, if the execution is possible, (rather than in cases which permit it) to specific performance of the contract...." [...] S. Litvinoff, Obligations, s 168 in 7 Louisiana Civil Law Treatise 310–315 (1975); Comment, Louisiana Law of Specific Performance: Codal Provisions and Methods of Enforcement, 40 Tul.L.Rev. 340, 343–345 (1966). Article 1927's restriction of specific performance to cases where damages would be "inadequate compensation" is consistent with the idea that recovery of damages is never an adequate remedy when specific performance is possible. S. Litvinoff p. 312; Comment, 40 Tul.L.Rev. p. 344. Article 1927's provision that, in "ordinary cases," a breach of contract entitles the creditor "only to damages," only implies a reference to nemo praecise cogit ad factum, that is, only damages should be granted when specific performance would require a violation of the obligor's freedom. S. Litvinoff, p. 313. Article 1928, which allows the obligee to require that anything which has been done in violation of a contract, "may be undone, if the nature of the cause will permit," shows greater care for the procedural aspects of the remedy of specific performance than does its French equivalent. S. Litvinoff, p. 313.

[16] We agree with the distinguished doctrinal writers that Articles 1926 through 1929 were intended to give first rank to the obligee's right to performance in specific form, consistently with other provisions of the Code. See 2 S. Litvinoff, Obligations, s 168, n. 77. Therefore, we reject the common law view that the obligee must

first clear the inadequacy of damage-irreparable injury hurdle before invoking the remedy.[4]

[17] A reading of the articles as a whole, however, implies that courts are empowered to withhold specific performance in some exceptional cases even when specific performance is possible. The phrases, "if the nature of the cause will permit" and "in ordinary cases," suggest a reference to a traditional civilian concept. The civil law systems, i.e., those descended from Roman law, have by and large proceeded on the premise that specific redress should be ordered whenever possible, unless disadvantages of the remedy outweigh its advantages. Farnsworth, Legal Remedies for Breach of Contract, 70 Columbia L.Rev. 1145 (1970). The main reservations have been for cases where specific relief is impossible, would involve disproportionate cost, would introduce compulsion into close personal relationships or compel the expression of special forms of artistic or intellectual creativity. Dawson, Specific Performance in France and Germany, 57 Mich.L.Rev. 495, 520 (1959). Professor Litvinoff has described the French jurisprudence as allowing courts to deny specific performance whenever the inconvenience of such forced execution would exceed the advantage, as when the cost of performing in kind is disproportionate to the actual damage caused, or when it is no longer in the creditor's interest, or when it would have a negative effect upon the interest of third parties. 2 Litvinoff, Obligations, s 166; See also, 2 M. Planiol, Civil Law Treatise pt. 1, no. 171A at 103 (11th ed. La. St. L. Inst. trans. 1959); Szladits, The Concept of Specific Performance in Civil Law, 4 Am.J.Comp.L. 208, 217 (1955).[5]

[18] For the foregoing reasons, we conclude that the legislative aim of the redactors of the code was to institute the right to specific performance as an obligee's remedy for breach of contract except when it is impossible, greatly disproportionate in cost to the actual damage caused, no longer in the creditor's interest, or of substantial negative effect upon the interests of third parties.[6] Applying this interpretation to the present case, we conclude that its nature will not permit specific performance.

---

4. For discussions distinguishing the civil and common law approaches to specific performance and critiques of Louisiana jurisprudence see: 2 S. Litvinoff, Obligations, ss 162–171 in 7 Louisiana Civil Law Treatise (1975); Jackson, Specific Performance in Louisiana, Past and Future, in Essays in the Civil Law of Obligations 195 (J. Dainow ed. 1969); Jackson, Specific Performance of Contracts in Louisiana, 24 Tul.L.Rev. 401 (1950); Krassa, Interaction of Common Law and Latin Law: Enforcement of Specific Performance in Louisiana and Quebec, 21 Can. Bar Rev. 337 (1943); Comment, Louisiana Law of Specific Performance: Codal Provisions and Methods of Enforcement, 40 Tul.L.Rev. 340 (1966).

5. Twentieth century French commentators argue that courts are justified in not granting specific performance only when it is materially or morally impossible. "Moral impossibility refers to a case 'when satisfaction in nature can by the hardest be procured from the defendant, but at the price of an act of violence which would be scandalous. Colin & Capitant, Cours EelEementaire [sic] de droit civil fran cais [sic] II (3 e ed. 1921) p. 17ff.; Planiol & Ripert, TraitEe Pratique de droit civil fran cais [sic] VII (1931) 69 f. f.'" Jackson, Specific Performance of Contracts in Louisiana, 24 Tul.L.Rev. 401, 415 (1950).

6. Even when a valid agreed remedy provision such as stipulated damages is included in the parties' contract, the court retains some discretion to modify that provision when circumstances such

[19] The evidence clearly reflects that that the cost of tearing down most of the $4 million building and doing incalculable damage to the remainder of the shopping center greatly outweighs any actual damage caused to the plaintiff. It is dubious that the devastation of such a building in a shopping center built with the hope of competing with a neighboring market complex is in Weingarten's real interest. It is evident that the third persons not party to the contract or to this lawsuit would be negatively affected. Shopping center tenants in the new building would lose their store space and risk losing their investments. H.J. Wilson Company, which occupies over 63,000 square feet of the building, would be particularly disadvantaged. The owners of the land and John Hancock Mutual Life Insurance Company, whose long term loan is secured by a mortgage on the shopping center and pledges of the leases of the five major tenants, would suffer a substantial negative effect. Although perhaps not controlling, additional considerations weighing against specific performance and its consequent destruction of a major commercial building are the potential negative effects upon the community in the form of economic waste, energy dissipation, and possible urban blight.

[20] Although the contractual provisions involved here cannot be specifically enforced under the circumstances of this case, we hold that they could have been under different conditions. Indeed, unless exceptional conditions prevail as in this case anything which has been done in violation of the contract may be undone, including the destruction of a building. Moreover, plaintiff is not without a remedy because it is entitled to be compensated fully in damages for any loss it sustains as a result of the breach of contract. Because the record presently does not provide an adequate basis for the assessment of damages, however, the case will be remanded to the trial court for that purpose.

[21] REVERSED AND REMANDED.

[22] WATSON and MARCUS, JJ., concur.

[23] LEMMON, J., concurs and assigns reasons.

LEMMON, Justice, concurring.

[24] When construction began, Weingarten sought to enjoin Northgate's blatant violation of the contract, and injunctive relief should have been granted. When preliminary injunctive relief was denied, Weingarten did not seek review of that ruling.

[25] After construction was completed, the permanent injunction was tried on the merits. Of course, it was impossible at that point to prevent construction, and Weingarten's only relief was to undo the contractual violation by requiring removal of the building. By this time, however, the rights of third parties had become involved, such as the landowners and the mortgage holders (as well as new lessees,

---

as partial performance make the agreed remedy inappropriate or unjust. See, La.C.C. arts. 1934 (5), 2120, 2127; La.C.C.P. art. 2164; Comment, Judicial Modification of Penal Clauses A Survey of Recent Developments, 53 Tul.L.Rev. 523 (1979).

by the time the matter reached this court). Although Northgate's breach was no less culpable, the court's weighing process in determining the appropriate remedy was complicated by the involvement of the rights of innocent third parties.

[26] At this point in the litigation I agree with the majority's analysis. Northgate's trampling on other parties' rights should have been halted earlier, when all of the equities favored Weingarten. Because of inherent flaws in the judicial process Weingarten must now obtain its relief through an award of damages.

Questions

1. Paragraphs 1–26: After you have read the case in its entirety, ponder over the nature, purpose and usefulness of specific performance as the preferred remedy at civil law.

2. Paragraph 1: Was the Court of Appeal wrong in requiring that "approximately 60% of the building be torn down and removed within six months of the effective date" of the judgment? Do you see any benefit, not necessarily in this case only, in a court ordering specific performance? What kind of obligation (give, do, not do) was the Court of Appeal requiring the defendant to carry out? Would it have been impossible for the defendant to specifically carry out that obligation? Does the law require the courts to consider the cost of performing in relation to the "damages caused"? Why should the interests of third parties interfere with the rights and obligations of the parties to a contract? What could become of the civil law principle according to which "a contract is the law for the parties" just as much legislation is the law for all? Isn't the Supreme Court kind of rewriting the contract (against the will of one party, at least) on the basis of grounds or circumstances that were foreign to the parties at the time they entered into their contracts with their own economic and business grounds? Was their contract at all against the law? How reliable and predictable are the grounds on which the Supreme Court justifies its ultimate decision? Under these circumstances, what legal advice would you give to business parties to a contract? What about private parties to a contract? Is there any difference in your advice? Shouldn't the law of contract be the same for all?

3. Paragraphs 12–16: Note the Court's learned and effective integration of doctrine into the Code articles as the primary sources of law. What is the Court's conclusion as regards the remedy of specific performance? What do you think of the Court's statement in paragraph 14: is it a judgment of value or one of principle? Read now paragraph 16; what do you think? Could this difference in remedies between the civil law and the common law be indicative and illustrative of more fundamental differences between the civil law and the common law?

4. Paragraphs 17–18: What do you think of the Court's reading of the Louisiana Civil Code articles and particularly of the Court writing that "a reading of the

articles as a *whole*, however, *implies* that courts are *empowered* to withhold specific performance"? (Emphasis ours.) In paragraph 18, what is the *ratio legis* (reason for the legislation) that the Court singles out? Is there any reason why the Court identifies such a reason? Is the answer in the final line of that sentence, and aren't the coming holdings or grounds of the opinion summarized in this one sentence? (Note that the co-authors of this casebook do not share the statements attributed to the French jurisprudence in paragraph 15, particularly in case Cass. 5-22-1997, J C P ed. G. 1997. 1. 4070 # 26.)

5. Paragraph 19: Of what nature are all of the grounds or reasons advanced by the Court to deny specific performance? Are any of them legal grounds or reasons? Are any of them contractual grounds or reasons?

Glenn Edward Grezaffi
v.
R. Craig Smith

Court of Appeal of Louisiana
First Circuit
June 24, 1994
641 So.2d 210

CARTER, Judge.

[....]

Facts

[1] On June 16, 1988, plaintiff, Glenn Edward Grezaffi, entered into a purchase agreement with defendant, R. Craig Smith, for the sale of a 2.536-acre tract of land located in Pointe Coupee Parish for $60,864.00.[1] The sale was to take place on September 1, 1988. Among other things, the purchase agreement was contingent upon the rezoning of the property as "R-4" and the release of the existing mortgage upon the execution of the act of sale. On August 9, 1988, the 2.536-acre tract of property was rezoned as "R-4." Thereafter, Smith failed to execute the act of sale for the purchase of the property.

[....]

[2] [...] Smith filed an answer to Grezaffi's petition and alleged that Grezaffi had intentionally interfered with his rights to obtain zoning on other projects.[2]

[3] On July 22, 1992, Grezaffi filed a motion for summary judgment. [....]

---

1. The agreement provided that Smith would pay $15,000.00 cash at the time of the execution of the act of sale and that Grezaffi would finance $45,864.00 at 12% interest for eighteen months.
2. In his answer, Smith alleges, by appellation, the defenses of failure of consideration, estoppel, and set-off. However, his answer also alleges specific facts which give rise to the defense of duress.

[4] In opposition to Grezaffi's motion for summary judgment, Smith alleged that the purchase agreement was null and void because of lack of consent in that his consent had been induced by duress. [....]

[5] On September 18, 1992, the hearing on the motion for summary judgment was held. After considering the evidence and argument of counsel, the trial court rendered judgment on October 15, 1992, granting Grezaffi's motion for summary judgment and ordering Smith to pay Grezaffi $64,864.00 plus legal interest from September 1, 1988, until paid. The judgment also ordered Smith to appear at a specific time and place to execute the appropriate documents transferring title of the 2.536-acre tract from Grezaffi to Smith. The trial judge also cast Smith for all costs.

[6] Thereafter, Smith filed a motion for new trial, alleging that the judgment granted Grezaffi more rights than he had under the purchase agreement. The new trial was granted, and, on April 14, 1993, the trial court rendered judgment in favor of Grezaffi and against Smith as follows:

1. Smith was ordered to pay Grezaffi the sum of $15,000.00 on or before April 15, 1993, and $45,864.00 at 12% interest in eighteen months from April 15, 1993.

2. Smith was also ordered to appear on or before April 15, 1993, to execute an act of sale to effectuate a transfer of the property from Grezaffi to Smith.

3. Smith was ordered to pay Grezaffi legal interest on the $15,000.00 from October 26, 1988, until paid.

4. Smith was ordered to pay Grezaffi legal interest on the $45,864.00 from April 26, 1990 through April 15, 1993.

[7] From this adverse judgment, Smith appeals, assigning the following errors:

1. The trial court erred in granting plaintiff's Motion for Summary Judgment and finding that there existed no genuine issues of material fact.

2. The trial court erred in ordering specific performance of a contract which was invalid.

[....]

Discussion

[8] Two Civil Code articles expressly address sales and promises to sell.

[9] LSA-C.C. art. 2456 provides as follows:

The sale is considered to be perfect between the parties, and the property is of right acquired to the purchaser with regard to the seller, as soon as there exists an agreement for the object and for the price thereof, although the object has not yet been delivered, nor the price paid.

[10] LSA-C.C. art. 2462 provides, in pertinent part, as follows:

A promise to sell, when there exists a reciprocal consent of both parties as to the thing, the price and terms, and which, if it relates to immovables, is in writing, so far amounts to a sale, as to give either party the right to enforce specific performance of same.

[11] These articles clearly establish that a sale exists as between the parties when there is agreement as to the object and the price and that, even if there is only a promise to sell, it may be specifically enforced by either party. *Succession of Dunham,* 393 So.2d 438, 445 (La.App. 1st Cir.1980), *affirmed in part, reversed in part on other grounds,* 408 So.2d 888 (La.1981). The inquiry must always be whether or not there existed a reciprocal consent as to the thing, the terms, and the price. *Dunaway v. Woods,* 470 So.2d 574, 577 (La.App. 1st Cir.1985); *Wallace v. Lafourche Parish School Board,* 394 So.2d 1329, 1330 (La.App. 1st Cir.1981).

[12] A major requirement of one who seeks specific performance is proper performance of his part of the contract. *Thompson v. Johnson,* 602 So.2d 272, 274 (La. App. 2nd Cir.1992). In the absence of proper performance, plaintiffs must prove that they are and were ready to comply with whatever obligations devolved upon them to perform. *Thompson v. Johnson,* 602 So.2d at 274. The courts are bound to enforce the contract as written. *Cooper v. Olinde,* 565 So.2d 978, 983 (La.App. 1st Cir.), *writ denied,* 569 So.2d 966 (La.1990). The burden of proof in an action for breach of contract is on the party claiming rights under the contract. The existence of the contract and its terms must be proven by a preponderance of the evidence. *See Baxter v. Zeringue,* 501 So.2d 327, 329 (La.App. 5th Cir.), *writ denied,* 504 So.2d 879 (La.1987); *Phillips v. Insilco Sports Network, Inc.,* 429 So.2d 447, 449 (La.App. 4th Cir.1983); *North American Contracting Corporation v. Gibson,* 327 So.2d 444, 449 (La.App. 3rd Cir.1975), *writ denied,* 332 So.2d 280 (La.1976); *New Orleans Silversmiths, Inc. v. Wormser,* 258 So.2d 592, 593 (La.App. 4th Cir.1972); *Walters v. Edwards,* 212 So.2d 749, 754 (La.App. 1st Cir.1968).

[13] In the instant case, the record clearly reveals that Grezaffi and Smith entered into a written agreement for the purchase of the 2.536-acre tract in Pointe Coupee Parish. The agreement set forth the thing and the price. However, Smith contends that there was no mutual consent because his consent was vitiated by duress.

[14] Consent is vitiated when it has been obtained by duress of such a nature as to cause a reasonable fear of unjust and considerable injury to a party's person, property, or reputation. LSA-C.C. art. 1959; *Wolf v. Louisiana State Racing Commission,* 545 So.2d 976, 980 (La.1989); *Cagle v. Loyd,* 617 So.2d 592, 598 (La.App. 3rd Cir.), *writs denied,* 620 So.2d 877 (La.1993); *Adams v. Adams,* 503 So.2d 1052, 1057 (La. App. 2nd Cir.1987). Age, health, disposition, and other personal circumstances of a party must be taken into account in determining the reasonableness of the fear. LSA-C.C. art. 1959; *Adams v. Adams,* 503 So.2d at 1057.

[15] Duress results when "a person makes an improper threat that induces a party who has no reasonable alternative to manifest his assent. The result of this type of duress is that the contract that is created is voidable by the victim." LSA-C.C. art. 1959, official comment (b); *Wolf v. Louisiana State Racing Commission,* 545 So.2d at 980. The threat of doing a lawful act or a threat of exercising a right does not

constitute duress. LSA-C.C. art. 1962; *Adams v. Adams,* 503 So.2d at 1057. However, a threat of doing an act that is lawful in appearance only may constitute duress. *Wolf v. Louisiana State Racing Commission,* 545 So.2d at 980.

[....]

[16] The affidavit of Grezaffi reveals that he is the owner of the 2.536-acre tract of land in Pointe Coupee Parish. On June 16, 1988, he entered into a purchase agreement with Smith for the sale of the 2.536-acre tract of land. A copy of the purchase agreement was attached to Grezaffi's affidavit. Grezaffi further stated that the property was rezoned as "R-4" by the City Council and that the Bank of New Roads agreed to release the mortgage on the property upon execution of the act of sale. According to Grezaffi, prior to the date on which the act of sale was to be consummated, he informed Smith of these facts and advised Smith that he stood ready, willing, and able to fulfill his obligations under the terms of the purchase agreement. Grezaffi further stated that, to date, Smith has refused to comply with the purchase agreement.

[....]

[17] The affidavit of John Donald LeBlanc, loan officer at the Bank of New Roads, revealed that the bank held a mortgage on the Grezaffi property sought to be transferred to Smith. According to LeBlanc, prior to September 1, 1988, Grezaffi informed him that the mortgaged property was to be sold to Smith and requested that the mortgage on the property be released. LeBlanc stated that, upon the closing of the sale and application of the proceeds to the debt owed to the Bank of New Roads, the mortgage would be released.

[18] Smith's affidavit revealed that, in the fall of 1987, he entered into a purchase agreement with Luke J. Grezaffi for property in close proximity to the property which is the subject of the instant suit. Smith stated that he signed the purchase agreement with Luke Grezaffi to build a Farmers Home rental-assisted elderly housing complex. Smith further stated that he subsequently engaged numerous professionals to complete the necessary financing to acquire the property and fund the construction. Smith also stated that he filed an application with the Farmers Home Administration for financing and obtained approval to begin the project. Subsequent thereto, Luke Grezaffi filed an application for rezoning of the property with the City of New Roads. According to Smith, he was then contacted by Glenn Grezaffi, plaintiff in the instant suit, and Grezaffi's sister regarding their opposition to the rezoning application, which Smith stated was based upon internal strife within the Grezaffi family. Smith stated that Grezaffi and Grezaffi's sister threatened him in that "if Luke Grezaffi did not purchase the land owned by Glenn Grezaffi which was contiguous to the property ... [Smith] had previously agreed to purchase from Luke J. Grezaffi, then Glenn Grezaffi and his sister would use their influence with the New Roads Planning and Zoning Commission and City Council to oppose the rezoning requests filed" by Luke Grezaffi. Smith further stated that it was made clear to him that his application for rezoning would be denied if Grezaffi

and Grezaffi's sister opposed the application for rezoning. Smith also stated that, faced with the prospect of losing his ability to build and complete the development and the associated monetary losses caused by Grezaffi's threats, he executed the purchase agreement with Grezaffi.

[19] After reviewing the record and the evidence submitted, we find that no genuine issues of material fact exist and that reasonable minds must inevitably conclude that Grezaffi is entitled to judgment as a matter of law. The record reveals that Grezaffi showed that he is and was ready to comply with the obligations devolved upon him to perform. The property had been rezoned as "R-4," and the existing mortgage would be released upon the execution of the act of sale. Although Smith alleged that his consent to the agreement was vitiated because of duress, the record unequivocally established that the alleged economic duress was not of the type sufficient to vitiate his consent. As a landowner in the area, Grezaffi had a legal right to oppose the rezoning of the property. Informing Smith that he would oppose the rezoning was not a threat. Accordingly, we find that the trial judge properly granted the motion for summary judgment.

Conclusion

[20] For the above reasons, the judgment of the trial court, granting Grezaffi's motion for summary judgment is affirmed. Smith is cast for all costs of this appeal.

[. . . .]

Questions

1. How many and what kinds of obligations are created by a purchase agreement or an act of sale for the purchase of the property? Is it important, from the point of view of benefiting from the right of specific performance, to properly identify the kind of obligation created by a contract? Would you say that when a party enters into a contract, it should ask itself whether or not it definitely wants specific performance of its obligation by the other party to the contract or whether it would be satisfied by receiving damages instead? How does this decision have an impact on whether an obligation is to do, to give, or not to do?

2. Paragraphs 9–11: Note how the Court is approaching its discussion of the issues. It refers, first of all, to the law, i.e., the controlling Louisiana Civil Code articles. Then the Court applies the articles to the facts. This is the proper approach to take in a jurisdiction governed by a civil code. How should the Court have identified the nature or kind of obligation therein created by the parties (to give, to do, or to not do)?

3. Paragraph 12: Is a promise to sell a unilateral contract or a bilateral contract? What about a contract of sale? In this paragraph, is the Court making any kind of implicit reference to some means of defense or exception that can be raised by one first party against another second party who is seeking performance from the first party?

4. Paragraph 13: Explain the difference(s) between duress, on the one hand, and the threat of exercising a lawful right, on the other. What is the outcome of the "trial judge [having properly granted] the motion for summary judgment"? The price of the sale was $60,864.00 in 1988. In the trial court's summary judgment, the price was set at $64,864.00 (*see* line 29). From where does the difference in price come? A year later, in 1994, in affirming the trial court's summary judgment, is the Court of Appeal also affirming the price of $64,864.00? Shouldn't that price have been raised, as it was by the trial court, to take into account the five-year span between 1988 and 1993?

Larry G. Culp, et al.
v.
Eagle's Nest Church of Monroe, Louisiana, et al.

Court of Appeal of Louisiana
Second Circuit
November 19, 2004
887 So.2d 743

PEATROSS, J.

[....]

[1] For a breach of contract granting a right of first refusal, "specific performance is the appropriate remedy." *Robichaux v. Boutte*, 492 So.2d 521 (La.App. 3d Cir.1986), *writ denied*, 496 So.2d 352 (La.1986), citing *Price v. Town of Ruston*, 171 La. 985, 132 So. 653 (1931) [...].

[2] Further, Article 2625 states that:

A party may agree that he will not sell a certain thing without first offering it to a certain person. The right given to the latter in such a case is a right of first refusal that *may be enforced by specific performance.* (Emphasis added.)

[....]

In support of this position, Eagle's Nest points to Litvinoff, *Louisiana Civil Law Treatise, The Law of Obligations, Quantum of Damages*, 6 La. Civ. L. Treatise § 4.10, footnotes omitted, stating:

[I]t is not enough for a plaintiff to show that his interest has been injured because of the defendant's breach. He must also prove that there is some basis for the court to estimate how much that interest has been injured. That conclusion prevails in the Louisiana jurisprudence. [....]

[....]

[3] [T]he Civil Code states that the right given to the holder of a right of first refusal may be enforced by specific performance. This language indicates that specific performance is not the only remedy in such cases, i.e., damages are also available in certain situations [...]. [....]

[4] [A] trial court acts within its discretion by denying specific performance which otherwise may be feasible, where the inconvenience of the performance outweighs damage to an obligee. [. . . .]

[5] [S]pecific performance is the preferred contractual remedy under Louisiana jurisprudence, but, where . . . it is impractical to grant specific performance, damages are also available. [. . . .]

[. . . .]

Section III — Damages Resulting from the Inexecution of Conventional Obligations (Court Assessed Damages and Stipulated Damages)

Louisiana Sources of Law
Louisiana Civil Code

Art. 1994. Obligor liable for failure to perform.

An obligor is liable for the damages caused by his failure to perform a conventional obligation.

A failure to perform results from nonperformance, defective performance, or delay in performance. (Acts 1984, No. 331, § 1, eff. Jan. 1, 1985.)

Art. 1995. Measure of damages.

Damages are measured by the loss sustained by the obligee and the profit of which he has been deprived. (Acts 1984, No. 331, § 1, eff. Jan. 1, 1985.)

Art. 1996. Obligor in good faith.

An obligor in good faith is liable only for the damages that were foreseeable at the time the contract was made. (Acts 1984, No. 331, § 1, eff. Jan. 1, 1985.)

Art. 1997. Obligor in bad faith.

An obligor in bad faith is liable for all the damages, foreseeable or not, that are a direct consequence of his failure to perform. (Acts 1984, No. 331, § 1, eff. Jan. 1, 1985.)

Art. 1998. Damages for nonpecuniary loss.

Damages for nonpecuniary loss may be recovered when the contract, because of its nature, is intended to gratify a nonpecuniary interest and, because of the circumstances surrounding the formation or the nonperformance of the contract, the obligor knew, or should have known, that his failure to perform would cause that kind of loss.

Regardless of the nature of the contract, these damages may be recovered also when the obligor intended, through his failure, to aggrieve the feelings of the obligee. (Acts 1984, No. 331, §1, eff. Jan. 1, 1985.)

Art. 1999. Assessment of damages left to the court.

When damages are insusceptible of precise measurement, much discretion shall be left to the court for the reasonable assessment of these damages. (Acts 1984, No. 331, §1, eff. Jan. 1, 1985.)

Art. 2000. Damages for delay measured by interest; no need of proof; attorney fees.

When the object of the performance is a sum of money, damages for delay in performance are measured by the interest on that sum from the time it is due, at the rate agreed by the parties or, in the absence of agreement, at the rate of legal interest as fixed by Article 2924. The obligee may recover these damages without having to prove any loss, and whatever loss he may have suffered he can recover no more. If the parties, by written contract, have expressly agreed that the obligor shall also be liable for the obligee's attorney fees in a fixed or determinable amount, the obligee is entitled to that amount as well. (Acts 1984, No. 331, §1, eff. Jan. 1, 1985; Acts 1985, No. 137, §1, eff. Jul. 3, 1985; Acts 1987, No. 883, §1.)

Art. 2001. [omitted]

Art. 2002. Reasonable efforts to mitigate damages.

An obligee must make reasonable efforts to mitigate the damage caused by the obligor's failure to perform. When an obligee fails to make these efforts, the obligor may demand that the damages be accordingly reduced. (Acts 1984, No. 331, §1, eff. Jan. 1, 1985.)

Art. 2003. Obligee in bad faith.

An obligee may not recover damages when his own bad faith has caused the obligor's failure to perform or when, at the time of the contract, he has concealed from the obligor facts that he knew or should have known would cause a failure.

If the obligee's negligence contributes to the obligor's failure to perform, the damages are reduced in proportion to that negligence. (Acts 1984, No. 331, §1, eff. Jan. 1, 1985.)

Art. 2004. Clause that excludes or limits liability.

Any clause is null that, in advance, excludes or limits the liability of one party for intentional or gross fault that causes damage to the other party.

Any clause is null that, in advance, excludes or limits the liability of one party for causing physical injury to the other party. (Acts 1984, No. 331, §1, eff. Jan. 1, 1985.)

Art. 2005. Secondary obligation.

Parties may stipulate the damages to be recovered in case of nonperformance, defective performance, or delay in performance of an obligation.

That stipulation gives rise to a secondary obligation for the purpose of enforcing the principal one. (Acts 1984, No. 331, §1, eff. Jan. 1, 1985.)

Art. 2006. Nullity of the principal obligation.

Nullity of the principal obligation renders the stipulated damages clause null.

Nullity of the stipulated damages clause does not render the principal obligation null. (Acts 1984, No. 331, §1, eff. Jan. 1, 1985.)

Art. 2007. Stipulated damages or performance.

An obligee may demand either the stipulated damages or performance of the principal obligation, but he may not demand both unless the damages have been stipulated for mere delay. (Acts 1984, No. 331, §1, eff. Jan. 1, 1985.)

Art. 2008. Failure to perform justified.

An obligor whose failure to perform the principal obligation is justified by a valid excuse is also relieved of liability for stipulated damages. (Acts 1984, No. 331, §1, eff. Jan. 1, 1985.)

Art. 2009. Obligee not bound to prove damage.

An obligee who avails himself of a stipulated damages clause need not prove the actual damage caused by the obligor's nonperformance, defective performance, or delay in performance. (Acts 1984, No. 331, §1, eff. Jan. 1, 1985.)

Art. 2010. [omitted]

Art. 2011. Benefit from partial performance.

Stipulated damages for nonperformance may be reduced in proportion to the benefit derived by the obligee from any partial performance rendered by the obligor. (Acts 1984, No. 331, §1, eff. Jan. 1, 1985.)

Art. 2012. Stipulated damages may not be modified.

Stipulated damages may not be modified by the court unless they are so manifestly unreasonable as to be contrary to public policy. (Acts 1984, No. 331, §1, eff. Jan. 1, 1985.)

Doctrine

Louisiana Law of Conventional Obligations, A Précis

Section 8.3.2

The word "damages," without any adjective in front of the word, refers usually to "compensatory damages," i.e., damages meant to compensate an obligee for the loss he suffered from the non performance of his obligation by the obligor. [. . . .]

The parties know that, under the law of the civil Code, failure to perform an obligation will result in the "**obligor [being] liable for the damages caused by his failure to perform a conventional obligation.**" **Art. 1994(1).** That obligation to pay damages comes into existence if the obligor fails to perform without any lawful excuse, or if there is defective performance or delay in performance. **Art. 1994(2).** [. . . .]

We can refer to these compensatory damages as conventional or contractual damages to distinguish them from "delictual" damages. Such delictual damages find their source of law in **Arts. 2315 et seq.** [. . . .]

By contrast with "delictual damages" which are due as a consequence of a juridical fact, conventional damages find their justification in a juridical act, a contract. [. . . .]

Since we are focusing, here, on conventional obligations or contract, the parties to a contract may, at the time of formation of the contract and in anticipation of a party not performing, "**stipulate the damages to be recovered in case of nonperformance. . . .**" **Art. 2005** [. . .].

Art. 1995 gives this instruction to the court that the "**Damages are measured by the loss sustained by the obligee and the profit of which he has been deprived.**" [. . . .]

The contractual clause stipulating for damages creates an *accessory* or *secondary* obligation which will come into existence only in case of non performance by an obligor of his principal obligation. [. . . .]

Since a stipulated damages clause is included in a contract, the obligor knows in advance that his failure to perform will vest in the obligee the right to demand the payment of the stipulated damages. When "**An obligee . . . avail[s] himself of a stipulated damages clause [he] need not prove the actual damage caused by the obligor's nonperformance, defective performance, or delay in performance.**" **Art. 2009.** [. . . .]

As **Art. 2012** states: "**Stipulated damages may not be modified by the court unless they are so manifestly unreasonable as to be contrary to public policy.**" Furthermore, "**Stipulated damages for nonperformance may be reduced in proportion to the benefit derived by the obligee from any partial performance rendered by the obligor.**" **Art. 2011.** [. . . .]

The contractual obligation of the obligor to perform the principal obligation, first and foremost, and his accessory obligation to pay damages as a "back up" obligation are of such a paramount importance that the law issues, in **Art. 2004**, a stern warning to both parties to a contract: **"Any clause is null that, in advance, excludes or limits the liability of one party for intentional or gross fault that causes damage to the other party.**

Any clause is null that, in advance, excludes or limits the liability of one party for causing physical injury to the other party." [. . . .]

The principle stated in **Art. 1995** applies, as a general proposition, to obligations to give, to do and not to do: **"Damages are measured by the loss sustained by the obligee and the profit of which he has been deprived."** Since these concepts of loss sustained (*damnum emergens*) and deprivation of profit (*lucrum cessans*) which are the two component parts of the damages owed by the obligor are often not susceptible of precise measurement in advance [. . .].

One important first qualification is dictated by the obligor's good or bad faith. [. . . .]

It follows that **"An obligor in good faith is liable only for the damages that were foreseeable at the time the contract was made."** Art. 1996. *A contrario*, **"An obligor in bad faith is liable for all the damages, foreseeable or not, that are a direct consequence of his failure to perform."** Art. 1997. What damages are "foreseeable or not" and what damages "are a direct consequence" of the obligor's failure to perform will be for a court to determine following a **"reasonable assessment of these damages."** Art. 1999. [. . . .]

A second qualification attached to the principle takes into consideration the behavior of the other party to the contract, the obligee. Good faith is required of both parties. **Art. 2003.** [. . . .]

Good faith and a corollary duty of loyalty explain also why **"An obligee must make reasonable efforts to mitigate the damage caused by the obligor's failure to perform. When an obligee fails to make these efforts, the obligor may demand that the damages be accordingly reduced."** Art. 2002. [. . . .]

Art. 1998 applies to "non-pecuniary loss" or *"dommage/préjudice moral"* as are the legal expressions in French and Québec civil law. As a non-pecuniary loss, it affects a "value, a feeling, a belief" which has no patrimonial content or monetary value and which, therefore, is very personal to the party affected by the loss. [. . . .]

It is to this kind of loss, a non pecuniary loss, that Art. 1999 will be applied in most instances since such a loss will be difficult to evaluate. Therefore, the damages themselves will be difficult to measure precisely. That measurement will have to be given a **reasonable assessment** by a court exercising **much discretion**. (Art. 1999).

Cases

Bruce Meador and Gretchen Meador v.
Toyota of Jefferson, Inc., et al.

Supreme Court of Louisiana
May 17, 1976
332 So.2d 433

CALOGERO, Justice.

[1] May an automobile owner recover damages for aggravation, distress, and inconvenience from a repairman who has unnecessarily and excessively delayed completion of the vehicle's repair? This is the principal question presented in this case. It is to be answered by the construction to be given that portion of Civil Code article 1934(3) which allows the recovery of nonpecuniary loss '(w)here the contract has for its object the gratification of some intellectual enjoyment, whether in religion, morality or taste, or some convenience or other legal gratification. . . .'[1]

[2] Following a collision, an eighteen-year-old girl brought her first acquired automobile, a 1971 model Toyota, to defendant, Toyota of Jefferson, Inc., for repair late in February of 1972. It was returned to her on September 20, 1972, some seven months later. In her suit for damages (she was joined in the suit by her father), the trial court awarded her $1554.77, which included $602.77 as reimbursement for seven of her monthly car notes, $252 for seven monthly insurance payments, and $700 for aggravation, distress, and inconvenience. The Court of Appeal agreed that defendant had breached its contract, but concluded that the undue delay consisted of only five of the seven months' repair period. Accordingly, it reduced the $602.77 and the $252 portions of the award by two-sevenths, allowing, respectively, $430.55 and $180, for a total of $610.55. The Court of Appeal disallowed the $700 awarded by the trial court for aggravation, distress, and inconvenience, and in these particulars amended the judgment in favor of plaintiffs. Meador v. Toyota of Jefferson, Inc., 322 So.2d 802 (La.App.4th Cir. 1975).

[. . . .]

[3] We have reviewed the transcript and agree with the factual findings of the Court of Appeal. Defendant did indeed breach the implied obligation to repair

---

1. L.C.C. art. 1934(3) provides:
   'Although the general rule is, that damages are the amount of the loss the creditor has sustained, or of the gain of which he has been deprived, yet there are cases in which damages may be assessed without calculating altogether on the pecuniary loss, or the privation of pecuniary gain to the party. Where the contract has for its object the gratification of some intellectual enjoyment, whether in religion, morality or taste, or some convenience or other legal gratification, although these are not appreciated in money by the parties, yet damages are due for their breach; a contract for a religious or charitable foundation, a promise of marriage, or an engagement for a work of some of the fine arts, are objects and examples of this rule.'

within a reasonable time; the undue delay amounted to five months; $610.55 is a fair assessment of plaintiff's recoverable pecuniary loss. (As noted earlier, this element is no longer before us). Furthermore, if recoverable, $700 would be a reasonable and proper award for plaintiff's nonpecuniary damages, i.e., her aggravation, distress, and inconvenience. Accordingly, we direct our attention to the principal question posed at the outset of this opinion.

[4] Generally, recovery for damages upon the breach of a contract is limited to the loss a person has sustained or the profit of which he has been deprived.[3] However, in certain limited circumstances a person may, upon the breach of a contract, recover damages for nonpecuniary loss. It is this sort of damage which plaintiff herein seeks to recover. Plaintiff argues that she is due recovery for aggravation, distress, and inconvenience which resulted from her inability to use her automobile for the period during which defendant unreasonably delayed its repair. She argues that this damage is recoverable under Civil Code Article 1934(3) which, as we indicated earlier, allows recovery for nonpecuniary loss '(w)here the contract has for its object the gratification of some intellectual enjoyment, whether in religion, morality or taste, or some convenience or other legal gratification. . . .'She argues specifically that the disjunctive 'or' in the article means that nonpecuniary damages are allowed where the contract has for its object the gratification either of 'some intellectual enjoyment' Or of 'some convenience.' Thus she contends that to gain recovery under the article, one need not show that the contract contained any intellectual element whatsoever; one may recover even when the object of the contract is purely physical gratification. This liberal position is supported by language, at least, in the First Circuit Court of Appeal opinion in Jack v. Henry, 128 So.2d 62 (La.App.1st Cir. 1961).[4] An alternative, broader position which also supports plaintiff's recovery is that it suffices, to permit nonpecuniary damages, that the object or objects of the contract include elements of both intellectual and physical gratification. See Holland v. St. Paul Mercury Ins. Co., 135 So.2d 145 (La.App.1st Cir. 1961), Meyer v. Succession of McClellan, 30 So.2d 788 (La.App.Orl.1947), Melson v. Woodruff, 23 So.2d 364 (La.App.1st Cir. 1945).

[5] On the other hand, defendant contends that in order for plaintiff to recover nonpecuniary damages, the object of the contract must be exclusively intellectual enjoyment, as opposed to partially intellectual — partially physical, and as opposed to exclusively physical enjoyment. This strict interpretation is given support in

---

3. L.C.C. art. 1934 provides:
   'Where the object of the contract is any thing but the payment of money, the damages due to the creditor for its breach are the amount of the loss he has sustained, and the profit of which he has been deprived, under the following exceptions and modifications.'
4. In the Jack case, the court stated:
   '(W)e believe that a contract for the construction of a home . . . has as its object the convenience of the owner within the meaning and intendment of the phrase "or some convenience" as used in Paragraph 3, Article 1934, LSA-R.C.C. entitling the owner of a residence to damages for inconvenience resulting from a contractor's breach of the obligation. . . .' 128 So.2d at 72.

the jurisprudence by such cases as Rigaud v. Orkin Exterminating Co., 236 So.2d 916 (La.App.3d Cir. 1970), Baker v. Stamps, 82 So.2d 858 (La.App.Orl.1955), Lillis v. Anderson, 21 So.2d 389 (La.App.Orl.1945), and Sahuc v. United States Fidelity & Guar. Co., 320 F.2d 18 (5th Cir. 1963).

[6] This Court has never adopted a strict view but has reached results favoring the broader interpretation of Art. 1934(3).[5] In Lewis v. Holmes, 109 La. 1030, 34 So. 66 (1903) a bride had contracted with the defendant store for the manufacture, or sewing, of five dresses, one for her wedding and the others for her trousseau. She was allowed recovery for deprivation of intellectual enjoyment and for mental suffering in connection with defendant's non-delivery of the four dresses for her trousseau. The contract's object was not purely intellectual, but rather entailed features both physical (her need for comfortable clothing), and intellectual (her preference for style, or 'taste,' and concern with her appearance on her wedding day and on her honeymoon).

[7] Two other cases where the Court allowed recovery and where there existed elments [*sic*] of both intellectual and physical gratification were O'Meallie v. Moreau, 116 La. 1020, 41 So. 243 (1906) and Jiles v. Venus Community Center Benevolent Mutual Aid Assn., 191 La. 803, 186 So. 342 (1939). In O'Meallie, the Court awarded damages for annoyance and vexation to a social club for breach of a contract to lease a picnic area, and in Jiles the Court awarded plaintiff damages for mental anguish from watching her child die without proper medical attention because of defendant Association's breach of a contract to supply doctors' services and medicine.

[8] In none of the foregoing cases, however, has the Court historically viewed the source of Article 1934(3) and the origin thereof.

[9] The third paragraph of Article 1934 had no counterpart in the Code Napoleon or the Louisiana Civil Code of 1808. The paragraph first appeared in the Louisiana Civil Code of 1825.[6] That Code was drafted in French, translated into English. Both French and English versions are official texts of the Code.[7] To interpret the Article, then, where as [*sic*] here the articles of the 1870 Code is not entirely clear,[8] we deem

---

5. For an excellent comment on this subject, including the 'liberal,' 'broad,' and 'strict' interpretation in the jurisprudence see 'Damages Ex contractu: Recovery of Nonpecuniary Damages For Breach of Contract Under Louisiana Civil Code Article 1934,' by Henri Wolbrette, III, 48 Tul.L.Rev. 1160 (1974).

6. It has been suggested that the source of this paragraph was Toullier, 6 Droit Civil, Liv. III, Tit. III, Chap. III, Sec. IV, s III, n. 293 (305 seq.) and Domat, I Loix Civiles, Part. I, Liv. III, Tit. V, Sec. II, ns. XI, XII (270). Batiza, The Actual Sources of the Louisiana Project of 1823: A General Analytical Survey, 47 Tul.L.Rev. 1, 80 (1972). Neither of these sources, however, contained the precise idea contained in 1934(3), although Domat does include a passage suggestive of the principle incorporated in 1934(3). See 48 Tul.L.Rev., Supra at 1173.

7. I A General Digest of the Acts of the Legislature of Louisiana passed from the year 1804, to 1827, Inclusive 223 (1928); See generally Dainow, The Louisiana Civil Law, in Civil Code of Louisiana (Dainow ed., 1961).

8. 48 Tul.L.Rev., supra at 1174.

it helpful to examine the French and English versions of the article in the Code of 1825.

[10] In the French version of the 1825 Louisiana Civil Code, the pertinent clause of Art. 1928 read:

'Lorsque le contract a pour but de procurer a quelqu'un une jouissance purement intellectuelle, telle que celles qui tiennent a la religion, a la morale, augout, a la commodite ou a toute autre espece de satisfaction de ce genre, ...'

[11] Translated into English this passage reads:

'When the contract has for its object to confer to someone a purely intellectual enjoyment, such as those pertaining to religion, morality, taste, convenience or other gratifications of this sort, ...'[9]

[12] The foregoing French article was mistranslated to read in the English version of Article 1928 of the Louisiana Civil Code of 1825, as follows:

'Where the contract has for its object the gratification of some intellectual enjoyment, whether in religion, morality, or taste, or some convenience or other legal gratification, ...'

[13] The English passage was copied verbatim into the Code of 1870.[10] Thus we conclude that the clause should, as it may, logically, be read as follows: Where the contract has for its object the gratification of intellectual enjoyment, such as that pertaining to religion, or morality, or taste, or convenience, ...

[14] It is evident that the proper interpretation of Article 1934(3), is not, as plaintiff contends, that nonpecuniary damages are allowable where the object is exclusively physical gratification. On the contrary, 'convenience' in the source provision was not a contract object triggering the availability of nonpecuniary damages, but was, rather, along with religion, morality, and taste, one example of 'purely intellectual

---

9. While the disjunctive 'or' prefacing 'some convenience' or other legal gratification might arguably suggest that nonpecuniary damages are allowed 'where the contract has for its object the gratification' of 'some convenience,' the ambiguity in the language of the paragraph becomes apparent when article 1934 is read in its entirety and in conjunction with article 1926. Article 1926 provides that in breach of contract cases damages may be given 'according to the rules established in the following section.' Article 1934 appears in the following section of the Code. It provides at the outset that with an exception not here relevant damages due for breach of contract are the amounts of loss and deprived profits, except for exceptions and modifications related thereafter in three numbered paragraphs. The third numbered paragraph recites the general rule, and then there appears the exception which employs the language here at issue. See Footnote 1, second sentence of the quoted article 1934(3). If that sentence were intended to allow nonpecuniary damages where a contract has for its object 'some' (virtually every contract of which we can conceive) convenience there would be no sense to the outset language of article 1934 limiting damage to losses sustained and profits of which deprived as a general proposition.

10. Only the comma after 'morality' was deleted in the version of the passage in the 1870 Code.

enjoyment,' the intellectual enjoyment being necessary as a contract's object before nonpecuniary damages became available.

[15] We find the French source provision of 1934(3) in the 1825 Louisiana Civil Code, if not controlling, at least persuasive in our present interpretation of the article's ambiguous counterpart in our 1870 Civil Code. While the foregoing interpretation does not allow nonpecuniary damages where the sole object is physical gratification, a proper interpretation of the entirety of Article 1934(3) does not in our view bar such damages in all instances where there exists as an object physical gratification. We believe that a contract can have 'for its object' intellectual enjoyment, assuming that intellectual enjoyment is a Principal object of the contract, notwithstanding that a peripheral, or incidental, or even perhaps concurrent object of the contract may be physical gratification.

[16] Thus, we would interpret Article 1934(3) as follows: Where an object, or the exclusive object, of a contract, is physical gratification (or anything other than intellectual gratification) nonpecuniary damages as a consequence of nonfulfillment of that object are not recoverable.

[17] On the other hand, where a principal or exclusive object of a contract is intellectual enjoyment, nonpecuniary damages resulting from the nonfulfillment of that intellectual object Are recoverable. Damages in this event are recoverable for the loss of such intellectual enjoyment as well as for mental distress, aggravation, and inconvenience resulting from such loss, or denial of intellectual enjoyment.

[18] The foregoing principles are not at variance with the results obtained in the cases of Lewis v. Holmes, supra, O'Meallie v. Moreau, supra, and Jiles v. Venus Community Center Benevolent Mutual Aid Assn., supra.

[19] Applying these principles to the case at hand, we conclude that plaintiff is not entitled to recover damages for aggravation, distress, and inconvenience caused by the five month loss of use of her automobile, because the procuring of intellectual enjoyment, while perhaps an incidental or inferred contemplation of the contracting parties, was not a principal object of the contract to have the car repaired. The principal object of the contract, the overriding concern of plaintiff, evident to defendant at the time the contract was entered into, was the repair of plaintiff's automobile with its consequent utility or physical gratification.

[20] As noted, we clearly do not hold that the object of a contract must be exclusively intellectual enjoyment in order to trigger article 1934(3)'s nonpecuniary damages. We do hold, however, that such intellectual enjoyment must be a principal object of the contract, and that nonpecuniary damages, when allowed, are limited to those which compensate for, or are directly related to, nonfulfillment of the intellectual object.

[21] We also deem it worth noting, however fundamental, that unlike the rule which we are required by the Civil Code to apply in this action for breach of contract, damages for mental anguish, aggravation, distress and inconvenience, are

recoverable in an action sounding in tort. La.Civil Code art. 2315; 2 M. Planiol, Traite elementaire de droit civil, no. 252 at 152 (11th ed., La.State L.Inst.tranl.1959); 48 Tul.L.Rev., Supra at 1171.

[22] Perhaps it would be better if damages for mental anguish in breach of contract cases were allowable just as in tort actions. However, such a matter directs itself to the law maker. Our responsibility is to interpret and apply the law, not to enact it.

[23] For the foregoing reasons, the judgment of the Court of Appeal is affirmed. All costs of this appeal are chargeable to the plaintiff.

[. . . .]

MARCUS, Justice (assigning additional concurring reasons).

[24] While I join in the majority opinion, in my view, damages are not awardable for annoyance and emotional distress in breach of contract cases unless the gratification of purely intellectual enjoyment is The principal object of the contract. Where only an incidental or concurrent object of the contract is the gratification of purely intellectual enjoyment, damages for annoyance and emotional distress are not recoverable.

DIXON, Justice (dissenting).

[25] I respectfully dissent. We should not deny recovery for damages which are suffered, for which justice requires compensation, for the rather superficial reason that plaintiff's action is in contract, not tort. Nevertheless, even considering this a contract action, these damages are recoverable under the plain terms of C.C. 1934(1).

[26] When plaintiff brought her vehicle to defendant for repairs, she had the right to expect that the repairs be completed within a reasonable time. They were not. As a result, not only did she suffer pecuniary loss, but also the aggravation of not having her car, the distress of not knowing when she would get it back, and finally the inconvenience of having to find other methods of getting around. In a society as dependent on the automobile as ours, where a car is not only a convenience but often a necessity, a plaintiff should be able to recover damages representing the aggravation, distress and inconvenience suffered when the repairman breaches his duty to fix the car within a reasonable time. Such damages are reasonably within the contemplation of the parties at the time the contract was entered into, and are therefore compensable. C.C. 1934(1).

[27] This court has consistently awarded damages for mental anguish and inconvenience in tort suits where property damage is sustained. In Dodd v. Glen Rose Gasoline Co., 194 La. 1, 193 So. 349 (1939), in which defendant's plant operated in a manner that prevented plaintiff from getting a good night's sleep, this court awarded damages for inconvenience and discomfort. In McGee v. Yazoo & M.V.R. Co., 206 La. 121, 19 So.2d 21 (1944), this court awarded damages for mental anguish, worry and inconvenience caused by the depositing of soot, smoke and cinders into plaintiffs' houses by defendant's roundhouse operation. In Fontenot v. Magnolia

Petroleum Co., 227 La. 866, 80 So.2d 845 (1955), we awarded damages for inconvenience and mental anguish suffered by plaintiff as a result of defendant's blasting operations.

[28] There is no logical reason to allow recovery of such damages when property is involved in cases delineated as 'tort,' and yet deny recovery of similar damages when property is involved (as in this case), simply because the cause of action is delineated as 'contract.' Both involve a duty and a breach. Louisiana employs fact pleading. A plaintiff need only state facts, which, if true, authorize recovery. Cox v. W. M. Heroman & Co., 298 So.2d 848 (La.1974). In the instant case, plaintiff has proved, to the satisfaction of the trier of fact, that she suffered inconvenience, distress and aggravation because of defendant's breach of duty. She should recover therefor. As Planiol states:

> '... The big objection is that mental suffering can not be compensated with money. But that is done every day in the case of torts; why act differently in contract cases? There is no reason for not doing so, and as M. Boistel has well said, just because one can not do so better, is no reason for doing nothing at all.'[1]

Questions

1. Paragraphs 1–28: After you have the read the whole case, can you draw a (mental) picture of the two parties involved in the case? Do they have the same capacity? Do they have the same technical knowledge? Do they have the same negotiating ability? Do any of these questions matter as regards the formation of a contract, the nature of the obligations created, and their performance? What about the remedies in case of breach of contract by one party or the other?

2. Paragraphs 4–18: What is the major issue discussed by the Court? In this respect, read carefully the Court's analysis of former Louisiana Civil Code article 1934. What lesson should you learn about the translation of legal documents on the one hand, and the role of history on the other hand? Can comparative law be of any help? What role did the cases play in giving a meaning to former Louisiana Civil Code article 1934? Which one of the three possible interpretations of article 1934 does the Court adopt as its interpretation? (*See* paragraph 16.) Is it clear to you?

3. Paragraph 19: Can you restate the principles to which the Court is referring? In the Court's statement starting with "Applying these principles ... [to] ... physical gratification," is there any suggestion that the Court might use an objective standard or a subjective standard of this notion of intellectual enjoyment? In the next paragraph, starting with "As noted," is the Court giving

---

1. 2 M. Planiol, Traité Elémentaire de Droit Civil No. 252 (11th ed. La.State L.Inst.Trans. (1959)).

any indication as to the process that should be used by a court to ascertain whether and how "such an intellectual enjoyment must be a principal object of the contract"? In light of Question 1, could the kinds of persons involved in a contract, the age and ability of one party or the other, the type of transaction entered into (a sale rather than a lease), or the particular cause of the obligation of one party, have some impact on the principal object of the contract, rendering it more intellectual enjoyment for one party than for the other?

4. Paragraph 22: What do you think of the distinction the Court makes between mental anguish in tort as opposed to contract? Is the notion of mental anguish a purely legal question confined to the type of action brought (tort v. contract), or is it rather a human element that becomes a part of any legal transaction in which a person is involved? Why should Ms. Meador (young and buying her first car to go to work) be granted moral damages in a tort action and not in a contract action? Wasn't Ms. Meador in good faith all through her ordeal? Can you say the same thing about the Toyota Dealership? Shouldn't the Court have made an issue of good faith (*see* La. Civ. Code art. 1759)? What do you think of Justice Dixon's dissenting opinion?

Brenda Bourne

v.

Rein Chrysler-Plymouth, Inc. and Chrysler Corporation

Court of Appeal of Louisiana
First Circuit
December 28, 1984
463 So.2d 1356

JOHN S. COVINGTON, Judge pro tempore:

[1] This is a suit for reduction of the purchase price of an automobile. Judgment was rendered against Chrysler Corporation, the manufacturer, and it appealed [. . .].

[. . . .]

Assignments Of Error

[2] Defendant-appellant, Chrysler Corporation (Chrysler), assigns as errors by the District Court [**among others**] the awarding of damages for inconvenience and mental anguish "which is clearly not recoverable in this type of action" [. . .].

Issues

[3] The issue [. . .] presented for our resolution [**is** . . .] whether damages for inconvenience and mental anguish were properly awarded under the facts peculiar to the instant case [. . .].

Facts

[4] Brenda Bourne purchased a new 1981 Chrysler Cordoba automobile on February 27, 1981 from defendant Rein Chrysler-Plymouth, Inc. (Rein), for a total deferred sales price of $14,641.85. Rein's salesman did not disclose to Ms. Bourne that the automobile had any mechanical defects which would render it "either absolutely useless, or its use so inconvenient and imperfect" to give rise to the legal presumption that she "would not have purchased it" if she had "known of the vice." C.C. art. 2520. Ms. Bourne accepted delivery of the car on Friday, February 27, 1981 after Rein's service department had closed for the weekend. While enroute to her home, immediately after accepting delivery, Ms. Bourne noticed the sluggish performance of the motor. During the weekend the engine "died" several times while Ms. Bourne was driving so she took the vehicle to the service department on Monday morning so that Rein's service technicians could resolve the engine stalling problem but they did not attempt any repairs that day. She returned the next day and was informed to bring the car back on Thursday because that would be the earliest time the repairs could be made. Between Tuesday morning and Thursday morning, when she returned the car to the service department as instructed, the horn was activated spontaneously and had to be disconnected to silence it. The technicians set the timing so high the car "would get away from" Ms. Bourne and she was frightened by its engine racing tendencies. After the horn was "fixed" on Thursday it did not function

at all. The malfunctioning headlights were also repaired at that time. Within a few days after Ms. Bourne bought the car a part of the console and the door panel fell off and had to be reglued. During the second week following the date of the purchase the vinyl roof "was starting to bubble" so Ms. Bourne returned the car to the service department where it remained two days because of the many problems to be dealt with. During that two day stay at Rein's the timing was reset but after the resetting the car began stalling out again.

[5] From the very outset the cruise control never functioned. Early in April, 1981 the air pollution pump became partially disconnected and it drilled a hole through the sheet metal of the hood. About one month later the air pollution pump and pulley assembly were replaced but the hole in the hood was not repaired. Late in June, 1981 the air conditioner malfunctioned while Ms. Bourne was driving to New Orleans from Ponchatoula and "all of a sudden the water came pouring in over" her feet; the water was coming from "in the front under the dash" and even after she turned off the air conditioner "it still kept coming"; the water flooded the interior of the car to a depth "up past the shoe". The flooding ruined the carpet and resulted in an offensive odor which did not dissipate during the two months Ms. Bourne ceased driving the car because Rein refused to replace the carpet and because she was "already terrified of the car because of the pump" disengaging and drilling a hole in the hood.

[6] Chrysler issued three recall notices requesting owners of 1981 Chrysler Cordobas to take their autos to the dealers to correct specified mechanical problems, including engine sluggishness and the pump.

[7] The increasing frequency of taking the automobile to Rein for mechanical corrections made her the butt of much laughter and unkind jokes by Rein's service personnel and some other personnel. The many returns for repairs, with repeated failures in her endeavor to have the vehicle so it would provide her safe and reliable transportation, caused Ms. Bourne to suffer great embarrassment, humiliation, and inconvenience from the day she bought the car and accepted its delivery up to the time she stopped driving the car in early July, 1981. She was afraid to drive the car because of its shabby and unsafe condition.

[8] Although Ms. Bourne continued to pay the monthly installments to Chrysler Credit Corporation (Chrysler Credit) and was not delinquent with them, Chrysler Credit filed suit to seize and sell the car under executory process. Upon receipt of petition for the writ of seizure and sale, Ms. Bourne retained counsel to enjoin both the seizure and sale in order to preserve her credit reputation and undo some of the embarrassment and humiliation she suffered when the car was seized at her work place. The executory proceedings damaged Ms. Bourne's credit and she paid cash for a used car.

[. . .] Damages

[. . . .]

[9] Chrysler simply argues in its brief that the lower court committed reversible error by awarding plaintiff damages for mental anguish and inconvenience.

Chrysler relies on *Meador v. Toyota of Jefferson, Inc.,* 332 So.2d 433 (La.1976) as authority for its premise that because the record is devoid of any suggestion that Ms. Bourne "purchased the vehicle for any type of intellectual enjoyment" the lower court improperly awarded her non-pecuniary damages in her quanti minoris action based on C.C. art. 2520 et seq.

[10] *Meador,* supra, was not a suit for redhibition or quanti minoris. The litigation in *Meador* had its origin in defendant's alleged excessive delay in completing repairs to an automobile brought to defendant to repair collision damage. The contractual obligation undertaken by defendant in *Meador* was the obligation to repair the automobile in a workmanlike manner in as short a period as possible under the total facts and circumstances. The Supreme Court held that C.C. art. 1934(3), dealing with damages generally, precludes awarding non-pecuniary damages in a breach of contract context unless intellectual enjoyment is a principal object of the contract, and that non-pecuniary damages, when allowed, are limited to those which compensate for, or are directly related to, nonfulfillment of the intellectual object.

[11] The *Meador* rule is no longer applied inflexibly in contract actions. *Gele v. Markey,* 387 So.2d 1162 (La.1980); *Pike v. Stephens Imports, Inc.,* 448 So.2d 738, 743 (La.App. 4th Cir.1984).

[12] *Philippe v. Browning Arms Co.,* 395 So.2d 310, 318 (La.1981), on rehearing, stated the duty of a manufacturer as being "the obligation to produce a product which is reasonably safe for its intended use" and that "[b]reach of this obligation gives rise to a cause of action in favor of the purchaser of the product not only to demand the return of the purchase price, but also, because the manufacturer is presumed to know of defects in its products, to demand all damages caused by the defect and reasonable attorney's fees."

[13] The court, in *Philippe,* supra, reasoned that "[t]here is no compelling reason to require a person injured by a defective product he has purchased to proceed either in contract or in tort. The seller's (manufacturer's) act of delivering a defective thing, when he knows of the defect, gives rise to delictual, as well as contractual, liability. (citations omitted)." The Supreme Court, per Lemmon, J., held "that the right and the extent of recovery by the purchaser of a thing against the seller or manufacturer is governed by the codal articles providing for responsibility in the seller-purchaser relationship, as applied through C.C. art. 2315. Since C.C. art. 2545 clearly provides for recovery of damages caused by a defective product and for reasonable attorney's fees, we conclude the court of appeal correctly made such award."

[14] In reaching the conclusion stated above, the court in *Philippe* reasoned that: "The appropriate standard of conduct in this case is derived from the codal articles on sales, since the cause of action of the purchaser of a defective thing may be enforced against both the seller and the manufacturer of a thing"; "[o]ne of the obligations imposed on the seller (manufacturer) is the warranty against hidden defects of the thing sold"; and the manufacturer, imputed with knowledge of defects in his products, is liable not only for the return of the price and the expenses of the

sale, but "also (is) answerable for damages and reasonable attorney's fees." *Philippe,* supra, at 318.

[**15**] *Philippe v. Browning Arms Co.,* supra, in our opinion, is authority for the proposition that the purchaser who sustains damages because he or she purchased a redhibitorily defective product is entitled to be compensated for all provable damages, including inconvenience and mental anguish, if the causation link is established. *Philippe,* supra, mandates judicial repudiation of the blanket exclusion of damages for inconvenience and mental anguish in redhibition and quanti minoris actions. To knowingly sell a redhibitorily defective product, such knowledge being imputed to a manufacturer, is to do a tortious act. It is well settled that a tortfeasor's victim who sustains mental anguish as a result of the action or inaction of the tortfeasor is entitled to be compensated for it.

[**16**] While the Trial Judge did not assign detailed written reasons, he obviously believed that plaintiff's uncontradicted evidence established that plaintiff in fact suffered mental anguish, in addition to considerable inconvenience, because of the multiplicity of vices or defects cumulatively constituting grounds for redhibition, which were never resolved satisfactorily enough to defeat plaintiff's suit for quanti minoris. [....]

[....]

Questions

1. Paragraphs 1–8: Do you think there was any purpose in the Court giving such a detailed presentation of the facts of this case? Recall the *Meador* case earlier in this section; do you see any difference with this case and the Court's focus here on one party, Ms. Bourne as buyer, as Ms. Meador was the buyer of the Toyota? Is the fact that Ms. Bourne was buying a new car of any significance? How would you describe the seller's behavior? Would you make any reference to good faith or bad faith? Could it be relevant in computing the amount of damages? Could there be fraud on the part of the dealership? Read Louisiana Civil Code articles 2520, 2524 and 2545.

2. Paragraph 8: Would you say that Chrysler Credit Corporation made a lawful use of its rights under Louisiana Civil Code article 1962 or that it abused its rights?

3. Paragraphs 9–16: In what respects is this Court distancing itself from the *Meador* court? Is a difference between a delay in performing services resulting in mental anguish and inconvenience and the occurrence of defects in a thing sold resulting in mental anguish and inconvenience sufficient to justify a difference in the outcome of the respective legal actions? Aren't both actions concerned with non-performance or bad performance of obligations? *See* La. Civ. Code arts. 1994–1998. What do you think of the *Philippe v. Browning Arms* case, particularly where it states: "There is no compelling reason"? What do you think of this Court saying: "*Philippe* mandates judicial repudiation of the

blanket exclusion of damages for inconvenience . . . actions"? (*See* paragraph 15.) Is the Court saying that whatever the cause or source of the damage, it is all a matter of tort? Could that classification of the cause of action have an impact on the length of the prescriptive period applicable to one action and not to the other? (*See* La. Civ. Code arts. 3492 and 3499.) Did the *Philippe* court create law or did it merely interpret the law as written in the Louisiana Civil Code articles?

The Kroger Company
v.
L.G. Barcus & Sons, Inc., et al.

Court of Appeal of Louisiana
Second Circuit
June 17, 2009
13 So.3d 1232

WILLIAMS, J.

[1] The plaintiff, The Kroger Company ("Kroger"), appeals a judgment in favor of the defendant, SCA Consulting Engineers, Inc. ("SCA"). The district court found that plaintiff's claim against defendant arising from the attempted repair of the building was based in tort and had prescribed. For the following reasons, we affirm.

Facts

[2] This matter arises out of a lawsuit filed by Kroger against numerous defendants, seeking damages caused by settlement of the foundation and floor of the Kroger store located on Youree Drive in Shreveport, Louisiana. The defendants included L.G. Barcus & Sons, Inc. ("Barcus"), which drilled and poured the auger cast piles, Professional Services, Inc. ("PSI"), the project geotechnical engineer, Travelers Casualty and Surety Company and St. Paul Fire & Marine Insurance Company, the insurers of the bankrupt contractor, Whitaker Construction Company, and SCA.

[3] In its original petition filed in October 2002, Kroger alleged that the store's foundation was designed and constructed in 1996 and 1997 and that the store opened for business in 1997. Kroger further alleged that SCA's foundation design and specifications were substandard and inadequate, resulting in the cast piles not being installed to the correct depth. This allegation is referred to as the "design phase" claim. The petition also asserted that after the initial settling of the store, Kroger requested that SCA make recommendations to remedy the settlement problem, but the attempts at remediation had not been successful.

[4] More than three years later, in March 2006, Kroger filed an amended petition reiterating the design phase allegations of the original petition and asserting a "repair phase" claim against SCA and another defendant, Hayward Baker, Inc. Specifically, in paragraphs 25, 26 and 27 of the amended petition, Kroger alleged that

following completion of the original construction, Kroger retained the services of SCA to remedy the settlement problem, but that the engineering services provided by SCA were "ineffective, performed negligently, and their implementation caused additional damages to the Kroger Store."

[5] Subsequently, SCA filed a motion for summary judgment on the grounds that the plaintiff's claims had prescribed. The district court rendered judgment granting in part the motion for summary judgment, dismissing plaintiff's design phase claims against SCA as prescribed, but denying summary judgment as to plaintiff's repair phase claims. Kroger appealed the judgment, which was affirmed by this court in *The Kroger Company v. L.G. Barcus & Sons, Inc.*, 43,804 (La.App. 2d Cir.1/ 14/ 09), 2 So.3d 1163, *writ denied*, 09-0382 (La.5/ 15/ 09), 8 So.3d 571.

[6] In April 2008, while the appeal was pending, SCA filed an exception of prescription seeking dismissal of Kroger's repair phase claim. In response, Kroger asserted that its claim did not sound in tort, but in contract, and was thus subject to a ten-year prescriptive period. SCA argued that Kroger's claim was delictual and had prescribed, since the claim was not filed within the applicable one-year prescriptive period. After a hearing, the district court found that Kroger's claim was based on negligence and subject to the one-year prescriptive period. The court rendered judgment sustaining SCA's exception and dismissing Kroger's claims. Kroger appeals the judgment.

Discussion

[7] Kroger contends the district court erred in sustaining the exception of prescription. Kroger argues that the applicable prescriptive period is ten years because the dispute with SCA is based on the parties' contract.

[8] Delictual actions are subject to a liberative prescription of one year, running from the day injury or damage is sustained. LSA-C.C. art. 3492. An action on a contract is governed by the prescriptive period of ten years for personal actions. LSA-C.C. art. 3499. The nature of the duty breached determines whether an action is in tort or contract. *Roger v. Dufrene*, 613 So.2d 947 (La.1993); *Trinity Universal Insurance Co. v. Horton*, 33,157 (La.App. 2d Cir.4/ 5/ 00), 756 So.2d 637. The distinction between damages *ex contractu* and damages *ex delicto* is that the former flow from the breach of a special obligation contractually assumed by the obligor, whereas the latter flow from the violation of a general duty owed to all persons. Even when a tortfeasor and victim are bound by a contract, courts usually apply the delictual prescription to actions that are actually grounded in tort. *Trinity, supra; Harrison v. Gore*, 27,254 (La.App. 2d Cir.8/ 23/ 95), 660 So.2d 563, *writ denied*, 95-2347 (La.12/ 8/ 95), 664 So.2d 426.

[9] The mere fact that the circumstances arose in the context of a contractual relationship does not make the cause of action contractual. The courts are not bound to accept a plaintiff's characterization of the nature of his cause of action if unsupported by factual allegations. *Thomas v. State Employees Group Benefits Program*, 05-0392 (La.App. 1st Cir.3/ 24/ 06), 934 So.2d 753.

[10] In this case, the alleged repair contract includes a writing drafted by SCA, dated October 10, 2001, stating in part: "SCOPE OF WORK: Field observation to observe possible foundation movements and negative drainage on an existing Kroger Food Store." Kroger also points to an outline prepared by SCA that proposed measures to strengthen the cast piles as forming part of the contract for services. We will assume the existence of a repair contract as alleged for the purpose of reviewing whether Kroger's claim has prescribed.

[11] In its amended petition, Kroger does not allege that a specific contract provision was breached, but that SCA's services were ineffective and negligently performed. Thus, Kroger's petition states a cause of action for breach of a person's general duty to perform repair work in a non-negligent, prudent and skillful manner. *See* LSA-C.C. art. 2316. Liability for breach of this duty arises *ex delicto. Trinity, supra; K & M Enterprises of Slaughter, Inc. v. Richland Equipment Company, Inc.,* 96-2292 (La.App. 1st Cir.9/ 19/ 97), 700 So.2d 921. Accordingly, the district court was correct in finding that Kroger's cause of action was in tort and subject to the one-year liberative prescriptive period of Article 3492.

[....]

Conclusion

[12] For the foregoing reasons, the district court's judgment sustaining SCA's exception of prescription is affirmed. The costs of this appeal are assessed to the appellant, The Kroger Company.

[13] AFFIRMED.

[....]

BROWN, Chief Judge, Dissenting.

[14] All personal actions, including actions to enforce contractual obligations, are subject to a liberative prescription of ten years unless otherwise provided by legislation. La. C.C. art. 3499. La. R.S. 9:5607 now provides for a five-year liberative prescriptive/peremptive period in all actions, tort or contract, against, *inter alia,* professional engineers. This provision, however, was added by Acts 2003, No. 854, 51, and is therefore inapplicable to the instant case. Delictual actions are subject to a liberative prescription of one year, running from the day injury or damage is sustained. La. C.C. art. 3492. Proper characterization of the nature of Kroger's cause of action is crucial to determination of the issue before this court.

[15] *In re St. Louis Encephalitis Outbreak in Ouachita Parish,* 41,250 (La.App. 2d Cir.09/ 01/ 06), 939 So.2d 563, this court observed that it is well settled that the same acts or omissions may constitute breaches of both general duties and contractual duties and may give rise to both actions in tort and actions in contract. A plaintiff may assert both actions and is not required to plead the theory of his case. *Dubin v. Dubin,* 25,996 (La.App. 2d Cir.08/ 17/ 94), 641 So.2d 1036. When a person negligently performs a contractual obligation, he has committed an active breach of contract which may also support an action in tort. *Id.*

[**16**] In *Cameron v. Bruce*, 42,873 (La.App. 2d Cir.04/ 23/ 08), 981 So.2d 204, 207, *writ denied*, 2008-1127 (La.09/ 19/ 08), 992 So.2d 940, we stated:

> A home inspector has a duty to exercise reasonable care and skill in his undertaking. A breach of that duty constitutes a tort as well as a breach of contract. One has a prescriptive period of one year from date of injury and the other is subject to a liberative prescriptive period of ten years. In medical and legal malpractice as well as in products liability cases, the legislature has acted to reclassify the wrongful act to impose the shorter prescriptive period. The amendment to the petition adding Con-Claire as a defendant was within the ten-year prescriptive period applicable to contract claims.

[**17**] Kroger retained the professional engineering services of SCA in October 2001 to address the settlement problem its Bayou Walk store was experiencing. The parties entered into a three-page contract agreement drafted by SCA dated October 10, 2001, which outlined SCA's scope of work, fee, additional services, as well as additional general terms and conditions such as provisions for site access, indemnification, risk allocation, and termination of services. The record also contains evidence of a verbal agreement for changes in scope of work and/ or revisions to drawings and specifications, as well as an outline/ proposal prepared by SCA regarding additional work.

[**18**] Kroger alleged that SCA's services were ineffective, performed negligently, and that their implementation caused additional damage to Kroger's store. This is an allegation of a breach of a contractual duty. As such the ten-year prescriptive period applies.

[**19**] As to the *ex delicto* claim, an amending petition relates back to an original petition when the action asserted in the amending petition arises out of the conduct, transaction or occurrence set forth or attempted to be set forth in the original petition. La. C.C.P. art. 1153; *Reese v. State, Dept. of Public Safety and Corrections*, 03-1615 (La.02/ 20/ 04), 866 So.2d 244. Kroger's "design phase" claim, filed on October 18, 2002, provided allegations that gave SCA fair notice of Kroger's cause of action for negligence arising out of professional services performed by SCA during the "repair phase." In that 2002 petition, Kroger asserted that, upon discovery of the initial settlement, requests were made in 2001 and 2002 upon the general contractor and SCA to address, remedy, and make recommendations concerning the problem. Kroger sought damages in this 2002 petition for, among other things, the costs of repairs and remediation occurring in 2001 and 2002 of approximately $1,895,000.

[....]

Questions

1. Paragraphs 8–10: This case is particularly interesting in that it makes a very clear and well-justified distinction between two types of action which have in common a breach of an obligation (*see* statements in paragraph 8). Considering that obligations can arise from different sources of law, do you see any

major legal reason(s) in the distinction that the Court makes here? Is there any reason based on prescription? See, in this respect, the last sentence of paragraph 10 and La. Civ. Code arts. 3492 and 3499. What about the burden of proof? What about the types of damages?

2. Paragraph 9: How do you read these two statements in light of the rule of law which states that a contract has the force of law for the parties (*see* La. Civ. Code art. 1983)?

3. Paragraph 11: How logical or legally well-grounded are these statements? How can the Court refer to services and the duty to perform repair work in a non-negligent, prudent and skillful manner and quote only a Louisiana Civil Code article from the law of torts (art. 2316) when articles 2762 and 2769 could have applied just as well, if not better, because of the Court assuming the existence of a repair contract?

4. Paragraph 11: Would prescription have run had the Court found the cause of action for the failure to repair in a contract for repair or "other works by the Job" (*see* La. Civ. Code arts. 2756–2777)? What about Louisiana Civil Code article 1994?

5. Contrast the majority opinion with Chief Judge Brown's dissenting opinion. Do you see any substantial difference? Which opinion appears to you to be more logical and better grounded in law?

Gloria's Ranch, L.L.C.
v.
Tauren Exploration, Inc., Cubic Energy, Inc., Wells Fargo Energy Capital, Inc., and Exco USA Asset, Inc.[1]

Supreme Court of Louisiana
June 27, 2018
252 So.3d 431

CLARK, Justice.

[. . . .]

Discussion

[. . . .]

[1] Next, Tauren argues the lower courts erred in determining the amount of damages due under La. Mineral Code art. 140. Louisiana Mineral Code art. 140 provides:

> If the lessee fails to pay royalties due or fails to inform the lessor of a reasonable cause for failure to pay in response to the required notice, *the court may award as damages double the amount of royalties due*, interest on that

---

1. The facts of this case can be found in the "Cases" section of Part One, Chapter Seven.

sum from the date due, and a reasonable attorney's fee regardless of the cause for the original failure to pay royalties. The court may also dissolve the lease in its discretion. (Emphasis added).

[2] As argued by Gloria's Ranch, and as applied by the lower courts in the instant case, the legislature intended to give the court discretion to effectively award treble damages (the amount of royalties due plus a penalty of two times the amount of royalties due). Contrarily, Tauren argues the article allows a court to impose a maximum award of double the amount of royalties due.

[3] The interpretation of a statute is a question of law and is reviewed by this court under a *de novo* standard of review. *Red Stick Studio Dev., L.L.C. v. State ex rel. Dep't of Econ. Dev.*, 10-0193 (La. 1/19/11), 56 So.3d 181, 184. As we explained in *M.J. Farms, Ltd. v. Exxon Mobil Corp.*, 07-2371, p. 13 (La. 7/1/08), 998 So.2d 16, 27 (internal citations omitted):

> The function of statutory interpretation and the construction given to legislative acts rests with the judicial branch of the government. The rules of statutory construction are designed to ascertain and enforce the intent of the Legislature. Legislation is the solemn expression of legislative will and, thus, the interpretation of legislation is primarily the search for the legislative intent. We have often noted the paramount consideration in statutory interpretation is ascertainment of the legislative intent and the reason or reasons which prompted the Legislature to enact the law.
>
> The starting point in the interpretation of any statute is the language of the statute itself. When a law is clear and unambiguous and its application does not lead to absurd consequences, the law shall be applied as written and no further interpretation may be made in search of the intent of the legislature.

[4] Moreover, the words of a law must be given their generally prevailing meaning. La. Civ. Code art. 11. Louisiana Mineral Code art. 140 provides in pertinent part that "[i]f the lessee fails to pay royalties due ..., the court may award as damages double the amount of royalties due." We find this language is a clear authorization by the legislature for courts to award a maximum of two times the amount of unpaid royalties, not three times the amount.

[5] Gloria's Ranch argues we are to assume that the article's language implicitly excludes the original amount of royalties due since the original amount would be paid "as a sum of money that would be owed to [Gloria's Ranch] in any event, as [Gloria's Ranch] is the rightful owner of those royalty interests" (citing the court of appeal's holding in *Cimarex Energy Co. v. Mauboules*, 08-452, p.9 (La. App. 3 Cir. 3/11/09), 6 So.3d 399, 407).[14] Under this argument, La. Mineral Code art. 140 authorizes a "penalty" or "additional damages" of double that amount. Thus, Gloria's

---

14. This court granted writs in *Cimarex* and reversed on other grounds. *Cimarex Energy Co. v. Mauboules*, 09-1170 (La. 4/9/10), 40 So.3d 931, 952. However, Justice Knoll reached the issue of double versus treble damages in her dissent:

Ranch contends an award totaling three times the amount of unpaid royalties is authorized.

[6] However, if we are to give every word its generally prevailing meaning, we are to read the word "damages" as it is generally meant. "An obligor is liable for the damages caused by his failure to perform a conventional obligation." La. Civ. Code art. 1994. "Damages are measured by the loss sustained by the obligee and the profit of which he has been deprived." La. Civ. Code art. 1995. "The measure of damages for a breach of contract is the sum that will place plaintiff in the same position as if the obligation had been fulfilled." *Dixie Roofing Co. of Pineville, Inc. v. Allen Parish Sch. Bd.*, 95-1526 (La. App. 3 Cir. 5/8/96), 690 So.2d 49, 56, *writs denied*, 96-2084 (La. 11/8/96), 683 So.2d 276, and 96-2100 (La. 11/8/96), 683 So.2d 277. Damages, then, are the judicial remedy whereby money replaces the obligation that was not performed.

[7] Based on this generally accepted definition of damages as compensation for the loss sustained, we interpret La. Mineral Code art. 140 as authority to award up to double the amount of royalties due. Clearly, an award of the amount of royalties due is the compensation for the failure to perform that obligation. The use of the permissive word "may" gives the court the authority to double that amount if the court, in its discretion, finds the defendant's conduct so warrants. A contrary reading that assumes the unpaid royalties are something separate from "damages" ignores the plain meaning of the word "damages." We do not believe the law, as written, leads to any absurd results, and, thus, we conduct no further investigation as to the legislative intent. Accordingly, we amend the judgment to reflect that the damages due under La. Mineral Code art. 140 are equivalent to two times the amount of royalties due ($242,029.26 × 2 = 484,058.52).

[....]

Conclusion

[8] Based on the foregoing, we find the lower courts improperly held Wells Fargo liable as an "owner" under La. Mineral Code art. 207 and a "lessee" under La. Mineral Code art. 140. Thus, we reverse the judgment as to Wells Fargo. Second, we affirm the judgment of solidary liability against Tauren, finding the obligation to furnish a recordable act evidencing the release of the lease is an indivisible obligation under the facts of this case. Third, we amend the amount of damages awarded under La. Mineral Code art. 140 to reflect a maximum award of double the amount

---

The far more natural reading of article 212.23(C)[sic] is to permit the plaintiff a total award of double the amount of unpaid royalties. As a simplified example, if the unpaid royalties total $100, the court has discretion to "double" the award by adding an additional $100 in statutory damages, for a total of $200. If the Legislature had intended article [212.23C] to permit a treble damages award, it would have said so. Several Louisiana statutes unambiguously permit an award of treble damages. This is not one of them. Moreover, as Mineral Code article [212.23C] is in the nature of a penal statute, it must be strictly construed in favor of the defendant. *Louisiana Bag Co. v. Audubon Indemnity Co.*, 08-0453 (La. 12/2/08), 999 So.2d 1104, 1120.

of unpaid royalties. Last, we amend the amount of attorney fees awarded for work done on appeal.

[9] REVERSED IN PART; AMENDED IN PART; AND AFFIRMED AS AMENDED.

[10] WEIMER, J., concurring in part and dissenting in part.

[11] GENOVESE, J., dissents in part.

Jennie Lombardo

v.

Calvin Lee Deshotel

Supreme Court of Louisiana
November 30, 1994
647 So.2d 1086

DENNIS, Justice

[....]

Expanded Statement of Facts and Proceedings Below

[1] On October 1, 1985, the plaintiff, Jennie Lombardo as seller, and the defendant, Calvin Lee Deshotel as buyer, signed an agreement to purchase or sell a piece of property located in Franklin, Louisiana. The price agreed upon by the parties was $115,000. The contract contained a clause that provided that "[i]n the event the purchaser fails to comply with this Agreement within the time specified, the seller shall have the right to declare the deposit * * * fortified [sic] * * * or the seller may demand specific performance." Initially, the sale was to take place on or before November 15, 1985 but it was subsequently postponed by agreement to December 5, 1985. When the date of closing arrived Lombardo was prepared to tender title but Deshotel refused to purchase the property.

[2] On March 26, 1986, Lombardo filed suit against Deshotel for specific performance alleging Deshotel's breach of the contract. While the suit for specific performance was pending, Lombardo sold the property to third parties for $90,000. Thereafter, on September 12, 1986, Lombardo amended her petition to request damages from Deshotel, including the difference between the price agreed upon in the contract and the price she obtained in the subsequent sale. Lombardo alleged that she had sold the property in mitigation of her damages.

[....]

[3] After a trial on the Merits, the trial court rendered judgment in favor of Lombardo and against Deshotel for the sum of $25,000. The trial court found that the sale of the property was justified as fulfillment of Lombardo's duty to mitigate her damage, the sale made specific performance impracticable, and this in turn entitled Lombardo to court-determined damages rather than her stipulated damages. Deshotel appealed. The court of appeal reduced Lombardo's award to $1,000 in

damages, the retention of the deposit, and affirmed the trial court judgment in all other respects. The court of appeal reasoned that because Lombardo and Deshotel stipulated to the amount of damages to be recovered in case of Deshotel's nonperformance, the stipulated amount ($1,000), is the compensation provided by law for the damage sustained. *Lombardo v. Deshotel*, (unpublished) 92 CA 2182, 637 So.2d 182 (Table) (La.App. 1st Cir.1994).

[....]

[4] Certiorari was granted to consider whether the court of appeal was correct in strictly enforcing the stipulation of damages clause agreed upon by the parties and in rejecting the trial court's rationale that the seller was released from any obligation under the clause by her duty to mitigate damages and the impracticability of specific enforcement caused by her sale of the property to a third person. *Lombardo v. Deshotel*, 639 So.2d 1179 (1994). We conclude that the court of appeal's judgment is essentially correct.

Civil Code Principles

[5] Obligations and contracts are distinct legal concepts. The nature and effect of the obligation is that of a bond between two persons imposed by the Code or other law whereby one of them, the creditor or obligee, is entitled to demand from the other, the debtor or obligor, the performance of a duty. 1 Litvinoff, Obligations §1 (6 Civil Law Treatise 1969) The effect of contracts is to give birth to, to modify, or to extinguish obligations. Cf., 2 Planiol, Civil Law Treatise, Part 1 no. 163 (La.St.L. Inst. trans.,) The parties by their contract bring a legal bond into being between them, but the law supplies the substance of the obligation, except as validly modified by them, and the machinery in order to provide enforcement. 1 Litvinoff, Obligations §75 (6 Civil Law Treatise 1969), citing 6 Toullier, Le Droit Civil Francais Suivant L'Orde du Code 2 (6th ed. Durvergier undated) and discussing Civil Code Articles 1760 and 2292 (1870); *Id.* §45. The distinction between obligations and contracts is important to the interpretation of the Civil Code; especially, Book III, Title IV, Chapter 8 entitled "Effects of Conventional Obligations," which deals interchangeably with the effects of obligations and the effects of contracts. C.C. Arts. 1983–2021; 2 Litvinoff §1; 2 Planiol no. 163. The distinction is very important in the present case, also, because the contract involved here does not modify significantly the obligations imposed by the Code. Consequently, the present case is governed essentially by the normal obligations precepts of the Civil Code.

[6] The two major rights of the creditor of an obligation are: (1) The right to exact, insofar as practicable, specific performance. C.C. Art. 1986; 2 Planiol no. 164; 2 Litvinoff §7; (2) The right to obtain an indemnity in money, referred to as damages, in case of inexecution or delay in the execution. C.C. Art. 1994; 2 Planiol no. 164; 2 Litvinoff §8. In cases of non-performance, the monetary indemnity is for the damage suffered by the creditor as a result of the non-performance of the obligation; it is clear therefore, that such indemnity can never be cumulated with actual performance. C.C. Art. 2007; Cf. 2 Planiol no. 257; 2 Litvinoff §9.

[7] Above all others, the creditor enjoys the right to demand, insofar as is practicable, the specific performance of the obligation. Here, however, the distinction between obligations to do or not to do is of great moment, since an obligation to give a thing is always susceptible of forced execution — unless, of course, performance has become impossible or impracticable — while this is not always the case with an obligation to do, or one not to do, where the liberal principle of modern law that prevents laying hands on a person to force him physically to do something is always taken into account. Civil Code Article 1986; 2 Litvinoff § 7.

[8] When the creditor elects to sue the debtor for damages, when specific performance is impracticable, or when the court refuses within its discretion to grant specific performance of an obligation to do, the fixing of the amount of the indemnity accorded as damages is made in two ways: (1) By the court, after the nonperformance is established. C.C. Art. 1999; 2 Planiol no. 246; or (2) By the parties themselves, in advance, by a stipulated damages clause inserted in the contract. C.C. Art. 2005; Cf., 2 Planiol no. 246; see 4 Aubry et Rau, Droit Civil Francais, in 1 Civil Law Translations pp. 91–92 and pp. 120–122 (1965) The sum stipulated in the clause replaces the need for the damages to be set by the court. Stipulated damages may not be modified by the court unless they are so manifestly unreasonable as to be contrary to public policy, C.C. Art. 2012; cf., 2 Planiol nos. 255–266; 4 Aubry et Rau at 121–122; 2 Litvinoff § 9, or if the obligor has partially performed. C.C. Art. 2011.

Application of Principles to Case at Bar

[9] It is undisputed by the parties that the deposit provision of the purchase agreement is a stipulated damages clause. Moreover, the clause contains the essential ingredients of a stipulation of damages: it was stipulated in advance by the parties, provides the sum to be recovered in case of nonperformance, and gives rise to a secondary obligation for the purpose of enforcing the principal one. C.C. Art. 2005.

[10] In light of the foregoing, and applying the legal principles to the case at bar, we conclude that the seller was bound by the stipulation of damages unless it has been shown to be so manifestly unreasonable as to be contrary to public policy. According to the language and structure of the code, the interpretation of its articles in pari materia rather than disconnectedly, and the doctrinal commentary, the obligee who has entered a stipulation of damages (i) is bound by the stipulation of damages even though she preferred to seek specific performance and asked for enforcement of her right to damages only after performance became impracticable, unless the stipulated damages are so manifestly unreasonable as to be contrary to public policy; and (ii) is not required to mitigate the damage caused by the obligor's failure to perform because the obligor may not demand that the damages be reduced when the obligee fails to make these efforts.

(i)

[11] We see nothing in the Civil Code that makes the obligee's duty under a stipulation of damages any less binding when she chooses damages as her second rather than her first recourse among creditors' rights. Reading the words in context, the

articles in pari materia, and the code as a whole, C.C. Arts. 12 and 13; Yiannopoulos, Louisiana Civil Law System, Part 1 § 46(c); 2 Planiol no. 220; it is clear that the stipulation of damages fixes the amount recoverable regardless of the route by which the obligee comes to the enforcement of the right to damages. Civil Code Article 2007 provides that "[a]n obligee may demand either the stipulated damages or performance of the principal obligation, but he may not demand both unless the damages have been stipulated for mere delay." There is nothing in this article or the other code provisions to indicate that the obligee's unsuccessful demand of performance relieves him of his obligation and duty under the stipulation of damages articles. There are a number of instances in which the obligee's attempts to specifically enforce the obligation might be rebuffed because specific performance is impracticable or because the obligation the obligor has failed to perform is an obligation to do. For examples, see Civil Code Article 1986, Revision Comments — 1984 (b) & (c); *J. Weingarten, Inc. v. Northgate Mall, Inc.*, 404 So.2d 896 (La.1981). To interpret the Code Articles disjointedly so as to release obligees from their stipulation of damages simply because they have brought unsuccessful specific performance actions would lead to absurd consequences. Only obligors would be bound by stipulations of damages, rendering Articles 2005 — 2012 of the Code useless.

[12] The evident intent of the redactors and the legislators, on the other hand, was to make the stipulation of damages clause more useful and predictable than before the 1984 revision of the obligations provisions. Civil Code Articles 2117–2129 (1870) closely followed Articles 1226–1233 of the Code Napoleon based on nineteenth century laissez-faire ideas, including the notion that the parties to a contract should be held to their agreed estimate of damages no matter what the circumstances. Exposé Des Motifs, La.Civ.Code Ann., vol. 8–9 p. 45. Although early decisions followed the strict approach of the Civil Code, later cases moved toward the common-law distinction between penalties and liquidated damages by holding that penal clauses are enforceable only if they were reasonably related to actual damages. *Id.* at 47. Ultimately, this court's decision in *Pennington v. Drews*, 218 La. 258, 49 So.2d 5 (1949) said that the expression "penal clause" as used in the Civil Code of 1870, was synonymous with "liquidated damages." This led to Louisiana courts asserting their power, in the absence of an expression of legislative will, to modify stipulated damages clauses by equating them with common-law "liquidated damages." Esposé Des Motifs, La.Civ.Code Ann., vol. 8–9 p. 47. The 1984 revision articles attempt to put and end to the confusion and inconsistency that have resulted from the courts' virtual disregard of the Civil Code provisions on stipulated damages. At the same time, the redactors recognized some merit in the court's perception of the need to be able to modify clauses of this kind in certain situations. Therefore, Article 2012 (1985) provides that stipulated damages may not be modified by the court unless they are so manifestly unreasonable as to be contrary to public policy. Article 2012 thus gives legislative sanction to the judicial prerogative to modify stipulated damages clauses, but it limits and channels that discretion to situations in which the stipulated damages are so disproportionate as to be contrary to public policy. The main tenet of Article 2012 is in harmony with classic civilian theory, and it is

consistent with the solution adopted in modern codes and followed by recent Continental jurisprudence. Exposé Des Motifs, La.Civ.Code Ann., vol. 8–9 p. 47 (citations of authorities omitted).

[13] Neither Lombardo nor Deshotel has contended that the stipulated damages are so manifestly unreasonable as to be contrary to public policy. Therefore, we do not reach that issue in the present case.

(ii)

[14] Civil Code Article 2002 provides:

> An obligee must make reasonable efforts to mitigate the damage caused by the obligor's failure to perform. When an obligee fails to make these efforts, the obligor may demand that the damages be accordingly reduced.

[15] This Article adjusts the conflict of interests that would otherwise exist when an obligee neglects to mitigate his damages and thereby exposes the obligor to further liability for consequences resulting from the obligor's failure to perform that were reasonably avoidable by the obligee. When the parties have stipulated the damages to be recovered in case of inexecution of an obligation, however, this conflict does not arise. The obligee can recover no more nor less than the stipulated damages regardless of the amount of the damage or the consequences caused by the obligee's neglect. Consequently, because the seller, Lombardo, could not suffer a reduction of her stipulated damages and therefore owed no duty to mitigate her damage to the purchaser, Deshotel, the doctrine of mitigation did not afford Lombardo any justification for selling the property to a third person, for aborting the specific performance action, or for avoiding her obligation or duty under the stipulation.

[16] Finally, we agree with the court of appeal that the clause in the real estate purchase agreement relating to the real estate agent's commission and fees and costs incurred in enforcing collection and damages does not override the stipulation of damages or release the seller from her reciprocal obligations and duties thereunder. Clearly, the commission, fees and costs clause is auxiliary to the enforcement of the stipulation of damages clause and other major provisions of the contract and does not supersede them.

[17] Consequently, we conclude that the seller, Lombardo, was bound by the stipulation of damages clause that she agreed to in advance with the purchaser, Deshotel. She was not excused from her reciprocal duty under this obligation simply because she sought to enforce her right to performance of the obligation before resorting to her right to damages.

[18] For the reasons assigned, the judgment of the court of appeal is affirmed.

[19] AFFIRMED.

[20] LEMMON, J., concurs and assigns reasons.

Questions

1. Paragraphs 1–2: What kind of obligation is here entered into by the parties? What kind of modality, such as "term," "condition," etc., can you identify behind the dates?

2. Paragraphs 1–2: Read La. Civ. C. arts. 2022, 2013, 2015, and 2017. What is, now, your opinion of Lombardo's action?

3. Paragraphs 3–17: Does the $25,000 represent the *damnun emergens*, the loss suffered, or the *lucrum cessans*, the profit denied? Under Section 5 Stipulated Damages, Civ. C. arts. 2005-2012, there is no article that confines the measurement of stipulated damages to the loss suffered and the profit denied; do you think that art. 1995 on the measure of damages in Section 4 Damages, which measures damages "by the loss sustained by the obligee and the profit of which he has been deprived" should be applicable to parties who include a stipulated damages clause in their contract? When art. 2012, under Stipulated Damages, allows the court to modify stipulated damages when "they are so manifestly unreasonable as to be contrary to public policy," should the court be guided by art. 1995 in modifying the amount of the stipulated damages?

4. Paragraphs 3–17: Under La. Civ. C. art. 2011, a court may reduce the amount of "stipulated damages for nonperformance . . . in proportion to the benefit derived by the obligee from any partial performance rendered by the obligor." What if the obligor has not performed at all? Reading *a contrario sensu*, shouldn't the court be allowed to increase the stipulated damages when there is no benefit derived by the obligee but there is a loss, a *damnun emergens*, suffered by him?

5. Paragraphs 3–17: Is the Court properly reading and interpreting arts. 2005, 2007, and 2011? What about the phrase "absurd consequences": what could such consequences be such as to render Civ. C. arts. 2005–2012 "useless"? Was the obligor in good faith? Shouldn't the Court have referred to art. 1997, which is applicable to an obligor in bad faith?

6. Paragraph 12: What is, in your opinion, the role given to the common law in this matter of "damages"? Isn't the Court a little too "absolute and definite" in its reading of art. 2012? Is "public policy," as used in art. 2012, the same as "public interest," as used in art. 7? Haven't the courts ruled that a "tough bargain" is still a bargain?

Betty McGee, et al.

v.

A C and S, Inc., et al.

Supreme Court of Louisiana
July 10, 2006
933 So.2d 770

KIMBALL, Justice.

[. . . .]

Facts And Procedural History

[1] Plaintiffs, the widow and children of James Edward McGee, filed the instant wrongful death and survival actions against many defendants, including James Edward McGee's former employers and manufacturers of asbestos-containing products used during his employment (collectively "defendants"), seeking to recover damages for injuries sustained as a result of James Edward McGee's exposure to asbestos, from which he died on January 28, 2000.

[2] In their petition, plaintiffs sought damages for, among other things, James Edward McGee's loss of enjoyment of life. Thereafter, defendants filed a motion *in limine* seeking to preclude plaintiffs from asserting a claim for loss of enjoyment of life. [. . . .] The district court remarked that it had allowed a separate category for loss of enjoyment of life in previous cases and denied defendants' motion *in limine*.

[3] [. . . .] [T]he court of appeal reversed the district court and granted defendants' motion *in limine* to prohibit plaintiffs from asserting a claim for loss of enjoyment of life. From that decision, plaintiffs applied for supervisory writs to this court, stating that the court of appeal erred in reversing the district court and holding that a separate award for loss of enjoyment of life is erroneous as a matter of law. We granted plaintiffs' writ application to determine whether loss of enjoyment of life is recoverable as a separate element of general damages that may be reflected as a line item on a jury verdict form.

Discussion

[4] Loss of enjoyment of life, sometimes known as hedonic damages, refers to the detrimental alterations of a person's life or lifestyle or a person's inability to participate in the activities or pleasures of life that were formerly enjoyed. See *Day v. Ouachita Parish Sch. Bd.*, 35,831, p. 8 (La.App. 2 Cir. 8/8/02), 823 So.2d 1039, 1044.

[5] In Louisiana, delictual actions are governed by La. C.C. art. 2315, which states that "[e]very act of man that causes damage to another obliges him by whose fault it happened to repair it." Thus, under La. C.C. art. 2315, a tortfeasor must compensate a tort victim for all of the damages occasioned by his act. The term "damages" refers to "pecuniary compensation, recompense, or satisfaction for an injury sustained." *Fogle v. Feazel*, 201 La. 899, 909, 10 So.2d 695, 698 (1942). In the delictual context, La. C.C. art. 2315 authorizes compensatory damages. Compensatory

damages encompass those damages "designed to place the plaintiff in the position in which he would have been if the tort had not been committed." Frank L. Maraist & Thomas C. Galligan, Jr., LOUISIANA TORT LAW § 7-1 (Michie 1996) (footnotes omitted).

[6] Compensatory damages are further divided into the broad categories of special damages and general damages. Special damages are those which have a "ready market value," such that the amount of the damages theoretically may be determined with relative certainty, including medical expenses and lost wages, while general damages are inherently speculative and cannot be calculated with mathematical certainty. *Id.* § 7-2 (footnotes omitted).

[7] This court has previously defined general damages as "those which may not be fixed with any degree of pecuniary exactitude but which, instead, involve mental or physical pain or suffering, inconvenience, the loss of gratification of intellectual or physical enjoyment, or other losses of life or life-style which cannot really be measured definitively in terms of money." *Duncan v. Kansas City S. R.R.*, 00-0066, p. 13 (La.10/30/00), 773 So.2d 670, 682; *Boswell v. Roy O. Martin Lumber Co., Inc.*, 363 So.2d 506, 507 (La.1978); *Anderson v. Welding Testing Lab., Inc.*, 304 So.2d 351, 352 (La.1974).

[8] Loss of enjoyment of life falls within the definition of general damages because it involves the quality of a person's life, which is inherently speculative and cannot be measured definitively in terms of money. "The loss of gratification of intellectual or physical enjoyment" included in the definition of general damages directly results from a person's "inability to participate in the activities or pleasures of life that a person formerly enjoyed" as set forth in the definition of loss of enjoyment of life. Similarly, "the loss of life or life-style" included in the definition of general damages is substantially similar to the "detrimental alteration of a person's life or lifestyle" as included in the definition of loss of enjoyment of life. Thus, loss of enjoyment of life is clearly encompassed within "the loss of gratification of intellectual or physical enjoyment, or other losses of life or life-style" component of this court's existing definition of general damages.

[9] La. C.C. art. 2315 authorizes a tort victim to be compensated for the damage sustained as a result of the delict, including those for loss of enjoyment of life, if proven. Moreover, this court has clearly defined general damages to include loss of enjoyment of life. Consequently, loss of enjoyment of life is a compensable component of general damages under both La. C.C. art. 2315 and this court's existing definition of general damages. Therefore, the only remaining issue is whether loss of enjoyment of life may be separated from other elements of general damages, such as mental and physical pain and suffering, and whether that separation may be reflected by having a line for loss of enjoyment of life on a jury verdict form. See *Joseph v. Broussard Rice Mill, Inc.*, 00-0628, p. 1 (La.10/30/00), 772 So.2d 94, 106–107 (Victory, J., assigning additional reasons) (stating "this Court has never squarely addressed the issue of awarding hedonic damages for loss of enjoyment of life as a separate element of damages").

[10] As established above, loss of enjoyment of life is a component of general damages and therefore loss of enjoyment of life is not separate and distinct from general damages. Nevertheless, general damages in Louisiana are routinely dissected. Courts commonly list different elements of general damages, including mental anguish and physical pain and suffering, both past and future, separately. In addition, general damages for permanent scarring and/or disfigurement are often listed separately. See, e.g., *Joseph*, 00-0628 at p. 17 (La.10/30/00), 772 So.2d at 106–107, n. 6; *Degruise v. Houma Courier Newspaper Corp.*, 95-1862, p. 9 (La.11/25/96), 683 So.2d 689, 694. Thus, allowing a separate award for loss of enjoyment of life would not offend the existing concept of general damages and would reflect the accepted method of listing elements of general damages separately.

[11] Moreover, loss of enjoyment of life is conceptually distinct from other components of general damages, including pain and suffering. Pain and suffering, both physical and mental, refers to the pain, discomfort, inconvenience, anguish, and emotional trauma that accompanies an injury. Loss of enjoyment of life, in comparison, refers to detrimental alterations of the person's life or lifestyle or the person's inability to participate in the activities or pleasures of life that were formerly enjoyed prior to the injury. In contrast to pain and suffering, whether or not a plaintiff experiences a detrimental lifestyle change depends on both the nature and severity of the injury and the lifestyle of the plaintiff prior to the injury.

[....]

[12] Given the conceptual difference between pain and suffering and loss of enjoyment of life, a separate award for loss of enjoyment of life is warranted and is not duplicative of the award for pain and suffering, if the damages resulting from loss of enjoyment of life are sufficiently proven. When given the proper jury instructions, jurors can comprehend the difference between the pain and suffering of being in a hospital, undergoing treatment, etc. and the loss of enjoyment of life that occurs because the injured party can no longer participate in a vocation or avocation that the party enjoys.

[13] A majority of the lower courts have supported this position by allowing separate awards for loss of enjoyment of life. [....]

[14] The Third Circuit Court of Appeal first recognized a separate award for loss of enjoyment of life in *Andrews v. Mosley Well Serv.*, 514 So.2d 491, 498–99 (La.App. 3 Cir.1987), after the jury awarded the plaintiff $75,000 for loss of enjoyment of life. [....]

[....]

[15] In addition, the First Circuit Court of Appeal has consistently held that loss of enjoyment of life is a separate item of damages independent from pain and suffering. *In re Medical Review Panel on Behalf of Laurent*, 94,1661, p. 13 (La.App. 1 Cir. 6/23/95), 657 So.2d 713, 722 (upholding an award for loss of enjoyment of life as warranted by the evidence [...]) [...]. [....]

[16] Similarly, the Second Circuit Court of Appeal has upheld separate awards for loss of enjoyment of life. *Varnell v. Louisiana Tech Univ.*, 30,260, pp. 9–10 (La. App. 2 Cir. 2/25/98), 709 So.2d 890, 896 (stating that "[t]aken as a whole, the record supports the District Court's award of damages for loss of enjoyment of life as a separate element from the rest of general damages") [. . .]. [. . . .]

[17] The Fifth Circuit has likewise followed the other circuits in holding that loss of enjoyment of life is a separate element of compensable general damages. *Stevenson v. Louisiana Patient's Comp. Fund*, 97-709, p. 6 (La.App. 5 Cir. 4/9/98), 710 So.2d 1178, 1182 [. . .]. [. . . .]

[18] In contrast, the jurisprudential development from the Fourth Circuit Court of Appeal has diverged from that of the other circuits. The Fourth Circuit has declined to follow the other circuits and remains the only circuit in Louisiana to have declared a separate recovery for loss of enjoyment of life erroneous as a matter of law.

[. . . .]

[19] However, we reject the Fourth Circuit's conclusion that a separate award for loss of enjoyment of life is erroneous as a matter of law. Although we are mindful that there is a conflict among the state and federal courts nationwide on this issue,[3] we agree with the courts, including the Louisiana First, Second, Third, and Fifth Circuit Courts of Appeal, that have held loss of enjoyment of life to be a separate compensable element of general damages. We conclude that loss of enjoyment of life constitutes damage that is compensable under La. C.C. art. 2315 and accordingly that the jury may be allowed to give a separate award for loss of enjoyment of life. Nevertheless, whether or not loss of enjoyment of life is recoverable depends on the

---

3. Courts across the country have taken varied approaches, and as many states' highest courts have yet to consider the issue of loss of enjoyment of life, the trend nationwide remains unclear. Nevertheless, states that have weighed in are sometimes either constrained or empowered to disallow or to allow a separate recovery for loss of enjoyment of life by their specific statutory scheme for tort, wrongful death, and survival actions. For instance, the Supreme Court of New Hampshire found that its wrongful death statute, allowing recovery for "the probable duration of his life but for his injury," authorized a separate award for decedent's loss of enjoyment of life, i.e. decedent's inability to carry on and enjoy life as if he would have lived. *Marcotte v. Timberlane/Hampstead Sch. Dist.*, 143 N.H. 331, 733 A.2d 394, 399 (1999). Similarly, the Supreme Court of Connecticut has "long held that loss of life's enjoyments is compensable in personal injury and wrongful death cases," *Mather v. Griffin Hosp.*, 207 Conn. 125, 540 A.2d 666, 678 (1988), while the Supreme Court of South Carolina has held that loss of enjoyment of life and pain and suffering are separately compensable elements of damage. *Boan v. Blackwell*, 343 S.C. 498, 541 S.E.2d 242, 244 (2001). In contrast, the Supreme Court of Nebraska has held that loss of enjoyment of life is not a separate category of damages but may be considered as an element of pain and suffering and/or disability. *Anderson v. Nebraska Dep't of Soc. Serv.*, 248 Neb. 651, 538 N.W.2d 732, 739 (1995). The Supreme Court of Washington, however, has upheld a jury instruction regarding plaintiff's loss of opportunity to become a professional dancer only because the court found that it did not mislead the jury or foster a double recovery in that particular case. *Kirk v. WSU*, 109 Wash.2d 448, 746 P.2d 285, 293 (1987).

particular facts of the case, and should be left to the district court's discretion on a case-by-case analysis.

[20] Furthermore, although a separate award for loss of enjoyment of life may be recoverable by the primary tort victim for the loss of enjoyment of life sustained during the victim's lifetime, it is not recoverable by the primary tort victim's family members who are eligible to recover for loss of consortium, service and society under La. C.C. art. 2315(B). Loss of consortium is a harm to relational interest which occurs when the other party to the relationship suffers physical harm (invasion of an interest or personality). *Ferrell v. Fireman's Fund Ins. Co.*, 96-3028, p. 8 (La.7/1/97), 696 So.2d 569, 574. Thus, under La. C.C. art. 2315(B), family members of the primary tort victim have an action, loss of consortium, that will compensate them for their diminished relationship with the primary tort victim. A family member's detrimental alteration in lifestyle, i.e. loss of enjoyment of life, results from the diminished relationship with the primary tort victim and therefore is already compensated with an award for loss of consortium. Hence, a wife's claim that she is unable to engage in activities that she formerly enjoyed prior to her husband's injury, such as taking vacations, attending sporting events, or dancing, is compensated under loss of consortium and need not be compensated again under loss of enjoyment of life. Allowing family members to recover for both their loss of consortium and their loss of enjoyment of life would be duplicative and would not be authorized by La. C.C. art. 2315(B).

[21] Turning to the instant case, we note that it arises in the context of wrongful death and survival actions. Because this issue is being resolved on a motion *in limine* and in advance of trial, it is unclear whether plaintiffs, the widow and children of James Edward McGee, are attempting to assert a claim for their own loss of enjoyment of life caused by James Edward McGee's illness under the wrongful death action or whether plaintiffs are attempting to assert James Edward McGee's claim for his own loss of enjoyment of life under the survival action. Thus, we must examine whether loss of enjoyment of life is recoverable in wrongful death and survival actions.

[22] In determining whether plaintiffs may assert a claim for loss of enjoyment of life in either a survival or wrongful death context, we begin with the premise that although both actions arise from a common tort, survival and wrongful death actions are separate and distinct. *Taylor v. Giddens*, 618 So.2d 834, 840 (La.1993). The survival action comes into existence simultaneously with the existence of the tort and is transmitted to beneficiaries upon the victim's death. *Id.* The survival action permits recovery only for the damages suffered by the victim from the time of injury to the moment of death. Id. It is in the nature of a succession right. *Id.* On the other hand, the wrongful death action does not arise until the victim dies and it compensates the beneficiaries for their own injuries which they suffer from the moment of the victim's death and thereafter. *Id.* In addition, a wrongful death claim is like a loss of consortium claim insofar as it clearly compensates the beneficiaries for their own injuries, separate and distinct from the primary victim's injuries. *Landry v. Avondale Indus., Inc.*, 03-0719, p. 10 (La.12/3/03), 864 So.2d 117, 126.

[23] Since we have determined that recovery is precluded for the loss of enjoyment of life suffered by the primary victim's family members as it is duplicative of their loss of consortium claim, we likewise conclude that recovery is precluded for the loss of enjoyment of life suffered by the primary victim's family members as it is duplicative of their wrongful death claim. Therefore, we find that plaintiffs are limited to asserting James Edward McGee's loss of enjoyment of life during his lifetime under the survival action, and are precluded from asserting their own loss of enjoyment of life caused by James Edward McGee's illness.

[24] Accordingly, we conclude that the court of appeal erred in holding that loss of enjoyment of life is erroneous as a matter of law. Instead, we find that loss of enjoyment of life is a separate compensable element of general damages that the jury may award separately from pain and suffering. However, plaintiffs may only assert a claim for the loss of enjoyment of life sustained by James Edward McGee, the primary tort victim, during his lifetime.

Decree

[25] For all the above reasons, we find that loss of enjoyment of life may be recoverable as a separate element of general damages that may be included on a jury verdict form. Therefore, we reverse the court of appeal's ruling granting the motion *in limine* and reinstate the district court's ruling denying the motion *in limine* to preclude plaintiffs from asserting a claim for loss of enjoyment of life.

[26] REVERSED.

[27] VICTORY and WEIMER, JJ., dissent and assign reasons.

[28] KNOLL, J., additionally concurs with reasons.

VICTORY, J., dissenting.

[29] I respectfully dissent from the majority's opinion for the same reasons given by Justice, then Judge, Knoll when she gave her view of hedonic damages, while sitting on the Third Circuit in 1987:

> ... in my view the jury verdict form contained a duplicitous item, namely, "Loss of enjoyment of life, past and future" and awarded plaintiff $75,000. For physical pain and suffering, past and future, the jury awarded plaintiff $250,000, and for mental pain and suffering, past and future, the jury awarded $75,000. After making awards for physical and mental pain and suffering, the award for loss of enjoyment of life is duplicitous. Therefore, I respectfully dissent, finding the damage award excessive and duplicitous.

Andrews v. Mosley Well Service, 514 So.2d 491, 501–2 (La.App. 3 Cir.1987), (Knoll, J., *781 dissenting), writ denied, 515 So.2d 807 (La.1987), *superseded by statute on other grounds as stated in Steers v. International Paper Co.*, 540 So.2d 1236 (La.App. 3 Cir.1989).

[30] Across the nation, the term "hedonic damages" did not make its debut until the 1980s, when economists began using the term to refer to certain aspects

of an injured party's non-pecuniary losses. See Victor E. Schwartz and Cary Silverman, *Hedonic Damages: The Rapidly Bubbling Cauldron*, 69 Brooklyn Law Rev. 1037, 1040–1041 (2004). In Louisiana, courts had not traditionally recognized "loss of enjoyment of life" as a separate element of damages and, in fact, such "hedonic damages" were not treated as a separate element of damages by any Louisiana appellate court before 1987, when the Third Circuit, over the dissent of then Judge Knoll, opined that "loss of enjoyment of life" damages could be awarded separate and apart from a general damages award. See *Andrews v. Mosley Well Service, supra*; see also *Hernandez v. Continental Casualty Insurance Company*, 615 So.2d 484, 492 (La.App. 4 Cir.1993) (Plotkin, J., dissenting). Instead, the traditional Louisiana approach was to include such "hedonic damages" within the broader scope of a unified general damages award, which extends to such non-pecuniary issues as "pain and suffering" and "loss of gratification." *Boswell v. Roy O. Martin Lumber Company, Inc.*, 363 So.2d 506 (La.1978) (affirming a general damages award which included damages for mental pain and anguish over the loss of timber on plaintiff's land). Notably, this traditional Louisiana approach continues to be followed by at least the Fourth Circuit Court of Appeal, which has consistently and explicitly rejected all efforts to separate "hedonic damages" from the more generalized concept of general damages.[1]

[31] Moreover, a nationwide survey of cases·shows that while state courts are split on this issue, the majority of state courts have held that hedonic damages are included in general damages such as pain and suffering, mental anguish, and physical impairment, and may not be considered as a separate element of general damages.[2]

---

1. See *Washington v. Aetna Life Insurance Company, et al.*, 04-0135 (La.App. 4 Cir. 10/13/04) 886 So.2d 572, 587, *writ denied*, 04-2799 (La.3/11/05), 896 So.2d 63, *reconsideration denied*, 04-2799 (La.4/27/05), 901 So.2d 1047 (holding that an award for loss of enjoyment of life and disability and/or disfigurement was duplicative of an award for past physical and mental pain and suffering); *Brown v. Southern Baptist Hospital*, 96-1990, 96–1991 (La.App. 4 Cir. 3/11/98), 715 So.2d 423, *on rehearing clarifying judgment* (La.App. 4 Cir. 4/15/98), *writ denied*, 98-959 (La.5/29/98), 720 So.2d 335, (explaining that an award for loss of enjoyment of life is included in the concept of general damages, and is duplicative of an award for past and future pain and suffering); *Mistich v. Volkswagon of Germany, Inc., et al.*, 94-0226 (La.App. 4 Cir. 6/25/97) 698 So.2d 47, *writ denied*, 97-1858 (11/14/97), 703 So.2d 623, (holding that hedonic damages are included in the concept of general damages, and do not constitute a separate claim or cause of action); *Smith v. Juneau*, 95-0724 (La. App. 4 Cir. 4/9/97), 692 So.2d 1365 (holding that a jury's award for permanent disability, scarring and permanent disfigurement, and past loss of enjoyment of life were duplicative of the pain and suffering awards and reducing the judgment accordingly); *Koepp v. Sea-Land Service, Inc.*, 93-2562 (La.App. 4 Cir. 11/17/94), 645 So.2d 1269 (denying recovery of hedonic damages as a distinct category of damages, stating that it was only a factor of pain and suffering, and held that the award of loss of enjoyment of life damages by the trial court was duplicative).

2. See *Loth v. Truck-A-Way Corporation, et al.*, 60 Cal.App.4th 757, 763, 70 Cal.Rptr.2d 571 (1998) (holding that in California, a pain and suffering award may include compensation for the plaintiff's loss of enjoyment of life but it may not be calculated as a separate award; however a plaintiff's attorney is not restricted from arguing this element to a jury); *Frito-Lay, Inc., v. Cloud*, 569 N.E.2d 983, 989 (Ind.Ct.App.1991), (holding it "is error to instruct the jury on the loss of quality and enjoyment of life as an element of damages separate from other elements of damage, such as pain and suffering

[32] Louisiana's unified concept of general damages serves to balance the potentially competing public policies of making the victim whole under Louisiana Civil Code art. 2315 et seq., along with avoiding the inequitable outcome of the injured party securing a "double recovery" for a single element of harm-a recovery that

---

or permanency of injury"); *Poyzer v. McGraw* 360 N.W.2d 748 (Iowa 1985) (holding that loss of enjoyment of life is a factor to be considered as a part of future pain and suffering and that it would be plainly duplicative to allow a separate award for loss of enjoyment of life); *Gregory v. Carey*, 246 Kan. 504, 791 P.2d 1329 (1990) (finding that evidence regarding loss of enjoyment of life was admissible, but allowing the jury to consider it as a separate element of general damages was in error); *Leonard v. Parrish*, 420 N.W.2d 629 (Minn.App.1988) (holding that the trial court did not abuse its broad discretion in rejecting plaintiff's request for a specific instruction on loss of her enjoyment of life damages to her sense of smell and taste, instead submitting that loss as a general element of damages); *Banks ex rel. Banks v. Sunrise Hospital*, 120 Nev. 822, 102 P.3d 52 (2004) (acknowledging the differences in opinion among jurisdictions regarding hedonic damages, and agreeing with California and those jurisdictions permitting plaintiffs to seek compensation for hedonic loss as an element of the general award for pain and suffering, but not separately in order to reduce the possibility of confusion or duplication of awards by the jury); *Nussbaum v. Gibstein*, 73 N.Y.2d 912, 914, 539 N.Y.S.2d 289, 536 N.E.2d 618 (1989), and *McDougald v. Garber*, 73 N.Y.2d 246, 538 N.Y.S.2d 937, 536 N.E.2d 372 (1989) (each holding that "loss of enjoyment of life is not a separate element of damages deserving a distinct award but is, instead, only a factor to be considered by the jury in assessing damages for conscious pain and suffering"); *First Trust Company of North Dakota v. Scheels Hardware & Sports Shop, Inc.*, 429 N.W.2d 5, 13–14 (N.D.1988) (holding that the trial court did not err in refusing the plaintiff's request to instruct on the loss of enjoyment of life as a separate element of damages as "[i]t would have been appropriate for the plaintiffs to have argued loss of enjoyment of life as a component of pain, discomfort, mental anguish, and impairment of health, mind, or person, all of which were set forth in the trial court's instructions as recoverable elements of damage in this case"); Will*inger v. Mercy Catholic Medical Center of Southeastern Pennsylvania, Fitzgerald Mercy Division, et al.*, 482 Pa. 441, 447, 393 A.2d 1188 (1978) (stating "[e]ven where the victim survives a compensable injury, this Court has never held that loss of life's pleasures could be compensated other than as a component of pain and suffering. Indeed, the two types of loss are interrelated"); *Corcoran v. McNeal*, 400 Pa. 14, 23, 161 A.2d 367, 372–73 (Pa.1960) (holding that "[t]he loss of well-being is as much a loss as an amputation. The inability to enjoy what one has heretofore keenly appreciated as a pain which can be equated with the infliction of a positive hurt. The conscious loss of a benefit to which one is entitled hurts as much as a festering wound"); *Judd v. Rowley's Cherry Hill Orchards, Inc.*, 611 P.2d 1216, 1221 (Utah 1980) (ruling that "[t]he pain and suffering for which damages are recoverable in a personal injury action include not only physical pain but also mental pain or anguish, that is, the mental reaction to that pain and to the possible consequences of the physical injury. Included in mental pain and suffering is the diminished enjoyment of life, as well as the humiliation and embarrassment resulting from permanent scars and disability"); *Bulala, M.D. v. Boyd, et al.*, 239 Va. 218, 232, 389 S.E.2d 670 (1990), (holding that they have not recognized "loss of enjoyment of life" as a separately compensable element of damages in personal injury cases because the term is duplicative of other elements contained in the damage instruction); *Wooldridge v. Woolett*, 96 Wash.2d 659, 638 P.2d 566 (1981), (rejecting plaintiff's assertion that a qualitative loss of life's pleasures is a separate element of damages apart from pain and suffering, as well as declining to follow plaintiff's argument that such a recognition of qualitative loss of life's pleasures should give rise to a separate element of damages for a quantitative loss of those same pleasures); *Wilt v. Buracker*, 191 W.Va. 39, 443 S.E.2d 196 (1993), *cert. denied*, 511 U.S. 1129, 114 S.Ct. 2137, 128 L.Ed.2d 867 (1994) (holding that the loss of enjoyment of life resulting from permanent injury is part of the general measure of damages flowing from the permanent injury and is not subject to an economic calculation)[.]

would be more in the nature of exemplary or punitive damages that are not allowed under Louisiana law unless expressly provided for by statute. *Gagnard v. Baldridge*, 612 So.2d 732 (La.1993). Allowing hedonic damages as a separate item upsets this delicate balance and gives rise to multiple recovery, as "loss of enjoyment of life" fits squarely within the traditional scope of general damages, usually mental pain and suffering, for purposes of Louisiana law. [....]

[....]

[33] The inability to enjoy certain things that were once enjoyed is almost always part of mental pain and suffering, which is already routinely awarded by judges and juries as a separate item of general damages.[3] Just as there is no need to separate "pain" and "suffering" from each other, there is no need to distinguish a lost enjoyment of life that is already included within the definition of general damages. [....]

[....]

[34] Contrary to the majority's opinion, allowing a separate award for loss of enjoyment of life allows a plaintiff to recover more than once for the same damage and gives rise to an endless array of potential subcategories for these losses. [....]

[....]

[35] Further, when the Louisiana legislature has found a need for separate and distinct elements of compensation to victims, it has provided for such by statute. For instance, in 1991, the legislature enacted La. Civil Code art. 2315.6 to include recoverable bystander damages for those who happen upon the scene of an event causing injury to another person. Interpreting the strict limitations of La. Civil Code art. 2315.6, this Court stated:

> The Legislature apparently intended to allow recovery of bystander damages to compensate for the immediate shock of witnessing a traumatic event which caused the direct victim immediate harm that is severe and apparent, but not to compensate for the anguish and distress that normally accompany an injury to a loved one under all circumstances.

Trahan v. McManus, et al., 97-1224 (La.3/2/99), 728 So.2d 1273 at 1279. Thus, the legislature decided to allow recovery of bystander damages, and created them as an element separate and apart from general damages. Similarly, in 1982, the Legislature amended La. Civil Code art. 2315 by Act 202 to add the second paragraph, which reads, in pertinent part: "[d]amages may include loss of consortium, services and society, and shall be recoverable by the same respective categories of persons who would have had a cause of action for wrongful death of an injured person." This amendment allows recovery for loss of consortium. Conversely, it is apparent that the Legislature sees no reason to create "loss of enjoyment of life" as a separate

---

3. Certainly, every reason one would not "enjoy life" would fall into one of the three categories of general damages already allowed-physical pain and suffering, mental pain and suffering, or disability.

element of damages, as it is already covered by the categories of general damages routinely allowed.

[36] I agree with the Fourth Circuit and the majority view of the other states' courts and find that allowing a separate award for hedonic damages is a duplication of what is already provided for in a general damages award, specifically mental pain and suffering, and sets a dangerous stage for double recovery of damages.

[37] For all of the above reasons, I respectfully dissent.

WEIMER, J., dissenting.

[38] There is no dispute that an injured party has a cause of action in tort to collect damages for loss of enjoyment of life and for mental pain and suffering, past and future. The real issue before this court is whether a line on a jury verdict form designated for loss of enjoyment of life, when coupled with a separate line on the same verdict form designated for mental pain and suffering, results in the plaintiff obtaining a duplicative award.[1]

[39] I respectfully dissent because I find that a damage award for mental pain and suffering can adequately compensate for hedonic[2] damages. The award for pain compensates an individual for no longer having a physical or mental condition that formerly was free of pain. The award for loss of enjoyment of life compensates an individual for the absence of a physical or mental activity that formerly was a part of his or her lifestyle. Thus, "pain" and "pleasure" are merely two sides of the same coin, making an award for pain the equivalent of an award for loss of pleasure. In the terms of a jury verdict that makes specific awards for pain and suffering and loss of enjoyment of life, the injured party is potentially compensated for the same deprivation twice.

---

1. Although not directly before us, the issue may be moot depending upon what the legislature meant when, in 1996, it amended LSA-C.C.P. art. 1812. In particular, paragraph C provides that in a case for damages for injury, death, or loss, the court, at the request of any party, shall submit to the jury special written questions inquiring as to:

   (4) The total amount of special damages and the total amount of general damages sustained as a result of the injury, death, or loss, expressed in dollars, and, if appropriate, the total amount of exemplary damages to be awarded.

Whether the 1996 amendment to Article 1812 was intended to require a single award for general damages and a single award for special damages as opposed to itemization has not been resolved. See 1 Frank L. Maraist & Harry T. Lemmon, Louisiana Civil Law Treatise: Civil Procedure (1999), § 11.12 at 310, citing this court's earlier opinion in *Guillory v. Avondale Shipyards, Inc.*, 448 So.2d 1281, 1286 (La.1984), wherein this court held the requirement that the jury award a total dollar figure as then provided in Article 1812 did not necessarily preclude interrogatories about specific items of damages. Citing LSA-C.C.P. art. 1812(C)(4), the treatise says that "[a]rguably, the court may permit itemization of the total amount." (Emphasis supplied.) Maraist & Lemmon, § 11.12 at 310 n. 18.

2. The word "hedonic" originated in the mid 17th century, from the word "hedonikos," which derived from the earlier Greek word for "pleasure." The New Oxford American Dictionary 788 (2001).

[40] When one suffers a loss of enjoyment of life, this loss refers to, in the words of the majority, "detrimental alterations of the person's life or lifestyle or the person's inability to participate in the activities or pleasures of life that were formerly enjoyed prior to the injury." Slip op. at 5. However, "alteration" or "inability" is generally caused by physical pain and suffering accompanied by mental pain and suffering. If one's lifestyle is altered or one's ability to participate in activities is changed, there is a commensurate physical or mental anguish component. Any distinction between or separation of the two, although existing theoretically, is far too fine a distinction to observe practically. As such, to award compensation for both results in duplication.

[41] I propose a very practical solution. Depending on the facts of the case, the jury verdict form should have a line for loss of enjoyment of life or a line for mental pain and suffering, but not both. In the alternative, the jury verdict form could include a single line for loss of enjoyment of life and mental pain and suffering, which would serve the purpose of allowing the jury to consider both components of general damages without having to draw a fine line distinguishing between the two. This resolution would serve the goal of making the plaintiff whole and would avoid duplication.

[42] Despite my faith in juries, a jury verdict form that itemizes both mental pain and suffering and loss of enjoyment of life in separate considerations forces a jury to slice too finely the distinction between the two. In theory, the jury is capable of making separate awards, but from a practical standpoint such is unrealistic. Juries are fully capable of adding to the mental anguish award if the injured party suffers a change of lifestyle. One who suffers a change in lifestyle need only convince the jury that this loss has increased his or her mental anguish.

[43] The traditional categories for general damages have served us for decades,[3] despite the fact that the whole area of general damages is defined as damages which cannot be calculated with pecuniary exactitude. Thus, exactitude cannot be expected. To avoid duplication, the trial court should allow an itemization of mental pain and suffering or an itemization of loss of enjoyment of life, but not both, on the jury verdict form. Alternatively, the jury verdict form could include a single line for loss of enjoyment of life and mental pain and suffering.

[. . . .]

Questions

NOTE: The Court is reasoning first *pro subjecta materia* to draw a distinction between different kinds of prejudices that can be caused to a human being and,

---

3. In Louisiana, courts had not traditionally recognized loss of enjoyment of life as a separate element of damages until 1987, when the Court of Appeal, Third Circuit opined that such damages could be awarded separate and apart from a general damages award. *Andrews v. Mosley Well Service*, 514 So.2d 491 (La.App. 3 Cir.), *writ denied*, 515 So.2d 807 (1987).

second, *in pari materia* to establish a common relationship between these kinds of prejudices, as well as, third, reasoning *a pari ratione* in pointing out that these diverse prejudices are all grounded in the same reason that dictates that they be compared.

1. Paragraphs 4–12: In this excerpt, the Court is providing us with a good civil law illustration of the process of the legal characterization of a legal concept.

2. Paragraphs 4–11: Although the Supreme Court has been considering "general damages" in the context of "torts-delicts," could the Court's evaluation and understanding of general damages be carried over or extended to a "contractual relationship" in which one party would suffer "a loss of gratification of intellectual or physical enjoyment" as a result of the other party breaching the contract? What if the latter party is in bad faith?

3. Can the distinction between the "primary tort victim" and the "primary tort victim's family members" be made in a contractual relationship wherein a party to a contract could suffer a loss of enjoyment of life and his/her family members, who are third parties to the contract, be entitled to "loss of consortium, service and society"?

4. Paragraphs 4–25: Notice that neither art. 2315A nor 2315B mention "loss of enjoyment of life" as a component part of general damages. It appears that the "courts" have created this concept of "loss of enjoyment of life" in interpreting art. 2315A and that "doctrine" has built upon that creation and made a distinction with art. 2315B, according to which "damages may include loss of consortium. . . ." Do you think it would be acceptable and reasonable to have two different understandings of "loss of enjoyment of life," one for tort and one for contract?

5. Paragraphs 29–37: What do you think of J. Victory's dissenting opinion? What does this opinion say about the role of a court, like the Third Circuit Court's decision in 1987?

6. Paragraphs 32–37: Notice the statement "Louisiana's unified concept of general damages" and the reference to Civ. C. arts. 2315, *et seq.* as "written law" or "legislation." (See La. Civ. C. arts. 1-3.) Notice also this statement: "the legislature sees no reason to create 'loss of enjoyment of life' as a separate element of damages, as it is already covered by the categories of general damages routinely allowed."

7. Paragraphs 38–43: Where the majority was attempting to find a separate *ratio legis* for the different items in recovery, Justice Weimer relied on one and the same *ratio legis*, or reason for the law as written legislation — or, very likely, on a reason of a higher level, the *ratio juris* or reason for the unwritten Law.

Preis, PLC
v.
Jane "Megan" Daily

Court of Appeal of Louisiana
Third Circuit
March 25, 2020
297 So.3d 853

SAVOIE, Judge

[. . . .]

Factual And Procedural Background

[1] In January 2017, while Jane "Megan" Daily (Daily) was a senior law school student, she was offered a full-time associate attorney position with Preis PLC (Preis). Employment was to begin no later than September 1, 2017, and it was contingent upon her passage of the Louisiana bar examination. Daily was presented with a "Letter Agreement For Employment with Preis PLC" (employment contract) on January 12, 2017, and she signed the contract on January 17, 2017. It provided for a starting annual salary and certain benefits, and further provided as follows:

[. . . .]

16. <u>YOUR COMMITMENT</u> — In consideration of the resources that have and will be expended by the Firm in your training and the fringe benefits provided, you agree to a term of employment of Three (3) years, commencing on the date you report to work to begin permanent full time employment. Should you fail to report to work to begin permanent full time employment on or before September 1, 2017 or should you terminate your employment with Preis PLC prior to the completion of the Three (3) year term, other than for health reasons of yourself, your spouse, and/or your children, the Firm will be entitled to liquidated damages of TEN THOUSAND AND NO/100 ($10,000.00) DOLLARS.

17. <u>FIRM'S COMMITMENT</u> — The Firm makes a corresponding commitment, assuming satisfactory performance, to employ you for a term of Three (3) years. In the event that your performance is unsatisfactory, the Firm shall have the right to terminate this contract of employment upon providing Thirty (30) days written notice to you.

. . . .

19. <u>CONFIDENTIALITY</u> — You agree to keep the terms of this offer, the conditions of employment, and your compensation confidential and will not disclose them to anyone outside of your immediate Family without the written permission of Edwin Preis, Robert Kallam, or Frank Piccolo.

Thereafter, Daily successfully completed the bar examination and began full-time employment at Preis as an associate attorney on or around September 1, 2017. [. . . .] However, she later resigned from the firm in November 2018. According to Daily, she had indirectly heard from other attorneys in the firm that her supervising attorney, Catherine Landry (Landry) was frustrated with her performance, and she felt she could be fired from the firm. Therefore, Daily sought employment elsewhere and resigned from Preis after securing a position at a different law firm.

[. . . .]

[2] On January 29, 2019, Preis filed a Petition for Breach of Contract and Damages against Daily seeking $10,000.00 in stipulated damages contemplated by the employment contract as a result of Daily's resignation prior to three years of employment. Preis's Petition ultimately sought an award of $7,408.05, explaining:

> The last payroll payment owed . . . was the November 18, 2018 payroll. After deducting payroll deductions, taxes, and the outstanding loan amount of $1,875.00 and stipulated liquidated damages due to Ms. Daily's breach of the three-year employment contract, Ms. Daily has an outstanding debt to Preis LLC of $7,408.05. Preis PLC seeks Judgment in this amount against Ms. Daily.

The Petition further sought a "Declaratory Judgment that the amounts owed herein may be offset against any amounts owed by Preis PLC to Ms. Daily[.]"

[. . . .]

[3] Thereafter, the trial court took the matter under advisement. On June 17, 2019, it issued a written Ruling. Therein, the trial judge noted that "considering that Daily's collections covered the expenses demonstrated to be directly attributable to her employment plus an additional sum of $84,394.74, [Daigle's] profitability analysis fails to approximate an actual loss to Preis." It went on to conclude that the $10,000.00 stipulated damages provision in the employment contract was not enforceable because it did not reasonably approximate Preis's loss in the event of a breach, as required by *Keiser v. Catholic Diocese of Shreveport, Inc.*, 38,797 (La. App. 2 Cir. 8/18/04), 880 So.2d 230. Therefore, the stipulated damages provision was equivalent to a forfeiture of wages prohibited by La.R.S. 23:634 and unenforceable as violation of public policy. *Id.*

[. . . .]

[. . . .] [O]n July 17, 2019, the trial court signed a Judgment awarding Daily $2,591.95 for past wages, $26,590.50 for penalty wages, and $15,036.50 for attorney fees, plus expenses and interest.

[4] Preis filed a suspensive appeal seeking a reversal of the trial court's ruling and a judgment awarding it $7,408.05 in damages owed under the employment contract. [. . . .]

[. . . .]

Analysis

Preis's Claim for Stipulated Contractual Damages:

[5] This case involves two competing claims: (1) Preis's claim against Daily for contractual damages as a result of her early resignation from the firm, and (2) Daily's claim under La.R.S. 23:631-23:653 for past wages owed as a result of her employment with Preis, penalty wages, and attorney fees. We will address Preis's claim first.

[6] On appeal, Preis seeks review of the trial court's ruling that the $10,000.00 stipulated damages provision in its employment contract with Daily was unenforceable and resulting conclusion that Daily does not owe damages as a result of her early resignation from the firm.

[. . . .]

[7] As the party seeking to enforce the stipulated damages provision, Preis bears the burden of proving that it is entitled to have the employment contract enforced against Daily. See *Service Investors Ltd. v. Scully*, 08-1062 (La.App. 3 Cir. 3/4/09), 9 So.3d 910. It therefore bears the burden of proving the essential elements of a valid contract, which includes a lawful cause — that is, one that is not unlawful or prohibited by public policy. *Id.*

[8] "The employer-employee relationship is a contractual relationship. As such, an employer and employee may negotiate the terms of an employment contract and agree to any terms **not prohibited by law or public policy.**" *Newsom v. Global Data Systems, Inc.*, 12-412, 12-413, p. 4 (La.App. 3 Cir. 12/12/12), 107 So.3d 781, 785, *writ denied*, 13-429 (La. 4/5/13), 110 So.3d 595 (emphasis added). Similarly, "[s]tipulated damages may not be modified by the court **unless they are so manifestly unreasonable as to be contrary to public policy.**["] La.Civ.Code art. 2012 (emphasis added).

[9] However, La.R.S. 23:634(A) expressly prohibits employers from including terms in their employment contracts that require employees to forfeit their wages in the event of their resignation; therefore, any such provision in an employment contract would necessarily be unlawful and against public policy. Specifically, La.R.S. 23:634(A) states:

> No person, acting either for himself or as agent or otherwise, shall require any of his employees to sign contracts by which the employees shall forfeit their wages if discharged before the contract is completed or if the employees resign their employment before the contract is completed; but in all such cases the employees shall be entitled to the wages actually earned up to the time of their discharge or resignation

[. . . .]

[10] As we recognized in *Service Investors Ltd.*, 9 So.3d at 915 (emphasis added):

> [S]tatutes such as La.R.S. 23:634-36 indicate a strong desire by our legislature to "take a good look" at employment contracts. Further evidence of this public policy to protect our state's employees while contracting with

employers can be found in La.R.S. 23:921, regarding nullity of noncompetition, choice of forum, or choice of law provisions unless specific criteria are met that protect the employee.

. . . .

Due to the clear public policy of our state to protect its employees when they enter into a contract for work with an employer, . . . **stipulated damage provisions must be scrutinized more closely than in typical contracts.**

[11] Provisions in employment contracts that do not expressly state that an employee must forfeit wages upon resignation prior to the term of the contract, but rather require the employee to pay stipulated damages upon resignation, have consistently been held to be de facto forfeiture of wages clauses in violation of La.R.S. 23:634(A), and therefore unenforceable, when the stipulated damages clause does not "reasonably approximate the obligee's loss in the event of a breach." *Keiser*, 880 So.2d at 236. "To determine the reasonableness, the court should inquire as to **whether the parties attempted to approximate the actual damages in confecting the agreement.**" [. . . .]

[. . . .]

[12] On appeal, Preis does not point to any case law wherein a stipulated damages provision in an employment contract was found to be enforceable against an employee. Rather, it attempts to distinguish the cases holding that a stipulated damages provision in an employment contract was unenforceable, arguing that the stipulated damages provision at issue here was reasonable under the circumstances, not penal in nature, and related to actual damages Preis sustained.

[13] Again, "[t]o determine the reasonableness, the court should inquire as to whether the parties attempted to approximate the actual damages in confecting the agreement." *Keiser*, 880 So.2d at 236. The stipulated damages provision at issue was part of a standard employment contract drafted by Preis. It required Daily to pay $10,000.00 in damages in the event she resigned prior to the three-year term "[i]n consideration of the resources that have and will be expended by the Firm in your [Daily's] training and the fringe benefits provided." Therefore, on its face, the employment contract does not attempt to approximate damages that Preis would sustain as a result of Daily leaving the firm prior to the three-year term. Rather, it seeks to compensate, or reimburse, Preis for resources, training, and fringe benefits expended to or on behalf of Daily during her employment.

[. . . .]

[14] We find that the evidence in the record reasonably supports the trial court's conclusion that the stipulated damages clause does not reflect an attempt by the parties to approximate actual damages in the event Daily resigned prior to the three-year commitment. Therefore, because the parties did not attempt to approximate actual damages when confecting the agreement, the stipulated damages provision requiring Daily to pay Preis $10,000.00 in the event of her early resignation is a de

facto forfeiture of wages clause prohibited by La.R.S. 23:634(A) and unenforceable. *Keiser*, 880 So.2d 230.

[....]

[15] Preis also argues on appeal that the stipulated damages provision should be upheld because Daily failed to establish that Preis did not suffer damages. It directs us to Comment (d) to La.Civ.Code. art. 2009, which states that a defendant is not prevented "from proving that a plaintiff who seeks to avail himself of a stipulated damages provision actually has sustained no loss. It merely shifts the burden of proof on the issue of damages from the plaintiff to the defendant."

[16] We disagree. First, we note that Preis's argument assumes the stipulated damages provision is otherwise enforceable; however, we have affirmed the trial court's ruling that it was not. Further, as previously noted, the trial court made a factual finding that Preis sustained no loss as a result of Daily's early resignation, because Preis profited from Daily's employment. Specifically, the trial court concluded that "Daily's collections covered her salary and benefits plus $84,394.74 of general expenses," and found that there was insufficient evidence establishing that Preis incurred over $84,394.74 in general expenses directly related to Daily's employment. Therefore, regardless of which party bore the burden of proof, the evidence in the record supports the trial court's finding that Preis did not suffer any damages as a result of Daily's early resignation.

[17] We therefore affirm the trial court's ruling that the stipulated damages provision in the employment contract was unenforceable and that Preis is not entitled to damages.

[....]

See also Chaudoir v. Porsche Cars of North America, 667 So.2d 569 (La.App. 3 Cir. 1995).

Questions

1. Nowhere do the Code articles on stipulated damages state that stipulated damages must "approximate the loss in the event of breach." Isn't it up to the parties, consenting freely, to set the amount of the stipulated damages so that their stipulated damages would be "measured by the loss sustained by the obligee and the profit of which he has been deprived," as stated in La. Civ. C. art. 1995? Shouldn't the stipulated damages be as measured by art. 1995, as some kind of lawful threat (art. 1962) against the obligor to motivate him not to act in bad faith (art. 1997) but to perform his obligation as per the contract he freely entered into, presumably in good faith?

2. Paragraphs 3–7: Relying on the cases of *Keiser* and *Service Investors*, the court refers to a "court-made" criteria of reasonableness of the loss resulting from the breach. Isn't it the purpose and justification of art. 1995 to lay down a "reasonable measure" of the damages owed an obligee? If so, then where does the

court find the source of their criteria of "reasonableness"? Is it likely that an obligor in bad faith would be concerned with causing on a "reasonable" loss or *damnum emergens* to his obligee? What about compensating the *lucrum cessans* expected by the obligee?

Comparative Law Perspective

— Civil Law—

Jean-Louis Baudouin & Pierre-Gabriel Jobin, *Les Obligations*

(5th ed. 1998), translated by John Randall Trahan

Damages and Penal Clause

846 — General observations — [. . . .] This clause contractually fixes the amount owed to the creditor in the event of nonperformance for which the debtor is at fault. It has the advantage of avoiding the risks of legal action and it dispenses the creditor from having to provide proof of the prejudice that he has effectively experienced. [. . . .]

Penal clauses assume varied forms. It can, for example, provide for the payment of a lump sum in the event of a pure and simple nonperformance or of a penalty (calculated as so much per day) for a delay in performance. [. . . .]

847 — Notion. Distinctions — [. . . .] A penal clause must [. . .] be distinguished from an alternative obligation [. . .]. The putting into work of a penal clause for the benefit of the creditor is [. . .] subordinated to the nonperformance of the obligation of his debtor and appertains to the creditor.

848 — General rules — A penal clause represents conventional damages with interest and takes the place of judicial damages with interest. It thereby exempts the creditor from proving the damage he has experienced and gives him the right to a stipulated sum based on the sole fact of nonperformance for which the debtor is at fault [. . .]. In this regard, it is therefore submitted to the majority of general rules that concern judicial compensation of the prejudice. [. . . .] The creditor [. . .] is never obligated to avail himself of a penal clause and can, in his discretion, opt for it or for the performance of the obligation in kind [. . .]. A penal clause is a secondary obligation, accessory to the principal obligation for the performance of which it is designed to provide assurance. [. . . .]

In the event of partial performance, the stipulated penalty must be reduced proportionately if the partial performance has benefitted the creditor.

François Terré, Philippe Simler, Yves Lequette & François Chénedé, *Droit Civil: Les Obligations*

at 957-67 (12th ed. 2019), translated by John Randall Trahan

Damages and Penal Clauses

§ 3. Penal clauses

887. Definition. Validity. A penal clause is that by which the contracting parties assess in advance the damages and interest owed by the debtor in the event of delay or nonperformance. [. . . .]

The Civil Code recognizes the validity of these clauses, which, since the reform of 2016, are regulated by Article 1231-5 of the Civil Code. [. . . .]

888. Advantages and disadvantages. A penal clause, in as much as it fixes by anticipation the amount of the indemnity owed by the debtor should he default, presents diverse advantages:

1. It permits the parties to avoid legal actions on the magnitude of the damage; thus, it dries up one source of litigation.

2. It enables the creditor to avoid the delays and the difficulties fixing the amount of damages and interest entails: the creditor does not even have to prove the reality of the damage.

3. By agreeing on a moderate amount (but not derisory [. . .]), the liability of the debtor can be lightened by the play of the penal clause [. . .].

4. Conversely, a penal clause permits the parties to give to their agreement an enhanced obligatory force, by stipulating, for a case of nonperformance, an elevated penalty (as long as it is not excessive [. . .]); the debtor will have the greatest interest in respecting his engagements, the nonperformance of which would risk being more burdensome for him. [. . . .]

889. Characteristics of the penal clause. A penal clause presents two characteristics: 1) it takes the place of damages and interest; 2) it involves a flat-rate forfeiture.

890. 1) A penal clause takes the place of damages and interest. [. . . .] Several consequences follow from this:

a) A penal clause implies the existence of an "illicit nonperformance", of a failure of the debtor to fulfill his obligations. [. . . .]

b) A penal clause implies the existence of an indemnity that takes the place of damages and interest. [. . . .]

c) A debtor is bound to bear the burden of a penal clause only in a case in which he can be condemned to pay damages and interest. This presupposes, first of all, that the debtor was previously put in default. [. . . .]

d) The creditor is not confined to asserting the penal clause against the debtor should he be in default; if he prefers, the creditor can pursue the execution of the obligation in kind, [. . .] just as he can demand the resolution of the contract on account of the nonperformance of obligations.

891. A penal clause involves a flat-rate forfeiture. [. . . .] As a result, the judge cannot grant the creditor a sum that is greater or lesser. [. . . .]

Depending on the circumstances, penal clauses, by reason of their flat-rate character, can benefit the creditor and not only the debtor. [. . . .]

893. Reduction or augmentation of the penalty by the judge. [. . . .]

a)   Former Article 1152 of the Civil Code specified that the creditor could not be allowed a sum greater or lesser than that provided for in the contract[.] [**The reform**] added a second line that authorizes the judge to reduce the penalty agreed to, if it is manifestly excessive or derisory. This power of moderation is not provided for in new Article 1231-5, according to which "the judge can, even on his own motion, reduce or augment the penalty thus agreed to if it is manifestly excessive or derisory.

[. . .] [T]he power of the judge is subordinated to the existence, at the time of his decision, to the manifestly excessive or manifestly derisory character of the penalty agreed to in relation to the prejudice effectively experienced. [. . . .]

The range within which the judge can maneuver is situated between the penalty and the damage/prejudice. If he decides to use his power, he is not obligated to align the amount of the penalty with that of the prejudice [. . .]. If he augments a manifestly derisory penalty, he cannot raise it to an amount that is superior to the prejudice experienced and if he reduces a manifestly excessive penalty, he cannot reduce it to an amount that is inferior to the prejudice, but he is permitted, at the extreme, to totally exonerate a contracting party from the weight of a penal clause by noting the absence of prejudice.

François Terré, Philippe Simler, Yves Lequette & François Chénedé, *Droit Civil: Les Obligations*

(12th ed. 2018)

Damages for Fraud

B. The sanctions for fraud

308. Nature of the sanctions. — Insofar as fraud vitiates the consent of the victim, the normal sanction is the *relative nullity* of the contract. [. . . .]

But fraud is also a fault that can be sanctioned by *damages*. The victim of fraudulent maneuvers can bring a delictual action to obtain compensation from the author of the fraud for the victim's prejudice suffered when declaration of nullity does not suffice for removing such prejudice. Besides, nothing obliges the victim to demand the nullity of the contract, if he prefers to limit himself to recovering damages. Unlike the nullity action, the delictual action brought by the victim of fraud does not require proof of an intentional act by the other party. In fact, [in] this action [. . .] simple negligence is sufficient for finding liability. Due to the public policy character of this delictual liability, it cannot be reduced contractually by a limitation of liability clause. [. . . .]

The extent of the damages varies depending on whether the victim of the fraud had chosen to maintain the contract or not. When the victim of fraud chooses to seek nullity, his reparable damages covers the cost of concluding the contract, since these have become useless because the contract has been annulled, as well as the loss of chance of concluding a contract with a third party, if this chance is serious. The request for nullity of the contract prevents the plaintiff from seeking compensation for lost profits from the contract. [. . . .] When the victim of fraud chooses not to request the nullity of the contract, his reparable damages consist of the loss of the chance of having been able to contract under more advantageous conditions. [. . . .]

Moreover, damages constitute the sole sanction in the case of fraud caused by a third party. It is the same with the sanction for incidental [non-material] fraud.

One can conceive of still another sanction for fraud — the *refusal of nullity*. An incapable who has dissimulated his condition by means of fraudulent maneuvers will not be able to obtain the nullity of the contract on account of his incapacity.

Alain Levasseur, *Comparative Law of Contracts*
at 125–45 (2008)

Performance — Damages

"[. . .] [C]ourts in civilian legal systems, routinely grant specific performance by ordering parties to perform their contracts. But courts in common law systems, for reasons that are largely historical, regard specific performance as an "extraordinary" remedy, to be granted only when an award of damages would not be "adequate." (I might add here that we Americans sometimes rationalize the denial of specific performance on the ground that this permits a party to a contract to commit an "efficient breach," but that concept of law and economics is one that not only does not travel well, but that struck most of my civilian colleagues as bordering on the immoral.) [E. Allan Farnsworth, A common lawyer's view of his civilian colleagues, 57 La.L.Rev.227, at 235.]

"[. . . .] The consequences of a binding promise at common law are not affected by the degree of power which the promisor possesses over the promised event. If the promised event does not come to pass, the plaintiff's property is sold to satisfy the damages, with certain limits, which the promisee has suffered by the failure. The consequences are the same in kind whether the promise is that it shall rain, or that another man shall paint a picture, or that the promisor will deliver a bale of cotton. If the legal consequence is the same in all cases, it seems proper that all contracts should be considered from the same legal point of view. [. . . .] If it be proper to state the common law meaning of promise and contract in this way, it has the advantage of freeing the subject from the superfluous theory that contract is a qualified subjection of one will to another, a kind of limited slavery. It might so regarded if the law compelled men to perform their contracts, of if it allowed promisees to exercise such compulsion. [. . . .] It is true that in some instances equity does what is called compelling specific performance. But, in the first place, I am speaking of the common law, and, in the next, this only means that equity compels the performance of certain elements of the total promise which are still capable of performance. [. . . .] The only universal consequence of a legally binding promise is, that the law makes the promisor pay damages if the promised event does not come to pass. In every case it leaves him free from interference until the time for fulfillment has gone by, and therefore free to break his contract if he chooses. [. . . .] [O.W. Holmes, Jr., The Common Law, 1881 at 299 et seq.]

"[In an American law school . . .] [w]e are trained to find ways of getting around or out of contracts, and, as lawyers, we occasionally even counsel clients to breach them. Civil lawyers, on the other hand, are much more committed to elaborating a legal mechanism to enforce as precisely as possible those promises that are actually made and intended. This part of their law is more systematized and coherent than is ours. These differences suggest that more is at stake than simply deciding where a particular loss should fall."

Civilians justify their system by reference to the maxim *pacta sunt servanda*. This "basic and it seems universally accepted principle of contract law" means, in the civil law, that promises are binding. [. . . .] As René David has explained, "the principle satisfies our philosophical and moral views; it is proper for individuals to be bound by their promises." [. . . .] To the civilian mind, the maxim is entirely self-evident [. . .]. René David believed the proper translation to be this: "commitments that have been made must be performed." [. . . .] American courts, however, generally adopt a translation that applies the maxim only to agreements: "agreements must be obeyed" [. . .]; "agreements must be respected" [. . .]; "agreements must be observed" [. . .]. [Richard Hyland, *Pacta Sunt Servanda*: A Meditation, 34 Va. J. Int. L. 405 et seq.]

"[. . . .] The binding nature of a promise is of utmost importance to the civil law, and the courts accordingly bind individuals to their promises. [. . . .] As Professors Flour and Aubert write [. . .] 'morality dominates civilian contract law. They state unequivocally that "the legal obligation incumbent on the contracting party to perform is none other than the moral duty to honor one's word, once given." The civilian focus on morality contrasts with the common law's concern for efficiency as the primary priority. [. . . .]

"This moral conception was translated into the civil codes of Europe by making specific performance the normal remedy for breach of contract, and monetary damages the exception, in contradistinction to the common law system of monetary remedies as the norm and specific performance as the exception. . . ." [Vivian Grosswald Curran, *Comparative Law, An Introduction*, Carolina Academic Press 2002, p. 25–26].

See La. Civ. C. articles: 1756, 1983, 1986, 1989, 1994–1998, 2002.

Fr. Civ. C. 1804 (before the revision of 2016–2017)

> **Art. 1134:** Conventions legally formed [. . . .] must be performed in good faith.

> **Art. 1136:** The obligation to give carries with it the obligation to deliver the thing and to preserve it until delivery, under the penalty to have to pay damages to the creditor.

> **Art. 1138:** The obligation to deliver is perfected by the mere exchange of consent between the contracting parties. The creditor becomes the owner of the thing [. . .].

> **Art. 1142:** Any obligation to do or not to do, in case of non-performance by the obligor, is transformed into an obligation to pay damages.

> **Art. 1144:** The creditor may also, in case of non-performance, be authorized to have the obligation performed on his own at the expense of the obligor.

> **Art. 1146:** Damages are due only after the obligor has been put in default to perform his obligation, except when the thing the obligor was bound to give or do could only be carried out within a certain time that has expired.

> **Art. 1149:** Damages owed the obligee are, in general, in an amount equal to the loss incurred and the gain of which he has been deprived, unless one of the following exceptions apply.

BGB (German Civil Code)

> **Section 242.** The obligor must perform in a manner consistent with good faith taking into account common usage.

> **Section 241.** (1) By virtue of the obligation the obligee is entitled to demand performance from the obligor. The performance may also consist of an omission.

> **Section 249.** (1) Anyone liable in damages must restore the condition that would exist if the circumstance obliging him to pay damages had not occurred.

> **Section 252.** The damage to be compensated also comprises the lost profits. Those profits are considered lost that in the normal course of events [. . .] could in all probability be expected.

C.C.Q. (Québec)

> **Art. 1590:** An obligation confers on the creditor the right to demand that the obligation be performed in full, properly and without delay.

> Where the debtor fails to perform his obligation without justification on his part and he is in default, the creditor may, without prejudice to his right to the performance of the obligation in whole or in part by equivalence, (1) force specific performance of the obligation; (2) obtain, [. . .]; (3) take any

other measure provided by law to enforce his right to the performance of the obligation.

Art. 1601: A creditor may, in cases which admit of it, demand that the debtor be forced to make specific performance of the obligation.

Art. 1602: In case of default, the creditor may perform the obligation or cause it to be performed at the expense of the debtor. [. . . .]

Art. 1607: The creditor is entitled to damages for bodily, moral or material injury which is an immediate and direct consequence of the debtor's default.

Art. 1611: The damages due to the creditor compensate for the amount of the loss he has sustained and the profit of which he has been deprived. Future injury which is certain and able to be assessed is taken into account in awarding damages.

Art. 1613: In contractual matters, the debtor is liable only for damages that were foreseen or foreseeable at the time the obligation was contracted, where the failure to perform the obligation does not proceed from intentional or gross fault on his part; even then, the damages include only what is an immediate and direct consequence of the nonperformance.

Philippe Malaurie, Laurent Aynès, Philippe Stoffel-Munck, *Les Obligations*, Defrénois 2003

§ 1. Specific performance of Obligations in kind

1. — Direct constraint

[. . . .] English law does grant specific performance only in exceptional cases, because, in general, it infringes upon individual freedom.

On account of the difficulties raised by specific performance by means of direct constraint, French law devised different measures of indirect constraint, the only surviving one being 'astreinte' (a daily penalty for delay in performing).

1129. [. . . .] In reality, it is impossible to have an obligation to do specifically enforced by public authorities, for fear of satisfying the private interest of the creditor at the expense of the debtor's freedom. It is only in the case of the transfer of ownership of a thing that the creditor may obtain specific performance by constraint: seize a movable, expulsion from a building [. . .]. In other cases, the creditor may be allowed to perform himself at the expense of the debtor [. . .] (see Civ. C. art 1144) [. . .] which suggests that the obligation is not *intuitus personae*.

1130. [**Civ. C. Art. 1142**], this text is an application of the rule *nemo precise cogi ad factum* (which) protects one's individual freedom. [. . . .] Specific performance in kind is denied today when it would offend a moral, material or legal impossibility. Either because of the personal nature of the obligation; thus, one could not specifically and forcefully compel an artist to carry out his obligation (a painting, for instance); or because one would face too many and major material obstacles; or because of a legal impossibility to enforce the obligation which would not otherwise prevent an 'equivalent' performance (damages, for example).

1131. [. . . .] Anytime an obligation to do can be enforced by constraint, performance in kind must be ordered. Thus, a buyer should be compelled to take delivery of the thing sold to him and delivered by the seller; [. . .] a tenant who refuses to leave the premises at the end of the lease can be expelled; [. . .].

2. — Astreinte

1132. Indirect but effective. — Astreinte [. . .] targets the debtor's wallet to compel him to perform. Astreinte has for its purpose the execution of a judicial decision of which it is the accessory; the judge can, even of his own motion, sentence the debtor to pay a sum of money, for each day of delay in general; it is, therefore, in the interest of the debtor to perform as soon as possible. [. . . .] Astreinte is 'personal' to the debtor in the sense that the debtor cannot pass it on to his sureties.

1134. Scope of application. Almost any court decision can have an astreinte attached to it, even when the object of the obligation is tainted with *intuitus personae*. [. . . .] However very strictly personal obligations, such as an artist's obligation, cannot be enforced by way of an astreinte (a capricious artist would act poorly under any constraint [. . .]; damages are a better remedy [. . .])[. . .].

1135. [. . . .] Astreinte is different from damages and has for its main purpose to 'crush' the obligor's resistance to the court's decision; it is a kind of *contempt of Court*.

— Common Law —

Restatement, 2d of Contracts (1981)

§ 235. Effect of Performance as Discharge and of Non-Performance as Breach

(1) Full performance of a duty under a contract discharges the duty.

(2) When performance of a duty under a contract is due any non-performance is a breach.

§ 236. Claims for Damages for Total and for Partial Breach

(1) A claim for damages for total breach is one for damages based on all of the injured party's remaining rights to performance.

(2) A claim for damages for partial breach is one for damages based on only part of the injured party's remaining rights to performance.

§ 243. Effect of a Breach by Non-Performance as Giving Rise to a Claim for Damages for Total Breach

(1) With respect to performances to be exchanged under an exchange of promises, a breach by non-performance gives rise to a claim for damages for total breach only if it discharges the injured party's remaining duties to render such performance, other than a duty to render an agreed equivalent under § 240.

(2) Except as stated in Subsection (3), a breach by non-performance accompanied or followed by a repudiation gives rise to a claim for damages for total breach.

(3) Where at the time of the breach the only remaining duties of performance are those of the party in breach and are for the payment of money in installments not related to one another, his breach by non-performance as to less than the whole, whether or not accompanied or followed by a repudiation, does not give rise to a claim for damages for total breach.

(4) In any case other than those stated in the preceding subsections, a breach by non-performance gives rise to a claim for total breach only if it so substantially impairs the value of the contract to the injured party at the time of the breach that it is just in the circumstances to allow him to recover damages based on all his remaining rights to performance.

UCC

§ 2-703. Seller's Remedies in General.

(2) If the buyer is in breach of contract the seller, to the extent provided for by this Act or other law, may:

(a) withhold delivery of such goods; [. . .]

(h) recover damages for nonacceptance or repudiation under Section 2-708(1);

(i) recover lost profits [. . .]

(k) obtain specific performance under Section 2-716; [. . .]

(m) in other cases, recover damages in any manner that is reasonable under the circumstances.

§ 2-714. Buyer's Damages for Breach in Regard to Accepted Goods.

(1) The measure of damages for breach of warranty is the difference at the time and place of acceptance between the value of the goods accepted and the value they would have had if they had been as warranted [. . .].

§ 2-716. Specific Performance; Buyer's Right of Replevin.

(1) Specific performance may be decreed if the goods are unique or in other proper circumstances. In a contract other than a consumer contract, specific performance may be decreed if the parties have agreed to that remedy. However, even if the parties agree to specific performance, specific performance may not be decreed if the breaching party's sole remaining contractual obligation is the payment of money.

(2) The decree for specific performance may include such terms and conditions as to payment of the price, damages, or other relief as the court may deem just.

(3) The buyer has a right of replevin or similar remedy for goods identified to the contract if after reasonable effort the buyer is unable to effect cover for such goods or the circumstances reasonably indicate that such effort will be unavailing or if the goods have been shipped under reservation and satisfaction of the security interest in them has been made or tendered.

G.H. Treitel, *The Law of Contract,* Seventh Edition, Stevens & Sons, 1987. (Reproduced with permission of the Licensor through PLSclear.)

Section 2. Effects of Breach

A breach of contract may entitle the injured party to claim damages, the agreed sum, specific performance or an injunction, in accordance with the principles discussed. [. . . .] In appropriate circumstances he may be entitled to more than one of these remedies: e.g. to an injunction and damages. [. . . .]

Chapter 21. Remedies

A breach of contract is a civil wrong. To break a contract can also occasionally be a criminal offence [. . .]. In most cases, however, a breach of contract will involve only civil liability [. . .]. A claim for specific relief is one for the actual performance of the defaulting party's undertaking. Where that undertaking is one to do, or to forbear from doing, some act, a claim for specific relief is made by the equitable remedies of specific performance or injunction; where the undertaking is one to pay a sum of money, a claim for specific relief is made by the common law action for an agreed sum. In an action for damages, the injured party claims compensation in money for the fact that he has not received the performance for which he bargained. [. . . .] A person who has performed his part of the contract but has not received the agreed counter-performance may, finally, claim back his performance or its reasonable value. [. . . .]

Section 1. Damages

The action for damages is always available, as of right, when a contract has been broken. It should, from this point of view, be contrasted with claims for specific relief and for restitution, which are either subject to the discretion of the court or only available if certain conditions are satisfied. An action for damages can succeed even though the victim has not suffered any loss: in that event, it will result in an award of nominal damages. In such a case, the purpose of the action may simply be to establish what the rights and liabilities of the parties under a contract are. [. . . .] Generally the victim will claim damages for a substantial loss; [. . .].

Section 3. Equitable Remedies

1. Specific Performance

The common law did not specifically enforce contractual obligations except those to pay money. Specific enforcement of other contractual obligations was available only in equity. It was (and is) subject to many restrictions. These are based partly on the drastic character of the remedy, which leads (more readily than an award of damages or of the agreed sum) to attachment of the defendant's person. But this is an important factor only where the contract calls for "personal" performance, *i.e.* for acts to be done by the defendant himself. Where the contract is not of this kind, it can be specifically enforced without personal constraint: for example, by sequestration, by execution of a formal document by an officer of the court, or by a writ of delivery. [. . . .] The more recent authorities [. . .] support some expansion in the scope of the remedy.

(1) Granted where damages not "adequate"

The traditional view is that specific performance will not be ordered where damages are an "adequate" remedy. [. . . .]

(2) Discretionary

Specific performance is a discretionary remedy: the court is not bound to grant it merely because the contract is valid at law and cannot be impeached on some specific equitable ground such as misrepresentation or undue influence. [. . . .] The discretion is, however, "not an arbitrary [. . .] discretion, but one to be governed as far as possible by fixed rules and principles."

E. Allan Farnsworth, *Contracts* (2d ed. 1990)

B. Enforcement by Specific Performance and Injunction

§ 12.4. Historical Development of Equitable Relief. [. . . .] The common law courts did not generally grant specific relief for breach of contract. The usual form of relief at common law was substitutional, and the typical judgment declared that the plaintiff recover from the defendant a sum of money. [. . . .]

§ 12.5. Forms: Specific Performance and Injunction. The most direct form of equitable relief for breach of contract is specific performance [. . .]. A court will not order a performance that has become impossible, unreasonably burdensome, or unlawful, nor will is issue an order that can be frustrated by the defendant through exercise of a power of termination or otherwise. Specific performance may be granted after there has been a breach of contract by either nonperformance or repudiation. [. . . .]

C. Enforcement by Award of Damages

§ 12.8. Basic Principles of Damages. The award of damages is the common form of relief for breach of contract. Virtually any breach gives the injured party a claim for damages for at least nominal damages, "to which," as a distinguished federal judge put it "for reasons we do not understand every victim of a breach of contract, unlike a tort victim, is entitled." Thus, even if the breach caused no loss [. . .] the injured party can recover as damages a nominal sum, commonly six cents or a dollar, fixed without regard to loss. [. . . .] In most successful actions for breach of contract, however, substantial damages are awarded.

The basic principle for the measurement of those damages is that of compensation based on the injured party's expectation. [. . . .] At least in principle, a party's expectation is measured by the actual worth that performance of the contract would have had to that party, not the worth that it might have had to some hypothetical person. [. . . .]

A court will not ordinarily award damages that are described as "punitive," intended to punish the party in breach, or sometimes as "exemplary," intended to make an example of that party. [. . . .] Punitive damages may, however, be awarded in tort actions, and a number of courts have awarded them for a breach of contract that is in some respect tortious. [. . . .]

International Law

UNIDROIT Principles of International Commercial Contracts (2016)

Article 5.1.4 (Duty to achieve a specific result, Duty of best efforts)

(1) To the extent that an obligation of a party involves a duty to achieve a specific result, that party is bound to achieve that result.

(2) To the extent that an obligation of a party involves a duty of best efforts in the performance of an activity, that party is bound to make such efforts as would be made by a reasonable person of the same kind in the same circumstances.

Article 7.2.1 (Performance of monetary obligations)

Where a party who is obliged to pay money does not do so, the other party may require payment.

Article 7.2.2 (Performance of non-monetary obligation)

Where a party who owes an obligation other than one to pay money does not perform, the other party may require performance, unless (a) to (e) [. . .].

Article 7.2.4 (Judicial penalty)

(1) Where the court orders a party to perform, it may also direct that this party pay a penalty if it does not comply with the order.

(2) The penalty shall be paid to the aggrieved party unless mandatory provisions of the law of the forum provide otherwise. Payment of the penalty to the aggrieved party does not exclude any claim for damages.

Article 7.4.2 (Full compensation)

(1) The aggrieved party is entitled to full compensation for harm sustained as a result of the non-performance. Such harm includes both any loss which it suffered and any gain of which it was deprived, taking into account any gain to the aggrieved party resulting from its avoidance of cost or harm.

(2) Such harm may be non-pecuniary and includes, for instance, physical suffering or emotional distress.

Article 7.4.4 (Foreseeability of harm)

The non-performing party is liable only for harm which it foresaw or could reasonably have foreseen at the time of the conclusion of the contract as being likely to result from its non-performance.

Section IV — What Contracts Shall Be Avoided by Persons Not Parties to Them; Simulation, Revocatory (Pauliana) Action, Oblique Action

Louisiana Sources of Law

Louisiana Civil Code

Art. 2025. Definition; simulation and counterletter.

A contract is a simulation when, by mutual agreement, it does not express the true intent of the parties.

If the true intent of the parties is expressed in a separate writing, that writing is a counterletter. (Acts 1984, No. 331, § 1, eff. Jan. 1, 1985.)

Art. 2026. Absolute simulation.

A simulation is absolute when the parties intend that their contract shall produce no effects between them. That simulation, therefore, can have no effects between the parties. (Acts 1984, No. 331, § 1, eff. Jan. 1, 1985.)

Art. 2027. Relative simulation.

A simulation is relative when the parties intend that their contract shall produce effects between them though different from those recited in their contract. A relative simulation produces between the parties the effects they intended if all requirements for those effects have been met. (Acts 1984, No. 331, §1, eff. Jan. 1, 1985.)

Art. 2028. Effects as to third persons. [*Amended*]

A. Any simulation, either absolute or relative, may have effects as to third persons.

B. Counterletters can have no effects against third persons in good faith. Nevertheless, if the counterletter involves immovable property, the principles of recordation apply with respect to third persons. (Acts 1984, No. 331, §1, eff. Jan. 1, 1985; Acts 2012, No. 277, §1.)

Revocatory Action

Art. 2036. Act of the obligor that causes or increases his insolvency.

An obligee has a right to annul an act of the obligor, or the result of a failure to act of the obligor, made or effected after the right of the obligee arose, that causes or increases the obligor's insolvency. (Acts 1984, No. 331, §1, eff. Jan. 1, 1985; Acts 2003, No. 552, §1; Acts 2004, No. 447, §1, eff. Aug. 15, 2004.)

Art. 2037. Insolvency.

An obligor is insolvent when the total of his liabilities exceeds the total of his fairly appraised assets. (Acts 1984, No. 331, §1, eff. Jan. 1, 1985; Acts 2003, No. 552, §1; Acts 2004, No. 447, §1, eff. Aug. 15, 2004.)

Art. 2038. Onerous contract made by the obligor.

An obligee may annul an onerous contract made by the obligor with a person who knew or should have known that the contract would cause or increase the obligor's insolvency. In that case, the person is entitled to recover what he gave in return only to the extent that it has inured to the benefit of the obligor's creditors.

An obligee may annul an onerous contract made by the obligor with a person who did not know that the contract would cause or increase the obligor's insolvency, but in that case that person is entitled to recover as much as he gave to the obligor. That lack of knowledge is presumed when that person has given at least four-fifths of the value of the thing obtained in return from the obligor. (Acts 1984, No. 331, §1, eff. Jan. 1, 1985.)

Art. 2039. Gratuitous contract made by the obligor.

An obligee may attack a gratuitous contract made by the obligor whether or not the other party knew that the contract would cause or increase the obligor's insolvency. (Acts 1984, No. 331, §1, eff. Jan. 1, 1985.)

Art. 2040. Contract made in course of business.

An obligee may not annul a contract made by the obligor in the regular course of his business. (Acts 1984, No. 331, § 1, eff. Jan. 1, 1985.)

Art. 2041. Action must be brought within one year.

The action of the obligee must be brought within one year from the time he learned or should have learned of the act, or the result of the failure to act, of the obligor that the obligee seeks to annul, but never after three years from the date of that act or result. (Acts 1984, No. 331, § 1, eff. Jan. 1, 1985.)

Art. 2042. Obligee must join obligor and third persons.

In an action to annul either his obligor's act, or the result of his obligor's failure to act, the obligee must join the obligor and the third persons involved in that act or failure to act.

A third person joined in the action may plead discussion of the obligor's assets. (Acts 1984, No. 331, § 1, eff. Jan. 1, 1985.)

Art. 2043. Assets transferred must be returned.

If an obligee establishes his right to annul his obligor's act, or the result of his obligor's failure to act, that act or result shall be annulled only to the extent that it affects the obligee's right. (Acts 1984, No. 331, § 1, eff. Jan. 1, 1985.)

Oblique Action

Art. 2044. Insolvency by failure to exercise right.

If an obligor causes or increases his insolvency by failing to exercise a right, the obligee may exercise it himself, unless the right is strictly personal to the obligor.

For that purpose, the obligee must join in the suit his obligor and the third person against whom that right is asserted. (Acts 1984, No. 331, § 1, eff. Jan. 1, 1985.)

Doctrine

Louisiana Law of Conventional Obligations, A Précis
Sections 11.1.1 to 11.1.6

An obligee who watches over his own interest has two actions available to him to protect "indirectly" his right to obtain some form performance from his obligor. One action is known as the "Revocatory Action" and the other is the "Oblique Action." [. . . .]

Revocatory Action

The action, named *revocatory* in the Louisiana civil Code, is also known in civil law jurisdictions as the "paulian action" or "pauliana action." It is described in

LSA-CC. **Art. 2036** in the following terms: "**An obligee has a right to annul an act of the obligor, or the result of a failure to act of the obligor, made or effected after the right of the obligee arose, that causes or increases the obligor's insolvency.**" [....]

Art. 2036 suggests that two sets of conditions must be met: one set of conditions concerns the obligee's right against his obligor and the second set focuses on the obligor's act or failure to act.

As regards the obligee's right, it is necessary that this right be either in existence and vested in the obligee or that this right be at least 'potential' before the obligor, by his act or failure to act, causes or increases his insolvency. [....]

As regards the obligor's act or result of a failure to act it must have caused or increased the insolvency of the obligor. **Art. 2037** provides an explanation of the meaning of insolvency for the purpose of the revocatory action: "**An obligor is insolvent when the total of his liabilities exceeds the total of his fairly appraised assets.**"

Furthermore, the act or result of a failure to act on the part of the obligor must not be or have been *strictly personal* to that obligor. [....]

A reading of Articles 2036, 2038, 2040 leads one to state that the effect of a revocatory action is to have a juridical act or contract *annulled.* Therefore the rules governing nullity or dissolution of contracts should apply.

Actually, the outcome of a revocatory action is not to "annul" an act or contract between the obligor and a third person but, rather, to declare that the act or contract cannot be "opposed" to the obligee who brings the revocatory action. [....]

Art. 2038 provides as follows: "**An obligee may annul an onerous contract made by the obligor with a person who knew or should have known that the contract would cause or increase the obligor's insolvency. In that case, the person is entitled to recover what he gave in return only to the extent that it has inured to the benefit of the obligor's creditors.**

An obligee may annul an onerous contract made by the obligor with a person who did not know that the contract would cause or increase the obligor's insolvency, but in that case that person is entitled to recover as much as he gave to the obligor. That lack of knowledge is presumed when that person has given at least four-fifths of the value of the thing obtained in return from the obligor." [....]

As regards "gratuitous contracts," **Art. 2039** states very clearly, in a few words, that "**An obligee may attack a gratuitous contract made by the obligor whether or not the other party knew that the contract would cause or increase the obligor's insolvency.**" [....]

[A]n obligee could not bring a revocatory action whenever he would interfere with his obligor's strictly personal rights *vis-à-vis* a third person.

Art. 2040 adds explicitly the following exception: "**An obligee may not annul a contract made by the obligor in the regular course of his business.**" [....]

One additional requirement is the proper timing of the exercise of his right by the obligee. Under **Art. 2041** "**The action of the obligee must be brought within one year from the time he learned of the act, or the result of the failure to act, of the obligor that the obligee seeks to annul, but never after three years from the date of that act or result.**" [. . . .]

In addition, "**In an action to annul either his obligor's act, or the result of his obligor's failure to act, the obligee must join the obligor and the third persons involved in that act or failure to act.**" **Art. 2042(1)**. As such, the third person will be allowed to raise the defense of the benefit of discussion as stated in **Art. 2042(2)**: "**A third person joined in the action may plead discussion of the obligor's assets.**"

As regards an important additional effect of a revocatory action, it is stated in **Art. 2043**: "**If an obligee establishes his right to annul his obligor's act, or the result of his obligor's failure to act, that act or result shall be annulled only to the extent that it affects the obligee's right.**" [. . . .]

Oblique Action

A single Article, **Art. 2044**, provides an obligee with an additional remedy against his obligor in the event the "**obligor causes or increases his insolvency by failing to exercise a right. . . .**" In that case "**the obligee may exercise it himself, unless the right is strictly personal to the obligor. For that purpose, the obligee must join in the suit his obligor and the third person against whom that right is asserted.**" This right of action of the obligee is known as the "oblique action." [. . . .]

Once an obligee can ascertain that his obligor has caused or increased his insolvency, that obligee will have to select that right or those rights of his obligor that the latter "fails to exercise." Not every right of an obligor can be exercised by his obligee because the obligor is still in charge of his patrimony and no "stranger" should be allowed, without limitations, to interfere with the obligor's management of his patrimony. [. . . .]

Thus, rights which are "personal" to the obligor cannot fall in the hands of the obligee. [. . . .]

As to the outcome of the oblique action, it is the opposite of the outcome of the revocatory action. Should an obligee be successful in bringing an oblique action, the benefit of the action will be shared by *all* the obligees.

Cases

The National Bank of Bossier City et al. v. Kenneth R. Hardcastle et al.

Court of Appeal of Louisiana
Second Circuit
October 30, 1967
204 So.2d 142

BARHAM, Judge.

[1] This is a revocatory action by two creditors of Willis H. Hardcastle, deceased. The defendants are the surviving widow of the deceased, Mrs. Ora Hopkins Hardcastle, the two sons of the deceased, Kenneth R. Hardcastle and Willis S. Hardcastle, and the Succession of Willis H. Hardcastle.

[2] Plaintiffs allege that on October 30, 1964, the deceased transferred the only real estate he owned to his two sons; that one of the sons was a creditor of the deceased; that deceased was insolvent at the time of transfer; that the transfers were for the purpose of defrauding the creditors; and that the creditors were injured by the transfers. Plaintiffs urged that the transfers were simulations, and, in the alternative, that they were subject to a revocatory action. They have abandoned their claim of simulation and appeal from the lower court judgment denying their right to revocation. Their suit for revocation is joined with an action to liquidate their debts as provided by LSA-C.C. art. 1975.

[3] The two pieces of property involved in this action are the home of the deceased and a business lot upon which was situated a small office building and which was used in deceased's used car business. The stated consideration in the deeds was the assumption of mortgages. However, the sons delivered to their father approximately $1,600.00 as a part of the overall transaction. It is not disputed that the actual value received by the two sons exceeds the consideration which was paid for the properties. At the time of the transfer the deceased was recovering from a severe stroke, was, in fact, insolvent, was overdrawn approximately $800.00 at the plaintiff bank, and was unable to meet the monthly payment on the obligations assumed by the two sons.

[4] It is the testimony of Kenneth Hardcastle that he and his brother had no knowledge of their father's business affairs and did not know that he was insolvent at the time of the transfer. They did know he was hard pressed temporarily for ready cash. Kenneth further testified that the motive for the transfer was to relieve their father of the monthly obligations attendant upon the mortgages they assumed, and to provide for his immediate need of cash. Mrs. Hardcastle attests to the fact that the family had no knowledge of the business situation of the deceased. None of the defendants participated in the operation of deceased's business at any time.

[5] The claim of the plaintiff, The National Bank of Bossier City, is predicated upon an unsecured promissory note for $2,500.00 dated May 11, 1964. The claim of

the plaintiff, Shreveport Auto Finance Corporation, is founded upon several notes secured by chattel mortgages representing a total debt of $12,733.03 after applying credits to the original indebtedness of $25,077.50.

[6] The revocatory action in Louisiana is established by LSA-C.C. art. 1970 et seq.

LSA-C.C. art. 1971:

'This action can only be exercised when the debtor has not property sufficient to pay the debt of the complaining creditor, or of all his creditors where there has been a cession, or any proceeding analogous thereto.'

LSA-C.C. art. 1978:

'No contract shall be avoided by this action but such as are made in fraud of creditors, and such as, if carried into execution, would have the effect of defrauding them. If made in good faith, it can not be annulled, although it prove injurious to the creditors; and although made in bad faith, it can not be rescinded, unless it operate to their injury.'

LSA-C.C. art. 1993:

'No creditor can, by the action given by this section, sue individually to annul any contract made before the time his debt accrued.'

[7] The prerequisites for the revocatory action are: (1) insolvency of the debtor; (2) injury to the creditor; (3) intent to defraud the creditors; (4) pre-existing and accrued indebtedness. See the discussion of the revocatory action in Louisiana in 9 Tul.L.Rev. 422.

[8] The defendants contend that the Shreveport Auto Finance Corporation debt was not pre-existing because of a refinancing maneuver which occurred after the transfer. Without a lengthy discussion as to the merits of this argument, we simply conclude that the debt was such as was 'accrued' and which would give rise to an action for revocation when liquidated.

[9] Appellants strongly urge that Kenneth Hardcastle, one of the defendants, is a creditor and that the presumption of fraud contained in LSA-C.C. art. 1984 should apply.

LSA-C.C. art. 1983:

'But if such fraud consisted merely in the endeavor to obtain a preference over other creditors, for the securing of payment of a just debt, under circumstances in which by law the endeavor to obtain such preference is declared to be a constructive fraud in such case the party shall only lose the advantage endeavored to be secured by such contract, and shall be reimbursed what he may have given or paid, but without interest; and he shall restore all advantages he has received from the transaction.'

LSA-C.C. art. 1984:

'Every contract shall be deemed to have been made in fraud of creditors, when the obligee knew that the obligor was in insolvent circumstances, and when such contract gives to the obligee, if he be a creditor, any advantage over other creditors of the obligor.'

[10] Plaintiffs contend that a previous loan of $800.00 from Kenneth Hardcastle to his father should categorize him as a 'creditor' under the above articles. However, the deeds do not in any way attempt to satisfy or cancel this obligation, and it is the positive evidence in the case that the transfers were not motivated by or made with any consideration for that obligation. We also conclude that the transferees did not, at that time, have knowledge of deceased's insolvency. Construing Articles 1983 and 1984 together, we are constrained to hold that Kenneth Hardcastle is not such a 'creditor' as would give rise to the presumption of fraud. We hold that plaintiff is not relieved from the burden of proof in relation to all of the elements necessary to maintain a revocatory action.

[11] That deceased was in fact insolvent is admitted. However, neither the creditors who complain nor the sons who purchased the property had real, factual and actual knowledge of the insolvency until after his death. Mr. Ashworth, Secretary-Treasurer for the largest creditor in this action, testified that his company did not consider the collection of deceased's indebtedness to be in 'jeopardy' until several days after his death. He further testified that Mr. Hardcastle's financial reverses had existed for several months before the transfer; that other used car dealers were in similar financial straits; and that the loan to Mr. Hardcastle was secured as much by his 'integrity' as it was by legal security devices. Upon the occasion of the renegotiation of Hardcastle's loan, which occurred after the transfers which are sought to be revoked, Ashworth was of the opinion that Mr. Hardcastle could solve his financial problems.

[12] All of the testimony supports a finding by this Court that Mr. Hardcastle was a man of great integrity and that he would not and did not, in fact, act to defraud his creditors. The Court just as easily concludes that the sons of the decedent had no intent to defraud the creditors of their father by their purchase of these properties. Contrarily, it was their intent to assist their father in finding a solution to his financial problem. This was the single and only motivation for their acceptance of the transfers.

[13] We could belabor this opinion with great detail as to testimony and in a comparison of cases involving the revocatory action. We simply cite cases and conclude that the factual situation in the instant case is far stronger for denial of the remedy than that which exists in any of the following: J. Grossman's Sons v. Chachere, 136 La. 666, 67 So. 545 (1915); Price v. Florsheim, 174 La. 945, 142 So. 135 (1932); Standard Plumbing, Heating & Supply Co. v. Dupree, La.App., 157 So. 759 (1934); Hendricks v. Phelps, La.App., 62 So.2d 185 (2d Cir., 1952).

[14] We conclude herein that although the deceased was insolvent in fact, and although the transfer did injure creditors who had pre-existing and accrued debts, that neither the transferor nor the transferees had any intent to defraud the creditors of the deceased, Willis H. Hardcastle. Under our conclusion the denial of the

presumption provided by LSA-C.C. arts. 1983 and 1984 is of no consequence since we believe the defendants have so affirmatively countered the allegation of fraud.

[15] The judgment of the district court is affirmed and appellant is taxed with the cost of this appeal.

Questions

1. Identify the many different legal relationships that exist in this case. Why could it be important to properly identify each one of these relationships?

2. Paragraph 6: Compare the articles from the Louisiana Civil Code of 1870 with the new Code articles 2036–2043. Have the prerequisites for a revocatory action changed? Are they more or less strict today? What could be a reason for the change and what consequence could it carry with it?

3. Paragraph 10: On which ground for the formation of contracts is the "loan" to be distinguished from the "deeds"? Is good faith somewhat relevant here?

4. Paragraph 11: According to the Court, what was the principal cause that motivated the sons?

5. What would be or should be the ruling of a court under the Louisiana Civil Code articles of today? Under these new articles, would the 4/5th rule of article 2038 have found room for application?

Succession of Mrs. Alice Boning, Widow of Joseph P. Henican

Court of Appeal of Louisiana
Fourth Circuit
May 10, 1971
248 So.2d 385

CHASEZ, Judge.

[1] On August 12, 1968 Mrs. Alice Boning Henican departed this life, leaving an olographic testament. During the term of her marriage with her husband, Joseph P. Henican, the testator gave birth to two sons who are by virtue of law her forced heirs. One son, Joseph, Jr., predeceased his mother while the other son, C. Ellis Henican, is still alive, although not mentioned in the will of the deceased. Rather the testator bypassed C. Ellis Henican entirely in favor of his five children, her grandchildren. Pursuant to the terms of her will, one half of the property of the deceased was bequeathed to the children of Mrs. Henican's son, Joseph, Jr. The other one half was bequeathed to the children of her other son, C. Ellis Henican.

[2] C. Ellis Henican is not contesting any portion of his mother's will. Although the testament deprives him of his forced portion, i.e., one quarter of his deceased mother's estate, he is making no attempt to have his reserved portion recognized. To the contrary, it is the National American Bank, hereinafter referred to as the Bank, that has so petitioned the court.

[3] The Bank has alleged that it is the creditor of C. Ellis Henican and that its rights as a creditor are being prejudiced 'by an obvious attempt to avoid the payment to C. Ellis Henican of the legitime due to him in said succession' and 'by (the) failure of said C. Ellis Henican to assert his claim to the legitime due to him with reference to said succession.' The Bank therefore prays that it be authorized as a creditor of C. Ellis Henican to accept the succession of Mrs. Alice Boning Henican in the name of her son and forced heir, C. Ellis Henican, and that it be placed in possession of the legitime due C. Ellis Henican to the extent of his indebtedness.

[4] Exceptions of no cause of action and/ or no right of action were filed by C. Ellis Henican and C. Ellis Henican, Jr. executor of the estate of Mrs. Alice Boning Henican. The exceptions were maintained by the lower court and the suit of the National American Bank was dismissed at its costs. From this adverse judgment the Bank has appealed to this court.

[5] The question thus squarely presented for our determination is whether or not a creditor of a forced heir may exercise the right of the forced heir to reduce a legacy which infringes on the forced portion of the debtor. We are of the opinion that the creditor has no such right.

[6] LSA-C.C. art. 1504 enunciates the right of reduction and provides as follows:

'On the death of the donor or testator, the reduction of the donation, whether *inter vivos* or *mortis causa*, can be sued for *only by forced heirs, or by their heirs or assigns*; neither the donees, legatees, nor creditors of the deceased can require that reduction nor avail themselves of it.' (Emphasis added)

[7] As may be seen from the literal terms of the article the right to compel a reduction does not extend to the creditor of the forced heir. Furthermore, the Supreme Court has refused to interpret the article so as to bring creditors of the forced heir within its terms and scope.

[8] In Tompkins v. Prentice, 12 La.Ann. 465 (1857), one Joseph Prentice died testate, survived by his mother and father, one brother and one sister. In his will, Joseph Prentice conveyed his entire estate to his mother, brother and sister to the complete exclusion of his father. Moreover, the father of the deceased executed a notarial act of renunciation of any interest which he might have had in his son's succession. The creditors of the father and forced heir of the deceased instituted suit to set aside the renunciation on the ground that it was in defraud of their rights and to have their debtor's share of the succession determined and pro rated among them to satisfy the indebtedness. In that case the court specifically held that the wording of codal article 1504 did not create a right in the creditor of the forced heir to assert the action to reduce a legacy. The court concluded that the term 'assign' used in the article did not include creditors but only 'those to whom rights have been transferred by particular title: such as sale, donation, legacy, transfer or cession.' LSA-C.C. art. 3556.

[9] The result of the Tompkins case is further substantiated by the wording of LSA-C.C. art. 1991 which provides:

'There are rights of the debtor, however, which the creditor (creditors) can not exercise, even should he refuse to avail himself of them.

'They can not require the separation of property between husband and wife; nor can they oblige their debtor to accept a donation Inter vivos made to him, nor can they accept it in his stead. Neither can they call on a coheir of the debtor to collate, when such debtor has not exercised that right.'

[10] The rights of the debtor enumerated in paragraph two of the above quoted article are illustrative in nature rather than exclusive. Therefore when Article 1991 is read in pari materia with Article 1504, the result is to recognize the right to reduce a legacy as right, personal in nature, which may not be exercised by a creditor of the forced heir-debtor. In fact, the right to bring an action for reduction is closely analogous to the right to call on a coheir to collate which article 1991 treats as a right personal to the debtor. Moreover, LSA-C.C. art. 1991 must be considered as a modification of the terms of LSA-C.C. art. 1990, which provides as follows:

'In case the debtor refuse or neglect to accept an inheritance to the prejudice of his creditors, they may accept the same, and exercise all his rights in the manner provided for in the title of successions, and they are authorized, by virtue of the action given by this section, to exercise all the rights existing in favor of the debtor for recovering possession of the property to which he is entitled, in order to make the same available to the payment of their debts.'

[11] When the two articles are read in conjunction, it is apparent that a creditor may exercise all rights of the debtor to obtain possession of property to which the debtor is entitled, except those rights which are personal to the debtor. The right to bring an action to reduce a legacy like the right to force a co-heir to collate is a personal right which a creditor may not assert. As was stated in the Tompkins case:

'Possibly the law-giver may have preferred to give effect to the wishes of the testator and allow his estate to take the direction he had indicated, rather than subject it to the seizure of creditors of an heir who did not feel himself aggrieved by the universal legacy to another.'

[12] After a careful review of the jurisprudence of the state, we find that the Tompkins case has not been modified by subsequent legislation or jurisprudence and that the principle of law enunciated therein is dispositive of the case at bar. This court is aware of the fact that under the French Code Napoleon the result of this matter would be different — that a creditor would have the right to assert the action to reduce a legacy if his debtor refused to do so. However, the law of the state of Louisiana on this matter differs from the French. As was stated in Cox v. Von Ahlefeldt, 105 La. 543, 30 So. 175 (1900):

'(The legislature) framed the law by which we are governed in language which expressly authorizes the bringing of the action to reduce the donations of the testator within the disposable quantum 'by forced heirs, or by their heirs or assigns.' Rev.Civ.Code, art. 1504. And in this respect the Civil Code differs also from the Code Napoleon, which authorizes the bringing of such action by the forced heirs, or 'par leurs heritiers ou ayants cause'; the term 'ayants cause' including creditors, a class not necessarily included in the term 'assigns.' Code Nap. art. 921; Fuzier-Hermann, vol. 11, p. 526, No. 11; Rev.Civ.Code, art. 3556, verbo 'Assigns'; Tompkins v. Prentice, 12 La.Ann. 465. We have no authority, then, to exclude collateral heirs from the right here claimed because they were excluded by the Spanish law, nor to include creditors because they are included under the French law.'

[13] Accordingly, unless and until the legislature sees fit to make the appropriate changes, the creditor of a forced heir has no right to assert the right of reduction of a legacy absent a specific assignment from the debtor.

[14] For the foregoing reasons the judgment of the lower court is affirmed. Costs of this proceedings to be borne by plaintiff-appellant.

Questions

NOTE: You must read and understand this case in the legal context that prevailed in the 1970s, particularly the matters of succession and forced heirship.

1. Paragraphs 2–5: What legal adjectives would you use to describe the son Ellis' right to his mother's succession? Do you see any reason or, rather, any necessity to accurately legally describe this right before addressing the issue of the Bank's right of action? *See*, in this respect, the question the Court is asking in paragraph 5. Is the answer the Court gives, i.e. "We are of the opinion that the creditor has no such right," the logical outcome of your legal description of Ellis' right?

2. Paragraphs 6–14: What method or methods of reasoning is the Court using when it refers to Louisiana Civil Code articles 1504 and 1991 and the *Tompkins* case?

3. Paragraphs 11–12: Is the Court making a purely legal statement derived from the legal analysis that precedes, or is the Court engaging in something more, such as a policy statement? Is the fact that French law would be different of some relevance to the nature of the Court's statement?

4. What was the proper Louisiana Civil Code name of the action the Banks attempted to exercise: oblique or revocatory? Explain. What would be the outcome of this case under today's Civil Code?

Succession of Elizabeth E. Terral and J. R. Terral
Supreme Court of Louisiana
April 24, 1975
312 So.2d 296

SUMMERS, Justice.

[1] Although other issues were presented in the trial and appellate courts, on this review we are solely concerned with an action in declaration of simulation involving one sale by James R. Terral dated December 2, 1943, purporting to convey 83 acres of land in Winn Parish to his son George Terral.

[2] According to the record, a rule was filed in this succession proceeding on February 2, 1972 by four of the eleven forced heirs, children and grandchildren, of decedents James R. Terral and his wife Elizabeth Eldridge. The object of the rule was to compel George Terral, who was then the administrator of the succession, to amend the descriptive list of property composing the succession assets by including the 83 acres purportedly conveyed to him by the deed of December 2, 1943.

[3] The rule is based upon the contention of the petitioning heirs that the sale of 83 acres by James R. Terral to George Terral was a simulation. The simulation took place, it is alleged, because the consideration was never paid. The deed, a cash sale in authentic form, executed before a notary public and two witnesses, is signed by James R. Terral as vendor and George Terral as vendee. It recites that the consideration was $581 'cash in hand paid, the receipt of which is hereby acknowledged.'

[4] In addition, the deed contains the following stipulation:

'It is understood and agreed that the said James R. Terral shall have the right to remain on said property as long as he lives and have the management of said lands sold herein and the said George Terral binds himself to (sic) not to sell said land as long as the said James R. Terral lives.'

[....]

[5] Evidence to support the charge of simulation was entirely inadequate. [....]

[6] [T]he clause in the deed whereby the vendor James R. Terral reserved the right to manage and remain on the property as long as he lived, and the stipulation binding George Terral not to sell the land as long as James R. Terral lived, constituted a reservation of a usufruct. This reservation vested in James R. Terral, the vendor, the right of enjoying the land, the property of which was by the deed ostensibly in the vendee George, and, to thereby draw from the same all the profit, utility and advantages it may produce. La.Civil Code art. 533.

[7] Where the seller has reserved to himself the usufruct, the case falls within the contemplation of Article 2480 of the Civil Code.[1] And when the seller reserves the usufruct 'there is reason to presume that the sale is simulated, and with respect to third persons, the parties must produce proof that they are acting in good faith, and establish the reality of the sale.' There is, moreover, evidence which is essentially undisputed that James R. Terral remained upon the property in the family home until his death in 1957. His widow survived him and continued in residence there until two years prior to her death in 1967. In a sense, therefore, 'the thing sold remains in the possession of the seller.' La.Civil Code art. 2480.

[8] As is usual in these cases the burden of establishing the reality of a sale many years after the fact is an onerous one. The burden is compounded when the party so charged must overcome a legal presumption that the purported sale is a simulation. Here the notary and witnesses were deceased; and George Terral possessed no checks, receipts, bank accounts or other documentation to support his contention that the price was in fact paid. His only evidence was the deed and his self-serving statements that he paid the price with funds he had saved and which he kept 'in his pocket.'

[9] He is apparently a man of limited education. At the time of the trial he was 74 years of age. His income from a simple farming operation was meagre. His testimony, given on two occasions in [*sic*] contradictory and at times incoherent.

[. . . .]

[10] Forced heirs have the right to annul absolutely and by parol evidence the simulated contracts of those from whom they inherit, and shall not be restricted to the legitime. La.Civil Code art. 2239.

[11] Charges of simulated contracts are principally governed by Article 2480 of the Civil Code. See footnote 1, supra.

[12] Although these articles are somewhat explicit, there is no effort in the code to define the doctrine of simulation. And there are no articles in the French Civil Code on this subject save Article 1321,[2] which is not one upon which we can rely for a definition. There is, however, an elaborate doctrinal edifice of simulation long recognized by the French Courts and text writers. See Aubry et Rau, Cours de droit civil francais XII (5e ed. 1922), no 756 bis., p. 184: 'Il n'y a pas de contre-lettre la o u il n'y pas simulation.' Cf. also Baudry-Lacantinerie, Precis de droit civil II (12E ed 1921), nos 295–96, p. 299; Baudry-Lacantinerie et Barde, Traite de droit civil XV,

---

1. La.Civil Code art. 2480 provides:
   'In all cases where the thing sold remains in the possession of the seller, because he has reserved to himself the usufruct, or retains possession by a precarious title, there is reason to presume that the sale is simulated, and with respect to third persons, the parties must produce proof that they are acting in good faith, and establish the reality of the sale.'
2. French Civil Code art. 1321 provides: 'Counter letters can only have effect between the contracting parties; they have no effect against others.'

Des Obligations III (3e ed 1908), nos 2385–2418, pp. 111–138; Demolombe, Traite des contracts IV (1878) nos 303–49, pp. 270–298.

[13] Simulation, according to Planiol, is an understanding between the parties against third persons. Ordinarily one of the parties, by means of the simulated act, proposes to deceive someone, and the simulation is thus a means of fraud. Planiol, Traite Ele me ntaire [*sic*] de Droit Civil, Vol. 2-part 1, nos 1185–1208.

[14] To some extent our decisions have discussed simulation and a definition of sorts may be derived from these expressions. For instance, in Viguerie v. Hall, 107 La. 767, 31 So. 1019 (1902) the Court said:

> 'It is no unusual occurrence for parties to place their property and rights in the name and under the control of others, without any consideration whatever, and without the intention of ownership being actually transferred. Such acts are permissible, and cannot be gainsaid, unless they carry injury to some one. A simulation is not necessarily a fraud. It is only so when injury to third persons is intended. Gravier's Curator v. Carraby's Ex'r, 17 La. 118, 36 Am.Dec. 608.'

[15] Where the alleged sale is a mere simulation, it may be set aside as a nullity by the heirs of the seller, for a simulated sale does not transfer the property. The fraudulent simulation, a mere pretense, without reality, conveys no title. Olivier, Voorhies & Lowrey v. Majors, 133 La. 764, 63 So. 323 (1913).

[16] A simulated contract is one which, though clothed in concrete form, has no existence in fact, and it may at any time, and at the demand of any person in interest, be declared a sham and may be annulled by the heirs of the apparent vendor. Maddox v. Butchee, 203 La. 299, 14 So.2d 4 (1943); Hibernia Bank and Trust Co. v. Louisiana Ave. Realty Co., 143 La. 962, 79 So. 554 (1918); Interstate Trust and Banking Co. v. Louisiana Ave. Realty Co., 143 La. 971, 79 So. 557 (1918).

[17] Each case involving simulation must be decided on its peculiar facts. And where the issue is primarily dependent upon the credibility of a single witness, as here, the decision of the trial judge is entitled to considerable weight. In this case the trial judge was unimpressed by George Terral's testimony, and properly so. A legal presumption established in law to shield the legitime of forced heirs from fraudulent transactions must be rebutted by convincing evidence which preponderates in favor of the reality of the sale. This has not been accomplished by George Terral's testimony; and the judgment of the trial court nullifying the sale of December 2, 1943 as a simulation is affirmed. The following described property is therefore ordered returned to the succession:

> 'S 1/ 2 of SW 1/ 4, Section 14, and beginning at the Northwest corner of Section 23, and run South 70 yards, thence East 210 yards, thence North 70 yards and thence West 210 yards to place of beginning. All in Township 13, North of Range 3 West, La.Mer., together with all improvements and appurtenances thereto belonging, containing 83 acres more or less.'

[. . . .]

Questions

1. Paragraph 1: Is the purpose of an action in simulation to declare the nullity of a juridical act? Can you reconcile Louisiana Civil Code articles 2025 and 2028 on simulation with article 1983?

2. Paragraph 4: Compare the stipulations in the deed with the Louisiana Civil Code articles on usufruct, particularly arts. 535 and 550, *et seq*. Do you agree with the Court that the reservation of a usufruct in a contract of sale is reason to presume a simulation? Where does the Court find this presumption?

3. Paragraph 9: Does it appear from this *in concreto* description of the son that the Court had its mind pretty much set on finding a simulation?

4. Paragraphs 10–17: What important statements does the Court make about "simulation and fraud" and "simulation and the legitime"?

J. B. Owen et al.
v.
W. H. Owen et al.

Supreme Court of Louisiana
June 21, 1976
336 So.2d 782

CALOGERO, Justice.

[1] This is a lawsuit by six of the seven children of I. M. and Henrietta Owen, including one J. B. Owen, against their brother (the seventh child W. H. Owen) and his vendees (Wayne S. Bush and Charles Wayne Bush) to have two transfers from their father, I. M. Owen, one to W. H. Owen and the other to W. H. Owen and J. B. Owen jointly, declared simulations, or, alternatively, nullified because they were donations in disguise and donations Omnium bonorum, or, alternatively, to have such property collated in a partition.[1]

[2] On March 22, 1957, I. M. Owen executed three separate deeds of sale covering tracts composed respectively of 40 acres, 40 acres, and 15 acres. He conveyed 40 acres to his son W. H. Owen for a stated consideration of $100, 40 acres to a second son J. B. Owen for a stated consideration of $720, and 15 acres to both W. H. Owen and J. B. Owen for a stated consideration of $300. The property descriptions are more fully given in the Court of Appeal opinion, Owen v. Owen, 325 So.2d 283 (La. App.2nd Cir. 1975), and are incorporated herein by reference. The properties are here referred to respectively as tracts one, two, and three. Ownership of tracts one and three are those at issue in this lawsuit.

---

1. Petitioners do not attack the transfers as being in derogation of Henrietta Owen's community rights (see C.C. art. 2404), presumably because she signed the deeds along with her husband.

[3] In October 12, 1957, I. M. Owen died intestate, and on February 1, 1970 his widow, Henrietta Owen, died intestate. In 1972, following the deaths of Mr. and Mrs. Owen and, of course, subsequent to the execution of the three deeds mentioned above, one of the plaintiffs, J. B. Owen, conveyed all of his interest in tract three to his brother W. H. Owen for $1500. Thereafter, on January 29, 1973, W. H. Owen conveyed the acreage made up of tracts one and three in the following manner: twenty-seven and one-half acres comprising the western half thereof to defendant, Wayne S. Bush for $7,837.50, and twenty-seven and one-half acres comprising the eastern half thereof to defendant Charles Wayne Bush, Wayne S. Bush's son, for $7,837.50. Some nine months thereafter this suit was instituted by six of the Owen children against the seventh child, W. H. Owen, and his vendees Wayne and Charles Bush. Plaintiffs asked that the court set aside the transfers from I. M. Owen to his sons, and order the property returned to the decedent's estate or declare that each of the forced heirs own an undivided one-seventh interest in the property. Alternatively, plaintiffs asked that the property be collated under the provisions of Article 1227 Et seq. of the Civil Code.

[. . . .]

[4] We granted writs upon defendants' application. 326 So.2d 376 (La.1976). In this Court, defendants allege that the Court of Appeal erred in finding that the conveyances by I. M. Owen were donations in disguise and donations Omnium bonorum, that they erred in concluding that a donation Omnium bonorum is an absolute nullity, and that they erred in decreeing that the seven heirs of Mr. and Mrs. I. M. Owen were owners each of an undivided one-seventh interest in the subject property.

[5] The following facts are borne out by the record and are not seriously contested. In March 1957, at the time I. M. Owen purported to sell the land in question to his sons, he sold tract number three, comprising 15 acres, for $300, although the property was worth $45 per acre, or $675.[2] On that same date he purported to sell tract one, comprising 40 acres, for a stated consideration of $100, although it was worth $45 per acre, or $1800.

[6] In 1970 the fifty-five acres owned by W. H. Owen were valued at $10,725. He sold the land to the Bushes in 1973 for approximately $16,000. In 1975, that same property was worth $18,700. Although neither of the courts below reached this issue, it is clear that the Bushes purchased the disputed property for a fair price.

[7] The acts of sale by which I. M. Owen conveyed the three tracts in 1957 identified the vendor as I. M. Owen and the vendees as W. H. Owen and J. B. Owen. The deeds, in authentic form, recite that the properties were sold to the respective vendees for the stated consideration 'cash in hand paid, the receipt of which is hereby acknowledged.' The deeds do not indicate that I. M. Owen was the father of W. H.

---

2. The property values quoted here were established by expert evidence at the trial and were uncontroverted.

and J. B., nor that these three properties constituted all of the property owned by Mr., or by Mr. and Mrs., Owen.

[8] The only contested issue of fact in the case is whether the sons actually paid their father for the property. J. B. judicially confessed that he paid nothing for the property. W. H. claimed that he did pay for the property which was transferred to him, but could produce no evidence to support his assertion. The trial court found that nothing was paid by either brother for the land, a finding the Court of Appeal upheld. There is no error in this finding, and we agree with the courts below that the March 22, 1957 sales of tracts one and three to W. H. Owen and to J. B. Owen and W. H. Owen, respectively, were not sales but were disguised donations under Article 2444 of the Civil Code.[3]

[9] It was established at the trial that before the Bushes purchased the property in question from W. H. Owen they were told by J. B. Owen that there was some question as to whether W. H. Owen could transfer a 'clear deed,' but they were given no reason for J. B.'s assertion. Wayne Bush also learned from W. H. Owen that he had bought the property from his father. However, there is no evidence that the Bushes ever had any knowledge of Mr. and Mrs. I. M. Owen's financial condition (at any time) nor any knowledge of the value of the property in March of 1957, some fifteen years before their purchase of the property.

[10] The plaintiffs established at trial that at the time of the transfers in question Mr. and Mrs. Owen were living on social security and welfare payments, and that they owned no immovable property other than the three tracts transferred; but there was no evidence as to the amount of income they were receiving, nor was there any evidence as to what their living expenses were. It was established that I. M. Owen had $600 when he died in late 1957, a sum W. H. Owen kept in an account 'for his mother.'[4]

[11] The plaintiffs contend, and the courts below found, that when I. M. Owen sold these two tracts he had divested himself of all of his property without reserving to himself enough for subsistence. Article 1497 prohibits such a donation in the following language:

'The donation Inter vivos shall in no case divest the donor of all his property; he must reserve to himself enough for subsistence; if he does not do it, the donation is null for the whole.'

3. Article 2444 provides in full that:
'The sales of immovable property made by parents to their children, may be attacked by the forced heirs, as containing a donation in disguise, if the latter can prove that no price has been paid, or that the price was below one-fourth of the real value of the immovable sold, at the time of the sale.'
4. W. H. Owen also testified that he put aside $1400 for his mother, money he received from a mineral lease, presumably sometime after his father's death in 1957.

[12] In order to sustain an attack on a gift as a donation Omnium bonorum, the heirs must prove conclusively that the donation divested the donor of all of his property. Whitman v. Whitman, 206 La. 1, 18 So.2d 633 (1944); Potts v. Potts, 142 La. 906, 77 So. 786 (1918); Hearsey v. Craig, 126 La. 824, 53 So. 17 (1910); Hinton v. May, 241 So.2d 583 (La.App.2nd Cir. 1970). In light of the stringent requirements set forth in the aforementioned cases, we are not as certain as were the lower courts that the requirements of Article 1497 were met so as to brand I. M. Owen's disguised donations as donations Omnium bonorum. We nonetheless accept the finding of the lower courts, for, even assuming the donations were Omnium bonorum, the decision of the Court of Appeal in our view must be reversed for the reasons we relate thereinafter.

[13] The plaintiffs allege first that the transfers from parent to sons were simulations. In our law, a simulation is a transfer of property which is not what it seems. Simulations are of two types: pure simulations, and disguised transfers.[5] In a pure simulation, sometimes called a non-transfer, the parties only pretend to transfer the property from one to the other, but in fact both transferor and transferee intend that the transferor retain ownership of the property. When this type of simulation is successfully attacked, the true intent of the parties is revealed, which was that no transfer had in fact taken place. In a contest between a vendor and vendee in this situation the true intent of the parties is effectuated and the courts hold that no transfer took place because the simulated sale is an absolute nullity. Successions of Webre, 247 La. 461, 172 So.2d 285 (1965); Schalaida v. Gonzales, 174 La. 907, 142 So. 123 (1932); Milano v. Milano, 243 So.2d 876 (La.App.1st Cir. 1971). The other type of simulation is a disguised transfer which seems on its face to be a valid sale, but which is intended by the parties to be a gift rather than a sale. When this sort of simulation is attacked successfully, as it has been here under Article 2444, the true intent of the parties is likewise effectuated by the law. A valid transfer has taken place, but its form is a donation rather than a sale and the Code articles on donations apply to the transfer. Stevens v. Stevens, 227 La. 761, 80 So.2d 399 (1955); Carter v. Bolden, 13 La.App. 48, 127 So. 111 (La.App.2nd Cir. 1930); 35 La.L.Rev. 192 (1974); 25 La.L.Rev. 313 (1965).

[14] However, when the property is no longer held by the original vendee but has passed into the hands of an innocent third party who has purchased for value and in reliance on the public records, the result is much different. In the case of Chachere v. Superior Oil Co., 192 La. 193, 187 So. 321 (1939), this Court upheld the rights of third party purchasers to retain the land in question even though the transfer to their vendor had been a disguised donation. The Court held that because the transfer from the original vendor (the parent of the plaintiff-forced heirs) to the original vendee (who in turn sold to the defendant-third party purchasers) was on its face

---

5. For discussions of the legal concept of simulations, See Lemann, Some Aspects of Simulations in France and Louisiana, 29 Tul.L.Rev. 22 (1954) and 35 La.L.Rev. 192 (1974).

a valid sale, the plaintiffs were not allowed, after the property had passed into the hands of third parties, to introduce evidence that the transfer was not a sale. The Court stated that:

> 'It is the well settled jurisprudence of this state that third persons dealing with immovable property have a right to depend upon the faith of the recorded title thereof and are not bound by any secret equities that may exist between their own vendor and prior owners of the land.' 187 So. 321.

[15] In the case of Thompson v. Thompson, 211 La. 468, 30 So.2d 321 (1947), this Court reaffirmed Chachere and held that, when a third person acquires title to land prior to the assertion by forced heirs of their rights to have the disguised donation annulled, and third party who had purchased for value on the strength of the public records will defeat the claim of the forced heir. The Court stated that:

> '(W)hereas our system of law has protected the forced heirs against acts designed to deprive him of his legitimate portion, the rights granted to such forced heir cannot be extended so as to defeat the subsequently acquired rights of third persons who have bought property on the faith of the public records and under the belief that their vendor acquired a valid title by purchase. In fine, considerations of public policy, respecting a stability of titles, makes it necessary that innocent third parties prevail over the forced heir even though it results in the denial of the heir's right which our law has so carefully guarded.' 30 So.2d at 329.

[16] Likewise, when immovable property which has been the subject of a 'pure' simulated sale is later sold to third persons who rely on the public records, in a case where the records show that the transfer was a proper sale, and where the records reveal no counterletter, the rights of the third party cannot be affected by subsequent proof that the original transfer was a pure simulation. Beard v. Nunn, 172 La. 155, 133 So. 429 (1931); Jackson v. Creswell, 147 La. 914, 86 So. 329 (1920); Vital v. Andrus, 121 La. 221, 46 So. 217 (1908); Gordon v. Culbertson, 296 So.2d 401 (La. App.2nd Cir. 1974); Redmann, The Louisiana Law of Recordation: Some Principles and Some Problems, 39 Tul.L.Rev. 491 (1965); 35 La.L.Rev. 192 (1974); 17 Tul.L.Rev. 457 (1943). It is clear then from the jurisprudence that in the situation where the original transfer was a pure simulation (and not therefore effective to pass title) And in the situation where the original transfer was a disguised donation (and Did therefore effectively pass title to the transferee) that the rights of a third party are protected if he purchased on the basis of a public record evidencing an apparently valid sale. Since the third party purchasers here, the Bushes, did purchase for value and in reliance on public records which evidenced a valid sale, they are protected against the claims of the plaintiff forced heirs notwithstanding the fact that the transfer was actually a donation in disguise.

[17] However, plaintiffs urge alternatively that the transfer was a disguised donation which purported to give away all that the donor (I. M. Owen) had, without retaining enough for his subsistence, in contravention of Article 1497, and therefore

'null for the whole.' Plaintiff argues that if the vendee received only a null title, one that was ineffective to transfer title, he could not validly pass title on to the Bushes.

[18] We find, however, that even if the title which passed to the sons could be declared absolutely null while the property remained in their hands,[6] when the property passed into the hands of an innocent third party purchasing in reliance on the public records, the claimants could no longer recover the property. In the case of Rocques v. Freeman, 125 La. 60, 51 So. 68 (1909), a widow transferred to her children through a partition her undivided interest in her community property. The children subsequently sold the property to third parties. The mother later attempted to nullify her transfer as a donation in disguise and as a donation Omnium bonorum, but this Court affirmed the dismissal of her petition. The Court found that her transfer was null because it was a donation in disguise and a donation Omnium bonorum, but held that the nullity could be asserted only against the donees, not against innocent third parties who had dealt with the property on the faith of the public records.

[19] The Court stated:

> 'The act which is sought to be annulled in this case as a donation does not appear on its face to possess that character. On its face, it is a partition between Charles F. Metoyer and his sister (plaintiffs' children). It was no more calculated to put innocent third parties on their guard against defects in the title than would have been a donation in the form of a sham sale. *And we do not imagine any one would say that a donation in the form of a sham sale could be annulled to the detriment of innocent third persons who had dealt with the property in the faith of the public records.*' 51 So. at 70. (emphasis added)

[20] We hold, therefore, that where there is nothing of record to indicate that the transfer to the original vendee could have been annulled as a donation Omnium bonorum and when an innocent party has purchased the land for valuable consideration relying upon the public records, the third party takes the property free of these unrecorded and secret equities.

[21] Plaintiffs, however, claim that the Bushes were not innocent third party purchasers because they had certain actual knowledge about the original transfers, namely, that the transfers were from father to children and that one of the brothers felt there was some doubt as to whether they (the Bushes) could get a 'clear deed.'

[22] It is uncontroverted that the Bushes were arms length purchasers who were buying the property for value, and that they were not participants or co-participants in any attempt at fraud. The legal issue here is whether the actual knowledge which they had of the previous transfer placed them in such a position that they could not rely on the public records. We hold that it did not.

---

6. For discussions of the area of donations Omnium bonorum, see 34 Tul.L.Rev. 228 (1974); 23 La.L.Rev. 433 (1963); and 6 La.L.Rev. 98 (1944).

[23] A third party purchaser can rely on the public records so long as he does not participate in fraud. Jackson v. Creswell, 147 La. 914, 86 So. 329 (1920); Kinchen v. Kinchen, 244 So.2d 316 (La.App.1st Cir. 1970), writ not considered, 257 La. 854, 244 So.2d 608; Dugas v. Talley, 109 So.2d 300 (La.App.1st Cir. 1959). Even if he has some actual nonrecord knowledge of a preceding transfer which might have made him suspicious of a deed's validity, he may still rely on the public records if they reveal an apparently valid sale. In the case of Prather v. Porter, 176 La. 324, 145 So. 675 (1933), this Court upheld the dismissal of a suit by the forced heir of the original vendor on defendants' exception of no cause of action (defendants were third party purchasers) where the plaintiff contended that defendants were chargeable with knowledge that the transfer was a donation, because the defendants knew the following things: the original vendees were stated in the recorded instrument to be the daughter-in-law and grandson of the vendor; the consideration was stated to be 'whatever amount'; and the transfer actually divested the transferor of all of his property. The Court held that these allegations were insufficient to charge the defendants with bad faith because, as it stated:

> 'the conveyance records are the only things to which one dealing with real estate or real rights needs to look. Notice or knowledge dehors the public records on the part of a third person is not equivalent to registry.' 145 So. at 677.

[24] As to plaintiffs' contentions as to the family relationship and the price, the Court stated:

> 'There is no law prohibiting the owner of real property from selling the property to his daughter-in-law and grandson. The price as finally expressed in an act of sale represents the stated consideration for the sale. And a vendee who has paid an adequate price cannot be dispossessed of his property because a prior vendor has chosen to part with his title for an inadequate consideration.' Id.

[25] The actual knowledge which the Bushes had of the transfer to their vendor was far less than the Court in Prather assumed that the defendants had there. Of record, defendants Bush knew only that the vendor and vendee had a common surname, and that fifteen acres had been sold ostensibly for $300 and forty acres ostensibly for $100. Although the price of the forty-acre tract might have seemed unusually low (had the Bushes known the land values some fifteen years before), the stated consideration of the smaller tract was later established as a full 44% Of its true fair market value,[7] and, as this Court stated in Prather, 'a vendee who has paid an adequate price cannot be dispossessed of his property because a prior vendor has chosen to part with his title for an inadequate consideration.' Beyond the record, the Bushes were aware that the original vendor-vendees were father and sons, and

---

7. It is not a matter of record in this case as to which twenty-seven and one-half acre tract encompasses the fifteen acres.

that one of the sons felt they could not get a clear deed. However, no suggestion has been made that the Bushes had any reason to believe that the sons had not paid for the property or that the sales in March of 1957 comprised all that the father had for his subsistence. It can therefore hardly be said that the Bushes were put on notice, either by the record or in fact, that the sales in question were donations, much less donations Omnium bonorum.

[26] Therefore we conclude that a third party, who is not participating in fraud, and who plans to purchase for value property which according to the public records was properly Sold to his prospective vendor, may rely on those records even though he has some actual knowledge on which he could speculate that a timely prosecuted legal attack upon his vendor's title might be successful.

[. . . .]

Questions

1. Paragraphs 1–12: What is a donation *omnium bonorum*? *See* La. Civ. Code art. 1498. Why is it reasonable to prohibit this type of donation?

2. Paragraph 13: Where does the Court find the adjective "pure" in "pure simulation"? Is it proper for the Court to state that "simulations are of two types" and to then refer only to a pure simulation, and,instead of using another adjective for the second type of simulation, referring to it as actually being a "disguised transfer"? Look at the adjectives used in the 1984–85 version of Louisiana Civil Code articles 2025 to 2028. Has a disguised transfer become a relative simulation?

3. Paragraph 13: Is the Court going too far in declaring that "the simulated sale is an absolute nullity"? Is it really an issue of nullity or one of a juridical act which, because it is simulated, can have no effect against third parties (*see* La. Civ. Code art. 2028)? Do you see the difference between nullity of a juridical act and lack of effect against third parties?

4. Paragraphs 13–18: What do you think of this public record doctrine? What goals do you think it is meant to achieve? Can you think of any possible unfairness, particularly when third parties had knowledge outside of the public records (*see* paragraph 18)? In the first sentence of paragraph 18, the Court refers to the title as "absolutely null," and yet, third parties would be protected. Can you identify any inconsistency in the Court's choice of words (*see* Question 3, above)?

London Towne Condominium Homeowner's Association
v.
London Towne Company, et al.

Supreme Court of Louisiana
October 17, 2006
939 So.2d 1227

VICTORY, J.

[1] We granted this writ application to resolve a split among the circuits as to the correct interpretation of Louisiana Civil Code Article 2041, which provides the prescriptive and peremptive periods for bringing a revocatory action. After reviewing the record and the applicable law, we reverse the judgment of the court of appeal and hold that, where the obligee seeks to annul an act of the obligor, the relevant date for prescriptive purposes is the date the obligee knew or should have known of the act, and that the date of recordation of the act does not, standing alone, commence the running of prescription.

Facts And Procedural History

[2] On August 28, 2001, the London Towne Homeowner's Association (the "Association") filed suit against the London Towne Condominiums (the "LTC") in the 24th Judicial District Court to collect amounts due for association dues and for defects in the condominiums (the "Lawsuit"). On May 24, 2004, the 24th Judicial District Court signed a judgment in favor of the Association and against LTC in the principal amount of $281,899.16, plus legal interest, expert witness fees and attorney's fees. LTC did not appeal the judgment, which has not been satisfied.

[3] On August 19, 2000, LTC acquired Unit 9 of 1201 Chartres Street in New Orleans for $202,000.00. On February 1, 2002, after the Lawsuit was filed, but prior to the entry of judgment against LTC, LTC executed an Act of Sale by which it purportedly sold the property to Millennium Group I, LLC ("Millennium") for $202,000.00. The February 1, 2002, Act of Sale was recorded in the Orleans Parish conveyance records on February 19, 2002.

[4] The Association alleges that shortly after obtaining its judgment against LTC, the Association learned of the 2002 transfer of the Chartres Street property. Believing that the transfer was part of a scheme to place LTC's assets out of the reach of its creditors, the Association filed a Petition for Declaratory Judgment in Orleans Parish on November 18, 2004, challenging the transfer under both the revocatory action and simulation articles of the Civil Code,[1] and seeking to have the transfer adjudged either an absolute or relative nullity. On June 2, 2005, Millennium filed

---

1. In support of its claims, the Association alleged that the transfer by LTC to Millennium was made for less then the amount stated in the Act of Sale or for no consideration at all, that the parties to the transfer intended for different effects to flow from the transaction than those stated in the Act of Sale or for the transaction to produce no effects between them, and that the transfer caused

peremptory exceptions of no cause of action and no right of action in response to the action in simulation and a peremptory exception of prescription in response to the revocatory action. Millennium argued that the Association's revocatory action was prescribed on its face under La. C.C. art.2041 because it was filed more than one year after the date the document evidencing the transfer was recorded.

[5] By judgment dated July 13, 2005, the trial court denied Millennium's exceptions. LTC sought supervisory review of the denial of its exception of prescription. The court of appeal granted LTC's writ and reversed the judgment of the trial court, holding that "Millennium met its burden of proof to show that the Association's revocatory action had prescribed, since over a year has passed from the date on which the Association received constructive notice of the sale," which the court of appeal ruled was the date the Act of Sale was recorded. *London Towne Condominium Homeowner's Association v. London Towne Company, et al.,* 05-1243 (La.App. 4 Cir. 1/ 18/ 06). We granted this writ application to resolve a split in the circuits as to commencement of prescription of a revocatory action under La. C.C. art.2041. *London Towne Condominium Homeowner's Association v. London Towne Company, et al.,* 06-0401 (La.5/ 5/ 06), 927 So.2d 298.

Discussion

[6] Louisiana Civil Code articles 2036–2043 provide the rules applicable to the revocatory action, pursuant to which "[a]n obligee has a right to annul an act of the obligor, or the result of a failure to act of the obligor, made or effected after the right of the obligee arose, that causes or increases the obligor's insolvency."[2] La. C.C. art.2036. These code articles dictate the type of relief to which an obligee is entitled and the procedures which must be followed in a revocatory action.[3] Civil Code article 2041 provides as follows:

---

or increased LTC's insolvency. The Association also alleged that the purported transfer was made to place the Chartres Street property beyond the reach of LTC's creditors.

2. "An obligor is insolvent when the total of his liabilities exceeds the total of his fairly appraised assets." La. C.C. art.2037.

3. La. C.C. art.2038 provides:

An obligee may annul an onerous contract made by the obligor with a person who knew or should have known that the contract would cause or increase the obligor's insolvency. In that case, the person is entitled to recover what he gave in return only to the extent that it has inured to the benefit of the obligor's creditors.

An obligee may annul an onerous contract made by the obligor with a person who did not know that the contract would cause or increase the obligor's insolvency, but in that case that person is entitled to recover as much as he gave to the obligor. That lack of knowledge is presumed when that person has given at least four-fifths of the value of the thing obtained in return from the obligor.

La. C.C. art.2039 provides:

An obligee may attack a gratuitous contract made by the obligor whether or not the other party knew that the contract would cause or increase the obligor's insolvency.

La. C.C. art.2040 provides:

An obligee may not annul a contract made by the obligor in the regular course of his business.

La. C.C. art.2042 provides:

The action of the obligee must be brought within one year from the time he learned or should have learned of the act, or the result of the failure to act,[4] of the obligor that the obligee seeks to annul, but never after three years from the date of that act or result.

[. . . .]

[7] In reversing the judgment of the trial court, the court of appeal relied on its prior holding in *Allied Shipyard, Inc. v. Edgett*, 03-1315 (La.App. 4 Cir. 2/ 11/ 04), 868 So.2d 189, *writ granted*, 04-0503 (La.4/ 23/ 04), 870 So.2d 281 (case settled after writ grant). *Allied Shipyard* held that prescription under La. C.C. art.2041 begins to run when the obligee-creditor knew or should have known of the donation which they alleged created or increased the insolvency of the debtor, which is when the donation sought to be set aside was recorded in the public record. 868 So.2d at 192. Based on *Allied Shipyard*, the court of appeal held:

> La. C.C. art.2041 clearly provides for constructive notice to trigger the running of prescription based on its express provision that a revocatory action shall be brought within one year from the time the creditor learned or **should have learned of the act.** Although the Association argues and the trial court reasoned that prescription should not commence until the Association learned that it had been damaged by the transfer, we find nothing in the record supporting an alternative date from which the Association claims that prescription should have run. Millennium met its burden of proof to show that the Association's revocatory action had prescribed, since over a year has passed from the date on which the Association received constructive notice of the sale.

[8] *London Towne Condominium Homeowner's Ass'n*, 95-1243, p. 3.

[9] The court in *Allied Shipyard* made clear its disagreement with the view of the Third Circuit, which has held that prescription does not begin to run until the creditor has constructive knowledge of the damage caused by the act which increases the insolvency of the debtor, rather than the date of the act itself. *First Federal Savings & Loan Ass'n of Lake Charles v. Jones*, 620 So.2d 408 (La.App. 3 Cir.), *writ denied*, 629 So.2d 347 (La.1993); *Jeme, Inc. v. Gold Coast Carpets, Inc.*, 94-182 (La.App. 3 Cir. 10/ 5/ 94), 643 So.2d 898. The Third Circuit reasoned in *First*

> In an action to annul either his obligor's act, or the result of his obligor's failure to act, the obligee must join the obligor and the third persons involved in that act or failure to act.
>
> A third person joined in the action may plead discussion of the obligor's assets.

La. C.C. art.2043 provides:

> If an obligee establishes his right to annul his obligor's act, or the result of his obligor's failure to act, that act or result shall be annulled only to the extent that it affects the obligee's right.

4. "The expression, '. . . the result of a failure to act of the obligor' contemplates situations in which an obligor becomes insolvent, or his insolvency increases, because of his failure to act, or when the obligor fails to defend himself in a lawsuit, and the resulting judgment creates or increases his insolvency." La. C.C. art. 2036, Official Revisions Comment (e) (1984).

3 · EFFECTS OF CONVENTIONAL OBLIGATIONS

Federal that "before First Federal could exercise its right to the revocatory action, it first had to be able to prove that it had been damaged by its debtor's actions." 620 So.2d at 411. Thus, "[t]he trial court's reliance on the recordation date of the trust instrument in the public records as the date prescription began to run was clearly misplaced." *Id.*

[10] The First Circuit has reached yet another conclusion as to the interpretation of La. C.C. art.2041. In *Parish Nat. Bank v. Wilks,* 04-1439 (La.App. 1 Cir. 8/ 3/ 05), 923 So.2d 8, 15, a case with essentially the same facts for prescription purposes as the case *sub judice,* the court "decline[d] to find that the time of the filing of the act of donation in the conveyance records was the date when [the creditor] knew or should have known of the act of donation, so as to commence the prescriptive period on its revocatory action." In so holding, the First Circuit correctly relied on our holding in *Phillips v. Parker,* 483 So.2d 972 (La.1986), which explained the public records doctrine as follows:

> The fundamental principle of the law of registry is that any sale, mortgage, privilege, contract or judgment affecting immovable property, which is required to be recorded, is utterly null and void as to third persons unless recorded. When the law of recordation applies, an interest in immovable property is effective against third persons only if it is recorded; if the interest is not recorded, it is not effective against third persons, even if the third person knows of the claim. . . .

[11] Thus, the law of registry does not create rights in a positive sense, but rather has the negative effect of denying the effectiveness of certain rights unless they are recorded. The essence of the public records doctrine is that recordation is an essential element for the effectiveness of a right, and it is important to distinguish between effectiveness of a right against third persons and knowledge of a right by third persons. An unrecorded interest is not effective against anyone (except the parties). A recorded interest, however, is effective both against those third persons who have knowledge and those who do not have knowledge of the presence of the interest in the public records. From the standpoint of the operation of the public records doctrine, knowledge is an irrelevant consideration. *Any theory of constructive knowledge which imputes knowledge of the contents of the public records to third persons forms no part of the public records doctrine.* (Emphasis added.)

[12] *Phillips,* 483 So.2d at 975–76 (footnotes and citations omitted). Thus, based on our holding in *Phillips,* the court of appeal in *Parish Nat. Bank* held:

> Since the public records doctrine allows the parties to rely on the absence of documents in the public records and does not impute knowledge of the contents of the public records to third persons, the public records doctrine cannot be used to charge an obligee (creditor) with constructive knowledge of documents in the public records for purposes of determining whether he knew or should have known of the act so as to commence the prescriptive period under La. C.C. art.2041.

[13] *Parish Nat. Bank, supra* at p. 15. In that case, because the defendant's motion for summary judgment was supported only by the recordation of the donation in the public records on March 4, 2002, and the plaintiff admitted in its petition that it learned of the donation on January 16, 2003, the court held that prescription began to run on January 16, 2003. *Id.*

[14] We have consistently held that the starting point in interpreting any statute is the language of the statute itself. *Touchard v. Williams,* 617 So.2d 885, 888 (La.1993); *Theriot v. Midland Risk Ins. Co.,* 95-2895 (La.5/ 20/ 97), 694 So.2d 184, 186. In reading the clear language of La. C.C. art.2041, it is evident that there are two possible prescriptive dates and one peremptive date for bringing a revocatory action. An action must be brought: (1) within one year from the time the obligee learned or should have learned of the act of the obligor that the obligee seeks to annul; (2) within one year from the time the obligee learned or should have learned of the result of the failure to act of the obligor that the obligee seeks to annul; or (3) never after three years from the date of the act or the result of the failure to act.

[15] In this case, what we have is an *act,* i.e., the sale of Unit 9 of 1201 Chartres Street in New Orleans, that the obligee seeks to annul. La. C.C. art.2041 clearly states that under these circumstances, the relevant date is one year from the time the obligee learned or should have learned of the act. The result of the act, or the harm caused as a result of the act, is not a relevant consideration because a result is only significant when there has been a failure to act.[5]

[16] Therefore, where an obligee is seeking to annul an *act* of an obligor, the relevant date is when the obligee learned or should have learned of the act. Granted, an obligee only has the right to bring an action to annul an act "that causes or increases the obligor's insolvency." La. C.C. art.2036. However, according to the clear language of La. C.C. art.2041, prescription begins to run from the date the obligee learned or should have learned of the act, not the date the obligee knows the act has caused or increased the obligor's insolvency. While this may, in theory, result in a cause of action prescribing before the obligee has the right to bring the action, we do not believe this was contrary to the intent of the legislature, as they have cut off the right

---

5. The Revision Comments to this article state:
   (a) This Article is new. As "insolvency" is substituted from "fraud" as the criterion for availability of the revocatory action, the prescriptive period should be one year from the day the obligee learned of the harm. Otherwise, a devious obligor could prejudice his obligee's claim and conceal his actions for a year, thereby escaping liability altogether.
La. C.C. art.2041, 1984 Revision Comments (a). In light of the clear wording of the statute, which provides a different commencement date depending on whether the obligee is seeking to annul an act of the obligee or the result of a failure to act on the part of the obligee, we reject the Comment's blanket statement that "the prescriptive period should be one year from the day the obligee learned of the harm." Clearly, this is not true where the obligee is seeking to annul an act of the obligor. As clearly expressed by the legislature, prescription begins to run in that case when the obligee learned or should have learned of the act.

to file a revocatory action by setting a peremptive period, regardless of the obligee's knowledge or lack thereof, three years from the date of the act or the result. As we held in *Reeder v. North,* 97-0239 (La.10/ 21/ 97), 701 So.2d 1291, 1296, in interpreting the legal malpractice prescriptive and peremptive period under La. R.S. 9:5605, "while the terms of the . . . statute of limitations statute may be unfair in that a person's claim may be extinguished before he realizes the full extent of his damages, the enactment of such a statute of limitations is exclusively a legislative prerogative." Just as in *Reeder,* the legislature has clearly stated the terms of this prescriptive/ peremptive statute of limitations and we are bound to interpret it as written.

[17] Thus, the remaining issue is whether the date of recordation in the public records *ipso facto* constitutes constructive notice to the obligee of the act itself. Based on our explanation of the public records doctrine in *Philips v. Parker, supra,* we reject that legal conclusion. As we stated in *Philips,* "[a]ny theory of constructive knowledge which imputes knowledge of the contents of the public records to third persons forms no part of the public records doctrine." 483 So.2d at 975–76. Therefore, recordation in the public records does not constitute constructive notice to third parties under La. C.C. art.2041.

[18] In light of the above, we need to determine if the trial court was manifestly erroneous in denying Millennium's exception of prescription. [. . . .] As our holding indicates, the date of recordation does not, standing alone, prove actual or constructive knowledge of the act. Constructive knowledge sufficient to trigger the running of prescription exists when a party has sufficient information or notice to excite inquiry regarding a possible claim. *Id.* at 510–11. Such information or knowledge as ought to reasonably put the victim on notice is sufficient to start the running of prescription. *Id.* The date upon which an obligee learned or should have learned of the act is a factual determination to be made by the trial court considering all the facts and circumstances of the case.[6]

[. . . .]

Conclusion

[19] Under the clear wording of La. C.C. art.2041, prescription on a revocatory action begins to run from (1) the time the obligee learned or should have learned of the act of the obligor that the obligee seeks to annul, or (2) the time the obligee

---

6. The date of recordation may be a relevant consideration if, based on the facts and circumstances of the case, the obligee knew or should have known of the recordation. Further, if it is found that the obligee knew about the recordation, the date he found out about the recordation would commence the running of prescription. Thus, while the date of recordation is not the determinative factor in ascertaining the commencement of prescription, it may be a relevant factor depending upon the facts and circumstances of the case. One example of an act that would provide constructive notice where an transfer has been recorded would be a judgment debtor examination where the creditor learns of the debtor's property but fails to investigate whether it has been transferred to a third party.

learned or should have learned of the result of the failure to act of the obligor that the obligee seeks to annul. However, in all cases, a revocatory action is perempted three years from the date of the act or the result of the failure to act. The date the obligee learned or should have learned of the act or the result of the failure to act is determined by considering all the relevant facts and circumstances of the particular case. Where the obligee is seeking to annul an act of the obligor, the act of recordation in the public records, does not, standing alone, provide constructive knowledge of the act. In this case, Millennium bore the burden of proving that one year had passed since the Association learned or should have learned of the transfer of the Chartres Street property. Because the only evidence it presented in support of its exception was the date of recordation of the transfer, it did not carry its burden of proof.

[. . . .]

Questions

1. Paragraphs 1–5: Why is the plaintiff Association bringing a revocatory action in conjunction with an action in simulation? Are the grounds of the two actions the same? Are the grounds for a revocatory action met in the facts of the case? We have seen in the *Owen v. Owen* case the importance of the public records doctrine and its effects as regards third parties; how does the court's statement in paragraph 1 fit with that doctrine? What is the difference between "prescription" and "peremption"? *See* La. Civ. Code arts. 3447 and 3458.

2. Paragraphs 6–10: Because the Louisiana Supreme Court must resolve a split among the circuits as to the correct interpretation of Louisiana Civil Code article 2041, notice that in its "Discussion," the Supreme Court starts with a list of the Louisiana Civil Code articles as the binding sources of law, to turn then to the jurisprudence. How many different interpretations of the same article 2041 were co-existing? *See* question below.

3. Paragraph 16: How can the Louisiana Supreme Court speak of "the clear language of La. C. C. art. 2041" when the Courts of Appeal had different interpretations of that article?

4. Paragraph 16: Do you see the distinction that the Louisiana Supreme Court makes between "the date of recordation" of an act, "constructive notice or knowledge of the act," and "imputed knowledge of the act"?

5. Paragraph 19: Can you restate in your own words the "Conclusion" given by the Court? Consider footnote 6: does it make "the clear wording of La. C.C. art. 2041" clearer? Did the Court spend its time clarifying the public records doctrine or the determination of that time (knowledge) that triggers the computation of the prescriptive or peremptive period of the revocatory action, or were the two intimately tied together?

Section V — Interpretation of Contracts

Louisiana Sources of Law
Louisiana Civil Code

Art. 2045. Determination of the intent of the parties.

Interpretation of a contract is the determination of the common intent of the parties. (Acts 1984, No. 331, §1, eff. Jan. 1, 1985.)

Art. 2046. No further interpretation when intent is clear.

When the words of a contract are clear and explicit and lead to no absurd consequences, no further interpretation may be made in search of the parties' intent. (Acts 1984, No. 331, §1, eff. Jan. 1, 1985.)

Art. 2047. Meaning of words.

The words of a contract must be given their generally prevailing meaning.

Words of art and technical terms must be given their technical meaning when the contract involves a technical matter. (Acts 1984, No. 331, §1, eff. Jan. 1, 1985.)

Art. 2048. Words susceptible of different meanings.

Words susceptible of different meanings must be interpreted as having the meaning that best conforms to the object of the contract. (Acts 1984, No. 331, §1, eff. Jan. 1, 1985.)

Art. 2049. Provision susceptible of different meanings.

A provision susceptible of different meanings must be interpreted with a meaning that renders it effective and not with one that renders it ineffective. (Acts 1984, No. 331, §1, eff. Jan. 1, 1985.)

Art. 2050. Provisions interpreted in light of each other.

Each provision in a contract must be interpreted in light of the other provisions so that each is given the meaning suggested by the contract as a whole. (Acts 1984, No. 331, §1, eff. Jan. 1, 1985.)

Art. 2051. Contract worded in general terms.

Although a contract is worded in general terms, it must be interpreted to cover only those things it appears the parties intended to include. (Acts 1984, No. 331, §1, eff. Jan. 1, 1985.)

Art. 2052. Situation to which the contract applies.

When the parties intend a contract of general scope but, to eliminate doubt, include a provision that describes a specific situation, interpretation must not restrict the scope of the contract to that situation alone. (Acts 1984, No. 331, §1, eff. Jan. 1, 1985.)

Art. 2053. Nature of contract, equity, usages, conduct of the parties, and other contracts between same parties.

A doubtful provision must be interpreted in light of the nature of the contract, equity, usages, the conduct of the parties before and after the formation of the contract, and of other contracts of a like nature between the same parties. (Acts 1984, No. 331, §1, eff. Jan. 1, 1985.)

Art. 2054. No provision of the parties for a particular situation.

When the parties made no provision for a particular situation, it must be assumed that they intended to bind themselves not only to the express provisions of the contract, but also to whatever the law, equity, or usage regards as implied in a contract of that kind or necessary for the contract to achieve its purpose. (Acts 1984, No. 331, §1, eff. Jan. 1, 1985.)

Art. 2055. Equity and usage.

Equity, as intended in the preceding articles, is based on the principles that no one is allowed to take unfair advantage of another and that no one is allowed to enrich himself unjustly at the expense of another.

Usage, as intended in the preceding articles, is a practice regularly observed in affairs of a nature identical or similar to the object of a contract subject to interpretation. (Acts 1984, No. 331, §1, eff. Jan. 1, 1985.)

Art. 2056. Standard-form contracts.

In case of doubt that cannot be otherwise resolved, a provision in a contract must be interpreted against the party who furnished its text.

A contract executed in a standard form of one party must be interpreted, in case of doubt, in favor of the other party. (Acts 1984, No. 331, §1, eff. Jan. 1, 1985.)

Art. 2057. Contract interpreted in favor of obligor.

In case of doubt that cannot be otherwise resolved, a contract must be interpreted against the obligee and in favor of the obligor of a particular obligation.

Yet, if the doubt arises from lack of a necessary explanation that one party should have given, or from negligence or fault of one party, the contract must be interpreted in a manner favorable to the other party whether obligee or obligor. (Acts 1984, No. 331, §1, eff. Jan. 1, 1985.)

Doctrine

Louisiana Law of Conventional Obligations, A Précis

Sections 10.1.1 to 10.2.2

A contract being, presumably, the outward manifestation of the parties' intent, the Code Articles which lay down the "rules" of interpretation of contracts can only have for their purpose to provide guidelines to ascertain and extract the intent of the parties out of the contract. This is the whole meaning of Art. 2045: "Interpretation of a contract is the determination of the common intent of the parties." [. . . .]

The majority of the Code Articles on this issue of interpretation focus on the words of the contract and the provisions of the contract. **Art. 2046, Art. 2047, Art. 2048.**

The words of a contract must be read also within the context of the provisions of the contract. [. . . .]

Articles 2049, 2050, 2051 and 2052 [. . .]. [. . . .]

It remains however, that in relating a provision of a contract to another provision in the same contract the courts must strive to **"determine the common intent of the parties." Art. 2045.** Ascertaining that "common intent" should be the goal to reach.

This is particularly important in those instances where one party to a contract is in a weaker bargaining position than the other party. The civil Code gives the courts two special rules to use for the purpose of protecting that party presumed to be the weaker of the two in any one of two situations contemplated in Articles 2056 and 2057. [. . . .]

Whenever the performance of the obligations created by a contract spreads over any length of time there exists the risk that the actual performance of the obligations may not match the performance as expected or as anticipated by the common intent of the parties when they entered their contract. The many different kinds of "surrounding circumstances" that prevailed at the time the contract was entered into may or, rather, are likely to be different from the circumstances that will surround the actual performance of the obligations created by the contract. [. . . .]

The question then raised is: what of the situation of the party negatively affected by a subsequent change in the circumstances? Can a court "re-write" the contract to adapt it to present day surroundings and claim, still, to "interpret" the contract as per the presumed "common intent" of the parties as it was at the time of formation of their contract? [. . . .]

A few specific Articles in the civil Code invite the judge to "re-write" a contract in specific circumstances. Such is the case of Art. 1861(2), Art. 1877, Articles 1951 and 1952. However, in all other circumstances, a contract being the "law" between the parties it should not be revised by a court under the guise of "interpretation."

Cases

Charles Ray Sanders, et al. v.
Ashland Oil, Inc., et al.

Court of Appeal of Louisiana
First Circuit
June 20, 1997
696 So.2d 1031

CARTER, Judge.

[....]

Background

[1] On December 8, 1990, employees of Protech Environmental Services, Inc. (Protech) were performing asbestos abatement services in connection with the renovation of Grandison Hall dormitory at Southern University in Baton Rouge, Louisiana. A fire began in the dormitory where two Protech employees, Charles Ray Sanders and Jesse Wayne Bickford, were removing mastic tile adhesive from the floors. As a result of the fire, Charles Ray Sanders sustained serious injuries, and Jesse Wayne Bickford was killed. The fire also caused substantial damage to the dormitory.

[2] On December 6, 1991, Charles Ray Sanders and Bobbie O. Bickford, individually, as administratrix of the Estate of Jesse Wayne Bickford, and as tutrix of the minor children, Brian Wayne Bickford and Travis Dan Bickford, filed the instant action **for personal injuries and punitive damages**, under docket number 376,039. Numerous defendants were named in the petition, including the State of Louisiana, through the Office of Risk Management, Division of Administration, Office of the Governor, and Southern University (the State); Protech; Roy Eschette, President of Protech; and Aetna Life and Casualty Company (Aetna Life), the liability insurer of Protech. Aetna Casualty and Surety Company (Aetna Casualty), the workers' compensation insurer of Protech, subsequently intervened in the action to exercise its right of subrogation.

[3] In a separate action, the State filed suit against Protech and its building loss insurer, Great American Insurance Company (Great American), under docket number 376,088, for **property damages** sustained to the dormitory. This suit was subsequently settled, and the State entered into a "General Release and Indemnity Agreement" with Protech and Great American for the sum of $10,000.00.

[4] On June 29, 1995, in the action for personal injuries and punitive damages, Eschette, Protech, Aetna Life, and Aetna Casualty (hereafter collectively referred to as Protech) filed a cross-claim and third-party demand against the State. Protech alleged that, under the second paragraph of the "General Release and Indemnity Agreement" executed in the property damage suit, the State agreed to indemnify

Protech for any amounts for which it may be cast, together with legal interest and costs. Additionally, Protech alleged that Aetna Casualty had paid substantial sums to defend and protect Eschette and Protech in connection with the claims for which the State agreed to provide indemnity, and, therefore, it was entitled to reimbursement by the State.

[5] The State answered, contending that, in entering into the release and indemnity agreement, the parties intended to settle *only* those claims arising out of the State's suit for property damage, not claims arising out of the suit for personal injuries and punitive damages.

[6] On September 26, 1995, the State filed a motion for summary judgment on the cross-claim/ third-party demand, contending that the release and indemnity agreement did not grant Protech indemnification by the State because the parties to the agreement did not intend for the indemnification to extend to any suit other than the State's suit for property damage. [....]

[7] On October 23, 1995, a hearing was held on the State's motion for summary judgment. At the conclusion of the hearing, the trial court, for oral reasons assigned, granted the motion for summary judgment, dismissing, with prejudice, Protech's contractual indemnity claims against the State and assessing costs to Protech. A judgment was signed on November 16, 1995.

[8] Protech appealed, assigning the following specifications of error:

1. The trial court erred in interpreting the agreement contrary to the clear and unambiguous meaning of its terms.

2. The trial court erred in considering parol evidence purporting to show the parties' intent.

[....]

Contract Interpretation

[9] Generally, legal agreements have the effect of law upon the parties, and, as they bind themselves, they shall be held to a full performance of the obligations flowing therefrom. *Belle Pass Terminal, Inc. v. Jolin, Inc.*, 92-1544, 92-1545, p. 16 (La.App. 1st Cir. 3/ 11/ 94); 634 So.2d 466, 479, *writ denied*, 94-0906 (La.6/ 17/ 94); 638 So.2d 1094; *Spohrer v. Spohrer*, 610 So.2d 849, 851–52 (La.App. 1st Cir.1992). In other words, a contract between the parties is the law between them, and the courts are obligated to give legal effect to such contracts according to the true intent of the parties. LSA-C.C. art.2045; *Martin Exploration Company v. Amoco Production Company*, 93-0349, p. 4 (La.App. 1st Cir. 5/ 20/ 94); 637 So.2d 1202, 1205, *writ denied*, 94-2003 (La.11/ 4/ 94); 644 So.2d 1048; *Spohrer v. Spohrer*, 610 So.2d at 852. This intent is to be determined by the words of the contract when they are clear, explicit, and lead to no absurd consequences. LSA-C.C. art.2046; *Woodrow Wilson Construction Company, Inc. v. MMR-Radon Constructors, Inc.*, 93-2346, p. 3 (La.App. 1st Cir. 4/ 8/ 94); 635 So.2d 758, 759, *writ denied*, 94-1206 (La.7/ 1/ 94); 639 So.2d 1167; *Belle Pass Terminal, Inc. v. Jolin, Inc.*, 634 So.2d at 479.

[10] When the words of a contract are clear and explicit and lead to no absurd consequences, no further interpretation may be made in search of the parties' intent. LSA-C.C. art.2046; *Belle Pass Terminal, Inc. v. Jolin, Inc.,* 634 So.2d at 479; *Stafford v. Jennings-Norwood Farm and Irrigation Company, Inc.,* 586 So.2d 735, 737 (La.App. 3rd Cir.1991), *writ denied,* 590 So.2d 590 (La.1992); *Investors Associates Ltd. v. B.F. Trappey's Sons Inc.,* 500 So.2d 909, 912 (La.App. 3rd Cir.), *writ denied,* 502 So.2d 116 (La.1987). The rules of interpretation establish that, when a clause in a contract is clear and unambiguous, the letter of that clause should not be disregarded under the pretext of pursuing its spirit. LSA-C.C. art.2046, comment (b); *Cashio v. Shoriak,* 481 So.2d 1013, 1015 (La.1986); *Belle Pass Terminal, Inc. v. Jolin, Inc.,* 634 So.2d at 479; *Spohrer v. Spohrer,* 610 So.2d at 852.

[11] In such cases, the meaning and intent of the parties to the written contract must be sought within the four corners of the instrument and cannot be explained or contradicted by parol evidence. LSA-C.C. art. 1848; *Belle Pass Terminal, Inc. v. Jolin, Inc.,* 634 So.2d at 479; *Investors Associates Ltd. v. B.F. Trappey's Sons Inc.,* 500 So.2d at 912. Contracts, subject to interpretation from the instrument's four corners without the necessity of extrinsic evidence, are to be interpreted as a matter of law, and the use of extrinsic evidence is proper only where a contract is ambiguous after an examination of the four corners of the agreement. *Martin Exploration Company v. Amoco Production Company,* 637 So.2d at 1205; *Investors Associates Ltd. v. B.F. Trappey's Sons Inc.,* 500 So.2d at 912.

[12] When the terms of a written contract are susceptible to more than one interpretation, or there is uncertainty or ambiguity as to its provisions, or the intent of the parties cannot be ascertained from the language employed, parol evidence is admissible to clarify the ambiguity or show the intention of the parties. *Martin Exploration Company v. Amoco Production Company,* 637 So.2d at 1205; *Belle Pass Terminal, Inc. v. Jolin, Inc.,* 634 So.2d at 480. In cases in which the contract is ambiguous, the agreement shall be construed according to the intent of the parties. LSA-C.C. art.2045. Intent is an issue of fact which is to be inferred from all of the surrounding circumstances. *Kuswa & Associates, Inc. v. Thibaut Construction Co., Inc.,* 463 So.2d 1264, 1266 (La.1985); *Commercial Bank & Trust Company v. Bank of Louisiana,* 487 So.2d 655, 659 (La.App. 5th Cir.1986). A doubtful provision must be interpreted in light of the nature of the contract, equity, usages, the conduct of the parties before and after the formation of the contract, and other contracts of a like nature between the same parties. LSA-C.C. art.2053; *Allen v. Burnett,* 530 So.2d 1294, 1301 (La.App. 2nd Cir.1988).

[13] Whether a contract is ambiguous or not is a question of law. *Spohrer v. Spohrer,* 610 So.2d at 853; *Myers v. Myers,* 532 So.2d 490, 494 (La.App. 1st Cir.1988); *Aycock v. Allied Enterprises, Inc.,* 517 So.2d 303, 309 (La.App. 1st Cir.1987), *writs denied,* 518 So.2d 512, 513 (La.1988). However, where factual findings are pertinent to the interpretation of a contract, those factual findings are not to be disturbed unless manifest error is shown. *See G/ O Enterprises, Inc. v. Mid Louisiana Gas Company,* 444 So.2d 1279, 1286 (La.App. 4th Cir.), *writ denied,* 446 So.2d 318 (La.1984);

Universal Iron Works, Inc. v. Falgout Refrigeration, Inc., 419 So.2d 1272, 1274 (La. App. 1st Cir.1982). When appellate review is not premised upon any factual findings made at the trial level, but instead is based upon an independent review and examination of the contract on its face, the manifest error rule does not apply. *Spohrer v. Spohrer,* 610 So.2d at 853; *Conoco, Inc. v. Tenneco, Inc., Tennessee Gas Pipeline Company,* 524 So.2d 1305, 1312 (La.App. 3rd Cir.), *writ denied,* 525 So.2d 1048 (La.1988). In such cases, appellate review of questions of law is simply whether the trial court was legally correct. *Spohrer v. Spohrer,* 610 So.2d at 853.

[14] In the instant case, the trial court, in oral reasons for judgment, stated, in pertinent part, as follows:

> The court finds that [the State] was referring to the suit for building damages, suit number 376,[0]88, when it signed the release indemnity agreement for $10,000.[00]. The court is also of the opinion that Pro-Tech could not possibly believe that the State would release them from a wrongful death [or] a personal injury action for this small amount. The second paragraph clarifies the language in the first paragraph, and this court interprets the language aforesaid to mean the State or Southern University and claims they may have means the State and Southern University. Furthermore, this is the standard release and indemnity agreement, and it's [sic] purpose is to protect Pro-Tech from the claims of those who are subrogated to the rights of the releasor, in this case the State. Clearly, the State did not sign this agreement to protect Pro-Tech from any and all claims made by anyone and everyone. Furthermore, this court feels that had the parties intended to included [sic] the pending personal injury suit 376,039, it would have been referenced. However, there's [*sic*] ample facts, I believe, before this court to render summary judgment. . . .

[15] From these reasons, it is unclear whether the trial court looked only at the four corners of the agreement and found it to be unambiguous or whether he found it to be ambiguous and then reviewed the parol evidence to determine the intent of the parties. Regardless of what the trial court reviewed, the threshold issue on appeal is whether the terms of the agreement are clear and unambiguous. If the language of the agreement is explicit and unambiguous, the contract must be enforced as written. However, if the language of the agreement is unclear and ambiguous, the contract must be construed in light of the intent of the parties.

A. Ambiguity

[16] The "General Release and Indemnity Agreement" at issue in this case provides, in pertinent part, as follows:

> That WE, THE STATE OF LOUISIANA THROUGH THE OFFICE OF RISK MANAGEMENT, DIVISION OF ADMINISTRATION, OFFICE OF THE GOVERNOR, AND SOUTHERN UNIVERSITY, for the sole consideration of the sum of $10,000.00, the receipt whereof is hereby acknowledged, do hereby release and forever discharge PRO-TECH ENVIRONMENTAL

SERVICES, INC. AND GREAT AMERICAN INSURANCE COMPANY, and any related and/or affiliated company of and from any and all claims or demands of whatsoever kind or nature, including strict liability, for or because of any matter or thing done, omitted or suffered to be done by any officer, agent, employee, successor or assigns of said parties, prior to and including the day hereof, and particularly on the [sic] account of any and all claims which they may have for personal injuries, smoke damage, cost of clean-up, removal of asbestos, air monitoring services, construction costs, painting, damage to terrazzo floors in Grandison Hall, as a result of a[sic] explosion/fire on December 8, 1990, at Grandison Hall, SOUTHERN UNIVERSITY Campus, Baton Rouge, Louisiana.

We do hereby further agree to indemnify and hold harmless said parties, together with all employees, agents, officers, or assigns thereof of and from any and all further claims and/ or punitive damage claims that may be made or asserted by the aforesaid or by anyone because of the aforesaid injuries, damages, loss or expenses suffered as a result of the aforesaid explosion/ fire, whether such claim is made by way of indemnity, contribution, subrogation or otherwise.

The foregoing payment is also received in full compromise and settlement of any and all claims that we have or may have against the insurers under any policy of insurance issued to any defendant, whether under the liability, medical payment or any other portion of said policy as a result of the aforesaid accident.

We further recognize that the injuries may be worse than they now appear to be, or may grow worse later, and that we accept this settlement with said knowledge. (Emphasis added.)

[17] The first paragraph of the agreement is a release clause, wherein the State agreed to release Protech and Great American and any related and/ or affiliated company from any and all claims resulting from the actions or inactions of Protech or Great American (or any officer, agent, employee, successor, or assign of Protech or Great American), particularly, any and all claims which they (the State) may have for personal injuries, smoke damage, cost of clean-up, removal of asbestos, air monitoring services, construction costs, painting, or damage to terrazzo floors in Grandison Hall, resulting from the December 8, 1990 fire.

[18] The second paragraph of the agreement is an indemnity clause, wherein the State agreed to indemnify Protech, Great American, and their employees, agents, officers, or assigns from any and all *further* claims which may be asserted by the "aforesaid" (the State) or by "anyone" because of the aforesaid injuries, damages, loss or expenses suffered as a result of the "aforesaid" fire.

[19] After carefully reviewing the agreement, we conclude that it is neither explicit nor unambiguous. Initially, we note that the agreement is poorly drafted and that

the use of legalese, such as "aforesaid," makes the meaning of the contract terms unclear. The agreement fails to reference the suit which is affected by the agreement and is signed by only one party to the agreement, the State. The indemnity clause utilizes the term "parties," but it fails to specify which "parties" are indemnified, i.e., the parties to the contract or the parties to the lawsuit. Additionally, we find that the indemnity clause, as written, is subject to more than one reasonable interpretation. It could be interpreted to provide indemnity for **all** claims arising from the fire filed by **anyone**, including those for personal injuries suffered by the petitioners in the personal injury suit filed against Protech. On the other hand, it could be interpreted to provide indemnity for only those claims listed in paragraph one to which the release was applicable. Because the agreement is neither explicit nor unambiguous, we will review the extrinsic evidence to determine whether the parties intended for the indemnity to extend to claims besides those involved in the State's suit for property damage.

B. Intent

[20] The extrinsic evidence in this case consists of various pleadings, correspondence between counsel for Protech and counsel for the State, and the transcript of a stipulation to settle between the State and Protech.

[21] In answers to a request for admissions propounded by the State, Protech admits that a series of letters exchanged between counsel (its attorney and counsel for the State) constitute the entirety of the settlement negotiations in suit number 376,088, the property damage suit. A review of those letters reveals that none of the letters discussed suit number 376,039, the suit for personal injuries. A November 23, 1993 letter from Protech's attorney to counsel for the State, states that "[o]ur client contacted us recently and requested that we obtain a reasonable settlement demand from you in hopes that we can close the *State of Louisiana versus Pro Tech Environmental* portion of this case." The letter then discussed figures relevant to the damage to Grandison Hall. A January 21, 1994 letter from Protech's attorney to the State's counsel states "[w]e confirm our telephone conversation on Wednesday, January 19, 1994 wherein you past [sic] along a settlement demand on behalf of the State of Louisiana as [a] result of its suit against Great American Insurance Company for a total of $32,552.98." On January 27, 1994, Protech's attorney wrote to counsel for the State, indicating as follows:

> After reviewing the entire file in this matter, it is apparent that there was no damage to the physical structure itself as a result of the fire since the building had been completely gutted prior to the fire taking place. . . .

> Accordingly, we ask that you pass along our settlement offer of $9,500.00, each party to bear its own expenses. . . .

[22] On February 4, 1994, the attorney for Protech wrote to counsel for the State, offering to settle the property damage suit for $10,000.00. Moreover, the exchange of letters resulted in an oral stipulation to settle which was transcribed by the court

reporter at the May 26, 1994 deposition of George Bigelow. The stipulation provides as follows:

> [Counsel for Protech]: This is a matter entitled *State of Louisiana through the Office of Risk Management versus Pro-Tech and Great American Insurance Company.* We were here today for the deposition of the State of Louisiana through its representative George Bigelow.
>
> Prior to the start of the deposition, we had some discussions and are in a position to settle **this matter** on the following terms and conditions:
>
> Great American Insurance Company and Pro-Tech will pay to the State of Louisiana the total sum of $10,000.[00], each party to bear some expenses, in full and final settlement of **this case**. (Emphasis added.)
>
> Agreed?
>
> [Counsel for the State]: Agreed.

[23] Based on the foregoing evidence, we conclude that the State showed that there is no genuine issue of material fact concerning the parties' intent that the State provide indemnification only for the claims set forth in suit number 376,088, the suit for property damage. The correspondence and the stipulation show that the settlement would encompass **only** that part of the case dealing with the State's suit for property damage against Protech. There is nothing to indicate that any other suit was to be included. The agreement does not reference any particular suit, and there is no caption on the agreement. Additionally, in the release portion of the agreement, the State releases Protech, Great American, and their employees, agents, officers, or assigns for the damages it (the State) sustained; there is no reference to anything else. In opposition to the motion for summary judgment, Protech failed to submit any affidavits or other documentation to contradict the State's evidence regarding intent and, thus, failed to raise a genuine issue of material fact as to the intent of the parties. There is not one scintilla of extrinsic evidence to support Protech's position. Therefore, we conclude that the trial court appropriately granted summary judgment in favor of the State.

[. . . .]

Questions

1. Paragraphs 1–4: What types of persons are involved in this case? Are they pretty much on an equal level to negotiate with each other? Should this be relevant if some disagreement occurs between them? Are they professionals in the same line of business? Is a "State" or "state institution" in a somewhat unusual or different negotiating position *vis-à-vis* the other party, whether the other party is a legal entity or a physical person? Could the State, in the "General Release and Indemnity Agreement," have waived its delictual liability? Could it have waived its contractual liability?

2. Paragraph 10: Is this paragraph a logical consequence of the Court's statement that the meaning of a contract must be sought within the four corners of that contract even when parol evidence is admissible?

3. Paragraph 11: Why is it a question of law whether a contract is ambiguous or not?

4. Paragraph 20: Since Louisiana Civil Code article 2046 does not allow a court to search for the parties' intent unless there is ambiguity, absurd consequences, etc., isn't a court rather free to decide whether or not to search for the common intent of the parties under article 2045? Do articles 2045–2057 give the courts any guidance as to how to determine the common intent of the parties? Where does the word and concept of "equity," mentioned in articles 2053–2055, fit in the four corners of a contract, its words, or the parties' intent?

Kathy Prejean
v.
Walter Guillory, et al.

Supreme Court of Louisiana
July 2, 2010
38 So.3d 274

PER CURIAM.

[....]

[1] On February 15, 1995, by written contract, the Broussard Housing Authority (BHA) hired [Kathy] Prejean as executive director of its Section 8 Housing Program[1] for an initial five-year term, with an extension period of another five years.[2] [....] [A susbsequent addendum to her employment contract] provided, in pertinent part:

1—That the [BHA] hereby retains and employs Kathy Prejean to be its Executive Director for a term of four (4) years commencing with the *1st* day of *January, 2002* and expiring *January 1, 2006*. In addition, it is further agreed by the parties hereto that this contract shall be extended for an additional four (4) years (the "extension period") upon the same terms and conditions at the option of [Prejean], unless the [BHA] gives [Prejean] by *October 1, 2005,* notice in writing that it will not extend the contract due to the inadequate performance of [Prejean]. The Board may make a finding of inadequate performance, after providing [Prejean] with written notice and an opportunity to be heard, upon a determination that a significant adverse

---

1. Section 8 housing is a tenant-based program financed with vouchers consisting of federal funds through the Department of Housing and Urban Development (HUD) to provide suitable housing for tenants in homes offered by approved homeowners/ landlords.

2. Prejean actually began working for the BHA without contract in October of 1994.

audit finding (or adverse management review) by federal or state funding agencies has gone uncorrected for more than sixty (60) days due to action or inaction by [Prejean].

2—That [Prejean] hereby accepts employment and hereby agrees that for the consideration hereinafter set forth, he/ she shall perform the duties as the Executive Director in conducting the business of said [BHA] and perform the duties of Secretary to the Board Members at their regular, special and annual meetings.

[2] In early 2004, without Prejean's knowledge, the BHA decided to transfer its Section 8 Housing Program to the LHA. [. . . .]

[3] Immediately following the adjournment of the BHA meeting, members of the BHA and LHA, along with Guillory, proceeded to the BHA office in Broussard. There a confrontation occurred between Guillory and Prejean concerning the keys to the office, which Prejean refused to relinquish to Guillory, for the purpose of securing the building to commence a final audit of the BHA's financial records. Eventually, Prejean and her staff left the building. That evening Prejean contacted the HUD offices in New Orleans. Upon returning to the BHA office the next morning, Prejean discovered the locks had been changed. After a phone conversation in which HUD officials, Prejean, and Guillory participated, Guillory gave Prejean the new keys to the building and left. Prejean then had the locks re-changed.

[. . . .]

[4] On October 5, 2004, Prejean filed suit against Guillory and the LHA for damages resulting from the "hostile takeover" of the BHA by the LHA. In her petition, Prejean sought[, **among other things,** . . .] "a declaratory judgment that her employment contract with [BHA] is valid and enforceable and will become the lawful obligation of the [LHA][, according to its terms] after any formal consolidation occurs."

[5] By November 2004, with HUD's approval of the transfer, Guillory assigned Tim Declouet to head the Broussard office. That same month, Prejean was diagnosed with cancer of her right breast, for which she underwent a mastectomy. By note dated November 2, 2004, Prejean's physician stated Prejean was scheduled for surgery on November 3, and excused her from work until November 22, 2004. By note dated November 11, 2004, Prejean's physician explained Prejean was scheduled for surgery on November 17, 2004, and would return to work after four weeks. Prejean was released to work on January 10, 2005, by noted dated December 9, 2004. In February 2005, Prejean was diagnosed with cancer of the left breast, for which she underwent a second mastectomy. By note dated February 10, 2005, Prejean's physician excused her from work for eight weeks following her surgery scheduled for February 16, 2005. Prejean was released to work on May 2, 2005, by her physician's note dated March 29, 2005, but that release date was extended to July 25, 2005, as stated in her physician's note dated April 25, 2005.

[6] On May 16, 2005, Prejean was called by her staff to the Broussard office regarding the presence of IRS agents inquiring about the BHA's third quarter 941 Form, which should have been filed in late December of 2004 or early January of 2005. By May 17, 2005, Prejean had remedied the situation by filing the necessary form with the IRS.[5]

[7] During that same month, Guillory, with knowledge of Prejean's illness, looked into the Prejean's medical file with the LHA's human resources department, which contained her physician's notes, and discovered Prejean was excused from work until July 25, 2005. He then brought her absenteeism to the attention of the LHA's Board of Commissioners. On May 17, 2005, the LHA passed a resolution to terminate Prejean due to excessive absences and sent Prejean a letter informing her of her termination effective May 31, 2005. The letter, dated May 17, 2005, stated:

RE: Permanent Termination

Please be advised that the Lafayette Housing Authority Board of Commissioners voted unanimously in favor of terminating your employment for failure to perform effective May 31, 2005. Enclosed you will find a copy of the resolution, background, and a check for May 2005.[6]

The Board's decision is based on your being absent from your position of employment for over sixty (60) continuous days and uninterrupted days after exhausting all sick and annual leave days. During your absence you did not contact this Board to make any type of arrangements concerning your continued and interrupted absence from work.

[8] In her First Supplemental and Amending Petition filed on February 22, 2008, Prejean sought damages for the LHA's breach of her employment contract by its wrongful termination of her employment.

[....]

Law And Discussion

[9] "[W]hen a contract can be construed from the four corners of the instrument without looking to extrinsic evidence, the question of contractual interpretation is answered as a matter of law." *Sims v. Mulhearn Funeral Home, Inc.,* 07-0054, p. 10

---

5. On the facsimile transmittal letter, Prejean wrote the following note of explanation for the late filings:

Yesterday I was told by IRS that the attach forms where [sic] not sent into there [sic] office. So this morning I went and turned in the 941 forms to I.R.S. [sic]. I was the one to do them before Lafayette Housing took over in Oct. 2004. But not a soul (person) ever gave them to me. At these times I was into the hospital battling the cancer. So I took care of there [sic] work for them.

6. From April 2004 through May 2005, Prejean's salary was paid by check drafted from the BHA's bank account. However, from around November 2004 and onward, the checks were signed by Guillory and Jonathan Carmouche. Prior to that time, the checks had been signed by Prejean and the chairwoman of the BHA, Gertrude Batiste.

(La.5/ 22/ 07), 956 So.2d 583, 590. "Interpretation of a contract is the determination of the common intent of the parties." La. Civ.Code art. 2045. The reasonable intention of the parties to a contract is to be sought by examining the words of the contract itself, and not assumed. *Sims,* 07-0054 at p. 7, 956 So.2d at 589; *McConnell v. City of New Orleans,* 35 La. Ann. 273 (1883). "When the words of a contract are clear and explicit and lead to no absurd consequences, no further interpretation may be made in search of the parties' intent." La. Civ.Code art. 2046. Common intent is determined, therefore, in accordance with the general, ordinary, plain and popular meaning of the words used in the contract. *Louisiana Ins. Guar. Ass'n v. Interstate Fire & Cas. Co.,* 93-0911, p. 5 (La.1/ 14/ 94), 630 So.2d 759, 763. Accordingly, when a clause in a contract is clear and unambiguous, the letter of that clause should not be disregarded under the pretext of pursuing its spirit, as it is not the duty of the courts to bend the meaning of the words of a contract into harmony with a supposed reasonable intention of the parties. *See Maloney v. Oak Builders, Inc.,* 256 La. 85, 98, 235 So.2d 386, 390 (1970); *McConnell,* 35 La. Ann. at 275. Most importantly, a contract "must be interpreted in a common-sense fashion, according to the words of the contract their common and usual significance." *Lambert v. Maryland Cas. Co.,* 418 So.2d 553, 559 (La.1982).

[10] With these basic principles in mind, we examine the relevant provisions of the contract at issue, particularly the extension provision, which as noted above provided in pertinent part: "That the [BHA] hereby retains and employs Kathy Prejean . . . for a term of four (4) years . . . *expiring January 1, 2006.* In addition, . . . this contract shall be extended for an additional four . . . *unless* the [BHA] gives [Prejean] by *October 1, 2005, notice in writing* that it will not extend the contract due to the *inadequate performance* of [Prejean]." (Emphasis added).

[11] The language of Prejean's employment contract is explicit. Prejean's contract expired on January 1, 2006. However, the addendum also contained an extension period of four years, which would take effect *unless* the BHA provided Prejean written notice of its intent not to extend the contract due to her inadequate performance by October 1, 2005.

[12] While the written notice provision posed no interpretative problems, the Court of Appeal took exception with the ambiguity of the phrase "inadequate performance." However, in accord with the longstanding rules of contractual interpretation, the general, ordinary, plain and popular meaning of the words "inadequate performance" is insufficient fulfillment of an obligation according to its terms. *See Webster's New International Dictionary Unabridged,* "Inadequate" (2d Ed.1955); *Webster's,* "Performance"; *Black's Law Dictionary,* "Inadequate" (6th Ed.1991); *Black's,* "Performance." Thus, under the terms of the contract at issue, Prejean's employer could refuse to extend her contract due to her insufficient fulfillment of an obligation arising from her employment.

[13] The Court of Appeal was further critical of the sentence directly succeeding the extension provision and found it could not even determine whether a finding by the board of an adverse audit was the only form of inadequate performance

justifying Prejean's termination or whether the language was merely illustrative of inadequate performance. Under our civilian tradition, however, "may" is permission. *Jacobs v. City of Bunkie*, 98-2510, p. 6 (La.5/ 18/ 99), 737 So.2d 14, 19; *Underwood v. Lane Memorial Hosp.*, 97-1997, p. 4 (La.7/ 8/ 98), 714 So.2d 715, 717; La.Rev.Stat. § 1:3. Therefore, by the general, ordinary, plain and popular meaning of the word, this provision should be read as merely illustrative, not mandatory. Nevertheless, as the appellate court correctly noted, any ambiguity in a contract is construed against the drafter thereof. *See Robinson v. Robinson*, 99-3097, p. 18 (La.1/ 17/ 01), 778 So.2d 1105, 1122; *Williams Engineering, Inc. v. Goodyear*, 496 So.2d 1012, 1018 (La.1986). Because Prejean drafted the contract, inadequate performance by Prejean in any form would have justified her termination.

[14] Therefore, to prevent the activation of the extension period under the terms of the contract, the LHA, as the BHA's successor, had to provide written notice of its intent not to extend the contract due to her inadequate performance. Through its letter dated May 17, 2005, the LHA provided Prejean with written notice of its intent not to extend her contract, clearly satisfying the addendum's written notice requirement well within the October 1 deadline.

[15] Moreover, the record reflects three grounds upon which the LHA could have based its finding of inadequate performance. First, the record definitively shows Prejean was medically excused from work from November 2, 2004 through January 10, 2005, and from February 16, 2005 through July 25, 2005, both of which periods far exceeded the LHA's uncontested two-week paid sick leave policy.[9] Significantly, the only records of Prejean's attendance were the medical excuses contained

---

9. Contrary to the Court of Appeal's finding, the record contains no evidence Prejean did not exceed her two-week paid leave allotment. Of the three co-workers/employees, who testified on Prejean's behalf, only Linda Anderson was employed during the "excused from work" time period in question, and although she testified Prejean came into work and work was delivered to Prejean's home, she did not know what Prejean's duties were nor could she say when or for how long Prejean was in the office during that period.

Prejean, herself, testified she could not work full days during this period and admitted she was not in contact on the days of her surgeries or the three to four days thereafter:

> Two (2) weeks after my surgery in November, I was cutting the checks for the [BHA]. And I was doing my recertifications. And I was doing the input into the computer. I may not have stayed the full eight (8) hours, but I was at the office. . . .
> * * *
> The only time I was not in contact is when I was undergoing surgery or recouping the three (3) to four (4) days after surgery.

Moreover, given the numerous surgeries, follow up procedures, treatments, and doctors' visits Prejean endured and as documented in the medical excuses and records admitted into evidence, even viewing the testimony in a light most favorable to Prejean, a reasonable person could not find Prejean did not exceed her allotted sick leave time, at the very least during the latter six-month period.

Additionally, LHA policy as testified to by both Prejean and Guillory required a person medically excused from work not be allowed to work for liability reasons. Prejean presented to the LHA numerous medical excuses in which her physicians ordered her not to work over a period of six months with each excuse further extending the prescribed "no work" period.

in her LHA medical file, and Prejean conceded to "someone looking at [her] file the beginning of May, it would look like [she] hadn't been at work from . . . February 16th . . . [a]nd [she wasn't] 'scheduled to come back until July 25th."[10] Therefore, based on her attendance record, the LHA had grounds for its finding of inadequate performance due to excessive absenteeism in that Prejean failed to fulfill her basic employment obligation of attendance. Second, according to the addendum's second paragraph, Prejean "shall . . . perform the duties of Secretary to the Board Members at their regular, special and annual meetings." The record irrefutably shows Prejean never attended any LHA board meeting from April 2004 through May 2005, and, therefore, never performed her duties of secretary to the board at its meetings. Third, Prejean testified she was responsible for filing the BHA's 941 Forms with the IRS, which she failed to do in January 2005, prompting a visit from the IRS to the BHA office in May of that year. Therefore, the record supports the LHA had grounds for finding inadequate performance on the part of Prejean in failing to sufficiently fulfill her contractual obligations and did not breach her contract by its termination.[11]

[16] Prejean, herself, testified she could not work full days during this period and admitted she was not in contact on the days of her surgeries or the three to four days thereafter:

> Two (2) weeks after my surgery in November, I was cutting the checks for the [BHA]. And I was doing my recertifications. And I was doing the input into the computer. I may not have stayed the full eight (8) hours, but I was at the office. . . .
>
> * * *
>
> The only time I was not in contact is when I was undergoing surgery or recouping the three (3) to four (4) days after surgery.

[17] Moreover, given the numerous surgeries, follow up procedures, treatments, and doctors' visits Prejean endured and as documented in the medical excuses and records admitted into evidence, even viewing the testimony in a light most favorable to Prejean, a reasonable person could not find Prejean did not exceed her allotted sick leave time, at the very least during the latter six-month period.

[18] Additionally, LHA policy as testified to by both Prejean and Guillory required a person medically excused from work not be allowed to work for liability reasons. Prejean presented to the LHA numerous medical excuses in which her

---

10. Notably, the record is silent concerning any contact between the LHA and Prejean regarding arrangements for her continued absences, although Prejean did testified she asked Guillory, during her November 2004 assessment meeting held at his request, "for some time because I knew I was fixing to have another surgery." Both Guillory and Prejean testified, however, they never met in 2005 regarding her job performance, her ability to perform, or her illness and medically necessitated leave time. The record is further silent regarding any discussion between Prejean, Guillory, or the LHA concerning her February diagnosis. Prejean admittedly did not seek extended leave under the federal Family Medical Leave Act.

11. Finding no breach, we pretermit discussion of all other assignments of error.

physicians ordered her not to work over a period of six months with each excuse further extending the prescribed "no work" period.

[19] We find, therefore, by its own terms, Prejean's contract expired on January 1, 2006, upon written notice of the LHA of its intention not to extend her contract due to inadequate performance. Consequently, Prejean is entitled to judgment awarding her seven months of salary for June through December 2005, plus interest from the date of judicial demand. We render judgment accordingly. Further, we render judgment dismissing Prejean's claims against Walter Guillory with full prejudice. The judgment of the Court of Appeal contrary to this holding is hereby reversed.

[. . . .]

Questions

1. Paragraph 9–10: At the beginning of paragraph 10, the Court states: "with these basic principles in mind. . . ." Nowhere in the preceding paragraph does the Court identify these principles. Can you identify them? Aren't they stated, after all, in some articles of the Louisiana Civil Code? So why give the impression that without the cases these principles could not be taken from legislation?

2. Paragraph 11: Can you describe the type of person Prejean is in relation to the other persons involved, BHA in particular? Do you know what a contract of adhesion is? What nominate contract was in existence between BHA and Prejean? What kind of obligations (give, do, not do) does such a contract create for Prejean, for instance?

3. Paragraph 12: The issue revolves around performance and inadequate performance. Before looking into the particular named contract at issue here, couldn't the Court have looked at the Louisiana Civil Code articles on "Obligations," such as 1756, 1758 and 1759, as well as the articles on "Damages," articles 1994–1995 in particular? What about articles 2746–2750?

4. Paragraph 13: Even though Kathy Prejean was a mere natural person, she "drafted the contract" and, therefore, "any ambiguity in a contract is construed against the drafter thereof." Do you think Kathy Prejean contemplated such a ruling when she drafted the addendum to her employment contract? In the following paragraphs, how does the Court read the contract and, particularly, Prejean's understanding of inadequate performance and the giving of adequate notice? Didn't LHA have sufficient grounds to justify an inadequate performance of her obligations by Prejean? Did the Court give an objective interpretation of inadequate performance, in the sense that objective circumstances beyond Prejean's control (medical reasons, mostly) prevented her (or anybody else) from performing her obligations in an objectively adequate or inadequate manner? Or did the Court give a subjective interpretation of inadequate performance and blame Kathy Prejean as a person for not performing her obligations in an adequate manner? Can you suggest any ground on which the Court of Appeal had ruled in favor of Kathy Prejean and against LHA?

Chapter 4

Manners in Which Obligations May Be Transferred and/or Extinguished

Section I — Assumption of Obligations

Louisiana Sources of Law

Louisiana Civil Code

Art. 1821. Assumption by agreement between obligor and third person.

An obligor and a third person may agree to an assumption by the latter of an obligation of the former. To be enforceable by the obligee against the third person, the agreement must be made in writing.

The obligee's consent to the agreement does not effect a release of the obligor.

The unreleased obligor remains solidarily bound with the third person. (Acts 1984, No. 331, §1, eff. Jan. 1, 1985.)

Art. 1822. Third person bound for amount assumed.

A person who, by agreement with the obligor, assumes the obligation of the latter is bound only to the extent of his assumption.

The assuming obligor may raise any defense based on the contract by which the assumption was made. (Acts 1984, No. 331, §1, eff. Jan. 1, 1985.)

Art. 1823. Assumption by agreement between obligee and third person.

An obligee and a third person may agree on an assumption by the latter of an obligation owed by another to the former. That agreement must be made in writing. That agreement does not effect a release of the original obligor. (Acts 1984, No. 331, §1, eff. Jan. 1, 1985.)

Art. 1824. Defenses.

A person who, by agreement with the obligee, has assumed another's obligation may not raise against the obligee any defense based on the relationship between the assuming obligor and the original obligor.

The assuming obligor may raise any defense based on the relationship between the original obligor and obligee. He may not invoke compensation based on an obligation owed by the obligee to the original obligor. (Acts 1984, No. 331, §1, eff. Jan. 1, 1985.)

Doctrine

Louisiana Law of Obligations in General, A Treatise

Sections 5.1 to 5.1.3-E

218. Preliminary observations. [. . . .]

The Revision Comments clearly indicate that the word "assumption" was taken from an English translation of the German Civil Code and from translations in English of the Italian and Greek Civil Codes, both influenced by the Burgerliches Gesetzbuch (BGB) or German Civil Code.[7]

The word "Assumption" is defined in *The Dictionary of English Law*[8] as follows: "Assume, assumption, in Scots law, to assume is to adopt, as of a new trustee." In *Black's Law Dictionary*, assumption is: "2. the act of taking (esp. someone else's debt or other obligation) for or on oneself; the agreement to so take <assumption of a debt>. -assume,vb."

219. Assumption or delegation? In light of the above, we are wondering why the word "Delegation" was not chosen in lieu of "Assumption"? The French Civil Code (Art. 1275) and the Civil Code of Quebec (Art. 1667) have opted for "Delegation" instead of "Assumption" to describe the same mode of transfer of obligations. The Louisiana Civil Code states in **art. 1886-1** that "**A delegation of performance by an obligor to a third person is effective when the third person binds himself to perform.**" Strangely enough, this description of delegation resembles very much the "assumption of debt" of the BGB![9] And in the *Dictionary of the Civil Code* we read that a "delegation" is a "triangular operation wherein on the order of a person the délégant-delegator, another person, the délégué-delegate, undertakes an obligation towards a third person, the délégataire-delegatee, who accepts the latter as debtor."

In other words, our preference would have been to use the word "delegation" instead of the word "assumption" and not much would have been changed in the legal regime of "assumption of obligations." Be that as it may, an assumption of an obligation is a juridical act which involves three parties at least. Two of these parties are already bound to each other when a third one agrees to take upon herself the debt or obligation of one of the original two parties. [. . . .]

---

7. The "Fifth Section" of Book 2 of the BGB is entitled "Assumption of debt." Strangely enough it follows the Fourth Section which is entitled "Assignment of claims." The German Civil Code, as amended to January 1973, Ian S. Forrester, Simon L. Goren, Hans-Michael Ilgen, Fred Rothman 1975.

8. *The Dictionary of the English Law*, Earl Jowitt (Clifford Walsh, Sweet & Maxwell Ltd 1959); *Black's Law Dictionary*, (9th ed., West 2010).

9. BGB, Fifth Section: Assumption of Debt § 414 [Contract between creditor and third party]. A debt may be assumed by a third party by agreement with the creditor in such a manner that the third party takes the place of the former debtor.

Assumption of Obligation by Agreement between an Obligor and a Third Person

222. Two requirements. The first paragraph of La. Civ. Code **art. 1821** states that, "**an obligor and a third person may agree to an assumption by the latter of an obligation of the former. To be enforceable by the obligee against the third person, the agreement must be made in writing.**" The two requirements mentioned in this Article are the "parties" to the assumption and the "form" of the assumption.

223. Requirements regarding the parties: a contract. To be binding between the obligor and the third person, the juridical act of assumption must meet all the requirements for a valid contract. [. . . .]

225. A written instrument. Although the agreement of assumption is entered into between the obligor and the third person, it is necessary that the instrument be in writing so that the agreement of assumption can be submitted to the obligee who, in turn, can enforce it against the third person. In a sense, the obligee becomes a party to a contract or agreement that includes a type of stipulation for his benefit making him a "third party beneficiary." The agreement is submitted to the obligee for his consent so as to vest in him the benefit of having now two obligors on whom he may call and who, in addition, are bound *in solido.*

226. Requirement of form. Article **1821** of the Civil Code requires that this agreement of assumption be in writing in order to be enforceable by the obligee-beneficiary against the third person/co-obligor. [. . . .]

Effects of an Assumption between the Obligor and the Third Person

229. Effects between the obligor and the third person [assuming obligor]. This bilateral relationship gives rise to two sub-sets of effects, some taking place between the third person and the obligor and others occurring in the relationship between the obligee and the obligor.

230. Extinction of the debt. As far as the third person and the obligor are concerned, the former may have entered into the assumption in order to extinguish a debt he himself owes to the latter on account of some prior juridical act or fact. [. . . .]

231. Right of contribution? [. . . .]

In contrast with the above situation wherein the third person-assuming obligor is himself a debtor of the original obligor, it may happen that an assumption of obligation will be entered into by the third person-assuming obligor in order to make a donation to the original obligor. [. . . .]

232. Original obligor not released. The second sub-set of effects of this form of assumption illustrates the originality of this means of transfer of obligations. Such an assumption of an obligation does not release the original obligor of his own debt *vis-à-vis* the obligee.[27] An assumption does not amount to a remission of debt,[28] nor is it the equivalent of a novation.[29] The original obligor remains bound to his obligee. [. . . .]

233. Effects between the obligee and the co-obligors (original and assuming obligors): solidarity. It is in this particular relationship that an assumption has its most important effects and where, actually, one can best grasp the *raison d'être* of this institution.

The third person-assuming obligor agrees to take upon himself the obligation of the original obligor and to stand as an obligor *vis-à-vis* the obligee. Moreover, this third person-assuming obligor becomes, by law, solidarily liable with the original obligor. "**The unreleased obligor remains solidarily bound with the third person**," states La. Civ. Code **art. 1821-3.**

Assumption of Obligation by Agreement between the Obligee and a Third Person

237. La. Civ. Code art. 1823. La Civ. Code **art. 1823** states that "[a]n obligee and a third person may agree on an assumption by the latter of an obligation owed by another to the former. That agreement must be made in writing. That agreement does not effect a release of the original obligor."

This form of assumption involves only two parties and, because it amounts to an agreement to pay the debt of another, it must be in writing,[34] as La. Civ. Code **art. 1823** emphasizes in this particular instance. [. . . .]

238. An agreement: the parties. An assumption of the original obligor's obligation by an agreement between the obligee and the third person-assuming obligor is a unilateral onerous contract between the latter two parties.[35] The involvement of the original obligor is not necessary and, actually, this form of assumption may take place without the original obligor's knowledge.

By such an agreement the third person-assuming obligor binds himself towards the obligee to substitute his own performance to that which was to be rendered by the original obligor.[36] This agreement must, therefore, meet all the requirements for a valid contract, the requirement of cause in particular.[37] [. . . .]

---

27. La. Civ. Code art. 1821 [. . .].
28. La. Civ. Code art. 1888 *et seq.: on Remission of Debt, see infra* Ch. 7, #405-420.
29. La. Civ. Code art. 1879 *et seq.;* on Novation, see *infra* Ch. 7, #368-398.
34. La. Civ. Code art. 1847 [. . .].
35. La. Civ. Code art. 1907 [. . .].
36. La. Civ. Code art. 1855 [. . .].
37. La. Civ. Code Art. 1966 *et seq.*

Effects of an Agreement of Assumption between Obligee and Assuming Obligor

246. Two sets of effects. The effects of such an agreement must be examined from two different perspectives since the agreement of assumption will have effects with respect to three parties at least: the obligee, the third person-assuming obligor, and the original obligor. [. . . .]

247. Original obligor not released. One most important effect or consequence of this agreement is that it does not release the original obligor of his debt towards the obligee.[50] [. . . .] [A]lthough the agreement of assumption could, in most instances, benefit the original obligor, he must remain free to reject that benefit if he has good reasons to object to it, so as to remain personally bound toward his original obligee only.

248. Original and assuming obligors not solidary. A second important effect of this form of agreement of assumption is that it does not make the original obligor and the assuming obligor solidarily bound to the obligee. [. . . .]

251. Two different situations. [. . . .]

[T]he effects of the relationship between the two obligors are determined by the particular nominate or innominate, gratuitous or onerous, contract that binds them.

Louisiana Law of Obligations in General, A Précis
Sections 5.1.1 to 5.1.3

An assumption of an obligation is a juridical act which involves three parties at least. Two of these parties are already bound to each other when a third one agrees to take upon himself the debt or obligation of one of the original two parties. [. . . .]

The first paragraph of **LSA-C.C. Art. 1821** provides that "**an obligor and a third person may agree to an assumption by the latter of an obligation of the former. To be enforceable by the obligee against the third person, the agreement must be made in writing.**" [. . . .]

To be binding between the obligor and the third person, the juridical act of assumption must meet all the requirement for a valid contract. [. . . .]

Although the agreement of assumption is entered into between the obligor and the third person, it is necessary that the instrument be in writing so that the agreement of assumption can be submitted to the obligee to be enforceable by him against the third person. [. . . .]

LSA-C.C. Art. 1823 states that "**[A]n obligee and a third person may agree on an assumption by the latter of an obligation owed by another to the former. That**

---

50. La. Civ. Code art. 1823 [. . .]. A "novation" would release the original obligor of his debt. See *supra* Ch. 3, #138.

agreement must be made in writing. That agreement does not effect a release of the original obligor."

This form of assumption involves only two parties and, because it amounts to an agreement to pay the debt of another, it must be in writing as **LSA-C.C. Art. 1823** emphasizes in this particular instance. [. . . .]

An assumption of the original obligor's obligation by an agreement between the obligee and the third person-assuming obligor is a unilateral onerous contract between the latter two parties. The involvement of the original obligor is not necessary and, actually, this form of assumption may take place without the original obligor's knowledge.

By such an agreement, the third person-assuming obligor binds himself towards the obligee to substitute his own performance to that which was to be rendered by the original obligor. This agreement must, therefore, meet all the requirements for a valid contract, the requirement of cause in particular.

Cases

Beverly B. McCrory, Wife of/and Gerard L. McCrory v. Terminix Service Co., Inc., and XYZ Insurance Company

Court of Appeal of Louisiana
Fourth Circuit
November 13, 1992
609 So.2d 883

ARMSTRONG, Judge.

[1] The plaintiffs, Beverly and Gerard McCrory ("McCrorys"), filed suit against defendant, Terminix Service Co., Inc. ("Terminix"), and its insurer claiming property and personal injury damages.[1] On Terminix's motion, the trial court granted partial summary judgment. The judgment limited the McCrorys' property damage claim to $5,000 in accordance with a provision in the parties' termite protection contract. The McCrorys appeal from that judgment, claiming the trial court erred in granting the partial summary judgment because the contractual provision interpreted by the court is ambiguous and because doubt exists as to the parties' intent to limit Terminix's liability to $5,000. We disagree.

[2] In 1962, the McCrorys' predecessor in interest, W.D. Fowler, contracted with Terminix for termite protection for the residence and garage located at 4763 Marigny Street, New Orleans. (Bruce-Terminix Protection Contract No. 72PRO62208-5.) Under the terms of this contract, for an annual fee, Terminix obligated itself to perform annual re-inspections and future applications of termiticides necessary for the

---

1. The McCrorys' claim for personal injury damages, arising from Terminix's use/misuse of termiticides on the McCrorys' residence, is not relevant to this appeal.

continued protection of the property against subterranean termites. Additionally, the contract provided that:

> The Terminix company further agrees that in the event of new subterranean termite damage to the structure or contents repairs will be performed with the approval and at the expense of the Terminix company. The liability of the Terminix company is not to exceed five thousand dollars ($5,000.00).

[3] The McCrorys assumed the terms of this contract when they purchased 4763 Marigny Street from Fowler.

[4] During a routine inspection of the McCrorys' residence in June of 1989, Terminix discovered termite activity and damage. Through this suit, the McCrorys contend that the termite damage to their home resulted from Terminix's failure to properly treat and/or annually inspect their property. They claim Terminix is liable for the full cost of repairing the property damage caused by the termites.

[5] Terminix's motion for partial summary judgment claimed that, under the clear and unambiguous terms of the parties' termite protection contract, its obligation to the McCrorys for property damage caused by termites does not exceed $5,000. Terminix contended that the contract's provision which unambiguously limits its liability must be enforced as written and, under well-settled Louisiana law, cannot be varied because it was not procured by fraud, accident or mistake. As the contract has the effect of law as between the parties, Terminix further argued that its terms could not be repudiated for economic or imprudent reasons, citing LSA--C.C. arts. 1971 and 1983.[2]

[. . . .]

[6] On appeal, the McCrorys assert that the contractual provision which purports to limit Terminix's liability to $5,000 is ambiguous because it does not specifically state the liability limitation of $5,000 is for property damage. The McCrorys argue that the contract clearly states that in the event of new termite damage to the structure or contents of 4763 Marigny Street, repairs will be performed at the expense of Terminix. They further claim that the contract does not place a dollar limit on those structure and contents repairs. Alternatively, the McCrorys assert that doubt exists as to the parties' intent regarding the contract provision. They claim that because Terminix has written post-1962 termite protection contracts for other clients, providing them with property damage liability limits of $25,000, Terminix intended to increase the liability limitation in their contract.

---

2. The cited Civil Code articles provide as follows:
Art. 1971. Freedom of parties
    Parties are free to contract for any object that is lawful, possible, and determined or determinable.
Art. 1983. Law for the parties; performance in good faith
    Contracts have the effect of law for the parties and may be dissolved only through the consent of the parties or on grounds provided by law. Contracts must be performed in good faith.

[7] Subject to the limits imposed by law, parties are free to contract as they choose. *Zeigler v. Pleasant Manor Nursing Home,* 600 So.2d 819 (La.App. 3d Cir.1992). The terms of the contract then have the effect of law on the parties. LSA-C.C. art. 1983 (former C.C. art. 1901). Interpretation of a contract is the determination of the parties' common intent. LSA-C.C. art. 2045 (former C.C. arts. 1945, 1950). When the words of a contract are clear and explicit and lead to no absurd consequences, no further interpretation may be made in search of the parties' intent. LSA-C.C. art. 2046 (former C.C. arts. 13, 1945). However, when the terms of a contract are susceptible to more than one interpretation, it is ambiguous, and parol evidence may be used to show the true intent of the parties. LSA-C.C. art. 2045, *et seq.; Dixie Campers, Inc. v. Vesely Co.,* 398 So.2d 1087 (La.1981); *Carter v. BRMAP,* 591 So.2d 1184 (La. App. 1st Cir.1992). Words susceptible of different meanings must be interpreted as having the meaning that best conforms to the object of the contract. LSA-C.C. art. 2048 (former C.C. art. 1952).

[8] Whether a contract is ambiguous or not is a question of law. *Carter v. BRMAP, supra.; Borden, Inc. v. Gulf States Utilities Co.,* 543 So.2d 924 (La.App. 1st Cir.1989), *writ den.,* 545 So.2d 1041 (La.1989). When a contract is to be interpreted by the court as a matter of law, a motion for summary judgment is the proper procedural vehicle to present the question to the court. *Carter v. BRMAP, supra.* Appellate review of the question(s) of law, is simply whether the trial court's interpretive decision is legally correct. *O'Neill v. Louisiana Power & Light Co.,* 558 So.2d 1235 (La.App. 1st Cir.1990).

[9] The McCrorys urge the trial court erred by determining that the contract they have sued upon limits Terminix's liability for property damage to $5,000. We disagree. The terms of this liability provision, taken as a whole, are not susceptible to more than one interpretation. The rule of strict construction does not authorize perversion of a contract's language or the creation of ambiguity where none exists. *Ransom v. Camcraft, Inc.,* 580 So.2d 1073 (La.App. 4th Cir.1991). The contract's provisions clearly and explicitly suggest that in the event of new subterranean termite infestation, Terminix's maximum liability for property damage, structure and/or contents repairs, is limited to $5,000.

[10] When the McCrorys purchased Fowler's residence and assumed the terms of his termite protection contract, they became bound by its terms. See LSA-C.C. arts. 1764, 1765, 1821 *et seq.* The contract became the law between them. The McCrorys cannot be given relief merely because they assumed a bad and/or outdated bargain. *Groom v. W.H. Ward Lumber Co., Inc.,* 432 So.2d 984 (La.App. 1st Cir.1983); *Louisiana Power & Light Co. v. Mecom,* 357 So.2d 596 (La.App. 1st Cir.1978). Hence, the McCrorys' initial claim of error is without merit.

[11] As the parties' contract is clear and unambiguous, there is no need to go outside the document to discover the parties' intent. *American Waste and Pollution Control Co. v. Jefferson Davis Parish Sanitary Landfill Com'sn,* 578 So.2d 541 (La. App. 3d Cir.1991), *writ den.,* 581 So.2d 694 (La.1991). The McCrorys are not entitled to present extrinsic, parol evidence on the issue of intent. It is therefore not

consequential that their neighbor has a termite protection contract with Terminix, dated 1968, providing property damage liability limits of $25,000. The letter of the McCrorys' contract clause cannot be disregarded under the pretext of pursuing its spirit. LSA-C.C. art. 2046, comment b (former C.C. arts. 13 and 1945(3)); *O'Neill v. Louisiana Power & Light Co., supra.* Thus, the McCrorys' second claim of error is also without merit.

[....]

Questions

1. Paragraphs 1–11: Clearly identify the number of parties and kinds of parties involved in this case. Identify the legal or types of relationships, if any, between these parties: are they legal, contractual, delictual, etc.? Identify the kinds of obligations that were created: are they personal or heritable? Is this form of identification of obligations important? How many relationships can you come up with and how do they relate to one another, particularly if they are contractual in nature? Is there any type of relationship between the contract of sale of the house and the contract for services between the seller and Terminix? Is there any direct relationship between the buyer and Terminix? In the negative, how could a relationship between the buyer and Terminix be created? Are the dates of these relationships somewhat or very relevant? Remember the principles which govern contracts; how do they apply here?

2. Paragraphs 7–9: Which rules of interpretation of contracts are relied on here? Remember the previous questions on the number of legal relationships existing here and the types of these relationships; do you see, now, any justification for asking the above preliminary questions?

3. Paragraphs 10–11: The Court uses the verb "assumed" (after "purchased") in paragraph 10 and refers to Louisiana Civil Code articles 1765 & 1821, *et seq.* Are the two sets of articles intimately tied together? Are they stating one and the same thing? If assumption there is, what type of assumption took place? Notice that the Court does not name the type of assumption that occurred in this case, whereas the Louisiana Civil Code mentions two types of assumptions: so?

Linda Brown
v.
Connecticut General Life Insurance Company, ABC Contractor, and DEF Architect

Court of Appeal of Louisiana
Fourth Circuit
March 7, 2001
793 So.2d 211

LOVE, Judge.

[. . . .]

Facts And Procedural History

[1] Linda Brown ("Ms. Brown") was employed by Mervyn's Department Store of California, Inc. ("Mervyn's"), located in the Lake Forest Shopping Center in New Orleans, Louisiana. On November 14, 1994, while in the course and scope of her employment, Ms. Brown fell down a flight of stairs. Ms. Brown filed a claim against Mervyn's under the Louisiana Worker's Compensation Act, seeking payment for medical treatment and weekly indemnity benefits.

[2] As a result of her worker's compensation claim, Mervyn's paid Ms. Brown compensation benefits and medical expenses in the amount of twenty-six thousand eight hundred twenty-four dollars and twenty-six cents ($26,824.26).

[3] On September 1, 1995, Ms. Brown filed a petition for damages against CIGNA Corporation, which is the owner of the land leased by Mervyn's, Audubon Construction Company and Sizeler Architects. In response to the lawsuit, on September 29, 1997, CIGNA Corporation filed a Third Party Demand against Mervyn's alleging that in the lease agreement, Mervyn's agreed to defend and indemnify CIGNA against claims such as Ms. Brown's.

[4] On or about May 7, 1998, Mervyn's filed a Motion for Summary Judgment alleging that CIGNA's Third Party Demand should be dismissed because as Ms. Brown's employer, Mervyn's is statutorily immune from suit under LSA-R.S. 23:1032.

[. . . .]

Discussion

[5] In this appeal, the defendant argues that Louisiana's Worker's Compensation statute, La. R.S. 23:1032, bars the claim filed by CIGNA. In response, CIGNA argues that, although La. R.S. 23:1032 does provide statutory immunity from tort claims filed by an employee for on the job injuries, the statute does not preclude an employer from contractually agreeing to indemnify another party for claims brought by employees.

[6] In part, Louisiana's worker's compensation statute, La. R.S. 23:1032, provides as follows:

A. (1)(a) Except for intentional acts provided for in Subsection B, the rights and remedies herein granted to an employee or his dependent on account of an injury, or compensable sickness or disease for which he is entitled to compensation under this Chapter, shall be exclusive of all other rights, remedies and claims for damages, including but not limited to punitive or exemplary damages, unless such rights, remedies and damages are created by a statute, whether now existing or created in the future, expressly establishing same as available to such employee, his personal representatives, dependents, or relations, as against his employer, or any principal or any officer, director, stockholder, partner or employee of such employer or principal for said injury, or compensable sickness or disease.

(b) The exclusive remedy is exclusive of all claims, including any claims that might arise against his employer, or any principal or any officer, director, stockholder, partner or employee of such employer or principal under any dual capacity theory or doctrine.

[7] In applying La. R.S. 23:1032, Louisiana case law is clear that an employee may not sue his employer in tort for non-intentional injuries sustained during the course and scope of employment. [. . . .]

[8] In this case, pursuant to the terms of the lease, the employer/lessee agreed to indemnify the building owner/lessor for any claims due to defects on the property. In Louisiana, the general rule is that the owner/lessor bears responsibility for the condition of the leased premises. See *La. Civ.Code Ann., Arts. 2695, 2317, 2322*; *Roberts*, 610 So.2d at 1100. However, the Louisiana legislature enacted an exception to this rule, which enables the lessee to assume responsibility for the condition of the premises in the lease contract. *La. R.S. 9: 3221*; *Mendoza v. Seidenbach*, 598 So.2d 404, 405 (La.App. 4 Cir. 3/31/92); *Dorion v. Eleven Eleven Building*, 98-3018 (La.App. 4 Cir. 5/12/99), 737 So.2d 878. Specifically, La. R.S. 9:3221 provides:

The owner of premises leased under a contract whereby the lessee assumes responsibility for their condition is not liable for injury caused by any defect therein to the lessee or anyone on the premises who derives his right to be thereon from the lessee, unless the owner knew or should have known of the defect or had received notice thereof and failed to remedy it within a reasonable time.

[9] The issue that this Court must decide is, when an employee is injured in the course and scope of employment and asserts a worker's compensation claim against his employer, is his employer immune from all other liability arising out of such injuries, even if the employer has agreed to indemnify the owner/lessor of the employment premises.

[10] This Court addressed this precise issue in *Norfleet v. Jackson Brewing Market, Inc.*, 99-1949 (La.App. 4 Cir. 11/17/99), 748 So.2d 525. In *Norfleet* an employee was injured during the scope of her employment, due to alleged dangerous conditions on leased premises. The employee brought a personal injury action against

the owner of the property from whom the employer leased the premises. In turn, the property owner and its liability insurer filed a third party demand against the employer and the employer's liability insurer, seeking indemnity pursuant to the terms of the lease. Thereafter, the employer filed an exception of no cause of action against the third-party demand, arguing that under worker's compensation laws, it was statutorily immune against non-intentional tort claims of its employee. The trial court granted the employer's exception of no cause of action. However, on application for supervisory writ, this Court reversed the trial court and found that the petition did state a cause of action.

[11] In the writ application, the employer argued that if forced to indemnify the building owner, then he was being held "indirectly" liable for the non-intentional tort claims of his employee that he could not be held directly liable for under worker's compensation laws. *Norfleet*, 748 So.2d at 526. In response to this argument, this Court stated:

> Perhaps it is true in a sense, but the short answer to this argument is that Premier Concepts contractually agreed to such "indirect" liability in its lease with Jackson Brewery. In other words, having voluntarily obligated itself to indemnify Jackson Brewery, Premier Concepts cannot renege upon that obligation to Jackson Brewery simply because the claim against Jackson Brewery was made by a Premier Concepts employee. *The exclusive remedy provision of the worker's compensation laws, which regulate liability as between employer and employee, do not strip Jackson Brewery, a stranger to the employment relation of Premier Concepts and Norfleet of its contracted-for right to indemnify.* [Emphasis added]

Id. at 526.

[12] Similarly, in this case, Mervyn's contractually assumed responsibility for liability resulting from defects in the leased premises. In Louisiana, parties may contract for any lawful cause. *La. Civ.Code art. 1971.* This provided, Louisiana courts have held that an employer is not prohibited from entering into an indemnification agreement with a potential third party tortfeasor, such as a lessor. See *Miller v. Louisiana Gas Serv. Co.*, 95-874 (La.App. 5 Cir. 6/25/96) 680 So.2d 52, 55; *Berninger v. Georgia-Pacific Corp.*, 582 So.2d 266, 267 (La.App. 1 Cir.1991). Thus, there is no Louisiana statute which prohibits the indemnification agreement entered into between Mervyn's and the building owner. As such, the indemnification provision contained in the lease contract is lawful. See *La.Civ.Code art. 1971.*

[13] Additionally, it is well settled that the provisions of a lease can affect third parties and govern the rights between the parties. See *Roberts*, 610 So.2d at 1100. Consequently, the lease agreement constitutes the law between the parties. See *K & M Ent. Slaughter, Inc. v. Pennington*, 99-0930 (La.App. 1 Cir. 5/12/00, 764 So.2d 1089), *writ denied*, 766 So.2d 548 (La.2000). Therefore, in this case, the lease contract dictates the rights between Mervyn's, the building owner and third parties. In the lease contract, Mervyn's agreed to indemnify and defend the building owner for all

claims filed by third parties injured on the leased premises. As the Court in *Norfleet* determined, Mervyn's cannot relinquish this obligation solely because the third party who made the claim against the building owner happened to be a Mervyn's employee. See *Id.*, 748 So.2d at 526. Admittedly, the indemnification agreement contained in the lease exposes Mervyn's to liability in excess of its' [*sic*] worker's compensation obligation. However, as in *Norfleet*, since Mervyn's voluntarily agreed to this arrangement, it is bound to honor this commitment.

[. . . .]

Questions

1. Go through the same general questions asked in Question 1 under the previous case, *McRory v. Terminix Service Co., Inc.*

2. In the *McCrory* case, a principal contract of sale had been entered into; in this case, what was the name of the contract (if any) between CIGNA and Mervyn's Department Store? Read the relevant Louisiana Civil Code articles, particularly articles 2696, *et seq.* What kinds of obligations are created by this kind of contract? What are the sources of liability of both the lessee, Mervyn's Store, and the lessor, CIGNA? If, under the law (Louisiana Civil Code articles and Louisiana Revised Statutes), delictual liability cannot be waived, can contractual liability be waived or limited? *See* La. Civ. Code art. 2004. In this case again, the Court lays down one very important principle of the law of contract: can you identify it? How is this principle relevant to the outcome of the case? The Court writes that "Mervyn's contractually assumed responsibility for liability resulting from defects in the leased premises." What kind of contractual assumption is the Court referring to? Are the conditions for this kind of assumption, as listed in the Louisiana Civil Code, met in this case?

Section II — Payment with or without Subrogation

Louisiana Sources of Law

Louisiana Civil Code

Art. 1825. Definition.

Subrogation is the substitution of one person to the rights of another. It may be conventional or legal. (Acts 1984, No. 331, § 1, eff. Jan. 1, 1985.)

Art. 1826. Effects.

A. When subrogation results from a person's performance of the obligation of another, that obligation subsists in favor of the person who performed it who may avail himself of the action and security of the original obligee against the obligor, but is extinguished for the original obligee.

B. An original obligee who has been paid only in part may exercise his right for the balance of the debt in preference to the new obligee. This right shall not be waived or altered if the original obligation arose from injuries sustained or loss occasioned by the original obligee as a result of the negligence or intentional conduct of the original obligor. (Acts 1984, No. 331, §1, eff. Jan. 1, 1985; Acts 2001, No. 305, §1.)

Art. 1827. Conventional subrogation by the obligee.

An obligee who receives performance from a third person may subrogate that person to the rights of the obligee, even without the obligor's consent. That subrogation is subject to the rules governing the assignment of rights. (Acts 1984, No. 331, §1, eff. Jan. 1, 1985.)

Art. 1828. Conventional subrogation by the obligor.

An obligor who pays a debt with money or other fungible things borrowed for that purpose may subrogate the lender to the rights of the obligee, even without the obligee's consent.

The agreement for subrogation must be made in writing expressing that the purpose of the loan is to pay the debt. (Acts 1984, No. 331, §1, eff. Jan. 1, 1985.)

Art. 1829. Subrogation by operation of law.

Subrogation takes place by operation of law:

(1) In favor of an obligee who pays another obligee whose right is preferred to his because of a privilege, pledge, mortgage, or security interest;

(2) In favor of a purchaser of movable or immovable property who uses the purchase money to pay creditors holding any privilege, pledge, mortgage, or security interest on the property;

(3) In favor of an obligor who pays a debt he owes with others or for others and who has recourse against those others as a result of the payment;

(4) In favor of a successor who pays estate debts with his own funds; and

(5) In the other cases provided by law. (Acts 1984, No. 331, §1, eff. Jan. 1, 1985; Acts 1989, No. 137, §16, eff. Sept. 1, 1989; Acts 2001, No. 572, §1.)

Art. 1830. Effects of legal subrogation.

When subrogation takes place by operation of law, the new obligee may recover from the obligor only to the extent of the performance rendered to the original obligee. The new obligee may not recover more by invoking conventional subrogation. (Acts 1984, No. 331, §1, eff. Jan. 1, 1985.)

Doctrine[1]

Louisiana Law of Obligations in General, A Précis

Sections 5.2.1 to 5.2.3

Concept of Subrogation

Article 1825 of the Civil Code defines subrogation in these terms: "**Subrogation is the substitution of one person to the rights of another. It may be conventional or legal.**"

Subrogation can then be described as a legal device meant to cause a person to be placed in the shoes of another. A legal fiction is thus created whereby an obligation is declared to survive in a person other than the original party and despite the performance of the original obligation. This is why "subrogation" amounts to the transfer of an obligation. For example, an obligee-creditor called subrogee-solvens (**subrogee** because he is subrogated and **solvens** because he has performed an obligation) can be substituted to another creditor, the original obligee-accipiens, (**accipiens** because he has received the benefit of the performance of an obligation), so that the obligor is now indebted to the subrogee-solvens who extinguished the obligation owed the accipiens by performing in the place of the original obligor. Subrogation is, therefore, both a mode of extinction of an obligation and a method of transfer of that same obligation. [. . . .]

The *raison d'être* and justification for this concept of subrogation are to be found in the shifting of the rights of action available to an obligee-accipiens to the benefit of the subrogee-solvens against the obligor. Whenever a third person pays the debt of another, unless that third person was motivated by a gratuitous intent (*animus donandi*) and meant, therefore, to make a gift to the obligor by extinguishing his debt, the third person will have a right of action for reimbursement against the obligor. [. . . .]

Article 1825 of the civil Code states that "**Subrogation is the substitution of one person to the rights of another. It may be conventional or legal.**" [. . . .]

A conventional subrogation can result from a contract between the obligee-accipiens and the third person-solvens. Such a conventional subrogation granted by the obligee or creditor is known as *ex parte creditoris* (on the part of the creditor). The second type of conventional subrogation can be the outcome of a contract between the obligor-debtor and the third person; in this case the subrogation is described as *ex parte debitoris* (on the part of the debtor). [. . . .]

---

1. The authors of this casebook, and the civil law doctrine in general, have views on the topic of "subrogation" that are substantially different, even contrary, to the views expressed in the "Revision Comments" that follow Code article 1825, as exemplified in the Thomson Reuters edition of the La. Civ. C. For that reason, we have given here doctrinal views of our own.

Article 1827 [. . . .] : "An obligee who receives performance from a third person may subrogate that person to the rights of the obligee, even without the obligor's consent. That subrogation is subject to the rules governing the assignment of rights." [. . . .]

Article 1828 [. . .] "An obligor who pays a debt with money or other fungible things borrowed for that purpose may subrogate the lender to the rights of the obligee, even without the obligee's consent.

The agreement for subrogation must be made in writing expressing that the purpose of the loan is to pay the debt." [. . . .]

Article 1829 of the civil Code lists four specific instances of subrogation by operation of law and adds a fifth catch all category. [. . . .]

There are two essential effects attached to a payment with subrogation: a) a transfer of the obligee-creditor's right to the third person-solvens and b) limitations on the extent of that right. [. . . .]

According to civil Code **Article 1826**, the **"obligation subsists in favor of the person who performed it who may avail himself of the action against the obligor and security on the assets of the same obligor that the original obligee had against the obligor. . . ."** Thus the action and the security as a whole are transferred with their particular modalities be they a term, a condition etc. [. . . .]

The second paragraph of civil Code **Article 1826** states, in part, that: **"B. An original obligee who has been paid only in part may exercise his right for the balance of the debt in preference to the new obligee. . . ."** It follows that subrogation takes place only up to the amount of the debt paid by the third person-subrogated solvens to the original obligee in discharge of the obligation of the obligor. [. . . .]

This same limitation applicable to conventional subrogation governs also subrogation by operation of law as stated in **Article 1830: "When subrogation takes place by operation of law, the new obligee may recover from the obligor only to the extent of the performance rendered to the original obligee. The new obligee may not recover more by invoking conventional subrogation."**

Louisiana Law of Obligations in General, A Treatise

Section 5.2.2

Conventional Subrogation

1. Conventional Subrogation by the Creditor (Ex Parte Creditoris)

263. Timing issues. The question which necessarily arises is the following: at which point in time in the relationship between the *obligee-accipens* and the *third party-solvens* can or must subrogation be granted?

[. . . .] What is of paramount importance in the performance of an obligation susceptible of conventional subrogation is that it is the payment or the performance which extinguishes the obligation and which becomes the *raison d'être*, the justification, of the subrogation. Indeed, under the La. Civ. Code **arts. 1826** *et seq.*, in itself and by itself *subrogation* cannot exist without a support on which it can rest, that support being the obligation itself. Subrogation exists because it is an accessory right brought into existence by the payment or the performance of an obligation. There is no reason to be "substituted" into the rights of an obligee-creditor unless that obligee-creditor is willing to consent to the substitution or subrogation because she has received some satisfaction or benefit, i.e., the payment or performance of the obligation of which she is the obligee. Logic and reason dictate, therefore, that subrogation <u>cannot take place before the performance</u> or payment of the obligation does occur, since subrogation would lack the necessary support or *raison d'être* for its existence [...]. [....]

A conventional subrogation <u>should not be available</u> to a *third person-solvens* at a point in time <u>after that</u> *third person solvens* <u>has performed the obligation</u>. The reason is that once the obligation has been performed or paid, no debt exists any longer and there are no rights remaining into which the *third person solvens* could be subrogated. The *obligee-accipens* can no longer subrogate someone into something, an obligation, that has been extinguished and, therefore, no longer exists. [....]

With respect to this particular requirement of the timing between the subrogation and the performance of an obligation, we disagree with a Comment given in the West edition of the Civil Code. This Comment, under **Code art. 1827**, states: "Under this Article, the agreement for subrogation may be made at any time."[73] Such a suggestion, we believe, is nonsensical, illogical and unfounded because it fails to pay due consideration to the relationship between the "obligation" on the one hand, and "subrogation" on the other hand. [....]

2. Conventional Subrogation by the Obligor (Ex Parte Debitoris)

265. La. Civ. Code art. 1828. La. Civ. Code **art. 1828** describes this type of subrogation as follows: "**An obligor who pays a debt with money or other fungible things borrowed for that purpose may subrogate the lender to the rights of the obligee, even without the obligee's consent.**

The agreement for subrogation must be made in writing expressing that the purpose of the loan is to pay the debt."

The validity of this type of conventional subrogation, because of its unusual nature, is subject to some stringent requirements.

266. Formality. Because of the far-reaching consequences of this type of subrogation which, actually, allows an obligor to dispose of a credit-claim or right which belongs to his obligee and to transfer that credit-claim or right into the patrimony of the third person-solvens, it is reasonable to subject it to a formality. The reason

---

73. La. Civ. Code art. 1827, Comment (f).

is that the obligor himself removes a right, a claim or credit from his obligee's patrimony to transfer it into the patrimony of a third person, the third party-solvens. [. . . .]

267. Express. This transaction between the third party-solvens and the obligor who transfers to the former the benefit of subrogation into the rights of the obligee-accipiens, (a third party to that transfer) amounts to that third party-solvens, first, making a loan to the obligor of the amount he paid to the obligee and, second, seeking to be subrogated by the obligor into the rights of the obligee as a sort of security device. It follows that this subrogation must, in addition to being in writing, also stipulate expressly that the purpose or "cause," or "reason" for the loan made by the third person was to pay off the obligor's debt.[83] [. . . .]

Legal Subrogation or Subrogation by Operation of Law

269. La. Civ. Code art. 1829. La. Civ. Code **art. 1829** lists four specific instances of subrogation by operation of law and adds a fifth "catch-all" category.[84] With this fifth category a major problem that existed under the Civil Code of 1870 has been resolved. Under the previous Code article 2161[85] there was no such general provision. The problem was, then, one of determining the scope of application of the article by interpreting it as being either exclusive or illustrative of any other instance of subrogation by operation of law. The new version of the article, La. Civ. Code **art. 1829**, now solves the issue.

Cases

Standard Motor Car Company et al.
v.
State Farm Mutual Automobile Insurance Company

Court of Appeal of Louisiana
First Circuit
October 4, 1957
97 So.2d 435

[See this case in PART THREE: QUASI-CONTRACTS.]

---

83. La. Civ. Code art. 1828-2.
84. La. Civ. Code art. 1829. . . .
85. La. Civ. Code of 1870, art. 2161.

St. Paul Fire & Marine Insurance Company
v.
Verry Gallien et al.

Court of Appeal of Louisiana
First Circuit
April 27, 1959
111 So.2d 571

LANDRY, Judge ad hoc.

[1] Plaintiff, St. Paul Fire and Marine Insurance Company, subrogee of its assured Willard L. Calloway, has taken this appeal from the judgment of the lower court rejecting plaintiff's demand against said assured Calloway and one Verry Gallien for the sum of $597.50 paid Calloway pursuant to a policy of collision insurance covering a 1954 Plymouth Tudor automobile belonging to Calloway and which said vehicle was totally destroyed in a collision with a 1956 Ford pickup truck owned and being operated by Gallien. The accident in question occurred March 1, 1957.

[2] Following said accident, plaintiff insurance company, on March 25, 1957, paid its assured Calloway the sum of $597.50 (the value thereof less an amount obtained for its salvage and the sum of $50 deducted from its value according to the policy provisions), and obtained from its said assured a subrogation agreement wherein Calloway subrogated plaintiff to all his rights against the third party, Gallien.

[3] Subsequent to signing the subrogation agreement in favor of plaintiff, Calloway granted Gallien a release on a form provided by the Department of Public Safety, Responsibility Division, State of Louisiana, discharging Gallien from responsibility for all claims arising from said accident, said release from Calloway to Gallien being dated April 19, 1957.

[4] Plaintiff's claim against the third party Gallien is predicated on the theory that the release from Calloway is null and void considering Calloway had previously subrogated plaintiff to all his rights against Gallien and Gallien's negligence being the sole cause of the accident, plaintiff is entitled to recover from him the amount paid plaintiff's assured Calloway.

[5] As against its assured Calloway, plaintiff's demand is founded on the principle that the subrogation agreement executed by Calloway prohibits his releasing from liability anyone who may be responsible in damages for destruction of the insured vehicle and, granting of such discharge by Calloway constitutes an active breach of plaintiff's antedated subrogation contract thereby conferring upon plaintiff the right to recover from Calloway the amount paid him.

[. . . .]

[6] The law of our state relative to subrogation is found in Articles 2159–2162 L.S.A. Revised Civil Code. The term subrogation has been defined by the courts of this state as the right of a person secondarily liable for a debt or obligation which he is

compelled to discharge, to assume all the rights of the principal creditor against a third party who may be legally responsible for the amount paid. Motors Insurance Corporation v. Employers' Liability Assurance Corporation, La.App., 52 So.2d 311.

[7] Although it possesses some attributes and characteristics of a sale, an act of subrogation is not a sale, transfer or assignment but rather a substitution of one claimant for another. As between an insurer and its assured, subrogation takes place by operation of law in those instances in which the insurer pays its assured a sum of money pursuant to a policy covering damages to property of the assured. Motors Insurance Corporation v. Employers' Liability Assurance Corporation, supra.

[8] Travelers Fire Ins. Co. v. Ackel, 29 So.2d 617 (relied upon by the court below) was decided by the Court of Appeal, Second Circuit, and held that a release granted by an assured to a third party prior to execution of an act of subrogation to his insurer, operates as a valid cancellation and discharge of all rights which the assured possessed against the third party thereby extinguishing the obligation of the third party to both insurer and assured. This case further held that an assured who executes a release to a third party prior to subrogating his rights to his insurer, violates his contractual obligation to the insurer thereby rendering the assured liable to the insurer for any amount paid.

[9] For reasons hereinafter set forth, we deem it unnecessary to consider either the applicability of the Ackel case, supra, or the validity of the release herein relied upon by plaintiff as the basis of its suit against its assured Calloway.

[10] The purpose of a contract of subrogation is to afford the subrogee the opportunity of a day in court to seek recovery from the third party allegedly answerable for such loss as the subrogee has been called upon to pay. Under the terms of the policy issued Calloway and the subrogation agreement received from him, plaintiff acquired the right and privilege of seeking reimbursement from Gallien of the amount paid Calloway. Among the rights thus acquired by plaintiff was that of instituting legal action against Gallien to seek to establish his liability to plaintiff for the amount plaintiff has been compelled to pay its assured Calloway.

[11] A determination of this case does not require decision on the issue of whether the release by Calloway constituted an active breach of his contractual obligation to plaintiff. Assuming arguendo the release to Gallien was valid (an issue upon which we refrain from ruling herein), plaintiff has in no way been aggrieved thereby considering Gallien has not urged said release as a defense to plaintiff's claim against him.

[12] In the case at bar, both the assured and third party were sued in a single action. The third party, Gallien, has not resisted plaintiff's demand against him despite his holding a release from plaintiff's assured. Said third party has not offered or urged the release in opposition to plaintiff's claim. No substantive or procedural right of plaintiff arising from the policy and subrogation agreement between plaintiff and its assured has been denied or adversely affected in any manner whatsoever.

[. . . .]

Questions

1. Paragraphs 1–7: What type of subrogation was created between the insured Calloway and its insurer St. Paul? Was that subrogation conditioned upon the occurrence of some event or was it always vested in the insurer regardless of any prior event occurring (*see*, in this respect, paragraph 6)? Under the collision insurance contract, since the insurer St. Paul was bound to pay its insured, Calloway, isn't the insurer paying the debt of another, the tortfeasor, Gallien? If that is the case, how are St. Paul and Gallien bound together, if at all? Could that relationship fit under any one of the five instances of "subrogation by operation of law," per Louisiana Civil Code article 1829 (*see* paragraph 7)? What important legal consequences would flow from this legal subrogation? What impact would it have on the release? What particular type of a legal or contractual relationship does the insurance contract create between the insured and its insurer? How are these two parties bound *vis-à-vis* a tortfeasor? Can one party do whatever it wants without thinking about the other party's rights?

2. Paragraphs 6–10: Do these two paragraphs answer some of the questions asked above? Do you understand the true meaning of subrogation, as distinguished from an assignment of rights, for example? *See* La. Civ. Code arts. 2642–2654.

Pringle-Associated Mortgage Corporation
v.
Ernest R. Eanes, Jr., et al.
Supreme Court of Louisiana
February 24, 1969
226 So.2d 502

On Rehearing

SANDERS, Justice.

[1] Because of the importance of this case, we granted a rehearing to reconsider the following question: Is a subcontractor who pays wages to his employees as they become due for labor on a building project subrogated under Article 2161 of the Louisiana Civil Code to the superior privilege granted laborers by LSA-R.S. 9:4801 and LSA-R.S. 9:4812?

[2] The facts are clearly and completely stated in our original opinion, and we condense them here: In 1965, Ernest R. Eanes, Jr. purchased a lot in East Baton Rouge Parish, for the purpose of subdividing the property and constructing apartment buildings. To secure funds for the construction, Eanes executed a promissory note for $335,000 in favor of plaintiff mortgage corporation, secured by a collateral mortgage affecting the land upon which the development project was to be erected. Eanes also entered into an agreement with Buddy Eanes Homebuilders, Incorporated, of which he was president, to construct apartments on the mortgaged property.

Pursuant to this agreement, Buddy Eanes Homebuilders let variou [*sic*] subcontractors to other firms to supply the labor and material necessary for construction. Although it did considerable work, Buddy Eanes Homebuilders defaulted as prime contractor. At the time of the default, plaintiff had advanced Eanes $263,615.70 for the project.

[3] On April 20, 1966 plaintiff sued Eanes in this proceeding on his promissory note and was awarded judgment for the amount then due. A writ of fieri facias issued under which the property subject to the collateral mortgage was seized and sold and, on June 8, 1966, plaintiff purchased the property at the sheriff's sale. This sale was made subject to certain previously recorded privileges.

[4] Now competing with the mortgage holder, the claimants to these privileges are Livingston Roofing & Sheet Metal Company, Inc. for $2,961.74, representing wages paid by it for labor; J. R. McFarland, d/b/a United Masonry Company, for $5,606.86, representing wages paid to his employees ($3,214.24) and wages of $2,396.62 for labor personally performed by McFarland, as subcontractor of the masonry work involved; and Capitol Detective Agency, Inc. for $1,446.26, representing salaries paid two night watchmen who were assigned to protect the project during its construction.

[5] The parties concede that no laborer, except McFarland, filed a lien or privilege, but the subcontractors timely filed a claim for the privilege of their laborers.

[6] The Court of Appeal, rejecting the subcontractors' right of subrogation under Article 2161, LSA-C.C., held plaintiff's mortgage primed all liens filed by the subcontractors, except the lien for labor personally performed by J. R. McFarland for $2,396.62. On original hearing, we upheld the subcontractors' right of subrogation under our decision in Tilly v. Bauman, 174 La. 71, 139 So. 762 (1932), and reversed the holding of the Court of Appeal.

[7] Subrogation is an ancient concept, having its origin in Roman law. It was more fully developed and refined in France and became part of the Code Napoleon of 1804.[1] The Louisiana Civil Code Articles on this subject are almost identical to the corresponding articles of the French Civil Code. See Comment, 25 Tul.L.Rev. 358, 359.

[8] As to legal subrogation, Article 2161 of the Louisiana Civil Code provides:

'Art. 2161. Subrogation takes place of right:

'1. For the benefit of him who, being himself a creditor, pays another creditor, whose claim is preferable to his by reason of his privileges or mortgages. * * *

'3. For the benefit of him who, being bound with others, or for others, for the payment of the debt, had an interest in discharging it.'

---

1. Arts. 1249–1252.

[9] The foregoing article enumerates exceptions to the general rule of Article 2134, that when a third person pays the debt of another, no subrogation takes place and the debt is extinguished. Under familiar principles of statutory construction, these exceptions should be strictly construed. Succession of Andrews, La.App., 153 So.2d 470, cert. denied 244 La. 1005, 156 So.2d 57; 50 Am.Jur., Statutes, s 431, pp. 451–452; 82 C.J.S. Statutes s 382, pp. 891–894.

[10] Subparagraph 1 of Article 2161 declares that subrogation takes place 'for the benefit of him who, being himself a creditor, pays another creditor, whose claim is preferable to his by reason of his privileges or mortgages.'

[11] The subcontractors in the present case, of course, are creditors of the prime contractor, Buddy Eanes Homebuilders, and we can assume they are creditors of the owner. For subrogation to occur, however, the laborers must also be creditors of the owner at the time their wages are paid.

[. . . .]

[12] Since the laborers had no contractual relation with the owner, they can be the owner's creditors only if they are accorded that status by the foregoing statute. The statute provides, however, that a laborer shall have a personal right of action against the owner 'from the filing of his claim.' Until the laborer files this claim, he never achieves the status of creditor. At best, he has only an inchoate right to become a creditor of the owner. Concededly, the laborers in the present case never filed an affidavit under the statute; their employers, the subcontractors, paid their wages as they became due. Hence, the laborers cannot be considered creditors of the owner to fulfil the conditions of subrogation.

[13] Another equally valid principle bars application of the first Subparagraph of Article 2161. No subrogation takes place under this provision when the creditor and potential subrogee acquits a debt for which he is primarily liable.

[. . . .]

[14] The modern French authorities support this principle. See 2 Aubry and Rau, Obligations, s 321, pp. 187, 203 (English Translation by the Louisiana State Law Institute, 1965); 2 Planiol Civil Law Treatise, No. 491, Footnote 27, p. 278 (English Translation by the Louisiana State Law Institute, 1959); 2 Baudry-Lacantinerie, Obligations, s 1560, pp. 670–671 (3d ed. 1907).

[15] The basic theory of this type of subrogation is that payment must be made by another creditor for the beneit [*sic*] of the debtor. When such a payment is made, the debtor is not liberated. Instead, the credit paid is in effect transmitted to the paying creditor, who assumes the preferred status of the creditor who has been paid. A creditor who pays his own debt has done no more than he was obligated to do. He has given nothing for the benefit of the debtor. Hence, subrogation is normally disallowed.

[16] To permit the subcontractors to invoke legal subrogation for the payment of their employees' wages would in effect award them a first ranking privilege for their own credit against the owner.

[17] We conclude subrogation must be rejected under Subparagrah 1 of Article 2161.

[18] The subcontractors maintain, however, they fulfil all requirements for subrogation under Subparagraph 3, declaring that subrogation takes place of right in favor of him, who 'being bound with others' pays the debt that he had an interest in discharging.

[19] Clearly this language presupposes the existence of a solidary obligation. If no solidary obligation exists, subrogation does not take place.

[20] In denying subrogation under this clause, the Court of Appeal held:

> '(T)he subcontractors and owners were not and indeed could not have been solidarily liable to the laborers whose claims are herein asserted. Under the circumstances herein the owner was never liable to the laborers as no liens were filed by any party occupying such status. Under the lien law, no liability arises on the part of the owner until the lien is recorded. Since the owner was never liable to the laborers, it necessarily follows he was not liable for such wages, solidarily or otherwise, with those priamrily [*sic*] obligated for the wages earned.

> 'In the instant case when the subcontractors herein involved paid the wages for which they now claim subrogation, said subcontractors were the sole debtors and prime obligors of the laborers concerned.'

[21] After reconsideration, we conclude the Court of Appeal correctly disposed of this issue. It is now apparent we erred in holding the owner became a debtor of the laborers 'as soon as the services are performed.' As we have demonstrated, the personal liability of the owner comes into existence only when laborers file their claim. Since the owner was no debtor, there can be no solidary obligation.

[. . . .]

[22] We hold, as did the Court of Appeal, that subrogation is unavailable to the subcontractors for their wage payments.

[. . . .]

Questions

1. Paragraphs 14–15: Carefully read these two paragraphs. Of particular importance is the statement in paragraph 15: "The basic theory of this type of subrogation (legal subrogation) is that payment must be made by another creditor *for the benefit of the debtor.*" (Emphasis ours.)

2. Paragraphs 16–17: Notice how the Court justifies (explains on legal grounds) its ruling: "subrogation must be rejected" for the reasons here given. Does this case explain the foundation and purpose of subrogation?

Charles W. Cox

v.

W. M. Heroman & Co., Inc., and American Employers Insurance Co.

Supreme Court of Louisiana
June 10, 1974
298 So.2d 848

TATE, Justice.

[1] A subcontractor ('Cox') sues his general contractor ('Heroman') for the balance due on the subcontract. The general contractor claims a credit for a payment made directly by Heroman to a supplier ('Reulet') of the subcontractor. [. . . .]

[2] The issue before us is two fold:

(1) Was Heroman entitled to pay Cox's creditor Reulet directly, over Cox's protect, thus (under Civil Code Article 2134) extinguishing Cox's debt to Reulet as to the extent of the payment and also giving Heroman a right to receive reimbursement of this payment from Cox?;

(2) If Heroman was Not entitled to pay Cox's debt to Reulet, nevertheless was not Heroman (by his payment and express agreement with Reulet) subrogated to recover Reulet's debt against Cox (Article 2159), thus entitling Heroman in the present suit to reduce the balance due by Heroman to Cox under the subcontract to the extent that it is extinguished (through the compensation of two debts, Article 2207) by the subrogated (Reulet) debt due by Cox to Heroman?

Facts

[3] Heroman as general contractor entered into a construction contract with a university in the amount of over five hundred thousand dollars. Heroman and Cox entered into a subcontract by which Cox agreed to perform the electrical work for $37,590.00.

[4] In the course of construction, progess [*sic*] payments were made by Heroman to Cox totalling $27,681.27. (An additional ten percent of the total of the progress estimates was retained by Heroman, in accordance with the subcontract agreement, for payment upon final acceptance.)

[5] As the completion of both the general contract and the subcontract neared, the present controversy arose. Heroman was informed by several suppliers of Cox on the job that Cox had not paid them, and Reulet (Cox's principal supplier) informed Heroman that it would lien the job.

[6] The facts forming the basis of the litigation occurred when on April 14, 1971 Heroman paid Reulet directly $4,349.74 to credit against Cox's debt due Reulet for supplies on the job. This sum was the total balance then due by Heroman to Cox. (It did not include the ten percent retained per the contract.) The payment was

specifically made for the account of Cox due for supplies on the present contract. Cox was sent a carbon copy of the letter by which payment was made.

[7] Prior to this payment of April 14, 1971, Reulet had conferred with Heroman about an unpaid amount of $8,360.55 due for supplies furnished Cox for the contract. Heroman had then sent to Cox a check for $4,439.74, payable to Cox and Reulet jointly. (This was the same amount later paid Reulet directly, being the then total unpaid balance due by Heroman to Cox.)

[8] Cox returned the check to Heroman. He stated that he considered this direct payment improper and unacceptable. He alleged that there were considerable overcharges claimed by Reulet amounting to over twenty-five hundred dollars.[1]

[9] Reulet then wrote Heroman that it would place a lien on the job unless the amount due was paid at this time. Reulet's letter concluded, that, if Heroman would pay the unpaid invoices due by Cox, Heroman 'is subrogated to all rights that we have against Cox in connection with this job and such payment.'[2]

[10] Upon receipt of this letter, Heroman immediately paid Reulet the full balance then due Cox ($4,349.74) by progress estimates, as stated above. Reulet accepted this payment, credited Cox's account, and did not lien the job.

[11] Cox then on April 22, 1974 filed a lien for the unpaid balance due on the job. Correspondence introduced by Cox shows that unsuccessful negotiations were subsequently conducted between Cox, Reulet, and other suppliers in an effort to allocate the remaining amount due by Heroman to Cox to unpaid accounts of Cox resulting from his performance of his subcontract.

[12] On December 27, 1971, Cox filed the present suit against Heroman and its surety (American Employers) to recover $10,016.62, then allegedly due under the contract, together with ten percent statutory attorney fees. The suit alleged that the unpaid balance included the sum of $4,349.74 which had been paid by Heroman to Reulet. In the suit, Cox specifically alleges that he was contesting the total amount claimed by Reulet ($8,360.55) because he estimates 'Reulet overcharges and errors in the amount of $2,500.00' See Art. 9 of petition.

---

1. Cox, in failing circumstances, was at this point claiming that all his suppliers had overcharged him.

2. Reulet's letter to Heroman provides:
    'We enclosed herewith our unpaid invoices for materials purchased by Mr. Cox and installed on the above captioned job. The total amount of these unpaid invoices is $8,360.55. I hereby certify that the amounts shown on these invoices are true and correct.' As we have previously told you, we have been unable to collect the $8,360.55 from Mr. Cox. Accordingly, we have no alternative buy to place a lien on this job unless the amount due us is paid at this time. You have told us that under the circumstances you will pay our unpaid invoices on this job, and this is to acknowledge that *upon receipt of said payment from you, your Company is subrogated to all rights that we have against Cox in connection with this job and such payment.*' (Italics ours.)

[13] Cox alleged that Heroman owed him: $5,448.99 representing the final draw and retainage (which Heroman in its answer conceded owing, except for back charges of $304.45), an alleged add-on due of $107.89 (which both previous courts found not owing), and the $4,349.74 previously paid by Heroman to Reulet.

[14] Heroman's answer pleaded the facts of the dispute, and acknowledged liability for only the final draw and retainage of $5,254.54.

[15] The trial court held that Heroman was not entitled under its contract to pay Reulet, Cox's creditor, directly. It therefore disallowed credit to Heroman for such payment and awarded Cox judgment for that sum, plus the amount due for the final draw and retainage, for a total amount of $9,908.73.[3]

[16] As earlier noted, the court of appeal concluded that the trial court was in error in refusing to allow Heroman credit against Cox's claim for the amount paid by Heroman to extinguish pro tanto Reulet's claim against Cox for supplies furnished for the present job. The court of appeal essentially held that Heroman was entitled to pay the debt due by Cox to Reulet and to be reimbursed by Cox for this payment, by reason of Civil Code Article 2134.[4] See Standard Motor Car Company v. State Farm Mutual Automobile Insurance Co., 97 So.2d 435 (La.App.1st Cir. 1957).

1. 'Payment' under Article 2134

[17] We granted certiorari primarily because of our doubt that, under the circumstances here shown, the debtor Heroman could extinguish a debt due to its creditor Cox by paying, not Cox, but Cox's creditor. We entertained this doubt because: (a) Cox expressly opposed such payment by Heroman of His debt due Reulet; instead, Cox expressly desired to receive amounts due him by Heroman for purposes of negotiating the payment due by him to Reulet in connection with certain disputed items; (b) The subcontract between Heroman and Cox expressly provided for Heroman's remedy, in the event of Cox's non-payment of suppliers on the job, namely, Heroman was to withhold payments due Cox until the grounds for nonpayment were removed.

[18] Article 2134 (quoted in full in Footnote 5) provides that an 'obligation may even be discharged by a third person in no way concerned in it', provided that, 'if he act in his own name, he be not *subrogated* to the rights of the creditor.' (Italics ours.)

---

3. We may say at this point that the questions of the disallowance of the ten percent attorneys fees for nonpayment when due of the subcontract price, and of the $107.89 add-on, as well as of Heroman's claim that the final draw and retainage was subject to a credit for $304.45 back charges, are not before us. The parties apparently accepted the determinations of the previous courts as to them, and they did not and do not seek further review of them.

4. Article 2134 provides:
'An obligation may be discharged by any person concerned in it, such as a coobligor or a surety.' The obligation may even be discharged by a third person no way concerned in it, provided that person act in the name and for the discharge of the debtor, or that, if he act in his own name, he be not subrogated to the rights of the creditor.'

[19] Although not subrogated to the rights of the creditor (such as to receive a stipulated interest or attorney's fees in the event of non-payment), a third person acting in his own name is entitled to be reimbursed by the debtor for the sum used to discharge the latter's debt. See Article 2299; Roman v. Forstall, 11 La.Ann. 717, 720 (1856); Standard Motor Car Company v. State Farm Mutual Automobile Insurance Co., 97 So.2d 435 (La.App.1st Cir. 1975). See also Hutchinson v. Rice, 105 La. 474, 29 So. 898 (1901); Weil v. Enterprise Ginnery & Mfg. Co., 42 La.Ann. 492, 7 So. 622 (1890); Gernon v. McCan, 23 La.Ann. 84 (1871); Nicholls v. His Creditors, 9 Rob. 476 (1845). The creditor cannot even refuse to receive the payment tendered by the third person, State ex rel. John Klein & Co. v. Pilsbury, 29 La.Ann. 787 (1877), unless perhaps the creditor has some special interest in having the obligation fulfilled by the debtor himself, Article 2136.[5]

[20] Articles 2134 and 2136, literal translations of French Civil Code Articles 1236 and 1237, are in accord, as thus interpreted, with traditional civilian obligations theory. 1 Litvinoff on Obligations, Section 27, p. 47, and Section 49 (Louisiana Civil Law Treatise, Vol. 6; 1969); Planiol, Civil Law Treatise, Vol. 2, Section 401 (LSLI translation, 1959); 1 Civil Law Translations (Aubry & Rau, Obligations), Sections 315, 316 (1965).

[21] As summarized in the last-cited translation of Aubry & Rau, at pp. 156–58: 'In general, the creditor cannot refuse payment offered by a third person whether or not interested in the extinction of the obligation . . . A payment made by a third person and accepted by the creditor extinguishes the obligation as definitively as one effected by the debtor personally, Except where the third person is legally or contractually subrogated to the rights of the creditor. In the last case, the debtor is discharged toward the original creditor, but the obligation continues to exist in favor of the third person who has been subrogated thereto.' (The italics are supplied to emphasize a legal distinction between 'payment' under Article 2134 and 'subrogation' under Articles 2159–2161, a distinction which is of decisional importance in this case.)

[22] The right of the third person to pay the creditor in his own name, and the obligation of the creditor to receive such payment for the benefit of the debtor's account, is not unqualified:

---

5. Article 2136 provides in full:
   'The obligation of doing can not be discharged by a third person against the will of the creditor, when it is the interest of the latter that it be fulfilled by the debtor himself.'
This article literally refers to an obligation to Do, as distinguished from an obligation to Give (which includes an obligation to Pay.) Articles 1883, 1905. The French interpretations of French Civil Code Article 1237 (of which Louisiana's Article 2136 is a literal translation) are in disagreement whether the provision permits the creditor to reject Payment as distinguished from Doing tendered by a third person. See 1 Civil Law Translations (Aubry & Rau, Obligations), Section 316 at footnote 2 (1965).

[23] Where, for instance, it is done to harm the debtor's interest, it may be an abuse of the third person's right to make the payment. See Comment, Abuse of Rights in Louisiana, 7 Tul.L.Rev. 426 (1933). Further, when the debtor opposes the payment, some decisions hold that the third person's payment, In the absence of subrogation, cannot be recovered, since the third person cannot conceptually be held to have acted on behalf of the debtor.[6] Woodlief & Legendre v. Moncure, 17 La.Ann. 241 (1865). See also Succession of Mulligan v. Kenny, 34 La.Ann. 50 (1882). See Comment, 7 Tul.L.Rev. 253, 256 (1933). Finally, where the third person and the debtor have a contractual relationship which regulated the former's right to pay the debts due by the debtor to others,[7] this contractual right may limit the third person's right to extinguish such debt due by the debtor to another. See Civil Code Article 1901: 'Agreements entered into have the effects of laws on those who have formed them. * * *.' Cf. Hardin v. Federal Rice Mill Co., 164 La. 49, 113 So. 760 (1927).[8]

[24] Without at this time attempting to determine what weight, if any, shall be accorded to any of these particular factors, it is sufficient for us to hold that, by reason of the totality of circumstances (including the contractual relationship between Heroman and Cox), Heroman did not have the right under Article 2134 to Extinguish Cox's debt to Reulet by directly paying Reulet despite Cox's opposition to such payment.

2. Subrogation under Articles 2159, 2160

[25] This does not end our inquiry, however. Heroman argues that, even though it was not entitled to entinguish [*sic*] Cox's debt and to receive reimbursement under Article 2134, it was by its payment expressly subrogated to recover from Cox this amount paid by it and to receive credit against its liability due Cox under the subcontract. For the reasons to be stated, we find this last contention to be well-founded.

[26] To recapitulate:

On the date of the April 14, 1971 payment, Two debts were involved: (a) that between Heroman and Cox, by which Heroman owed Cox $4,349.74, payable immediately, but subject to Heroman's contractual right to withhold

---

6. Here, however, the principle of unjustified enrichment may permit the third person to recover for benefits received by the person enriched. Police Jury v. Hampton, 5 Mart., N.S., 389 (1827).

7. The subcontract between Heroman and Cox provided that, when the subcontractor (Cox) failed to pay his suppliers on the job as required by the contract, then the general contractor (Heroman) had the right to withhold payments due Cox until Cox paid his suppliers. This might be regarded as a contractual substitution limiting the right of Heroman under Article 2134 to extinguish by direct payment any debt owed by Cox to his suppliers.

8. A rice broker paid the freight-charges on rice shipped by the owner-consignor. The rice had been sold upon the express agreement that the Purchaser would be liable for shipping costs. The broker paid the freight charges and then, when the purchaser became insolvent, sued the seller-consignor. He was denied recovery. Although the consignor-seller was ordinarily primarily liable, under the contract the shipping charges became the debt of the purchaser. Whatever the broker's rights against the purchaser, he was not entitled to recover the shipping charges from the seller because, under the contract, the shipping charges were to be paid otherwise than by it.

payment to Cox until Cox paid his debt due Reulet (see debt B); and (b) Cox's debt due Reulet for supplies received on the Heroman-Cox job, which totalled $8,360.55 by Reulet's invoices, of which amount Cox contested $2,500 as overcharges.

If Heroman's payment to Reulet did not entitle Heroman to extinguish pro tanto Heroman's debt to Cox, then as (at least) of the date of the trial court judgment of June 20, 1972 there are also Two debts at issue in this litigation, both equally liquidated and demandable: (a) the debt due Cox by Heroman in the amount of $9,908.73, being due for the final progress estimate and the retainage; (b) the debt due Heroman by Cox for $4,349.74, Heroman's expressly subrogated right to recover this amount of the debt previously due by Cox to Reulet.

[27] For reasons we will set forth, debt (b) exists as well as debt (a). The debts being equally due and demandable, at least as of the time of the judgment, they are mutually extinguished by the compensation. See Articles 2207–2209.[9]

[28] The subrogated debt of $4,349.74 is due by Cox to Heroman, for the following reasons:

Article 2159 provides: 'Subrogation to the right of a creditor in favor of a third person who pays him, is either conventional or legal.' Article 2160(1) provides that a conventional subrogation shall take place, 'When the creditor, receiving his payment from a third person, subrogates him in his rights, actions, privileges, and mortgages against the debtor; this subrogation must be expressed and made at the same time as the payment.'

[29] In urging that an express conventional subrogation took place, Heroman relies upon: (a) the offer by Reulet to receive payment of invoices due it by Cox and 'upon receipt of said payment, your Company (i.e., Heroman) is subrogated to all rights that we have against Cox in connection with this job and such payment',[10] Cox further offering not to lien the job if Heroman would make such direct payment;

---

9. These articles provide:

'Art. 2207. When two persons are indebted to each other, there takes place between them a compensation that extinguishes both the debts, in the manner and cases hereafter expressed.'

'Art. 2208. Compensation takes place of course by the mere operation of law, even unknown to the debtors; the two debts are reciprocally extinguished, as soon as they exist simultaneously, to the amount of their respective sums.'

'Art. 2209. Compensation takes place only between two debts having equally for their object a sum of money, or a certain quantity of consumable things of one and the same kind, and which are equally liquidated and demandable. The days of grace are no obstacle to the compensation.'

10. The letter is quoted in full at Footnote 2. It was introduced in evidence as D-1 without objection in connection with Reulet's testimony. The pre-trial order previously noted Heroman's intention to offer this letter in evidence.

(2) Heroman's acceptance of such offer by paying all the money then due Cox to Reulet, whereupon Reulet ratified the qualified acceptance by crediting Cox's account with payment and desisting from liening the job.

[30] Heroman's contention is well founded. By the acceptance of the offer, Heroman was subrogated to Reulet's right to recover Reulet's debt against Cox. A third person 'having agreed to pay the debt only on condition that he should be subrogated, he was ipso facto subrogated when he made the payment. The thing having been understood and agreed upon, it was not necessary to have any further agreement on the subject at the time of payment. The payment was made in accordance with the agreement; that is to say, with subrogation.' Cooper v. Jennings Refining Co., 118 La. 181, 183, 42 So. 766 (1907).

[31] A creditor (Reulet) has the right to receive payment on a debt owed him and, by contract, to subrogate his payor (Heroman) to his claim. The debtor (Cox) cannot, by prohibiting the payor (Heroman) to make such payment, thus limit the creditor's legal right to make such a contract in order for the latter to receive payment. Subrogation is thus permitted in the interest of the creditor rather than of the debtor. This is distinguishable from a payment made by a third person under Article 2134, which theoretically is an act done in the debtor's interest; the debtor, by prohibiting the act, can deny the third-person payor the right to act allegedly in the former's interest.

[32] Cox argues that subrogation is not at issue and did not occur because[, **among other things, . . .**] partial subrogation is not permitted without the consent of the debtor.

[. . . .]

[33] [. . .] In contending that partial Subrogation is not permitted, as dividing the debt without the consent of the debtor, Cox relies upon a line of decisions holding that partial assignment is not permitted without the consent of the debtor.[11] There is a substantial conceptual difference between, on the one hand, an 'assignment', which has the nature of the sale and acquisition of a credit so as to permit its enforcement of the assignee, and, on the other hand, a conventional 'subrogation', which has for its primary purpose the negotiated discharge of a debt due to the creditor. Civil Law Translations (Aubry & Rau, Obligations), Section 321 b (1965); Comment, 25 Tul.L.Rev. 358, 368–69 (1951). Thus, in a subrogation the interest of a creditor (here, Reulet) in receiving payment of his debt in return for subrogating the third party to his right to recover it, outweighs the interest of the debtor (here, Cox)

---

11. Red River Valley Bank & Trust Co. v. Louisiana Petrolithic Const. Co., 142 La. 838, 77 So. 763 (1918); Meyer v. Vicksburg, Shreveport & P. Railway Co., 35 La.Ann. 897 (1883); LeBlanc v. Parish of East Baton Rouge, 10 Rob. 25 (1845); Cantrelle v. LeGoaster, 3 Rob. 432 (1943); Miller v. Brigot, 8 La. 533 (1835); King v. Havard, 5 Mart., N.S., 193 (1826); Stein v. Williams Lumber Co., 36 So.2d 62 (La.App.Orl.Cir. 1948); Lane v. Deas Co., 12 La.App. 382, 125 So. 514 (1929). All of these cases involved Assignments rather than subrogation. Stein, however, itself an assignment case, included the dictum that subrogation, as well as assignment, was prohibited without the debtor's consent, erroneously citing the other above-noted assignment cases as authority.

in avoiding the division of the debt he owes into multiple claims, the policy preventing partial assignments (see decisions cited in Footnote 4 above).

[34] No authority is cited to us which prevents partial subrogation. The Civil Code, in fact, recognizes that a partial subrogation can take place in the case of a legal subrogation, Article 2161, and that, in the case of both legal and conventional subrogation, a partial subrogation may take place, Article 2162.[12]

[35] Planiol notes: 'Subrogation by consent of (the) creditor . . . is always possible. The creditor, on receiving payment from a person other than the debtor, can always accord to him a subrogation to assure his recourse, and he is also free to refuse it.' Vol. 2, Section 479. 'The subrogation, resulting exclusively from the creditor's will, may, at his pleasure, be total or partial.' Section 482. 'When the creditor has received from the subrogee a partial payment only, the credit is divided between them; the original creditor remains creditor for the unpaid portion and the subrogee becomes creditor to the extent of the payment he has made.' Section 515. Planiol also notes that the only conditions required to effect a conventional subrogation are that it be express and that the creditor should consent to it, at the latest, at the time that the creditor receives his payment. Section 480.[13]

[36] We could find no decisions which held that the consent of the debtor was necessary for the creditor to subrogate part of the debt due by receiving payment from a third person. On the other hand, we found decisions such as R. M. Walmsley & Co. v. Theus, 107 La. 417, 31 So. 869 (1901) and numerous collision insurer subrogation cases which without discussion allowed a partial subrogation by the creditor unconsented—to by the debtor.

[37] We therefore find valid the partial subrogation to Heroman resulting from the express agreement of Reulet at the time Heroman made payment to Reulet upon Cox's debt.

[38] When a subrogor sues the debtor, the latter has the right to raise all defenses available. Here, the evidence is uncontradicted that Cox owed Reulet in excess of the amount paid to Reulet by Heroman, the claim against Cox to which Reulet was expressly subrogated to such payment. If Cox seriously contended he did not owe Reulet the amount to which Heroman was subrogated, Cox had the right under the pleadings to prove such opposition to Heroman's claim of credit for such amount.

---

12. Article 2162 in full provides:
'The subrogation established by the preceding articles, takes place as well against the sureties, as against the debtors. It can not injure the creditor, since, if he has been paid but in part, he may exercise his right for what remains due, in preference to him from whom he has received only a partial payment.'
13. We should note that there is a difference between a subrogation by the creditor, Article 2160(1), and a subrogation by the debtor, Article 2160(2)—the latter requiring the consent of the creditor affected. See Planiol, Vol. 2, Sections 484–490.

3. Conclusion

[39] In summary, we hold that Heroman is entitled to reason of compensation to receive a credit against the debt Heroman owes Cox arising out of the equally liquidated and demandable debt due Heroman by Cox by reason of Heroman's subrogated claim.

[40] At the time Heroman made the payment to Reulet, it was not entitled to credit against its debt due Cox, by reason of the stipulations in the contract between Cox and Heroman and of Cox's expressed opposition to such payment. However, whatever right Cox may have had under its contract to secure penalties from Heroman for non-compliance with the contract terms, this issue has passed out of the case (see Footnote 4).

[41] The only issue thus before us is whether, when both claims are equally liquidated and demanded, Heroman is entitled to compensate its subrogated claim owed by Cox against its debt owed to Cox. We hold that it is.[14] We thus reach, for different reasons, the same result as the court of appeal.

[42] Accordingly, for the reasons assigned, we affirm the court of appeal decree.

[43] Court of appeal decree affirmed.

[44] DIXON, J., dissents with reasons.

DIXON, Justice (dissenting).

[45] I respectfully dissent. The Code provides that the subrogation agreement must be made at the same time as the payment.

[46] C.C. 2160 provides:

'The subrogation is conventional:

1. When the creditor, receiving his payment from a third person, subrogates him in his rights, actions, privileges, and mortgages against the debtor; this subrogation must be expressed and made at the same time as the payment. * * *'

[47] This provision requires that the subrogation be clear, definite and that the subrogation be made at the time of payment. The French article is the same. (C.N. 1804, Art. 1250).

[48] Translations of French commentators that are available to us are even more specific. Planiol says the subrogation 'must be conferred at the same time as payment.' Planiol, Civil Law Treatise, Vol. 2, No. 480 (Louisiana State Law Institute Translation 1959). Aubry and Rau say the subrogation 'must be made simultaneously with the payment.' Aubry and Rau, Cours de Droit Civil Francais, s 321, Vol. I, Civil Law Translations, La.Law Inst. 1965.

---

14. If we were to hold otherwise, then Heroman would have to sue Reulet to recover back the money paid to it in error, and Reulet would have to sue Cox to recover such amount, which until now it has credited on its unpaid claim for supplies against Cox.

[49] From the meager resources at hand, it appears that the modern French view has not departed from the very explicit codal provisions.

[50] Carbonnier says:

'Condition de temps: la subrogation doit e tre consentie au moment mem du paiement (en pratique, dans la quittance me me, quittance subrogatoire).' Droit Civil, Vol. 2, No. 130 (1956).

[51] A report of the most recent jurisprudence states:

'La date de la subrogation doit e tre contemporaine du paiement (Com. 14 de c. 1965, Rec. Gaz. Pal. 1966. 1. 278).' Repertorie De Droit Civil (Mise A Jour 1974).

[52] For whatever reason, conventional subrogation agreements in anticipation of payment are not sanctioned by our statutes. The subrogation must be consented to at the time of payment.

[53] Dicta in Cooper v. Jennings Refining Co., 118 La. 181, 42 So. 766 is contrary. That case, however, did not necessarily involve conventional subrogation, in spite of the discussion of conventional subrogation in the opinion. The claimant guaranteed payment for a load of pipe — the debt of another — and became a surety. C.C. 3035. Upon payment, the surety had recourse against the debtor (C.C. 3052) and, in addition, was subrogated to the rights of the creditor by operation of law. C.C. 2161(3).

[54] The Court was distracted in Cooper v. Jennings, Supra, because the surety did not agree In writing to pay the debt of another. C.C. 2278. Nevertheless, when the surety recognized his obligation and paid the debt, that problem of proof no longer existed. See C.C. 2133.

[55] The case before us could be decided with less violence to the law under C.C. 2161(3) as a legal subrogation. In spite of toobroad [*sic*] language in Pringle-Associated Mtg. Corp. v. Eanes, 254 La. 705, 226 So.2d 502, the contractor is obligated to pay the materialman if the subcontractor does not. (In Pringle, the subcontractor did not pay the debt of another. He paid his own debt, for which he was primarily liable-wages of his workmen-and sought legal subrogation to their lien rights.)

[56] Nevertheless, there is something fundamentally wrong in allowing a debtor (Heroman) to pay another person instead of his creditor (Cox) over the strong protest of the creditor.

[. . . .]

[57] The preferred solution to the problem in the case before us is to allow the creditor Cox to prevail, and collect from his debtor Heroman, reserving to Heroman whatever rights he might have to reimbursement from Reulet.

Questions

1. Paragraphs 1–16: To attempt to understand this case as clearly as possible, we suggest that, after you have read the "Facts," you draw a diagram of the

relationships created between the three major parties involved; then, identify and name the contracts that may exist in the case. Since several 'bilateral' contracts exist here, be sure to single out which party may be a 'third party' to a particular contract between two other parties. This exercise will be essential to an understanding of the Court's opinion. In addition, you should read the Louisiana Civil Code articles on Performance/Payment (arts. 1854–1863), Subrogation (arts. 1825–1830), Assumption (arts. 1821–1824), and Assignment of Rights (arts. 2642–2654, particularly art. 2653).

2. Paragraphs 17–19: In paragraph 19, how can the Court bring in former Louisiana Civil Code article 2299 (now articles 2292–2293) when Heroman is bound by a contract with Cox? On the basis of current article 2134, shouldn't Heroman be denied subrogation if he pays Reulet "in his own name" and against the will of Cox? Would the law be the same today under current articles 2292–2293 and 1855?

3. Paragraph 22: How do these limitations to the right of a third person to pay for the benefit of his debtor's account apply to the case at hand? To the extent that a subrogation is a transfer of a right and, thereby, has much in common with an assignment of rights, of what relevance is Louisiana Civil Code article 2653? Could Cox's objections be equal to a prohibition under article 2653?

4. Paragraph 25: Heroman acknowledges that he was not entitled to extinguish Cox's debt; thus was the payment lawful? Either Heroman had a "right" to pay Cox's debt to Reulet or he didn't, right? Under the facts of the case, Reulet claimed to be Cox's obligee, but didn't Cox claim that he had been overcharged and, therefore, was himself possibly an obligee of Reulet to some extent? So if Reulet is Cox's creditor and if Cox is, in turn, Reulet's creditor, how can these two reciprocal debts be extinguished up to the amount of the lesser? *See* La. Civ. Code arts. 1893–1902 on Compensation. Notice that the Court refers to Heroman "receiving credit against its liability due Cox. . . . ." In other words, the amount of Heroman's payment to Reulet on behalf of Cox will be deducted from Heroman's debt to Cox. The Court imposed on Cox the method of payment called compensation *(see supra)*. Could compensation be a legal obstacle to Heroman paying Cox's debt to Reulet? *See* La. Civ. Code art. 1824-2 by analogy or on the basis of reasoning *ubi eadem ratio idem jus*, "where the reason is the same the law must be the same." What about Cox's objections, which could be based on redhibitory defects (*see* La. Civ. Code arts. 2520–2548) or disproportionate price (*see* La. Civ. Code art. 2464)? In an action between Cox and Reulet, Cox could raise such defenses. What happened to these defenses once the Court allowed compensation to take place in the relationship between Heroman and Cox? Could Cox still raise against Heroman the same defenses he could have raised against Reulet? If Cox could prove that he had been overcharged by Reulet in the amount of $X (or that there were defects of that amount), does it mean that Cox could get that amount from Heroman, who would then have to pay that $X amount on top of

the balance of his debt to Cox? If so, could Heroman then turn against Reulet for having paid too much to the latter when subrogation took place?

5. Paragraph 31: From the above, Heroman's payment of Cox's debt to Reulet by way of compensation should not be allowed because Heroman should not have the right to make that payment. What then is the Court saying in the sentence: "A creditor (Reulet) has the right . . . claim"? And the Court continues with this statement: "The debtor (Cox) cannot . . . limit the creditor's legal right to make such a contract (of subrogation). . . ." In conclusion, the Court states: "Subrogation is thus permitted in the interest of the creditor rather than of the debtor. This is distinguishable from a payment made by a third person under Article 2134, which . . . interest." Is the Court saying that Heroman was not a third party to the contract between Cox and Heroman? Where does the Court find this law? Do you agree with the Court's statement on subrogation in paragraph 33: "Thus, in a subrogation the interest of a creditor (here, Reulet). . . . outweighs the interest of the debtor"? Is the Court really finding this kind of holding or statement of the law in the Louisiana Civil Code? Is this issue of partial division of the debt for the benefit of the creditor that important so as to justify, in a sense, subrogation? Remember your diagram from Question 1, above: where did you place Heroman in relation to the contract between Cox and Reulet? Was Heroman a third party to that contract or not?

6. On this issue of the simultaneous timing of a payment of a debt with subrogation, do you agree with the majority or with the dissenting opinion, and the doctrine quoted here? Considering the foundation and *raison d'être* of subrogation, which opinion makes more sense?

Bruce Martin
v.
Louisiana Farm Bureau Casualty Insurance Company, et al.

Supreme Court of Louisiana
July 5, 1994
638 So.2d 1067

WATSON, Justice.

[1] The issue is whether a health and accident insurer, which pays its insured's medical expenses after an automobile accident, is entitled to legal subrogation against the tortfeasors.

Facts

[2] On October 27, 1987, guest passenger Bruce Martin was injured in a two-vehicle collision. Martin sued the drivers, the owners, and the insurers of both vehicles. Golden Rule Insurance Company, Martin's health and accident insurer, paid his medical expenses and intervened to recoup the sums paid under Martin's policy.

[. . . .]

Law and Discussion

[3] Golden Rule's claim for legal subrogation rests on Civil Code article 1829(3), which provides:

Art. 1829. Subrogation by operation of law.

Subrogation takes place by operation of law:

* * * * * *

3) In favor of an obligor who pays a debt he owes with others or for others and who has recourse against those others as a result of the payment.

[4] Article 1829(3) is an exception to the general rule that subrogation does not take place when a third person pays the debt of another. LSA-C.C. art. 1855 states the general rule that " . . . performance rendered by a third person effects subrogation only when so provided by law or by agreement." Legal subrogation derogates from the principle that no one may acquire another's right without that person's concurrence. 1 Saul Litvinoff, Obligations, § 11.51, at 289–90 (5 Louisiana Civil Law Treatise 1992); 7 Planiol & Ripert, *Traité Pratique de Droit Civil Français* nos. 632–33 (2e ed. 1954). Due to the exceptional nature of subrogation by operation of law, the right is strictly construed. *Pringle-Associated Mortgage Corporation v. Eanes*, 254 La. 705, 226 So.2d 502 (1969).

[5] The initial inquiry under article 1829(3) is whether Golden Rule is bound "with . . . or for others."

[6] An obligor is bound with others when the obligation is solidary. LSA-C.C. art. 1794. Obligors are also bound with others when the obligation is indivisible. LSA-C.C. art. 1815; LSA-C.C. art. 1818. Co-sureties of the same debt are bound with each other. LSA-C.C. art. 3056. Sureties for debtors, who bind themselves or their property to secure performance, are subsidiary obligors and bound for others. LSA-C.C. art. 3048; LSA-C.C. art. 3295. These applications are supported by leading civil law commentators. *See* 2 Planiol & Ripert, *Traité Elémentaire de Droit Civil*, pt. 1, no. 501, at 282 (La.St.L.Inst. trans., 11th ed. 1959); Aubry & Rau, *Droit Civil Français*, in 1 Civil Law Translations § 321, at 202 (1965); 1 Saul Litvinoff, Obligations, § 11.54-56, at 297–301 (5 Louisiana Civil Law Treatise 1992); 12 Duranton, *Cours de Droit Français* no. 166-70 (3e ed. 1834); 7 Toullier, *Droit Civil Français* no. 147-153 (5e ed. 1839). Comments of French authors interpreting articles adopted from the French Civil Code are entitled to great weight. *Orleans Parish Sch. Bd. v. Pittman Construction Co.*, 261 La. 665, 260 So.2d 661 (1972); *Rials v. Davis*, 212 La. 161, 31 So.2d 726 (1947).

[7] None of these relationships are present in this case. First, Golden Rule is not solidarily bound with the defendants. An obligation is solidary among debtors when they are obliged to the same thing, so that either may be compelled to perform the whole obligation, and payment by one exonerates the other. LSA-C.C. art. 1794; *Hoefly v. Government Employees Ins. Co.*, 418 So.2d 575 (La.1982). Solidary liability is never presumed and arises only from a clear expression of the parties' intent or

from the law. LSA-C.C. art. 1796. An insurer bound to repair the damage caused by a tortfeasor is solidarily liable with the tortfeasor because both are obliged to the same thing — repair of the tort damage. *Fertitta v. Allstate Ins. Co.*, 462 So.2d 159 (La.1985). See LSA-R.S. 22:1406(D)(1)(a); LSA-R.S. 22:655(B)(1). Medical insurers are not obligated to repair tort damages. A medical insurer contracts to pay stipulated medical expenses, regardless of whether there is a tortfeasor and tort liability. The medical insurer thus pays its own debt, not that of the tortfeasor, and the two are not obligated to "the same thing." *See Fertitta*, 462 So.2d at 164, n. 7; 2 Planiol & Ripert, *Traité Elémentaire de Droit Civil*, p. 1, no. 491 n. 27, at 278 (La.St.L.Inst. trans. 11th ed. 1959).

[8] Golden Rule's obligation is not indivisible. An obligation is indivisible when the object of performance is not susceptible of division, for example an obligation to deliver a specific thing. LSA-C.C. art. 1815. The obligation to pay money at issue here is susceptible of division and thus provides no basis for legal subrogation.

[9] A health and accident insurer is principally liable for the insured's medical expenses within the policy limits. Golden Rule is therefore not a subsidiary obligor or surety whose purpose is to secure the tortfeasors' debt.

[10] *Aetna Ins. Co. v. Naquin*, 488 So.2d 950 (La.1986), allowed the insurer of rental property subrogation recovery against a negligent roofing contractor. In *Naquin*, both the insurer and the negligent roofer were bound for payment of the leaky roof damages. *Naquin* was a property damage exception to the general rule, which should not be extended to health and accident insurance. See the *Naquin* dissent by Dixon, C.J.

[11] Golden Rule argues that legal subrogation should obtain because a contrary result would produce dual recovery. The possibility of a plaintiff's dual recovery alone does not overcome the weight of authority against legal subrogation. A tortfeasor is barred from raising collateral sources as a defense. See e.g., *American Indemnity Co. v. New York F. & M. Under. Inc.*, 196 So.2d 592 (La.App. 1 Cir.1967); *Peacock's, Inc. v. Shreveport Alarm Co.*, 510 So.2d 387 (La.App. 2 Cir.), writ denied, 513 So.2d 826, 827, 828 (La.1987); *Dixie Trucks, Inc. v. Davis*, 530 So.2d 107 (La.App. 2 Cir.1988); *Brannon v. Shelter Mut. Ins. Co.*, 520 So.2d 984 (La.App. 3 Cir.1987); *Weir v. Gasper*, 459 So.2d 655 (La.App. 4 Cir.1984), writ denied, 462 So.2d 650 (La.1985); *Teague v. Barnes*, 519 So.2d 817 (La.App. 5 Cir.1988). Consequently, plaintiffs will occasionally have insurance reimbursements for certain elements of damages and recover some of the same elements from tortfeasors.

[12] Legal subrogation would bestow a windfall on Golden Rule, which did not bargain for that benefit. Health and accident insurers can readily protect themselves by stipulating reimbursement rights or conventional subrogation in their policy contracts. See, for example, *Miller v. Sauseda*, 611 So.2d 831 (La.App. 3d Cir.1992), writ denied, 614 So.2d 1254 (La.1993).

Conclusion

[13] A health and accident insurer is not "bound with ... or for" a tortfeasor whose actions give rise to medical expenses. Consequently the insurer does not

become legally subrogated to its insured's cause of action simply by making the medical payments called for in its insurance contract.

$$[\,\ldots\,]$$

MARCUS, Justice (dissenting).

[14] I disagree with the majority's holding that a health and accident insurer does not become legally subrogated to its insured's cause of action against a tortfeasor by making medical payments. La.C.C. art. 1829(3) provides for legal subrogation:

> in favor of an obligor who pays a debt he owes with others or for others and who has recourse against those others as a result of the payment.

[15] Golden Rule, as the insurer, is responsible for plaintiff's medical expenses. Defendants are also liable for those expenses as a result of the accident. This is sufficient to satisfy the requirement in art. 1829(3) that the obligor owe a debt "with others." It is not necessary to examine the nature of the relationship between the obligors as the article does not require solidarity. *See Aetna Insurance Co. v. Naquin*, 488 So.2d 950, 954 (La.1986) (interpreting similar language in old La.C.C. art. 2161(3), the predecessor of art. 1829). Since the tortfeasor has not yet paid the plaintiff, the insurer still has recourse against the tortfeasor, thus satisfying the second requirement of art. 1829(3). Therefore, the insurer should be legally subrogated to the rights of the plaintiff against the tortfeasor for the medical expenses it has paid. Accordingly, I respectfully dissent.

Questions

1. Properly identify and describe, in legal terms, the relationships created before and after the accident. Describe the obligations resulting from these relationships. For example, was there any condition? Was there any heritable or personal obligation? Was there any joint or solidary obligation?

2. Read the Louisiana Code articles on "Subrogation" and contrast the distinctive features of the two forms of subrogation. On the basis of those articles, which form of subrogation, if any, could take place in this case?

3. Paragraph 7: How do the statements of the Court fit with your description of the legal relationships (Question 1)? How important, and even determinant, is the Court's emphasis on "the same thing"?

4. Paragraph 8: Why is the Court referring to indivisible obligation? Is there any connection between solidarity and indivisibility? Could either one lead to an instance of legal subrogation?

5. Paragraph 10: What do you think of the Court rejecting an *a pari ratione* reasoning? Does it make sense?

6. Paragraph 11: Would Golden Rule really be bestowed a windfall? What kind of windfall is the Court talking about? According to the Court, "Golden Rule did not bargain for that benefit"; with whom should Golden Rule have bargained?

Lionel Lorio Smith

v.

Kathleen Hebert Smith

Court of Appeal of Louisiana
First Circuit
December 20, 1996
685 So.2d 649

PARRO, Judge.

[. . . .]

Facts and Procedural History

[1] [This case involves the partition of the community property. More specifically, it addresses, among other issues, the husband's claims of reimbursement due to his use of separate funds to purchase the first family home, which was later sold, whereupon the proceeds of that sale were deposited by husband into an account and later used to purchase the family's replacement home.]

[. . . .]

Applicable Law

[2] Under Louisiana law, property is generally characterized as either community or separate. LSA-C.C. art. 2335. The classification of property as separate or community is fixed at the time of its acquisition. *Terry v. Terry*, 565 So.2d 997, 999 (La.App. 1st Cir.1990). In proving whether an asset is community or separate, the parties are guided by the following principles.

[3] LSA-C.C. art. 2338 provides that community property comprises: property acquired during the existence of the legal regime through the effort, skill, or industry of either spouse; property acquired with community things or with community and separate things, unless classified as separate property under Article 2341; property donated to the spouses jointly; natural and civil fruits of community property; damages awarded for loss or injury to a thing belonging to the community; and all other property not classified by law as separate property. Things in the possession of a spouse during the existence of the community are presumed to be community, but either spouse may prove that they are separate property. LSA-C.C. art. 2340.

[4] Regarding the classification of property as separate, LSA-C.C. art. 2341 provides, in part, that a person's separate estate comprises: property acquired by a spouse prior to the establishment of a community property regime; property acquired by a spouse with separate things or with separate and community things when the value of the community things is inconsequential in comparison with the value of the separate things used; and property acquired by a spouse by inheritance or donation to him individually. In order to transfer separate property to the community with the stipulation that it shall be part of the community, a transfer by

onerous title must be made in writing or a transfer by gratuitous title must be done by authentic act. LSA-C.C. art. 2343.1.

Lionel's Claims for Reimbursement

[5] Lionel contended the trial court erred in failing to recognize his right to reimbursement for the use of his separate funds to make a down payment on the first family home [. . .] following the termination of the marriage.

A. Down Payment on the First Family Home

[6] Kathleen admitted Lionel had used his separate funds in the acquisition of their first home, which was community property. Even the trial court believed Lionel had sold his separate stock and used the proceeds for the down payment on the first home. Although Lionel claimed in his detailed descriptive list that he expended approximately $50,000 of his separate funds toward the purchase of the home, his list of reimbursements introduced at trial itemized the amount expended at only $11,000, which coincided with the amount withdrawn from Lionel's separate passbook savings account on May 28, 1975 (the date the first home was purchased). Although no other specific evidence of this amount was introduced at trial, there is nothing in the record to indicate the parties disputed the amount of separate funds expended.

[7] Following the sale of the first home, the proceeds were placed into an account and later used to acquire the family's replacement home. The trial court concluded that the sale of the community asset resulted in a contribution to the community of the separate funds used in acquiring the first home.[2] Such a finding presupposes the separate identity of the funds expended in acquiring the first home was reestablished after the sale of the first home. We disagree. Under the principle of real subrogation, which is applicable to both separate and community property, the funds derived from the sale of the first home remained community property.[3] *See* LSA-C.C. art. 2341, comment (c); *Albert v. Albert*, 625 So.2d 765, 768 (La.App. 1st Cir.1993).

[8] The parties do not dispute that the first home belonged to the community and that Lionel's separate funds were used for the acquisition of this community property. Since Lionel used his separate funds in acquiring community property, obviously, he would have had a claim for reimbursement for the use of his separate funds pursuant to LSA-C.C. art. 2367. Thus, the issue presented to this court is whether Lionel's right to reimbursement was affected as a result of the subsequent sale of the first home. We think not.

---

2. There is no evidence that the requirements of LSA-C.C. art. 2343.1 were ever satisfied. Therefore, the separate funds of Lionel were never given to the community. See Landry v. Landry, 610 So.2d 1045, 1047 (La.App. 3rd Cir.1992).

3. There is no codal authority to support a finding that the funds derived from the sale of a community asset is part community and part separate based on the original classification of the things used to acquire the community asset.

[9] Under LSA-C.C. art. 2367, a spouse is entitled to reimbursement upon proof that his or her separate property was "used for the acquisition, use, improvement, or benefit of community property." The right to reimbursement is not peculiar to any particular property or its proceeds. Thus, Lionel's right to reimbursement was not affected by the sale of the first home. Therefore, the trial court was legally incorrect in denying Lionel's right to reimbursement under LSA-C.C. art. 2367 for the use of his separate property in the acquisition of community property. Accordingly, Lionel is entitled to reimbursement from Kathleen in the amount of $5,500.[4]

[. . . .]

Questions

1. What kind of "subrogation" is occurring in this case? What is the root of the word "real"? What is the opposite?

2. Paragraph 7: What is the source of this form of subrogation? Does the Court refer specifically to a Louisiana Civil Code article as is the case of personal subrogation (*see* La. Civ. Code arts. 1825–1830)? What is a principle of law? Where and how do you find it (or them)? Can you think of some other form of real subrogation? Aren't monetary damages a substitute thing for the destruction of the principal object of a contract of sale, for example, and isn't this a form of real subrogation?

Safeway Insurance Company of Louisiana
v.
State Farm Mutual Automobile Insurance Company

Court of Appeal of Louisiana
Second Circuit
March 5, 2003
839 So.2d 1022

KOSTELKA, Judge Pro Tempore.

[1] State Farm Mutual Automobile Insurance Company ("State Farm") appeals a judgment by the Shreveport City Court against it in the amount of $1,394.99 and in favor of Safeway Insurance Company of Louisiana ("Safeway"). For the following reasons, we affirm.

Facts

[2] On November 2, 2000, Jopawnna Baines ("Baines") borrowed, with permission, the vehicle of her friend, Jackie Holloway ("Holloway") while Baines' vehicle was being repaired. Holloway's vehicle was insured by an insurance policy issued by

---

4. However, Kathleen's liability for one-half of the funds used would be limited to the value of her share in the community after deduction of all community obligations. LSA-C.C. art. 2367.

Safeway (the "Safeway policy"). Baines' vehicle was insured by a policy of insurance issued by State Farm (the "State Farm policy").

[3] As Baines was operating Holloway's vehicle in Shreveport, Louisiana, the vehicle came in contact with a child, Tori Ladd, who was walking along the street upon which Baines was traveling. As a result of the accident, the child was injured and received medical treatment for which medical expenses were incurred. Safeway (Holloway's insurer) paid Ladd's parents, $1,394.99 in full and final settlement of any and all claims for the injuries and expenses incurred on behalf of their child as a result of the accident.

[4] Subsequently, Safeway filed its Petition of Subrogation against State Farm, asserting that the State Farm policy which covered Baines' vehicle, provided primary liability coverage for the accident. Safeway further claimed that it was subrogated for the amount of $1,394.99 it paid in settlement. [. . . .]

[5] After issuing its written Opinion, which included its findings and reasons for judgment, the trial court rendered Judgment in favor of Safeway and against State Farm in the amount of $1,394.99. This appeal by State Farm ensued.

Discussion

[6] The minimal monetary amount at issue in this appeal truly belies the interesting and complex issues of law before us. [. . . .]

[. . . .]

Safeway's Subrogation Claim

[7] Concluding that State Farm was primarily obligated to the Ladds despite Safeway's payment to them, we must next ascertain whether Safeway had a valid claim against State Farm for the amount of the payment made to the Ladds.

[8] Subrogation is the substitution of one person or entity to the rights of another. La. C.C. art. 1825. As stated by the Louisiana Supreme Court in *A. Copeland Enterprises, Inc. v. Slidell Memorial Hosp.*, 94-2011 (La.06/30/95), 657 So.2d 1292, "[S]ubrogation is the legal fiction established by law whereby an obligation, extinguished with regard to the original creditor by payment which he has received from a third person, or from the original debtor but with funds that a third person has provided, is regarded as substituting in favor of this third person who in essence steps into the shoes of the original debtor and is entitled to assert, in the measure of what he has paid, the rights and actions of the former creditor." Subrogation may be either conventional or legal. La. C.C. art. 1825. It may result from either the agreement of the obligor or the obligee or both with a third person (i.e., conventional subrogation), or directly from the operation of law (i.e., legal subrogation). Thus, the intention of subrogation is to protect such persons who perform certain acts. *A. Copeland Enterprises, Inc., supra.*

[9] When subrogated to the rights of the insured, the insurer stands in the shoes of the insured and thereby acquires the independent right to assert the actions and rights of the insured. *Barreca v. Cobb*, 95-1651 (La.02/28/96), 668 So.2d 1129; La. C.C.

arts. 1825 and 1826; *Bailsco Blades & Casting, Inc. v. Fireman's Fund Ins. Co.*, 31,876 (La.App.2d Cir.05/05/99), 737 So.2d 164.

[10] In its Petition of Subrogation, Safeway alleged to be subrogated to the rights of Holloway, its insured, as a result of its payment of settlement proceeds to the Ladds. Clearly, its policy provides such. It did not claim any other rights of subrogation as to Baines or the Ladds. After a hearing [...], the trial court ruled in favor of Safeway, noting that Safeway could be potentially subrogated to (1) "its insured's rights against State Farm for not paying the claim" or (2) the Ladds. We determine that Safeway properly made a subrogation claim; however, it was neither subrogated to the rights of Holloway, as claimed, or the Ladds, as the trial court determined. Instead, we determine that Safeway is subrogated to the rights of Baines, for the following reasons.

[11] Although not specifically claimed by Safeway, it clearly would be subrogated to the rights of Baines in the case *sub judice*. Baines operated Holloway's vehicle with permission, which, under the clear terms of the Safeway policy, made Baines its insured.[3] State Farm concedes that Baines was also Safeway's insured under the Safeway policy. The Safeway policy further provides "[I]n the event of any payment under this policy, [Safeway] shall be subrogated to all the insured's rights of recovery therefor against any person or organization. . . ."[4] Thus, Safeway had the right to assert any claim of Baines arising from the collision with the Ladd child — another fact conceded by State Farm.

[12] However, State Farm argues in brief that Safeway could not assert subrogation rights as to Baines, because she had no rights or claims against State Farm as a result of her collision in Holloway's vehicle, as she suffered no damages to her person or property. However, State Farm overlooks the rights Baines has against it arising from the contractual relationship between her and State Farm vis-à-vis the State Farm policy issued to Baines. Obviously, she had a right to assert a claim against State Farm in the event it failed to provide coverage as stated in the policy. *See,* La. C.C. art.1994.[5] So considering, Safeway, as subrogee of Baines, and under La. R.S. 22:1406(F), clearly has a subrogation claim against State Farm in this proceeding.

[13] Moreover, we are not constrained by the fact that Safeway failed to specifically claim that it was subrogated to the rights of Baines in this case. The appellate

3. The Safeway policy defines "Persons Insured" as "(1) the named insured" or "(2) any other person using such automobile to whom the name insured has given permission, provided the use is within the scope of such permission."

4. Notably, the right of subrogation is not limited to the "named insured."

5. Also, La. R.S. 22:1220(A) imposes a duty of good faith and fair dealing in performance of the insurance contract. *See also,* La. C.C. art.1983; *Williams v. Louisiana Indem. Co.*, 26,887 (La.App.2d Cir.06/21/95), 658 So.2d 739, 742. Breach of this particular duty by the insurer renders it liable for any damages, foreseeable or not, that are a direct consequence of its failure to perform. La. C.C. art.1997; La. R.S. 22:1220(A). No allegations of bad faith were made against State Farm by Safeway; however, the statute is illustrative to show that Baines potentially had rights against State Farm.

court shall render any judgment which is just, legal, and proper upon the record on appeal. La. C.C.P. art. 2164. The purpose of this article is to give the appellate court complete freedom to do justice on the record regardless of whether a particular legal point or theory was made, argued, or decided by the court below. *Id.*, Comment (a); *see also, Rachal v. Rachal*, 35,074 (La.App.2d Cir.10/12/01), 795 So.2d 1286. Considering the record before us, including the policy of insurance issued by Safeway and La. R.S. 22:1406(F) making State Farm primary insurer, it is clear that Safeway was subrogated to the rights of Baines against State Farm. It is only fair and equitable that Safeway be able to recoup the monies paid to the Ladds, which, under the statute, were primarily owed by State Farm.

Direct Action Statute

[14] Finally, State Farm argues that the trial court erred in allowing a cause of action by Safeway directly against State Farm. It argues that pursuant to La. R.S. 22:655 (the "Direct Action Statute"), there is no provision therein that would allow Safeway to proceed directly against State Farm. However, as determined by the Louisiana Supreme Court in *Cacamo v. Liberty Mut. Fire Ins. Co.*, 1999–3479 (La.06/30/00), 764 So.2d 41, 43:

> The Direct Action Statute is designed to grant a procedural right of action against an insurer where the plaintiff has a substantive cause of action against the insured. It was enacted to give special rights to tort victims, not to insureds with contract claims against a defendant. In this case, plaintiffs do not purport to file their claims under the Direct Action Statute and have no need to do so. . . . (Citations omitted).

[15] Here, as discussed, Safeway's claim against State Farm is as subrogee of Baines — whose own rights against State Farm derive from the terms of the State Farm policy of insurance. Just as the *Cacamo* plaintiffs, any right of action Baines had against State Farm was in contract, giving her and Safeway, as subrogee, the right to make claims directly against State Farm. So considering, State Farm's reliance on the Direct Action Statute is misplaced, and the trial court was not in error finding that the Direct Action Statute was inapplicable in this particular proceeding.

[. . . .]

Questions

1. Clearly identify the sources and types of legal relationships created between all of the parties involved. In the final analysis, where do the two insurance companies stand in relation to each other?

2. Paragraphs 8–9: Notice how the Court introduces the concept of subrogation: the Court cites the Louisiana Civil Code article first and then illustrates its application. Notice the sentence "Subrogation may be either conventional or legal." Is it in the nature of a policy statement? How does the next sentence fit in the nature of the previous sentence?

3. Paragraphs 10–11: Into whose rights is Safeway subrogated? Does your analysis of the sources and types of obligations created here fit with the Court's ruling on Safeway's right of subrogation?

4. Paragraph 12: How important is the statement made by the Court in this paragraph? Is the Court saying that, for whoever has a lawful right to be compensated, no procedural hindrance should stand in the way of that right? In fact, isn't the Court saying, in its own words, what Louisiana Civil Code article 2298 states: "A person who has been enriched without cause at the expense of another person is bound to compensate that person"? Thus, shouldn't a court find a way to make whole someone who would otherwise be unjustly or unfairly (i.e., without cause or reason) impoverished? Is subrogation in the law of contract (conventional subrogation) or under the law (legal subrogation) nearly the equivalent of what a direct action would be in torts?

Starr Surplus Lines Insurance Company and Lexington Insurance Company
v.
Bernhard MCC, L.L.C., et al.

Court of Appeal of Louisiana
Fifth Circuit
December 2, 2020
308 So.3d 372

CHAISSON, ROBERT, J.

[. . . .]

[1] [. . . .] It is well settled in Louisiana law that a subrogee can have no greater rights than those possessed by its subrogor and is subject to all limitations applicable to the original claim of the subrogor. *Certified Cleaning & Restoration, Inc. v. Lafayette Ins. Co.,* 10-948 (La. App. 5 Cir. 5/31/12), 96 So.3d 1248, 1251. [. . . .]

[. . . .]

[2] [T]he waiver of subrogation is an essential part of the realtor's argument [. . .].

[3] [. . . .] The purpose behind such a waiver is to assure that, in instances of losses covered by the policy, the insurer is to bear the risk of loss regardless of any fault on the part of the identified parties, as well as to prevent a potential windfall to the insurer subrogated to the rights of an insured against other parties to the contract.[7] [. . . .]

---

7. Few Louisiana courts have addressed mutual waivers of subrogation in the context of construction projects, but the issue has been addressed by courts in other jurisdictions. In *School Alliance Ins. Fund v. Fama Const. Co.,* a New Jersey court, after analyzing nearly identical mutual waiver of subrogation language from a previous iteration of an AIA contract, found in favor of the

[. . . .]

[4] [W]e find as a matter of law that the mutual waiver of subrogation provisions found in the Prime Contract signed by TMG, the subrogor, preclude Starr Surplus and Lexington, the subrogees, from bringing claims against BMCC, the subcontractor, for the recovery of damages caused by a risk of loss covered by the builder's risk policy.

[. . . .]

Old Republic Life Insurance Company
v.
Transwood Inc., Tuthill Corporation, Axiall, LLC previously known as Georgia Gulf Chemicals & Vinyls, LLC, TRG, Inc. previously known as Delta Process Equipment, Inc., Christopher Fontenot, Westside Truck and Auto, et al.

Court of Appeal of Louisiana
First Circuit
June 2, 2017
222 So.3d 995

THERIOT, J.

[. . . .]

[1] Generally speaking, legal subrogation does not take place simply because a third person pays the debt of another. *See* La. C.C. art. 1855; Martin v. Louisiana Farm Bureau Cas. Ins. Co., 94-0069 (La. 7/5/94), 638 So.2d 1067, 1068; Watters v. State, Dep't of Transp. & Develop., 33,870 (La.App 2 Cir. 9/27/00), 768 So.2d 733, 737. Louisiana Civil code art. 1829(3) sets forth an exception to this general rule that applies when an obligor pays a debt he owes with others or for others. However, because legal subrogation is in derogation from the principle that no one may acquire another's rights without that person's concurrence, the right is strictly construed. *See* Martin, 638 So.2d at 1068.

[2] In assessing whether legal subrogation occurs under La. C.C. art. 1829(3), the initial inquiry is whether the obligor is bound with or for others. [. . . .]

[. . . .]

[3] Under Louisiana law, although an insurer which pays claims on behalf of its insured is not entitled to legal subrogation, it may still be entitled to conventional subrogation if appropriately provided in the contract of insurance. *See* Watters, 768

---

subcontractor against the insurer which issued the builder's risk property insurance policy for a school construction project. *Sch. All. Ins. Fund v. Fama Const. Co.*, 353 N.J.Super. 131, 140, 801 A.2d 459, 464 (Law. Div. 2001); see also *Chadwick v. CSI, Ltd.*, 137 N.H. 515, 517, 629 A.2d 820, 822 (1993).

So.2d at 737. Conventional subrogation occurs when an obligee who receives performance from a third person subrogates that person to his rights, even without the obligor's consent. La. C.C. art. 1827. The third person, or conventional subrogee, is substituted to all of the rights of the original obligee and is entitled to recover the full amount of the debt from the obligor, regardless of the amount he paid to the original obligee. *See* A. Copeland Enterprises, Inc. [v. Slidell Mem'l Hosp.], 657 So. 2d 1292, 1296., 657 So.2d at 1298. Although the obligor's consent is not required for conventional subrogation, the obligee's intention to subrogate must be clearly indicated; furthermore, if subrogation is disputed, the obligee's intention must be shown by "clear proof of acts of the obligee. . . ." *Id.*

[. . . .]

See also *Thibaut v. Thibaut*, 915 So.2d 883 (La.App. 1 Cir. 2005).

Section III — Imputation of Payment

Louisiana Sources of Law
Louisiana Civil Code

Art. 1864. Imputation by obligor.

An obligor who owes several debts to an obligee has the right to impute payment to the debt he intends to pay.

The obligor's intent to pay a certain debt may be expressed at the time of payment or may be inferred from circumstances known to the obligee. (Acts 1984, No. 331, §1, eff. Jan. 1, 1985.)

Art. 1865. Imputation to debt not yet due.

An obligor may not, without the obligee's consent, impute payment to a debt not yet due. (Acts 1984, No. 331, §1, eff. Jan. 1, 1985.)

Art. 1866. Payment imputed to interest.

An obligor of a debt that bears interest may not, without the obligee's consent, impute a payment to principal when interest is due.

A payment made on principal and interest must be imputed first to interest. (Acts 1984, No. 331, §1, eff. Jan. 1, 1985.)

Art. 1867. Imputation by obligee.

An obligor who has accepted a receipt that imputes payment to one of his debts may no longer demand imputation to another debt, unless the obligee has acted in bad faith. (Acts 1984, No. 331, §1, eff. Jan. 1, 1985.)

Art. 1868. Imputation not made by the parties.

When the parties have made no imputation, payment must be imputed to the debt that is already due.

If several debts are due, payment must be imputed to the debt that bears interest. If all, or none, of the debts that are due bear interest, payment must be imputed to the debt that is secured.

If several unsecured debts bear interest, payment must be imputed to the debt that, because of the rate of interest, is most burdensome to the obligor.

If several secured debts bear no interest, payment must be imputed to the debt that, because of the nature of the security, is most burdensome to the obligor.

If the obligor had the same interest in paying all debts, payment must be imputed to the debt that became due first.

If all debts are of the same nature and became due at the same time, payment must be proportionally imputed to all. (Acts 1984, No. 331, § 1, eff. Jan. 1, 1985.)

Doctrine

Louisiana Law of Obligations in General, A Précis

Section 7.1.2

When an obligor owes his obligee several obligations bearing on fungible things or when he owes several debts of money to the same obligee-creditor, it is important to determine which one of the many obligations or debts he owes the obligor wishes to extinguish when making a payment. Such is the purpose of the codal provisions outlining the regime of imputation of payment. [. . . .]

The parties to an obligation may, by common agreement, decide which one of the debts owed by the obligor will be extinguished first when a payment is made. Unless the law raises an obstacle of public order to the goal pursued by the parties, a conventional imputation agreed upon by the parties should be fully enforceable.

When the parties involved have not specifically provided for this situation, preference of choice will then be given to the obligor since he is the party bearing the burden of the obligation. This preference is expressed in a principle stated in **Article 1864.** [. . . .]

In the event that neither the obligor nor the obligee have exercised their right to state which debt is to be discharged by imputation, the law lays down rules which supplement the wills of the parties by providing different ways in which that imputation of payment is to take place. These different ways are listed in civil Code **Article 1868.**

Cases

Gilbert M. Porche and Theresa Landry Porche
v.
Thomas S. Waldrip, et al.

Court of Appeal of Louisiana
First Circuit
March 6, 1992
597 So.2d 536

SHORTESS, Judge.

[1] Gilbert Porche (plaintiff) was injured in an automobile accident. He sued the other motorist, Thomas Waldrip; Waldrip's employer, Forshag; Forshag's insurer, United States Fidelity & Guaranty Company (USF & G); and his own uninsured motorist carrier, Louisiana Farm Bureau Mutual Insurance Company (Farm Bureau). Prior to trial, plaintiff settled with USF & G for $100,000.00, and Farm Bureau tendered $50,000.00.

[2] The trial court found plaintiff's damages totaled $426,917.42.[1] The court imputed the payments made by USF & G and Farm Bureau to the principal due and entered judgment in favor of plaintiff against Farm Bureau in the sum of $276,917.42, together with legal interest on that sum from date of judicial demand. The court also awarded plaintiff interest on the $50,000.00 tendered by Farm Bureau from date of judicial demand until the date of tender.

[3] Plaintiff's appeal is limited[, **for purposes herein, to . . .**] whether the $50,000.00 tendered made by Farm Bureau prior to trial should have been imputed first to principal rather than interest.

[. . . .]

[4] Plaintiff contends the trial court erred in applying the tender made by Farm Bureau prior to trial to the principal sum due plaintiff for damages rather than to accrued interest. The trial court subtracted $150,000.00 (the tender plus USF & G's payment) from the total damages awarded of $426,917.42 and entered judgment in that amount. At the time of judgment, accrued interest exceeded $50,000.00. Plaintiff contends the court should have entered judgment for $326,917.42, together with legal interest from date of judicial demand until paid, subject to a credit of $50,000.00, to be applied first to accrued interest.

[5] Plaintiff bases this contention on Louisiana Civil Code article 1866 and the case of *Payton v. Colar*, 518 So.2d 1104 (La.App. 4th Cir.1987). Article 1866 provides:

> An obligor of a debt that bears interest may not, without the obligee's consent, impute a payment to principal when interest is due.

---

1. The trial court also awarded plaintiff's wife $7,500.00 for loss of consortium.

A payment made on principal and interest must be imputed first to interest.

Payton involved a post-judgment tender. In that case, the court held a "tort judgment bearing judicial interest" is a "debt that bears interest" within the meaning of article 1866. 518 So.2d at 1106.

[6] In this case, however, we have a pre-judgment tender. At the time the tender was made, there was no "debt that bears interest" within the meaning of article 1866. In *McElrath v. Dupuy*, 2 La.Ann. 520 (1847), the court held that when the debt was not yet due at the time of payment, this article did not apply.[3] The court stated that the credit was to be applied "to that part of the debt which the debtor had the greatest interest in discharging, which was the principal, as upon that interest was accruing." 2 La.Ann. at 523.

[7] We note article 1865 provides a creditor may not impute payment to a debt not yet due without the debtor's consent. In this case, the plaintiff accepted Farm Bureau's tender and thus consented to imputation of payment to the debt. Since the debt was not yet due, the payment must be imputed to the principal, the part of the debt Farm Bureau had the greatest interest in discharging. Thus, the trial court properly credited the pre-trial tender by Farm Bureau to the principal due.

[. . . .]

Questions

1. Paragraph 3: The focus of your attention should be on the Court's statements regarding whether the $50,000.00 paid (tendered: *see* La. Civ. Code arts. 1869–1872) by Louisiana Farm Bureau *"prior to trial"* should have been imputed to the principal rather than to the interest (emphasis ours). What is the nature of an obligation before a trial on that obligation? Does it exist and, if it does, what is its nature? How would you qualify or describe in legal terms a judgment in conclusion of a trial? Is it a term and if so, what kind? Is it a condition and if so, what kind? Is there any significance to assigning a legal qualification or description to such an event as judgment?

2. Paragraphs 5–7: Read all of the Louisiana Civil Code articles on "imputation" (arts. 1864–1868). What is the purpose of imputation? Which party should it benefit and under what circumstances? *See* La. Civ. Code arts. 1864 and 1867. As far as imputation is concerned, how relevant was the question above about the proper legal qualification of a judgment as a term or as a condition? Likewise, as concerns imputation, was it relevant to make a distinction between

---

3. At the time of this decision, the court was interpreting article 2160 of the 1825 Civil Code, which contained substantially the same language as current article 1866, as follows:

> The debtor of a debt, which bears interest or produces rents, can not, without the consent of the creditor, impute to the reduction of the capital any payment he may make, when there is interest or rent due.

Every payment which does not extinguish both the principal and the interest must be imputed first to the payment of the interest.

a principal obligation and a secondary obligation? Do you see a difference between the word "due" used by the Court in paragraph 7, and the word "owed"? Which one should the Court have used?

Andrew Payton
v.
Wendell Colar, et al.

Court of Appeal of Louisiana
Fourth Circuit
December 15, 1987
518 So.2d 1104

GULOTTA, Chief Judge.

[1] Plaintiff appeals from a judgment dismissing his rule to calculate and compel the payment of the remaining balance due on a partially paid personal injury judgment. The issue to be decided is whether funds deposited as partial payment by a judgment debtor are to be first applied to principal or interest. Because LSA-C.C. Art. 1866 provides that, in the absence of the obligee's consent, the obligor of an interest bearing debt may not impute payment to the principal when interest is due, we conclude that partial payments by the judgment debtor must be applied first to reduce outstanding judicial interest before they can reduce the principal amount of the judgment.

[2] In October, 1984, plaintiff recovered a personal injury judgment against Wendell A. Colar, New 77 Club, Inc., and Insurors Indemnity and Insurance Company, in solido, in the sum of $711,000.00 plus costs and interest from date of judicial demand (February 21, 1979). On February 4, 1985, the defendant insurer delivered to plaintiff's attorney a check for $305,610.00. This check was offered under the terms of "payment in full" and represented the insurance policy limits plus post judgment interest on the total judgment. Plaintiff's attorney rejected the amount as full settlement and returned the check. On March 1, 1985, defendant deposited $305,610.00 in the registry of the court. On April 9, 1985, plaintiff filed a "Motion to Withdraw the Funds from the Registry of the Court", stating that there was a substantial dispute about other funds being due in excess of the amount deposited. Pursuant to an order on April 12, 1985, plaintiff withdrew the funds.

[3] On May 12, 1986, in *Payton v. Colar*, 488 So.2d 1271 (La.App. 4th Cir.1986), writ denied 494 So.2d 332 (La.1986), this court held that Insurors Indemnity was liable in solido with other defendants to the plaintiff for the full amount of the judgment of $711,000.00, plus interest from the date of the judicial demand and all costs. After writs were denied by the Supreme Court, the defendant insurer tendered $931,586.30 to plaintiff, who refused to accept this amount as full satisfaction. On October 15, 1986, defendant filed a motion to deposit the funds in the registry of the court, and on that same day plaintiff withdrew the funds.

[4] On October 28, 1986, plaintiff filed a "Rule to Compel Satisfaction of Judgment and Calculate and Assess Interest". In this rule, plaintiff disputed the "calculation

and application of funds" paid by the insurer, and asked for the principal amount of $56,735.93, plus interest, which plaintiff contended was the remaining balance still unpaid. Without written reasons, the trial judge dismissed the rule with prejudice.

[5] Appealing, plaintiff contends that under LSA-C.C. Art. 1866 all payments made to an interest bearing debt must first be applied to interest unless otherwise agreed to by the obligee. According to plaintiff, when defendant deposited the $305,610.00 into the registry of the court on March 1, 1985, the amount of judicial interest due at that time was $444,335.98. Plaintiff argues that the $305,610.00 payment should have first been applied to satisfy the interest, leaving $138,725.89 in interest and the entire $711,000.00 principal still unpaid after the partial payment. As a result, plaintiff contends that until defendant deposited $931,586.30 in the court registry, interest continued to be calculated on the $711,000.00 judgment. Furthermore, according to plaintiff, after the $931,586.30 payment was made, the full amount of interest owed at the time of payment was satisfied, and the principal was reduced to $56,735.93. Plaintiff thus argues that defendant still owes that judgment balance plus interest from date of judicial demand, costs, and attorney's fees.

[6] On the other hand, defendant contends that when a debtor makes a good faith tender of an undisputed portion of a judgment to a plaintiff, the plaintiff is not entitled to recover legal interest on the amount tendered after it has been either presented to plaintiff or deposited in the court's registry. Because the insurer never disputed that it was liable for at least $300,000.00 of the judgment principal, plus post judgment interest, defendant argues that its initial tender of $305,610.00 was in good faith, and that the deposit of that amount in the court registry reduced the judgment principal to $411,000.00 and the interest by $5,610.00. Defendant contends that after the March 1, 1985 deposit, interest is calculated on $411,000.00 of the judgment principal. According to defendant, the subsequent payment of $931,586.30 fully satisfied all outstanding principal and interest, and the trial judge properly dismissed plaintiff's rule for additional interest. We disagree.

[7] LSA-C.C. Art. 1866, relied on by plaintiff, provides as follows:

> An obligor of a debt that bears interest may not, without the obligee's consent, impute a payment to principal when interest is due.
>
> A payment made on principal and interest must be imputed first to interest.

This article is found in Title III of Book III of the Civil Code, which is entitled "Obligations in General". LSA-C.C. Art. 1757, which is also included in Title III, provides that obligations can arise from contracts as well as from the law, as in instances of wrongful acts.[1] Thus, an offense or quasi offense under LSA-C.C. Arts. 2315 et seq. creates an obligation on the part of the wrongdoer in favor of the injured party.

---

1. LSA-C.C. Art. 1757 provides:
   Obligations arise from contracts and other declarations of will. They also arise directly from the law, regardless of a declaration of will, in instances such as wrongful acts, the management of the affairs of another, unjust enrichment and other acts or facts.

[8] It is well settled that an obligation, when reduced to judgment, is merged therein and no longer exists as a distinct obligation, but it is deemed as having acquired the status of the thing adjudged. *Sailing Wiping Cloth Co. v. Sewell, Inc.*, 419 So.2d 112 (La.App. 2nd Cir.1982); *Glazer Steel Corp. v. LaRose Shipyard, Inc.*, 372 So.2d 250 (La.App. 1st Cir.1979); *Agricultural Enterprises, Inc. v. Morgan*, 147 So.2d 40 (La.App. 2nd Cir.1962); *Mackee v. Cairnes*, 2 Mart., M.S. 599 (1824); *Abat v. Buisson*, 9 La. 417 (1836); *West Feliciana Railroad Co. v. Thornton*, 12 La.Ann. 736 (1857); *The Citizens Bank of Louisiana v. Hancock*, 35 La.Ann. 41 (1883); *Lalanne v. Payne*, 42 La.Ann. 152, 7 So. 481 (1890); *Cassiere v. Cuban Coffee Mills*, 225 La. 1003, 74 So.2d 193, (1954). Likewise, a debt reduced to a judgment also acquires the status of the thing adjudged. *Cassiere v. Cuban Coffee Mills,* supra; *Mackee v. Cairnes,* supra; *Abat v. Buisson,* supra; *West Feliciana R. Co. v. Thornton,* supra; *Citizens Bank of Louisiana v. Hancock,* supra; *Lalanne v. Payne,* supra. LSA-C.C. Art. 2924, which is also found in Book III of the Civil Code, defines "judicial interest" as legal interest on a sum that is the object of a judicial demand.[2]

[9] Reading these codal provisions *in pari materia*, we conclude that a tort judgment bearing judicial interest is a "debt that bears interest" within the meaning of LSA-C.C. Art. 1866 and that a judgment debtor may not, without the obligee's consent, impute a payment to principal when interest is due. Thus, a partial payment on a tort judgment must be imputed first to judicial interest before it can be applied to reduce the principal amount of the judgment.

[10] In *Lambert v. Cronvich*, 373 So.2d 554 (La.App. 4th Cir.1979), writ denied 376 So.2d 960 (La.1979), we applied former LSA-C.C. Art. 2164, the precursor to present LSA-C.C. Art. 1866, to a money judgment rendered on promissory notes that contained specific provisions for interest and attorney's fees. In *Lambert*, the trial judge applied partial credits to reduce the principal amount of the judgment. Although we agreed with the application of certain credits, we amended the judgment after concluding that the credits should be applied in accordance with LSA-C.C. Art. 2164,[3] i.e., if the payment does not extinguish both interest and principal, it should be

---

2. LSA-C.C. Art. 2924 provides, in pertinent part:
   A. Interest is either legal or conventional.
   B. (1) Legal interest is fixed at the following rates, to wit:
       (a) At twelve percent per annum on all sums which are the object of a judicial demand, whence this is called judicial interest; and * * * *
   (2) The rate of judicial interest resulting from a lawsuit pending or filed during the indicated periods shall be as follows:
       (a) Prior to September 12, 1980, the rate shall be seven percent per annum.
       (b) On and after September 12, 1980, until September 11, 1981, the rate shall be ten percent per annum.
       (c) On and after September 11, 1981, the rate shall be twelve percent per annum.
3. LSA-C.C. Art. 2164 provides that:
   "The debtor of a debt, which bears interest or produces rents, cannot, without the consent of the creditor, impute to the reduction of the capital any payment he may make, when there is interest or rent due.

applied to the interest first. Thus implicit in *Lambert* was a conclusion that a money judgment containing interest is a debt bearing interest within the meaning of the codal article. Applying the *Lambert* rationale, we conclude that LSA-C.C. Art. 1866 applies to the money judgment in our case, even though we are dealing with a tort judgment rather than a judgment on a promissory note.

[11] Having determined that LSA-C.C. Art. 1866 applies in the instant case, we conclude that the payment made by defendant on March 1, 1985 should have first been applied to satisfy the interest owed, and the remainder, if any, applied to reduce the principal. According to our calculations set out below, the $305,610.00 did not reduce the principal but merely reduced the interest owed on March 1, 1985. Consequently, Insurors Indemnity still owes plaintiff the remaining judgment principal of $57,538.60 plus judicial interest until paid. [. . . .]

[12] Although the cases[4] relied on by defendant do apparently stand for the proposition that judicial interest ceases to run upon an amount tendered in partial payment of a judgment, none of the cited opinions discusses LSA-C.C. Art. 1866 or its precursor, former LSA-C.C. Art. 2164, which specifically provides that a partial payment must be credited first to interest before it can be applied to reduce the principal.

[13] In *Schmidt v. Holmes*, 487 So.2d 577 (La.App. 4th Cir.1986), one of two solidary judgment debtors forwarded a check for his one half virile share of the tort judgment including interest and costs. The plaintiffs in *Schmidt* refused to accept the payment on the grounds that they were entitled to full satisfaction of the judgment from either or both of the solidary judgment debtors and that the acceptance would prejudice their rights to the full satisfaction of the judgment. The debtor then sent a letter to the plaintiff stating that it was not its intention that plaintiffs should waive any rights to ultimately collect the full judgment against them in the event the other debtor would not be able to pay. Two months later, after the second solidary debtor tendered its one-half of the total judgment principal plus costs and interest, the plaintiffs then accepted the earlier tender by the first obligor. Because the first debtor's tender did not include the interest accrued from the original date of that tender to the date of the second debtor's tender, plaintiffs thereafter filed a "Rule to Compel Satisfaction of Judgment and To Assess Interest against Defendant". The trial court in *Schmidt* dismissed plaintiffs' claims for the additional interest, and we affirmed the trial court's decision.

"Every payment which does not distinguish both the principle and the interest must be imputed first to the payment of the interest."

4. *Schmidt v. Holmes*, 487 So.2d 577 (La.App. 4th Cir.1986); *Williams v. Hanover Insurance Company of New York*, 351 So.2d 858 (La.App. 2nd Cir.1977); *Boudreaux v. Riley Buick, Inc.*, 415 So.2d 970 (La.App. 2nd Cir.1982); *Carlyon v. Aetna Casualty and Surety Company*, 413 So.2d 1355 (La.App. 3rd Cir.1982), and *Mamou Farm Service, Inc. v. Hudson Insurance Company*, 488 So.2d 259 (La.App. 3rd Cir.1986).

[14] By allowing a solidary debtor to pay less than the full amount of a judgment and thereby interrupt the accrual of interest on the amount paid, *Schmidt* and the cases there directly conflict with our interpretation and application of LSA-C.C. Art. 1866 in the instant case. The *Schmidt* opinion is silent as to LSA-C.C. Art. 1866, however, and an argument based on this codal article was apparently not presented to the court. Nonetheless, to the extent that our earlier opinion conflicts with our reasoning in the instant case, we hereby overrule Schmidt.[5]

[....]

KLEES, Judge, dissenting in part and concurring in part.

[15] I do not agree that our decision in the instant case necessitates the overruling of *Schmidt v. Holmes* and accordingly dissent from that part of the opinion. In *Schmidt*, one of two solidary debtors tendered payment of one-half the total principal, costs and interest due on the date of the tender. Plaintiffs refused to accept this amount until six weeks later, at which time they received a check from the other debtor for one-half the total judgment, costs and interest due on the date of the second tender. After accepting both checks, plaintiffs filed a Rule against the debtor who had made the initial tender seeking to recover the interest that had allegedly accrued on his half of the principal from the date of the original tender until the date that plaintiffs actually accepted the payment. We held that plaintiffs were not entitled to the additional interest because they could have accepted the initial tender without prejudicing their rights to collect the entire judgment from either defendant. *Schmidt, supra* at 578.

[16] *Schmidt* is distinguishable from the instant case because the plaintiffs in *Schmidt* did not contend that the initial payment should have been imputed to interest before principal, but rather that they were entitled to additional interest because they chose not to accept the payment until six weeks after it was originally tendered.

[17] Civil Code article 1866, upon which the majority relies, states that "[t]he obligor of a debt that bears interest may not, *without the obligee's consent*, impute a payment to principal when interest is due." (Emphasis added). In *Schmidt*, the plaintiffs and defendants were in agreement as to which portion of each payment constituted principal and which portion constituted interest; at issue was the date at which the interest ceased to accrue. By not making an argument under article 1866, the *Schmidt* plaintiffs tacitly consented to the defendants' allocation of the funds. Accordingly, the court's interpretation of article 1866 in the instant case does not conflict with *Schmidt*.

[18] While I agree with the majority's holding in this case, I can foresee potential problems with the application of C.C. Art. 1866 to solidary obligations which this case does not address.

---

5. In accordance with our internal rules, our opinion in the instant case has been submitted to all judges of this court, and a majority of them have voted to overrule the *Schmidt* decision.

On Application for Rehearing

PER CURIAM.

[19] In a petition for rehearing, the defendant insurer contends that LSA-C.C. Art. 1866 applies only to debts bearing "conventional interest", i.e., a charge by an obligee for the obligor's right to use the obligee's money over a period of time. According to defendant, legal interest on a judicial demand is a form of "moratory" damages or penalty that is a separate debt from the principal amount of the judgment, and a judgment debtor can therefore choose to apply his partial payment toward either the judgment principal or the judicial interest pursuant to LSA-C.C. Art. 1864.[1]

[20] In support of this contention, defendant cites the 18th Century French legal scholar, Pothier, as follows:

> "The rule which we have established, that the application ought to be made to the interest before the principal, does not hold with regard to interest due by a debtor, from the time of a judicial demand being made, as a penalty for his delay; such interest is awarded by way of damages, and forms a distinct debt from the principal; and what the debtor pays is applied rather to the principal than to this interest. . . . This is established by an arrêt [decision] of 1649 and another of 1706."[2]

[21] Although Pothier's works are influential as a source of the Code Napoleon, we do not find this passage persuasive in our case. Article 1254 of the Code Napoleon of 1804, which is the French counterpart to our present LSA-C.C. Art. 1866, makes no exception for moratory interest in stating the rule for imputing payments.[3] The 19th Century commentators Aubry and Rau have noted that the French redactors did not adopt Pothier's distinction between the two types of interest:

> "Pothier (No. 571) teaches that this rule [of applying payment to interest before principal] applied in the past to compensatory interests only and not to moratory interests. Since Article 1254, however, did not reproduce this distinction it seems that it should not be admitted today. Delvincourt,

---

1. LSA-C.C. Art. 1864 provides:

"An obligor who owes several debts to an obligee has the right to impute payment to the debt he intends to pay.

"The obligor's intent to pay a certain debt may be expressed at the time of payment or may be inferred from circumstances known to the obligee."

2. Pothier, *A Treatise On The Law of Obligations, or Contracts*, trans. William David Evans (Philadelphia: 1826).

Although the passage cited by defendant is numbered "534" in the Evans translation, it is numbered "571" in the French edition of Pothier's works. See II *Oeuvres De Pothier*, Nouvelle Edition (Paris: 1821).

3. C.N. 1804, Art. 1254 provides:

"The debtor of a debt which bears interest or produces arrearages, cannot, without the consent of the creditor, impute the payment which he makes on the capital, in preference to the arrearages or interest; a payment made on the capital and interest but which is not integral, is first imputed to the interest."

II, p. 556; Favard, *Rép.*, Imputation, § 3; Larombière, III, Art. 1254, No. 4; Zachariae, § 320, note 5. But see: Duranton, XII, 192; Marcadé, on Art. 1254, No. 3."[4]

[22] In addition to this authority, we note that Jean Domat, another French legal scholar whose writings influenced the redactors of the Code Napoleon and the Louisiana Civil Code, has recognized that interest can arise from four causes: by contract, by the nature of an obligation, by law, or " . . . as a punishment of the debtor who defers payment after the creditor has made his demand in a court of justice, both of his principal, and of the interest due for default of payment."[5] Unlike Pothier, Domat notes that a payment on a debt should be applied first to the discharge of the interest, even if the interest is "due by a sentence of a court of justice":

> "If a debtor makes a payment to discharge debts which of their nature bear interest, such as that of a marriage portion, or what is due by virtue of a contract of sale, *or the same be due by a sentence of a court of justice*, and the payment be not sufficient to acquit both the principal and the interest due thereon; the payment will be applied, in the first place, to the discharge of the interest, and the overplus to the discharge of a part of the principal sum. [Emphasis ours]."[6]

[23] Based on these authorities, we reaffirm our interpretation of LSA-C.C. Art. 1866 as expressed in our initial opinion. As we have noted, LSA-C.C. Art. 1866 is found in Title III ("Obligations in General") of Book III of the Louisiana Civil Code. LSA-C.C. Art. 1866 makes no distinctions between contractual debts or judgment debts, or between conventional interest and judicial interest. Pothier's observations of early French law on this issue have not been incorporated in either the Code Napoleon or the Louisiana Civil Code, and do not persuade us to reach a different result in our case.

[. . . .]

[24] Accordingly, defendant's petition for a rehearing is denied.

[. . . .]

Questions

1. Design a diagram of all the relationships existing in this case and describe in legal terms the obligations created. Identify, for example, any principal obligor v. secondary obligor, sources of obligations (contract v. tort), etc.

2. Paragraph 5: What are the legal arguments made by plaintiff as regards the different amounts of money he claims are owed to him? As regards the interest

---

4. Aubry and Rau, *Cours de Droit Civil Français*, § 320, Footnote 4, trans. Louisiana State Law Institute (1965). See also Fuzier-Herman, *Code Civil*, Art. 1254, Footnote 2, (Paris: 1896), citing similar authorities on this issue.

5. Domat, *The Civil Law in Its Natural Order*, § 1958, trans. by William Strahan (Boston: 1850).

6. Domat, § 2284.

that plaintiff claims is owed to him, how does plaintiff look upon this interest: does he look upon it as an additional compensation for his inability to have used the principal amount of money; does he look upon it as damages for some loss?

3. Paragraph 6: What do you think of defendant's statement that "when a debtor makes a good faith tender of an undisputed portion . . . the plaintiff is not entitled to recover legal interest"? Isn't "good faith" a strong argument? How does defendant look at the interest he claims he should not pay: does he look at it as a penalty; does he look at it as damages not due because there was no loss or prejudice suffered by plaintiff?

4. Paragraphs 7–8: Note that the Court first states the law in the form of Louisiana Civil Code articles 1866, 1757, and 2315. In the first part of the first sentence in paragraph 8, is the Court saying that the judgment *creates* the obligation or is it only acknowledging the existence of an obligation as arising from the sources of law mentioned at the outset? What does the later phrase "thing adjudged" mean? Does it mean case law or *jurisprudence constante*?

5. Paragraph 20: What are the defendant's views on the legal nature of interest, particularly conventional interest, and moratory damages? What do you think of the Court searching for support in comparative law? Should it look to "any" comparative law?

Don J. Chaisson and Diane Chaisson
v.
Matthew Chaisson
Court of Appeal of Louisiana
Second Circuit
February 26, 1997
690 So.2d 899

STEWART, Judge.

[. . . .]

Facts

[1] From March, 1989, through December, 1991, Mr. and Mrs. Chaisson advanced money to their youngest son Matthew for a car, college expenses, furniture, etc. When Matthew graduated Louisiana Tech University and obtained full-time employment, he began making payments to his parents in the amount of $300.00 per month from September, 1991, through September, 1992. In July, 1993, the amount of the payments were reduced to $200.00 per month by agreement between Matthew and his parents. Matthew made five payments in the amount of $200.00. After November, 1993, all payments from Matthew ceased.

[2] Mr. and Mrs. Chaisson retained counsel who wrote Matthew demanding repayment on the money lent him by the Chaissons. Once Matthew obtained

counsel, all further contact regarding the debt was made with Matthew's attorney. Matthew disputed that any money was owed his parents, except on the loan with which Matthew purchased a car.

[3] Thereafter, on May 19, 1995, Mr. and Mrs. Chaisson filed suit in Shreveport City Court to recover the amount they allegedly loaned Matthew for a car and college expenses. Trial was held on January 18, 1996. At trial, Mr. and Mrs. Chaisson introduced a handwritten document listing money loaned to Matthew for numerous reasons, including summer school tuition, rent, furniture, housewares, spending money, etc. That document also indicated several payments made by Matthew and included a detailed repayment schedule. At trial, Matthew's siblings testified as to their agreement with their parents regarding payment of college expenses. Matthew's sister, Audra, did not owe her parents any amount when she graduated college. However, Matthew's brother, Peter, did owe his parents some amount of money and made payments until he had paid his parents back on those loans. A family friend, Anna Ratcliff, testified regarding her personal knowledge of Mr. and Mrs. Chaisson's policy of advancing money to their children for various reasons and of requiring repayment of those advances.

[4] On April 1, 1996, the trial court rendered written reasons and found that there was an oral agreement between Matthew and his parents to repay the advances of money, that, upon his securing full-time employment after graduation, Matthew did begin making payments "without imputation as to which of these debts would be paid first," and that, as the debts were of the same nature and were due at the same time, payment was proportionally imputed to all debts pursuant to La.C.C. art. 1868. The court further found that the debts had not prescribed nor had Mr. and Mrs. Chaisson violated the Fair Debt Collection Act. The court rendered judgment in favor of Mr. and Mrs. Chaisson in the amount of $10,006.12 plus legal interest from the date of judicial demand. Judgment was prepared by counsel for Mr. and Mrs. Chaisson, approved by counsel for Matthew Chaisson, and signed on April 15, 1996.

Discussion

Assignment of Error #1

[5] Matthew asserts that the trial court erred in finding that an agreement existed between he [*sic*] and his parents concerning the repayment of money advanced by Mr. and Mrs. Chaisson, except for the amount advanced for purchase of a car.

[. . . .]

[6] In any action based on contract, three elements must be proven: 1) an offer, 2) an acceptance, and 3) the consent of the parties. *La.C.C. art. 1927.* Absent any formalities as may required by law, an offer and acceptance may be made "orally, in writing, or by action or inaction that under the circumstances is clearly indicative of consent." *La.C.C. art. 1927.*

[7] Matthew contends that Mr. and Mrs. Chaisson failed to prove that they made an offer to Matthew which he accepted and that, therefore, there was never any consent or "meeting of the minds" regarding the terms of the alleged loan agreement.

See *Eagle Plumbing, Heating and Air Conditioning, Inc. v. Ragusa*, 517 So.2d 280 (La. App. 1 Cir.1987).

[8] Included in the evidence adduced at trial was a hand written document listing the advances of money made to Matthew for various reasons, indicating any payments made by Matthew and the balance owed, and including computation of a monthly payment amount and a payment schedule. Further, the testimony of Mr. and Mrs. Chaisson, Audra, and Peter clearly established that Mr. and Mrs. Chaisson advanced money to their children during their college years for personal needs and that Mr. and Mrs. Chaisson intended these advances to be loans which would be repaid by the individual child upon graduation and obtaining full-time employment. Matthew also testified that this was the family policy and admitted that he and his parents had discussed, on more than one occasion, the money advanced to him and their intention that the advances were to be considered a loan.

[9] Although Matthew, by his own admission, understood his parents' intent, he contends that he did not explicitly agree to their terms but that he merely took the money. The trial court questioned Matthew extensively concerning this aspect of his testimony and whether Matthew considered any options for funding his college education other than his parents, such as student loans, National Guard, etc. The colloquy between the trial court and Matthew clearly establishes that Matthew knew that his parents intended the advances to be loans which he was responsible for repaying upon obtaining full-time employment after graduation and that, although the specific details of the agreement, i.e., interest rate and term of repayment were not determined at the time he accepted the loans, he knew there would be a term for repayment of the balance of the money advanced plus interest.

[10] Contrary to Matthew's contention, we find an offer and an acceptance under the circumstances of this case. Matthew's parents made him a standing offer to lend him money for his tuition and other things during his college years on the understanding that he would be obligated to pay the loans in installments once he was out of college and gainfully employed. He accepted their offer from time to time by accepting from them specific amounts of money for particular purposes for which he needed money. An offer may be accepted other than by sacramental words such as "I accept your offer." *North Louisiana Milk Producers Ass'n, Inc. v. Southland Corp.*, 352 So.2d 293 (La.App. 2 Cir.1977).

[11] Based on the evidence and testimony presented, we do not find that the trial court was clearly wrong or manifestly erroneous in finding that an agreement existed between Matthew and his parents concerning repayment of money advanced for college expenses by Mr. and Mrs. Chaisson to Matthew. This assignment is without merit.

[. . . .]

Assignments of Error #3 and #4

[12] Matthew contends that his parents failed to file suit for repayment timely. He asserts that the money advanced was not "of the same nature" as found by the trial

court and that a three year prescriptive period applied so that his parents should have filed suit within three years of his graduation from college on May 18, 1991.

[13] Mr. and Mrs. Chaisson argue that the trial court did not err in finding that the money advanced Matthew were loans "of the same nature" and that the debts had not prescribed because Matthew made payments by check with no reference to payment on the car loan.

[14] *La.C.C. art. 1868* provides, in pertinent part, that "if all debts are of the same nature and became due at the same time, payment must be proportionally imputed to all." An action on money lent is subject to a three-year prescriptive period which commences to run from the day payment is exigible. *La.C.C. art. 3494; La.C.C. art. 3495.*

[15] The record establishes that the loans were used to purchase such items as a car, gifts, and household necessities and to pay such expenses as rent, utilities, and insurance premiums. All these loans were for expenses incurred during the time Matthew attended college and were related to his college attendance. We find that the trial court was not clearly wrong in finding that, pursuant to *La.C.C. art. 1868*, the debts were of the same nature and became due at the same time and that, therefore, payment on one debt must be imputed proportionally to all.

[16] As previously discussed, the agreement between Matthew and Mr. and Mrs. Chaisson provided that Matthew was not obligated to begin repaying the amounts advanced for his college expenses until he obtained full-time employment after graduation. Matthew graduated on May 18, 1991. Matthew made payments sporadically until November 6, 1993. Each payment was made by check referenced only as a monthly payment such as "June payment" or "August payment." Mr. and Mrs. Chaisson filed this lawsuit on May 19, 1995.

[17] Prescription is interrupted by acknowledgment of the debt. *La.C.C. art. 3464.* Payment on the debt constitutes an acknowledgment which interrupts prescription. *Marr v. Johnson*, 204 So.2d 806 (La.App. 2 Cir.1967). As we agree with the trial court that these debts are of the same nature and due at the same time and that payment must be proportionally imputed to all the debts, Matthew's payments on these loans interrupted prescription until the last payment on November 6, 1993. Clearly, Mr. and Mrs. Chaisson timely filed this action within three years of that date. We find that the trial court was not clearly wrong in finding that the debts had not prescribed. Therefore, this assignment is without merit.

[. . . .]

Questions

NOTE: To better prepare to discuss this case, you should read the Louisiana Civil Code articles on "donations" (particularly arts. 1467–1567 and most particularly arts. 1526–1567) and "Loan" (arts. 2891–2912).

1. Paragraph 1: Describe in legal terms the nature of things for which money was advanced to Matthew. Was graduating from college any kind of condition

for the parents advancing money to Matthew or for Matthew paying it back? What about securing employment?

2. Paragraph 2: Does the Court identify the source or sources of Matthew's payments to his parents? What name, if any, could or should the court have given to the (legal?) relationship between Matthew and his parents? Was there a legal duty on the part of the parents to advance money to Matthew?

3. Paragraph 4: What name is the Court giving to the bond of law created between the parents and Matthew? Is there any legal reason or ground for Matthew to refer to his sister Audra, "who did not owe her parents any amount"?

4. Paragraph 12: Do you have any comment on whether or not there was a meeting of the minds? What would have been the effect of having the agreement in writing?

5. Paragraph 14: After you have read the Code articles on "Imputation," what is your comment on the Court's application of the requirements for imputation, particularly under Louisiana Civil Code article 1868?

Section IV — Tender & Deposit

Louisiana Sources of Law
Louisiana Civil Code

Art. 1869. Offer to perform and deposit by obligor.

When the object of the performance is the delivery of a thing or a sum of money and the obligee, without justification, fails to accept the performance tendered by the obligor, the tender, followed by deposit to the order of the court, produces all the effects of a performance from the time the tender was made if declared valid by the court.

A valid tender is an offer to perform according to the nature of the obligation. (Acts 1984, No. 331, §1, eff. Jan. 1, 1985.)

Art. 1870. Notice as tender.

If the obligor knows or has reason to know that the obligee will refuse the performance, or when the object of the performance is the delivery of a thing or a sum of money at a place other than the obligee's domicile, a notice given to the obligee that the obligor is ready to perform has the same effect as a tender. (Acts 1984, No. 331, §1, eff. Jan. 1, 1985.)

Art. 1872. Sale of a thing and deposit of proceeds.

If performance consists of the delivery of a perishable thing, or of a thing whose deposit and custody are excessively costly in proportion to its value, the court may order the sale of the thing under the conditions that it may direct, and the deposit of the proceeds. (Acts 1984, No. 331, §1, eff. Jan. 1, 1985.)

Doctrine

Louisiana Law of Obligations in General, A Précis

Section 7.1.3

Although an obligor may be willing and ready to perform, it is still conceivable that his obligee might refuse to receive the performance offered. Whether the obligee's objections to the performance are valid or unreasonable, it remains that the obligor who is in a position to perform might suffer a prejudice should he have no alternative means of carrying through with his performance.

Taking into account the concerns and interests of both the obligee and the obligor, the law has devised the institution of *tender and deposit* as a means of providing a temporary solution to the conflicting rights of the two parties involved. [. . . .]

The civil Code provides for two forms of *tender and deposit* at the same time it outlines the effects, both general and particular, of each one. [. . . .]

In the event an obligee has, unequivocally and without apparent justification, refused to accept the performance offered by his obligor, the latter may, thereafter, make a *tender* followed by a *deposit* to the order of the court. [. . . .]

A *tender and deposit* is meant to amount to the performance of the object or item of the obligation involved rather than be a substitute for it. [. . . .]

It is possible that the thing tendered and deposited be a perishable product to be consumed or used within a relatively short period of time. A long storage might lead to the destruction of that thing despite all the diligence exercised by the obligor. To prevent such a useless outcome, **Article 1872** offers the depositor, and the court, an alternative solution which will protect the interest the obligee has in the performance. [. . . .]

The second form of tender available to an obligor is outlined in **Article 1870** [. . .]. [. . . .]

The importance of this rule of law is that it makes a mere notice of readiness to perform equivalent to a tender and vests in it the same legal effects.

See *Payne v. Hurwitz*, 978 So.2d 1000 (La.App. 1 Cir. 2008).

Section V — Impossibility of Performance

Louisiana Sources of Law
Louisiana Civil Code

Art. 1873. Obligor not liable when failure caused by fortuitous event.

An obligor is not liable for his failure to perform when it is caused by a fortuitous event that makes performance impossible.

An obligor is, however, liable for his failure to perform when he has assumed the risk of such a fortuitous event.

An obligor is liable also when the fortuitous event occurred after he has been put in default.

An obligor is likewise liable when the fortuitous event that caused his failure to perform has been preceded by his fault, without which the failure would not have occurred. (Acts 1984, No. 331, §1, eff. Jan. 1, 1985.)

Art. 1874. Fortuitous event that would have destroyed object in hands of obligee.

An obligor who had been put in default when a fortuitous event made his performance impossible is not liable for his failure to perform if the fortuitous event would have likewise destroyed the object of the performance in the hands of the obligee had performance been timely rendered.

That obligor is, however, liable for the damage caused by his delay. (Acts 1984, No. 331, §1, eff. Jan. 1, 1985.)

Art. 1875. Fortuitous event.

A fortuitous event is one that, at the time the contract was made, could not have been reasonably foreseen. (Acts 1984, No. 331, §1, eff. Jan. 1, 1985.)

Art. 1876. Contract dissolved when performance becomes impossible.

When the entire performance owed by one party has become impossible because of a fortuitous event, the contract is dissolved.

The other party may then recover any performance he has already rendered. (Acts 1984, No. 331, §1, eff. Jan. 1, 1985.)

Art. 1877. Fortuitous event that has made performance impossible in part.

When a fortuitous event has made a party's performance impossible in part, the court may reduce the other party's counterperformance proportionally, or, according to the circumstances, may declare the contract dissolved. (Acts 1984, No. 331, §1, eff. Jan. 1, 1985.)

Art. 1878. [omitted]

Doctrine

Louisiana Law of Obligations in General, A Précis
Sections 7.2.1 to 7.2.2

Whenever a legal relationship requires that a performance be undertaken in the future, be it a day, a month or a year, or when the performance itself spreads over a period of time, there always exists the danger that the expectations of the parties will be upset, betrayed or altered in one way or another. Events may occur which will interfere with the proper planning and anticipation of the parties. [. . . .]

Civil Code Article 1875 defines a fortuitous event in these terms:

> "A fortuitous event is one that, at the time the contract was made, could not have been reasonably foreseen."

The simplicity of this definition is misleading, in particular when one is asked to weigh the meaning of the requirement of *reasonableness*. [. . . .]

To ensure the stability of contracts, the security of business transactions and the reliability of the promises given, the courts should make use of certain criteria to test the reasonableness of the parties' failure to foresee a fortuitous event and plan accordingly their contractual obligations. [. . . .]

The legal effects resulting from the occurrence of a fortuitous event that affects an obligor's performance will vary in extent with the time of that occurrence and its factual impact. In this respect one can distinguish between an absolute impossibility for the obligor to perform and a partial impossibility to do so. [. . . .]

Civil Code **Article 1873-1** formulates the general principle as follows:

> "An obligor is not liable for his failure to perform when it is caused by a fortuitous event that makes performance impossible." [. . . .]

The legal consequence of this absolute impossibility to carry out an entire performance because of a fortuitous event is that **"the contract is dissolved"** and **"the other party may then recover any performance he has already rendered."** [. . . .]

Civil Code **Article 1877** formulates an equitable rule in these terms:

> **"When a fortuitous event has made a party's performance impossible in part, the court may reduce the other party's counterperformance proportionally, or, according to the circumstances, may declare the contract dissolved."**

Cases

City of New Orleans; Blake G. Arata et al., representatives, etc.; and New Orleans Public Service, Inc.

v.

United Gas Pipe Line Company

Louisiana Power & Light Company

v.

United Gas Pipe Line Company and Pennzoil Company

Court of Appeal of Louisiana
Fourth Circuit
April 30, 1987
517 So.2d 145

REDMANN, Chief Judge.

[1] United Gas Pipe Line Company appeals from judgments for breach of contract damages in favor of Louisiana Power and Light Company for $40,309,142 and New Orleans Public Service, Inc. (and the class of persons paying the latter's electric rates during the breach) for $44,403,106. LP & L and NOPSI [New Orleans Public Service, Inc.] were obliged by the contracts to buy, and United was obliged to supply to them, their requirements (or part-requirements) of natural gas for electric power plants over periods of up to 25 years. United raises many issues [. . . **but its** . . .] principal argument is that a national gas shortage and governmental distribution orders reduced or excused its contractual delivery obligations, both because the contracts so provide in cases of gas shortage, governmental orders, or force majeure, and because of a variety of other defenses.

[. . . .]

[2] We conclude that the record supports the trial judge's factual conclusion that United did not prove its affirmative defenses for its conceded failure to deliver the contracted gas. United did not prove that, if it had not released gas reserves that it already had (and had acted with reasonable diligence to acquire additional available gas reserves to meet its already existing contractual commitments and had not further committed itself to new sales of gas), the shortage would still have occurred (or to what extent) on its interstate and New Orleans area intrastate pipelines. United did not prove that its actions did not cause its shortage and were not, at the least, a breach of its implied contractual obligations under its contracts to provide gas. We reason that the contractual impairment of deliveries clause does not purport to exonerate United from liability; that the governmental orders would not have been necessary as to United but for United's self-caused shortage; and that the force majeure clause is inapplicable because United did not prove that the shortage was not within its control. [. . . .]

[3] It is undisputed that United did not supply the gas that, unless somehow excused, it was obliged to supply for LP & L's and NOPSI's power plants under the long-term contracts. United is therefore liable for the damages caused by its failure to deliver the contracted gas, unless it proves that its delivery obligation is reduced or excused by one of its several defenses.

[4] Essentially, all of United's defenses partake of the nature of impossibility of performance because of a nationwide gas shortage and federal commission and court orders adopted because of that shortage. Essentially, the trial court's response, which we deem not manifestly erroneous but supported by the evidence, is that United bound itself to perform its contracts with LP & L and NOPSI, and that United did not prove that it did perform those contracts reasonably and in good faith: did not prove that it acted reasonably, in view of its performance obligations, to acquire and maintain sufficient gas reserves to satisfy its contractual obligations. The trial court's reasoning is that United itself brought about its shortage, which therefore does not exonerate United from liability.

United's Appeal

[5] [**Among other things, United argues that . . .**] liability was imposed on United without any consideration of the effect of the well-recognized gas shortage of the 1970s on United's ability to serve its customers and without reasoned analysis of the prudence of United's management of its gas supplies [. . . **and that . . .**] damages were awarded for reductions in deliveries brought about entirely by federal order rather than by United's shortage of gas[. . .]. [. . . .]

[. . . .]

III. The Gas Shortage as Exoneration

[6] That gas in ample quantity was unavailable from 1970 or so is not gainsaid. Beginning in 1968 and continuing through the 1970s, nationwide gas reserves declined as usage exceeded additions. But the shortage did not produce the results United claims by its many defenses, some of which overlap (as do this opinion's discussions).

III(a). Industry Conditions and United's Actions

[7] United's basic contention is that it did seek to perform, reasonably and in good faith, its contractual commitments; that its purportedly imprudent or improvident management decisions were in fact reasonable and blameless, given the conditions existing at the time and the knowledge available at the time, including the expectations regarding the size and accessibility of underground reserves of natural gas. The genuine shortage of natural gas during the 1970s in Louisiana and throughout the nation, United claims, was unforeseeable and beyond the control of any individual pipeline company.

[8] The trial court concluded that United's management of its gas supplies, including releases, acquisitions and sales, was imprudent and constituted the sole cause of its shortage. United claims that the trial court's evaluation of United's conduct was

flawed because the court did not identify what was imprudent, based its findings on a purely retrospective analysis, and ignored the practices and expectations of the pipeline industry.

[9] United claims that its expectations about the future availability of natural gas were reasonable and consistent with industry expectations; that it had no reason to believe in the period of 1960–66 that it faced a possible shortage. United asserts that it first became aware of possible peak-day shortages in 1969, and that its maintenance of its gas reserve inventory was reasonable and responsive to changing supply and market conditions.

[10] United contends that it could not reasonably maintain the reserves it had because its contracts obliged it to take certain proportions of production annually or else pay for them, and that increasingly high levels of penalty payments for failure to take the contracted gas, caused by its inability to increase sales meaningfully until 1965, coupled with the continual increase in proved reserves in take-or-pay fields boding yet higher penalties, made it impossible for United to maintain existing reserves or make major new gas acquisitions for its interstate system until after 1965. In late 1965 and early 1966, as its system-wide oversupply problems were in the process of being resolved, United contends it recommenced the acquiring of major new reserves.

[11] United asserts that it was not until 1970, when it began to experience a sudden unavailability of new reserves, combined with continued delays in the construction of an ambitious offshore project and unforeseen downward revisions of estimates of its remaining reserves, that United realized that it would not be able to get sufficient new reserves to avoid some system-wide curtailments.

[12] Another element contributing to United's predicament was that customers varied their level of takes during the year, at differing percentages of their maximum contract levels. The ratio of actual deliveries to the maximum contract limit is known as the annual load factor. The load factor of United's pipeline customers increased from 81% in 1965 to 94% in 1969. United's power plant customers also increased their load factors. United claims that the increases within existing maximum daily quantities under contracts were not predicted by customers or by United. According to United, new or enlarged commitments entered into after Jan. 1, 1968, account for less than 1% of total sales (excluding sales by facilities transferred to Pennzoil) during 1968–1970, and, by comparison with increasing load factors and other problems (increased sales on prior contracts were 14% of total sales), new sales were not, as the trial judge had found, a significant factor in its ultimate curtailment of deliveries.

[13] In short, United contends that when considered in light of the problems it had to address, the information available to it at the time, and the accepted industry custom and practice, United's business decisions regarding the management of its gas supplies were reasonable and designed to ensure adequate supplies for United's customers.

[14] We conclude, as amplified in the discussion below of United's more particularized defenses, that United's actions, however reasonable in other contexts, were not reasonable in the context of firm requirements contracts, because they did not constitute a reasonable effort to perform those contracts, especially in their implied obligations to have and maintain, or to acquire, at whatever cost, the gas necessary to fulfill the explicit delivery obligations.

[15] On its New Orleans intrastate line, which supplied LP & L's Ninemile Point plant and NOPSI, for example, in the years 1962 through 1969, United released massive reserves of gas under contract. These releases were the result of United's contractual attempts (some allowing the producer the right to cancel United's rights) to avoid costly and escalating penalty payments, under "take or pay" contracts, for failure to take gas as United had contracted to do. [....]

[16] The releases of those reserves (over half to Humble Oil as a result of an "omnibus agreement" of October 1, 1962) had business considerations as their purpose, and in that sense may well be described as reasonable. [....] United argues that its releases of reserves were reasonable responses to problems such as these. One may well accept that reserve releases were reasonable for United's purposes, but the releases, and the intrastate system shortage they caused, simply were not beyond United's control — as is required for the applicability of the contract's force majeure provision and the Civil Code's impossibility defense.

[17] United's conversion of the New Orleans intrastate system into part of the interstate system (by injecting interstate gas), United argues plausibly, was more beneficial than harmful to intrastate system customers, in that the gas that had been still attached to the former intrastate system (after the releases) was used in that lower-pressure ("locked-in") system only, which also received additional gas from the higher-pressure remainder of the interstate system. Also plausible is that United's sales to new intrastate system customers would, by themselves, not have created any problem for old customers (had the releases not occurred).

[18] Even so, United's efforts as a whole to deal with (to escape) increasing costs of performance do not constitute good faith performance of its obligations, explicit and implicit, under its gas delivery contracts.

[19] Thousands of times greater by absolute count, although less dramatic in proportion to usage, were the releases affecting United's interstate system, which served LP & L's Sterlington plant near Monroe. That system's annual usage was about 1,300 to 1,500 billion cubic feet between 1960 and 1968, with a growth trend of over 3% a year and with a total usage during that period of about 12,454 Bcf. During that period United released almost 4,590 Bcf while adding only about 4,083 Bcf. Thus, over that nine-year period, that system suffered a continuing and increasing decline of reserves of over 1,300 Bcf a year from usage plus a slight further decline because additions to reserves were more than offset by releases of reserves. Had reserves simply been maintained at the 1960 level, United could have met its delivery obligations under its contracts for well beyond another nine years. LP & L's Sterlington

contract only ran about eight years from the first curtailment. The record shows that there was no gas shortage in the early 1960s, and the trial judge's conclusion was therefore reasonable that United could have acquired additional reserves that, coupled with the reserves it released, would have maintained its reserve position and its ability to fulfill its contractual obligations over the lives of the contracts at issue. United does show that take-or-pay costs and other considerations prompted its business decisions, but increased costs to perform do not excuse nonperformance of contracts. In perspective, penalty pre-payments for gas of $7,000,000 a year (or their balance of $15.3 million by 1963 or even $21.3 million by 1965) to assure ability to comply with its contracts, although truly a substantial amount of money, are not so excessive a "prepayment [of] working capital" (as the Federal Power Commission deemed them) as to justify nonperformance by an enterprise whose annual sales of 1,300,000,000 thousand cubic feet of gas, if all sold at a minimum price of $.175 per Mcf (its 1956 contract prices for LP & L were from $.175 to .745) would bring annual gross income of $227,500,000.

III(b). Contract Construction

[20] United argues (and the trial court agreed) that the contracts authorize certain curtailments, and that those curtailments would therefore not constitute a breach of the contracts. United argues that the trial court erred, however, by improperly identifying the circumstances authorizing curtailments and by finding that those circumstances were not present.

[21] In particular, United argues that the "impairment of deliveries" clause should operate to allow curtailments without liability if a shortage exists, provided only that the shortage was not brought about through United's bad faith. The trial court ruled that in addition to there being a shortage, the shortage has to be the result of force majeure and United has to have "prorated its gas supplies between its customers in the order of priorities enumerated," before the impairment of deliveries clause would reduce or suspend United's delivery obligations. United argues that its curtailment priorities differed from those enumerated only because federal commission curtailment orders required curtailment priorities as mandated under the Natural Gas Act and that those orders superseded contract priorities because of the contracts' "duly constituted authorities" clause. Furthermore, United claims that the impairment of deliveries clause is not dependent on the "force majeure" clause, but is intended to be operative with respect to any system-wide shortages that would impair deliveries. Finally, United argues that the trial court erred in determining and applying the appropriate fault standard under the impairment of deliveries clause.

[. . . .]

Force Majeure

[22] The contracts also contained force majeure clauses, which suspended the obligations of a party when "rendered unable wholly or in part by force majeure to carry out its obligations. . . ." The contracts define force majeure as

"acts of God, strikes, lockouts or other industrial disturbances, acts of public enemy, wars, blockades, insurrections, riots, epidemics, landslides, lightning, earthquakes, fires, storms, floods, washouts, arrests and restraints of governments and people, civil disturbances, explosions, breakage or accident to machinery or lines of pipe, the necessity for making repairs or alterations to machinery or lines of pipe, freezing of wells or lines of pipe, partial or entire failure of wells, and any other causes, whether of the kind herein enumerated or otherwise, not within the control of the party claiming suspension and which by the exercise of due diligence such party is unable to prevent or overcome. . . ."

[23] The trial judge's factual conclusion, reasonably supported by the record, was that by the exercise of due diligence, in not releasing reserves, in acquiring reserves when it could have done so, and in not committing itself to further deliveries by added sales atop its preexisting contractual obligations, United could have prevented the shortage that its own actions caused. In such a factual situation, the force majeure clauses by their own definition do not apply and therefore did not suspend United's obligations.

[. . . .]

III(d). Louisiana Code Defenses

[24] United also argues that the trial judge erred in rejecting its separate defenses, under the Louisiana Civil Code, of fortuitous event or irresistible force, failure of cause, error as to motive, and implied condition.

Fortuitous Event

[25] United contends that the nationwide gas shortage was a "fortuitous event or irresistible force" within C.C. 1933(2) (1870). United cites cases of performance excused by flood (*Viterbo v. Friedlander*, 120 U.S. 707, 7 S.Ct. 962, 30 L.Ed. 776 (1887)) and very heavy rainfall (*Davis v. Tillman*, 370 So.2d 1323 (La.App. 2 Cir.1979)). But those were not cases in which, for example, a contractor was held not liable for the failure of a flood-wall or roof because of flood or rain — that is, was exonerated by the occurrence of the risks that his contract undertook to protect against. United's contracts undertook to provide gas requirements over specified periods of many years and, by necessary implication, to do what was necessary to have the gas to be able to provide it. Had United done the necessary, there would have been no "fortuitous" shortage on its lines here involved. United's fortuitous event or irresistible force defense, C.C. 1933(2) (if applicable despite United's arguably "active" breach, C.C. 1931, by release of reserves), is not different in substance or in result from its contractual force majeure defense.

Lack or Failure of Cause; Error; Condition

[26] United also argues that there was a lack or failure of cause in the contracts in question and therefore they can have no effect; that the error of the parties in assuming the continued availability of natural gas was an error as to the principal

cause, thereby vitiating consent to the contracts; and that the availability of gas was at least an implied condition of the contracts.

[27] United argues that civil law "cause," C.C. 1893 (1870) (largely analogous to common law consideration), for United's obligation to deliver LP & L's and NOPSI's requirements was lacking or failed. United cites art. 1897's declaration that a contract is without cause "when the consideration for making it was something which, in the contemplation of the parties, was thereafter expected to exist or take place, and which did not take place or exist." Art. 1897 itself exemplifies its meaning: "A gift in consideration of a future marriage is void by this rule, if the marriage do not take place." The record suggests that United, in failing to put itself into a position of ability to perform its long-term contracts, may have relied on a "contemplation" that gas would always be available; but it does not suggest that LP & L and NOPSI, in obtaining firm 20-year contracts for requirements, relied on that contemplation. That is not the tenor of the contracts. United did not contract only that, as long as gas were freely available, it would transport it through its pipelines to LP & L and NOPSI. United's argument from art. 1897 would transform United's obligation from one to supply requirements into one to supply what it might have available, and that was not the intent of the contracts. The utility companies did not commit themselves to buy the contracted requirements exclusively from United for 20 years for the "principal cause" that gas was assumed to be readily available, nor in exchange for a conditional obligation that United would sell if gas were available. The utilities committed themselves to buy exclusively from United for the described contract prices in exchange for United's commitment that it would have and deliver gas. The utilities' commitment was the cause for United's obligation (not conditioned on the availability of gas), just as United's commitment was the cause for the utilities' obligation. The contracts were ordinary requirements contracts that are not invalid for lack or failure of cause or consideration.

[. . . .]

Questions

1. *City of New Orleans* was decided prior to the Revision of the law of *force majeure* and "impossibility of performance." Which part(s) of new Louisiana Civil Code article 1873 seem(s) to be the most pertinent to disputes of the kind presented in this case? The first paragraph, which states the "general principle" of impossibility of performance, is, of course, pertinent, but isn't there another one that's even more directly "on point"? Explain.

2. Was the supposed "fortuitous event" on the basis of which United sought to exonerate itself—an acute shortage of natural gas—truly "fortuitous"? Why or why not? *See* La. Civ. Code art. 1875.

3. In order for an obligor to be relieved of liability due to impossibility of performance, the fortuitous event must render performance "truly," or as it is sometimes said, "absolutely" impossible. *See* La. Civ. Code art. 1873. Did the acute natural gas shortage of which United complained in fact have that effect?

Hanover Petroleum Corporation
v.
Tenneco Inc.

Court of Appeal of Louisiana
Third Circuit
March 2, 1988
521 So.2d 1234

GUIDRY, Judge.

[1] In this suit, Hanover Petroleum Corporation (hereafter Hanover) seeks relief from Tenneco Inc.'s alleged breach of a Gas Purchase Contract (hereafter the "Kaplan Contract") relating to Hanover's interest in the production from three gas wells located in the Kaplan Field, Vermilion Parish, Louisiana. The trial court granted summary judgment in favor of Hanover finding that the Kaplan Contract is a valid and enforceable contract; the defenses raised by Tenneco in opposition to the motion for summary judgment are issues of law which have no merit; Tenneco breached its "take or pay" obligations under the contract; and, a separate evidentiary hearing should be held to determine the quantum of Hanover's damages and the availability of the remedy of specific performance. [. . . .]

Facts

[2] The Kaplan Contract is dated June 8, 1981. The terms of the contract, as amended, obligate Hanover to sell and Tenneco to buy a quantity of "deep gas" produced from three wells in the Kaplan Field equal to 85% of the delivery capacity of the wells.[1] Under the terms of the contract, Tenneco agreed to annually take, or pay for if not taken, the aforementioned quantity of gas. Where gas is paid for but not taken, Tenneco is given the right, under the contract, to make up such volumes, during the term of the contract, by taking volumes of gas, at a later date, above the minimum contract volume without charge. The obligation assumed by Tenneco under the Kaplan Contract is commonly referred to in the industry as a "take or pay" obligation.

[3] The record establishes that, for a considerable period of time prior to the institution of this suit, and continuing thereafter, Tenneco has not taken nor has it paid for the volume of gas which it is required to take or pay for annually under the terms of the Kaplan Contract. In fact, in the spring of 1983, Tenneco notified its producer-suppliers, including Hanover, in a document styled "Emergency Gas Purchase Policy" (EGPP), of its inability to, in substantial part, comply with its "take or pay" obligations under existing gas contracts because of events occurring subsequent to

---

1. The contract covers only gas produced from a subsurface interval below 15,000 feet, i.e., gas classified as "deep gas" which was deregulated under Section 107 of the Natural Gas Policy Act of 1978 (NGPA).

the contracts allegedly constituting force majeure. Hanover repudiated the EGPP announced by Tenneco as a unilateral breach of the Kaplan Contract and this suit followed.

[4] On appeal Tenneco contends, as a basic proposition, that the trial court erred in granting summary judgment despite the presence of genuine issues of material fact with regard to the applicability of the affirmative defenses of Force Majeure, Commercial Impracticability, Imprevision, Mistake and Error, Failure of Cause or Consideration etc., all of which were urged by it at the trial level and all or any one of which, it suggests, would excuse its failure to perform under the Kaplan Contract. Stated another way, Tenneco urges that the trial court erred in striking the affirmative defenses urged by Tenneco without regard to the presence of genuine issues of material fact regarding their applicability. [. . . .]

[5] At the outset, we address a threshold issue before consideration of this appeal on its merits.

[. . . .]

Force Majeure

[6] The Kaplan Contract contains a force majeure provision which reads in pertinent part as follows: "In the event of either party being rendered unable, wholly or in part, by force majeure to carry out its obligations under this Contract, other than to make payments due for gas delivered prior to such force majeure, it is agreed that on such party giving notice and reasonably full particulars of such force majeure in writing or by telegraph to the other party within a reasonable time after the occurrence of the cause relied on, then the obligations of the party giving such notice, so far as they are affected by such force majeure, shall be suspended during the continuance of any inability so caused, but for no longer period, and such cause shall so far as possible be remedied with all reasonable dispatch. The term 'force majeure,' as employed herein, means act of God, strikes, lockouts or other industrial disturbances, acts of public enemy, wars, blockades, insurrections, riots, epidemics, landslides, lightning, earthquakes, fires, storms, floods, high water, washouts, arrests and restraints by government or persons, civil disturbances, explosions, breakage or accident to machinery, wells, or lines of pipe, the necessity for making repairs or alterations to machinery, wells or lines of pipe, freezing of wells or lines of pipe, partial or entire failure of any wells, and any other causes, whether of the kind herein enumerated or otherwise, not reasonably within the control of the party claiming suspension."

[7] Tenneco principally contends that the following events, subsequent to the confection of the Kaplan Contract, constitute force majeure within the meaning of the quoted clause and excuses their failure to fully perform the contract: the economic recession; the pricing scheme of the Natural Gas Policy Act of 1978; the abundance of and the drop in the price of competitive fuels; the mild 1982–1983 winter; the increase in deliverability of fields committed to Tenneco under gas purchase

contracts; and, the delivery by producers of greater quantities of higher cost gas rather than lower cost gas under contracts which involve the sale of gas in more than one price category. Additionally, Tenneco contends that, at the very least, the meaning of the force majeure clause, particularly the catch-all provision "any other causes, whether of the kind herein enumerated or otherwise" and the intent of the parties in adopting same constitute genuine issues of fact which preclude the rendition of summary judgment. The trial court determined otherwise, presumably finding no ambiguity in the force majeure clause and Tennecos [*sic*] affirmative defense based thereon a meritless issue of law.

[8] Our research discloses that these issues are res nova at the state appellate level. See *Universal Resources Corporation v. Panhandle Eastern Pipe Line Company,* 813 F.2d 77 (5th Cir.1987). However, these precise issues have been considered at the trial level by both the State and Federal Judiciary. Judge Parker in *Koch v. Columbia Gas Transmission Corporation,* No. 83990-A (M.D.La.1985); Judge Duhe in *Exxon Corporation v. Columbia Gas Transmission Corporation,* 624 F.Supp. 610 (W.D.La.1985); and, Judge Brunson in *The Stone Petroleum Corporation et al v. Tenneco, Inc.,* No. 84-5072, Div. "F", 15th Judicial District Court, Parish of Lafayette, Louisiana (Jan. 1987), respectively, refused to grant summary judgment on the contractual force majeure issue concluding that (1) the scope of force majeure in the contracts is considerably broader than the statutory concept of force majeure; and, (2) genuine issues of fact as to whether the events cited actually prevented performance and are encompassed by the force majeure clause existed which precluded summary judgment. On the other hand, Judge Dirosa in *Amoco Production Company v. Columbia Gas Transmission Corporation,* No. 83-11570, Div. "L", Civil District Court for the Parish of Orleans, Louisiana (June 1985), and Judge Gonzales in *Preston Oil Company v. Transcontinental Gas Pipeline Corporation,* No. 294491, Div. "L", 19th Judicial District Court, Parish of East Baton Rouge, Louisiana (Dec. 1986), decided otherwise, as did the learned trial judge in the instant case. We find the analysis in *Preston* by Judge Gonzales of the force majeure issue compelling and persuasive and take the liberty of quoting same:

> "In light of this *broad* language and in response to their apparent breach of the contract, the defendant adopts several of the same "force majeure"-type factual defenses used by other defendants to this kind of litigation involving 'take-or-pay' contracts. The three most significant are: 1) increased capacity of Preston to deliver gas; 2) reduced market demand for defendant's product; 3) fundamentally changed governmental regulations transforming the industry from a regulated to an unregulated one.

[9] However, shifting supply and demand and changing governmental regulations are normal factors considered in any business transaction. By the clear and unambiguous terms of the remainder of the contract, the plaintiff accepts the supply risk, the defendant accepts the market risk, and both parties adopt the risk of changed governmental regulations. These three factual defenses certainly do not constitute the same type of catastrophic events enumerated in the first part of the 'force majeure'

article. Although these are forces or events beyond the defendant's control, no court has ever brought them within the ambit of the 'force majeure' defense.

[10] The defendant would have the court interpret the clause 'whether of the kind herein enumerated or otherwise' which modifies the phrase 'or any other cause,' to mean any other cause *whatsoever* beyond the control of the defendant in addition to the specifically named ones. If this interpretation were correct, the contract would state that either party could escape responsibility if events beyond the party's control made performance either difficult or unprofitable. An obscure, modifying phrase, buried in an exhibit, would be the most important writing in the entire contract. However, a party would never sign a contract, if this interpretation were correct, because the remainder of the contract would become meaningless. Instead, the court unequivocally interprets the 'or otherwise' phrase to not include the specific promises and provisions in other parts of the contract. In other words, the remainder of the contract clearly and unambiguously states that the plaintiff assumes the supply risk while the defendant assumes the market risk, and these are not the events contemplated by the 'force majeure' escape valve. The basis commitments of the other parts of the contract remain in force despite the 'or otherwise' phrase. The contract must be interpreted consistently; otherwise, defendant's interpretation would render the bulk of the contract meaningless.

[11] Moreover, defendant's strained interpretation of the obscure 'force majeure' clause cannot mean that changed governmental policy or regulation will suspend obligations under the contract. There are absolutely no criteria in the 'force majeure' provisions by which to judge when or how such changes would affect the contractual obligations. What degree of shifting governmental policy is required? Must the change be unfavorable? The 'force majeure' provisions do not address these issues because they were never intended to do so. Modifications in governmental policy and regulation are economic facts of life and are not a basis for suspending a contract. *Superior Oil Co. v. Transco Energy Co.* [616 F.Supp. 98] C.A. No. 84-2138, mem. (W.D.La., Feb. 13, 1985); *Universal Resources Corp. v. Panhandle Eastern Pipeline Co.*, mem. (N.D.Tex., April 1, 1986). Finally, because a contract is law between the parties, this court believes that interpretation of a contract is solely a matter of law, and thus, no material issue of fact must be decided in reaching the conclusions outlined above."

[12] In a similar vein, the learned trial judge in the instant case stated:

"Tenneco claims that due to prevailing economic conditions resulting in a dramatic drop in natural gas prices it was necessary to repudiate its contracts with natural gas producers-suppliers. Tenneco, accordingly, instituted its Emergency Gas Purchase Policy (EGPP), thereby unilaterally modifying the quantity and pricing provisions of its purchase contracts effective May 1, 1983, and the take or pay provisions effective January 1, 1983. Hanover filed this suit for specific performance seeking to invalidate the EGPP and to enforce the original quantity, pricing and take or pay provisions of the contract.

[13] Historically Louisiana jurisprudence has recognized these type [*sic*] of requirements contracts which have been viewed as a veritable constitution between the parties to govern future sales. See 6 S. Litvinoff, Louisiana Civil Law Treatise § 119 n. 32, § 284 n. 47 (1969); Hopkins, 49 Tulane Law Review 605 (1975). In fact, take-or-pay provisions are commonplace in the natural gas industry and are not unconscionable or unfair. *Sid Richardson Carbon & Gasoline Co. vs. Internorth, Inc.*, 595 F.Supp. 497 (N.D.Tex.1984). The seller's obligation is twofold: (1) insuring that the buyer receives all the goods he requires and (2) supplying the goods at the fixed contract price regardless of market fluctuations. The buyer thereby is assured of his supply and is insulated from increases in the market price. In return, he assures the seller a ready market for his goods at a fixed price. 'Under such a provision, the buyer must assume the market risk; that is, that it may not find a market for all the gas it is obligated to purchase under the contract. If the gas does, in fact, expire during the pendency of the contract, the buyer would then have an action against the seller for its failure to perform under the contract. The buyer thus takes the market risk, while the seller takes the supply risk . . . The market risk implicit in take-or-pay provisions is the burden of the [buyer], which must be accepted along with the benefits of the contract. Changing market conditions cannot rewrite an unambiguous and evenly negotiated contract.' *Universal Resources Corporation vs. Panhandle Eastern Pipeline Company*, No. CA 3-85-0723-R (April 1, 1986); see also *Sid Richardson Carbon & Gasoline vs. Internorth*, supra."

[14] Our careful consideration of this issue prompts us to conclude that the events relied on by Tenneco as excusing its failure to fully perform the Kaplan Contract do not constitute force majeure within the meaning of the force majeure clause of the contract and no issue of fact material to this determination exists.

[15] It is a cardinal rule that in construing a contract, it must be considered as a whole, and all clauses of the agreement are to be interpreted in reference and relation to each other giving to each that meaning which results from the entire act. *Farrell v. Hodges Stock Yards, Inc.*, 343 So.2d 1364 (La.1977). As noted by Judge Gonzales in *Preston*, the construction of the force majeure clause advocated by Tenneco cannot be squared with the other provisions of the contract and, in particular, the mutual obligations assumed by the parties under the take or pay provisions thereof. Although the circumstances relied upon by Tenneco are forces or events beyond its control, adverse economic conditions and modifications in governmental regulations and policy which tend to render performance burdensome and unprofitable do not constitute force majeure. As stated in *Northern Indiana Public Service Company v. Carbon County Coal Company*, 799 F.2d 265 (7th Cir.1986):

> "The whole purpose of a fixed-price contract is to allocate risk in this way. A force majeure clause interpreted to excuse the buyer from the risk he expressly assumed would nullify a central term of the contract."

[16] For these reasons, we conclude that Tenneco's reliance on force majeure is without merit as a matter of law.

Whether Tenneco's Performance is Excused Because of the Affirmative Defenses of Commercial Impracticability and Imprevision

[17] Tenneco first urges that, under Texas law, commercial impracticability excuses its failure to perform under the contract. We previously concluded that Louisiana law rather than Texas law governs this proceeding. The common law doctrine of commercial impracticability has no application under Louisiana law. See *The Superior Oil Company v. Transco Energy Company, et al.,* supra.

[18] We reject Tenneco's defense of imprevision for the same reason. This essentially French doctrine which permits judicial reformation of contracts whenever a drastic change in circumstances renders performance for one of the parties harsh has not been recognized or accepted by the courts of this state. Although reference to this doctrine appears in *Armour v. Shongaloo Lodge No. 352, Etc.,* 342 So.2d 600 (La.1977), the doctrine is not discussed and the result reached in that case would indicate that if considered our Supreme Court rejected same.

The Defense of Error

[19] Tenneco urges that the unforeseen collapse of the natural gas market and governmental restructuring of the industry has rendered its performance under the contract untenable. From this premise, it argues that the doctrine of mutual or unilateral error requires the voidance of the contract. In effect, what Tenneco argues is that, had it anticipated the mentioned events, it would never have agreed to the terms of the Kaplan Contract, therefore its consent was the result of error.

[20] The language of the Kaplan Contract is plain and unambiguous. Tenneco's claim of error is founded on nothing more than an error in judgment founded upon its own evaluation of future market conditions.

[21] Our Civil Code declares that consent may be vitiated by error only when it concerns the principal cause or motive and that cause or motive was known or should have been known to the other party. La.C.C. arts. 1948 and 1949. In *Caddo Parish School Board v. Cotton Baking Company,* 342 So.2d 1196 (La.App. 3d Cir.1977), our brethren rejected a claim of error based upon a change in market conditions stating: "The alleged error is not an error in mathematical calculation, but an error in judgment which does not entitle [the seller] to rescind the agreement. In addition, Article 1825 requires both parties to be aware of an error before a contract can be voided. There is no evidence that the [plaintiff] had any knowledge of the effect the Russian wheat sales would have on the price of bread products. The fact that [the seller's] bid on the item was much less than the other bid is not in itself sufficient to impute knowledge of an error to the [plaintiff]. 342 So2d at 1198."

[22] It is not within the province of the courts to relieve parties of their bad bargains. *Kenny v. Oak Builders, Inc.,* 256 La. 85, 235 So.2d 386 (1970). The principal cause of the Kaplan Contract was the sale and concommittant [*sic*] purchase of a certain volume of gas at a fixed price. There is no error alleged in regard thereto.

The expectations of the parties as to the profitability of the contract are irrelevant to a determination of error. As stated by Judge Duhe in *Superior Oil Company,* supra. "Undoubtedly, Pipeline [Transcontinental Gas Pipeline Company] was in error as to its motive for entering into this obligation. The market has simply not evolved in the manner anticipated. But this error is far from an error in the obligation itself. And Pipeline has failed to establish an issue of fact as to whether there was error as to the principal cause of the contract, i.e., a certain price for a certain quantity of gas. *The Superior Oil Co., supra,* p. 109."

[23] For these reasons we reject Tenneco's claim of error.

Failure of Cause or Consideration

[24] Tenneco argues that the consideration for its obligation to pay for gas not taken was the ability to make up the gas at a later time and, since make up is no longer possible because of changes in market conditions, there is no cause or consideration for Tenneco's take or pay obligation. In this connection, Tenneco argues alternatively that its inability to make up the gas at a later time renders the take or pay obligation an unlawful stipulated damage clause rather than an alternative obligation. We find merit in neither of these contentions.

[25] The Kaplan Contract specifically mandates that for each contract year Tenneco will either take and pay for, or pay for if not taken, a specified quantity of gas. The contract establishes a limited makeup period after which Tenneco loses its right to make-up. Take-or-pay obligations are common-place in the natural gas industry and are not unconscionable or unfair. *Sid Richardson Carbon & Gasoline Co. v. InterNorth, Inc.,* 595 F.Supp. 497 (N.D.Tex.1984). Tenneco and Hanover bargained for a certain allocation of risks. Tenneco cannot now be heard to complain of lack of cause based on its projections of future market conditions which apparently turned out to be incorrect.

[26] The take or pay obligation assumed by Tenneco is not an unlawful stipulated damage clause but an alternative obligation. We so held in *Pogo Producing Co. v. Sea Robin Pipeline Co.,* 493 So.2d 909 (La.App. 3rd Cir.1986), writ denied, 497 So.2d 310 (La.1986).

[. . . .]

Questions

1. Paragraph 2: As the *Hanover Petroleum* court explained, the "take or pay" contract into which the parties entered obligated Tenneco to either (1) buy a certain amount of gas per term ("take") or (2) pay a certain sum of money representing a percentage of the price of that gas ("pay"). In terms of "classification of obligations," how should the kind of obligation that Tenneco undertook be described? Hint: *see* La. Civ. Code art. 1807, *et seq.*

2. Paragraphs 6–16: The *Hanover Petroleum* court concludes that, in the end, the *force majeure* clause in the contract under examination provided no greater

protection for the parties than did the "law" of *force majeure* (now called the law of impossibility of performance). Does that seem plausible to you? Why or why not?

3. Paragraph 10: Did the "shifting supply and demand and changing governmental regulations" of which Tenneco complained in fact render the performance of its obligations "truly" or "absolutely" impossible? *See* La. Civ. Code art. 1873.

4. *Hanover Petroleum* was decided prior to the Revision of the law of *force majeure*/"impossibility of performance." Which part(s) of the new Louisiana Civil Code article 1873 seem(s) to you the most pertinent to disputes of the kind presented in this case? The first paragraph, which states the "general principle" of impossibility of performance, is, of course, pertinent, but isn't there another one that's even more directly "on point"? Explain.

Dollar Thrifty Auto Group, Inc. & Dollar Systems, Inc.
v.
Bohn-DC, L.L.C., d/b/a Don Bohn Dodge and ABC Insurance Co.

Court of Appeal of Louisiana
Fifth Circuit
September 30, 2008
23 So.3d 301

WALTER J. ROTHSCHILD, Judge.

[. . . .]

LAW AND DISCUSSION

[1] [. . . .] [A] depositary is not an insurer of the deposit, and is not liable for loss or deterioration of the thing deposited that has resulted from an irresistible force or "force majeure," in the absence of a special undertaking. [. . . .]

[. . . .]

[2] [. . . .] Clearly, Hurricane Katrina, with its unprecedented flooding and devastation, was a force majeure or Act of God that was unforeseen and unavoidable.

[. . . .]

[3] [. . . .] Considering the circumstances, including the mandatory evacuation order in New Orleans and the surrounding areas, the time constraints involved, and the number of vehicles on Bohn's premises, we find that Bohn's failure to move Dollar's vehicles to a different location was not unreasonable.

[. . . .]

[4] Dollar further asserts that Bohn should have informed Dollar that its premises could flood, because it had previously flooded on May 8, 1995. Flooding is a common occurrence during a major storm. Failure to give warning of the obvious

may not be a cause in fact of an injury. [. . . .] [W]e find that it was difficult, if not impossible, to know prior to the storm what areas would and would not flood, due to the unforeseen and unprecedented extent of the flooding in the aftermath of Hurricane Katrina.

[. . . .]

Comparative Law Perspective

Alain Levasseur, *Comparative Law of Contracts*

at 165–84 (2008)

[B]etween the time the contract is negotiated and entered into on the basis of the circumstances that exist at that time and the time specified for the performances to be carried out, many different, unexpected or unforeseen events may occur in such a manner as to upset and disrupt the parties' plans as laid down in the contract. [. . . .]

These events may fit under a variety of adjectives: 'political', 'economic', 'financial', 'natural'. . . . Yet, they all have in common the fact that they may serve as a justification for a party not to perform her side of the bargain, or carry out a modified and adjusted performance of the original obligation. [. . . .]

— Civil Law —

See La. Civ. C. articles: 1873–1877.

Fr. Civ. C. 1804 (revised in 2016)

> **Art. 1137(1):** An obligation to preserve the thing, whether the contract has for its object the benefit of one party only, or whether it has for its object the common interest of the parties, imposes on the party in charge of preserving the thing the duty to act as a prudent administrator (*bon pere de famille*).

> **Art. 1147:** Should it be the case, an obligor is liable to pay damages either on account of his failure to perform, or on account of his delay in performing, whenever he is unable to prove that the non-performance was caused by a fortuitous event for which he cannot be held liable, or that he did not act in bad faith.

> **Art. 1148:** No damages are owed when, because of force majeure or a fortuitous event, an obligor was prevented from giving or doing what he was bound to give or do, or when he did what he was forbidden from doing.

> **Art. 1302:** When a certain and identified thing which was the object of an obligation, has perished, is out of commerce, or is lost in such a manner that one absolutely cannot know of its existence, the obligation is extinguished is the thing has perished or has been lost without the obligor's fault and

before he had been put in default [. . .]. The obligor must prove the fortuitous event he alleges.

BGB (German Civil Code)

Section 275. Exclusion of the duty of performance.

(1) A claim for performance cannot be made in so far as it is impossible for the obligor or for anyone else to perform.

(2) The obligor may refuse to perform in so far as performance requires expenditure which, having regard to the subject matter of the obligation and the principle of good faith, is manifestly disproportionate to the obligee's interest in performance. When determining what may reasonably be required of the obligor, regard must also be had to whether he is responsible for the impediment to performance.

(3) Moreover, the obligor may refuse to perform, if he is to effect the performance in in person and, after weighing up the obligee's interest in performance and the impediment to performance, performance cannot be reasonably required of the obligor.

C.C.Q. (Québec)

Art. 1693: A debtor is released where he cannot perform an obligation by reason of a superior force and before he is in default, or where, although he was in default, the creditor could not, in any case, benefit by the performance of the obligation by reason of that superior force, unless, in either case, the debtor has expressly assumed the risk of superior force.

The burden of proof of superior force is on the debtor.

Art. 1694: A debtor released by impossibility of performance may not exact performance of the correlative obligation of the creditor; if the performance has already been rendered, restitution is owed.

Where the debtor has performed part of his obligation, the creditor remains bound to perform his own obligation to the extent of his enrichment.

Ph. Malaurie, L. Aynès, Ph. Stoffel-Munck, *Droit Civil, Les Obligations* (10th ed. LGDJ 2018)

§ 3. Grounds for exoneration

[. . . .] An obligor cannot be held liable when the non-performance of his obligation can be imputed to a fortuitous event (force majeure) to which are assimilated the 'fact' of the obligee, the fact of a third person, or the prince. These 'causes' (grounds) exonerate the obligor, unless they have only a temporary effect, in which case they merely suspend the contract.

I. — Force majeure

952. Reasonable. — [. . .]. Just as the English theory of *frustration* is now used in reference to the notion of a 'reasonable person', in France force majeure tends to be defined by an event which is reasonably irresistible, unforeseeable and exterior which, most often requires a case by case appraisal. [. . . .]

953. Suppletive. — The rules concerning force majeure are not mandatory rules (rules of public order): these rules can be modified by contract, to the extend that the parties may freely delimit the content of the obligations. [. . . .]

954. Irresistible: no one is obligated to perform the impossible. — The event must be irresistible; it is the main requirement; if it could have been overcome, even though the performance would have been more difficult and onerous, the obligor would still be held liable for not having performed [. . .]. The difficult question is to determine at which point in time there is 'irresistibility.' It is obvious that law is not absolute and cannot expect the obligor to be a 'superman,' Tarzan . . . Rambo . . . All is necessarily relative. The real question to ask is the following: should irresistibility be evaluated *in abstracto* or *in concreto*? There are cases on both sides [. . .]. The Court of Cassation has confirmed that there does not exist any financial force majeure (force majeure does not exist for obligations of sums of money). [. . . .]

955. Unforeseeable. — [. . .]. [T]he event [. . .] must have been reasonably unforeseeable at the time of perfection of the contract. If the obligor could have foreseen the event when the contract was concluded, he will be at fault for not having taken the necessary precautions. [. . . .] ([S]ame comment with respect to "absolute" unforeseeability as for "irresistibility" above). As with irresistibility, unforeseeability also depends on the circumstances [. . .].

956. Exterior. — Lastly, the event traditionally must be 'exterior' to the obligor, otherwise he should be liable. Exteriority is implied by the expression of "a cause (source) foreign to the obligor" so that the event cannot be imputed to the obligor. [. . . .] The 2016 revision to the law of obligations did not include this condition in the definition that new article 1218 gives to force majeure in contractual matters. However, it echoes the idea on which it was based, by providing that the exemption presupposes an event "outside the obligor's control." [. . . .]

II. — Fact of the creditor, of a third person or of the prince

958. Fact of the creditor. — The fact of the creditor (the victim) exonerates the obligor. This is a rational view: if the damage was caused by the victim, it cannot be held against the obligor. [. . . .]

959. Fact of a third person or the prince. — [There is there also a ground for not holding the obligor liable] if the fact was irresistible, unforeseeable and if the obligor was not to be held liable in one way or another. It is a type of force majeure. [. . . .]

— Common Law—

England

William Blackstone, *Commentaries on the Laws of England*

Chapter XXII. Of Proceedings in the Courts of Equity.

3. With respect to the mode of *relief.* [. . . .] A court of equity will compel them [**executory agreements**] to be carried into strict execution, unless where it is improper or impossible; instead of giving damages for their non-performance [. . .].

G.H. Treitel, *The Law of Contract,* Seventh Edition, Stevens & Sons, 1987. (Reproduced with permission of the Licensor through PLSclear.)

Chapter 20 Frustration

(7) Impossibility and impracticability

(a) Impracticability distinguished from impossibility. The doctrine of frustration originated in cases where performance was said to have become "impossible."

That, in itself, is something of a relative term. What is "impossible" depends partly on the current state of technology, and partly on the amount of trouble and expense to which one is prepared to go to achieve it. [. . . .] For this reason the current trend in the United States is to abandon the very words "impossible" and "impossibility" and to use instead the terms "impracticable" and "impracticability." [. . . .]

(b) Impracticability generally no excuse. [. . .] [I]t appears that "impracticability" is not generally sufficient to frustrate a contract in English law. [. . . .] Lord Radcliffe said: "It is not hardship or inconvenience or material loss itself which calls the principle of frustration into play. There must be as well a change in the significance of the obligation that the thing undertaken would, if performed, be a different thing from that contracted for. . . ." Where performance would, in view of changed circumstances, cause not merely extra expense but acute personal hardship to one party, it has been said that "equitable relief may . . . be refused because of an unforeseen change of circumstances not amounting to legal frustration." But in such cases the contract is not discharged: the defendant remains liable in damages even though specific performance is refused on the ground of severe hardship. [. . . .]

2. Frustration of Purpose

Frustration of purpose is, in a sense, the converse of impracticability. The two ideas resemble each other in that neither is concerned with cases in which performance has become impossible. Impracticability is said to arise when a *supplier* of goods, services or other facilities alleges that performance of his own promise has become so burdensome to him that he should no longer be bound to render it. The argument of frustration of purpose, on the other hand, is put forward by the recipient of the goods, services or facilities: it is that supervening events have so greatly reduced the value to him of the other party's performance that he should no longer be bound to accept and to pay the agreed price. [. . . .]

The more recent authorities show that "the frustrated expectations and intentions of one party to a contract do not necessarily, or indeed usually, lead to the frustration of that contract," They make it difficult to establish the defence of frustration of purpose; but they do not make it impossible. [. . . .]

Restatement, 2d of Contracts (1981)

§ 261. Discharge by Supervening Impracticability

Where, after a contract is made, a party's performance is made impracticable without his fault by the occurrence of an event the non-occurrence of which was a basic assumption on which the contract was made, his duty to render that performance is discharged, unless the language or the circumstances indicate the contrary.

§ 265. Discharge by Supervening Frustration

(1) Where, after a contract is made, a party's performance under it is impracticable without his fault because of a fact of which he has no reason to know and the non-existence of which is a basic assumption on which the contract is made, no duty to render that performance arises, unless the language or circumstances indicate the contrary.

(2) Where, at the time a contract is made, a party's principle purpose is substantially frustrated without his fault by a fact of which he has no reason to know and the non-existence of which is a basic assumption on which the contract is made, no duty of that party to render performance arises, unless the language or circumstances indicate the contrary.

UCC

§ 2-613. Casualty to Identified Goods.

Where the contract requires for its performance goods identified when the contract is made, and the goods suffer casualty without fault of either party before the risk of loss passes to the buyer, or in a proper case under a "no arrival, no sale" term (Section 2-324) then

(a) if the loss is total the contract is avoided; and

(b) if the loss is partial or the goods have so deteriorated as no longer to conform to the contract the buyer may nevertheless demand inspection and at his option either treat the contract as avoided or accept the goods with due allowance from the contract price for the deterioration or the deficiency in quantity but without further right against the seller.

§ 2-614. Substituted Performance.

(1) If without fault of either party the agreed berthing, loading, or unloading facilities fail or an agreed type of carrier becomes unavailable or the agreed manner of performance otherwise becomes commercially impracticable but a commercially reasonable substitute is available, the substitute performance must be tendered and accepted.

§ 2-615. Excuse by Failure of Presupposed Conditions.

Except to the extent that a seller may have assumed a greater obligation and subject to section 2-614:

> (a) Delay in performance or nonperformance in whole or in part by a seller that complies with paragraphs (b) and (c) is not a breach of the seller's duty under a contract for sale if performance as agreed has been made impracticable by the occurrence of a contingency the nonoccurrence of which was a basic assumption on which the contract was made or by compliance in good faith with any applicable foreign or domestic governmental regulation or order whether or not it later proves to be invalid.

E. Allan Farnsworth, *Contracts* (2d ed. 1990)

C. Impracticability and Frustration

§ 9.5. Growth of Impossibility as an Excuse. The common law was slow to give effect to the maxim *impossibilium nulla obligatio est* ("there is no obligation to do the impossible"). Courts were less receptive to claims of excuse based on events occurring after the making of the contract than they were to claims of excuse based on facts that existed at the time of the agreement. [. . . .]

§ 9.6. A New Synthesis: The Doctrine of Impracticability. The common law development [. . .] is synthesized in UCC 2-615, Excuse by Failure of Presupposed Conditions. [. . . .]

Under the new synthesis, the party that claims that a supervening event or "contingency" prevented performance must meet four requirements. First, the event must have made "performance as agreed . . . impracticable." Second, the nonoccurrence of the event must have been "a basic assumption on which the contract was made." Third, the impracticability must have resulted without the fault of the party seeking to be excused. Fourth, that party must not have assumed a greater obligation than the law imposes. Although these requirements involve questions of fact, courts have sometimes been reluctant to entrust the granting of excuse on this ground to a jury. [. . . .]

§ 9.9. Effects of Impracticability and Frustration. The effect of *supervening* impracticability or frustration on the excused party is usually to discharge that party's remaining duties of performance. The effect of *existing* impracticability or frustration on the excused party is usually to prevent any duty of performance on that party's side from arising. [. . . .]

A prospective failure of performance due to impracticability or frustration has a similar effect. The fact that one party's anticipated failure to perform will be excused on the ground of impracticability or frustration does not prevent the other party from justifiably suspending performance and from terminating the contract. But the other party cannot recover damages for breach. [. . . .]

UNIDROIT Principles of International Commercial Contracts (2016)

Article 6.2.1 (Contract to be observed)

Where the performance of a contract becomes more onerous for one of the parties, that party is nevertheless bound to perform its obligations subject to the following provisions on hardship.

Article 6.2.2 (Definition of hardship)

There is hardship where the occurrence of events fundamentally alters the equilibrium of the contract either because the cost of a party's performance has increased or because the value of the performance has increased or because the value of the performance a party receives has diminished, and

(a) the events occur or become known to the disadvantaged party after the conclusion of the contract;

(b) the events could not reasonably have been taken into account by the disadvantaged party at the time of the conclusion of the contract;

(c) the events are beyond the control of the disadvantaged party; and

(d) the risk of the events was not assumed by the disadvantaged party.

Article 6.2.3 (Effects of hardship)

(1) In case of hardship the disadvantaged party is entitled to request renegotiations. The request shall be made without undue delay and shall indicate the grounds on which it is based.

(2) The request for renegotiation does not in itself entitle the disadvantaged party to withhold performance.

(3) Upon failure to reach agreement within a reasonable time either party may resort to the court.

(4) If the court finds hardship it may, if reasonable,

(a) terminate the contract at a date and on terms to be fixed, or

(b) adapt the contract with a view to restoring its equilibrium.

Article 7.1.7 (Force majeure)

(1) Non-performance by a party is excused if that party proves that the non-performance was due to an impediment beyond its control and that it could

not reasonably be expected to have taken the impediment into account at the time of the conclusion of the contract or to have avoided or overcome it or its consequences.

(2) When the impediment is only temporary, the excuse shall have effect for such period as is reasonable having regard to the effect of the impediment on the performance of the contract.

(3) The party who fails to perform must give notice to the other party of the impediment and its effect on its ability to perform. If the notice is not received by the other party within a reasonable time after the party who fails to perform knew or ought to have known of the impediment, it is liable for damages resulting from such nonreceipt.

(4) Nothing in this article prevents a party from exercising a right to terminate the contract or to withhold performance or request interest on money due.

Section VI — Novation

Louisiana Sources of Law
Louisiana Civil Code

Art. 1879. Extinguishment of existing obligation.

Novation is the extinguishment of an existing obligation by the substitution of a new one. (Acts 1984, No. 331, §1, eff. Jan. 1, 1985.)

Art. 1880. Novation not presumed.

The intention to extinguish the original obligation must be clear and unequivocal. Novation may not be presumed. (Acts 1984, No. 331, §1, eff. Jan. 1, 1985.)

Art. 1881. Objective novation.

Novation takes place when, by agreement of the parties, a new performance is substituted for that previously owed, or a new cause is substituted for that of the original obligation. If any substantial part of the original performance is still owed, there is no novation.

Novation takes place also when the parties expressly declare their intention to novate an obligation.

Mere modification of an obligation, made without intention to extinguish it, does not effect a novation. The execution of a new writing, the issuance or renewal of a negotiable instrument, or the giving of new securities for the performance of an existing obligation are examples of such a modification. (Acts 1984, No. 331, §1, eff. Jan. 1, 1985.)

Art. 1882. Subjective novation.

Novation takes place when a new obligor is substituted for a prior obligor who is discharged by the obligee. In that case, the novation is accomplished even without the consent of the prior obligor, unless he had an interest in performing the obligation himself. (Acts 1984, No. 331, §1, eff. Jan. 1, 1985.)

Art. 1885. Novation of solidary obligation.

A novation made by the obligee and one of the obligors of a solidary obligation releases the other solidary obligors.

In that case, the security given for the performance of the extinguished obligation may be retained by the obligee only on property of that obligor with whom the novation has been made.

If the obligee requires that the other co-obligors remain solidarily bound, there is no novation unless the co-obligors consent to the new obligation. (Acts 1984, No. 331, §1, eff. Jan. 1, 1985.)

Art. 1886. Delegation of performance.

A delegation of performance by an obligor to a third person is effective when that person binds himself to perform.

A delegation effects a novation only when the obligee expressly discharges the original obligor. (Acts 1984, No. 331, §1, eff. Jan. 1, 1985.)

Doctrine

Louisiana Law of Obligations in General, A Précis
Sections 7.3.1 to 7.3.4

Novation is one of these legal devices meant, at the same time, to extinguish and to transfer an obligation. [. . . .]

As a general rule, a novation is a juridical act, the creation of the wills of two parties at least, which brings about **"the extinguishment of an existing obligation by the substitution of a new one."** (LSA-C.C. Art. 1879). It follows necessarily that a new obligation is substituted to a previously existing one through a change in one of the *essential* requirements constitutive of an obligation. There takes place then a true legal metamorphosis of obligations.

A novation amounts, actually, to a merger into one legal concept, that of novation, of two separate juridical acts: one juridical act extinguishes an existing obligation while the other juridical act creates a new obligation. This dual effect of novation requires that some conditions be met for novation to take place and carries with it some important practical consequences. [. . . .]

Two fundamental conditions must be met for a novation to take place under whatever form it might appear. [. . . .]

The first condition required is that of a succession of obligations and the second is that of the intent to novate (*animus novandi*). [. . . .]

A novation is the outcome of a change in an *essential* component part of an obligation (parties, cause, object) or in the substitution of a modality which affects the very existence of an obligation. [. . . .]

An objective "**novation takes place when, by agreement of the parties, a new performance is substituted for that previously owed, or a new cause is substituted for that of the original obligation. If any substantial part of the original performance is still owed, there is no novation.**

Novation takes place also when the parties expressly declare their intention to novate an obligation." [. . . .]

LSA-C.C. Art. 1882 provides expressly for one form of subjective novation by substitution of an obligor to another. [. . . .]

Novation of obligees. **LSA-C.C. Art. 1882** does not mention this form of subjective novation as a possibility open to parties to an obligation.

Louisiana Law of Obligations in General, A Treatise
Section 7.5.1

389. Novation of obligees: an issue. La. Civ. Code **art. 1882** does not mention this form of subjective novation as a possibility open to parties to an obligation. However, one can find in comment (d)[133] to that article a statement that explains briefly why a novation of obligees was not mentioned in **art. 1882**. The comment states: "subjective novation by substitution of a new obligee is not provided for because the effects of such a novation are readily achieved through an assignment of credit."

390. Novation and assignment: a difference. Not only is this statement far too broad to be accurate and, thus, convincing, but it also fails to take into consideration both the *raison d'être* of a novation of obligees and the *raison d'être* of an assignment of credit, as well as some of the fundamental differences between these two institutions.

For example, an assignment of credit (or assignment of right)[134] is a transfer that takes place between the obligee-assignor and the third-party assignee without the involvement of the obligor, the latter receiving merely a notice of the transfer. On the other hand, in a novation of obligees the existing obligor must consent to the agreement of novation contemplated by his obligee so as to create a new obligation and a right of action for the benefit of the new obligee against him. Furthermore, an assignment of credit does not alter the nature of the obligation thus transferred; the same obligation that existed before the transfer or assignment remains in existence

---

133. La. Civ. Code art. 1882 (West ed.).

134. La. Civ. Code arts. 2642 to 2654, Sale of a Right or Assignment of a Right; see Levasseur & Gruning, *Louisiana Law of Sale and Lease, a Précis*, §2.3.5.

after the transfer. It means, therefore, that the obligor can raise against the assignee the same exceptions and defenses he could have raised against the original obligee-assignor. In a novation of obligees, on the other hand, because a new obligation results from the substitution of a new obligee to the original one, the obligor who has consented to the novation may not raise against the new obligee the defenses he had available against the original obligee. In other words, in a novation, a new and different obligation is substituted to the original obligation. Furthermore, an assignment of credit transfers an obligation with all its accessory rights of security that guarantee the performance of that obligation. On the contrary, in a novation of obligees, the obligation that is created is a new one and none of the accessory rights attached to the former obligation are transferred to the new obligee. In addition, because the obligation is new, it will be subject to its own (and new) prescriptive period.

Louisiana Law of Obligations in General, A Précis
Sections 7.3.1 to 7.3.4

In a novation of obligees, the obligation which is created is a new one and none of the accessory rights attached to the former obligation are transferred to the new obligee. In addition, because the obligation is new, it will be subjected to its own (and new) prescriptive period. [. . . .]

"The immediate effects of novation are two, essentially: 1) extinction of an existing obligation and 2) its replacement by a new one." [. . . .]

LSA-C.C. Art. 1879 states unequivocally that "**novation is the extinguishment of an existing obligation by the substitution of a new one.**" It follows from the creation of a <u>new</u> obligation that all the accessory rights which ensured the performance of the <u>original</u> primary obligation are also extinguished as is suggested, furthermore, by **LSA-C.C. Art. 1884: "Security given for the performance of the extinguished obligation may not be transferred to the new obligation without agreement of the parties who gave the security."** [. . . .]

The new obligation which emerges from the juridical act of novation is free of all the rights of action and exceptions which were attached to the former and original obligation. The new obligation takes on its particular legal features and a legal existence of its own. [. . . .]

[A] delegation is a juridical act whereby the debtor-obligor instructs another, the third person or delegated debtor, to become a debtor and perform an obligation for the benefit of the obligee. Under these circumstances the consent of the obligee is not necessary as his right of action against his original obligor is preserved. [. . . .]

[A] personal obligation on the part of the obligor cannot be delegated as long as the obligee has not agreed to make that same obligation personal on the part of the delegated obligor. [. . . .]

On the order or request of the original obligor, the delegated obligor binds himself *vis-à-vis* the obligee and, thereby, creates an obligation which is totally independent and distinct from the obligation still binding the original obligor towards the obligee. [. . . .]

[A] delegation does not create a bond of solidarity between the original obligor and the delegated obligor as an assumption of obligations between an obligor and a third person would establish. [. . . .]

A perfect delegation amounts to a novation when the obligee expressly discharges the original obligor. [. . . .]

An imperfect delegation does not amount to a novation because the oblige does not wish to discharge the original obligor.

Cases

Polk Chevrolet, Inc.
v.
Vince J. Vicaro

Court of Appeal of Louisiana
First Circuit
April 6, 1964
162 So.2d 761

LANDRY, Judge.

[1] This appeal is by defendant, Vince J. Vicaro, from a deficiency judgment rendered against him, as co-maker of a promissory note, in favor of appellee, Polk Chevrolet, Inc., in the sum of $1,010.32, together within interest at the rate of 8% Per annum from April 1, 1961, until paid, plus the additional sum of 25% On both principal and interest, as attorney's fees, and costs.

[2] The note in question, dated April 30, 1959, was signed by present defendant, Vince J. Vicaro, and his son, Samuel J. Vicaro, and represented the balance due on the sale price of an automobile purchased by said Samuel J. Vicaro which said vendee simultaneously granted a chattel mortgage on the vehicle as security for the note. Appellee subsequently transferred the note to General Motors Acceptance Corporation (sometimes hereinafter referred to simply as 'GMAC'), said transfer being by full or special endorsement.

[3] On December 29, 1960, Samuel J. Vicaro executed another promissory note made payable to the order of GMAC, the primary purpose of which was to effect a rearrangement of the installments due under the prior note of April 30, 1959. The latter note, which was not signed by defendant herein, expressly provided that the terms of the former instrument, except as to the modification and rearrangement of installments, were to remain in full force and effect.

[4] Subsequently, plaintiff herein obtained judgment against Samuel J. Vicaro in a suit brought on both said notes for the unpaid delinquent balance due on the

indebtedness. In execution of said judgment plaintiff caused the mortgaged property to be sold, with appraisement, and instituted the present action against defendant as co-maker of the initial note, for the aforesaid deficiency.

[5] Although defendant, for all practical purposes, concedes the correctness of the pertinent facts as hereinabove set forth, [**presents the defense, among others, that plaintiff has . . .**] no cause of action predicated upon the alleged extinguishment of the note sued upon by novation[. . .]. [. . . .]

[. . . .]

[6] Novation is a contract consisting of two stipulations; one to extinguish an existing obligation, the other to substitute a new one in its place. To constitute a novation there must simultaneously occur both the cancellation of a present or outstanding obligation and the substitution in its place of a new obligation with the consent of the parties concerned. LSA-C.C. Article 2185.

[7] It is clear that defendant's obligation on the note, being that of co-maker, was in solido. Therefore, if, as contended by defendant, execution of the second note by his solidary obligor, Samuel J. Vicaro, operated as a novation of the first note, defendant was released and discharged from all obligation thereon. LSA-C.C. Article 2198.

[8] Novation, however, is never presumed. Johnson v. Johnson, 235 La. 226, 103 So.2d 263; Hayes v. Claterbaugh, La.App., 140 So.2d 737. For novation to result the discharge of the original debtor or obligor must be express. LSA-C.C. Articles 2185, 2187, 2190, Hayes v. Claterbaugh, supra.

[9] It is equally well settled that modification of an obligation does not effect a novation unless the intention of the parties to novate the obligation is clear and explicit. Rex Finance Co. v. Cary, La.App., 145 So.2d 672 (affirmed on other grounds, 244 La. 675, 154 So.2d 360). The taking of a new note in partial renewal of an old one, does not operate a novation or extinguish the original debt or the pledge securing same. Davis v. Welch, 128 La. 785, 55 So. 372.

[10] In the case at bar there was patently no intention to novate the preexisting indebtedness by the execution of the second note by Samuel J. Vicaro alone. On the contrary, the latter instrument, in referring to the mortgage of April 30, 1959, states "the terms and provisions of which document except as modified by this rearrangement of installments, remain in full force and effect." Such language clearly refutes an intention to novate the original indebtedness. Inasmuch as there was no intention on the part of either obligor or obligee to cancel the existing indebtedness, execution of the second note did not operate as a novation. The asserted defense of release by novation is therefore without merit.

[. . . .]

no novation

☞ - language refutes novation

Questions

1. Describe clearly and in legal terms the many relationships involved here, particularly the relationship between Vince Vicaro and his son, Samuel, as co-makers of the promissory note.

2. Paragraph 3: After you have read the Code articles on "Novation" (arts. 1879–1887) compare the contents of the two notes, the 1959 note and its transfer with the 1960 note. Do you have any comment? Is the Court's statement about the "latter note" of any importance? What fundamental distinction does it make between the types of requirements for a contract to exist? Does the distinction between essential requirements versus accessory requirements mean anything to you?

3. Paragraph 5: What do you think of the defendant's arguments, particularly (1), (3), and (4)?

4. Paragraphs 6–9: Can you see any difference between former Louisiana Civil Code article 2185, as cited by the Court, and new Louisiana Civil Code article 1879? How does the Court's statement in paragraph 8 match your description of the legal relationships above? To what kind of novation is the Court referring (subjective or objective) in paragraph 9? How relevant is the third paragraph of Louisiana Civil Code article 1881? What is a partial renewal? Is there a danger in using renewal next to novation? Isn't novation creating a new obligation? *See* La. Civ. Code art. 1879.

5. Paragraph 10: How does this statement fit your distinction between essential requirements versus accessory requirements in Question 2?

Crescent Cigarette Vending Corporation
v.
Alvin J. Toca

Court of Appeal of Louisiana
Fourth Circuit
December 19, 1972
271 So.2d 53

BOUTALL, Judge.

[1] This is a suit on a promissory note made by the defendant, Alvin Toca, in the principal sum of $1,000.00, alleging a balance due of $507.95. The defendant filed his answer pleading extinguishment of the obligation. He alleged that the obligation was extinguished by the delivery of a new note executed by a third party in the amount of the balance due at that time, pursuant to an agreement between the parties. The trial court rendered judgment in favor of the defendant, and from this adverse judgment, plaintiff appeals.

[2] The record shows that the defendant admitted making the note and further admits that he did not make all of the payments thereon. He contends, however, that he is not obligated to make any further payments because of the following facts. Defendant was the operator of a lounge called "Laura's Playroom", and in connection with that business had installed in the premises a cigarette machine belonging to plaintiff. Defendant needed some money for stock and other purposes, and as a consequence borrowed from the plaintiff $1,000.00 for which he signed the note in question. The note was payable out of the defendant's commission received from the operation of the cigarette machine plus $10.00 weekly. The defendant on or about October 17, 1969, sold the business "Laura's Playroom" to a certain Sam Jones without benefit of the Bulk Sales Act.

[3] The defendant contends that at the time he sold the business to Sam Jones, there was an agreement between Jones, Crescent Cigarette, and himself that Jones would assume the outstanding obligation on the note by signing another promissory note in which Jones alone was responsible. In effect, defendant is contending that a novation has taken place and is relying on LSA-C.C. art. 2185 which states:

> "Art. 2185. Novation, definition
>
> "Art. 2185. Novation is a contract, consisting of two stipulations; one to extinguish an existing obligation, the other to substitute a new one in its place."

[4] In the present situation we should also observe LSA-C.C. art. 2192 which states:

> "Art. 2192. Discharge of original debtor
>
> "Art. 2192. The delegation, by which a debtor gives to the creditor another debtor who obliges himself towards such creditor, does not operate a novation, unless the creditor has expressly declared that he intends to discharge his debtor who has made the delegation."

Express declaration of intent to discharge the defendant is denied by the representative of plaintiff, and Jones was not a party to the suit, nor was he called as a witness. The issue in the case thus becomes one of preponderance of evidence, burden of proof, and credibility of witnesses. *In Midlo & Lehmann v. Katz*, 195 So.2d 383 (La.App.4th Cir., 1967), the court stated that a novation is never presumed, and the burden of proof to establish a novation is on the person who claims it. The court also stated in Midlo that the intention of parties to substitute a new obligation for the original one may be shown by the character of the transaction and the facts and circumstances surrounding the transaction, as well as by the terms of the agreement itself.

[5] The only evidence in the case is the testimony of the representative of Crescent Cigarette and the testimony of the defendant. The testimony of the representative of Crescent Cigarette is that Jones did not make a promissory note to be substituted for the note in question, but that Jones borrowed some money from Crescent Cigarette in an independent transaction and executed a note for the money borrowed. The

Evidence

conditions or terms of the note are not in evidence. The representative of plaintiff testified that he handled the transaction personally and that the new note signed by Jones had nothing to do with the note sued upon. As opposed to this, the defendant testified that he talked to Jones about buying the business, but because Jones did not have as much money as defendant wanted, Jones agreed to assume defendant's note with plaintiff; that defendant then contacted Crescent Cigarette and spoke to a person known only as "Tommy" who told him that he had to get "the OK from Mr. Moore." Defendant then testified that he never heard any further from Crescent until the building burden down in March, 1971.

[6] The trial judge rendered judgment in favor of the defendant with the following statements:

– Trial Judge

> "The defendant impresses the court as being a fundamentally honest and good man. He probably did the very best he could for his situation in life. Plaintiff's suit is dismissed at plaintiff's cost."

While the reasons given by the trial judge would indicate that this is a question simply of credibility of the witnesses, such is not the situation here. If it were simply a question of credibility of the witnesses, it would appear that the statement of the trial judge quoted above would indicate that he believed one witness and disbelieved the other witness, and hence, we would not interfere with his judgment in such a matter. However, this is a suit on a promissory note and a special affirmative defense of extinguishment of the obligation is set forth in the answer in accordance with LSA-C.C.P. art. 1005. Our jurisprudence has consistently held that a person pleading an affirmative defense bears the burden of proving such a defense, and of course it must be established by a preponderance of the evidence. B. F. Goodrich Company v. Ryan Tire Service, Inc., 203 So.2d 863 (La.App.1st Cir., 1967); Barbari v. Fireman's Insurance Co., 107 So.2d 480 (La.App.1st Cir., 1958). In B. F. Goodrich, the court stated that novation is an affirmative defense and the party claiming it must establish it by positive proof.

[7] It is noted in the case at bar that along with the testimony of the parties, there is in evidence the promissory note itself, which contains nothing upon it to show that it was cancelled or in any other way extinguished or modified. Under the facts as related by the defendant, he did not establish that there was another promissory note signed by Jones, relating to the same debt, nor that Jones bound himself for the debt, nor that Crescent consented to release him from the obligation. Except for the reference to a conversation with a clerk named 'Tommy', who announced to him that transferring the debt would require approval of Mr. Moore, defendant's testimony is devoid of any conversation or agreement with any representative of Crescent that approval was granted or a binding contract was entered into. In this regard it is noteworthy that although he alleges that he sold the place to Jones and that Jones assumed the obligation of the note, Jones was not called to testify. While it may be presumed that Jones could just as easily have been called by the plaintiff as well as the defendant, we must note that the burden is upon the defendant of

establishing the affirmative defense. The record does not disclose to us the preponderance of evidence necessary for the defendant to overcome the plaintiff's demand, and we are of the opinion that the judgment should be reversed.

[8] For the foregoing reasons, it is ordered that there is judgment herein in favor of appellant annulling and reversing the judgment appealed from. It is further ordered that there is now judgment rendered in favor of plaintiff-appellant, Crescent Cigarette Vending Company, and against defendant-appellee, Alvin Toca, in the full sum of $507.95, together with 8% Per annum interest from date of demand until paid, plus 25% Of said amounts as attorney's fees. Appellee to pay all costs of these proceedings.

[. . . .]

Questions

1. Establish and describe in legal terms the relationships existing in this case.

2. Paragraph 3: Jones "would assume the outstanding obligation on the note. . . ." What is an assumption of obligation? *See* La. Civ. Code arts. 1821–1824. The Court states: "In effect," and refers to then Louisiana Civil Code article 2185 (current Louisiana Civil Code article 1879) on novation. Are novation and assumption one and the same thing? The Court refers to then Louisiana Civil Code article 2192 (current article 1886) on delegation. What are the differences between a novation and a delegation?

3. In your legal opinion, and on the basis of the evidence considered by the Court, was the right decision reached by the Court? What kind of novation did the defendant fail to establish: subjective or objective?

First National Bank of Abbeville
v.
Donald Greene, et al.
Court of Appeal of Louisiana
Third Circuit
December 21, 1992
612 So.2d 759

STOKER, Judge.

[1] This is an appeal from a judgment recognizing certain in rem collateral mortgages on defendants' property which secure two collateral mortgage notes. The main issues in this case are whether there was a proper pledge of the collateral mortgage notes to secure a hand note and whether the hand note was novated without a repledging of the collateral mortgage notes. We affirm.

Facts

[2] In 1984, Hardy Tractor of Gueydon, Inc. sought financing for the construction of a new building. Ruby Linscomb Hair LeBlanc and Delores Hair Dietz were

relatives of the company's president in 1984, Keith Hair. LeBlanc and Dietz owned the tract of land which Hardy Tractor leased for its business operations. LeBlanc and Dietz agreed to put in rem collateral mortgages on their property in order to secure two loans to Hardy Tractor from First National Bank of Abbeville. Dietz, who lived out of state, executed two powers of attorney in favor of LeBlanc for the sole purpose of confecting the collateral mortgages to secure the two loans to Hardy Tractor (for $100,000 and, later, an additional $20,000).

[3] The collateral mortgage for $100,000 was executed on January 11, 1984 and signed by Keith Hair on behalf of Hardy Tractor and by Ruby Linscomb (now LeBlanc) on behalf of herself and Dietz. However, the collateral mortgage note and the collateral pledge agreement were signed only by Keith Hair for Hardy Tractor. The pledge agreement states that the collateral is pledged by the borrower (Hardy Tractor).

[4] On June 1, 1984, a collateral mortgage for $20,000 was executed and signed by Keith Hair for Hardy Tractor and by Ruby Linscomb for herself and Dietz. Again, the collateral mortgage note and the collateral pledge agreement were signed only by Keith Hair for Hardy Tractor. The pledge agreement states that the collateral is pledged by the borrower (Hardy Tractor).

[5] The debtors delivered both of these notes to the First National Bank of Abbeville (Bank), and these two collateral mortgage notes have remained in the Bank's possession at all times pertinent to the lawsuit.

[6] Hardy Tractor executed five hand notes in 1984 up to the $120,000 total limit, against which the collateral mortgage notes were pledged as security. The hand notes each matured in sixty or ninety days. Subsequently, the hand notes were consolidated and renewed in one note for $120,000, with eleven monthly payments plus a final balloon payment due in August 1985. This note stated that it was also secured by the original pledges. It was signed by Keith Hair and Donald Greene for Hardy Tractor. Donald Greene was a director of Hardy Tractor.

[7] In September 1985, the hand note was again renewed for the balance due of $113,463.96, payable in eleven monthly installments plus a final balloon note due in September 1986. This note was signed for Hardy Tractor by Wayne Zaunbrecker, Donald Greene and Burton Hardy, all directors of Hardy Tractor. A new collateral pledge agreement was drawn up, pledging the two 1984 collateral mortgage notes to secure the new hand note. The 1985 pledge agreement states that it does not have the effect of releasing the original 1984 pledge agreements. The 1985 pledge agreement is signed by Wayne Zaunbrecker, on behalf of himself, Hardy Tractor and three other principals in Hardy Tractor, and by Donald Greene and Burton Hardy. Also, Wayne Zaunbrecker, Donald Greene and Burton Hardy signed a continuing guaranty for the Hardy Tractor note on September 30, 1985.

[8] Sometime in 1986, Hardy Tractor of Gueydon, Inc. became defunct. Donald Greene, Wayne Zaunbrecker and Burton Hardy agreed to divide and personally assume the corporate debts. Donald Greene assumed the debt owed to First National Bank of Abbeville.

[9] In February 1987, First National Bank accepted a new hand note signed by Donald Greene for $108,339.55, for which it renewed the loan for the balance due on the 1985 Hardy Tractor hand note. The new note was payable in eleven monthly installments with a balloon payment due in February 1988. The note stated, "Collateral securing other loans with us may also secure this loan." Also, on February 17, 1987, Burton Hardy and Wayne Zaunbrecker signed a continuing guaranty on the note given by Donald Greene.

[10] Finally, in July 1988, the Bank made the last renewal of the loan on the basis of a note given by Donald Greene for $104,920.92, payable on demand or on January 25, 1989, plus one quarterly interest payment on October 25, 1988. The note states that it is secured by the two 1984 collateral mortgage notes. It is signed by Donald Greene.

[11] Donald Greene became delinquent in payment of the 1988 hand note. The Bank placed him in default and sent a notice of the default to LeBlanc and Dietz, as required by the collateral mortgage. On June 22, 1989, the Bank filed this suit against Donald Greene, Delores Hair (Dietz) and Ruby Linscomb (LeBlanc) for the balance due on the 1988 hand note plus accrued interest ($112,301.83), plus interest until paid, attorney fees and costs, and for recognition of the two 1984 collateral mortgages.

Trial Court Action

[12] [**After losing on an exception of no cause of action, . . .**] Dietz and LeBlanc then answered with a general denial.

[13] At trial, the Bank introduced evidence of the debt, the in rem collateral mortgages, and the pledges. The loan officer who handled the loan, Steve Griffin, testified that Donald Greene personally took over Hardy Tractor's debt after Hardy Tractor went out of business. Donald Greene testified that neither he nor Hardy Tractor ever released the collateral mortgages on the property which secured the debt.

[14] Dietz, LeBlanc, and their attorney failed to appear at trial, due to having overlooked the notice of the trial date which was sent to them.

[15] The trial judge held in favor of the Bank, granting a judgment against Greene for $113,759.29 and recognizing the collateral mortgages and the in rem collateral mortgage notes pledged to the Bank.

[. . . .]

Assignments of Error

[16] On appeal, Dietz and LeBlanc [. . .] argue[, **among other things,**] that the hand note issued to Hardy Tractor was extinguished by novation. Therefore, the new hand note to Donald Greene was not secured by the pledge securing the Hardy Tractor note.

[. . . .]

Novation

[17] Appellants argue that the hand notes executed by Hardy Tractor were novated, thereby extinguishing the ancillary obligation of pledge with the discharge of the principal obligation. This argument is founded on the contention that the collateral mortgage notes were only pledged as security for the original $120,000 loan to Hardy Tractor.

[18] Appellants further argue that the hand notes executed by Hardy Tractor were novated either by the creation of a new debt and coincidental payment of the original debt, through the 1987 hand note executed by Donald Greene or by the substitution of Donald Greene as the debtor on the hand note after Hardy Tractor had become defunct.

[19] The principles of novation are well settled and understood. The Louisiana Supreme Court has set forth an excellent discussion of these principles in *Scott v. Bank of Coushatta*, 512 So.2d 356 (La.1987). As provided in LSA-C.C. art. 1882, novation takes place when a new obligor is substituted for a prior obligor who is discharged by the obligee. The facts and circumstances of a given case must clearly evidence an intent by the creditor to release the prior debtor. See the 1984 Revision Comments under LSA-C.C. art. 1882 and the discussion in *Scott*.

[20] In the case before us, we find no evidence that the parties to the loan contract intended to extinguish existing debt and substitute a new one in its place. The Bank permitted one of the guarantors of Hardy Tractor's debt to assume responsibility for its continued payment. No new obligation was created by accepting payment from one of Hardy Tractor's guarantors. The Bank merely renewed Hardy Tractor's loan as it had done annually since the loan was originated. It is not reasonable to believe the Bank intended to substitute an unsecured debt for one secured by collateral mortgage notes and personal guarantees. Therefore, the debt was not novated by payment.

[21] Moreover, we do not find that the Bank intended to release Hardy Tractor when it accepted payment by Donald Greene and renewed the loan in his name. Such an intention was never discussed by the parties to the loan, nor was it expressed by the Bank. Since Donald Greene was one of the guarantors of the Hardy Tractor loan, we cannot justifiably assume that the Bank intended to release Hardy Tractor from liability when it accepted payments by Donald Greene.

[22] Therefore, we hold that the hand notes executed by Hardy Tractor were not novated.

[....]

Conclusion

[23] Therefore, we hold that the trial judge did not err in rendering a judgment in favor of the Bank, recognizing the collateral mortgage notes secured by the collateral mortgages on the property of Dietz and LeBlanc.

[. . . .]

Questions

1. Before focusing on novation, it is essential, once again, to ascertain the number, the sources and the kinds of relationships created in this case.

2. Consider the facts: assuming obligations have been created, identify the legal component parts of these obligations. For example, is an obligation personal or real? Is one obligation a principal obligation and another a secondary obligation? How are the parties bound if they are obligors? How are they bound if they are obligees? What are the sources of these obligations: the law or a contract or more than one contract? Is the contract or are the contracts nominate contracts?

3. Paragraph 16: How would you phrase the novation issue? Would you phrase it in terms of subjective novation? If so, what are the requirements for such a subjective novation to take place? Isn't a note a thing? Could the novation, if there is one, be an objective novation (*see* paragraph 18)? On what particular requirement of a novation is the Court focusing?

4. Paragraph 20: In the sentence starting with "In the case before us" and ending with "in its place," is the Court listing the requirements for a type of novation? What are these requirements and to what type of novation is the Court referring? In the fourth sentence, the Court uses the verb "renewed": is there any difference, in terms of effects, between a renewal and a novation? What weight would you give to the fact that the loan had been renewed annually since it originated? If you had to take the side of Ruby H. LeBlanc and Delores H. Dietz, who signed the collateral mortgage notes, could you make an argument (strong?) on the basis of Louisiana Civil Code article 1884?

Comparative Law Perspective

— Civil Law —

Robert J. Pothier, *A Treatise on the Law of Obligations or Contracts*

vol. 1, n°s 546–565 at 380–94 (William David Evans trans., 1806)

§ I. Of the Nature of a Novation and its Several Kinds

[546] A Novation is a substitution of a new debt for an old. The old debt is extinguished, for which reason, a novation is included amongst the different modes, in which obligations are extinguished.

[547] A novation may be made in three different ways, which form three different kinds of novations. The first takes place, without the intervention of any new person, where a debtor contracts a new engagement with his creditor, in consideration

of being liberated from the former. This kind has no appropriate name, and is called a novation generally.

[548] The second is that which takes place by the intervention of a new debtor, where another person becomes a debtor in my stead, and is accepted by the creditor, who thereupon discharges me from it. The person thus rendering himself debtor for another, who is in consequence discharged, is called expromissor; and this kind of novation is called *expromissio.*

The expromissor differs entirely from a surety, who is sometimes called in law, *adpromissor.* For a person by becoming a surety does not discharge, but accede to, the obligation of his principal, and becomes jointly indebted with him.

[549] The third kind of novation takes place by the intervention of a new creditor, where a debtor, for the purpose of being discharged from his original creditor, by the order of that creditor, contracts some obligation in favour of a new creditor.

There is a particular kind of novation called delegation, which frequently includes double novation. [. . . .]

[550] It results from the definition which has been given, that there can be no novation without two debts being contracted, one of which is extinguished by the substitution of the other.

It follows that if the debt, of which it is proposed to make a novation by another engagement, is conditional, the novation cannot take effect until the condition is accomplished.

Therefore, if there is a failure in the accomplishment of the condition, there can be no novation, because there is no original debt to which the new one can be substituted.

Also, if the conditional debt, of which it is intended to make a novation by a new engagement, is a specific thing, which has been destroyed or perishes, before the condition is accomplished, there will be no novation even if the condition should exist; for, since the accomplishment of the condition cannot confirm a debt of a thing which has no existence, there is no original debt to which the new one can be substituted. [. . . .]

§ II. Of the Intention to Make a Novation

[559] In order to constitute a novation, the consent of the creditor, or of some person having authority from him, or a quality to make a novation for him, is requisite. [. . . .]

The reason of this law is, that a person should not easily be presumed to abandon the rights which belong to him. Therefore, as a novation implies an abandonment by the creditor of the first claim, to which the second is substituted, it ought not to be easily presumed, and the parties ought expressly to state it. [. . . .]

[563] The effect of a novation is, that the former debt is extinguished in the same manner as it would be by a real payment.

Where one of several debtors in solido alone contracts a new engagement with the creditor, as a novation of the former debt, the first debt being extinguished by the novation, in the same manner as it would have been by a real payment, all his co-debtors are equally liberated with himself. And as the extinction of principal obligation induces that of all accessary obligations, the novation of the principal debt extinguishes all accessary obligations, such as those of sureties.

If the creditor wished to preserve the obligations of the other debtors and sureties, it would be necessary for him to make it a condition of the novation, that the co-debtors and sureties should accede to the new debt; in which case, in default of their acceding to it, there would be no novation, and the creditor would preserve his ancient claim. [. . . .]

§ III. Of Delegation

[564] Delegation is a kind of novation, by which the original debtor, in order to be liberated from his creditor, gives him a third person, who becomes obliged in his stead to the creditor, or to the person appointed by him. [. . . .]

It results from this definition, that a delegation is made by the concurrence of three parties, and that there may be a fourth.

There must be a concurrence, 1st, of the party delegating, that is, the ancient debtor who procures another debtor in his stead.

2d, Of the party delegated, who enters into an obligation, in the stead of the ancient debtor, either to the creditor or some other person appointed by him.

3d, Of the creditor, who, in consequence of the obligation contracted by the party delegated, discharges the party delegating.

Sometimes there intervenes a fourth party, *viz.* the person indicated by the creditor, and in whose favour the person delegated becomes obliged, upon the indication of the creditor, and by the order of the person delegating. [. . . .]

[565] A delegation includes a novation, by the extinction of the debt from the person delegating, and the obligation contracted in his stead by the person delegated. Commonly, indeed, there is a double novation; for the party delegated is commonly a debtor of the person delegating, and in order to be liberated from the obligation to him, contracts a new one with his creditor. In this case there is novation both of the obligation of the person delegating, by his giving his creditor a new debtor, and of the person delegated, by the new obligation which he contracts.

Robert Pothier, *Traité Des Obligations*

2 Œuvres de Pothier, n° 594 at 65–66 (ed. 1825).

Unless it appears clearly that the obligee has had the intention of making a novation, novation is not presumed. [. . . .] It is so if, since the debt was contracted, some act has been passed between the obligee and the obligor (i) whereby a term for payment has been granted; or (ii) whereby they have agreed on a new place for the performance; or (iii) whereby the obligor has been accorded the privilege (a) of rendering performance to someone other than the obligee or (b) of giving a thing in lieu of the money that was due [i.e., a *dation en paiement*]; or (iv) even whereby the obligor obligates himself to pay a larger or a smaller sum than that to which the obligee would have wanted to restrain himself. In all these cases, and in others like them, it is necessary to decide, on the basis of our principle — novation is not presumed — that there has been no novation and that the parties have wanted only to modify, diminish, or augment the debt rather than to extinguish it so as to substitute another for it, if they have not explained themselves.

Section VII — Remission of Debt

Louisiana Sources of Law
Louisiana Civil Code

Art. 1888. Express or tacit remission.

A remission of debt by an obligee extinguishes the obligation. That remission may be express or tacit. (Acts 1984, No. 331, §1, eff. Jan. 1, 1985.)

Art. 1889. Presumption of remission.

An obligee's voluntary surrender to the obligor of the instrument evidencing the obligation gives rise to a presumption that the obligee intended to remit the debt. (Acts 1984, No. 331, §1, eff. Jan. 1, 1985.)

Art. 1890. Remission effective when communication is received by the obligor.

A remission of debt is effective when the obligor receives the communication from the obligee. Acceptance of a remission is always presumed unless the obligor rejects the remission within a reasonable time. (Acts 1984, No. 331, §1, eff. Jan. 1, 1985.)

Art. 1891. Release of real security.

Release of a real security given for performance of the obligation does not give rise to a presumption of remission of debt. (Acts 1984, No. 331, §1, eff. Jan. 1, 1985.)

Art. 1892. Remission granted to sureties.

Remission of debt granted to the principal obligor releases the sureties.

Remission of debt granted to the sureties does not release the principal obligor.

Remission of debt granted to one surety releases the other sureties only to the extent of the contribution the other sureties might have recovered from the surety to whom the remission was granted.

If the obligee grants a remission of debt to a surety in return for an advantage, that advantage will be imputed to the debt, unless the surety and the obligee agree otherwise. (Acts 1984, No. 331, §1, eff. Jan. 1, 1985.)

Doctrine

Louisiana Law of Obligations in General, A Précis

Sections 7.4.1 to 7.4.2

A remission of debt can be defined as a bilateral juridical act or contract, gratuitous or onerous, whereby an obligee gives up the right to demand the performance of an obligation owed by his obligor. Civil Code **Article 1888** states that "**A remission of debt by an obligee extinguishes the obligation. That remission may be express or tacit.**" [. . . .]

For a remission to be valid two wills must coexist, the obligor in particular must agree to the remission offered to him by his obligee. LSA-C.C. **Art. 1890** states, in part, that "**acceptance of a remission is always presumed, unless the obligor rejects the remission within a reasonable time.**" [. . . .]

An obligor who would want to reject a remission of his debt would have to expressly manifest his opposition or rejection. One cannot be forced to accept a "gift," a "gratuity," which is often the case of a remission of debt. In a sense, the obligee "forgives" the debt owed by his obligor. [. . . .]

The effectiveness of a remission of debt, its binding effect and its proof are contingent upon the obligor receiving the communication of the obligee's intent. As **LSA--C.C. Art. 1890** states: "**A remission of debt is effective when the obligor receives the communication from the obligee. Acceptance of a remission is always presumed unless the obligor rejects the remission within a reasonable time.**" The selection of the *receipt theory,* as the time of effectiveness of the remission, is quite reasonable since it assumes that the obligor will accept the benefit of the remission of debt. [. . . .]

Besides this tacit acceptance by the obligor, the law has provided for instances of presumption of remission of debt. One such example is referred to in **LSA-C.C. Art. 1889** in these terms: "**An obligee's voluntary surrender to the obligor of the instrument evidencing the obligation gives rise to a presumption that the obligee intended to remit the debt.**" [. . . .]

Once an obligor has had his obligation remitted, he is discharged of any performance. The extinction of the primary obligation will carry with it the discharge of any accessory obligation by virtue of the principle *accessorium sequitur principale.* [. . . .]

When obligors are joint obligors each one owes a share of the whole performance. [. . . .]

The remission of debt benefits only the joint obligor who was offered, and who accepted, the discharge granted to him. [. . . .]

Departing from the law of solidarity as it existed before 1984, the new Code Articles have opted for a rational principle by providing that "**Remission of debt by the obligee in favor of one obligor, or a transaction or compromise between the** obligee and one obligor, benefits the other solidary obligors in the amount of the portion of that obligor." (LSA-C.C. Art. 1803-1). [. . . .]

In its first paragraph, **Article 1892** states that "**A remission of debt granted to the principal obligor releases the sureties.**" This rule is but an application of the principle that the accessory follows the fate of the principal (*accessorium sequitur principale*).

However, "A remission of debt granted to the sureties does not release the principal obligor." (LSA-C.C. Art. 1892-2). [. . . .]

The third paragraph of **LSA-C.C. Art. 1892** states that "**Remission of debt granted to one surety releases the other sureties only to the extent of the contribution the other sureties might have recovered from the surety to whom the remission was granted.**" [. . . .]

Lastly "If the obligee grants a remission of debt to a surety in return for an advantage, that advantage will be imputed to the debt, unless the surety and the obligee agree otherwise." (LSA-C.C. Art. 1892-4).

Cases

Frank Arender, d/b/a Farm Realty Company
v.
Jess Carr Gilbert

Court of Appeal of Louisiana
Third Circuit
March 4, 1977
343 So.2d 1146

CULPEPPER, Judge.

[1] This is a suit filed by Frank Arender, a real estate broker, to enforce the bonus clause of a 30-day 'exclusive listing agreement' between him and defendant, Jess Carr Gilbert. The exclusive listing agreement provided that plaintiff would receive a commission of $35,000 plus a bonus of one-half of any amounts received in excess of the price set by Gilbert for the sale of certain woodland and timber on the 'Black Hawk Plantation'. Defendant reconvened against plaintiff seeking return of a $35,000 payment which he made to plaintiff for his services. The basis of the reconventional demand is that plaintiff allegedly breached his fiduciary duty to defendant by representing and having an ownership interest in Three Rivers Farm, Inc., the corporation which purchased the subject property. The trial judge rendered a judgment rejecting the claims of both parties, and both parties appealed.

[2] The litigation arises from a very complex land sale transaction. The trial record and briefs of counsel suggest several issues. The decisive issue, however, is whether the following letter from Arender to Gilbert dated 8/18/1973 constitutes and 'accord

and satisfaction' which estops Arender from claiming any futher [*sic*] compensation under the terms of the July 11, 1973 exclusive listing agreement:

> 'RE: Agreement between you and myself dated 7/11/73 relative to sale of Black Hawk Plantation-land and timber 'Dear Sir: 'I acknowledge my fee to be in the sum of $35,000.00 as a result of the sale to Three Rivers Farm, Inc. dated 8/17/73. 'I hereby accept a note from you in the amount of $35,000.00 to be paid 1/10/1974 (one line of type is marked out at this point) and is full compensation for my services.
>
> /s/ Frank L. Arender'

[3] This letter was introduced into evidence without objection.

[4] The record shows that Gilbert purchased Black Hawk Plantation for approximately $1,200,000 in February of 1973. It consisted of 9,615 acres of woodland and cleared land situated in the southern part of Concordia Parish along the Mississippi River.

[5] On July 11, 1973, Gilbert entered into an 'exclusive listing agreement' with Arender to secure a purchaser for the woodland and timber on Black Hawk Plantation. The agreement specified that 7,532 acres of woodland were to be sold at $140 per acre. The standing timber on Black Hawk Plantation was to be sold for an additional $650,000. The total proposed selling price, therefore, was $1,704,480.

[6] The listing agreement set the credit terms of the sale at '29% Down and the balance in January, 1974. 'The agreement provided further that Arender was to receive a commission of $35,000, to be paid in January, 1974. Also, the following bonus clause was contained in the listing agreement: 'In the event the selling price is more than the above figure, Frank (Arender) is to receive one-half of all over this figure.' The agreement was to run 30 days from July 11, 1973.

[7] After securing the exclusive listing, Arender immediately began contacting potential purchasers. One of these, Dale Rogers, was interested in purchasing only a portion of the plantation for use in his farming operation. He was not interested in purchasing the entire tract offered.

[8] Arender also contacted a Lake Providence attorney, Captan Jack Wyly. Wyly, as Rogers, was interested in purchasing only portions of the land offered. Through the efforts of Arender, Wyly and Rogers met and formed a corporation to purchase the subject property. The corporation was formed on July 19, 1973 under the name Three Rivers Farm, Inc. Its president was Dale Rogers. A total of 300 shares of stock were issued on three certificates. 100 shares were issued to Rogers, 100 shares to his wife, and 100 shares to Wyly's secretary, who held the shares for him. Arender owned no stock in the corporation.

[9] A round of negotiations between Wyly, Gilbert, Rogers and Arender followed. Gilbert's attorney, George Griffing, was also involved in these negotiations. Wyly and Rogers trusted Arender, and often Arender acted as 'middle man' between representatives of Three Rivers and Gilbert. Offers and counteroffers were communicated

to both parties through Arender. Finally, on July 26, 1973, Three Rivers and Gilbert executed a contract whereby Three Rivers acquired an option to purchase a certain portion of Black Hawk Plantation (about 7,100 acres) for the total sum of $1,798,560. The option price, $50,000, was paid by Three Rivers on July 26, and applied toward the purchase price.

[10] The option agreement stated that the act of sale was to be passed on August 17, 1973, at which time an additional $450,000 was to be paid in cash to Gilbert. The remainder of the purchase price, $1,298,560, was to be represented by a promissory note due on January 5, 1974.

[11] The property described in the option to purchase was not the same property described in the exclusive listing agreement between Gilbert and Arender. During the course of negotiations, Rogers stated that in order to secure financing for the purchase, some cleared land would have to be included in the property sold. In response to Rogers' financing difficulties, Gilbert added about 550 acres of cleared land, but in return, Gilbert retained several hundred additional acres of woodland which he originally intended to sell.

[12] The act of sale was passed on August 17, 1973 substantially in accordance with the terms of the 'Option To Purchase.' The $450,000 cash payment was in the form of a check drawn on the account of J. E. Jones Lumber Company payable to Three Rivers, which was endorsed to Gilbert by Three Rivers. J. E. Jones Lumber Company stopped payment on its check, however, when its attorney discovered a notice of lis pendens affecting the subject property had been filed by Ricks Lumber Company on August 17. In its petition, Ricks alleged that Arender, acting as Gilbert's agent, had promised to sell certain timber located on Black Hawk Plantation to Ricks for a specified price. The Ricks' suit was eventually dismissed on an exception of no cause of action, but the stop payment order on the check brought the subject sale transaction to a halt.

[13] All of the parties were concerned about the future course of the transaction. On the day after the act of sale was passed, August 18, 1973, Arender, Rogers, Gilbert and his attorney, George Griffing, met at Gilbert's house to determine what course of action they should follow. The initial purpose of the meeting was to determine how the Ricks suit could be dismissed and the notice of lis pendens removed from the record. Other types of negotiations also took place at the meeting, including some negotiations concerning Arender's fee. It is the negotiations regarding Arender's fee that we are concerned with.

[14] Prior to the meeting, Gilbert had become dissatisfied with Arender. Apparently, he thought that Arender was not entitled to his fee. For example, Gilbert testified he considered the listing agreement to be terminated because the land actually sold was not the land described in the listing agreement. The credit terms of the final sale were also different from those specified in the listing agreement. Additionally, Gilbert testified that shortly after the option to purchase was executed, Arender told him that he had an ownership interest in Three Rivers. (The evidence shows,

however, that Arender had no such interest in Three Rivers.) Gilbert testified, and the trial judge concluded, that shortly after the option agreement was executed, Gilbert began negotiating for himself and no longer considered Arender his agent. In summary, Gilbert entered the August 18 negotiations with Arender and others believing that Arender had not fulfilled the terms of the listing agreement, had represented Three Rivers to Gilbert's detriment, and was not entitled to his fee.

[15] The atmosphere at the August 18 meeting was tense. Gilbert testified, and the trial judge concluded, that Arender demanded payment of his $35,000 commission at this meeting. The listing agreement of July 11, 1973 provided that the commission was not due until January, 1974. Gilbert and his attorney, George Griffing, drafted the letter quoted at the outset of this opinion in response to Arender's demand. By way of review, Arender acknowledged in the letter that his fee for the sale of Three Rivers was $35,000. Arender further stated in the letter that he accepted a note from Gilbert in the amount of $35,000 to be paid 1/10/74, the note being 'full compensation for my services.' The letter made specific reference to the exclusive listing agreement of 7/11/73, but did not mention the 'one/half over' bonus provision. The question before us is whether this letter constitutes an 'accord and satisfaction', which would bar Arender's claim to any further compensation under the terms of the July 11 exclusive listing agreement.

[16] Our courts have adopted the common law doctrine of accord and satisfaction. Each of these three conditions must be present for its application: (1) An unliquidated or disputed claim. (2) A tender by the debtor. (3) An acceptance of the tender by the creditor. Young v. White Stores, Inc., 269 So.2d 266 (La.App.3rd Cir. 1972) and cases cited therein. An additional prerequisite to settlement by accord and satisfaction is that the creditor must understand that if the reduced payment is accepted his claim will have been paid in full. Antoine v. Elder Realty Company, 255 So.2d 625 (La.App.3rd Cir. 1971). If the tender itself clearly sets forth that the lesser sum is offered in full payment of the disputed or unliquidated debt, however, acceptance of the tender constitutes acceptance of the debtor's offer. Charles X. Miller, Inc. v. Oak Builders, Inc., 306 So.2d 449 (La.App.4th Cir. 1975).

[17] The August 18 letter executed by Arender, accompanied by Arender's acceptance of the tendered note for $35,000, constitutes an accord and satisfaction. The requirements of tender of payment by the debtor and acceptance by the creditor are obviously satisfied. The further requirement that the debt be unliquidated or disputed is also satisfied.

[18] The debt was, in fact, unliquidated and disputed. Though there is some question as to whether Gilbert informed Arender of all of the reasons that he felt would prevent Arender from receiving the full amount of the fee contemplated by the listing agreement, there is no doubt that the fee was disputed.

[19] The fee was the subject of negotiations between Gilbert and Arender at the August 18 meeting. It was Arender who first brought up the subject by demanding payment of the $35,000 commission at the meeting. By the terms of the exclusive

listing agreement, the commission payment was not due until January, 1974. Apparently, Arender opted to take a $35,000 note as full compensation for his services rather than risking both his commission and his 'one-half over' on successful resolution of the transaction in accordance with the terms of the original listing agreement. In other words, Arender bargained away his chances to collect a commission plus a bonus by accepting a $35,000 note tendered as full compensation before any compensation was due under the terms of the listing agreement. The note was paid at maturity.

[20] The present case is not one of those where the debtor scrawls 'in full settlement' or other similar words on his check and sends it off to the distant creditor, hoping that the creditor will unwittingly cash it and effect an accord and satisfaction. Arender and Gilbert were literally negotiating at arms' length when the tender was made. The tender was apparently the subject of some discussion between the two. The bargaining process was operative. Its end product was the accord and satisfaction agreement.

[21] Arender argues that no dispute as to the amount of money owed to him existed when Gilbert tendered the $35,000 note as full compensation for his services. The record supports this argument to the extent that there was no discussion as to the 'one-half over' provision of the contract at the August 18 meeting. There was, however, a dispute as to whether any portion of Arender's fee, either the commission or the one-half over bonus, was due.

[22] Even if we assume that Arender was not aware of any dispute concerning the amount of his fee before August 18, he would have been put on notice that such a dispute existed by the very terms of the letter which he signed on that day. The letter made specific reference to the exclusive listing agreement of July 11, 1973. In unambiguous terms, Arender acknowledged in the letter that his Fee as a result of the sale to Three Rivers Farm, Inc. was $35,000. It is significant that he acknowledged his Fee to be in the amount of $35,000 rather than acknowledging his Commission to be in that amount. The term 'fee' is much broader than the term 'commission'. 'Fee' can reasonably be deemed to include all of the compensation to be earned by Arender as a result of the sale, including the 'one-half over' bonus stipulated in the listing agreement. The broad scope of the letter and its intended effect become even clearer when the second paragraph of the letter is considered along with the first paragraph. In the second paragraph, Arender acknowledges acceptance of the note as 'full compensation' for his services.

[23] Though the letter does not mention the 'one-half over' provision, its intent could hardly be more clearly expressed. The letter was intended as an 'accord and satisfaction' to bar any future claim for compensation based upon the terms of the July 11 exclusive listing agreement.

[24] In the Charles X. Miller case, supra, the court quoted from 1 C.J.S. Accord and Satisfaction s 6, P. 479, to explain that an accord and satisfaction could be effected even though the creditor may have acted under a misapprehension as to the

legal effect of his acceptance or may not have understood or believed that it would have the effect of accord and satisfaction, provided that the creditor acted knowingly or with knowledge of all the pertinent facts. Arender was intimately involved in all aspects of the transaction and had knowledge of all of the pertinent facts. Furthermore, any fact or opinion unknown to him could have been easily ascertained by simply asking one of the parties present at the August 18 meeting.

[25] The question of whether a debt is 'disputed' is a factual one which must be decided on a case by case basis by reference to the record as a whole. In the present case, we determine a dispute existed. Under a similar factual situation in Hancock v. Lincoln American Life Insurance Company, 278 So.2d 561 (La.App.1st Cir. 1973), the court determined that no dispute existed and held the doctrine of accord and satisfaction was inapplicable. In Hancock, the court quoted at length from the decision of our Supreme Court in Pontchartrain Park Homes v. Sewerage & Water Board, 246 La. 893, 168 So.2d 595. A portion of the quotation from Pontchartrain Park dealing with the requirement of a 'dispute' for accord and satisfaction follows: 'Unquestionably the creditor must have knowledge, actual or imputed, of the existence of a dispute regarding the amount due. It is not necessary, however, that there be haggling over a fixed contract price to either constitute a dispute or impute knowledge thereof to the creditor. It suffices that actual knowledge be shown *or circumstances demonstrated from which knowledge may reasonably be inferred.*' (Emphasis added) 278 So.2d 561 at 564[.]

[26] In the present case, it was Arender who provoked the dispute concerning his fee by demanding its payment four months before it would have been due. There was no haggling over the exact amount due, but Arender had knowledge of the facts upon which Gilbert based his contention that Arender was not entitled to a fee. Furthermore, the contents of the letter signed by Arender on August 18 charged him with imputed knowledge that some dispute concerning the amount of his fee existed. The answers to any questions he may have had were within his grasp. He failed, either intentionally or unintentionally, to avail himself of these answers.

[27] 'Accord and satisfaction' is an affirmative defense which must be pleaded in the answer. LSA-C.C.P. Art. 1005 and Official Comment E to that article. Defendant pleaded facts constituting the basis for the defense of accord and satisfaction in paragraphs 4 and 15 of his answer, though he did not label the defense 'accord and satisfaction.' Furthermore, the letter which affected the accord and satisfaction was introduced into evidence without objection, thereby enlarging the pleadings to include the defense. LSA-C.C.P. Art. 1154; Conques v. Hardy, 337 So.2d 627 (La. App.3rd Cir. 1976); Edwards v. Edwards, 282 So.2d 858 (La.App.1st Cir. 1973), writ refused, 284 So.2d 777 (La.1973). Therefore, Arender's assertion that Gilbert cannot urge the affirmative defense of accord and satisfaction because he failed to plead it in his answer is without merit.

[28] The same result could be reached through application of the provisions of our Civil Code dealing with voluntary remission of debt. LSA-C.C. Art. 2199, et seq. The application of the principle of remission in cases such as the present one

is explained in Obligations, J. Denson Smith, 26 La.L.Rev. 497 and 498. There, Professor Smith explains that under the common law theory, the significance of the 'dispute' requirement for accord and satisfaction lies in the fact that in the absence of a dispute, the receipt by the creditor of less than the amount due will not serve as consideration to discharge the remainder. In our civilian system, however, although a disputed claim may be compromised by way of settlement, an undisputed claim may also be discharged in whole or in part by voluntary remission. No consideration is required and the absence of a dispute is wholly unimportant. All that is required under the remission articles is a finding that the creditor intended to remit his claim or that he estopped himself to claim the contrary.

[29] In the present case, the letter of August 18 shows a clear and convincing intent to effect a voluntary intentional remission of any part of the debt (broker's fee) beyond the acknowledged total fee of $35,000.

[30] Having disposed of Arender's claim, we move now to Gilbert's reconventional demand for return of the $35,000 fee paid to Arender pursuant to the terms of the August 18 accord and satisfaction agreement. The alleged grounds for the reconventional demand are that (1) Arender breached his fiduciary duty to Gilbert by representing Three Rivers in negotiation preceding the July 26 'Option To Purchase', and (2) Arender allegedly acquired an ownership interest in Three Rivers prior to execution of the option to purchase. The evidence in the record supports neither of these assertions. To the contrary, the evidence shows that Arender had no ownership interest in Three Rivers and received no compensation from them.

[31] The most conclusive answer to Gilbert's reconventional demand is that he is also barred by the accord and satisfaction between the parties stated in the August 18, 1973 letter quoted above.

[32] We conclude there is no merit to Gilbert's reconventional demand for return of the $35,000 fee which he paid to Arender.

[. . . .]

Questions

1. The *Arender* court, without explanation, notes that the Louisiana courts had long ago "adopted the common law doctrine of accord and satisfaction." *See* paragraph 16. By what authority did they do so? Regardless whether what the courts did was authorized, was it needed? Did the civil law of Louisiana not already possess an analogous institution, one through which interested parties could have obtained the same effects as those that arise from accord and satisfaction? *See* La. Civ. Code art. 3071, *et seq.*

2. Since *Arender* was decided, Louisiana's "law" of accord and satisfaction has been codified. *See* Civ. Code art. 3079. Would the "accord and satisfaction" issue presented in *Arender* be decided any differently under the codified law?

3. The *Arender* court states that "[n]o consideration is required" for a valid remission of debt. *Arender* was decided under the old law of remission. Is the

Arender court's statement consistent with the new law? *See* La. Civ. Code art. 1888. If consideration is not required for a valid remission, then what kind of juridical act is a remission? Hint: *see* La. Civ. Code arts. 1909 & 1910; then *see* La. Civ. Code art. 1888.

Alvin J. Arledge as Administrator of the Succession of Joseph Alton Arledge

v.

Arlen C. Bell

Court of Appeal of Louisiana
Second Circuit
January 23, 1985
463 So.2d 856

SEXTON, Judge.

[1] Arlen C. Bell appeals a declaratory judgment finding that he is indebted to the succession of Joseph Alton Arledge in the amount of $9,000, representing the unpaid balance of a loan from decedent to defendant. We reverse and remand for a new trial.

[2] Decedent, Joseph Alton Arledge, was a single man with no children who died intestate on November 17, 1982. One sister, Willie Travis Arledge Bell, predeceased Joseph. He was survived by one brother, Alvin Julius Arledge, the duly qualified administrator of this succession. Defendant herein is one of the three children born to Willie Bell and is therefore a nephew to the decedent.

[3] The administrator of the succession brought suit for declaratory judgment separately against defendant, and his sister Charlotte Bell, seeking declarations of the amounts of their respective indebtedness to the succession. Arlen Bell's answer alleged that the transaction was a gift and, in the alternative, that if the initial transaction was characterized as a loan, the debt was extinguished by remission in a long distance telephone call between Arlen C. Bell and the decedent. In interrogatories which were admitted into evidence, appellant conceded that the money was originally advanced from his uncle as a loan. The cases were consolidated for trial. Judgment was rendered in favor of the succession and against both defendants. Only Arlen C. Bell has appealed.

[4] At trial Arlen Bell testified that in 1980 he borrowed $10,000 from his uncle in order to place a down payment on a home for his family. He subsequently paid ten installments of $100 each on the loan, reducing the unpaid balance to $9,000.

[5] On appeal, defendant urges the applicability of LSA-C.C. Art. 1888, et seq.,[*] claiming that the debt had been remitted by his uncle.

---

[*] Prior to the revision of the "Obligations" articles of the Civil Code by Act No. 331 of 1984, the remission articles were contained in Article 2199, et seq. As the redactors comment to the new

[6] All that is required under the remission articles is a determination that the creditor intended to remit his claim or that he has estopped himself to claim the contrary. *Cowley Corporation v. Shreveport Packing Co.,* 440 So.2d 1345 (La.App. 2d Cir.1983), writ denied, 444 So.2d 122 (La.1984). While the remission of a debt cannot be revoked by a creditor, remission is never presumed unless it clearly appears that the creditor intended it. The burden of proving remission, express or tacit, rests with those claiming the benefit. *Cowley, supra; Succession of Martin,* 335 So.2d 494 (La.App. 2d Cir.1976), writ denied, 337 So.2d 516 (La.1976). No particular form for remission is necessary and the remission may either occur by oral declaration or in writing. *Gulf States Finance Corporation v. Moses,* 56 So.2d 221 (La.App. 2d Cir.1951).

[7] At trial, defendant's attorney attempted to elicit testimony concerning the substance of the long distance telephone conversation. Counsel for the succession objected on hearsay and relevancy grounds. The objection was sustained, and the evidence was admitted by proffer. Appellant contends that the trial court erred in refusing to admit and consider this evidence.

[8] In regard to his relevancy argument, appellee contends that LSA-C.C. Art. 1536 precludes the admission of this evidence. Appellee claims that the alleged conversation relative to forgiveness of Arlen Bell's debt constituted a gift of a credit, an incorporeal thing. Thus, he asserts that LSA-C.C. Art. 1536, which stipulates formal requirements for the donation of incorporeal movables, is controlling, thus rendering appellant's evidence irrelevant.

[9] Our initial inquiry, then, must be directed to the character of the transaction here involved to determine whether the formal requirements of Article 1536 are pertinent. It is clear from the testimony and answers to interrogatories of the defendant Arlen C. Bell that this transaction was originally intended to be a loan and not a donation. Therefore, if the deceased acted as the defendant asserts, that action forgave an existing obligation.

[10] While the forgiveness of a debt may in some respects appear to be a donation because of the gratuitous intent manifested by the act of forgiveness, in specific terms it is the remission of a previous obligation. It therefore must be considered within the context of our law on remission.

[11] As Professor Levasseur explains:

> When remitting a debt, the creditor is usually motivated by a gratuitous intent (animus donandi). Such a gratuitous juridical act is tantamount to a donation and should, therefore, be subjected to the conditions of substance applicable to liberalities (collation, reduction, revocation . . .). However, the

---

Article 1888 indicates, that Article does not change the law. While some changes were made in the remission articles, these changes primarily deal with the effects of remission on sureties and have no effect on the instant litigation. See generally, Section 4, Chapter 6 of the Exposé Des Motif of the Project of Titles III and IV of Book III of the Civil Code of Louisiana.

conditions of form pertaining to donations are not applicable (LCC 1536 et seq).

A. Levasseur, *Précis in Conventional Obligations: A Civil Code Analysis,* at 84 (1980). Accord, S. Litvinoff, 6 *Louisiana Civil Law Treatise: Obligations,* §371 (1969). See also *Hicks v. Hicks,* 145 La. 465, 82 So. 415 (1919).

[12] The redactors comment (b) to the new Article 1888 is succinctly in accord with Professor Levasseur: (b) Although *remission* is an act gratuitous in principle, it *is considered a sort of indirect liberality not subject to the requirements of form prescribed for donations.* See 4 Aubry et Rau, Cours de droit civil francais-Obligations 223 (Louisiana State Law Institute trans. 1965); 2 Colin et Capitant, Cours elementaire de droit civil francais 403 (10th ed. 1953); 7 Planiol et Ripert, Traité pratique de droit civil français 716 (2nd ed. 1954); 1 Litvinoff, Obligations 627–628 (1969). See also *Hicks v. Hicks,* 145 La. 465, 82 So. 415 (1919); *Reinecke v. Pelham,* 199 So. 521 (La. App.Orl.1941). [Emphasis ours]

[13] Therefore, while a remission may involve a donative intent on the part of the creditor, the authentic form requirements of LSA-C.C. Art. 1536 do not apply. A remission may be perfected by an oral agreement and appellant's evidence which sought to establish an oral remission was relevant.

[. . . .]

Question

1. As the *Arledge* case correctly notes, a remission, though it is a donation, is nevertheless excepted from the ordinary "form" requirements for donations. But why should that be so? Does Louisiana Civil Code article 1888 help? Can you think of any other kinds of "indirect liberalities" that may be excepted from the donative form requirements? *See* La. Civ. Code arts. 1243 & 1248.

Comparative Law Perspective

— Civil Law —

Georges Ripert & Jean Boulanger, *Traité de droit civil*

vol. 2 (1957)

1933. Definition. — The remission of debt is a renunciation by the obligee of his rights. By its nature, such a renunciation is voluntary. [. . . .]

1934. Contractual nature of remission. — Remission of debt is not a unilateral juridical act. If the obligee wishes to keep to himself his willingness to forgive the obligor, then the obligee can only do one thing: not pursue the obligor and wait until prescription of the action accrues. An immediate extinction of the debt presupposes an agreement between obligee and obligor. It follows that a declaration of remission of debt made by the obligee is not binding on him and it can be withdrawn as long as it not accepted. [. . . .] However, the obligor can accept an offer to remit at any time and in any manner. As the remission of the debt is in his interest, the obligor's acceptance will be easily admitted according to the circumstances. [. . . .]

1935. Onerous and gratuitous character. — Remission of debt can be made by onerous or gratuitous title; it is a mistake to say that remission always constitutes a liberality. The obligee is free to consent to a release of his obligor in exchange for an equivalent; in our law we have the example of a transaction (or compromise): the "equivalent" may be an advantage of some kind received by the obligee, such as the waiver of a right that the other party has [. . .].

1936. General rules [on form]. — [. . . .] Remission is no longer a formal act [. . .]. It can be written or verbal. [. . . .] Remission of debt can be *express* or *tacit*. Express remission can be verbal, but the obligor may face difficulties regarding proof. Tacit remission results from any act that implies the obligee's will to renounce his credit right. [. . . .] Generally, when remission is tacit, it may take the form of a simulated receipt singed by the obligee who confirms that he has been paid even though no payment was made. [. . . .] But [. . .] nothing prevents the obligee from executing a waiver of his credit rights [. . .].

1939. Legal presumption (of proof). — Remission is a juridical act and is subject to the general rules of proof of obligations. [. . . .]

1945. Extinction of the obligation. — Remission of debt produces a completely liberative effect: whether it is granted gratuitously or in exchange for some advantage, it extinguishes the debt together with all its accessories. [. . . .]

1946. Effects of a gratuitous remission. — When remission is made by gratuitous title, it constitutes a liberality. As such it is subjected to the rules peculiar to donations (except for the rules on formal validity): it can be reduced if it impinges on the forced portion of the obligor's succession; it can be revoked in the same way as a donation can be revoked (ingratitude of the donee [. . .]); it can be collated if the obligor is one of the presumptive heirs of the obligee [. . .].

Victor Marcadé, *Explication Théorique et Pratique du Code Civil*

vol. 4, n° 802 at 642 (7th ed. 1873)

Passive Solidary: Distribution of Loss Caused by Post-Release[1] *Insolvency*

When the obligee [. . .] declares that he is remitting the debt of a co-obligor only *for his part* or *while conserving his rights against the other obligors*, he always has an action against the others, but only with a deduction for the part of the first. If, for example, the debt was 12,000 francs, with four solidary obligors, the credit, after a remission had been given to one of them, would thereafter be only 9,000 francs and there would thereafter be solidary among the other three only for these 9,000 francs. And if one of these three became insolvent, the portion that the discharged co-obligor would have had to bear of this insolvency would find itself, too, as a necessary consequence, lost for the obligee, and it could not be recovered from the other two. It is obvious, then, that a remission made to one of the co-obligors can never aggravate the position of the others.

But if the obligee had declared that he was remitting not the *debt* (whether absolutely and without restriction or only for the part of one obligor), but simply *solidarity* [i.e., **if the obligee had merely "renounced" solidarity**], he would then conserve his action for the totality of the 12,000 francs against each of the three others and for 3,000 francs against him as to whom solidarity had been remitted [**i.e., renounced**] [La. Civ. Code art. 1806].

Jacques Mestre & Marie-Ève Tian, *Solidarité Passive*

in *Contrats et Obligations: Obligations Conjointes et Solidaires: Solidarité*, n°s 126–27 at 28 (1995)

126. — Solidarity continues to weigh on the other co-obligors for the ensemble of the debt, with a deduction made for the contributive part of the beneficiary of the remission [**renunciation**] of solidarity. The contribution of each to the debt will be fixed according to the principles exposed [. . . **above**] and the following. Suppose,

---

1. There are two distinct kinds of "release" with which we are concerned here: (i) a remission *of the debt* and (ii) a renunciation of solidarity, formerly called "discharge from solidarity" or, even more confusingly, "remission *of solidarity*." The distinction turns on the *intent of the parties to the release*, in particular, on precisely *from what* the obligee intends to release the obligor. If the obligee intends to release the obligor from any further liability whatsoever, so that the obligee could not thereafter demand anything else from that obligor, then the release is a "remission of debt." If the obligee intends to release the obligor only from solidarity, in other words, to relieve him of the unique burdens associated with being a *solidary* obligor, thereby transforming him into an "ordinary" obligor (that is, a *joint* obligor), then the release is a "renunciation of solidarity." *See* 1 Saúl Litvinoff, The Law of Obligations § 7.83, at 189–90, *in* 5 Louisiana Civil Law Treatise (1992).

It is imperative not to confuse these two types of release. As you will see, in Louisiana and France, each has profoundly different effects from the other.

for example, a debt of 60,000 francs that must be repaid in parts that are equal among four obligors A, B, C, and D. If A [...] benefits from a remission [renunciation] of solidarity, each of the three others is exposed to paying 60,000–15,000 = 45,000. But he who pays that sum can exercise an action in contribution against the two others, for 15,000 from each of them.

127. — The exercise of the contribution action can become complicated by the insolvency of one of the co-obligors. This hypothetical case is provided for in article 1215 of the Civil Code [**La. Civ. Code art. 1806**]. [....]

Taking up again the previous example, one supposed that the [...] obligee has granted A an individual remission [**renunciation**] of solidarity; that the obligor B, having been pursued by the obligee, paid the 45,000 francs that constituted the balance of the debt; and that the obligor D finds himself in a state of insolvency. The question is onto whom, at the end of the day, the charge of 15,000 francs that represents the contributive part of the insolvency falls.

[...] [U]pon remitting [**renouncing**] the solidarity of one of the obligors, the obligee did not have the intention of assuming the risk of the insolvency of another obligor. He should never bear the consequences of that insolvency. [....] The result, in the same example, is that the obligor B, having been condemned to pay 45,000, can exercise his contribution action against C not only for 15,000, by also for a third of the contributive part of the insolvency (5,000), that is, for 20,000. An[other] third of the contributive part of the insolvency will be reclaimed from the obligor who was discharged from solidarity. And the paying obligor B will retain a final charge of 15,000 + 5,000 = 20,000. This interpretation is altogether conformed to the text of article 1215 [**La. Civ. Code art. 1806**].

Section VIII — Compensation

Louisiana Sources of Law

Louisiana Civil Code

Art. 1893. Compensation extinguishes obligations.

Compensation takes place by operation of law when two persons owe to each other sums of money or quantities of fungible things identical in kind, and these sums or quantities are liquidated and presently due.

In such a case, compensation extinguishes both obligations to the extent of the lesser amount.

Delays of grace do not prevent compensation. (Acts 1984, No. 331, § 1, eff. Jan. 1, 1985.)

Art. 1894. Obligation not subject to compensation.

Compensation takes place regardless of the sources of the obligations.

Compensation does not take place, however, if one of the obligations is to return a thing of which the owner has been unjustly dispossessed, or is to return a thing given in deposit or loan for use, or if the object of one of the obligations is exempt from seizure. (Acts 1984, No. 331, §1, eff. Jan. 1, 1985.)

Art. 1895. [omitted]

Art. 1896. [omitted]

Art. 1897. Compensation extinguishes obligation of surety.

Compensation between obligee and principal obligor extinguishes the obligation of a surety.

Compensation between obligee and surety does not extinguish the obligation of the principal obligor. (Acts 1984, No. 331, §1, eff. Jan. 1, 1985.)

Art. 1898. Compensation between obligee and solidary obligor.

Compensation between the obligee and one solidary obligor extinguishes the obligation of the other solidary obligors only for the portion of that obligor.

Compensation between one solidary obligee and the obligor extinguishes the obligation only for the portion of that obligee.

The compensation provided in this Article does not operate in favor of a liability insurer. (Acts 1984, No. 331, §1, eff. Jan. 1, 1985.)

Art. 1899. Rights acquired by third parties.

Compensation can neither take place nor may it be renounced to the prejudice of rights previously acquired by third parties. (Acts 1984, No. 331, §1, eff. Jan. 1, 1985.)

Art. 1900. Assignment by obligee.

An obligor who has consented to an assignment of the credit by the obligee to a third party may not claim against the latter any compensation that otherwise he could have claimed against the former.

An obligor who has been given notice of an assignment to which he did not consent may not claim compensation against the assignee for an obligation of the assignor arising after that notice. (Acts 1984, No. 331, §1, eff. Jan. 1, 1985.)

Art. 1901. Compensation by agreement.

Compensation of obligations may take place also by agreement of the parties even though the requirements for compensation by operation of law are not met. (Acts 1984, No. 331, §1, eff. Jan. 1, 1985.)

Art. 1902. Compensation by judicial declaration.

Although the obligation claimed in compensation is unliquidated, the court can declare compensation as to that part of the obligation that is susceptible of prompt and easy liquidation. (Acts 1984, No. 331, §1, eff. Jan. 1, 1985.)

Doctrine

Louisiana Law of Obligations in General, A Précis
Sections 7.5.1 to 7.5.3

LSA-C.C. Art. 1893 describes compensation by operation of law in these terms: "Compensation takes place by operation of law when two persons owe to each other sums of money or quantities of fungible things identical in kind, and these sums or quantities are liquidated and presently due.

In such a case, compensation extinguishes both obligations to the extent of the lesser amount.

Delays of grace do not prevent compensation."

Compensation by operation of law is circumscribed, however, by a series of four conditions which limit its scope of application. [. . . .]

The first condition is that the two persons must be indebted to each other in the same capacity as principal obligors and entitled to claim a performance from each other in the same capacity as principal obligees. Thus each part must be, at the same time, principal obligor and principal obligee. [. . . .]

Compensation by operation of law may occur only between obligations of sums of money or between obligations bearing on things which are fungible and of the same kind. This form of compensation by operation of law is, therefore, circumscribed to obligations to give things which are fungible. [. . . .]

A debt is liquidated when it is certain and its amount determined. A debt which is contested, as when it is being litigated, is not liquidated and, in addition, its amount is not fixed or determined.

An obligation is due whenever it is demandable so that the creditor can obtain its immediate performance. [. . . .]

LSA-C.C. Art. 1894-2 lists two important exceptions to the right of compensation by operation of law: "Compensation does not take place, however, if one of the obligations is to return a thing of which the owner has been unjustly dispossessed, or is to return a thing given in deposit or loan for use, ..."

Occurrence by operation of law means simply that, in this case, compensation takes place automatically even unbeknownst to the parties. As soon as the requirements for compensation by operation of law are met, the two obligations involved are extinguished either entirely or *pro tanto;* "Compensation extinguishes both obligations to the extent of the lesser amount." (LSA-C.C. Art. 1893-2). [. . . .]

There exists this paradox that, although compensation takes place by operation of law, still it must be demanded, claimed or pleaded. Under **LSA-C.C. Art. 1900,**

An obligor who has consented to an assignment of the credit by the obligee to a third party may not claim against the latter any compensation that otherwise he could have claimed against the former.

An obligor who has been given notice of an assignment to which he did not consent may not claim compensation against the assignee for an obligation of the assignor arising after that notice.

Once compensation has occurred as a result of all its conditions being met, the parties, or a party, may renounce it. [. . . .]

LSA-C.C. Art. 1901 lays down a very reasonable rule which is but an illustration of the general principle of freedom of contracts: "Compensation of obligations may take place also by agreement of the parties even though the requirements for compensation by operation of law are not met." [. . . .]

The third form of compensation is the judicial compensation.

A court may allow compensation to take place despite the non existence of all the conditions required for compensation by operation of law. "Although the obligation claimed in compensation is unliquidated, the court can declare compensation as to that part of the obligation that is susceptible of prompt and easy liquidation." (LSA-C.C. Art. 1902)

Cases

In re Canal Bank & Trust Co.
Intervention of Wainer

Supreme Court of Louisiana
January 2, 1934
152 So. 578

LAND, Justice.

[1] On December 27, 1932, H. Wainer & Co. borrowed from Canal Bank & Trust Company $20,000, for which H. Wainer & Co. gave its promissory note indorsed by H. Wainer, individually, payable ninety days after date.

[2] H. Wainer & Co. is a trade-name under which H. Wainer, individually, is doing business.

[3] The note is made payable at the Canal Bank & Trust Company, New Orleans, La.

[4] There is a provision in the note that: 'At the maturity of this note, or when otherwise due, as above provided, any and all money, stocks, bonds or other securities or property of any nature whatsoever on deposit with, or held by, or in the possession of, said bank as collateral or otherwise, to the credit or for account of the makers, endorsers or other parties hereto, or any of them, shall be and stand applied forthwith to the payment of this note, or any other indebtedness due said bank by said parties hereto, or any of them. * * *'

[5] On March 1, 1933, H. Wainer & Co. had on deposit with the Canal Bank & Trust Company the sum of $18,490.45, and H. Wainer, individually, had on deposit with that bank the sum of $5,551.02.

[6] From March 1, 1933, until March 20, 1933, the Canal Bank & Trust Company remained closed and did no business, except that on Friday March 3, 1933, pursuant to a resolution adopted by the New Orleans Clearing House Association, with the approval of the state banking commissioner and the acting Governor of the state, permitted withdrawals by its depositors not exceeding 5 per cent. of the balance to the credit of the depositors as of March 1, 1933. During this period the Canal Bank & Trust Company remained closed, except as above stated, acting under the orders of the state authorities and the Proclamations of the President of the United States, of date March 6 and March 9, 1933 (see 12 USCA § 95 note), declaring and extending a national banking holiday.

[7] On March 10, 1933, the President by Executive Order (see 12 USCA § 95 note) authorized the Secretary of the Treasury, under such regulations as he may prescribe, to permit any member bank of the Federal Reserve System to perform any and all of its usual banking functions.

[8] The President in this Executive Order further directed that all banks who are members of the Federal Reserve System, desiring to reopen for the performance of all of their usual or normal banking functions, should apply for a license therefor to the Secretary of the Treasury.

[9] The Canal Bank & Trust Company was at that time a member of the Federal Reserve System, and promptly applied for a license to be permitted to reopen for the performance of all its usual and normal banking functions, but was refused a license by the Treasury Department.

[10] On March 18, 1933, the Secretary of the Treasury issued and promulgated a regulation, designated as No. 27, in which he authorized any bank which was a member of the Federal Reserve System, and which was not licensed to reopen for the purpose of its usual banking functions, to permit withdrawals by depositors and payments to creditors of such percentage of amount due to them, not exceeding 5 per cent., as it may determine with the approval of the appropriate state authorities.

[11] Thereafter the Canal Bank & Trust Company, with the approval of the state banking commissioner, permitted withdrawals by depositors not exceeding 5 per cent. of the amount to their credit as of the close of business on March 1, 1933.

[12] Prior to March 27, 1933, H. Wainer & Co. withdrew all of the 5 per cent. balance to its credit as of March 1, 1933, $924.52.

[13] The Canal Bank & Trust Company notified its depositor that it would not permit the withdrawal of the remaining 95 per cent. of its balance, $17,537.85.

[14] On March 27, 1933, the Canal Bank & Trust Company made available and permitted H. Wainer, individually, to withdraw 5 per cent. of the balance to his credit as of March 1, 1933, namely, $277.50. All of this amount the depositor withdrew, except the sum of $57.65.

[15] The remaining 95 per cent. to his credit as of March 1, 1933, $5,273.47, the Canal Bank & Trust Company notified him he could not withdraw.

[16] On the date on which the note of H. Wainer & Co., indorsed by H. Wainer, fell due, March 27, 1933, H. Wainer & Co. sent the Canal Bank & Trust Company two checks, one for the sum of $2,500 and the other for the sum of $17,500, claiming that they were entitled to pay, compensate or offset the note with these checks. The offer of H. Wainer & Co. and H. Wainer was refused, and the checks were subsequently returned to them without prejudice to the rights of either party.

[17] At no time during the period beginning March 2, 1933, and ending May 20, 1933, did the Canal Bank & Trust Company pay out more than 5 per cent. to any depositor of the balance to the credit of such depositor as of March 1, 1933, and did not pay out any gold or gold certificates whatever.

[18] The bank did not lend any money, but did collect on notes and extend notes and did borrow cash on its assets from the Reconstruction Finance Corporation for the purpose of setting up the fund to pay the 5 per cent. due depositors and creditors.

[19] The amount borrowed from the Reconstruction Finance Corporation is as follows:

$1,000,000 on March 3, 1933.

$2,300,000 on March 20, 1933.

$1,100,000 on March 22, 1933.

[20] The Canal Bank & Trust Company was placed in liquidation on May 20, 1933, and it is not now and has not been since May 20, 1933, in a position to pay all creditors and depositors in full in cash, and the amount that will ultimately be paid to creditors and depositors, or the time at which payment or payments will be made, is indefinite and not capable of ascertainment.

[21] The facts above stated are in accordance with the statement of facts agreed upon by counsel, and found at pages 24 to 27, inclusive, in the transcript in this case.

[22] At the date of the maturity of the note, H. Wainer & Co. had a balance in the Canal Bank & Trust Company of $17,537.85, and H. Wainer a balance of $5,331.12, a total balance of $22,868.97, or $2,868.97 over and above the amount due the bank on the note, in which it is expressly stipulated that the deposits of intervener in the bank, at the maturity of the note, 'shall be and stand applied forthwith to the payment of this note.'

[23] The Canal Bank & Trust Company having refused on March 27, 1933, when the note fell due, to accept the check of H. Wainer & Co. for $17,500 and the check of H. Wainer for $2,500 in compensation or offset of the note, the intervener, H. Wainer, filed the present suit against the liquidators of the bank to compel them to deliver to him as paid and canceled the note for $20,000 and also a dividend of $842.70 on the balance of deposit remaining in the bank.

[24] The trial judge held that the Canal Bank & Trust Company was solvent on March 27, 1933; that the note for $20,000 was compensated on that date, when it fell

due, by virtue of the waiver provision therein that the deposit should be applied to the discharge and extinguishment of the debt evidenced by the note; and that the proclamations and orders of the President of the United States and the regulations of the Secretary of the Treasury did not affect plaintiff's right to compensate and offset the note with his deposits in the bank.

[. . . .]

[25] From this judgment intervener has appealed.

[. . . .]

[26] 3. The general law as to compensation or set-off, as it prevails in this state, is found in the following articles of our Civil Code:

Article 2207. 'When two persons are indebted to each other, there takes place between them a compensation the extinguishes both the debts, in the manner and cases hereafter expressed.'

Article 2208. 'Compensation takes place of course by the mere operation of law, even unknown to the debtors; the two debts are reciprocally extinguished, as soon as they exist simultaneously, to the amount of their respective sums.'

Article 2209. 'Compensation takes place only between two debts, having equally for their object a sum of money, or a certain quantity of consumable things of one and the same kind, and which are equally liquidated and demandable.

[27] 'The days of grace are no obstacle to the compensation.'

[28] There can be no doubt that the bank was indebted to intervener in the amount of the deposits, and that intervener was indebted to the bank in the amount of the note.

[29] These debts existed simultaneously on March 27, 1933, when the note fell due, and they were equally liquidated and demandable on that day.

[30] The two debts, therefore, became reciprocally extinguished at that date, 'by the mereoperation [*sic*] of law, even unknown to the dobtors [*sic*].'

[31] The general American rule is that: 'Where a depositor is indebted to the bank and his indebtedness is due, he may set off his deposit against his indebtedness * * * and this right of set-off exists without any previous demand being made for the deposit.' Ruling Case Law, vol. 3, par. 157, p. 529.

[32] Colin and Capitant, in discussing this subject, say:

'C'est en matière commerciale que la compensation trouve ses plus importantes applications. Cela se comprend sans peine. Il est rare que des rapports réciproques d'obligations se forment entre personnes non commercantes. Au contraire, ces rapports mutuels entre deux négociants, par exemple entre un commercant et son banquier, entre unfabricant et un commissionnaire, sont de tous les jours. Or, le commerce vit surtout de crédit; ilévite le plus possible l'emploi du numéraire, il a besoin de simplifier le plus possible les paiements.

'De là est né l'usage du compte courant dont nous avons déjà parlé et qui est fondé sur le principe de la compensation. Toutes les opérations commerciales qui se font entre les deux parties, viennent se fondre dans le compte courant, et le solde constaté lors la clôture de ce compte fait seul l'objet d'un paiement effectif. * * *'

[33] The translation of the above is as follows: 'It is in commercial matters that compensation finds its most important applications. That is easily understood. It is rare that reciprocal accounts of obligations are formed between persons who are not merchants. On the contrary, these mutual accounts between two merchants, for example, between a merchant and his banker, between a manufacturer and an agent, occur every day. Now, commerce subsists above all on credit; it avoids as much as possible the use of cash, it needs to simplify payments as much as possible.

[34] 'From this was born the custom of the account *current*, of which we have already spoken, and which is founded on the principle of compensation. All the commercial operations which occur between the two parties become blended in the account current, and *the established balance* at the time of the closing of this account *alone* is the object of a *real payment*. * * *' (Italics partly ours.) Colin & Capitant, Cours Élémentaire De Droit Civil Francais, Tome II, Septième Édition (1932), pp. 319, 325, n° 336, 346.

[35] No *real* payment being necessary as the basis of the right of intervener to compensate the note with his deposits, the contention of the liquidators of the bank that intervener in this case cannot plead compensation, because he could not draw more than 5 per cent. of his deposits in bank, an amount insufficient to pay the note, is not sound in law.

[36] Compensation, at all events, is but a *fictitious* payment, the balancing of accounts, the extinction of one debt by another, by mere operation of law.

[37] We are not impressed, therefore, with the contention of the liquidators in this case that the universal law of compensation, or set-off, prevailing in the various states of the Union was set aside, either by the prohibition in the President's promulgations against 'paying out' bank deposits after the national banking holiday had been declared, or by the limitation in Regulation No. 27 of the Secretary of the Treasury of payment of 5 per cent. to depositors and creditors.

[....]

[38] Neither the proclamations of the President, nor the regulation of the Secretary of the Treasury changed, or could change, the indisputable fact that mutual indebtedness between the bank and intervener existed simultaneously on March 27, 1933, when the note of intervener fell due, and that this indebtedness on that date

was equally liquidated and demandable. Necessarily, the law of compensation or set-off applies to the case.

[....]

[39] In the second place, the provision in the note applying intervener's deposits on the note is not a contract, but is a mere waiver by the intervener of the obstacle of article 2210 of our Civil Code, in providing that compensation does not take place where one of the demands is for the restitution of a deposit.

[40] The exception provided by article 2210 of the Civil Code as to irregular deposits is in favor of the depositor and not of the bank.

[41] In France, where the Code contains articles similar to ours, it is universally recongized [*sic*] that, where the obstacle preventing compensation is in favor of one of the parties, that similar to ours, it is universally recognized this kind of compensation being designated by the French commentators as 'facultative compensation.'

[42] In discussing this subject Planiol says. 'Définition et Utilité-La compensation facultative est celle qui s'opère *par la volonté des parties*, quand l'une d'elles lève un obstacle résultant des dispositions de la loi. Une des conditions manque pour la compensation légale: par exemple, l'une des deux dettes n'est pas liquide, ou bien elle est suspendue par un terme, ou bien encore il s'agit d'une créance née d'un dépôt: si les parties sont d'accord pour accepter en compensation la dette non liquide, ou si celle qui y avait droit renonce au bénéfice du terme, ou enfin si le déposant consent á être réglé par compensation, leur volonté doit être respectée et la compensation s'opérera (Cass. 25 nov. 1891, D. 92, 1 296).'

[43] The translation of the above is as follows: 'Facultative Compensation is that which operates by the will of the parties, when one of them removes an obstacle resulting from the dispositions of the law. One of the conditions is lacking for legal compensation: for example, one of the two debts is not liquidated or perhaps it is suspended by a term, or perhaps it involves a credit arising out of a deposit: if the parties agreed to accept in compensation the non liquidated debt, or if the one who had the right, renounces the benefit of the term, or finally, if the depositor agrees to be governed by compensation, there will ought to be respected and compensation will operate (Cass. Nov. 25, 1891, D. 92. 1 296).' M. Planiol, Droit Civil, vol. 2, Troisième Édition (1905) n. 594, pp. 194, 195.

[44] 5. Article 2215 of our Civil Code also provides that: 'Compensation can not take place to the prejudice of the rights acquired by a third person; therefore, he who, being a debtor, is become creditor since the attachment made by a third person in his hands, can not, in prejudice to the person seizing, oppose compensation.'

[45] This article is a literal reproduction of article 1298 of the Code Napoleon, and has no application to the present controversy.

[46] It refers to the case where a third person 'acquires' rights to one of the obligations, by attachment, assignment, or in any other legal way, before the other claim comes into existence, or before it has become demandable. See in this connection

Colin & Capitant, Cours Élémentaire De Droit Civil Français, Tome II Septième Édition (1932) p. 325, n. 346.

[. . . .]

Questions

1. In order for a debt to be compensable, it must be "presently due." *See* La. Civ. Code art. 1893. After the Secretary of the Treasury, implementing the President's Executive Order, effectively prohibited Canal Bank from paying out any more than 5% of what it owed to Wainer, was Canal Bank's obligation to refund Wainer's deposit truly "due"? What does it mean for a debt to be "due"? Is "due" something different from "payable"?

2. At the time at which Canal Bank was decided, there was no legislation in place in Louisiana that recognized the French doctrinal principle of "facultative compensation." Is that true under the Revision? *See* La. Civ. Code art. 1901; *see also* La. Civ. Code art. 1894.

First National Bank of Commerce
v.
Arthur Dufrene[1] and Kim Dufrene dba Dufrene Super Market

Court of Appeal of Louisiana
First Circuit
April 19, 1988
525 So.2d 298

CARTER, Judge.

[1] This is an appeal from the judgment of the trial court in favor of First National Bank of Commerce (Bank) and against defendant Kim Dufrene d/b/a Dufrene Super Market (Dufrene) awarding the Bank $3,100.00 and denying set-off and/or compensation.

Facts

[2] The Louisiana Grocers' Co-Operative, Inc. (Co-op) was a cooperative of grocery stores organized as a Louisiana corporation. Its purpose was to purchase items in volume for resale to its various members. There were two primary sources of financing, i.e., "members' buying deposit" and loans by the Bank. The Co-op owed the Bank several million dollars in loans, which were secured by an assignment of accounts receivable and a mortgage affecting the inventory of the Co-op. The Co-op subsequently filed for relief under Chapter 11 of the United States Bankruptcy Code,

---

1. On October 13, 1986, Arthur Dufrene was dismissed as a party defendant pursuant to a motion to dismiss.

and the United States Bankruptcy Court authorized the Bank to collect the accounts receivable due the Co-op.

[3] Defendant was a member-stockholder in the Co-op and had a balance in the "members' buying deposit," as defined by the bylaws, in the amount of $9,954.00. Dufrene was also indebted to the Co-op for $3,100.00 in receivables. Dufrene did not give notice of withdrawal from membership in the Co-op, in accordance with the bylaws, until after his receipt of the notification of the assignment of his account to the Bank by the Co-op.

[4] Thereafter, the Bank filed suit against Dufrene for the $6,387.63 in receivables owed to the Co-op. After trial, the trial judge rendered judgment in favor of the Bank and against Dufrene for $3,100.00, but denied the Bank's claim for attorney's fees. From this adverse judgment, Dufrene appeals.

Issue

[5] The primary issue raised is whether Dufrene is entitled to the legal defense of compensation or set-off. Dufrene reasons that any indebtedness to the Co-op should be set-off against the funds in Dufrene's "members' buying deposit," which was stipulated to have been $9,954.00 as of the date Dufrene received notice of the assignment of accounts receivable from the Bank.

Discussion

[6] The trial court found as follows, and we agree that:

This matter involves the claim of First National Bank of Commerce to collect the indebtedness of Kim Dufrene, doing business as Dufrene's Supermarket, due to Louisiana Grocers Cooperative, Incorporated. The facts have been stipulated to and filed as a joint exhibit by both the plaintiff and defendant. No witnesses were presented to the Court due to the stipulations. The Court has considered the arguments of counsel and the brief submitted by plaintiff's attorney. The Court notes for the record that defendant's attorney did not submit a pre-trial memorandum as ordered by the Court.

The parties argue Article 1893 of the Civil Code which states in pertinent part that compensation takes place by operation of law when two persons owe to each other sums of money or quantities of fungible things identical in kind, and these sums or quantities are liquidated and presently due. The key language in that Article seems to be "liquidated and presently due."

In this case there's no question that Mr. Kim Dufrene was a member of Louisiana Grocer's Cooperative, Incorporated and that he had established a buying deposit account with the corporation which amounted to $9,954. The Court does not feel that that account is a "liquidated and presently due" account since the bylaws set forth certain prerequisites before a member can withdraw that money. Furthermore, Article 1894 of the Civil Code states in pertinent part that compensation does not take place, however, if one of the obligations is to return a thing given in deposit or loan for use.

In this case there seems to be no question in this Court's mind that the members' buying deposit is exactly what it says it is and that's a deposit, or, as counsel for the defendant argues, a loan for use. In either case, it's covered by Article 1894 of the Civil Code (it seems to this Court) and therefore, compensation does not take place by operation of law.

In light of this Court's oral reasons and the reasons set forth in the plaintiff's pre-trial memoranda, the Court will render a judgment in this matter in favor of First National Bank of Commerce against Kim Dufrene, doing business as Dufrene's Supermarket, in the sum of $3,100. [. . . .]

[7] From the above, it is clear that the financial purpose of the "members' buying deposit" was to provide operating capital for the Co-op and not to pay receivables due the Co-op from its members. The "members' buying deposit" represented part of the "members' equity" in the corporation (along with Class A and Class B stock, patronage dividends, and retained earnings) rather than a current liability or a short term debt. Since the "members' buying deposit" was an equity of the Co-op and not a current liability of the corporation, compensation and/or set-off are not available to Dufrene.

[8] We further note that the burden of proof is upon Dufrene to establish by a preponderance of the evidence his right to set-off or compensation. *See Coburn v. Commercial National Bank*, 453 So.2d 597 (La.App. 2nd Cir.1984), *writ denied*, 457 So.2d 681 (La.1984).

[9] LSA-C.C. art. 1893 provides as follows:[2]

Compensation takes place by operation of law when two persons owe to each other sums of money or quantities of fungible things identical in kind, and these sums or quantities are liquidated and presently due.

In such a case, compensation extinguishes both obligations to the extent of the lesser amount.

Delays of grace do not prevent compensation.

[10] In the instant case, at the time of the notice, the "members' buying deposit" did not constitute an equally demandable debt of the Co-op, and compensation was not available. *See Beninate v. Licata*, 473 So.2d 94 (La.App. 5th Cir.1985), *writ denied*, 477 So.2d 1124 (La.1985). Dufrene had not withdrawn from the Co-op at the time of his receipt of notice of the assignment to the Bank. According to Article 4.4.2 of the bylaws, Dufrene was not entitled to receive any funds from the "members' buying deposit" until he withdrew from the Co-op. Therefore, the debt was not liquidated and presently due at the time of the assignment.

---

2. *See also* LSA-C.C. art. 1900 which deals with an assignment of an obligation and provides that an "obligor who has been given notice of an assignment to which he did not consent may not claim compensation against the assignee for an obligation of the assignor arising after that notice."

[11] Therefore, compensation and/or set-off were not available to Dufrene for three reasons: the "members' buying deposit" was not liquidated and presently due since the bylaws provided certain prerequisites before a member could withdraw the money; secondly, the "members' buying deposit" represented an equity contribution of the respective members of the Co-op; and compensation is precluded under LSA-C.C. art. 1894[3] in that the "members' buying deposit" was a deposit or loan for use.

[. . . .]

Questions

1. The *First National Bank* court concludes that the Co-op's obligation to pay out Dufrene's deposit was not "due" because, under the terms of the agreement between the Co-op and Dufrene, he was not yet entitled to "withdraw" any of the deposited funds. And yet the *Canal Bank* court concluded that, notwithstanding that Wainer, thanks to the federal Treasury Department's order, was not entitled to "withdraw" but 5% of his deposited funds, Canal Bank's obligation to pay out Wainer's deposit was fully "due." Is it possible to reconcile these conclusions?

2. What do you think of the *First National Bank* court's argument that compensation was unavailable to Dufrene because Co-op's debt to him was "to return a thing given in deposit"? What of the *Canal Bank* court's assertion that the rule that compensation does not take place if one of the debts of this kind "is in favor of the depositor and not of the bank" (or other depositary)? *See* paragraph 40 of the previous case, *Canal Bank*. If that is true, then shouldn't the depositor, in this case Dufrene, be able to "waive" the benefit of the rule unilaterally? *See Canal Bank*, paragraph 43, quoting Planiol ("if the depositor agrees to be governed by compensation, there [sic: their] will ought to be respected and compensation will operate"). And wasn't that precisely what he tried to do when he claimed that compensation had taken place?

3. The *First National Bank* court states that the "deposit" arrangement between the Co-op and Dufrene could be classified as a "loan for use." Given that the deposit consisted of money, which is a "consumable" thing, is this classification correct? *See* La. Civ. Code art. 536.

---

3. LSA-C.C. art. 1894 provides as follows:
   Compensation takes place regardless of the sources of the obligations.
   Compensation does not take place, however, if one of the obligations is to return a thing of which the owner has been unjustly dispossessed, or is to return a thing given in deposit or loan for use, or if the object of one of the obligations is exempt from seizure.

A Confidential Limousine Service, Inc.
v.
London Livery, Ltd.

Court of Appeal of Louisiana
Fourth Circuit
January 8, 1993
612 So.2d 875

ARMSTRONG, Judge.

[1] This case involves a suit on an open account.

[2] Plaintiff, A Confidential Limousine Service, Inc. ("A Confidential") filed suit against London Livery, Ltd. ("London Livery") for money due for certain limousine services rendered on an open account. The petition asked for $13,565. The record reflects that London Livery had contracted with A Confidential to provide limousine services to it in January 1990. A Confidential alleged that London Livery refused to pay for these services after amicable demand.

[3] London Livery answered the petition pleading defenses of failure and/or want of consideration and setoff. It also filed a reconventional demand against A Confidential raising factual allegations under the Louisiana Unfair Trade Practices Act, LSA-R.S. 51:1401, *et seq*, and the Uniform Trade Secrets Act, LSA-R.S. 51:1431, *et seq*. [....]

[4] After various discoveries took place, A Confidential filed a motion for summary judgment contending that based upon its original petition[1] its attached documents and the sworn affidavit of its owner, Jamie Obermeyer, no genuine issue of material fact existed and it was entitled to summary judgment on the open account as a matter of law. LSA-C.C.P. arts. 966, 967. A Confidential contended that London Livery had not contested that services were rendered and its claims are for unliquidated damages and/or do not constitute a defense to a liquidated claim. In support of its argument A Confidential cited *Gulf Fed. Sav. and Loan Ass'n v. Nugent*, 528 So.2d 782 (La.App. 3d Cir.1988), *writ den.*, 533 So.2d 19 (La.1988), for the position that London Livery is not entitled to set off and/or compensation since it does not occur when two debts are not equally liquidated and contemporaneously demandable.

[5] In its opposition to the motion, London Livery argued that A Confidential was not legally entitled to summary judgment since it was contesting the correctness of the quantum of the debt and did not admit it. London Livery contended that the affidavit of Alan B. Fisher, its president, contains an analysis of A Confidential's invoices, and reveals billing errors totalling $1,410. On those grounds, it claimed the debt was not liquidated.

---

1. In response to an exception filed by London Livery, A Confidential filed a first amending and supplemental petition adding Jamie and Kurt Obermeyer as parties plaintiff.

[6] After a hearing, the trial court granted partial summary judgment in favor of A Confidential in the amount of $10,835 plus legal interest from date of judicial demand. London Livery appeals.

[. . . .]

[7] [. . .] London Livery claims summary judgment should not have been granted because the quantum of A Confidential's claim is disputed and therefore not liquidated. Since it proved overbilling, it contends A Confidential's claim is not liquid. Therefore, summary judgment should not have been granted and London Livery's claims should have offset A Confidential's after both were liquidated and demandable.

[8] We disagree. While the trial court did not provide its rationale for entering judgment for $10,835, an amount $1,410 less than was prayed for in the petition, the parties' memoranda, written contract and A Confidential's computerized trip sheets favor the explanation that the amount of the judgment reflects the portion of the debt which was certain and liquid. A liquid debt is one whose existence is certain and its quantity determined. *American Bank v. Saxena*, 553 So.2d 836 (La.1989), citing 4 Aubry & Rau, Cours de Troit Civil Francais, s. 326 (6th ed. 1965); Litvanoff [*sic*], The Law of Obligations in Louisiana Jurisprudence (1979), p. 646. The portion of the debt which was capable of ascertainment by mere calculation in accordance with accepted legal standards was therefore liquid. *American Bank v. Saxena, supra.*; *Sims v. Hays*, 521 So.2d 730 (La.App. 2d Cir.1988).

[9] For a debt to be liquidated, acknowledgment by the debtor is not required. Litvanoff [*sic*], *supra*. Nevertheless, we note that London Livery has not denied receiving the limousine services for which it was billed. The documents corroborate that the disputed $1,410 correlates to the parties' varied interpretations of the contractual term "daily rental rate" and not to billings for services which were not rendered. Thus, the trial court did not err in finding $10,835 of the debt liquid and determinable.

[10] London Livery's claim for offset and/or compensation was not sufficient to prevent summary judgment of this liquidated debt. The statutory requirements of setoff, or compensation as it is called in the Civil Code, are set forth in LSA-C.C. art. 1893 as follows:

Art. 1893. Compensation extinguishes obligations

Compensation takes place by operation of law when two persons owe to each other sums of money or quantities of fungible things identical in kind, and these sums or quantities are liquidated and presently due.

In such a case, compensation extinguishes both obligations to the extent of the lesser amount.

Delays of grace do not prevent compensation.

[11] For compensation to apply, two distinct debts equally liquidated and demandable must exist contemporaneously. *American Bank v. Saxena, supra.*;

Hartley v. Hartley, 349 So.2d 1258 (La.1977); *Rauch v. Rauch,* 535 So.2d 1317 (La. App. 5th Cir.1988); *Gulf Fed. Sav. & Loan Ass'n v. Nugent, supra.* Louisiana jurisprudence has barred the application of compensation to tort claims. *American Bank v. Saxena, supra.* Thus, at the time judgment was entered, London Livery's reconventional demand did not constitute an equally demandable debt of A Confidential. *Cf. First Nat. Bank of Commerce v. Dufrene,* 525 So.2d 298 (La.App. 1st Cir.1988), writ den., 530 So.2d 567 (La.1988); *Van Hoosen v. First Nat. Bank of St. Martin,* 583 So.2d 106 (La.App. 3d Cir.1991); *Project Square 221 v. Salles,* 557 So.2d 345 (La.App. 4th Cir.1990), *writ den.,* 560 So.2d 12 (La.1990). But see *Rosenthal v. Oubre,* 504 So.2d 1102 (La.App. 5th Cir.1987) [applied/defined terms of "mutuality of obligors" and "equally liquidated and determinable debt" very loosely.] London Livery's unliquidated claim for tort damages could not be pleaded in compensation against A Confidential's liquidated claim based on an open account. *Cf. American Bank v. Saxena, supra; Gulf Fed. Sav. & Loan Ass'n v. Nugent, supra.* London Livery's second assignment is also without merit.

[....]

[12] The trial court entered partial summary judgment in favor of A Confidential in the amount of $10,835, the portion of the obligation which was liquid and determinable. As the judgment is in accord with the above cited provisions and the intent of the summary judgment statutes, it was not error for the trial court to grant summary judgment on that portion of the debt.

[13] For the foregoing reasons, the judgment of the trial court is affirmed. Costs of this appeal are assessed against appellant.

[....]

Question

1. The *Confidential Limousine* court rules, in the end, that though the debt London Livery owes A Confidential is liquidated in part and, therefore, is to that extent compensable, nevertheless compensation cannot take place because the debt that A Confidential owes back to London Livery—a "tort" debt—is entirely unliquidated. Does this mean that a delictual obligation can never be subject to compensation, not even in part? What if the tort victim in a personal injury case were to claim, say, $50,000 in lost wages and the tortfeasor were to acknowledge, first, that he was liable for the tort and, second, that the tort victim's lost wages damages amounted to at least $40,000?

Comparative Law Perspective

— Civil Law —

Marcel Planiol, *Treatise on the Civil Law*

vol. 2, pt. 1, nᵒs 562–67 at 314–22 & nᵒs 594–97 at 324–25
(Louisiana State Law Institute trans., 11th ed. 1939)

562. Definition

When two persons mutually owe each other similar objects, it is not necessary that each of them pay to the other that which he owes; it is more simple to consider them both liberated up to the amount of the lesser of the two debts, so that the excess of the greater alone can become the object of an effective enforcement (Art. 1289). Compensation may therefore be defined as a special mode of extinguishing reciprocal obligations, which mutually dispense the two debtors of effective performance. Thus each one of them possesses at the same time (1) a means of liberating himself by renouncing his credit; (2) a guaranty for his credit, in refusing to pay what he owes. [. . . .]

566. Definition

Compensation is legal when it operates by effect of the law and under conditions fixed by it. It is the only one with which the Code is concerned.

567. Enumeration

Five conditions, of which three only are indicated by the law (Art. 1291) are necessary: (1) reciprocity of obligation; (2) fungible nature of their objects; (3) liquid estate of the two debts; (4) exigibility of the credit opposed in compensation; (5) seizability of the right extinguished by the compensation.

588. Extinction of the Two Debts

Compensation is equivalent to a double payment: it extinguishes the two debts, up to the amount of the lesser. The two debts are extinguished with all their accessories, mortgages, sureties, etc. Interest ceases to run.

If there are several debts owing by one of the parties to the other, the rules as to imputation of payments are followed in determining which will be extinguished by compensation. [. . . .]

594. Definition and Usefulness

Facultative compensation is that which operates by the will of the parties, when one of them raises an obstacle resulting from the provisions of the law. One of the conditions for legal compensation may be lacking: for example, one of the debts may be unliquidated, suspended by a term, or created by virtue of a deposit; if the parties agree to accept the unliquidated debt in compensation, or if the party who is entitled to the term renounces the benefit thereof, or if the depositor consents to a settlement by compensation, there is no reason why their wishes should not be respected and no reason why the compensation should not take place.

595. Effects

Facultative compensation being the work of the will of the parties, naturally cannot exist and produce its effects except from the day it was agreed upon. It is not endowed with any retroactivity. [. . . .]

597. Definition

There is judicial compensation when a debtor who is sued for the execution of a debt files a reconventional demand against the plaintiff pleading a credit in opposition to the original demand, which credit does not have or fulfill the conditions required for legal compensation.

Section IX — Confusion

Louisiana Sources of Law
Louisiana Civil Code

Art. 1903. Union of qualities of obligee and obligor.

When the qualities of obligee and obligor are united in the same person, the obligation is extinguished by confusion. (Acts 1984, No. 331, §1, eff. Jan. 1, 1985.)

Art. 1904. Obligation of the surety.

Confusion of the qualities of obligee and obligor in the person of the principal obligor extinguishes the obligation of the surety.

Confusion of the qualities of obligee and obligor in the person of the surety does not extinguish the obligation of the principal obligor. (Acts 1984, No. 331, §1, eff. Jan. 1, 1985.)

Art. 1905. Solidary obligations.

If a solidary obligor becomes an obligee, confusion extinguishes the obligation only for the portion of that obligor.

If a solidary obligee becomes an obligor, confusion extinguishes the obligation only for the portion of that obligee. (Acts 1984, No. 331, §1, eff. Jan. 1, 1985.)

Doctrine

Louisiana Law of Obligations in General, A Précis

Section 7.6.1 to 7.6.2

Confusion is the merging in the same person of the qualities of obligee and principal obligor with respect to the same obligation. As **Article 1903** states: "**When the qualities of obligee and obligor are united in the same person, the obligation is extinguished by confusion.**"

For confusion to occur one must assume the existence of an obligation and a party who is, at the same time, obligee and obligor of that obligation. A typical example of confusion would occur in matters of succession where an obligee could inherit from his obligor. [. . . .]

Confusion thus creates an obstacle to a legal action by the party involved against himself. [. . . .]

LSA-C.C. Art. 1904-1 provides another illustration of the principle according to which the fate of an accessory obligation is determined by the fate of the principal obligation: "**Confusion of the qualities of obligee and obligor in the person of the principal obligor extinguishes the obligation of the surety.**" When the principal obligation is extinguished by confusion the accessory obligation will also disappear. [. . . .]

A confusion may be only partial where a part of an obligation is not susceptible of performance. Such could be the case in the event an obligation involves solidary obligors or solidary obligees. **LSA-C.C. Art. 1905**.

Cases

Noah Deshotel
v.
Travelers Indemnity Company

Supreme Court of Louisiana
January 18, 1971
243 So.2d 259

BARHAM, Justice.

[. . . .]

[1] The plaintiff in this case, Noah Deshotel, was injured in an accident while riding in a car owned by him and driven by his unemancipated minor son, Ronald. It is conceded in this court that Ronald's negligence caused the injuries suffered by his father. The father has sued his insurer, Travelers Indemnity Company, under the direct action statute, R.S. 22:655, because his son is an insured under the omnibus clause of the policy. The trial court gave judgment for the policy limits, $5000.00, with legal interest and costs, and the Court of Appeal affirmed.[1]

[2] The principal contention of the defendant is that under Article 2318 of the Civil Code the negligence of the minor son must be imputed to the father, who is thus effectively barred from recovery.

[3] If the father has a cause of action against his minor son for his personal damages resulting from the son's delicts, it is found under Civil Code, Article 2315: 'Every act whatever of man that causes damage to another obliges him by whose fault it happened to repair it.' Article 2318 makes the father, or after his death the mother or the tutor, of the minor responsible for the damage occasioned by the minor's delicts. However, Article 2318 does not relieve the minor of his responsibility for his tortious conduct, and other codal provisions expressly recognize the minor's responsibility for his own delicts. Article 1785 provides: 'The obligation arising from an offense or quasi offense, is also binding on the minor.' Article 1874 reads: 'He (the minor) is not relievable against obligations resulting from (his) offenses or quasi offenses.' This same provision is found in Article 2227. Additionally, our jurisprudence has recognized that there is a cause of action in others against the minor for his delicts. The procedure for exercising this cause of action is through suit against the minor's legal representative.

[4] Since others have a cause of action against a minor for his offenses and quasi-offenses, the question then arises as to whether the father of a minor child is excepted and denied a cause of action for his personal damage resulting from the

---

1. On rehearing by per curiam that court noted the conflict with Funderburk v. Millers Mutual Fire Insurance Company of Texas, 228 So.2d 169, decided by that same circuit on October 30, 1969, only a few months previously, writs refused 255 La. 158, 229 So.2d 735; 255 La. 159, 229 So.2d 736.

delicts of that minor. Article 2315 makes no exception as to those who are entitled to recompense for the damages occasioned them by others. There is no article in the Civil Code, no article in the Code of Civil Procedure, and no statutory provision which deprive the father of a Cause of action against his minor child for the child's delicts which cause damage to the father.

[5] Moreover, nowhere is there any provision of law which deprives the father of the Right of action against the child for his delicts. However, R.S. 9:571 (formerly Article 104 of the Code of Practice) bars a suit by an unemancipated minor child against either parent during their marriage, and R.S. 9:291 prohibits a suit by a wife against her husband during marriage except for certain specified purposes. These Code ancillaries necessarily recognize the existence of a Cause of action but deny the Right of action during the existence of the particular familial relationship. We have allowed a child to sue the estate of his deceased father for the wrongful death of his mother resulting from the negligence of the father. Ruiz v. Clancy, 182 La. 935, 162 So. 734. Although as between husband and wife during marriage there is no right of action, we have repeatedly held that the wife has a cause of action against the husband for his delicts which cause her damage, and we have held under the direct action statute that the defense against the accrual of a right of action during marriage is personal to the husband and is not a defense available to the husband's insurer. Edwards v. Royal Indemnity Co., 182 La. 171, 161 So. 191; Le Blanc v. New Amsterdam Casualty Co., 202 La. 857, 13 So.2d 245.

[6] From all this legislation and jurisprudence we conclude that the father has a Cause of action against his minor son for damages resulting from the minor's delictual acts. Moreover, there now exists no bar, either legislative or jurisprudential, to a Right of action in the father during the minority of the child.[2] If the child has a defense of no right of action, it would be personal to him and could not be relied upon by his insurer. Edwards v. Royal Indemnity Co., and LeBlanc v. New Amsterdam Casualty Co., both cited above.

[7] As previously stated, the defendant's principal contention is that Article 2318 is applicable to the case at hand and bars a father's recovery from his son for the minor's negligent acts because those negligent acts are imputed to the father. The Court of Appeal correctly concluded that Article 2318 is inapplicable here, and that it determines only the responsibility of the father for the delicts of the minor child in relation to third parties. Article 2318 does not create negligence in the father because of the minor's negligent acts; it merely attaches financial responsibility to

---

2. We express no opinion at this time on whether public policy would deny the father a right of action directly against a minor son. Since the present suit is against the insurer, that question is not presented. We are cognizant of a problem in semantics in using 'right of action', the exception which raises absence of interest in the plaintiff. 'Immunity from suit' is more descriptive and precise. Regardless of terminology, the issue would be raised by a peremptory exception and not by the dilatory exception of lack of procedural capacity. We use 'right of action' advisedly here since Code of Civil Procedure Article 927 allows the court, on its own motion and at all levels, to note failure to disclose a right of action. If this defense is available here, it should be accorded this legal dignity.

the father for the delicts of his minor child. See Williams v. City of Baton Rouge, 252 La. 770, 214 So.2d 138; Johnson v. Butterworth, 180 La. 586, 157 So. 121; Barham, Liability Without Fault, XVII La.Bar. J. 271 (1970). Article 2318 has no application to the instant case in which the father's claim is against the insurer of his son for damages which inure directly and only to his own benefit as compensation for his personal losses.

[8] It has also been urged that the father becomes here both debtor and creditor, and that when the qualities of debtor and creditor are united in the same person, confusion extinguishes the obligation; that where confusion takes place in the person of the principal debtor, it also avails the surety. La.Civ.Code, Arts. 2217, 2218. In the instant case, under Article 2315 the debtor is the minor son, and the damage sued for is a debt due only to the father. There is one debtor, and one creditor; they are separate entities.[3]

[. . . .]

Question

1. The *Deshotel* court's assertion that the father is only a creditor of, and not a debtor to, his son rests on the Court's conclusion, stated earlier in the opinion, that the father has no liability to the son under Louisiana Civil Code article 2318. What, then, should be the result in a case in which that article would impose liability on the father? Consider this example: a minor child, through his negligence, injures a third person who, it so happens, is already obligated to repay to the child's father a sum of money that the father had previously loaned to him. Let's ignore the fact that the third person's tort claim is unliquidated — a fact that, by itself, would preclude compensation. Under these circumstances, could compensation take place between the tort victim's loan debt to the father, on the one hand, and the father's tort debt to the tort victim under Louisiana Civil Code article 2318, on the other? Does Louisiana Civil Code article 1905 help you to answer this question?

---

3. This suit does not involve a claim for a debt which could inure to the benefit of the negligent child, such as a debt for that child's medical expenses for which the father is responsible. In such a case we might be concerned with derivative negligence rather than with imputed negligence. To avoid confusion, we note that in Funderburk v. Millers Mutual Fire Insurance Company of Texas (La.App.3rd Cir. 1969), 228 So.2d 169, the father was suing for his damages which were the medical expenses of One of his minors incurred because of the negligence of Another of his minors. The principles laid down in this opinion are applicable to Funderburk, and that case is specifically overruled.

Hibernia National Bank
v.
Continental Marble and Granite Company, Inc., et al.

Court of Appeal of Louisiana
Fifth Circuit
March 17, 1993
615 So.2d 1109

GRISBAUM, Judge.

[1] This appeal concerns a dation en paiement. From the trial court's judgment recognizing defendant Doyle Coulon's judicial mortgage against defendant Continental Marble and Granite Company, Inc. (Continental), Hibernia National Bank (Hibernia) appeals. We affirm.

Issues

[2] We are called upon to determine [... **among other things** ... w]hether the trial court erred in holding Hibernia's collateral mortgages on the subject immovable property were extinguished by confusion as the result of the dation.

Facts

[3] The facts are basically undisputed.

[4] From 1982 to 1984, Hibernia lent Continental various sums of money, evidenced by 12 promissory notes. As a part of the security therefor, Continental granted Hibernia two collateral mortgages on certain movable and immovable property owned by Continental. In 1987, Continental, because it experienced difficulties paying its debt to Hibernia, entered into a partial dation with Hibernia. In consideration for its agreement to relieve Continental of part of the financial obligations owed, Hibernia bargained to receive from Continental the transfer, conveyance, and delivery of certain movable and immovable property "free from any lien, mortgage or encumbrance whatsoever" other than the two mortgages in favor of Hibernia. The parties (Hibernia and Continental) executed the dation on August 3, 1987. Hibernia recorded the dation in the conveyance records in Jefferson Parish at 10:50 a.m. on August 5, 1987. It is undisputed by either party that, at the time the dation was executed, no liens, mortgages, or other encumbrances were recorded against the immovable property other than Hibernia's two collateral mortgages. Unbeknownst to either party, at 10:01 a.m. on August 5, 1987, shortly before Hibernia recorded the dation, defendant Doyle Coulon recorded a civil judgment in Jefferson Parish against Continental.

[....]

[5] Hibernia claims the trial court erred in holding Hibernia's mortgages were extinguished by confusion when Hibernia did not receive unencumbered title to the immovable as bargained.

[6] The Civil Code articles concerning confusion read as follows:

Art. 1903. **Union of qualities of obligee and obligor**

When the qualities of the obligee and obligor are united in the same person, the obligation is extinguished by confusion.

Art. 3411. **Methods of extinction**

Art. 3411. Mortgages are extinguished:

1. By the extinction of the thing mortgaged.

2. By the creditor acquiring the ownership of the thing mortgaged.

3. By the extinction of the mortgagor's right.

4. By the extinction of the debt, for which the mortgage was given.

5. By the creditor renouncing the mortgage.

6. By prescription.

[7] In light of our finding regarding the initial issue, we commonsensibly conclude that when the dation was executed, Hibernia, the creditor, received unconditioned ownership of the property. Thus, by operation of law, the two collateral mortgages were extinguished by confusion.

[8] For the reasons assigned the trial court's judgment is hereby affirmed. All costs of this appeal are to be assessed against the appellant.

[. . . .]

Questions

1. What, precisely, is a *dation en paiment* (in English, "giving in payment")? *See* La. Civ. Code art. 2655, *et seq.*

2. According to Louisiana Civil Code article 1903, confusion takes place "[w]hen the qualities of obligee and obligor are united in the same person." In what sense does this "union" of the qualities of "obligee" and "obligor" take place when the mortgagee acquires ownership of the mortgaged thing? In other words, what is the "obligation" as to which the mortgagee is now, at once, supposedly both obligee and obligor? *See* La. Civ. Code arts. 3279 and 3319.

Section X — Dissolution and Nullity

Louisiana Sources of Law
Louisiana Civil Code
Dissolution

Art. 2013. Obligee's right to dissolution.

When the obligor fails to perform, the obligee has a right to the judicial dissolution of the contract or, according to the circumstances, to regard the contract as dissolved. In either case, the obligee may recover damages.

In an action involving judicial dissolution, the obligor who failed to perform may be granted, according to the circumstances, an additional time to perform. (Acts 1984, No. 331, § 1, eff. Jan. 1, 1985.)

Art. 2014. Importance of failure to perform.

A contract may not be dissolved when the obligor has rendered a substantial part of the performance and the part not rendered does not substantially impair the interest of the obligee. (Acts 1984, No. 331, § 1, eff. Jan. 1, 1985.)

Art. 2015. Dissolution after notice to perform.

Upon a party's failure to perform, the other may serve him a notice to perform within a certain time, with a warning that, unless performance is rendered within that time, the contract shall be deemed dissolved. The time allowed for that purpose must be reasonable according to the circumstances.

The notice to perform is subject to the requirements governing a putting of the obligor in default and, for the recovery of damages for delay, shall have the same effect as a putting of the obligor in default. (Acts 1984, No. 331, § 1, eff. Jan. 1, 1985.)

Art. 2016. Dissolution without notice to perform.

When a delayed performance would no longer be of value to the obligee or when it is evident that the obligor will not perform, the obligee may regard the contract as dissolved without any notice to the obligor. (Acts 1984, No. 331, § 1, eff. Jan. 1, 1985.)

Art. 2017. Express dissolution clause.

The parties may expressly agree that the contract shall be dissolved for the failure to perform a particular obligation. In that case, the contract is deemed dissolved at the time it provides for or, in the absence of such a provision, at the time the obligee gives notice to the obligor that he avails himself of the dissolution clause. (Acts 1984, No. 331, § 1, eff. Jan. 1, 1985.)

Art. 2018. Effects of dissolution.

Upon dissolution of a contract, the parties shall be restored to the situation that existed before the contract was made. If restoration in kind is impossible or impracticable, the court may award damages.

If partial performance has been rendered and that performance is of value to the party seeking to dissolve the contract, the dissolution does not preclude recovery for that performance, whether in contract or quasi-contract. (Acts 1984, No. 331, §1, eff. Jan. 1, 1985.)

Art. 2019. Contracts for continuous or periodic performance.

In contracts providing for continuous or periodic performance, the effect of the dissolution shall not be extended to any performance already rendered. (Acts 1984, No. 331, §1, eff. Jan. 1, 1985.)

Art. 2020. [omitted]

Art. 2021. Rights of third party in good faith.

Dissolution of a contract does not impair the rights acquired through an onerous contract by a third party in good faith.

If the contract involves immovable property, the principles of recordation apply to a third person acquiring an interest in the property whether by onerous or gratuitous title. (Acts 1984, No. 331, §1, eff. Jan. 1, 1985; Acts 2005, No. 169, §2, eff. Jan. 1, 2006; Acts 2005 1st Ex. Sess., No. 13, §1, eff. Nov. 29, 2005.)

Art. 2022. Refusal to perform.

Either party to a commutative contract may refuse to perform his obligation if the other has failed to perform or does not offer to perform his own at the same time, if the performances are due simultaneously. (Acts 1984, No. 331, §1, eff. Jan. 1, 1985.)

Art. 2023. Security for performance.

If the situation of a party, financial or otherwise, has become such as to clearly endanger his ability to perform an obligation, the other party may demand in writing that adequate security be given and, upon failure to give that security, that party may withhold or discontinue his own performance. (Acts 1984, No. 331, §1, eff. Jan. 1, 1985.)

Art. 2024. Contract terminated by a party's initiative.

A contract of unspecified duration may be terminated at the will of either party by giving notice, reasonable in time and form, to the other party. (Acts 1984, No. 331, §1, eff. Jan. 1, 1985.)

Nullity

Art. 2029. Nullity of contracts.

A contract is null when the requirements for its formation have not been met. (Acts 1984, No. 331, §1, eff. Jan. 1, 1985.)

Art. 2030. Absolute nullity of contracts.

A contract is absolutely null when it violates a rule of public order, as when the object of a contract is illicit or immoral. A contract that is absolutely null may not be confirmed.

Absolute nullity may be invoked by any person or may be declared by the court on its own initiative. (Acts 1984, No. 331, § 1, eff. Jan. 1, 1985.)

Art. 2031. Relative nullity of contracts.

A contract is relatively null when it violates a rule intended for the protection of private parties, as when a party lacked capacity or did not give free consent at the time the contract was made. A contract that is only relatively null may be confirmed.

Relative nullity may be invoked only by those persons for whose interest the ground for nullity was established, and may not be declared by the court on its own initiative. (Acts 1984, No. 331, § 1, eff. Jan. 1, 1985.)

Art. 2032. Prescription of action.

Action for annulment of an absolutely null contract does not prescribe.

Action of annulment of a relatively null contract must be brought within five years from the time the ground for nullity either ceased, as in the case of incapacity or duress, or was discovered, as in the case of error or fraud.

Nullity may be raised at any time as a defense against an action on the contract, even after the action for annulment has prescribed. (Acts 1984, No. 331, § 1, eff. Jan. 1, 1985.)

Art. 2033. Effects.

An absolutely null contract, or a relatively null contract that has been declared null by the court, is deemed never to have existed. The parties must be restored to the situation that existed before the contract was made. If it is impossible or impracticable to make restoration in kind, it may be made through an award of damages.

Nevertheless, a performance rendered under a contract that is absolutely null because its object or its cause is illicit or immoral may not be recovered by a party who knew or should have known of the defect that makes the contract null. The performance may be recovered, however, when that party invokes the nullity to withdraw from the contract before its purpose is achieved and also in exceptional situations when, in the discretion of the court, that recovery would further the interest of justice.

Absolute nullity may be raised as a defense even by a party who, at the time the contract was made, knew or should have known of the defect that makes the contract null. (Acts 1984, No. 331, § 1, eff. Jan. 1, 1985.)

Art. 2034. Nullity of a provision.

Nullity of a provision does not render the whole contract null unless, from the nature of the provision or the intention of the parties, it can be presumed that the contract would not have been made without the null provision. (Acts 1984, No. 331, § 1, eff. Jan. 1, 1985.)

Art. 2035. Rights of third party in good faith.

Nullity of a contract does not impair the rights acquired through an onerous contract by a third party in good faith.

If the contract involves immovable property, the principles of recordation apply to a third person acquiring an interest in the property whether by onerous or gratuitous title. (Acts 1984, No. 331, §1, eff. Jan. 1, 1985; Acts 2005, No. 169, §2, eff. Jan. 1, 2006; Acts 2005 1st Ex. Sess., No. 13, §1, eff. Nov. 29, 2005.)

Doctrine

Louisiana Law of Conventional Obligations, A Précis
Sections 9.1.1 to 9.2.2

"Dissolution", in the civil Code, is the "undoing" of an existing bond of law such as a contract, for example. The essence of the word "dissolution" means that something that exists or has existed is or was "dissolved" and, thus, ceases or has ceased to exist.

The word "dissolution" is not the only one used in the civil Code to convey the same meaning that the word "dissolution," in a legal sense, carries. [. . . .]

Words such as "termination," "extinction," or "rescission" are also often used in the place of 'dissolution' to mean the same thing as dissolution. [. . . .]

All this to say that a variety of words are used, unfortunately not consistently, in the civil Code to instruct us that some existing legal relationships come to an end for reasons provided by law or as per the intent of parties. What is essential and most important to state here is that these different words, whichever one is selected, are all to be contrasted with, and differentiated from, the concept and word "nullity." As will be discussed below, "nullity" prevents the coming into existence of a juridical act because an essential requirement for that act is lacking or because the act is against public order.

The concept of "dissolution" and, therefore, the legal meaning of the word itself is that a legal bond has been created and has been in existence and that, most likely, it has had effects or could have had effects. However, because of circumstances that have occurred during the existence of the bond of law, the latter must now be dissolved or considered as having been dissolved. For example, **Art. 2013** provides that **"When the obligor fails to perform, the obligee has a right to the judicial dissolution of the contract. . . ."**

One can identify two different sets of grounds that justify the dissolution of a contract. One set includes grounds which are outside the control of the obligor to bring about or not and the other set includes grounds which are within the control of the obligor to bring about or not. Obviously, the consequences of a dissolution resulting from one set of grounds will be different from the consequences resulting from the other set of grounds. [. . . .]

[A]n obligor who cannot perform his contractual obligation because of some circumstance outside his control, will be relieved of any performance because of the dissolution of the contract; the contract has ceased to exist. [. . . .]

The legal nature or identity of a contract may give either party the right, when exercised in good faith, to 'terminate' the contract. Art. 2024 [. . .]. Art. 2747 [. . .]. Art. 3025.

The fact that the obligor may have contributed to the breach of his own principal obligation will have consequences for that obligor. **Art. 2013.** [. . . .]

[A] failure to perform by the obligor may also result from the breach of performance of a secondary obligation in such a manner that the future performance of the principal obligation will be endangered. **Art. 2023.** [. . . .]

An obligor who fails to perform, besides being granted, maybe, an additional time to perform, may have a lawful reason not to perform at all as explained in **Art. 2022.** [. . . .]

Dissolution can be "judicial" when declared by a court of law, or it can be left to the parties to a contract.

Judicial dissolution may be declared by a court "**when the obligor fails to perform**" because "**the obligee has a right to the judicial dissolution of the contract . . .**" and he "**may recover damages.**" Art. 2013(1). [. . . .]

Dissolution can be claimed by the obligee to have occurred "automatically," "of right," where, "**according to the circumstances**" he may "**regard the contract as dissolved.**" **Art. 2013.** This same Article goes on to say that "**the obligee may recover damages.**" It is obvious that the obligor will be somewhat reticent to pay, willingly, 'damages' to the obligee in addition to having to accept that the contract "is" dissolved. It is most likely that only a court will be in a position to grant damages to the obligee. [. . . .]

The situation that is most likely to occur is described in **Art. 2015.** [. . . .]

The effects of dissolution between the parties are governed by one principle and some exceptions to that principle.

The principle is that the parties must be returned to the situation they were in before the contract was entered into. To state the principle otherwise, the parties must be returned to the *status quo ante.* There are exceptions to that principle on account of an impossibility or impracticability to restore the parties to their pre-contract situation. [. . . .]

The principle is stated in the first sentence of **Art. 2018** "**Upon dissolution of a contract, the parties shall be restored to the situation that existed before the contract was made. . . .**" It follows that the contract is 'retroactively' undone, erased, as if it had never existed. [. . . .]

The second sentence of this first paragraph of Art. 2018 takes into consideration the fact that the 'restoration in kind' is not always, actually very seldom, possible. Damages will be awarded by the court to prevent one party from being enriched at the expense of the other. [. . . .]

As regards **Art. 2019,** it addresses another situation in which 'restoration' is impossible, impractical or simply useless. "**In contracts providing for continuous** or periodic performance, the effect of the dissolution shall not be extended to any performance already rendered." [. . . .]

Article 2021 [. . .] states that "Dissolution of a contract does not impair the rights acquired through an onerous contract by a third party in good faith. If the contract involves immovable property, the principles of recordation apply to a third person acquiring an interest in the property, whether by onerous or gratuitous title." [. . . .]

Nullity of a juridical act is the sanction resulting from the non-existence or the failure in the integrity of an essential requirement <u>at the time the juridical act is entered into</u>. As **Art. 2029 states very clearly: "A contract is null when the requirements for its formation have not been met."** [. . . .]

There lies the distinction between *"nullity"* and *"caducity."* [. . . .]

"Caducity" operates only in the future, it *has no retroactive* effect; it does not erase the past of a juridical act. The consequences of "caducity" are simply that the legacy or donation will have no effect in the future. [. . . .]

There are two broad kinds of Nullity, absolute or relative, depending on the type of cause or ground that justifies the nullity of a juridical act. [. . . .]

LCC Art. 2030 describes an absolute nullity in these words: "A contract is absolutely null when it violates a rule of public order, as when the object of a contract is illicit or immoral. A contract that is absolutely null may not be confirmed. Absolute nullity may be invoked by any person or may be declared by the court on its own initiative." Article 2031 describes a relative nullity as follows: **"A contract is relatively null when it violates a rule intended for the protection of private parties, as when a party lacked capacity or did not give free consent at the time the contract was made. A contract that is only relatively null may be confirmed. Relative nullity may be invoked only by those persons for whose interest the ground for nullity was established, and may not be declared by the court on its own initiative."**

Article 2030 suggests that a juridical act is absolutely null when the violation of the law is of great concern and so major that it is "absolutely" necessary to protect, by the absolute nullity of the juridical act, the general interest or public order of the societal group at the expense of the private interest of the parties involved in the unlawful juridical act. [. . . .]

The lesser effects of relative nullity are explained by the fact that the 'nullity' of the juridical act occurs in the relation between the parties because only their private interest, as opposed to 'public,' is at stake; that private interest of the parties deserves some degree of protection. It follows that, because of the private nature of this kind of nullity, the relative nullity of a juridical act can be 'waived' by the party or parties or it can be 'cured' by the party protected by the nullity. In addition, whereas an action to have a juridical act declared absolutely null does not prescribe, an action in relative nullity does prescribe. [. . . .]

In some instances, the courts are guided in their evaluation of the nature of a nullity and, therefore, in the amount of discretion they may have. [. . . .] **Art. 94** [. . .]. **Art. 1965.**

Art. 2034 limits the "presumptive" nullity of a contract to one provision of a contract: **"Nullity of a provision does not render the whole contract null unless from the nature of the provision or the intention of the parties, it can be presumed that the contract would not have been made without the null provision."** [. . . .]

[A] relative nullity can be claimed only by that party whose interest is meant to be protected. Such is the case in the most common instance of relative nullity, i.e. vices of consent in the formation of a contract. Because a private interest is at stake, the party protected by the relative nullity can "cure" the ground of nullity by such juridical acts as "confirmation" and "novation." [. . . .]

As regards the absolute nullity of a juridical act, it is obvious that more plaintiffs should be granted the right of action than only those who may seek the relative nullity of a juridical act. The protection of the public interest needs for the circle of potential plaintiffs to be enlarged to include anyone who has a "legitimate interest" because of some legal relationship he or she has with the parties to the absolutely null juridical act. [. . . .]

Art. 2032 speaks for itself: **"Action for annulment of an absolutely null contract does not prescribe.**

Action of annulment of a relatively null contract must be brought within five years from the time the ground for nullity either ceased, as in the case of incapacity or duress, or was discovered, as in the case of error or fraud.

Nullity may be raised at any time as a defense against an action on the contract, even after the action for annulment has prescribed." [. . . .]

It is important to point out here that if an action may prescribe, particularly for a relative nullity, the defense or exception of nullity itself never prescribes. Such is the meaning of the third paragraph of Art. 2032. [. . . .]

A principle common to both kinds of nullity is that of the retroactive effect of the nullity. The first sentence of the first paragraph of **Art. 2033** is very clear: **"An absolutely null contract, or a relatively null contract that has been declared null by the court, is deemed never to have existed. . . ."** If the contract is *deemed never to have existed*, it follows that anything that has been done "in the past," any of the performances that have been carried out by a party or the parties have to be erased, wiped out, as if nothing had ever occurred. The problem is practical: how to restore the past to what it was before the parties entered their contract and performed, in total or in part, their obligations. Somewhat of an answer is given in Arts. 2033 and 2035, which draw a distinction between the effects of retroactivity between the parties themselves, on the one hand, and *vis-à-vis* third persons, on the other hand. [. . . .]

As regards the principle of the retroactive effect of nullity, whether relative or absolute, it has the same effects as the retroactivity of a resolutory condition the purpose of which is to wipe out the effects of whatever performance may have occurred. Thus, each party must return to the other the performance received because that performance has become "undue." [. . . .]

The exception described in **Art. 2033-2**, is a standard application of the civil law maxim: *Nemo auditur suam propriam turpitudinem allegans.* This maxim is somewhat equivalent to the common law maxim of "clean hands." [. . . .]

[**T**]he nullity of a contract between two parties should not have detrimental effects against good faith third persons, i.e. persons who did not know and could not have known of the ground of nullity of a contract to which they were not parties. "Good faith" once again will protect those third persons who can claim its benefit. Hence **Art. 2035: "Nullity of a contract does not impair the rights acquired through an onerous contract by a third party in good faith. If the contract involves immovable property, the principles of recordation apply to a third person acquiring an interest in the property whether by onerous or gratuitous title."**

Cases

Opal Mennella
v.
Kurt E. Schon E.A.I., Ltd., et al.
United States Court of Appeals
Fifth Circuit
December 2, 1992
979 F.2d 357

POLITZ, Chief Judge.

[1] In these consolidated appeals, the parties dispute the ownership of a masterpiece painted by Sir Anthony Van Dyck. Mrs. Opal Mennella complains of the district court's summary judgment dismissal of her claim of conversion and denial of sanctions; Kurt E. Schon, E.A.I., Ltd., et al., complain of the court's award to Mrs. Mennella of certain payments she made on the painting and of the dismissal of their claim of defamation. Concluding that the question of ownership is controlled by basic principles of property and contract law as adopted and codified in the Louisiana Civil Code, and concluding that Schon's defamation suit is without merit, we affirm the district court except as relates to recovery of interest by Mrs. Mennella.

Background

[2] This *mise en scene* began in the Spring of 1988 when Mrs. Mennella agreed to purchase a painting from Schon's New Orleans art gallery. She previously had purchased two paintings from Schon and had admired this piece on previous visits. The painting, entitled "Princess Mary, Eldest Daughter of King Charles I, Mother

of King William III" by the Flemish Master Sir Anthony Van Dyck, was more than 300 years old.[1] Princess Mary married William of Orange; it is their names which identify one of America's first and finest colleges. The purchase price was $350,000. Motivated to purchase, she paid Schon $50,000 with the $300,000 balance, according to the invoice, to be paid on June 1, 1988.

[3] The painting never left Schon's possession. Mrs. Mennella, experiencing cash-flow problems, amicably secured an agreement to pay the balance over a six-month period. By Christmas of 1988, however, she had managed to pay only an additional $90,000. At that point she demanded authentication of the painting to be used to secure a loan to pay the balance of the purchase price. Schon sent an expert's appraisal stating that the portrait was "one of five copies by Sir Anthony Van Dyck."[2] Concerned that the portrait might be a counterfeit, Mrs. Mennella enlisted the aid of her attorneys who moved to void the sale and recover the sum paid. Acting through counsel, Mrs. Mennella repudiated the painting's value, refused to make further payments, and demanded return of the $140,000 paid.

[4] Schon responded by letter on April 25, 1989, a full year after the ostensible sale, that Mrs. Mennella should be satisfied with the authenticity of the painting after receiving a second appraisal. In that letter Schon demanded performance within five days, absent which he would be forced to place the painting back in the active sale stock of the gallery. Mrs. Mennella made no apparent effort to reply or to enforce her rights under the contract. She did not make or tender the agreed price or object to the time period in which Schon demanded payment. Instead, she and her attorneys insisted on referring to the contract as "an agreement to purchase" rather than as a sale, obviously seeking to distance her from ownership and the obligation to pay the balance of the purchase price.

[5] On May 2, 1989, Schon wrote Mrs. Mennella, informing her that he regarded her silence and inaction as a default and that he considered the sale canceled. No money was refunded. Instead, in September Schon offered to either refund $95,000, representing the consideration paid less $45,000 for the cost of authentication and commission paid to Schon's salesman, or to give Mrs. Mennella $140,000 in store credit. Mrs. Mennella rejected both offers.

[6] Without Mrs. Mennella's knowledge, the painting was shipped to Christie's in London where, in November 1989, it sold for more than $1.4 million.

[7] The following month, unaware of the London sale, Mrs. Mennella filed the instant suit seeking recision of the sale and damages, claiming that she only agreed to buy the painting upon "proper authentication and verification." She complained

---

1. Van Dyck is, after Rubens, the most prominent Flemish painter of the 17th Century. Under the appointment of King Charles I he served as "principal paynter in ordinary of their Majesties." It was during this period that Van Dyck was Knighted and presumably painted the portrait in question.

2. The appraisal was conducted in January of 1989. The conclusion was confirmed by a Dr. Erik Larsen in March and reduced to writing in April of 1989.

that the painting she agreed to purchase was a fraud and was worth far less than she had agreed to pay.[3] Schon answered and counterclaimed, alleging defamation. Informed of the London sale, Mrs. Mennella's attitude markedly changed. Her lawyers, presumably somewhat chagrined, amended the complaint, claiming that the sale was complete from the start and, as a result, the painting was Mrs. Mennella's and the London sale constituted a conversion.[4]

[8] Based on the pleadings, depositions, and affidavits, the district court concluded that Mrs. Mennella, though entitled to her payments and interest from the day of her demand, was not entitled to the proceeds of the London sale. Schon's counterclaim for defamation was rejected. Mrs. Mennella apparently thought this claim to be frivolous and moved for sanctions against Schon for presuming to advance it. The district court denied the motion for sanctions. Both parties timely appealed.

Analysis

[. . . .]

[9] The controlling principles of Louisiana law are neither complex nor mysterious. This dispute is readily resolved by resort to its chronology. That the parties formed some manner of contract on April 5, 1988 is not disputed. Rather, the dispute concerns the more remote question of whether the painting belonged to Mrs. Mennella so as to lend credence to her claim that Schon's sale of the painting constituted conversion.[5] We must first decide whether the contract supports her claim to ownership.[6]

1. The nature of the obligation

[10] Whether the contract provided for a present transfer of title depends on the objectively determined intentions of the parties.[7] If the sale was intended to be contingent on adequate authentication and verification, as Mrs. Mennella originally

---

3. In her original complaint, Mrs. Mennella claimed that she "made verbal demands in early 1989 which were followed by written demand . . . for the return of [her $140,000]."

4. The amended complaint sought to "amend her [complaint] to state that: Plaintiff is and has been the owner of the [portrait]."

5. Conversion is a common-law tort recognized by Louisiana courts as a quasi-offense under Civil Code article 2315. *See, e.g., Holley v. Singletary*, 464 So.2d 410 (La.App.1985).

6. Mrs. Mennella's claim to the proceeds flows from her right to the painting. That right is defined by the Civil Code and the contract. One must recall the boundaries of common-law conversion before applying it to the unique relation created by Civil Code sales. Conversion, as the action has evolved, is predicated on (1) the plaintiff's right to possession, and (2) the defendant's exercise of dominion or control over the goods which is in fact inconsistent with the plaintiff's rights. W. Page Keeton, et al., *Prosser and Keeton on the Law of Torts*, §15, at 92, 104–05 (5th ed. 1984). If the April contract transferred title and Schon was not within his rights to sell the painting, only then would he be liable in damages under a conversion theory. The key is whether Schon, based on Mrs. Mennella's conduct, had the right to sell the painting.

7. La.Civ.Code art. 2045 (West 1987); *M.O.N.T. Boat Rental Serv., Inc. v. Union Oil Co. of Cal.*, 613 F.2d 576 (5th Cir.1980); *Kuswa & Assoc., Inc. v. Thibaut Constr. Co., Inc.*, 463 So.2d 1264 (La.1985).

claimed, or on the payment of the purchase price and tender of delivery, as the district court determined, then the obligation would have been "suspensive" under the Louisiana Civil Code. The Code defines a suspensive obligation as one which is "dependent on an uncertain event."[8] Article 2471 of the Code provides: "A sale, made with a suspensive condition, does not transfer property to the buyer, until the fulfillment of the condition." If, on the other hand, the sale was not conditioned "on an uncertain event," then title would pass under article 2456 of the Code which provides:

> The sale is considered to be perfect between the parties, **and the property is of right acquired to the purchaser** with regard to the seller, as soon as there exists an agreement for the object and the price thereof, although the object has not yet been delivered, nor the price paid [emphasis added].

After reviewing all relevant indicia of the parties' intentions, we conclude that they did not intend to create a suspensive obligation.

[11] Because we do not have the luxury of a fully comprehensive written contract[9] we must glean the intention of the parties from other sources. The Civil Code commands our consideration of the "nature of the contract, equity, usages, the conduct of the parties before and after the formation of the contract, and of other contracts of a like nature between the same parties."[10] We find the conduct of both parties, before and after April 5, 1988, to be instructive.

[12] It is clear that Schon regarded the transaction as a perfected sale, one not contingent on authentication or anything else. The day after Mrs. Mennella paid the gallery $50,000, Kurt Schon wrote to congratulate her on the "purchase of the painting." Equally telling, Schon immediately paid his salesman a substantial sales commission.[11] The invoice was straightforward; it described the transaction as a sale without reference to any condition. There was only the notation of the initial payment, amount and due date of the balance, and identification of the portrait.

[13] Similarly, Mrs. Mennella never made any claim to a right to authentication until December, when she was facing financial difficulties and already had paid $140,000 for the painting. We are mindful of and consider significant the fact that the parties had executed two similar contracts without any authentication requirement. Though the present efforts to reverse an earlier position may be the cause of uplifted eyebrows, it appears consistent with the original understanding and prior dealings.

---

8. La.Civ.Code art. 1767.
9. A written contract is not required to accomplish a sale of a movable. La.Civ.Code art. 2441. Where the price or value exceeds $500, however, proof of the contract must be proved by at least one witness and other corroborating circumstances. La.Civ.Code art. 1846. The summary judgment record contains ample proof of the making of the contract.
10. La.Civ.Code art. 2053.
11. Schon later sought to withhold this commission from the refund of Mrs. Mennella's payments.

[14] The district court found the sale to be conditioned on both the delivery of the painting and the payment of the purchase price. We find that this reading creates unnecessary tension with the literal language of article 2456 and fails to comport with the accepted civilian rubrics.

[15] Article 1767 defines a conditional obligation as "one dependent on an uncertain event." If the anticipated performance were treated as an uncertain event virtually every bilateral contract would be a conditional obligation and venerable article 2456 would be rendered meaningless. Indeed, if the performance was so "uncertain" as to create a conditional obligation, it would be nigh impossible to treat the exchange of promises as a contract. Louisiana courts long have recognized that the Civil Code does not allow the parties to condition the transfer of title on the payment of the purchase price.[12] Instead, in credit sales, Louisiana courts consistently have held that when the parties consent and agree as to the price and the thing, title passes instanter. So sayeth article 2456.

[16] Therefore we are compelled to hold that title to the painting passed to Mrs. Mennella in April of 1988. We must now consider whether that title was divested prior to the London sale.

2. The execution of the duties under the contract

[17] In support of her claim of ownership of the painting, Mrs. Mennella seizes upon the transfer of title and would ignore all of her subsequent actions. Legal title is not so barren a concept. The Civil Code clearly portends a transfer of title subject to the execution of the contract. For example, the seller may wrongfully sell and deliver the object to an innocent third party who would acquire title, provided he has paid fair value.[13] The seller retains a security interest in the property[14] pending tender of the purchase price and has the concomitant duty of due care towards the object.[15] The seller has the right to put the buyer in default and to dissolve the contract upon the buyer's failure to perform, and under certain conditions to simply regard the contract as dissolved.[16] That divestment is the principal issue presented by this appeal.

[18] Mrs. Mennella was obliged to carry her end of the bargain, timely payment, just as Schon was obliged to care for and ultimately deliver the painting.

---

12. *Haymon v. Holliday*, 405 So.2d 1304 (La.App.1981).

13. The Code explicitly accommodates such a result: "The sale is considered to be perfect and the property is of right acquired to the purchaser **with regard to the seller.** . . ." La.Civ.Code art. 2456. *See also* La.Civ.Code art. 518 ("when possession has not been delivered, a subsequent transferee to whom possession is delivered acquires ownership provided he is in good faith"); Yiannopoulos, 2 *Louisiana Civil Law Treatise* § 354 (1991).

14. La.Civ.Code art. 3227; *C & A Tractor Co. v. Holland American Ins. Co.*, 445 So.2d 1286 (La. App.), *cert. denied*, 449 So.2d 1348 (La.1984).

15. La.Civ.Code art. 2468.

16. La.Civ.Code art. 2013. *See e.g., Texala Oil & Gas Co. v. Caddo Mineral Lands Co.*, 152 La. 549, 93 So. 788 (1922); *Hay v. Bush*, 110 La. 575, 34 So. 692 (1903). Comment (a) of the 1984 addition of article 2013 cites both opinions.

Mrs. Mennella's erroneous conclusion that the painting was not authentic caused her to repudiate the transaction, demand a return of her partial payment, and refuse to pay the balance due. This is a course of action she would have been entitled to follow had she been correct in her assumption.[17] That assumption was not correct, however. Indeed, in forming her belief that the painting was a fraud she relied on an appraisal which clearly indicated that the painting was executed by Van Dyck. She received repeated assurances from the seller that he would perform, accompanied by repeated demands for her performance. Further, from January to May she made no effort whatever to authenticate the painting or to investigate the credentials of the experts from whom she had received appraisals. Instead, through counsel, Mrs. Mennella made manifest that she had no intention of performing[18] and demanded a return of her money, refusing a "net" refund or a full store credit.

[19] Whether she claims to have been exercising her right to receive adequate authentication under the contract, or an effort to enforce a warranty, there is no excusing Mrs. Mennella's express repudiation and continued refusal to perform after receiving two appraisals. Mrs. Mennella comes before the courts burdened with the troublesome albatross of her repudiation. We may not ignore it.

[20] Mrs. Mennella now offers a somewhat tortured explanation of the legal significance of her failure to perform. Essentially, the argument turns on what she characterizes as Schon's failure to formally accept her offer to rescind the contract. Such obfuscation need not long detain us. That argument ignores the fact that Mrs. Mennella was in default by January of 1989, at the very latest, when the voluntary extension expired. The communication from counsel refusing to proceed and demanding a refund cannot be construed as anything but a definitive refusal to perform. The lamb of her so-called "offer to rescind" cannot lie peacefully beside the lion of her refusal to perform. The fact that she may have based her actions on a mistaken belief that the painting was not genuine[19] does not change the character of her actions; failure to perform does not presuppose a fraudulent intent, only an inexcusable failure to do that which was promised.[20]

[21] If accepted at face value, the argument by counsel for Mrs. Mennella would stand the law of contracts on its ear. Contracts bind persons to the assigned risks and benefits. Mrs. Mennella would blithely shift the benefits and the corresponding burdens as best suits her most immediate interests. She may not do so.[21]

---

17. When both parties to a contract share a mistake of fact involving the essence of a party's consent "the granting of relief presents no problem." La.Civ.Code art. 1949, cmt. (d); *see generally*, La.Civ.Code arts. 1948–50.

18. Counsel for Mrs. Mennella concedes that this is the weakest part of their argument: "that it appears as though she didn't want it."

19. Neither may her failure to receive what, by her estimation, was sufficient evidence of authentication — a right she did not have — serve as an adequate excuse for her failure to perform.

20. *See generally, Robertson v. Buoni*, 504 So.2d 860 (La.1987).

21. La.Civ.Code art. 2055; *see also Douglas Oil Tools, Inc. v. Demesnil*, 552 So.2d 77 (La.App.1989) (representations which are relied upon to a party's detriment give rise to estoppel). *See also Ranger*

[22] We conclude that Mrs. Mennella's written communication through counsel refusing to perform may justly be treated as an anticipatory repudiation[22] and that her failure to pay the balance in the extended period allowed for same constituted an active repudiation of the contract.

3. Dissolution

[23] Dissolution of the contract would terminate Mrs. Mennella's property rights in the painting. Indeed, this was the prayer of Mrs. Mennella's initial lawsuit. The final question before us is whether Schon secured a dissolution before the London sale.

[24] When faced with Mrs. Mennella's refusal to perform Schon had three choices. He could: (1) sue to enforce performance or to secure a judicial dissolution; (2) continue to seek performance albeit in an untimely manner; and/or (3) put Mrs. Mennella in default and, if she failed to correct same, regard the contract as dissolved.

[25] Initially, Schon opted for the second choice; he invited untimely performance. Seeking to accommodate Mrs. Mennella's cash-flow problems, he agreed to a modification of the contract, extending the $300,000 payment from June until the following January. He then provided two appraisals to assuage her voiced concerns regarding the painting's origin.[23] Schon informed Mrs. Mennella she had five additional days to perform; otherwise he would have to consider the sale dissolved. Finally, when Mrs. Mennella made clear that she would not perform, Schon gave her notice that he was treating the sale as canceled and was returning the painting to the active stock for sale.

[26] Recently, revisions to the Civil Code formally adopted a practice the Louisiana courts have long recognized: extrajudicial dissolution.[24] Schon's letters were sufficient to put Mrs. Mennella in default, a prerequisite to dissolution by notice.[25] We find them sufficient, under the circumstances, to dissolve the contract.

Nationwide Ins. v. American Cas. Co., 658 F.Supp. 103, 108 (D.Del.1987) ("A party who breaches a contract may not rely on the benefits of that same contract."), aff'd, 833 F.2d 307 (3d Cir.1987).

22. Litvinoff, *Law of Obligations in the Louisiana Jurisprudence,* 371 (2d ed. 1985) ("[A] situation that could be characterized as an anticipatory breach at common law can be regarded as an active violation of the contract in Louisiana.").

23. There is some dispute as to when the Larsen appraisal was sent. It is clear, however, that it was sent by April when Schon still demanded performance. Mrs. Mennella complains that this communication by Schon included a demand for two different prices, one which included interest and one for the contract price. In either event she refused to perform at any price and then waited, saying nothing after receiving Schon's next letter which informed her that the sale was dissolved; indeed, she was still seeking dissolution and disavowing ownership, as late as March, 1990.

24. Mrs. Mennella cites cases from the 1940s and 1950s suggesting that judicial dissolution was Schon's exclusive remedy. In light of much earlier precedents and the recent amendments to the Civil Code, we can hardly view those decisions as persuasive. *See* n. 16, *supra.*

25. La.Civ.Code art. 1991. "An obligee may put the obligor in default by a written request of performance . . . or by filing suit for performance. . . ."

[27] The Civil Code provides that the obligee has a right, in certain cases, to treat the contract as dissolved.[26] The "unilateral, non-judicial dissolution provided for in the revised articles is not a novelty."[27] Under the civilian tradition, the obligor must be notified of his default, given a certain time to perform, and warned that the contract will be considered dissolved if performance is not rendered.[28] The time set must be reasonable according to the circumstances,[29] and the breach must be substantial to justify the dissolution.[30]

[28] The Civil Code is not exhaustive in its description of the circumstances that will entitle the obligee "to regard the contract as dissolved" without litigation. Because the pertinent articles are relatively new, the Louisiana courts have not yet expounded on the issue. Whether a repudiation is sufficiently clear to allow dissolution without litigation undoubtedly will pose a difficult question in some cases. Fortunately for this *Erie* court, this is not one of those cases. Schon prudently waited until Mrs. Mennella unequivocally refused to perform and demanded the return of her money before notifying her of the default and dissolution.[31] Article 2013, when read in harmony with related articles, such as articles 2014[32] and 2018,[33] allows extrajudicial dissolution where the obligee has received partial payment. The Code makes clear, however, that the obligee is liable for the return of any partial payments unless he has a right to retain them.[34]

[29] Schon's notice is not rendered ineffective by his failure to simultaneously return the partial payments. Article 2018 provides the obligor in default with an action to recover partial payments to the extent they exceed the damages incurred. Article 2013[35] states that the obligee who regards the contract as dissolved has the right to pursue a remedy in damages. The comments to article 2015 (non-judicial dissolution by notice) likewise state that "[a]fter such notice is given, the obligor will be liable for any delay damages that accrue." At the same time, the obligee is duty bound to mitigate his damages.[36] We conclude that article 2013, when read *in*

---

26. La.Civ.Code art. 2013.

27. Litvinoff, *supra*, at 389.

28. Id.

29. La.Civ.Code art. 2015.

30. La.Civ.Code art. 2014.

31. If extrajudicial dissolution were not appropriate in this case we have difficulty conceiving of a case in which it would be. Such a result would be intolerable as litigation would have to result from every failed sales agreement to clear title.

32. The article allows dissolution where the obligor has partially performed but the part not rendered substantially impairs the obligee's interest.

33. That article provides: "If partial performance has been rendered and that performance is of value to the party seeking to dissolve . . . , the dissolution does not preclude recovery for that performance, whether in contract or quasi-contract."

34. *See, e.g.*, La.Civ.Code art. 2018.

35. "In either case [judicial or non-judicial dissolution] the obligee may recover damages." La. Civ.Code art. 2013.

36. La.Civ.Code art. 2002.

pari materia with other articles,[37] allows the seller to regard the contract as dissolved and temporarily retain partial payments when the buyer is in breach. The seller, of course, is limited in his actions by operation of article 1759, which provides that "Good faith shall govern the conduct of the obligor or obligee in whatever pertains to their obligation."[38] Thus he may hold only the funds necessary to compensate for the loss he reasonably believes he will suffer. Under the prevailing circumstances, we conclude that Schon's actions were reasonable and that they were executed in good faith.

[30] We hold that Schon validly dissolved the contract by notice of default after it became obvious that Mrs. Mennella would not perform. Consistent therewith, we therefore hold that Schon had legal title to the painting when it was sold in London.

[. . . .]

Questions

1. Paragraph 4: The Court assumes, without much explanation, that the "notice to perform" that Schon gave Manella, an essential prerequisite to extra-juridical dissolution in most cases, was adequate under Louisiana Civil Code article 2015. What, precisely, does that article require of such a notice? What is meant in the second paragraph of the article by "the requirements governing a putting . . . in default"? *See* La. Civ. Code art. 1989, *et seq.*

2. Paragraphs 27–30: The Court addresses the question whether Schon was entitled to regard the sale contract as dissolved once Manella refused to pay the balance of the purchase price using an impressive interpretative methodology. Can you identify the various interpretative methods and techniques that the Court employed?

3. Paragraphs 29–30: What is the "source" (in the sense of La. Civ. Code art. 1757) of Schon's obligation to refund to Manella the payments she had made of the sale price? Is it a "contract" or is it something else? *See* La. Civ. Code art. 2018, par. 2; *see also* La. Civ. Code art. 2298.

---

37. La.Civ.Code art. 13.
38. *See also* La.Civ.Code art. 1983.

Kenneth David Jones
v.
Ezeb Chevalier

Court of Appeal of Louisiana
Third Circuit
May 22, 1991
579 So.2d 1217

FORET, Judge.

[1] Plaintiff and appellant, Kenneth David Jones, appeals from a judgment in favor of Ezeb Chevalier, defendant and appellee herein.

[2] Jones brought this action, alleging that Chevalier was liable to him for what appears to be a claim for breach of an illegal contract. Jones claims that Chevalier was responsible for his arrest and ensuing damages because Chevalier did not warn him of the police investigation into his activities, as agreed.

[3] Chevalier filed an exception of no cause of action in response to Jones' petition, which was granted by the trial court.

[4] By this appeal, Jones contends that he was not given notice of the hearing, and an opportunity to present evidence at the hearing on the exception of no cause of action. The record supports his contention. Although the record contains a notice of the hearing on the exception, the record does not reflect that Jones was personally served pursuant to La.C.C.P. art. 1314 and 1231, et seq.

[5] Jones was not prejudiced by the lack of notice because evidence may not be introduced to support or controvert the exception of no cause of action. La.C.C.P. art. 931. Nor was Jones entitled to notice as a matter of constitutional due process: the failure to disclose a cause of action is a peremptory objection which may be noticed by either the trial or the appellate court on its own motion. La.C.C.P. art. 927. When either the trial or the appellate court notices the failure to disclose a cause of action, no hearing is required. Conversely, when notice is not given and no hearing is conducted, it must be presumed that the court, in granting the exception, has acted on its own motion.

[6] Moreover, a contract which violates a rule of public order, as does this alleged agreement, is absolutely null, and unenforceable. La.C.C. art. 2030. The absolute nullity of such a contract may be declared by the court on its own initiative. *Id.*

[7] The trial court's judgment was proper.

[. . . .]

Question

1. In this case, the disappointed party—Jones—had not yet rendered his performance (paying of money) as of the time at which the other party—Chevalier—breached the contract. But what if Jones had paid Chevalier for

his services "in advance"? Under those circumstances, would Jones have been entitled to recover this performance? Why or why not? *See* La. Civ. Code art. 2033, pars. 1 & 2.

M. Robert Voitier, Sr.
v.
Antique Art Gallery, et al.

Court of Appeal of Louisiana
Third Circuit
April 6, 1988
524 So.2d 80

GUIDRY, Judge.

[1] On May 15, 1984, plaintiff, M. Robert Voitier, Sr., filed this suit seeking rescission of a contract of sale of a painting entitled "Wooded Farmland Glade", supposedly an original work of art by George Inness. Voitier purchased the painting, which was owned by Fred Rotondaro, on June 26, 1982 at an auction sale conducted by Morton's Auction Exchange, Inc., in New Orleans, Louisiana. Plaintiff seeks a rescission of the sale and a return of the sale price because of an error of fact which he alleges was the principal cause for making the contract, i.e., the painting is not an original work of art by George Inness. Plaintiff, in addition, sought the recovery of attendant damages.

[. . . .]

[2] After a trial on the merits[. . . **found, among other things, that . . .** t]he painting owned by Rotondaro which was sold to Voitier was not an original George Inness.

[3] [T]he trial court rendered judgment in favor of plaintiff [. . .] for the sum of $23,610.93, which included a return of the purchase price of $17,500.00 and all damages sustained by the purchaser, Voitier. [. . . .]

Facts

[4] In early 1982, Fred Rotondaro, a resident of the state of Maryland, purchased the painting at issue, which was reputed to be an original George Inness work of art from David Harrison, d/b/a Antique Art Gallery. Prior to the purchase, Rotondaro had the painting authenticated and was satisfied that it was an original George Inness painting. [. . . .]

[. . . .]

[5] [**Subsequently, at an auction,** . . .] M. Robert Voitier, Sr. was the successful bidder on the painting at issue which was alleged to be an original work of art by the early American artist, George Inness. The bid price was $17,500.00. Voitier had seen the painting prior to the auction and on the day of sale made his bid telephonically. In addition to the purchase price, Voitier paid a 10% hammer fee, $1,750.00, and 3%

sales tax. He was also required to pay freight and insurance fees to transport the painting to his residence. Upon delivery to his residence, Voitier noticed the absence of the letter of authenticity which he had been assured would accompany the painting. [**He immediately requested . . .**] and was eventually sent a letter of authenticity written by a Rosalyn Mikesell, owner/director of the Webberly Galleries in Chicago, Illinois. Voitier was not satisfied with Mikesell's letter of authenticity and engaged the services of Nicolai Cikovsky, an expert on the works of George Inness. Cikovsky, after studying the painting, rendered a written opinion to Voitier stating that the painting was not a George Inness original. [**After unsuccessful attempts to recover the purchase price,** . . .] Voitier then instituted this suit.

[. . . .]

Sufficient Cause for Rescission of Sale [. . .]

[6] The trial court determined that the painting in question was not an original George Inness work of art. Appellants do not seriously question this fact determination. They contend that this fact determination will not support a cause of action for rescission on the ground of error. [. . . .]

[7] Our brethren of the Fourth Circuit in *Deutschmann v. Standard Fur Company, Inc.*, 331 So.2d 219 (La.App.1976), succinctly stated the law regarding the invalidation of contracts for unilateral error as follows:

> "Our jurisprudence is well settled that a contract may be invalidated for a unilateral error as to a fact which was the principal cause for making the contract, where the other party knew or should have known it was the principal cause. LSA-C.C. art. 1845; *Savoie v. Bills*, 317 So.2d 249 (La.App. 3d Cir.1975); *West Esplanade Shell Service, Inc. v. Breithoff*, 293 So.2d 595 (La.App. 4th Cir.1974). Error as to the nature or object of a contract may be with regard to either the substance or the object of the agreement, or substantial quality of the object, or some other quality of the object if such quality is the principal cause of making the contract. *Jefferson Truck Equipment Co. v. Guarisco Motor Co.*, 250 So.2d 211 (La.App. 1st Cir.1971)."

[8] The record discloses that the painting in question was advertised [. . .] as a George Inness original work of art. The record establishes that Voitier had previously purchased an original George Inness painting and was anxious to add another original to his collection. In other words, the record makes crystal clear that Voitier was not interested in just any painting but rather that his principal motive was to acquire a George Inness original. In furtherance of this desire, Voitier paid the substantial price of $17,500.00 for the painting. It is equally clear from the record that [**the seller** . . .] was fully aware of plaintiff's motive. Before submitting a bid, Voitier viewed the painting and exacted assurances [**from Morton's**], albeit made in good faith, that the painting was an authentic original and that a letter of authenticity would accompany the painting. Under the circumstances present in this case and considering the applicable legal principles, we have little difficulty concluding that

plaintiff has established his right to a rescission of the contract on the basis of unilateral error.

[....]

Questions

1. The *Voitier* court, curiously enough, did not cite any legislative authority in support of its conclusion that Voitier was entitled to recover the purchase price he had paid. Can you find any such authority? *See* La. Civ. Code art. 2033.

2. Though the *Voitier* opinion is silent on the matter, one must suppose that Antique Art Gallery sustained damages of some sort as a result of this sale-gone-bad, e.g., costs of appraisement of the painting. If Antique Art Gallery had, in fact, sustained such damages, should it have been entitled to recover them from Voitier? Why or why not? *See* La. Civ. Code art. 1952.

Chapter 5

Proof of Obligations and Payment

Louisiana Sources of Law

Louisiana Civil Code

Art. 1831. Party must prove obligation.

A party who demands performance of an obligation must prove the existence of the obligation.

A party who asserts that an obligation is null, or that it has been modified or extinguished, must prove the facts or acts giving rise to the nullity, modification, or extinction. (Acts 1984, No. 331, § 1, eff. Jan. 1, 1985.)

Art. 1832. Written form required by law.

When the law requires a contract to be in written form, the contract may not be proved by testimony or by presumption, unless the written instrument has been destroyed, lost, or stolen. (Acts 1984, No. 331, § 1, eff. Jan. 1, 1985.)

Art. 1833. Authentic act.

A. An authentic act is a writing executed before a notary public or other officer authorized to perform that function, in the presence of two witnesses, and signed by each party who executed it, by each witness, and by each notary public before whom it was executed. The typed or hand-printed name of each person shall be placed in a legible form immediately beneath the signature of each person signing the act.

B. To be an authentic act, the writing need not be executed at one time or place, or before the same notary public or in the presence of the same witnesses, provided that each party who executes it does so before a notary public or other officer authorized to perform that function, and in the presence of two witnesses and each party, each witness, and each notary public signs it. The failure to include the typed or handprinted name of each person signing the act shall not affect the validity or authenticity of the act.

C. If a party is unable or does not know how to sign his name, the notary public must cause him to affix his mark to the writing. (Acts 1984, No. 331, § 1, eff. Jan. 1, 1985; Acts 2003, No. 965, § 1, eff. Jan. 1, 2005.)

Art. 1835. Authentic act constitutes full proof between parties and heirs.

An authentic act constitutes full proof of the agreement it contains, as against the parties, their heirs, and successors by universal or particular title. (Acts 1984, No. 331, § 1, eff. Jan. 1, 1985.)

Art. 1836. Act under private signature duly acknowledged.

An act under private signature is regarded prima facie as the true and genuine act of a party executing it when his signature has been acknowledged, and the act shall be admitted in evidence without further proof.

An act under private signature may be acknowledged by a party to that act by recognizing the signature as his own before a court, or before a notary public, or other officer authorized to perform that function, in the presence of two witnesses. An act under private signature may be acknowledged also in any other manner authorized by law.

Nevertheless, an act under private signature, though acknowledged, cannot substitute for an authentic act when the law prescribes such an act. (Acts 1984, No. 331, § 1, eff. Jan. 1, 1985.)

Art. 1837. Act under private signature.

An act under private signature need not be written by the parties, but must be signed by them. (Acts 1984, No. 331, § 1, eff. Jan. 1, 1985.)

Arts. 1838 to 1841. [omitted]

Art. 1842. Confirmation.

Confirmation is a declaration whereby a person cures the relative nullity of an obligation.

An express act of confirmation must contain or identify the substance of the obligation and evidence the intention to cure its relative nullity.

Tacit confirmation may result from voluntary performance of the obligation. (Acts 1984, No. 331, § 1, eff. Jan. 1, 1985.)

Art. 1843. Ratification.

Ratification is a declaration whereby a person gives his consent to an obligation incurred on his behalf by another without authority.

An express act of ratification must evidence the intention to be bound by the ratified obligation.

Tacit ratification results when a person, with knowledge of an obligation incurred on his behalf by another, accepts the benefit of that obligation. (Acts 1984, No. 331, § 1, eff. Jan. 1, 1985.)

Art. 1844. Effects of confirmation and ratification.

The effects of confirmation and ratification are retroactive to the date of the confirmed or ratified obligation. Neither confirmation nor ratification may impair the rights of third persons. (Acts 1984, No. 331, § 1, eff. Jan. 1, 1985.)

Art. 1845. [omitted]

Art. 1846. Contract not in excess of five hundred dollars.

When a writing is not required by law, a contract not reduced to writing, for a price or, in the absence of a price, for a value not in excess of five hundred dollars may be proved by competent evidence.

If the price or value is in excess of five hundred dollars, the contract must be proved by at least one witness and other corroborating circumstances. (Acts 1984, No. 331, § 1, eff. Jan. 1, 1985.)

Art. 1847. Debt of a third person and debt extinguished by prescription.

Parol evidence is inadmissible to establish either a promise to pay the debt of a third person or a promise to pay a debt extinguished by prescription. (Acts 1984, No. 331, § 1, eff. Jan. 1, 1985.)

Art. 1848. Testimonial or other evidence not admitted to disprove a writing. [*Amended*]

Testimonial or other evidence may not be admitted to negate or vary the contents of an authentic act or an act under private signature. Nevertheless, in the interest of justice, that evidence may be admitted to prove such circumstances as a vice of consent or to prove that the written act was modified by a subsequent and valid oral agreement. (Acts 1984, No. 331, § 1, eff. Jan. 1, 1985; Acts 2012, No. 277, § 1.)

Art. 1849. [omitted]

Arts. 1850–1852. [Repealed]

Art. 1853. Judicial confession.

A judicial confession is a declaration made by a party in a judicial proceeding. That confession constitutes full proof against the party who made it.

A judicial confession is indivisible and it may be revoked only on the ground of error of fact. (Acts 1984, No. 331, § 1, eff. Jan. 1, 1985.)

Doctrine
Louisiana Law of Obligations in General, A Précis
Sections 6.1.1 to 6.1.3

An authentic act is defined as a writing executed before a notary public or an officer **"authorized to perform that function, in the presence of two witnesses and signed by each party who executed it, by each witness and by each notary public before whom it was executed."** (LSA-C.C. Art. 1833). [. . . .]

Although a notary is the most likely officer who will preside over the formalities of the act, other public officers are authorized to stand in the place of a notary to perform the latter's functions. As illustrations, the laws allows commissioned officers in the active service of the Armed Forces or the Coast Guard of the U.S. (R.S. 35:7) as well as ambassadors, consuls (R.S. 35:9) or recorders (R.S. 44:101) to perform the functions of a notary. [. . . .]

The role played by the written instrument itself (*instrumentum*) in the prerequisites of a valid authentic act explains why the contents of such an act are given a binding force which admits of few exceptions. Oral evidence, if freely admitted, could so tamper with the contents of an authentic act as to deprive the latter of any value, at the same time it would seriously discredit the role and authority of notaries or other qualified public officers. [. . . .]

An act under private signature is defined as an act **"which need not be written by the parties, but must be signed by them."** (LSA-C.C. Arts. 1837).

The legal weight attached to such an act rests, as a consequence, upon the validity of the signatures of the parties, or party to it. It follows that a party against whom an act under private signature is asserted may attempt to deny his signature by any available means of proof. Conversely, any means of proof may be used to establish that the signature belongs to that party. [. . . .]

An act under private signature facilitates the burden of proof of the party who claims its benefit even though the evidentiary weight of such an act is limited. [. . . .]

"Confirmation is a declaration whereby a person cures the relative nullity of an obligation." (LSA-C.C. Art. 1842-1). Confirmation is, therefore, a unilateral juridical act, express or tacit, enabling a person to make *retroactively* valid a juridical act which was defective when first entered into. [. . . .]

"Ratification is a declaration whereby a person gives his consent to an obligation incurred on his behalf by another without authority." (LSA-C.C. Art. 1843). [. . . .]

Ratification is, therefore, a unilateral juridical act, express or tacit, enabling a person to give her consent to a juridical act entered into on her behalf by another who had no authority to do so. In a sense, to ratify another person's juridical act is to vest power and authority in that person after the juridical act has been carried out [ex *post facto*] or retroactively in a sense. [. . . .]

The difference between confirmation and ratification is, therefore, that confirmation erases a ground for nullity of a contract whereas ratification adds to a juridical act a necessary requirement for its validity. [. . . .]

A juridical act which is confirmed or ratified is fictitiously considered to have been perfect, and therefore valid, as of the time it had been entered into (*ex tunc* or "as of then"), since it is cured retroactively of its defect. [. . . .]

Whenever a written instrument is required, or where written proof is prescribed, an exception to these legal dispositions can be found in civil Code **Article 1853** which provides for a judicial confession.

Section I — Literal Proof

Cases

Sunray Services, Inc.
v.
The City of Minden

Court of Appeal of Louisiana
Second Circuit
February 28, 1997
690 So.2d 970

GASKINS, Judge.

Facts

[1] [Plaintiff, garbage hauler, who had provided commercial and industrial garbage hauling services under exclusive contract with city brought action against the city for breach of contract. The city council motioned to extend the plaintiff's contract for an additional seven years. The mayor vetoed the action as being contrary to the provisions of the statute dealing with city trash collection contracts and sent the plaintiff written notice of the city's intent to terminate the contract. The plaintiff contended that its contract was still in effect because the mayor was not authorized by the city council to act alone in terminating contract. The city asserted that by its subsequent actions in receiving bids and awarding the contract to another company, it ratified the mayor's letter of termination.]

Ratification

Law

[2] As a general rule, a mayor acting alone is without power to execute a contract binding on the city in the absence of an ordinance or resolution by the governing

council authorizing him to do so. *Smith v. Town of Vinton*, 209 La. 587, 25 So.2d 237 (1946); *Daspit v. City of Alexandria*, 342 So.2d 683 (La.App. 3d Cir.1977), writ denied, 344 So.2d 1056 (La.1977).

[3] Ratification is a declaration whereby a person gives his consent to an obligation incurred on his behalf by another without authority. An express act of ratification must evidence the intention to be bound by the ratified obligation. Tacit ratification results when a person, with knowledge of an obligation incurred on his behalf by another, accepts the benefit of that obligation. La.C.C. Art. 1843.

[4] An unauthorized contract of an agent may be ratified by the subsequent action or inaction of the principal upon being apprised of the facts. *Louisiana Consumer's League, Inc. v. City of Baton Rouge*, 431 So.2d 35 (La.App. 1st Cir.1983), writ denied, 435 So.2d 431 (La.1983). The general theory of ratification of the unauthorized acts of an agent is that the principal, with full knowledge of the facts, consents to the unauthorized actions and adopts the contract as if it had been previously authorized. *Everett v. Foxwood Properties*, 584 So.2d 1233 (La.App.2d Cir.1991).

Discussion

[5] In late 1989, the Minden City Council appointed a committee to study the privatization of both residential and commercial trash collection. Although the 1982 contract with Sunray functionally privatized commercial collection, there was an apparent consensus that opening commercial collection to a free market would allow bidders on the residential collection to offer better prices if they had the chance to offer both types of collection. [. . . .]

[6] When the city council voted at its April 2, 1990 meeting to accept the recommendation of the sanitation committee, it specifically referred to privatizing both residential *and* commercial sanitation. [. . . .] The testimony of members of the city council and/or the sanitation committee reveals that they understood that the termination of the Sunray contract flowed from their decision to privatize both residential and commercial collection and that they approved the contents of the mayor's notice letter to Sunray. They were fully aware of the termination notice, and no effort was ever made to repudiate it. To the contrary, the city council proceeded ahead and awarded the contract for the residential collection to Waste Management.

[7] Inasmuch as we find that Mayor Brown's termination notice was tacitly ratified by the Minden City Council, we find no basis for rendering judgment against the City of Minden. Accordingly, we reverse the trial court judgment awarding damages in favor of Sunray.

[. . . .]

Questions

1. Did Sunray involve a case of "ratification," properly so called as that term is defined in Louisiana Civil Code article 1843? Why or why not? If not, was it

proper for the Court to apply the principles established in that and related articles in order to resolve the dispute before it? In doing so, what kind of "methodology" was the Court employing?

2. Problems of ratification most commonly arise in connection with the nominate contract of "mandate" (comparable to Anglo-American "agency"); to be more specific, in cases where the mandatary ("agent") "exceeds" the "authority" that has been conferred on him by his principal. *See* La. Civ. Code art. 2989, *et seq.* As a general rule, the principal is not bound to perform contracts that the mandatary, acting in excess of his authority, makes for him (*see* La. Civ. Code art. 3020) and, in such a case, the principal is not liable to the mandatary for any loss he may sustain (*see* La. Civ. Code art. 3008) unless the principal thereafter "ratifies" the contract.

State ex rel. Hebert

v.

Recorder of Mortgages et al.

Supreme Court of Louisiana
May 23, 1932
143 So. 15

ST. PAUL, J.

[1] Relator was the owner of certain real estate on which there was a homestead mortgage of $4,000. He made a nominal sale thereof to one Thiberville for the recited consideration of $1,500 cash and the assumption of said mortgage, which deed was duly recorded. In point of fact, this sale was simulated and made for convenience only. The supposed purchaser paid no cash and paid nothing on the mortgage which he nominally assumed, nor was he expected to do so. The vendor remained in possession of the property and continued to make his payments to the homestead. The supposed purchaser at once gave relator a counter letter acknowledging that he had no interest in the property and that same belonged to relator. But this counter letter was not registered.

I

[2] For some three years and more the property stood on the public records as belonging to Thiberville, who then retransferred it to relator, reciting the circumstances as above stated.

[3] But in the meanwhile, certain creditors of Thiberville had obtained judgments against him and had recorded same as judicial mortgages against all his property.

[4] It is not shown that Thiberville's creditors gave him credit or took judgments against him and recorded them with actual knowledge that the property stood in his name, or that they had any other knowledge than that which the law presumes from the fact that it stood as his upon the public records.

II

[5] This is a proceeding to cancel and erase from the records the inscription of said judicial mortgages in so far as they affect this property on the ground urged by relator that "recorded judgments against a simulated transferee of property do not operate as judicial mortgages against the property in the absence of circumstances creating an estoppel against the owner"; which seems to be an established principle in courts of equity and common law, but which the defendants contend is not the law of this state.

[6] The trial judge held with the defendants, and the relator appeals.

III

[7] Rev. Civ. Code, article 2239, reads as follows: "Counter letters can have no effect against creditors or bona fide purchasers. * * *"

[8] Rev. Civ. Code, article 2266, reads as follows: "All sales, contracts and judgments affecting immovable property, which shall not be so recorded [i.e. in the proper office], shall be utterly null and void, except between the parties thereto. The recording may be made at any time, but shall only affect third persons from the time of the recording. * * *"

[9] The creditors meant in Rev. Civ. Code. article 2230, are, of course, the creditors of the party giving the counter letter, and in whose name the property stands.

[10] And a counter letter relating to immovable property is, of course, a contract affecting immovable property, since it is the immovable property, since it is the acknowledgment of a natural obligation to restore the property to its true owner and a promise, express or implied, to do so.

IV

[11] Articles 2239 and 2266, Rev. Civ. Code, must therefore be read together. Counter letters duly recorded affect all persons even creditors from the time of the recording. Counter letters not recorded are "utterly null and void" except between the parties thereto.

[12] In Slark v. Broom, 9 La. Ann. 69, this court held that a counter letter (unrecorded) acknowledging that the price of a ship had not been paid in full, though the bill of sale so recited, could not be opposed to other creditors of the purchaser, or avail to claim a vendor's lien on the ship.

[13] In Tulane v. Levinson, 2 La. Ann. 787, this court held that the creditors of the vendor of an immovable could, by recording their judgment against him, obtain a valid judicial mortgage against the property, and could validly seize, sell, and buy in the property, although knowing that the property had been sold to another who had failed to record his deed in the proper office.

[14] In Harang v. Plattsmier, 21 La. Ann. 426, this court overruled Swan v. Moore, 14 La. Ann. 833, wherein it had been held that actual knowledge of an unrecorded title on the part of a creditor is equivalent to knowledge or notice resulting from

the registry of such title; and, referring to Acts of 1855, p. 335 (now Rev. Civ. Code, art. 2266), held that: "The lawgiver, it would seem, was determined to settle the vexed question, whether knowledge was equivalent to registry in Louisiana, and he declared that it was not." In First Nat. Bank v. Ft. Wayne Artificial Ice Co., 105 La. 133, 29 So. 379, 381, this court said: "We take it to be well settled under our law that, while a sale of immovable property may be good as between the parties by virtue of their agreement, it is void as to third persons until registered."

[15] In McDuffie v. Walker, 125 La. 152, 51 So. 100, this court held, that as to third persons, unrecorded acts affecting immovable property were so far nonexistent, that they might be deliberately ignored with entire good faith; for "It cannot, however, be said that a third person perpetrates a fraud merely by treating as void, as to himself, a contract which the law in terms declares 'shall be utterly null and void, except between the parties thereto;'" (just as had actually been done, and approved of by the court, in Tulane v. Levinson, supra). "To hold such doctrine is necessarily to hold that one who knows a particular contract to be denounced by the law as utterly void is bound in spite of the law to respect it as valid and binding, a paradox to which a court of justice would be unwilling to commit itself as an interpretation of law." And the court said further: "It is evident that whether a person acquires an interest in real estate to the extent of its value or part of its value as a mortgagee or as a vendee the principle involved in the application of the law of registry is the same; and hence if it be true that one may acquire a valid first mortgage, though he know at the time that as between the mortgagor and another there already exists an unrecorded mortgage upon the same property, it must also be true that one may acquire a valid title to such property, though he know that as between his vendor and another an unrecorded title has already been passed. The law makes no distinction between mortgages and sales or between creditors and vendees or mortgagees; nor does it discriminate between those who acquire property with knowledge of unrecorded contracts and those who acquire without such knowledge. Its purpose is to establish and enforce as a matter of public policy upon the subject of the most important property right with which it deals the rule that unrecorded contracts affecting immovable property "shall be utterly null and void, except between the parties thereto." No language could be plainer or more emphatic, and the courts have no more power to read into the rule established by it an exception, not contained in it, than they would have to read such an exception into the rule that a verbal sale of immovable property shall not affect third persons."

V

[16] We have cited these few cases out of the very large number holding to the same effect, because these case [*sic*] show that in this state registry is not a mere matter of notice alone, but a matter of public policy upon a "most important property right"; and that considerations of equity cannot prevail against it. "With us, those laws [of registry] are considered as founded on public policy, and the want of registry cannot be supplied. In the other States they are viewed differently, and notice in any form is held to be equivalent to registry." Lockett v. Toby, 10 La. Ann. 713, 715.

[17] The only case in which the contrary was held, to wit, that registry was only a matter of notice and not of public policy (Swan v. Moore, supra), was emphatically repudiated by legislative act in 1855 (Harang v. Plattsmier, supra), and by the uniform jurisprudence of this court ever since that time.

[18] Hence, all consideration of equity being banished, the creditors of a vendor who record judgments against him after he has sold the property but before the purchaser records his deed may not only ignore the purchaser with the unrecorded title, but acquire a judicial mortgage superior in rank to that of all judgment creditors of the purchaser without exception; since "there can be no actual owner of immovable property, so far as third persons are concerned, other than the owner of record; for, except as between the parties thereto, an unrecorded conveyance is 'utterly null and void,' and conveys no title." Baker v. Atkins, 107 La. 490, 32 So. 69, 70.

VI

[19] The equity doctrine on which relator relies is that a judgment creditor acquires no lien against property standing in the name of his judgment debtor, but in which that debtor has no beneficial interest, unless the judgment creditor can successfully plead an estoppel in pais against the actual owner of the property.

[20] But, as we have endeavored to show, registry is a matter of public policy in this state, against which considerations of equity cannot prevail; and "there can be no actual owner of immovable property, so far as third persons are concerned, other than the owner of record."

[21] It is true there are a few cases apparently out of harmony with the otherwise uniform jurisprudence of this court.

[22] Peters v. Toby, 10 La. Ann. 408, was decided in 1855 on a state of facts existing, and in litigation which had begun, long before the legislative act of that year. It is not authority under that legislation.

[23] The other cases (Broussard v. Le Blanc, 44 La. 880, 11 So. 460; Succession of Manson, 51 La. Ann. 130, 25 So. 639; Douglass v. Douglass, 51 La. Ann. 1455, 26 So. 546) were examined and distinguished in Baker v. Atkins, 107 La. 490, 32 So. 69, 72, in which it was said: "There is, no doubt, some language in these opinions which sustains the views which have been here considered [substantially those herein urged by relator], but we are of opinion that its application should be confined to the cases in which it was used, it being much safer at times to reason from general propositions to particular cases than the reverse."

[24] This case is governed by articles of the Louisiana Civil Code as they existed before the Civil Code revision of 1984, as all acts pertinent to this case occurred before the revision.

Questions

1. Paragraph 1: The *Hebert* court states that the sale out of which the case arose was "simulated." We studied the concept of "simulation" earlier in the

casebook. Which kind of simulation was involved in Hebert? What is the significance of that classification?

2. Paragraph 10: The court states that a counter-letter signed by the ostensible buyer of a simulated sale constitutes an "acknowledgment of a natural obligation to restore the property to its true owner," that is, the ostensible seller. We studied the concept of "natural obligation" earlier in the casebook. What do you think of the *Hebert* court's statement regarding the ostensible buyer's "natural obligation" to restore the property to the ostensible seller? Is this among the examples of natural obligations listed in Louisiana Civil Code article 1762? Does this supposed natural obligation conform to the account of natural obligations provided in Louisiana Civil Code article 1760?

3. The *Hebert* case concerns what is known as the "public records doctrine," a body of principles to which you have already been exposed. The public records doctrine is an important aspect of the law of "Sales and Leases." Since *Hebert* was decided, this body of principles has been codified. *See* La. Civ. Code art. 3338, *et seq.* Looking at the *Hebert* case, what would you say the "public records doctrine" has to do with the topic you are presently studying, that is, "proof of obligations"? Is it that, when juridical acts involving immovable property are involved, proof of the existence of rights and duties pertaining to that property requires that there be some written evidence of their existence in the public records? *See* La. Civ. Code art. 1839, par. 2.

Succession of Mrs. Allena Rogers Montgomery

Court of Appeal of Louisiana
Second Circuit
May 6, 1987
506 So.2d 1309

LINDSAY, Judge.

[1] On January 9, 1984, William Johnson, executor of the Succession of Allena Rogers Montgomery, filed with the succession a descriptive list of assets and liabilities. Listed under the liabilities is an unsecured note in the original amount of $128,525 executed by Allena Montgomery in favor of Thomas Montgomery. The amount of liability for the aforementioned note was recorded in the descriptive list as $0.00.

[2] On December 17, 1985, Thomas Montgomery filed a motion to traverse the descriptive list, seeking to have the descriptive list amended to include the amount allegedly remaining due on the note. The executor filed an opposition to the motion to traverse, claiming that the promissory note was issued without consideration. A hearing was held on January 2, 1986. At the conclusion of the hearing, the trial judge denied Thomas Montgomery's motion to traverse, and dismissed the action with prejudice, ruling that the note had been issued without consideration.

[3] Mr. Montgomery has appealed, raising the issues of whether the trial court properly admitted certain parol and documentary evidence, whether the evidence

supported the conclusion of the trial court and whether the trial court erred in rendering a judgment dismissing plaintiff's motion to traverse "with prejudice." For the following reasons, we affirm the trial court judgment.

[4] The record reveals that at the hearing on the motion to traverse the descriptive list, counsel for Mr. Montgomery introduced into evidence the promissory note in question, and an attached affidavit which had been executed by the decedent. In the affidavit, the affiant, Allena Montgomery, states that she has executed a promissory note in favor of her son, Thomas Montgomery, in the amount of $128,525 and that the consideration for the note is the money, groceries and other items furnished by her son since the death of her husband in 1959. Additionally, the affidavit recites that her son has also paid her accounts, paid taxes on real estate, provided transportation and managed her affairs. The notary before whom the affidavit was executed testified that the affidavit expressed the desires of the affiant. Mr. Montgomery did not testify, nor was he present at the hearing.

[5] William Johnson, the executor of the succession and the grandson of the deceased, testified that the note should not be listed in the descriptive list because he felt there was no real debt involved; i.e., there was no consideration for the note. To substantiate his belief, Mr. Johnson testified that Mrs. Allena Montgomery and her previously deceased husband donated land and a store to Thomas Montgomery in 1959 to compensate him for services rendered and to be rendered in caring for Mrs. Allena Montgomery. Mrs. Allena Montgomery's husband died five days after the act of donation was passed. Furthermore, on January 3, 1981, eight lots in Benton, Louisiana were sold by Mrs. Allena Montgomery to Thomas Montgomery for $2,000. Mr. Johnson felt that this price was substantially inadequate. Likewise, on June 6, 1981,[1] Allena Montgomery sold approximately 130 acres of land in Bossier Parish to Thomas Montgomery for $37,650. Mr. Johnson also felt that this was a substantially inadequate price. Certified copies of the various transactions were filed in evidence.

[6] Appellant contends that copies of the documents and the testimony of William Johnson were inadmissible. [....] [A]ppellant contends that the affidavit and note together constitute an act under private signature duly acknowledged which, at the time of execution, was equivalent to an authentic act and therefore full proof of its contents against the parties, their heirs or assigns. Thus, any evidence presented which would contradict the facts as established in the authentic act should be excluded as parol evidence.

---

1. Allena Montgomery's will and the note at issue are also dated June 6, 1981.

I. Admissibility of Evidence

[....]

[7] [**Appellant contends, among other things,**] that the note and affidavit constitute an act under private signature, duly acknowledged, and therefore other evidence cannot be admitted to contradict this "authenticated document."

[8] Under former Civil Code Article 2242,[2] an act under private signature, duly acknowledged has, between those who have subscribed to it, and their heirs and their assigns, the same credit as an authentic act. An authentic act is full proof of the agreement contained in it, against the contracting parties and their heirs or assigns, unless it be declared and proved a forgery. LSA-C.C. Art. 2236.[3]

[9] However, appellee contends that evidence of simulation and failure of consideration were admissible by virtue of former LSA-C.C. Art. 2239.[4] That article of the Code provides that forced heirs shall have the right to annul absolutely and by parol evidence the simulated contracts of those from whom they inherit, and they shall not be restricted to the legitime.

[10] Appellee is correct in asserting that LSA-C.C. Art. 2239 allows him, as executor of the succession and a forced heir, to attack an act of the deceased, even though in authentic form, by parol evidence to prove that the act is a simulated contract. *Smelley v. Ricks*, 174 La. 734, 141 So. 445 (1932); *Succession of Broussard*, 306 So.2d 399 (La.App. 3rd Cir.1975).

[11] The evidence was also admissible to show that the deceased has acted to deplete her estate through the use of a simulation to defeat the forced heirship laws of this state. *Smith v. Smith*, 239 La. 688, 119 So.2d 827 (1960).

[12] For the foregoing reasons, we conclude that the trial court correctly admitted Mr. Johnson's testimony concerning a lack of consideration, as well as the evidence of the other donations which the deceased made to Thomas Montgomery.

[....]

Questions

1. Throughout its opinion, the *Montgomery* court proceeds on the assumption that what it calls "lack of consideration" is an adequate "defense" to the enforcement of a "promissory note." Was that assumption correct? *See* La. Civ. Code art. 1966 & art. 1967. If "lack of consideration" is not a *per se* defense to the enforcement of the note, does it not, nevertheless, lay the basis for another attack on the enforceability of the note, for example, that the note was not in "proper form"? If the promissory note was not given "for consideration," then

---

2. This case is governed by articles of the Louisiana Civil Code as they existed before the Civil Code revision of 1984, as all acts pertinent to this case occurred before the revision

3. Id.

4. Id.

what kind of contract did it represent? Hint: *see* La. Civ. Code arts. 1909 &
1910. What does one call a gratuitous contract that transfers a thing? *See* La.
Civ. Code art. 1468. What form is required for such a contract? *See* La. Civ.
Code art. 1541.

2. *Montgomery* was decided under the "old law" of "proof of obligations." Under
the "new law," may one still use parol evidence in an effort to show that a
juridical act that has been documented in an authentic act was simulated? *See*
La. Civ. Code art. 1848.

Lane N. Meltzer
v.
Sarah A. Meltzer

Court of Appeal of Louisiana
Fourth Circuit
September 28, 1995
662 So.2d 58

WALTZER, Judge.

[. . . .]

Statement of Facts

**[1] [In connection with their divorce proceedings, Lane M. Meltzer (Lane) and
Sarah Allen Meltzer (Sarah) litigated the validity of a marriage contract entered
into by the parties prior to their marriage and later recorded. In this marriage
contract, Lane and Sarah rejected the community property regime. The litigation
is based on Sarah's denial]** that it was executed in the presence of a notary public
and two witnesses.

[. . . .]

[2] At the hearing on 26 July 1994, the parties to the contract, the notary public
before whom it was executed and the two witnesses testified.

[3] Louis G. Shushan, the notary and Lane's first cousin, testified that he has prac-
ticed law for forty-one years. He recognized the contract when it was shown to him,
but had no independent recollection of the contract from the time of its execution,
eighteen years previous. He identified his signature, and identified witness Linda
Condon as Lane's secretary at the time the contract was executed and identified witness Carol Lazaro as his own secretary for the last twenty-eight years. He recalled
that Sarah was represented at the time by attorney, now United States District Judge
Martin L.C. Feldman. He did not recall whether all parties were in his office at the
time the contract was executed. He said it was not unusual at the time for all the
parties not to be present at the same time when acts were executed. He testified that
if he signed this act, all of the signatories came into his office and signed it. He testified that he had no reason to believe that he did not follow the requisite procedure of
having each party and witness sign before him.

[4] Sarah testified that Lane presented the contract to her about two weeks before their wedding date, and suggested she take it to a lawyer to "have him check it out." Sarah testified that she took the contract to Feldman, whom she described as her lawyer and a friend. She admitted having had the opportunity to obtain legal advice in connection with the contract. She admitted having signed the contract, but testified that she did so outside the presence of Mr. Shushan, in "Shepard's office"[1] on the 31st floor 1010 Common Street in New Orleans. She testified that Mr. Shushan's office was on the 5th floor of the same building, but that her first visit to Mr. Shushan's office occurred after her marriage to Lane in conjunction with the sale of a parcel he had acquired with his first wife. Sarah denied that Linda Condon was present when she signed the contract, and denied ever having met Carol Lazaro.

[5] Sarah testified that during her marriage to Lane she maintained a separate account into which she deposited the income she received from her property, and to which Lane had no access. It is uncontroverted that during the entire seventeen year existence of their marriage, Lane and Sarah conducted their financial affairs in conformity with the terms of the Matrimonial Agreement.

[6] Lane testified that the contract was prepared by Mr. Shushan's office. He gave it to Sarah, to be reviewed by her attorney. Sarah told him she had talked to her attorney about the contractual provisions and was prepared to sign it. It was Lane's understanding that the contract provided that his and Sarah's properties were separate, and what was his remained his, and what was hers would remain hers. Lane could not recall who was present when the contract was signed, and recalled that it was signed in Shepard's office. Lane testified, and Sarah admitted, that she eventually left him. He testified that he had feared she would leave him as she had left her two former husbands.

[7] Linda Condon testified that in 1976 she was secretary of a partnership in which Lane had an interest. Her recollection was that she signed the Marriage Contract in Lane's office. She did not recall if Mr. Shushan or Ms. Lazaro were present, although she did recall Mr. Shushan's coming to Lane's office from time to time. She testified that Mr. Shushan's office was on the 15th floor and Lane's office was on the 31st floor of the 1010 Common Street Building.

[8] Carol Lazaro testified that she has been Mr. Shushan's legal secretary for twenty-seven years, and had no recollection of the actual signing of the Marriage Contract. She testified that she was sure she met Sarah when the contract was signed. Ms. Lazaro testified that she believed the Marriage Contract was executed by the parties in front of the witnesses. According to Ms. Lazaro, Mr. Shushan was careful that all requisites for a notarial act were met, particularly after his involvement in the Louis Johnson case in late 1975 or early 1976 wherein Mr. Shushan was required to prove in court that he had met the codal requirements for the execution of an authentic act.

---

1. The reference is to Shepard Latter. According to Mr. Shushan, Latter died in 1973.

[9] In its Reasons for Judgment, the trial court found:

> Of the five [witnesses], Mrs. Meltzer was the only one to claim that she recalled the circumstances surrounding the execution of the document nearly seventeen years ago. She stated that she signed the document in the office of Shepard Latter at 1010 Common Street with only Lane Meltzer present. However, this testimony was weakened by her failure to recall another incident which occurred soon after the execution of the Marriage Contract.

SPECIFICATION OF ERROR: *The trial court was clearly wrong in finding that Sarah Meltzer did not prove the Marriage Contract was null.*

[10] Sarah contends that she offered sufficient proof that the execution of the Marriage Contract did not comply with the formal requisites set forth in La.C.C. art. 2328, which provided in 1976 that every matrimonial agreement must be made by an act before a notary and two witnesses.

[11] Plaintiff's burden of disproving the validity of an authentic act is indeed heavy. Planiol wrote:

> The person who produces an authentic act, regular in appearance, does not need to prove its authenticity. The act comes accompanied by exterior signs difficult to imitate . . . These exterior signs suffice. As Dumoulin said in speaking of this kind of writing: "*Scripta publica probant se ipsa.*" As a result, the public act which is regular in appearance, enjoys a presumption of authenticity, which reverses on this point the burden of proof: if the attribution of the act to its apparent author is contested, the latter who offers it has nothing to prove; it is for his adversary who denies the authenticity to demonstrate the falsity of the act, and he *cannot make this proof except by the perilous means of the "inscription de faux" (above Nos. 83–85).*[2] Planiol, *Traité Elémentaire de Droit Civil*, Vol. 2, No. 88. (Emphasis added.)

[12] In the case at bar, Sarah does not contend that the Matrimonial Agreement was forged. Neither does she contend that she or Lane or the witnesses or the notary did not sign the document, nor that it was procured through any vice of consent such as duress, fraud or error. She admits that she had two weeks within which to consult with her own able counsel, Judge Feldman, and to determine whether she would renounce during this, her third marriage, the benefits and responsibilities of the community property regime then in effect in Louisiana. Sarah's only basis for reversing seventeen years of financial activity based upon a separate property regime is not that any signature, including her own, on the document is forged or fraudulently obtained or otherwise not authentic, but rather that she signed the document in the presence only of her then fiancé.

---

2. The "*inscription de faux*" is the name of a special procedure which serves to establish that an instrument has been forged. Planiol, *supra*, Vol. 2, No. 83.

[13] Historically, the reason for the requirement of execution of the marriage contract before a notary and for its recordation was to protect the sanctity of the agreement from the danger that a contract under private signature, not recorded, could easily be destroyed and the matrimonial agreement inevitably changed through the obligatory application of statutory community. Planiol, *supra*, Vol. 3, No. 806.[3]

[14] Planiol notes the significance of predictability in his discussion of the effect of these contracts on third parties dealing with married persons. Absent a recorded contract, "people were afraid to deal with married persons who claimed they had marriage contract [sic]; thus even spouses in good faith had their credit jeopardized." Planiol, *supra*, Vol. 3, No. 809. In the instant case, where the parties owned, bought and sold substantial real estate holdings, this aspect, the immutability of the marriage contract, is most significant.

[15] The Louisiana Civil Code defines an authentic act:

> An authentic act is a writing executed before a notary public . . . in the presence of two witnesses, and signed by each party who executed it, by each witness, and by the notary public before whom it was executed.

> To be an authentic act, the writing need not be executed at one time or place, or before the same notary public or in the presence of the same witnesses, provided that each party who executes it does so before a notary public, . . . and in the presence of two witnesses and each party, each witness, and each notary public signs it. . . . La.C.C. art. 1833.[4]

[16] This Court interpreted these formal requirements in the context of an antenuptial marriage contract, holding:

> All that the law requires [for the validity of an authentic act] is that the notary and witnesses be present, C.C. 2328, when each contracting party signs the act, C.C. 2234, and that notary and witnesses themselves also sign the act, although not necessarily at the time that any party signs it. Accordingly, the act before us is not invalid because of the simple facts that the husband and wife in this case did not execute the act in the presence of each other, and that the notary and witnesses did not sign the act at the time that one (or either) party signed it.

> Our basic reasoning is that substance should prevail over form unless the law unmistakably requires a contrary result. Here the mature spouses-to-be must be presumed to have desired and consented to the exact agreement contained in the written instrument. The law only requires that the

---

3. This immutability of the matrimonial agreement in French law was a fundamental principle: the will of the parties expressed prior to the marriage was regarded as sacred and worthy of protection against subsequent assault by a party seeking institution of the statutory community system. *See,* Planiol, *supra,* Vol. 3, Nos. 813–814.

4. Acts 1984, No. 331, sec. 1, effective 1 January 1985. According to Comment (a) to the present article, this Article reproduces the substance of C.C. Art. 2234 (1870), and does not change the law.

agreement be "made by an act before a notary and two witnesses," C.C. 2328: such an act is an authentic act, C.C. 2234, "executed before a notary public . . . , in the presence of two witnesses. . . ." Nowhere does the law expressly require that the notary and the witnesses sign the act in the presence of the parties,. . . .

[17] *Rittiner v. Sinclair*, 374 So.2d 680, 685 (La.App. 4th Cir.1978). *See also, Nunez v. Nunez*, 436 So.2d 682, 683 at footnote 1 (La.App. 4th Cir.1983).

[18] An authentic act in Louisiana, as under the French Code, is presumed to be valid, and this presumption is established in the interest of public order, to maintain peace among men and to prevent contestations concerning the proof or evidence of their conventions. *Succession of Tete*, 7 La.Ann. 95, 96 (La.1852).

[19] Where, as here, the memories of the signatories are blurred by the passage of time, one seeking to invalidate an apparently authentic act must present strong and convincing proof of such magnitude as to overcome the presumption of verity of notarial acts. *DiVincenti v. McIntyre*, 611 So.2d 140, 142 (La.App. 1st Cir.1992), *writ denied* 614 So.2d 1264 (La.1993).

[20] Sarah does not contend that any of the five signatories failed to sign the Marriage Contract or that any of the signatures were obtained by fraud, mistake or duress. Neither did she offer any proof that Lane's signature was not signed in the presence of the notary and two witnesses. As to her own signature, only Sarah testified to an exact recollection of the signing process, and her testimony standing alone, even if accepted by the trier of fact, would be insufficient to overcome the presumption of validity. *See, DiVincenti*, 611 So.2d at 141–143.

[21] We are mindful that a marriage contract should be maintained if possible. *Id.* At the time of the execution of the Marriage Contract, Sarah was thirty-seven years old, twice divorced, and represented by able independent counsel. Lane, seventeen years her senior, was likewise represented. The notary was an experienced practitioner who had recently been required to offer proof in court that another of his notarial authentic acts had been properly executed. The record is devoid of any proof, even were we to consider Sarah's testimony, which was rejected by the trial court, that the Rittiner standard was not met.

[22] The trial judge, who observed the witnesses, chose not to accept Sarah's testimony. This credibility determination can virtually never be manifestly erroneous, and we find it to have been within the sound discretion of the trier of fact. *Stobart v. State of Louisiana, through Dept. of Transp. and Development*, 617 So.2d 880, 882 (La.1993); *Rosell v. ESCO*, 549 So.2d 840, 844 (La.1989). We will not disturb that credibility choice.

[23] Sarah's testimony having been rejected by the trial court, we turn to the testimony of the remaining witnesses. The trial court accepted Mr. Shushan's testimony that he had no reason to believe he did not follow the requisite procedure in the execution of the Marriage Contract, and found support in Ms. Lazaro's testimony that she was sure that the parties and other witness came to Mr. Shushan's

office to execute the document because it was his practice to have everyone present in his office when notarized documents were executed. The trial court found this testimony to have been bolstered by Mr. Shushan's participation in prior litigation concerning the validity of an authentic act. The trial judge found that Ms. Condon did not recall the circumstances of the execution. We find these conclusions to be supported by the record taken as a whole. Sarah relies on Lane's testimony that he could not refute her testimony as an admission by Lane of the truth of her version of the signing; however, a careful reading of the record shows that Lane testified that he had no specific recollection of the signing, and, therefore, could not conscientiously say that her testimony was incorrect. We cannot equate a failure to remember with corroboration of an adverse party's testimony.

[24] The trial court concluded that the evidence offered by Sarah as a whole did not support by a reasonable preponderance of the evidence that the Marriage Contract was not an authentic act. We find this conclusion to be supported by the record as a whole, and find no manifest error in the trial court's determination.

[25] We affirm the trial court's judgment finding that Sarah A. Meltzer failed to prove by a reasonable preponderance of the evidence that the Marriage Contract executed by and between Lane Meltzer and Sarah Allen on 10 November 1976 was invalid.

[26] *AFFIRMED.*

Questions

1. From the point of view of the *Meltzer* Court, what was the fundamental "problem" with Sarah's case? Was it (1) that the "defect" in the creation of the act that she alleged — that she had not signed the act in the presence of the notary and witnesses — was not, by itself, sufficient to render the act invalid or (2) that she simply lacked sufficient proof of this alleged defect? If it is the latter, then what is one to make of the Court's repeated statements that Sarah alleged neither "forgery" nor "vice of consent"?

2. The *Meltzer* Court seems to have assumed that an act that purports to be in authentic form carries with it a presumption that the process whereby the act was produced was, in fact, "regular" — that is, that it was signed by each party before the notary and witnesses, etc. Does the applicable legislation support this assumption? Consider, in particular, Louisiana Civil Code article 1835, which provides that an authentic act constitutes "full proof of the agreement it contains." Is the process for preparing an authentic act part of "the agreement" the act contains? If not, then what is the basis for the Court's assumption? Is it "doctrine," as represented by Planiol? Prior jurisprudence?

Section II — Testimonial Proof

Case

Snow-White Roofs, Inc.
v.
Frank Boucher and Robert Coppage

Court of Appeal of Louisiana
Fourth Circuit
February 7, 1966
182 So.2d 846

SAMUEL, Judge.

[1] [Plaintiff contractor sued owners of residence for, among other things, the contract price. Defendant denied liability and asked, alternatively, for a reduction of the contract price for roof repair work not completed by the plaintiff.]

[. . . .]

[2] The fact that in performing its work under the contract plaintiff did "snow white" the roof (a process discussed later in this opinion) and did not repair the leaks is undisputed. The appeal is based on plaintiff's contention that under the terms of the contract it was not obligated to repair leaks in the roof, that the contract must be enforced as written and that the trial judge was in error in admitting parol evidence which had the effect of placing plaintiff under that added obligation. Plaintiff had made timely objections to that evidence.

[3] Under our Civil Code and jurisprudence parol evidence cannot be admitted against or beyond what is contained in a written contract; such evidence is inadmissible to vary, alter or add to the contract's terms. LSA-C.C. Art. 2276; Dufrene v. Tracy, 232 La. 386, 94 So.2d 297; Rosenthal v. Cauthier, 224 La. 341, 69 So.2d 367; Reuter v. Reuter's Succession, 206 La. 474, 19 So.2d 209. However, where there are ambiguities in a written contract, parol evidence is admissible to clarify those ambiguities by showing the intention of the parties. See Rosenthal v. Gauthier, supra; Rudman v. Dupuis, 206 La. 1061, 20 So.2d 363; Holloway Gravel Co. v. McKowen, 200 La. 917, 9 So.2d 228.

[4] The contract in the instant case is on one of plaintiff's printed forms. It does state that "Snow-White is not a water proofing" and it does make reference to a plaintiff brochure which accompanied the contract. The brochure sets out the work to be done in connection with the "Snow White Service". The repair of roof leaks is not included as part of the work as set out in the brochure. There appears in handwriting (all unprinted portions of the contract are in handwriting) on the first page of the contract, immediately below the name of the defendant-agent and the address of the premises upon which the work was to be done, the phrase "Residence to be Repaired and Snow White Coated". The approximate area to be covered by the work

is stated as being the "Entire Roof Area". The contract was signed by the defendant-agent, a realtor, and by a representative of the plaintiff.

[5] The president of the plaintiff corporation, that party's only witness, testified relative to the purposes of "snow whiting" a roof and that testimony appears to be consistent with the printed terms of the contract and brochure. His testimony was to the effect that the process beautifies, reduces the cost of air conditioning, and secures gravel on the type of roof here involved; it does not waterproof or repair leaks. However, this witness also testified that the plaintiff corporation occasionally did do other types of roofing work, including the repairing of leaks, when called for by the contract.

[6] Clearly the contractual phase, "Residence to be Repaired and Show White Coated", calls for more than the snow whiting process. The word "Repaired" is in addition to that process and is ambiguous in that the type of repair is not specified. This case therefore falls under the exception to the rule we have set out above and parol evidence was properly admitted to explain the repairs intended by the parties.

[7] The evidence admitted for this purpose consisted only of testimony given by witnesses on behalf of the defendants. Those witnesses were the defendant-agent, his secretary, and the tenant who occupied the premises. The plaintiff's representative, who had negotiated and signed the contract on behalf of plaintiff, was deceased at the time of trial. The testimony thus adduced establishes the fact that the parties intended to enter into a contract which included repairing leaks in the roof. In short summary that testimony was to the following effect:

[8] The defendant-agent was informed by the tenant that the roof was leaking and needed repairs. He contacted several roofing contractors asking for bids or prices. He also contacted plaintiff, obtaining his information as to that corporation from the classified section of the local telephone directory and eventually entered into the contract here involved. At the time he discussed the matter with plaintiff's representative he informed that person he wished to have the leaks repaired and was told by the representative that the leaks would be repaired as a part of the contract. The leaks were not repaired and the roof continued to leak after plaintiff's work had been completed. The leaks were later repaired by another contractor at a cost of $165.

[9] Our conclusion is that, insofar as plaintiff's appeal is concerned, the judgment must be affirmed.

[....]

Question

1. Does the jurisprudential rule on which the *Snow-White* court based its analysis — "where there are ambiguities in a written contract, parol evidence is admissible to clarify those ambiguities by showing the intention of the parties" — constitute an "exception," properly so called, to the general legislative rule that "[t]estimonial or other evidence may not be admitted to negate or vary the contents of an authentic act or an act under private signature"

(*see* La. Civ. Code art. 1848, sent. 1)? If so, then why is it not included among the legislative exceptions to that general rule that are collected in the second sentence of that same article? If not, then what is the nature of the relationship between the jurisprudential rule and the general legislative rule?

Section III — Presumptions

Case

Lloyd Jackson, Sr., et al.
v.
Gulf Insurance Company et al.

Supreme Court of Louisiana
June 5, 1967
199 So.2d 886

SANDERS, Justice.

[1] This action for damages Ex delicto poses the question of whether the disserving testimony of a plaintiff as to the circumstances of an automobile accident bars his recovery as a judicial confession or conclusive admission, despite other preponderating evidence supporting the liability of the defendant. [. . . .]

[2] On November 3, 1962, Lloyd Jackson, Sr., Lena Porea, and Kathleen Lee, plaintiffs herein, were guest passengers in an automobile driven by Lloyd Jackson, Jr. and insured by Gulf Insurance Company. The automobile collided with a pickup truck owned by H. A. Folse Sons and insured by Maryland Casualty Company. At the time of the accident, a Folse employee was driving the truck. He was accompanied by two boys, who were distributing circular advertisements.

[. . . .]

[3] Lloyd Jackson, Sr. and Kathleen Lee, who were riding in the front seat of the automobile, testified they first saw the truck approaching when the two vehicles were about a block apart. At that time each vehicle was moving at a reasonable speed in its proper lane. After the vehicles were very close to each other, so they testified, the truck suddenly swerved across the center of the highway, striking the automobile in its lane of travel.

[4] The testimony of plaintiff Lena Porea corroborated that of the other plaintiffs in some respects, but her testimony failed to completely absolve the automobile driver from negligence.

[5] The three occupants of the truck testified at the trial. Having been injured in the collision, one of the delivery boys was unable to recall the details of the accident. But the combined testimony of the driver and the other delivery boy was to the effect that at the time of the collision the truck was stopped partially off the highway

on the proper side, while one of the delivery boys picked up some circulars that had blown off the truck. The approaching automobile drove across the highway and hit the stopped truck. The record contains other testimony showing that after the collision there were skid or tire marks running from the automobile's travel lane to the impact point on the truck's side of the road.

[6] The trial court found that the automobile crossed the highway and hit the stopped truck, as related by the truck driver and his corroborating witnesses. The court dismissed the suit against the truck driver's insurer, Maryland Casualty Company. The court also dismissed the plaintiffs' suit against the other defendant, Gulf Insurance Company, insurer of the automobile driver, on the ground that the plaintiffs were "precluded from recovery * * * because they testified to no acts of negligence" on the part of the automobile driver. The court held that their testimony operated as a judicial confession under LSA-C.C. Article 2291, barring recovery since it exonerated the automobile driver from negligence. The plaintiffs appealed.

[7] In the Court of Appeal, the plaintiffs attacked the trial court judgment rejecting their demands against Gulf Insurance Company, the insurer of the automobile driver. The Court of Appeal partially reversed and granted recovery to plaintiff Lena Porea, finding that her testimony did not completely exonerate the automobile driver from negligence. The Court of Appeal affirmed the judgment insofar as it rejected the demands of the other plaintiffs, finding that their testimony did exonerate their host driver from negligence. The court held this testimony was a judicial confession under LSA-C.C. Article 2291, barring the plaintiffs' recovery despite a finding that the host driver was at fault in the accident. See La.App., 188 So.2d 84. On application of the unsuccessful plaintiffs, we granted certiorari to review the Court of Appeal judgment. See 249 La. 771, 191 So.2d 144.

[8] We agree with the Court of Appeal's finding of fact and find the collision resulted from the fault of the automobile driver. The Court of Appeal also found that plaintiffs-relators testified that the truck suddenly swerved into the automobile's lane and struck the automobile, contrary to the court's finding. From our review of the testimony, we conclude the plaintiffs testified to facts which, if accepted by the court, would exonerate their host driver from fault.

[9] Article 2291 of the Louisiana Civil Code provides:

"The judicial confession is the declaration which the party, or his special attorney in fact, makes in a judicial proceeding.

"It amounts to full proof against him who has made it.

"It can not be divided against him.

"It can not be revoked, unless it be proved to have been made through an error in fact.

"It can not be revoked on a pretense of an error in law."

[10] The defendant-respondent contends that this Article applies to the present case and that plaintiffs' factual testimony exonerating the automobile driver from

fault is a judicial confession which bars their recovery. The respondent relies upon a series of cases in the intermediate courts of appeal, including Thompson v. Haubtman, 18 La.App. 119, 137 So. 362 (1931); Stroud v. Standard Accident Insurance Co., La.App., 90 So.2d 477 (1956); Bowers v. Hardware Mutual Casualty Co., La.App., 119 So.2d 671 (1960); and Franklin v. Zurich Ins. Co., La.App., 136 So.2d 735 (1962).

[11] The plaintiffs-relators contend Article 2291 is inapplicable to an automobile accident suit. They assert the Article applies only to proof of conventional obligations, or contracts, since it is found in Title IV of the Civil Code relating to conventional obligations and in a chapter entitled, "Of the Proof of Obligations and of That of Payment." Alternatively, they assert that the disserving testimony of the plaintiffs does not bar their recovery, because the court found the host driver was in fact guilty of negligence causing the accident.

[12] The initial question framed by these contentions is whether LSA-C.C. Article 2291 applies to a suit for damages arising from a delict, or tort.

[13] The Article, of course, is in Title IV of the Louisiana Civil Code dealing with conventional obligations. It forms part of Chapter 6, entitled, "Of the Proof of Obligations and of That of Payment." This chapter, however, contains a number of articles of general application. For example, Article 2282 deals with the competency of witnesses; Article 2283, with the attorneyclient [*sic*] privilege; Article 2284, with legal presumptions; and Article 2286, with res judicata. See, generally, Saunders' Lectures on the Civil Code (Bonomo ed., 1925) p. 460.

[14] Article 2291 contains no language delimiting it to proof of conventional obligations. The Article refers generally to "a judicial proceeding." This Court has long recognized that the Article applies to judicial proceedings other than those involving the proof of a contractal [*sic*] obligation. See, e.g., Penn v. Burk, 244 La. 267, 152 So.2d 16 (suit to enjoin executory process); D'Antoni v. Geraci, 224 La. 818, 70 So.2d 883 (divorce action); and Sanderson v. Frost, 198 La. 295, 3 So.2d 626 (petitory action). We conclude that Article 2291 applies to the present delictual action.

[15] More difficult is the question of whether the disserving factual testimony of a party-witness is a judicial confession under Article 2291, barring recovery despite a contrary judicial finding of facts consistent with the defendant's liability.

[16] Some appellate decisions, without analyzing the history and purpose of the Article, have assumed that a party's disserving factual testimony amounts to a judicial confession, inexorably binding the party irrespective of preponderating evidence to the contrary. The underlying notion seems to be that a party who has testified incorrectly against himself should lose his case. See Franklim v. Zurich Insurance Co. and Thompson v. Haubtman, supra. This Court has never passed upon the question, though in the recent case of Reynolds v. Hardware Mutual Casualty Company, 249 La. 268, 186 So.2d 588, we expressed serious doubt that Article 2291 applies to a party's testimonial recitation of facts.

[17] The codal text relating to the judicial confession (l'aveu judiciaire) emanates from Article 1356 of the Code Napoleon. Imported from that code, the text became

part of Louisiana's first Civil Code, See C.C.1808, p. 314, Art. 257. Succeeding codes retained the test without substantial change.

[18] Like the Code Napoleon, the Louisiana Codes classified the judicial confession as a distinct method of proof. C.N. 1804, Art. 1316; C.C.1808, p. 304, Art. 216; C.C.1825, Art. 2230; C.C.1870, Art. 2233. Article 2233 of the present Code classifies the methods of proof as the literal proof, the testimonial proof, the presumption, and the confession of the party.

[19] Under the original Code Napoleon, only a witness could give Testimony. A party litigant could offer proof only by Admissions and Oaths. 2 Planiol, Civil Law Treatise (Translation by Louisiana State Law Institute) No. 17.

[20] The judicial admission, or confession, was a party's express acknowledgement of the correctness of "the fact or the act charged against him" by his adversary. 2 Planiol, supra, No. 24. In practice, the judicial confession was incorporated in a formal act. See 20 Laurent, Droit Civil Francois, s 166, p. 196 (3d ed. 1878). Such a confession amounted to full proof and dispensed with testimony. 2 Planiol, supra, Nos. 22–29.

[21] Party oaths under the Code Napoleon represented a formal system designed to test the truth when the testimony was unsatisfactory. Planiol, supra, Nos. 31–35. This system was never fully adopted in Louisiana.

[22] At the time Louisiana adopted the judicial confession principle, the Civil Code disqualified a party litigant as a witness, because of his interest in the cause. C.C.1808, p. 312, Art. 248; Pugh, Evidence, 23 La.L.Rev. pp. 407–408. The Code restricted proof by party oath to interrogatories on facts and articles. C.C.1808, p. 316, Art. 258. Article 259 of the Louisiana Civil Code of 1808 specifically defined the interrogatory on facts and articles as written questions propounded to the opposite party endeavoring to obtain from the party's avowals (les aveux) some proof respecting the object of the litigation. Article 263 provided that the answer, that is, the avowal elicited by this formal procedure, formed complete proof against the responding party. Thus, the avowal dispensed with the production of evidence.

[23] The disqualification of a party litigant as a witness continued in Article 2260 of the Civil Code of 1825. See Beer v. Word, Asher & Co., 13 La.Ann. 467 (1858); Baudoin v. Nicholas, 12 Rob, 594 (1846); and Brander v. Ferriday, Bennett & Co., 16 La. 296 (1840). By 1867, witness disqualification because of interest in the cause had been removed through amendment of the Code Article. See Act 71 of 1867 and Act 204 of 1868.

[24] The Civil Code of 1825 omitted Articles 258 to 264 of the 1808 Code, dealing with proof by oath of a party through interrogatories on facts and articles. The codifiers relegated this series of articles to a code of evidence then being prepared. See Volume I, Louisiana Legal Archives, p. 290. At the same time, they retained in the Civil Code the judicial confession article, which immediately preceded the articles suppressed. See C.C.1825, Art. 2270.

[25] This historical analysis clearly points to a conclusion that the judicial confession is distinct from a party's factual testimony. The Louisiana codes have distinguished the confession of a party from testimonial proof. Furthermore, during the formative period of the confession rule, a party litigant was generally incompetent to testify as a witness.

[26] As a legal concept, the judicial confession is designed to dispense with evidence. It has the effect of withdrawing the subject matter of the confession from issue. See Sanderson v. Frost, 198 La. 295, 3 So.2d 626 and Farley v. Frost-Johnson Lumber Co., 133 La. 497, 63 So. 122, L.R.A.1915A, 200. In the landmark case of Frost-Johnson Lumber Co., supra, this Court pointed out that Article 2291 refers only to the confession made in the suit, that is, in the pleadings or note of evidence, "for the purpose of dispensing from taking evidence * * *."

[27] As noted in Coleman v. Jones & Pickett, 131 La. 803, 60 So. 243, it is of the nature of this kind of admission that it be, by intention, an act of waiver relating to the opponent's proof and not merely an assertion made for some independent purpose, such as a statement made for the purpose of giving testimony.

[28] See also Pugh, Evidence, 23 La.L.Rev. 406–408. For the common-law view of this subject, see McCormick On Evidence, ss 239, 243 (1954) and 9 Wigmore, Evidence, ss 2588, 2594A (3d ed. 1940).

[29] A judicial confession under Article 2291 is a party's admission, or concession, in a judicial proceeding of an adverse factual element, waiving evidence as to the subject of the admission. A party's testimony is offered as evidence, not as a waiver of it. To be an effective agency of truth, the trier of fact must be allowed to weigh the disserving testimony of a party, as well as other evidence. When the truth is found elsewhere, the party's disserving testimony must yield in order to achieve the ends of justice. Hence, we reject as unsound the several expressions of the Courts of Appeal tending to equate a party's disserving factual testimony with a judicial confession.[2]

[30] We hold that the plaintiffs' disserving testimony is not a judicial confession or conclusive admission. Hence, they are entitled to recover.

[31] Heretofore, we have remanded cases to the Court of Appeal to fix damages when that court has failed to pass upon the issue. See Felt v. Price, 240 La. 966, 126 So.2d 330, and the cases therein cited. We will remand this case to permit the Court of Appeal to fix damages.

[32] For the reasons assigned, the judgment of the Court of Appeal is reversed. Judgment is rendered in favor of the plaintiffs against the defendant, Gulf Insurance Company, in such sums as may hereafter be fixed, and the case is remanded to the

2. These cases include *Thompson v. Haubtman*, 18 La.App. 119, 137 So. 362 (cert. denied 1932); *Stroud v. Standard Accident Ins. Co.*, La.App., 90 So.2d 477; *Bowers v. Hardware Mutual Casualty Co.*, La.App., 119 So.2d 671; and *Franklin v. Zurich Ins. Co.*, La.App., 136 So.2d 735 (cert. denied 1962). The results reached in these cases are not necessarily erroneous.

Court of Appeal, Fourth Circuit, for the assessment of damages according to law. The defendant is condemned to pay all costs of court.

Questions

1. The first issue presented in *Jackson* is whether the rule of former Louisiana Civil Code article 2291 (*see* current La. Civ. Code art. 1853) applied to proof of delictual obligations. The plaintiffs, who contended that the article did not so apply, constructed an argument based on the structural arrangement of the Code: their premise was that this article appears in the part of the Code that pertains to "conventional obligations"; their conclusion, therefore, was that this article applies only to conventional, as opposed to delictual, etc., obligations. What kind of methodological argument is this? *Jackson* was decided under the old law of proof of obligations; under the new law, which side — the plaintiffs or the defendants — would the structure-of-the-code argument favor? In what part of the Code is the new article situated?

2. Paragraphs 16-25: The second issue presented in *Jackson* is whether a party's "disserving" testimony may constitute a judicial confession against him. How would you characterize, methodologically speaking, the first argument that the *Jackson* Court makes in support of its answer to this question? Once again, *Jackson* was decided under "old law"; would the case be decided the same way under "new law"?

Part Three

Quasi-Contracts

Chapter 1

Quasi-Contracts

Section I — Contract and Quasi-Contract

Doctrine

Louisiana Law of Obligations in General, A Précis

Section 1.1.2

Some obligations arise without an agreement between persons when they result from the lawful and voluntary act of one person, from which an obligation may be created for the benefit of a third person or, sometimes, a reciprocal obligation between two or more persons. **LSA-C.C. Art. 1757** lists two quasi-contractual obligations: the management of the affairs of another (*negotiorum gestio*) and unjust enrichment. The latter is then rephrased under the more technical civil law title of "Enrichment Without Cause." One will find under "Enrichment Without Cause," the statement of a general principle and the legal regime of another quasi-contractual relationship known as the "Payment of a Thing Not Owed" (*condictio indebiti*).

Cases

National Crankshaft Company
v.
Natural Gas Industries, Inc., James H. Hoag, Liquidator, and James H. Hoag, Individually, in Solido

Supreme Court of Louisiana
June 8, 1964
165 So.2d 1

HAWTHORNE, Justice.

[1] National Crankshaft Company instituted this suit against Natural Gas Industries, Inc., James H. Hoag, Liquidator, and James H. Hoag, individually, in solido, seeking judgment for $923.18, the purchase price of a crankshaft alleged to have been sold and delivered to Natural Gas Industries. The defendants deny that this crankshaft was purchased from the plaintiff and averred that it was purchased from

a different company, National Welding & Grinding Company, with which they had a 25 per cent discount arrangement and which owed them an adjustment for work previously done. The Court of Appeal, Second Circuit, affirmed a judgment of the city court of Shreveport rejecting plaintiff's demand, 158 So.2d 370, and plaintiff's application for writ of review was granted by this court.

[2] John N. Brantley, superintendent of the defendant Natural Gas Industries, by a telephone call from Tatem, Texas, on January 11, 1962, placed an order for a crankshaft, with instructions that it be shipped to Olla, Louisiana. He called the listed telephone number of National Welding & Grinding Company in Dallas, Texas, and assumed that he was speaking to John H. Hudson, sales engineer of National Welding. Mr. Hudson, however, denied that he had received the call or that National Welding & Grinding Company had sold the defendant the crankshaft; he stated that the defendant corporation did not owe National Welding any sum whatever for the crankshaft, and that his company and the plaintiff National Crankshaft Company are separate corporations. The general manager of the plaintiff National Crankshaft testified that the telephone order was placed with him, and explained that the call was transferred to him because National Welding was in the business of repairing crankshafts but not of selling them.

[3] In due course the crankshaft was received and accepted by defendant at Olla, Louisiana. The crankshaft was shipped via Braswell Freight Lines and was accompanied by a freight bill to which was attached a duplicate invoice of National Crankshaft. The freight bill disclosed that the shipper was the plaintiff National Crankshaft, and the invoice which accompanied the freight bill showed this company to be the seller. According to the testimony, the freight receipt was signed by an employee of the defendant Natural Gas, and the invoice was delivered to him at the time of the delivery of the crankshaft. Mr. Brantley, superintendent of defendant Natural Gas Industries, admitted receiving the invoice, which passed over his desk, and admitted noticing that it was from National Crankshaft, but said that he refused to approve it for payment because his company was not allowed a 25 per cent discount.

[4] On May 25, 1962, plaintiff wrote the defendant Natural Gas that its account of $923.18 was more than 90 days past due. Again on June 28 plaintiff advised defendant that its previous letter concerning the past due account had gone unanswered, and demanded payment or satisfactory arrangements within 10 days of receipt of this last letter.

[5] Defendants admit the receipt of the crankshaft, and testified that it had been incorporated into their machinery and was actually in use at the time the case was tried below.

[6] As stated by the Court of Appeal, how the mixup occurred in receiving and handling the order is not satisfactorily explained by the record; but the evidence is convincing that the defendant Natural Gas intended to place the order with National Welding and Grinding and believed that it had done so, and is equally convincing

that the order was actually filled by National Crankshaft, a company with which the defendant had no intention of contracting.

[7] The Court of Appeal was correct, under the authorities cited in its opinion, in holding that plaintiff could not recover on the basis of the telephone order of January 11, 1962; but that court failed to recognize that under the circumstances of this case there was liability on the part of the defendant under the doctrine of quasi-contract — that is, a promise to pay implied from keeping the goods after notice. 1 Williston on Contracts, 3rd ed., sec. 80, pp. 264–265; 5 Williston on Contracts, rev'd ed., sec. 1575, p. 4404; *Barnes v. Shoemaker*, 112 Ind. 512, 14 N.E. 367; to the same effect, La.Civ.Code Arts. 2293, 2294; see Planiol, Treatise on the Civil Law (La. State Law Institute tr.), V. 2 pt. 1, nos. 810A et seq., pp. 432 et seq. We consider that the following quotation from Williston states the law applicable here:

> "* * * if after an offer is made to one person only, performance is tendered by another, though the offeror may refuse the tendered performance, yet if he does receive performance knowing that it is not tendered by or on behalf of the offeree, he will be bound. * * *" 1 Williston, *supra*.[1]

[8] In the instant case when the crankshaft was delivered with the accompanying invoice clearly indicating that plaintiff National Crankshaft, and not National Welding, was filling the order — an invoice which was received by an employee of the defendant and seen and noted by the defendant's superintendent —, defendant had the choice either of accepting the goods, thereby implying a promise to pay and establishing a quasi-contractual relationship, or of refusing them under the theory that it had no contract with the plaintiff. Rather than refusing the crankshaft, the defendant incorporated it into its machinery, and it was actually being used, as already stated, at the time of the trial.

[9] For the reasons assigned the judgment of the Court of Appeal is annulled and set aside, and it is now ordered that there be judgment in favor of plaintiff, National Crankshaft Company, and against the defendants, Natural Gas Industries, Inc., James H. Hoag, Liquidator, and James H. Hoag, individually, in solido, for $923.18 with 5 per cent per annum interest thereon from judicial demand until paid. All costs are to be paid by the defendants.

Questions

1. Paragraph 6–7: The Court applies the "doctrine of quasi-contract" to this case, in which there was a "promise to pay *implied* from keeping the goods after notice" (emphasis added). Does this mean that an "implied contract" is a "quasi-contract"? To support its holding, the Court cites an excerpt from

---

1. Although plaintiff's suit is based on the contract of sale of January 11, under the authority of Article 2164 of the Code of Civil Procedure the appellate court may render any judgment which is just, legal, and proper on the record on appeal.

Professor Williston's treatise on contract law. *See* paragraph 7. However, immediately after the quoted passage, Williston goes on to say, "The tender of performance is, in effect, a *new offer*, and receipt of the performance an *acceptance of this new offer*" (emphasis added).

2. Paragraph 7: According to the Court, defendant had two options — either to accept the goods, thus becoming liable under quasi-contract, or to refuse them under the theory of an absence of contract. Do these alternatives seem logical to you, especially given the fact that liability in quasi-contract presupposes the absence of a contract? If defendant accepts the goods, is this not a contract, which can be formed either by express or implied consent? *See* Louisiana Civil Code articles 1927, 2053–2057.

Mr. and Mrs. Vincent Stelly, Individually, and on Behalf of Madonna Lee Stelly, Minor Child
v.
Gerber Products Company

Court of Appeal of Louisiana
Fourth Circuit
June 6, 1974
299 So.2d 529

REDMANN, Judge.

[. . . .]

[1] C.C. art. 2293 defines quasi-contracts as "the lawful and purely voluntary act of a man, from which there results any obligation whatever to a third person, and sometimes a reciprocal obligation between the parties."

[2] The meaning of art. 2293 is clearer from its Code context. Art. 1760 states the origin of civil obligations as either the operation of law or the consent of the parties. The latter source is contract. As to the former, art. 2293 declares that, while some obligations are imposed by the law alone, others arise "from an act done by the party obliged, or in his favor . . . (and) result either from quasi contracts, or from offenses and quasi-offenses."

[3] Litvinoff, Louisiana Civil Law Treatise, Obligations § 59, describing this traditional civilian classification, writes:

> "Within the context of this classification, contracts are Willful and Lawful acts of agreement productive of obligations. Quasi-contracts are Willful and Lawful acts also, but without the concurrence of the wills required for the formation of an agreement. Delicts and quasi-delicts (offenses and quasi-offenses) are Unlawful acts, which is the feature which distinguishes these sources (of obligations) from the two preceding ones."

Aubry & Rau, Droit Civil Francais, Obligations, § 305 (La.Law Inst. trans.), observe:

> "Obligations of the second kind (founded on an act of man; cf. La.C.C. art. 2292) may be founded either on a lawful or an unlawful act.

> "In the first case, they derive from contract . . . or a quasi contract . . . : In the second case, from an offense or a quasi offense. . . ."

[4] Toullier, Droit Civil Francais, II, iv, Of Obligations Which are Formed without Agreement, § 113 (trans. Miller, ed. Polack), 16 La.Bar.J. 147 (1968), similarly characterizes the French Code's division as into those obligations occasioned by "licit acts and agreements . . . (and) those which arise from illicit acts. These (latter) are divided into two categories, offenses and quasi-offenses."

[5] The Louisiana Civil Code is express in defining quasi-contract as resulting from "lawful" and voluntary act, art. 2293. Our Code does not expressly define offense and quasi-offense as "unlawful" acts from which obligations arise, but this word is used in art. 2324, in the chapter "Of offenses and quasi offenses", to characterize the tortious act:

> "He who causes another person to do an unlawful act, or assists or encourages in the commission of it, is answerable, In solido, with that person, for the damage caused by such act."

[6] *Hartman v. Greene*, 1934, 193 La. 234, 190 So. 390, 391, concludes that "unlawful" in art. 2324 means simply "wrongful" and not criminal.

[7] We conclude that the word "lawful" in art. 2293 is a word of art in the civilian tradition of dividing acts into those which one has the right to do and those which the law, in its most general sense, denies one the right to do. See Toullier, *supra,* §§ 119–120.

[8] In our case, the act of defendant from which an obligation is argued was the manufacture of food for human consumption or its advertising as fit for human consumption. These are indeed "lawful" acts if the food is wholesome, but no obligation arises toward the consumer from manufacturing etc. wholesome food.

[9] Plaintiffs seek damages because, allegedly, defendant manufactured Unwholesome food that made plaintiff infant seriously ill. It is not lawful, in the sense of art. 2293, to make and sell food which contains harmful substances. Such an act is unlawful, in the sense of art. 2324. The manufacture of Unwholesome food is therefore not a lawful act from which a quasi-contractual obligation may arise.

[10] Thus neither the lawful act of manufacturing etc. wholesome food, nor the unlawful act of manufacturing unwholesome food, can result in any quasi-contractual obligation to the consumer.

[. . . .]

See also *Duggan Machine Co., Inc. v. Consolidated Well Serving Co. Inc.,* 187 So.2d 124 (La. App. 2 Cir. 1966), and *Smith v. Hudson,* 519 So.2d 783 (La. App. 1 Cir. 1987).

Comparative Law Perspective

— Civil Law —

Alain Levasseur, *Louisiana Law of Unjust Enrichment in Quasi-Contracts*

at 7–8, 51–52 (1991)

In the time of Justinian [....] the notion of quasi-contracts resulted from a desire to establish a transition between the original and broad concept of contractual obligations and the new, more restrictive one, which we have inherited today under the name of conventional obligations. Unexpectedly, however, this concept of obligations arising *quasi ex contractu* found within itself enough of an impetus to become a new and independent source of obligations through a simple, and apparently innocuous, mistranslation of its original name. Indeed, instead of articulating the source of that obligation as one binding the parties *as if there existed a contract* between them (*quasi ex contractu*), the legal expression now commonly used consists in saying that one is bound *quasi-contractually* or by a *quasi-contract*, as if the Latin name of that source of obligations had been *ex quasi contractu*. This simple switch or shift in the position of the prefix ex from one side of quasi (*quasi ex*) to the other side (*ex quasi*) is responsible for much controversy and uncertainty.

It has actually raised the generic notion of *quasi-contracts* to a ranking equal to that of contracts and *delicts* (torts) as sources of obligations when, in reality, its original and historical meaning was lacking in substance and legal implications. It was merely a convenience means of bringing under one label a variety of obligations whose sources did not have much in common as evidenced by the fact that they arose from a variety of sources (*ex variis causarum figuris*). [....]

A *quasi contract* is, therefore, the source of an obligation which is created without any agreement. By contrast, "a contract is an agreement by two or more parties whereby obligations are created, modified, or extinguished." Such a contract "is formed by the consent of the parties established through offer and acceptance" which can "be made orally, in writing, or by action or inaction that under the circumstances is clearly indicative of consent."

The line of separation between a contract and a quasi-contract is thus clearly drawn in Louisiana statutory law: whenever consent can be found, under whatever form, a contract was meant to bind one party or another. The courts should always give preference to a contractual remedy over a quasi-contractual one. There are two fundamental reasons: 1) a contractual remedy expresses and carries out the original and true intent of the parties who meant to be bound by the laws of their own contract and that law ought to be upheld; and 2) our courts would find more guidance in the articles of the Civil Code on conventional obligations as to when it is appropriate to grant the parties the full enforcement of their rights and remedies. A quasi-contractual remedy should never be considered as an alternative to a contractual remedy since the latter is to be considered as a part of the law of the contract between the parties; furthermore, a contractual remedy is always more beneficial to a party who claims to have been impoverished by the other party's breach of an obligation. A quasi-contractual remedy should be contemplated only as a last resort in order to avoid upsetting the predetermined and well-balanced scheme of the legal and contractual remedies available to both parties under the law. Where a judge cannot resort to equity when legislation or custom is controlling, likewise he should not be able to resort to a quasi-contractual remedy when there is a law or a contract controlling the subject matter under consideration.

Nikolaos Davrados, *Demystifying Enrichment Without Cause*
78 La. L. Rev. 1223, 1249–53 (2018)

Scholars have advanced several theories concerning the legal nature of enrichment without cause (as well as *negotiorum gestio* and payment of a thing not due). [. . . .] The real difficulty with [**these theories**] lies in the imperfect, and much debated definition of the term "quasi-contract." [**French scholars have notably said that**] quasi-contract is a "legendary monster that should be banished from the juridical vocabulary." [. . . .] A more accurate and systematic approach is to characterize enrichment without cause (as well as *negotiorum gestio* and payment of a thing not due) as a type of *juridical fact*. [. . . .] A juridical fact is a conduct or event to which the law attaches legal consequences regardless of whether those consequences are in fact desired. The conduct of a person can be licit or illicit. Capacity and fault of the obligor in licit juridical facts are irrelevant factors, whereas culpability and liability are usual factors in the case of illicit juridical facts. "Quasi-contracts," including *negotiorum gestio*, payment of a thing not due, and enrichment without cause, are licit juridical facts.

Philippe Malaurie, Laurent Aynès & Philippe Stoffel Munck, *Droit des Obligations*
n° 1015 at 595 (10th ed. 2018)

1015. The quasi-contract is a spontaneous act of a person ("purely voluntary act," article 1300, line 1, old article 1371 [**of the French Civil Code**]), that results in an advantage for a third person and an impoverishment of the maker of the act; the third person is thus obligated to compensate the maker of the act. The method of this compensation is modeled on a supposed contract, as if ("quasi") such a contract for compensation existed between the enriched person and the impoverished person. Unlike a contractual obligation, however, an obligation arising from quasi-contract is not at all based on the will of the debtor. Unlike a delictual obligation, the quasi-contractual obligation of the debtor is not based on his illicit act. Quasi-contract has thus become an autonomous source of obligations, which finds its origins in equity.

More so than other institutions, quasi-contract is a product of history, but also a topic of frequent controversy. Its evolution can be summarized in three stages: a

Roman origin; a crisis at the beginning of the 20th century; and a contemporary renaissance.

— Common Law —
Arthur Corbin, *On Contracts*
vol. 1, § 19, at 44 (1963) and 58 (1990 Pocket Part)

A distinction has long been suggested between contracts implied-in-fact and contracts implied-in-law. [....] Something very different is meant by the term "contract implied-in-law;" it is an obligation that is created by the law without regard to expressions of assent by either words or acts. Some confusion was caused by the use of the term "implied contract" to refer to such different kinds of obligation; and the tendency is now strong to substitute the term "quasi-contract" in place of the term "contract implied-in-law."

[....] Quasi-contract analysis tends to be somewhat undisciplined, depending to the extent that it does on policy considerations and on the doing of "substantial justice." This does not mean that there are not principles that can be applied by the courts. The key to understanding quasi-contract is the realization that, while contract law in the modern setting seeks to fulfill the reasonable expectations of the parties, quasi-contract seeks to fulfill reasonable expectations of society. The closely allied term "unjust enrichment," that finds its way into most quasi-contract cases stands as evidence of the heavy public policy orientation of the law of quasi-contract. "Reasonable expectation," then, is the term that unifies contract and quasi-contract. A formal statement of quasi-contract might be that it is the theory of recovery by which courts give a remedy similar to that historically available for breach of contract when they find that justice requires such a remedy.

Section II — Management of Another's Affairs (Negotiorum Gestio)

Louisiana Sources of Law
Louisiana Civil Code

Art. 2292. Management of affairs; definition.

There is a management of affairs when a person, the manager, acts without authority to protect the interests of another, the owner, in the reasonable belief that the owner would approve of the action if made aware of the circumstances. (Acts 1995, No. 1041, § 1, eff. Jan. 1, 1996.)

Art. 2293. Application of rules governing mandate.

A management of affairs is subject to the rules of mandate to the extent those rules are compatible with management of affairs. (Acts 1995, No. 1041, § 1, eff. Jan. 1, 1996.)

Art. 2294. Duties of the manager; notice to the owner.

The manager is bound, when the circumstances so warrant, to give notice to the owner that he has undertaken the management and to wait for the directions of the owner, unless there is immediate danger. (Acts 1995, No. 1041, §1, eff. Jan. 1, 1996.)

Art. 2295. Duties of the manager; liability for loss.

The manager must exercise the care of a prudent administrator and is answerable for any loss that results from his failure to do so. The court, considering the circumstances, may reduce the amount due the owner on account of the manager's failure to act as a prudent administrator. (Acts 1995, No. 1041, §1, eff. Jan. 1, 1996.)

Art. 2296. Capacity.

An incompetent person or a person of limited legal capacity may be the owner of an affair, but he may not be a manager. When such a person manages the affairs of another, the rights and duties of the parties are governed by the law of enrichment without cause or the law of delictual obligations. (Acts 1995, No. 1041, §1, eff. Jan. 1, 1996.)

Art. 2297. Obligations of the owner.

The owner whose affair has been managed is bound to fulfill the obligations that the manager has undertaken as a prudent administrator and to reimburse the manager for all necessary and useful expenses. (Acts 1995, No. 1041, §1, eff. Jan. 1, 1996.)

Doctrine

Louisiana Law of Unjust Enrichment in Quasi-Contracts
at 66–69 (1991)

In order to clearly understand and easily identify the relationships created in the management of another's affairs, it is important to place the proper label on the parties involved: the party who volunteered to act for the benefit of another will be referred to as the gestor or as the manager, and the party for whose benefit the act was undertaken will be known as the principal or owner.

How, then, is it possible for one person acting of her own accord to create "certain obligations . . . without any agreement, either on the part of the person bound, or of him in whose favor the obligation takes place"? What possible foundation could offer enough of a justification to explain why a gestor's interference in the affairs of another can eventually compel the latter to incur obligations towards the former? [. . . .]

Equity, justice, and reason [**is where**] we can find the rationale for the institution of *negotiorum gestio*. Altruism, the duty or need to help and assist others, appears to be the true foundation of the rights and obligations flowing to the parties bound under *negotiorum gestio*. How else can one explain that the gestor is entitled to recover only his useful and necessary expenses but no profit or salary at all? How to explain that, even if the principal does not eventually derive any actual benefit from the management of his affairs by another, that principal must nevertheless reimburse the gestor if the principal's affairs were wellmanaged at one time in the past? How to explain otherwise that "where the circumstances of friendship or of necessity have induced a person to undertake the management," the judge may mitigate the damages arising from the faults or the negligence of the manager/gestor? [. . . .]

The rights and obligations of both the gestor and principal are tailored or fashioned both by the altruistic intent of the gestor and on account of the real need that exists on the part of the principal, although the gestor does not wish to go as far as suffering a loss himself. It is for those same reasons that the Roman praetor granted the *actio negotiorum contraria* to a gestor.

This moral foundation of *negotiorum gestio* explains to a large extent why the Louisiana Civil Code provisions are so few, and so broad, in their regulation of this institution. It is somewhat difficult to legislate morality. The jurisprudence, on the other hand, must contend with daily practical issues which need to be answered against the general background of statutory law. The courts will have to proceed by way of deductive reasoning, from the existing general principles of the law down to the formulation of specific rules so as to allow *negotiorum gestio* to fulfill its human, moral, and legal meaning.

Cases

Standard Motor Car Company et al.
v.
State Farm Mutual Automobile Insurance Company

Court of Appeal of Louisiana
First Circuit
October 4, 1957
97 So.2d 435

TATE, Judge.

[1] Plaintiffs appeal from judgment dismissing their suit upon exception of no right and cause of action.

[2] The petition alleges: A car left by a customer of the plaintiff, Standard Motor Car Company, Inc. ('Standard'),[1] for servicing was involved in an intersectional collision while being road-tested by Standard's employee in the course and scope of his employment. The negligence of a driver insured by defendant, State Farm Mutual Insurance Company, was the sole proximate cause of the accident. Standard paid for

---

1. Standard's collision insurer is co-plaintiff for the portion of the damage paid by it.

repair of the damages and by this tort suit seeks recovery of same from the insurer of the tortfeasor.

[3] Defendant contends that, in the absence of a conventional subrogation by the Owner of the damaged car in favor of Standard, Standard as Possessor has no right or cause of action for the damage caused to its customer's car, even though Standard paid for the repair of same. This contention is based upon the doctrine that 'subrogation will not generally be decreed in favor of a mere volunteer or intermeddler who, without any duty, moral or otherwise, pays the debt or discharges the obligation of another,' 50 Am.Jur. 696, 'Subrogation', Section 21. See also 83 C.J.S., Subrogation s 9, p. 601. See LSA-Civil Code Article 2161, especially 2161(3).

[. . . .]

[4] Plaintiffs urge most forcefully that the garageman is at least under a moral duty to repair the cars of his customers injured while in his custody. It is argued that the garageman cannot morally or as a matter of sound business practice return his customer's car to the latter in a damaged condition with the observation that it is up to the customer to collect for the loss from an allegedly negligent third party. We are reminded that the garageman, as depositary or bailee, is under a duty to return the car deposited with him in the same condition as received, and that — as between him and his customer, the depositor — injury to the car during the garageman's custody establishes a prima facie case in favor of the customer against the garageman. *Hazel v. Williams*, La.App. 2 Cir., 80 So.2d 133; Articles 1908, 2937, 2938, 2944, 2945, LSA-Civil Code. The garageman thus has at least a prima facie duty to repair the vehicle damaged while in his custody before returning it to his customer. Furthermore, should be refuse to repair the vehicle on the ground that the damages resulted from the negligence of a third party tortfeasor, the prescriptive period applicable to his customer's action against him for the damages to the car, while in the garageman's custody is that of ten years, Article 3444, LSA-C.C., *Reehlman v. Calamari*, La.App.Orleans, 94 So.2d 311; far longer than the peremptive one year for tort actions during which either party must seek to hold the negligent third person.

[5] The contentions of the plaintiffs-appellants are sustained by the jurisprudence; although in fairness we must add that the authorities cited below were not called to the attention of the learned trial judge.

[. . . .]

[6] The result we have reached is consistent with the common law principles surrounding a 'bailment', which is quite similar in many respects to a civil law 'deposit'. [. . . .]

[7] The jurisprudence specifically pertaining to deposit and bailment has thus readily furnished a rationale for this decision. But it is not inappropriate to note that although the garageman in this case may be not subrogated to rights of the customer against the tortfeasor nevertheless he may have acquired by the payment to the creditor (i.e., the owner of the car) a right of action to recover the payment

from the person legally obligated for the debt (i.e., the tortfeasor). This arises under Article 2134, LSA-C.C., which provides that the obligation is discharged by payment by another party 'no way concerned in it' (i.e., the garageman), even if the latter 'act in his own name', although it also provides that the latter 'be not subrogated to the rights of the creditor'.

[8] While there are no Louisiana cases on the subject the equivalent article of the French Civil Code, CN 1236, was explained in the report of Monsier Jaubert presented to the Tribunal (8 Fenet, Discussions, p. 341–342), in part as follows: 'Quoique le tiers qui offre le paiement n' ait pas un intérêt direct et civil à l'acquittement de l' obligation, le créancier ne pourra non plus refuser de recevoir, puisqu'en dernière analyse le créancier n' a d'autre intérêt que d'être payé; mais dans ce cas le tiers ne peut forcer le créancier a le mettre a son lieu et place pour les privilèges, les hypothèques et la contrainte par corps. La loi ne veut pas, avec raison, que contre le gré du créancier un tiers vienne s' interposer pour acquérir le droit de vexer le débiteur; *le tiers que paie qui paie n'acquiert alors qu'une action simple contre le débiteur qui entièrement libre de l'obligation primitive.*'[5]

[9] As was recently stated by one of the main treatises on French Civil law: 'Celui qui a effectué un paiment pour le compte d'un tiers sans ne lui ayant donné aucun mandat a cette fin, ne saurait en réclamer le remboursement audit tiers qu'à la condition de prouver l'obligation de celui-ci dans la dette ainsi acquitté par lui,'[6] IV Aubry et Rau, Droit Civil Francais (Supplement permanent, p. 1. 1957) Section 316, citing Cass. civ. 13 novembre 1939 (Gaz.Pal.1940, 1, 8 Sir.1940, 1, 27; J.C.P. 40, II, 1956).

[10] Or as stated in Planiol et Ripert, Droit Civil Francais, Tome VII (2, 2 ed, 1954), Section 1150, p. 352: '* * * (U)n tiers quelconque, même non intéressé et agissant de son proper gré, a qualitè pour payer. Mais le tiers qui paie ne peut exiger à son profit le bénéfice de la subrogation de la part du créancier (art. 1236); il ne pourra exercer contre le de biteur que la recours fonde sur la gestion d'affaires ou l'enrichisement

---

5. Roughly translated:
  'Although the third person who offers the payment has not a direct civil interest in extinguishing the obligation, the creditor cannot refuse to receive it, for in the last analysis the creditor has no other interest than to be paid; but in this case, the third (party) cannot force the creditor to put him in his (the creditor's) place with regard to the privileges and mortgages he may have or to his right to cause the arrest of the debtor. The law rightly does not allow a third party to interpose himself against the will of the creditor in order to acquire the right to harass the debtor; *the third party who pays then acquires only a simple action for reimbursement against the debtor who is then entirely free of the original obligation.*' (Italics ours.)
6. Roughly translated:
  'He who has effected a payment for the account of a third person without having been given any authority for that purpose, will be allowed to demand reimbursement from the said third person only on the condition of proving that the latter was bound to pay the debt thus discharged by him.'

sans cause.[7] The footnote to this sentence in the French text is the citation to the decision of the Civil Chamber of the Court of Cassation, Feb. 12, 1939 (D.He 1929 180), in which the court reversed a lower court judgment which had held that the stranger or volunteer could not recover in the absence of a legal or conventional subrogation. See also Cass. req. Feb. 3, 1879 (S.79.1.365; D.79.1.231), in which by way of dictum, remarking that 'Ce principle est incontestable', the court of cassation said: 'Le tiers qui a payé la dette d'autrui de ses propres deniers, a, bien que non subroge aux droits du créancier, un recours contre le debiteur (c. civ. 1236.).'[8]

[11] See also 2 Baudry-Lacantinerie, Précis De Droit Civil, II (13e Ed.) 149, Section 324 'Recours du tiers qui a payé.'

[12] Furthermore, the civil law does not share the hostility of the Anglo-American common law to the 'volunteer', and as stated above quite possibly recovery in the present case is allowable under the theory of negotiorum gestio, Articles 2295–2300, LSA-Civil Code, see Comment, 'Negotiorum Gestio in Louisiana', 7 Tulane Law Review 254, the quasi-contractual obligation arising from the situation where a person voluntarily manages the business of another without any authorization whatsoever.

[13] The action of the garageman in repairing the damage to its customer's automobile might be considered to be in satisfaction of the third party tortfeasor's obligation to the customer for the damage to the latter's car, and therefore an act of negotiorum gestio as to said third party defendant tortfeasor herein. For all that is required for an instance of negotiorum gestio is that one person (the gestor) manage, of his own accord, the 'affair' of another (the principal) LSA-Civil Code, Article 2295. The garageman attended to the 'affair' of the defendant herein when he fulfilled defendant tortfeasor's obligation to the owner of the car existing by reason of his negligently damaging said vehicle. LSA-Civil Code, Article 2316.[9]

---

7. Roughly translated:
   'Any third person whatever, even though not interested and acting of his own inclination, has the capacity to pay (the debt of another). But the third person who thus pays cannot demand subrogation to the creditor's interest (art. 1236); he can exercise against the debtor only the remedy founded on negotiorum gestio or unjust enrichment.'

8. Roughly translated:
   'The principle is incontestable * * * (that) The third person who pays the debt of another from his own funds has, although not subrogated to the rights of the creditor, a remedy against the debtor (CN 1236).'

9. In this regard, it is of no consequence that the plaintiff garageman herein must have intended to favor its customer, the car owner, or to preserve or foster his own business good will in fulfilling the defendant tortfeasor's obligation to the owner of the car damaged through its negligence. Although the institution of Negotiorum gestio is often associated with an act Motivated by the desire to render a Service to the principal whose affair is managed, this motivation is said not to be an essential of its application. All that is required is that the gestor be aware of the fact that he is attending to another's business, in this case the defendant tortfeasor's obligation to repair the damage caused to the owner of the car, and his motive may be to benefit (a) another or even (b) himself. For instance, the Italian Civil Code of 1942, the newest of the major Codes, specifically reflects this thought with the formula requiring no more than that the gestor act Knowing he is managing or

[14] For the above and foregoing reasons the judgment of the District Court herein sustaining defendant's exceptions of no right and cause of action is reversed, and the cause is remanded for further proceedings according to law. The costs of this appeal are assessed against defendant-appellee; all further costs to await final disposition of this matter.

[15] Reversed and remanded.

Questions

1. Paragraph 2: Clearly identify all the parties involved in this case. Identify, in legal terms, the relationships existing between sets of parties; is each based in contract, delict/tort, etc.? Can you phrase precisely the issue raised in the case?

2. Paragraph 3: How strong is the defendant's argument that the plaintiff was not subrogated into the rights of the car owner? What kind of subrogation is the defendant referring to? Is the word or the concept of "intermeddler" in the Louisiana Civil Code applicable? Notice the references given by the Court: are they persuasive sources of law in Louisiana?

3. Paragraph 4: Why is the defendant arguing that plaintiff is a "depositary"? After you have read the Louisiana Civil Code articles on deposit (*see* arts. 2926–2940), is it possible for the plaintiff to fit the legal profile of a depositary? Is it in the plaintiff's interest to argue the existence of a "moral duty" to repair the cars of his customers? Would a "natural obligation" have been a better legal argument? Could the concept of moral duty be, here, a borrowing from the common law which does not know of natural obligations? How would the different prescriptive periods (10 years for deposit compared to 1 year for torts/delicts) negatively affect the plaintiff? In the last sentence, does the Court really mean "peremptive one year for tort actions"?

---

attending to another's affair. Italian Civil Code, Article 2028; Pandolfelli, Codice Civile illustrato con i lavori preparatori (Libro d lle Obligazaioni) (1942) 658, 659. And Negotiorum gestio is often used in France (according to the jurisprudence and doctrine) and in Germany (under German Civil Code, Article 679) to permit recovery by a person (the gestor) who supplies food, clothing, or money to dependents of the principal. Certainly in these cases the motive is to help the dependent rather than the principal. On the French law, see Picard, La gestion d'affaires dans la jurisprudence contemporaine, Revue Trimestrielle de Droit Civil (1942) 419, 446 seq.

Besides, the mere fact that one protects his own interest or even advances his own welfare does not of itself take the action out of the scope of Negotiorum gestio. Thus French jurisprudence admits that a seller, whose buyer could not take delivery of grain because of the rise of a war, could sell the grain both in his own and his buyer's interests and still be a gestor. (Req. 19 juin 1872, Dalloz Periodique 1872.1.471.) Similarly, a co-owner may be a gestor in repairing property or attending to a common obligation; and the surety and co-debtor who pay to fulfill their own obligations as well as those of the principal are treated as negotiorum gestors. See generally on the matter of motive, Picard, La gestion d'affaires dans la jurisprudence contemporaine, Revue Trimestrielle de Droit Civil (1922) 5, at 23; Gore, L'enrichissement sans Cause (1949) No. 261.

4. Paragraphs 7–13: Judge Tate makes a distinction between subrogation and payment of the debt of another: is this the proper distinction to make? Are these two concepts two different ways or modes of paying another's debt? Carefully read the Code articles on "Payment" or "Performance" (*see* arts. 1854, *et seq.*) and on "Subrogation" (*see* arts. 1825–1830). Judge Tate cites then to Louisiana Civil Code article 2134 (now art. 1855) and refers extensively to French doctrine. Is this a legitimate and proper approach for a Louisiana court? Pay particular attention to the text translated from French into English in footnote 8. Is the second sentence relevant to the case? Keep this sentence in mind as you read Judge Tate's opinion. Compare the Louisiana Civil Code articles on payment (article 1855, particularly) with the Louisiana Civil Code articles on the Management of the Affairs of Another (*see* arts. 2292–2297). Do you see any difference?

5. Paragraph 12: What do you think of the statement made here by Judge Tate? Is he finding this feature of the civil law in some *ratio juris* (reason for the law) which is then incorporated in some institutions of the civil law, such as the Management of the Affairs of Another, Unjust Enrichment, or Louisiana Civil Code article 1855? What about the concept of good faith which is different at civil law from what it is at common law?

H. C. Hobbs et al.
v.
Central Equipment Rentals, Inc., et al.

Court of Appeal of Louisiana
Third Circuit
March 5, 1980
382 So.2d 238

FORET, Judge.

[1] The basic facts upon which this lawsuit is based were succinctly set out by the trial court and we take the liberty of quoting therefrom:

> "On November 6, 1974, the plaintiffs filed this suit against Central Equipment Rentals, Inc., Sam Hance and Bonnie Rose Crawford Hance, seeking $329,811.86, alleging that they were the owners of a two-thirds interest in a mineral lease executed by the St. Martin Land Company on June 20, 1950. They claim that the defendants arranged for the removal of certain property and equipment located on three wells affected by this lease belonging in part to the plaintiffs and in part to the defendants, and converted the materials to their own use, which had a value insofar as the two-thirds interest of the plaintiffs is concerned of the amount claimed.

> "The defendants brought into this lawsuit Fred Setoon and Condor Pipe Company but after the trial on the merits, by consent they were dismissed from the case.

"The defendants filed an answer on April 14, 1975, and a reconventional demand alleging that it was necessary to employ certain parties to salvage the three wells and clean them up, and that the defendant paid $19,951.60 for this, as well as $2,024.82 to the tax collector of St. Martin Parish for the 1973 ad valorem taxes, showing that Mrs. Hance, a defendant, was in partnership with the two Hobbs plaintiffs, and she spent that money on their account and should be reimbursed by them in the amount of two-thirds of the money spent."

[2] The trial court rendered judgment in favor of defendants-appellees granting their reconventional demand and against plaintiffs-appellants, rejecting their claims. From this judgment, plaintiffs have appealed.

[....]

ASSIGNMENTS OF ERROR # 3 AND # 4.

[3] Plaintiffs-appellants allege that the trial court erred in applying Civil Code Articles 2292, 2298, 2868, and 2862 since the acts of the defendants-appellees in contracting to alienate the wellsite equipment went beyond the powers of an administrator and further erred in applying the partnership article since we are dealing with immovable property, thus requiring the partnership to be in writing and any transactions of the partners to be in writing. Appellants cite as authority Civil Code Articles 2836 and 2870. Additionally, appellants allege that the trial court erred in finding that Sam and Bonnie Hance were prudent administrators.

[4] As previously noted, these contracts in question do not involve immovables, but instead involve movable property. For this reason, assignment of error #3 is without merit.

[5] We think, as did the trial court, that the actions of Mrs. Hance are governed by the Civil Code articles relating to quasi contracts. LSA-C.C. Article 2292 reads:

"Certain obligations are contracted without any agreement, either on the part of the person bound or of him in whose favor the obligation takes place.

Some are imposed by the sole authority of the laws, others from an act done by the party obliged, or in his favor.

The first are such engagements as result from tutorship, curatorship, neighborhood, common property, the acquisition of an inheritance, and other cases of a like nature.

The obligations, which arise from a fact, personal to him who is bound, or relative to him, result either from quasi contracts, or from offenses and quasi-offenses."[1]

---

1. We observe in passing that C.C. Article 2292 apparently contains at least three errors in the English translation of the French text. The word "contracted" in the first paragraph of Article 2292 should be "formed", and the words "common property" in the second paragraph should be "co-ownership". See editorial comments under Article 2292 Translation of RCC 1870.

[6] Quasi contracts arise without agreement from the lawful and purely voluntary act of a man from which there results any obligation whatever to a third person, and sometime a reciprocal obligation between the parties. LSA-C.C. Articles 2292, 2293, 2294. The essential elements of quasi contracts are a benefit conferred on the defendant by the plaintiffs, an appreciation by defendant of such benefits, and acceptance and retention by the defendant of such benefits under circumstances such that it would be inequitable for him to retain the benefits without payment of the value therefor. *Teche Realty & Investment Co., Inc. v. A.M.F., Inc.*, 306 So.2d 432 (La.App. 3 Cir. 1975), writ denied, 309 So.2d 681 (La.1975).

[7] Once a quasi contract is formed, Civil Code Article 2298 gives the standard to which the negotiorum gestor is held in the management of the affairs of another. LSA-C.C. Article 2298 states in pertinent part:

> "In managing the business, he is obliged to use all the care of a prudent administrator."

[8] We are of the opinion that the Hances did exactly what a prudent administrator would have done. Upon learning that the Hobbs were unable or unwilling to contribute to the clean-up operations, they took it upon themselves to locate contractors with the necessary expertise to perform the cleaning, plugging and abandoning of the wells. This was done at a minimal cost, as can be seen by comparison to the first bid which was submitted [...]. [....]

[9] Mrs. Hance was in the position of a partner with regard to the wells in question. LSA-C.C. Article 2868 states:

> "When several partners are intrusted with the administration without their duties being pointed out, or when it is not expressed that one shall not be able to act without the other, they may do separately all the acts relating to such administration."

It is clear from the record that the duties of the partners were not clearly delineated. Each partner was therefore empowered or free to act on behalf of the partnership with regard to the administration of the partnership business. The record shows Mrs. Hance was of the belief that she could expect no help, financial or otherwise, from the Hobbs in having the wells plugged and abandoned. She was therefore empowered to act on behalf of the partnership of her own volition. LSA-C.C. Article 2862 provides that:

> " ... no partner shall be held liable for any loss which has happened in consequence of any thing *bona fide* done or omitted by him in the legal exercise of his power, either as administrator or partner, although such act or omission should be injudicious and injurious to the partnership."

[10] Mrs. Hance's actions were both bona fide and those of a prudent administrator. Not only were they prudent and bona fide, but they were not injudicious or injurious to the partnership. Mrs. Hance acted in what was at the time a very fair manner. For these reasons, assignment of error #4 is without merit.

[. . . .]

[11] AFFIRMED.

Questions

1. Paragraphs 6–9: The Court notes that *negotiorum gestio* is a type of quasi-contract, which arises "without agreement." Was there no agreement between the parties in this case? Take a look at Louisiana Civil Code articles 2801 and 2802.

2. Paragraph 10: The Court discusses the obligation of the manager of another's affairs to act as a "prudent administrator." Is this standard objective (with reference to what a reasonable person would do) or subjective (with reference to what that particular manager did)? Look at Louisiana Civil Code article 2295 and the revision comments thereto.

D.H. Overmeyer Co., Inc.
v.
Blakeley Floor Covering, Inc.

Court of Appeal of Louisiana
Fourth Circuit
September 15, 1972
266 So.2d 925

SAMUEL, Judge.

[1] This appeal involves the breach of a written contract of lease and the credit to which the defaulting lessee is entitled from rent the lessor collected from a second tenant following defendant's abandonment of the leased premises.

[2] The facts are not in dispute. Plaintiff rented defendant warehouse space for the period beginning July 15, 1968 and ending July 14, 1969 for $460 per month. Upon signing the agreement, defendant gave plaintiff a check for $920 in advance to cover rent for the first and last month. The check was not honored by defendant's bank because of insufficient funds on deposit.

[3] Plaintiff received no rent whatsoever. On November 20, 1968 it filed a petition for a writ of sequestration of defendant's property located in the leased premises to protect its lessor's privilege. The petition alleged defendant then owed $5,520, which included rent unpaid for more than four months of occupancy and future rents for the remainder of the one year lease term. The claim for future rents was based on a lease provision permitting the lessor to accelerate payment for future rents if the lessee did not make timely payment of the monthly rent.

[4] On January 1, 1969 plaintiff leased the same premises to another tenant at a monthly rental of $800. The second tenant's occupancy extended beyond the expiration date of the lease. At the trial on June 29, 1971, plaintiff reduced its claim to $2,530, being the amount of unpaid rent from July 15, 1968 through December 31, 1968.

[5] After trial there was judgment in favor of plaintiff in the amount of $320. Plaintiff has appealed. Defendant has answered the appeal asserting it has no liability on the lease whatsoever.

[6] In arriving at the amount of the judgment, the trial court allowed defendant a credit of $5,200 ($800 per month collected by plaintiff from the second tenant for a period of six and one-half months) against $5,520, the total amount due for the full one year lease term (twelve months at $460 per month). Thus the defaulting lessee profited from plaintiff's re-letting the premises at a higher rental by applying funds derived from the second tenant not only to reduce defendant's liability during the second occupancy, but also retroactively to offset unpaid rent owed by defendant prior to the beginning of the second lease.

[7] Plaintiff concedes it is obligated to credit the rent it collected from the second tenant against the amount it claims from the defaulting lessee. However, it contends: the credit is limited to the period for which the second tenant paid that rent; when the lessor obtained a higher rental from the second tenant, the amount greater than the rent due by the defaulting lessee could not be applied retroactively to offset the latter's indebtedness for the time it occupied or had possession of the premises.

[8] Defendant relies on a line of decisions involving mitigation of damages in a contract of lease. As a general rule, our courts have stated a lessor need not mitigate damages by reletting his premises when the original lessee breaches his contract by abandoning them.[1] However, if the lessor does re-let his property for the unexpired term, he must credit his lessee with funds collected from the new tenant.[2] It has been reasoned that in re-letting to a second tenant the lessor acts as a negotiorum gestor for the defaulting lessee or as an agent acting without authority of his principal.[3] In our view, this de facto agency principle is limited to a mandate for the purpose of mitigating damages In *Bernstein v. Bauman*, 170 La. 378, 389, 127 So. 874, 877, the court stated:

> "Plaintiff did not lease the premises to Gordon until defendants had abandoned them and after he made due demand upon defendants. He took possession of the premises and leased them to Gordon *as a negotiorum gestor for defendants and for the purpose of minimizing the damages.*" [(]Emphasis ours).

[9] We have not been cited to, nor have we found, a case where a lessor obtained higher rent from the second lease than he did from the first. It is our opinion that the implied agency must be limited to the principle of mitigation of damages and the rents collected from the second tenant should only be credited against that amount the defaulting lessee would have been required to pay from the time of the second occupancy to the expiration of the lease.

---

1. Meyers v. Drewes, La.App., 196 So.2d 607.
2. Weil v. Segura, 178 La. 421, 151 So. 639.
3. See LSA-C.C. Art. 2295.

[10] In this case defendant occupied plaintiff's warehouse for more than four months without paying anything and it abandoned the leasehold in haste when sequestration was imminent. The property remained vacant approximately six weeks after defendant vacated. Thereafter, plaintiff found a new tenant at a higher rental which gave the defendant the benefit of a six and one-half month rental credit. While it is true plaintiff benefitted from re-letting the property, we cannot permit the additional rent collected from the second tenant to apply retroactively to offset that portion of defendant's debt which accrued prior to the second lease. Defendant had had the use of the property during that time and the full rent had been earned by its occupancy and possession. The credit to which defendant is entitled is limited to its rental obligations during the existence of the second lease. In *Wilson v. G. Brian Corporation*, 244 La. 433, 437, 152 So.2d 550, 551, the court stated:

> "... the accrued rent is unqualified and definitely owing to the lessor ... it having been earned by the lessee's past occupancy and possession of the premises."

[11] For the reasons assigned, the judgment appealed from is amended to increase the plaintiff's award from $320 to $2,530. As thus amended, and in all other respects, the judgment is affirmed. Defendant is to pay all costs of this litigation.

[12] Amended and affirmed.

Questions

1. Paragraphs 2–4: In this case, did the lessor lease the property to the second lessee in order to "protect the interests" of the first lessee, or to protect his own interests, or to protect the interests of both? Is this determination made subjectively or objectively? In other words, should it matter what the lessor had in mind or does it suffice that re-letting the property objectively benefits the first lessee? Take another look at Louisiana Civil Code article 2292 and revision comment (c) thereto.

2. Paragraph 8. Take a look at the actual opinion of the case cited by the court. Now, assume that the lessor managed to lease the property to a second lessee for *less rent* compared to the rent charged to the first lessee. If we follow the court's reasoning, would the lessor (manager) be liable to the first lessee (owner) for poorly "managing the affair"? Or should we resolve this issue with reference to other provisions? See, for example, Louisiana Civil Code article 1886.

3. Paragraphs 9–11: The court notes the absence of "cases" on the issue before it. Is such an absence important? Does the court cite to any positive law (legislation or custom) in its opinion? Is the court's finding substantiated under any provisions in the Civil Code? Can you locate these provisions?

Jerry Tyler, d/b/a Jerry Tyler & Son Towing & Recovery
v.
Sam Haynes, Jr., Haynes Motor Lines, Inc. and McKoin Trucking Co., Inc.

Court of Appeal of Louisiana
Third Circuit
May 3, 2000
760 So.2d 559

THIBODEAUX, Judge.

[. . . .]

Facts

[1] On January 7, 1998, a tractor-trailer owned by the defendants, Sam Haynes, Jr. (hereinafter "Haynes"), Haynes Motor Lines and McKoin Trucking Company, was involved in an accident; the rig of the trailer ran off the road. Approximately twenty to thirty gallons of diesel leaked out of the tractor's tank into a ditch.

[2] The Louisiana State Police Department was called to the scene of the accident. The State Police then contacted Jerry Tyler, d/b/a Jerry Tyler & Son (hereinafter "Tyler"), to tow the tractor-trailer. Tyler subsequently dispatched and subcontracted Courtney Construction Company of Alexandria, Inc. (hereinafter "Courtney") to contain the diesel fuel and debris and to keep the fuel from contaminating the surrounding area and the water system. The services totaled $27,674.71.

[3] Pursuant to orders of the State Police, the tractor-trailer was towed to Tyler's salvage yard in Pineville, Louisiana and stored there for approximately one week until the proper owners could be notified. It was not until January 14, 1998 that it was established that Haynes was the owner of the 1983 Strick Trailer.

[4] The rig was stored at Tyler's yard for about one week without payment of any costs. Tyler made demand upon Haynes and City National Bank of Baton Rouge, the lienholder, by letters dated January 16, 1998 and February 12, 1998, to pay the costs. Tyler threatened to retain the tractor-trailer rig as security until the costs were paid.

[5] Haynes instituted suit in East Baton Rouge Parish and sought release of the tractor-trailer rig. Shortly thereafter, Haynes paid Tyler $2,500 and retrieved the rig from Tyler's yard.

[6] Tyler then sued Haynes in Grant Parish for $27,674.71, which represented the costs for towing and cleanup, together with judicial interest from date of judicial demand until paid, reasonable attorney fees and all costs of the proceedings.

[. . . .]

Law and Discussion

[. . . .]

[7] The case before us has an abnormal realm of facts. A tractor-trailer rig was found in a ditch in Grant Parish. The driver of the rig was surprisingly not present. At the time the rig was found on January 7, 1998 until January 14, 1998, the owner of the rig was not known. Two State troopers saw the rig, which was not overturned, and contacted Tyler. Tyler then contacted Courtney to clean up the diesel fuel that had leaked from the rig's tank into the ditch.

[8] The State Police had a duty to have the wreckage removed from the roadway. Louisiana Revised Statutes 32:2 authorizes the Department of Transportation to supervise and regulate traffic on the highways in Louisiana. Louisiana Revised Statutes 48:347(C) empowers the Department of Transportation to remove obstacles from the highway at the expense of the responsible person. Based on these provisions, the troopers contacted Tyler to remove the rig from the ditch to insure safe travel on the roadway. Tyler likewise had a duty to remove the diesel from the ditch; this required him to subcontract Courtney. The troopers had definite authority to have the tractor-trailer removed and Tyler had apparent authority to remove it from the ditch. Tyler also had apparent authority to contact someone who was capable of cleaning up the diesel and the other debris which resulted from the rig's accident, all at the expense of the responsible party, Haynes, the owner of the trailer.

[9] Predicated upon these facts, we conclude the trial court was correct in its assessment that a quasi-contract exists in this case.

[10] A quasi-contract evolves from the theory of *negotiorum gestio,* or the unauthorized management of affairs of another. Louisiana Civil Code Article 2292 provides an individual in Tyler's position to manage the affairs and to protect the interests of another, Haynes (the owner), without the authority of the owner, in the reasonable belief that the owner would approve of the action if he were made aware of the circumstances. The management is purely voluntary. The evidence is sufficient to connote that Tyler's actions were primarily in the interest of managing Haynes' affairs — towing Haynes' tractor-trailer which possibly prevented it from sustaining additional damage if it were left stranded on the roadway. *See* La.Civ.Code art. 2292, comment (c). Also, we have no reservations that Haynes would have desired services, such as those provided by Tyler, to have the tractor-trailer towed and to have the debris removed from the accident scene.

[. . . .]

Questions

1. Paragraphs 1–6: Identify clearly all the parties involved in this case. Identify, in legal terms, the relationships existing between sets of parties. Is there a contract between some of the parties? With regard to *negotiorum gestio*: Can you identify: (1) what is the "affair managed"; (2) who is the manager of the affair; (3) who is the owner (whose affair is managed)? How did the manager manage the affair? Did the manager make any juridical acts (e.g., contracts with third

persons) or was the affair managed merely by material acts? Take a look at Louisiana Civil Code articles 2293 and 2297.

2. Paragraph 10: The court notes that the acts of the manager were "purely voluntary." Is that true? Doesn't the court note earlier, in paragraph 8, that the parties involved had a *duty* to clear the accident site? What kind of duty was this? Was it a legal obligation based on contract or based on law (or both)? When a "manager" has a pre-existing duty, do the provisions on *negotiorum gestio* even apply? If not, what other remedies could the "manager" pursue against the "owner"? *See* Louisiana Civil Code article 2298.

Craig Burns
v.
Sabine River Authority

Court of Appeal of Louisiana
Third Circuit
May 5, 1999
736 So.2d 977

PETERS, J.

[1] Sabine River Authority appeals a judgment that denied its peremptory exception of prescription and ordered that a mandatory injunction issue to require it to remove a roadway that had been erected across an inlet of the Toledo Bend Reservoir and to provide Craig Burns water access to his property within thirty days. [....]

[....]

[2] In reversing the trial court, we stated:

> The management of another's affairs gives rise to a quasi contract. LSA-C.C. Art. 2295.[1] Whether the owner be acquainted with the undertaking or ignorant of it, the quasi contractual relationship of *negotiorum gestio* occurs. *Id.* When the manager assumes the agency, he contracts the tacit engagement to continue the management he has begun and to complete it. *Id.* Planiol states that a *gestion d'affaires* is created in every case where a person accomplishes a juridical act in the interest of another without having been charged to do so. 2 M. Plainol [sic], *Civil Law Treatise* pt. 2, no. 2273 at 308 (11th Ed.La.St.L.Inst.trans.1959).

> It is essential to *negotiorum gestio* that the manager be doing another's business, not his own business. *Tate v. Dupuis,* 195 So. 810 (La.App. 1st Cir. 1940); *Chance v. Stevens of Leesville, Inc.,* 491 So.2d 116 (La.App. 3rd Cir. 1986), writ denied, 495 So.2d 302 (La. 1986).

---

1. Our cite in *Burns* was to former La.Civ. Code art. 2295. New La.Civ.Code art. 2292 is in accord with former La.Civ.Code art. 2295, and new La.Civ.Code art. 2293 is based on former La.Civ.Code art. 2295.

Based on the facts alleged in Burns's petition and reported in the *Lucius* decision [*State, Sabine River Authority v. Lucius*, 335 So. 2d 95 (La.App. 3rd Cir.1976)], we find that the case *sub judice* presents a classic case of *negotiorum gestio*. At the time Sabine sued [. . .] to remove the illegal roadway, it was acting to preserve the juridical rights of the landowners whose property lay beyond the road and bordered the inlet. Now Sabine is obliged to complete the management of that affair by enforcing the judgment it obtained as the *gestor* of the owners. Since Burns's ancestor in title, an active participant in the prior litigation [. . .], directly benefitted from Sabine's legal action, we find it of no moment that Burns's identity was not known when Sabine undertook its management of the affairs of others. See, Comment, Management of the Affairs of Another, 36 Tul.L.Rev. 108(1961). Accordingly, as a result of the quasi contract between Sabine and Burns, Sabine may now be required to remove the road.

[. . . .]

[3] Actions sounding in quasi contract are subject to the ten-year liberative prescription period for personal actions under La.Civ.Code art. 3499. *Kilpatrick v. Kilpatrick*, 27,241 (La.App. 2 Cir. 8/23/95); 660 So.2d 182, *writ denied*, 95-2579 (La.12/15/95); 664 So.2d 444; *Taylor v. Smith*, 619 So.2d 881 (La.App. 3 Cir.), *writ denied*, 625 So.2d 1038 (La.1993). Sabine filed the initial suit [. . .] in 1973 and obtained judgment in 1975. The judgment in *State, Sabine River Authority v. Lucius*, 335 So.2d 95 (La.App. 3 Cir.1976), became final in 1976. The Burnses did not file the instant suit until 1990, well over ten years after the final judgment in *Lucius*. Therefore, we find that the trial court erred in failing to sustain the exception of prescription.

[. . . .]

[4] REVERSED AND RENDERED.

See also *Philip Darce v. One Ford Automobile* (La.App. 2 Cir. 185 1925) and *Kirkpatrick v. Young*, 456 So.2d 622 (La. 1984). Also see *Dean v. Hercules, Inc.*, 314 So.2d 430 (La.App. 1 Cir. 1975), reversed on other grounds, 328 So.2d 69 (La.1976), which held that in the third paragraph an error of translation occurred: the French word "fait" is better translated as "act" and not "fact."

Comparative Law Perspective

— Civil Law —

Marcel Planiol & Georges Ripert, *Traité Pratique de Droit Civil Français*

vol. 7, n° 723 at 6–7 (Paul Esmein rev., 2d ed. 1954)

723. By obligating the owner to compensate the manager, the doctrine of management of affairs prevents the owner from enriching himself at the manager's expense. It is therefore understandable that one could confuse management of affairs with enrichment without cause, and one could also suggest that management of affairs, which is regulated in the Civil Code, paved the way for the jurisprudential recognition of the *actio de in rem verso*.

Nevertheless, these two institutions differ with regard to the obligations they create: The manager is entitled to full compensation, even when the profit for the management no longer exists, while the *actio de in rem verso* obligates the enriched person to compensate only for any currently remaining enrichment.

— Common Law —

John P. Dawson, *Unjust Enrichment, A Comparative Analysis*

at 140–41 (1951)

The *negotiorum gestio*, in short, is a characteristic civil-law institution, appearing substantially everywhere. This very widespread acceptance suggests that altruism does not deserve the opprobrium that our [**common law**] courts have heaped upon it.

In fact, we have already gone some distance in approving unsolicited intervention. The clearest ground is the preservation of the intervenor's own interest, usually a limited or contingent interest in some specific asset. But a public interest will sometimes suffice, as with medical services in an emergency, burial of the dead, the supplying of necessaries to a person entitled by law to support from the defendant. [....] But our whole attitude is that we require excuse and insist that it be good. There is of course the sharpest contrast in the attitude toward waterborne altruists. Our law of maritime salvage not only permits but encourages intervention by giving it a generous reward. Our good neighbor policy applies on the sea but not on land.

E. Allan Farnsworth, *Contracts*

at 104–105 (2d ed. 1990)

The Restatement of Restitution lays down the broad principle that a "person who has been unjustly enriched at the expense of another is required to make restitution." We shall confine this preliminary consideration of that principle to a single inquiry: when does the law require one who has not requested a benefit to make restitution for it?

To begin, the person claiming restitution must have conferred a benefit of some kind on the other party. [. . . .] Furthermore, even if a benefit as been conferred, a court may deny recovery on any of several grounds: the benefit may have been conferred "officiously;" it may have been conferred "gratuitously;" or it may not be "measurable."

"Officiousness" is the term traditionally used to describe interference in the affairs of others that is not justified in the circumstances. Recovery is denied for benefits officiously conferred so that one will not have to pay for something forced upon one against one's will.

Although the gist of the notion of officiousness is not difficult to grasp, the precise line between the "officious intermeddler" or "volunteer" and the deserving claimant is difficult to draw, and no attempt will be made to draw it here.

Section III — Payment of a Thing Not Due

Louisiana Sources of Law
Louisiana Civil Code

Art. 2299. Obligation to restore.

A person who has received a payment or a thing not owed to him is bound to restore it to the person from whom he received it. (Acts 1995, No. 1041, §1, eff. Jan. 1, 1996.)

Art. 2300. Obligation that does not exist.

A thing is not owed when it is paid or delivered for the discharge of an obligation that does not exist. (Acts 1995, No. 1041, §1, eff. Jan. 1, 1996.)

Art. 2301. Obligation under suspensive condition.

A thing is not owed when it is paid or delivered for discharge of an obligation that is subject to a suspensive condition. (Acts 1995, No. 1041, §1, eff. Jan. 1, 1996.)

Art. 2302. Payment of the debt of another person.

A person who paid the debt of another person in the erroneous belief that he was himself the obligor may reclaim the payment from the obligee. The payment may not be reclaimed to the extent that the obligee, because of the payment, disposed of the instrument or released the securities relating to the claim. In such a case, the person who made the payment has a recourse against the true obligor. (Acts 1995, No. 1041, §1, eff. Jan. 1, 1996.)

Art. 2303. Liability of the person receiving payment.

A person who in bad faith received a payment or a thing not owed to him is bound to restore it with its fruits and products. (Acts 1995, No. 1041, §1, eff. Jan. 1, 1996.)

Art. 2304. Restoration of a thing or its value.

When the thing not owed is an immovable or a corporeal movable, the person who received it is bound to restore the thing itself, if it exists.

If the thing has been destroyed, damaged, or cannot be returned, a person who received the thing in good faith is bound to restore its value if the loss was caused by his fault. A person who received the thing in bad faith is bound to restore its value even if the loss was not caused by his fault. (Acts 1995, No. 1041, §1, eff. Jan. 1, 1996.)

Art. 2305. Liability when the thing is alienated.

A person who in good faith alienated a thing not owed to him is only bound to restore whatever he obtained from the alienation. If he received the thing in bad faith, he owes, in addition, damages to the person to whom restoration is due. (Acts 1995, No. 1041, §1, eff. Jan. 1, 1996.)

Doctrine

Louisiana Law of Unjust Enrichment in Quasi-Contracts

at 152–155 (1991)

[T]he Louisiana Civil Code articles governing the quasi-contract of the payment of a thing not due reflect the dualism of the Roman law description of the same concept. A payment may not be due when the payor, known in civil law terminology as solvens, made a payment by mistake or when the payment was made without a cause to justify its validity. Following the guidance of the Civil Code, the Louisiana jurisprudence has implemented this historical division of *condictio indebili* into two separate actions.

One line of cases stands for the proposition that a solvens's remedy can be based on the ascertainment that he made an error. [. . . .] Another line of cases acknowledges the existence of a *condictio indebiti* quasi-contract in the absence of a cause justifying the performance of an obligation and where no error was made by the solvens/payor. [. . . .] In conclusion, under both Louisiana Civil Code and the jurisprudence, the quasi-contractual remedy of *condictio indebiti* is available, first to a person who has paid a sum of money or carried out a performance under the mistaken belief that she owed such a sum or such a performance and second, to a person who performed an obligation which existed at the time the performance took place but which has been subsequently rescinded or nullified for failure or absence of cause.

Cases

Bossier Parish School Board
v.
Pioneer Credit Recovery, Inc.

Court of Appeal of Louisiana
Second Circuit
January 14, 2015
161 So.3d 1007

MOORE, J.

[1] Pioneer Credit Recovery Inc., a collection agency, appeals a judgment ordering it to repay the Bossier Parish School Board ("BPSB") $5,055.93, the amount BPSB erroneously sent to Pioneer pursuant to a federal order of withholding (administrative wage garnishment) after the order was released. We affirm.

Factual and Procedural Background

[2] Nancy White, a former BPSB employee, defaulted on her United Student Aid Funds student loan. United Student Aid retained Pioneer, a subsidiary of Sallie Mae, to collect. In June 2010, Pioneer sent BPSB the order of withholding, directing it to withhold from Ms. White's earnings an amount sufficient to pay off her defaulted $1,339.09 loan, and to forward the withheld funds to Pioneer each pay period. BPSB complied, taking $459.63 out of Ms. White's paycheck each month starting in August 2010. By October 10, the default amount was paid off. On October 27, Pioneer sent BPSB a federal release order of withholding, authorizing it to stop withholding and forwarding funds. BPSB stopped withholding money from Ms. White's check, but through clerical error continued sending $459.63 a month, out of BPSB's funds, to Pioneer. By the time the error was detected, in September 2011, BPSB had overpaid $5,055.93 to Pioneer. In October, BPSB finally advised Pioneer of the error and demanded a refund; Pioneer responded that it had already "refunded" the overpayment directly to Ms. White.

[3] BPSB filed this suit in January 2012 to recover the overpayment. In later pleadings, it argued that recovery was based on the theory of payment of a thing not owed, La. C.C. arts. 2299 and 2300. Pioneer admitted that it had received the overpayments but argued that BPSB was solely at fault for failing to comply with the federal guidelines for withholdings, 20 U.S.C. § 1095a and 34 C.F.R. 682.41(b)(9), and for disregarding the release of order of withholding. Pioneer's director of portfolio management stated by affidavit that it had refunded all overpayments directly to Ms. White, under the mistaken belief that the money was hers. BPSB argued that in point of fact, the overpayments were public funds.

[4] The matter proceeded to trial on joint stipulations. The district court rendered a written opinion citing La. C.C. art. 2299, "A person who has received a payment for a thing not owed to him is bound to restore it to the person from whom he received it[,]" and Revision Comment (b) to that article, "Louisiana courts interpreting this

provision have correctly ordered persons who received things or payments not owed to return them to the persons who made the delivery or the payment." The court found that the person who made the payment was BPSB, not Ms. White. It further found that Pioneer's direct payments to Ms. White were made "under Pioneer's sole discretion in an attempt to remedy the overpayment," but did not amount to restoring it to the person from whom Pioneer received it. The court concluded that Pioneer's obligation was to restore the $5,055.93 to the original sender, BPSB, and rendered judgment to that effect.

Discussion

[5] Pioneer has appealed, raising four assignments of error. By its first assignment, it urges the court erred in failing to find BPSB negligently failed to follow the law of garnishment, La. C.C.P. arts. 2411 et seq.; that any loss was solely the fault of BPSB; and that BPSB had "unclean hands" in pursuing the claim. By its second assignment, it urges the court erred in failing to find BPSB's actions grossly negligent in continuing to send funds after the release of order of withholding in October 2010. Framing the issue as payment of the debt of another, La. C.C. art. 2302, Pioneer again argues that equitable relief is not available to any party with "unclean hands," *Metropolitan Life Ins. Co. v. Mundy,* 167 So. 894 (La.App. 1 Cir.1936); *Pioneer Bank & Tr. Co. v. Dean's Copy Prods.,* 441 So.2d 1234 (La. App. 2 Cir.1983). Pioneer submits that BPSB had unclean hands because it failed to monitor its own bookkeeping department and verify that it was forwarding funds that belonged to the debtor instead of public money. By its third assignment, Pioneer reiterates that the court erred in failing to find BPSB's conduct grossly negligent, and its hands unclean, for failing to notify Pioneer that the funds paid under garnishment were actually public funds until after Pioneer had already mistakenly refunded the overpayment to Ms. White. By its fourth assignment, Pioneer urges that not only was BPSB grossly negligent in continuing to pay over one year after receiving the release of order of withholding, but, under the predecessor (pre-1996) version of Art. 2302, former Art. 2310, by paying the excess to Ms. White, Pioneer "parted with title" to the overpayment and is no longer liable to restore it to BPSB.

[6] Cases of enrichment without cause have been regulated by La. C.C. arts. 2298–2305 since January 1, 1996. 1995 La. Acts No. 1041, effective January 1, 1996. Article 2299 specifically provides the obligation to restore:

> A person who has received a payment or a thing not owed to him is bound to restore it to the person from whom he received it.

[7] This article clearly governs the instant case. Pioneer received a thing not owed to it, an overpayment of garnishment funds; Pioneer is thus bound to restore it to the entity, BPSB, from whom it received the thing not owed. The district court was not plainly wrong in finding to this effect.

[8] We are unpersuaded by Pioneer's reliance on the "unclean hands" doctrine throughout its first three assignments of error. We recognize the maxim that "a suitor who engaged in his own reprehensible conduct in the course of the transaction at

issue must be denied equitable relief because of unclean hands," *McKennon v. Nashville Banner Pub. Co.,* 513 U.S. 352, 360, 115 S.Ct. 879, 885, 130 L.Ed.2d 852 (1995). The law is clear, however, that courts may resort to equity only when "no rule for a particular situation can be derived from legislation or custom," La. C.C. art. 4. The existence of positive law on the subject precludes the application of equitable concepts. *Wier v. Glassell,* 216 La. 828, 848, 44 So.2d 882, 889 (1950); *Commercial Nat'l Bank v. Rowe,* 27,800 (La.App. 2 Cir. 1/24/96), 666 So.2d 1312. Even if the equitable doctrine of "unclean hands" applied, the jurisprudence uniformly interprets it as "reprehensible conduct," *McKennon v. Nashville Banner Pub. Co., supra;* "any illegal or immoral act or transactions to which he is a part," *Allvend Inc. v. Payphone Comm'ns Co.,* 2000-0661 (La.App. 4 Cir. 5/23/01), 804 So.2d 27, and citations therein; or as "a course of conduct naturally calculated, if not deliberately intended, to cause the very conditions that led [the other party] to seek equitable relief," *City of New Orleans v. Board of Directors of La. State Museum,* 98-1170 (La.3/2/99), 739 So.2d 748. While BPSB's bookkeeping standards in this instance appear surprisingly relaxed, they are far from reprehensible, illegal, immoral or naturally calculated to induce Pioneer's conduct. BPSB's conduct is much closer to the mere mistake which this court found insufficient to block equitable recovery in *Carter v. Flanagan,* 455 So.2d 689 (La.App. 2 Cir.1984). In fact, BPSB's error appears only slightly more serious than Pioneer's conduct in "refunding" over $5,000 to Ms. White without ascertaining that she had paid it in the first place. These assignments of error lack merit.

[9] By its fourth assignment of error, Pioneer cites the former La. C.C. art. 2310, urging that by paying the excess to Ms. White, it "parted with" title, thus extinguishing BPSB's right to claim restitution.[1] Pioneer contends that BPSB's only right is against Ms. White.

[10] As noted, since January 1, 1996, La. C.C. art. 2302 has provided the remedy for payment of the debt of another person:

> A person who paid the debt of another person in the erroneous belief that he was himself the obligor may reclaim the payment from the obligee. The payment may not be reclaimed to the extent that the obligee, because of the payment, disposed of the instrument or released the securities relating to the claim. In such a case, the person who made the payment has a recourse against the true obligor.

[11] The first sentence of this article excludes its application from the instant case. In mistakenly sending the overpayments to Ms. White, Pioneer was not paying the debt of another person; only Pioneer owed the obligation to restore the excess to BPSB. Moreover, this record does not show that any instrument or securities relating to the claim were disposed of, released, destroyed or parted with. Under the

---

1. Former Art. 2310 provided, in part, "This right [to claim restitution] ceases, if, in consequence of the payment, the creditor has destroyed or parted with his title; but the recourse still remains to the person paying against the true debtor."

principles of La. C.C. art. 2299, Pioneer appears to have a cause of action against Ms. White, but it did not join her as a defendant or bring a third-party claim against her in the instant suit. We decline to rule on a claim that has never been asserted. This assignment of error lacks merit.

Conclusion

[12] For the reasons expressed, the judgment is affirmed. All costs are to be paid by Pioneer Credit Recovery Inc.

[13] **AFFIRMED.**

Questions

1. Paragraphs 1–3: Identify the parties in this case. How many "payments of a thing not due" were made? Who was the payor (solvens) and who was the payee (accipiens)? Was payment made by mistake? Can you identify the mistake(s)?

2. Paragraphs 4–5: What is the legal source of the "unclean hands doctrine"? Can you find legislative expression of this doctrine in the Civil Code? *See*, for example, at Louisiana Civil Code article 2033. Can you think of circumstances where this doctrine would apply as a defense to a claim for "payment of a thing not due"?

3. Paragraphs 8–11: Do you agree with the court's conclusion that this case did not present an issue of "mistaken payment of a debt of another person"? *See* Louisiana Civil Code articles 1855 and 2302.

4. Paragraphs 8–11: Assume that the object of the payment was an individualized thing (e.g., a corporeal movable). What defenses could the defendant payee raise? *See* Louisiana Civil Code articles 2304–2305.

Whitehall Oil Company, Inc.
v.
Mrs. Marie Celeste Delaureal Boagni et al.

Court of Appeal of Louisiana
Third Circuit
December 5, 1968
217 So.2d 707

CULPEPPER, Judge.

[1] This case is consolidated for trial and appeal with Whitehall Oil Company, Inc. v. Heard et al., 217 So.2d 717, in which a separate decision is being rendered by us this date. The plaintiff seeks to recover from the defendants certain overpayments of gas royalties not due under the respective leases. From an adverse judgment in both cases, the plaintiff has appealed.

[2] There is no dispute as to the facts. They are set forth in a joint stipulation by the parties. The defendants are lessors in two oil, gas and mineral leases covering

certain lands in St. Landry Parish, Louisiana. The lease in the present case is dated December 13, 1959 and the one in the companion case December 7, 1959. There is also an assignment of overriding royalty, pertaining to the lease of December 1, 1959, to certain of the defendants. These leases were acquired by plaintiff by assignment on April 4, 1960.

[3] On September 13, 1961, the Federal Power Commission granted plaintiff temporary authority to sell the gas produced from the two leases at a price of 23.25¢ per m.c.f. However, this temporary authority was conditioned on plaintiff's agreement to restore to the pipeline purchasers any difference between the price temporarily authorized and the price finally approved by the Federal Power Commission.

[4] On July 23, 1964, the Federal Power Commission established the final authorized price at 20¢ per m.c.f. pursuant to the terms of the temporary authority, plaintiff then refunded to the pipeline purchasers the difference between the price temporarily authorized and the final price established.

[5] Plaintiff actually paid royalties to the defendants, based on the temporary price of 23.25¢ per m.c.f., until the final price of 20¢ was established on July 23, 1964. However, the joint stipulation of the parties states: "The defendants were not notified in any way prior to July 23, 1964, that they could be subjected to a retroactive demand for excess royalty payments in the event the gas sales price was reduced." Early in 1965 plaintiff demanded reimbursement from the royalty owners for their respective portions of the overpayments which plaintiff had refunded to the pipeline purchasers. Defendants refused and this suit followed.[1]

[6] Plaintiff argues first that under the very language of the two leases, and the overriding royalty assignment, the defendants are entitled only to their proportionate parts of the amount "realized" by the plaintiff from the sale of the gas.[2] And, since it finally "realized" only 20¢ per m.c.f., there was an overpayment of royalty not due which must be refunded. Plaintiff relies on the general equitable principles of unjust enrichment, LSA-C.C. Articles 21 and 1965, and particularly the articles of our Civil Code dealing with "Payment Of A Thing Not Due".[3]

---

1. Two royalty owners, Mrs. Susan B. Gardiner and Richard O. Eckhart, voluntarily remitted the alleged overpayments made to them, but the defendants in the present suit refused.

2. The lease dated December 13, 1959 provides that on gas the royalty is "the market value free of cost of production and delivery of one-eighth of the gas so sold or used. * * *" This lease further states: "In any case where lessee sells gas or plant products of his and lessor's, lessor shall receive the same price and terms as lessee and in such cases the gas of both parties shall be measured in the same manner." The assignment of overriding royalty dated December 13, 1959 pertains to this lease and states that the overriding royalty shall be calculated and paid in the same manner that is provided in the lease.

The royalty clause in the lease dated December 7, 1959 is somewhat different, as it provides: "The royalty on gas sold by lessee to be one-fourth of the amount realized at the well from such sales."

3. Art. 2301. He who receives what is not due to him, whether he receives it through error or knowingly, obliges himself to restore it to him from whom he has unduly received it.

Art. 2302. He who has paid through mistake, believing himself a debtor, may reclaim what he has paid.

[7] These latter articles are found in Title V, Chapter I of our Civil Code entitled "Of Quasi Contracts". The rationale of the articles is that, even without an express agreement to that effect, every payment presupposes a debt. Consequently, if a thing has been paid without it being due, it can be recovered.[4]

[8] In construing these articles, the first question is the requirement of error. Article 2301 provides that, as to the person who receives the payment, it is immaterial whether he had knowledge the payment was made through error. In the present case, the defendants had no knowledge whatever that the alleged overpayments were made subject to a condition that they might have to refund them. In any event, this is immaterial, for even if they had known the payments were not due, this would not affect their obligation to refund them.

[9] Article 2302 states that "he who has paid through mistake, believing himself a debtor, may reclaim what he has paid." Thus, our Civil Code allows recovery of payment through error of a thing not due.[5] In the present case, the alleged overpayments were not made through error on the part of the plaintiff. It knew that under the terms of the leases it was obligated to pay royalty on the basis of the price for which it sold the gas to the pipeline purchasers. The lease provisions to this effect are clear and were so understood by the plaintiff. At the time these payments were made, they were actually due. Hence, there can be no contention that they were paid through error.

[10] Since the payer was not in error, defendants make a strong argument that the above quoted codal articles, regarding payment of a thing not due, can have no application. However, this is not the end of our inquiry of the statutory materials. In discussing "repetition", the French action to recover payment of a thing not due, Planiol, Civil Law Treatise, an English Translation by the Louisiana State Law Institute, Vol. 2, Part I, pg. 449, Sec. 837 states:

Art. 2303. To acquire this right, it is necessary that the thing paid be not due in any manner, either civilly or naturally. A natural obligation to pay will be sufficient to prevent the recovery.

Art. 2304. A thing not due is that which is paid on the supposition of an obligation which did not exist, or from which a person has been released.

Art. 2305. That which has been paid in virtue of a void title is also considered as not due.

Art. 2306. The payment from which we might have been relieved by an exception that would extinguish the debt, affords ground for claiming restitution.

Art. 2307. But this exception must be such that it shall extinguish even all natural obligation. Thus he who, having the power to plead prescription, shall have made payment, can not claim restitution.

Art. 2308. It is considered that a thing has been paid, when not due, if the payment was made by virtue of an agreement, the effect of which is suspended by a condition, the event of which is uncertain.

Art. 2309. This principle must not be extended to things due on a day certain, nor to conditions which must certainly happen.

4. Planiol, Vol. 2, Part I, pgs. 448–454, Secs. 835–846; Great American Indemnity Co. v. Dauzat, 157 So.2d 308 (La. App., 3d Cir. 1963); Ark. Fuel Oil Co. v. Williams, 183 So. 128 (La.App.2d Cir. 1938); LSA-C.C. Art. 2133.

5. See the Case Note in 20 Tul.Law Rev. 618 for a review of the history of Article 2302 and its interpretation.

"Repetition always presupposes that what was paid was not due, but in order to determine precisely the conditions under which repetition can be exercised, it is necessary to distinguish between three different situations: (1) where there was no obligation whatever between the payer and the payee; (2) where the payment was made in view of an actual obligation which has since ceased to exist; and (3) where the obligation paid had an illicit or an immoral cause."

[11] Planiol takes the position that error by the payer is required in situation (1) listed above, but not in situations (2) and (3). The present case falls within situation (2), of which Planiol says in Vol. 2, Part I, pg. 452, Sec. 843:

"It is required that there be something not due: the plaintiff in repetition must prove that his debt was resolved or annulled, or that the future debt did not arise; *but the condition of error is not required, and it cannot be exacted.* There is an act other than payment, and that is the annulment, the resolution or failure of a condition, which renders necessary the reestablishment of things in the state they would have been in if the agreement had not been made." (Emphasis added)

[12] We note that Planiol's discussion concerns Code Napoleon Article 1376, which is almost identical to our own LSA-C.C. Article 2301. These two articles do not attempt a further definition of "a thing not due", nor do they expressly provide for recovery of a payment made through error. Our own Louisiana Civil Code has added Articles 2302 through 2309, which have no corresponding source articles in the Code Napoleon. The purpose of these additional articles is to expressly allow recovery where there is error on the part of the person making the payment and to further define "a thing not due".

[13] LSA-C.C. Article 2304 is particularly applicable to the present situation. It provides that "a thing not due is that which is paid on the supposition of an obligation which did not exist, or from which a person has been released." The first part of the article pertains to the situation where a person pays through error a debt which actually does not exist at the time of the payment. (This is in effect the same as Article 2302.) However, the latter part of the article applies to the situation where an actual obligation exists at the time of the payment, but the debt is later released. Although Article 2304 does not expressly stated that in this latter situation error on the part of the payer is not required, we think this is necessarily implied. For, if there is an actual legal obligation at the time of the payment, it cannot be made through mistake. As Planiol says, in Vol. 2, Part I, Sec. 843, quoted above, there is an act which takes the place of the payment through error, and that is the subsequent resolution or failure of the contract. Under our Code, this would be a resolutory condition.[6]

---

6. LSA-C.C. Article 2308 affords similar relief where the condition is suspensive. See also Articles 2021, 2023, 2042 and 2045 on suspensive and resolutory conditions.

[14] From the statutory materials, it is our conclusion that in the present case, error on the part of the plaintiff at the time of the payment is not required. Plaintiff need only show that subsequent to the payment the debt was released by the occurrence of a resolutory condition. The Code, Article 2304, provides no further limitation or condition. However, our courts have applied equitable considerations in many cases for recovery of payment of a debt not due.

[15] For instance, the courts have considered the following equity factors in suits to recover payment of a thing not due: (1) Was the payer guilty of fault such as fraud or duress, or of negligence in failing to protect his own interests or in failing to treat fairly the interests of the payee, Pennsylvania Casualty Co. v. Brooks, La.App., 24 So.2d 262; Metropolitan Life Ins. Co. v. Mundy, La.App., 167 So. 894; New Orleans & N.E.R.R. Co. v. La. Construction & Improvement Co., 109 La. 13, 33 So. 51; Rivers v. New Orleans Waterworks Co., 35 La.Ann. 822; Ducros v. Missouri State Life Ins. Co., Orl.App. No. 7996. (2) Would recovery result in injury to the party to whom the payment was made, Continental Oil Co. v. Jones, La.App., 191 So.2d 895; Central Surety & Ins. Corp. v. Corbello, La.App., 74 So.2d 341. (3) Would the party who made the payment receive some benefit from the payment by error, Morse v. Oates, 11 La.App. 462, 123 So. 439.

[16] Jurisprudence in common law jurisdictions has developed many other equitable factors to be considered in a suit for recovery of payment of a debt not due. Some of these mentioned in 40 Am.Jur. 820-872, Verbo Payments, Secs. 155 through 235 are: (1) was the payment made under business duress (Sec. 171), i.e., was it necessary to make the payment to preserve the payer's property or protect his business interests; (2) was the payment made under protest (Sec. 180, et seq.); (3) did the payer have another remedy in lieu of payment (Sec. 183); (4) was the payment induced by fraud (Sec. 185); (5) was there mutuality of mistake (Sec. 191); (6) has the payment caused such a change in the position of the payee that it would be unjust to require him to refund (Sec. 201). We see no reason why equity factors, such as the ones developed in common law jurisdictions, should not be applied where appropriate by the courts of Louisiana. Actually many have been discussed and some applied. For instance, the concept of business duress was discussed in New Orleans & N.E. R.R. Co. v. La. Construction & Improvement Co., 209 La. 13, 33 So. 51, but the court found under the facts of that case that it should not apply. However, the decision of the court shows the extent to which equitable considerations are taken into account. The court said:

> "The question narrows to what is in law a voluntary payment. The distinction to be made between payments voluntary and payments under duress has been a fruitful theme of discussion in the courts. Where the parties were not on equal terms; where the payer had no choice; where the only alternative was to submit to an illegal exaction or discontinue business — these and other like circumstances evidencing pressure or duress under which money or other value is parted with have never been regarded as embraced within the rule of voluntary acts within the meaning of the maxim 'Volenti

non fit injuria.' Swift Co. v. U.S., 111 U.S. [22] 28, 4 Sup. Ct. 244, 28 L.Ed. 341. But where dispute arises and the debtor, who pays under protest, has at hand other means of immediate relief than by making the payment, his act is not one done under coercion and his protest does not take the case out of the category of voluntary payment."

[17] Now let us examine the facts of the present case to determine where the equity lies. Plaintiff contends the payments were made under "business duress".[7] The argument here is that, in order to protect its leases, plaintiff had to make the overpayment of royalty based on the price fixed by the Federal Power Commission. Hence, that the payments were made under business duress and the defendants should not be allowed by equity or good conscience to retain them. This is a persuasive argument. Plaintiff could charge no more than the price authorized by the Federal Power Commission and, in order to protect its leases, it had to pay royalty on the basis of this price. In seeking the highest possible price plaintiff was attempting to protect not only its own but the payee's interests. There was no way for plaintiff to determine in advance whether the final price authorized would be lower. In the interim, it paid the full royalty to defendants who had the use of the money. Hence, up to this point, the equity seems to favor the plaintiff.

[18] Defendants' principal argument is that plaintiff should have notified them that the overpayment of royalties might have to be refunded. Defendants say that the plaintiff could have sought an agreement, whereby the excess royalty could have been placed in escrow until the final authorized price was determined by the Federal Power Commission; or that plaintiff could have sought to obtain from defendants an amendment of the lease; or at least that plaintiffs could have filed a suit for declaratory judgment to determine their rights under the leases. Defendants contend that by not pursuing one of these alternatives, the plaintiff has been guilty of negligence in the protection of its own interest and has failed to mitigate its losses. Of course, defendants also argue that they were misled into using the funds for a period of three years and now it would cause them injury if they had to make restitution.

[19] It is our conclusion, after considering all of the facts, that the equities favor the plaintiff. The only substantial equitable argument against its position is that it failed to notify the defendants in some way, either through an attempted escrow agreement, a suit for declaratory judgment, payment under protest or by some other means that part of the royalty payments might have to be refunded. However, this lack of notice to the defendants is offset to some extent by the fact that the

---

7. 40 Am.Jur. 831, Verbo Payments, Sec. 171 defines this exception to the general rule of voluntary payment as a situation "where by reason of the peculiar facts a reasonably prudent man finds that in order to preserve his property or protect his business interest it is necessary to make a payment of money which he does not own and which in equity and good conscience the receiver should not retain. * * *"

overpayments received are not large sums[8] and the defendants have failed to show their circumstances are such that they will be injured by the return of these over-payments which were not due.

[20] The plaintiffs pray for refund of both the principal and interest which it had to pay to the pipeline purchasers under its agreement. We find no case which considers the question of interest on recovery of a payment not due. However, under the facts of this case, we think interest should be denied.

[21] The defendants also argue that under LSA-C.C. Art. 2671 the rent due under a lease must be "certain and determinative". They argue that if a refund of the rent (in this case the royalties) is required, the price would then be uncertain and the lease violated. The answer to this argument is that the present action is based on a quasi contractual obligation authorized by our Civil Code as discussed hereinabove.

[22] The arguments made by defendants under the heading of "estoppel" in their brief, are substantially the same as those discussed above in considering the equities of the case.

[23] For the reasons assigned, the judgment appealed is reversed and set aside. It is now ordered, adjudged and decreed that there be judgment herein in favor of Whitehall Oil Company, Inc. against Mrs. Marie Celeste Delaureal Boagni in the amount of $1752.91; against Mrs. Gladys Mae Pitre Boagni in the amount of $536.44; against Mrs. Gladys Boagni Waterbury in the amount of $152.27; against Christopher Dietlein Boagni in the amount of $274.72; against Vincent Boagni, Jr. in the amount of $1727.28; against Edward M. Boagni, III in the amount of $1752.88, and against the following, in the proportions stated for each, out of the sum of $1883.67 formerly held in the registry of the court in proceedings numbered 44352 on the docket of the Twenty-seventh Judicial District Court for the Parish of St. Landry:

Marie Celeste D. Boagni	33.333%
Edward M. Boagni, III	33.333%
Gladys M. Pitre Boagni	22.200%
Vincent D. Boagni, Jr.	7.423%
Christopher D. Boagni	3.711%

[24] It is further ordered that the defendants pay legal interest from the date of judicial demand until paid, together with all costs in the district court and in this court of appeal.

[25] Reversed and rendered.

TATE, Judge (dissenting).

[26] The writer respectfully dissents.

---

8. The amounts of principal to be refunded by the respective royalty owners vary from about $2380.80 down to $152 and aggregate about $9,458.37 in the two cases.

[27] From 1961 to 1964 the plaintiff Whitehall unconditionally paid royalties to the defendant landowners. In 1965, Whitehall informed them that the payments so made unconditionally had, in reality, been made subject to a resolutory condition. Whitehall stated that the landowners owed them refunds (of about 1/8 of the royalties previously paid) because Whitehall had been forced to reimburse such amounts to the purchaser of the mineral products, pursuant to a side-agreement between it and the purchaser (which provided for a temporary price pending a final Federal Power Commission ruling with reimbursement to be pursuant to the final price approved by the F.P.C.) It is conceded that the defendant landowners were totally ignorant of this agreement, and that Whitehall had never informed them of it nor that the royalties unconditionally paid during these three years were subject to refund upon later claim.

[28] In its scholarly opinion, the majority concedes that the general rule is to the effect that payments voluntarily made with full knowledge of the facts cannot subsequently be recovered; that it is only payments made through error which can as a general rule be subsequently recovered. However, the majority suggests that Civil Code Article 2304[1] permits, as an exception, the recovery of payments voluntarily made subject to a resolutory condition. In the writer's opinion, for the reasons to be set forth more fully below, this is neither the express nor the implied meaning of the article.

[29] The exception sought to be applied here does violence to the general legal principle that, for the stability of society and of transactions, voluntary payments made with full knowledge of all the facts and not under duress may not subsequently be recovered, even though the amount so paid is not actually owed. New Orleans & N. E.R. Co. v. Louisiana Construction & Imp. Co., 109 La. 13, 33 So. 51 (1902); Fuselier v. St. Landry Parish, 107 La. 221, 31 So. 678; Rivers v. New Orleans Water Works Company, 35 La.Ann. 822; Hicks v. Levett, 2d Cir., 19 La.App. 836, 140 So. 276; Ducros v. Missouri State Life Ins. Co., 4 Peltier's Orleans Appeals 463 (Orl. No. 7996). See also Strange v. Continental Supply Co., 165 La.Ann. 20, 115 So. 353.

[30] Similar rules are applied by the common law also. See 70 C.J.S. Payment §§ 133–144. This ancient and universal legal principle is expressed by the maxim, "Volenti non fit Injuria" ("That to which a person assents is not esteemed in law an injury"). Broom's Legal Maxims (5th ed., 1870).

[31] This universal principle, however, has its equitable limitations. One of these is that he who pays through error what is not due, may reclaim what has been paid. Civil Code Article 2302.[2] Thus, the provision of Code Article 2301, permitting recovery of payments made when not owed to the receiver, must be understood as subject to the requirement of Article 2302 that they have been paid through mistake. Rivers

---

1. Article 2304 provides: "A thing not due is that which is paid on the supposition of an obligation which did not exist, or from which a person has been released."

2. Article 2302 provides: "He who has paid through mistake, believing himself a debtor, may reclaim what he has paid."

v. New Orleans Water Works Company, 35 La.Ann. 822 (1883). See also Planiol, Civil Law Treatise, Volume 2, Section 840 (LSLI translation, 1959).

[32] In refusing to apply this general principle, the majority relies upon Civil Code Article 2304: "A thing not due is that which is paid on the supposition of an obligation [a] which did not exist, or [b] from which a person has been released." The majority interprets the latter ("b") part of this article to mean that a payor is entitled to recover a payment made for a debt due at the time which is later released through a resolutory condition.

[33] I respectfully submit that such an interpretation is erroneous. Pertinently, the article provides that recovery is permitted of payments made "on the *supposition* of an obligation * * * from which a person *has been released.*"

[34] The intended meaning of "supposition" in this context must be in the dictionary sense of something which is *mistakenly* believed to be an obligation, but one which has actually been released.[3] To hold otherwise deprives the word "supposition" of any meaning in the article, so that article is amended to omit the phrase and as if it read: "A thing not due is that which is paid on an obligation which did not exist, or from which a person has been released."

[35] Likewise, the article does not apply to a payment made upon an obligation valid at the time which is *subsequently* annulled or avoided. The article applies only to a payment on an obligation "from which a person *has been* released." This is the present perfect tense of the verb, and "The present perfect tense shows that an act has been completed prior to the present". The Macmillan Handbook of English, p. 245 (1963).

[36] In holding that repetition lies for the present voluntary payment, the majority relies upon Planiol's statement that the action is permitted where the payment is voluntarily made without mistake in view of an actual obligation which has since ceased to exist. Planiol Sections 837, 842-844. As to this type of obligation, it is suggested that no "error" is required because the annulment or resolution of a condition upon which the contract has been made takes the place of error. Section 843. The example given is when the buyer voluntarily paying the price to mortgage creditors at execution sale is evicted by a third party with a superior title. Section 844.

[37] The majority's reasoning is forceful and persuasive. If payment is made upon an obligation subject to a resolutory condition, I have no doubt that it should be restored should the resolving condition occur (a) when both parties knew of the resolutory condition or (b) when the payor did not know of it, such as where unknownst to him there was a defect in his purchaser's title so the sale was subsequently rescindable through this resolutory condition. Indeed, I think this to be the thrust of the Planiol discussion, although there is much reason to accept the majority's interpretation of it.

---

3. Webster's Seventh New Collegiate Dictionary (1967): *verbo* "supposition": "something which is supposed"; *verbo* "supposed": "Believed; *also:* mistakenly believed".

[38] In any event, I do not think this sort of reasoning should apply here. The payor unconditionally paid an amount only conditionally owed. Insofar as the payee is concerned, the belated claim for refund is generically identical to a claim based upon a contention of no obligation at all at the time (instead of upon an obligation unknown at the time to be subject to resolution), for years later the return is now claimed of money he has received and spent in the belief he is entitled to keep it. Generically, the stabilizing social principle should apply that the equities favor the innocent recipient rather than the one who voluntarily paid with full knowledge that he might not owe it.

[39] Under such circumstances, the party who paid with full knowledge of the facts should not have recovery. To protect himself and to avoid the disruptive effects upon the finances of the innocent recipients of a subsequent claim for refund, the payor could simply have put the payee upon notice that such payments were made subject to a later claim for refund.

[40] Insofar as the plaintiff debtor now claims that payments were made under duress, our jurisprudence is clear that under circumstances such as the present one cannot voluntarily make the payments with full knowledge of the facts, and without protest, and yet later claim that business duress forced them. The decisions earlier cited rejected similar claims of duress under circumstances where actual coercive tactics by the payees were at issue.

[41] Whitehall's petition pleads for reimbursement because of unjust enrichment.

[42] This claim for unjustified enrichment is essentially founded upon Civil Code Article 1965. This article provides for application of the principle preventing unjust enrichment only, however, in the instances where the law or the contract is silent as to the rights of the parties as to the recovery sought. Moore v. Housing Authority of City of Opelousas, La.App. 3 Cir., 125 So.2d 504, 508; Clark v. Shaffett, La.App. 1 Cir., 37 So.2d 56, 58–59.

[43] Thus, for the doctrine of unjustified enrichment to apply, there must not only be an enrichment of one person and the impoverishment of another, but also an absence of a legal cause for the enrichment of one at the expense of the other. Thompson v. Taylor, La.App.3rd Cir., 192 So. 2d 609, Nicholas, Unjustified Enrichment in the Civil Law and Louisiana, La., 36 Tul.L.Rev. 605 (Part 1) (1962), 37 Tul. L.Rev. 49 (Part II) (1962); Planiol, Civil Law Treatise, Volume 2, Sections 932-938 (LSLT Translation, 1959); 2 Dalloz Repertoire de Droit Civil, "Enrichissment sans Cause", Section 3, Nos. 71-131 (1952). "* * * The action will not lie if the enrichment and impoverishment is justified by a rule of law." Nicholas, cited above, at 37 Tul.L.Rev. 605, 635.

[44] In the present instance, the plaintiff is not entitled to recover on the grounds of unjustified enrichment. The payees are entitled to keep what has been paid to them voluntarily and with full knowledge of the facts, because of the stabilizing legal principle preventing payors from disturbing the status quo by demanding reimbursement subsequently of payments made by them voluntarily with full knowledge of the facts justifying them to withhold or to condition their payment.

[45] For the reasons assigned, I respectfully dissent.

[. . . .]

Questions

1. Do you find the majority's reasoning more convincing, or do you agree with Judge Tate's dissent?

2. This case was decided under the Louisiana Civil Code of 1870. The provisions on "payment of a thing not due" were revised in 1995. Review revised Civil Code articles 2299–2305. According to revision comment (c) to Louisiana Civil Code article 2299: "Article 2302 of the Louisiana Civil Code of 1870 declares: 'He who has paid through mistake, believing himself a debtor, may reclaim what he has paid.' This provision derives from the 1825 Revision and has no counterpart in the French Civil Code or in the Louisiana Civil Code of 1808. The provision has been suppressed. *Under Article 2299, a person who knowingly or through error has paid or delivered a thing not owed may reclaim it from the person who received it.*" (emphasis added). Is this comment accurate? If payment was made voluntarily, can the payor (solvens) always recover that payment from the payee (accipiens)?

Michael Joseph Gallo
v.
Brenda Ann Conner Gallo
Supreme Court of Louisiana
December 3, 2003
861 So.2d 168

WEIMER, Justice.

[1] Upon initial inspection, this case presents an issue regarding reimbursement of money. Upon closer scrutiny, one finds issues which explore the underpinnings of the parent-and-child relationship. An ex-husband is asserting a right to recover monies he paid to his ex-wife for the support of a minor child, born during the marriage, who for many years he believed was his biological child. Years after the couple's divorce, it was determined another man was actually the biological father. The trial court denied the ex-husband's claim for reimbursement from his ex-wife. Reversing, the court of appeal awarded the ex-husband reimbursement for the child support paid to the ex-wife. For the reasons that follow, we reverse the court of appeal's ruling and deny the ex-husband's demand for reimbursement.

[. . . .]

Discussion

[2] The issue in this case is not whether the law *prohibits* reimbursement of the child support payments, as the court of appeal indicated, but whether the law *allows* reimbursement. The question calls for consideration of how the legislature and the

courts have dealt with the concepts of child support in light of fluctuating mores and trends in family law. *See, T.D. v. M.M.M.,* 98-0167, p. 4 (Knoll, Justice, concurring) (La.3/2/99), 730 So.2d 873, 878-879; *see also,* LSA-R.S. 9:305, quoted *infra.* The historical background of child support principles is explained in CHRISTOPHER L. BLAKESLEY, LOUISIANA FAMILY LAW § 16.02 at 16-2, 16-3 (Louisiana Civil Code Series Issue 1, 1996):

> Louisiana's Civil Law tradition,[6] from its French and Spanish beginnings, provided for the parental obligation of child support. The Common Law did not have such an auspicious beginning. The Elizabethan Poor Laws in England during the 16th century were the initial weak and ulteriorly motivated attempt to make the father pay the parish . . . for child support given his child. . . . Louisiana's and continental Codes influenced child support legislation in the rest of the United States. [Original footnotes omitted.]

[3] "The sources of law are legislation and custom." LSA-C.C. art 1. In Louisiana, as in all codified systems, legislation is the superior source of law. LSA-C.C. art. 1, cmts. (a) and (c). Legislation cannot be abrogated by custom. LSA-C.C. art. 3. Accordingly, the starting point of our analysis is with the codal articles to determine the status of the parties and their reciprocal rights and obligations.

---

6. Family solidarity was one of the three ideological pillars of the Code Napoleon, along with freedom of contract and private property; these ideological pillars were considered necessary to overthrow the complex restraints of feudalism. Shael Herman, "The Louisiana Civil Code: A European [sic] Legacy for the United States" (1993) at p. 38.

> The drafters of the [Louisiana] Civil Code considered the family the basic cell of society and the protector of the future of society. The Civil Code provisions were influenced by middle class values and specifically by a sense that the family was a closely knit group under the authority of . . . strong parents. These values are reflected particularly in provisions concerning the economic rights of a family to the wealth accumulated by a family member. When one considers the financial shakiness of the public institutions designed to keep the family afloat (welfare, social security, etc.), it is heartening to find a private law concerned with the material well-being of the family. If the Civil Code rules we describe appear anachronistic, perhaps it is because we no longer share the code drafters' assumptions about the centrality of the family's role in society.

> In the disposition of property, the Civil Code promotes family solidarity. Although in other states familial financial responsibilities do not routinely go beyond what is necessary for periodic support of dependent children and spouses, Louisiana law has traditionally imposed support obligations on a parent and has generally insured that a spouse will receive family capital in the form of community property and that minor and incompetent children will receive fixed shares. Although responsibility to a person's family restricts his autonomy, the code's restrictions permit considerable latitude to dispose of property outside the family circle, to favor one minor child over another, and even to alter the share of capital to which a spouse is entitled. These features of code regulation permit the conclusion that the Civil Code stresses family responsibility over individual autonomy to a greater extent than the law of other states in which the balance tips towards autonomy. [Footnote omitted.]

Id. at 53–54.

[4] "The husband of the mother is presumed to be the father of all children born or conceived during the marriage." LSA-C.C. art. 184.[7] "A suit for disavowal of paternity must be filed within one year[8] after the husband learned or should have learned of the birth of the child; but, if the husband for reasons beyond his control is not able to file suit timely, then the time for filing suit shall be suspended during the period of such inability." LSA-C.C. art. 189. The policy embodied in the restrictive provisions of the Louisiana Civil Code dealing with the action to disavow is to protect innocent children, born during marriage, against scandalous attacks upon their paternity by the husband of the mother, who may be seeking to avoid paternal obligations to the child. *Williams v. Williams,* 230 La. 1, 7-8, 87 So.2d 707, 709 (1956).[9] Thus, the traditional and historical position of Louisiana jurisprudence was to zealously guard and enforce the presumption created by Article 184. *Pounds v. Schori,* 377 So.2d 1195, 1200 (La.1979). The fundamental ends achieved by such court action were preservation of the family unit, avoidance of the stigma of illegitimacy, and aversion to the disinheritance that resulted from a successful disavowal action. There is a public interest in dispelling doubts as to legitimacy which demands the establishment of a relatively short time for bringing challenges. These considerations contributed to this court's holding, in 1979, that the period of time in which a husband must file a suit for disavowal to defeat the presumption of his paternity is peremptive. *Id.*

[. . . .]

[5] [. . . .] This court's recognition of peremption as a concept distinct from prescription formed the basis of enactment by the legislature in 1982 of LSA-C.C. arts. 3458–3461. *See* LSA-C.C. art. 3458, Revision Cmts. — 1982(b), *citing Pounds,* 377 So.2d 1195. "Peremption is a period of time fixed by law for the existence of a right. Unless timely exercised, the right is extinguished upon the expiration of the peremptive period." LSA-C.C. art. 3458. "The provisions on prescription governing computation of time apply to peremption." LSA-C.C. art. 3459. "Peremption may be pleaded or it may be supplied by a court on its own motion at any time prior to final judgment." LSA-C.C. art. 3460. "Peremption may not be renounced, interrupted, or suspended." LSA-C.C. art. 3461.

[6] The one-year peremptory time limitation for bringing a challenge to the paternity of a child born during a marriage begins on the date of the child's birth

---

7. For a thorough history of this presumption *see T.D. v. M.M.M.,* 98-0167 at 1–4 (Kimball, Justice, dissenting), 730 So.2d at 880–882.

8. Previous to a 1999 amendment to Article 189, the time period had been one hundred and eighty days. Although that time period was in effect at the time of M.L.G.'s birth in 1985, the legislature specified that the amendment was to have retroactive effect.

9. In *Williams,* the husband of the mother requested an order requiring the mother and the daughter he was attempting to disavow to submit to blood testing. The order was denied, and thus, the husband was unable to rebut the presumption of LSA-C.C. art. 184, which at that time was a conclusive presumption. The rationale of *Williams* is still viable although, since 1989, the law has allowed a husband, in a disavowal action, the use of negative blood tests as proof that he is not the biological father of the child born during his marriage to the mother. LSA-C.C. art. 187(1).

rather than when the husband becomes aware of the wife's alleged fraud and alleg-edly learns that he is not the father of the child. *See Pounds v. Schori*, 369 So.2d 1090, 1092 (La.App. 1 Cir.1979),[11] *aff'd*, 377 So.2d 1195; *accord, Brugman v. Prejean*, 288 So.2d 702, 704 (La.App. 3 Cir.1974.) Thus, being unaware of misrepresentation or fraud by the mother is not the "inability" to file suit to disavow which LSA-C.C. art. 189 allows as a bar to the commencement of the peremptive period.

[. . . .]

[7] Accordingly, we hold *sua sponte*[12] that Mr. Gallo's right to rebut the LSA-C.C. art. 184 presumption of paternity was perempted because he did not file an action for disavowal within a year of M.L.G.'s date of birth, April 27, 1985. Thus, the "Peti-tion to Disavow Paternity" will be dismissed with prejudice as being perempted.

[. . . .]

[8] Next, we must determine if there is any other legal basis which, absent dis-avowal, allows reimbursement to Mr. Gallo.

[9] Louisiana Civil Code, article 2299, provides, "A person who has received a payment or a thing not owed to him is bound to restore it to the person from whom he received it." This court recently held that when monies were paid while a judgment in a plaintiff's favor was being appealed devolutively and, after payment, the judgment was reversed, the payor could recover the monies pursuant to Arti-cle 2299. *Gootee Construction, Inc. v. Amwest Surety Insurance Company*, 03-0144 (La.10/10/03), 856 So.2d 1203. Although a final judgment relieves Mr. Gallo of future child support, the "debt" of child support he paid prior to that judgment was not rescinded or annulled as was the debt in *Gootee Construction, Inc.*

[10] An examination of the child support jurisprudence reveals the courts of appeal have struggled with the issue of what circumstances cause a father's payment of child support to be "a thing not owed" so that LSA-C.C. art. 2299[16] would be appli-cable and reimbursement would be owing. [. . . .]

[11] "Fathers and mothers, by the very act of marrying, contract together the obligation of supporting, maintaining, and educating their children." LSA-C.C. art. 227.[17] Thus, proof of birth during marriage establishes the obligation of support. *State v. Kiper*, 408 So.2d 1312, 1314 (La. 1982) (Husband of the mother was presumed to be

---

11. The court of appeal stated there was nothing in the record or pleadings to suggest that the time limitation commenced at any date other than the date of the child's birth. This observation was made despite the husband's allegation in his petition to disavow that he did not cohabit with his wife at a time when she could have conceived a child. We note Mr. Gallo has made no such allegation.

12. *See* LSA-C.C. art 3460, quoted *supra*, which allows this court to notice peremption on its own at any time prior to final judgment.

16. The lower courts have seldom cited Article 2299.

17. Child support legislation is now "vast, various and spread out over numerous codes and stat-utes." BLAKESLEY, LOUISIANA FAMILY LAW §16.01 at 16-1. A list of pertinent legislation given by Professor Blakesley is a helpful resource for statutory authority regarding child support. *Id.*

the father of her children born during the marriage and was obligated to support them even pending his actions to disavow paternity.). [. . . .]

[. . . .]

[12] Proper analysis recognizes that it is not the adults but the child who is at the center of this unfortunate controversy. A father's obligation to support his children is a "primary, continuous obligation," based during marriage on parental authority and after divorce on tutorship. Blakesley, Louisiana Family Law § 16.02 at 16-5. The child is the veritable creditor of each parent's unilateral obligation for the child's upbringing with the special expenses it entails. *Id.* at 16-6. This father-child relationship between Mr. Gallo and M.L.G. did not end with blood testing that showed Mr. Gallo was not the biological father of M.L.G. He remained her legal presumptive father and was identified as such in the three-party acknowledgment. Fatherhood rests on something more than genes. *See, T.D. v. M.M.M.,* 98-0167 at 2 (concurring opinion), 730 So.2d at 878, *citing Lehr v. Robertson,* 463 U.S. 248, 103 S.Ct. 2985, 77 L. Ed.2d 614 (1983). Furthermore, Louisiana has recognized dual fatherhood. In *Smith v. Cole,* 553 So.2d 847, 854, (La.1989), this court held that the failure of the husband of the mother of the child to exercise his right to disavow paternity timely established the child as his legal and legitimate child. The legal tie of paternity would not be affected by subsequent proof of the child's actual biological tie. [. . . .]

[. . . .]

[13] Other benefits Mr. Gallo received stem from the fact that for four years following the couple's separation, Mr. Gallo had custody of the child he petitioned to disavow. [. . . .] Mr. Gallo was entitled to all of the many benefits of fatherhood, not the least of which are the love and affection of this child he considered his and reared as his for so many years. There is nothing in the record to indicate that Mr. Gallo did not receive the love and affection of this child, that he did not feel the special, precious bond a father enjoys with a daughter. In this respect, Mr. Gallo has received much from this child.

[14] Although Mr. Gallo finds himself in an unfortunate situation, which includes adultery by his former wife and the realization this child is not biologically his, he cannot recover the monies he has paid as child support because they were not wrongfully paid (LSA-C.C. art. 2299) [. . .].

[. . . .]

Conclusion

[15] Accordingly, we hold the court of appeal's reversal of the denial of Mr. Gallo's reimbursement claim was erroneous for several reasons. First, Mr. Gallo's attempted disavowal action, asserted in his "Petition to Disavow Paternity," was perempted because it was not brought within a year of the child's birth as required by LSA--C.C. art. 189. [. . . .] Finally, Ms. Gallo was not required to make reimbursements because she did not receive "a thing not owed" as required by LSA-C.C. art. 2299; child support payments are made for the benefit of the child, not the mother.

[16] For these reasons, we dismiss with prejudice the "Petition to Disavow Paternity" as having been perempted; we reverse the judgment of the court of appeal, and we deny Mr. Gallo's motion for reimbursement.

[17] **PETITION DISMISSED WITH PREJUDICE; JUDGMENT REVERSED.**

[18] VICTORY J., concurs.

[19] JOHNSON, J., dissents and assigns reasons.

Questions

1. Paragraph 3: The court points out the correct civilian methodology of applying the positive law (legislation and custom). Can you locate the legislation (Civil Code articles) that the court applied? Did the court identify all the applicable provisions? Now, take a look at Louisiana Civil Code article 2300. According to civilian methodology, shouldn't this provision apply before resorting to the jurisprudence that the court discussed in this paragraph? From reading this provision, does the court's reasoning make more sense?

2. Paragraphs 8–15: Assume that the father in this case had successfully disavowed his paternity. Can you think of another defense to his action for reimbursement of paid child support as "payment of a thing not due"? *See* Louisiana Civil Code articles 1760–1762.

Comparative Law Perspective

— Civil Law —

Gabriel Marty & Pierre Raynaud, *Droit Civil — Les Obligations*

vol. 2, n° 623 at 656 (1962)

623. [. . . .] We have endeavored to define payment of a thing not due as a particular quasi-contract, akin to a quasi-loan for consumption (*pro mutuum*), the obligation to give restitution arising from the will of the payee (accipiens). Nevertheless, the problematic idea of "quasi-contract" might lead us to abandon such a characterization and to adopt an approach that places payment of a thing not due as a subcategory of the general principle of enrichment without cause — the action for restitution of the undue payment thus would be a form of the *actio de in rem verso*. Such an approach based on the principle of enrichment without cause could be justified by the fact that the impoverishment of the payor (solvens) and the correlative enrichment of the accipiens are without cause from the moment that the payment was not due.

Keeping in mind that the enrichment here consists of a payment, the abovementioned approach seems valid if we consider such payment as a simple act [**i.e., not a legal act**]. However, if we consider payment as a juridical act, and more precisely as a contract, the foundation of payment of a thing not due seems less closely situated in the law of enrichment without cause and more closely related to the law of contract. Restitution of an undue payment thus presents itself as a consequence of nullity of the contract of payment due to lack of cause, because the extinction of a debt is the cause for payment and the payment of a thing not due is without cause in the sense of article 1131 [**of the French Civil Code**].

Although cause in the context of conventional obligations and cause with regard to unjust enrichment perform very similar functions, a choice between the two to establish the basis for the action for recovery of a thing not due is important when it comes to specifying and explaining the conditions of this action.

Section IV — Enrichment Without Cause

Louisiana Sources of Law
Louisiana Civil Code

Art. 2298. Enrichment without cause; compensation.

A person who has been enriched without cause at the expense of another person is bound to compensate that person. The term "without cause" is used in this context to exclude cases in which the enrichment results from a valid juridical act or the law. The remedy declared here is subsidiary and shall not be available if the law provides another remedy for the impoverishment or declares a contrary rule.

The amount of compensation due is measured by the extent to which one has been enriched or the other has been impoverished, whichever is less.

The extent of the enrichment or impoverishment is measured as of the time the suit is brought or, according to the circumstances, as of the time the judgment is rendered. (Acts 1995, No. 1041, §1, eff. Jan. 1, 1996.)

Doctrine
Louisiana Law of Unjust Enrichment in Quasi-Contracts
at 347–348 (1991)

The Louisiana Civil Codes have always recognized the power of the courts to decide on the basis of equity in those instances where there exists no express law governing the legal issue under consideration. As early as the Digest of 1808, and thereafter in the Civil Codes of 1825 and 1870 as well as in the amendments of the 1980s, a Louisiana court was instructed, "when no rule for a particular situation can be derived from legislation or custom, ... to proceed according to equity. To decide equitably, resort is made to justice, reason, and prevailing usages." Furthermore

766 PART III · QUASI-CONTRACTS

[. . . .] [t]he 1984 legislative amendment to Article 1965 of the Code of 1870 has rephrased the wording of the definition of equity without deviating from its original substantive meaning. It describes equity as: "being based on the principles that no one is allowed to take unfair advantage of another and that no one is allowed to enrich himself unjustly at the expense of another." [. . . .] It is obvious that the courts of this state have been given mandatory legislative authority to bring into Louisiana law any equitable remedy they see fit and proper to introduce. Beyond the two [. . .] forms of quasicontracts [*negotiorum gestio* **and payment of a thing not due**] they could have given their judicial sanction to [**the Roman law**] statement dictating that "by the law of nature it is fair that no one become richer by the loss and injury of another." And yet, despite the substantial parallelism between [**this**] moral principle and the Louisiana Civil Codes and statutory rules, the courts of Louisiana have not utilized, until rather recently the creative audacity to incorporate into the Louisiana civil law tradition the civilian quasi-contractual remedy of *de in rem verso* [**enrichment without cause**]. Had the courts looked back into the history of the civil law tradition and resorted to civilian legal methodology, they could have accomplished much earlier than the French courts what the latter did in the absence of any legislative mandate.

The judicial creation and the history of *de in rem verso* in Louisiana started with some hesitancy, almost reluctance, [. . . .] in the second half of the 19th century. Thereafter, following several decades in oblivion, the *actio de in rem verso* reemerged suddenly and abruptly into a fully grown remedy in the landmark case of *Minyard v. Curtis Products, Inc.*

Nikolaos Davrados, *Demystifying Enrichment Without Cause*

78 La. L. Rev. 1223 to 1225 (2018)

Enrichment without cause was introduced into the Louisiana Civil Code as revised Article 2298. As indicated in the revision comments, this provision codified preexisting jurisprudence that had imported the theory of action *de in rem verso*, together with the mysteries of this theory's jurisprudential past.

Generally, liability for enrichment without cause requires a displacement of wealth in favor of the enriched obligor at the expense of the impoverished obligee. Moreover, this displacement is not justified by the will of the parties or by operation of law. The remedy provided is subsidiary. It is intended to restore this patrimonial imbalance while at the same time rectifying the inequity of the situation pursuant to the moral directives of equity and commutative justice.

Cases

E. F. Minyard

v.

Curtis Products, Inc.

Supreme Court of Louisiana
December 11, 1967
205 So.2d 422

SUMMERS, Justice.

[1] This action was initiated when E.F. Minyard d/b/a Rockwood Insulation Company (Minyard) filed a "Petition for Indemnity" against Curtis Products, Inc., (Curtis) on November 17, 1965. Curtis filed peremptory exceptions based upon pleas of prescription of one year for actions in redhibition under Civil Code Articles 2534 and 2546 and of ten years for personal actions under Article 3544. The trial court and the Court of Appeal have sustained Curtis' peremptory exceptions and have dismissed Minyard's suit. See Minyard v. Curtis Products, Inc., 192 So.2d 208 (La. App.1966). Writs were granted to review this action. 250 La. 104, 194 So.2d 99 (1967).

[2] The sole issue presented for this Court's consideration is whether or not appellant's cause of action as set forth in the "Petition for Indemnity" has prescribed under Articles 2534 and 2546 or 3544 of the Civil Code.

[3] On March 3, 1953 the Housing Authority of New Orleans (HANO), as owner, entered into a construction contract with Pittman Construction Company (Pittman) for the construction of Section I of the Desire Street Housing Project (Project). For the purposes of this construction, Pittman entered into a subcontract with Minyard whereby the latter became bound for the application of caulking materials under Pittman's general contract with HANO. Minyard was to receive $3,000 for the work and for furnishing the materials. The subcontract restated those portions of the general contract which were pertinent to the required application of caulking materials; it read in part as follows:

> "Caulking compound shall be Kuhl's Plastoid, Pecora, or equal. Compound shall be of proper consistency to be readily worked and not be affected by vibrations or long exposure to outside climate or temperature changes. Compound shall form a thin tough elastic film on surface but remain permanently plastic underneath * * *."

[4] In an effort to comply with the requirements of his subcontract, Minyard decided upon a "regular Plastoid" caulking compound, which is not the name of a specific material, but, instead, is a generic term and the trade name of several grades of caulking compound manufactured by Plastic Products, Inc., and distributed by a subsidiary corporation Plastoid Products Company, Inc.

[5] As required by the contract, Minyard submitted to HANO's architects a sample of the "regular Plastoid" caulking compound, together with a chemical and physical

analysis of the compound which had been submitted to Minyard by Plastoid Products, Inc., from whom Minyard was buying the caulking compound. The analysis and representations concerning the compound submitted by Plastoid Products, Inc., had in turn been prepared by Plastic Products, Inc., the manufacturer from whom Plastoid Products, Inc., was to purchase the material for resale to Minyard.

[6] In its transmittal of the analysis and representations concerning the compound to Pittman, Minyard endorsed the properties of the compound and guaranteed it would comply with the specifications.

[7] The sample submitted by Minyard was approved by HANO's architects and Minyard commenced the caulking work. Shortly thereafter HANO's clerk-of-the-works noted that the caulking was beginning to pull away from the aluminum. This fact was brought to Minyard's attention, and it was suggested to Minyard that there be an inspection of the work by representatives of the caulking compound manufacturer. The manufacturer did inspect the work and stated that the "pulling away" was not due to any defect in the caulking compound material. A supervising architect was called in, and he decided that the caulking was "not too objectionable provided it didn't develop into anything worse."

[8] Minyard proceeded with the caulking job. Then on January 26, 1955 the clerk-of-the-works complained in writing to Pittman that "the caulking used is pulling away from wood, brick, aluminum and iron and does not appear to be elastic underneath" and that it was not in compliance with the specifications.

[9] Thereafter, at HANO's request, a test was run on a sample of the compound by the Pittsburg Testing Laboratory. The test revealed that the shrinkage of the compound was 23.55% rather than the 8.9% which had been certified by the manufacturer and endorsed and guaranteed by Minyard. Pittsburg Testing Laboratory also tested a sample of the caulking which had been applied on the houses by Minyard and found it to be hard on the surface but nonplastic underneath. It was also found that the caulking which Minyard had applied showed cracks ranging from hairline to 1/16 inch.

[10] HANO, in compliance with the provisions of the general construction contract, caused the removal of the "regular Plastoid" caulking compound and had it replaced with a suitable material. The cost incurred by HANO in correcting this defective condition amounted to $16,994.42.

[11] On November 15, 1955, Pittman, the general contractor, filed suit against HANO, as owner, for materials furnished and work performed by Pittman in constructing the Project. HANO filed a reconventional demand against Pittman for the costs it had incurred in remedying the defective caulking job. Pittman, in a third party proceeding, prayed for judgment over against Minyard, its subcontractor, for the amount Pittman might be held to pay to HANO under the reconventional demand.

[12] After trial the District Court held Pittman liable to HANO for $16,994.42 as HANO's cost for correcting the caulking work and gave judgment in favor of

Pittman for this amount over against Minyard, the caulking subcontractor. The judgment was affirmed by the Court of Appeal (Pittman Const. Co. v. Housing Authority of New Orleans, 169 So.2d 122), and writs were refused in this Court, 247 La. 344, 170 So.2d 865 (1965).

[13] Both courts found that the "pulling away" and cracking were due solely to the fact that the "regular Plastoid" caulking compound had failed to meet the requirements of the specifications. There was no question of improper workmanship on the part of Minyard, the subcontractor. Minyard's liability was predicated upon his endorsement and guarantee of the physical and chemical analysis and properties of the caulking compound.

[14] Minyard satisfied the judgment against him by paying Pittman $24,100 on March 29, 1965. Minyard filed this present suit approximately eight months later on November 17, 1965 against Curtis the successor of Plastic Products, Inc., manufacturer of the caulking compound, for "Indemnity" claiming the amount it, Minyard, had paid to Pittman, the costs and expense incurred in that suit, attorneys fees and the sum of $20,000 for loss of reputation and business due to the suit in which Minyard had been involved with Pittman and the Housing Authority. Minyard styled this claim "Petition for Indemnity". It seems also to be cumulated with a claim against Curtis Products, Inc., as the successor of Plastoid Products, Inc.

[15] It was to this petition that Curtis Products, Inc., the successor of the manufacturer, interposed the pleas of prescription of one and ten years based upon the theory that Minyard's claim, although labeled a petition for indemnity, was in fact a suit for redhibition prescribed in one year under Articles 2534 and 2546 of the Civil Code. Alternatively, it is asserted that it is a suit for breach of contract and, as such, is a personal action prescribed in ten years under Article 3544 of the Civil Code.

[16] The trial court found the prescription of one year under Articles 2534 and 2546 of the Civil Code applicable for it considered this to be a suit in redhibition between the buyer, Minyard, and the seller, Curtis as the successor of Plastoid Products, Inc., for which a remedy was provided by law which was prescribed in one year from the sale (La.Civ.Code art. 2534), or at the latest within one year from the discovery of the vice in the thing sold. (La.Civ.Code art. 2546). January 26, 1955 was found to be the date when the vice in the caulking compound was "discovered" for it was on this date, it will be recalled, that the clerk-of-the-work called attention to the "pulling away" of the caulking compound.

[17] On appeal to the Fourth Circuit the judgment was affirmed. The Court of Appeal announced, moreover, that because the suit was instituted on November 17, 1965, more than ten years after the cause of action accrued on January 26, 1955, recovery is barred by the prescription of ten years provided for in Article 3544 of the Civil Code.

[18] We are of the opinion that a basic error occurred in both the trial court and the Court of Appeal brought about, perhaps, by the deceptive similarity in the names of Plastoid Products, Inc., and Plastic Products, Inc., two business corporations.

Although one may have been the distributor of the products of the other, as Plastoid Products, Inc., was indeed the distributor of the products and of the caulking compound manufactured by Plastic Products, Inc., they must, nevertheless, in legal contemplation, be considered as separate entities, Plastoid Products, Inc., being the seller of the compound to Minyard and Plastic Products being the manufacturer of the compound. Plastic Products, Inc., the manufacturer, had no express contractual relation with Minyard the buyer.

[19] The confusion occasioned by the similarity in the names of these two corporations is further compounded by the fact that Curtis is the successor to both Plastoid Products, Inc., and Plastic Products, Inc. A suit against Curtis, the successor of Plastoid Products, Inc., the seller, by Minyard, the buyer, would therefore be subject to the pleas of prescription applicable to actions in redhibition advanced by Curtis; but those prescriptive pleas would not necessarily bar a suit by Minyard for indemnity against Curtis, the successor of Plastic Products, Inc., the manufacturer with whom Minyard had no contractual relationship.

[20] It is obvious from the above facts that the judgment against Pittman for the cost of replacing the faulty caulking compound was not brought about through any fault on the part of Minyard. Both the trial court and the Court of Appeal so found. Minyard's responsibility to Pittman was purely technical, vicarious or derivative because it endorsed the physical and chemical analysis and representation of the manufacturer in whose stead Curtis stands in this suit. The real fault or cause of the expense or damage incurred in the recaulking work on the project was the defective material of the manufacturer, the predecessor of Curtis. There was no contract between Minyard and Curtis as the successor of the manufacturer. Minyard's contract was with the seller. Thus, Minyard seeks indemnity against the manufacturer, not the seller, and since there was no buyer-seller relationship the prescription applicable to suits in redhibition or for suit on an express contract are not applicable.

[21] Even though Minyard has been compelled to pay the amount it paid in satisfaction of the judgment against it because of its technical or constructive liability, when the real fault or cause of damage to Pittman was the manufacturer's defective caulking compound, the law provides no express statutory remedy for Minyard in this situation.

[22] The courts have, however, since early times, sought to grant relief in such a situation. These cases have not been definitive in their treatment of the theoretical basis for a recovery.

[23] The device employed by the courts to grant relief has sometimes been the civil law action de in rem verso, which is an action for unjust enrichment. (Garland v. Scott's Estate, 15 La.Ann. 143 (1860); Payne & Harrison v. Scott, 14 La.Ann. 760 (1859)). More often, however, the courts have employed the action in indemnity. As early as 1814 the principle emerged in a decision of this court (Meunier v. Duperron, 3 Mart., O.S., 285) that if one not actually at fault, i.e., one who was in good faith, is made to answer for the injury sustained by another, then the party not actually at

fault has a cause of action to recover against the party whose fault caused the injury. Cf. Fitzgerald v. Ferguson, 11 La.Ann. 396 (1856).

[24] In Brannan, Patterson & Holliday v. Hoel, 15 La.Ann. 308 (1860) the Court determined that Brannan, Patterson & Holliday, who paid the damage caused by a collision in which their steamboat was involved, were entitled to reimbursement from one Hoel, who was piloting the steamboat and whose negligence caused the damage. This result was obtained without stating the legal principles upon which the reimbursement was allowed. Note, 7 La.L. Rev. 592 (1947). In the case of Sincer v. Heirs of Bell, 47 La.Ann. 1548, 18 So. 755 (1895), the principle that the party not at fault who has paid the damage can recover from the person actually at fault is restated by inference when the Court disallows Sincer's recovery against Bell finding that Bell was not at fault in causing the injury to the third parties.

[25] After the Brannan v. Hoel Case, supra, the courts considered a number of cases for indemnity arising out of tort. Indemnity was allowed in Costa v. Yochim, 104 La. 170, 28 So. 992 (1900) where an employer has been compelled by judgment to pay the injured person and then sued the negligent employee, and in Appalachian Corporation v. Brooklyn Cooperage Co., 151 La. 41, 91 So. 539 (1922), where the plaintiff owner recovered from the occupier of premises after paying a judgment of the injured third party. See 7 La.L.Rev. 592 (1947).

[26] The case of Sutton v. Champagne, 141 La. 469, 75 So. 209 (1917), while not adding to our understanding of the basis upon which indemnity is allowed by the courts, does give us a better general understanding of its nature. The facts upon which the decision rests are stated in the opinion:

> "This suit is against the parents of two 14 year old boys, Charles Champagne and Leo Sill, in damages for the death of a colored boy, the little 9 year old son of the plaintiffs, who was killed in one of the streets of the city of New Orleans, in the built-up part of the city, by a bullet out of a 22-caliber Remington rifle * * * with which the two boys and four other boys of about the same age had just been shooting birds in the street.

> "The rifle and the cartridges had been given to young Champagne by his father, and on the occasion in question young Champagne was shooting birds with it in a large tree in the street; the other boys being with him. Leo Sill begged to have the gun to shoot, and Champagne let him have it; and just then the gun went off, as Leo Sill was trying to ascertain whether it was cocked."

Discussing the liability of the parent of young Sill and the question of whether she might seek reimbursement from Champagne's father, the Court said:

> "We meet with * * * difficulty in solving the legal problem as to the liability vel non of the mother of young Sill. It seems illogical and hard that a mother should be liable in damages for the consequences of the act of somebody else in intrusting a dangerous instrument to her inexperienced child

out of her presence and without her knowledge. At the same time the plaintiffs make out a case against her, under the hereinabove quoted codal provisions (La.Civ.Code arts. 2316, 2317, 2318), when they show that, owing to the unskillful and careless handling of a rifle in the street by her boy, their child was killed. The solution of the problem must be that, while she is liable to the plaintiff, she has her recourse over against the person who by his act brought the responsibility upon her; and we shall so decide."

[27] The case of South Arkansas Lumber Co. v. Tremont Lumber Co., 146 La. 61, 83 So. 378 (1919) decided the important question that the claim of a party entitled to indemnity does not commence to run until he has been condemned by judgment of court to pay the damage out of which his cause of action arises.

[28] Appalachian Corporation v. Brooklyn Cooperage Co., 151 La. 41, 91 So. 539 (1922), announced the concept of indemnity with some clarity and allowed recovery under that theory, but it wrongfully formulated the basis of recovery when it announced that the claimant of compensation, Appalachian, had a cause of action in tort for contribution from a joint tort-feasor.[1]

[29] Subsequent decisions which followed the Appalachian rule reasoned that the exception to the general rule, prohibiting contribution between joint tort-feasors not cast in solido, operates a *legal subrogation,* the effect of which is to allow the "joint tort-feasor" who is only technically or constructively liable to assert the injured third parties" claim against the party actually at fault. Johnson v. Housing Authority of New Orleans, 163 So.2d 569 (La.App.1964).

[30] Although the Appalachian Case properly permitted recovery, the "joint tort-feasor" not really at fault who paid the claim of the injured party was given a right to seek "contribution" for the full amount which he paid. The use of this concept has frequently been questioned. This injury was caused, not by any act of negligence on the part of Appalachian but because of the "actual fault" of Brooklyn Cooperage Co. Appalachian's liability to Lincoln, its employee, is a liability imposed because of the employer-employee contractual relationship and by its obligation to furnish him a

---

1. American Employers' Ins. Co. v. Gulf States Utilities Co., 4 So.2d 628, 630, 631 (La.App.1941). "* * * the Louisiana Courts have recognized the right of one tort-feasor to indemnity from another when the claimant is guilty of no fault and has been subjected to liability only because of some arbitrary rule of law * * * the claimant of indemnity must show that he discharged an existent obligation which, as between him and defendants, should in good conscience have been shouldered by the latter." Note, 7 La. L.Rev. 255 (1947).
"Joint Tortfeasors — Right to Indemnity
"The Louisiana courts have consistently recognized that a tort-feasor who is obliged to satisfy a judgment against him may seek indemnity from a third party who, as between himself and the indemnity claimant, was primarily responsible for the injury to the victim." Malone, "Torts and Workmen's Compensation". 17 La.L.Rev. 345, 348–349 (1956). See also, Note, 9 Tul.L.Rev. 125 (1934–1937); 4 La.L.Rev. 451 (1941 & 42); Holloman, "Contribution Between Tort-Feasors: Treatment By the Courts of Louisiana", 19 Tul.L.Rev. 255 (1944).

safe place to work. Appalachian, then, is only "technically or constructively at fault", while Brooklyn Cooperage Co. is "actually at fault". Brooklyn Cooperage alone has caused an injury or damage, under Article 2315 of the Civil Code, which Appalachian is under a "legal duty" to repair.

[31] Contribution was the incorrect concept to employ, in this context; first, because a joint tort-feasor cannot seek contribution unless the tort-feasor against whom he seeks contribution has been cast in solido with him; second, because Appalachian and Brooklyn Cooperage are not joint tort-feasors who have both acted to "cause" an injury to Lincoln; third, Appalachian is allowed to recover the total amount which it has been made to pay to Lincoln, not just a pro rata share allowed a joint tort-feasor who seeks contribution; and, fourth, the prescription applied to the case is the one year tort prescription reckoning from the day Appalachian is condemned to pay the judgment obtained against it by Lincoln. This delay in the commencement of prescription is sought to be justified on the theory that only at that instant does Appalachian sustain an injury under Article 2315 of the Civil Code, which Brooklyn Cooperage is obliged under the same codal article to repair. In short, under this theory Appalachian is legally subrogated to Lincoln's cause of action and at the same time acquires a separate cause of action of its own in tort against Brooklyn Cooperage. Under the strict rules applicable to contribution among joint tort-feasors through legal subrogation which existed when the Appalachian Case was decided, however, the subrogee Appalachian acquires only the right of the subrogor Lincoln; and if the latter's claim against Brooklyn Cooperage has prescribed, then Appalachian's cause of action would also be lost. There is an irreconcilable inconsistency in the reasoning of the Court on this aspect of the case. Williams v. Marionneaux, 240 La. 713, 124 So.2d 919 (1960); Marquette Casualty Co. v. Brown, 235 La. 245, 103 So.2d 269 (1958); Forcum-James Co. v. Duke Transportation Co., 231 La. 953, 93 So.2d 228 (1957); Cox v. Shreveport Packing Co., 213 La. 53, 34 So.2d 373 (1948); Quatray v. Wicker, 178 La. 289, 151 So. 208 (1933); and Garvey v. Great Atlantic & Pacific Tea Co., 125 So.2d 634 (La.App.1961).

[32] Though the decisions in these cases point out the error of the theory employed in the Appalachian decision, they do not offer an alternative theory or legal justification for allowing recovery against the party actually at fault by a party who has been compelled to pay for the damage caused by that fault and who is only technically, vicariously, derivatively or constructively at fault.

[33] Later in the year when the Appalachian Case was decided, the Court also decided Foster & Glassell Co. v. Knight Bros., 152 La. 596, 93 So. 913 (1922) in which it interpreted the Appalachian Case. At that time it redefined the basis of the action for indemnity as a cause arising out of "implied or quasi contract."

[34] The cause of action arose when Foster & Glassell Co., as employer, satisfied the workmen's compensation claim of one of its employees Morris, who had sustained injuries caused by the negligent fault of Knight Bros. Having satisfied the compensation claim, Foster & Glassell Co. initiated suit for reimbursement against Knight Bros. To this action against it, the defendant filed a plea of prescription of

one year under the theory that the claim for reimbursement rested on Article 2315 of the Civil Code. The Court in its opinion discussed the nature of the action:

> "It is said by defendant that the action is one ex delicto, and that plaintiff can have no greater rights than those of Pink Morris against defendant, a third person, through whose fault the injury is alleged to have occurred. This is undoubtedly true, in so far as the claim is for and on behalf of Morris; but plaintiff had two causes of action under the law, the one for and on behalf of Morris [under the Workmen's Compensation Act], and the other for indemnification, as upon an implied or *quasi contract* to be reimbursed for money which it was compelled to pay on account of the fault of defendant, for which, under the allegations of the petition, it was in no wise responsible. * * *
>
> "* * * where two persons are liable to another for injuries received, the one because of fault or negligence, and the other merely because of statutory requirements or duty, but without actual fault, the latter, upon paying for the injury so inflicted, may recover of the tort-feasor as indemnity the sum so paid as upon an *implied or quasi contract*." (Emphasis added.)[2]

[35] We again sought to find a proper basis for a claim for indemnity in Plummer v. Motors Insurance Corporation, 233 La. 340, 96 So.2d 605 (1957) saying:

> "* * * in this third-party action what the insurance company is saying to the third-party defendant is, in effect: 'Your act caused the breach of my obligation to plaintiff, and as a result of this breach you should pay or indemnify me for any sum for which I may be cast.' In other words, the insurance company in its action against third-party defendant is not seeking an award in damages for the wrongful and unlawful conversion of the property, but is only seeking *indemnification in quasi-contract* for any sum for which it may be cast in plaintiff's suit because of the breach of its obligation. * * * Under these circumstances the prescription provided in Article 3536 is without application (that is, the prescription for a tort)." (Emphasis and parentheses added.)

[36] In Edward Levy Metals, Inc. v. New Orleans Public Belt Railway, 243 La. 860, 148 So.2d 580 (1963) the Court again reaffirmed the classification of a claim for indemnity as an action in quasi contract. We declared there:

---

2. The holding of this case has been overruled by Marquette Casualty Co. v. Brown, 235 La. 245, 103 So.2d 269 (1958) insofar as it applies to the case of an employer's attempted recovery from a tort-feasor of the amount which he has been made to pay an injured employee in workmen's compensation. Marquette Casualty Co. v. Brown held that under special provisions of the Workmen's Compensation Act, the employer's action was in legal subrogation. The reasoning in the Foster & Glassell Case, nevertheless, remains relevant to a consideration of the rights of a party to claim reimbursement for the payment of damages where it is only technically liable and the damage is due to the fault of the party against whom reimbursement or indemnity is sought, where the remedy in such a situation is not specifically defined and prescribed by statute.

"* * * We think the claim is one in indemnity, which is quasi contractual and governed by the prescription of Article 3544 of the Civil Code. The obligation that the third party plaintiff is seeking to enforce here is one for *unjust enrichment* to be enforced in the future in that third party plaintiff is to be indemnified in the event he is compelled to pay the principal plaintiff on account of the (unjust enrichment) * * * of third party defendant.

"The allegations of the third party petition sounding only in *quasi contract* we need not determine their sufficiency otherwise — only that they do not sound in tort and are therefore not prescribed in one year." (Parentheses and emphasis added.)

Thus it may be seen that the principles supporting the action for indemnity have undergone an interesting development. A reference to civil law authorities should be helpful in our effort to more thoroughly coordinate this relief with the principles upon which the Civil Code is founded.

[37] In all civil matters, where there is no express law, the judge is bound to decide according to equity. La.Civil Code art. 21 (1870). There is, moreover, in our law the moral maxim "that no one ought to enrich himself at the expense of another." La.Civil Code art. 1965 (1870). This latter article announces the principle of unjust enrichment.

[38] These principles apply to the facts of the case at bar. Although not always referred to, they were the underlying reasons for the decision of those cases which have allowed recovery under the concept of indemnity to which we have referred; the later cases cited, we have already noted, having more properly characterized the action for indemnity as an action or claim in quasi contract for unjust enrichment.

"Certain obligations are contracted without any agreement, either on the part of the person bound, or of him in whose favor the obligation takes place.

"Some are imposed by the sole authority of the laws, others from an act done by the party obliged, or in his favor.

"The obligations, which arise from a fact, personal to him who is bound, or relative to him, result either from quasi contracts, or from offenses and quasi-offenses." La.Civil Code art. 2292 (1870).

"Quasi contracts are the lawful and purely voluntary act of a man, from which there results any obligation whatever to a third person, and sometimes a reciprocal obligation between the parties." La. Civil Code art. 2293 (1870).

"All acts, from which there results an obligation without any agreement, in the manner expressed in the preceding article, form quasi contracts. But there are two principal kinds which give rise to them, to wit: The transaction of another's business, and the payment of a thing not due." La.Civil Code art. 2294 (1870).

Thus the general concept of quasi contractual obligations is clearly and succinctly stated. Article 2294 does not purport to enumerate the exclusive factual situations which can give rise to quasi contractual obligations; it only enumerates the "two principal kinds", the transaction of another's business (negotiorum gestio), and the payment of a thing not due (condictio indebitati). The implication is that there are others, Colin et Capitant, Cours Elementaire De Droit Civil Francais, T. 2, n° 10, p. 8 (10th ed. 1953); Dalloz, 10 Jurisprudence Generale Du Royaume, "Obligations", Ch. 7, Sect. 1, p. 777 (1830); Planiol et Ripert, Traite Pratique De Droit Civil Francais, T. 7, "Obligations," n° 719, p. 1, 2 (2d ed. 1954).

[39] There is a general concept of quasi contractual obligations;[3] it is a concept based upon the principle that where there is an unjust enrichment of one at the expense or impoverishment of another, then the value of that enrichment or else, in some cases, the amount of the impoverishment must be restituted. Planiol, Traite Elementaire De Droit Civil, T. 2, n° 812, n° 813 (8th ed. 1939).

[40] Under this general theory of quasi contractual obligations founded upon an unjust enrichment we find the civil law action *de in rem verso*. See Nicholas, Unjustified Enrichment in Civil Law, Part I, 36 Tul.L. Rev. 605 (1962), Part II, 37 Tul.L.Rev. 49 (1962). The *actio de in rem verso*, although recognized by this Court long ago, was not treated definitively and was only applied in the two cases to which we referred above. Garland v. Scott's Estate, 15 La.Ann. 143 (1860); Payne & Harrison v. Scott, 14 La.Ann. 760 (1859).

[41] The action, however, has been well developed in France, influenced in large measure by the French Civil Code articles from which our own are copied. See Nicholas, supra. Nicholas says: "Among the essentials of the civil law remedy are its generality and its corrective or supplementary character."

[42] An early statement of the *actio de in rem verso* is to be found in Patureau-Miran v. Boudier, Cour de Cassation (Ch.req.) June 15, 1892, (1893) S.I. 281, (1892) D.I. 596 (Fr.). Speaking of the derivation and nature of the action, the Court said:

> "* * * It derives from the principle of equity which forbids enrichment at the expense of another, and since it has been regulated by no provision of the enacted law, its exercise is subject to no precise rules; it is sufficient that the plaintiff allege and undertake to prove that as a result of some sacrifice or act on his part he has procured an advantage to the defendant."

[43] As Nicholas points out, in France the action has rightfully been subjected to limitations by the courts in its application. For, as he observes, "unregulated discretion is ultimately the negation of law." There are now five prerequisites to the successful suit by actio de in rem verso: (1) there must be an enrichment, (2) there must be an impoverishment, (3) there must be a connection between the enrichment and

---

3. Planiol having enumerated the two types of quasi contractual obligations specifically mentioned by the Code Napoleon, concludes that these categories are not exclusive. Planiol et Ripert, Traite Pratique De Droit Civil Francais, T. 7, Obligations, n° 719, p. 2 (1954).

resulting impoverishment, (4) there must be an absence of "justification" or "cause" for the enrichment and impoverishment, and finally (5) the action will only be allowed when there is no other remedy at law, i.e., the action is subsidiary or corrective in nature. 36 Tul.L.Rev. 605, 610.

[44] As to the first three prerequisites, these are operable in any other recognized action for unjust enrichment in Louisiana, such as negotiorum gestio or condictio indebitati. As to the fourth prerequisite to the action, this same requirement of an absence of a "justification" would apply in Louisiana under the general provisions of our codal articles which announce the principle of unjust enrichment; that there is no "justification" is inherent in the definition of "unjust". The fifth requirement, that there be no other remedy available at law, is simply an aspect of the principle that the action must not be allowed to defeat the purpose of a rule of law directed to the matter at issue. It must not, in the language of some writers, "perpetrate a fraud on the law." Article 21 of the Louisiana Civil Code prohibits a reference to principles of equity in cases which would allow application of more specific legal action.

[45] The remedy afforded by the actio de in rem verso is not unlike that allowed by the action for indemnity under Louisiana jurisprudence. The remedies and prerequisites of the action de in rem verso are also found to be compatible with the principles of our Civil Code and we will apply them to this case allowing recovery by Minyard against Curtis in the amount of the judgment paid by Minyard to Pittman only, with legal interest on that amount from the date of judicial demand in this suit until paid, and for all costs of this suit.

[46] Since, under the principles announced, the cause of action does not come into being until the party seeking recovery for unjust enrichment has been compelled to discharge the obligation which forms the basis for the unjust enrichment claim, the prescriptive period in the case at bar will be reckoned from the day Pittman obtained judgment over against Minyard. And we shall apply to that situation the prescription of ten years provided by Article 3544 of the Civil Code applicable to quasi contracts, for the claim is one in quasi contract. Clearly, under this theory, the claim is not prescribed.

[47] For the reasons assigned, the judgment of the trial court and the Court of Appeal maintaining the pleas of prescription filed herein are reversed and set aside, and this cause is remanded to the trial court to be proceeded with in accordance with law and the views expressed herein.

[48] HAMITER, J., concurs in the result.

[49] HAWTHORNE, J., concurs in the decree.

[50] McCALEB, J., dissents being in accord with the views of the Court of Appeal. See La.App., 192 So.2d 208.

[51] HAMLIN, J., dissents being of the opinion that the result reached by the Court of Appeal is correct.

Questions

1. Paragraphs 3–47: Identify the parties in this case and their legal relationships. These parties are juridical persons, some of whom are successors of previous parties. Was there a contract between the parties? Now, take a look at the five requirements for the *actio de in rem verso* that the court identifies in paragraph 43. Are all these requirements met here? Does the court convincingly explain that all these requirements were met?

2. Current Civil Code article 2298 did not exist when this opinion was written. On what sources of law does the court base the *actio de in rem verso*? What is the relation of this action with the other two quasi-contracts — *negotiorum gestio* and payment of a thing not due?

Grace Q. Edmonston
v.
A-Second Mortgage Company of Slidell, Inc., et al.

Supreme Court of Louisiana
January 14, 1974
289 So.2d 116

SUMMERS, Justice.

[1] Plaintiff Grace Q. Edmonston owned a house and lot in Pearl River, Louisiana, as part of her separate estate acquired prior to her marriage to Lucien E. Edmonston. After they were married she and her husband applied for and obtained a $16,000 loan from Standard Life Insurance Company of the South. As a condition precedent to the loan, Standard required plaintiff and her husband to insure their lives for $8,000 each in whole life policies with double indemnity benefits in the event of accidental death. These policies were assigned by the Edmonstons to Standard under an "assignment of collateral security" agreement. The assignment, dated January 7, 1964, was executed contemporaneously with a first mortgage in favor of Standard securing the $16,000 loan bearing upon the Pearl River property.

[2] Terms of the assignment agreement provided that, upon the death of either Mr. or Mrs. Edmonston, Standard would apply the proceeds to discharge the mortgage, or, at their option, pay the proceeds to the beneficiary. The policy insuring Lucien E. Edmonston's life named Grace Q. Edmonston as beneficiary.

[3] Later, on September 24, 1964, plaintiff and her husband negotiated a $4,000 loan from A-Second Mortgage Company of Slidell, Inc. To secure the payment of this loan, the Edmonstons executed a second mortgage in the principal sum of $7,200 in favor of A-Second affecting the Pearl River property.

[4] Two years later the Edmonstons experienced financial difficulties. To alleviate the problems involved, they agreed to convey the Pearl River property to A-Second for the satisfaction of their mortgage indebtedness to A-Second, as well as the indebtedness in favor of Standard. To evidence this agreement the Edmonstons executed

a *dation en paiement* conveying the property to A-Second. In turn A-Second declared the mortgage note of $7,200 in its favor satisfied, granting to the Edmonstons, at the same time, due acquittance and discharge of all indebtedness affecting the property. By this transaction, and by further agreements, A-Second assumed payment of the mortgage note held by Standard, agreeing to make all payments as they came due, and to maintain the life insurance policies in effect by premium payments. Although not objecting to the transfer of title to A-Second, Standard would not and did not release the Edmonstons from the effects of the mortgage obligation owed to Standard.

[5] Lucien E. Edmonston was accidentally killed on March 28, 1967. According to the terms of the policy on his life, this event made the $16,000 double indemnity proceeds payable to his wife as beneficiary. On April 26, 1967 the balance due on Standard's mortgage loan was $14,512.87. At that time Standard prevailed upon Mrs. Edmonston to apply $14,512.87 of the $16,000 policy proceeds to the payment of the mortgage note which they held and to accept the balance of $1,487.13 in cash in full satisfaction of her claim as beneficiary. To manifest her agreement to this transaction, Mrs. Edmonston executed a document titled "Release of Claimant" on May 1, 1967 wherein she acknowledged receipt of the $16,000 due her as named beneficiary in the policy. From this amount she applied $14,512.87 to the satisfaction of the mortgage note in favor of Standard, and the mortgage and the note secured thereby were cancelled in full. A check for the $1,487.13 balance was issued to Mrs. Edmonston, duly endorsed by her and deposited to her account.

[6] This suit followed on March 7, 1968 in which Mrs. Edmonston, as plaintiff, seeks judgment against Standard for $14,512.87, plus penalties, attorneys' fees, interest and costs. Alternatively, she prays for judgment in the same amount against A-Second and its successors C. A. Corporation and U.S. Thrift and Loan Corporation. Defendant A-Second and its successors (to whom we shall refer individually and collectively as A-Second) filed a third party petition against Standard for recovery of any amounts which they were adjudged to owe Mrs. Edmonston. Standard in turn third partied A-Second.

[7] The trial court denied relief to Mrs. Edmonston. On appeal to the First Circuit the judgment was affirmed. La.App., 273 So.2d 707. We granted certiorari to review these judgments. La., 277 So.2d 440.

I

[8] Mrs. Edmonston's principal demand against Standard is based upon allegations that she was distressed by her husband's death and did not knowingly and voluntarily pay the balance due on the mortgage note held by Standard; hence, she alleges, Standard was not authorized by the policy assignment or otherwise to apply the proceeds to the satisfaction of the balance due on the mortgage note it held.

[9] It is unnecessary in this connection to consider the enforceability of the policy assignment, for the record does not adequately support the contention that Mrs. Edmonston was unaware of her rights or obligatons at the time she agreed with

Standard that the policy proceeds could be applied to the satisfaction of the balance due on the mortgage note. We do not agree with her contention that she did not act freely and voluntarily. As already noted, she accepted the balance due and signed the "Release of Claimant" agreement. She had been furnished a full statement of the proposed disposition of the funds. In addition, she was knowledgeable, had some experience in affairs of this kind, and was fully aware of the fact that she and her husband had not been discharged from the obligation to Standard. She concedes she was aware of the fact that she was primarily liable on the note held by Standard despite the fact that A-Second had assumed its payment.

[10] With this finding we dismiss Mrs. Edmonston's principal demand against Standard for return of the $14,512.87 paid on the balance due on the mortgage note.

II

[11] Mrs. Edmonston's alternative demand is, however, the central issue argued in briefs to this Court. The contention is that the trial court and Court of Appeal erred in not invoking and applying the *actio de in rem verso* to permit her to recover $14,512.87 against A-Second. This restitutionary remedy is founded upon principles of unjust enrichment embodied in Civil Code articles 21 and 1965.[1] The action derives from the maxim that natural justice requires that no one should be enriched at the expense of another. It is used to fill a gap in the law where no express remedy is provided. According to this position, A-Second was, in fact, relieved of the payment of that amount and thereby enriched to that extent while, at the same time, Mrs. Edmonston was impoverished by her discharge of an obligation which A-Second had assumed to pay on her behalf.

[12] This Court set out the requirements to be met before the *actio de in rem verso* was applicable in Minyard v. Curtis Products, Inc., 251 La. 624, 205 So.2d 422 (1967). The case concerned an action by a subcontractor, as buyer of a faulty caulking compound, against the successor to the manufacturer of the compound for the amount the subcontractor was cast in judgment to pay to the contractor as damages incurred in recaulking made necessary by the faulty compound. This Court applied

---

1. La.Civil Code art. 21:
     "In all civil matters, where there is no express law, the judge is bound to proceed and decide according to equity. To decide equitably, an appeal is to be made to natural law and reason, or received usages, where positive law is silent."
   La.Civil Code art. 1965:
     "The *equity* intended by this rule is founded in the Christian principle not to do unto others that which we would not wish others should do unto us; and on the moral maxim of the law that no one ought to enrich himself at the expense of another. When the law of the land, and that which the parties have made for themselves by their contract, are silent, courts must apply these principles to determine what ought to be incidents to a contract, which are required by equity."
   See also La.Civil Code articles 501, 507, 1793, 2147, 2301, 2302, 3407 for examples of legislation based on principles of unjust enrichment.

the *actio de in rem verso* to the subcontractor's claim for indemnity against the successor to the manufacturer, which it held was unjustly enriched by this payment.

[13] To deter courts from turning to equity to remedy every unjust displacement of wealth with unregulated discretion, certain limitations are applicable to the *actio de in rem verso*. The Minyard decision set forth five prerequisites which must be satisfied to successfully invoke the action: 1) There must be an enrichment; 2) there must be an impoverishment; 3) there must be a connection between the enrichment and the impoverishment; 4) there must be an absence of "justification" or "cause" for the enrichment and impoverishment; and 5) the action will only be allowed when there is no other remedy at law, i.e., the action is subsidiary or corrective in nature.

1) Enrichment

[14] There must be an enrichment.

[15] A-Second by the *dation en paiement* executed on October 18, 1966 acquired the Edmonston house and lot for a recited consideration of $5,178.24 — the balance due on the Edmonston obligation to A-Second — and the assumption by A-Second of the balance due on the first mortgage to Standard in the sum of $14,512.87, a total $19,691.11 paid for a property valued by Standard's appraisers at $24,100. Thus, when Mrs. Edmonston discharged the $14,512.87 obligation to Standard, A-Second was relieved of the payment of that debt which it had assumed and therefore A-Second's patrimony was enriched to that extent.

[16] There is no merit to A-Second's contention that it acquired the Edmonston property subject to the encumbrances and for that reason it was entitled to all benefits derived from the life policies since it paid the premiums. At the time of the *dation,* no contract was entered into which would entitle A-Second to the proceeds of the life insurance. There was, moreover, no legal requirement between Mrs. Edmonston and A-Second that Mrs. Edmonston discharge A-Second's obligation to pay the mortgage note due Standard. To the contrary, A-Second had, by the *dation,* given the Edmonstons full acquittance and discharge of all encumbrances affecting the property. That is to say, Mrs. Edmonston owed A-Second nothing, still A-Second was the beneficiary of $14,512.87 when Mrs. Edmonston paid the mortgage note held by Standard. Thereby A-Second received a benefit they had never bargained for, the discharge of its obligation to Standard. To that extent A-Second was unquestionably enriched and in our view the case falls within the meaning of enrichment as that term is contemplated by the *actio de in rem verso*.

2) Impoverishment

[17] There must be an impoverishment.

[18] The Court of Appeal was of the opinion that Mrs. Edmonston suffered no impoverishment. By paying the mortgage note held by Standard, on which she was personally liable, the court reasoned, Mrs. Edmonston was released from this debt to her benefit.

[19] This point of view overlooks the fact that Mrs. Edmonston gave up her house and lot to A-Second in the *dation en paiement* to satisfy *all* debts bearing against the property. When she paid Standard, therefore, she was paying an obligation of A-Second. Actually, she paid the $14,512.87 twice: once in the *dation en paiement* by conveying her house to A-Second with the understanding that A-Second would pay that debt and again when she paid Standard. She was thus impoverished when her patrimony was diminished by the amount paid to Standard.

3) There must be a connection between the enrichment and the resulting impoverishment

[20] There was a causal connection between Mrs. Edmonston's impoverishment and A-Second's enrichment as our discussion demonstrates. When Mrs. Edmonston paid the balance due to Standard and the mortgage and note were cancelled, A-Second immediately became the beneficiary to the exact extent of the payment. Mrs. Edmonston's one act of payment therefore simultaneously enriched A-Second and impoverished her. Unless Mrs. Edmonston prevails here, A-Second gets a $24,100 home for $5,178.24 as a direct consequence of the payment. These facts meet the test which requires that "It must be clear that the defendant would not have been enriched unless the plaintiff has been impoverished." Guttridge and David, The Doctrine of Unjustified Enrichment, 5 Cambridge L.Jour. 204, 214 (1933–35).

4) There must be an absence of "justification" or "cause" for the enrichment and the impoverishment

[21] "Cause" is not in this instance assigned the meaning commonly associated with contracts, but, rather, it means that the enrichment is justified if it is the result of, or finds its explanation in, the terms of a valid juridical act between the impoverishee (Mrs. Edmonston) and the enrichee (A-Second) or between a third party (Standard) and the enrichee. A valid juridical act with the enrichee is essential to a finding of "cause". Nicholas, Unjustified Enrichment in the Civil Law and Louisiana Law, Part I, 36 Tul.L.Rev. 622 (1962).

[22] The issue, then, is whether there is a contract, express or implied, between Mrs. Edmonston and A-Second or Standard and A-Second which would justify the enrichment of A-Second. If there is such, the contract is the law between them and it serves as a legal cause or justification for the enrichment. If cause is found, the enrichment is not unjustified and the attempt to invoke the *actio de in rem verso* must fail. For it is not every unjust enrichment which warrants the resort to equity; only the unjust enrichment for which there is no justification in law or contract allows equity a role in the adjudication.

[23] A-Second argues that justification or cause does appear on the face of the policy assignment from the Edmonstons to Standard. But this does not suffice to satisfy the requirement. The French law requires an act between the impoverishee and the enrichee or the third party and the enrichee. This is the better test. See Nicholas, Id., at 625, 628, 631.

[24] The contract of assignment relied upon by A-Second is an agreement between the Edmonstons and Standard, not with A-Second the enrichee. A-Second is neither mentioned nor contemplated in this contract. And the *dation* was the only juridical act between Mrs. Edmonston and A-Second even remotely associated with the facts at issue. The *dation* concerned the giving in payment of the Edmonston house and lot in satisfaction of A-Second's mortgage and the assumption by A-Second of the obligation to discharge the Standard mortgage and pay the policy premiums. No element of this agreement entitles A-Second to the policy proceeds utilized by Mrs. Edmonston to satisfy the Standard mortgage.

[25] Moreover, the assignment by Mrs. Edmonston to Standard has no real bearing on the issues, for its validity is extremely questionable. Mrs. Edmonston is not permitted under this Court's jurisprudence to assign her beneficiary rights before they actually accrue, for at the time of the assignment Mr. Edmonston had the right, by the terms of the policy on his life, to change the beneficiary at any time. Dorset v. Thomas, 152 La. 60, 92 So. 734 (1922); Douglass v. Equitable Life Assur. Soc., 150 La. 519, 90 So. 834 (1922); 2A Appleman, Insurance Law and Practice, ¶¶ 1257, 1282 (1966).

5) The action will only be allowed where there is no other remedy at law, i.e., the action is subsidiary

[26] Civil Code Article 21 expressly states that the judge can turn to equity (*actio de in rem verso*) only where there is no express law. The action must not be allowed to defeat the purpose of a rule of law directed to the matter at issue. It must not "perpetrate a fraud on the law." Minyard v. Curtis Products, Inc., 251 La. 624, 205 So.2d 422 (1967).

[27] There is no remedy available to Mrs. Edmonston other than the *actio de in rem verso*. She has, in effect, paid the debt of another and the actual benefit to A-Second cannot be questioned. Principles of negotiorum gestor are inapplicable, for she had no intent to benefit A-Second. La.Civil Code arts. 2295–2300. There is no remedy by which she can recover the money paid to Standard for she was obligated to them. But she owed no obligation to A-Second, and there was no requirement in law or by contract, that she discharge A-Second's debt to Standard; and there is no contract or rule of law which permits Mrs. Edmonston to reclaim from A-Second the $14,512.87 enrichment resulting to A-Second by the payment of that amount to Standard.

[28] It follows, therefore, that the action here is subsidiary in character; it will defeat no rule of law and equity will prevail by allowing Mrs. Edmonston to recover from A-Second.

[29] And, since we are doing equity, A-Second will be allowed a credit for insurance premiums paid on the life policies. Douglass v. Equitable Life Assur. Soc., 150 La. 519, 90 So. 834 (1922).

[30] For the reasons assigned the judgments of the trial court and Court of Appeal are reversed, and judgment is rendered in favor of Grace Q. Edmonston and against A-Second Mortgage Company of Slidell, Inc., C.A. Corporation, and U.S. Thrift and

Loan Corporation, individually, jointly and in solido, in the amount of $14,512.87, plus legal interest from the date of judicial demand until paid, and for all costs of these proceedings, less a credit of $321.70, the amount paid on policy premiums, with legal interest thereon from date of judicial demand.

[31] All other demands of plaintiff, and all third party demands asserted herein are denied.

[32] CULPEPPER, J., dissents, being of the opinion that the judgment of the Court of Appeal is correct.

[33] DIXON, J., dissents.

Questions

1. Paragraphs 1–13: Carefully identify the parties in this case and their legal relationships. Focus especially on the legal relationship between the Edmonstons and A-Second Mortgage based on their second contract. *See* Louisiana Civil Code article 1821 and 1794. Now, take a look at the five requirements for the *actio de in rem verso* that the court analyzes in paragraph 13. Are all these requirements met here? Focus especially on the last requirement. Did Mrs. Edmonston not have another remedy against A-Second Mortgage based on their contract?

2. Paragraphs 14–31.: The court thoroughly analyzed the five requirements for the *actio de in rem verso*. On the basis of this analysis, take another look at the opinion in the previous case, *Minyard*, and try to apply these requirements to the facts of that case.

Coastal Environmental Specialists, Inc.
v.
Chem-Lig International, Inc., Chem-Lig International Industries, Inc. & David Stutz

Court of Appeal of Louisiana
First Circuit
November 9, 2001
818 So.2d 12

WHIPPLE, J.

[1] Plaintiff, Coastal Environmental Specialists, Inc. (hereinafter "Coastal"), appeals the grant of partial summary judgment in favor of defendant, the Greater Baton Rouge Port Commission (hereinafter "the Port"). For the following reasons, we affirm.

Facts and Procedural History

[2] Chem-Lig International, Inc., later Chem-Lig International Industries, Inc., leased a portion of land from the Port of Greater Baton Rouge where Chem-Lig

housed a chemical plant and warehouse. Chem-Lig processed, manufactured, and sold sodium lignosulfate, an anionic water soluble chemical used as drilling mud.

[3] In March of 1996, Chem-Lig personnel discovered that a 20,000 gallon frac tank, containing "wash water" had been leaking on the Chem-Lig premises over a period of time. [. . . .]

[4] Chem-Lig then hired Coastal to perform the remediation and clean the areas affected by the spill. [. . . .] On March 26, 1996, [an inspection of] the Chem-Lig facility [. . .] determined that the work had been performed satisfactorily. The material from the March clean-up was stored in roll-off boxes rented daily from Coastal on the Chem-Lig site.

[5] In May of 1996, after a hard rain, the same material spilled in March was again found on Chem-Lig's plant facility. By this time, Chem-Lig had experienced financial problems and was in the process of closing its business. [. . . .] Chem-Lig subsequently shut down all operations in May of 1996. Ultimately, the Port utilized their own maintenance staff, rented the necessary equipment, and hired Rust Environmental, an environmental engineering firm, to clean up the spill. [. . . .]

[6] On December 5, 1996, Coastal filed suit against the Greater Baton Rouge Port Commission seeking to recover the balance of $85,842.00 due from Chem-Lig for the rental fees and work performed in connection with the clean-up of the March spill. In its petition, Coastal also alleged that [. . .] the Port was unjustly enriched by the services performed by Coastal.

[7] In response, the Port filed a motion for partial summary judgment seeking to dismiss plaintiff's claims for payment of expenses incurred pursuant to its contract with Chem-Lig, contending that [. . .] plaintiff also has no remedy under any theory of unjust enrichment.

[8] By judgment dated March 22, 2000, the trial court granted partial summary judgment in favor of the Port, dismissing Coastal's claims against the Port for payment for work that Coastal had performed pursuant to its contract with Chem-Lig. [. . .] Coastal appeals [. . .].

Discussion

[. . . .]

Unjust Enrichment

[. . . .]

[9] Coastal further contends that the trial court erred in dismissing its claims against the Port under the theory of unjust enrichment. The action for unjust enrichment is addressed in LSA-C.C. art. 2298, which provides as follows:

> A person who has been enriched without cause at the expense of another person is bound to compensate that person. The term "without cause" is used in this context to exclude cases in which the enrichment results from a valid juridical act or the law. The remedy declared here is subsidiary and

shall not be available if the law provides another remedy for the impoverishment or declares a contrary rule.

The amount of compensation due is measured by the extent to which one has been enriched or the other has been impoverished, whichever is less.

The extent of the enrichment or impoverishment is measured as of the time the suit is brought or, according to the circumstances, as of the time the judgment is rendered.

[10] The root principle of unjustified enrichment is that the plaintiff suffers an economic detriment for which he should not be responsible, while the defendant receives an economic benefit for which he has not paid. *See Scott v. Wesley,* 589 So.2d 26, 27 (La.App. 1st Cir.1991). An action for unjust enrichment is allowed only when the plaintiff has no other remedy at law. However, where there is a rule of law directed to the issue, an action must not be allowed to defeat the purpose of said rule. *Carriere v. Bank of Louisiana,* 95-3058, p. 12 (La.12/13/96), 702 So.2d 648, 657. Stated differently, unjust enrichment principles are only applicable to fill a gap in the law where no express remedy is provided. *Louisiana National Bank of Baton Rouge v. Belello,* 577 So.2d 1099, 1102 (La.App. 1st Cir.1991).

[11] In *Minyard v. Curtis Products, Inc.,* 251 La. 624, 652, 205 So.2d 422, 432 (1967), the Louisiana Supreme Court set forth five prerequisites that must be satisfied to successfully invoke the action, noting that there must be: (1) an enrichment, (2) an impoverishment, (3) a connection between the enrichment and the impoverishment, (4) an absence of justification or cause for the enrichment and the impoverishment, and (5) no other remedy at law available to the impoverishee. *Commercial Properties Development Corp. v. State Teachers Retirement System,* 2000-0392, p. 2 (La.App. 1st Cir.3/28/01), 808 So.2d 534, 539. To recover under the doctrine of unjust enrichment, a claimant must prove all five elements; if any one is not proven, the claimant's recovery is barred. *Bernard v. First Republic Life Insurance Company,* 510 So.2d 97, 102 (La.App. 1st Cir.1987).

[12] The fifth requirement, that there be no other practical remedy at law available to the impoverishee, is critical to the resolution of this case. In *Morphy, Makofsky & Masson, Inc. v. Canal Place 2000,* 538 So.2d 569 (La.1989), the Louisiana Supreme Court held that the existence of a claim on an express or implied contract precludes application of the unjust enrichment theory, because the potential claim constitutes a practical remedy at law available to the impoverishee. Furthermore, in cases where a claim has been exercised and a judgment obtained, it is most apparent that there is a practical remedy available at law. *See Pilgrim Life Insurance Company of America v. American Bank and Trust Company of Opelousas,* 542 So.2d 804, 807 (La.App. 3rd Cir.1989); *Central Oil & Supply Corporation v. Wilson Oil Company, Inc.,* 511 So.2d 19, 21 (La.App. 3rd Cir.1987), *writ denied,* 535 So.2d 747 (La.1989).

[13] In *Scott v. Wesley,* Scott, a home builder, obtained a judgment against Wesley, the person with whom he contracted to build the home. After unsuccessful attempts to collect on the judgment, Scott filed suit and obtained a judgment against the

landowner under the theory of unjust enrichment. On review, this court reversed the trial court's award against the landowner, stating:

> In *Royal Oldsmobile Co., Inc. v. Yarbrough,* 425 So.2d 823 (La.App. 5th Cir. 1982), plaintiff's claim in unjust enrichment was denied because the court found that he had a practical remedy at law, even though his purchaser had moved to another state. The court explained: "Because appellants chose not to further pursue [purchaser] in California is not sufficient reason to impose liability on [enrichee]. The ease of attaining a remedy is not a sufficient reason to apply unjust enrichment". *Royal,* 425 So.2d at 825.

Scott v. Wesley, 589 So.2d at 28.

[14] In the instant case, Coastal has a remedy at law against Chem-Lig. In fact, as noted previously, Coastal has already instituted suit against Chem-Lig International, Inc., Chem-Lig Industries, Inc., and David Stutz in the Eighteenth Judicial District Court, Docket No. 27,855. In that suit, Coastal seeks to recover the balance of $85,842.00 for the clean-up work performed and rental fees on the bases of Coastal's initial proposal to Chem-Lig [. . .]. Coastal clearly admits throughout its petition filed in that suit and in its brief to this court that the nature of its relationship with Chem-Lig was contractual. Yet, in brief, Coastal complains that "any judgment obtained [against Chem-Lig] would be worthless," and states that "[i]t is of no moment that the Port's contract with Chem-Lig required Chem-Lig to pay for the clean up," thereby asking this court to completely ignore the legal remedy available to it. Applying the above-stated legal precepts that we are bound to follow, we find no support for Coastal's arguments. Whether Coastal can succeed in recovering and collecting in its suit against Chem-Lig is not determinative. Clearly, a legal remedy is available to Coastal. There is no "gap in the law" that prevents Coastal from recovering from Chem-Lig.

[15] Inasmuch as another remedy at law was available to Coastal, under the above law and jurisprudence, an action by Coastal premised upon an unjust enrichment theory likewise must fail.

[16] Accordingly, we find no merit to these assignments.

Quasi-Contract / Negotiorum Gestio

[. . . .]

[17] In this assignment, Coastal claims that the trial court erred in failing to recognize its cause of action pursuant to LSA-C.C. art. 2297, obligations of the owner, which provides as follows:

> The owner whose affair has been managed is bound to fulfill the obligations that the manager has undertaken as a prudent administrator and to reimburse the manager for all necessary and useful expenses.

[18] Louisiana Civil Code article 2292, defines management of affairs as follows:

> There is a management of affairs when a person, the manager, acts without authority to protect the interests of another, the owner, in the reasonable

belief that the owner would approve of the action if made aware of the circumstances.

[19] A quasi-contract evolves from the theory of negotiorum gestio, or the unauthorized management of affairs of another. This quasi-contract comes about when a person, the gestor, voluntarily undertakes to manage another's affairs, whether the recipient of the benefit of this management is aware of it or not. *Kirkpatrick v. Young*, 456 So.2d 622, 624 (La. 1984). The gestor is under the obligation to act as a prudent administrator, and the one whose business has been well-managed is under an obligation to indemnify the manager in all personal engagements he has contracted and to reimburse him all useful and necessary expenses. LSA-C.C. arts. 2298, 2299; *Taylor v. Taylor*, 97-1565, p. 6 (La.App. 1st Cir.6/25/99), 739 So.2d 256, 261, *writ denied*, 99-2202 (La.11/5/99), 750 So.2d 188. The management is purely voluntary. *Tyler v. Haynes*, 99-1921, p. 7 (La.App. 3rd Cir.5/3/00), 760 So.2d 559, 563. It is essential to negotiorum gestio that the manager be doing another's business, not his own business. *Burns v. Sabine River Authority*, 614 So.2d 1337, 1340 (La.App. 3rd Cir.), *writ denied*, 617 So.2d 935 (La.1993).

[20] Coastal claims that it is entitled to recover its expenses under the theory of negotiorum gestio. In the case sub judice, Coastal was acting under the authority vested in it by Chem-Lig pursuant to its contract with Chem-Lig. The contract gave Coastal full authority to incur expenses concerning the clean-up of Chem-Lig's facility, in return for which Coastal was to receive payment from Chem-Lig. The management was not "purely voluntary," but rather, was pursuant to its contract with Chem-Lig. At the time Coastal performed the services contracted for by Chem-Lig, Coastal fully expected payment as the parties previously agreed.

[21] The Port argues in brief that "the law of quasi contract does not extend to elevate the contractual rights of The Port against Chem-Lig, nor does the law transform The Port into a surety to protect the appellant from losses on an account receivable created in the course of the appellant's business operations." On review, we agree.

[22] Thus, this assignment likewise is without merit.

Conclusion

[23] Accordingly, the March 22, 2000 judgment of the trial court is affirmed. Costs in this matter are assessed against the plaintiff/appellant, Coastal Environmental Specialists, Inc.

[24] **AFFIRMED.**

Questions

1. Paragraphs 2–15: Identify the parties in this case and their legal relationships. Now, take a look at the five requirements for the *actio de in rem verso* that the court analyzes in paragraph 11. Are all these requirements met here? The court focuses specifically on the fifth requirement (subsidiarity principle). Do you identify any other requirement not being met?

2. Paragraphs 17–22: Assume that a claim of *negotiorum gestio* existed in this case. Would this finding preclude liability based on the *actio de in rem verso*?

Dumas and Associates, Inc.
v.
Lewis Enterprises Inc., Fred M. Bayles and Todd Kaplan

Court of Appeal of Louisiana
Second Circuit
December 22, 1997
704 So.2d 433

STEWART, Judge.

[. . . .]

Quantum Meruit

[. . . .]

[1] Clearly, the trial court has confused the two situations wherein *quantum meruit* has been applied by Louisiana courts. *Quantum meruit* has existed in our jurisprudence since the early part of the 19th century. The term *quantum meruit* has been employed in several contexts, both as a civilian concept and as an import from the common law. Our jurisprudence has distinguished "a *contractual quantum meruit,* when a contract is implied from the circumstances, but no agreement as to price has been reached" from a "a *quasi contractual quantum meruit,* when the plaintiff has conferred a benefit on defendant in pursuance of a contract supposedly valid but in truth void." *Howell v. Rhoades,* 547 So.2d at 1089. See also Comments, *Quantum Meruit in Louisiana,* 50 Tul.L.Rev. 631 (1976); Comments, *Actio De In Rem Verso in Louisiana: Minyard v. Curtis Products, Inc.,* 43 Tul. L.Rev. 263 (1969); Nicholas, *Unjust Enrichment in Civil Law and Louisiana Law,* 37 Tul.L.Rev. 49 (1962).

[2] Confusion has arisen due to our courts' use of the term *quantum meruit* both in contract cases without stipulated compensation or price and in unjust enrichment cases. The civilian concept of *quantum meruit* is the measure of compensation or price unstated in a contract whereas the common law substantive claim of *quantum meruit,* similar to the civilian *actio de in rem verso,* is geared toward equity and unjust enrichment. *Baker v. Maclay Properties Co., supra; Morphy, Makofsky & Masson, Inc. v. Canal Place 2000,* 538 So.2d 569 (La.1989). In the former, a contract exists, and the court merely supplies a price. In the later, no contract exists, and the court must supply a substantive basis for recovery.

[3] When *quantum meruit* is used as descriptive term, "descriptive of the equitable principles of contract interpretation," plaintiff must show only the reasonable value of his services regardless of whether defendant's patrimony is commensurately enriched. *Morphy, Makofsky & Masson, Inc. v. Canal Place 2000,* 538 So.2d at 574–575. Conversely, both *quantum meruit* as a substantive law basis of recovery and *actio*

de in rem verso both require that plaintiff prove the degree of his impoverishment and the extent of defendant's enrichment, and neither theory applies where a contract exists. *Baker v. Maclay Properties Co., supra; Morphy, Makofsky & Masson, Inc. v. Canal Place 2000, supra; Howell v. Rhoades, supra.* In *Baker v. Maclay Properties Co.,* the court discussed "Baker's possible confusion of the common law and civil law meanings of quantum meruit" and determined that Baker had asserted a claim for unjust enrichment, or *actio de in rem verso.* 94-1529 at p. 18, 648 So.2d at 897. Recent cases indicate that Louisiana courts have attempted to alleviate the "confusion and inconsistency" in use of the term quantum meruit and that *quantum meruit* as a substantive basis of recovery is viewed with disfavor. *Fogleman v. Cajun Bag & Supply Co.,* 93-1177 at pp. 4–5 (La. App. 3rd Cir. 6/15/94), 638 So.2d 706, 709. See also *SMP Sales Management, Inc. v. Fleet Credit Corp.,* 960 F.2d 557 (5th Cir. 1992).

[. . . .]

[4] When one avails himself of the services of another in performance of a task, he is obligated to compensate that person. *Morphy, Makofsky & Masson, Inc. v. Canal Place 2000, supra; Doll v. Albert Weiblen Marble & Granite Co.,* 207 La. 769, 22 So.2d 59 (1945). A contract may be implied "from facts and circumstances showing a mutual intention to contract." *Morphy, Makofsky & Masson, Inc. v. Canal Place 2000,* 538 So.2d at 573; *V-8 Taxi Cab Service, Inc. v. Hayes,* 322 So.2d 442 (La.App. 2nd Cir.1975). When a contract is implied from the circumstances (all other elements of a contract are present), but no agreement as to compensation has been reached, the missing term is supplied by the court, and the measure of damages, under what has been termed *quantum meruit,* is the reasonable value of claimant's services. *Morphy, Makofsky & Masson, Inc. v. Canal Place 2000, supra; Howell v. Rhoades, supra.*

[. . . .]

Comparative Law Perspective

— Civil Law —

Fr. Civ. C. 1803 (as revised in 2016–2017)

> Art. 1303. Except for cases of management of affairs of another and payment of a thing not due, a person who benefits from an unjustified enrichment to the detriment of another person must indemnify the impoverished person to an amount that is equal to the lesser of the two values of the enrichment and the impoverishment.

> Art. 1303-1. The enrichment is unjustified when it does not result from the fulfillment of an obligation by the impoverished person, nor from his liberal intent (intention to confer a gratuitous benefit).

> Art. 1303-2. Compensation is excluded if the impoverishment is the result of an act performed by the impoverished person with a view to a personal profit.

The amount of compensation can be reduced by the judge if the impoverishment was preceded by a fault of the impoverished person.

Art. 1303-3. The impoverished person has no action on this basis if another action is available to him or is legally barred, as in the case of as prescription.

Art. 1303-4. [The Court] assesses on the date of the judgment the impoverishment with reference to the date of the expenditure and the enrichment that still exists on the date of the demand. If the enriched party is in bad faith, the compensation due is equal to the higher of these two values.

C.C.Q. (Québec)

Art. 1493. A person who is enriched at the expense of another shall, to the extent of his enrichment, indemnify the other for the latter's correlative impoverishment, if there is no justification for the enrichment or the impoverishment.

Art. 1494. Enrichment or impoverishment is justified where it results from the performance of an obligation, from the failure of the person impoverished to exercise a right of which he may avail himself or could have availed himself against the person enriched, or from an act performed by the person impoverished for his personal and exclusive interest or at his own risk and peril, or with a consistent liberal intention.

Art. 1495. The indemnity is due only if the enrichment continues to exist on the day of the demand.

Both the enrichment and the impoverishment are assessed on the day of the demand; however, where the circumstances indicate the bad faith of the person enriched, the enrichment may be assessed as at the time he benefited therefrom.

Art. 1496. Where the person enriched disposes of his enrichment gratuitously, with no intention of defrauding the person impoverished, the action of the person impoverished may be taken against the third person beneficiary if the latter could have known of the impoverishment.

— Common Law —

Restatement 3d of Restitution and Unjust Enrichment (2011)

§ 1. Restitution and Unjust Enrichment

A person who is unjustly enriched at the expense of another is subject to liability in restitution.

§ 2. Limiting Principles

(1) The fact that a recipient has obtained a benefit without paying for it does not of itself establish that the recipient has been unjustly enriched.

(2) A valid contract defines the obligations of the parties as to matters within its scope, displacing to that extent any inquiry into unjust enrichment.

(3) There is no liability in restitution for an unrequested benefit voluntarily conferred, unless the circumstances of the transaction justify the claimant's intervention in the absence of contract.

(4) Liability in restitution may not subject an innocent recipient to a forced exchange: in other words, an obligation to pay for a benefit that the recipient should have been free to refuse.

§ 3. Wrongful Gain

A person is not permitted to profit by his own wrong.

§ 4. Restitution May Be Legal or Equitable or Both

(1) Liabilities and remedies within the law of restitution and unjust enrichment may have originated in law, in equity, or in a combination of the two.

(2) A claimant otherwise entitled to a remedy for unjust enrichment, including a remedy originating in equity, need not demonstrate the inadequacy of available remedies at law.

Index